# ATOMS for PEACE and WAR
# 1953-1961

# ATOMS
## FOR
# PEACE
## AND
# WAR
## 1953-1961

### Eisenhower
### and the Atomic Energy Commission

**Richard G. Hewlett
and Jack M. Holl**

**With a Foreword by Richard S. Kirkendall
and an Essay on Sources by Roger M. Anders**

**University of California Press**
Berkeley     Los Angeles     London

Published 1989 by the
University of California Press
Berkeley and Los Angeles, California

University of California Press, Ltd.
London, England

Prepared by the Atomic Energy Commission; work made for hire.

Library of Congress Cataloging-in-Publication Data

Hewlett, Richard G.
  Atoms for peace and war, 1953–1961.

  (California studies in the history of science)
  Bibliography: p.
  Includes index.
    1. Nuclear energy—United States—History.
2. U.S. Atomic Energy Commission—History.
3. Eisenhower, Dwight D. (Dwight David), 1890–1969.
4. United States—Politics and government—1953–1961.
I. Holl, Jack M.   II. Title.   III. Series.
QC792.7.H48   1989        333.79'24'0973        88-29578
ISBN 0-520-06018-0 (alk. paper)

Printed in the United States of America
1   2   3   4   5   6   7   8   9

# CONTENTS

# *ILLUSTRATIONS*

*(following page 374)*

# *FIGURES AND TABLES*

# FOREWORD

This volume, the third in the official history of the Atomic Energy Commission, makes sizable contributions in several areas, including the Eisenhower presidency. During the years in which work on the book has moved forward, that presidency has been one of historiographical frontiers, an area of exciting explorations and new developments. A "revisionism" has emerged to challenge a conception that had taken shape earlier and was quite negative in its appraisal of Eisenhower. Some findings of the revisionists now seem quite firmly established, but the new interpretation has not swept the field. Challenges to it have also appeared. A volume focusing on nuclear energy cannot make contributions to all aspects of the controversy over President Eisenhower, but this book can and does have much to say about some main features of the debate. In the process, the book illustrates, as did the earlier volumes in the series, how very good "official history" can be.

Early on, American historians were not enthusiastic about Eisenhower as president.[1] Journalists and other writers outside the historical profession, including Samuel J. Lubell, Robert J. Donovan, Arthur Krock, Merlo J. Pusey, Arthur Larson, and Clinton Rossiter, had developed positive appraisals in the mid-1950s, but by the 1960s most historians endorsed the more negative views first presented by Norman Graebner, Hans J. Morgenthau, Richard Rovere, Marquis Childs, William V. Shannon, Walt W. Rostow, Richard Neustadt, James MacGregor Burns, and Emmett John Hughes from 1956 to 1963. A poll by Arthur M. Schlesinger in 1962 and a much larger one conducted by Gary M. Maranell in 1968 revealed that historians ranked Eisenhower in a low position among American presidents, far below the great and near great.

Several themes characterized this interpretation of the president from Abiline. His critics in and out of the historical profession portrayed him as a man who neither dominated nor controlled his own administration and its policies. Instead, people such as John Foster Dulles ran things, often badly. Moreover, the president had little understanding or liking for his job, was weak and passive rather than energetic, muddled rather than intelligent. Dulles, a pious dogmatist, damaged U.S. relations with other nations and nearly precipitated World War III; the administration's fiscal and military policies weakened the United States. Although Eisenhower, in spite of his close ties with corporate executives and conservative Republicans, did preserve the New Deal and Containment, the domestic and international programs of Democratic administrations, he failed to take advantage of his popularity, supply needed innovations, and define and act on problems. Instead, he left them for solution by his more intelligent and energetic successor.

Before the end of the 1960s, however, a new view began to take shape and gain support. It emerged first outside the historical profession in essays by Murray Kempton, Gary Wills, and Richard Rhodes from 1967 to 1970. It moved into historical scholarship in 1972, chiefly in a large work by Herbert S. Parmet, and advanced in that world over the next several years in essays and books by Barton J. Bernstein, Blanche Wiesen Cook, Gary W. Reichard, and Charles C. Alexander. By the early 1980s, Richard H. Immerman, Douglas Kinnard, Allen Yarnell, Elmo Richardson, and R. Alton Lee had made various contributions to what was by then called "Eisenhower Revisionism." It reached a high point in works by Robert Divine, Fred I. Greenstein, and Stephen Ambrose, published from 1981 to 1984. Since then, this revisionist movement has continued to roll forward in writings of Mary S. McAuliffe, Anna K. Nelson, Walter A. McDougall, and David Allan Mayers, among others. And such writings have had an impact on the profession as a whole, for polls in this decade indicate that Eisenhower has moved toward greatness in the eyes of many historians.

Why has the change taken place? The publication of a new round of memoirs, including ones by Arthur Larson, Arthur Krock, and Milton S. Eisenhower, made some contributions; the opening of new sources, especially the file developed by Eisenhower's personal secretary, Ann Whitman, contributed even more, doing so by revealing features of his presidency that had been hidden or unclear before. The times, however, deserve most of the credit. Vietnam, Watergate, riots, high inflation, the economic slowdown, soaring government spending, short-term presidencies, unprecedented deficits in the federal budget, and other ills of American life since 1965 provided new perspectives. Looking at Ike from those angles, many observers found much to admire.

The revisionism produced by these forces had several major features. One that links all the authors and justifies placing them in a group was the portrayal of Eisenhower as a strong, active president. The writers presented him as a person of intellectual strength with a point of view (although one they defined in varied ways), desire to push it forward, and skill in doing so. He was self-confident, a good judge of people, possessed detailed knowledge of what was going on, controlled his administration, and used his subordinates for his own purposes. Providing what Greenstein labeled "hidden hand leadership," he often concealed the ways in which he was working and frequently allowed his lieutenants to take the flak so as to preserve his prestige and strength. Although his critics often lampooned his speaking habits, revisionists insisted that he used language skillfully and was clear when he wished to be, unclear when that served his purposes.

Although not a solid bloc, many revisionists are united by admiration of the results of Eisenhower's efforts as well as his methods. Some see him as a calm, quiet contributor to the destruction of Senator Joseph R. McCarthy. Some present him as working effectively with the politicians to reshape the Republican party and preserve the New Deal. Some argue that he exerted a restraining influence on both right-wing Republicans and the "military-industrial complex," thereby avoiding both inflating prices and an escalating arms race.

Above all, the most enthusiastic revisionists, such as Divine, see Eisenhower as a man of peace. In their view, he, unlike his predecessor and his successors, was restrained, moderate, and prudent in using power and active and effective in promoting peace, his area of greatest concern. Knowing how to act in a nuclear age, he ended the Korean War, avoided military involvement on the side of the French in Vietnam, rejected "Liberation" for "Containment," and sought to end nuclear testing. Although the times offered many opportunities to go to war, he did not seize any of them, and he worked with some success to lower Cold War tensions, though doing so often pitted him against hard-line Cold Warriors in his own party, including Dulles. At the same time, the president did not back away from action when an international situation demanded it. And he treated allies with respect for he recognized that the U.S. needed their cooperation.

Although the revisionists exerted substantial influence, they did not gain a monopoly on interpretations of Eisenhower. Even some of those who contributed to the rise of the movement, such as Immerman and Cook, parted company with their associates on important points. Nearly all writers came to see Eisenhower as a strong president, at least in international affairs, but many, such as Peter Lyon in 1974, and Stephen Schlesinger, Stephen Kinzer, Thomas J. Noer, Bryce Wood, Stephen G. Rabe, George Herring, and Robert J. McMahon more recently, dislike ways in which he used his strength; at least one historian, Robert F. Burk, has reaffirmed after much research the old view of this president as weak and seriously inadequate in one major area: black civil rights.

Thus, recently opened sources now sustain antirevisionist as well as revisionist interpretations. The former, in addition to criticizing Eisenhower for giving little help to efforts to destroy racial injustices inside the United States, charge that he lacked a coherent philosophy, failed to reshape the Republican party, and tolerated "McCarthyism" in his administration, thereby damaging the State Department as well as individuals. Antirevisionists maintain that he was a vigorous Cold Warrior, threatened nuclear war more than once, and made defective disarmament proposals. While often agreeing that the president sought to avoid nuclear war, they demonstrate that he employed covert action by the Central Intelligence Agency and other parts of the government to subvert or attempt to subvert governments and reshape the world. He did so in Iran, Guatemala, Vietnam, Indonesia, Egypt, Laos, Eastern Europe, Cuba, and the Congo.

Just as antirevisionists portray Eisenhower as weak on race relations at home, they object to his roles in the Third World. They maintain that he made the United States the foe of revolution in Southeast Asia, brought the Cold War to South Asia, failed to appreciate the strength of and adjust to Arab nationalism, and was insensitive to and distrustful of nationalist movements in Latin America and Africa and did not deal successfully with them. By failing to give enough attention to Eisenhower's failures in the Third World, the revisionists have presented, Robert McMahon argues, "a distorted and oversimplified view of American foreign relations during a critical eight-year period."[2]

There is significant disagreement among the antirevisionists. It concerns the sources of Eisenhower's actions. Some, such as Lyon, Schlesinger, Kinzer, and Cook, see him as a captive of big business, seeking to serve its interests, such as the interest of United Fruit in Guatemala. Others, Immerman, for one, emphasize ideology, presenting the president as dominated by anticommunism.

Out of the clash of points of view and the industrious exploration of the sources, a complex portrait of Eisenhower is taking form. The early book by Alexander, more recent articles by Thomas F. Soapes and Robert Griffith, monographs by Burton I. Kaufman and H. W. Brands, Jr., and a biography by Burk paint the man as complex and not easily appraised. Ambrose, in his biography of 1983–1984 and also his 1981 book with Immerman, on Eisenhower's use of "spies," makes an especially strong effort to strike a balance.

Although Eisenhower historiography is still in an early stage, some matters do appear settled, and the biggest problems seem defined. Clearly, Eisenhower was an important president—an active rather than a passive one. He was also a man of several parts who was working in a complex period and engaging in varied activities. Scholars now face the difficult tasks of weighing the different sides of his presidency. How important was each? What deserves the most weight? Should we stress his avoidance of war or his promotion of covert activities? Should we emphasize his efforts to re-

duce conflicts with the Soviet Union or his Cold Warriorism and his relations with Third World nationalisms?

The new volume by Hewlett and Holl taps the recent writing on
Eisenhower and adds to our understanding of his presidency. The citations,
and also the good essay on sources by Roger M. Anders, indicate that the
authors and their team found the revisionists especially helpful. Thus, this
work cites Parmet, *Eisenhower and the American Crusades* (1972) and Ambrose, *Eisenhower: The President* (1984), with Anders defining the first
as "a well-balanced, detailed study of Eisenhower's first administration
but . . . much less thorough on the second" and pointing out the harmony
between Ambrose and Hewlett and Holl in interpreting the president.
Hewlett and Holl also draw upon Divine, including *Eisenhower and the
Cold War* (1981), "an excellent study, although limited to specific topics,"
according to Anders, as well as *Blowing in the Wind: The Nuclear Test Ban
Debate* (1978), which the essay on sources labels the best single-volume
study of the fallout controversy.

Although the revisionists provided more help than the antirevisionists, Hewlett and Holl are not uncritical in using any of their predecessors
and depend chiefly on primary materials. Like other recent works, this one
draws significantly on the now rich resources of the Eisenhower Library,
especially the Whitman file, and also rests upon other sources, including
congressional materials and records of the Department of State, the Federal
Bureau of Investigation, and, above all, the Atomic Energy Commission.
Even though some sources cannot yet be seen by historians, even ones with
the privileges that Hewlett and Holl enjoyed, the massive quantity of materials available for substantial topics in recent history provides a rationale,
as Anders points out, for team research.

This book on the Atomic Energy Commission is not a narrow history
of a government agency. Dealing with the AEC during the period when
issues concerning nuclear weapons and nuclear power emerged as large
public concerns, the volume ranges well beyond the commission. Much of
the work deals with Eisenhower. Although not uncritical, the authors find
much to admire in him.

Hewlett and Holl offer support for the conception of Eisenhower as
a strong, active president, determined to supply leadership. Subordinates,
such as Dulles, Lewis Strauss, and John McCone, did not dominate him.
Instead, he exerted a powerful influence on them, bringing them around to
his point of view or restraining, even frustrating them. He concealed his
"withering temper" from the public but not from his aides. He kept in
touch with developments, considered programs thoughtfully, searched for
answers, initiated his own ideas, acted both tough and flexible, engaged
in give and take with members of his administration and with outsiders,
and battled for his convictions. He played the political game with skill,
concealing at times his motives and moves from the press and the public

as Greenstein suggested, while appealing boldly for support on other occasions.

Eisenhower was not a shadowy figure in his administration. He was prominent, easy to see, at least for those who could and can get behind the scenes. In this book, we see him playing many crucial roles. Determined to have an impact, he participated vigorously in the affairs of government in order to accomplish his purposes.

And one of his main purposes, Hewlett and Holl indicate, was peace. Here, too, as in their conception of Eisenhower as an active president, they are in harmony with the revisionists and contribute to developing the revisionist interpretation. These historians of the AEC present this president as passionately interested in and very active on behalf of peace, and their issue area, which includes the bomb, provides one of the best ways of illustrating these aspects of his presidency. Knowing little about the destructiveness of nuclear weapons before he came to office, he quickly learned what these new tools could do, was deeply troubled by what he learned, and sought from the beginning to the end of his administration to reduce the danger of nuclear war. He supplied leadership in developing and promoting a series of proposals and programs: Operation Candor, Atoms for Peace, disarmament negotiations with the Soviet Union, a worldwide ban and an American moratorium on nuclear testing. And he suffered deep disappointment over the narrow limits on his accomplishments. He avoided a nuclear war in his time, but the danger of one still existed when he left office.

The book also illustrates other sides of Eisenhower's presidency. It supplies some evidence of the influence of business leaders on him, more on his preference for private rather than government enterprise. Here, the issue was who would develop nuclear power, private corporations or public agencies. The book also offers evidence on his interest in the unification of Western Europe and the development of closer ties between that region and the United States as means to peace, prosperity, and security.

Hewlett and Holl lend some support to antirevisionist themes. The book illustrates Eisenhower's difficulties in reshaping the Republican party as an instrument of internationalism, and, while they do not advance our knowledge of the president's relations with Senator McCarthy, the authors do show Eisenhower behaving in McCarthy-like ways. Even though he came out for Operation Candor, an effort to give the public the facts about the dangers of nuclear war, the president worried greatly about security and had a strong bias in favor of secrecy where weapons were concerned, and he played a major part in a sad story that featured the removal of J. Robert Oppenheimer's security clearance, thereby barring the physicist from further contributions to the nuclear program.

Although these authors give less attention than the antirevisionists to Eisenhower's acceptance of Cold War assumptions, they do note that he was a Cold Warrior. They see him as less of one than were some other members of his administration, including Lewis Strauss, the AEC's chairman through much of the period. Compared with some other people of importance, Eisenhower was less fearful and more willing to compromise, but he did have a quite negative view of the Soviet Union and its ambitions. Unlike some other historians, Hewlett and Holl neither challenge that view nor argue that it was the key to the president's failures as a champion of peace. They merely point out that his concern about Soviet military strength did hamper his efforts to end the arms race.

Eisenhower's relations with the Third World, a topic of large significance according to some recent writers on his presidency, are largely beyond the scope of this book, yet it does touch upon the subject and, in doing so, does not challenge the antirevisionists. Hewlett and Holl have no need to discuss covert activities, but they do call attention to the Europe-first orientation of Eisenhower's Atoms-for-Peace program. Also, they note the importance for the nuclear enterprises of the United States and its European allies of uranium deposits in such places as the Belgian Congo and South Africa. And they point out that one motive for promoting nuclear power in Western Europe, a major part of Atoms for Peace, was a desire to reduce the region's dependence on the oil of Third World countries.

Thus, the volume contributes many points to our understanding of the Eisenhower presidency. Also, by the way in which it is written, the book challenges critics of official history. Note the willingness to report negative as well as positive sides of the agency's record. See, for good examples, the discussion of the Oppenheimer affair and especially the conclusion reached. See the discussions of radiation, of the conflict between arms control and Atoms for Peace, of the AEC's efforts to develop nuclear power, and of the agency's critics, such as Senator Clinton Anderson. Note the penetrating essays on personalities, such as the comparison of Strauss and McCone in Chapter 18. Above all, consider what is written about the agency and disarmament. In this and other parts of the book, the authors give their readers, including other scholars, the evidence and arguments required to form opinions of their own. By doing so, the book establishes bases for new advances on the Eisenhower frontier.

Richard S. Kirkendall

# *PREFACE*

This book begins with a surreptitious briefing of Dwight D. Eisenhower on the status of nuclear technology in the United States a few days after his election as President in 1952. So secret was the occasion that only Eisenhower himself and two government officials knew at the time that the meeting had taken place, much less what was revealed. Some of the information conveyed was considered too sensitive to be committed to paper, and the official who spoke with the President-elect destroyed all his notes as soon as he left the room.

The book ends in autumn 1960, just eight years later, as Eisenhower was completing his second term. By that time he had become a central figure in a growing national and international debate on the terrifying issues that could lead to nuclear war or world peace. The place of nuclear power in the world economy and in military strategy was no longer the concern of a few thousand scientists, engineers, and government officials living in secret conclaves sealed off from the rest of the world by elaborate security barriers. Nuclear technology had now become a part of the political, the economic, and even the social fabric of the United States and the industrialized nations of the West.

How this remarkable change occurred in less than a decade is a question that historians have only begun to probe, and when they do they will find it a subject of extraordinary complexity and interest. As one would expect, some aspects of the emergence of nuclear technology are recorded in the conventional records of national and international politics. But for an adequate understanding of the subject, historians must also dig into complex issues of economic policy, including the role of national governments and private industry in developing nuclear and conventional power sources, the changing prospects of economic use of nuclear power in different parts of the world, and the impact of technological development on these prospects.

Another area of critical importance is the perceived impact of nuclear technology on military strategy and tactics, on national defense systems, and ultimately on national security itself. Related to these military issues are such difficult questions as the consequences of testing nuclear weapons and the potential impact of nuclear warfare, not just on the structures of national governments but also on biological systems on which human existence depends. Even more difficult to assess are the subtle, long-term social and psychological effects of the nuclear threat.

We touch upon all these themes in greater or lesser degree in this book, and we make no pretense that all of them have been either adequately introduced or fully explored. Rather this volume should stand among the first of many that will need to be written before historians can presume to understand the full implications of the evolution of nuclear technology. As an initial study, this book focuses upon the role of the United States government in this evolution. Other nations, of course, have had a critical part in this development, but as the first nation to use nuclear power for military purposes and as a world leader in applying this energy source to civilian uses, the United States is a reasonable place to start. Moreover, we have not attempted to follow the evolution of nuclear technology in other countries, except to view that development from the American perspective.

In our research we soon concluded that even the American story was too big to compress within the pages of a single volume. We also saw that in some instances the problems of obtaining adequate documentation for the whole story were insurmountable so soon after the events we were attempting to describe. It was obvious that a fully balanced account of the effort to build a nuclear industry in the United States would have to include the activities of many corporations and industrial leaders as well as those of elected officials and government administrators. But for many reasons the records documenting the role of private industry are not now available to historians and probably will not be for many years. Therefore, we describe events only from the government perspective.

We also made a conscious decision not to enter the vast and arcane world of delivery systems for nuclear weapons, which involve technologies far different from those associated with nuclear warheads themselves. To follow the tortuous evolution and proliferation of delivery systems and their relation to military organization and doctrine would have required another volume at least as long as this one.

Thus, we chose to write this book primarily from the perspective of the United States Atomic Energy Commission, the federal agency established in 1946 with unprecedented authority that gave it a virtual monopoly over all aspects of the development of nuclear technology for both military and peaceful purposes. The history of the Commission before the Eisenhower years has already been addressed in two earlier volumes: *The New World, 1939–1946*, published in 1962, and *Atomic Shield, 1947–1952*, published in 1969. As a third volume in the series, *Atoms for Peace and War* carries forward the story from the end of the second volume but with a somewhat different approach and emphasis. The earlier volumes were written as institutional histories and included chapters on organization and management. Now that the Commission no longer exists, it seems more useful to focus on its role in formulating domestic and international policy in the nuclear field, particularly the Commission's relationships with the Eisenhower White House, than to probe the agency's internal structure.

Practical considerations also influenced our decision to take this new course. Most obvious, all the Commission's official files were placed under our control as official historians of the Commission and its successor agencies. Thus, we had not only free access to the records but also responsibility for organizing and maintaining the large collection of policy documents that make up the Commission's archives.

Because we were among the first historians with security clearance to seek access to the large and rich collection of classified files in the Eisenhower Presidential Library, we were among the few able to use these records before they were closed to research. Access to the detailed summaries of meetings of the National Security Council and to the President's classified correspondence made it possible to examine policy issues for both Eisenhower's and the Commission's perspectives and thus to gain an insight into the decision process that offered an exceptional opportunity for contemporary historians. As government historians we were also given full access to classified nuclear policy records held by the Department of State. This privilege enabled us often to add a third perspective to our analysis of White House meetings on international affairs.

Thus, in exploring the evolution of nuclear technology during the Eisenhower Administration we have built our narrative around the activities of the successive chairmen of the Atomic Energy Commission and their fellow commissioners as they strove to resolve the perplexing issues that confronted them during these critical years. Never far from the scene, however, were the President's senior advisers and Eisenhower himself. Indeed, looking back on what we have written, we can only conclude that Eisenhower dominated the formulation of nuclear policy in a way that no other President has before or since. In essence, then, this book records the actions of the President and the Commissioners with only enough technical and administrative detail to keep policy considerations in context.

The opening chapter, which describes the first two secret briefings of the President-elect, not only explains what Eisenhower learned about the new technology but also gives the reader the background needed to follow the narrative. Chapter 2 recounts how Eisenhower reacted to this information, how he recognized the unprecedented threat to national security posed

xxi

by nuclear weapons, especially the hydrogen bomb, and how he began to give high priority to reformulating both domestic and foreign policy as a response to this threat.

In Chapter 3 we follow the President's long and frustrating search for a new approach to the nuclear dilemma, beginning with hopes for Operation *Candor* early in 1953 and ending with his historic address on Atoms for Peace before the United Nations General Assembly at the end of the year.

Growing out of the bitter controversies emerging from efforts to understand the significance of the bomb in 1953 was the agonizing chain of events that ultimately resulted in revoking the security clearance of J. Robert Oppenheimer, one of the nation's most distinguished and influential advisers on nuclear policy. In Chapter 4 we describe in detail for the first time the actions taken by the President, members of his cabinet, the Commission under Chairman Lewis L. Strauss, and J. Edgar Hoover of the Federal Bureau of Investigation in this tragedy. The Oppenheimer case marked the beginning of a new chapter in the Commission's history and in the process revealed to the public more about the life-and-death issues of the nuclear era than Operation *Candor* ever could have done.

Chapter 5 describes the efforts of the Administration, the Commission, and the Congress to revise the Atomic Energy Act of 1946, a process that raised serious questions about the role of the federal government in developing nuclear energy as an electric power source and the degree to which the Commission would be permitted to cooperate with other nations in promoting the President's Atoms-for-Peace proposal. The new Atomic Energy Act of 1954 provides the statutory basis for the rest of the volume.

In Chapter 6 the narrative moves away from the nation's capital to describe the growing sophistication and destructive capability of testing nuclear weapons, culminating in the Pacific test on March 1, 1954, that forced a sweeping reassessment of the implications of nuclear warfare. The chapter also includes an overview of the Commission's nationwide complex of mills, laboratories, and production plants built to transform uranium ore and other special materials into nuclear weapons.

Chapter 7 examines the Commission's plans to build experimental nuclear reactors for generating electric power and its attempts to encourage private industry to take part. The power demonstration reactor program is explained in the context of the growing policy debate between a Republican Administration and a Democratic Congress over the government's role in promoting nuclear technology.

Chapter 8 returns to the President's Atoms-for-Peace speech in December 1953 and follows the initial proposals by the Commission and the Department of State for realizing Eisenhower's dream. Eisenhower, Commission Chairman Lewis L. Strauss, and Secretary of State John Foster Dulles are the leading characters in this drama. The scene shifts from

Washington to Geneva and back to the United Nations in New York as Western scientists and diplomats seek a workable formula for international cooperation, with or without the Soviet Union.

Caught up in the worldwide enthusiasm over the peaceful atom, the Commission in 1955 tried to concentrate its resources on projects that appeared feasible in light of existing technology. Fending off proposals from both the Administration and the Congress for full-scale development of nuclear power reactors, the Commission opted for more modest, long-term projects involving power reactor experiments, research in high-energy physics, preliminary studies of controlled thermonuclear reactions, and research on the biological effects of radiation. These activities are described in Chapter 9.

The staggering dimensions of the thermonuclear test in the Pacific on March 1, 1954, both in terms of destructive power and radioactive fallout, required a full-scale reassessment of nuclear weapon strategy and the hazards of nuclear testing. Chapter 10 traces initial attempts to comprehend the implications of the test within the Administration and then the Commission's efforts to translate technical data into information the public could understand. Before the end of 1955, fallout had become a national and then an international issue on which the Great Debate of future years would be based.

The Atoms-for-Peace plan posed an intractable dilemma: the need to safeguard technical information on nuclear weapons against dissemination to unfriendly nations and the President's desire to promote the use of nuclear technology for peaceful purposes. Chapter 11 follows the evolution of Administration policy to resolve the dilemma and the impact of the proposed International Atomic Energy Agency and the EURATOM plan on this policy.

By late 1955 the Eisenhower Administration was facing a wide range of perplexing issues related to both the domestic and international aspects of nuclear policy, and under the threat of increasing fallout from testing and the power of the hydrogen bomb these were becoming issues of great public concern. During the first half of 1956, as described in Chapter 12, the President pushed both Strauss and Dulles to respond to this growing concern with practical proposals for limiting or banning nuclear tests. At the same time, Strauss and the Administration beat back attempts by the Democratic Congress to launch a massive federal program to build full-scale nuclear power plants.

Nuclear technology became a significant issue in presidential politics for the first time in the 1956 election. Building on Chapter 12, Chapter 13 shows how the H-bomb became an issue in the campaign and how Eisenhower used it to his own advantage.

After the 1956 election the President returned to his quest for an end to the nuclear arms race. Chapter 14 recounts both the activities of

Harold E. Stassen, the President's adviser on disarmament, in drafting a plan and the objections raised by Strauss and Dulles.

Building on the mandate that he saw in the President's reelection victory, Strauss launched out boldly in 1957 to entice private industry into building and operating nuclear power plants. A part of this strategy was creating a market for American power reactors in Europe through the EURATOM plan. As Chapter 15 reveals, the prospects for nuclear power had already begun to fade in the face of economic realities. By the end of the year Strauss stood almost alone in his dogmatic fight for a private power industry.

By 1957 the International Agency and EURATOM had become key elements in Eisenhower's grand plan to use nuclear technology to forge strong economic bonds with Europe and to provide markets for American reactors abroad. Chapter 16 examines the conflicts that the Commission and the State Department encountered in promoting these organizations as they tried to reconcile requirements for adequate safeguards with the President's plan, heralded in the United States' impressive demonstration of technical achievement at the second international conference on the peaceful uses of atomic energy in Geneva in 1958.

Chapter 17 describes the growing public opposition to nuclear testing both in the United States and abroad in 1957 and early 1958. As Eisenhower continued to press for a test ban and a flood of publications sensationalized the health hazards of fallout, Strauss and the Commission justified further testing as a means of developing a "clean" weapon. International pressure for a test ban reached new heights in the United Nations in September 1957, and the shocking news of *Sputnik* the following month brought into positions of influence a new group of scientists with a new approach to a test ban. By the time Strauss left the Commission in June 1958, the President was considering a proposal to ban atmospheric testing.

With the appointment of John A. McCone as Strauss's successor in July 1958, the Commission began to take a more realistic and less dogmatic approach to the development of nuclear power. Chapter 18 shows how McCone worked with both the Congress and representatives of industry to develop a new set of priorities. McCone's efforts brought into public debate for the first time some of the practical problems facing nuclear power development.

During the last three years of the Eisenhower Administration the Commission supported a broad range of projects to develop nuclear propulsion systems for aircraft, rockets, and submarines and auxiliary power systems for satellites. On the civilian side, the Commission continued to finance basic research in high-energy physics, controlled fusion, and peaceful uses of nuclear explosives. As Chapter 19 shows, McCone tempered support for these projects with hard-headed appraisals of their cost and effectiveness. The chapter also relates his personal efforts to broaden the exchange of scientific and technical information with the Soviet Union.

Chapter 20 describes Eisenhower's final attempts to end the nuclear arms race, culminating in his decision in 1958 to announce a unilateral moratorium on nuclear testing and his continuing support of negotiations with the Soviet Union until the end of his term in 1961.

Although most documentation for this book has been declassified, some narrative covering significant policy issues rests on classified materials cited in the notes but unavailable to the public. Because we have had free access to records regardless of their classification, we can be confident that our interpretations are based on all the sources available to us. At the same time, we have not always been able to present all the relevant facts, particularly on issues related to nuclear weapon technology, testing, and test-ban negotiations. In a few instances, we have had to delete material considered diplomatically sensitive in our description of negotiations with the United Kingdom. We regret that we cannot point out where these deficiencies occur, but we can assure our readers that we have tried to convey the essential truth, if not all the details upon which it rests. As we suggested at the beginning of this preface, this book represents more the first than the last word on a subject of major significance in the recent history of the United States. We trust that in time other historians and scholars will ferret out the remaining details and examine other aspects of the subject.

xxv

Richard G. Hewlett
Jack M. Holl
Germantown, Maryland

# ACKNOWLEDGEMENTS

For eighteen years, until the agency was abolished in 1975, the Atomic Energy Commission supported this history project, which has resulted, along with other publications, in the three books published in this series. During those years all the Commissioners and senior staff provided the support and encouragement needed to accomplish this task. We owe a special debt of gratitude to Woodford B. McCool, who served as Secretary of the Commission from 1956 until 1973; he took the initiative to establish the history program and provided the resources and the staff that made the first two volumes possible. His successor, Paul Bender, continued that support during the early research for this book. From Velma E. Lockhart, who for more than twenty-five years maintained the Commissioners' official files, we inherited the primary source material for this book. Each Commission chairman—Lewis Strauss, John McCone, Glenn T. Seaborg, and James R. Schlesinger—personally supported the history project. Dixy Lee Ray, chairman during the Commission's final years, also took a personal interest in the historians and helped us to gain control of the historical records that now constitute a large part of the Department of Energy's archives.

While the project was a part of the Energy Research and Development Administration, we received continued support from Robert C. Seamans, Jr., the administrator; Robert W. Fri, his deputy; and Sam Hale, special assistant to the administrator. They made it possible not only to continue research for this book but also to collect historical records on a variety of energy projects. Jack King and Robert Newlin, successive directors of public affairs, provided program support that enabled us to accept new responsibilities beyond the work of writing this book.

When the Department of Energy was created in 1977, the history program was assigned to the Department's executive secretariat. Since then, each Secretary of Energy, including James R. Schlesinger, Charles W. Duncan, Jr., James B. Edwards, Donald Paul Hodel, and John S. Herrington, has maintained the history program. Helping us to find a place in the new department were Raymond Walters, Frank R. Pagnotta, Christina L. Rathkopf, Gene K. Fleming, and Carole J. Gorry. In the midst of a sweeping reorganization in 1981, William S. Heffelfinger, director of administration, rescued the project from lassitude and placed it once again in the executive secretariat under the strong leadership of William V. Vitale. A protégé of W. B. McCool in the Atomic Energy Commission, Vitale has not only fostered and defended the history program but has also helped shape its larger mission and goals. Lawrence F. Davenport, assistant secretary for management and administration, and Harry L. Peebles, director of administration, have continued Heffelfinger's support. Other Department of Energy officials who have been especially encouraging include W. Kenneth Davis, John F. Bagley, John A. Griffin, Robert T. Duff, Jill Ellman Lytle, Roy G. Boger, Jr., and Thomas F. Cornwell.

xxviii

No government historian can complete a large research project without the assistance of numerous fellow workers. Lester Koogle, Denise Diggin, Dave Farace, Jim Kelly, Eric McDonnell, Paul Landau, Thomas J. Murray, and Hannah King helped us with library reference and interlibrary loans. Cathy Hutzell, Annette Black, Arthur Ballou, and Robert Kelbaugh assisted us in gaining access to agency records, while Richard Peabody, Louis Hicks, and Jack Schneider provided guidance to photo collections. I. L. Cucchiara, Lenard Safranski, Doug Hughes, Leo Sullivan, Charles Reichardt, and Charles Knesel helped us with classification problems. Robert Tharp provided important advice on security matters.

We received help from the Department's field offices and national laboratories as well. Because we focused more on President Eisenhower's nuclear policies than on the Commission's technical programs, we used field and laboratory records less than in previous volumes, but they still proved invaluable. David A. Heimback, Gilbert Ortiz, Walter Bramlett, and Anthony Riveria at Los Alamos National Laboratory, Floyd Beets and William Hatmaker at Oak Ridge National Laboratory, Dennis DeFord at the Department's Richland Operations Office, and E. Newman Pettitt at Argonne National Laboratory aided us in finding pertinent records and locating former officials.

Except for the Commission's records, our most extensive research was conducted at the Dwight D. Eisenhower Presidential Library in Abilene, Kansas. James P. Leyerzapf, assistant director for archival services, coordinated our access to records and made special arrangements that speeded the course of our research. We also appreciated the help of David Haight, Hazel Stroda, and other members of the library staff.

At the Herbert Hoover Presidential Library in West Branch, Iowa, Director Robert S. Wood and Archivist Dwight Miller efficiently met our research needs. At the National Archives in Washington, D.C., we received invaluable assistance from Edward J. Reese in modern military records. George Hobart in prints and photographs at the Library of Congress helped us in our search for photographs. We are also grateful for the help provided by the Princeton University Libraries professional staff and the Columbia University Oral History Project. Before his retirement from the State Department, Wilmer Sparrow provided essential documentation.

As part of a government economy measure, our volunteer historical advisory committee was abolished in 1977. Fortunately, before its demise, this group of distinguished historians and other scholars helped us lay a solid foundation for our research and reviewed several early chapters in draft form. We are grateful to Alfred D. Chandler, Jr., Harvard University; Thomas P. Cochran and Thomas P. Hughes, University of Pennsylvania; Richard S. Kirkendall, Iowa State University; Richard W. Leopold, Northwestern University; Nancy J. Weiss, Princeton University; Davis T. Stanley, then at the Brookings Institution; and the late Shields Warren, New England Deaconess Hospital, for their brief but helpful service.

Our greatest debt is to the professionals and staff of the History Division who have worked with us on this project. Roger M. Anders and Alice L. Buck served as research assistants, editors, critics, and even drafted portions of the manuscript, including all the work on the appendices and illustrations. Mrs. Buck's skillful management of production details and Mr. Anders's incomparable knowledge of the Commissioner's records were indispensable to our success. Terrence Fehner spent long hours editing the manuscript and footnotes and offered valuable suggestions for improving style. Prentice Dean and Travis Hulsey also provided valuable research assistance from time to time. As she had done on previous volumes, Betty J. Wise typed the earliest draft chapters. Later Sheila Convis assumed both typing and word processing support for the project. As the book manuscript neared completion, Jeannie Raines, Pauline Robarge, Marian Scroger, and Joyce Forrest typed various draft chapters and assisted with preparation of the manuscript for publication. We cannot express sufficient gratitude to the History Division team who worked skillfully and loyally to produce this book.

Finally, we wish to acknowledge the generous help provided by Richard S. Kirkendall, Iowa State University; Gerald F. Tape, former Atomic Energy Commissioner; and George T. Mazuzan, chief historian at the Nuclear Regulatory Commission, who read the entire manuscript in final form and offered their criticisms and suggestions for improving the text. As with all our advisers, they are not responsible for the errors or flawed interpretations that may appear in the text, but their efforts have made this a better book.

xxix

## CHAPTER 1

# A SECRET
# MISSION

It was almost nine o'clock on a rainy November morning in 1952. Remnants of a heavy ground fog still clung to the sodden terrain of the Augusta National Golf Club in Georgia. Two men in the rear seat of a nondescript sedan watched anxiously as the driver felt his way over the narrow road to the clubhouse. The fog might have seemed a convenient cover for what was a highly secret mission, but in fact it had almost prevented the travelers from making their appointment. As the car stopped at the clubhouse entrance, the two men hurried inside. After a brief conversation one of them was given a seat in the manager's office, a small room on the ground floor. He was Roy B. Snapp, the Secretary of the United States Atomic Energy Commission. His mission was to brief General of the Armies Dwight D. Eisenhower, who seven days earlier had been elected President of the United States.

Snapp was a natural choice for this delicate assignment. As Secretary of the Commission he was privy to the most closely held secrets of the nation's atomic energy program, those sensitive and sometimes extraordinary bits of information that were reserved for the five Commissioners themselves. As a naval officer in World War II, Snapp had been deeply involved in military intelligence and planning when he served with the secretariat of the Joint Chiefs of Staff. At the end of the war he was special adviser to Brigadier General Leslie R. Groves, who had spearheaded development of the atomic bomb in the Manhattan Project. He had organized the Commission's secretariat in 1947 and was also serving as liaison officer with the National Security Council.[1]

While waiting for the President-elect to arrive, Snapp had an opportunity to compose himself after the harried flight from Washington. The heavy fog had sent the small commercial airliner on a circuitous route, which terminated in Columbia, South Carolina, rather than Augusta. Fortunately Bryan F. LaPlante, the director of the Commission's Washington security operations, had accompanied him and was able to keep in touch with the Commission's Savannah River Operations Office near Augusta. Prompt dispatch of a government car had made it possible for Snapp to keep his nine o'clock appointment with Eisenhower. He also had time to reflect on the incongruity of the situation: a meeting with the future President in this small unpretentious office with carefree golfers on vacation chattering and joking just outside the two open doors leading to the room.

A few minutes later Snapp heard familiar voices in the hall outside. Suddenly he realized that he had a pistol under his jacket for safeguarding a top secret document he was carrying. He leaned around the doorpost at the rear of the office and alerted the Secret Service agent. By the time the agent had reassured him that "we're all carrying guns," Eisenhower was in the room. He recognized Snapp from his visits to the Joint Chiefs' headquarters in Washington. As Eisenhower took a chair at the manager's desk, Snapp seated himself at the general's elbow.

Before Snapp could open the double envelopes containing his top secret message, Eisenhower launched into a discussion of atomic energy.[2] The President-elect said he had been talking with Charles A. Thomas, president of Monsanto Chemical Company, who had suggested that private industry build nuclear reactors that would produce both electric power for commercial purposes and plutonium for weapons.[3] As a well-known industrialist with a firsthand knowledge of nuclear technology, Thomas could command attention within both the new administration and American industry. Now, six years after the Commission had assumed responsibility for the nation's atomic energy program, industry was becoming restive over the delay in realizing the commercial application of nuclear power. While most of the nation was preoccupied with the election campaigns during autumn 1952, a clamor for a greater role in the development of atomic energy was rising among power equipment manufacturers and the electric utility industry.

Eisenhower quizzed Snapp on the feasibility of Thomas's proposal for a dual-purpose reactor. Completely unprepared for this line of questioning, Snapp had heard enough about the idea during the preceding year to assure Eisenhower that the Commission had considered Thomas's suggestion. In large part, the feasibility of dual-purpose reactors depended upon whether the military services increased their requirements for nuclear weapons. Without going into details, Snapp reminded the general that the Commission's existing production complex, plus the very large additions then under construction, would provide a truly impressive capacity. Only in recent months, when this larger capacity was nearing reality, had a dual-purpose reactor become feasible in a technical sense.

At this point the general philosophized a bit, declaring his approach to government in economic matters allowed private industry to do as much as it could. Snapp assured him that the Commission expected private industry to take the lead in developing civilian nuclear power. The Commission, in Snapp's opinion, was already vigorously pursuing the development of nuclear reactors for a variety of purposes. Work was well advanced on nuclear propulsion systems for submarines and naval ships. Snapp also pointed out that many of the nation's largest corporations, including du Pont, General Electric, Union Carbide, and Westinghouse, were engaged in operating production facilities and laboratories for the Commission. Snapp wanted to remind Eisenhower that under the Atomic Energy Act of 1946 the Commission was still required to maintain ownership over all nuclear facilities and fissionable material used to fuel reactors. Unless the law were changed, it would be difficult for industry to have a major role in nuclear development.

By this time, however, Eisenhower's mind was moving in other directions. He was reading the top secret memorandum that had required the special security precautions LaPlante had arranged for the mission.[4] The memorandum from Gordon E. Dean, the chairman of the Commission, related the extraordinary developments that had occurred during the nuclear weapon tests then being conducted by the Commission and the military services at the Enewetak[5] proving grounds in the Pacific. So awesome was the information that President Truman had asked Dean to convey the news at once to Eisenhower. "The significant event to date," Dean wrote, "is that we have detonated the first full-scale thermonuclear device," which for security reasons the Commission referred to as *Mike*. Snapp predicted that the United States would not have a deliverable thermonuclear weapon for at least a year. When Eisenhower asked why, Snapp explained in deliberately oversimplified terms that *Mike* had been designed as a scientific experiment to determine whether heavy isotopes of hydrogen could be "burned" in the fusion process. The experiment required a large device, many times bulkier and heavier than could be carried in a bomber, plus extensive associated equipment.

What made *Mike* exceptional was the awesome power of the fusion reaction. Scientists at Enewetak estimated the blast as equivalent to more than ten million tons of TNT, or five hundred times the power of the fission weapon that devastated Hiroshima. "The island of the Atoll," Dean wrote, "which was used for the shot—Elugelab—is missing, and where it was there is now an underwater crater of some 1,500 yards in diameter."

Eisenhower paused to contemplate the significance of these gruesome statistics. He was troubled about the growing power of the nuclear weapons being added to the American arsenal. He favored scientific research and understood the scientists' interests in developing more powerful and efficient weapons, but he thought there was no need "for us to build enough destructive power to destroy everything." "Complete destruction,"

3

he said somewhat enigmatically, "was the negation of peace." Certainly the United States needed enough force to counteract the Soviet threat, but he neither feared the Russians nor thought this kind of fear should influence American foreign policy.

As Eisenhower read on, he paused occasionally to ask Snapp for an explanation of a technical term. He was reassured to learn that the Commission had so far released no information about *Mike.* In fact, the weather had cooperated by keeping the remnants of the mushroom cloud over the Pacific for seven days, thus making it difficult for the Soviet Union to obtain samples and determine the nature of the explosion. Some information about the test, however, would inevitably leak out, if only because of the size of the detonation and the brightness of the flash, visible for several hundred miles. The large number of military personnel and scientists involved in the *Mike* operation would also result in some leakage of information about the test. There had already been a speculative story reported in Los Angeles to the effect that the United States had detonated a hydrogen bomb. The Commission had decided, however, to issue no statement about the test until the entire series was completed. Then the Commission would release only the cryptic words used after the 1951 series: "the test program included experiments contributing to thermonuclear weapons research."[6]

This proposal disturbed Eisenhower. He saw no reason to tell the Russians anything about the tests. Only when Snapp had assured him that the statement would be exactly the same as that used in the past did Eisenhower relent. Then in a reflective way he added that one of the greatest problems in the military services was that they all wanted to publicize their accomplishments. He thought it was a crime that air space reservation maps for the Commission's Hanford plant and other installations had been issued to the public.

The last portion of Dean's letter informed Eisenhower that the Commission had prepared a top secret report describing the stockpile of nuclear weapons, the organization and operation of the agency, relationships with the President, the Department of Defense, and the Congress, and a summary of current problems facing the Commission. Eisenhower expressed a strong interest in this information, but he observed that he would have no place to store classified material until he set up his office in the White House. In place of the written report he suggested a briefing by the Commissioners, preferably in New York because it would be "very awkward" for him to be in Washington before the inauguration. When Snapp assured him that the Commissioners would be glad to go to New York, Eisenhower called his secretary and scheduled a two-hour meeting for the morning of November 20 at his temporary headquarters in the Commodore Hotel.

Snapp had completed his mission, but the relaxed President-elect had still more questions about the Commission's facilities. Snapp described the complex production chain from uranium ore to finished metal. The expansion program, Snapp stressed, was a truly ambitious commitment on the Commission's part, one that did involve some risk. The Commission at that time had assured supplies of uranium ore sufficient to satisfy only half the capacity of the production chain when the expansion program was completed.[7]

Eisenhower was obviously pleased, observing that he had always had high regard for the Commission. He thought the present Commission under Gordon Dean was doing an excellent job, and he looked forward to the meeting in New York. The Commission's program involved some of the most difficult and far-reaching issues facing the new administration, and Eisenhower intended to give it high priority. His interest in the Thomas proposal showed that he recognized the peaceful potential of nuclear power. Although he accepted the key role of nuclear weapons in national defense, he did not overlook the enormous dangers that the existence of the nuclear stockpile posed. From Snapp's comments about the size of the Commission's budget and the growth of the stockpile, Eisenhower detected the fact that nuclear weapons were relatively cheap and getting cheaper. He expressed to Snapp his concern that some junior officer might decide that they could be used like other weapons. To Snapp such a statement carried special weight when it came from one of Eisenhower's background.

The first thing Snapp did after the meeting was to burn the top secret document. On the plane back to Washington he tried to jot down the details of the conversation. Immediately after his return he would have to report to the Commissioners and begin preparations for the briefing in New York on the following Wednesday.

Dean was encouraged by Eisenhower's reaction to his letter. He understood how important it was for the President-elect to understand the Commission's activities and especially its role in policy formulation. Dean had cut his teeth as a Commissioner on the painful decisions that followed the detonation of the first Soviet nuclear device in August 1949. In formulating a response to the Soviet challenge Dean had demonstrated his ability for clear thinking and independent action. Although a majority of his colleagues opposed accelerating development of a thermonuclear weapon, Dean had concluded that the project was imperative, if regrettable. With Dean's support, forces in Congress and the Executive Branch convinced Truman to make his historic decision on January 31, 1950, to give the thermonuclear weapon top priority.[8] In addition to being a law professor, Dean had served in the criminal division of the Department of Justice during the New Deal years and as executive assistant to two Democratic attorneys general. The fact that he had been a partner in a Washington law firm with the late Senator Brien McMahon, chairman of the Joint Committee on Atomic Energy, also explained his appointment to some veterans of the Washington scene. Dean, however, had justified the confidence the President had expressed in him by appointing him chairman in summer 1950.

5

Dean had proved himself an uncommonly able administrator, one who could find his way through the snarls and snags of controversy that entangled the Commission and come up with reasonably clear policies. He could also hold his own with Cabinet officers and the President's staff. But with Republicans in control of the White House and the Congress, Dean's power was in eclipse. He expected to leave the Commission when his term expired on June 30, 1953, if not before.

In preparing for the New York meeting, Dean relied upon Snapp and Edward R. Trapnell to gather materials from the staff. Trapnell had worked in Washington as a newspaper reporter and government public information officer before World War II. He then entered the atomic energy project in 1945 as a public relations adviser to General Groves, helped to set up the Commission's public information staff in 1947, and took charge of congressional relations in 1952. With all the charm of a Virginia gentleman, Trapnell could use his excellent knowledge of the Commission to accomplish the most sensitive of missions.

Because he had heard of Eisenhower's preference for terse, graphic presentations, Trapnell elected to prepare a briefing book that would summarize the essential facts on large poster cards.[9] Early in the presentation Trapnell included a budget summary:

| Fiscal Year | Atomic Energy Commission (in billions of $) | Department of Defense (in billions of $) |
|---|---|---|
| 1951 | 2.0 | 47.8 |
| 1952 | 1.6 | 61.0 |
| 1953 | 4.1 | 52.1 |

Trapnell placed on the same display card the explosive equivalent of the nuclear stockpile as it had existed at the end of World War II, as it stood at the time of the briefing, and as it was projected for 1956 and 1966. The top secret figures supported Eisenhower's observation that nuclear weapons were relatively cheap and getting cheaper.

Other charts explained the principal features of the implosion type of fission weapon as consisting of a spherical core of fissionable material (either plutonium or uranium-235) surrounded by concentric spheres of natural uranium and high explosives. The latter consisted of shaped charges or "lenses" of different kinds of explosives so designed that the shock wave initiated on the outside of the weapon would uniformly implode the core and set off the chain reaction. A chart of the six weapon types then being produced for the stockpile revealed that the yields could be varied by changing the nuclear components. Because the recent test of the thermonuclear device was considered the most sensitive bit of information on weapon development, the chart showed only that *Mike* was twenty feet high, almost eight feet in diameter, and weighed eighty-two tons.

Another chart presented a simplified version of the vast complex of plants and laboratories that produced the stockpile: uranium mills and sampling stations, feed material plants, huge reactors for producing plutonium and tritium, and mammoth gaseous-diffusion plants for producing uranium-235. Oak Ridge fabricated the uranium parts for weapons while a new Commission facility in Colorado finished the plutonium parts and assembled the nuclear cores for weapons then in the stockpile.

The nonnuclear components were produced by contractors and suppliers too numerous to mention in the Eisenhower briefing. But Trapnell's chart did include several plants: Burlington, Iowa, and Amarillo, Texas, produced the shaped charges of high explosives; the Mound Laboratory at Miamisburg, Ohio, manufactured the high-explosive detonators and neutron initiators; and the Kansas City plant assembled most mechanical and electrical components. Overseeing the entire weapon production chain, the Los Alamos Scientific Laboratory and the Sandia Laboratory, both in New Mexico, were responsible for all research and development of nuclear and nonnuclear components, respectively. The chart did not even mention the new weapon laboratory at Livermore, California, which with Los Alamos would conduct all tests of new weapon designs at both the Pacific and Nevada sites.

For at least five years, if not from the very beginning of the Commission's existence, the production of fissionable materials and nuclear weapons for military purposes had been the primary mission. But the Commission also had broad responsibilities for generally developing nuclear science and technology and making available the results of this work for a wide range of industrial, medical, and scientific applications. A few of these applications, particularly the development of nuclear power, would contribute obviously and directly to the military and civilian objectives of the federal government. Thus, Dean asked Trapnell to give substantial attention to the Commission's reactor development efforts. The Eisenhower presentation included a photograph and diagram of the first generation of nuclear power in an experimental breeder reactor in 1951, a photograph of the land-based prototype of a nuclear-powered submarine nearing completion at the national reactor testing station in Idaho, and descriptions of several approaches to a nuclear-powered aircraft that were being studied at the Oak Ridge National Laboratory.

Dean made certain that the briefing contained a clear statement on the Commission's plans for stimulating industrial development of nuclear power. With the Commission's encouragement, four industrial teams had already completed feasibility studies of nuclear power and had submitted proposals for joint ventures with the Commission in building nuclear power

7

plants. A fifth industrial team was just then starting its own study, and other groups were interested. In addition to amending the Atomic Energy Act of 1946, the Commission faced a critical policy question in determining how the first companies having favored access to nuclear technology would be prevented from obtaining an unfair advantage over others.

Although the long-term outlook for producing economic electric power from nuclear fuel was good, the Commission made clear in the briefing materials that this goal would not be reached easily or quickly. The first practical use of electrical power would be in a submarine, where cost was not controlling. The development of submarine propulsion systems and other reactors for the military, however, would advance the technology of civilian power systems. As for the suggestion that industry build dual-purpose reactors, the Commission reiterated Snapp's judgment that feasibility of the idea would depend upon a continuing demand for nuclear weapon materials. The Commission proposed to place a much heavier investment in developing breeder reactors that would substantially improve the economics of nuclear power and the use of raw materials.

For the purposes of the Eisenhower briefing, the Commission found it more difficult to describe its basic research in the physical and biomedical sciences. The Commission saw its first responsibility in biology and medicine as safeguarding the health of atomic energy workers and the civilian population in general from the harmful effects of radiation, whether from normal Commission operations, weapon tests, or enemy attack. But beyond this, the Commission felt an obligation to exploit the beneficial uses of atomic energy in studying and treating such diseases as cancer, in improving soil management and crop yield for agriculture, in developing new varieties of useful plants, in studying growth, nutrition, and the biological functions of plants and animals, and in using radioactive tracers to study living systems. Research was performed in the Commission's Oak Ridge, Argonne, and Brookhaven national laboratories and was supported by the Commission in 250 colleges, universities, hospitals, and private research institutions.

The Commission predicated its far-reaching research efforts in the physical sciences on the assumption that scientific knowledge provided the essential foundation for future technology. A better understanding of the physical universe would stimulate more economical production processes and new scientific applications. The research process itself would enhance the nation's scientific and technical capabilities and thus contribute to national security. As these statements appeared on the briefing charts, they smacked of platitudes; but they did reflect the honest assumptions on which the Commission's physical research program rested. The Commission's six laboratories engaged in physical research employed nearly one thousand scientists using facilities costing $200 million. Fifteen hundred scientists worked on projects of interest to the Commission in ninety universities and private research institutes provided with government-owned equipment worth $4 million. The preeminence of the United States in the nuclear sciences by 1952 was almost entirely the result of the magnitude and effectiveness of Commission support.

Even this brief survey of Commission activities both in production and research made clear the exceptional diversification of resources in at least three senses. Organizationally the Commission was highly decentralized as a result of the conscious efforts of David E. Lilienthal, the first chairman, and his associates when they created the agency. The field managers of the nine operations offices exercised a large degree of independent authority and actually supervised most of the Commission's employees. Of the 6,600 employees on the Commission's rolls in November 1952, only 1,600 were stationed in Washington. Almost as many reported to the director of the Santa Fe operations office, which directed the Commission's weapon activities in the field, and more than one thousand were assigned at Oak Ridge.[10]

Diversification also took the form of geographical dispersion. Although many old-line executive departments, such as the Departments of the Army and Agriculture, had employees in all forty-eight states, few had major installations in such widely separated regions of the nation. The Army had established the pattern of dispersal during World War II in the interests of secrecy and military security. In a day before air travel had become commonplace, it was no easy task for headquarters officials to maintain effective communications and management control over the huge but remote installations in Tennessee, New Mexico, and Washington State. Since taking over the atomic energy project in 1947, the Commission, if anything, had further dispersed its activities to include key installations in Idaho, Nevada, South Carolina, Kentucky, and the atolls of the Pacific.

Another form of diversification rested upon the Commission's decision to continue the Army's policy of relying mostly upon private contractors working in government-owned facilities to perform both production and research functions. Employment figures demonstrated the extent of the Commission's reliance on contractors. Compared to the 6,600 government employees in November 1952, there were more than 137,000 contractor employees, of whom 62,000 were engaged in operational activities and 75,000 were working on construction projects. Among the contractors were some of the largest and best known corporations in the country (see Table 1).

Dean's busy schedule left him little time to review the briefing cards that Snapp and Trapnell were preparing, but he did find a few moments to dictate three pages as an introduction.[11] Dean's first concern was that the new President understand the roles that the White House, the Department of Defense, and the Commission had in determining national policy on nuclear weapons. He wanted to stress that the Commission had never at-

9

### Table 1
### Major AEC Contractors

PRODUCTION

| Contractor | Installation | Job |
|---|---|---|
| General Electric | Hanford, WA | Plutonium |
| Union Carbide and Carbon | Oak Ridge, TN<br>Paducah, KY | U-235 |
| Western Electric–Bell Lab. (AT&T) | Sandia Lab., NM | Weapons |
| Bendix Aviation | Kansas City, MO | Weapon Parts |
| Monsanto Chemical | Mound Lab., OH | Weapon Initiators |
| E. I. du Pont de Nemours | Dana, IN | Heavy Water |
| American Cyanamid | Reactor Testing Station, ID | Operate Chemical Processing Plant |
| Phillips Petroleum | Reactor Testing Station, ID | Operate Materials Testing Reactor |
| Dow Chemical | Rocky Flats, CO | Weapon Parts |

RESEARCH AND DEVELOPMENT

| Contractor | Installation | Job |
|---|---|---|
| University of California | Los Alamos Scientific Laboratory, NM | Weapons |
| | Radiation Laboratory, Berkeley, CA | Basic Research |
| Union Carbide and Carbon | Oak Ridge National Laboratory, TN | Research and Development |
| University of Chicago | Argonne National Laboratory, IL | Reactor Development |
| Associated Universities | Brookhaven National Laboratory, NY | Basic Research |
| Westinghouse Electric | Pittsburgh, PA | Reactor Development |

tempted to judge what weapon requirements should be in terms of numbers. The Joint Chiefs of Staff initiated requirements for review by the Secretary of Defense and the President. The Commission simply advised the Secretary and the President whether it would be feasible to meet the requirements in terms of dollars, manpower, and critical materials. At the same time, Dean noted, the Commission did have an important function in providing the basic weapon designs that ultimately became the source of military requirements.

In the production and allocation of special nuclear materials such as plutonium, uranium-235, and tritium, the Atomic Energy Act required

**Table 1, cont.**

**Major AEC Contractors**

*RESEARCH AND DEVELOPMENT*

| Contractor | Installation | Job |
|---|---|---|
| California Research and Development Co. (sub. of S.O. of CA) | Livermore, CA | Reactor Development |
| General Electric | Knolls Atomic Power Laboratory, NY | Reactor Development |
| Iowa State College | Ames Laboratory, IA | Metallurgy |
| University of Rochester | Rochester, NY | Biology and Medicine |

*CONSTRUCTION*

| Company | Site | Project | Estimated Cost in Millions |
|---|---|---|---|
| du Pont | Savannah River, SC | 6 Heavy Water Reactors | $ 1.5 |
| Peter Kiewit & Sons | Portsmouth, OH | U-235 Gaseous Diffusion Plants, X 25–33 | 1.3 |
| F. H. McGraw | Paducah, KY | U-235 Gaseous Diffusion Plants, C 31–37 | 922.0 |
| Maxon Construction | Oak Ridge, TN | U-235 Gaseous Diffusion Plant, K-33 | 462.0 |
|  |  | Alloy Development Plant | 35.0 |
| Henry J. Kaiser Co. | Hanford, WA | 2 Graphite Reactors | 260.0 |
| Girdler Corp. | Dana, IN | Heavy Water Plants | 104.0 |
| George A. Fuller | Fernald, OH | Feed Materials Production Center | 78.0 |
| Atkinson-Jones Construction Co. | Hanford, WA | 1 Graphite Reactor | 64.0 |
| Austin Company | Rocky Flats, CO | Weapon Facility | 45.0 |
| Bechtel Corp. | Reactor Testing Station, ID | Chemical Processing Plant | 34.0 |

a presidential determination annually. The Commission used the military requirements from the Joint Chiefs and its own estimates of how much material could be produced in drafting the determination, which was submitted jointly by the Commission and the Secretary of Defense. Although the chairman of the Commission was not a member of the National Security Council, he had served from time to time on a special committee of the council that had included the Secretaries of Defense and State. The special committee had advised the President on such important matters as the acceleration of thermonuclear weapon development in 1950 and the $3-billion expansion of production facilities approved in January 1952. Without explicitly claiming a role in policy formulation in the White House, Dean wanted to make clear that there was a precedent for Commission participation.

Dean hurried from one appointment to another on Tuesday, November 18. That evening he spoke to the Kiwanis Club in nearby Rockville, Maryland, and then took the overnight sleeper train to New York.[12] Also riding on the train were Snapp, Trapnell with the clumsy leather portfolio containing the briefing charts, and LaPlante, who served as a security escort. To avoid the possibility that someone might recognize them and guess that the entire Commission was going to New York to see Eisenhower, the Commissioners had decided to travel separately.

There was something bizarre about the members of the Atomic Energy Commission sneaking off to New York for a meeting with the President-elect. In this instance, as in Snapp's trip to Augusta, the reason lay in the Enewetak test. The Commissioners had hoped that even the simple fact that the test had occurred would be concealed from the Soviet Union, if only to avoid providing a stimulus for a similar effort in that country. At the very least, it was important to conceal the information as long as possible so that scientists in other countries would miss the fleeting opportunity to collect samples of airborne debris that would provide information about the nature of the test. But even beyond these considerations, a curious silence surrounded anything related to the hydrogen bomb. The enormous magnitude of its implications was almost too terrifying to contemplate. Even the Commissioners and those few members of the staff used to discussing the subject could not speak casually in the awesome presence of the bomb. This partially subconscious restraint, as well as the more obvious security considerations, caused the Commissioners to hope that they could meet Eisenhower without arousing further public curiosity about the Enewetak event.

Commissioner Henry D. Smyth, the Princeton physicist who had written the famous Smyth report on the wartime atomic energy program, boarded the train alone. Appointed to the Commission with Dean in May 1949, Smyth by reason of seniority and his extensive knowledge of nuclear science and technology was an especially influential member of the Commission. The son of a university professor, Smyth had spent almost his entire life at Princeton, first as a child, then as a Princeton student, and later as a member of the physics department. Smyth's Ivy League background and his standing in the academic world as much as his capabilities as a physicist made him a valuable asset to both the wartime Manhattan Project and the current Commission. His soft-spoken and reflective manner marked him as a scholar who could exercise the detached judgment of a scientist. But he was also a man of strong principles. More than once, especially on the thermonuclear weapon decision, he had proved himself capable of fighting tenaciously for his convictions.

12

In the morning the members of the group made their separate ways from Pennsylvania Station to 686 Park Avenue, the apartment of Commissioner Thomas E. Murray. At sixty-one, Murray was the oldest member of the Commission. Thin, sober, and tight-lipped, Murray personified the gray eminence. His stern sense of morality grounded in an intense loyalty to the Roman Catholic Church influenced all his thoughts and actions; he saw his Commissioner duty as one of defending his nation and his church against atheistic communism. A Yale graduate in 1911, Murray had established himself as a highly successful engineer and business executive in New York. He had two hundred patents to his credit, and by the time he was appointed to the Commission in March 1950 he had been president of his own company, board member of his family company and several large corporations, trustee of several banks, and receiver of the Interborough subway system. A conservative Democrat, Murray brought to the Commission a shrewd, analytical mind, the hard-headed practicality of an engineer, and an unswerving determination to keep the United States second to none in nuclear technology.

13

Breakfast at Murray's apartment gave Dean and his colleagues a chance to discuss the strategy for their meeting with Eisenhower. Shortly before nine they left for the Commodore Hotel, where they were to meet the fourth Commissioner, Eugene M. Zuckert. Like Murray a Democrat, a New Yorker, and a Yale alumnus, Zuckert was the youngest member of the Commission. After a few years as an attorney with the Securities and Exchange Commission, Zuckert had joined the faculty of the Harvard business school and organized the first advanced management course ever offered there. During most of World War II Zuckert directed a training program in statistical control for Air Force officers and served briefly as a naval officer in a management position. After the war Zuckert became a protégé of W. Stuart Symington and served as his special assistant in the Surplus Property Administration, the War Department, and the Department of the Air Force, where he became assistant secretary in 1947. As a member of the Commission since February 1952, Zuckert had taken a strong interest in management. Still young and aggressive, he could be blunt and outspoken with both his fellow Commissioners and the staff.

By the time the Commissioners had reached the Commodore, Snapp, Trapnell, and LaPlante had already arrived at the service entrance and had taken a freight elevator to the seventh floor. After the Commissioners arrived, the entire group used a back stairway to reach the Eisenhower suite on the sixth floor. Only in this way could they avoid the horde of reporters stationed in the lobby.

While Trapnell put the charts in order, Snapp introduced the Commissioners.[13] Dean remarked that the Commission had nothing of paramount importance to present, but he thought he should bring Eisenhower up-to-date on the thermonuclear test. Dean expressed his regret that there had been so many security leaks about the recent test. Some military personnel attached to the operation at Enewetak had written letters home describing the tests, and the newspapers had picked up the story. This comment triggered an outburst from Eisenhower, who did not even wait for Snapp and Trapnell to leave the room. He said he could not understand why security could not be better, citing "that Smith report" in summer 1945 that gave away much vital information about the atomic energy project and particularly the exact location of the production plants. Perhaps trying to save Eisenhower from embarrassment, Dean mentioned that Smyth, the author of the report, was in the room. This information did not deter Eisenhower at all as he continued to denounce the report for giving away too many details to no purpose.

By this time Snapp and Trapnell had left, and Dean pulled out his three pages of opening remarks. In a conversational style he gave a few words of background about each Commissioner and noted one vacancy to be filled. Then Dean turned to his presentation.

Many of Eisenhower's reactions were similar to those he had expressed in Augusta. When Dean explained the thermonuclear test, Eisenhower returned to the question of secrecy. He said he wished the Commission could keep all information about the test out of print. He would have preferred that the Russians find out about it on their own; his theory was that it would upset the Russians if they came to the conclusion that the United States had progressed so far in weapon development without boasting about it. The Russians, in Eisenhower's opinion, expected the Americans to brag about everything they did, and silence would throw them off balance.

During most of the briefing Eisenhower took no particular exception to the Commission's presentation. He thought the projection of a $4-billion budget in fiscal year 1953 was reasonable in terms of an $80-billion federal budget. He again expressed his doubts that the Russians were looking for a chance to start a war or to use nuclear weapons. Only when Dean came to the chart on nuclear-propelled aircraft did Eisenhower react. He was dismayed that the Commission was spending so much money on such a fanciful idea. Zuckert attempted to reply by suggesting that the Commission was merely trying to provide what the Air Force wanted. Eisenhower interrupted and pulled himself out of his chair. Looking out the window he declared that this kind of reasoning was wrong. If a civilian agency like the Commission thought a military requirement was untenable or wasteful in terms of existing technology, there was an obligation to oppose it. He hoped to establish a board of outstanding industrialists and scientists who could review projects like this one. Nuclear propulsion for submarines was a different matter—that made sense.

The last few briefing charts described the Commission's plans for encouraging industrial development of nuclear power plants. Eisenhower again mentioned his conversation with Charles Thomas and his interest in involving private participation as much as possible. Toward the end, Eisenhower again brought up the general question of security and expressed great confidence in J. Edgar Hoover, director of the Federal Bureau of Investigation (FBI). It was almost eleven o'clock when the Commissioners took their leave after a full and useful briefing.

The following Monday Dean called Truman to report on the session with Eisenhower. Dean explained that no one except those present knew about the briefing and he was trying to keep it quiet. Truman said he was pleased to hear about it because he wanted the incoming President to have as much information as possible.[14]

Certainly the session with the Commission had been helpful to Eisenhower. From the nature of his questions, it was apparent that he had had very little understanding of either the military or civilian aspects of the atomic energy program before the election. From the briefing the Commissioners could conclude that the new President now had some conception of the size and nature of the nuclear weapon stockpile and the growing capacity for producing special nuclear materials and weapons. On the peaceful side, Eisenhower now had some comprehension of the wide-ranging capabilities of the scientists and engineers supported by the Commission for exploiting the beneficial aspects of nuclear technology. One of the most intriguing possibilities was using nuclear power to generate electricity.

For their own part, the Commissioners also acquired some helpful intelligence during their visit to New York. They could not help but be impressed by Eisenhower's intense interest in atomic energy. The subject had been high on his agenda during his stay in Augusta, and he had given the Commissioners two hours in New York when prospective cabinet officers and leading Republican senators could command only a few minutes of his time. It was also clear that Eisenhower fully supported the Commission's efforts rapidly to enlarge the arsenal of nuclear weapons and to maintain that strength as a bastion of national security.

At the same time, the new President displayed a remarkable ambivalence about nuclear energy. Perhaps only a man with Eisenhower's experience in leading his nation in what was believed its greatest military operation could be as sensitive as he was to the extraordinary dangers inherent in the possession of so much physical power. Eisenhower seemed to understand the possibilities for human failure, misdirected ambition, intrigue, treachery, and death in the nuclear era. Thus, behind Eisenhower's realism was an intense concern with secrecy and security. This penchant of the new President would manifest itself in other parts of his Administration, but nowhere else would it have greater impact than in the Commission's programs. Finally, Eisenhower had demonstrated his dedication to economy in government, in terms of both funding and federal power. Surely this attitude had profound implications for an agency with unprecedented authority and largess in the development of a new and frightening technology. Eisenhower seemed determined to see the atom developed for both peaceful and military uses, but in a way counter to some of the strongest trends toward the aggrandizement of power in the federal government during twenty years of Democratic administrations. With the Eisenhower victory in 1952, a new day was dawning for both the nation and the Commission. To that change and challenge the Commission would have to respond.

16

CHAPTER 2

# THE EISENHOWER
# IMPRINT

The Commission's secret session with the President-elect on November 19, 1952, provided a valuable insight into Eisenhower's character and interests. It left on the Commissioners an indelible impression of the exceptional import the new chief executive would attach to both the military and civilian uses of atomic energy. But the brief session in New York did not give the Commissioners any degree of permanent entrée to the new President or his Administration. After twenty years in the political wilderness, Republican leaders, especially in the Congress, eagerly anticipated the opportunity to overhaul the vast bureaucracy they attributed to five Democratic administrations. Whatever personal confidence Eisenhower may have had in the Commissioners, as Truman holdovers they were not to be welcomed into the new Administration's official family. Roy Snapp, the Commission's secretary, had to go hat in hand to the Republicans for invitations that would permit the Commission to participate in the inauguration.[1]

Reading the newsclips during the seven weeks between the election and the inauguration, the Commissioners could get some sense of the imprint Eisenhower was attempting to make on the bureaucracy and the nation. The announcement of most Cabinet posts two days after the Commodore meeting made clear that American industry with its conservative economic principles would have a strong voice in the new Administration. President of General Motors Charles E. Wilson, named Secretary of Defense, reinforced that theme a few weeks later by selecting four industrialists to fill the positions of the deputy secretary and the three service secretaries. The nomination of John Foster Dulles to Secretary of State and the President-elect's trip to Korea early in December revealed a determination to take new and decisive initiatives in international affairs. On the cruiser *Helena* returning from Guam to Honolulu, Eisenhower discussed possible ways of cutting the Truman budget. His "team" included Dulles and Wilson; Treasury Secretary-designate George M. Humphrey; Douglas McKay, who would become Secretary of the Interior; Joseph M. Dodge, the future director of the Bureau of the Budget; and General Lucius D. Clay.[2] The geographical distance between the *Helena* and the Commission's headquarters building on Constitution Avenue in Washington was no greater than the figurative displacement of the Commissioners from the center of power in the new Administration.

## NEW PRIORITIES

Even before the November conference with Eisenhower, Dean and his fellow Commissioners had understood the need for new priorities in a new Administration. Their secret conference with the President-elect and more public evidence of the course Eisenhower intended to follow reinforced Dean's impression that a major reorientation in the Commission's programs would be necessary, but such adjustments were never easy. Additional resources in terms of larger budgets and more personnel seldom accompanied new requirements. Somehow the Commission would have to produce more with the same or smaller resources.

By late January 1953, Dean could almost guess what the Eisenhower impact would be. First, the President obviously desired to build a strong nuclear arm as part of the nation's defense; that interest would require more nuclear weapons and materials. At the same time Dean could not overlook the Republicans' interest in reducing federal expenditures and reversing what they saw as an invasion of the sphere of private industry by the government in two decades of Democratic rule. Although Dean and most of his fellow Commissioners were conservative in terms of economic policy, this latter concern of the Republicans posed potential difficulties. Since October 1950, the Commission had been engaged in a vast expansion of its facilities for producing special nuclear materials and weapons. The budget for fiscal year 1954, which Truman had approved late in 1952, included $1.156 billion for operating expenses and $436 million for plant and equipment, compared to the 1950 figures of $414 million for operations and $256 million for plant and equipment. The almost threefold increase in operating expenses reflected only the beginning of the heavy funding requirements that the Commission would face as new plants still under construction were completed.[3]

Huge plants were under construction to increase capacity at each step in the production chain: the new feed materials production center at Fernald, Ohio; a plant to produce large quantities of lithium-6 at Oak Ridge; a third and fourth gaseous-diffusion plant at Paducah, Kentucky; a whole new gaseous-diffusion complex at Portsmouth, Ohio; two "jumbo"

18

reactors and a separation plant for producing plutonium at Hanford; and five heavy-water reactors at the Savannah River site in South Carolina for producing tritium from lithium-6 as well as plutonium. In the nationwide weapon production network, there was much activity: the new weapon assembly plant at Rocky Flats, Colorado; a major expansion of research facilities at Los Alamos; new buildings at Albuquerque, New Mexico, Burlington, Iowa, Livermore, California, and Amarillo, Texas. Plans had already been completed for testing eight weapon devices at the Nevada Proving Ground in spring 1953 and for another series including full-scale thermonuclear weapons in the Pacific beginning late in the year. The Commission's expansion program represented one of the greatest federal construction projects in peacetime history.[4]

The astronomical figures in the President's 1954 budget were still more than $800 million below the Commission's original request, the largest dollar cut falling on production facilities. Most significant, however, was the $176-million cut in obligations for reactor development facilities, which represented a reduction of 77 percent in the Commission's request. This substantial reduction reflected a lack of confidence in the Commission's efforts to reorient its reactor development efforts from plutonium production units to civilian power reactors.

19

Within a few days after Truman sent his budget to the Congress, the Bureau of the Budget announced its intention to review the entire document against the new Administration's own priorities. On February 3, 1953, Budget Director Dodge informed all executive departments and agencies of the need not only to set new priorities but also to balance the federal budget.[5] A few discreet inquiries by the Commission's budget staff indicated that Dodge's admonitions were not to be taken literally; the Commission would be permitted to increase its personnel ceiling to meet the needs of its expanding program.[6]

The Commission's primary defense against budget cuts was to cite the rapid growth of the military program. As Dean explained to the National Security Council in February, it was not possible to reduce expenditures and at the same time continue to produce nuclear materials and weapons at ever increasing rates in the new production plants that would be coming into operation. On this point the Commission presented a united front with the military services. A week earlier Dean had told the military liaison committee, the statutory group of officers charged with advising the Commission on military applications of nuclear energy, that recent improvements in the operation of the Hanford reactors and design changes in the Savannah River plants would enable the Commission to exceed the original goals of the 1952 expansion program. The Commission thus had been able to save funds, as Dodge had ordered, by cancelling a sixth reactor at Savannah River. The members of the military liaison committee, however, bristled at the idea of reducing fissionable material production for weapons and assured Dean that if they had known that greater production would be possible, they would have raised the production targets for the expansion program.[7]

For several years Dean had been irritated by the unwillingness of the Department of Defense to set firm requirements. Now that the Commission was faced with substantial budget cuts, it was imperative for the Department of Defense to make firm commitments. If cuts were required, how large should they be in materials for weapons, nuclear submarines, the nuclear-powered aircraft carrier, and the nuclear-powered bomber? Dean complained to Defense Secretary Wilson: "To assume . . . that some arbitrary figure must be taken from the atomic energy program would seem to run counter to the principle that choices must be made." Yet Dodge, perhaps at the suggestion of Wilson, took just this approach in a proposal that Eisenhower approved in March 1953. Because the Commission's budget was "essentially determined by the Defense Department requirements," the National Security Council should evaluate the Defense and Commission budgets together. The study was to be coordinated by the new assistant to the President for atomic energy matters, Lewis L. Strauss.[8]

Strauss had been one of the original Commissioners appointed by Truman in 1946. The son of a shoe merchant in Richmond, Virginia, Strauss had made his own way in the world. At the age of twenty in 1917, he talked himself into a position on Herbert Hoover's staff in organizing the Food Administration and later served as Hoover's personal secretary on the Belgian relief mission. Strauss then made his mark on Wall Street with the international banking firm of Kuhn, Loeb & Company. During World War II he served in the naval reserve on James V. Forrestal's staff and retired in 1945 with the rank of rear admiral. During his three years on the Commission Strauss established himself as hard-working and conscientious, if somewhat overbearing in advancing his opinions. He took a great interest in matters of security and intelligence, took credit for establishing the long-range detection system that had revealed the Soviet nuclear test in August 1949, and led the uphill fight with Dean to accelerate the development of the hydrogen bomb. With that accomplished, Strauss returned to his financial career in New York but continued to serve as a consultant to the Joint Committee on Atomic Energy in evaluating the adequacy of the Commission's production efforts. Although a conservative Republican in the Taft wing of the party, Strauss maintained his friendship with Dean. The two occasionally had lunch together and kept in touch by telephone.

Strauss had no desires or expectations to return to federal service even after Eisenhower's election. He had scarcely known Eisenhower and had not supported Eisenhower's drive for the Republican nomination. Strauss was therefore surprised when the President called him home from a Caribbean vacation in late February 1953 and asked him to make an independent study of the atomic energy program. Within a few weeks Eisenhower suggested that Strauss take over the chairmanship of the Commission from Dean, who had announced on February 10 that he would retire within three months. Strauss refused the offer on the grounds that the Commission's chairman was necessarily involved in a large number of routine matters that prevented him from giving full attention to larger policy issues. Strauss thought he could better serve the Administration as special assistant to the President for atomic energy matters, and Eisenhower approved the appointment on March 7, 1953.[9]

Dean was delighted with Strauss's appointment. Not only did the two men understand each other, but Strauss was also knowledgeable about the Commission. Furthermore his interest in the expansion program suggested that he would fight for an adequate Commission budget. Dean offered Strauss full cooperation in preparing his report to the National Security Council.[10] In the meantime, Dean was turning his attention to the difficult question of formulating a policy for developing nuclear power.

21

## NUCLEAR POWER: SEARCH FOR A POLICY

Long before the budget uncertainties of 1953 arose, Dean and his fellow Commissioners had seen the need for a clear-cut policy on nuclear power development. The sharp cuts that the Truman Administration had made in the Commission's reactor development budget reflected the failure to formulate a coherent plan in the face of the extraordinary pressures and conflicting demands of the expansion program. Dean himself recognized these shortcomings a few days before the inauguration. He wrote the other Commissioners that "we have been too indecisive" in responding to proposals from industry,[11] and the lack of direction in the Commission's reactor program was in part a result of that indecision. The fact was that public interest in nuclear power had overtaken the Commission's diffuse and largely ineffective efforts to formulate a policy.

The Commission's own accomplishments in developing new types of power reactors were in part responsible for the rise in public interest. In June 1952, Truman had caught the nation's attention in laying the keel for the world's first nuclear-powered submarine, an event that seemed to bring nuclear power close to reality. In October the Commission released the hitherto classified information that a small experimental breeder reactor, designed and built by the Commission's Argonne laboratory, had actually generated electricity from nuclear power and was proceeding to test the principle of breeding.[12] These accomplishments, plus the enthusiastic reports of the four industrial study groups that had been admitted behind the Commission's security barriers, gave public interest in nuclear power a stimulus it had not experienced since 1945.

Reflecting this new enthusiasm, the Joint Committee on Atomic Energy had been proposing for six months to hold hearings on the Commission's plan for industrial development of nuclear power. During autumn 1952, the committee staff had compiled a four-hundred-page volume of information, *Atomic Power and Private Enterprise*.[13] The committee's own statement reflected the conviction that the Commission's activities in developing plutonium production reactors, power reactor experiments, and military propulsion reactors had demonstrated the feasibility of nuclear power. The great question was how much it would cost.

The Joint Committee summarized industry's role since 1947 in developing nuclear power, largely under Commission contracts; but most interesting of all were the results of an informal opinion survey of "company executives, government officials, scientists, lawyers, and others" in fall 1952. There was general agreement that the Commission should develop prototype reactors, but opinion on the government's role in building full-scale units ranged from full support to no support. There were three alternatives for ownership of reactors, fissionable material, and handling facilities: exclusive government ownership; permissive, licensed private ownership; or mandatory exclusive private ownership subject to government regulation. Government financing of reactor development at least through the prototype stage was generally accepted. Some scientists believed that complete government financing would bring the quickest results, but many business executives thought industry could build the full-scale plants if the government offered reasonable tax advantages and subsidies. Within industry some feared that the Commission under existing legislation would compete with private efforts to build power reactors. Industry spokesmen in general advocated revising the existing law to permit more nearly normal operation of the free enterprise system. Others, including many lawyers and government officials, opposed changing the law until the Commission had built a prototype power reactor and the needs for revision were clearer; some argued that revising the law would cause all planning to stop for six months while Congress debated the issue and another twelve months while the new legal provisions were being studied.

The Joint Committee report made clear several points: first, technological developments had created a broad interest in nuclear power; second, development of nuclear power would require administrative and financial arrangements not possible under the existing Atomic Energy Act; and third, the new interest in nuclear power was becoming the principal incentive for a fundamental revision of the act. Redefining the relationships between government and industry in the atomic energy enterprise, however, involved a host of political, economic, and social issues that only extended discussion and debate could settle.

Even in summary form, *Atomic Power and Private Enterprise* indicated the extraordinarily complex issues facing the Commission in devising a nuclear power policy. The Commission's staff was not well equipped to handle issues of this nature. Reactor development had been approached almost entirely as a technical problem by scientists and engineers. The division of reactor development, headed by physicist and engineer Lawrence R. Hafstad, had been forced to concentrate its efforts almost entirely on production and military propulsion reactors. Not much more than one-tenth of the operating funds for reactor development were going directly into power reactor projects. Even if Hafstad and his engineers had been able to give more thought to power reactor systems, they would have found it hard to address the relevant political and economic questions. That fact was clear in late 1952 when Hafstad presented to the Commission a plan for reorienting the Commission's efforts. Essentially an engineering analysis, the proposal did not consider many larger issues raised in the Joint Committee report. [14]

William Lee Davidson, who for seven months had been director of industrial development, came closer to the mark in January 1953, when he briefed the Commissioners. Davidson was also a scientist, having come to the Commission from the research division of the B. F. Goodrich Company, but he at least had an industrial perspective if not the talents of an economist. [15] Working with Hafstad, Davidson proposed a "moderately expedited development program," intended to promote reactors capable of producing significant amounts of commercially competitive power within a decade. The existing Commission program of working through industrial study groups would take at least fifteen years. Davidson's proposal, costing about $100 million over ten years, would encourage private projects without offering direct financial support, government financing of small pilot plants, and possibly Commission construction of one nuclear power plant for its military or prestige value. [16]

By late February 1953, Davidson's ideas had been transformed into a succinct Commission policy statement for the President. [17] In lieu of high-flown language about the historical significance of nuclear power, the Commissioners attributed the need for a policy statement to budgetary expediencies and to pressure from the Joint Committee. The Commission found "the attainment of economically competitive nuclear power to be a goal of national importance." It would be a major setback for the nation if its leadership in nuclear power development should pass to other countries. The Commission would help industry by continuing to support research and development and by promoting the construction of experimental reactors.

The Commission suggested to Eisenhower several forms of assistance. The Commission proposed to finance construction of an experimental power reactor using sodium as a coolant and graphite as a moderator. The sodium-graphite reactor was expected to generate 7,500 kilowatts of electricity. Private industry would then be invited to build a full-scale reactor (100,000–200,000 kilowatts) with private funds on the condition that the

23

Commission would protect the owners against excessive losses. Finally, the Commission would offer private industry technical assistance from the national laboratories in building a full-scale power-breeder reactor. The price tag was identical to the Davidson-Hafstad proposal: $10 million per year over ten years.

The suggestions did not receive a warm reception from the National Security Council when Dean presented them a week later. Eisenhower did not want to approach Congress until the Executive Branch had agreed on Administration policy. Furthermore, after his discussions with Charles Thomas of Monsanto, Eisenhower doubted that industry would agree to participate without a heavy government subsidy. In Eisenhower's estimation the subsidy might go as high as $100 million; Dodge guessed it might be even higher. Secretary Wilson thought the Commission was moving too fast and should wait at least six months before making a commitment on subsidies. Secretary Humphrey went even further and urged construction of a pilot plant before any subsidies were considered. Dean shrewdly suggested that it would be unwise to limit the plan to one government-built pilot plant. He thought nuclear power development would come more quickly with industrial participation, but that would require changes in the Atomic Energy Act. Jumping on this point, Eisenhower declared that modification of the act should come first; in the meantime, he would consider only a small subsidy. In the end, the council agreed to refer the report to its group of outside consultants and hold funds for the sodium-graphite reactor to the $3 million included in the budget.[18]

During the last three weeks in March 1953, Dean had numerous opportunities to assess the Commission's position on nuclear power. There were several discussions of a preamble to the policy statement that would help the consultants from the National Security Council to put the statement in proper context. Most Commissioners, including Dean, met with the consultants to brief them on the fundamentals of nuclear technology. Dean took pains to see that Strauss had all the information he needed for his report on the Commission's budget, not only because Strauss represented the President but also because Dean had heard from the National Security Council staff that Strauss might be his successor.[19]

Dean again encountered stiff resistance to his proposed budget cuts when the National Security Council reconsidered them on March 31. He failed to restore earlier reductions in funds for the sodium-graphite reactor, but Eisenhower reaffirmed his desire to amend the act in order to make industrial participation easier. Strauss had investigated various possibilities for wringing another $200 million out of the Commission's budget, but he admitted that none of these seemed prudent. Secretary Humphrey expressed his reluctance to abandon any hopes of cutting the expansion program. What could the council do? Then Charles Thomas, one of the consultants, came up with an idea: why not eliminate the project for building nuclear propulsion plants for aircraft and for the aircraft carrier? This action would save $254 million in the first two years. Eisenhower thought the idea had merit; these projects could be delayed until the success of the first nuclear submarine had been determined. The President was not ready to make a final decision, but no one had given him any solid reasons why these projects should be continued.[20]

## NUCLEAR POWER AND PRIVATE ENTERPRISE

When the March 31 decision of the National Security Council filtered back to the Commission and the Department of Defense, the instinctive reaction in the bureaucracy was to gird up for a battle of the budget, but some astute observers saw a more fundamental issue at stake. Commissioner Murray wrote Dean that he considered the cuts in the reactor budget "merely a symptom" of the differing views of the Commission and the council. The Commission had proposed government development of nuclear power with private assistance; the National Security Council had reversed these roles by calling for private development with government assistance. Murray was convinced from two years of experience in consulting with industry on nuclear power projects that development would be much too slow to maintain American leadership in nuclear technology if the nation relied upon anticipated private profits for incentive. "Although I have consistently urged private *construction* and *operation* of nuclear power plants, I am convinced that successful and rapid *development* demands retention of Government leadership at this time."[21]

Because almost every issue discussed by the National Security Council was considered top secret, few people in the atomic energy establishment besides the Commissioners themselves could appreciate the significance of the March 31 action. Not even the Commissioners were privy to the warning of the seven consultants who had submitted to the council a strongly worded, almost alarming analysis of the government's ability to support national security programs. The consultants expressed "grave doubt that our national substance will stand the strain of its protracted diffusion over the world in the form principally of nonproductive munitions of war." The costs of rearmament during the Korean conflict had been excessive, and the consultants "deplored the profligate use of scientific and engineering manpower in military programs."

At the same time, the consultants recognized a growing need to strengthen American defenses. This need could be met, not by pouring resources into military projects in a conventional way but by restructuring military preparedness. The consultants advocated more stress on production capacity as a military reserve than on stockpiling military hardware. Defense should depend more heavily on "more powerful nuclear weapons

25

and increasingly effective means of delivery." The consultants also recommended more attention to tactical nuclear weapons and their deployment to NATO forces. Through careful planning and stern measures of economy it would be possible to achieve adequate material security with a balanced budget in 1954.[22]

Eisenhower and his advisers did not take such an extreme position on the need for economy, but the consultants had some influence. "The survival of the free world," in the National Security Council's opinion, depended upon "a sound, strong economy" in the United States and that rested in turn on balancing the budget, if not in 1954 or 1955, then as soon thereafter as possible. Within these financial limitations the United States would "continue to assist in building up the strength of the free world" and would seek "to contain Soviet expansion and to deter Soviet power from aggressive war." The Commission could contribute both to increased security and to the balanced budget by effecting the expenditure reduction suggested by Strauss and Thomas and by advancing the development of nuclear power "primarily by private, not government, financing." In addition to reducing government spending, private financing would "tap the great scientific laboratories of private enterprise," stimulate competition between government and private laboratories, automatically disperse nuclear production plants, and "create new industries, new employment, and new sources of taxes."[23]

Implicit in this argument for industrial development of nuclear power was a corollary that did not appear in government memorandums: if industry lost the initiative in developing this energy source of the future, then the last hope for keeping electrical energy generation in private hands would go down the drain. Late in winter 1953 few politicians or government officials were anxious to begin a new round in the old battle between public and private power interests, a struggle going back to the establishment of the Tennessee Valley Authority (TVA) in 1933 and the epic victory of the New Deal over the power trust, a triumph embodied in the Public Utility Holding Company Act of 1935. Harry S. Truman, who as a freshman senator had voted for the act, kept the issue alive during his presidency by denouncing "the million-dollar propaganda campaigns" of the private power lobby. One trade magazine for the electric utilities industry responded by calling Truman's talk of cheap public power a political "lollipop" in the presidential campaign of 1952; that publication welcomed Eisenhower's victory as a blow to the "planned drive toward socialization" of the industry.[24]

Most enthusiasm for nuclear power in spring 1953 arose from sincere convictions, as *Newsweek* put it, that "atomic power is at the finger tips of this generation." The Joint Committee's *Atomic Power and Private Enterprise* demonstrated clearly the broad base of optimism about nuclear power within American industry. The addition of a fifth industrial study group to the Commission's cooperative nuclear power program in April 1953 suggested a growing and even impatient interest, even if the Commissioners and the staff privately discounted the significance of such arrangements. Four days later former Commissioner T. Keith Glennan, who for more than a year had spurred industry to enter the nuclear field, announced the incorporation of the Atomic Industrial Forum, an organization of businessmen, engineers, scientists, and educators interested in the industrial development and application of atomic energy. Based in New York, the forum was to serve as both a clearinghouse for information and a stimulant to industrial participation. The board of directors included the presidents or atomic energy executives of thirteen large corporations and institutions of higher education. Later that same week Walker L. Cisler, president of the Detroit Edison Company, and eight other executives representing the Dow Chemical–Detroit Edison study group, met with the Commissioners to offer amendments to the Atomic Energy Act that would enable private industry to invest in nuclear projects. The following week Congressman James E. Van Zandt, a Republican from Pennsylvania and member of the Joint Committee, introduced in the House of Representatives a bill authorizing private industry to own or hold nuclear fuel on long-term lease.[25]

27

Imbedded in this mass enthusiasm, however, were some indications that nuclear power could become a pawn in the endless struggle between public and private power interests. The same trade magazine that had welcomed Eisenhower's election as a boost to the defenders of private utility companies looked upon strong industry initiative in nuclear power development as a way of getting the government out of the power business. Van Zandt announced in the *Congressional Record* that one purpose of his bill was "to prevent an atomic TVA by prohibiting the Atomic Energy Commission from selling power except as produced in conjunction with manufacture of weapons materials." Public power advocates voiced their own anxieties in letters to the Commission. The American Public Power Association opposed any change in the Atomic Energy Act until steps could be taken "to prevent any monopolistic advantage accruing to any private person or corporations." The association advocated Commission development of pilot plants and participation by publicly owned electric utilities in development contracts. Using even stronger language, the Congress of Industrial Organizations supported the proposition that "the Atomic Energy Act should be strengthened by requiring that the actual operation of all facilities can be handled by the government itself and not by large monopolistic corporations like DuPont and Monsanto."[26]

Within the Eisenhower Administration the public-versus-private power issue was not stated in such stark terms, but it was evident that important elements within the Administration were determined to see that nuclear power was developed as a private enterprise. Addressing the National Security Council on April 22, 1953, Roger M. Kyes, Deputy Secretary of Defense, argued for canceling altogether, rather than merely post-poning development of, the nuclear bomber and the nuclear aircraft carrier. Kyes justified his proposal as an economic measure, but Dean immediately recognized it as a threat to the Commission's reactor development effort. He reminded the council that, by eliminating the sodium-graphite reactor and now the aircraft and carrier reactors, the Commission would no longer have a single nuclear power experiment. Because the Department of Defense had rescinded its requirements for the two military reactor projects, the Commission could no longer justify them in terms of national security. But Dean suggested that portions of the projects helpful to producing an economical power reactor might be continued. Eisenhower said he would be happy to consider such a recommendation from the Commission.[27]

Dean's ploy may have seemed like a slender reed to Kyes and others at the meeting, but Dean was acting on more than a hunch. A week earlier Murray had proposed that it might be possible to transform the carrier project into a central station power reactor. The carrier reactor itself was to be a land-based prototype capable of generating a substantial amount of power. The project had been set up largely at Murray's insistence in April 1952. Because Westinghouse had been working on the reactor under the close scrutiny of Captain Hyman G. Rickover and his naval reactors branch for more than a year, the Commission could hope to move ahead quickly on a scaled-down version of the plant after some naval features had been eliminated.[28]

Rickover had occasion to explore Kyes's reasons for opposition to the carrier project in a lively discussion at the Pentagon on April 30. The feisty naval officer, who never hesitated to speak his mind in defending the naval reactors program, found Kyes philosophically opposed to any project that remotely threatened to give the federal government a place in nuclear power development. Kyes, a young General Motors executive whom Wilson had brought to the Pentagon from Detroit, was convinced that American industry was ready to invest in nuclear power and that industry could complete a power reactor much more quickly than Rickover could build the carrier prototype. There was no possibility, Kyes said, of reopening the decisions of the National Security Council.[29]

Although the carrier reactor was dead, the Commission saw a real possibility of converting it into a nuclear power project. While Dean was out of town, Murray and Smyth took up the cause. In a firm letter to the President on April 29, Smyth expressed the heart of the argument for the civilian power project. The Commission recognized the importance of industrial participation, but all the Commissioners were convinced that "even after statutory obstacles are removed, private industry will not assume a major part of the expensive, long-term development work that must precede the attainment of civilian power." Two days later Smyth and Murray discussed with Strauss how best to approach the President in a meeting Strauss

28

had arranged for May 4. When Smyth and Murray entered the Oval Office that day, they found that Strauss had laid the groundwork for a favorable reception. The President seemed impressed with Murray's argument that the new version of the carrier reactor would assure the United States the world's first large-scale nuclear power plant at a cost of $50 to $60 million less than the estimate for the carrier reactor. Eisenhower told the two Commissioners that the Department of Defense had already proposed a new version of the aircraft propulsion reactor, keeping that project alive at a lower cost.[30]

With the President's support Smyth had no trouble selling the new reactor project to the National Security Council on May 6, 1953. In addition to approving a new and scaled-down approach to the aircraft reactor, the council agreed to use Westinghouse's work on a pressurized-water reactor for the carrier in a new central station nuclear power plant; the total cost would be $100 million, "unless private financing should become available before completion." That same afternoon Murray turned in a masterful performance before the Joint Committee in making clear why private financing was not likely. Reading from letters he had received from Cisler and others, Murray declared that private industry had no money available for power reactor development. Unless the government stepped in with something like the new pressurized-water reactor, the nation would lose as much as ten years in attaining commercial nuclear power.[31] This kind of argument was certain to win the support of committee members who questioned either the wisdom or feasibility of turning nuclear power development over to private industry.

By dropping casual references to National Security Council documents Murray was able without violating executive privilege to signal the committee that the council had come to some decision on a nuclear power policy; but by not saying so specifically, Murray left to the committee the option of requesting once again the briefing that Dean and the Commissioners had so long postponed. The committee was quick to invite the Commission to testify on May 26 and to provide further information on the National Security Council's action.[32]

Dean was sharp enough to see great possibilities in the situation. The White House could not very well object to the Commissioners' presenting the nuclear power statement that the National Security Council had approved on April 22. Nor would the President be displeased if the Commission offered draft legislation amending the act to permit greater participation by industry; the President himself had given that project top priority. But Dean was also careful not to mention to the White House staff anything about the Commission's own power statement. Thus, when Dean appeared before the Joint Committee on May 26, he was free to read the entire Commission statement into the record. When the time came to present the policy statement adopted by the National Security Council, however, Dean

29

carefully omitted the references to the Administration's preference for "private, not government, financing." He thereby left the impression that the Commission and the council were essentially in agreement; the main difference was how much load the government would have to carry. Dean covered himself by later submitting the full text of the National Security Council statement for the record.[33]

Likewise, Dean took advantage of the opportunity to present the Commission's version of new legislation on industrial participation before the Bureau of the Budget and the Administration were able to revise it. He admitted that the proposal was no more than a draft, but he hoped to give the committee a starting place. The Commission favored a separate act, not a series of amendments to the Atomic Energy Act. Industry, under Commission license, could own power reactors, processing facilities, and fissionable materials used or produced in such operations. The Commission would regulate the safety and security aspects of licensed activities and could make long-term commitments for the sale or lease of nuclear materials to licensees. The Commission could but would not be required to purchase fissionable and by-product materials produced by licensees.[34]

Dean realized that he was cutting corners in not being completely candid with either the White House or the Joint Committee, but he saw no other way out of a difficult situation.[35] He rightly concluded that Wilson and Kyes, among others who had recently taken positions in government, did not fully appreciate the subtleties of policy formulation, especially given the tendency of new government officials to attempt sweeping reforms with simplistic measures. Dean also knew that he had avoided a head-on collision between the new Administration and the Joint Committee, a result he could rationalize as a potentially creative act. Much of Dean's success as chairman had resulted from his pragmatic view of events and his tendency to avoid theoretical arguments. But there was an inherent danger in Dean's attempt to finesse the philosophical differences over the government's role in developing nuclear power. Postponing the debate might mean that the issue would never be raised in a constructive context. Dean himself would be leaving the Commission and the government in a few weeks, and he had assurances that his successor, probably Strauss, would pursue the course he had so adroitly established.

## THE NEW CHAIRMAN

Despite the rumors that Strauss would succeed him as chairman, Dean had received no official notice from the White House as late as June 1 and decided to raise the question in a formal letter to the President. The next day Eisenhower confirmed the rumors. Because Strauss had not yet severed all his business connections in New York, the appointment was not to be announced for several weeks. Dean was pleased with the choice not only because he thought Strauss well qualified for the position but also because his successor's knowledge of the atomic energy program would make the transition easier than it might have been.[36]

Not until June 19 did Strauss inform the President that he was prepared for an announcement of the nomination "if you continue so disposed." By the time the news broke on June 24, Strauss had drafted a brief statement for the press. He noted that he had never intended to return to public life after his resignation from the Commission in 1950, but he could not fail to respond to a call from the President. He recalled his interest over two decades in the therapeutic uses of nuclear energy and expressed the hope that his return to the Commission would "coincide also with an era of vigorous progress in the benign uses of this great natural force—that is to say, for industrial power, for healing, and for widespread research."[37]

31

The press and members of Congress applauded Strauss's nomination without exception. Citing Strauss's interest in nuclear science, his previous service on the Commission, his promotion of the detection system that provided evidence of the first Soviet nuclear detonation, and his fight for the thermonuclear weapon, many editorial writers and columnists found Strauss "uniquely qualified," a "wise choice," "the right man for the job." General Groves called the appointment "the best thing that could have happened for the country." Strauss, the general said, "knows the subject and he's a 100 percent American." Only the newspapers in the nation's capital questioned Strauss's penchant for security, "a kind of intellectual isolationism" that would suggest his opposition to broadening access to nuclear technology. The Senate section of the Joint Committee, meeting three days later, voted unanimously to recommend Strauss's confirmation without asking him a single question.[38]

Strauss received a warm welcome in his first appearance before the Joint Committee on July 20, 1953. He took advantage of the occasion to introduce Joseph Campbell, who just four days earlier had been nominated as the fifth member of the Commission. A New York accounting executive, Campbell had served as treasurer of Columbia University during Eisenhower's presidency there. Strauss had urged the President to appoint Campbell, whom Strauss admired for his "meticulous judgment" and "personal loyalty."[39]

Just as Dean had opened the series of fourteen hearings on atomic power development and private enterprise on June 24, Strauss closed them by appearing as the last witness. Claiming that he had not been on the job long enough to have fixed opinions on the subject, Strauss did little more than read the Commission's policy statement into the record. He foresaw difficulties in formulating a new patent policy that would give industry a larger role in developing atomic energy than was possible under the existing provisions of the Atomic Energy Act, but he hoped to be able to present proposed amendments before the end of 1953.[40]

The hearings demonstrated widespread concurrence in the Commission's evaluation of the status of nuclear power. Despite the Eisenhower Administration's initial hopes for early production of nuclear power by private industry, it was clear from the hearings that industry was not yet prepared to assume the full cost and that Commission support of research and development and its regulation of nuclear activities would have to continue indefinitely.

If the Administration accepted this fact in the abstract, it was not yet prepared to take any positive action on a government reactor project. Only the direct intercession of Congressman Cole, the new chairman of the Joint Committee, provided the House appropriations committee with the information it needed to add $12 million to the Commission's 1954 budget for the project. Cole, a Republican lawyer from upstate New York, had proven himself a conscientious and effective member of the Joint Committee since 1949. He seemed determined to demonstrate that a member of the House of Representatives could be as dynamic and influential in advancing the cause of atomic energy as his famous predecessor, Brien McMahon, had been.[41]

For the immediate future the Commission's principal reactor project would be the pressurized-water reactor, the civilian version of the prototype propulsion system for an aircraft carrier. After a heated debate within the Commission's staff during July, Rickover and his naval reactors branch were given full responsibility. Initially Strauss had questioned whether the reactor would gain public acceptance as a civilian effort if Rickover's group were in charge, but Rickover and Murray had convinced the new chairman that the project was truly civilian. Some members of the reactor development staff and the general advisory committee argued that the proposed reactor was neither large enough nor novel enough in design to offer a promising demonstration of nuclear power. Some electric utility executives attempted to keep the new venture out of Rickover's control on the grounds that Rickover would give industry little real chance to participate. Murray, however, resolutely countered these arguments and induced the Commission to settle the issue in Rickover's favor. Although the Commission did not announce the decision until October, Rickover's group and the Westinghouse team at the Bettis laboratory near Pittsburgh were already at work on the new project.[42]

In the July hearing before the Joint Committee, Strauss had been able to avoid specific commitments to a plan for developing nuclear power, but the Congressional concession was only temporary. The bright promise of the nuclear age had swept over Republicans and Democrats alike in the Congress. If Strauss intended to gain the initiative, he would have to move quickly before Congress reconvened in January. Less obvious to the public but more telling to Strauss than the Congressional pressure was the President's determination to find some redeeming value in nuclear technology. Nuclear power for civilian purposes seemed an obvious answer, but only under certain conditions. The Administration's economic and budgetary policies would not condone large federal expenditures for that purpose. Rather, Eisenhower looked to Strauss and the Commission to break the government monopoly by proposing amendments to the Atomic Energy Act so that private industry could take the lead. The new President had left his imprint on Commission policy; it was Strauss's task to see to it that his imprint was observed.

33

## CHAPTER 3

# THE PRESIDENT
# AND THE BOMB

In his inaugural address on January 20, 1953, President Eisenhower said nothing explicit about atomic energy, but there were unmistakable overtones in his careful phrases. He asked the nation:

> Are we nearing the light—a day of freedom and of peace for all mankind? Or are the shadows of another night closing in upon us? . . . This trial comes at a moment when man's power to achieve good or to inflict evil surpasses the brightest hopes and sharpest fears of all ages. . . . Science seems ready to confer upon us, as its final gift, the power to erase human life from this planet.[1]

The recent test of *Mike* at Enewetak must have been on Eisenhower's mind as he read these words.

## THE THERMONUCLEAR QUESTION

Eisenhower's veiled reference to the hydrogen bomb showed that he recognized the significance of *Mike*, but the new President could not have suspected that on the very next day he would be faced with a profound disagreement among leading nuclear scientists, a controversy that raised serious questions about the adequacy of the Commission's thermonuclear program. The day after the inauguration Representative Carl T. Durham, acting chairman of the Joint Committee on Atomic Energy, told the President that the Joint Committee staff had compiled a massive chronology purporting to document the argument that the Commission had been less than enthusiastic in its efforts to develop a hydrogen bomb. Eisenhower expressed interest and a few days later asked Durham for a copy of the study.[2]

The disagreement had its origins deep within the atomic energy establishment, in life-and-death issues that aroused passions and emotions. Like most things related to the hydrogen bomb, however, the debate over the scope and pace of the thermonuclear program was known to relatively few people, even among those who worked behind the security barrier that sealed off the world of atomic energy from the rest of American life. Old-timers in atomic energy development like Edward Teller could trace the dispute back to the early 1940s. Teller was an extraordinary theoretical physicist whose creative imagination had many times proven invaluable in developing ideas for nuclear weapons. He had long been intrigued with the idea of a bomb that would draw upon the enormous amounts of thermonuclear energy that powered the stars. But Teller was also a passionate individualist driven by strong emotions and original conceptions that raced far beyond the realm of existing reality. After the announcement of the first Soviet nuclear weapon test in September 1949, Teller had been a leader in the successful attempt to convince President Truman that the United States should answer the Soviet challenge by accelerating the work at the Los Alamos weapon laboratory on a hydrogen bomb.[3]

Despite aggressive efforts at Los Alamos, Teller was not convinced that either Los Alamos or the Commission was doing enough to assure the earliest possible achievement of a thermonuclear weapon. Teller's contribution had been crucial in supplying the design principle that would make the Enewetak test possible, but he continued his criticisms of Los Alamos and the Commission, even to the point of leaving Los Alamos and openly advocating early in 1952 the establishment of a new laboratory for thermonuclear research.[4]

In this new venture Teller drew upon old allies in the thermonuclear dispute; Senator Brien McMahon, chairman of the powerful Joint Committee on Atomic Energy, and William L. Borden, the committee's executive director. McMahon and Borden, like Teller, were men of passionate beliefs who lived in daily fear of the Soviet menace. McMahon, with his energetic leadership and the assistance of Borden's keen intellect, had dominated the Joint Committee since 1949. Their constant concern was whether the Commission was moving fast enough in developing and producing weapons.

Perhaps with Teller's prodding, perhaps on their own initiative, McMahon and Borden launched two further inquiries into the adequacy of nuclear weapon development in February 1952. In the first hearing, with the Secretary of Defense and the Joint Chiefs of Staff, McMahon raised the question that Klaus Fuchs, the German-born British scientist who had been convicted of Soviet espionage in 1950, had acquired during his stay at Los Alamos some essential principles of the thermonuclear weapon. Convinced that American efforts had been less than expeditious, McMahon feared that the Russians might already be ahead of the United States in the thermonuclear field.[5] In a second hearing two weeks later Borden presented the

35

Commissioners with an alarming interpretation of recent intelligence reports about the nature of the third Soviet test, information that suggested a dangerous underestimation of Soviet capabilities in producing both fissionable and thermonuclear materials by isotope separation.[6]

In both instances the attempts by McMahon and Borden to accelerate weapon development failed. In the first, the Department of Defense found no grounds for concluding that the Commission's efforts were inadequate.[7] In the second, Commissioner Smyth displayed his command of production and weapon technology by convincingly discounting the significance of the reports about the Soviet test. A few weeks later, however, in March 1952, the same stories about Fuchs and the recent Soviet test stirred up enough concern in the new Deputy Secretary of Defense William C. Foster to result in a meeting of the National Security Council's special committee on atomic energy. After Teller had briefed the committee on the history of weapon development, Dean with considerable difficulty convinced the Secretaries of Defense and State that there was nothing new or particularly significant in Teller's fears.[8]

Although Dean succeeded in keeping the thermonuclear question out of the National Security Council, he could not contain Teller within the atomic energy establishment. The issue of whether to create a second laboratory inevitably embroiled the Commission's general advisory committee and its chairman, J. Robert Oppenheimer. A man of exceptional ability as a physicist, administrator, and leader, Oppenheimer had built and directed the Los Alamos laboratory during World War II, had sparked much of the United States' effort to establish international control of atomic energy after the war, and, as chairman of the Commission's principal advisory committee since 1947, perhaps more than any other individual had influenced the Commission's course in its formative years. Oppenheimer also served on important committees in other executive departments. Like most members of the general advisory committee, Oppenheimer was not convinced that a second laboratory would necessarily enhance weapon development.[9] Indirectly Oppenheimer criticized Teller for promoting the second laboratory for political rather than technical reasons. The committee members also complained among themselves that they were being blamed for deficiencies at Los Alamos that they had tried to correct much earlier.

One scientist with whom the committee consulted on the second laboratory was Hans A. Bethe, the distinguished theoretical physicist from Cornell University who had long been associated with weapon development at Los Alamos. Bethe was disturbed by what he heard at the committee meeting, particularly by Dean's reports of growing dissatisfaction within the Defense Department over the thermonuclear project. He decided to write the Secretary of the Air Force a letter setting the record straight. His summary of thermonuclear development since 1946 was designed to show that Fuchs was not exposed to vital information about design of the hydrogen

36

bomb and that Teller's conception in April 1951 was essential to the American success. Teller, when he read Bethe's summary, came to exactly the opposite conclusion. [10]

Borden's reaction to Bethe's analysis and Teller's critique was one of frustration and alarm. In Borden's opinion the Bethe analysis was nothing but a "white wash," perhaps even the result of a conspiracy by Oppenheimer and the Commission to hide the inadequacy of the thermonuclear program. [11] There was no consolation for Borden in the fact that Oppenheimer had retired from the general advisory committee on June 30, 1952; Oppenheimer still had ample means of exerting what Borden considered a negative influence on military developments. Borden had also been disheartened by McMahon's death a few weeks after Oppenheimer's retirement. With McMahon's strong voice silenced, Borden felt that he alone would have to shoulder the leadership for awakening the nation to the lagging development of nuclear weapons, especially the hydrogen bomb.

Borden decided first to set the record straight by compiling a "history" or "chronology." For this task he recruited John T. Walker, like himself a Yale law graduate, who would serve also as the Joint Committee's counsel. From the committee's voluminous files Walker compiled a compendium of excerpts from correspondence, reports, and hearing transcripts that seemed to demonstrate the failure of the Commission, the general advisory committee, defense officials, and military officers to understand the overwhelming importance of thermonuclear weapons. The excerpts were arranged in chronological order with a minimum of editorializing; but, like a lawyer's summary of evidence, the chronology moved inexorably to its intended conclusion.

The nature of Walker's assignment made it impossible for him to turn to the Commission staff or to Los Alamos for technical assistance. Instead, he relied on John A. Wheeler, the theoretical physicist who directed Project *Matterhorn* as a part of the Commission's thermonuclear effort at Princeton University. Wheeler not only had expert knowledge of the subject but also as a Commission consultant was cleared for access to highly classified information. He had the further advantage of being close to Teller's views, thus generally sympathetic with Borden's purpose. In addition to reviewing the chronology, Wheeler also agreed to comment upon a reexamination of the Fuchs question that Walker had prepared as part of his study. [12]

37

## THE WHEELER INCIDENT

By New Year's Day, 1953, the chronology was in final form, presumably incorporating Wheeler's latest suggestions, [13] but Walker was still deeply immersed in the Fuchs question. Walker, with Borden's encouragement, attempted to outline in detail how Fuchs might have picked up the germ of the thermonuclear principle as early as 1946. During the first week in January Walker mailed Wheeler his analysis of the evidence. The press of business did not give Wheeler time to read the Walker document, and he finally took it with him on a trip to Washington, when he would have an opportunity to discuss it with Walker.

Thus the stage was set for the calamity that threw the thermonuclear debate into the lap of President Eisenhower. Although Wheeler took special precautions to keep this and other highly classified documents in his possession during his overnight train ride to Washington, the following morning he inadvertently misplaced the envelope containing the documents. He was able to retrieve the envelope, but the Walker document was missing. After a frantic search Wheeler reported the loss to the Joint Committee. Borden personally called railroad and Pullman officials to impound the sleeping car and all laundry and trash from the train. Not until sometime before noon did Borden call the FBI. An exhaustive search, including partial dismantling of the Pullman car, failed to locate the document.

The loss seemed certain to hold awesome consequences for both Wheeler and Borden. In the first place, the document contained a succinct summary of the American thermonuclear program, including the design and operating principles of the *Mike* device, important code names, and a summary of the Bethe-Teller "debate."[14] It was hard to imagine how anyone could have selected a more sensitive document of so few pages concerning the hydrogen bomb. Second, a document of this sensitivity should have been handled as top secret material, which, according to Commission security regulations, was to be transported only by an armed courier in a private compartment. Third, Wheeler, while serving under a Commission contract and traveling on Commission funds, had lost the document in the process of compiling material that would reflect unfavorably on the Commission's management of the project.

Whether by design or circumstance, the loss of the Walker document did not immediately come to the attention of the Commission. Not until January 13, almost a week after the incident, did John A. Waters, the Commission's director of security, receive a routine letter from J. Edgar Hoover, director of the FBI, informing the Commission that Wheeler had lost a "confidential document . . . summarizing the Atomic Energy Program."[15]

Because Hoover's letter did not suggest the true significance of the lost document, Waters handled it as a routine matter.[16] Nine days later, when Waters learned that the FBI had not yet obtained a copy of the lost document from the Joint Committee, he became concerned and notified the Commission's general manager, Marion W. Boyer. After several discussions with Borden, Waters finally arranged to see a copy of the Walker report on February 4, but even then Borden would not permit the Commission to have a copy. Waters and a Commission classification officer who saw the document were aghast at its contents and immediately informed the Commissioners. Dean personally called the FBI to alert the agency to the extreme sensitivity of the lost information, and Commissioner Murray briefed Hoover on the serious nature of the loss. Not until that day did Borden give the Commission a copy of the Walker document.

Borden had every reason to try to avoid confrontation over the Wheeler debacle. At last realizing the full implications of the case, Hoover decided to report the loss to the White House. Eisenhower, appalled by such an incredible security lapse in the waning days of the Truman Administration, seized an opportunity before a scheduled meeting of the Commissioners with the National Security Council to demand an explanation of the incident. Lined up like five school boys before the master's desk, Smyth later recalled, the Commissioners meekly witnessed an extraordinary display of presidential anger. Murray had never in his life seen anyone more agitated. In the Army, Eisenhower observed, a security offender was dealt with swiftly and surely. At first Eisenhower was convinced it was an "inside job," purposely designed to get the papers into Russian hands.[17] Dean attempted to explain the complexities of the case: that the lost paper was not a Commission document, that Wheeler was no ordinary physicist, and that the Joint Committee was deeply implicated in the affair.

Why was it necessary for the Joint Committee to have such sensitive materials in the first place? Eisenhower's inquiry unwittingly echoed the question some Commissioners had been asking themselves. Dean patiently explained that under the terms of the Atomic Energy Act the Commission was required to keep the committee "fully and currently informed."[18] Eisenhower thought this provision was a mistake and expressed doubts about the committee's leadership. Dean explained that since McMahon's death the preceding summer the committee had been effectively without a chairman. Durham, the ranking Democrat on the committee, had taken McMahon's place; but now that the Republicans controlled the Congress, it was not clear who would be chairman. Until Durham had taken over the chairmanship, the committee had always elected a senator as chairman, but now there was a bitter dispute within the committee over whether Senator Bourke B. Hickenlooper of Iowa or Congressman W. Sterling Cole of New York would get the post. Dean also mentioned to the President that neither he nor any of his fellow Commissioners had seen a copy of the Walker paper; he was not even certain that the Joint Committee staff had informed all committee members about the loss.

The President, clearly shocked by the affair and not satisfied with Dean's reply, announced that he would call Hickenlooper and Cole to his office the following morning and demand that they decide at once the question of the chairmanship. He was also going to recommend reorganizing staff functions to prevent a similar loss in the future. Still unnerved by the

39

incident two days later, Eisenhower discussed the problem with the National Security Council on February 18.[19] He understood that the technical staff of the committee was to be abolished when the new chairman was selected, but this action would not lessen the appalling danger created by the loss of the Walker paper. Several council members expressed their opinions that the incident could not be attributed to carelessness but to nothing less than treason and espionage. Vice-President Richard M. Nixon suggested a complete FBI investigation of every member of the committee staff, and there was some discussion about whether Hoover and the FBI could take custody of the committee's classified files.

The strong reactions of Eisenhower and the National Security Council may have been stimulated by the growing pressure of the Rosenberg case. When Wheeler had made his ill-fated trip to Washington on the night of January 6, many Rosenberg sympathizers were coming to the nation's capital to demonstrate at the White House for presidential clemency for Julius and Ethel Rosenberg, the convicted atomic spies whose execution had been stayed until the President could act. On February 11, just a week before Eisenhower learned of the loss of the Walker document, the President had denied clemency on the grounds that the Rosenberg's betrayal of the nation's atomic secrets to Russia "could well result in the deaths of many, many thousands of innocent citizens."[20]

In the face of this decision, how could Eisenhower have viewed the loss of the Walker document with less concern? After all, the Rosenbergs had presumably passed on unevaluated information about the early designs of atomic weapons; the Walker paper was a detailed and authentic description of the operating principles of the hydrogen bomb. There was, however, a certain irony in the outcome of the Wheeler affair: Wheeler, who admitted his carelessness, suffered no public embarrassment; moreover, no one who really knew him or anything about the incident ever questioned his loyalty or integrity. In a most serious predicament, which might have resulted in the loss of Wheeler's security clearance, the Commission's chairman had defended Wheeler before the President as a scientist of exceptional abilities, a man so gifted that the nation could not afford to lose his services. Wheeler received an oral and written reprimand from Dean, but the incident was completely concealed behind the security barriers.

Borden, on the other hand, stood to lose most of the influence he had come to wield over national policy on nuclear weapons. Before McMahon's death Borden had been one of the most powerful and effective spokesmen for nuclear weapons in the atomic energy establishment, but he now realized that his days with the Joint Committee were numbered. Even before the Republican victory in the November elections Borden had consulted Strauss and others about a position in private industry. The Wheeler incident now made the inevitable more imminent. Dean seized the opportunity afforded by Wheeler's lapse to break Borden's grip on the committee.

By bringing the incident to the attention of the President and some committee members before Borden reported it, Dean undermined confidence in Borden in places that counted most. In spring 1953 Borden began in earnest to wind up his affairs on the Hill.

If Borden had any regret over leaving his committee post, it was that he might not have time to complete his campaign for the thermonuclear weapon. The planning and hard work of the preceding three years had culminated in the thermonuclear chronology, which he considered a massive indictment of the Commission's efforts. Walker had worked day and night to complete the study before he left the Joint Committee staff in early 1953. No doubt Borden had paved the way for Congressman Durham to raise the thermonuclear issue with Eisenhower the day after the inauguration. The new president had acknowledged receipt of the chronology on February 14, 1953,[21] but could hardly have grasped the significance of the bulky and somewhat turgid document before he heard the alarming news of the Walker paper. The irony was that Borden, who had tried with all his considerable powers to speed the building of a thermonuclear arsenal, had through the Wheeler incident destroyed his own effectiveness in advancing that cause.

41

## THE SHADOW OF THE BOMB

Since Roy Snapp's secret visit to Augusta in November 1952, Eisenhower had been struggling with the staggering implications of a weapon that could destroy not only an entire city but perhaps civilization itself. Dean and his colleagues had explained the hydrogen bomb in a technical sense, as a piece of hardware that could be produced if sufficient materials were available. They had outlined the Commission's plans for testing components of a deliverable thermonuclear weapon at the Nevada Proving Grounds during the spring and achieving an emergency capability after a full-scale test in the Pacific early in 1954. The President still had faith in the Commission's technical competence in these matters, despite the indictment set forth in the Joint Committee chronology.

From his very first exposure to the subject, however, Eisenhower saw the hydrogen bomb as much more than a matter of weapon technology. He focused immediately on the enormous power of the new weapon, the falling ratio of cost to destructive capability, and the desperate problems of control in a hostile world. However competent the atomic energy establishment might be, the Commissioners did not speak to these larger considerations; at least they had not (and perhaps could not) in the limited context of a presidential briefing. Outside the Commission virtually no one had enough facts to discuss the situation knowledgeably.

A rare opportunity to wrestle with some larger issues presented by the hydrogen bomb came in February 1953 when the President received a report on "Armaments and American Policy" prepared by a group of State Department consultants.[22] The report had originated in a request from Secretary of State Dean G. Acheson in April 1952 that a group of consultants take a fresh look at the strategy that the United States was using in the increasingly meaningless sessions of the United Nations Disarmament Commission. Because Acheson was thinking of a wide-ranging, original study similar to that prepared by the Acheson-Lilienthal group in 1946, he appointed two members of that group to the disarmament panel: Oppenheimer and Vannevar Bush, the eminent electrical engineer and administrator who had had a key role in formulating government policy on science and atomic energy for more than a decade. The other members of the panel were John S. Dickey and Joseph E. Johnson, both former State Department officials who were now prominent in academic circles, and Allen W. Dulles, deputy director of the Central Intelligence Agency. McGeorge Bundy, then on the Harvard faculty, served as secretary and Oppenheimer as chairman.

The Oppenheimer disarmament panel did not take a narrow view of its assignment but rather chose "to consider the problem of arms limitation in the context of a general study of the political meaning of modern weapons in the present deeply divided world." In this broader context the panel soon became convinced that the proper center of study was not arms regulation itself but the larger range of problems that came under the general heading of armaments and American policy. Reviewing the history of arms control since the time of the Acheson-Lilienthal study, the panel saw no real sign of likely agreement, largely because of the intransigent and deceitful attitude of the Soviet Union. The differences between the "free world" and the Soviet Union were "so deep-seated that no genuine, large-scale political settlement seems likely within the present generation."

The panel was convinced, however, that something had to be done about the frightening acceleration of the arms race in which devastating power was accumulating on both sides at an unprecedented rate and in a way that would put the heart of both nations, not just international borders and armies, on the front lines of any future war. Even more dangerous was the fact that few people, even inside the government, understood the special character of the nuclear arms race. Because nuclear weapons were so dangerous, men hesitated to think hard about them, and the resultant high level of security reduced "the quantity and quality of responsible discussion."

What most people, both inside and outside the government, failed to understand, the disarmament panel claimed, was not only that the nuclear stockpiles on both sides were growing at a phenomenal rate but also that the destructive force of the weapons in the stockpiles was increasing rapidly as new models replaced old. The panel saw no real long-term shortage of fissionable material for any major power and considered nuclear weapons relatively cheap. The Soviet Union might never have as many bombs as the United States at any given time, but the panel pointed out that the Russians easily could have as many as the Americans had had a few years earlier. In a matter of five or ten years the Soviet Union would have enough nuclear weapons to destroy American society beyond hope of recovery.

Because few Americans understood the unprecedented implication of the nuclear arms race, the panel believed that the United States government had reacted to the growing Russian threat with the knee-jerk response of trying to stay ahead of the Soviet Union in weapon development and in building the capability for a massive nuclear attack in case of war. The United States, in the panel's opinion, had backed itself into a rigid policy of massive nuclear retaliation that left the nation without flexibility for response.

43

To provide more flexibility, the disarmament panel first recommended "a policy of candor toward the American people—and at least equally toward its own elected representatives and responsible officials—in presenting the meaning of the arms race." Public understanding was essential to the American system, and Americans did not show a responsible awareness of the dangers of nuclear weapons. There should be a straightforward statement from those who knew the facts, including quantities of weapons and rates of increase. The State Department advisers did not believe that the facts would cause hysteria; the present danger in the United States was not hysteria but complacency. Americans should understand the rate and impact of the Soviet danger, and the government should go beyond the point of just keeping ahead of the Russians.

The panel's other recommendations were not spelled out in as much detail, but they were firmly stated. The United States, in the consultants' opinion, should help other nations in the free world to understand the nuclear threat and their relationship to America's nuclear strength so that some sense of responsibility might be shared outside the Soviet bloc. The panel urged much more attention to continental defense of the United States, not to prevent entirely a Soviet nuclear attack, but rather to minimize its effects and to give the United States more freedom to act in a crisis. Finally, the consultants recommended that the United States disengage itself from the hopeless and misleading disarmament discussions in the United Nations and develop better communications with the Soviet Union.

Unlike many reports by consultants, Bundy's final draft of the panel study reflected a broad understanding of the subject, careful analysis, a judicious balance of the ideal and the practical, and above all succinct and direct language. Eisenhower was so impressed with the report that he discussed it at some length with the National Security Council on February 18, 1953.[23] He was particularly taken with the first recommendation—more candor in explaining the nature of the arms race to the American people. The President asked the council members to read the report and be prepared to discuss it the following week.

The council meeting on February 25 gave Dean and all the members an opportunity to express their views on the report. Dean had arranged to discuss it with Allen Dulles, a panel member, before going to the meeting. Dean favored the first recommendation on the grounds that better understanding of the growing power of nuclear weapons would have a salutary effect on both the Kremlin and the American people. Secretary Wilson led the opposition to the panel's recommendations, primarily on the grounds that a candid explanation of the arms race would frighten the American people rather than reassure them. Eisenhower was now concerned about the first recommendation for Operation *Candor*. He could see that a better understanding of the catastrophic implications of nuclear warfare both in the United States and throughout the world would be a step toward peace. At the same time, the President was deeply impressed with the importance of secrecy and particularly its value in keeping the Russians off balance.[24] Like many things in government, candor was good in theory but hard to put into practice.

## THE BATTLE REJOINED

Eisenhower's favorable reaction to the panel report represented no small accomplishment for Oppenheimer and his colleagues. In the hostile and strident atmosphere of the Cold War, it was not easy to sound the note for openness and public discussion of policies affecting the national security. By catching the President's attention, Oppenheimer had reason to hope that the deadly issues surrounding the development and production of ever more efficient nuclear weapons would not be buried once again from public view. To bring the issues into public debate Oppenheimer presented an unclassified version of the panel report at a meeting of the Council on Foreign Relations in New York on February 17.[25]

Oppenheimer's very success, however, increased the likelihood that adversaries who had been trying to drive him from the government since 1949 would join forces once again to challenge him as the panel report raised old issues in a new form. Just as the President had seized on the *Candor* proposal as the most intriguing idea in the panel report, so others would use *Candor* as a symbol encompassing the complex of philosophical arguments that arose from the contemplation of thermonuclear war. Thus, *Candor* served as a lightning rod that inevitably drew old rivals back to the great debate over thermonuclear strategy.

For Oppenheimer nothing was more fateful than the circumstances that made it possible for two of his most skillful and dedicated adversaries to join forces once again just as the *Candor* breakthrough occurred in February 1953. Although Borden was on his way out as executive director of the Joint Committee, he had the determination and fortitude to hold on for one more skirmish with Oppenheimer on national security issues. In his lonely battle as a Democratic holdover in a Republican Administration he had the immense good fortune of acquiring the support of a former ally who was to become the President's closest adviser on atomic energy. On March 7, two weeks after Oppenheimer's meeting with the President, Lewis Strauss became Eisenhower's special assistant on atomic energy.

Development of the hydrogen bomb had been the common interest that first brought Borden and Strauss together. In 1949 both men had felt strongly enough about the urgency of the weapon to look upon the reservations of Oppenheimer and the general advisory committee with incomprehension and dismay. The two men had worked together to redirect the trend of events that Oppenheimer's committee had set in motion, and they had emerged victorious when President Truman decided to accelerate research on the hydrogen bomb in January 1950. After Strauss left the Commission a few weeks later, Borden arranged to have Strauss serve as a special adviser to the Joint Committee on the expansion of the Commission's capacity for producing fissionable material, and the two men kept in touch after that assignment ended. During summer 1952 Strauss had helped Borden and Walker in providing information from his personal records for the thermonuclear chronology.[26]

Strauss and Borden were also drawn together by their growing distrust of Oppenheimer's motives, integrity, and judgment, particularly after their experience during the hydrogen bomb debate in 1949. Borden probably first learned about the derogatory information in Oppenheimer's security file a few weeks after President Truman's hydrogen bomb decision, when J. Edgar Hoover testified before the Joint Committee; he also had an opportunity to review the file briefly in November 1950.[27]

The FBI's file on Oppenheimer went back to March 1944, when an FBI investigation revealed that Oppenheimer had belonged to several organizations infiltrated or dominated by communists. The FBI also learned that early in the 1940s Oppenheimer's brother, wife, and former mistress had been communists. Even after he became involved in the Manhattan Project, Oppenheimer continued to associate with members of the Communist party. Strauss had known about the contents of the file at least as early as March 1947, when as a Commissioner he had reviewed it and agreed that it contained no new information warranting further consideration of Oppenheimer's clearance.[28]

Strauss's attitude toward Oppenheimer was ambivalent at best. On the one hand, he was impressed by Oppenheimer's intelligence and ability as an administrator and scientist. As a trustee of the Institute for Advanced Study, Strauss had urged Oppenheimer's appointment as director; and as a

45

Commissoner, Strauss had offered Oppenheimer assistance in his work as chairman of the general advisory committee.[29] On the other hand, the two men disagreed on many issues in addition to those related to the thermonuclear weapon: the merits of exchanging nuclear information and material with other nations, the need for rigid security in research activities, and the feasibility of Operation *Candor*. Common among Commission staff members was a story, based on one dramatic incident, that Oppenheimer had earned Strauss's undying hatred by ridiculing him before the Joint Committee in a public hearing for his opposition to the shipment of iron isotopes to Norway in 1949. The event had occurred, but it hardly seemed a sufficient explanation for Strauss's feelings about Oppenheimer. Strauss was sensitive to personal slights, but he was also sophisticated enough to consider many factors in making any decision.[30]

46

Both Strauss and Borden were able in 1951 and 1952 to suspend any personal judgments about Oppenheimer's loyalty, but they continued to worry about his effect on thermonuclear development. In August 1951 they had shared exasperation over what they saw as Oppenheimer's efforts to discourage scientists from working on the hydrogen bomb. The decision led inevitably to speculation about Oppenheimer's motivations, and the two men once again mulled over some of the troubling information in Oppenheimer's security file. In spring 1952 Borden was among those who attempted to remove Oppenheimer's influence from the atomic energy program by making certain that he was not reappointed to the general advisory committee when his term expired on June 30. There is no evidence that Strauss was directly involved, but he was probably aware of the successful efforts by Teller, Murray, and Willard F. Libby to prevent Oppenheimer's reappointment.[31]

Oppenheimer's decision not to seek another term in the face of the opposition did not end the matter. Although no longer a member of the general advisory committee, Oppenheimer did obtain a consultant's contract from the Commission and several government boards. Hence Borden had no reason to relax his concern about Oppenheimer. Probably at Borden's suggestion, Senator McMahon invited Francis P. Cotter, a former FBI specialist in Soviet espionage techniques, to join the committee staff. Cotter's sole function was to dig into every scrap of evidence, to check out every lead in the Oppenheimer file. Both Borden and Cotter followed with interest the government's case against Joseph W. Weinberg, at one time a graduate student in physics at the University of California, for perjuring himself in testifying that he had never attended a communist meeting in Berkeley in 1941, when one such meeting was allegedly held in Oppenheimer's residence. Perhaps Borden's suspicions were further aroused when the case against Weinberg was suddenly dropped.[32]

During summer 1952 Cotter continued to run down snippets of information in Oppenheimer's security file. In November he completed a working paper presenting a fair and straightforward distillation of Oppenheimer's record. Then came Walker's round-the-clock efforts to complete the thermonuclear chronology, the successful plan to bring the chronology to the attention of the new President, and the Wheeler incident, which continued to haunt Borden into the spring of 1953, as both J. Edgar Hoover and Gordon Dean faulted the Joint Committee (and by implication Borden) for lax security practices revealed by the Wheeler case.[33] In one way or another, all the issues with which Borden had been struggling for four years seemed to be coming to a head.

## SECURITY AND CANDOR

During Strauss's first six weeks at the White House he had little time for Borden, Oppenheimer, or *Candor* as he tried to protect the Commission's nuclear projects from the Administration's efforts to balance the budget. Because Borden was persona non grata in Administration circles after the Wheeler incident, any contacts with Strauss must have been informal and discreet. The first recorded contact between the two men in 1953 occurred on April 28, when Borden called Strauss's office at the White House and arranged to bring over "a paper," which he delivered personally on the afternoon of April 30. Borden's call may have been related to launching an open attack upon Oppenheimer. That same day Strauss had telephone conversations with six other men who were deeply involved in the movement.[34]

The medium of attack was to be an anonymous article in the May issue of *Fortune* magazine. The author, the public was to learn months later, was Charles J. V. Murphy, an editor of *Fortune* who had served as an Air Force reserve officer with Secretary Thomas K. Finletter. Murphy's article purported to summarize over a period of six years Oppenheimer's pernicious influence on the development of nuclear weapons, especially the hydrogen bomb. Rife with inaccuracies and oversimplifications, the article cast a sinister connotation on many events familiar to those in the atomic energy establishment: the lack of progress on thermonuclear development at Los Alamos during the years when Oppenheimer dominated the Commission's weapon development policies through the general advisory committee; Oppenheimer's opposition to Teller's demand for a second weapon laboratory; Oppenheimer's leadership in opposing an accelerated thermonuclear program in 1949; and his subtle efforts to discourage scientists from joining the project after 1950.[35]

Murphy, however, gave much more attention to another conflict less familiar to those in atomic energy circles. This dispute involved Oppenheimer's disagreements with Air Force officials over the role of air power in nuclear war. As Murphy explained it, "a life-and-death struggle" had developed over national military policy "between a highly influential group of

47

American scientists and the military." The "prime mover among the scientists" was Oppenheimer, who had "no confidence in the military's assumption that SAC [Strategic Air Command] as a weapon of mass destruction is a real deterrent to Soviet action." Murphy supported his thesis with a facile and oversimplified account of Oppenheimer's alleged success in subverting a series of study projects financed by the military to investigate some strategic and tactical implications of nuclear war. These studies included Project *Charles* at the Massachusetts Institute of Technology to evaluate defense systems against atomic attack, the creation of the Lincoln Air Defense Laboratory in 1951 to study air defense systems, the *Vista* study at the California Institute of Technology in 1951 to investigate the tactical uses of nuclear weapons, and the Lincoln Summer Study in 1952 to determine the feasibility of a continental air defense system against a Soviet nuclear attack.[36]

48          In what appeared to be an accurate description of the fears and suspicions circulating at the highest levels of the Air Force at that time, Murphy explained how Oppenheimer and other scientists close to him allegedly undermined the original intent of these studies and transformed them into clever repudiations of the Air Force doctrine of strategic bombing. By summer 1952, Murphy declared, Oppenheimer and his associates were united in a sinister conspiracy calling itself ZORC (based on the initials of the four alleged conspirators). ZORC, Murphy alleged, was determined to strip the United States of its nuclear superiority in a misguided and naive hope that such action would reduce the threat of nuclear war.[37]

Strauss was not the only man of influence in Washington to be aroused by Murphy's innuendoes. On May 12 Senator Joseph R. McCarthy called on J. Edgar Hoover to discuss the possibility of starting an investigation of Oppenheimer. McCarthy hinted at bipartisan support when he noted that Senator Stuart Symington, a Democrat and former Air Force Secretary, was concerned enough about Oppenheimer's controversy with the Air Force to consider an investigation. Hoover tried to discourage McCarthy by suggesting that such a move might involve a jurisdictional dispute with the Joint Committee on Atomic Energy or the Jenner committee. But Hoover's main concern was Oppenheimer's broad popularity, especially among scientists. Whatever the committee decided to do about Oppenheimer, Hoover advised, "should be done with a great deal of preliminary spade work" so that, when the investigation became public knowledge, the committee "would have substantive facts upon which to predicate its action."[38] Strauss, who was in close contact with the FBI at the time, must have found the threat of a McCarthy investigation alarming. Not only would it put the Administration on the defensive on the Oppenheimer case, a position Strauss would not have relished, but it could also stir up enormous popular support for Oppenheimer if the case presented against him was not convincing.

By this time *Candor* was beginning to enter Strauss's field of vision, perhaps for the first time, and with it came a deepening concern about Oppenheimer's influence on Administration policy. In February, when Eisenhower had first discussed the report of the disarmament panel with Oppenheimer, *Candor* was a fresh idea, if somewhat naive and impractical. But since the death of Stalin in March, the President had taken a more optimistic view toward relations with the Russians and in a speech to newspaper editors on April 16 had invited the new Soviet leadership "to awaken . . . to the point of peril . . . and to help turn the tide of history." The more seriously the President and others within the Administration took it, the more worried Strauss became. The planning board of the National Security Council had appointed a special committee to meet with Vannevar Bush, a member of the disarmament panel, to draw up recommendations for implementing the panel's report. On May 8 the committee endorsed most ideas of the Oppenheimer report in a paper distributed as NSC 151 to members of the council, its staff, and most likely to Strauss.[39]

49

The committee thought that the government could acquaint the American people with the nature of the arms race without causing them "to lose heart in the present struggle or to seek a solution through preventive war." Neither could the proposal require any release of technical data on nuclear weapons or any compromise of intelligence sources. At the same time, the committee noted, the *Candor* proposal would require an important change in existing policies. The government would be releasing not only certain facts about the arms race but also its official analysis of those facts. And to be effective the release could not occur on just one occasion; it would have to take place over a period of time. Such a plan would require some understanding by the Congress and some mechanism for deciding what information should be released and how.

The committee then proceeded to outline the kinds of information to be released; the essential principle was that the government would not continue its "negative" policy of releasing fragments of information only when pressed but rather would adopt a "positive" policy of continuous publication of information. "It would mean that the President and his principal officers would regularly take the people into their confidence in the conviction that in a democracy an informed public is the best safeguard against extreme public reactions." The committee recommended that specific information be released on the degree of defense possible and that the statement be tied to the panel's recommendations on continental defense.

One of the touchiest topics was the proposed description of the United States stockpile of nuclear weapons. Stopping far short of the panel's recommendations, the committee did not propose to release actual numbers of weapons but to speak rather of the growing destructive power of stockpiled weapons, perhaps only in terms of the number of square miles that would be devastated by such a weapon. The American people would be told that the feasibility of thermonuclear weapons had been demonstrated, but it was not yet clear how thermonuclear weapons would alter the nature of atomic warfare in view of the already enormous destructive capability of fission weapons. As for Soviet capabilities, the nation would learn that within two years the Soviet Union would have "a stockpile numbered in the hundreds, and not many years thereafter in excess of a thousand."

## OPPENHEIMER AND CANDOR

Now that *Candor* was becoming the centerpiece in the Administration's plans for responding to the dangers of thermonuclear war, Strauss did not dare to attack the proposal directly, although his every instinct must have rebelled at any significant release of weapon information that might help the Soviet Union. One recourse was to point to the disadvantages of *Candor* in his discussions with the White House staff. Another was to undermine Oppenheimer's influence and, by raising questions about the scientist's security record, perhaps remove him from the Administration's policy councils altogether. The latter course suggested that Strauss and Borden might cooperate in seeking an answer to the old question of Oppenheimer's reliability.

By mid-May 1953 Borden was devoting most of his time at the Joint Committee to the Oppenheimer case and continuing salvos against the Commission in the Wheeler security controversy. Perhaps at Strauss's instigation, the FBI asked the Commission's security office to forward any information it received about Oppenheimer's plans for foreign travel, a move suggesting that Oppenheimer's activities abroad might somehow risk a compromise of classified information. One week later Borden called Waters at the Commission's security office to ask whether there was "anything new" in the Oppenheimer case. Before ending the call Borden asked Waters to send him Oppenheimer's security file.[40]

With Cotter's working paper on Oppenheimer already in hand, Borden did not need Oppenheimer's file for a quick review of the facts but rather for a thoughtful study of every shred of evidence, every implication and nuance that might shed some light on the Oppenheimer mystery. Except for a brief interruption on May 19 and 20 for another acrimonious exchange of correspondence with the Commission on the Wheeler incident, Borden buried himself in the Oppenheimer case. After wrestling in his mind one more time with each scrap of evidence, he compiled fifteen pages of questions ranging from serious to frivolous. His questioning, legitimate, improper, and silly, implied that Oppenheimer had been unjustly shielded from the requisites of a thorough security review.[41]

Gradually Borden began to see the Oppenheimer case in the same light in which he viewed the whole hydrogen bomb development. That is, just as he believed that the thermonuclear program had been neglected through lack of attention, so he thought that the Oppenheimer case had been ignored by being "kicked under the rug." The more he thought about them, the more Borden analyzed the two issues in the same vein, concluding that the same kind of attitude, almost the same kind of conspiracy, was working with respect to the H-bomb issue and Oppenheimer. But the Oppenheimer question needed, Borden thought, a single document, like the thermonuclear chronology, that pulled together all the disparate facts to show the Commission's reluctance to face the Oppenheimer question squarely.

Strauss in the meantime was becoming more and more preoccupied with Oppenheimer and *Candor*. On May 25 he confided to an FBI official his suspicion that Oppenheimer's communist sympathies were not yet dead. A Commission report, which Strauss had requested, revealed that David Hawkins, a physicist and former member of the Communist party, had been hired to work at Los Alamos during the war at Oppenheimer's instigation and had remained there until July 1947. Strauss also described in detail his opposition to Oppenheimer's attempt to bring Felix Browder, the son of the American Communist party leader, to the Institute for Advanced Study on a fellowship. Strauss's anxieties had been aroused because Browder was reportedly not an outstanding scholar and because Oppenheimer, in Strauss's estimation, had employed questionable tactics in trying to push through the appointment.[42]

51

Just the week before, Strauss had discovered that Oppenheimer had called the White House to request a meeting with Eisenhower on an urgent matter that he would reveal to no one but the President.[43] Privately, Strauss could only guess that the request had something to do with the forthcoming meeting of the National Security Council to discuss the Administration's plans for *Candor*. Or was it possible that Oppenheimer had caught wind of the renewed interest in his security file and was trying to protect himself? Strauss asked the FBI whether it would cause any difficulty if he mentioned his concerns about Oppenheimer to the President when Strauss saw him that afternoon; the FBI had no objection. Strauss's misgivings about Oppenheimer were also heightened by a report from the Commission that Oppenheimer had written a letter to the New York security office outlining his plans to visit Brazil in June and Japan in September.[44] Could these trips conceivably be designed to provide Oppenheimer a chance to talk freely with scientists abroad or possibly even with communist agents? Strauss requested a copy of the letter immediately.

Strauss could take some satisfaction in the fact that he had been alert enough to prevent Oppenheimer from catching the President unaware either at his private session with Eisenhower, now scheduled for May 29, or at the council meeting on *Candor* on May 27. But the results of that meeting were hardly comforting to Strauss, who saw *Candor* as foolishness at its best and a threat to national security at its worst. Much discussion at the council meeting reiterated the positions taken on February 25: the President's infatuation with the *Candor* idea despite its incompatibility with his strong instinct for secrecy and the opinions of Secretaries Wilson and Humphrey that *Candor* would scare the American people. In the end the argument seemed to move the President in the direction of *Candor*, but he still had reservations. These led him to the idea, and then to a decision, that all government statements in the future should avoid any reference to thermonuclear weapons and should use only the generic term "atomic weapons." Before making a final decision, Eisenhower wanted to see a draft of a speech that he might use to launch the project.[45]

Oppenheimer's new success in promoting *Candor* with the President must have heightened Strauss's anxiety about the scientist's influence over national security policy. If Oppenheimer was a security risk—a possibility Strauss had been unable to reject—his support of *Candor* could be interpreted as an attempt to compromise atomic secrets. The gnawing doubts that Oppenheimer's security file had raised in the minds of Strauss and Borden were now more pertinent than ever before.

For information on security matters Strauss had well-established lines of communication with both the Commission and the FBI. Not only could he telephone Dean and J. Edgar Hoover directly, but he also had informal contacts at the working level in both agencies through Bryan LaPlante and Charles Bates, Hoover's liaison agent with the Commission. During the next year Bates would be an inconspicuous but almost daily visitor to the Commission's headquarters building.

On June 4 Strauss called the FBI and asked once again to see the bureau's summary of the Oppenheimer file. When Bates arrived at Strauss's White House office a few hours later with the summary, Strauss told him that Eisenhower had drafted him against his wishes to serve as chairman of the Commission. Strauss had warned the President that "he could not do the job" if Oppenheimer were connected in any way with the program. Strauss had spoken very frankly to the President about Oppenheimer and intended to do the same with Robert Cutler, who handled national security affairs for the President. Approaching Cutler would be tricky, Strauss said, because Cutler served with Oppenheimer on the Harvard Board of Overseers and "did not like to hear criticism of his 'friends.' "[46]

Strauss would have been even more concerned had he known about a new development in the Oppenheimer affair. During Oppenheimer's visit to Washington the previous week, the scientist had asked Dean to extend his consultantship with the Commission for another year beyond its expiration date of June 30. Time was short; Oppenheimer would be leaving for Brazil within two weeks, and by the time he returned Dean would no longer be chairman. It was also quite likely that Dean and Oppenheimer knew that Strauss would by then be in charge of the Commission, a situation that would end all chances for Oppenheimer's reappointment. In light of the strong opposition to Oppenheimer revealed by Murphy's article, continuation of his Commission consultantship was the only way of retaining Oppenheimer's voice in the government in national security affairs, and specifically *Candor*. Without taking time to discuss the issue with the Commission or the staff, Dean instructed the general manager's office to renew Oppenheimer's contract. The renewal was dated June 5, perhaps the most fateful day in Robert Oppenheimer's life. As Strauss wrote nine years later: "It was this contract which involved the AEC in the clearance of Dr. Oppenheimer and which required that the Commission, rather than some other agency of the Government, be made responsible to hear and resolve the charges against him."[47]

By the first week in June the future looked promising for *Candor*. Oppenheimer's renewed contract assured that *Candor* would continue to be well represented in national policy councils. There was also every assurance that the President's speech launching *Candor* would be drafted quickly and efficiently. The task had been assigned to Charles D. Jackson, the ebullient editor of *Time* magazine who had joined the Eisenhower campaign as a speech writer in 1952. Far more imaginative and adventuresome than his boss, Jackson was constantly bombarding the President with all sorts of ideas for selling the Administration's policies to the American public. Operation *Candor* had struck a resonant chord in Jackson, and he took up the cause with enthusiasm. He even went so far as to sound out his friends in the advertising business in New York on how the job might be done. As Jackson often discovered, however, he quickly moved far beyond the President's wildest expectations. Eisenhower refused Jackson's suggestion that he use the dedication of the nuclear submarine prototype in Idaho as an occasion for announcing *Candor*. The President was no more receptive to a State Department draft of a *Candor* kick-off speech that Jackson submitted about the middle of June.[48]

While Jackson was trying to bring the President's thoughts on *Candor* into focus, the idea of informing the American people about the arms race was gaining public currency. For one thing the informed public knew that the study by the State Department panel existed although the full contents of the report had not been released.[49] Oppenheimer, however, known to be chairman of the panel, removed some ambiguity in June, when *Foreign Affairs* published an article based on his February speech before the Council on Foreign Relations.[50] Oppenheimer had been careful to separate his personal views from any government policy discussions, and he had cleared a draft of the article with the White House. But anyone who knew anything about the situation could see that Oppenheimer was not writing in a vacuum. In describing the arms race, Oppenheimer complained that "I must tell about it without communicating anything. I must reveal its nature without revealing anything."

53

Oppenheimer did relate information that had already been released about the Soviet program, namely that the Russians had accomplished three nuclear explosions and were producing fissionable material in substantial quantities. He also stated his own personal guess that the Russians were about four years behind the United States and that their scale of operations was not as big as that of the United States four years earlier. The American people, however, should know "quantitatively and, above all, authoritatively where we stand in these matters." Oppenheimer confessed that he had never discussed the classified facts about the nuclear arms race with any responsible group "that did not come away with a great sense of anxiety and somberness at what they saw." The United States' four-year lead over the Russians would mean little as the nuclear stockpile grew; America's twenty-thousandth bomb would be of small comfort when the Russians had their two-thousandth. Then he added the sentence that would long outlive him: "We may be likened to two scorpions in a bottle, each capable of killing the other, but only at the risk of his own life."

One obvious frustration Oppenheimer encountered in writing his article was that he could say nothing at all about thermonuclear weapons, which lay at the center of the panel's original concern and undoubtedly sparked Eisenhower's interest in the panel report. The frustration was the same for Eisenhower, Dean, or anyone else in the government who was privy to the facts. On the one hand, there was a natural tendency to withhold information about the thermonuclear test as much as possible; on the other, the results were so obviously significant to national security that others had to know.

Dean had sensed this feeling late in May 1953, when he saw for the first time a special film prepared by Joint Task Force 132 on the Enewetak test in November 1952. The film explained in detail the physical principles involved, the working components of the *Mike* device, and the elaborate preparations taken to gather technical data about the detonation. Although the film contained enough Hollywood clichés to annoy many viewers, it did effectively build suspense for more than an hour as the spine-tingling moment of detonation approached. The climax came in the extraordinary technicolor shots of the detonation, supported by statistical data that helped to put the incredible scale of the explosion in perspective.[51]

Dean was so impressed that he immediately called Robert Cutler at the White House to urge that the President see the film. On June 1, the President, the Cabinet, the National Security Council, the Joint Chiefs of Staff, and the Commissioners assembled in the East Wing theater to view the uncut, top secret version. The following day Dean and the President discussed how some of the more sensitive technical information in the film could be deleted so that a shorter version, still classified secret, could be shown to a larger audience.[52] Within the Administration the film probably

54

did far more than Oppenheimer's article to stimulate interest in Operation *Candor*.

Dean took up the *Candor* theme in the closing moments of his vale-dictory press conference as chairman of the Commission on June 25, 1953. Always the practical man, Dean cited the need to amend the Atomic Energy Act to give the Commission more flexibility in dealing with other nations and the need to release more technical information to industry. But most important of all in Dean's estimation was the release of information about atomic weapons in order to develop an informed public opinion, "which is the only realistic base upon which our defense and foreign policies can be built in the atomic age." Both Oppenheimer's and Dean's statements received wide attention in the American press. As the *Christian Science Monitor* noted, "A strong current has begun to flow in the direction of less secrecy and more information for the American people about the atom."[53]

55

## *STRAUSS AND* CANDOR

The current of public opinion running in favor of *Candor* continued to pick up speed during the first week of July 1953. In response to a question about the Oppenheimer article and the Dean valedictory, the President admitted at a press conference on July 8 that

> personally I think the time has arrived when the American people must have more information on this subject, if they are to act intel-ligently. . . . I think the time has come to be far more, let us say, frank with the American people than we have been in the past.

As the new chairman of the Commission and as a member of Eisenhower's inner circle of advisers on national security, Strauss could not entertain for a moment the idea of contradicting the President, but he was not ready to give up the fight. He would not, as the *Washington Post* hoped in an edi-torial on his appointment, move with the *Candor* current.[54]

Even within the Commission Strauss had to be careful not to oppose *Candor* openly, but he did do so indirectly. His first opportunity came when he received a comprehensive analysis of the Commission's policy on secu-rity and classification, which Smyth had prepared in the closing weeks of the Dean administration. Smyth had concluded that it would be in the na-tional interest to permit a greater exchange of technical information with Belgium, Canada, and the United Kingdom and to release much more data on reactor technology to American industry. In some areas, like thermo-nuclear weapons, continuing the most severe security restrictions was in order, but Smyth accepted the general thesis of the Oppenheimer panel that the public should know more about the nature of the arms race.[55]

Strauss had also received a letter from the Joint Committee on Atomic Energy citing the favorable comments by the President and Dean on *Candor* and requesting a detailed study of the need to revise the Atomic Energy Act to permit a wider dissemination of technical information. Without expressing his views on these specific questions, Strauss suggested that both the Smyth paper and the Joint Committee letter involved the same general issues, which he proposed to discuss in September, when he planned to take his fellow Commissioners on a weekend retreat at White Sulphur Springs, West Virginia.[56]

Some hint of Strauss's current views on security appeared in his correspondence with Senator Alexander Wiley, chairman of the Senate Foreign Relations Committee. Wiley wrote Strauss of his deep concern about American vulnerability to a Soviet nuclear attack, commenting that until the American people were acquainted with the given facts of the nuclear arms race they would be living in a "fool's paradise." In his reply Strauss did not mention *Candor*, but he was quick to stress the need for balancing the value of such information to the American people and the value of the same information to potential enemies. "All of us pray," he wrote Wiley, "that history will vindicate the wisdom of our judgments, both as to what is revealed and what is continued secure."[57]

The Commission's staff had numerous occasions during Strauss's first month as chairman to observe his sensitivity to all matters dealing with security and the control of information. On July 14 he questioned an earlier Commission decision authorizing the transmittal of unclassified drawings of a Brookhaven accelerator to a group of high-energy physicists in Europe. Strauss and Murray were both fearful that the drawings, although unclassified, would help other nations build accelerators to produce fissionable material. When Smyth assured him that this was not likely, Strauss still did not believe that the Commission would receive any direct benefit from the release and chose to delay a decision until he could discuss the problem with Ernest Lawrence. The clear implication was that the Commission was unlikely to benefit from research performed by other countries with American materials or technical data. Reaching back to the period of his earlier service on the Commission, Strauss requested information on whether a technical report had been received from Norway on research conducted with a radioactive iron isotope that the Commission had released over Strauss's objection in 1949. Strauss also opposed releasing an unclassified report on the Commission's reactor development program to the Joint Committee and expressed grave concern over the numbers of emergency clearances and missing top secret documents.[58] For old-timers on the staff Strauss's readiness to pounce on security matters reminded them of earlier days.

Strauss was careful to make no public statements about *Candor* but he worked behind the scenes to counter the Oppenheimer and Dean statements and even, in a subtle way, the remarks by the President himself. After April 28, when he apparently first discussed with Charles Murphy the article exposing the alleged Oppenheimer conspiracy, Strauss was in frequent contact with Murphy and most probably helped him to prepare a second article, which appeared in the August 1953 issue of *Fortune*. More temperate and accurate than the first article, the second attempted to refute Oppenheimer's main arguments in *Foreign Affairs* without mentioning the insinuations of conspiracy in the May article. By reporting the President's remarks in the opening paragraphs without comment, Murphy gave his readers an opportunity to apply his criticisms of Oppenheimer's position indirectly to the President. The Murphy article contained arguments typically used by Strauss to support rigid security for weapon information and particularly for stockpile figures. Also like Strauss, Murphy placed information about nuclear power plants in a separate category as potentially suitable for release to the public. On July 16, the day Murphy sent his manuscript to the printer, he called Strauss's office for some last-minute advice. Almost as a credit, the article included one photograph, a portrait of Strauss with the caption: "Strauss believes in keeping a tight lid on information about U.S. atomic weapons."[59]

57

Although Murphy and Strauss had been too circumspect in the *Fortune* article to be accused of challenging the President, the article left no doubt about Strauss's position in the minds of Administration leaders. C. D. Jackson brought up the subject over cocktails with Strauss on August 4. Strauss reassured Jackson that he was neither involved in a feud with Oppenheimer nor opposed to the President's speaking to the nation on *Candor* but that he did object to the use of "any comparative arithmetic" on American and Soviet nuclear stockpiles.[60]

## JOE 4

Any relaxation of security that Operation *Candor* might have inspired was suddenly blocked by new developments in the international arms race during August 1953. On August 8, in a speech before the Supreme Soviet in Moscow, Premier Georgi M. Malenkov announced that the United States no longer had a monopoly of the hydrogen bomb. In response to press inquiries Strauss blandly replied that the United States had never assumed that the bomb was beyond Soviet capabilities and for that reason had embarked on its own project three years earlier.[61]

On August 12 Strauss and the Administration received from the Air Force long-range detection system the first fragmentary evidence that Malenkov's statement was not a hollow claim. The Soviet Union had apparently conducted its fourth nuclear weapon test, which the Americans called *Joe 4*. Because the detonation had been quite powerful, the Americans thought it was possibly a thermonuclear device, but direct evidence would not be available until airborne samples of radioactive debris from the test could be collected and analyzed. In the meantime it was extremely important for intelligence reasons to prevent the information from becoming public; the longer that event could be postponed, the more easily could the government conceal the degree of efficiency and accuracy of the long-range detection system. Perhaps for this reason, Strauss did not immediately inform his fellow Commissioners but chose rather, as special assistant to the President, to work with the White House staff in drafting announcements that might be used under a variety of circumstances.[62]

Strauss and Jackson met with the President in New York on the morning of August 19 to discuss both *Candor* and the Soviet test. Eisenhower, although reluctant to make any announcement, finally approved for later release a simple statement to the effect that the Russians had conducted an atomic test. Later the same day in Washington, after conferring with the other Commissioners and State Department and CIA officials, Strauss decided not to release any announcement until information from the first samples arrived later in the evening. In Strauss's office at the Commission headquarters at eight o'clock, scientists from the Air Force long-range detection system stated conclusively that "a fission and thermonuclear reaction had taken place within Soviet territory." Despite State Department assurances that the Russians were not likely to elaborate on Malenkov's statement of August 8, Strauss learned at ten-thirty that evening that Moscow radio had announced a Soviet test involving a hydrogen reaction several days earlier. After redrafting the public announcement to contain a reference to thermonuclear reactions, Strauss decided that he would have to clear the release with the President in view of Eisenhower's order not to mention the hydrogen bomb in public statements. Because the President was at that time flying to Denver, Strauss was unable to clear the release until almost midnight. The next day some of the nation's newspapers carried the headline: "REDS TEST H-BOMB."[63]

For most Americans, perhaps even for Strauss and others in the Administration, that simple statement sufficiently described Soviet capabilities. The hydrogen bomb was more than a weapon; it was a symbol of military capability that gave Oppenheimer's analogy of "two scorpions in a bottle" a new and more terrible significance. As Congressman Cole of the Joint Committee pointed out to the American Legion in October 1953, the Russians had detonated a hydrogen weapon "only nine months after our own hydrogen test." Although Strauss, like all other members of the Administration, was enjoined by the President from public comment on hydrogen bombs, Strauss did confide to others in classified discussions his fears that the Soviet Union had bypassed some earlier refinements of fission weapons and had concentrated on thermonuclear designs several years earlier, probably before the United States accelerated its own thermonuclear program in 1950. The President himself in a press conference on September 30, 1953, had referred to the Soviet achievement as the creation of a hydrogen bomb.[64]

The fact was, however, that neither the Commission nor the Administration had any incontrovertible evidence on August 20 or even on October 12 that the Soviet Union had developed a thermonuclear weapon. As the Commission's original statement carefully put it, the initial evidence on August 20 merely confirmed that the detonation involved both fissionable and thermonuclear materials. It was apparent that the general statements made in 1953 and later years about Soviet superiority in thermonuclear weapon development were far from the whole truth. The Soviet scientists had *not* detonated a "true" hydrogen weapon within nine months after *Mike*. They had *not* developed an airborne thermonuclear weapon before the United States. And it was *not* true that the Americans had taken the wrong path in using deuterium while the Russians had struck out directly for the more practical lithium-deuteride approach.

Why then did these misconceptions arise and then persist in discussions of national security issues? First, the inherent limitations of intelligence-gathering systems made it impossible in 1953, or even many years later, for American scientists to construct an authoritative description of all features in *Joe 4*. The nation's most experienced and talented scientists could and did disagree in interpreting some evidence. Second, and more important, the extreme secrecy that surrounded both the American thermonuclear program and the intelligence reports on Soviet developments caused much confusion. Some Commissioners apparently were not apprised even of the simple facts deduced by the scientists.[65] Although some facts did leak into the public press, distortions inevitably occurred as reporters speculated on the fragmentary evidence and the Commission for security reasons refrained from confirming or denying the accuracy of such speculations. For more than two decades the most elementary facts about *Mike* and *Joe 4* were unconfirmed, and a full description of these devices will probably not be revealed in this century. Lacking a full understanding of the qualitative differences between the Soviet and American devices, Strauss and others in the Administration had no compunctions in assuming the worst about the Soviet thermonuclear challenge.

59

## THE QUEST FOR CANDOR

During summer 1953, Jackson by his own admission had had little success in producing an acceptable draft of the *Candor* speech for the President. No matter what approach he took to the meaning of the thermonuclear weapon, Jackson found that he ended up with a gruesome story of human destruction. Unless the Administration could find some positive hope to present to the American people and the world, the horrifying consequences of nuclear warfare would simply generate fear, and, as the President remarked, the public could not be expected to reach an intelligent understanding in an atmosphere of fear.[66]

*Joe 4* seemed to heighten the tension that the threat of thermonuclear weapons had already created in both the government and the nation. On one side, *Joe 4* represented a massive increase in the Soviet Union's nuclear capability, a trend that seemed to make the arguments for *Candor* even more urgent. There now seemed to be that much less information about American weapons to conceal from the Russians, and it was all the more imperative to acquaint the American people with the truth of their predicament, however unpleasant that knowledge might be. On the other side, it was possible to argue, as some did, that *Joe 4* required a tightening of belts, a new dedication to enlarging the United States' own nuclear capabilities, and a need to protect every technical secret that still remained in American hands.

Eisenhower himself apparently felt these same kinds of tensions. Although he was among the most conservative of his Administration in wanting to seal off the details of weapon technology from the nation's potential enemies, the President refused to abandon his initial conviction that the world needed to understand the awesome dangers of the thermonuclear age if unspeakable disaster was to be avoided. Thus, despite his dissatisfaction with Jackson's drafts, Eisenhower continued to push for *Candor*. By early September, Jackson, with help from his friends in the National Advertising Council, had proposed an elaborate scheme for a series of seven television programs beginning in October. The President himself would lead off with his own statement on "The Safety of the Republic in the Atomic Age." On successive Sundays Cabinet officers and other Administration officials would participate in round-table discussions similar to those Eisenhower and some of his Cabinet members had presented on June 3, 1953. These discussions would cover international affairs, the capabilities of the Soviet bloc, the need for strengthening the free world, the dangers of subversion at home, and the role of civilians in an age of peril.[67]

From the outset Jackson's television series seemed doomed to failure. Some government officials, J. Edgar Hoover for example, were reluctant to participate; of equal concern to Jackson were those anxious to speak their minds. Jackson had been careful to exclude Defense Secretary Wilson, who had already demonstrated his vulnerability to baited questions in press conferences. Even with careful selection of participants and preparation of a script, it would be difficult to predict the impact of the programs in the still relatively unfamiliar medium of television. Given the exceptional sensitivity of the subject, it was frightening to contemplate the potential damage of a casual remark in a series of relatively unstructured discussions.[68]

In the end two developments during September 1953 killed the television series. First, the idea itself inevitably leaked to the press with disastrous consequences; now, no matter what the President decided, some of the press would probably accuse him of being less than candid about *Candor*. Second, "a Babel of conflicting statements," as columnist Arthur Krock put it, developed about the imminence of the Soviet thermonuclear threat. Strauss himself, in a speech before the National Security Industrial Association on September 30, voiced publicly for the first time his fears that the Soviet Union had bypassed research on fission weapons to beat the United States to the punch in developing the hydrogen bomb. Arthur S. Flemming, director of the Office of Defense Mobilization and an advocate of industrial dispersion, had stated in a public report on October 4 that "Soviet Russia is capable of delivering the most destructive weapon ever devised by man on chosen targets in the United States." Congressman Cole, remarking that he preferred "financial ruination" to "atomic devastation," urged the expenditure of $10 billion for air defense. Val Peterson, whose Federal Civil Defense Administration budget had been severely cut by the Eisenhower Administration, saw no hope for a peaceful settlement of the Cold War. But Secretary Wilson thought the Soviet Union was three or four years behind the United States in developing both thermonuclear weapons and the aircraft to carry them.[69]

61

These and other contradictory statements on the threat posed by *Joe 4* had reached epidemic proportions in the nation's press by the second week in October. After a long discussion of the problem at the National Security Council meeting on October 7, 1953, Eisenhower decided to accept Strauss's proposal that all statements about thermonuclear weapons by Administration officials first be cleared with the chairman of the Atomic Energy Commission.[70]

The next day at his weekly press conference, Eisenhower read a carefully prepared statement on *Joe 4*. The Soviet Union had tested "an atomic device in which some part of the explosive force was derived from a thermonuclear reaction." The Soviet Union now had "the capability of atomic attack on us, and such capability will increase with the passage of time." The President did not "intend to disclose the details of our strength in atomic weapons of any sort, but it is large and increasing steadily." The statement, repeating words used by Strauss in his September 30 speech and by Senator Hickenlooper, a conservative Republican member of the Joint Committee, seemed to kill a central proposal by the Oppenheimer panel for Project *Candor*. That statement, plus the President's assignment of Strauss as the Administration's watchdog over thermonuclear information, led the press to conclude that *Candor* was now dead.[71]

The President, strangely enough, did not seem to share that view. Because he believed that the people of the United States and of the world could be given the facts they needed about the dangers of nuclear warfare without revealing such details, he had never considered detailed revelations about thermonuclear capabilities or the weapon stockpile an essential element of *Candor.* But Eisenhower wanted some positive suggestion that would give hope for the future. He was intrigued with developing an idea that had occurred to him during his vacation in Denver during August. When he had returned to Washington briefly for Chief Justice Fred M. Vinson's funeral on September 10, he had asked General Robert Cutler, who handled national security affairs, to convey his idea to Strauss and Jackson. "Suppose," the President suggested, "the United States and the Soviets were each to turn over to the United Nations, for peaceful uses, X Kilograms of fissionable material." [72]

## STRAUSS AND OPPENHEIMER

62

Strauss may well have taken some comfort in the President's suggestion as a move away from what he saw as Oppenheimer's dangerous and naive proposal for *Candor.* But were Oppenheimer and his friends merely naive, or were there sinister motives behind their continuing efforts to promote *Candor* even in the face of the terse Soviet announcement of *Joe 4?* How could an intelligent person like Oppenheimer support such a hair-brained idea when the Soviet Union was obviously out to overtake the United States in nuclear weapon development? The gnawing doubts about Oppenheimer's loyalty that Strauss had shared with Borden since 1950 continued to haunt both men.

Borden seemed to drop out of Strauss's world after leaving the Joint Committee at the end of May 1953. Except for one telephone conversation on July 16, there is no evidence that the two men communicated during the remainder of that year. Borden, unable to fathom the Oppenheimer mystery posed in the scores of questions that he had assembled on the subject, left Washington for his vacation retreat near the St. Lawrence River. There he would continue to ponder the shadowy record of Oppenheimer's past and the scientist's impact on the development of nuclear weapons. [73]

Strauss had no such opportunity to retreat from the Oppenheimer enigma. As chairman of the Commission, he was now directly responsible for protecting what he saw as the little that was left of the nation's supremacy in nuclear weapon technology, and he now knew to his dismay that his future as a government official was closely linked to Oppenheimer's. Dean's action in extending Oppenheimer's consultant contract had seen to that, and for Strauss there was no easy escape. He and J. Edgar Hoover had agreed that it would be dangerous to attack Oppenheimer directly unless there was convincing evidence against him. [74] Strauss was not eager to risk his cordial relations with America's scientific giants, something he greatly cherished, and his leadership of the Commission in a dramatic showdown with a scientist as popular and prestigious as Oppenheimer. Patience and the expiration of Oppenheimer's contract on June 30, 1954, might take care of the Oppenheimer problem. But in the meantime Strauss could not afford to overlook any scrap of evidence that might convince the public that Oppenheimer could not be trusted. If such information should fall into his hands, Strauss would have no choice but to risk his political future to protect the national security.

During summer 1953, Strauss pursued his discreet inquiries of Oppenheimer's activities with the help of Bryan LaPlante, now his security aide, and Charles Bates of the FBI. Strauss continued to be concerned about Oppenheimer's plans for foreign travel, presumably because trips abroad would offer him a chance to contact communist agents or even to slip behind the Iron Curtain. When the first intelligence reports on *Joe 4* arrived, Strauss's level of anxiety rose. On August 18, the day before the Soviets announced *Joe 4*, Strauss asked for Oppenheimer's security file, which had remained at the Joint Committee since Borden requested it on May 14. The next day, before meeting with the President to discuss *Joe 4* and *Candor*, Strauss complained privately to his fellow Commissioners about Oppenheimer's request for classified defense documents. The Commission could refuse Oppenheimer only with difficulty because Dean had extended Oppenheimer's consultant contract in June. Strauss was further annoyed to learn on August 31 that Oppenheimer had been seeking information from the Commission staff about the recent Soviet test series, apparently in disregard of Strauss's instructions that all such information would be disseminated only through his office. In an attempt to head off Oppenheimer, Strauss told the staff that he would speak to Oppenheimer personally on September 2. [75]

63

Unknown to his fellow Commissioners, Strauss had already been in direct contact with Oppenheimer, who had called Strauss at his Virginia farm on August 28 for an appointment in Washington on September 1. When Strauss had suggested an afternoon meeting on that day, Oppenheimer had begged off, saying that he had an important appointment at the White House. Anxious to know what Oppenheimer was up to, Strauss asked LaPlante to arrange to have Oppenheimer put under FBI surveillance during his visit to Washington. The bureau dutifully reported back on September 2 that Oppenheimer had not gone to the White House but had spent the entire afternoon in the men's bar of the Statler Hotel with columnist Marquis Childs. The surveillance also revealed that Joseph Volpe, Jr., a former general counsel of the Commission and Oppenheimer's lawyer in the Weinberg case, had visited Oppenheimer at the hotel for a half hour that evening. Volpe had then been trailed to a food store, where he purchased groceries and took them to the home of a former Commission employee who had worked as a special assistant to Chairman Lilienthal. Strauss guessed that Oppenheimer was giving Childs information for articles in the *Wash-*

*ington Post* supporting Oppenheimer's views on national security. The information that Volpe had visited the former Commission associate, a woman who, the FBI said, had a record of some association with communist-front organizations, conjured up images of illicit and possibly treasonable relationships reminiscent of those in which Oppenheimer had been involved during the 1930s. Oppenheimer's obvious lie to Strauss about his commitments for September 1 reinforced Strauss's conviction that Oppenheimer and his friends fell short of acceptable standards of morality and to that extent were less than fully trustworthy.[76]

## NICHOLS AND OPPENHEIMER

64

After his morning conference with Oppenheimer on September 2, Strauss looked forward to a more pleasant meeting. He had invited Commissioners Murray and Zuckert to lunch with Major General Kenneth D. Nichols, Strauss's candidate to replace Marion W. Boyer as general manager. Nichols, a West Point graduate and a career Army officer with a Ph.D. in engineering, had served with General Groves in the Manhattan Project. Following World War II Nichols had been a consultant to the Joint Committee. Nichols already had a reputation for being tough, principled, and opinionated. Rejected outright for any position on the Commission staff in 1947 because of his strong ties to the Manhattan Project, Nichols had continually challenged the Commission's authority in military matters. With Oppenheimer, Nichols had raised the ire of the Air Force by advocating greater emphasis on tactical weapons; but in contrast with the Princeton physicist, Nichols was also counted among the staunchest proponents of the hydrogen bomb.[77]

The luncheon began with some reminiscences about the Manhattan Project, and then conversation turned to Oppenheimer's position on the hydrogen bomb and the renewal of his clearance in June. Murray seized the opportunity to explain how the contract with Oppenheimer had been executed. According to Murray, Dean had not consulted the other Commissioners before renewing the contract. Murray's inference was clear: once again in the interest of expediency unwarranted shortcuts had been taken to maintain Oppenheimer's clearance.[78]

The luncheon meeting cleared the way for Nichols to assume the office of general manager on November 1, 1953, with a clear mandate to carry out the atomic energy policies of the Republican Administration as interpreted by Strauss. For over a decade Nichols's position on the Oppenheimer case, although complex, had remained consistent. Intimately familiar with Oppenheimer's record, Nichols never shared Strauss's and Borden's fears that Oppenheimer might be a Soviet agent. Nevertheless Nichols maintained that Oppenheimer was a major security risk and should not be granted clearance. Nichols had opposed granting Oppenheimer's clearance in 1942; when the war ended and the need for taking chances was past, Nichols attempted to instigate a review of all questionable clearances, including Oppenheimer's. Whenever possible Nichols encouraged officials, particularly in the Department of Defense, to discontinue consultation with Oppenheimer. Nichols was more or less satisfied with the progress made in gradually terminating Oppenheimer's various clearances. Now, as general manager, Nichols was in a position to complete the process.[79]

## TOWARD THE PEACEFUL ATOM

During September and October 1953 the Oppenheimer case was a matter of chronic but not paramount concern for Strauss. Much higher on his agenda was the President's suggestion that the United States and the Soviet Union might divert equal amounts of fissionable material to peaceful purposes. At first Strauss did not see any practical advantage in Eisenhower's suggestion. What good would it do to contribute fissionable materials to peaceful uses if the United States and the Soviet Union both retained large amounts in the form of weapons? And how would it be possible to protect the contributed material from falling into the hands of an aggressor nation? Not willing to take his fellow Commissioners into his confidence on so sensitive a matter, Strauss confined his discussion of the subject to breakfast meetings with Jackson at the Metropolitan Club in Washington. From these sessions the new effort took the name of Project *Wheaties.*[80]

65

By mid-September Strauss began to think better of the idea and suggested that it be considered by an ad hoc committee on disarmament within the National Security Council. With the President's approval Strauss set out to put his ideas on paper. Starting with the assumption that any agreement with the Soviet Union "would be presently unenforceable by any known means," he concluded that any plan for partial or total atomic disarmament would have to be "clearly and unequivocally advantageous" to the United States and that any proposal would have to benefit the United States, even if the Soviet Union rejected it. Such an agreement would have to be "independent of reliance upon continued good faith or enforcement" because absolute accountability for all fissionable material produced would be impossible. The agreement would have to be acceptable to nonnuclear nations and could not rely on international ownership, control, or operation of any facilities within the United States or the Soviet Union.[81]

Building on Eisenhower's idea, Strauss proposed that all uranium and thorium mines be shut down for ten years. All plutonium production reactors would cease operation except for one facility in each country for producing radioactive isotopes for research. Each nuclear nation would deliver a fixed amount of fissionable material each month to a "World Atomic Power Administration." To provide maximum protection for the material, Strauss proposed that it either be stored as a highly diluted solution in underground tanks at some isolated location, such as Ascension Island, or be dispersed to a large number of scattered sites. Strauss acknowledged that the plan would not immediately reduce the threat of biological, nuclear, or conventional warfare, but it did offer "a means of impounding gradually the devastation of atomic warfare and, by its simplicity and plausibility, it would be likely to attract the adherence of the small neutrals and the enthusiastic support of plain people."

Strauss's preoccupation with the security aspects of the proposal was not likely to appeal to Eisenhower or Jackson, but the plan did embody the President's basic strategy—to approach world disarmament, not in one dramatic proposal, but in small steps in tune with existing realities and simple enough for the public to understand. Complex plans for balanced reductions of both nuclear and conventional armaments, such as those the State Department proposed in October 1953, were not amenable to presentation in a presidential address but would require months, if not years, of secret diplomatic negotiations. In autumn 1953 Eisenhower had no intention of limiting the Administration's efforts to diplomatic channels.[82]

Despite the debacle that had overtaken Operation *Candor* in September, Eisenhower had never abandoned the idea of speaking out on the growing dangers of nuclear warfare. Always before, the overwhelming pessimism of the *Candor* drafts had caused the President to hold back; but Strauss's plan, which offered small but positive hope for a way out of the nuclear dilemma, now seemed to make *Candor* possible. A special opportunity lay in the fact that the United Nations General Assembly was then meeting in New York. A speech there would give Eisenhower a world, rather than just a national, platform.

Late in October Jackson began to assemble the ingredients for a speech before the General Assembly. From the dozen drafts of the *Candor* speech, he could extract the grim statistics on the nuclear arms race: the destructive capability of the United States' nuclear stockpile compared to that of all the munitions used in World War II and the fact that the Soviet Union had the hydrogen bomb. From the State Department's latest proposal he could borrow material that would describe the trouble spots in Europe, Korea, and Southeast Asia that were breeding grounds for new global conflicts. From Strauss's paper he could extract the proposal for a positive contribution to world peace.

The essential structure and tone of the speech were fixed on November 6 when Jackson read his second draft aloud to the President, Strauss, and United Nations Ambassador Henry Cabot Lodge, but revisions continued apace. The fifth draft completed on November 28 barely survived a sustained attack by Secretary of Defense Wilson and his deputy, Roger M.

Kyes. Undaunted, Jackson immediately began work on a sixth draft, which he expected to have ready in a few days.[83]


## THE BORDEN LETTER

Although both Strauss and Nichols would have been happy to see Oppenheimer excluded from national security information, neither man wanted to precipitate that action in a way that would damage the atomic energy program or their own effectiveness as government officials. They had bided their time too long on the Oppenheimer case to take any rash or ill-considered action. Yet, within a week after Nichols took over as general manager, William Borden, most likely without contacting either Strauss or Nichols, dispatched to the FBI a letter destined to change the lives of all four men.

On November 12, Lou B. Nichols, an FBI official in Washington, received a letter addressed to J. Edgar Hoover from Borden, whom he had known as executive director of the Joint Committee. After reviewing the extraordinary scope of Oppenheimer's activities in national security affairs since World War II, Borden concluded that Oppenheimer was and for some years had been "in a position to compromise more vital and detailed information affecting the national defense and security than any other individual in the United States." As chairman or as a member of "more than thirty-five important Government committees, panels, study groups, and projects, he [had] oriented and dominated key policies involving every principal United States security department and agency except the FBI." Then without so much as a sentence of transition, Borden went to the purpose of his letter: "to state my own exhaustively considered opinion, based on years of study of the available classified evidence, that more probably than not J. ROBERT OPPENHEIMER is an agent of the Soviet Union."[84]

Borden's charges were so serious that they could not be ignored, but Agent Nichols and his associates at the FBI received the letter with some skepticism. Why had Borden waited so long after leaving the Joint Committee to make his charges? Did he really have some evidence against Oppenheimer, or was he merely trying to put his worst fears on the record? Borden had not backed up his letter with any solid evidence of Oppenheimer's alleged treason but merely summarized in single sentences some twenty instances purporting to show Oppenheimer's ties with communists. The FBI staff noted that Borden's allegations followed the FBI summary of Oppenheimer's file, "except Borden has included his own interpretations and conclusions, which are not factual in every instance." Because Borden's reliability was in doubt, the FBI staff proposed to Hoover that he send a special agent to Pittsburgh to interview Borden to determine whether he had any concrete evidence. In the meantime the FBI wanted to keep Bor-

67

den's letter from leaking to Oppenheimer or the press, but the FBI felt compelled to warn all departments and agencies that had granted Oppenheimer access to classified information. Painstaking review of the draft within the FBI delayed dispatch of the letter until November 27.[85]

## BORDEN AND MCCARTHY

Concurrent events explained the extreme sensitivity that the FBI exercised in handling the Borden letter. On November 6, the day before Borden mailed his letter, Herbert M. Brownell, Jr., Eisenhower's Attorney General, accused former President Truman of nominating Harry Dexter White to be director of the International Monetary Fund despite the fact that he knew White had been a communist spy. Thereafter Truman went on nationwide radio and television to defend himself, accusing Brownell and the Eisenhower Administration in turn of "McCarthyism."

As the issue of McCarthyism boiled up in the nation's press, Murray became increasingly concerned about Strauss's growing tendency to immerse himself in security matters. As he told J. Edgar Hoover on November 23, he was shocked that Strauss had employed as his special assistant David S. Teeple, a former aide to Senator Hickenlooper and former security investigator for the Manhattan Project, a man known around Washington for his excessive zeal in security matters. Teeple, at Strauss's behest, was reportedly digging around in old files and launching "many investigations into things that had happened in the past." Murray asked Hoover whether the FBI had given Strauss any information that had caused him to employ Teeple and step up security activities. At first Hoover could think of nothing out of the ordinary, but then he recalled somewhat nonchalantly the Oppenheimer case. He mentioned to Murray his efforts during spring 1953 to head off Senator McCarthy and his special investigator, Roy Cohn; Hoover was convinced that McCarthy had been successfully contained. Almost as an afterthought, Hoover mentioned the Borden letter. Hoover could not explain why Borden had written the letter, but he supposed that Borden "had a lot of these things on his mind and decided more or less to dump them into the lap of the FBI." Giving Murray no indication he was particularly alarmed by the Borden letter, Hoover promised to send Murray copies of all important FBI communications with the Commission, including special reports to the chairman and a copy of the Borden letter.[86]

Hoover was correct in asserting that he had steered McCarthy away from the Oppenheimer case. On the day after Murray's visit to the FBI, McCarthy demanded and received equal time over radio and television to respond to Truman. According to C. D. Jackson, McCarthy's sensational speech, aside from announcing an open season on lambasting Truman, openly "declared war on Eisenhower."[87] While the Borden letter was still in FBI channels, Eisenhower and his staff at the White House discussed the President's response to McCarthy. C. D. Jackson and others in the Administration argued that appeasing McCarthy would wreck the Republican party and lead it to defeat in 1954 and 1956. Eisenhower, however, was adamant; on December 2 he declared he would not "get in the gutter" with McCarthy.[88]

On that same day Hoover began to receive responses to his memorandum forwarding the Borden letter and the Oppenheimer summary to the White House and the heads of seven departments and agencies. The first to call was Secretary of Defense Wilson, who was "shocked" by the news. He recalled the Wheeler incident and wondered whether Oppenheimer might have been involved with Wheeler in the loss of the top secret document. Wilson had already talked to Brownell and Strauss, who had said he did not know whether Oppenheimer was a communist but he knew that the scientist was a "liar." Wilson wanted to be certain that Oppenheimer was cut off from any access to classified defense information. Hoover suggested that Wilson consult General Cutler at the White House and Strauss before taking any formal action. Hoover also reminded Wilson that the FBI had not yet interviewed Borden about his letter.[89]

Apparently dissatisfied with Hoover's cautious approach, Wilson called Eisenhower directly. Because Cutler had not yet brought the matter to the President's attention, Eisenhower did not at first know what Wilson was talking about. But as the Secretary proceeded to describe the FBI summary of the Oppenheimer case and the charges in the Borden letter, which both he and Strauss had received, the President became greatly concerned. "Jolted" by the news about Oppenheimer, Eisenhower bravely professed not to be worried about the McCarthy threat, but his subsequent action that day showed that he did not take the matter lightly.[90] The President sent immediately for Strauss, who found Cutler and others gathered in the Oval Office when he arrived at the White House. The President was determined to act quickly, but he wanted to check first with Attorney General Brownell to make certain that the evidence against Oppenheimer was solid. The next morning, before the meeting of the National Security Council, Eisenhower met with Wilson, Strauss, Under Secretary of Defense Kyes, and Cutler to decide what should be done. Still deeply troubled, the President directed that, pending further investigation, "a blank wall" should be placed between Oppenheimer and any sensitive or classified information.[91]

Just how that "blank wall" was to be constructed the President allowed Strauss and others to decide. The most obvious measure was to revoke Oppenheimer's clearance for atomic energy information, a step Strauss immediately explored. Hoover saw two dangers in this approach. First, he worried that Oppenheimer, then traveling in Europe, might defect to the Soviet Union if he learned of the action against him before he returned to the United States. Second, Hoover warned that lifting Oppenheimer's clearance would give him the opportunity to request a public hearing. Unless the evidence against Oppenheimer was convincing, Hoover feared that he might use clever lawyers to vindicate himself and "then a martyr would have been made of an individual who we know morally is a security risk." Much of the evidence against Oppenheimer, Hoover contended, could not be introduced in a public hearing without revealing confidential sources. Furthermore, Hoover was not at all confident of Borden's reliability. He had dispatched an FBI agent to Pittsburgh to interview Borden that evening; unless Borden had some solid evidence against Oppenheimer, Hoover was not sure that the government would have a good case.[92]

Hoover much preferred the alternative of disbanding the one government committee of which Oppenheimer was still a member (in the Office of Defense Mobilization) so that his clearance would automatically lapse. Abolishing that committee, however, was found impractical, and Strauss noted that merely allowing the clearance to lapse would not be sufficient to cut Oppenheimer's many lines of communication with scientists in the atomic energy establishment. In fact, Strauss on the afternoon of December 3 considered notifying the directors of all the Commission's laboratories that Oppenheimer's clearance had been suspended. But both LaPlante and Hoover warned Strauss that such a directive would likely leak to Oppenheimer, who might then decide to defect. Thus, Strauss decided to revoke the clearance but to issue no instructions to the field and to delay informing Oppenheimer until he returned to the United States on December 13. Running through all these discussions on December 3 was the pressure to act quickly. As Cutler told Strauss, "he wanted a record established of very prompt action."[93] Such a record would presumably protect the President in any subsequent investigation by McCarthy, and the best way to take prompt action was to suspend Oppenheimer's clearance.

As Nichols astutely observed, there was an important coincidence between the Harry Dexter White–McCarthy incident and the Oppenheimer case.[94] Indeed, McCarthy had forced the President's hand in dealing with Oppenheimer, but not for the reasons generally assumed. Eisenhower had little reason to fear that McCarthy would exploit the Oppenheimer case, but, in the atmosphere created by Brownell's charges against Truman and then McCarthy's accusations against the Administration, Eisenhower knew that he faced a crisis of confidence with his immediate staff. McCarthy had presented the inexperienced President a delicate political problem to which he instinctively responded with caution approaching timidity. The Oppenheimer case, however, lay in the familiar area of national security where, cloaked in secrecy, the former general could react with the same kind of dramatic swiftness that he had demonstrated in the Wheeler affair. In short, with Dulles, Jackson, and others worried about presidential leadership, it was almost inevitable that Eisenhower would respond boldly to Borden's challenge.

Strauss may have been correct when he said that the President wanted to get rid of Oppenheimer. But as Eisenhower wrote in *Mandate for Change*, the charges against Oppenheimer "were brought not by an unknown citizen," but by Borden, who had directed the Joint Committee staff "under the preceding Democratic administration, and who obviously was aware of the gravity of his charges." Under the circumstances, which included the fact that the President was due to leave for an international conference in Bermuda, Eisenhower had few alternatives. There was no time for a calm and leisurely deliberation. Finally, because Eisenhower had no direct knowledge of the Oppenheimer file except through Hoover's report and no authority to revoke the physicist's clearance by presidential order, he could only suspend Oppenheimer's access to classified information pending a hearing by the Atomic Energy Commission. Thus, almost before anyone knew it, events had advanced to the point where few viable options were left.[95]

71

## ATOMS FOR PEACE

On the morning of December 3, 1953, before the meeting of the National Security Council that decided Oppenheimer's fate, the President reviewed C. D. Jackson's sixth draft of the United Nations speech with Strauss, Wilson, Dulles, and Kyes. Jackson later wrote that Wilson was "still mumbling around in his cave," but Kyes had reversed himself after his bitter attack on November 30. The session resulted in a few more changes that Jackson managed to complete later that day.[96]

Eisenhower probably would have addressed the General Assembly in November had it not been for the Bermuda conference with Prime Minister Winston Churchill and Premier Joseph Laniel of France. Because the British and French leaders had not been told of the plan, the President decided not to seek an invitation from the United Nations until he had arrived in Bermuda. Strauss explained his proposal for a nuclear pool to Lord Cherwell, Churchill's scientific adviser. Although Cherwell predicted that the pool would be difficult to establish, he agreed to support the plan. Churchill, who had already read the speech, then approved it with only a few suggestions for minor changes, which Eisenhower accepted.[97]

Arrangements had been made for the presidential party to fly directly from Bermuda to New York, where Eisenhower was to address the General Assembly on December 8. As soon as the President boarded the plane, he called Dulles, Strauss, Jackson, and James Hagerty, his press secretary, to his cabin and began to edit the speech line by line. As each page was completed, it was retyped on stencils and reproduced on a mimeograph machine in the rear luggage compartment. As the plane approached La Guardia Field, Dulles, Strauss, and others helped to staple copies that would be distributed at the United Nations.[98]

As Eisenhower mounted the rostrum at the General Assembly that December afternoon, he was realizing a hope he had been pursuing since the first weeks of his Administration—to arrest and, if possible, reduce the growing danger of a world holocaust made possible by the development of fission and thermonuclear weapons. The United States proposed that the nuclear nations "begin now and continue to make joint contributions from their stockpiles of normal uranium and fissionable materials to an International Atomic Energy Agency" to be established under the aegis of the United Nations.[99]

In nine weeks the President had moved far beyond Strauss's proposal for an international pool of fissionable material. Instead of isolating the material in underground tanks, Eisenhower was now proposing to use it to develop power for peaceful purposes. "Who can doubt," the President asked, "if the entire body of the world's scientists and engineers had adequate amounts of fissionable material . . . , that this capability would rapidly be transformed into universal, efficient, and economic usage." Nuclear power itself was to save the world from nuclear devastation.

Balancing the nuclear threat with nuclear power was an idea that Eisenhower seemed to have vaguely in mind in his very first comments to Snapp in Augusta more than a year before. The idea's simplicity and directness were appealing. It electrified the United Nations General Assembly and the world as few political statements had done since Bernard Baruch's address in June 1946.[100] But in the very simplicity of the idea lay its limitations. Could atomic energy, which had heightened world tensions and distrust, now become a unifying force for peace? And was nuclear power as imminent as the President seemed to think? These were questions the Atomic Energy Commission would have to answer.

CHAPTER 4

# THE OPPENHEIMER
# CASE

When Lewis Strauss returned to Washington on December 8, 1953, following the President's speech at the United Nations, he plunged back into the Oppenheimer case. Because Oppenheimer's only significant access to classified information was through his consultant contract with the Commission, Strauss knew that he and his fellow Commissioners would have to undertake on behalf of the government whatever formal action was brought against Oppenheimer. The extreme sensitivity of atomic energy information had prompted the Commission to develop detailed procedures for handling personnel security cases. Since 1947 these procedures had been tested in numerous cases and had come to be regarded by many security experts as a model that other government agencies might well follow.[1] In two respects, however, the Commission's security procedures were not well designed for the impending Oppenheimer case: they had been used almost exclusively at the Commission's field offices rather than at headquarters, and they had never been applied to a person of Oppenheimer's prestige and influence.

## TROUBLE AT HOME

Strauss's first priority was to set things right with his fellow Commissioners, who knew only that the President had ordered Oppenheimer's clearance suspended. During the hectic hours on December 3, when Strauss was trying both to respond to the President's order and to prepare for the Bermuda conference, there had been no opportunity for a Commission meeting. Although Smyth had technically served as acting chairman during Strauss's absence in Bermuda, he had been bedridden with a sinus infection and sore throat during that week and had the benefit of only one brief and guarded telephone conversation with Strauss before the chairman's departure. To bring the Commission up-to-date, Strauss scheduled an executive session for December 10.[2]

Murray was the only Commissioner who had already responded to the events of the previous week. While Strauss was in Bermuda, Murray completed a memorandum that set forth his views on the Oppenheimer case. Reminding Strauss that he had known of Oppenheimer's record since joining the Commission, Murray wanted to make clear that he had not been ignorant of or complacent about the matter. But it had been his understanding that Oppenheimer's record "was not sufficiently derogatory to call for stopping his access to restricted data."[3] Nevertheless, after reviewing Oppenheimer's "strong negative position" on the hydrogen bomb, Murray believed that the physicist's usefulness had been severely reduced. Murray had been especially determined to eliminate Oppenheimer's unhealthy "excessive influence" over the general advisory committee and had argued in 1951 against the reappointment of Enrico Fermi to the committee in order to establish a strong precedent against Oppenheimer's reappointment a year later. In fact, since he also believed that the paramount interest of the country outweighed "any possible question of equity to an individual," Murray agreed that Oppenheimer's access to classified information should be terminated if there were "any shadow of doubt on the security of vital information accessible to Oppenheimer," and "from a reading of the FBI report, I would like to record that I don't reach the conclusion that Borden does."[4]

Thus, Murray served Strauss notice that he, although in sympathy with the move to dump Oppenheimer, would not support the use of the security system to achieve that end. Unfortunately Murray's voice was somewhat muted because circumstances prevented him from developing his statement fully. In a memorandum ultimately sent to Strauss, Murray confessed that for the past three years he had discussed various security matters with Hoover, who had briefed him on the Oppenheimer case. What Murray could not tell Strauss was Hoover's earlier statement that "there was not sufficient derogatory evidence in the FBI files to call for AEC's ending Oppenheimer's access to restricted data," a considerably stronger reservation than the one ultimately given to Strauss. Rejecting Murray's statement in the draft memorandum, Hoover denied that he had ever expressed such a definite opinion and requested Murray to eliminate specific mention of their conversations about Oppenheimer, particularly those that had taken place during the Weinberg case in November 1952. After negotiating with two of Hoover's agents, Murray agreed to amend his statement by deleting "the fact that Mr. Hoover expressed any opinions about Oppenheimer," but he retained reference to his special knowledge of the Oppenheimer case.[5]

Originally Murray intended to recommend that the Oppenheimer

74

case be referred to the special committee on atomic energy of the National Security Council, a maneuver that would obviously diminish Strauss's role in any future proceedings against Oppenheimer. Without success Murray sought support for his proposal from Smyth and Zuckert, the other Truman appointees to the Commission. The three men convened prior to the December 10 executive session; Murray read his memo but failed to receive the approval of either colleague. Without promising their support or disagreeing with Murray, they left the whole matter in limbo. At the moment another issue seemed even more important than the Oppenheimer case. They had just learned that Strauss had been working on Eisenhower's Atoms-for-Peace speech without their knowledge. This information not only damaged their pride but also suggested that Strauss was usurping their functions as Commissioners. Thus the "Bermuda crisis," as they called it, loomed as large as the Oppenheimer case itself. Just before the three Commissioners entered the executive meeting, Smyth and Zuckert both spoke openly of resigning.[6]

75

From the outset the Oppenheimer case threatened to become a partisan issue. Joseph Campbell, Eisenhower's other Republican appointee, was the only Commissioner with whom Strauss really confided on December 3. Campbell met Strauss at the airport on December 8 and accompanied by two aides drove to Strauss's apartment at the Shoreham to brief the chairman. Strauss told Campbell that he had an appointment the morning of December 9 to discuss the Oppenheimer case with the President, Brownell, and Authur S. Flemming, director of the Office of Defense Mobilization. Strauss met again with Brownell and Flemming at the Department of Justice the following day after the conclusion of the National Security Council meeting.[7]

Strauss opened the executive session on December 10 by reviewing the events of December 3 but omitting his meeting with the President. On receiving the President's directive, Strauss explained, he had immediately called a meeting of the Commission, which had been attended only by Campbell. The chairman did not tell them that he had met with Flemming and Brownell, but he did note that he intended to consult with Brownell. There were no objections. Then Strauss took cognizance of Murray's independent contacts with Hoover by announcing that he intended to ask Hoover to keep all the Commissioners advised.[8]

## THE STATEMENT OF CHARGES

The first step in a personnel security investigation was to prepare a statement of charges. Usually a field office attorney performed this task, but, because of the exceptional nature of the Oppenheimer case, Strauss asked William Mitchell, the Commission's general counsel, to draw up the statement himself. Mitchell, fifty years old, had been educated at Princeton and Harvard and had practiced law in Minnesota and the District of Columbia. His service in the Army Air Force during World War II had led to his appointment in the Truman Administration as special representative of the President to negotiate civil air transport agreements with several Latin American countries and as special assistant to the Secretary of the Air Force on overseas bases. As the son of Herbert Hoover's attorney general, however, Mitchell's credentials as a conservative Republican were impeccable. Mitchell's quiet and judicious manner and his unquestioned integrity made him an effective legal adviser to Strauss.

Although Mitchell had broad experience as a lawyer in both private practice and government, he had never before been directly involved in preparing a security case. After several unsuccessful attempts to draft the statement of charges himself, Mitchell obtained Strauss's permission to give the assignment to Harold P. Green, a young lawyer who had worked in the general counsel's office for three years. Green had never read the Oppenheimer file, but he had learned something of Oppenheimer's "checkered past" as an official observer at the Weinberg trial. On Friday afternoon, December 11, Mitchell gave Green two thick volumes of the Oppenheimer file and a copy of the Borden letter. Mitchell explained the background of the "blank wall" directive and the need for secrecy. He asked Green to prepare a statement of charges against Oppenheimer that weekend.[9]

Green was given few instructions except that he was not to focus on Borden's allegations concerning Oppenheimer's opposition to the hydrogen bomb. Green knew from the outset that he was involved in a matter of historic proportions, but he did not suspect that the Oppenheimer case would be handled any differently from routine personnel security reviews conducted by the Commission. Arriving at the Commission at 6:00 a.m. on Saturday, Green began his systematic review of Oppenheimer's file, only to be interrupted twice by Commission General Manager Nichols, who summoned him to his office to talk about the case.[10] Well aware that under Commission regulations Nichols would probably make the final decision about Oppenheimer's fate, Green was disconcerted by Nichols's apparent enthusiasm for the prosecution and the seeming impropriety of taking a position against Oppenheimer's interests.

Green worked steadily throughout the day, reading the FBI files that contained a monotonous rehash of ancient events and stale investigations.[11] The only fresh information of any interest consisted of recent interviews with Teller and Kenneth W. Pitzer, who criticized Oppenheimer for his opposition to the hydrogen bomb; but this material was outside the scope of Mitchell's vaguely defined guidelines. Unable to identify substantial grounds for challenging Oppenheimer's loyalty, Green decided to take a tack common to personnel security cases: to draft charges primarily designed to test Oppenheimer's veracity. Green had no qualms about his

76

strategy. Confident that an experienced and eminent board would review the charges, he selected thirty-one items from the file, almost all of which would allow the prospective board to match Oppenheimer's memory and truthfulness against known and established facts.

When Green finally finished his draft statement of charges at noon on Sunday, he called Mitchell, who wanted to review the draft before submitting it to Strauss, Nichols, and Hoover for concurrence. Thereafter followed what has been described as the "most crucial two-hour period in the entire Oppenheimer affair." [12] Green, waiting alone at the Commission, mulled over his work, becoming increasingly dissatisfied with ignoring the FBI interviews of Teller and Pitzer. Oppenheimer should not be punished because of his opposition to the hydrogen bomb, Green understood, but could not his alleged disingenuousness on the hydrogen bomb issue serve as a pertinent and more timely basis for testing his veracity? With nothing else to do, Green decided to cast several additional charges based on the material found in the unused FBI interviews. Concentrating on the Teller interview, which he found most useful, Green added seven more charges. Teller himself, as the FBI interview made unmistakably clear, did not doubt Oppenheimer's loyalty and thought it wrong to remove him from any office on the grounds of disloyalty. Nevertheless, Teller hoped that Oppenheimer would be removed from all responsibilities connected with military preparedness because of the mistaken advice he had given in recent years. Using the same words as Borden, Teller accused Oppenheimer of "whitewashing" the record of the general advisory committee in an attempt to show that, once the weapon had become an inevitability, the committee had favored its development all along. Here was sufficient grist for Green's veracity mill. When he was done, Green had extended the charges from thirty-one to thirty-eight, producing by coincidence, perhaps, seven H-bomb charges, the same number that Borden had included in his November 7 letter to Hoover. [13]

Satisfied with his draft at last, Green relinquished the manuscript to Mitchell, who made no changes and offered no objections to the paper, including the hydrogen bomb allegations. The next morning Mitchell sent the draft to Nichols, who forwarded it to Hoover without comment. The FBI carefully checked Green's work for accuracy, making certain that its files confirmed all the charges. Hoover subsequently recommended that two charges be dropped entirely and eleven others be amended either to correct misspellings and incorrect data or to eliminate accusations that could not be substantiated by available witnesses. Hoover mostly confined himself to editorial chores, avoiding substantive comment on the hydrogen bomb charges and the other allegations. [14]

It is tempting to conclude that the hydrogen bomb charges were included in the statement almost as an afterthought and inexplicably were endorsed by the Commission virtually unnoticed and unchallenged. Unfor-

77

tunately including the H-bomb charges was far less accidental than it seemed on the surface. Mitchell had not told Green that he had given up the assignment after Smyth and Zuckert had criticized his attempts to include the H-bomb charges. In fact, all the Commissioners except Campbell had strong opinions on this question, and Smyth had relented on December 14 only with great reluctance.[15]

## THE MEETING WITH OPPENHEIMER

Strauss kept the President fully informed of developments in the case and solicited advice from Eisenhower in turn. Oppenheimer's request for an appointment with Strauss precipitated the issue, and in the President's office they decided that Strauss should see Oppenheimer, tell him about the President's directive, and give Oppenheimer a chance to resign; should he decide to carry his case further, Strauss could hand him the statement of charges and offer him the regular hearing procedure. Thus, when Strauss convened an executive session on the afternoon of December 15, the Commission was presented with another fait accompli: this time presidential concurrence in procedures the Commission itself had not yet approved.[16]

Although Smyth and Murray knew that they could not oppose actions approved by the President, both had deep reservations about the decision. Smyth believed that a formal suspension of clearance would not only be a severe blow to Oppenheimer's reputation but would also tend to prejudice the evidence. There was some chance, in Smyth's opinion, that Oppenheimer's consultant contract could be terminated without raising the clearance question, but Smyth finally decided not to press his objections with his fellow Commissioners because he feared that the case might become a political football in the hands of McCarthy. Murray shared a similar concern after he had met privately with Joint Committee on Atomic Energy security officer Francis Cotter, who told him that he knew all about the Oppenheimer case and Borden's role in it. Cotter urged that the Commission consider using a specially appointed presidential panel to hear the Oppenheimer case, and he intimated that Joint Committee Chairman Cole would support such a move. A few days later Herbert S. Marks, a former general counsel at the Commission, insisted on seeing Strauss to warn him that Senator William Jenner was considering an investigation of Oppenheimer.[17] None of these developments would make it any easier for the Commission to drop the case.

When Oppenheimer kept his appointment with Strauss on December 21, the chairman explained to him that the Commission faced a difficult problem in continuing his clearance. Without naming Borden, the chairman told Oppenheimer how a former government official had called attention to Oppenheimer's record, an action that resulted in an FBI report to the President, who had directed the Commission to subject Oppenheimer's clearance to a formal hearing pursuant to the President's recent executive order. Strauss explained that the first step would be to suspend Oppenheimer's clearance by giving him a letter from the general manager informing the scientist of his rights and the nature of the derogatory information occasioning the suspension of his clearance.[18] Handing Oppenheimer a draft of the letter, Strauss and Nichols waited tensely while Oppenheimer read the charges. Obviously impressed and shaken by the evidence accumulated against him, Oppenheimer inquired whether a board had ever cleared anyone with a similar record. Strauss conceded that he did not believe a comparable case had ever been heard before and could not venture an opinion on the probable outcome.

Oppenheimer's resignation was an obvious alternative to a formal hearing, and the two men discussed that option at some length.[19] It became evident to Oppenheimer that Strauss believed a simple resignation was the better course to follow, but Strauss stopped short of making an outright recommendation. Sensitive to possible future accusations that he and Nichols had used "star chamber" tactics on Oppenheimer, Strauss was careful not to force Oppenheimer into any prescribed course of action. At first reflection Oppenheimer was inclined to offer his resignation, a move that might have ended the matter then and there; but the more he thought about the specter of the Jenner committee investigation, the more he became troubled by the prospect of resigning his consultantship prior to the putative investigation by the Congressional committee. To quit without a fuss, as Strauss plainly wanted him to do, would also be interpreted as evidence of guilt whenever the President's order and the Commission's unsigned charges were brought to light, as they surely would be.

When Oppenheimer asked how much time he had to think the matter over, Strauss replied that, because implementing the President's order had already been delayed nearly three weeks, he could only give the scientist until the next day to make up his mind. Nevertheless, Oppenheimer thanked Strauss for his consideration and indicated he would consult with Marks. Desiring to study the statement of charges carefully with his lawyer before coming to a decision, Oppenheimer asked if he could take a copy of Nichols's letter with him. Strauss refused the request on the grounds that it would be unwise to circulate the unsigned letter, but he promised to dispatch the statement of charges immediately should Oppenheimer choose to go through the normal hearing procedure rather than request termination of his contract.

Oppenheimer apparently had had no intimation of the government's proposed action before he walked into Strauss's office, and the shock of his experience was evident as he rose to leave. He regretted, the scien-

79

tist remarked to Strauss, that he had to sever his relationship with the government under either alternative, but he understood that given the circumstances the Commission had little recourse but to offer him the two painful choices. As Oppenheimer prepared to leave, Strauss told him about Marks's visit earlier that morning. When Oppenheimer indicated he would like to consult Marks immediately, Strauss lent the scientist his car so that he could drive directly to Marks's office. It was 3:35 p.m.; the entire meeting had lasted only slightly more than thirty minutes.[20]

That evening Oppenheimer met briefly with Marks and another friend, former General Counsel Joseph A. Volpe, Jr., before returning to Princeton by train. Shortly after noon the next day Nichols called Oppenheimer in Princeton to ask whether he had reached a decision. Oppenheimer had not had time to recover from the blow of the previous day's meeting, much less give very much thought to the decision, but Nichols insisted upon an answer that afternoon. Under this pressure Oppenheimer decided to return at once to Washington, and he spent the evening in Volpe's office discussing the strategy of a reply. Volpe, experienced in the ways of the bureaucracy, urged Oppenheimer to seek an accommodation with the Commission: Oppenheimer would quit if the Commission accepted his resignation without prejudice, that is, on the basis that his services were no longer needed without mentioning the security aspect. But cold reflection reminded them that neither the Borden letter nor the Commission's statement of charges would disappear. From Oppenheimer's point of view, it was one thing to resign under pressure when one's services were no longer wanted or needed but quite another to be forced out by the security system, sacrificing both integrity and honor while leaving the charges unchallenged. He decided to accept the Commission's statement of charges with all the risks and uncertainties it entailed.[21]

Even before Oppenheimer accepted the statement of charges, Strauss inquired whether the FBI could set up a "full-time surveillance" of Oppenheimer, which would have required agents to monitor Oppenheimer's every movement and contact around the clock. Hoover objected that such an operation would be too costly in manpower and money, but he did order the FBI office in Newark, New Jersey, to maintain a "spot check" on Oppenheimer. This meant assigning two agents to follow Oppenheimer and members of his family when they left his residence and to observe visitors. Hoover also authorized taps on Oppenheimer's home and office telephones; these were installed on January 1, 1954. The Newark office reported that the taps made the spot check quite efficient and permitted the FBI to plan surveillance operations when Oppenheimer indicated that he planned travel outside the Princeton area. Thus, after January 1 the only privacy accorded Oppenheimer by the FBI were conversations within his own home.[22]

## A STRATEGY FOR DEFENSE

Buoyed up and encouraged by his friends, Oppenheimer set about after the New Year to obtain competent legal assistance in his confrontation with the Commission. Far from complacent about his situation, Oppenheimer would have been even more concerned had he known that Strauss, Nichols, and Mitchell were privy to his every move in selecting counsel. When the FBI agent in Newark first began to pick up conversations about legal matters, he called his supervisors in Washington to ask whether the tap should be continued "in view of the fact that it might disclose attorney-client relations." He was assured that the tap was appropriate because Oppenheimer was involved in a security case, not a criminal action; moreover, the FBI's chief concern, the agent was informed, was to learn immediately of any indication that Oppenheimer was planning to flee the country. Under the circumstances the surveillance was "warranted." Strauss in turn reassured Bates that the surveillance was "most helpful" to the Commission in that "they were aware beforehand of the moves he [Oppenheimer] was contemplating." Strauss confided to both Bates and Mitchell that the importance of the case "could not be stressed too much." If the Commission lost the case against Oppenheimer, Strauss thought that the atomic energy program would fall into the hands of "left-wingers" and the scientists would take over the whole program. Strauss warned that if Oppenheimer were cleared, then "anyone" could be cleared regardless of the information against them.[23]

81

The FBI office in Newark provided Strauss and Mitchell with almost daily reports on Oppenheimer's efforts to find counsel. Volpe advised Oppenheimer to find a tough trial lawyer experienced in the rough and tumble of courtroom cross-examination; but selection of appropriate, able, and available counsel on short notice was a difficult task. It took Oppenheimer almost two weeks, with Marks's help, to assemble his legal staff. His chief counsel would be Lloyd K. Garrison, a New York attorney whom Oppenheimer knew as a member of the board of trustees of the Institute for Advanced Study. Garrison offered Oppenheimer legal distinction well-matched to the physicist's scientific reputation. Like Oppenheimer, Garrison was also drawn to liberal causes and had served as president of the National Urban League and as a member of the American Civil Liberties Union. Described as "Lincolnesque in appearance" and "mild of manner," Garrison seemed an excellent complement to Oppenheimer, both temperamentally and intellectually. Assisting Garrison were Marks and Samuel J. Silverman, an attorney in Garrison's law firm.[24]

Shortly after accepting the assignment as Oppenheimer's chief counsel, Garrison realized that he would need a security clearance. Not only would Oppenheimer's FBI files and materials relating to the hydrogen bomb be denied him without a clearance, but Garrison feared he could not even talk freely with his client without compromising classified information. Garrison's application for clearance for himself, Marks, and Silverman gave Nichols some concern. Although the FBI had no substantially derogatory information on Silverman or Garrison, there had been several allegations going back many years against Marks. Much material in Marks's file was hearsay, vicious, and unverified, but it seemed serious enough to preclude a quick reinstatement of Marks's clearance without a full background investigation. There was a real danger that the Commission might become involved in a personnel security hearing for Marks as well as Oppenheimer. [25]

Trying to be as diplomatic as possible, Nichols suggested limiting clearance to Garrison alone on the grounds that one clearance would be sufficient for handling Oppenheimer's case. After considering the question for several days, Garrison decided that he would not request a clearance for either himself or his associates but would present the case as best he could on the basis of unclassified evidence. Nichols had no choice but to accept Garrison's decision, but he told Garrison he had made a serious mistake. Nichols assured Garrison that he would try to declassify all documents relevant to the case, but Garrison's decision left him standing with Oppenheimer outside Eisenhower's "blank wall" of security. [26]

During the third week of January 1954, Garrison and others explored with Nichols and Strauss a variety of procedures that might have avoided a formal hearing. In every case Strauss was careful not to appear to be forcing Oppenheimer's hand, but with good reason he could not promise that the proposed alternatives would save Oppenheimer from later embarrassment. [27] In fact, when Garrison and his colleagues had thought better of their own suggestions, Strauss offered Garrison an idea of his own. It was always possible for Oppenheimer, as it would be for any respondent, to terminate his contract, thus removing the "need to know" and making further proceedings unnecessary. In this connection, if the Commission had Oppenheimer's letter of resignation in hand, Strauss would try to reinstate the scientist's clearance temporarily before the resignation was accepted and, against his better judgment, withdraw the letter of charges before accepting the resignation. Again Strauss could offer no absolute guarantees, especially against Congressional hearings or publicity attendant to the case, but his solution would have allowed Oppenheimer to save some face, avoid a hearing, and minimize the impact of his troubles on the Commission's program.

Given the pendency of the hearings, Garrison doubted whether it would be possible for Oppenheimer to tender his resignation without appearing to concede the substance of the charges, even if they were withdrawn. Marks suggested that Oppenheimer's clearance could be reinstated

82

and the proceedings dropped, allowing the physicist's contract to expire on June 30, 1954; but in view of the President's orders it was not possible for the Commission to do this. As they parted, the lawyers indicated they would discuss the matter with Oppenheimer while Strauss reported the negotiations to the full Commission. At the end of the day, Garrison and Marks returned to report bad news; they had spent the afternoon discussing alternatives with Oppenheimer, and the scientist had decided it was necessary to go through with the hearing.[28] The negotiations having failed, both sides had no choice but to continue their preparations for a hearing.

## THE SECURITY BOARD

Because the Washington headquarters did not have a regularly constituted personnel security board as did the Commission's operations offices, it was necessary either to bring in a board from the field or to appoint an ad hoc board for the sole purpose of judging the evidence against Oppenheimer. It was also apparent to Commission officials that should Oppenheimer demand a hearing, no ordinary panel would be competent to review the case. Thus, after conducting an exhaustive field survey, General Counsel Mitchell recommended the ad hoc board. Mitchell suggested the Commission recruit a board of tough but honest men who were Oppenheimer's peers; if possible the board should be composed of a lawyer, a university scientist, and an individual with a national reputation in private life. It was also desirable, Mitchell noted, to have at least one Republican and one Democrat on the board.[29]

83

Gordon Gray was the Commission's choice to head the board. From a wealthy and prominent North Carolina family, Gray brought to the board a stature that easily matched Oppenheimer's. A graduate of Yale Law School, Gray had practiced law in New York, had become a publisher in North Carolina, and had been active in state politics. After serving in the Army during World War II, he became Assistant Secretary of the Army in 1947 and had served as a presidential assistant until he was elected president of the University of North Carolina in 1950. Gray was the only member of the board to be recruited personally by Strauss.

The staff recommended the second member, Ward V. Evans, a professor of chemistry at Loyola University in Chicago. Evans had earned a reputation as a conscientious member of security review boards appointed by the Chicago operations office. He scarcely matched Oppenheimer in scientific reputation, but he was a respected teacher. To balance Evans, a conservative Republican, the Commission hoped to find another Democrat so that the board would not seem stacked against Oppenheimer. After at least four candidates refused the position, Mitchell secured the consent of industrialist Thomas A. Morgan of New York. The son of a North Carolina farmer, Morgan had worked his way up through the trades to become a naval technician during World War I. His ability to repair gyrocompasses earned him a position with the Sperry Gyroscope Company after the war, and he became president of the company in 1933 at the age of forty-six. In 1949 he had served in the Truman Administration as an adviser on management improvement.[30]

Although neither Oppenheimer nor Garrison expressed any dissatisfaction with the Commission's choices for the board, the selection of Roger Robb as counsel for the board proved one of the Commission's most controversial decisions. First, the selection of an attorney from outside the general counsel's staff to assist the board in a personnel security matter was unprecedented, representing another clear departure from the Commission's normal procedures. But that fact alone would not have raised questions were it not for Robb's perception of his task. In contrast to Garrison, whose experiences in labor arbitration had taught him the arts of compromise and conciliation, Robb had earned distinction as a prosecutor during his seven years as Assistant United States Attorney in Washington between 1931 and 1938. Thereafter in private practice he developed a local reputation for being a combative and resourceful trial lawyer.

Like Gray, Robb was first approached personally by Strauss. When the Commission decided to seek outside assistance in the Oppenheimer case, Strauss obtained Robb's name from Deputy Attorney General William P. Rogers. Robb's selection as the personnel security board's counsel was later interpreted as evidence of Strauss's determination to "get Oppenheimer." Strauss, Stewart and Joseph Alsop charged, "had the final responsibility for the curious decision that the AEC counsel should be Roger Robb, a man best known as the lawyer for Senator Joseph R. McCarthy's chief journalistic incense-swinger, Fulton Lewis, Jr."[31] Although there was no evidence that Robb was Strauss's or the Administration's hand-picked hatchet man, the fact that Robb was employed for his trial skills was evident even to Robb himself. Thus, Robb's subsequent handling of the Oppenheimer case before the Gray board helped create the suspicion that he had been specifically chosen to carry out Strauss's alleged vendetta against the scientist.[32]

## PREPARING FOR THE HEARINGS

Garrison's decision to present the defense on an unclassified basis by foregoing a security clearance for himself meant that he could inspect no classified material in Oppenheimer's file. Garrison and Marks requested the Commission to declassify certain documents entirely. These included 1946

FBI reports containing derogatory information about Oppenheimer, letters from leaders of the Manhattan Project, and specific Commission records on Oppenheimer's 1947 clearance and his views on the hydrogen bomb. Nichols informed Garrison that Oppenheimer could read any classified document Oppenheimer himself had signed. If Oppenheimer came to Washington for that purpose, Nichols promised to make the documents available to him in the general manager's office. Although there were no verbatim minutes of the Commission's action in 1947, Mitchell was willing to stipulate for purposes of the Gray board hearings that "on August 6, 1947, the Commission recorded clearance of Dr. J. Robert Oppenheimer, which it noted had been authorized in February 1947."[33] But Nichols reported that the Commission was unable to go beyond that.

Garrison's disadvantage was obvious but far greater than even he suspected. The FBI had not only provided the Commission with investigative reports relative to the Borden letter and Nichols's statement of charges, but between December 22, 1953, and April 12, 1954, the first day of the Gray board hearings, the FBI sent the Commission more than 110 reports concerning Oppenheimer, of which more than 50 were transmitted as personal letters from Hoover to Strauss.[34] Hoover was careful not to reveal the source of his information, but it was evident even from his letters that the FBI had either bugged or wiretapped Oppenheimer's home and office or had successfully secured an informant among Oppenheimer's inner circle of friends and associates. As a consequence, the Commission knew of the defense lawyers' plans and strategy, their discussions with potential witnesses for Oppenheimer, and their conferences with their client, as well as Oppenheimer's other business, both personal and mundane.[35]

It is difficult to assess the influence of Hoover's communiqués on the outcome of the Oppenheimer case, and it is not known when Hoover's letters to Strauss were added to Oppenheimer's official file. If they were placed in the file before the hearing, or were added during the hearing, the Gray board would have had access to them. If not, possibly the Gray board did not know of their existence. Robb probably knew about them and Nichols certainly did, as perhaps did Murray, who boasted that he received everything from Hoover that Strauss did.

If the Hoover letters accomplished nothing else, they allowed the Commission to follow the progress of Oppenheimer's preparations. During February Hoover reported in detail Oppenheimer's telephone conversations with his brother; the activities of Garrison and Marks; a private discussion with Robert Cutler, administrative assistant to the President; and conversations of Oppenheimer's wife's at social events. Even more important for Robb were Hoover's reports on Oppenheimer's strategy and the reasons behind his selection of defense witnesses.[36]

On February 4, 1954, Robb settled down to study the Oppenheimer

85

file and plan his presentation to the personnel security board. Strauss and Mitchell had explained that the hearing would not be a trial, but Robb realized that the proceedings would have many elements of a trial and prepared his case accordingly. Working steadily between eight and ten hours a day, Robb plowed through Oppenheimer's thick Manhattan District file, which at the time was in the possession of the FBI. Although he had known virtually nothing about Oppenheimer when he accepted the assignment, Robb quickly assumed command of the case.

To begin with, Robb discovered that he worked most easily with C. Arthur Rolander, Jr., his chief assistant from the division of security, Charles Bates of the FBI, and Bryan LaPlante and David Teeple, special assistants to Chairman Strauss. Teeple was especially helpful in providing Robb concise personality profiles of all the major characters involved on both sides. Bates not only provided liaison with the FBI but also suggested new aspects of the case. For the most part, however, because the matter was held in such strict secrecy, Robb and Rolander worked on the case alone.[37]

Robb's task was made difficult by the magnitude of Oppenheimer's file, but he had help from other sources. Corbin Allardice, Borden's successor as executive director of the Joint Committee, offered Robb and Rolander important assistance by providing copies of relevant documents that the FBI had culled from the committee's files. Allardice also suggested that Robb interview Borden and Teller and gave Robb a transcript of an interview in May 1950 with Teller, who deplored Oppenheimer's impact on the hydrogen bomb project. The FBI provided Robb and Rolander with the greatest volume of information on Oppenheimer, going back to the contents of the trash from Oppenheimer's residence at Los Alamos during World War II. Because many of these sources could not be compromised—by agreement with the FBI—much of the file was withheld from Oppenheimer and his attorneys, but not from Robb, Rolander, the Gray board, Nichols, and the Commissioners, who were to decide Oppenheimer's fate.[38]

By prior agreement with the FBI, Robb and Rolander agreed not to interview persons outside the Commission who had already been interviewed by the FBI; they would rely upon Bates to furnish transcripts from the FBI files. Robb insisted, however, on the right to interview employees and consultants, including scientists such as Teller, Ernest O. Lawrence, and Luis W. Alvarez, even if they had recently talked to the FBI. The only exception to this rule was Borden, neither an employee nor a Commission consultant when interviewed by Robb and Rolander on February 20, 1954. Borden expressed his opinion that "in terms of his capacity to compromise information" no other scientist was potentially more dangerous than Oppenheimer. After three and one-half hours of telling Robb and Rolander all he knew about the subject, Borden offered the investigators a list of twenty-eight individuals able to furnish additional information concerning Oppenheimer's influence on the atomic energy program.[39]

John Lansdale, Jr., and Boris T. Pash, both Army security officers during World War II, and General Groves freely discussed Oppenheimer's wartime security status, offering the same opinions in private or in sworn testimony before the Gray board. Unfortunately, some academic scientists, such as Wendell M. Latimer, a professor of chemistry at the University of California, were not that consistent. Accustomed to speaking openly and freely about associates in offices, laboratories, and closed faculty meetings but circumspect and correct when discussing professional colleagues in public, Oppenheimer's academic critics, with the exception of Teller, compiled a poor record of candor during the Gray board proceedings. Teller was fearful that the proceedings might develop into a fight that could adversely affect the nuclear program. Nevertheless, he insisted that any information supplied by him to the Commission or the FBI and used in the hearing be identified with his name, not as furnished by an unidentified informant.[40] Others were not so insistent.

Although Ernest Lawrence did not appear before the Gray board to testify in person, his interview with Robb and Rolander was placed in the record beyond the reach of Garrison's cross-examination. After relating the oft-told story of his own efforts to accelerate the development of the hydrogen bomb in fall 1949, Lawrence concluded that Oppenheimer was largely responsible for the growing resistance to the project. Even worse in Lawrence's opinion were Oppenheimer's attempts to wreck research projects on new weapons. He concluded that Oppenheimer had become so arrogant and had been guilty of so much bad judgment that "he should never again have anything to do with the forming of policy."[41]

## MCCARTHY AND THE PRESS

Late in January 1954 James Reston of the *New York Times* received information "from a reliable source" that the Commission had started proceedings against Oppenheimer. Unable to obtain any confirmation from either Oppenheimer or Strauss, Reston attempted to persuade both sides to release the story by playing on their mutual fears that Senator McCarthy might seize the Oppenheimer issue. Reston was in a strong position because both sides would have preferred to release the story through the relatively responsible *New York Times* rather than gamble on the unpredictable effects of a McCarthy disclosure. Reston told Oppenheimer that the *Times* would print the story eventually, but he promised to withhold publication as long as possible.

The Reston threat was bound to exacerbate suspicions on both sides

87

that the other party was attempting to play politics with the case through the newspapers. The initial reaction in both camps, however, was to join forces to keep Reston quiet. To prepare for the inevitable, the Commission prepared a press release on January 29, 1954, and authorized Mitchell to alert Garrison to Reston's intentions. Garrison acknowledged that Reston had approached Oppenheimer. Whether or not Garrison reciprocated Mitchell's reading of the Commission's proposed press release over the telephone, the Commission soon had a copy of Oppenheimer's proposed statement from J. Edgar Hoover.[42] During February Garrison continued to discuss with Strauss and Nichols the Commission's response to press inquires.

As the Army-McCarthy feud moved toward its climax, Garrison became more worried that Oppenheimer might become McCarthy's next target. Garrison knew that McCarthy had already come across Oppenheimer's name in another investigation. Until he received Reston's warning, however, Garrison considered an investigation by the Jenner committee the greater threat. It seemed likely that the Joint Committee would rise to any challenge to its own prerogatives from Jenner, but Garrison could get no assurances from Strauss that the Commission would back the committee in such a position.[43]

The situation became even more dangerous on March 31 when Strauss, just back from the Pacific weapon tests, announced that the United States had developed a hydrogen bomb that could destroy an entire city. McCarthy, who had obtained time on Edward R. Murrow's television program to reply to the newsman's attack upon his investigating methods, used the occasion to launch an unexpected blast at the Commission's thermonuclear program. McCarthy charged that there had been an eighteen-month delay in the project as a result of foot-dragging by communist sympathizers.[44] The charge suggested to those in the atomic energy establishment that McCarthy had obtained access to Borden's chronology. For Garrison, who knew nothing of Borden's paper, the charge came dangerously close to Oppenheimer. Whether McCarthy had any solid information or was merely lashing out against his enemies, the attack did come just three days before the formal hearings were to begin on April 12. It was not likely that the Oppenheimer case could be kept secret much longer.

From the FBI, Strauss learned that Oppenheimer was now discussing the possibility of a news release with both the Alsop brothers and Reston. The Alsops were indignant to learn of Oppenheimer's difficulties and were determined to write an essay exposing the government's duplicity in "persecuting" Oppenheimer. Perhaps frightened by the Alsops' enthusiasm, Oppenheimer seemed to prefer working with Reston, who suggested that Garrison give him, in strictest confidence, a copy of the statement of charges and Oppenheimer's reply. Reston was to prepare a story and hold it until it could no longer be kept secret. Garrison appreciated Reston's forbearance as well as the value of the story breaking in an accurate article by a newsman of Reston's stature. But Garrison also knew that subsequent articles in other papers were not likely to tell the full story, and these might damage Oppenheimer's case. Garrison was also reluctant to break his news embargo agreement with the Commission and did not want to offend the members of the Gray board before the hearings began.[45]

At the same time both the White House and the Commission were wary of McCarthy's exploitation of the Oppenheimer case. In a White House meeting on April 9, 1954, Strauss told Sherman Adams and others that he had learned from the publisher of the *Times* that the editorial board had voted not to publish Reston's story until the news broke elsewhere. Strauss had expressed his gratitude and had promised to alert the *Times* if he learned that anyone else was about to use the story. James C. Hagerty, the President's press secretary, feared that the Eisenhower Administration might get caught in crossfire between McCarthy and Oppenheimer as each tried to use the White House to his own advantage. To avoid that danger, Hagerty suggested that Strauss withdraw his commitment to alert the *Times*. Then, Hagerty reasoned, the *Times* would run the Reston story using Garrison's documents. In so doing, the *Times* would undercut McCarthy and make it unnecessary for the White House to leak the story. Hagerty then assisted Strauss in drafting a press release that would be issued "on the spot" when the story finally broke. In reviewing the draft release on April 10, Eisenhower stressed the importance of sticking to the facts in the Oppenheimer case so that the government could assure "orderly procedure." "We've got to handle this so that all our scientists are not made out to be Reds," the President warned, because "that Goddamn McCarthy is just likely to try such a thing."[46]

89

As a final effort to neutralize McCarthy, Hagerty sought the senator's pledge to keep silent on the Oppenheimer matter for security reasons. When Hagerty learned that Vice-President Nixon had supposedly extracted such a promise from McCarthy, he suggested that Strauss, Everett M. Dirksen, the Senate majority leader, or perhaps even Nixon himself, should remind McCarthy of the need to respect his previous commitments. Later that same day Strauss tried to reassure a still unconvinced Hagerty that McCarthy had been silenced. Everything seemed to be under control for opening the Gray board hearings on Monday morning, April 12.

## THE GRAY BOARD CONVENES

During the week of anxiety at the White House and the Commission over the possibility that McCarthy might capitalize on the Oppenheimer case, the personnel security board began its review of the scientist's clearance file. On the morning of April 5, 1954, Gray, Morgan, and Evans gathered in their makeshift headquarters for a briefing on security criteria and procedures. Thereafter, with Robb and Rolander close at hand to answer questions or provide technical assistance, they worked meticulously through the file. Throughout the week they remained as anonymous as possible, avoiding the public and eating together at lunch and dinner, where they were often joined by Robb. Not surprisingly, they soon enjoyed a close and personal rapport.[47]

At the outset Morgan reported a profoundly disturbing incident that had occurred just before he left New York. On March 30 he had been approached by Trevor Gardner, a special assistant to the Secretary of the Air Force for research and development, who told Morgan he knew all about the forthcoming hearing. Gardner related that many of the nation's leading scientists were deeply concerned about the government's actions, and he warned that great damage could be done to American scientific morale and defense efforts should Oppenheimer's clearance not be reinstated. Gardner also cautioned Morgan that, in addition to Reston and the Alsops, McCarthy had the story and might use it to everyone's detriment. Morgan, who misunderstood neither Gardner's intentions nor his veiled threats, reported the contact to Gray, who passed the information on to Strauss. Strauss, in turn, informed the President and the Secretary of Defense.[48]

The impact of the Gardner incident on the Oppenheimer case was subtle. Mitchell assured Morgan he could dismiss the matter from his mind, secure in the knowledge that the government had matters well in hand. But the incident, which had involved a serious leak of classified information, left a residue of suspicion with Gray and Morgan on the eve of the hearings. At a minimum they were distressed by the improper advances made on Oppenheimer's behalf. More seriously, perhaps, the incident provided firsthand evidence that Oppenheimer and his friends disregarded the ordinary constraints of the security system and intimidated opponents and critics. By the end of the week, Gray was no longer passively analyzing Oppenheimer's file but was contributing derogatory evidence that he had heard about the scientist.[49]

Gray's suspicions of Oppenheimer and his friends significantly increased following the publication of Reston's story on the second day of the hearing. Apparently ignorant of Hagerty's strategy to force publication in the *New York Times*, Gray had accepted Garrison's pledge that he would do everything possible to keep the story out of the press. Unfortunately, Garrison did not tell Gray that he had already given Reston copies of the statement of charges and Oppenheimer's reply. Thus, when the *Times* accompanied its story with full texts of these documents, it was painfully clear to Gray that Garrison had been less than candid with the board. No one at the Commission seriously questioned Oppenheimer's right to release the charges, and even Gray did not regard the publication a breach of security.

Nevertheless, given Garrison's prior assurances of confidentiality, the episode provided the Gray board still another example of how Oppenheimer and his associates placed their personal judgment above the "rules" by which everyone else had agreed to be governed. Inexcusably, no one at the White House or at the Commission had bothered to tell Gray that the "rules" had been changed.[50]

After weeks of preparation the hearings began on Monday morning, April 12. Perhaps to avoid reporters, perhaps because of the shortage of space in the Commission's headquarters building, Gray convened the hearings in a converted office on the second floor of a dilapidated temporary building that the Commission occupied on Constitution Avenue, near the Washington Monument. In accordance with Commission practice, the security hearing was closed, and attendance was strictly limited. The only Commission personnel were the three members of the board, Robb, Rolander, a classification officer, a court reporter, and a transcriber. With Oppenheimer and his wife were Garrison and his legal associates—Silverman, Allen B. Ecker, and sometimes Marks. Before this group appeared a steady stream of forty witnesses, including Oppenheimer. The list of witnesses included prominent government officials who had known Oppenheimer during and after World War II, two former Commission chairmen and three former Commissioners, several members of the general advisory committee, Nobel laureates, some of Oppenheimer's academic colleagues at Berkeley, leaders of the American scientific community, and former Army security officers. Beginning at nine-thirty each morning, the sessions lasted with few exceptions until well after five, usually for five days each week over a period of four weeks.

Gray opened the first session by reading the statement of charges and Oppenheimer's autobiographical reply.[51] In his moving response, Oppenheimer admitted all but three of Nichols's allegations. He was, by his own admission to the board, a fellow traveler, whose brother Frank, sister-in-law Jacquenette, friend Jean Tatlock, and wife Katherine had all been members of the Communist party. Oppenheimer's confession, however, was hardly startling or incriminating. Army and Commission officials had known about the uncontested derogatory information for years and twice, in 1942 and 1947, had passed favorably on Oppenheimer's clearance despite the record. In fact, Gray was deeply troubled that most of the allegations placed Oppenheimer in double jeopardy, contrary to the American system of justice.[52]

Ironically the members of the board were much more concerned about the three allegations Oppenheimer denied: that he had attended a communist meeting in his home in 1941; that he had obstructed progress on the thermonuclear weapon; and that he had lied about contacts with Soviet agents. Thousands of words and many weeks later, the board's deliberations would focus on the second and third of these allegations; they were, in fact, to determine Oppenheimer's fate, whatever public reasons the board and the Commission might give.

## ALLEGATIONS: THE CROUCH INCIDENT

Of the first controverted allegation, the Commission and the FBI had known for more than a year that the so-called "Crouch incident" could not be substantiated. In May 1950 Paul Crouch and his wife had testified before the California committee on un-American activities that they had attended a Communist party meeting at Oppenheimer's Berkeley residence. Now before the Gray board, Oppenheimer explained what Gordon Dean had long known: Oppenheimer could not have attended such a meeting because he was on vacation with his wife in New Mexico at the time, a fact that was confirmed by their guest, Hans Bethe.[53]

## ALLEGATIONS: THE HYDROGEN BOMB

The second controverted charge, which contended that Oppenheimer had obstructed the development of the hydrogen bomb, was at the same time a central issue in the minds of Oppenheimer's critics and one of the most difficult allegations to substantiate. Aside from noting Oppenheimer's well-known reservations about the hydrogen weapon, Nichols cited only two specific incidents of alleged obstruction. The first was that Oppenheimer had sent reports to Los Alamos about the October 1949 meeting of the general advisory committee, which had recommended against accelerating thermonuclear development. The second was that he had discouraged other scientists (unnamed in the charges) from participating in the project. On the first charge, the Gray board easily determined that the reports in question were not circulated by Oppenheimer but rather had been sent to Los Alamos at the request of the Commission's general manager in preparation for a Congressional visit.[54] But even with this minor charge refuted, the larger question remained: Had Oppenheimer's opposition to the thermonuclear program jeopardized the security of the United States?

Evidence presented to the Gray board established that Oppenheimer had opposed the hydrogen bomb in 1949 on moral and technical grounds, but there was little to indicate that he had obstructed the development of the weapon after Truman had authorized it. Major General Roscoe C. Wilson and David T. Griggs, testifying for the Air Force, recalled Secretary Thomas K. Finletter's suspicious reaction to Oppenheimer's preference for tactical atomic bombs over thermonuclear weapons. Furthermore, there was a belief within the Air Force, Griggs reported, that Oppenheimer led a group of scientists determined to clip the wings of the Strategic Air Command by advocating deployment of tactical weapons in Europe and the establishment of continental air defense in North America.[55]

Although the plot against the Strategic Air Command could not be proven, Air Force officials had found some of their misgivings reinforced in April 1952, when Luis Alvarez shared with Finletter and others his recollections of Oppenheimer's left-wing activities during the prewar period at Berkeley. Alvarez had learned, however, that this information was already in FBI files. As was often true in the Oppenheimer affair, the only "new" information Alvarez could offer concerned Oppenheimer's apparent duplicity on thermonuclear matters.[56]

Despite their suspicions, it was difficult for Oppenheimer's critics, whether in 1952 during the fight for the second weapon laboratory or in 1954 before the Gray board, to demonstrate conclusively that Oppenheimer had actually impeded the thermonuclear project. It proved impossible to link his evident lack of enthusiasm for the hydrogen bomb with their suspicions of his disloyalty. In April 1952, when Alvarez saw Finletter, the FBI was also questioning four other nuclear scientists about Oppenheimer's attitude toward the hydrogen bomb. Of the four, only one, who requested anonymity, openly expressed his doubts about Oppenheimer's loyalty.[57] On the other hand, Hans Bethe, one scientist Oppenheimer supposedly discouraged, denied that his friend had ever tried to influence him not to work on the hydrogen bomb, although he had agreed in principle with Oppenheimer that the weapon should not be developed.[58]

In the final analysis, the significance of the hydrogen bomb charges brought against Oppenheimer must be measured against their ultimate source, Edward Teller. To Robb, Teller conceded that neither did he know what motivated Oppenheimer to oppose the thermonuclear program nor could he prove that Oppenheimer had not acted in good faith. Teller believed, however, that Oppenheimer had given a good deal of "harmful" advice so as deliberately to impede the project. Skirting the assessment of Oppenheimer's loyalty, Teller speculated that Oppenheimer, not wanting to see his achievements surpassed, might have become a victim of his own vanity. Whatever the reason, Teller thought Oppenheimer should never again have influence over the American thermonuclear program, although he hoped Oppenheimer's clearance would not be revoked "for a mere mistake of *judgment*."[59]

When Teller arrived in Washington to testify he was depressed and troubled, as Strauss no doubt noticed during a private visit just before the hearing. To counteract Teller's doubts and to prepare him as an effective "rebuttal" witness, Robb provided Teller with excerpts from the hearings and a digest of materials from Oppenheimer's security file. The tactic worked when Teller, only vaguely aware of Oppenheimer's left-wing background, shared the alarm of those who read Oppenheimer's file for the first

93

time. Furthermore, in one instance, he identified testimony that was at variance with his recollection of an earlier conversation with Oppenheimer. Teller seemed to think that Oppenheimer was up to his old tricks, and Robb did nothing to disabuse Teller of this assumption.

On the witness stand, Teller offered substantially the same testimony he had earlier given Robb and the FBI. When Robb inquired about Oppenheimer's loyalty, Teller replied unequivocally, "I have always assumed, and I now assume that he is loyal to the United States." But to Robb's question whether he believed Oppenheimer was a security risk, Teller answered:

> In a great number of cases I have seen Dr. Oppenheimer act—I understand that Dr. Oppenheimer acted—in a way which for me was exceedingly hard to understand. I thoroughly disagreed with him in numerous issues and his actions frankly appeared to me confused and complicated. To this extent I feel that I would like to see the vital interests of this country in hands which I understand better, and therefore trust more.
>
> In this very limited sense I would like to express a feeling that I would feel personally more secure if public matters would rest in other hands.[60]

Afterwards Teller realized he had virtually condemned Oppenheimer for his opinions and advice. Trying to clarify his thinking for Gray, Teller speculated that Oppenheimer would not knowingly or willingly endanger the safety of the United States. To that extent, he advised, there was no reason to deny clearance. But in contradiction to his earlier statement to Robb, Teller continued, "If it is a question of wisdom and *judgment*, as demonstrated by actions since 1945, then I would say one would be wiser not to grant clearance." Understandably, Teller admitted he was a "little bit confused on this issue, particularly as it refers to a person of Oppenheimer's prestige and influence."[61] Nevertheless, he successfully summed up the substance of the hydrogen bomb charges, which Green had drawn from Teller's FBI interview.

## ALLEGATIONS: THE CHEVALIER AFFAIR

The third controverted allegation related to the well-known Chevalier incident. This allegation was disputed, not because there was any doubt that the incident had taken place but rather because there was uncertainty about the facts of the case and the significance of subsequent meetings between Oppenheimer and Haakon Chevalier at Princeton in 1950 and in Paris in 1953. Although the Chevalier incident stood as the single most important issue raised by the statement of charges, the facts of the matter have never been fully disclosed, nor has the importance of this single incident in bringing about Oppenheimer's ultimate downfall been fully understood.

Sometime in 1942 when Russian armies were battling for their very existence, Peter Ivanov, secretary to the consulate-general of the Soviet Union in San Francisco, asked George C. Eltenton, a British citizen employed by the Shell Development Corporation, to assist the Russians in obtaining information concerning the secret atomic research conducted at the University of California Radiation Laboratory. Ivanov suggested that Eltenton might contact either Lawrence, Oppenheimer, or perhaps Alvarez.[62] Later in 1946, when interviewed by the FBI, Eltenton was not certain that the third scientist was Alvarez, although that was his best recollection. In fact, Alvarez was not at Berkeley at the time, but Ivanov may not have known this. Of the three, Eltenton knew only Oppenheimer slightly but not enough to approach him. Instead, he suggested that Chevalier, a Berkeley professor known to be a close friend of Oppenheimer's, might serve as a contact with the scientists. Subsequently, Eltenton approached Chevalier with the same request on the grounds that the Soviet armies needed the information in their struggle against the Nazis. Chevalier was uneasy about Eltenton's request, but he agreed to keep the matter confidential even from his wife.[63]

Later Oppenheimer invited the Chevaliers to dinner. While both men were in the kitchen mixing drinks, Chevalier casually mentioned his conversation with Eltenton. It is uncertain whether Chevalier merely reported his meeting with Eltenton or mentioned details of the scheme, including the proposed contacts with Lawrence and perhaps Alvarez. But Oppenheimer stated in no uncertain terms that the idea was terribly wrong, and thereupon Chevalier dropped the subject immediately. Thus, Oppenheimer saw no danger in the incident, and, because he was confident Chevalier was no spy, he neglected to report it to security officers at the laboratory. Besides, he was soon swept up in events that demanded his utmost attention. On March 25, 1943, Oppenheimer left California for New Mexico to establish the Los Alamos laboratory.

Having assumed command at Los Alamos, Oppenheimer became more sensitive to security requirements. Concerned now that Eltenton bore watching, he alerted Lieutenant Colonel John Lansdale, Jr., Manhattan Project security officer, to the fact that Eltenton had tried to contact scientists on the project. Not surprisingly, the security officers wanted more details, and on August 23, 1943, Oppenheimer was cross-examined about this matter by Lt. Colonel Boris T. Pash, an Army counterintelligence officer stationed at the Presidio in San Francisco. Unknown to Oppenheimer, the interview was recorded.

Oppenheimer had not anticipated Pash's interrogation and thus was unprepared for the grilling he received. Pash was particularly interested in

95

indentifying Eltenton's confederate and the other scientists who might have been approached, but Oppenheimer, wanting to protect himself, Lawrence, and Alvarez, as well as his friend Chevalier, refused to divulge any more names. Again and again Pash probed, but each time Oppenheimer demurred by responding only that approaches had been made to three persons, two of them (presumably Alvarez and himself) located at Los Alamos. Oppenheimer's story, although misleading, was accurate as far as it went; unfortunately, thereafter, it became confused and twisted.[64]

Determined to ferret out the truth after additional unsuccessful interviews with Oppenheimer, Lansdale and Pash asked Groves to order Oppenheimer to name the intermediary. Groves eventually complied, but only after a preliminary conversation with Oppenheimer failed to elicit the information voluntarily. Groves thought Oppenheimer was acting like a schoolboy in protecting his friends, but on December 12, 1943, he learned that Oppenheimer had family concerns as well: apparently Chevalier had also talked to his brother, Frank. As the plot thickened, the truth was irretrievably lost. Had Chevalier actually approached both Oppenheimer brothers, or had he spoken only to Frank, who then turned to his older brother for advice? Was Oppenheimer trying to shoulder the entire burden for his brother and friends? Obviously, a great deal was at stake, including the project. Thus, whatever his motives, Oppenheimer secured Groves's pledge not to report his brother's name to the FBI, thereby incredibly implicating the head of the Manhattan Project in his story. Back in Washington, Groves wondered whether he was bound by his promise to Oppenheimer. Advised by his aides that he had a higher obligation to national security, Groves nevertheless omitted Frank Oppenheimer's name from the dispatches alerting the field officers to the chain leading from Eltenton to the nuclear scientists.[65]

There, for the moment, the matter rested. Oppenheimer had been forthcoming in all details of the incident except the names of the other scientists, for which he was not pressed. With no immediate threat to the project and with the principals all under surveillance, Groves saw no need to challenge Oppenheimer further. Besides, the FBI and Army security preferred to make no move until an overt act of espionage had been committed. Premature questioning of either Eltenton or Chevalier might not only drive the suspected spy ring further underground but would also confirm for the Russians the key figures in the American atomic bomb project.

In 1946, when the FBI finally interviewed Eltenton, Chevalier, and Oppenheimer, the truth became even more confused. Picked up and questioned simultaneously, Eltenton and Chevalier were cross-checked during their interrogation. At first Chevalier admitted nothing but ultimately confessed he had been approached by Eltenton. He insisted, however, he had talked to no one besides Oppenheimer, to whom he did not mention Eltenton's name. Eltenton, on the other hand, offered important additional information. He recalled that Ivanov had suggested contact with three scientists: Oppenheimer, Lawrence, and a third whom he could not remember but guessed was Alvarez. After the unsuccessful meeting with Robert Oppenheimer, Eltenton dropped the matter but did try to help Chevalier to obtain a government position. By then, however, information in Chevalier's security file precluded his employment with the government.[66]

On September 5, 1946, the FBI interviewed Oppenheimer, after Chevalier had warned him of the government's investigation. Believing that his old friend was in trouble for his wartime involvement with Eltenton, Oppenheimer tried to explain to the FBI how he had wanted to warn security officers about Eltenton's spying without identifying his innocent friend. To emphasize the importance of Eltenton's threat, he told the special agents, he had concocted a "complicated cock-and-bull story" about three scientists whom Eltenton sought to contact; actually he thought that he had been the only person contacted by Chevalier. He implied that in this matter the FBI need investigate no further. Significantly, no mention was made of Frank Oppenheimer at this time by his brother, Eltenton, Chevalier, or the FBI.[67]

Oppenheimer's repudiation of his "cock-and-bull story" created serious questions concerning his veracity in 1946, and later in 1954, when he offered essentially the same explanation to the Gray board. He did not know, obviously, about Eltenton's identification of the three scientists. But what explained his backing down from the original story, which seems to have been authentic? It is always possible, but unlikely, that Oppenheimer had concocted his original story without knowing how closely it conformed to the actual facts. If this were true, then he had intended to lie in 1943 but attempted to tell the truth in 1946 and after. Alternatively, perceiving his friend's trouble but confident that Chevalier had given the FBI no additional information, he may have changed his story in 1946 to protect the identity of the scientists, and more particularly, that of his brother. Under this scenario, he would have told the truth in 1943 but would have lied to the FBI and the Gray board thereafter. Finally, Oppenheimer may have been trying to tell the truth all along. Like Eltenton, however, he may have forgotten most details that Chevalier did not help him reconstruct. In 1943, he was obviously alarmed about the prospects of Soviet espionage, and in a possible allusion to Alvarez's work at MIT, warned Pash that the Russians were interested in all kinds of information, including radar. By 1946, however, it was evident that neither Lawrence nor Alvarez had been tainted by the Chevalier affair, which had never gone beyond Oppenheimer. Thus, whether out of forgetfulness or because he was embarrassed by his exaggerated warning, Oppenheimer may have tried to adjust his 1946 story to fit the facts as he understood them. But once he came to believe he had lied to Pash, his only explanation was that his story had been a "fabrication and tissue of lies." His shame and contrition are apparent throughout the

97

transcript of the hearing.[68] Unquestionably, Oppenheimer's revised explanation would have been more convincing had he both avoided social contact with Chevalier after 1943 and mentioned his brother; as it was, he did neither.

It was perhaps significant that Lansdale recalled but one contact; Oppenheimer was not the only witness subject to forgetfulness about this issue. But Lansdale's recollection was of no assistance because the one person he remembered was Oppenheimer's brother, Frank.[69] Also appearing as a friendly witness, Groves nevertheless testified that he believed Frank Oppenheimer had been one link in the chain that Robert had tried to conceal. Understandably, Groves did not reveal fully the substance of Robert Oppenheimer's confession or the part he had played in keeping Frank Oppenheimer's name from the FBI.[70] Robb did not press Groves or Lansdale for this information but simply left it in the classified files beyond Garrison's reach.

98

Additional derogatory evidence, not included in the Nichols letter and not examined here, was developed during the hearings. For the most part, this information dealt with Oppenheimer's associations with suspected left-wingers such as David Bohm, Giovanni Rossi Lomanitz, Bernard Peters, and Rudi Lamert. One item dealt with Oppenheimer's handling of Glenn Seaborg's ambivalent recommendation to the general advisory committee in 1949 concerning the development of the hydrogen bomb. Believing that fairness to Oppenheimer required that he be confronted with his accuser, Robb subpoenaed Borden toward the end of the hearings. By the time Borden took the witness stand, however, those present at the proceedings were benumbed by more than 2,800 pages of testimony. Except for squabbling over whether Borden should be allowed to read his November 3 letter into the record, Oppenheimer's lawyers did not challenge or ask to cross-examine the person who had instigated the suspension of clearance. After only three more sessions the hearings concluded on May 6, 1954.

## THE GRAY BOARD DECISION

On May 27, 1954, the personnel security board, in a two-to-one decision with Gray and Morgan in the majority, recommended against restoring Oppenheimer's security clearance. With most allegations uncontested and only the Crouch incident denied and unproven, the board's principal task was evaluating the evidence rather than finding the facts. In that respect, the board found that Oppenheimer was loyal and discreet but nevertheless a security risk. The board acknowledged that it had received convincing testimony of Oppenheimer's devotion to his country and volunteered that "Dr. Oppenheimer seems to have had a high degree of discretion reflecting an unusual ability to keep to himself vital secrets." But the board also asserted that in times of peril, the requirements of national security were absolute. Because there were reasonable doubts in their minds concerning Oppenheimer, they could not recommend reinstatement.

Gray and Morgan ultimately outlined four controlling considerations leading them to their conclusion. First, they found that Oppenheimer's "continuing conduct and associations" reflected a serious disregard for the requirements of the security system. Principally, Gray was disturbed by the arrogance with which Oppenheimer placed his own judgment above that of more responsible persons. Gray and Morgan perceived Oppenheimer's arrogance firsthand in the Trevor Gardner incident and the news "leaks" to Reston. More particularly, Gray noted his concern about Oppenheimer's behavior in the Chevalier affair and the hydrogen bomb controversy and his opinions on tactical weapons, nuclear submarines, nuclear-powered aircraft, continental defense, and long-range detection.[71] Oppenheimer's continuing contacts with Chevalier in 1950 and 1953 also reflected a disregard for the need to keep his associations above suspicion. With the exception of Chevalier, however, the hearings and the security file revealed no significant contact between Oppenheimer and his prewar left-wing associates after 1943. Of course, he had continued to live with his wife and to see his brother and sister-in-law, and once he met Bohm and Lomanitz on a Princeton street corner while on the way to the barbershop. But unless one was willing to read something sinister into these associations, Oppenheimer committed only one indiscretion—continuing his friendship with Chevalier. No doubt for the board that was serious enough.

The board also found Oppenheimer susceptible to influence that could have serious implications for the security of the United States. This finding, perhaps, was the most ironic of all. More than one witness had attacked Oppenheimer for his Svengali-like influence over friends and subordinates. Instead, Gray and Morgan seized on two isolated incidents as proof of the exact opposite—that Oppenheimer was unduly susceptible to the influence of others. In 1943, at the insistence of Edward U. Condon, Oppenheimer and Lawrence had unsuccessfully tried to obtain a draft deferment for Lomanitz. Again, supposedly under pressure from Condon, Oppenheimer had publicly modified his criticism of Peters before the House Un-American Activities Committee in 1949. Furthermore, even though he had been openly attacked by Condon in the press, Oppenheimer indicated to the board his willingness to support Condon. Apparently the board considered it a sign of weakness that Oppenheimer would vouch for someone who had criticized him personally. Even Gray and Morgan were uncertain whether these inconclusive incidents demonstrated a susceptibility to influence. As a supplement, therefore, they added that the incidents also reflected bad judgment, a conclusion that clearly raised the question of Oppenheimer's "understanding, acceptance, and enthusiastic support of the security system." Again, Oppenheimer's relations with Reston during the

99

hearings indicated either that he was susceptible to the journalist's influence or that he used extremely bad judgment. Either way, Oppenheimer's assurances were not to be trusted.

The most unsettling of the board's conclusions related to Oppenheimer's "conduct" in the hydrogen bomb project. In response to Nichols's charges that Oppenheimer had slowed down thermonuclear development, the board found specifically that he had neither circulated the reports in question nor discouraged other scientists from working on the project. As to the more general allegation concerning Oppenheimer's opposition, the board found that "because of technical questions involved," it could not categorically state that the project had definitely been delayed. Thus, with the specifications discredited, why did the charge not fall? Rather than dismiss the charge, the board accepted Teller's reasoning and found that Oppenheimer's lack of enthusiasm had delayed the initiation of a concerted effort on the hydrogen bomb. Consequently, whatever the motivation, Oppenheimer had damaged the security interests of the United States. The board's finding, stripped of Teller's qualification, in effect condemned Oppenheimer for his sincerely offered, if incorrect, opinion. [72]

Finally, Gray and Morgan "regretfully concluded" that Oppenheimer had been less than candid in his testimony before the board. As Garrison noted in his brief to the Commission, this subjective finding was perhaps the most difficult of all to refute. It was also the most damaging to Oppenheimer's case. Without access to the classified files, Oppenheimer's lawyers and most subsequent commentators have assumed the board was referring to the scientist's testimony about the meeting of the general advisory committee in October 1949 and other matters relating to the hydrogen bomb controversy. No doubt these matters were in the minds of the board members, but from the board's perspective a more serious lack of candor was revealed in Oppenheimer's testimony on the Chevalier affair, when he had failed to be forthcoming about his brother. This failure became a major factor in Nichols's recommendation to the Commission.

When the hearings were over, Gray believed that the proceedings had been as fair as circumstances allowed. He granted that Oppenheimer and his counsel did not have full access to the documentation in possession of the board, but he did not believe that the deficiency had appreciably disadvantaged Oppenheimer. Gray admitted to some discomfort about Robb's aggressive cross-examinations and his piecemeal and surprise references "from various documents." But because Oppenheimer's veracity was a major issue, Gray ultimately justified Robb's prosecutorial methods on the grounds that only a vigorous and effective cross-examination could get at the truth. [73] Curiously, Robb had been inexplicably gentle when it came to pressing Oppenheimer, Groves, and Lansdale for the facts concerning Frank Oppenheimer's involvement in the Chevalier affair.

Whatever doubts Gray may have had concerning the fairness of

Robb's tactics were laid to rest when Robb volunteered to help Evans write his dissenting opinion. Evans's original pencil draft had alarmed Gray, who was less concerned by the dissent than he was by the prospect that the statement, if filed as written, would reflect unfavorably on Evans and probably on the work of the board itself. Thus, after completing his work on the majority decision, Robb in turn assisted Evans in preparing his brief. Evans could find no basis for denying Oppenheimer clearance. The charges relating to his left-wing past were old and twice evaluated; those pertaining to the hydrogen bomb controversy were utterly unproven. Evans observed that many of Oppenheimer's statements before the board still showed him to be naive but nevertheless extremely honest. But more than Oppenheimer's clearance was at stake. Evans expressed greatest concern about the impact a decision against Oppenheimer would have on scientific development in the United States and on American scientific prestige abroad. Hailed by some as an eloquent defense of Oppenheimer and science, in truth Evans's dissent was barely adequate, not even beginning to refute the arguments that Gray and Morgan had developed in detail.[74]

101

## NICHOLS'S RECOMMENDATION

Under established Commission procedures, either the manager of the field office or the deputy general manager at headquarters was responsible for handling security cases in his area. The manager appointed the personnel security board and received its findings. Then the manager notified the subject of the board's recommendation, the manager's decision, and the subject's right to appeal the findings to a personnel security review board. In addition, the manager also had the right of appeal. Should the case be appealed, the review board, if it chose, could take additional testimony, hear oral arguments, or receive supplemental briefs from counsel. Again, the manager made the final decision, based on the files, the boards' recommendations, and his own judgment about the impact upon the atomic energy program if the clearance were denied.[75]

The Oppenheimer case presented the Commission an anomaly, not only because of the importance of the case but because it was heard at headquarters. Because the Commission had no deputy general manager at the time, the responsibility devolved on Nichols, who of necessity worked very closely with the Commissioners. Furthermore, as Murray, Smyth, and Zuckert argued, the Commission could not avoid accepting direct responsibility in this matter. Under these circumstances, the Commissioners rather than the manager would exercise final judgment in the Oppenheimer case.[76]

Garrison advised Oppenheimer to waive his appeal to a review board so that the case could go directly to the Commission, as he had always wanted. With Oppenheimer's contract due to expire on June 30, there was always danger that a delay would render the case moot and damagingly unresolved. Unfortunately, having sacrificed his appeal to a review board, Oppenheimer no longer had a forum in which to argue his case. Garrison's request to appear before the Commission to present oral arguments on Oppenheimer's behalf was refused without explanation. This move left Garrison absolutely in the dark about Nichols's recommendation to the Commission. While preparing his rebuttal, Garrison also felt more keenly than ever his failure to secure a clearance. The Commission was required to reject his request for access to the pertinent file material because, at Robb's suggestion, the staff had discontinued processing Garrison's application for clearance during the Gray board hearings.[77]

102

Nichols's recommendation, presented to the Commission on June 12, 1954, was a forceful document in which the general manager showed his long distrust of Oppenheimer. From the earliest days of the Manhattan Project, Nichols had been uncertain of Oppenheimer's loyalty and had opposed giving him a security clearance. Even without evidence of disloyalty, Nichols believed Oppenheimer had endangered American security by both recruiting questionable people for the program and seriously disregarding the security system. Candidly, he confessed to the Commission that not until he was appointed general manager had he been in a position to "take action" regarding Oppenheimer.[78] He presented the Commission with a brief that might be called the Nichols model for justifying suspension of Oppenheimer's clearance. According to Nichols, the situation could be described with mathematical curves. While Oppenheimer's access to classified information remained high and constant, his usefulness to the government had been steadily declining since the end of World War II. Nichols also charted Oppenheimer's "Communist associations" on a downward curve between 1943 and 1954, but as associations decreased, the risk from those associations increased. In other words, although usefulness and left-wing associations had decreased as a consequence of the Cold War, the danger from Oppenheimer actually increased.[79] Finally, Nichols was not troubled by the intimation that Oppenheimer's clearance had been suspended on the basis of old information. Quite the contrary, he told the commissioners, never before had the facts of the files been comprehensively reviewed; indeed, evaluating all the derogatory information together rendered the old material new.

For obvious reasons, Nichols indicated that he concurred in the findings and recommendations of the board, but in fact his letter to the Commission contained a significant shift in emphasis. First, Nichols rejected the findings concerning the hydrogen bomb controversy except "as evidence bearing on Dr. Oppenheimer's veracity." Nichols said that technical opinions could have no security implications unless they were coupled with sinister motives, and "the evidence establishes no sinister motives on the part of Dr. Oppenheimer in his attitude on the hydrogen bomb, either before or after the President's decision." In effect, he rejected one of the board's "controlling considerations."

Nichols recommended rejecting Oppenheimer's clearance on three grounds: the Chevalier incident, his lack of veracity, and his past and continuing associations. Nichols thus altered substantially the grounds for decision. With susceptibility to influence and the hydrogen bomb controversy eliminated as considerations, the Commission's refusal to allow oral argument became manifestly unfair. As Smyth prophetically warned: "If we give Dr. Oppenheimer's attorneys no opportunity to comment on the Nichols's letter, we will be open to grave criticism when the letter is published."[80] The Nichols brief, Smyth realized, was an important document in the proceeding, not a simple letter of transmittal.

Nichols, with Robb's assistance, briefed the Commission on his analysis of the case; he emphasized that he had focused on the Chevalier affair, with the rest supplemental. "If you feel I am wrong on the Chevalier incident," he told the Commissioners, "then you can say I have gone overboard on some of these other things." Nichols had hoped that Oppenheimer could clarify the Chevalier incident during the hearings, instead of leaving the situation as confused as ever. If Oppenheimer was truly attempting to protect his friend in 1943, Nichols wondered why he had told the "cock-and-bull story," which was far more damaging to Chevalier than his subsequent version given to the FBI in 1946. Although Nichols was upset that Oppenheimer had not been forthcoming, he did not explain why Robb failed to cross-examine Oppenheimer, Groves, or Lansdale on this point. Nor did he explain why the man with the clearest recollection of the events—William A. Considine, Groves's chief legal adviser—was not called to testify.[81]

Nichols thought the Chevalier incident provided the principal evidence for Oppenheimer's lack of veracity. However the uncertainty was resolved, Nichols believed Oppenheimer a liar. But because the unchallenged evidence in the files indicated strongly that the 1943 version of the incident was more accurate than the later less damaging 1946 account, Nichols and Robb saw the possibility that Oppenheimer had lied to the Gray board when he repudiated the "cock-and-bull story." Oppenheimer's motive, Nichols assumed, was the same that had prompted him to request Groves's confidence—to protect his brother Frank. Shortly after Oppenheimer's clearance had been suspended by the President, Frank Oppenheimer had denied any involvement in the Chevalier affair.[82] Assuming his confession to Groves was accurate, Oppenheimer obviously could not confirm it without directly impugning his brother. The situation was similar to that in 1946 when FBI agents confronted him with a story that he could not repudiate without hurting Chevalier. In both instances, the simple and more innocent version shifted the burden away from his friend and brother to

103

himself; to some that might have appeared noble, but to Nichols it represented an inexcusable breach of the security system as well as outright lying.[83]

Finally, Nichols was alarmed at the sinister implications of Oppenheimer's visit to Chevalier in Paris in December 1953. The issue was officially labeled "continued associations" in his briefing to the Commission. Nichols expressed his personal fear that Oppenheimer's visit was not entirely social or innocent. "The non-charitable view is this," he explained to the Commissioners, "why would Oppenheimer of his own initiative come here to Washington to see Ken Fields to get a briefing on weapons, go out to Los Alamos on a briefing of weapons, just prior to going to Paris to see Chevalier?"[84] For Nichols the implication was self-evident and unacceptable. As he had told the Commission, if they accepted his premise concerning the relationship between Oppenheimer and Chevalier, all else would fall into place.

104

## WHITE HOUSE REACTION

At the White House, Eisenhower agreed with Nichols's assessment of the impropriety of Oppenheimer's Paris visit with Chevalier. "How can any individual report a treasonable act on the part of another man and then go and stay at his home for several days?" the President asked. "It just doesn't make any sense to me."[85] Although Eisenhower had his facts garbled—the Chevaliers had only entertained the Oppenheimers for dinner—the President harbored no second thoughts about his suspension of clearance. When informed that Oppenheimer and Garrison under pressure from Reston were contemplating release of both the Gray board findings and Garrison's rejoinder to the Commission, Eisenhower commented that Oppenheimer was acting just like a communist, using all the rules to win public sentiment through martyrdom. Nevertheless, the President was determined above all else that the Commission "must act decent on this and must show the people of the country that we are more interested in trying to find out the facts than to get headlines like McCarthy does."[86]

In addition to the squeeze between Oppenheimer and McCarthy, Strauss reported that the Truman appointees to the Commission—Murray, Smyth, and Zuckert—were playing politics with the Oppenheimer case. Murray, especially, was suspected of leaking the Commission's discussion to several newspapers as part of his continuing fight against Strauss. As late as June 10, Strauss estimated that the three Commissioners would vote to restore Oppenheimer's clearance in order to embarrass the Republican Administration. Strauss cited the Commission's decision to rule on the case and its haste to decide the matter before Zuckert's term expired on June 30 as evidence of their determination to save Oppenheimer at the chairman's expense. Eisenhower sympathized with Strauss and assured him that he was more determined than ever to secure a Republican majority on the Commission following Zuckert's retirement.[87]

Suspicions and acrimony deepened over the debate whether to publish the Gray board hearings. Strauss learned from the FBI that Garrison and Oppenheimer feared publication of the transcript would greatly harm Oppenheimer's case. In order to mitigate the damage, Oppenheimer again discussed with Reston the possibility of releasing prior to the Commission's decision excerpts from the transcript most favorable to Oppenheimer.[88] Strauss, who naturally wanted to beat him to the punch with a full disclosure of the hearings, encouraged Gray to request publication of the unclassified version of the hearings. Unfortunately for Strauss, Gray had previously assured each witness that the proceedings, in accordance with Commission regulations, would be kept strictly confidential; furthermore, Gray had promised that the Commission would take no initiative to release information on the hearings. It would seem that the Commission could do nothing but wait for Oppenheimer to act.[89]

105

Fortuitously, Strauss found his excuse for publication of the hearings. Overwhelmed by the massive transcript and files, Smyth had asked two Commission officials to prepare a summary of the case listing each of Nichols's charges along with Oppenheimer's reply, pertinent file material, and related testimony. The summary of evidence condensed the entire case into 241 convenient pages. Also pressed to review the transcript and evidence, Zuckert obtained a copy of the summary and took it with him on the train to Boston on Saturday, June 12. In the confusion of disembarking his family from the train in Boston, Zuckert forgot to pick up the summary, which was later recovered by the FBI. Strauss, reporting the incident to the White House, relayed his suspicions that Zuckert had actually passed the document on to Oppenheimer's friends. With the material compromised, Strauss believed there was no choice but to publish the hearings as quickly as possible. Murray and Smyth blocked immediate action, principally on the grounds that the Commission had an obligation to protect the confidential testimony of the witnesses. But after Nichols secured releases from the board and witnesses, only Smyth held out against publication, on the grounds that the testimony should not be released until the Commission had made its own decision.[90]

## THE COMMISSION DECISION

Strauss did not realize it, but the vote to publish the Gray board hearings anticipated the Commission's ultimate division in the Oppenheimer case. Uncertain of the vote until three days before Oppenheimer's contract was due to expire, Strauss reported to the White House on June 27 that the

President's suspension would be upheld by a vote of four to one, with Smyth dissenting. Strauss accepted White House congratulations for doing "a wonderful job," but it is problematical whether he personally influenced any decision other than Campbell's.[91]

Actually, the Commission delivered five opinions in the Oppenheimer case. Strauss wrote the majority opinion in which Zuckert and Campbell concurred. Both Zuckert and Campbell, however, also submitted separate opinions of their own. In addition, Murray and Smyth submitted independent opinions in the matter; Smyth's, of course, was a dissent. The decision was officially made on June 28, 1954.[92]

Smyth's dissent offered a logical and sympathetic explanation of the derogatory information in the files. Noting the "clear conclusion" of the board that Oppenheimer was completely loyal, Smyth could not concur that he was nevertheless a security risk. With respect to the Chevalier episode, Smyth found the incident inexcusable but understandable and without serious consequence for American security. Furthermore, he failed to find any pattern of "continuing association" beyond minor "occasional incidents of a complex life." As for Oppenheimer's alleged lack of veracity, Smyth concluded: "Unless one confuses a manner of expression with candor, or errors in recollection with lack of veracity, Dr. Oppenheimer's testimony before the Gray board has the ring of honesty." According to Smyth, the only question to be determined by the Commission was whether Oppenheimer might intentionally or unintentionally reveal classified information to persons who should not have it. His character and associations were important only insofar as they indicated the likelihood of security violations. If one began with the assumption that Oppenheimer was disloyal, Smyth continued, the derogatory information might arouse suspicion. But, if the entire record were read objectively, Smyth argued, Oppenheimer's loyalty and trustworthiness emerged clearly, and the various disturbing incidents became understandable and unimportant. Smyth evaluated the whole man: Oppenheimer's contributions to the nation, his disassociation from subversive organizations after 1942, his mature view of the communist threat expressed repeatedly in high government councils between 1945 and 1953, and, finally, the high tribute and expressions of confidence given by some twenty-five witnesses of impeccable character and high responsibility in Oppenheimer's behalf. He weighed all this information, the favorable and the unfavorable, and decided that Oppenheimer's employment would not endanger American security but rather was "clearly consistent with the interests of the national security."

In sharp contrast to Smyth's opinion, Murray was the only person involved in the case to find Oppenheimer "disloyal." Murray offered a legalistic and extremely rigid definition of loyalty. After tracing the derivations of the concept, Murray concluded that a person's loyalty must be judged against obedience to the security system. Such a standard provided

106

the decisive measure of one's loyalty to one's government. In addition, the communist conspiracy had created special problems for the United States, which had been forced to erect a system of laws and executive orders designed to protect the government "against the hidden machinery of subversion." When applying his loyalty test to Oppenheimer, Murray found a frequent and deliberate disregard for those regulations that restricted associations and a seriously deficient cooperation with the security system. On this basis, he determined that Oppenheimer was "disloyal."

Murray's opinion was deficient in several respects. In contrast to every other opinion, he did not specify or allude to any evidence to support either of his findings. In his only reference to the facts of the case, Murray reversed his original position by placing no significance at all on the evidence relating to the thermonuclear controversy. Instead, he eloquently rejected the idea that any influence of disloyalty could be drawn from opinions offered in good faith to the government. Thus, one must read between the lines to find the evidence that disturbed Murray. In doing so, it would appear that he based his decision almost entirely upon the Chevalier affair and particularly on the meetings between Oppenheimer and Chevalier in 1950 and 1953. In strictly following Nichols's logic, however, Murray failed to balance "the whole man" against deviation from the norm of conduct revealed in Oppenheimer's contacts with Chevalier. Murray's opinion was a syllogism founded on a false premise: the security criteria established norms for loyal citizens; Oppenheimer deviated from the norm; therefore, Oppenheimer was disloyal. It is evident that once the hydrogen bomb charges were swept away Murray had difficulty finding adequate ground for denying clearance. His inflexible standard allowed him to focus on the derogatory facts without evaluating their importance.

107

On the other hand, Campbell's opinion was ambiguous. In general, he viewed his responsibility as the narrowest possible appellate review. After summarizing the proceedings against Oppenheimer, he concluded that the board had conducted a fair hearing with honesty and integrity. Campbell not only sustained the recommendations of the board and the general manager, but by signing the majority opinion he also concurred in the Commission's wide-ranging review and reevaluation of the evidence. Given the striking differences between the board's findings and Nichols's recommendations, Campbell's position made it impossible to determine just which opinion he accepted. His confusion, however, pointed up the injustice of denying Oppenheimer a chance to answer Nichols's recommendations. Oral arguments before the Commission might have helped to clear the confusion apparent in Campbell's opinion.

Zuckert's statement also differed sharply from Murray's. He rejected Murray's idea that any deviation from the security system amounted to disloyalty. Obviously referring to the Chevalier affair, he stated that no single act of lying or isolated disregard of security considerations and obstruction of security inquiries would by themselves have been decisive. But when he perceived "a combination of seriously disturbing actions and events" as reported in the Oppenheimer case, he decided that risk to security had passed acceptable bounds. Zuckert correctly understood that his task was to weigh the risks presented by the individual against what was "at stake and the job to be done." Zuckert's opinion might be criticized for its failure to state the need for weighing favorable information, which in Oppenheimer's case was considerable, but perhaps this was implicit in his duty "to determine how much of a risk is involved in respect to any particular individual." Zuckert's statement is logical and convincing, subject to criticism only by applying Zuckert's standards against the facts of the Oppenheimer case; this is done in Strauss's analysis of the majority opinion.

The majority decision, Strauss said, stood on two legs: "fundamental defects in character" and Oppenheimer's "associations." Following Nichols's recommendation, Strauss rejected categorically any inference that the Commission's decision was based in any way on Oppenheimer's role in the thermonuclear controversy. As to "character," the majority cited six incidents in which Oppenheimer had behaved improperly. Not surprisingly, the Chevalier affair headed the list. Strauss reflected the same ambivalence toward the evidence as Nichols, and he arrived at essentially the same conclusion. Whether Oppenheimer lied to Pash and Groves in 1943 or to the Gray board in 1954 was virtually academic because the results were about the same: on the one hand, he had lied to federal security officers; on the other, he had committed perjury before the board.

The remaining five illustrations merely supplemented the main example. Strauss reiterated the evidence concerning Lomanitz, Peters, the Seaborg letter, and other incidents. He noted that Oppenheimer had told the FBI in 1950 that he did not know that Joseph Weinberg had been a communist until the fact became public. As the recording of his 1943 interview with Lansdale revealed, however, Oppenheimer knew Weinberg to be a communist much earlier. Yet how was this an illustration of his defect in character? What deception could Oppenheimer hope to accomplish by lying to the FBI in 1950 when he had admitted knowing Weinberg to be a communist in 1943? Clearly, the whole interview revealed nothing but a failure in recollection; but viewed against the Chevalier incident, the lapse suggested to the majority a pattern in which Oppenheimer mitigated his stories after 1946. Significantly, the majority opinion stated that its findings on Oppenheimer's "fundamental defects of character" were not limited to six examples cited but that "the work of Military Intelligence, the Federal Bureau of Investigation and the Atomic Energy Commission—all at one time or another have felt the effect of his falsehoods, evasions and misrepresentations." The charge was sweeping and tantalizing in that it suggested large reservoirs of information yet untapped in the file. In fact, as Harold Green knew, there was nothing more, unless one looked at the material relating to the hydrogen bomb charges. Perhaps, in a backhanded way, that was what the Commission meant to imply.

To substantiate the second leg of the majority opinion, Strauss cited Oppenheimer's left-wing associations prior to 1942 but was careful to state that these well-known associations were not in themselves a controlling reason for the Commission's decision. Not surprisingly, Oppenheimer's meeting with Chevalier in Paris provided the main basis for this finding. Here the failure to underscore favorable information was particularly damaging because the majority neglected to point out that one meeting had included André Malraux, an important adviser to Charles De Gaulle. The most intelligent view of this episode was expressed in the hearings by George F. Kennan, who believed that senior government officials must be permitted maturity of judgment to know when and under what circumstances they can see a person:

> If they come to you sometimes, I think it is impossible for you to turn them away abruptly or in a cruel way, simply because you are afraid of association with them, so long as what they are asking of you is nothing that affects your governmental work. I myself say it is a personal view on the part of Christian charity to try to be at least as decent as you can to them. [93]

Kennan's plea for Christian charity succumbed to Nichols's fears of communist conspiracy. In its decision, the majority made no mention of Oppenheimer's work at Los Alamos or to his years of faithful service and devotion to duty. The Commission's decision read like a judgment in a criminal case demanding punishment for misconduct in the past rather than a security evaluation predicting Oppenheimer's future behavior, based upon all relevant data. This failure to evaluate the "whole person" was the Commission's most fundamental error. In the final analysis, even the Commissioners apparently realized the flimsiness of their rationale for denying clearance. They could not in good conscience say that Oppenheimer's clearance would "endanger the national security" or be inconsistent with the requirements of the security system. Instead, they declared that "concern for the defense and security of the United States requires that Dr. Oppenheimer's clearance should not be reinstated." Ironically, neither the Atomic Energy Act nor the regulations required such a finding.

## AFTERMATH AND CONSEQUENCES

Decades later, the Oppenheimer case continued to haunt those who participated in it and to fascinate those who discovered it as either history or legend. It involved primarily one of the most celebrated scientists of modern times, a man whose career seemed to epitomize the awesome role that science had come to play in American life. And, as the Commission's formal opinions made clear, the case did not involve mere political opinions or scientific judgments but more fundamental matters of morality, loyalty and service to one's country, and ultimately the role of the scientist in a democracy. The very terms in which the issue was cast suggested themes that transcended both twentieth-century America and modern science. Some observers could not help thinking of a modern-day Galileo on trial for speaking the truth about nature or even a new Socrates accepting the judgments of lesser men. In more contemporary terms, some believed that Oppenheimer, as a victim of McCarthyism, shared a martyrdom similar to Scopes, Sacco and Vanzetti, or the Rosenbergs and Hiss.

If such large implications of the Oppenheimer case did not assure it a place in American consciousness, the publication of the transcript surely did. The transcript, with its hundreds of pages of testimony ranging over the whole history of nuclear development in America since 1942, provided an extraordinary insight into the hitherto secret world of the atomic energy establishment. As one journalist remarked, "The Oppenheimer transcript is Operation *Candor*."[94] The debate over the hydrogen bomb, the fight among the nuclear scientists and with the Air Force over national defense policy, and the scores of other previously classified episodes were outlined in vivid and often embarrassing detail. The human foibles of petty falsehood, pride, misunderstanding, self-deception, and envy were preserved for all to see. Given the rich human quality of the material and the dialogue from the transcript, it was not surprising that playwrights soon saw the dramatic possibilities of the Oppenheimer case.

For those whose lives were touched directly, the case had added dimensions. No participant would ever be the same again. For Oppenheimer and his family, the impact was obvious and devastating, and it did not end with the Commission's decision. The Commission and the FBI were frightened by intelligence reports in August 1954 that Soviet agents were trying to arrange for Oppenheimer's defection and even more by Oppenheimer's decision to take his family on a sailing vacation in the Virgin Islands.[95] Obviously the case had not closed with the stripping of Oppenheimer's clearance and credentials as a government official. For more than a decade, Oppenheimer would linger in exile, cut off from a world that had been the center of his career, a world he had done much to create.

For others the repercussions were long-lasting if not so severe. Strauss, Teller, Borden, Green, Robb, Garrison, Smyth, Murray, and Zuckert would never in the eyes of the public be able to shake off their identification with the case. All would share in varying degrees public criticism and vindication for their roles in the drama. An episode that under other circumstances would have soon passed from public memory would indelibly mark their careers, taint their subsequent achievements, and embitter relationships among them for years to come.

Vexing and painful as the scars on individuals were, the institutional effects of the Oppenheimer case were probably more significant. Initially the Commission as a federal agency drew relatively little criticism from the public. For the most part, press reaction was not hostile; nor, with the exception of the Alsops' diatribe, *We Accuse!*, did journalists take up Oppenheimer's cause after the Commission's final decision. Slightly more than three hundred individuals outside the establishment took time to express their opposition to the decision while almost fifty approved.[96]

The greatest criticism came from scientists, especially those within the atomic community. Even before the hearings were concluded, twenty-seven physicists from the University of Illinois signed a statement in the *Bulletin of the Atomic Scientists* protesting the hydrogen bomb charges against Oppenheimer. In the same issue, thirteen prominent scientists, including Linus Pauling and Albert Einstein, affirmed their faith in Oppenheimer. Hans Bethe, president of the American Physical Society, telegraphed the society's denunciation of the Gray board's decision before the Commission's final vote. Petitions signed by eleven hundred scientists and staff from the national laboratories and leading universities expressed indignation at the action against Oppenheimer and warned of damage to Commission programs. Nichols was so concerned about the protest from Argonne that he considered going to Chicago personally, as he had done under similar circumstances in 1945, to explain the government's action to the scientists. He was dissuaded only when Walter H. Zinn, director of the laboratory, assured him that the visit was unnecessary.[97]

111

Strauss was troubled if not surprised by the scientists' reactions and attempted to explain the Commission's position at the July meeting of the general advisory committee. Recognizing that almost half of the petitioners had worked at Los Alamos, where Oppenheimer had been the wartime director, Strauss decided to present a presidential citation to the laboratory for its extraordinary achievement. The gesture, dubbed "Operation Butter-Up" by one newspaper,[98] was too transparent to be effective. There was also some concern expressed through the general advisory committee that the Commission would launch a massive review of security clearances using questionable associations as derogatory evidence. Such fears stemmed directly from the formal opinions of Murray and Zuckert in the Oppenheimer case.[99]

Despite warnings from the general advisory committee of low morale in the Commission's laboratories, no mass exodus of disenchanted scientists occurred. Neither did recruitment for Commission projects lag, nor did vital programs suffer from a lack of qualified scientists. How the Oppenheimer case affected the career decisions of individual scientists has never been determined in any systematic way. Some saw the Commission's action as outrageous and sickening; in the minds of others, Oppenheimer got what he deserved. There was, however, a subtle but permanent shift in many scientists' perception of the Commission. Eight years earlier the scientists had seen the Commission as their agency, a new and enlightened institution that could, among other things, free the scientist from the restraints and indignities of military control. The Commission had justified that faith, but the Oppenheimer case had planted seeds of doubt. It was not likely that an agency that had destroyed the career of a leader like Oppenheimer could ever again enjoy the full confidence of the nation's scientists. To that extent, the effects of the Oppenheimer case were permanent and damaging.

CHAPTER 5

# THE POLITICAL
# ARENA

James R. Newman, one author of the Atomic Energy Act of 1946, described the law as establishing "in the midst of our privately controlled economy a socialist island with undefined and possibly expanding frontiers."[1] Newman was referring to the sections of the act that gave the Commission absolute control over all fissionable materials, all facilities using or producing such material, and all information related to nuclear technology. Under the almost inflexible provisions of the law, the Commission had virtually dominated the development of nuclear technology in the five years since 1947. Other sections of the act exempted the Commission from the civil service system and from many administrative laws and regulations that applied to other government agencies. These exemptions gave the Commission an unusual degree of flexibility in administration and made possible the recruitment of a staff with capabilities exceptional in the civil service. Furthermore, the enormous sums appropriated by the Congress for military applications of atomic energy insured the agency a "standard of living" that few Cabinet departments enjoyed.

Living in this rarified atmosphere, the Commission could afford to exercise an unusual degree of independence from both the Executive and Legislative branches of the government, from the pressures of lobbyists and special interest groups, and from the political process as a whole. Before 1953 the Commissioners could say with more truth than could most government executives that their agency was untouched by the stain of politics. The golden days of privilege and isolation, however, were beginning to fade in 1953. The rising interest in nuclear energy within American industry, the determination of the Eisenhower Administration to reverse the trend toward greater governmental control of the economic system, the growing opportunities to use nuclear energy for civilian purposes and to encourage international cooperation as a way to world peace—all these forces stimulated public interest in liberalizing the Atomic Energy Act of 1946.

These efforts would in part establish at least some bridges between the "island of socialism" and the mainland of the nation's "free enterprise system," open new channels for disseminating nuclear technology, and reduce the extent of the government monopoly. The process of amending the act would itself begin to lead the Commission and its staff out of the secret, sealed-off world of the atom. The points at issue in the legislative debate involved not so much the special considerations of nuclear technology but rather such broad policy questions as the role of government and private industry in the nation's energy economy. Such a debate alone would have inevitably entangled the Commission in the web of partisan politics. As it happened, the Dixon-Yates controversy, as Commissioner Zuckert put it, was "to deflower the AEC in a political sense."[2] By summer 1954, when the new legislation took effect, the Atomic Energy Commission would find itself in the middle of the political arena.

114

## LEGISLATION FOR PRIVATE INDUSTRY

In formulating a nuclear power policy for the Eisenhower administration in spring 1953, the Commission had drafted legislation intended to remove some legal obstacles to participation by private industry.[3] The bill would have permitted, under license by the Commission, the private ownership of both power reactors and the fissionable material used as fuel in or produced by the reactors. Even the Commission, however, recognized that the bill was preliminary in several respects. It did not speak to such important matters as patents and contained no provision for international cooperation. Because Dean had no time to clear the draft within the Executive Branch before presenting it to the Joint Committee on May 26, 1953, the Bureau of the Budget asked the committee not to release the bill to the public.[4]

Review of the proposal within the bureau and other executive agencies quickly revealed major issues that went to the heart of Administration policy, not only on nuclear power but on other economic matters as well. There was general agreement within the Executive Branch, for example, that the government monopoly of reactors and fissionable materials would have to be relaxed in some way. But would such a relaxation weaken controls that seemed essential for safety and security reasons? And what would prevent the few large corporations like du Pont, General Electric, and Union Carbide, which had already attained a high degree of competence in nuclear technology as Commission contractors, from monopolizing the infant industry as licensees? Congressmen Chet Holifield and Melvin Price, two Democratic members of the Joint Committee, voiced concerns of public-power advocates, calling the Administration's proposal a vast "giveaway" of the public treasure. In their minds the federal government had invested more than twelve billion dollars in developing nuclear technology while industry had provided little financial support. Now the Administration proposed, they argued, to let a few giant corporations monopolize the technology developed at government expense. Holifield and Price would have been fascinated to know that within the Administration Sinclair Weeks, the conservative Secretary of Commerce, had expressed similar reservations. Weeks favored continuing government controls, not only to protect the national economy but also to reimburse the government for private use of a "national treasure" of fissionable materials.[5]

## THE PATENT QUESTION

Not until summer 1953 did the Commission face the perplexing question of what to do about the patent provisions of the 1946 act. Under its terms no private patent rights could be obtained for any invention used in the production or utilization of fissionable material or atomic weapons. The act also required the Commission to declare certain patents affected by the public interest and therefore subject to compulsory licensing. Such a finding was required when the Commission determined that an invention utilized fissionable material or atomic energy and that licensing was necessary to effectuate the purposes of the act. In such cases, the owner was entitled to a reasonable royalty fee.

The government monopoly of nuclear technology since 1946 had been so complete that the Commission had had very little opportunity to apply the patent provisions of the act in nuclear power development. For contracts with the industrial study groups established in 1952 the Commission had insisted upon its right to determine the disposition of all patent rights to any invention that might result from the study projects. This restriction not only protected the government from the possibility of having to pay royalties for inventions made by the companies but also prevented these companies from securing a preferred patent position. Several industrial groups had already told the Commission that they would not accept this restriction on any activities subsequent to their initial studies.[6]

Lacking any special knowledge of patents, the Commissioners were reluctant to rush into a decision on new legislation. During three meetings in June 1953 they preferred to examine the broad implications of such legislation. On the one hand, they might err by not being liberal enough in encouraging industrial participation; on the other, they might open the doors to industry too quickly with disastrous results for the future. Zuckert feared that eliminating the compulsory licensing requirement for inventions related to utilizing atomic energy might be unwise. Although economic nuclear power appeared to be the first goal of industry, there was no guarantee that the situation would not change. Zuckert thought that royalties paid under compulsory licensing would offer industry sufficient incentive for the time being.[7]

As a scientist, Smyth had less feel for patent law and administration than did any of his colleagues. He asked why a company should be entitled to a profit from an invention developed with government funds simply because the specific application of that invention lay outside the field of atomic energy, as the staff recommendation proposed. He was not impressed with the argument that the Department of Defense used such an arrangement in contracts with aircraft manufacturers. Smyth held that the situation was quite different in the case of nuclear energy: virtually all technology had been developed at government expense.

Dean, during the last weeks of his term as chairman, took a different view. He thought it was time to open up the broad area of atomic energy use to the normal operation of the patent system. As long as the government was assured a royalty-free right to use these inventions, he thought it would advance development to permit broad patent rights. Marion W. Boyer, who had enjoyed a long career in industry before he became the Commission's general manager, agreed with Dean. He even went so far as to suggest that it might be necessary to risk giving some companies a preferred position in the industry in the interests of promoting rapid development of nuclear technology. As Dean warned, there might never be a nuclear power industry if the government continued to restrict the dissemination of technical information and denied industry the profit incentive for innovation.

Zuckert rejected the suggestion that he lacked enthusiasm for industrial development, but he did confess to deep concern about the possibilities of monopoly by a few large companies, particularly those holding major operating contracts at Commission facilities. He was worried that in the course of their work some of these companies might have developed inventions that technically lay outside the production or utilization of fissionable material. It was possible that some of these inventions were being withheld pending a liberalization of the act's patent provision. Zuckert suggested that instead of giving broad patent rights in a virtually unexplored field of technology, the Commission should advocate some form of compulsory licensing in the entire field of atomic energy.[8]

A few weeks later, after Strauss had become chairman, the Commissioners resumed the discussion with their patent advisory panel. All five members were authorities on patent matters and members William H. Davis and Casper W. Ooms had influenced the drafting of the patent provisions of the 1946 act. The advisory panel advocated a middle ground between complete freedom and complete restriction on patent matters. Davis thought the Commission should retain the right to find a specific invention affected with the public interest and should be able to require licensing of such an invention. John A. Dienner, a Chicago patent attorney,

116

supported Davis and suggested compulsory licensing for as long as twenty years. Commissioner Murray, who believed the panel was being too conservative, suggested that a five-year limit on compulsory licensing would be sufficient. Without venturing an opinion on that point, Ooms advocated compulsory licensing in principle, although he warned that industry would strongly object.[9]

The Commissioners took all these ideas under advisement in an executive policy conference at White Sulphur Springs, West Virginia, late in September. There were no records of the discussion, but the decisions were clear enough. The Commission's legislative proposal in October 1953 would have permitted private ownership of fissionable material as well as reactors, but there would be provisions spelling out the safeguards and recovery rights necessary to protect the national interest. No private patent rights would be permitted for inventions relating to the military uses of atomic energy, and all other inventions relating to the use of atomic energy would be subject to compulsory licensing at the Commission's discretion for five years.[10]

117

## INFORMATION AND SECURITY

The Commission's proposal was designed to open the way for industrial participation in nuclear development, but it would not affect other provisions of the 1946 act that restricted the flow of technical information on several levels. Not only did the act severely limit the exchange of technical information with other nations, but it also posed troublesome obstacles to disseminating classified information within the atomic energy establishment and to allied governments in Europe. The Commission had been proposing revision of these restrictive sections of the 1946 act for several years. Although some of these proposals were not much more than "housekeeping" amendments, their total effect would have significantly opened up nuclear technology.[11]

Section 10 had become one of the most awkward sections of the 1946 act. It provided for a special category of information, called "restricted data," inflexibly defined to include virtually all atomic energy information of any security significance. The act also imposed special restrictions on disseminating restricted data to foreign nations and required a full background security investigation for all Commission employees, contractors, and persons receiving restricted data from Commission contractors. This last restriction was especially burdensome because it prevented Commission contractors from giving restricted data to military officers or employees of the Department of Defense, although the latter could receive such data directly from the Commission. Section 10 even required a full investigation for construction workers and others who had access only to relatively non-sensitive information that was legally in the restricted data category. In autumn 1953 the Commission staff gave some thought to recommending elimination of the restricted data provisions of Section 10 altogether but concluded that repeal would weaken security unless uniform and more effective regulations were established for the federal government as a whole.[12]

Perhaps no provision of the 1946 act had caused the Commissioners more anguish than the restrictions of Section 10 on the exchange of information with foreign nations. The act provided that until Congress declared by joint resolution that effective and enforceable international safeguards against the use of atomic energy for destructive purposes had been established, no exchange of information on industrial uses of atomic energy was permitted, although the exchange of basic scientific and technical information was encouraged. In an effort to preserve at least a semblance of the cooperative arrangements that had developed during World War II with the British and the Canadians, the Commission had agreed to exchange basic scientific data in nine specified areas under a formal modus vivendi signed in 1948. As a Commissioner, Strauss had opposed anything but the narrowest possible interpretation of the nine technical areas, and Senator Hickenlooper had led an attack on the technical cooperation program when he learned that information on plutonium was being provided to the British under the modus vivendi. Following the bruising treatment the Commission received during the Hickenlooper investigation in summer 1949, and the revelation of Klaus Fuchs's treachery early in 1950, the modus vivendi was applied only in the strictest terms, much to the disappointment of the British and the Canadians.[13]

In 1951 the urgent need for feed materials to supply the rapidly expanding production of nuclear weapons had led the Congress to adopt an amendment to Section 10 that authorized exchanges of information on all manufacturing operations from the processing of feed materials through the production of fissionable materials. Although the amendment theoretically established a legal basis for exchanging reactor information, it did prescribe a cumbersome process involving review by the National Security Council, approval by the President, and a thirty-day waiting period before the Joint Committee before the proposed exchange could take place. The amendment also required a finding by the Commission that the recipient nation had adequate security standards to protect the information to be exchanged, but the Commission thought this provision would be very difficult to apply in any general exchange to technical data. Instead, the staff proposed an amendment that "there shall be no exchange of restricted data with other nations, except as authorized by the Commission upon a finding that the common defense and security will not be adversely affected." This amendment would obviate the review process and the waiting period and

118

would also permit the exchange of weapon information. The same determination by the Commission would be added to Section 5 of the act to permit distributing fissionable material to other nations and to permit persons to engage in producing such materials outside the United States.

## THE COMMISSION BILLS

On November 18, 1953, the Commission dispatched the two draft bills to the Bureau of the Budget: the first, the "peaceful uses bill," would broaden the legal basis for industrial participation in nuclear technology; and the second, the legislative program, would provide for a freer flow of information. In sending a summary of the legislation to Eisenhower, Strauss informed the President that the Commission had hereby complied with his request of the previous March for recommendations on amending the 1946 act.[14]

119

By this time the President was reviewing a third or fourth draft of his Atoms-for-Peace speech and was moving rapidly toward proposals for international cooperation in industrial development of atomic power, which would require amendment of the 1946 act. The Bureau of the Budget promptly circulated the Commission bills to other executive agencies and departments, but White House demands for a quick response allowed insufficient time for careful analysis, especially by the departments most directly concerned. By December 11, 1953, the White House deadline for completing departmental review, only the Department of State, the Federal Trade Commission, and the Federal Power Commission had submitted comments; of these, the most substantive were the views of the Federal Power Commission. Jerome K. Kuykendall, the commission's chairman, raised the fundamental question of whether the rather general and unrestricted authority granted to the Atomic Energy Commission in matters of licensing, the sale of by-product power, and the purchase of by-product plutonium from power reactors would not constitute an abrogation of Congressional authority in the policy area. Kuykendall reminded the Commission that the Supreme Court had invalidated Franklin Roosevelt's National Industrial Recovery Act on this ground. Furthermore, Kuykendall argued, there was plenty of legislative precedent establishing precise criteria for executive departments and agencies to use in determining sale and purchase prices.

Kuykendall also criticized the vague language of the peaceful uses bill, giving the Commission discretion in issuing licenses. Instead he proposed mandatory conditions for issuing licenses to protect the Commission from charges of arbitrary denial or preferential treatment of licensees. Likewise, Kuykendall criticized the failure of the bill to provide specific standards for determining the adequacy of safety and security measures proposed by licensees. Both regulatory commissions warned of potential difficulties in the vague and, to some extent, conflicting provisions intended to prevent violation of antimonopoly laws. The trade commission questioned the adequacy of the proposed five-year limitation on compulsory licensing of inventions and urged that the bill provide for mandatory review by the Attorney General of all licenses prior to issuance.[15]

These and other comments from the regulatory commissions reflected an impressive degree of administrative knowledge and experience that the Atomic Energy Commission and its staff would do well to heed. Although the Commission's legal staff did not precisely accept every suggestion, most comments were adopted in one form or another. In any case, it was valuable for the Commission to be exposed to the kinds of questions raised. As William Mitchell, the general counsel, reminded the Commissioners on December 7, 1953, the comments from the regulatory agencies raised some of the more important issues that the Commission would face in later stages of the legislative process.

120

Although the bills in their final form were still very similar to the Commission's early drafts, the legislative proposals were now closely identified with Eisenhower. The Atoms-for-Peace speech on December 8, 1953, had raised nuclear policy to the presidential level, and, in the public mind at least, the proposals for amending the 1946 act stemmed naturally from Eisenhower's statements before the United Nations. Both the State of the Union and budget messages in January 1954 stressed the importance of nuclear energy for both peaceful and military purposes and notified the Congress that the Administration was drafting legislation for greater international cooperation in atomic energy development. The draft prepared by the Commission staff did serve as a rough outline for the presidential message sent to Congress on February 17, but the message had been completely redrafted in the White House during the preceding two weeks. The legislative proposals were in a very real sense those of both the Administration and the Commission.[16]

## THE JOINT COMMITTEE BILL

Although the President's message was a public document, the White House did not release the draft bills, which the Commission sent directly to the Joint Committee. It did not take Executive Director Corbin Allardice long to determine that, despite all the Commission's careful drafting, the bills could never be introduced as written because they were still cast as amendments to the 1946 act. The amendment approach had served well a year earlier when the Commission was taking its initial steps toward revision, but as the number of amendments increased, the rationale for the basic structure of the act disappeared. It was now apparent to Allardice that the bills should be completely restructured as new legislation.

Chairman Cole and Allardice also perceived that whatever legislation the committee introduced should be embodied in a single bill. Holifield and Price had already attacked the 1953 industrial participation bill as giving a few large corporations a monopoly of nuclear technology. It seemed likely that other Democrats in Congress would take up that theme; then the large Democratic minority would succeed in defeating the bill. On the other side, a bill liberalizing the dissemination of information, particularly to foreign nations, seemed certain to come under attack by members of both parties who were wary of international cooperation and who insisted upon protecting the "secret" of the atomic bomb. If, however, one bill combined the two aims, then both groups would have to risk losing those parts of the bill they favored when they attacked the provision they opposed.

121

Although Allardice favored a completely new bill, drafting legislation from scratch would be a heavy and relatively unfamiliar task for the Joint Committee. Most mechanical aspects of drafting would fall on George Norris, Jr., who had replaced John T. Walker as committee counsel. Norris, dogmatic on the matter of private enterprise, had extensive experience in industry. Norris's professional background and ideological leanings suggested that he would be especially helpful in drafting legislation that would bring industry into atomic energy development. Norris was not only intensely interested in removing what he considered the serious infringement of the patent system accomplished in the 1946 act, but he also had strong views on licensing and other administrative procedures. Once Norris had the assignment to draft a new bill, he selected as his model the format and numbering system of the Federal Communications Act of 1934 and copied the licensing provisions of that act almost verbatim.[17]

The Joint Committee draft, however, was by no means the product of Norris and the staff. Cole and Hickenlooper both took a personal interest in the bill and committed themselves to long sessions, sometimes going into the evening, in drafting sections of the bill line-by-line with Allardice and Norris. When the preliminary draft was completed early in March, Allardice distributed copies to other committee members, and discussions in the larger group continued behind closed doors over the next five weeks. Although Edward Trapnell, as the Commission's liaison officer with the committee, was able to follow the general directions of the committee's thinking through his conversations with Allardice, some of the bill's provisions surprised the Commissioners when they received a draft on April 5.[18]

With only three days to review the bill before it was introduced in Congress, Strauss could suggest only that the Commission would present its views on the bill in executive hearings that were scheduled for early

May. By that time Mitchell and Trapnell had discussed the bill with the committee staff, and Mitchell had drafted a detailed commentary that Strauss presented at the closed hearings beginning on May 3, 1954.[19]

## THE HEARINGS: INFORMATION AND SECURITY

Strauss began his commentary by focusing first on the sections of the Joint Committee bill dealing with information and security. Section 144 of the bill followed the Commission's draft in many respects by providing greater latitude in international cooperation, but the Joint Committee had made changes the Commission found troublesome. The Joint Committee version prohibited the communication of restricted data relating to the design or fabrication of atomic weapons, except external size, weight, and shape. Strauss told the committee that the Department of Defense objected to this restriction as seriously inhibiting the development of defense plans with the North Atlantic Treaty Organization.

122

Section 123 of the Joint Committee bill would apply to all international exchanges, for either peaceful or military purposes, the cumbersome review procedures that the Commission had found objectionable in the 1951 amendment to the 1946 act. The section would require an agreement for cooperation with each nation or regional defense organization, to be approved by the Commission and the President and then to be submitted to the Joint Committee for a thirty-day review. Under questioning, Strauss had to admit that the thirty-day waiting period had never delayed approval of a cooperative arrangement with the British and Canadians. The objection, he said, came from the Administration, presumably on the grounds that the thirty-day waiting period constituted a restriction on the executive powers of the President.

Strauss also expressed strong reservations about the Joint Committee's definition of restricted data, which reinstated the phrase "utilization of atomic weapons," a term the Commission had agreed to drop after a series of negotiations with the Department of Defense. He also objected to Section 145(c) that would have required automatic declassification of all restricted data after three years unless the Commission took positive action to retain classification. Strauss held that the millions of classified documents held by Commission employees and contractors made this provision administratively unworkable.[20]

## THE "PRINCIPAL OFFICER" ISSUE

On the afternoon of May 3, Strauss turned from his prepared statement to a special problem that had been raised by the proposed language in Section

21. The Joint Committee draft stated that "the Chairman shall be the principal officer of the Commission." Strauss was concerned because the question of the respective roles of the chairman and the other Commissioners had been disrupting the harmony of the Commission for several months. In January 1954, when the Commission was attempting to sort out the many problems raised by the Oppenheimer case, Strauss had asked both Mitchell and the Attorney General whether he as chairman or the Commission as a whole could function as the "head of the agency" in personnel security matters. Failing to get any very helpful legal opinion, Strauss apparently kept the matter to himself; but when the Commission received the Joint Committee draft of the bill in April, the "principal officer" provision of Section 21 reopened the question of the chairman's role. Commissioner Murray immediately took up the issue, and, as Strauss reported to Cole, there had been "prolonged discussion" of Section 21 within the Commission. During April personal animosities between Strauss and Murray over this issue had risen to the flash point as Murray attempted to obtain copies of Strauss's January correspondence with Mitchell and the Attorney General.[21]

123

In the executive hearing on May 3, 1954, Strauss told the Joint Committee that the Commissioners had all agreed that the 1946 act was unclear in defining the responsibilities of the chairman in relation to those of the Commissioners, but there was still no consensus on how the situation might be remedied. Strauss himself suggested that an institution as large and complex as the Commission needed a chairman with more affirmative responsibility than the 1946 act provided, but he preferred to let his fellow Commissioners speak first on the issue.

Smyth, the senior member of the Commission, agreed that the chairman's role was ambiguous in the 1946 act, but he was not sure that ambiguity was undesirable; it had provided a certain flexibility, permitting the several chairmen and acting chairmen to establish various working relationships with their colleagues. Smyth admitted that the Commission form of operation was clumsy and inefficient at times, but he still preferred it to having a single "head of the agency." Smyth's real concern was that if the chairman's position were "too greatly strengthened," the other Commissioners might not have all the information required to exercise their legal responsibilities.[22]

The heart of the dispute became apparent when Commissioner Murray presented his case. Murray said he was concerned about the "trend toward centralization of authority in the Chairman" and that the proposed Section 21 accelerated that trend. He would accept a change making the chairman "the chief administrative agent and spokesman of the Commission" but only if the bill provided that all members of the Commission would have equal authority and responsibility and would have "full access to all information relating to the performance of these responsibilities."[23]

Murray's statement carried two implications: first, Strauss had proposed the "principal officer" provision in an attempt to dominate the Commission; second, Strauss was withholding information from his colleagues. Cole himself attempted to refute the first charge by assuring the committee that the phrase had originated, not in a suggestion from Strauss, but in Norris's research for the Joint Committee bill. The phrase, Cole contended, was common in organic statutes for regulatory commissions. Knowledgeable persons, however, including members of both the Joint Committee and Commission staff, believed that Strauss had proposed the idea. As the hearing proceeded, the committee could begin to appreciate why Strauss might have suggested the provision, if only informally. After considerable prodding by Senator Clinton P. Anderson, Commissioner Zuckert admitted that he believed he had been deprived of information relating to his responsibilities, specifically atomic energy matters discussed in the National Security Council. Zuckert was careful to deny any personal criticism of Strauss; the problem, he said, lay rather in the complexities of administrative structure.

In response, Strauss reminded the committee that the Commission had never had regular representation on the National Security Council. As special assistant to the President, Strauss had attended council meetings before he became chairman, and the President had continued to invite him to attend in that capacity even after his appointment to the Commission. Strauss did not think that under the circumstances he could reveal to his colleagues all the atomic energy matters discussed by the council. Senator Anderson agreed that Strauss could hardly do otherwise unless the President chose to give the Commission official representation on the council.

Zuckert, however, argued that the problem was not so easily resolved. The people of the United States had a right to expect that the Commissioners were fully competent to exercise their authority, but in fact they were not privy to all the information related to their responsibilities. The fault lay, not in the President, the National Security Council, or Strauss, but rather in the nature of the Commission's responsibilities and the structure of the Executive Branch. As Congressman Holifield put it, the Commission was no longer engaged simply in producing fissionable materials and weapons. Under the proposed bill, the agency would have wide influence on policy in both international affairs and domestic economic matters. Zuckert maintained that this new authority would inevitably involve the Commission in politics, and it was unrealistic to expect that the Commission could continue to maintain a nonpolitical or even a nonpartisan stance. The Commission in Zuckert's opinion would have to become part of the Administration. He even went so far as to suggest that the President be given authority in the law to appoint a majority of the Commissioners at the beginning of his term on a frankly partisan basis.

124

In response to a request from Senator Eugene D. Millikin, Zuckert offered an example of the kind of problem the Commission faced in the area of international affairs. The Commission, Zuckert said, had not been informed in advance about the contents of Eisenhower's Atoms-for-Peace speech. Strauss replied, not quite accurately, that the idea for the speech had crystallized in Bermuda and that the speech had been written on the flight to New York. The discussion then degenerated into a series of indirect exchanges between Murray and Strauss that clearly reflected the personal animosity between them.[24]

The significance of the "principal officer" debate, however, lay in Zuckert's observations that the Commission was heading (or was being led) into the political arena. The issues raised in the attempt to amend the legislation demonstrated that fact. So did the Commissioners' growing sense of responsibility in areas previously reserved for the President and his advisers. No less significant was Eisenhower's realization that atomic energy posed critical issues in both domestic and international policy. In fact, much Commissioner dissatisfaction with exclusion from such issues as the Atoms-for-Peace speech or Oppenheimer's access to classified information resulted from the President's determination to exercise his authority in matters clearly within the Commission's responsibilities.

125

## THE HEARING: INDUSTRIAL DEVELOPMENT

On May 4, Strauss was finally able to return to his prepared statement. On the provisions of the Joint Committee bill designed to encourage industrial participation Strauss cited a number of technical difficulties, but he mostly objected to the sections on patents and the ownership of fissionable materials. Closely following the Administration's own reasoning, Strauss held it impracticable to require the Commission, as the Joint Committee bill did, to retain government ownership of all fissionable material, whether produced by the government or by licensees in private facilities. Because the Joint Committee version would also require the government to pay the licensee just compensation for the material, the government would in effect be undertaking a long-term and open-ended commitment to purchase all commercially produced plutonium, whatever the price. If the committee insisted on government ownership, Strauss suggested that the Commission at least be given authority to decline to license reactors that would produce materials beyond the government's needs. Strauss also thought it wise to limit to its own maximum cost of production the price the government would have to pay.

Allardice, who knew Strauss well, did not hesitate to probe the reasoning behind the Commission's opposition to government ownership. After weeks of drafting, the committee had concluded that government ownership would be necessary to maintain adequate controls over fissionable materials, particularly plutonium, which could be used for weapons. The Commission had opted for private ownership mainly to avoid an open-ended government commitment to purchase plutonium produced in privately owned facilities, especially if military needs for plutonium should be satisfied at some time in the future. This concern had taken on new dimensions in July 1953, when Strauss had reopened the question of encouraging industry to build dual-purpose reactors, which would produce significant amounts of plutonium. Allardice doubted that dual-purpose reactors would have any important role or that military demands for plutonium would decline in the near future. He also claimed that private ownership would both require industry to invest large sums in fuel inventories and discourage private participation. As a practical matter, both Allardice and Holifield feared that the prospect of placing weapon quantities of fissionable material in private hands was enough to defeat the bill in either house. [25]

The patent question was always complicated, but the point at issue in the May hearings was clear-cut. The committee bill, largely reflecting the strong ideological views of Cole and Norris, abolished the special patent provisions of the 1946 act and failed to provide for a transition period of compulsory licensing of patents developed under government contract. Cole took the position that any infringement, even a five-year period of compulsory licensing of patents, violated constitutional rights and threatened the very root of American technological superiority. Strauss and the Eisenhower Administration were no less interested in preserving the patent system, but they were also concerned about preventing a monopoly of the new industry by a few large companies that already had an advantage as Commission contractors. Without support from either the Commission or the Republican administration, Cole faced a tough battle on the patent question, given the strong Democratic minority that advocated an even longer period of compulsory licensing. [26]

Predictably private ownership of reactors and fissionable materials received almost unanimous support at the public hearings beginning on May 10, 1954. Jerome D. Luntz, editor of *Nucleonics* magazine, cited an informal survey of business leaders to show that private ownership of reactors was the most popular feature of the Joint Committee bill. He admitted that an industry probably could be started with leased fuels, but he saw no disadvantages in private ownership of fissionable materials. Representatives of the American Bar Association, equipment manufacturers, electric utility companies, and the Federation of American Scientists all took the position that private ownership was essential if atomic energy was to join the private enterprise system.

Opinions were nearly as unanimous in opposing Section 102 of the bill, which required, as the 1946 act had, a report on the social, political, economic, and international aspects of any practical commercial use of atomic energy before the Commission could issue any licenses for this purpose. The opposition, mostly from equipment manufacturers and electric utilities, followed closely the reasoning expressed in private by the Commissioners six months earlier: the writing and clearance of such a report through the federal bureaucracy would be so difficult and time-consuming that it would greatly delay the entrance of nuclear power into the civilian economy. Throughout most of the hearings, Congressman Holifield stood alone in his insistence that the Commission had an obligation to inform the Congress of the potential impact of a new technology. Only in the closing hours of the hearings on May 19 did Leland Olds, a former chairman of the Federal Power Commission and now a public-power lobbyist, suggest that such a report would be vital if electric power from the atom was to be integrated "into the total power policy of the country." [27]

The question of compulsory licensing received the most prolonged discussion in the public hearings. Although the issue was directly associated with patent policy, the debate centered largely on the dangers of monopoly. Only the spokesmen for the patent law association examined the legal and constitutional questions of infringements on patent rights. Industry representatives saw little possibility of a patent monopoly in atomic energy, and representatives of small businesses saw no advantage at all in a compulsory system of cross-licensing. On the other side, spokesmen for organized labor, the public-power movement, and rural electric companies saw the absence of compulsory licensing provisions as extending the tight monopoly that private utility companies had allegedly established in the electric power industry. Holifield stressed the monopoly theme in questioning witnesses and pointed out two instances in which antimonopoly language in the 1946 act had been deleted. Even though the discussions of compulsory licensing were scattered through the hearings, Holifield succeeded in maintaining continuity in his attack on the industrial participation provisions of the bill. [28]

## DIXON-YATES: A POLITICAL DIVERSION

In a closed session with the Joint Committee on May 5, 1954, Casper Ooms, the patent authority, had reflected that both the committee and the Commission were probably placing too much stress on the patent issue. It was prudent to include provisions in the bill to meet all likely circumstances, but Ooms did not see the patent sections as determining the future of the nuclear industry. [29] The frequent discussions of patents, and particularly the merits of compulsory licensing, during the hearings were merely outward symptoms of a deeper concern: Would the federal government or private industry develop and then control this promising new source of energy?

Through most executive sessions and open hearings on the atomic energy bill, the Joint Committee had been able to steer away from this larger and highly volatile question. But already at work within the Administration were forces that would tie the bill to the public-versus-private power issue. On June 4, when the committee concluded its long discussion of the principal officer issue, Holifield raised a question about the proposed Section 164, which would extend the authority granted the Commission in the 1946 act to enter into contracts to provide electric utility services "in connection with the construction or operation of the Oak Ridge, Paducah, or Portsmouth installations." Holifield noted the difficulties that a group of private utility companies had encountered in completing a power plant at Joppa, Illinois, across the Ohio River from the Commission's Paducah gaseous-diffusion plant. The press and TVA supporters had come to refer to the sorry stories of construction delays and cost overruns at Joppa as the "Ebasco fiasco," a term that Holifield used in his remarks. He went on, however, to describe his concern over a proposed new contract between the Commission and "the Dixon-Yates group" to supply 600,000 kilowatts of power in the Memphis, Tennessee, area. Holifield noted that the Commission did not propose to use the power from the Dixon-Yates plant for its own facilities but rather to meet TVA requirements in the Memphis area. He announced his intention to involve the committee's right to analyze Section 164 as the basis for a full-scale discussion of the Dixon-Yates proposal.[30]

The bizarre proposal, which became infamous as "the Dixon-Yates contract," had its origins in the primary tenets of the Administration and, in fact, in Eisenhower's personal philosophy of government. In his remarks at the dedication of Garrison Dam in North Dakota on June 11, 1953, the President had spoken of the need to disperse the powers of the Executive Branch both functionally and geographically. By accepting the federal government's role in building giant dams, Eisenhower warned that it was "part of a great conservation work that all parts of our nation must benefit from and must participate in." The following week in a news conference, the President made clear that he was thinking of TVA when he had spoken of the dangers of "creeping socialism." He thought it was necessary to re-evaluate a situation in which general tax revenues could be used to provide cheap power to one section of the nation.[31] TVA, as a regional power system financed with federal funds, seemed to do just that. As the President saw it, there were only two alternatives. Either the federal government could establish more TVAs across the country until the nation's entire electric utility system was government-owned, or TVA would have to live on its own

128

resources without help from federal taxes; unquestionably, the President preferred the second alternative.

A perfect opportunity to launch the President's attack on "creeping socialism" came in autumn 1953, when TVA requested 1955 budget funds to begin work on a coal-fired power plant on the Mississippi River at Fulton, Tennessee, to supply the rapidly growing power needs of the Memphis area. The President and Budget Director Dodge opposed this request, not only as an unwise extension of TVA but also as a threat to the Administration's campaign for budget cuts. When the Bureau of the Budget asked TVA Chairman Gordon R. Clapp what the agency would do if the Administration refused the request, Clapp replied that the TVA board would probably recommend that some power then being provided for the Commission's gaseous-diffusion plants be released to meet TVA's growing needs.[32]

Clapp's reply was probably little more than a ploy to convince the Bureau of the Budget that building the Fulton plant was the only possible solution, but Dodge took the idea seriously. On December 2, 1953, he met with Strauss to discuss the possibility that the Commission could obtain additional power from private sources to operate the final sections of the Paducah plant still under construction. Strauss immediately asked a senior member of the Commission's staff to approach James W. McAfee, president of Electric Energy, Incorporated, which was already supplying private power at Paducah from the Joppa plant. Although McAfee did not think his own company could accept a contract, he suggested that the Commission consult Edgar H. Dixon, president of Middle South Utilities, which was interested in supplying the Memphis area. On Christmas Eve, Rowland R. Hughes, assistant director of the Bureau of the Budget, informed Strauss that the TVA budget would include no funds for the Fulton plant on the expectation that the Commission would find a private source to relieve TVA of 500,000 to 600,000 kilowatts of the Commission's power requirements. Hughes decided to include a statement to this effect in the President's budget message to Congress, with the proviso that the bureau would consider supplemental appropriation for the Fulton plant if the Commission's efforts failed.[33]

The President's reference to the possibility of a supplemental appropriation probably represented an attempt to disarm those who would claim that the Administration's plan was designed to kill TVA; but the reference also seemed to recognize the difficulties in carrying out the plan. Until January 6, no one at the Commission except Strauss and one staff member knew of the plan. Both Murray and Zuckert were outraged when they learned that Strauss had been involved in discussions for more than a month without their knowledge, and Nichols was less than enthusiastic about the proposal on the realistic grounds that it would cost the Commission more money for power under a contract less firm than that with TVA.

129

Furthermore, both McAfee and Dixon argued for a direct contract between TVA and a private utility to provide power at Memphis, where it was needed, rather than at Joppa, where it would be hard to dispose of excess power if the Commission contract were canceled. Clapp, however, refused to consider any plan that would require TVA to purchase power from a private utility. The only solution seemed that proposed in Hughes's office on January 20, 1954: namely, the Commission would negotiate a contract with a private utility to build and operate a power plant across the Mississippi River from Memphis, and the Commission would release an equivalent amount of power being supplied by TVA's Shawnee plant near Paducah. At Hughes's request, Nichols discussed the idea with both Dixon and Eugene A. Yates of the Southern Company. On February 20, Dixon and Yates agreed to submit a proposal that would accomplish the complex arrangement the Administration had devised.[34]

130

## THE COMMISSION AND DIXON-YATES

As in the origins of the Oppenheimer case and the Atoms-for-Peace speech, the Commission was in fact something less than an enthusiastic participant in devising the Dixon-Yates plan. Among the Commissioners probably only Strauss saw TVA as a threat to private enterprise,[35] and even he was not happy about the prospect of the Commission being used as an agent to accomplish a policy aim that had nothing to do with atomic energy. Strauss certainly would look with disfavor on any plan that would threaten the power supply to the Commission's production plants or raise costs substantially. Only Nichols saw real merits in the proposal, in an entirely technical sense. As an engineer, he thought it reasonable to build the plant near Memphis where the power was needed. Murray, as an engineer from the electric utility field, might conceivably have come to a position close to Nichols's and thus on Strauss's side of the question, but Strauss had once again aroused the suspicions of his colleagues by failing to apprise them of his discussions with the Bureau of the Budget. Perhaps Strauss in this instance and others had avoided his colleagues because he had his own reservations about the Administration's proposal and did not wish to be placed in a situation of defending his superiors. This explanation seemed likely in the Dixon-Yates case. Because it did not yet involve the President personally, Strauss could not hope to justify his independent action on the basis of his confidential role as a presidential adviser.

When the two utility executives received Hughes's invitation to submit a proposal, they were given only a few days to complete it. They proposed to form a corporation that would finance and construct a new power plant in the Memphis area under a twenty-five-year contract with the Commission (the limit of the Commission's authority under the Atomic Energy

Act). The annual capacity charge would be based on an estimated plant cost of $200 per kilowatt. The Commission would be required to pay the annual capacity and energy charges, to compensate the corporation for all taxes, and to arrange for interconnecting with the TVA system.

The Commission's reaction to the proposal was ambivalent at best. Although the proposal would save the federal government at least $120 million in capital costs, the Commission would have to pay about $4 million per year more than the existing TVA contract required, and less than $1 million of that amount would be returned to the government in federal taxes. Furthermore, because the power would come from a plant not yet built, it would be less reliable than the TVA power already available and under contract. Because these features of the proposal were distinctly disadvantageous to the Commission, any determination to accept the proposal would have to be made by "higher executive authority or the Congress" on the basis of overall advantages to the nation. The Commission's letter to the Bureau of the Budget on March 3 did not make clear that both Smyth and Zuckert were opposed to even conditionally accepting the proposal.[36]

131

But if Clapp or any Commissioners hoped that the relatively unfavorable provisions of the Dixon-Yates proposal would result in its rejection, they were to be disappointed. Hughes requested Nichols at once to work with the Federal Power Commission in negotiating a more favorable arrangement. The revised proposal submitted by Dixon and Yates on April 10 did scale down the proposed charges substantially, in part by reducing the estimated cost of construction from $200 to $149 per kilowatt. Nichols also succeeded in incorporating provisions that would require the corporation to accept half of any escalation in construction costs up to about $10 million more than the estimated $107 million and all added costs above $117 million. Under this proposal, the added annual cost would be less than $2 million above that of the existing TVA contract, all of which could be attributed to taxes.[37]

In commenting on the new proposal, the Commissioners reiterated to Hughes their concerns about assuring the reliability and continuity of power at Paducah. They argued that TVA should bear all costs for power above those in the existing TVA contract to avoid a Commission subsidy of TVA. Once again, Strauss requested that either the Budget Bureau or Congress determine whether the proposal was appropriate. Commission discussion of the contract, however, brought out new objections. Smyth and Zuckert pointed out in a letter to Hughes, now director of the bureau, that "not one kilowatt" from the Dixon-Yates plant would be used in Commission production facilities. The Commission would be assuming a twenty-five-year commitment to support a project "irrelevant" to its own mission. Smyth and Zuckert called the proposal "obviously incongruous" and "a reversal of the sound philosophy" incorporated in draft legislation recently sent to the Congress to remove from the Commission responsibilities not essential to its mission. The two Commissioners made clear, however, that "if the President or the Congress directs the Commission to accept such a responsibility, we will endeavor to discharge it fully."[38]


## DIXON-YATES: THE ISSUE DRAWN

As long as the discussion of the Dixon-Yates proposal remained within the Executive Branch of the government, the Administration could control the situation. But once the matter came to the attention of the Congress, Dixon-Yates would become a political issue. Although the Joint Committee learned of the Dixon-Yates idea early in January, probably from Commissioner Murray, there was no real basis for raising the issue until something specific appeared in written form. The inevitable occurred during the Congressional review of the 1955 budget. By the time the Commission submitted the revised Dixon-Yates proposal to the Bureau of the Budget in mid-April, the House Appropriations Committee had already approved both the Commission's and TVA's budgets, and the Senate subcommittee was waiting only for a decision on the Fulton plant to complete its action on the TVA budget. Although Nichols did everything he could to avoid a commitment until the Administration had had time to analyze the new proposal, he was forced to submit a short statement on the proposal to the Senate subcommittee on April 17. That provided Senator Albert Gore of Tennessee just enough ammunition to raise some questions about Dixon-Yates in the Senate on April 21. Gore asked why, in light of the poor performance of private industry in building the Joppa plant, the government had decided on a complicated arrangement to produce replacement power two hundred miles from the Paducah plant at a cost exceeding that of the existing TVA contract. The senator could see only three reasons: "to strike a death blow forever" at the Fulton plant, to move private utilities into the TVA area at Memphis, and to subsidize a private-power company through the Atomic Energy Commission. Gore alerted the Administration to the far-reaching implications of the proposal, warning "that it will be a story many times told if the proposal is accepted."[39] The Administration could have no clearer signal that Dixon-Yates would embroil the Commission in a full-fledged fight on the issue of private versus public power.

Congressman Holifield had fired the opening salvo at the Dixon-Yates proposal in the Joint Committee hearings on June 4. Having gained Cole's assent to probe the question in detail as a part of the committee's review of Section 164 of the proposed bill, Holifield launched a full-scale attack on Dixon-Yates on June 17. By that time two events had sharpened the issues. First, as Nichols revealed in the hearing, on June 16 the President had directed the Commission to start negotiations with Dixon and Yates. Second, there was almost no support for the proposal within the

Commission. The Smyth-Zuckert letter to Hughes had leaked to the press on June 4. In the afternoon session on June 17, Murray made clear his opposition to the proposal on the grounds that it was not a logical function for the Commission. Murray's testimony was of special significance because, as he noted, he had long supported private-power development and had been responsible in part for private building of the Joppa plant. Murray's statement also meant, as Senator Gore was quick to point out, that a majority of the Commissioners opposed the idea. Campbell, who squirmed under Holifield's persistent questioning, would say only that he agreed with Nichols's analysis of the proposal. That was not much of an endorsement because Nichols, as general manager, claimed only that the proposal was a technically sound approach to accomplishing the Administration's objectives, which were beyond his responsibility. Campbell's ambiguous stance left Strauss the proposal's sole supporter. Strauss based his support on the argument that government competition in "the power business" was unfair to private industry because of tax and investment advantages enjoyed by TVA. The savings claimed by TVA were illusory in Strauss's opinion because they were ultimately paid for by general tax revenues.[40] Thus, Strauss found himself virtually alone on the Dixon-Yates proposal, in a position resting almost entirely on a political argument.

133

## A NEW BILL FROM THE JOINT COMMITTEE

Once Holifield introduced the Dixon-Yates issue on June 4, 1954, the attention of not only the Joint Committee but also the full Congress gravitated quickly to the controversial issues that the proposal raised. Only with difficulty did Chairman Cole keep the discussion on the provisions of the Joint Committee bill for two more days. The final all-day sessions on June 17 and 18 were devoted exclusively to Dixon-Yates. Although the intrusion of Dixon-Yates posed obvious problems for further action on the bill, the hearings had proved useful. Relations between the Joint Committee members and the Commissioners had been good; the discussions had for the most part resulted in a free and open exchange of ideas without too much concern about prerogatives and established positions. Cole's patience as the presiding officer softened the impact of Holifield's sometimes strident and partisan inquiries.[41]

To the casual observer, the new bill that Cole and Hickenlooper introduced in the House and Senate on June 30, 1954, appeared almost identical to the earlier Joint Committee drafts. But close examination revealed significant changes in some sections. In the international area, the Commission could take some comfort in the softening of the provisions of Section 123, which had required Commission approval of the security procedures of foreign nations and which had given the United States a unilateral right to withdraw from bilateral agreements on peaceful uses of atomic energy. More ambiguous was the wisdom of other changes adopted at the suggestion of Senator Bricker. The words "or group of nations" had been deleted from every section relating to international cooperation so that such activities would be limited to single nations with which bilateral agreements had been negotiated under the conditions specified in Section 123.[42]

Also at Bricker's suggestion, the committee had added a new provision, Section 124, which authorized the President to negotiate an international arrangement establishing an atomic pool with a group of nations. The new section appeared to implement the President's suggestion in his Atoms-for-Peace speech, but any such arrangement would have to comply with the provisions of Section 123. In other words, membership in the international pool would be limited to nations with which bilateral agreements had been negotiated. Furthermore, any "international arrangement" for an atomic pool would have to take the form of a treaty, which would have to be approved by the Senate, or a joint resolution, which would have to be submitted to both Houses of Congress. As Holifield and other Democrats would point out, Section 124 would surely exclude the Soviet Union from the atomic pool and would make any pool under United Nations auspices impossible. In the eyes of Bricker and probably Strauss, Section 124 would retain rigid safeguards over distribution of fissionable materials and would keep any atomic pool firmly within Congressional control.[43]

On matters of security, the June 30 bill provided a clear-cut definition of restricted data that reverted to the position originally taken by the Commission in autumn 1953. The Joint Committee's definition would retain as restricted data all information related to the "design, manufacture, or utilization of atomic weapons" and eliminate the complicated provisions insisted upon by the Department of Defense for joint determinations by the two agencies in removing weapon information from the restricted data category. The new draft also abandoned the earlier provision for automatically declassifying restricted data.

Retaining the Commission's proposal to permit private ownership of production and utilization facilities, the committee draft excluded the private ownership of fissionable materials originally endorsed by the Commission. Apparently Allardice's contention that government ownership was necessary to assure effective control of the material was persuasive. Having opted for government ownership, the committee had to meet the Commission's valid objection that the bill in its original form would have required the government to provide "just compensation" for all fissionable materials produced in privately owned reactors. The committee addressed this problem by changing Section 52 to read that the government would pay "a fair price" for all such material; Section 56 set forth a number of considerations that the Commission could use in determining fair price in order to avoid open-ended commitments to purchase all material at whatever price might constitute "just compensation."

Section 53 of the revised bill was greatly expanded to cover another question raised by continuing government ownership: the distribution of fissionable materials for research and development, medical research, and therapy, and its licensing for industrial uses. The new section prescribed the uses for which material could be distributed, the criteria to be met before licenses could be issued, the basis for reasonable charges for using fissionable materials, and the conditions to be included in licenses. To reflect recent accomplishments in developing thermonuclear weapons, the committee substituted the words "special nuclear materials" for the more limited phrase "fissionable materials" wherever it appeared in the bill. The revised language of Section 51 would permit the Commission to declare other materials such as tritium or deuterium to be special nuclear materials if it so desired.

135

On two controversial points in the April draft the June 30 bill provided reasonable compromises. First, the Section 21 provision establishing the chairman as "the principal officer" of the Commission had been modified along the lines that Murray had suggested; now the chairman would be the "official spokesman" of the Commission, but the section also provided that each member of the Commission would "have equal responsibility and authority" in all actions of the Commission. The second point of contention involved Section 102, which required the Commission to file a report on the practical value of atomic energy for peaceful purposes before any license could be issued. As a compromise, the June 30 bill provided that the Commission would have to make a written finding that at least one facility had been sufficiently developed to be of practical value for industrial or commercial purposes before a license would be issued for that type of facility. But the Commission was no longer required to file a report that would predict "the social, political, economic, and international effects of such use." The mere finding of practical value would be much easier to make.

One of the most striking changes in the June 30 bill was the complete reversal of the patent position that Cole and Norris had set forth in the April draft. Although Cole continued to believe that compulsory licensing of patents was both unwise and unconstitutional, the majority of the committee was impressed by arguments for cross-licensing advanced by the Commissioners and their patent advisers. Once the Joint Committee had decided to introduce compulsory licensing, it was necessary to draft all the legal paraphernalia to cover patenting and licensing of inventions or discoveries in the nonmilitary field. For this purpose the committee staff made its only adoption of language from the Commission's own peaceful uses bill; the exact words of the Commission draft appear nowhere else except in

Sections 152(a) and 152(b) of the June 30 bill.[44] To this basic structure the committee added other provisions drafted by Ooms and the Commission's legal staff.[45] These sections covered the qualifications of license applicants, the Commission's procedures in granting licenses, the payment for royalty fees, and various patent technicalities. Compulsory licensing was to be in effect for a period of five years. Section 156 also reinstated the patent compensation board, which had earlier been rendered unnecessary by eliminating compulsory licensing.

The June 30 bill, running to more than one hundred pages, was long and complex. Not all members of the Joint Committee understood the implications of all its provisions, nor could they find their way through the labyrinth of nineteen chapters and dozens of cross-referenced sections. But the bill as it was presented to the Congress for debate did reflect to some extent the views of American industry and labor unions, public interest groups, scientists and engineers, the Administration and the Executive Branch, and finally the committee itself. The bill had resulted from more than a year of deliberations in the Commission, the Executive Branch, and the Joint Committee. In most respects it seemed to accomplish the original purpose of making nuclear technology a part of American life. The Dixon-Yates controversy, however, raised some doubt as to whether the very process of developing new legislation had brought into play forces that would destroy all chances for the bill's adoption. In any case, the fate of the bill and the future of the nation's atomic energy program now rested with the House of Representatives and the Senate.

## THE CONGRESSIONAL DEBATE

It was already apparent on June 30 that Cole and Hickenlooper would face a tough fight in guiding the bill through Congress. Although the two leaders could count on strong support from the Eisenhower Administration, the Republican majorities in both houses were razor-thin, four votes in the House and only one in the Senate. In addition to the four-vote margin, Cole did have the advantage of the rigid rules for House debate, which tended to give the majority the advantage. The Joint Committee chairman also had a good working knowledge of the bill and sufficient prestige and ability to lead the bill's supporters in the House.

Hickenlooper faced a much more difficult task in the Senate. On a purely partisan basis, his chances were no better than fifty-fifty after Wayne Morse, the Oregon independent, announced on June 18 that he saw the bill as an Administration attempt to give the nation's atomic energy program to American monopolies. Nor could Hickenlooper count on many conservative southern Democrats to support the Republican cause in this case. The Ad-

ministration's decision to pursue the Dixon-Yates contract had been interpreted in TVA country as an attempt to destroy the public-power enterprise.
Tennessee's two Democratic senators, Albert A. Gore and Estes Kefauver,
had already joined forces with Lister Hill and John J. Sparkman of Alabama
and with Warren G. Magnuson of Washington in a stated objective of using
the impending Senate debate on the atomic energy bill as a way of defeating
the Administration on Dixon-Yates.

The Joint Committee's decision to accept Senator Bricker's amendments to the international sections also threatened the future of the bill.
Not only did the Bricker amendments raise the charge that the "atomic
pool" provision in Section 124 was a "phony" but they also would inevitably
introduce into the debate the touchy subject of the United Nations. As the
State Department had warned, Section 124 could easily tie the bill to strong
sentiments in the Congress against the United Nations and international
cooperation in general. In fact, liberal Democrats like Holifield and Senator
John O. Pastore of Rhode Island saw Section 124 as a new form of the
recently rejected Bricker amendment to the Constitution, which would have
restricted the President's authority in international affairs.[46]

Although Hickenlooper served as principal spokesman for the bill
in the Senate, the fate of the measure rested mostly with William F. Knowland of California. As majority leader, Knowland determined the schedule
of debate in the closing weeks of the Eighty-third Congress, which planned
to adjourn on July 31. Working closely with the Administration, Knowland
wanted to delay action on the bill long enough so that he could use the
pressure for adjournment to limit debate while still leaving enough time to
complete action on the bill. Thus, Knowland did not strongly resist the
efforts of the TVA senators to prolong debate during the first two weeks of
July 1954, as they launched full-scale attacks on the Dixon-Yates proposal.
When Hickenlooper formally began debate on the Joint Committee bill on
July 13, Knowland still appeared willing to let the Dixon-Yates opponents
have relatively free rein.[47] Although Hill, Kefauver, Gore, Morse, and Magnuson were energetic and determined, they could not expect to stop Senate
action on the bill by themselves; Knowland anticipated that within a few
days the TVA group would run out of steam.

Knowland's hopes for passing the atomic energy bill, however, took
a decided downward turn on July 15, when "a liberal coalition," as the
press called it, began to form in opposition to the bill. On that Thursday
afternoon, a number of representatives of consumer, farm, and labor organizations met by chance in the corridors of the Senate office building and
discovered that they had a common interest in defeating the Dixon-Yates
proposal. This group quickly coalesced around the TVA senators led by
Lister Hill, and within a few days a hard core of opposition to Dixon-Yates
had been organized to include about twenty senators. The small group of

137

TVA senators had now been enlarged to include those who saw Dixon-Yates as a threat to public-power interests and to the old progressive fight against monopoly. [48]

The strength of the new coalition became evident on Friday, July 16, when Knowland was unable to keep the debate on the atomic energy bill from drifting off into prolonged attacks on Dixon-Yates. The proposal itself had become a legitimate issue in the debate when Senator Clinton P. Anderson, speaking for the Democratic minority of the Joint Committee, introduced an amendment that would have limited the Commission's contracting authority under Section 164 to the purchase of power to be used directly in Commission facilities. Homer Ferguson of Michigan countered with an Administration amendment that would specifically authorize arrangements like the Dixon-Yates proposal. [49]

By Saturday, July 17, the new coalition of Democrats began to take hold as senators from beyond the TVA area dominated the attack on Dixon-Yates. Responding to Democratic suggestions that the domestic development sections of the bill be dropped in favor of legislation enacting the Atoms-for-Peace plan, both Knowland and the President reiterated their determination to hold out for the entire bill, even if the Senate had to resort to twelve-hour sessions. On Tuesday, July 20, the Democratic threat took specific form when Herbert H. Lehman of New York introduced the Commission's original peaceful uses draft as a substitute for the Joint Committee bill. The February draft, which had not previously been printed in Congressional documents, contained none of the provisions for industrial participation in the Commission's original companion bill or in the measure before the Senate. Under Knowland's threat of round-the-clock sessions, the Democratic coalition controlled the floor all day Wednesday while they mustered support for a decisive vote that evening on the Dixon-Yates amendments. [50]

Adoption of the Ferguson amendment by a vote of fifty-six to thirty-five and defeat of the Lehman substitute showed that the Administration could drive the Joint Committee bill through the Senate without sacrificing the Dixon-Yates proposal. The vote also convinced the public-power coalition that its best weapon would be the filibuster, which would endanger not only the atomic energy bill but also the Administration's farm and foreign aid programs. As William H. Langer of North Dakota took the floor for a long disquisition on the dangers of monopoly, senators retired to cots set up in the cloak rooms. [51]

With the help of Wayne L. Morse, the record-holder for filibuster speeches, the coalition had more than enough resources to control the floor around the clock for the rest of the week. It also became clear on Thursday that the Democrats had enough votes to amend the bill on issues other than Dixon-Yates. Within a matter of hours late in the afternoon, the Senate adopted an amendment presented by Edwin C. Johnson of Colorado granting the Commission authority to produce and market electric power generated in its own plants and another by Guy M. Gillette of Iowa providing that public utilities and cooperatives be given preference in purchasing this power. Failing repeatedly to limit debate by unanimous consent agreement or to prevent minor amendments, Knowland early on Friday morning resorted to the tactic of tabling any amendment on which debate was not limited. Successful in this effort, Knowland also introduced a petition of cloture, to be voted on early in the following week.[52]

In an attempt to bring greater pressure on the Democratic opposition, the Administration decided to push the bill through the House on Friday, July 23, 1954. In contrast to the Senate debate, Cole and the Republican leaders in the House were able virtually to exclude extraneous matters such as Dixon-Yates. Members of the Joint Committee from both parties dominated the four hours of general debate and for the most part reiterated the arguments presented during the Joint Committee hearings. The debate on amendments under the five-minute rule telescoped into a few hours the days of argument in the Senate. Reflecting the Republicans' firmer control of the House, Cole and his associates were able to defeat House equivalents of the Anderson and Johnson amendments. The House also rejected several amendments proposed by Holifield to assure the Commission a commanding position in developing nuclear power for commercial purposes. The Democrats were successful only in adopting a preference clause in Section 44 on the sale of by-product power from Commission facilities and two amendments regulating leases of public lands for uranium mining.

139

By this time the debate was moving into the evening hours, a circumstance relatively rare in the House. With encouragement from Knowland and Vice-President Nixon, who had come over to the House side of the Capitol to lend support, Cole kept the debate on target. He quickly pushed through several technical amendments and then introduced the only substantive change he would propose: to strike the compulsory licensing provisions from the bill. Holifield and other Democratic members of the Joint Committee were quick to point out that the committee had already rejected Cole's proposal, but the House sustained Cole decisively by a vote of 203 to 159. By three o'clock on Saturday morning, the clerk read the last section of the bill; it was evident that the bill would pass with only the five amendments already adopted. Only a parliamentary maneuver delayed the vote until the following week.[53]

Prospects for the bill in the Senate now rested on breaking the filibuster. Knowland's threat of cloture was more a psychological than a practical instrument. Much more significant was a request late Saturday evening by Lyndon B. Johnson, the minority leader, for a unanimous consent agreement providing that no further amendments could be introduced after noon on Wednesday, July 28. Morse quickly killed the proposal by objecting, but Johnson's proposal suggested that the Democratic leadership in the Senate was growing impatient. Johnson, with strong influence over conservative Democrats, could threaten the public-power coalition. Gore and the TVA senators also faced pressure from southern Democrats willing to support some public-power amendments but unwilling to do so during the filibuster. Knowland and the Administration, sensing a shift of opinion on the Democratic side, stood firm for the bill.[54]

After the cloture petition was defeated on Monday morning, July 26, the coalition began to accept two- or three-hour limits on the debate on each amendment presented, and the Senate spent the rest of the day considering a dozen such proposals, eight of which were adopted. Only one, proposed by Senator Gore, related to the Dixon-Yates issue. The only other successful amendment of significance was proposed by Robert S. Kerr of Oklahoma to extend the period of compulsory licensing from five years to ten. Knowland's hopes for a vote on the bill, however, were dashed late on Monday, when Morse resumed the filibuster that he continued through the night. Not until Tuesday evening was Knowland able to bring the thirteen-day debate to an end after more than 180 hours of discussion, a Senate record for a two-week period. The first vote, fifty-seven to twenty-eight, was close to that on the Ferguson amendment, which specifically authorized the Commission to enter into the Dixon-Yates contract. Thirteen Democrats joined forty-four Republicans in voting for the bill. Opposing the bill were twenty-five Democrats, two Republicans (John Sherman Cooper of Kentucky and Langer of North Dakota), and Wayne Morse. Senator Anderson of New Mexico was the only member of the original Democratic opposition to vote for the bill.[55]

## THE BILL BECOMES LAW

The conference committee appointed to resolve differences in the Senate and House versions of the bill were with one exception members of the Joint Committee: for the House, Republicans Cole, James E. Van Zandt of Pennsylvania, and Carl Hinshaw of California and Democrats Holifield and Carl T. Durham of North Carolina; for the Senate, Republicans Knowland, Hickenlooper, and Bricker of Ohio and Democrats Johnson of Colorado and Anderson. Cole and the Republicans clearly dominated the conference sessions during the first week in August. The conference report released on August 6 retained the Ferguson amendment, which specifically authorized the Dixon-Yates contract and watered down the provisions granting public utilities and cooperatives a preference in purchasing by-product electric power produced in Commission facilities. The preference clauses sponsored by the Democrats and already adopted in both houses were to be effective "at all times"; in the conference report, they were applicable "insofar as possible." The conferees also eliminated the Johnson amendment, one of the public-power coalition's few victories in the Senate, which gave the Commission authority to produce and market electric power from its own facilities. Holifield and the public-power group envisioned that under the authority granted by the Johnson amendment the Commission would be able to build and operate full-scale nuclear power plants that would provide a "yardstick" for commercial plants, such as TVA facilities had done for private utilities using conventional fuels. It was precisely this kind of extension of the TVA idea that the Eisenhower Administration was fighting. The conferees also retained a provision sponsored by New England's two Democratic senators, John F. Kennedy of Massachusetts and John O. Pastore of Rhode Island, which would give private utilities in high-cost power areas, where public power was not available, a preference in purchasing by-product power from the Commission. All these changes stemmed directly from the public-versus-private-power fight and had only a marginal impact on the Commission.[56]

141

A second and equally psychological victory for the Republican members of the conference committee was the wholesale reincorporation of the Cole-Norris patent philosophy employing the identical language of the Joint Committee's April draft and the Cole amendment adopted in the House on July 26. The Cole-Norris approach deleted all the language in Section 152 and the following sections that provided for compulsory cross-licensing of patents on nonmilitary inventions determined by the Commission to be affected with the public interest. In place of the nonmilitary uses section, Cole substituted his original language, which would limit patent licensing to inventions made under Commission contracts. As a sop to the Democrats, Cole and the Republican conferees did accept the restoration of two provisions in Section 155 on eligibility and standards for patent licensing (now to be possible only in Commission-related activities) and a new Section 156, which specifically prohibited the monopolistic use of patents granted with the Commission's permission on nonmilitary inventions. The language was archaic, but both sides understood the issue—whether the government or private industry was to control the development of atomic energy for civilian purposes.

Representative Holifield and Senators Anderson and Johnson refused to sign the conference report, and the Democrats assailed it in both Houses. First to fall was the "insofar as practicable" restriction in the preference clauses. Cole disclaimed any "sinister" motive in the conference committee's action. The qualification, he maintained, merely recognized that preference could not be granted in every situation. The Democrats, asking who was to determine what was "practicable," attacked the qualification as a Republican attempt to wipe out the hard-fought and meager victory of the public-power coalition. Knowland, plainly hoping to avoid the delay that would be caused by a second conference, suggested a joint resolution deleting the objectionable phrase. The Democrats, however, obviously would not accept Cole's deletion of the compulsory licensing provisions, and the Senate voted on August 13 to reject the conference report.[57]

The second conference, during the second week of August, centered on the compulsory licensing question. Cole, who remained adamant in his opposition to compulsory licensing, finally saw that he was fighting for a lost cause. The public-power senators were determined to revive the filibuster over this issue, and the Administration was not willing to lose the entire bill over a point that seemed more symbolic than real. Because Norris remained as determined as Cole in his opposition, Allardice asked Francis P. Cotter of the Joint Committee staff to work out a compromise: Cole's version of Section 152 governing patents in Commission-related activities would stay in the act but so would the language providing for compulsory licensing for a period of five years. The compromise removed the last roadblock. Following House acceptance of the second conference report on August 17, President Eisenhower signed the act into law on August 30.[58]

In the narrow sense of partisan politics the outcome was a victory for the Republican Congress and for the President. Eisenhower had inspired the legislation. The Republican leadership of the Joint Committee had written a strong bill that would break the government monopoly of the atom and make possible some cooperation with other nations for both military and civilian purposes. With the bill well in hand, Eisenhower and his advisers had not hesitated to launch the Dixon-Yates proposal, which was intended to circumscribe the growth of federal power systems. Republican leadership in the Congress had, with the President's unflagging support, embodied the Dixon-Yates proposal in the law, fought off the filibuster, and then carried through every key provision of the legislation.

For the Commission as a government agency, the legislation accomplished virtually all the aims set forth by the staff in autumn 1953. In addition to the much-discussed provisions for industrial participation and international cooperation, the 1954 act effected many other revisions of the original law. Most of these never attracted attention in Congressional hearings or debates, but they were vital to the efficient administration of the agency's business. In the eyes of some veterans on the staff, the Commission had paid a high price for the new law. Along with the new authority for industrial and international cooperation came inevitably more restraints by both the Executive and Legislative branches. The President, and not the Commission, would have the final voice in approving international agreements, and the Joint Committee would have an opportunity to criticize, if not invalidate, international agreements before they became effective. The Commission also lost to the Joint Committee a measure of independence that only experienced administrators could appreciate. Never discussed in Congressional hearings or debates but strongly opposed by the Commission

142

was a provision in Section 261, which would require Joint Committee authorization of all appropriations for plant and equipment. To this degree, the Joint Committee acquired the power of the purse in addition to its already impressive influence on policy matters, and the Commission to the same degree lost a portion of its independence. The Commission, like nuclear technology, was beginning to move from its private world into the mainstream of American life.

Years later, former Commissioners would recall the passage of the 1954 Atomic Energy Act as the "high-water mark" of the Commission. Perhaps there were other events of equal or greater significance, but there is no question of the historical importance of this legislation. Old-timers would see it as the turning point in the history of the Commission—a unique moment full of hope and promise for the future.

143

CHAPTER 6

# NUCLEAR WEAPONS:
# A NEW REALITY

Two hours before dawn on a chilly March morning in 1953, *Newsweek* correspondent Leonard Slater huddled with nineteen other newsmen in a dirt trench on Yucca Flat within the Commission's Nevada Proving Grounds. Slater and the others had been selected to accompany an infantry unit into advance positions just 3,500 yards from a steel tower holding a test version of a full-scale atomic bomb. Like hundreds of observers before and after him, Slater endured hours of boredom as he awaited the detonation, but there was something special about this test: Slater and the troops were closer to ground zero than anyone had been since the Hiroshima and Nagasaki attacks.

Shivering more from the anticipation than from the cold, Slater heard the final countdown over the public address system, blinked in momentary shock as the nuclear fireball lit the trench brighter than the noonday sun, braced himself for the shock wave, and listened for what seemed like minutes for the dull roar generated by the detonation. Scrambling from the trench at the "all-clear" announcement, Slater and his companions watched in awe the purplish fireball swirling upward from the desert floor. Within minutes the familiar mushroom cloud, nearly five miles high, was forming where the shot tower had been.

At Alamogordo in 1945 the first atomic test had drawn from observers comparisons with scenes in the apocalypse. Little more than seven years later at Yucca Flat, Slater detected a tone of condescension among the troops. One officer thought the trip had not been worth the effort. Others compared the blast unfavorably with the flash and concussion produced by a standard artillery piece. In a matter of minutes soldiers with radiation monitoring equipment were calmly moving out in jeeps in the direction of ground zero.[1]

This striking change in reactions to the bomb was more than just a matter of time. Oppenheimer and his associates at Alamogordo had seen *Trinity* in terms of their own intimate experiences in building the bomb and their knowledge of its size and physical characteristics. It had been truly terrifying to witness what their groping with theory and experimental evidence had produced. For those who came to Yucca Flat, however, the bomb was not a finite experiment in physics. It had become in the popular mind a specter of enormous power, of superhuman dimensions, seemingly greater even than the ordinary forces of nature. For the troops the detonation of a very small atomic bomb, witnessed at a distance of about two miles, did not measure up to the image that popular literature had evoked in their minds. As with all physical phenomena, the meaning lay in the eyes of the beholder.

But the 1953 tests gave thousands of Americans an opportunity to witness the power of the atomic bomb directly, while millions of others around the world through the eyes of television, newsmen, and photographers could experience the bomb in terms they could understand. This time the bomb was not being tested solely on warships as at Bikini or on military equipment, but on such familiar objects as automobiles, white frame houses, fences, telephone poles, power lines, packaged foods, and aspirin. These artifacts from the everyday world provided a human scale against which both ordinary citizens and public officials could measure the significance of the bomb. Furthermore, the tests were being conducted in the continental United States, where their weekly progress would be reported in the press, on radio, and on television. The bomb would no longer be a vague, mysterious instrument of infinite disaster but rather a dangerous and immediate reality in American life.

145

## UPSHOT-KNOTHOLE

The test series that began on March 17, 1953, was the product of more than a year of planning by the Commission, the Department of Defense, and the Federal Civil Defense Administration (FCDA). Even before the *Tumbler-Snapper* series was concluded in spring 1952, Los Alamos began to formulate requirements for another continental test series designated as Operation *Upshot*. Although no one knew exactly what experimental devices would be tested, the Los Alamos scientists were certain that the first detonation of the thermonuclear device and the huge fission weapon called *King* would raise many questions that could be answered only by further experiments. The Nevada Proving Grounds was too close to urban areas (sixty-five miles from Las Vegas) for testing multimegaton devices like *Mike* or even fission devices, like *King*, which exceeded 100 kilotons; but it was far more economical and convenient than Enewetak for tests of smaller yields, which would provide essential information for designing the components of both thermonuclear and fission weapons. Twenty shots in two previous Nevada tests in 1951 and 1952 had demonstrated the value of a continental test site.[2]

The other half of the test series was Operation *Knothole*, which would include a variety of experiments for both the Department of Defense and the Federal Civil Defense Administration to determine the implications of nuclear detonations for both people and equipment. The enormous expense and complexity of nuclear tests made it imperative to integrate the objectives of both *Upshot* and *Knothole*. There were special advantages of a dual test series in Nevada, given the space to deploy thousands of troops and military equipment and the relative ease to set up civil defense experiments. But a dual test series also had disadvantages, particularly for the Commission's weapon laboratories. The efficient conduct of *Knothole* required firm schedules set long in advance; but Operation *Upshot* was essentially a series of field experiments in a rapidly developing technology and, therefore, constantly subject to change. As early as the *Greenhouse* tests in 1951, the Los Alamos scientists had discovered the inhibiting effect of dual operations when they were unable to take advantage of continuing research because a design change to increase yield would have upset plans for both tests of military effects and biomedical experiments. Dissatisfied as the scientists were with the prospects of a dual test series, there was no way to avoid it.[3]

By early 1953 the test program was set (see the following list of Operation *Upshot-Knothole* test shots). Los Alamos would have five shots primarily related to diagnostic experiments, although all would involve civil defense or military effects or both. The new weapon laboratory at Livermore had scheduled two specialized experiments to check novel design principles for weapons; neither test was encumbered with military or civil defense projects. Finally, Los Alamos had scheduled three shots primarily related to effects. Five of the six diagnostic shots would be fired on three-hundred-foot towers for precision in data collections. The sixth diagnostic shot was planned to verify yield only and could be air-dropped to fire at a relatively high altitude in order to reduce the uptake of ground dust in the radioactive cloud. Two of the tests of military effects were also to be air-dropped to simulate combat conditions for the troops; the third military shot was an atomic artillery shell to be fired from a 280-millimeter cannon.[4]

| Shot | Date 1953 | Type | Yield (Kilotons) |
|---|---|---|---|
| 1. Annie | March 17 | Tower | 16.0 |
| 2. Nancy | March 24 | Tower | 24.0 |
| 3. Ruth | March 31 | Tower | 0.2 |

| Shot | Date 1953 | Type | Yield (Kilotons) |
|------|-----------|------|------------------|
| 4. Dixie | April 6 | Airdrop | 11.0 |
| 5. Ray | April 11 | Tower | 0.2 |
| 6. Badger | April 18 | Tower | 23.0 |
| 7. Simon | April 25 | Tower | 43.0 |
| 8. Encore | May 8 | Airdrop | 27.0 |
| 9. Harry | May 19 | Tower | 32.0 |
| 10. Grable | May 25 | Gun | 15.0 |
| 11. Climax | June 4 | Airdrop | 61.0 |

## THE CIVILIAN DIMENSION

Along with the twenty newsmen and the troops in forward positions for the March 17 shot was Val Peterson, the newly appointed Federal Civil Defense Administrator. Peterson's presence was just one more way of demonstrating the importance of civil defense activities in the *Upshot-Knothole* tests. For more than a year the civil defense agency had been planning for this day. Originally hoping to have a shot of its own, the agency, like the Commission and the military services, had finally accepted the necessity for a combined operation.

The day before the first shot, Harold L. Goodwin, the director of FCDA's operations staff, briefed the press on the experiments set up on Yucca Flat. None had proved more fascinating during the press tour of the site than the two frame houses built 3,500 and 7,500 feet from ground zero. These two-story, center-hall dwellings with basements were typical of thousands of American homes. They were complete except for interior finish, plaster, and utilities. Government-surplus furniture, household items, and fully-dressed manikins were installed in the houses to measure damage. House No. 1, closest to ground zero, was expected to be completely destroyed by blast and had been equipped with reflective paint and venetian blinds to keep it from burning. The house at 7,500 feet would be damaged but probably not destroyed. Two types of blast shelters, located in the basements of the houses, were designed to protect occupants from the heavy debris load of the collapsing structure. Eight other shelters designed by FCDA for backyard use had been built nearby.

Also of great press interest were the fifty automobiles of various types, colors, and operating conditions placed at different distances and orientations from ground zero; some contained manikins. Goodwin told the reporters that these tests were especially important because they would indicate whether the family car would provide any effective protection against the radiation, heat, and blast of a nuclear bomb.[5]

The third major FCDA project was the testing of four types of calibrated instruments that would record the angle of incidence of thermal energy from the bomb and thus help to determine its exact air-zero position. Such information would be essential to civil defense officials in directing rescue teams and estimating damage and casualties. FCDA had also planned several classified projects for later shots in the series to test blast effects on standard wall panels and partitions, to determine the effects of radiation on lungs, and to measure the reliability of radiation survey instruments.

Important as the technical results of the civil defense experiments would be, they would have even greater value in giving the general public some impression of what an atomic attack could mean in everyday life. For this purpose the Commission and FCDA had jointly organized an elaborate public information plan for the March 17 test and several others later in the series. More than 250 newsmen, 360 state governors and mayors, and scores of county and civil defense officials had been invited to visit the site before the *Annie* shot, observe the test, and if possible inspect the results. Reporters and photographers would have an excellent vantage point from a rise dubbed "News Nob" on the edge of Yucca Flat, and there was to be live radio and television coverage.

148

The shot on March 17 was successful in both its technical and informational aspects. The countdown went smoothly, and the yield was close to the planned fifteen kilotons. House No. 1 was destroyed by blast as planned, and the high-speed camera shots of its destruction provided a series of dramatic photographs that were widely published in newspapers and magazines. House No. 2 suffered some damage but remained intact as predicted. The battered manikins provided graphic evidence of the weapon's vicious power. The basements afforded good protection against radiation, and the simple basement shelters were effective against debris. The family automobile would be relatively safe outside a ten-block radius for a small weapon of this type, provided that some windows were left open to prevent the roof from caving in on the passengers. Most heavily damaged cars that did not burn and were not radioactive could be driven away soon after the shot.[6]

News coverage of the shot was excellent, as expected. Most daily newspapers and weekly news magazines covered the story with special reports and photographs. A television audience estimated at eight million viewers had a somewhat less than satisfactory impression of *Annie*, particularly in establishing some sense of scale, but reporter Chet Huntley's somber descriptions of the drama from the forward trenches were judged impressive. Most newspapers gave their readers adequate factual accounts of the test and pointed up the implications for civil defense. Some even reminded readers that the absence of total destruction resulted from the relatively small size of the device and the long distances from ground zero to the experiments and the observers.

Probably more significant than the first news stories were the follow-up articles by state and regional civil defense officials in their local newspapers. These articles were important in translating the effects of *Annie* into terms that had meaning in neighborhood surroundings and stressed the substantial value of even the simplest precautions in the event of a nuclear attack. These local appeals were supported naturally by Peterson's hard-hitting plea for national action on civil defense with Eisenhower's strong endorsement.[7] With careful planning Peterson and his associates had been able to capture the nation's attention with the March 17 event, and they were able to sustain much of this interest as the tests proceeded during spring 1953.

149

## THE MILITARY SPHERE

Vital as the civil effects tests appeared to be for national security, the military implications for *Upshot* were even more critical. Largely hidden from public view was the vast complex of government organizations, military units, scientific laboratories, and private contractors that made the tests possible. Unlike the Pacific tests, directed by a joint military task force for the Commission, the continental tests at Nevada were entirely in the Commission's hands. The line of authority led through the headquarters division of military application, headed by Brigadier General Kenneth E. Fields, to Carroll L. Tyler, manager of the Commission's Santa Fe operations office, who served as test manager. Because all previous continental tests and all but two in *Upshot* depended on research at Los Alamos, officials of that laboratory under the direction of Alvin C. Graves were in charge of scientific aspects of the tests. Herbert F. York, a young physicist who would later be officially designated director of the new Livermore laboratory, worked with Graves in staging the two Livermore tests. Military operations were coordinated through the Albuquerque field command of the Armed Forces Special Weapons Project, established in the Pentagon soon after World War II to handle atomic energy matters for all three military services.[8]

Shots scheduled for *Upshot* and other series at the Nevada site in the 1950s typically involved various purposes, and as many as possible were incorporated in a single shot. Some shots included fundamental research in nuclear physics that would test the feasibility of new theoretical approaches to weapon design. Others provided technical data for full-scale production engineering of a new weapon. Often shots were planned to explore phenomena that could affect the efficiency and performance of weapons but that were not susceptible to theoretical analysis. Sometimes shots were designed to provide a basis for choice between two or more theoretical methods of weapon improvement or to gain time by eliminating the need for months of calculations and laboratory experiments. In the *Upshot* series several shots were designed to test components that would be used in new weapon designs. Only occasionally was it necessary to proof-test complete or stockpiled weapons, and such tests were combined whenever possible with studies of weapons effects, for both civilian and military purposes. In most instances the shots consisted of highly instrumented experimental devices rather than complete weapons.[9]

150

In terms of direct participation, the most important parts of *Upshot-Knothole* for the armed services were the weapon effects tests. Under the technical direction of the Armed Forces Special Weapons Project, these tests were designed to reveal tactical problems involved in the use of nuclear weapons, to determine the effects of radiation and blast on military equipment, and to give combat troops experience in maneuvers with nuclear weapons. Exercise *Desert Rock V* involved more than fifteen thousand ground troops of the Army, Navy, Marines, and Air Force. The placement of combat units in advanced positions, as was done for the *Annie* shot, continued during the series. In subsequent shots, officer volunteers occupied positions as close as two thousand yards from ground zero. Larger numbers of combat troops were stationed about twice that distance from the blast.

The military services also provided vital support functions for the tests as they had in all such exercises since the *Sandstone* tests in the Pacific in 1948. The Air Force furnished weather services, about twenty-five aircraft, and one thousand civilians and military personnel in direct support of the series. At least fifty combat and other operational aircraft were involved in dropping test devices, cloud sampling and testing, radiological terrain surveys, photography, training, and data collection.

## HAZARDS OF CONTINENTAL TESTING

The Nevada Proving Ground did offer substantial advantages over Enewetak or Bikini for testing nuclear devices and defense against nuclear attack, but the rapidly expanding use of the continental test site also posed an ever increasing threat to the American public. The potential hazards in continental testing had been weighed against defense requirements before the Alamogordo test in 1945 and had been considered again by the Commission before the first Nevada tests were authorized in 1951.

In planning and executing the twenty continental tests before *Upshot-Knothole*, the Los Alamos scientists had acquired considerable skill and experience in predicting the potential hazards and minimizing them. That these capabilities had reached a level of some sophistication was

clearly evident in the special fifty-page section on "Public Safety in Continental Weapons Testing," which the Commission published as part of its
thirteenth semiannual report to the Congress in January 1953. To be sure,
there was a certain amount of special pleading in the title of the report and
its contents. The purpose of the report, after all, was to reassure the American people, not to present an even-handed analysis candidly describing the
uncertainties involved. But in light of the extreme secrecy that still prevailed in Commission activities at that time, the report was surprisingly
detailed and informative. It reviewed the reasons for establishing the Nevada Proving Grounds in the first place; it described in a straightforward
manner the flash, airblast, and radiation effects of nuclear detonations; and
it clearly acknowledged radiation as the most serious hazard. The report
honestly discussed the origin and rationale for maximum permissible doses
of radiation, both on the surface of the human body and internally, and the
implications of fallout in terms of both somatic and genetic effects. The
report concluded,

> There is negligible hazard to property from blast; that proper warn-
> ings and patrolling have prevented any injury to humans from heat,
> light, or blast; and that the highest levels of radioactivity released
> by fall-out of particles are well below the very conservative stan-
> dards fixing the amounts of radiation that can be received externally
> or internally by the human body without harming the present or later
> generations.[10]

But the public report did not reveal the growing uneasiness within
the test organization over the difficulty of holding radiation effects below
the standards set forth in the report. About the time that the public report
was released, Tyler convened a special committee at Los Alamos to appraise the operational future of the test site. The committee included not
only Los Alamos scientists and military officers from Washington but also
the Commission's directors of public information and biology and medicine.
After concluding that the Nevada Proving Ground was "vital" to weapon
development, the committee found that considerations of public safety were
the major restriction on the type and size of devices tested at the site and
that this restriction was related mostly to yield, placement of the device or
mode of delivery, and resulting fallout near the site. There would have to
be "a very strong, overriding reason" to justify a surface or subsurface shot
exceeding one kiloton. A tower shot over thirty-five kilotons should be
fired "only under very stable, predictable [weather] conditions." Airbursts
should not exceed fifty kilotons until the laboratory could further assess the
probability that a fuse failure might turn an aerial device into a surface
shot. The committee admitted that luck as well as good planning had prevented fallout radiation from exceeding the established standards in past
tests. To reduce this possibility in the future the committee recommended

new firing sites, less frequent use of each site, aluminum towers, higher towers, and soil stabilization at the base of the towers.[11]

Because plans for *Upshot-Knothole* were virtually complete when the Tyler committee met, the report probably reflected an effort to evaluate the hazards posed by the series rather than an attempt to establish a ceiling for shots scheduled in the series. In any case, the report, an internal document, was not sent to the Commission in Washington until May 1953, when two-thirds of the series had been completed. Certainly Graves and the test group did not think it necessary to comply literally with the guidelines stated in the report. Of the seven tower shots scheduled for *Upshot-Knothole*, four were expected to reach or exceed the thirty-five kiloton ceiling recommended by the committee. Because all the shots were in several respects experimental, it was not possible to predict yield exactly, and the actual yields in some cases exceeded and in others fell short of the estimates.[12] The test group clearly expected substantial fallout beyond the test site, but drawing on experience in earlier series there was confidence that the monitoring teams could quickly detect fallout patterns after each shot in the *Upshot-Knothole* series. In theory, the plan was to warn people in communities to take shelter if significant fallout appeared to be heading in their direction; in fact, however, it was not always possible to contact isolated prospectors and ranchers.

Although offsite fallout was in some way related to yield, the relationship was not linear. It was possible to exceed the thirty-five kiloton limit without significant offsite fallout. The test group had greatly improved its ability to determine from weather data the probable direction and speed of the radioactive cloud and thus to select firing times that would result in a minimum of offsite fallout. Despite these precautions, however, some offsite fallout occurred from seven of the ten shots originally scheduled for the series.[13]

There was no easy way to determine the health hazard of this fallout, but with the intention of providing a conservative margin of safety the test group had established a maximum permissible weekly exposure of 0.3 roentgen (R), a physical unit of measure defined in terms of the ionizing effect of X-rays. This limit was derived from standards recommended by the National Committee on Radiation Protection and the International Commission on Radiological Protection in 1950 on the basis of data accumulated over several decades of industrial and clinical experience. The best authorities at that time believed that the human body was capable of repairing most if not all somatic damage produced by 0.3 roentgen over a one-week period. In fact, Commission scientists believed that a rapidly delivered dose of about 25 roentgens of whole-body radiation was required to produce permanent damage in humans. Because *Upshot-Knothole* was planned to occur over a period of three months, or thirteen weeks, the test

152

group simply extrapolated the 0.3-roentgen figure to cover that period. Thus, the guideline for the series became 3.9 roentgens.[14]

Also to be considered was the genetic damage that might be caused by this amount of radiation. As the Commission's semiannual report informed the public in January 1953, scientists agreed that genetic mutations were directly proportional to dose, with no recovery or repair processes at work. Daily or weekly repetitions of such doses could produce a noticeable increase in the number of mutations among offspring. The determination of the effects of radiation on mutation rates was a difficult process that required experiments with large numbers of laboratory animals over many years. Preliminary data then available on mice suggested that exposing the germ cells to 80 roentgens would double the natural rate of human mutations. Obviously the less radiation received by the genes, the better.

The test group never considered the 3.9-roentgen figure as an outside limit that could be approached without concern. The large uncertainties about the effects of radiation required that exposures be held to the lowest possible levels. The first precaution was to fire the shot only under weather conditions that would preclude the radioactive cloud from moving rapidly from the test site and in a direction that would carry it over populated areas. Second, the test group routinely used an elaborate system of fixed air-sampling stations and mobile teams to monitor fallout in the area within 200 miles of the test site. Beyond that distance mobile units and 121 stations manned by the U.S. Weather Bureau collected air samples for analysis at the Commission's Health and Safety Laboratory in New York City.[15]

153

## FALLOUT IN UPSHOT-KNOTHOLE

The test group's monitoring teams were able to determine fallout patterns very quickly after each shot. The radioactive cloud from the first shot, *Annie*, did move due east from the test site and dropped fallout on St. George, Utah, but the Commission reported that the maximum radiation level was no more than 0.026 roentgens per hour, far below the guidelines set for offsite exposures. *Nancy*, the second shot, was somewhat larger than *Annie* and apparently dumped substantial amounts of fallout in sparsely populated areas northeast of the test site. Because monitoring teams had been stationed only in communities and took only a limited number of readings along roads, it was impossible to know the precise radiation levels in the hinterland. In its public releases the Commission merely reported that there had been no fallout in populated areas, although it was admitted that the small number of residents at Lincoln Mine, Nevada, had been requested to remain indoors for two hours while radiation from fallout exceeded 0.5 roentgens per hour. The third through the sixth shots produced no radioactivity measurable in inhabited areas. [16]

More radiation exposures, however, did occur during the high-yield shots that concluded the series. A wind shift at the time *Simon* was detonated on April 25 carried the radioactive cloud over two highways in Nevada. When fallout reached 0.46 roentgens per hour, Graves ordered roadblocks set up, and about forty vehicles with interior readings of 0.007 roentgens per hour were washed at government expense. [17]

By far the most serious was the fallout from the *Harry* shot on May 19. Postponed three days because of unfavorable weather, *Harry* was fired under what seemed to be perfect conditions. But a wind shift and a slight increase in wind velocity spread fallout in a pattern about fifty miles square over populated areas east of the proving ground. For the second time in a month roadblocks were set up on major highways to monitor motor vehicles. At 9:10 a.m., about four hours after the shot had been fired, readings as high as 0.32 roentgens per hour were being recorded at the roadblocks. At that time Edward S. Weiss, the Public Health Service officer stationed in St. George, called the sheriff's office and radio station to warn people in the area to take cover. Local schools kept children indoors during the morning recess, and the washing of contaminated cars in St. George was suspended. By 9:40 a.m. most of the population in St. George was under cover, and the community came to a standstill.

The all-clear came before noon when the first officials from the test site arrived to look over the situation. Because of the understandable tension among the residents, Weiss was ordered to remain in the area for several more days. During that period he considered collecting milk samples from local dairies to check for radioactivity, but because of the uneasiness in the community Weiss concluded that such a survey might create alarm. For that reason he limited his investigation to a few samples of milk purchased in local stores. From measurements at St. George the test group later estimated that the maximum amount of external exposure that could have been received at St. George was 6.0 roentgens and 5.0 roentgens at Cedar City. Scientists later estimated that children living near the test site received thyroid doses from iodine-131 ranging from inconsequential levels to those possibly causing some thyroid abnormalities. [18]

## PUBLIC AND PRIVATE CONCERNS ABOUT FALLOUT

Although many people in these Utah communities were unnerved by the incident, they were reassured by statements from the test group that the radiation exposure had been below hazardous levels. Most people did not complain about having to remain indoors or waiting at roadblocks. There was neither public alarm nor open protest in the communities, but individuals did complain that fallout had caused physical injuries or disabilities. Only two very mild Congressional inquiries resulted from the *Simon* and *Harry* incidents, and both took the form of requesting reassurance rather than registering protest. In both instances, Commission officials and the test group were able quickly to convince the congressmen that adequate precautions had been taken to assure public safety. Very few newspapers outside the immediate area covered the incidents, and most of these stressed the Commission's reassurances. Incomparably more troublesome were the deluge of letters and flurry of newspaper and magazine articles speculating on whether the seemingly unusual number of severe tornadoes occurring across the nation that spring were caused by the Nevada tests. The Commission's public information staff was still answering tornado inquiries long after the fallout incidents had been forgotten.[19]

Public alarm had been avoided, but the Commissioners were privately concerned about the fallout from the larger shots in the series. On May 13, 1953, John C. Bugher, director of the Commission's division of biology and medicine, reported that the total potential integrated dose to inhabitants in thinly populated areas following the *Simon* shot had been as high as 10 roentgens. A new dimension to the fallout problem developed when a heavy rainout near Troy, New York, the following day delivered a potential integrated dose of 2 roentgens. The Commissioners expressed concern about the unexpected high yield of *Simon* (forty-three kilotons). Dean observed that there had been an understanding that high-yield shots would be fired outside the United States, but he admitted that the Commission had no firm criteria for deciding such issues.[20]

The Commissioners also received troubling reports that sheepmen who customarily wintered their herds north of the test site had encountered unusually heavy losses after trailing their sheep to an area west of Cedar City, Utah, for shearing during April. Losses ranged up to 30 percent for newborn lambs and 20 percent for ewes or mature sheep. Because the winter range had received substantial fallout from the *Nancy* shot on March 24, there was a possibility that radioactive fallout could have been a factor in the sheep deaths. Unfortunately most of the dead sheep had been disposed of before veterinarians and radiation specialists arrived on the scene, but many surviving sheep in the affected herds showed lesions on the face and back after shearing. State and local veterinarians were unable to diagnose the malady, and those from the Public Health Service and Los Alamos were not certain whether the lesions were caused by fallout. Arrangements were made to sacrifice some of the surviving sheep for detailed biological studies and further radiation experiments on sheep were started at the Commission's Los Alamos and Oak Ridge laboratories.[21]

The fallout question became more pertinent the following week when

155

the Commission considered a proposal to add an eleventh shot to the series. Design work had just been completed at Los Alamos on some new principles that would be used in the *Castle* series in the Pacific early in 1954 to develop a deliverable thermonuclear weapon. Because Los Alamos had completed this work earlier than expected, it would be possible to test the new principle at *Upshot-Knothole* rather than in a special single-shot series in the Pacific in autumn 1953.

Testing the device in Nevada would have significant advantages over a Pacific test in terms of saving time and money, but the yield would be more than sixty kilotons, about 30 percent greater than *Simon*. When Dean expressed grave concern about local fallout or more distant rainout, Graves could give the Commission only partial assurances. First, *Simon* had made possible a more reliable estimate of yield. Second, the proposed test would be an airdrop rather than a tower shot, a factor that would greatly reduce fallout. Third, because it would be the last shot in the series, the test group could afford to wait for the best possible weather conditions.[22]

The Commission approved the eleventh shot on May 18, but the decision was clouded in uncertainty the following day when the first reports of fallout from *Harry* were received in Washington. Zuckert immediately requested a statement of the weather criteria that would be considered the minimum acceptable for the eleventh shot and raised the whole question of the test policy at the Nevada site. He considered the fallout from *Simon* and *Harry* as posing "a serious psychological problem" that would require the Commission to consider alternatives to continental testing. Zuckert also noted that the Commission's request to the President for authorization to use additional fissionable material for the eleventh shot had not alerted Eisenhower of the magnitude of the shot or the possible dangers involved. At Zuckert's suggestion, Dean discussed these considerations with Strauss at the White House. Strauss expressed greatest concern over the possibility that heavy fallout or rainout might jeopardize future testing in Nevada, primarily because he was impressed by the substantial advantages of conducting the test there. Strauss took the matter to Eisenhower, who with some misgivings approved the test.[23]

The eleventh shot, *Climax*, fortunately performed close to predictions. Although the yield was sixty-one kilotons, offsite fallout was far below that of *Simon* and *Harry*, and the test provided the information needed for the *Castle* series. These results, however, did not end the matter for Zuckert. The weather criteria that he had requested for *Climax* were vague at best and did not reach the Commission until the day after the shot. A week later Zuckert suggested the need for a full-scale review of "the highly interrelated public relations and safety problems that we have created" at the Nevada site. The committee appointed to study these problems should, in Zuckert's opinion, include experts in public information as well as in weapon and related technologies.[24]

## THE QUESTION OF CONTINENTAL TESTING

To Zuckert and others the problems raised by the increasing size and number of Nevada tests were more a public relations concern than a safety problem. This was not to say that safety was considered unimportant—far from it. But safety could be managed by technology; public relations could not. Tyler, whom the Commission designated chairman of the study group, followed Zuckert's lead in giving public relations a prominent place in the investigation. He invited Morse Salisbury, the Commission's director of public information, to serve as a member of the committee, and Richard G. Elliott, the Commission's public information officer at Los Alamos, had a key role as secretary of the committee. Other members included Bradbury and Graves from Los Alamos, Bugher on radiation matters, and veteran specialists from other government agencies on weather and blast effects.

Without any written instructions from the Commission, Tyler assumed that his job was to produce a more detailed study than the one completed in January 1953 and that any conclusions should be supported by comprehensive reports or documentation. To get the committee started, Tyler proposed that it examine various questions under the general headings of the radiological problems of testing, both in the immediate test area and at greater distances: factors determining the amount of fallout; the blast and the shock problems; the need for the continental test site; public education; and the kind of conclusions the committee should expect to reach. Elliott saw the task as supplementing the earlier report with *Upshot-Knothole* experience, preparing a definitive study of the value of continental tests, and recommending guidelines for future continental testing, specifically in terms of public safety and education. Much groundwork was to be covered by eleven studies assigned to committee members and others for completion in August 1953.[25]

By late September, the Tyler committee had unanimously concluded that a continental test site was necessary and that the Nevada Proving Grounds was still the best site available. The committee was also confident that operational controls at the site could be strengthened "to provide continuing assurance of public safety" and believed that a better education and information program was necessary.

One issue to be resolved before Nevada testing could be resumed was whether the *Upshot-Knothole* series had caused the sheep kill. Commission personnel at the test site were fully aware that the future of continental testing might hang on the results of the investigations already started. The studies completed during autumn 1953 concluded that neither the level of external radiation, nor radiation burns on the sheep's skin, nor radiation of the sheep's thyroid from iodine-131 in the fallout could have caused the deaths. The supporting data presented by the Commission's laboratories were impressive and seemed conclusive. It seemed much more

157

likely at the time that the excessive number of deaths resulted from the extremely dry weather that left the herds badly undernourished that spring. Although the results were favorable, Commission officials in the field threw the best possible light on the findings, not only to show the general public that the tests could be conducted safely but also to reassure the Commissioners, some of whom remained unconvinced.

When a group of sheep owners brought suit for damages against the government in 1955, the court found in favor of the government on the basis of the unanimous opinion of expert witnesses that there was no evidence that the fallout had caused the sheep deaths. Twenty-seven years later, however, in 1982 the same judge who had tried the original case vacated his decision on the strength of evidence that the Commission officials had perpetrated a fraud upon the court by suppressing the contrary opinions of some scientists.[26]

158

Although the point was not made explicitly, the committee's task had obviously changed from that originally conceived by Tyler. No longer was the committee expected simply to assess Nevada operations; the Commission now was demanding a solid justification for continental testing at the Nevada site. Personnel at the test site had been cut back to a skeleton force, and the Commission had refused to authorize any further construction until the Tyler committee had completed its report. To make certain that the committee's findings were fully documented, Tyler requested committee members and others to prepare additional reports and expand those already written. When completed in February 1954, the report consisted of a 62-page document backed up by twenty-five studies totaling more than 220 pages.[27]

Although the Tyler committee reaffirmed its September recommendation that tests be continued at the Nevada site, the report did propose certain restrictions on test operations. First, the committee set forth guidelines for justifying the need for shots, controlling or reducing fallout from potentially hazardous shots, prohibiting marginal shots under questionable weather conditions, and imposing yield limitations on surface, tower, and airborne shots. Second, the committee proposed a "planning maximum" of ten to fifteen shots in one year at the Nevada site. Third, the committee advocated lowering the standard for offsite exposure from 3.9 roentgens over thirteen weeks to the same amount integrated over an entire year.

The Commissioners were inclined to accept all the recommendations of the Tyler committee, but all except Murray wanted the views of the Commission's principal advisory committees before taking final action. Murray could see no reason to delay preparations for the next series at Nevada. Consideration by the advisory committees centered on the planning maximum. The advisory committee on biology and medicine favored a maximum of ten shots per year with no more than three high-yield tower shots. The general advisory committee, on the other hand, could find no sound reason for limiting the number of shots. A better approach, the committee thought, was to exercise the greatest precautions possible to protect test personnel and the public but to let operational needs determine the number of shots. Finally, on June 30, 1954, more than a year after Zuckert first raised the issue and on the last day of his term, the Commission approved the continuation of Nevada tests, subject to the restrictions proposed by the Tyler committee but without limiting the number of tests in any one year.[28] On this basis Tyler would make plans for the next continental test series in 1955.

## RAW MATERIALS

*Upshot-Knothole* had helped to make nuclear weapons something of a reality for many Americans, particularly those living in the vicinity of the Nevada Proving Grounds, although the tests revealed almost nothing about the vast network of production and manufacturing plants that had been created to produce nuclear weapons. The far-flung complex of mines, ore-processing mills, feed material plants, gaseous-diffusion plants, production reactors, chemical separation plants, metal fabrication plants, and weapon component and assembly plants was still largely concealed behind the security barriers established by the Atomic Energy Act. Only cleared observers, and then only those with a real "need to know," were privy to concise information about the production chain.

159

Some of the most tightly held data related to the procurement of uranium ore. Production rates were top secret until mid-1953 and were available only to a few persons beside the Commissioners because the amount of uranium ore processed could be related in a rough way to the production of fissionable materials. Ore data were also considered especially sensitive in the early years because most uranium used in the American project came from overseas sources under secret agreements. Of the 3,700 tons of uranium concentrates ($U_3O_8$) that the Commission received in 1953, only about one-quarter (1,100 tons) came from mines in the United States; the rest was produced in the Belgian Congo (1,600 tons), South Africa (500 tons), Canada (400 tons), and Portugal (100 tons). Another reason for secrecy was that successful accomplishment of the expansion program was heavily dependent upon the availability of sufficient ore to feed the production plants then under construction. The plants then in operation or under construction would require 9,150 tons of uranium concentrates per year when in full operation. Thus, 1953 receipts were less than one-half the ultimately required amount, and that goal was not expected to be attained before 1957, more than a year after all the plants were to be completed.[29]

These facts justified the high priority the Commission put on ore procurement, but they did not tell the whole story. Prospects for new sources of ore were developing so rapidly that it was difficult to keep up with them. As for foreign sources, the leveling off of production from the Shinkolobwe mine in the Belgian Congo would be more than offset by projections of rapidly increasing deliveries later in the decade from the Union of South Africa and Canada. South African concentrate production could reasonably be expected to rise to five or six thousand tons per year by 1960 as leading plants were constructed to process uranium in residues from gold-mining operations in the Transvaal and the Orange Free State. Increased Canadian production was expected to come from new ore discoveries in northwestern Saskatchewan and northwestern Ontario.[30]

By far the most dramatic increase in concentrate production came from domestic sources in the western United States. In 1948 just over 100 tons of concentrates were delivered from domestic sources, principally from the Salt Wash member of the Morrison geologic formation in southwestern Colorado and southeastern Utah. By 1953 progressive exploration and Commission production incentives had extended the ore-producing area on the Colorado plateau to three times its original size and had led to the discovery of significant deposits in other types of geologic formations in New Mexico, South Dakota, and Wyoming. So rapidly had ore prospects improved in the western states that Jesse C. Johnson, the Commission's director of raw materials, was able to abandon earlier plans to extract very low-grade ore from Tennessee shales and Florida phosphates. Although hundreds of millions of tons of ore were potentially available from these sources, the concentrates would cost $40 to $50 per pound, compared to an average cost of $12 per pound for plateau ores.[31]

Uranium mining on the plateau, in fact, was taking on boom proportions, which the newspapers found reminiscent of gold-rush days. As often happened in the mining industry, intense exploration resulted in discoveries of large deposits of relatively high-grade ore where only scattered, small deposits had been found before. The 1953 boom added the names of Charles A. Steen and Vernon J. Pick to the list of rags-to-riches legends in American mining history.[32]

With ore receipts approaching one-half million tons per year in 1953, Johnson's highest priority was to see that mills were built on the plateau fast enough to process the ore into concentrates. All the mills on the plateau in early 1953, except the Commission mill at Monticello, Utah, were privately owned. The largest private mills, all in Colorado, were two operated by the U.S. Vanadium Company at Rifle and Uravan, two operated by the Vanadium Corporation of America at Naturita and Durango, and one at Grand Junction, operated by the Climax Uranium Company; Vitro Chemical Company also had a plant at Salt Lake City, Utah. These mills barely met 1953 requirements. Despite efforts to build new mills, specifi-

160

cally near the New Mexico discoveries, the Commission's ore stockpile grew to 775,000 tons by the spring of 1954, when ore was being delivered at a rate of 900,000 tons per year at an average grade of 0.3 percent $U_3O_8$. Ore deliveries, if not mill capacity, continued to outstrip requirements.[33]

The domestic procurement experience seemed to substantiate the position Commissioner Murray had consistently taken—namely, that in searching for supposedly ever scarcer minerals, strong incentives for private industry often produced generous supplies. In July 1952 Murray had urged the Commission to establish a procurement goal of 12,500 tons of concentrate per year, about 25 percent more than the 9,150 tons needed for all plants to be built under the expansion program. The Commission adopted the higher goal within a price ceiling of twenty-five dollars per pound. As the Colorado uranium boom developed in 1953 along with prospects for much larger deliveries from South Africa and Canada, the Commission had no difficulty in raising the goal to 15,000 tons in April 1954. Five months later, the Commission could adopt a firm target of 17,500 tons per year with a permissive target of 20,000 at a maximum price of fifteen dollars per pound. Continuing improvement in the raw material outlook was reflected in further increases in the procurement goal to about 25,000 tons in July 1955 and to 27,000 tons in February 1956. Although projections for both civilian and military uses were still uncertain, there was growing confidence within the Commission that ore procurement would not inhibit future development.[34]

161

## PRODUCTION PLANTS

The increasing amounts of uranium concentrates being delivered in the mid-1950s provided feed for the growing network of facilities that produced plutonium, uranium-235, and other materials for nuclear weapons. During most of this period the concentrates delivered from domestic and foreign sources were reduced to uranium metal at the Mallinckrodt Chemical Works in St. Louis, Missouri, or at the Feed Materials Production Center, a new facility the Commission had constructed at Fernald, Ohio, near Cincinnati. Slugs of metallic uranium were shipped to Hanford, where they were welded into aluminum cans and inserted in the six plutonium-producing reactors in operation in early 1953. The much larger stocks of "virgin" uranium to be produced in the feed plants in subsequent years would serve as fuel for the new "Jumbo" reactors (KE and KW) at Hanford and for the five huge heavy-water reactors at Savannah River.[35]

Under the expansion program the increase in uranium-235 production was to be even larger than that of plutonium. Some measure of magnitude of the expansion could be gained from the gigantic effort to construct new gaseous-diffusion plants for producing uranium-235. The original U-shaped building at Oak Ridge had been one of the largest industrial plants ever constructed in the United States. In 1953 the original facility was dwarfed by the construction of three much more efficient plants at Oak Ridge (K-29, K-31, and K-33). As the year began, the foundations for K-33 were completed. Roughly comparable in physical size to the Oak Ridge complex would be the gaseous-diffusion plants at Paducah, Kentucky, and Portsmouth, Ohio. Started early in 1951, the first unit (C-31) of the Paducah plant was in operation late in 1952, and the three other units were in various stages of construction. Site studies had just started for the three big units at Portsmouth.

Because of the severe shortage of feed materials, very little of the uranium hexafluoride to be processed in these plants would come from virgin uranium. Instead the Commission was forced to rely on the enormous quantities of slightly depleted uranium that would come from the Hanford and Savannah River reactors. Until recently all the uranium removed from the Hanford reactors since 1945 had been stored in a chemical soup with a variety of fission products in huge underground tanks at Hanford. After years of plodding development by several laboratories, the Commission had placed in operation the Redox plant, which recovered uranium as well as plutonium from the irradiated fuel slugs at Hanford. Although Redox was theoretically capable of extracting uranium from material in the underground tanks, a solvent-extraction process using tributyl phosphate (TBP) as the solvent showed greater promise for this process. After a long series of construction delays, the TBP plant was just coming into operation early in 1953, and Redox was just approaching capacity operation.

The rapidly improving prospects for developing a thermonuclear weapon during the early 1950s stimulated interest in producing the materials that would probably be used in such a weapon, especially the heavy isotopes of hydrogen: deuterium and tritium. The Commission already had an impressive production capacity for deuterium in the heavy-water plants at Dana, Indiana, and Savannah River, South Carolina, which had been built to supply moderator for the production reactors at Savannah River. Tritium, a radioactive isotope with a relatively short half-life, did not ordinarily exist in nature and had to be produced by irradiating the light element, lithium, in a production reactor. Although both the Hanford and Savannah River reactors would be capable of producing tritium, their use for this purpose would reduce their capacity for plutonium production. Unless additional reactors were built, the Commission would have to balance its needs for plutonium and tritium.

There was another approach to the thermonuclear weapon that could conceivably reduce the demand on reactor capacity for tritium production. This was the idea, first discussed at the Princeton conference in 1951, of

162

placing lithium in the weapon itself and using fission neutrons to produce tritium in place. For this purpose, however, it appeared necessary to use the lighter isotope of lithium, which made up only 7 percent of the element in nature. In 1949 there had been some interest in separating the lithium isotopes, not for lithium-6 but for lithium-7, which had some attractive properties for use as a reactor coolant and moderator. Preliminary research on methods of separating the lithium isotopes was thus available at Oak Ridge in 1951, when the Los Alamos laboratory first requested a small amount of highly enriched lithium-6 for thermonuclear research. This material was produced with the old electromagnetic equipment built at Oak Ridge during World War II. The gross inefficiency and high cost of this operation, however, prompted the development of a better method, for which an electric exchange process was selected. Elex, as it was called, consisted of large shallow trays in which mechanical agitators mixed an amalgam of lithium and mercury with an aqueous solution of lithium hydroxide. After counterflow through a series of stages, the lithium-6 tended to concentrate in the amalgam while the lithium-7 could be extracted by electrolysis from the hydroxide solution. Chemical reaction between lithium and water was prevented by placing anodes in the hydroxide solution and using the amalgam as a cathode.[36]

163

Although Oak Ridge had nothing more than laboratory data on the Elex process, the urgent need for lithium-6 for the thermonuclear program led the Commission in August 1951 to approve construction of a small plant to be in production by autumn 1952. Within a matter of weeks, however, this plan was overtaken by Los Alamos research, which suggested the possibility of a dry thermonuclear fuel using lithium deuteride. Late in September 1951 Oak Ridge had a new requirement: produce lithium deuteride by September 1953 in an Elex plant with twice the capacity of the original plant. Top priorities and special effort brought the first half of the plant into operation on August 14, 1953, and the second half came into operation a month later.[37]

## DRIVE FOR THE HYDROGEN BOMB

The steadily increasing tempo of the Commission's production and construction activities reflected in large part the evergrowing sense of urgency to achieve an operational hydrogen bomb. A formal military requirement laid down by the Joint Chiefs of Staff in June 1952 called upon the Commission to produce a thermonuclear weapon in the megaton range that would be compatible with delivery systems to be available in 1954.[38] There were two ways of approaching that goal. One was to develop a very large fission weapon using substantial amounts of thermonuclear fuel. Before the

*Mike* shot in November 1952, this "semi-thermonuclear" weapon seemed the shortest and surest route to the formal requirement, but it offered no other advantages. Besides being a very large and heavy weapon, it did not seem to point to promising avenues of future development. The second approach was the "true" thermonuclear weapon. Because it depended on a radical new design using the Teller-Ulam principle, it involved more risk than the "semi," but it opened a wide range of possibilities for thermonuclear designs, including weapons much smaller than the "semi" on the one hand or very much larger in yield on the other. Either approach seemed amenable to wet or dry thermonuclear fuels.[39]

Important as *Mike* was in verifying the Teller-Ulam principle, it was not the key to reaching the military requirement. *Mike* and other experiments conducted during the *Upshot* series merely increased the probability that the "true" weapon would work. The actual testing of models that could be turned into weapons would come in Operation *Castle*, originally scheduled for autumn 1953. To meet the military requirement on time, it seemed that *Castle* could be no later than that. The schedule would also have made it possible to use elements of Major General Percy W. Clarkson's Joint Task Force 132, which had conducted the *Ivy* series in 1952, to provide the logistics and support operations for *Castle*.

## PLANNING FOR CASTLE

The stunning success of the *Mike* shot resulted almost immediately in postponing *Castle* until early 1954. The postponement opened the opportunity to conduct in the *Upshot* series further experiments that would contribute directly to *Castle*. The delay also assured the availability of more lithium-6 for *Castle* devices and moved the tests to the late winter and spring, when favorable weather conditions were more likely in the central Pacific. There was one disadvantage: the military services would have to disband some support units at Enewetak and then assemble new teams for *Castle*.[40]

Long before *Mike* and the change of schedule, however, plans had been laid for a major revision of testing procedures in the Pacific. *Mike* would merely confirm what Alvin C. Graves, the scientific test director, and others at Los Alamos had already concluded: namely, thermonuclear shots in the megaton range were too powerful to be conducted at Enewetak without threatening the extensive facilities that had been constructed there for earlier tests. *Mike* had destroyed an entire island in the Enewetak atoll and had damaged facilities on other islands. With the much larger tests contemplated for *Castle*, even the permanent facilities at the southern rim of the atoll would be threatened by thermonuclear tests on the northern islands. After considering several alternatives, Graves recommended that

164

most shots in the *Castle* series, specifically the large thermonuclear tests, be conducted at Bikini, some 180 miles east of Enewetak. Bikini, the site of Operation *Crossroads* in 1946, was still uninhabited, but it offered no facilities that would be useful in 1954. Graves's plan was to keep the main operational base for *Castle* at Enewetak, where the low-yield tests would be conducted. For the large tests at Bikini it was necessary to construct only a tent camp for construction and test personnel, a power plant, and a runway for small cargo planes. The two atolls would be linked by aircraft, ships, and radio and telephone communications.[41] In a sense one could say that nuclear weapon technology had now reached such colossal dimensions that a test site more than 180 miles wide was required.

The unprecedented radioactive fallout during the *Upshot-Knothole* series, the public anxiety about the possible effects of testing on weather, and the Eisenhower Administration's interest in budget stringency all combined to prod the Commission to reduce the number of tests scheduled for *Castle*. From the other direction, the Commission heard persuasive arguments from the weapon laboratories for at least six shots. Graves told the Commissioners on July 23, 1953, that there were compelling reasons for all six tests. The first three were high-yield shots necessary to assure an emergency capability with thermonuclear weapons; they would lead to weapons that could be carried in a B-36 bomber. The fourth, also high-yield but somewhat smaller in size and weight than the others, was intended for use in the new B-47 bomber. As a Los Alamos leader, Graves could vouch for the value of the first four high-yield shots, just as Herbert F. York and others at Livermore could speak for the need for the two low-yield tests, which it was hoped would open the way to thermonuclear weapons much smaller in size and yield than *Mike*.[42]

165

There were the usual discussions of the relative merits of the proposed shots with some agonizing over how many should be devoted to assuring an emergency capability and how many to developing new and more promising designs. Beyond these concerns was always the dilemma of substituting for the recommended shots one or more highly experimental tests with new designs that might easily fail but that might also provide a giant step forward in weapon technology should they prove successful. Strauss asked Graves how long the Commission could postpone the decision without jeopardizing the February 15 start of the *Castle* series; Graves suggested the middle of September.

By that time the Soviet Union had detonated *Joe 4*, an event that raised the level of anxiety and urgency within the Commission and the laboratories. When Kenneth E. Fields, the director of military application, presented the revised shot schedule on September 22, 1953, he noted the need for one substitution and a delay in starting the series until March 1, mostly because of a lag in construction at Bikini but also in order to ease the strain on logistics. Again the Commissioners struggled with the need to assure emergency capability with pedestrian but reliable designs as opposed to testing more risky but also more promising concepts.

## NEW PRODUCTION REQUIREMENTS

A new issue appearing in September 1953 was the critical need for lithium deuteride and tritium. To the extent that any device designed to provide emergency capability relied on large amounts of these materials, the less probable it was that the laboratories would meet the required stockpile dates. And beyond that point, there was still no positive assurance that a dry weapon would work. If the first test in the series, which was to be a weapon using lithium deuteride, should fail, the test schedule would have to be revised, and the possibility would increase that Los Alamos would have to fall back for emergency capability on such unpromising systems as the weapon version of *Mike* with its great bulk and cumbersome cryogenic gear.[43]

Although the Commissioners were determined to give the highest priority to the emergency capability, they were also prepared to take a large risk that dry weapons would be successful, an assumption that dictated a much larger potential requirement for lithium deuteride than the recently completed plants at Oak Ridge would produce. On September 30 to meet this prospective demand the Commission authorized construction at Oak Ridge of a second plant, larger than the first, using a somewhat different process called Colex, which utilized countercurrent exchange in columns. As officials in the Bureau of the Budget found, to their consternation, the Commission had approved the new plant simply on the anticipation of need and with no firm requirement from the Department of Defense. Instead of following usual budget channels, Strauss obtained the required apportionment of funds directly from Budget Director Dodge while Defense proceeded to draft the requirement.[44]

Formal statement of the higher requirement came from the Joint Chiefs of Staff on December 15, 1953. The Joint Chiefs expressed the opinion that *Joe 4* threatened the "substantial lead in destructive capability" that the United States enjoyed over the Soviet Union. Because production of thermonuclear weapons was "the cheapest method to obtain high-yield weapons and more destructive capability," the Soviet Union could be expected to pursue this course. Unless the United States substantially accelerated its schedule for producing thermonuclear weapons, the Soviet Union would obtain nuclear superiority by 1958.

In this dangerous situation, the Joint Chiefs saw only two solutions: first, to build new production facilities at great expense; or, second, to shift production in order to increase the size of the thermonuclear stockpile more rapidly. The latter course seemed the better, although it would mean some reduction in requirements for fission weapons in the megaton range. Following this course the Joint Chiefs proposed new requirements for the composition of the stockpile that would allocate available production capacity mostly to high-yield thermonuclear weapons and low-yield fission weapons for tactical support, air defense, and demolition.[45]

Even before the Joint Chiefs sent the formal notification, the Commission's operating contractors were considering how best to meet the new requirements. It seemed likely that the military requirements could be met over the long range, but there were questions about the near term. With the existing reactors at Hanford and the new units just coming into operation at Savannah River it would be difficult to produce the large amounts of tritium needed for weapons in the proposed stockpile, but there were reasons to be hopeful. First, new methods of loading the reactors would substantially increase production of either tritium or plutonium, and, second, the *Castle* tests might significantly reduce the amount of tritium required for each thermonuclear weapon.[46]

If tritium requirements could be reduced, the Commission would have more capacity at Hanford and Savannah River for producing plutonium, which would also be in short supply. Plutonium was needed for not only low-yield fission weapons but also the fission component that would initiate thermonuclear reactions in the hydrogen bomb. The Commission's production staff undertook detailed studies to determine the optimum allocation of reactor capacity at both sites to tritium and plutonium formation.

Other nuclear materials needed to meet the new requirements from the Joint Chiefs would also be in short supply, but there were ways in which the Commission could close most gaps. The outlook for deuterium production was relatively good because the existing plants at Dana and Savannah River could produce all the heavy water required; but it would be necessary to enlarge the electrolytic plant at Savannah River and build a new one at Oak Ridge to extract deuterium from heavy water. Part of the near-term deficiency in uranium-235 production could be overcome by accelerating completion of the new gaseous-diffusion plants at Oak Ridge and Paducah. Beyond that, until the Portsmouth plant could be built, more production of uranium-235 could be accomplished only by either feeding more uranium to the Oak Ridge and Paducah plants or increasing the amount of electric power used to drive the compressors. In either case, the decision would rest ultimately upon how much the Commission was willing to pay for additional production. As for lithium-6, the expansion of the Oak Ridge facility authorized only a few weeks earlier would meet the Joint Chiefs' requirements if the amount of feed for one new Colex plant was increased.[47]

167

## THE QUESTION OF RESPONSIBILITY

It did seem possible to meet most Joint Chiefs' requirements, and there was no sentiment within the Commission on December 23, 1953, to delay the immediate actions that General Manager Nichols proposed on an emergency basis. The letter from the Joint Chiefs, however, did raise some old concerns about the nature and implications of military requirements, which the Commissioners had discussed many times over the preceding seven years.[48] Although Strauss favored quick action, he wanted to confirm his impression that the stockpile recommended by the Joint Chiefs was based on specific targeting plans, not just their estimates of the Commission's ability to produce.

168

Zuckert, who remained unconvinced on this point, spoke at some length about the enormous destructive capability of the proposed stockpile, which he estimated would be equivalent to several billion tons of TNT by 1957. He posed the frightening possibility that by then the United States might have the capacity to destroy the entire arable portion of the Soviet Union. Zuckert did not think the Commission should question military requirements on military grounds, but he believed that the Commissioners had individual responsibilities as civilian officials to make sure that the President understood the implications of a decision that clearly transcended military matters. The decision, in Zuckert's opinion, involved a determination by the highest civilian authority that the proposed size and composition of the stockpile were consistent with national objectives as well as military needs.

Although Strauss did not really question the validity of the requirements, he acknowledged the obligation to discuss the issue with the President. In addition to the points Zuckert had raised, Strauss shared Smyth's concern about the potential hazards from radioactive fallout if military plans for using thermonuclear weapons were ever carried out. Early in February 1954 the Commissioners reviewed the entire proposal in detail and discussed its implications. As a result, the question was presented to Eisenhower in a joint letter from Strauss and Secretary of Defense Wilson, and the President signed a formal directive approving the decision on February 6, more than two months after Nichols had alerted the staff to prepare for the new requirements.[49]

## BUILD-UP FOR CASTLE

Although the Commissioners did not begin to concentrate their attention on *Castle* until late 1953, preparations for the tests had started more than a year earlier. On October 2, 1952, within weeks after the Commission had approved the Bikini site, the first contingent of thirty-nine employees of

Holmes & Narver, Inc., the Commission's construction contractor at the Pacific Proving Grounds, landed on Bikini to begin site preparations. By the time the *Ivy* series began a month later, about two hundred people were working on the few essential facilities needed to accommodate air and sea transportation from Enewetak.[50]

As soon as the essential activities of Operation *Ivy* were completed early in 1953, General Clarkson established Joint Task Force 7, which included many components of the *Ivy* group, and began to build the complex of administrative arrangements that would enable the three military services to support the scientists in the *Castle* series. The first task was to reach agreement on the general conception of the operation. All high-yield tests would be conducted at Bikini, but the main base of operations would continue to be Enewetak. Activities at Bikini were to be limited to the minimum necessary to instrument and fire the devices. In fact, the devices themselves, with one exception, would not be assembled at Bikini but rather in the Enewetak Atoll. Placed on barges, the test devices would be towed to firing positions at Bikini.[51]

169

The plan reflected in many ways the incredible magnitude of the effects expected from large thermonuclear weapons. So enormous were the projected yields that it hardly seemed feasible to maintain habitable facilities at Bikini, even when the shots were fired on the opposite side of the atoll. In addition, experience with the *Mike* shot at Ivy made clear that the relatively small amount of land above sea level at Bikini would soon be destroyed if all future tests were to be land-based.

But the operation of the proving ground, which stretched over more than two hundred miles of open ocean, posed logistical and administrative problems for Clarkson and the Joint Task Force. Transportation requirements alone challenged the capabilities of the peacetime military services in moving thousands of personnel and tons of equipment between the atolls and between the islands composing each atoll. Communication needs were equally demanding, not only in terms of installing telephone, cable, and radio facilities but also in managing the networks. At Enewetak Island, which served as the base of operations, and Parry Island, where most test devices were assembled, the task force had to arrange for construction of machine shops, laboratories, warehouses, repair facilities, barracks, offices, and port facilities.

As in the *Ivy* series, Clarkson organized the Joint Task Force by task groups. The scientific task group (7.1) under William E. Ogle, a Los Alamos scientist, was responsible for all aspects of assembling, positioning, and firing the devices. The group also installed all related test instrumentation and managed the radiological safety program. Each military service operated as a task group. The Army group (7.2) was responsible for ground security and all base facilities at Enewetak. The Navy task group (7.3) provided security for the thousands of square miles of ocean within the danger area, operated the interatoll ship transport system, provided shipboard technical facilities, and moved the firing targets to Bikini. The Air Force task force (7.4) supplied aircraft for cloud sampling and tracking, technical photography, and weapon effects on aircraft. A major Air Force assignment was operating a network of weather stations on islands in the central Pacific that reported, along with Air Force weather reconnaissance planes, to Weather Control at Enewetak. The Air Force task group also operated the interatoll air transport system and provided search and rescue operations. A fifth task group, not included in the *Ivy* operation, was staffed by Commission personnel from the Santa Fe operations office to supervise construction operations by Holmes & Narver.[52]

170

The unprecedented yields projected for some *Castle* shots were something the military task group could understand. Very early the Air Force task group concluded that the aircraft used in *Ivy* for sampling airborne debris from the detonations lacked the speed, range, and altitude capabilities needed to track and sample the downwind movement of particles from the *Castle* tests. Acquiring suitable aircraft and developing effective procedures for cloud sampling thus became matters of special concern. Both the Air Force and the Navy recognized the growing importance of accurate weather forecasting as the yield of the shots increased. Wind patterns, not only on the surface but at all altitudes up to 100,000 feet, could conceivably carry clouds of radioactive particles over inhabited islands as far away as Enewetak or other islands in the Marshalls, where rainfall might cause substantial fallout. Despite extensive experience gained by the military weather services in earlier Pacific tests, the relative lack of good data, compared with those available for continental land masses, posed a special challenge for the weatherman.[53]

Likewise the military task groups had no trouble appreciating the security implications of an operation as big and dispersed as *Castle*. Lacking the authority to censor mail or other private communications, the Joint Task Force recognized that it would be almost impossible to prevent some information about the tests from seeping to the outside world, despite extensive measures for indoctrinating personnel on the importance of security. The enormous magnitudes of the projected yields in themselves threatened security. The flash and sonic shock wave might be observable fifty or more miles away, and, depending on weather conditions, some fallout might occur at even greater distances. Samples of fallout material picked up by Soviet spy ships could reveal important information about the nature of the test. Thus, it was deemed essential to conceal any information about the precise time or location planned for any test. It was also vital to establish an exclusion or "danger" area large enough to preclude obvious intelligence gathering by the Soviet Union or other nations.[54]

The military task groups, however, were less impressed with operational considerations posed by the less familiar characteristics of nuclear tests, specifically the dangers of radiation. Radioactive fallout was considered a potential but unlikely hazard beyond the immediate vicinity of Bikini. This attitude resulted from the *Ivy* experience, where extraordinary precautions were taken at considerable expense and to little purpose when virtually no local fallout occurred from the *Mike* shot. Graves and Commission officials had some difficulty convincing the military to make comparable plans for aerial surveys and emergency evacuation plans for *Castle*.[55]

The absence of any pressing concern about fallout was clearly reflected in the definition of the "danger" zone established for *Castle*. Obviously the *Ivy* exclusion area had to be enlarged eastward to include Bikini, but the question was how much further east. Extending east and south of Bikini were two long chains of atolls that composed the Marshall Islands. With unfavorable precipitation and wind patterns, significant fallout on some of these islands was theoretically possible. For that reason, the scientific task group intended to exercise every reasonable precaution within the limits of weather forecasting to see that radioactive debris from *Castle* shots would move in a northeasterly direction, away from Enewetak and the Marshalls. Recognizing the margins for error, the scientists insisted that the military services establish a capability for emergency evacuation of Enewetak and of the Marshall atolls immediately east of Bikini. The nearest of these atolls were Rongelap and Ailinginae, which lay scarcely more than fifty miles east-northeast of Bikini. If the exclusion area had been established with the fallout hazard as the primary concern, these atolls might well have been included within its boundaries. But in fact the eastern border of the exclusion zone was established, on the recommendation of the Department of the Interior, precisely to exclude the two atolls on the grounds that inclusion would require evacuation of the inhabitants for the duration of *Castle*. Thus, the eastern boundary at 166° 16' east longitude was fixed primarily for security reasons, and to that extent it was misleading to refer to the zone as a "danger area."[56]

171

By early 1954 more than ten thousand military and scientific personnel were pushing to meet the March 1 deadline for the first shot in the *Castle* series. Much activity related to the twenty experimental programs to be carried out with the detonations. Although many of these were directly related to weapon diagnostics, six experimental programs were sponsored by the Department of Defense and concerned weapon effects.[57] Actual assembly of the first device could not be completed until February 17, after the USS *Curtiss* arrived at Enewetak under destroyer escort with the nuclear components.[58]

The three military task groups conducted operational rehearsals during February, concluding with a general task force rehearsal on the morning of February 23. All task groups participated as fully as possible to test security and emergency evacuation procedures, the cloud sampling system, and communications. The scientific task group tested the readiness of in-

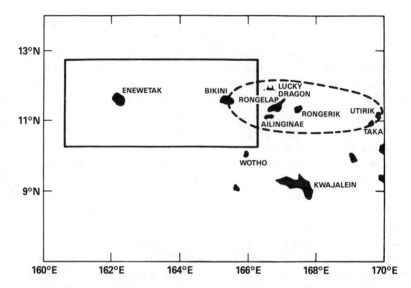

Figure 1. The exclusion area established for the March 1, 1954, *Castle Bravo* shot did not contain the Marshall atolls east of Bikini. The dotted lines indicate the path of the fallout cloud. Also shown is the position of the Japanese fishing vessel, the *Lucky Dragon*, at the time of the detonation.

strumentation and firing circuits as far as possible. Ogle encountered several technical problems that would have aborted an actual detonation on that day. During the last two days in February, small craft began evacuating the last 1,400 workmen and technicians from the island camps at Bikini to ships in the lagoon, which then moved southeast about thirty miles from ground zero. All usable equipment had been moved south to Eninman and Enyu Islands so that it would be the maximum distance (about twenty miles) from the point of detonation. Only the firing party remained ashore, in a specially constructed bunker on Enyu.[59]

## BRAVO

On February 22, 1954, the scientific task group under Ogle's direction completed the installation of the *Bravo* test device. Because it was to be the first shot in the series, the device had not been placed on a barge but in a small structure on a reef off Namu Island at the northwestern perimeter of the atoll. As the first test of a dry thermonuclear system, *Bravo* had special significance. Its performance would affect the subsequent agenda for *Castle* and could conceivably change the course of future development of thermonuclear weapons.

Once the final equipment checks were completed, the long countdown began to H-hour, at 6:54 a.m., local time, on March 1. The actual firing time now depended mostly upon weather conditions, which in the central Pacific could change significantly from hour to hour. Clarkson, Graves, Ogle, and several other task group commanders attended weather briefings at midnight and at 4:00 a.m. March 1. There was little concern about precipitation because the forecasts called for a relatively light cloud cover and only widely scattered showers. The group gave more attention to the ever changing complex of wind patterns at various altitudes. That morning surface and low-altitude winds were from the northeast while those above 20,000 feet tended to be from the west, an almost typical pattern. The variability and hence the cause for uncertainty lay in the wind pattern from 7,000 to 11,000 feet. At these altitudes the winds were light, but they had a decidedly northerly component. The more northerly the wind vectors, the more likelihood there was that the radioactive cloud would pass over the inhabited islands east of Bikini in the northern part of the Marshalls. At the moment the weather picture seemed favorable if not ideal. In fact weather conditions had been near perfect on February 27 and had deteriorated only slightly since then. To postpone the shot might well have pushed the beginning of the *Castle* series into a decidedly unfavorable period with the possibility of a long and expensive delay. At the end of the four o'clock briefing, Clarkson and his advisers decided to fire *Bravo* on schedule.[60]

173

From the moment of firing *Bravo* gave every sign of being a spectacular success. Even the crudest, most preliminary measurements indicated a yield far greater than the six megatons estimated as the most likely figure. Other and more ominous indications of large yield were the surprisingly high levels of radiation recorded. Aircraft approaching Eninman Island a few minutes after the detonation recorded radiation levels that would preclude immediate reopening of the airstrip. A few minutes later the firing party in the control bunker on Enyu Island reported rapidly rising radiation readings even after the doors of the bunker had been closed. Before eight o'clock the Navy ships, which carried the shore personnel from Bikini and served as floating laboratories and offices in the lagoon, began reporting dangerously high radiation levels. The ships, already thirty miles south of Bikini, were ordered to head south at best speed to a fifty-mile range, to activate washdown systems and to use maximum damage control measures. Radiation readings on the decks were as high as 5 roentgens per hour with maximum readings of 25 roentgens in deck drains. Personnel were forced to stay below decks in the stifling heat for more than four hours, until fallout declined to safe levels.

The ships were then ordered to return within ten miles of Bikini, but they could not enter the lagoon because of high levels of radioactivity. The firing party had been evacuated by helicopter from Enyu, and radiation levels on Eninman were too high to permit either landing on the island or operating the airstrip. Extensive physical damage to the equipment stored on Eninman and to other facilities on the island showed the enormous destructive power of *Bravo*. Examination of test data gave a yield of fifteen megatons, almost three times the most probable figure. Much more troublesome were the unexpectedly high radiation levels, which gave the Joint Task Force no choice but to double maximum permissible exposures of 3.9 roentgens for critical personnel such as helicopter pilots, flight deck personnel, and boatpool operators. Unable to enter the lagoon, the principal vessels of the Navy task group returned to Enewetak and prepared to resume operations at Bikini from a shipboard base of operations. Severe overcrowding of personnel on the ships, plus the unavailability of shore facilities, would hamper subsequent operations, but the earlier decision to use barge shots with instrumentation on buoys now seemed fortuitous.[61]

As radiation levels began to fall in the Bikini area late on March 1, reports of rapidly increasing readings trickled in from the atolls immediately to the east. These reports supported data collected by the Air Force cloud tracking teams that winds aloft were carrying the main body of *Bravo* debris in a direction just slightly north of east. As radiation levels climbed on March 2, the Air Force sent amphibious aircraft to Rongerik, 133 nautical miles from ground zero, to evacuate 28 military personnel who manned the weather station and other scientific equipment for the Joint Task Force. Later the same day the Navy task group dispatched destroyers from Bikini to rescue native populations on other atolls. Early the next morning a beaching party went ashore at Rongelap, only about one hundred nautical miles southeast of ground zero. Within hours the islanders had gathered their personal belongings for what they believed would be a temporary stay at Kwajalein and boarded the USS *Philip*, where radioactive fallout was removed by washing. Later in the day another 18 islanders were picked up at nearby Ailinginae Atoll before the ship proceeded overnight to Kwajalein. The second destroyer reached Utirik on March 4, and despite the heavy surf the Navy transferred 154 islanders by life raft and small boat to the USS *Renshaw*.[62]

At Kwajalein military physicians examined the islanders and treated them for radiation exposure. When the people from Utirik showed no signs of radiation injury, they were transported to another island in the Marshalls, where they stayed until they returned to their home island in June. The people from Rongelap and Ailinginae were less fortunate. Because they had been much closer to Bikini than had those from Utirik, they had received much more fallout. Average readings at Rongelap were 0.375 roentgens per hour, and some soil samples were as high as 2.2 roentgens. Taking into account the length of time the islanders remained on Rongelap after the fallout occurred, radiation safety personnel computed that the islanders received a whole-body gamma dose of 175 rad on Rongelap, 69 rad on Ailinginae, and 14 rad on Utirik. As could be expected from such exposures, the Rongelap islanders developed low blood counts and suffered some temporary loss of hair, skin lesions, and hemorrhages under the skin. In terms of blood count, the islanders suffered about the same degree of damage as did Japanese who were about 1.5 miles from ground zero at Hiroshima and Nagasaki. Equally distressing to the Rongelapese was that they were effectively exiled from their island home. Despite assurances of early repatriation, presumably by May 1955, the Rongelapese were not permitted to return to their home island until June 1957.[63]

## THE LUCKY DRAGON

The final and in many ways the most telling radiation incident from *Bravo* was not discovered until March 14, when a Japanese fishing vessel, the *Fukuryu Maru* (*Lucky Dragon*) *No. 5* arrived in Japan with all twenty-three members of the crew suffering from radiation exposure. The ship's log and interviews with the crew indicated that the vessel had been about eighty-two nautical miles from Bikini at the time of the *Bravo* shot, or just beyond the eastern boundary of the exclusion area. The crew had seen the flash and heard the detonation. Although the fishermen suspected that the blast was a nuclear weapon test, they did not know that tests were scheduled at that time or that there was any danger from fallout. In fact, only after skin irritation, nausea, and loss of hair developed on the return voyage to Japan did some of the crew begin to guess that the white powdery substance that had fallen from the clouds like snow was radioactive. Fearing that they might be detained by the Americans or even that their ship might be sunk if their presence near Bikini were detected, the crew members decided to give no hint of what had happened until they returned home. By the time the ship reached its home port of Yaizu, the effects of radiation had become so prominent and irritating that several members of the crew reported to the local hospital. The two who appeared most seriously injured were taken to the Tokyo University Hospital, and within a few days all the rest were in the hospital in Yaizu.[64]

 The Commission in Washington first learned of the *Lucky Dragon* tragedy on March 15 from commercial news reports. Without waiting to consult Strauss, who had already left for the Pacific to witness the second shot in the *Castle* series, the other three Commissioners asked Nichols to provide immediate technical assistance to the American ambassador in Tokyo and to the Japanese scientists and physicians treating the fishermen. John J. Morton, director of the Atomic Bomb Casualty Commission in Hiroshima, arrived in Tokyo on March 18 by military plane with a team of doctors and hematologists who had extensive experience in observing radiation effects in Hiroshima and Nagasaki survivors. Radiation physicists provided by the U.S. Air Force joined the team in Tokyo. The team examined the two crewmen in the university hospital and compiled full clinical

175

reports. The following week the team went to Yaizu, where they were permitted to board the *Lucky Dragon*, take some samples of fallout, examine some of the fish caught during the voyage, and use Geiger counters to measure radiation on the twenty-one crewmen in Yaizu.[65]

By this time the incident had received sensational treatment in the Japanese press. *Yomiuri Shimbun*, one of the largest Tokyo dailies, carried a series of frightening stories about "ashes of death." Another large Tokyo paper, *Shukan Asahi*, reported that the Japanese people were "terror-stricken by the outrageous power of atomic weapons which they [had] witnessed for the third time." *Asahi* editors speculated on the nature of the weapon tested and raised the possibility that the Americans had detonated a cobalt bomb, intentionally designed to spread poisonous radiation. Much to the discomfort of Strauss, Murray, and other security-minded Commission officials, *Shukan Asahi* also raised the possibility that a bomb using lithium had been tested.[66]

176

Although the Americans seemed sincerely to regret the incident and offered the Japanese full cooperation and assistance in treating the injured fishermen, the Commission was deeply concerned about what the remaining traces of radioactive ash on the ship might reveal about the design of *Bravo*. The Americans were especially sensitive about any evidence that might suggest the success of a dry thermonuclear weapon. For this reason the Americans refused to provide any information about weapon design or fallout content. The Japanese were especially offended by this refusal because they believed that the fishermen had been subjected to a new type of radiation and that it would be impossible to treat their injuries adequately without this information. The Japanese scientists and physicians simply could not accept the assurances of American experts that this information was unnecessary.

In this atmosphere of suspicion, the initial Japanese willingness to cooperate with the Americans quickly evaporated. When Merril Eisenbud, director of the Commission's health and safety laboratory in New York, arrived in Tokyo on March 21, he was greeted courteously but was not permitted to examine any of the fishermen. Only after much persuasion that urine tests were essential in determining the amount of ingested radiation received was he able to obtain samples from some patients. As the Japanese position stiffened, the Americans became more frustrated. They were convinced that the fishermen were not receiving the best possible treatment largely because, in Eisenbud's opinion, the Japanese did not wish to appear dependent on American help. The Americans were also disappointed that they were not permitted to make full biomedical studies of a group of people who had lived for two weeks in a high radiation environment. The Japanese, for their part, did not wish once again to be "guinea pigs" for American experiments.[67]

As the incident became a major issue in Japanese politics and continued to dominate the newspapers, the Japanese people reacted with an intense emotionalism. It was as if all the pent-up fears and anxieties engendered by Hiroshima and Nagasaki had suddenly burst into the open. For the third time in a decade Japanese civilians had been inflicted with the disfiguring and insidious injuries caused by nuclear weapons. The involvement of a fishing vessel was especially disturbing because it suggested that radioactive fallout from weapon tests might poison a major source of food for the Japanese people.

Both the State Department and John M. Allison, the American ambassador in Tokyo, at once sensed the full potential of the incident for damaging international relations. Allison had some success in conveying a sense of deep personal concern and in reassuring the Japanese government. He may also have been instrumental in keeping public criticism focused almost entirely on nuclear weapons while surprisingly little hostility was expressed against the United States. Within the Commission, however, there was much less evidence of compassion for the fishermen and more concern about the security and scientific implications. Eisenhower refused to say anything about the *Bravo* shot at his press conference on March 17, but he promised to answer questions the following week.[68]

From Enewetak Strauss sent Hagerty a report on *Bravo*. The tests, Strauss reported, were routine, but the results to date had been of great value and significance. The reports of radiation injuries to the Marshall Islanders were exaggerated, Strauss maintained, and claims about the fishermen were unverified. After describing how the danger area was established and patrolled, Strauss concluded: "The tests are continuing as planned." On March 24 the President relayed to the press only Strauss's statements about the exaggerated reports and deferred further comment until Strauss returned.[69]

After witnessing the second *Castle* shot, Strauss released a statement on March 31 summarizing unclassified portions of his report to the President. Going back to the first Soviet atomic explosion in 1949, Strauss justified the tests as part of the nuclear arms race and then set about to correct "exaggerated and mistaken characterizations" of the tests by the press. Although the statement did serve that purpose, it was cast in cold, almost imperious language that tended to belittle the implications of fallout on the Marshall Islanders or the Japanese fishermen. One clearcut misstatement in Strauss's report was that the *Lucky Dragon* "must have been well within the danger area." All available evidence was and is to the contrary. That Strauss chose to reject evidence of the ship's true position probably reflects his conviction, conveyed privately to Hagerty, that the *Lucky Dragon* was probably a "Red spy ship." Similar suspicions expressed earlier in Japan by Congressman Cole had outraged the Japanese.[70]

177

## COMPLETION OF CASTLE

For Clarkson and the Joint Task Force at Bikini the international implications of *Bravo* were more than overshadowed by the immediate logistical problems involved in completing the *Castle* series. The widespread devastation wrought by *Bravo* and the heavy fallout at Bikini required extensive changes in operational plans. *Bravo* had left Bikini all but uninhabitable so that logistical support and technical operations for the most part had to be based on Enewetak or on Navy ships assigned to Joint Task Force 7.3. The need to abandon even the limited base facilities at Bikini imposed a substantial transportation burden on shot preparations. Much equipment stored on Eninman Island before the *Bravo* shot now had to be loaded on ships and transported to Enewetak.

178     The disastrous fallout following *Bravo* required the imposition of much more stringent weather criteria for later shots in the series with attendant costly delays. *Romeo*, the second shot, was scheduled after *Bravo* for March 13 but could not be fired until March 27 because of unfavorable weather. Other shots in the series were also delayed as the frequency of favorable weather conditions declined during the spring. The exclusion area was greatly extended by adding a new sector centered on a point midway between Bikini and Enewetak and sweeping a huge semicircular area 450 miles in radius from west through north to the east. Both the new weather criteria and the expanded danger area recognized the unparalleled magnitude of both blast and fallout produced by thermonuclear weapons. The Nevada Proving Grounds, comprising about 500 square miles of desert, was a sizeable portion of the state, but it was miniscule compared to the exclusion area of 15,000 square miles at Enewetak for Operation *Ivy*. Then for *Bravo* the Commission had expanded the exclusion area to include Bikini and its size reached more than 67,000 square miles, or roughly the size of New England. After the *Bravo* fallout, the area was expanded to about 570,000 square miles, or twice the area of Texas. Thus, the testing of a single large thermonuclear weapon was beginning to require the exclusion of people from a significant portion of the earth's surface.

The most profound changes in *Castle* operations after *Bravo* resulted from the extraordinary nature of the technical information revealed by the tests. In addition to demonstrating the feasibility of a dry thermonuclear weapon, *Bravo* opened the way to other design improvements, of which the surprisingly high yield was only one indication. Following *Bravo* the sequence of shots was changed for a second time; some planned shots were canceled, and others were changed or added. Although such schedule changes in the middle of a series always introduced the possibility that some shots would not be used to the best advantages, the Los Alamos and Livermore scientists accepted the risk in order to capitalize on new opportunities for design improvement. As it turned out, four shots followed *Bravo* and *Romeo: Koon* on April 7, *Union* on April 26, *Yankee* on May 5, and *Nectar* on May 14.[71]

## THE NEW REALITY

Long before *Nectar* was fired, both the laboratories and the Commission realized that *Castle* had surpassed the most sanguine expectations for the series. In autumn 1953 the Joint Chiefs of Staff and the Commission had faced a given possibility of multiple failure. There had been no assurance that any shots would be successful; even if some devices were successful, they might not provide an emergency capability in megaton weapons that seemed essential to national security in meeting the Soviet challenge. And even if by chance one device offered that slim margin of emergency capability, there seemed even less chance that the Commission's production plants could turn out the special nuclear materials needed to meet stockpile requirements. For Strauss, Murray, Teller, and some Los Alamos scientists, the deadly race with the Soviet Union was very much in doubt. Possession of the hydrogen bomb alone could dangerously alter the balance in the Cold War.

179

But *Castle* changed all that. Even after *Bravo*, and certainly after *Romeo*, the future looked entirely different. It seemed that the American scientists had suddenly found the key to new realms of nuclear weapons. With a few notable exceptions, every new design principle incorporated in the *Castle* series seemed to work, often beyond the hopes of the most optimistic designers. By the time *Castle* was over, the United States had a choice of weapons for emergency capability. The feasibility of the dry thermonuclear weapon had been demonstrated so decisively that the Commission with confidence could cancel its contracts for cryogenics research for the wet device.

Equally important, the decision for dry weapons would immediately relieve the heavy pressure on the Commission's production complex. The plan to use a substantial portion of the neutrons in the Savannah River reactors for producing tritium could now be abandoned and that much more of the capacity devoted to plutonium formation. *Castle* also opened new possibilities for the more efficient use of all special nuclear materials, including lithium-6. Thus, even a heavy dependence on dry thermonuclear designs did not severely tax the capacity of the Alloy Development Plant, which was already producing beyond its design specifications at Oak Ridge.[72]

The design concepts demonstrated in *Castle* opened the way not only to multimegaton weapons of vast destructive capability but also to a whole "family" of thermonuclear weapons in a spectrum of yields, ranging from small tactical weapons to those matching the yields of much heavier and larger fission weapons already in the stockpile. In fact, *Castle* had rendered some stockpile weapons obsolete and seemed to be overtaking the utility of others. In explaining the significance of *Castle* to the general advisory committee on July 14, 1954, Bradbury went far beyond a description of specific design improvements. *Castle*, he said, had made possible a new philosophy for building the stockpile. Rather than try to achieve a balanced distribution of yields, Bradbury wanted both to concentrate on types in which large numbers of weapons would be needed and to develop the best possible weapons with optimum characteristics. This change alone would effectively enlarge the stockpile of ready weapons.

Isidor I. Rabi, the distinguished physicist who had replaced Oppenheimer as chairman of the committee, saw in Bradbury's remarks "a complete revolution" in nuclear weapons. Two years in the future, Rabi said, the stockpile would have little resemblance to what it had been two years earlier in 1952 before the *Mike* shot. These sweeping changes in weapon technology, Rabi suggested, reflected a growing maturity that would require a more sophisticated use of systems engineering. In this respect, the Sandia laboratories operated by Western Electric at Albuquerque could make an important contribution. The entire committee agreed that the performance of the Los Alamos scientists at *Castle* had been outstanding. Committee members sensed an increasing feeling of strength and experience that had been missing at Los Alamos a few years earlier.[73]

As for Livermore, the committee saw in the new laboratory an exciting potential for the future, despite the fact that the Livermore shots planned for *Castle* had proved no more successful than those at *Upshot-Knothole*. Both Rabi and John von Neumann, the metamathematician, agreed that the Livermore scientists had done a remarkable job of diagnosing data from *Castle* experiments. Herbert F. York and the young colleagues he had helped recruit for the new laboratory were talented and energetic. They were purposely concentrating on the more difficult, high-risk designs that they hoped would quickly establish the laboratory's reputation as second to none, including Los Alamos. While York and his associates reveled in the freedom and informality they enjoyed under Ernest Lawrence's protection, the more experienced and conservative members of the general advisory committee were concerned about the lack of organization at Livermore. Although York was scientific director, the laboratory still had no formal head. Teller still wielded an enormous and stimulating intellectual influence in the laboratory, but he could not give it the kind of stable management the committee thought it needed. York might be able to provide that stability, but he was young and relatively inexperienced. The committee hoped that the leadership question could be settled soon so that Livermore could reach its full potential.[74]

As results of the *Castle* series came in, the sense of accomplishment shared by the weapon laboratories and the Joint Task Force was certainly

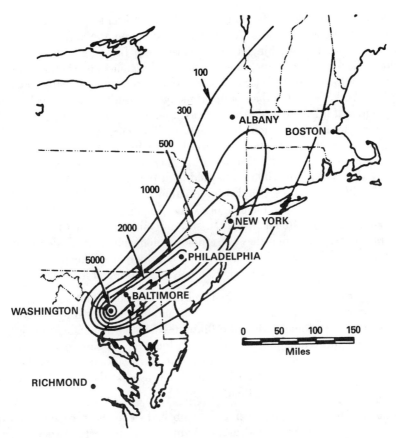

Figure 2. Fallout pattern from March 1, 1954. *Castle Bravo* detonation superimposed on the eastern United States.

justified. The weapon devices themselves were evidence of exceptional scientific ingenuity and imagination. The successful conduct of the tests, despite the unexpected difficulties created by *Bravo*, were a tribute to all three military services under Clarkson's command. But *Castle*, like *Upshot-Knothole*, did taint the sweet taste of success with a sickening reality: mankind had succeeded in producing a weapon that could destroy large areas and threaten life over thousands of square miles.

In fact, the hydrogen bomb was so enormous in its destructive power that it defied human description. The general public caught some sense of this dimension at the conclusion of the President's press conference on March 31, 1954, when in response to a question, Strauss said that the bomb could be made big enough "to take out any city," even New York. The remark made headlines in the nation's newspapers. More precise descriptions of the bomb's destructive power were not possible in unclassified statements. Much more frightening was General Fields's statement on the fallout effects of *Bravo* at a Commission meeting on May 24. If *Bravo* had been detonated at Washington, D.C., instead of Bikini, Fields illustrated with a diagram, the lifetime dose in the Washington-Baltimore area would have been 5,000 roentgens; in Philadelphia, more than 1,000 roentgens; in New York City more than 500, or enough to result in death for half the population if fully exposed to all the radiation delivered. Fallout in the 100-roentgen area, which might have been roughly comparable to the *Lucky Dragon* exposures, stretched northward in a wide band through New England toward the Canadian border. This diagram was classified secret and received very little distribution beyond the Commissioners.[75]

Although not privy to this information, knowledgeable scientists did not fail to grasp the significance of *Castle*. Eugene Rabinowitch, editor of the *Bulletin of the Atomic Scientists*, saw an ominous warning in the *Castle* results, especially when they were placed alongside John Foster Dulles's enunciation of "massive retaliation" as a principle of American foreign policy only a few months earlier. Rabinowitch expressed his alarm

> that statesmen (and ordinary citizens) discuss (and some of them advocate) "massive retaliation" as an answer to local aggression, at the very moment when the Bikini test should have taught them that "atomic retaliation" has become something no sane person should even consider as a rational answer to *any* political or military situation (short of direct Soviet aggression against the United States or Western Europe—if then).[76]

For four years the hydrogen bomb had been the preoccupation of hundreds of American scientists and engineers. In spring 1954 success had come in almost too heady a form. And just behind it were the frightening problems—some that threatened human existence itself—created by that success. The Atomic Energy Commission, the United States, and the world truly faced a new reality in the technology of war.

## CHAPTER 7

# NUCLEAR POWER
# FOR THE MARKETPLACE

In his testimony before the Joint Committee on July 31, 1953, Lewis Strauss was careful to avoid committing himself on any sticky issue arising from the development of civilian nuclear power and industry's potential role in it. In fact, Strauss told the committee, in the few weeks since he had become chairman, he had been able to do little more to prepare himself than to read portions of the transcript of the hearings that had begun on June 24 with Gordon Dean's farewell statement. The transcript presented new facts that, Strauss said, would cause him to approach the question of nuclear power with an open mind in the months ahead.[1]

Surely an open mind would be an asset in trying to cope with the tangle of policy issues produced by the sudden burst of interest in nuclear power. If nuclear energy were no longer to be an isolated, esoteric technology but a commodity in the American marketplace, significant adjustments had to be made in the nation's organic law and economic policies. But even in the more limited sphere of developing and introducing the new technology itself, Strauss and the Commission faced an impressive array of imponderables.

Many of these questions were related to the process of technological innovation: How does one best go about introducing a new technology into society? A familiar problem for large manufacturers, the management of technological innovation was hardly a common function for federal officials, except in the area of regulation. The application of radio broadcasting as a new technology in the United States, for example, did not depend upon promotional efforts by the federal government, although it did require federal regulation. The introduction of commercial air travel did require federal subsidies in several forms, but the technology itself was already in private hands. In the case of nuclear power, however, the entire technology was confined within the government in 1953. Thus, the Atomic Energy Commission faced an almost unprecedented situation in bringing nuclear reactor technology into the marketplace.

The Commission had already identified the principal vehicles of innovation. These included, first, the dissemination of technical information itself, a process severely restricted by classification rules and security procedures until the new Atomic Energy Act became law in 1954. Second, the Commission had an obvious responsibility to build experimental power reactors and to perform basic research on potential reactor materials and nuclear processes in the national laboratories. Third, it was conceivable that the Commission might build a full-scale nuclear power reactor that would provide private industry with realistic data on operational performance and costs. Fourth, the Commission might offer to assist private industry in designing, developing, and constructing full-scale power reactors. Lastly, the Commission could provide incentives for completely independent projects by private industry to construct and operate nuclear power plants. Most of these incentives were made available in the Atomic Energy Act of 1954.

## DISSEMINATING TECHNICAL INFORMATION

Ever since 1947 the Commission had been trying to establish effective channels for communicating technical data to private industry within the restrictions of the 1946 act. Some of the earliest efforts, which involved clearing a few corporate executives for access to classified data, were too small to be effective; but by 1950 some useful data were reaching industry through the Oak Ridge School for Reactor Technology and the distribution of classified technical reports. Later that same year, Charles A. Thomas had requested that industrial study teams, composed of engineers from equipment manufacturers and electric utilities, be given access to the Commission's reactor development files so that the companies could judge for themselves the feasibility of building nuclear power plants.[2] By spring 1953, three such studies had been completed, a fourth had been approved, and even more industrial groups had asked the Commission for similar arrangements.[3]

With good reason the Commissioners were reluctant to accept additional study agreements. Thomas and others had used them to promote the construction of dual-purpose reactors, which could lead to undesirable subsidies to industry by exposing the government to virtually open-ended commitments to purchase the plutonium produced in such reactors at the very time that the Commission's plutonium production capacity was beginning to catch up with military requirements. As Lawrence R. Hafstad, the director of reactor development, wrote the commissioners in September 1953, "the blunt fact seems to be that we are now too late for the 'dual purpose' approach . . . and too early for the 'power only' approach." In Hafstad's opinion, reactor technology simply was not yet well enough developed to justify large investments of private money. There was a limit to what industry could learn from paper studies, and more studies were unlikely to produce new information.[4] Not until the new act was passed in 1954 would it be possible to open new channels of technical information for industry.

## SEARCH FOR A PROGRAM

In opposing the encouragement of industrial study groups, Hafstad recognized that the Commission would have to respond in some other way to the growing public demand for rapid development of civilian nuclear power. A veteran administrator of government research and development projects, Hafstad had directed the Johns Hopkins Applied Physics Laboratory, which had produced the proximity fuse and other military technology during World War II. After the war he had served with Vannevar Bush as executive secretary of the research and development board in the Department of Defense before becoming director of the Commission's reactor development division early in 1949. Hafstad's ability and reputation as a physicist had enabled him to hold his own with the prestigious and influential members of the general advisory committee while his down-to-earth, practical approach as an engineer had assured him good relationships with the Commissioners and the staff.[5]

185

Since 1950 Hafstad had been steering a middle course between those who advocated a government-dominated reactor program, concentrating on military projects, and those who urged an accelerated civilian power program, relying heavily on private industry for reactor development. Hafstad had been caught in the cross-fire between these opposing views before, but never had his position been more uncomfortable than it was during the summer of 1953. While executives from large corporations spoke confidently of private industry's ability to take over development of civilian nuclear power at the public hearings before the Joint Committee in June and July, members of the committee openly questioned industry's willingness to invest substantially without some clear indication that nuclear power was economically feasible. Democratic members of the Joint Committee, led by Congressmen Chet Holifield and Melvin Price, pressed the Commission impatiently for a vigorous development effort that would lead to operating a full-scale nuclear power plant within a few years. At the end of the hearings Chairman Cole, in an essentially bipartisan action, requested the Commission formulate "a three to five year program consisting of specific research and development projects—perhaps including construction items."[6]

## REACTORS FOR THE MILITARY

Hafstad faced several difficulties in attempting to respond to the committee's request. The Commission's reactor development program was already heavily committed to military propulsion reactors for the Navy and Air Force. The military projects not only preempted a substantial portion of available funds as well as scarce resources in the national laboratories but also tended to preoccupy the reactor development staff, to the detriment of the civilian power program. Members of Hafstad's staff were sometimes intimidated by the uphill fight against the established military projects. So strong was the military emphasis, in fact, that the Commission commonly referred to the remainder of its reactor development projects as the "civilian power program."

186

The strong military orientation of the reactor program was largely the result of Captain Hyman G. Rickover's extraordinary impact as chief of the naval reactors branch. Since 1948, when Rickover had succeeded in establishing himself as both a Commission official and head of the Navy's nuclear propulsion program, he had carried within the Commission's headquarters as much weight as some division directors and certainly more than any other branch chief. Totally committed to the task of bringing nuclear propulsion to the fleet, Rickover worked relentlessly to assemble within his personal control all the elements of an effective development program. By skillfully capitalizing on his dual function for the Commission and the Navy, Rickover had won for himself an unusual degree of independence from both organizations before Hafstad became director of the division. Although Rickover was careful always to comply with the formal procedures of the bureaucratic system, he took full advantage of the inattention, indifference, or mistakes of other officials to build between the Commission and the Navy an independent and (except for funding) self-sufficient development enterprise.[7]

An important step in this struggle for autonomy was Rickover's success in acquiring Commission laboratories whose entire mission was tied to his program. In 1949 and 1950 he had had no choice but to use Argonne National Laboratory to generate the scientific and technical data needed to fix the basic design of the first submarine reactor, but by 1953 he had transferred almost all work to the Bettis Laboratory, which the Commission established near Pittsburgh exclusively for the navy project. In 1950 Rickover had helped the reactor development staff to terminate an unpromising project that General Electric had been pursuing to develop a power-breeder reactor and had used this opportunity to bring the company into the navy program as a second major development contractor. With General Electric and its staff of experienced engineers and managers came the Knolls Atomic Power Laboratory, which the company had established with Commission funds as a center for developing nuclear power reactors. Although the company fought to retain at least a portion of Knolls for this purpose, Rickover eventually succeeded in excluding all activities not related to his project.[8]

Although Westinghouse and General Electric performed their work under Commission contracts, all technical supervision and much contract administration came from Rickover's office in Washington. Rickover's staff even followed the work of Westinghouse and General Electric subcontractors and took a direct interest in negotiating and administering procurement contracts for critical materials. On major policy or budget issues, Rickover had the initiative; Hafstad and the Commissioners usually endorsed his recommendations. Even on routine administrative actions, the Commission staff learned to give Rickover's requests special attention.

Administrative control was not an end in itself for Rickover; it assured him an effective voice in technical matters. In the early years Rickover had devoted an enormous amount of his time and effort to building a staff that was fully competent in nuclear science and technology. He insisted that members of his staff be prepared to review every technical decision by Westinghouse, General Electric, or any other contractor and report back with comments or criticisms for further study. Rickover focused unrelentingly on the technical unknowns or obstacles that stood in the way of successful development, and this focus took precedence over organizational relationships or the status of individuals. Rickover did not relieve contractors of their responsibilities for producing according to their contracts, but he never hesitated to intervene at any point to make sure that wrong decisions and mistakes were not threatening scheduled programs. Rickover and his staff were as unyielding and unforgiving as was the technology they were attempting to master.[9]

This highly aggressive and uncompromising style of management did not win Rickover many friends among the reactor development staff, laboratory directors, field managers, naval officers, or company officials; but his extraordinary performance against the most challenging schedules made him a force that could not be denied. Rickover himself had played a part in establishing a Navy commitment to have a nuclear submarine ready for sea by January 1, 1955. This goal required him to accomplish in five years with a completely new technology a task that often had taken as many as fifteen years in the Navy. By eliminating small reactor experiments and mock-ups, Rickover had dared to strike out simultaneously to build land-based prototypes of two types of propulsion systems: the Mark I version of

187

the submarine thermal reactor, which Westinghouse developed at Bettis, and the Mark A version of the submarine intermediate reactor, which General Electric developed at Knolls. Because Mark I and Mark A had the same configurations and power capabilities of the proposed shipboard plants, their successful operation would provide some assurance that the shipboard units would work. Fighting against time, Rickover and his staff had the Mark I prototype operating at the Commission's Idaho test site in March 1953. Several months of testing revealed no major flaws, and on June 25 Mark I began a full-power test that Rickover continued until the plant had generated enough power to carry a submarine across the Atlantic. This magnificent achievement, perhaps more than any other single event, convinced government officials and members of the Joint Committee that nuclear power was a reality. Now it seemed possible that with some luck and hard work, Rickover might actually have the Mark II plant operating in the submarine *Nautilus* by late 1954. At the same time, General Electric was making good progress on the Mark A prototype at West Milton, New York, and Bettis had already started engineering studies for the submarine advanced reactor, which would include many improvements over the *Nautilus* plant.[10]

188

Although the Navy project caused Hafstad some headaches, it was by no means so troubling as the joint effort with the Air Force to develop nuclear propulsion systems for military aircraft. Since 1946 some Air Force officers had dreamed of using nuclear power to provide essentially unlimited range for a bomber carrying nuclear weapons. During the overly exuberant early days at Oak Ridge, aircraft companies under Air Force contracts were eager to design airframes and jet engines for such a plane even before any concept of the nuclear power plant had been developed. Designing a reactor with sufficient power and reliability and at the same time light enough and with sufficient shielding against radiation proved no easy task. By 1953 the Commission was spending more than $17 million per year on two types of propulsion systems: one by General Electric, in which air from the turbines would be heated directly in the reactor core, and a second at Oak Ridge National Laboratory, which would use as a heat source a reactor fueled with a liquid mixture of fused salts containing uranium. Liquid sodium would carry heat from the reactor to a heat exchanger. The Truman budget for fiscal year 1954 proposed a substantial increase that would have brought total expenditures by the Commission and the Air Force close to $54 million per year. The Eisenhower Administration, in its quest for budget reductions, had cut the project back to $15.3 million in Commission funds and $9.4 million from the Air Force, figures not much below actual costs in the previous year. The cuts moved the several projects back from pilot plants and prototypes to fundamental experiments.

The continuing lack of coherence in the aircraft program proved that there was nothing magical about the organization of the Navy project. In a deliberate effort to copy the Rickover pattern, the Air Force and the Commission had set up a joint project with an Air Force officer, Brigadier General Donald J. Keirn, to serve in a dual capacity much as Rickover did. By summer of 1953, however, it was evident that Keirn, despite his considerable abilities and experience, had probably taken the reins too late to bring order out of chaos. Lacking both a clear focus and a promising technical base, the aircraft program was doomed to continuing frustration.[11]

## REACTOR EXPERIMENTS

In responding to the Joint Committee's request for a short-term commitment on civilian power reactors, Hafstad had to consider the reactor experiments that the Commission was already planning or building. The problem was that, although some of these projects had been started years earlier, none could possibly lead to an economic power reactor in three to five years, no matter how much the Joint Committee insisted on quick results. In fact, as Hafstad pointed out to the Commissioners in September 1953, five years was too short a period for effective planning, much less constructing reactors.[12] The reactor experiments that the Commission had first authorized in 1948 were only the beginning of a long-term development process. In one sense, these experiments represented a judicious and commendably conservative approach to nuclear power. By building a series of small, relatively inexpensive reactor experiments, each using a theoretically promising approach to the design of a power reactor, the Commission hoped that it could evaluate the relative advantages of several designs before heavily committing to constructing full-scale reactors. Approaching innovation on a broad front in the early stages of development was precisely the strategy that Vannevar Bush and James B. Conant had advocated with stunning success in producing fissionable material for the first atomic weapon.

Despite the compelling inner logic of the broad front approach, it had substantial disadvantages for the Commission in summer 1953. Most obviously, none of these experiments could conceivably produce significant amounts of power. With luck, one of them might justify starting work on an actual power reactor in five or ten years. Coupled with the broad front, the experimental approach suggested to the uninitiated timidity and indecisiveness within the Commission. Second, the Commission's approach reinforced certain Joint Committee and public misconceptions about the nature of technological development. For example, some thought that a small reactor experiment would tell the engineers most of what they needed to know to build a power reactor; however, although the experiment often produced valuable clues, it almost never revealed a clear pathway to success. The

189

popular assumption, frequently expressed in Joint Committee hearings, was that the progression from reactor experiment, to pilot plant, and then to full-scale power reactor was not only direct but automatic. As many reactor engineers had already learned, even the successful operation of a reactor experiment did not necessarily warrant further development.

These misconceptions originated in another popularly accepted assumption: the familiar pathways of development in chemical engineering provided an adequate model for reactor technology. In the past, engineers had enjoyed notable success in translating the results of an experiment in a chemistry laboratory into an efficient industrial process. In reactor technology, however, the phenomena involved were just as complicated, and the number of nontechnical variables was much larger. As in chemical engineering, scientific data were essential to developing reactor technology, but they were far from sufficient. Still in its early stages, reactor technology also required a large measure of creative and imaginative engineering to make the transition from experimental reactor to proven reactor.

Most Commission experience since 1947 testified to these limitations of the reactor experiment. The most publicized effort of this type by 1953 was the experimental breeder reactor, which Walter H. Zinn and his Argonne team had built at the Commission's Idaho test site. The experiment, in generating token amounts of electric power in late 1951, had first suggested to the American public that nuclear power was imminent. The experiment also demonstrated that breeding was at least theoretically possible. But the reactor, despite its success as an experiment, did not open the way to a practical power source. The facility verified scientific principles; it did not address the host of extraordinarily difficult engineering problems involved in extracting useful energy from a power source of very high density with a liquid-metal coolant. In 1952, following the successful operation of the experiment, the Commission had approved simultaneous studies of an intermediate-scale breeder by Argonne and a full-scale breeder by the California Research and Development Company. The Commission, however, was unable to convince the Bureau of the Budget that this next step was likely to lead to concrete results, and the plan was dropped.[13]

The efforts of Alvin Weinberg and his staff at Oak Ridge to develop a homogeneous reactor had experienced a similar fate. Oak Ridge had built a homogeneous experiment, which in 1953 had generated a few watts of electric power and had demonstrated the principle of operation. The distinctive advantage of such a reactor was that it avoided the expensive process of fabricating fuel elements, moderator, control rods, and other high-precision core components by placing a fluid mixture of fissionable material, moderator, and coolant in a tank of proper configuration to produce a critical mass. Energy could be extracted simply by pumping the fluid through external heat exchangers, and, theoretically at least, the reactor could be refueled by continuously reprocessing the fluid without shutting down the system. Thus, the system held out the possibility of very low costs and high efficiency in heat transfer. In the eyes of many nuclear scientists and engineers these advantages made the homogeneous reactor potentially the most promising of all types under study, but once again the experiment did not reveal how the tricky problems of handling a highly radioactive and corrosive fluid were to be resolved. Weinberg's next step was not to be a power reactor but merely another experiment of slightly larger size with design improvements that might make continuous operation possible.[14]

Of all the promising reactor types, the Commission's laboratories had the most experience with water reactors, in which either ordinary water or heavy water served as both moderator and coolant. Argonne had taken the lead in developing heavy-water reactors, not for power generation, but for plutonium production at Savannah River. The high cost of heavy water and the availability of enriched uranium from the gaseous-diffusion plants, however, did not make this type attractive for power generation. Of much greater interest was the light-water reactor, which Weinberg and others had suggested at Oak Ridge during World War II. The materials testing reactor, developed cooperatively by Oak Ridge and Argonne, used the light-water system, and Rickover had adopted light water for the Mark I prototype (and, of course, for the Mark II as well).[15]

191

In all these light-water applications, the moderator-coolant was kept under pressure to prevent boiling, and special care was taken to design reactors so that no local boiling would occur. There was some concern among engineers that boiling within the reactor might either cause voids, "hot spots," that would affect reactivity or lead to oscillations that could produce destructive power surges. In his quest for a reliable propulsion system, Rickover had selected the pressurized water system for the aircraft carrier reactor as well as for Mark I, Mark II, and the submarine advanced reactor. The decision by the Eisenhower Administration to convert the carrier reactor into a civilian system meant that the Commission's first full-scale power plant would use pressurized water.[16]

Logic suggested, however, that a boiling-water reactor would have a higher thermal efficiency than a pressurized system. For that reason it was only a matter of time before someone investigated this possibility. Early in 1950 Samuel Untermyer at Argonne suggested that steam formation in the core of a light-water reactor during a power excursion might actually shut down the reactor. If this were true, it might be possible to build a power reactor actually using boiling as a control mechanism. A series of experiments at Argonne with electrically heated fuel elements immersed in water gave promising results on heat transfer and steam formation. To provide

data on the effect of steam voids on instability Untermyer proposed construction of a reactor experiment at the Idaho test site. Joseph R. Dietrich
and others at Argonne designed the boiling reactor experiment, called
Borax-I, that operated successfully at just about the time the Joint Committee issued its request for a reactor plan in summer 1953. Borax-I showed
not only that a boiling reactor had a high degree of inherent safety in its
ability to shut itself down, but also that it could operate stably.[17] When the
Commission came to formulating the five-year reactor program, the boiling
water reactor would certainly be an option to consider.

## THE ROLE OF INDUSTRY

192

The centerpiece of the Commission's five-year program as it developed in
autumn of 1953 was to be the pressurized-water reactor, which Murray and
Dean had managed to salvage from the demise of the carrier propulsion
project. With Eisenhower's approval and the National Security Council's
acquiescence, the Commission had decided in June that the quickest way
to build a full-scale nuclear power plant would be to give Rickover the
tasks of stripping the naval features from the carrier propulsion project,
which Westinghouse had already started at Bettis, and developing the basic
design for power purposes.

The decision, however, was inherently too controversial to be made
so easily. When Strauss succeeded Dean as chairman just two weeks later,
the issue was ripe for reopening, especially since the Commission had not
yet announced the decision. The first move for reconsideration came from
the reactor development staff itself at a Commission meeting on July 9,
1953. Hafstad's assistants made a plea for a reactor that would be large
enough to have a chance of being economical. Rickover countered that
argument by insisting that the power rating was limited by the size of the
pressure vessel, which approached the limits of power plant technology at
that time. He could not, however, respond so easily to the implications of
a letter that arrived from the Joint Committee by special messenger during
the course of the meeting. In the letter Cole notified the Commission that
his appeal to the House Appropriations Committee for construction funds
for the pressurized-water reactor had been approved. Thus, in Cole's
words, the project had been "*initiated* by the Congress," and for that reason
the Joint Committee had "a more than usual interest" in it. Cole also expressed concern about the "heavy emphasis" on naval aspects. The implications were clear: the Joint Committee intended to see that the Commission built a full-scale power reactor and that Rickover did not dominate it
for his own purposes.[18]

Rickover interpreted the letter as a challenge to his own role in the project, but he told Murray on July 13 that he was more concerned about rumors of industry opposition. Murray confirmed this report in a call to Willis Gale, chairman of the Commonwealth Edison Company of Chicago. Murray held firm on the Commission's decision to build the reactor under Rickover's direction, but he did invite Commonwealth Edison and other utilities to join the project. Gale made it clear that he was not interested in sending a few engineers to work under Rickover, but he was enthusiastic about Murray's earlier suggestion that several other electric utilities join Commonwealth Edison in building a nuclear power plant. At the moment, however, Gale and his associates seemed much more interested in a heavy-water reactor than in the Commission's proposal. [19]

Murray still believed that no one company could afford to build a nuclear power plant without some hope that it would be economically competitive, but he had to admit that Gale was assembling an impressive group of companies. The Nuclear Power Group, as it came to be called, included some of the largest electric utility companies in the nation: the American Gas and Electric Service Corporation of New York City, the Pacific Gas and Electric Company of San Francisco, and the Union Electric Company of St. Louis. Also part of the group was the Bechtel Corporation of San Francisco, one of the nation's largest construction firms for conventional power plants.

193

Although Murray was willing to entertain serious proposals from such groups, he was not ready to permit vague expressions of interest to undermine the Commission's decision to build a pressurized-water reactor under Rickover's control. To ratify that decision, Murray urged Strauss to issue a press release, preferably one from the White House. After Moscow radio on August 19 revealed the detonation of *Joe 4*, Murray urged the Commission not to lose the enormous propaganda advantage of responding to the Soviet saber rattling with a declaration of the United States' intention to develop nuclear power for peaceful purposes. Strauss, however, continued to procrastinate, perhaps as a caution against Murray's exuberance, perhaps to get a better feel for the Commission's policy stance during his first weeks as chairman. Strauss himself told Murray that he was simply trying to make sure that the plant was built at minimum cost. [20]

While Murray continued to press the Commission to announce its decision on the pressurized-water reactor, he also pursued discussions with the Nuclear Power Group in hopes that it would join the project. Murray could do this with the Commission's blessing following approval of a study agreement with the group on August 20. Further discussions with Philip Sporn of American Gas and Electric encouraged Murray to believe that the Nuclear Power Group might agree to build and operate the reactor at a site near Portsmouth, Ohio, where the facility might provide some of the enormous quantities of electric power needed to operate the new gaseous-diffusion plant. He predicted that, once the Commission announced its decision to build the plant, the Nuclear Power Group would offer to meet one-third of the costs for the steam system and turbogenerator, which might total $10 million.[21]

## NUCLEAR POWER AND NATIONAL SECURITY

By mid-October rumors of the Commission's decision were beginning to leak to the press, and Strauss could no longer put off Murray's insistence upon an announcement. In a dramatic speech before an electric utility convention in Chicago on October 22, 1953, Murray announced that the Commission would build a full-scale power reactor capable of producing at least 60,000 kilowatts of electricity. The drama of the speech, however, came, not from this statement of fact, but rather from Murray's effort to put the decision in context. He took the occasion to reiterate every argument he had used over the previous six months when internally discussing nuclear power policy and the role of industry. Attaining economical nuclear power, in Murray's opinion, was just as vital to national security as the United States' preeminence in nuclear weapons. Friendly nations were counting on the United States not only to protect them from Soviet aggression but also to supply them with nuclear power technology. In fact, Murray pointed out, some of these nations (he did not name Belgium and South Africa) provided the United States with uranium ores essential for building the nuclear arsenal. "Unless we embark on an all-out attack on our nuclear power program immediately, we may be deprived of foreign uranium ores." Thus "the atomic arms race and the nuclear industrial power race [were] strangely related."[22]

Having evoked this starkly pragmatic argument, Murray explained the background for the Commission's decision going back to the nuclear power statement in spring 1953. Murray assured his audience that as a business man in private life, no one was more anxious than he to end "nationalization" of atomic energy. But he was convinced, along with most of the Commission, that the federal government had to build the first full-scale plant; only then would the skills and competitive motivations of private industry be effective. Thus, the Commissioners' decision to build the pressurized-water reactor was only an interim measure, merely a first step toward establishing the new industry. In the meantime, the pressurized-water reactor would be America's answer to the recent Soviet thermonuclear test. "For years," Murray concluded, "the splitting atom, packaged in weapons has been our main shield against the Barbarians—now, in addition, it is to become a God-given instrument to do the constructive work of mankind." *U.S. News and World Report* summarized the message for the busy reader:

Atomic power for industry is on the way. An international race for supremacy has started. Britain, with one atomic-power project, is in the race. Russia probably is starting. Now the U.S. is jumping in. Plan is for a full-scale atom-power plant at a big atomic-materials center. If it works, as expected, U.S. will keep its atomic lead.

*Time* called the announcement "a new phase" of the atomic age, and the *New York Times Magazine* forecasted the age of atomic power.[23]

## THE FIVE-YEAR PROGRAM

By the time Murray delivered his Chicago speech, the Commissioners were already well on their way to formulating the five-year development program that the Joint Committee had requested. At the policy conference at White    195
Sulphur Springs in September 1953, Hafstad had presented the full scope of the issues that the Commission faced in developing nuclear power for the marketplace. Hafstad's alternatives ranged all the way from a plan for developing nuclear power by private industry, using as much as $200 million in federal funds over the five-year period, to a government-controlled program centered in the Commission's national laboratories.[24]

As Murray's speech revealed, Commission thinking was much closer to the second extreme than to the first. Three projects in the five-year program represented continuing efforts by the Commission's national laboratories and were completely under government control: the fast-breeder and boiling-water experiments at Argonne and the homogeneous reactor experiment at Oak Ridge. One concept, the sodium-graphite reactor, would be pursued by North American Aviation, Incorporated, as the only example of a private development effort financed by the Commission. The fifth project, the pressurized-water reactor, was government-sponsored and directed, with the degree of participation by private industry to be determined by the response to the Commission's invitation of December 7, 1953, for proposals to invest in the project.[25]

The classified report of more than 130 pages, which the Commission delivered to the Joint Committee in February 1954, outlined in detail the rationale for selecting the design concepts to be developed. The report included reasonably candid evaluations of the status of each concept. The pressurized-water reactor seemed most likely to be successful in the short term, by the end of 1957, but it offered a poor long-term prospect of producing economic nuclear power. Argonne's next step beyond the Borax tests would be an experimental boiling-water reactor to be built at the Illinois laboratory. Because the concept was new, the boiling-water reactor would not be ready for large-scale testing for at least five years, but it showed more promise of achieving competitive power than the pressurized-water reactor. The first step toward the sodium-graphite reactor was to be the sodium reactor experiment, which North American would build at the company's site in Santa Susana, California. Because, like the pressurized-water reactor, the sodium reactor experiment could take advantage of relatively well-developed technology, the experiment was likely to prove successful in the short term but did not hold great promise for generating economic nuclear power. As for the fast breeder, Argonne had scaled down its plan for developing medium- and full-size plants simultaneously and had decided to build a second experimental breeder reactor at the Idaho testing station, where the first breeder was still operating. Oak Ridge intended to take a similarly modest step toward a homogeneous reactor by building a second experiment at the Tennessee laboratory. Both the homogeneous and fast-breeder projects were unlikely to result in significant breakthroughs in the short term, but there was widespread agreement that these types were the most promising approaches to the commercial power plants of the future. The Commission expected to spend $8.5 million per year on research and development, while the five experimental plants would cost $200 million.[26]

196

## SHIPPINGPORT

A careful review of the proposed five-year program on February 5, 1954, led the Joint Committee to the conclusion that the plan was sound and deserved support. The only reservation concerned the wisdom of building the pressurized-water reactor as a full-scale plant when it had no chance of generating economic power. Holifield wanted to make certain that, if the project were terminated, Hafstad would not be tempted to substitute one of the more promising reactors. Hafstad assured him that other types, such as the homogeneous or boiling-water reactors, although more promising in the long run, were not ready for full-scale construction at that time. Holifield found more reassurance in the fact that Rickover had now scaled down the estimated cost of the pressurized-water reactor to $52 million, but he was still concerned that some scientists who opposed the Commission's decision to build the reactor might later accuse the Joint Committee of wasting the money on what the members knew was going to be an uneconomic reactor. With Hafstad's assurance that the project was sound, Holifield and the committee were willing to proceed, but they wanted to review the situation again after the responses to the Commission's invitation for proposals from industry had been evaluated.[27]

Even before the February 15 deadline, the Commission had eliminated the Nuclear Power Group, which in November had submitted an offer to provide trained personnel, build the conventional electrical generating portions of the plant, and operate the plant. The estimated financial contribution by the group, however, was so small that the Commission had no choice but to reject it. With that rejection, the last hope for construction of the nation's first commercial nuclear power plant by private industry disappeared.[28]

Of the nine offers received by the February deadline, the one from the Duquesne Light Company of Pittsburgh was clearly superior. The company offered to build a new plant on a site it owned in Shippingport, Pennsylvania, on the Ohio River twenty-five miles northwest of Pittsburgh. At no cost to the government, Duquesne offered to provide the site, build the turbogenerator plant, and operate and maintain the entire facility. The company also agreed to assume $5 million of the cost of developing and building the reactor, which Westinghouse would design and the Commission would own. For the steam delivered by the reactor the company was willing to pay the equivalent of eight mills per kilowatt-hour, a comparatively high price. Hafstad's staff estimated that over the course of the five-year contract Duquesne's contribution would be more than $30 million, compared to $24 million for the next most attractive proposal. Also, under the Duquesne offer the Commission could cancel the contract at any time without incurring termination charges.[29]

As General Manager Nichols told the Joint Committee on March 12, 1954, the Duquesne proposal was almost too good to believe. He was convinced that the company had extended itself to make an attractive offer simply because Duquesne wanted to get in on the ground floor in nuclear power. Patiently Nichols reviewed every project in the five-year plan and assured the committee that only the pressurized-water reactor was ready for full-scale construction. The decision to build the plant, however, did not mean that the other projects would be neglected. The decision, Nichols said, might actually spur the other projects to new efforts, and he did not rule out the possibility that in another year another approach might be ready for full-scale construction.

In the course of the discussion Representative Carl Hinshaw, the only engineer on the Joint Committee, raised a new and intriguing question: Had the Commission considered the international implications of the five-year program? As Murray had suggested in his Chicago speech, the Commission was developing power reactors not just for domestic use but also for friendly nations abroad. Had the Commission thought about what type of reactor would be best suited for export? Smyth replied that the Commission had discussed the subject without coming to any conclusion, but he did make some personal observations after determining that it was permissible to speak on classified matters. The facts were that the United States could offer to export either heavy-water or light-water reactors under the Atoms-for-Peace program. Heavy-water reactors might be more attractive to European nations because they could probably obtain supplies of heavy

197

water and natural uranium without depending on the United States. If, however, the United States selected light-water reactors for export, the Commission would have to supply the slightly enriched uranium fuel because no European countries were likely to make the heavy financial commitment necessary to build an enrichment plant. One advantage, then, of using light-water reactors for export, Smyth noted, was that the United States could control both the supply of uranium fuel elements and also reprocessing of spent fuel. This leverage could be important in assuring reliable safeguards against the diversion of fissionable material.[30]

## NUCLEAR POWER AND ATOMS FOR PEACE

While the Joint Committee continued to press the Commission on developing commercial power reactors, the Eisenhower Administration was exerting similar demands from the sanctuary of the National Security Council. In the summer of 1954 the council's planning board, on which Roy Snapp represented the Commission, began to formulate the specific measures for following through on the President's Atoms-for-Peace proposal. Efforts to create the International Atomic Energy Agency and to organize an international conference on the peaceful uses of atomic energy were high on the list. But the planning board expected nuclear power to offer a practical goal for international cooperation.

Snapp and his colleagues recognized that economic nuclear power was still at least a decade away and that most countries had neither the trained personnel nor the resources to support its development. It did seem feasible, however, that the United States could provide small experimental or training reactors with limited amounts of slightly enriched uranium as fuel. By suggesting that experience with research reactors was an essential step in achieving technical capability for building power reactors, the United States could gain time for resolving the difficult policy questions involved in selling power reactors abroad.[31]

As Strauss pointed out to the National Security Council on August 12, 1954, the United States could not avoid the issue for very long. Countries with critical shortages of power, like Sweden and Japan, might want to move quickly toward nuclear energy. How would the United States decide which countries would receive the limited assistance that the United States would be able to provide? And how could the United States prevent the diversion of fissionable material produced in power reactors to nonpeaceful purposes?[32]

To answer these and other questions the planning board appointed a subcommittee under Snapp's direction to draft a policy statement. Drawing heavily upon the Commission's staff for ideas and opinions, Snapp completed his paper before the end of 1954. Cautionary in tone, the statement first contained the warning voiced by Commissioner Murray and members of the staff that the operation of research reactors was not an essential step in the development of power reactors as the planning board's August draft had implied. Although a research reactor in a foreign country might help to train scientists and engineers in nuclear technology, the research reactor itself would not reveal much about the design of a power reactor. Second, Snapp and the Commission took a dim view of building a full-scale power reactor, like the Shippingport plant, in a foreign country; such a plant would be neither economical nor reliable for continuous and fault-free operation. In fact, the project might do the cause of nuclear power more harm than good.[33]

Throughout fall 1954 and into winter 1955, however, the Commission had to contend with the persistent hope expressed by State Department officials and other members of the planning board that nuclear power might be the key to a successful Atoms-for-Peace program. No sooner did the Commission deflate one idea than the planning board came up with another. By the time Snapp's policy paper reached the National Security Council itself, it advocated, not the construction of a Shippingport reactor abroad, but a cooperative effort by scientists and engineers from friendly nations to construct an experimental power reactor in the United States.[34]

Strauss rose in the National Security Council on February 10, 1955, to oppose this idea. Such a project would result in hopeless confusion, a "tower of Babel"; but even worse, it would give foreign scientists access to the most advanced United States designs for power reactors. This argument appealed to Secretary of Defense Wilson, who hoped that such advantages would be reserved for American industry. On the other side were Secretary of State Dulles and United Nations Ambassador Henry Cabot Lodge, who, although not questioning the Commission's technical appraisal of the idea, expressed concern that the Administration still had not come up with one solid project that would clearly support the President's commitment to nuclear power in his United Nations speech. Strauss argued that the training and assistance programs already launched would do much more for Atoms for Peace than would the experimental reactor. Eisenhower agreed that the reactor idea was just a "gimmick." No decision would be made until Strauss had completed a comprehensive report on the status of nuclear power.[35]

## NEW HORIZONS

International implications were not the Commission's only concern in reactor development policy in 1954. Equally pressing were the requirements of the new Atomic Energy Act, which became law in August. Nichols had already asked the staff to begin thinking about the administrative structure and regulations required to transform the government's near-monopoly of nuclear energy into a new commercial industry. Before the end of the summer, Nichols established several task forces within the staff to begin drafting the series of required regulations and procedures.[36] The task forces included one or more experienced attorneys from the general counsel's office and appropriate specialists from the program or staff divisions. To supervise and coordinate the work of the task forces, Nichols selected Harold L. Price, a crusty, conservative lawyer who had been a mainstay of the legal staff since Manhattan Project days at Oak Ridge. Thoroughly professional to the point of being impersonal, Price was not the sort who would have been picked to be general counsel, but he was a conscientious and reliable practitioner of the legal art.[37] He had drafted much of the atomic energy legislation enacted since 1947, including crucial sections of the 1954 act. Price could be relied upon to do the job right without yielding to pressures for expediency even if they came from the Commissioners, industry, or members of Congress.

200

The Commission had no intention, however, of waiting for Price to construct the new regulatory framework before encouraging direct private participation in nuclear power development. Strauss in particular was driven by the National Security Council directive, which placed a high priority on nuclear power to be developed with private rather than government funds. Although Strauss accepted the necessity of the five-year program and the Shippingport reactor to get commercialization started, the Commission had been criticized for recommending government control in these two instances. Beyond that, both Strauss and his fellow Commissioners were sensitive to the repeated claims by industry executives, particularly in the Nuclear Power Group, that private companies were ready to make the substantial financial commitments necessary to build a full-scale nuclear plant. The Commissioners were ready to call what they considered industry's bluff by soliciting proposals for joint or full participation.[38]

During autumn 1954, Nichols worked with Price, Hafstad, and Don S. Burrows, the Commission's controller, in designing an acceptable form of solicitation. Because Nichols and his associates entertained almost no hope that industry would undertake to build full-scale plants without some government support, Burrows had to make some provisions for funding in the 1956 budget, which was then in the final stages of preparation. Informal discussions at the Bureau of the Budget had encountered considerable skepticism about the Commission's request for $50 million in operating funds and $25 million for construction to stimulate industrial participation. Bureau officials wondered whether this kind of stimulation was warranted so soon after passage of the 1954 act, especially when Nichols admitted that there was no urgent domestic need for nuclear power. The motivation, Nichols said, was the Atoms-for-Peace program and the international race with the Soviet Union and the United Kingdom for world leadership in the new technology.[39]

To support the budget request, Nichols sent the Commissioners a brief staff paper on December 13, 1954. He suggested a power demonstration reactor program, under which private companies would be invited to design, build, and operate their own nuclear power plants with only limited assistance and funding from the Commission. The Commission would waive all fuel-use charges for seven years, although industry would be required to pay for fissionable material actually consumed in the reactors. The companies could perform some work in Commission laboratories and would enter into contracts that would provide fixed amounts of funding for development, fabrication, and experimental plant operation. All proposals were to be submitted by April 1, 1955, and would be evaluated in terms of their probable contribution to achieving economically competitive power, the cost to the Commission of fuels and materials, the risk assumed by industry, and the competence and responsibility of the proposer.[40]

201

Most discussion at the Commission meeting on December 21, 1954, centered on the April 1 deadline. Two Commissioners thought the short deadline would eliminate companies that were not already involved as contractors or members of industrial study groups. Nichols admitted this danger, but he thought it essential to have some replies in hand when he defended the $75-million budget request before Congressional committees in spring 1955. Informal discussions with industry leaders led Nichols to believe that there would be at least three proposals, an estimate on which he had based the $75-million request. He assured the Commissioners that they could issue a second invitation in autumn 1955 if all of the funds were not committed in response to the first.[41]

In retrospect it is difficult to understand how a paper with such far-reaching consequences could win Commission approval so easily. The power demonstration reactor program was, after all, the most decisive step the Commission had yet taken toward creating a nuclear industry. The plan was intended to draw private enterprise into the complex and usually controversial relationships that were part of the process of federal licensing and regulation. The five-year program had focused entirely on technological development; it did not involve private enterprise. Shippingport was really a government project with only a limited role for private industry. With power demonstration reactors the Commission would finally begin to cross the dividing line between government monopoly and private enterprise.

Yet the Commission approved Nichols's idea without considering its economic or political implications. Perhaps the quick decision was a tribute to Nichols's firm management of the staff, but more likely it resulted from the general manager's cool and competent presentation. Nichols reduced the decision to the practical perspective of the engineer-administrator. The plan seemed a sensible first step toward a distant goal, a step that the Bureau of the Budget and the Congress could understand and appreciate. It was not cast as a major policy decision. Certainly there was good common sense in Nichols's tactics, but there were dangers in this casual, almost tentative approach. It opened the possibility that the Commission would have to resolve in public many specific issues it had not settled in the comfortable confines of the conference room on Constitution Avenue.

## NEW FACES ON THE JOINT COMMITTEE

Strauss had every reason to anticipate controversy when he next met with the Joint Committee. Democratic victories in the 1954 fall elections deprived the Republicans of Congressional control after two short years. Within the Joint Committee the shift in power was reflected in both leadership and membership. Following the pattern established in 1953, the committee chairmanship now reverted from the House to the Senate, where the ranking Democrat was Clinton P. Anderson of New Mexico. A member of the Joint Committee since 1951, the former Secretary of Agriculture under Truman had become a prominent critic of the Eisenhower Administration for its efforts to enlarge private industry's role in nuclear power development at the expense of government projects. Although Anderson's initial impression of Strauss was favorable, that opinion had begun to deteriorate following the Democrats' failure to kill the Dixon-Yates proposal in summer 1953, and Murray's ever more pointed attacks on Strauss hastened the process. The Republican stalwarts on the Senate side were still to be reckoned with: Hickenlooper, Eugene D. Millikan of Colorado, Knowland, and Bricker. They were matched by Democrats John O. Pastore of Rhode Island, Albert Gore of Tennessee, and Henry M. Jackson of Washington, who was returning to the committee after previous service as a congressman. On the House side the leaders were the same—Holifield and Price for the Democrats and Cole and Hinshaw for the Republicans—but the 1954 elections gave the Democrats a dominant position.

The aggressive and experienced leadership already demonstrated by the Democratic members of the committee foreshadowed a sharp challenge to the Eisenhower Administration and its nuclear policies. Soon after the new Democratic Congress convened in January 1955, Senator Anderson set out to reverse the action of the lame-duck Republican majority, which in November 1954 had waived the thirty-day waiting period for Joint Committee consideration of all electric utility contracts so that the Dixon-Yates agreement could be signed before the Democrats took over. On January 28, 1955, the Joint Committee formally revoked the Republican resolution and recommended cancellation of the Dixon-Yates contract.[42]

202

## THE PUBLIC FORUM

The opportunity for direct confrontation between the Commission and the committee first appeared in the hearings that Anderson called for January 31, 1955, pursuant to Section 202 of the new act. In authorizing the committee to conduct hearings on "the development, use, and control of atomic energy" during the first sixty days of each session of Congress, Section 202 gave the committee license to probe ultimately into every aspect of the Commission's activities. That privilege, plus the mandate to pass on all authorizations for construction appropriations under Section 261, gave the Joint Committee two powerful tools with which it would influence national policy on nuclear power over the next decade.[43]

Anderson began the Joint Committee hearings on January 31 on a cordial note by extending Strauss best wishes on his birthday, and Strauss replied by discussing the power demonstration reactor program and its relationship to the five-year program, as the committee had requested. But later that afternoon Murray moved the hearing into a political context by charging that the Commission had been so preoccupied with the Dixon-Yates contract in recent months that important business had been neglected. Strauss refuted the charge the next day as "unfortunate and inaccurate," and both men proceeded to poll the staff on the actual amount of time spent on the Dixon-Yates matter since the contract had been approved in November. When Murray claimed a week later that the figure was more than two thousand hours, Strauss tried to put the facts into perspective by having a courier wheel into the hearing room a pile of boxes containing all the staff papers considered by the Commission since Dixon-Yates was first introduced a year earlier. As a contrast he showed the committee a small folder containing all the papers coming to the Commissioners on Dixon-Yates. This unseemly display, which caused Anderson to lose his patience, was but further evidence of the petty bickering and accusations of dishonesty that undermined relations between the two Commissioners. Under the circumstances, Anderson was not inclined to accept the charges of either antagonist, but the dispute did not enhance his confidence in Strauss. Trivial to the point of annoyance, the squabble did breed distrust and suspicion between the Commission and the Joint Committee.[44]

Despite the disruptive effects of the Dixon-Yates issue, Anderson and the committee were able to pursue a thoughtful and penetrating discussion of the power demonstration reactor program. Nichols provided a well-rounded justification for the Commission's invitation as a first effort to determine the amount of government assistance that industry might require before entering the nuclear power field. The Commission was convinced, Nichols said, that industry was not yet prepared to build nuclear power plants without financial help from the government, but at the same time the Commission was determined to hold government assistance to a minimum.

203

If the Commission's predictions were wrong and industry was willing to proceed alone, the Commission certainly would not stand in the way.

Very close questioning of industry witnesses during the hearing supported the Commission's rationale. Walker L. Cisler, spokesman for a group of midwestern electric utilities planning to submit a proposal under the new program, admitted that government assistance of this kind was needed to demonstrate the feasibility of nuclear power in full-scale facilities. But Cisler still maintained that industry was fully prepared after successful demonstration to take the next step on its own; he claimed that a large-scale government development program was unnecessary.[45]

Although the Commission's program, as Nichols argued, did attempt to respond to the realities of the situation, it had the disadvantage of most compromises: it was subject to attack from two directions. Holifield saw the program as an admission that the confident statements by private industry about the promising commercial prospects for nuclear power were merely window-dressing. Cole, however, saw the Commission's program as a subtle effort to use government contracts rather than licenses under the new act to develop nuclear power. Specifically, Cole questioned whether the Commission could provide assistance and funds for research on power demonstration reactors without violating the "no-subsidy" provision that the act applied to licensees. Nichols assured Cole that the Commission would be careful to see that no Commission money went into bricks and mortar for power demonstration plants and that funds for research would be limited to a predetermined amount.[46] Thus, the 202 hearings reinforced the Commission's determination to hold government assistance to a minimum.

Whether this kind of limitation was consistent with the aim of accelerating nuclear power development was another question. In fact, the general tenor of the hearings was that rapid development should take precedence over other considerations. Jerry Voorhis, executive director of the Cooperative League, once again criticized the 1954 act for encouraging monopoly in the electric power industry, but he too put nuclear power first. "In part the resolution of the present crisis in the world," Voorhis declared, "depends on the relative success of the free world, as contrasted with the totalitarian world, in building a quality of life that is good for all its people and I believe atomic energy can play a major role in this great enterprise." When Senator Pastore asked whether the United States was doing all it could to develop nuclear power, Cisler reminded him that the nation already had 40 percent of the world's electrical generating capacity, which was sufficient at the moment. But Pastore was unconvinced: "Are we not trying to win the hearts and minds of people in other parts of the world? . . . That is the great inspiration that was given to the world in the speech made by the President. Are we winning that race?"[47]

At least, the Joint Committee was prepared to await the results of the Commission's invitation. If attractive offers were received on April 1 and industry demonstrated a willingness to build reactors, perhaps no further government encouragement beyond the power demonstration program would be required. In the meantime, however, the Joint Committee was closely watching the Commission's activities, especially the five-year program for building reactor experiments. In early March 1955 the committee, anticipating inspection trips to the laboratories, asked the Commission for a progress report on the five reactor experiments. A few weeks later, just before the deadline for the power demonstration proposals, the committee announced the appointment of a special panel to study the impact of the peaceful uses of atomic energy. Such a panel would surely probe the Commission's nuclear power efforts, and the appointment of Robert M. McKinney, editor of the *Santa Fe New Mexican* and friend of Senator Anderson's, suggested the likelihood of political motivations in the study.[48] Clearly the public debate on nuclear power policy was just beginning.

205

## POWER DEMONSTRATIONS: DEFINING INDUSTRY'S ROLE

In spring 1955 the Commission pinned most of its hopes on the power demonstration reactors. After worrying for weeks that the response to the January invitation would be unimpressive, the Commission was mildly pleased to receive four proposals by the April 1 deadline. The Nuclear Power Group, which had bid unsuccessfully on the Shippingport project, offered to build a 180,000-kilowatt boiling-water reactor, to be completed near Chicago by 1960. A group of nine electric utilities headed by the Detroit Edison Company proposed to build a 100,000-kilowatt fast breeder, to be completed by 1958 in the Detroit area. The Yankee Atomic Electric Company of Boston, a consortium of thirteen utilities in New England, opted for a 100,000-kilowatt pressurized-water reactor, to be completed in western Massachusetts by late 1957. Finally, the Consumers Public Power District of Columbus, Nebraska, proposed a 75,000-kilowatt sodium-graphite reactor, to be completed in 1959. All four projects represented an extension into the demonstration phase of four of the five reactor types that the Commission was developing under the five-year program, and Strauss confidently expected in a few weeks a fifth offer, which never came, for a homogeneous reactor. In the weeks before the April 1 deadline, company officials were frequently in contact with Strauss, other Commissioners, Nichols, and the staff. The utility groups probably knew enough about each other's interests to match the Commission's program almost project for project.[49]

The almost casual way in which the Commission had approved the demonstration program in December 1954 and the very general selection criteria set forth in the invitation did not provide much guidance for evaluating the proposals. By the time the selection board and the director of reactor development reported back to the Commissioners in late June, Nichols had left the agency; he was replaced by Brigadier General Kenneth E. Fields, the director of the division of military application, who had retired from the Army to accept the general manager's position.[50] An experienced engineer with an outstanding military record, Fields had held several assignments in the atomic energy program since Manhattan Project days. Although he was as familiar as most Commission staff with the agency's activities, he could not have been privy to all the rationale and motives that underlay Nichols's advocacy of the power demonstration program.

Almost at once the Commissioners got bogged down in the details of the proposals, despite the fact that the selection board recommended accepting all four. A problem remained: no response strictly adhered to the kinds of assistance that the Commission offered to provide in the invitation. The Consumers and Yankee plans went so far beyond the rather narrow limits set forth in the invitation that they took on the nature of government projects in which industry would participate, rather than being industry efforts using limited government support.[51]

Even the limits on support had proved too liberal in light of questions raised by Congressman Cole during the Section 202 hearings in February. Cole challenged the Commission's authority to provide funds ostensibly for research and development if in fact such funds were to be used to offset construction and operating costs. This foray into the legislative history of the Atomic Energy Act was inconclusive, but it did make the Commissioners more sensitive to the fine points of administration than they had been in December. In some respects the Commission in July was making the kinds of policy decisions that should have been reached during the previous December, and some applicants under the demonstration program complained privately that the Commission was making up the rules after the contest had begun.[52]

The extended discussions within the Commission during July and August 1955 revealed the kinds of dilemmas that any federal agency found in moving a new technology from government control into the marketplace. Even as late as summer 1955 the Commission still had no real confidence that private industry was prepared to make sound decisions about the direction of nuclear power technology. Thus, evaluating the power demonstration proposals became not just a matter of matching them with the criteria in the invitation but also of appraising the technical merits of the reactor systems presented. Commissioner Libby struggled for weeks to find some way to bend the criteria to permit the selection of the Consumers offer, which he considered the most attractive technically but the least responsive to the invitation's terms. In the opposite direction, the Commission was not enthusiastic about the Yankee proposal, even if it could be brought into line with the terms of the invitation, because it seemed to offer nothing new beyond the Shippingport plant; hence, it was scarcely worth the expenditure of funds for research and development. Therefore, the Commission's dilemma was twofold: trying to maintain technical balance in the program while attempting to move the technology into the economy, where presumably economic as well as technical factors would influence the course of development.[53]

The Commission also faced what could be called the Shippingport dilemma. To the extent that the Commission agreed to furnish forms of assistance going beyond the terms of the invitation, the closer the power demonstration projects would come to being government enterprises of the Shippingport type. In fact, Congressman Cole's position suggested that once government support passed a certain point, at least the nuclear portion of the plants would have to be government property; this would defeat the very purposes of the power demonstration reactor program by eliminating the possibility of private ownership and control. Thus, the smaller the percentage of government support, the farther away from the Shippingport model the new projects would be. The trouble with pursuing this goal was that, as the projects became more independent of government support, the Commission would lose its hold on technical information developed in the course of design, construction, and operation of the demonstration plants. The prospect of losing access to the technical data produced in the projects worried the Commissioners. It seemed that while the technology was still in transition from government monopoly to marketplace conditions, some sort of middle course between government projects like Shippingport and the private construction of licensed facilities was in order.

Beyond these considerations the Commission was motivated by the simple desire to see the demonstration program, once launched, become a success. In the simplistic terms that often prevailed on Capitol Hill, success would be determined by the number of power reactors actually resulting from the invitation. The Commission also feared that it would discourage industry proposals in the future if it rejected any of the first four. Yet the staff kept reminding the Commissioners that two constraints made it virtually impossible to accept the Consumers and Yankee proposals: the limitation on funding authority stressed by Congressman Cole and the potential danger of the Shippingport dilemma.[54]

These reservations were responsible for both delaying announcement of a Commission decision until August and phrasing it as a compromise that revealed the Commission's two minds on the subject. The Commission found the proposals by the Nuclear Power Group and the Detroit Edison consortium acceptable for negotiation. The Yankee and Consumers offers as submitted were not acceptable, but the Commission authorized the staff to continue discussions that might result in revised submissions. The product of four months of deliberation would hardly impress either the Administration or the Congress as a bold and aggressive response to insistent demands for nuclear power.[55]

207

Since the beginning of the Eisenhower Administration the Commission had responded positively in its own way to the public demand for nuclear power. At the end of 1952 the new technology was still a military secret and a government monopoly. Even before the 1954 act became law, the Commission had taken steps to give private industry access to the technical data needed to evaluate the prospects for a nuclear power industry. In one short year since the passage of the new law, the Commission had launched an ambitious plan for private development and construction of nuclear power plants.

In terms of its technical dimensions, the power demonstration reactor program was a bold, and perhaps even an unwarranted, effort to make nuclear power common in the marketplace. Privately the Commissioners still questioned whether the technology would support the grandiose public vision of the nuclear age, and they hoped that the resources and ingenuity of private industry could find a shortcut to economical nuclear power. In summer 1955, however, the technology needed to achieve that goal did not exist. Nuclear power was not yet ready for the marketplace.

208

## CHAPTER 8

# ATOMS FOR PEACE:
# BUILDING AMERICAN POLICY

The scene was one Lewis Strauss would never forget. The President, his eyes glistening with emotion, sat almost meekly in his high-backed chair on the rostrum as delegates to the United Nations General Assembly filled the hall with applause. Throughout Eisenhower's twenty-minute statement the 3,500 delegates had listened in silence as the President pledged that the United States would devote "its entire heart and mind to find the way by which the miraculous inventiveness of man shall not be dedicated to his death, but consecrated to his life." Now that he had concluded, even the Soviet delegation joined the acclamation.[1] December 8, 1953, would be a memorable day in the history of the United Nations, but would it be more than a brief flash of idealism in a world drifting toward nuclear war?

## WORLDWIDE REACTIONS

The President's speech, broadcast worldwide by the Voice of America, received enthusiastic response from every continent. With the exception of communist governments and press, most officials and newspapers hailed Eisenhower's proposals as constructive, courageous, and a possible step toward improved East-West relationships. There was general agreement that Eisenhower had delivered one of the most significant speeches of the postwar era, a statement in the "grand design" tradition of the Marshall Plan. But there was also widespread recognition that Eisenhower's vision would become reality only if there were good faith on all sides, a requirement that some pessimists did not expect from the communists. Initial reactions from *Pravda* and other communist newspapers were almost predictable. Suspicious and hostile, communist editors charged that Eisenhower described the threat of atomic warfare without offering any suggestions for banning atomic weapons. The Soviet foreign ministry promised only to give the proposal "serious attention." For the moment the world pushed aside concerns about Korea, Trieste, and Berlin as millions reflected on the meaning of the President's words.[2]

The domestic response to Eisenhower's speech was highly favorable, although not unboundedly so. On Capitol Hill, reporters found a marked difference between public statements and private comments, but no one doubted the sincerity of Congressman Cole when he pledged support for the President's proposals "with all my heart" to secure Congressional approval of the plan. Senators from McCarthy of Wisconsin and Hickenlooper of Iowa to Mike Mansfield of Montana described the speech as "a good suggestion," "great," and "daring." Democrats and Republicans alike saw the speech as a master stroke of propaganda, but they divided on the feasibility of establishing an international atomic energy agency. Carl Durham of North Carolina raised the specter of another foreign "giveaway" program. Freed from attribution, some Congressional leaders doubted that the "nationalist bloc" would vote to share the United States' atomic energy technology with an international body. Still other senators complained that Eisenhower should have consulted them before launching such a fundamental departure in foreign policy.[3]

Like the miffed senators, no Commissioner except Strauss had known of the President's intention until the day of the speech. After accidentally finding a reference to the speech in newspaper reports from the Bermuda conference, Murray had obtained a preliminary draft from the State Department. Murray was furious over yet another example of Strauss's failure to keep the Commission informed of White House policy discussions about atomic energy matters. He was even more appalled that Strauss would confide in Lord Cherwell while keeping his fellow Commissioners in the dark. Murray was so angry that he even advocated cabling Strauss to request clearance of the President's speech. The Commissioners did not take this step, for obvious reasons, but Eisenhower's speech suggested, just as his unilateral action in the Oppenheimer case had, that they were outside the Administration's inner circle on atomic energy affairs. After these two experiences both Zuckert and Smyth gave serious thought to leaving the Commission. Murray, whose term still had more than three years to run, girded himself for a relentless and often bitter struggle with Strauss and the Administration.[4]

Although Strauss, as he did in the Dixon-Yates case, was careful to conceal any personal reservations about the Atoms-for-Peace proposal out of loyalty to the President, there was some scanty evidence that his enthusiasm was limited. In October, Strauss had worried about the risks to international security in collecting nuclear fuel in a United Nations pool. After the speech Strauss seemed to fear that the President's remarks might create false expectations over the prospects for nuclear disarmament and perhaps some lowering of America's defenses. Strauss thought the President should express his gratitude if the Russians unexpectedly accepted the President's proposals, but even then Eisenhower should warn the American people that

> it would be most unfortunate . . . if, despite the hope which a war-sick world will reasonably draw from this gleam of light, we of the United States assume that the present danger is diminished or that our military posture should meanwhile be affected to the slightest degree.[5]

Strauss said he did not oppose the President's proposal; he merely wished to warn that Atoms for Peace would not soon take precedence over Atoms for War.

211

## A NEW ROAD TO DISARMAMENT

The White House press conference was jammed with reporters on December 16, 1953. Even experienced hands on the White House press corps sensed unusual excitement because the President, reflecting his continued commitment to *Candor*, authorized for the first time direct quotation of all his remarks. Still tanned from the Bermuda sun and exhilarated from his United Nations triumph, Eisenhower met the press with full confidence and relaxed humor. He was not reticent in claiming the Atoms-for-Peace idea as his own. Granting that many people had contributed to the formulation of the final proposal, Eisenhower remarked that he had "originated the idea of a joint contribution to a central bank in an effort to get all people started on thinking in different terms about this whole business of atomic energy." Previous ideas, he explained, called for international inspection, which provided the Russians an automatic reason for rejecting them. The President hoped that his Atoms-for-Peace plan would sweep all previous proposals from the negotiating tables and thus "open up many lines of study."[6]

The President was undoubtedly referring to the years of frustration that the United States had endured in its quest for international control of atomic energy, ever since Bernard M. Baruch made his dramatic proposal in a similar appearance before the General Assembly in June 1946. By the end of that year, American hopes for effective action in the United Nations Atomic Energy Commission were all but dead; in 1947 discussions tapered off and finally stopped.[7] International control remained a dead issue in the United States until October 1950, when President Truman, in an address to the General Assembly, proposed a new disarmament commission to consider both conventional and nuclear weapons. The National Security Council directive (NSC 112 of July 6, 1951) gave evidence of the frustrations and disappointments encountered in five years of discussions with the Soviet Union. By the time the General Assembly finally established the new disarmament commission in January 1952, there was little reason for optimism.[8]

The United States delegation, lead by Benjamin V. Cohen, wanted to focus on the problems of disclosure and verification in 1952. The Americans probed the Soviet Union's willingness to accept effective inspection, presuming that any verification plan agreeable to the Soviets would also be acceptable to the United States; furthermore, a Russian rejection would have an obvious propaganda advantage for the United States. For its part, the Soviet Union continued to advance proposals already rejected: a one-third reduction of armed forces by the Big Five—the Soviet Union, the United States, the United Kingdom, France, and China; a prohibition of atomic weapons through a mere declaration that these weapons would be outlawed (the ban binding only after effective controls were established); and the disclosure of official data on armed forces and armament.[9]

To break the disarmament stalemate Secretary of State Acheson had appointed a panel of consultants, chaired by Oppenheimer, to take a fresh look at the full range of disarmament questions and their implications. The panel's report in January 1953, with its stress on *Candor*, had sparked Eisenhower's interest in developing an entirely new approach to the nuclear threat in international affairs. Other members of the National Security Council, notably Secretaries Wilson and Humphrey, were slow to follow the President's lead. But after the Russians fired *Joe 4* in August there was no doubt that the Soviet Union had gained the propaganda edge over the United States, which had a shopworn, dead-end disarmament policy.[10]

Formulating a new policy for the Administration was a complex operation that had to proceed simultaneously at both the presidential and the agency levels. While Eisenhower, Dulles, Jackson, and Strauss made their tortuous way through Operation *Candor* to the United Nations address, Walter Bedell Smith, the Acting Secretary of State, coordinated the extensive staff work necessary in developing the details of the new policy. It was logical for Smith to call upon the Commission to evaluate the technical factors on which the new policy would rest, and it was just as reasonable for Commissioner Smyth to head the technical committee.[11] Smyth had performed similar functions as far back as 1949, when the Truman Administration formulated its policy on thermonuclear weapons.

Smyth's committee found that the situation had changed radically since the days of severe uranium shortages that characterized the 1940s. Without hurting weapon production in the United States, sufficient uranium could now be supplied to satisfy the world's need for research and nuclear power, even if all the existing mines and production plants were shut down for ten or twenty years. On the debit side, with so much uranium available, there was no longer any way of assuring that all fissionable material had been declared, short of a system of continuous and unimpeded inspection in all countries.[12]

Although Smyth's (and the Commission's) role in the policy process may have seemed clear and logical to the State Department and the National Security Council, Strauss's special relationship to the President and the council did arouse distrust in his fellow Commissioners. Murray became so upset that he attempted to interject the Commission into the decision process in October 1953, by proposing that the United States release information about the location of its uranium mines and production plants and even admit United Nations observers to the *Castle* test series in the spring of 1954 as a way of embarrassing the Soviet Union.

By October 15 tensions within the Commission had risen so high that in Strauss's absence his colleagues had adopted a formal resolution stating that the agency "as a Commission" had a responsibility to participate in formulating United States policy in international control. Growing more impatient and frustrated, Smyth decided to drop all work on the technical committee because Strauss and Dulles were making the policy decisions. Only a personal appeal from Strauss on October 18 convinced Smyth to continue as head of the technical committee, although he was still seriously considering resigning from the Commission. Smyth might not have been so discouraged had he known that Strauss had actually forwarded his recommendations to the President through C. D. Jackson, but Strauss's sense of loyalty to Eisenhower would not permit him to reveal even this confidence.[13]

213

## INTERPRETING THE EISENHOWER PROPOSAL

Once the President decided, in October 1953, to address the United Nations, Eisenhower's conception of the Atoms-for-Peace plan became an important factor in any consideration of American disarmament policy. The United Nations speech was the product of the President and a few close advisers; it did not reflect the concerns and interests of the professional bureaucracy in Washington or of allied governments abroad. Enunciated by the President almost as a personal hope, the speech could not set forth specific proposals. American officials and foreign governments were all uncertain about the precise intentions of the President's noble sentiments. The glowing generalities were subject to many interpretations, and these in turn would ultimately determine the proposal's fate.

Among the first to face the problem of interpretation were the British, who had an opportunity to review the draft at the Bermuda conference just before Eisenhower went to New York. Churchill's first goal at Bermuda was to try to reestablish the full measure of cooperation on nuclear weapon development that the two nations had created in the early years of World War II. As diplomatically as possible, Eisenhower explained the inhibitions imposed by the 1946 Atomic Energy Act and pledged to do what he could to secure a number of amendments at the next session of Congress; however, Churchill was impatient with such vague reassurances. If the United States wanted the United Kingdom to be a full military partner, the British would need information on the weight, dimensions, and ballistics of American weapons adapted for the design of British planes. Cherwell assured the Americans that the British did not intend to develop a hydrogen bomb, but until the United Kingdom could build its own stockpile of atomic weapons, the Royal Air Force would have to rely upon the United States for atomic bombs.[14]

214

Eisenhower, perhaps embarrassed that he could not reply to Churchill's requests directly, launched a disquisition on atomic weaponry, which continued the following evening at dinner. To the discomfiture of his British hosts, Eisenhower concluded that "the atomic bomb has to be treated just as another weapon in the arsenal." Should hostilities resume in Korea, for example, there was a distinct possibility that the United States would use nuclear weapons against communist air bases, supplies, and troop concentrations. Churchill protested that such an action might touch off World War III and the consequent bombing of London with "the destruction of all we hold dear, ourselves, our families and our treasures." In a state approaching desperation, Churchill could not immediately comment on the draft of the Atoms-for-Peace speech. Eventually he suggested two changes to tone down overly belligerent passages. Cherwell accepted the idea of an atomic bank but predicted that the Russians would obstruct negotiations of any proposal.[15]

After Stalin's death in March 1953 and the end of the Korean War in July, Americans held a faint hope for some change in the Soviet Union's foreign policy toward the United States. Although Malenkov, speaking before the Supreme Soviet in August, did not stint on any usual criticism aimed at the United States, Ambassador Charles E. Bohlen had noted a greater frankness and realism than ever before in Russian discussions of internal affairs. C. D. Jackson, for one, was determined to remain as optimistic as possible "that the Soviet leaders will recognize the President's proposal as a serious and feasible first step toward atomic peace." Even the initial Russian reaction, Jackson added, need not be regarded as the Soviet government's considered decision.[16]

Jackson's caution was well advised. On December 21, 1953, Soviet Foreign Minister Vyacheslav M. Molotov informed Dulles that the Soviet government was prepared to discuss Eisenhower's plan, assuming that the United States would also agree to entertain Soviet proposals for the total ban of nuclear weapons. Although the Soviet note did not contain an unqualified endorsement of Eisenhower's speech and reiterated some old disarmament slogans, Jean Allary of the *Agence France Presse* observed that if the Soviets' demand for a nuclear ban was not a preliminary condition but a goal to be worked for, then agreement was possible. Other foreign observers noted that the lack of vituperation in the Russian reply gave hope that the Soviet Union really desired to negotiate.[17]

Within the American government interpretations of the President's intentions also differed, much to Jackson's annoyance. The State Department virtually accepted the Soviet construction that would have initiated negotiations on "atomic disarmament" without reference to general disarmament, including conventional weapons. The Department of Defense, on the other hand, argued that the State Department's position was not only counter to long standing United States policy, as confirmed by the National Security Council, but would also be tantamount to defense suicide. Atomic disarmament alone would reduce the United States to a position inferior to the Russians in conventional weapons. The dispute reflected both the hope of some State Department officials who argued that Eisenhower had successfully broken the disarmament stalemate and the fear of those in the Defense Department who worried that Atoms for Peace might be used to clip the wings of the Strategic Air Command.[18] Strauss pointed out that the purpose behind the atomic bank proposal had been to ease international tensions by reducing existing nuclear stockpiles. Nevertheless, if the Russians rejected the idea, the United States would still have won a substantial psychological victory. The President wanted to sidestep the disarmament issue, not confront it, Strauss argued.[19]

215

Ultimately, only Eisenhower himself could settle the fundamental questions concerning his intentions. Meeting with Dulles, Strauss, Jackson, and Deputy Secretary of Defense Roger Kyes, on January 16, 1954, the President stated his central point as simply and forcefully as possible: the distinction between total and atomic disarmament was largely academic because neither could be accomplished without the most rigid and comprehensive system of inspection. Surprisingly, Eisenhower did not oppose outlawing the atomic bomb without an agreement on conventional weapons and armies. The bomb, he ruefully observed, had really frightened America because it was the first weapon that could cripple American industry, the winning factor in all major conflicts since the Civil War. If atomic and hydrogen weapons were outlawed, the Russians would be left with a vastly superior conventional force, but American industrial capacity could readily cope with any military assault on the North American continent. No disarmament agreement with the Russians, however, could be effective in the current international climate, the President staunchly argued, without foolproof inspection safeguards.[20]

Dulles agreed, but he reminded Eisenhower that the Russians would press for nuclear disarmament no matter what the United States did. Consequently, with the President's concurrence, Dulles recommended two courses of action. First, the United States would "listen" to any proposal the Soviet Union cared to submit on control or abolition of nuclear weapons, but Dulles would not be drawn into negotiations on this subject. Second, the United States would press forward on discussions of peaceful uses entirely separate from any negotiations on weapons. To implement the latter, a joint working group from the Commission, State, and Defense had been appointed to develop issues that would serve as the basis for discussions and to explore whether the discussions should proceed privately with individual governments or be pursued through an international organization such as the United Nations.[21]

As part of the Administration's effort, Strauss asked Smyth and his committee to draft a charter for the international organization suggested in Eisenhower's speech. Smyth, still smarting from the sting of the "Bermuda crisis" while becoming increasingly worried by the Oppenheimer affair, reluctantly agreed to accept the assignment with the proviso that the Commission support his understanding of the President's speech. Because there were many interpretations of Atoms for Peace, Smyth asked the Commission to sponsor the most radical possibility—namely, that Eisenhower intended to look beyond peaceful uses to envision the eventual reduction of atomic stockpiles in the United States and the Soviet Union. After extensive discussion Smyth received his endorsement.[22]

Once disentangled from disarmament questions, Atoms for Peace faced three other policy questions, none of them insurmountable from the American perspective. The first concerned the amount of fissionable material each country would be expected to contribute to an international agency. Initially, Strauss had feared theft of the material unless it were stored in a highly dilute solution at a remote location. In fact, the question was whether the United States could induce the Russians to contribute anything at all to the bank. Smyth, who also served as chairman of the joint working group, asserted that the United States contribution should be large enough to launch the program but not so great as to make it impossible for the Soviets to participate, assuming they responded in good faith. It would be best, Smyth thought, to begin with small contributions of normal and partially enriched uranium, which could be gradually increased over time to the point where contributions actually began to reduce weapon stockpiles. Although all contributions ought to be made on a one-to-one ratio by the United States and Russia, the initial United States contribution might acceptably be two or three times that of the Soviet Union.[23]

There was also the question of how much information the Commission would provide the international agency. Everyone agreed that declassified information could be made available as a matter of routine; the agency would thus act as an international library and clearinghouse for nuclear information. It was also foreseen that as soon as the international agency moved into nuclear power, almost all reactor technology would have to be declassified. The most sensitive information would involve advanced military propulsion reactors, such as those designed for submarines, ships, and airplanes. But even in this area, Robert LeBaron from the Defense Department observed that the technology could be declassified once the military no longer needed to keep it secret.[24]

Finally, the working group debated whether it would be permissible for members of the international agency to exchange fissionable material or information outside the organization's jurisdiction. The question was of special interest to the United States, which had the option of negotiating directly with friendly nations. The working group saw that Congress would never allow the United States to work exclusively through a United Nations agency. On the other hand, the members believed that certain countries, such as India, might prefer to obtain reactors through a neutral agency rather than directly from either the United States or the Soviet Union. Consequently, the group decided that the agency should not have a monopoly on international negotiations but that bilateral arrangements between countries would also be acceptable. Thus, the agency would be a clearinghouse, for both nuclear materials and technical information, without authority to plan, finance, or conduct projects of its own. Membership in the agency would be open to all nations, regardless of their United Nations affiliation, and even nonmember nations that accepted its conditions would be eligible for its services.[25]

217

Thus did the joint working group set forth the outlines of a charter for the international agency. Now it was the State Department's responsibility to open the way for international discussions.

## APPROACHING THE RUSSIANS

On board the *Santa Isabel* cruising in the Caribbean, David Lilienthal also reflected on the Atoms-for-Peace idea. Initially, the former chairman of the Commission had been enthusiastic about Eisenhower's speech and had urged the United States to proceed immediately with the proposal without waiting for Soviet participation. Before leaving New York, however, Lilienthal had been told by a confidant, who had declined to lead the American team negotiating with the Russians, that "there was no substance in the proposal itself." Lilienthal concluded that the President's performance had been nothing but a propaganda ploy, a shocking deception, not only for the Russians but for the American people as well.[26]

Perhaps Lilienthal's judgment would not have been so harsh had he known of the Administration's determination to push ahead with Atoms for Peace, with or without cooperation from the Soviet Union. But neither the State Department nor anyone else was certain of how to proceed. Dulles favored private negotiations through normal diplomatic channels apart from the United Nations disarmament commission. In fact, he thought there was considerable logic to limiting initial discussions to the three countries that actually had nuclear weapons—the United States, the United Kingdom, and the Soviet Union. Although there was no way to avoid talking about disarmament in bilateral discussions with the Russians, Dulles thought it futile to work through a United Nations committee that could neither limit its membership nor keep its discussions pertinent.[27]

Strauss and Secretary of Defense Wilson agreed that bilateral negotiations with the Russians, and possibly with the British, would be best. Eisenhower's correspondence with Churchill, Strauss's conversations with Cherwell, and Dulles's meetings with Sir Roger Makins, the British ambassador, had already advanced British participation to the point where it would be impractical to exclude them.[28] There was even the risk, Dulles observed, that Churchill might undertake negotiations on his own initiative if left out of the discussion. Actually the Americans had few objections to including the British; however, the possibility of French involvement did concern them.

The American architects of the international agency who met on January 6, 1954, were unanimous that the French should be excluded as long as possible, largely for reasons of security. Dulles was not overly worried about alienating the French or driving them toward the Soviet Union. He underscored his preference by noting that Churchill had a similar attitude toward the French and would also resist including them in atomic discussions. Assistant Secretary Livingston T. Merchant pointed out that it would be difficult to exclude the French, particularly if the Canadians and Belgians were eventually brought into the discussions. Strauss seemed to concur with Merchant, for, although he hated to think of French participation, he remarked that most likely the Belgians, and therefore the French, would have to be included within a year. Since Bermuda, he reported, the Belgians' noses had been "out of joint," and with the uranium ore purchase agreements about to expire it might even be prudent to consider Brussels as the headquarters for the proposed international agency. For the present, the group decided to exclude the French from American planning for the international agency.[29]

The following day Dulles fully explained the American strategy to Ambassador Makins and stressed that the United States intended to conduct preliminary talks with the Soviet Union to determine when, where, and with whom the Russians wanted to meet. Dulles promised to keep Makins fully informed of developments; but alluding to the sensitive problem of excluding the French, he asked the British not to participate formally in the discussions until after the four-power conference scheduled for Berlin late in January. Makins assured Dulles that the British, aware of the French problem, had no intention of inserting themselves into the preliminary talks with the Russians. Indeed, British Foreign Minister Anthony

218

Eden was anxious that atomic discussions not get mixed up with the Berlin conference itself. Makins warned, however, that once the negotiations became multilateral, it would be difficult to proceed without Canada and the Union of South Africa, let alone France and Belgium.[30]

With assurance of British support, Dulles on January 11, 1954, presented Soviet Ambassador Georgi N. Zaroubin the United States' suggestion for private discussions of atomic energy, including the proposed international agency. In addition to urging early bilateral discussions of Eisenhower's plan, the United States expressed its willingness to consider any proposal that the Soviet Union wished to make concerning nuclear weapons, with the proviso that the first efforts would necessarily be modest in order to build "trust and confidence." The following week the Soviet Union accepted the proposal for confidential exchanges with the understanding that, at an appropriate stage, the negotiations would include Communist China. Until such time, the Soviet Union conditioned its acceptance of the American overture by insisting on the principle of rotation, under which one meeting would be devoted to the international agency and the next to the Soviet proposal for a ban on nuclear weapons.[31]

The Berlin conference in January and February 1954 had been convened by the Big Four to discuss Korea, Indochina, Germany, Austria, and other outstanding problems; but it also provided Dulles and Molotov an opportunity for further atomic energy discussions. Meeting after the plenary session on January 30, Dulles informed Molotov that the United States was preparing a memorandum that would set forth the United States' proposals for establishing an international atomic energy agency. Although the United States had consulted with certain allies, Dulles said he did not want to include other countries at this stage. Molotov was prepared to receive the American memorandum and offered a draft Soviet declaration also designed to counter the nuclear threat. Predictably the Russians pursued disarmament by advocating that the Big Five, including Communist China, join in an unconditional renunciation of using nuclear weapons. Molotov assumed that the five countries would also participate in subsequent atomic energy negotiations. Dulles could offer no comment, but he did not object to informing Eden and French Foreign Minister Georges Bidault of the Soviet document, provided American-Soviet talks remained private. Prudently, Dulles had already briefed Bidault on American intentions and had received his polite acquiescence in the American proposal.[32]

## THE ATOMS-FOR-PEACE PROPOSAL

While Dulles conducted his leisurely discussions with the Russians, Smyth's committee continued drafting an outline of the proposal. On at least one occasion prior to the Berlin conference Strauss had briefed the

219

Commissioners on the exchanges between Dulles and the Russians; but, as Smyth had noted, the Commission had never been assigned an official role in preparing or approving the draft. Consequently, except for those informal discussions, the Commission had no official voice in completing the memorandum sent to the State Department on February 12, 1954.[33]

Smyth's outline, more a checklist than a plan, highlighted the atomic bank by defining broad functions for the international agency: receiving, storing, and allocating nuclear materials and fostering technical information services. The agency's administrative machinery, its financing, and its relationship to the United Nations were left purposely vague to avoid prematurely rigid assumptions about its functions. As promised, the United States submitted the outline to the British, Canadians, and French for comment and to the Belgians, South Africans, and Australians for information.[34]

220

The reactions from the British and Canadian governments were generally favorable, while the French offered no substantive comments. The United States' atomic partners had so little part in the plan that it was easy to accommodate their suggestions by changing only a few sentences. When the British wondered whether the proposed agency had been tied too closely to the United Nations, the Americans changed the provision requiring the agency to report to the Security Council, where its work would be subject to veto. The Canadians, however, openly expressed resentment at not having been consulted more extensively. Sensitive to the Canadians' objections, R. Gordon Arneson, in charge of the atomic energy section of the State Department, expressed the United States' hope for consultation among the three governments as the negotiations proceeded.[35]

Although not overly optimistic about the possibilities of success with the Russians, American Kremlinologists had been searching for evidence of a softening in Soviet foreign policy. C. D. Jackson noted that the Russians had sent their first team to Berlin—Molotov, Gromyko, Malik, and Zaroubin. But apart from unusual personal friendliness, especially from Molotov, Jackson found no visible evidence of a new direction in Soviet foreign policy. More astutely, Jacob D. Beam of the policy planning staff and later ambassador to the Soviet Union observed that the Kremlin had engaged in an "Operation *Candor*" of its own since Eisenhower's United Nations speech. Malenkov's electrifying address of March 14, 1954, let the facts about the Soviet nuclear arsenal and its destructive power speak for themselves without resort to threat or bombast. Beam identified a subtle, but important, shift in Soviet rhetoric on international atomic problems made necessary by the latest developments in that field. Before the Russians had built their own nuclear weapons, they stood for abolition of all nuclear armaments. As they approached technical parity, the Russians stressed prohibition on use, not abolition, showing they had no more intention than the United States of totally scrapping such weapons. And for the first time the Kremlin admitted Russia's vulnerability in a nuclear war.[36]

The United States presented its plan for the international agency to Soviet Ambassador Zaroubin on March 19, 1954, but one month later in Geneva the Russians smashed any hope for an immediate acceptance. In his note to Dulles, Molotov virtually ignored the American outline. Purposely assuming that Eisenhower's atomic bank plan was primarily a disarmament scheme, the Soviets criticized the very point that Smyth had used to promote the idea—that the small amounts of nuclear materials allocated to the international agency would not in any significant way diminish the stock available for nuclear weapons. Instead, the American plan only created the illusion of a "peaceful atom" because growing electrical generation using nuclear reactors would actually increase the amount of nuclear material available for weapons.[37]

From a propaganda point of view, the Russian note was severe and perhaps damaging. In substance, the Russians charged that Eisenhower had spoken grandiosely before the United Nations, that he had frightened the world with the prospect of a nuclear holocaust while promising new solutions to the Cold War. Sadly, the Soviets implied, the vaunted new approach turned out to be a piddling American proposal for an insignificant international pool, which, if anything, would only accelerate the arms race. Furthermore, the Russians charged, the Americans privately evaded the problem of the "inadmissibility" of atomic weapons and thus failed to meet the President's own purpose—eliminating the threat of atomic war. The Kremlin ardently professed its support for the "peaceful atom," but the Russians claimed that the American proposals were so one-sided that they could only be considered as a supplement to a more fundamental agreement. In other words, Molotov would not negotiate the charter for the international agency until the United States had signed a disarmament agreement.[38]

Unfortunately, according to one State Department analyst, there seemed to be some basis for the Russian claim that the modest proposal submitted by the United States hardly met the expectations aroused by the President's eloquent speech. While striving to preserve the secrecy of the talks, the United States could offer only one response: it was necessary to take small steps showing good faith so that greater accomplishments could follow. Accordingly, on May 1 at Geneva, Dulles conferred informally with Molotov on the proposal. He stressed that the agency would not be able to solve the disarmament problems worrying the Russians. Dulles bluntly told Molotov that a greater degree of confidence had to exist between the countries before significant progress would be made on disarmament. In a curious reversal of roles, Dulles argued that the President's speech contained only a modest proposal for improving East-West relations. Molotov, on the

221

other hand, insisted that the United States plan was not so innocuous as the Americans assumed because power reactors could also produce materials that might be used to fabricate atomic bombs. The deficiency in the American plan, Molotov asserted, was neither political nor ideological but scientific—a fact Dulles could confirm by consulting directly with American scientists.

Nonplussed by Molotov's technical argument and clearly disadvantaged when discussing scientific matters, Dulles weakly promised to look into the matter fully, although he was skeptical about his ability to understand Molotov's point. Ultimately, the State Department answered Molotov by vaguely asserting that methods could be devised to prevent the diversion of nuclear materials from power reactors. Dulles did not assume that the Russians had rejected the international pool, but he informed Molotov that, unless the United States received a positive answer, the United States would consult other interested nations. To take it or leave it was the Soviet dilemma, and throughout the summer of 1954 no one in the Western world was certain of the Soviet Union's final decision.[39]

## A MORATORIUM ON TESTING

Concurrent with planning the international agency in winter and spring 1954, the Eisenhower Administration, at the prompting of Commissioner Murray, briefly explored the possibilities of adopting a moratorium on nuclear testing. Murray accepted Jacob Beam's view that the Russians had shifted from advocating abolition of nuclear weapons to proposing prohibition of their use. He believed that the Soviet Union had created the opportunity for another initiative by the United States, one that would further Eisenhower's atomic energy aims. Murray considered the atomic arms race unique because large-scale testing, which was necessary for weapon development but which could not be kept secret, only intensified world tensions and stimulated successive rounds in the race. Yet this very combination of circumstances offered the possibility of stopping the headlong rush toward world disaster. A moratorium on large-scale testing, in Murray's opinion, would not only sharply curtail weapon development to the point where it might even be halted, but it would also remove the need for inspections or interference with national sovereignty. Because the United States was well ahead of the Russians in thermonuclear technology, a moratorium on testing would not upset American superiority in nuclear weapons. If the Soviet Union rejected the idea, however, Murray thought the President would win another stunning propaganda victory.[40]

It was ironic that the suggestion to link a test moratorium with the Atoms-for-Peace program should come from within the Commission on the eve of the *Castle* test series in February 1954. Furthermore, despite

Strauss's encouragement, it was almost certain that Murray's proposal would have received little attention from the Administration had not Prime Minister Jawaharlal Nehru of India, supported privately by the British, also advocated a moratorium on testing hydrogen weapons. Nehru's pleas, made in April after the *Castle-Bravo* shot, indicated that the full impact of Eisenhower's warning about the consequences of thermonuclear warfare could only be understood in the shadow of the awesome Bikini explosion.[41]

Eisenhower had alluded to the destructive power of thermonuclear weapons in his United Nations speech; but his references to tons of TNT and "explosives equivalents," while frightening, did not convey the picture of a world in ruins. Two months later in Chicago, Congressman Cole completed the sketch that the President had outlined before the General Assembly. After *Bravo* every metaphor was obsolete. Cole had mentioned nothing about *Bravo* in his talk, but even the details of the comparatively primitive *Mike* shot of November 1952 had been sufficient to panic Winston Churchill, who apparently had little comprehension of the power of thermonuclear weapons before he went to Bermuda. Perhaps for the first time Churchill was aware that England was defenseless against a nuclear attack. Not only was he concerned that a single bomb could destroy London, but he also realized that a hydrogen bomb dropped in the sea to the windward side of Great Britain could poison the entire country with radioactive fallout. The *Bravo* shot brought Churchill under intense pressure from the Labour opposition for details of the test and launched a protest against further experimentation. Distraught at being personally attacked for Britain's lack of information concerning American policy, Churchill informed Eisenhower that he intended to publish the text of the 1943 Quebec Agreement in order to demonstrate that the leaders of the Labour government after the war, not the Conservatives, had failed to keep abreast of United States developments.[42]

223

In response to the mounting anxiety over American tests, from both inside and outside the government, Dulles obtained Eisenhower's approval in April 1954 to explore the possibility of ceasing all thermonuclear testing. The President appointed Dulles, Strauss, and Admiral Arthur W. Radford, chairman of the Joint Chiefs of Staff, to study the matter. Thereafter, in London, Dulles was able to reassure Eden that the United States was sensitive to world opinion about the Bikini tests and that the President had requested technical advice on the subject.

Once again the Commission was left officially in the dark about Strauss's special assignment from the President. On May 7, 1954, after the National Security Council had received a report from the Joint Chiefs of Staff opposing any agreement on a test moratorium, Strauss informed his fellow Commissioners that the President had reconstituted the special committee on atomic energy for the purpose of considering the possible suspension of thermonuclear weapon testing. Again Strauss's colleagues protested. Murray especially complained that Strauss had authorized an official agency position on Nehru's proposal without consulting the Commissioners.[43]

For Strauss, harried now by the Oppenheimer case and Dixon-Yates, the dispute with Murray was minor but irritating. As before, Strauss moved somewhat reluctantly under the President's direct orders, while attempting to keep the Commission informed without compromising the confidence of either the President or the National Security Council. Strauss informed his colleagues on May 21 that the special committee was meeting, but he did not relate the substance of the discussions during which he and Robert B. Anderson, the Acting Secretary of Defense, had strongly opposed the moratorium to the dismay of Robert R. Bowie of the State Department's policy planning staff.[44]

The struggle for a test moratorium, however, was all shadowboxing in early summer 1954. The moratorium stood no chance at all as long as the United States dominated the thermonuclear club. Initially Dulles had favored the idea as a means of improving United States relations with the British, a position that became unnecessary when Churchill personally informed Eisenhower of Britain's decision to proceed with thermonuclear development, contrary to what Cherwell had told the Americans at Bermuda. With the British vying for the thermonuclear weapon along with the Russians, the Americans were not about to sacrifice any real or imagined advantage. More sensitive to scientific questions after his embarrassment by Molotov in Geneva, Dulles asked for a thorough technical evaluation of the moratorium idea in comparison with its political and propaganda advantages. On the technical level, it was necessary to solicit the views of the Commission directly.[45]

To answer Dulles's questions, the Commission invited representatives of its two weapon laboratories, Edward Teller and Norris E. Bradbury, to comment on the feasibility of suspending United States tests. In the main, the scientists' technical advice was negative and with Oppenheimer's fate hanging in the balance, they refrained from offering political observations. If there were a total ban on tests, they noted, it would still be possible for the Russians to conceal low-yield tests. Furthermore, even if the moratorium were adequately policed, any ban that extended beyond 1957 would seriously impair weapon development in the United States.[46]

Not wishing to appear totally negative, Strauss had the concurrence of all the Commissioners, except Murray, in stating that a moratorium on large-weapon testing would be to America's advantage, an important step toward general disarmament if arranged by a dependable agreement; but such an agreement with the Russians was in Strauss's opinion "illusory." Furthermore, should the Administration decide that an unenforceable agreement with the Russians was desirable for propaganda purposes, Strauss warned that it might not be possible to resume testing thereafter.

224

The United States could then lose more international goodwill than could be gained by sponsoring the moratorium in the first place. Without exploring the matter further, the National Security Council accepted Dulles's and Strauss's recommendations and shelved the moratorium idea on June 24, 1954.[47]

## ATOMS FOR PEACE: WITH OR WITHOUT THE RUSSIANS

For the moment the path toward Atoms for Peace was obscured. With the moratorium and disarmament blocked, the international agency still unchartered, the Russians uncooperative, the British near panic, Oppenheimer cashiered, Dixon-Yates festering, and the atomic energy bill stuck fast in the Senate, the Administration was understandably uncertain about its next step. An obvious alternative was to plunge ahead with a modified international agency, with or without Russian partnership. The advantages of this course of action were clear enough. It would dramatize America's intention to promote internationally the constructive uses of atomic energy, even though Cold War tensions might not be lessened. To some extent, the step would counteract the adverse publicity following the *Lucky Dragon* fallout incident and counterbalance the communists' pleas for outlawing the use of nuclear weapons. Most important, the move would put the Russians in a bad light and tend to counteract centrifugal forces in the Western alliance. It would also be politically popular in the United States.

225

On the negative side officials worried about the consequences of Russian absence from an international agency. A Soviet boycott would frustrate Eisenhower's two main aims in proposing an atomic pool: to lessen Cold War tensions and to siphon off weapon-grade material from existing nuclear stockpiles. In addition to the possibility that the Cold War might even be intensified, there was fear that Soviet espionage would be aided to the extent that the United States provided classified or formerly classified information to the international agency. By proceeding without the Russians, the United States would lose the propaganda advantage of being able to state that Soviet rejections of the plan had scuttled Eisenhower's dream. At the same time, the Russians would be left with the option of joining the agency whenever it suited their interests. Finally, absent Russian participation, the State Department thought it advisable for the United States to negotiate nuclear power agreements directly with various countries, especially with those rich in uranium and thorium deposits, in return for their allegiance and material support.[48]

Characteristically, Eisenhower fretted over the indecision of his advisers. When Strauss appeared before the Joint Committee to testify on the atomic energy bill, the President directed Strauss to make it "abundantly clear" that the United States had no intention of giving up its Atoms-for-

Peace plan just because the Soviet Union had rejected it. By June 4, 1954, Eisenhower had decided to proceed without the Russians, if necessary. He ordered Dulles, Strauss, and Wilson to explore means of sharing atomic energy information through the North Atlantic Treaty Organization (NATO) and other channels in addition to intensifying United States planning efforts on the international bank. At his news conference on July 7, the President unambiguously served notice that he was "not going to let it die, if I can possibly help it." Later, when the Senate filibuster against the atomic energy bill also seemed to threaten Atoms for Peace, Eisenhower even considered introducing a special bill that would at least save the international plan. Although that was ultimately unnecessary, the President reiterated his determination to press forward with or without the Russians when he signed the Atomic Energy Act into law on August 30.[49]

226

Dulles had quickly endorsed the President's decision to proceed, although he knew this move would trouble the British, who were not enthusiastic about an atomic pool without Soviet contributions. Apparently the British feared getting caught shorthanded in an international agency that would dilute American interest in bilateral agreements and weaken Commonwealth obligations between the United Kingdom and uranium-rich South Africa and Australia. Eden expressed these concerns during his June meetings with Eisenhower in Washington, only to receive an eloquent presidential soliloquy on the virtues of the peaceful atom coupled with Eisenhower's vague assurances of American cooperation "within the limits of the law."[50]

Although Strauss also supported the presidential directive, he was not anxious to push plans for the international agency while the fight over the atomic energy bill continued in Congress. On July 12, Strauss, fearing the United States had been losing ground to Soviet delaying tactics, congratulated Eisenhower for his decision to move ahead with the Atoms-for-Peace plan; yet, on the same day, the chairman ordered Snapp to hold up everything on the international agency until after the atomic energy bill had passed. Strauss's motives were unclear, and his refusal to act apparently took the State Department by surprise. Perhaps Strauss wanted to mark time while waiting for passage of the act, with its restrictive international sections that forbade United States participation in a multilateral atomic pool. Certainly he was nervous about the membership in such an organization. He favored limiting membership in the international agency to countries recognized by the United States, a restriction that excluded Communist China. Nevertheless, Strauss continued to promote Eisenhower's program by including glowing references to it in his address before the Veterans of Foreign Wars on August 5.[51]

Most questions concerning the direction of the Atoms-for-Peace plan and the future of the nuclear material pool were resolved by the National Security Council on August 13, 1954. Assuming that the Russians would not participate in the international agency and that the atomic energy bill would become law, the council adopted a policy consistent with the proposed law. Dulles hoped to keep the relationship between the international agency and the United Nations as tenuous as possible in order to avoid criticism of the United Nations in Congress; he estimated that it would take at least two years to negotiate a multilateral agreement that would receive Senate ratification. In the interim, the United States was to maintain its leadership in the peaceful uses of atomic energy by sponsoring international scientific conferences, offering assistance in construction of small-scale research reactors, and providing training programs and technical information.[52]

Even more progress could be made through bilateral negotiations, which would salvage something of the spirit of the President's plan for an international atomic energy bank. In keeping with the agreements for cooperation, Section (123) of the 1954 act, the National Security Council stipulated in NSC 5431/1 that all bilateral agreements for sharing nuclear material would have to meet three requirements. First, no agreement could be inimical to the United States' security, and, where possible, any agreement should promote the United States' own atomic energy interests. In this respect, as Strauss had been recommending since December, the first bilateral agreement might be made with Belgium, which still controlled the uranium-rich Belgian Congo. Second, no agreement could be negotiated that either required weapon-grade materials or significantly diverted fissionable materials or trained personnel from nuclear weapon development in the United States. In every case where the United States provided nuclear materials for research or power reactors, whether by gift, lease, or sale, the Atomic Energy Commission would require the return of all spent fuel and nuclear by-products for reprocessing in the United States. Finally, the council wanted to insure that the United States gained the "maximum psychological and educational advantage" from its endeavors in this field. Dulles was particularly bothered about this point because he thought the directive of the National Security Council fell short of the President's United Nations proposal. Strauss and Robert Cutler allayed Dulles's concerns, however, by arguing that the proposed program would be well received, especially if it were announced by the President in conjunction with ground-breaking ceremonies for the nation's first commercial power reactor at Shippingport, Pennsylvania.[53]

227

Speaking from Denver via radio and television on Labor Day 1954, Eisenhower ended the Administration's long silence about its Atoms-for-Peace plan. Ignoring the Russians except to note that American initiatives had been "cynically blocked in the councils of the world," the President briefly outlined the United States' determination to work for an international agency while negotiating bilateral agreements. This time, however, no one was caught unprepared by the President's speech, which was made all the more dramatic when he used an "atomic wand" in Denver to set a bulldozer in motion at the Shippingport site. Not only was the Commission consulted closely about the contents of the speech, but Strauss had explained the matter carefully to Cole for the information of the Joint Committee. The State Department, in turn, briefed Canada, the United Kingdom, South Africa, France, Portugal, Belgium, and Australia. Subsequently, Eisenhower ordered Dulles and Strauss to implement NSC 5431/1, with the Atomic Energy Commission assigned leadership in formulating a definitive program of action while the State Department continued its diplomatic exploration.[54]


## THE RUSSIAN BOMBSHELL

228

Dulles was looking forward to the ninth session of the United Nations General Assembly in September 1954 as an occasion for announcing the steps the United States intended to take in giving life to the President's proposals. Dulles wished to address the General Assembly early in the session when he planned to propose establishing the international agency and calling an international scientific conference on the peaceful uses of atomic energy. In an effort to draw attention to the speech, Dulles planned to conclude with a dramatic and unexpected announcement that the United States would also extend invitations "to a substantial number of medical and surgical experts from abroad" to work in American cancer hospitals using atomic energy techniques. Leaving to Ambassador Henry Cabot Lodge the task of explaining why the United States had dropped the nuclear material pool from its proposal, Dulles would conclude with the pious assurance that the United States intended to exclude "no nation from participation in this great venture," including the Russians.[55]

On September 22, the day before Dulles was to deliver his address, the Soviet government ended five months of silence on Atoms for Peace by declaring its willingness to continue discussions with the United States. Although the Russians reiterated their desire to obtain an international ban on the use of nuclear weapons, they agreed to examine American ideas for safeguards against the diversion of nuclear materials from research and power reactors to military uses. Then, for the first time, the Russians outlined three "important principles" to be followed in creating the international agency. First, no state or group of states should be permitted to enforce its will on other states. Second, an international atomic energy agency should not jeopardize the security of any of its members. And third, the Russians explicitly agreed with the United States that the agency should report its activities to the Security Council and the General Assembly on the grounds that all matters affecting the security of member states were to be referred to the Security Council as provided in the United Nations' charter.[56]

The Soviet proposal to continue negotiations was a bombshell for Dulles and the Administration; they had assumed that the Russians would not be a party to such an international agreement. Already in its discussions with the British and Canadians the United States had virtually abandoned the March 19 outline in favor of an international agency without an atomic bank and only nominally associated with the United Nations. Passage of the Atomic Energy Act of 1954, as well as British and Canadian nervousness about losing their special nuclear relationship with the United States, had caused the Administration to reevaluate its original approach in favor of an agency planned and initiated by the United States, the United Kingdom, and Canada. France, South Africa, Australia, Portugal, and Belgium would be invited to review the plans and, if in agreement, join the organization as charter members. This approach, however, had its drawbacks. Although the eight member-nations of the "working group" could all be justified by their status as producers or consumers of raw materials, they also constituted the principal colonial powers, including Portugal, not a member of the United Nations, and South Africa, one of the most unpopular countries in Africa and Asia. Nevertheless, in order to satisfy its allies and the law and with a vague hope of ratifying an international agreement by mid-January 1955, the Administration decided to proceed without devising a formula to add acceptable and cooperative nations to the working group.[57] Thus, the Russians' unexpected agreement to continue discussions abruptly ended the Americans' brief consideration of founding a private nuclear club.

229

Not surprisingly, some State Department officials thought the Russian communiqué was only a troublesome propaganda ploy that did not represent serious intentions. For example, Gerard C. Smith, recruited from the Atomic Energy Commission in 1954 as Dulles's atomic energy adviser, put the matter succinctly: "Do we want the Russians in the Agency? and if so, do we want them in the Agency planning now?" Although only forty-one, Smith had an impressive background and wide experience. A graduate of the Yale Law School, he had served in the Navy during World War II and had practiced law in several prominent New York firms before coming to Washington in 1950 as special assistant to Commissioner Murray. Smith's four years in Murray's office exposed him to the intricacies of atomic energy policy at the highest levels. As a Republican, he was acceptable to the Administration. Mature and knowledgeable, Smith was a natural choice as the State Department's expert in atomic energy, which was still in 1954 an esoteric and intimidating subject within the department.

Smith realized that it would not be possible first to establish the agency on American terms and then accept Soviet membership at a later date. Nevertheless, it was also obvious that continuation of discussions with the Soviet Union might paralyze American negotiations with other countries or destroy the United States' momentum toward creating a functioning agency. Smith reflected somewhat bitterly that Americans should welcome Soviet obstruction if the United States ultimately decided it did not really want an international agency. In this fashion, Americans would gain all the good will necessary through bilateral arrangements and still control the situation while appearing to want multilateral international cooperation. The outcome would be the same as the fruitless disarmament negotiations, with all sides agreeing in principle that the goal was desirable but disagreeing on the means to achieve it.[58]

Despite the unresolved problem of responding to the Soviets, the United States presented the second "Preliminary Outline" of an international agency for review and comment by the French, South Africans, Belgians, Portuguese, and Australians. Predictably this outline, which became known as the October 6 plan, did not provide for pooling of nuclear materials as proposed in March. As critics of the pooling idea had stated, without Russian participation it was pointless for the United States and the United Kingdom alone to release weapon materials to an international agency when other purposes would be achieved without actual physical transfer of fissionable material. Even with the Russians in the picture again, the British and Canadians, who had never really liked the pooling concept, were opposed to returning to the original March 19 atom bank idea. More important, the National Security Council in NSC 5431/1 had determined that in keeping with the Atomic Energy Act the United States would "earmark" reasonable quantities of fissionable materials for use in approved projects without actually physically placing the material in an agency bank. Although no one was certain whether the Russians would be interested in the revised proposal, no serious thought was given to returning to the original plan.[59]

Consequently, the Administration was forced to explore a confusing contingency plan in the event the Soviets entered seriously into the eight-power discussions. There was no doubt in the Americans' minds that an international agency with the Russians would be far different from one without them. Strauss, for one, thought it naive to expect that the Soviet Union would honor any commitment merely to earmark material for an agency; he would not be satisfied unless the Russians actually "ponied up" the material to be held physically by the agency. The trouble with his demand, as Strauss knew full well, was that under the Atomic Energy Act it was impossible for the United States to do the same thing. In the face of the State Department's exasperation, Strauss shrugged off the dilemma by stating that he took a "pragmatic view" of the situation, assuming that in the agency the United States would cooperate with friendly nations first. To the State Department's suggestion that the United States might donate a re-

230

search reactor to the agency, Strauss replied that he had already been thinking about placing just such a reactor in Puerto Rico. The only question that Strauss seemed prepared to discuss with the Russians was how to prevent the diversion of nuclear materials from power reactors to weapons. On this score, he was even willing for Commission representatives to meet with Russian experts in Moscow, although Strauss thought the solution was simple enough: merely require all fuel elements from power reactors to be reprocessed under United Nations' auspices.[60]

When the State Department lamented the trend toward more shadow and less substance in the United States' plans for the international agency, Strauss replied that placing even a small amount of fissionable material at the disposal of the agency, rather than at the complete discretion of the United States, would be severely criticized by the Joint Committee as a serious security breach. Strauss, in turn, complained that there were too many "cooks" in the nuclear kitchen. He expressed concern over the divided responsibility among himself, Lodge at the United Nations, and Morehead Patterson, the New York industrialist appointed to negotiate the international agreement. Strauss's pique may have been prompted by Lodge's "freewheeling" on the peaceful uses issues at the General Assembly.

231

Lodge, who had been joined in New York by C. D. Jackson for the Atoms-for-Peace item, worried both the Commission and the State Department with his penchant for departing from the prepared script. In an effort to check Lodge's independence, the State Department had promised the British and the Canadians, as well as the Commission, that they would have prior review of Lodge's remarks. Dulles, however, who was equally worried about keeping "a rein on the combination of Lodge and C. D. Jackson," showed little inclination to suppress the publicity that the two men were generating at the United Nations. With the collapse of the atomic pool, Lodge and Jackson believed it was necessary for the United States to puff its international efforts with movies and atomic energy kits in order to offset Russian propaganda claims that the United States had abandoned its Atoms-for-Peace campaign. Subsequently when Andrei Y. Vyshinsky of the Soviet delegation charged that the President's great proposal of December 1953 had been reduced to isotopes and fertilizer, Lodge and Jackson clamored for approval to make a spectacular announcement that the Atomic Energy Commission had decided to allocate to the international agency 100 kilograms of nuclear materials for peaceful projects.[61]

The idea of announcing the allocation had been discussed before the opening of the General Assembly session, but neither the President nor the Joint Committee had authorized the announcement. Thus, when the initial draft became "lost" at the Commission, no action could be taken. Frantically, C. D. Jackson worked on the telephones from New York while Smith lobbied from within the government to get Strauss to act. In the meantime,

Lodge wrote directly to Eisenhower. He observed that the only way to bring the President's program back to life would be to issue a statement that the United States had set aside a specified quantity of fissionable material earmarked solely for the project.[62]

Whatever the reasons for his reluctance, Strauss could hold out no longer; in a last-minute call to Jackson in New York, Strauss informed him that the State Department had cleared the announcement with White House approval. At that, Jackson drafted a paragraph that he rushed to Lodge, who was just about to begin his remarks. Inserting the paper at the very end of the speech, Lodge dramatically concluded his outline of American proposals by stating, "I have just been authorized by the President of the United States to state to you that the Atomic Energy Commission has allocated 100 kilograms of fissionable material to serve as fuel in the experimental atomic reactors to which the Secretary of State and I have previously referred." Vyshinsky had been furiously scribbling notes as Lodge talked. Jackson later recalled, "When he heard the 100 kilograms statement, [he] shrugged his shoulders, gathered up his papers, and put them in his briefcase—and that was that."[63]

## PLANNING FOR GENEVA

Dulles's United Nations speech focused attention on the proposal for the international agency and the American offer to allocate fissionable material for peaceful purposes, but the text of the speech gave almost as much weight to calling an international scientific conference on the peaceful uses of atomic energy. Like the international agency, the conference had its origins in the events leading up to Eisenhower's United Nations address almost ten months earlier. Strauss had mentioned the idea to Cherwell at Bermuda; and when international discussion of Atoms for Peace reached a stalemate during spring 1954, Strauss had recalled his earlier suggestion as a way of giving substance to the President's proposal. Strauss discussed his idea with Isidor I. Rabi, the Nobel physicist who had replaced Oppenheimer as chairman of the Commission's general advisory committee. Although Rabi had been one of Oppenheimer's staunchest defenders during the security investigation, Strauss greatly respected Rabi as a scientist and sought his views. Rabi accepted Strauss's argument that an international conference might have propaganda value in winning worldwide support among scientists for the President's plan.[64]

Initially Strauss and Rabi were thinking in terms of a small, strictly scientific conference, to be held in the United States and sponsored by the National Academy of Sciences or the National Science Foundation. To keep things simple, Strauss and Rabi envisaged that the delegates would attend as scientists and not as official representatives of their nations. Strauss quickly obtained assurances that the National Science Foundation would consider sponsoring the conference. After checking with the White House, Strauss announced in a speech before the Los Angeles Foreign Affairs Council on April 19, 1954, that the President intended "to convene an international conference of scientists at a later date this year . . . [to explore] the benign and peaceful uses of atomic energy."[65]

Gerard Smith offered the State Department's full cooperation in arranging the conference; but a host of uncertainties, many of them the same as those delaying the whole Atoms-for-Peace plan, made it impossible to come to any final decisions during spring 1954. Would the Soviet Union and other communist countries attend the conference, and could it be held without Russian participation? Would the United States be pressured by other nations to release scientific information that was still classified under the terms of the 1946 act, and was there any possibility of a successful conference without the release of really substantive technical information on nuclear power reactors? Could such an international conference be held in the United States without imposing embarrassing restrictions on communist delegates and other scientists who held views unpopular with Americans? Should the conference be tied to the President's atom bank proposal, or should it deal with a broader range of scientific and technical questions?

233

Rabi discussed these and other considerations with the general advisory committee at its May meeting. Although the conference might well win worldwide support among scientists for the President's proposal, the committee members were even more enthusiastic about the opportunity for "a real forum for the exchange of information in biology, medicine, basic science, and engineering." There was general agreement that political issues should be excluded. Walter G. Whitman, a chemical engineer from the Massachusetts Institute of Technology and a veteran adviser to the Commission, was captivated by the bold approach the President had taken; he urged that the conference be organized around a series of sessions at which delegates would present technical papers on peaceful applications of atomic energy. The conference agenda, the committee agreed, should be drafted by an international working group.[66]

Through Smith at the State Department Strauss arranged for Rabi's appointment as head of the preliminary planning group and obtained permission for Rabi to discuss these suggestions with his counterparts in the United Kingdom and Canada. Even before going abroad, Rabi learned from embassy officials in Washington that both nations had reservations about the political nature of the conference, the wisdom of holding it in the United States, and the feasibility of convening it in 1954. When Rabi, however, took account of these criticisms in drafting a "prospectus" for the conference in July 1954, Smith and his associates at the State Department objected to holding the conference outside the United States. They questioned whether the conference could really avoid political issues; if it did not entertain political issues, the conference would lose its official status and would raise the sticky question of whether delegates from Communist China and East Germany could attend. One obvious solution would be to hold the conference under United Nations auspices, and the State Department was leaning in that direction.[67]

In August 1954 Rabi visited England and France, where his discussions with leading scientists greatly expanded his conception of the conference. In both formal and private meetings Sir John Cockcroft, head of the British nuclear research establishment, proposed a wide range of subjects for the conference agenda, including the social and economic aspects of nuclear energy, basic nuclear science, nuclear technology, research reactors, nuclear power, medical and biological applications, industrial uses of radioactive isotopes, health and safety, education and training, and an exhibition of nuclear information and equipment. Rabi and Cockcroft agreed that the conference would be valuable if the United States, Britain, and Canada all presented papers of real substance on the technical aspects of building nuclear power reactors. Rabi suggested that the conference probably could not be held before spring 1955 in order to give British and American officials time to declassify information that could now be released under the terms of the new Atomic Energy Act. It was also apparent that if their broad agenda was adopted, the conference would have to be sponsored by the United Nations. The French were not happy with United Nations sponsorship but agreed to follow the American lead.[68]

In his United Nations speech on September 23, 1954, Dulles committed the United States to a conference to be sponsored by the international organization. In working with the British and Canadians on the details of the agenda, Smith was joined by John A. Hall, director of the Commission's office of international affairs. A Harvard Ph.D. in government, Hall had joined the State Department after World War II as an adviser to the United States delegation to the United Nations, before going to the Commission in 1948 as its resident expert on liaison with the State Department. Urbane and debonair, Hall looked every inch the professional diplomat. The same age as Smith and with a comparable professional background, Hall had come to know and respect his State Department counterpart during Smith's four years at the Commission.

In planning for the conference on the international organization, Smith and Hall could draw on Cockcroft's memorandum, suggestions from a number of French scientists and representatives of the European scientific community, and strong staff support from the Commission. Robert A. Charpie, a physicist with Union Carbide at Oak Ridge, compiled drafts of the agenda with help from Hafstad, Kenneth Davis, and others. In planning the technical content of the agenda, the group was concerned that many proposed topics could not be discussed in American, British, or Canadian papers because important technical data on power reactor technology were still listed as confidential in the new tripartite classification guide drafted in England early in October; some data, relating to the costs of producing fissionable material and heavy water, were still classified secret or top secret.

After extensive discussion the Commission decided early in January 1955 that the conference papers would be permitted to go beyond the classification guide in only a few specific instances. American delegates could be permitted to discuss the economics of producing uranium concentrates for reactor feed but not actual costs of material from individual sources; the sales price but not the production cost of heavy water; the cost of uranium-235 but only up to a 20-percent enrichment; the general features only of one obsolescent type of reactor fuel element; and details of the aqueous fuel for a homogenous reactor unlikely to be of practical value. None of this information would reveal anything about the leading edge of power reactor technology in the United States. Still, the agenda was far broader than Rabi's original conception of it, and it seemed likely that many delegates, especially from smaller nations with no atomic energy program, would find much of substance in the papers to be presented by scientists from the western nations.[69]

235

By this time the United Nations General Assembly had approved the American proposal for the international conference, and Secretary-General Dag Hammarskjold had taken steps to create the official conference organization. In addition to the agenda, Rabi and Hall were also prepared to suggest appointments of conference officials and rules of procedure. Rabi would serve as the United States member of the United Nations advisory committee that would make formal arrangements for the conference. Rabi was also successful in obtaining the appointment of Walter Whitman of the general advisory committee as secretary-general of the conference. United States officials, especially Strauss, were relieved to have an American in this strategic position. The Americans were willing to concede appointing a scientist from a neutral nation as president of the conference. Over Strauss's strong opposition, the State Department accepted Britain's nomination of Homi J. Bhabha of India as president; but the department insisted that the conference be held in Geneva, Switzerland, largely because it would be more economical to use existing United Nations buildings there rather than build new facilities elsewhere.[70]

## BILATERAL AGREEMENTS

While the United Nations organized the international scientific conference to be held at Geneva, the United States pressed ahead with its own program for the international development of atomic energy. On November 4, 1954,

Eisenhower had appointed Morehead Patterson to be the principal United States Atoms-for-Peace negotiator. Patterson, who had directed development of equipment for classified projects at Savannah River and Hanford while he was president of American Machine and Foundry, had just completed his first major diplomatic assignment as United States representative at the 1954 disarmament talks conducted in London during May and June. He accepted the President's challenge to produce "deeds, not words" by directing a vigorous program of bilateral discussions while at the same time advancing negotiations to establish the International Atomic Energy Agency.[71]

The first agreements for cooperation concluded in 1955 modestly provided for American assistance in establishing research reactors abroad. The research bilaterals, as they were called, provided for the exchange of unclassified information on the design, construction, and experimental operation of research reactors. In addition, the Commission agreed to lease to each participating nation not more than six kilograms (at any one time) of uranium enriched to 20-percent uranium-235. The agreements also required cooperating countries to maintain adequate safeguards and accounting procedures as well as to permit American inspection of research reactors in which leased fuel was used. Finally, the research bilaterals mandated the reprocessing of all spent fuel elements by the United States. From the Commission's perspective, the military potential of such transactions was minor.[72]

By the time the Geneva conference was convened in August 1955, the Commission had negotiated two dozen research bilaterals. The first of these agreements was concluded with the government of Turkey on June 10, 1955, after the Joint Committee was assured that the Turkish bilateral was not "open ended" in its provisions for the lease of special nuclear materials. Typical of the agreements signed at this time, at the request of the Turkish government, American firms would be allowed to sell research reactors to Turkey and to provide other assistance including information related to health and safety problems, the use of reactors in medical therapy, and the use of radioactive isotopes in biological, agricultural, and industrial research. By 1961 the United States had negotiated thirty-eight research bilaterals with thirty-seven participating countries.[73]

The Commission also offered technical assistance to foreign countries developing research reactor plans, including advice in selecting an appropriate reactor and guidance in contacting United States industrial firms to obtain detailed assistance in solving design problems. Once a design was adopted, Commission staff experts assisted in preparing a hazard evaluation report. Although the United States did not assure operational safety of the foreign research reactor or assume liability for accidents, the Commission's technical committee reviewed the hazard report along with the research plans before offering financial assistance or allocating fuel.[74]

236

Of greater concern to the Administration and the Commission were the power bilateral agreements, negotiated at the same time, and often in conjunction with the research bilaterals. In January 1955 the Commission perceived a close relationship between United States foreign policies on nuclear power and nuclear weapons. To maintain American nuclear strength, the Commission advised the National Security Council that the United States had to obtain uranium abroad, establish overseas bases, and convince its allies that nuclear weapons could be legitimately used against communist aggression. Although the Atoms-for-Peace program could not reduce foreign anxiety concerning nuclear war, the Commission believed that atomic power contributing to the "peaceful well-being of the world" would greatly assist in attaining these objectives while at the same time refuting Soviet propaganda that the United States was concerned solely with the military atom.[75]

Thus, from the Commission's perspective, priority was given to aggressive implementation of the foreign power reactor program. Only secondarily did the Commission support multilateral projects such as the International Atomic Energy Agency. In fact, because power bilaterals offered political and economic advantages, as well as maximum supervision of foreign activities, Commissioner Murray hoped the United States would continue negotiating bilateral agreements even after the international agency was established. On the other hand, Murray, who had long advocated a more vigorous American program, did not object to framing bilateral agreements in such a way that they would be compatible with the international agency or any other multilateral group of nations that the United States approved.[76]

237

A year had now passed since the President had made his momentous speech at the United Nations. During those twelve months not only the American government but also its allies and the Soviet Union had attempted to respond, each in its own way, to the proposal that had captured world attention. With the failure to make any headway on either disarmament or a moratorium on thermonuclear tests, the urgency for some agreement on an international agency became more apparent. In the face of Soviet objections, Eisenhower had determined to press ahead without the Russians, even if that meant limiting international cooperation to a series of bilateral arrangements. The unexpected announcement of Soviet support in September, however, had revived the Administration's hopes for the international agency. The primary outlook for the new organizations and for the peaceful uses conference suggested that Atoms for Peace might be successfully launched on the diplomatic front in 1955. Still to be determined was the best course the Administration might take in pursuit of the peaceful atom at home and abroad.

## CHAPTER 9

# PURSUIT OF
# THE PEACEFUL ATOM

The efforts of John Foster Dulles in the State Department and Henry Cabot Lodge and C. D. Jackson in the United Nations in the closing weeks of 1954 at last had given the Eisenhower Administration some evidence of positive achievement in establishing the framework for international control of atomic energy. Unless the Russians balked again, the charter for the new international agency might be completed for ratification by the time the nations of the world convened in Geneva, Switzerland, in September 1955 for the opening of an international conference on the peaceful uses of atomic energy. Erecting the international framework, however, constituted only a small part of the President's proposal. It was equally important to the Administration that the United States produce something more tangible than draft charters, diplomatic notes, and grandiose plans for international meetings. Eisenhower sensed that his dreams for the peaceful atom would attain reality only when informed citizens in America and throughout the world had practical evidence of the peaceful uses of atomic energy. As 1954 produced more talk than solid results, the President became more impatient. He seemed determined in the new year that the nation should produce something, if only a symbol, that demonstrated the beneficial application of nuclear technology.

The President's determination sent ripples of influence through the National Security Council to several departments and agencies, but none was more directly affected than the Atomic Energy Commission. As the nation's manager and promoter of nuclear technology, the Commission was the one agency that could produce the hardware or other visible accomplishments that the President was seeking. In one respect, Eisenhower's personal interest offered the Commission an exceptional opportunity: It assured the agency a sympathetic ear, if not uncritical endorsement of its programs and budgets. In other respects, however, meeting the President's expectations posed a dilemma for Strauss and his associates.

On the one hand, no group could have been more eager to fulfill the President's hopes by demonstrating the practical benefits of the atom. All the Commissioners personally believed in the promise of atomic energy and were as anxious as the President to see that promise realized. They were not immune to the sense of moral compulsion that drove the President to seek some redeeming value in a new technology that threatened the future of civilization. They responded to the challenge posed by the British and the Russians in the international race for nuclear power. They shared the view that nuclear technology could be used as a benign force, demonstrating the superiority of the democratic system and a capitalistic economy, as well as a horrifying threat in the Cold War.

239

On the other hand, Strauss and his colleagues were also aware of their responsibility as managers and guardians of a new technology to see that it was developed wisely, safely, and economically. During the Eisenhower Administration, nuclear technology had caught the imaginations of both influential business leaders and many ordinary citizens at home and abroad. The almost unbridled enthusiasm over the potential uses of atomic energy raised the danger of heavy political and financial commitments to questionable projects. Precipitous decisions could result in embarrassing the Administration, imposing severe financial losses on American business, endangering the public safety, fostering monopolistic control of the new technology, undermining private ownership of electric utilities, damaging national prestige, and losing the Cold War. In short, the dilemma was how to promote and support the Administration's pursuit of the peaceful atom while at the same time exercising responsible control over its development.

## NUCLEAR POWER AND FOREIGN POLICY

No one was more sensitive to the relationships between nuclear power and foreign policy at the beginning of 1955 than was Lewis Strauss. For six months Strauss and Roy Snapp, his representative on the National Security Council's planning board, had been struggling to steer the council's foreign policy pronouncements in a direction that made sense in terms of nuclear technology. Fully convinced that the United States could employ the promise of nuclear power as a major instrument in foreign policy, the planning board had become impatient with the technical reservations and objections that Snapp relayed from the Commission. After listening to Snapp's arguments, the planning board had given up the idea that research reactors could be a credible expression of the Atoms-for-Peace program, but the board refused to abandon small reactors as the quickest way to demonstrate nuclear power abroad. This time the board recommended small power reactors producing up to 20,000 kilowatts, on the theory that reactors of that size might be economical in certain remote, high-cost power areas in foreign countries. The Commission considered the proposal risky because there was no solid evidence that a foreign market for small power reactors existed.[1]

240 The planning board's final version, sent to the National Security Council early in March 1955, represented the first formal restatement of the Administration's policy on the international atom since April 1953. The early development of nuclear power was still the key to maintaining the United States' lead in nuclear technology. The nation's nuclear facilities and technology were "a great asset in the effort to promote a peaceful world compatible with a free and dynamic American society." Promoting the peaceful uses of nuclear energy could "generate free world respect and support for the constructive purposes of U.S. foreign policy, . . . strengthen American world leadership and disprove the Communists' propaganda charges that the U.S. is concerned solely with the destructive uses of the atom." Both the Soviet Union and the United Kingdom, according to the policy statement, were challenging America's superiority for promoting nuclear power. More veiled in this version than in earlier drafts was the military justification for Atoms for Peace, but the Administration understood that assistance to other nations, particularly Belgium and South Africa, in developing nuclear technology could be vital in assuring continued American access to foreign sources of uranium ore.[2]

Early in the National Security Council meeting on March 10, 1955, Strauss questioned a statement in the policy paper that "private rather than government financing should be used to the maximum extent possible, without jeopardizing the early development of nuclear power." Strauss complained that the statement implied that private financing would delay development, but Eisenhower, probably to Strauss's consternation, took just the opposite view. The President thought that atomic power should be developed without too much concern about the role of private industry, although he said he firmly believed in private enterprise. He thought the council's first concern should be the national interest, not the demands of private industry. The council quickly agreed that peaceful uses would be developed "as rapidly as the interests of the United States dictate, seeking private financing wherever possible."[3] The new policy certainly would not help Strauss in promoting private development of nuclear power in the face of Joint Committee demands for a government program.

## STRAUSS BUILDS HIS TEAM

Despite his aggressive leadership as chairman during 1954, Strauss was not in the best position for the impending public debate as 1955 began. Three Commissioners—Zuckert, Smyth, and Campbell—had left office during the last six months of the year. To replace Zuckert and Smyth, the President had accepted Strauss's recommendations, nominating two distinguished scientists, both of whom had served on the Commission's general advisory committee. Willard F. Libby, a talented chemist, had been associated with the atomic energy project since the 1940s, first with gaseous-diffusion research during World War II and then as a scientist working under Commission research contracts at the University of Chicago. As a member of the general advisory committee since 1950, Libby had staunchly supported the Commission's activities in basic research and weapon development.[4]

241

Although Libby was later to win the Nobel prize in chemistry for his radiocarbon dating techniques, John von Neumann was even more renowned than Libby at the time of his nomination to the Commission. One of the nation's most respected physicists, a world authority in mathematics, and a pioneer in the theory of games, von Neumann had built at Princeton one of the first large electronic computers, which had helped to resolve some complex design problems associated with thermonuclear weapons.[5] Strauss had known von Neumann personally for many years and admired his friend for his intellectual brilliance and his unstinting devotion of his talents to national defense in the Cold War. Strauss could hardly have done better in choosing men with a broad understanding of nuclear science and technology, but both were relatively inexperienced in the rough and tumble of political life in Washington. Presumably they would confine themselves to technical matters and leave the initiative on policy to Strauss, as neither Zuckert nor Smyth had been willing to do.

As trusted members of the inner establishment, neither nominee seemed vulnerable to challenge by the Joint Committee. Libby, in fact, was confirmed speedily without a formal hearing, but Congress adjourned late in 1954 without acting on the von Neumann nomination. Strauss learned privately that there was some uneasiness in the Joint Committee about von Neumann's security record. There was some concern that von Neumann was a close friend of Oppenheimer's and that he held an appointment at the Institute for Advanced Study, where Oppenheimer was director. For years both men had kept their highly classified atomic energy files in a common vault at the institute, and there were rumors that Oppenheimer's secretary, who had maintained his classified files, would now work for von Neumann. Buried in von Neumann's security file was a notation that he had written a letter on behalf of one defendant in the Canadian atomic spy trials in 1946.

Strauss responded by noting that the accused person had been acquitted. No information in the file was new; nor had it prevented the government from using von Neumann on highly classified projects for almost a decade. The security problem at the institute had been resolved after removing all of Oppenheimer's classified files from the facility; and, Strauss assured the council, Oppenheimer's secretary would not be working for von Neumann. No one inside the establishment seemed concerned about von Neumann's personal integrity, much less his loyalty, but the potential for a second Oppenheimer case was frightening. Eisenhower agreed with Strauss that the Administration should stand firm on the nomination, and members of the Joint Committee cooperated by keeping the matter quiet and arranging to meet with von Neumann individually and privately to avoid giving hints to the press. So touchy was the whole affair, however, that von Neumann's confirmation was delayed until mid-March 1955.[6]

242

Strauss also had to accommodate the departure of several key members of the staff. Nichols privately told the chairman in September that he would be leaving in spring 1955 to set himself up as an engineering consultant.[7] Some members of the staff believed that having purged the staff of some of the "liberal," antimilitary holdovers from the Lilienthal period, Nichols considered his job essentially complete; the headquarters staff seemed fully in the control of former Army engineers from the Manhattan Project. Others guessed that Nichols was leaving because, with Strauss as chairman, he saw no possibility of exercising the kind of operational control over the agency that General Groves had enjoyed in the Manhattan Project.

Strauss was perhaps most reluctant to see Hafstad resign as director of reactor development. After five years on the job Hafstad was ready to move into a more lucrative position in business, which opened up at the Chase National Bank in New York with Strauss's recommendation. Over the years Strauss and Hafstad had become personal friends, and Strauss had come to rely heavily on Hafstad's judgment in technical matters.[8]

Replacing Hafstad was to be something of an ordeal for Strauss because the issue led to another round in his endless feud with Murray. In this case Murray was absolutely unyielding in his determination to see Rickover as Hafstad's successor. Strauss could hardly deny Rickover's technical qualifications on the basis of his record in developing naval propulsion reactors. The undeniable, if somewhat embarrassing, fact was that Rickover was the only Commission official who could lay claim to success in building power reactors. But Rickover's highly individualistic style, his close ties to the Joint Committee, and his hard-nosed approach to relations with private industry gave Strauss reason to seek other candidates. Strauss's friends in private industry and leading scientists in the national laboratories warned the chairman that Rickover's appointment would lead to mass defections from the Commission's reactor development program. Without committing himself too firmly, Strauss supported Richard L. Doan, a physicist who directed the nuclear activities of the Phillips Petroleum Company, which operated the Commission's national reactor testing station in Idaho. With Strauss and Murray at a stand-off, Libby refused to take sides, and Strauss was deprived of von Neumann's support pending his Congressional confirmation.[9]

Finally, late in February 1955, a compromise candidate emerged in W. Kenneth Davis, who had been serving as acting director of the reactor development division since Hafstad's departure.[10] Davis was a chemical engineer who had joined Hafstad's staff in April 1954. Just thirty-six years old, Davis had four years of experience in nuclear technology with the California Research and Development Company, a subsidiary of Standard Oil of California, where he had worked on the Commission's Livermore project to develop a large accelerator for producing plutonium and tritium. Like Hafstad, Davis was not a specialist in reactor technology, but he had demonstrated good judgment and administrative ability in his presentations to the Commissioners. He had quickly grasped the issues involved in bringing industry into nuclear power development, and he was a principal architect of the power demonstration reactor program. For technical support and a working knowledge of the division's activities, Davis recruited as his deputy Louis H. Roddis, Jr., a former naval engineering officer who had been a member of Rickover's senior staff since 1946.[11]

243

Strauss also lost the services of two other men who had been at the center of the Commission's activities since the 1940s. Roy Snapp had organized the secretariat and then had served as the Commission's representative on the planning board of the National Security Council. Edward R. Trapnell, after working in public information matters and special projects like the New York briefing of President-elect Eisenhower, had become director of Congressional relations. Both men found the agency under Strauss increasingly uncongenial and decided to leave government for the business world.[12]

Snapp was replaced as secretary of the Commission by Woodford B. McCool, whom Snapp had recruited in 1953. McCool, however, would never become one of Strauss's protégés. Intensely loyal to the Commission, always tough and hard driving, McCool would occasionally clear the Commission meeting room of all staff members so that Strauss and Murray could vent their anger and frustration in private. Nonetheless, McCool principally devoted himself to institutionalizing a professional secretariat that insured the accurate recording of the Commission's decision-making process. In time, it became well known throughout the Commission that one would "get it straight" from McCool, who could be distant and rigid but who above all protected the integrity of the decision process.

## THE NUCLEAR MERCHANT SHIP

During a long session of the National Security Council on March 10, 1955, the discussion drifted to the possibility of installing a nuclear propulsion plant in a merchant ship. Eisenhower was fascinated with this idea, which had come from Admiral Arthur W. Radford, chairman of the Joint Chiefs of Staff. The United States had been the first nation in the world to use nuclear power to propel warships, as the spectacular performance of the *Nautilus*, the world's first nuclear submarine, had just demonstrated. What could better promote Atoms for Peace than to use the same or a similar propulsion system in a commercial vessel?

Strauss assured the President that the Commission already had a contractor investigating the idea, but he was more than a little troubled by Eisenhower's half-serious suggestion that the Commission try to get a nuclear-powered commercial ship in operation within three months. When Strauss reported two weeks later that the ship would cost $12 million and take two years to build, he suggested that by that time the Atoms-for-Peace program would be so far along that the ship would have no great impact on world opinion. The ship could be completed sooner, Strauss admitted, with a high priority, but such a move would inevitably interfere with developing nuclear ships for the Navy. Even on a less pressing schedule, Strauss said, Rickover had reservations about the idea. Rickover doubted that a well-qualified crew could be trained in two years, and he thought it risky to rely on a power plant as new as that in the *Nautilus* to maintain scheduled sailing dates during a well-publicized world tour. [13]

Ignoring these warnings, the National Security Council reaffirmed its directive to the Commission to "make an urgent study, including estimates of cost and time of completion, of installing at the earliest possible date a nuclear reactor propulsion unit in a U.S. merchant ship, which ship might travel throughout the free world to dramatize" the Atoms-for-Peace program. Working almost around the clock with headquarters and field personnel, Davis completed the report on April 5. The next day, with no time to clear the draft with his fellow Commissioners, Strauss presented the report to the National Security Council. Although the time estimated to complete the project had now risen to thirty months and the cost to $31 million, both Eisenhower and Vice-President Nixon were enthusiastic. Strauss again warned that the project might delay Rickover's work on nuclear submarines, but the council approved high-priority construction of a ship using a standard dry-cargo hull and a reactor similar to that in the *Nautilus*. When Strauss conveyed this decision to the Commissioners a week later, they were faced with another fait accompli in formulating nuclear policy. [14]

Despite the President's endorsement in a New York speech in April 1955, the ship project foundered in Congress. Strauss and the Commission-

244

ers set aside their private misgivings and loyally supported the project before the Subcommittee on Authorizing Legislation of the Joint Committee,
but Holifield and the subcommittee skillfully used Rickover to slow it
down. The spectacular success of the *Nautilus* had vindicated the Joint
Committee's tenacious support of Rickover in his efforts in summer 1953
to obtain promotion to rear admiral and thereby remain head of the naval
propulsion project. Carefully avoiding any comment on the wisdom of the
President's decision to build the ship, Rickover testified in May 1955
that the project would inevitably interfere with his own efforts to build a
nuclear navy. Rickover's reservations were enough to derail the project, at
least temporarily, as Holifield's subcommittee deleted it from the authorization bill.[15]

## THE SMALL POWER REACTOR

Strauss and the Commission had just as much trouble curbing the Administration's enthusiasm for the small power reactor. In January 1955 Nelson A. Rockefeller, who had succeeded C. D. Jackson as the President's
special assistant, became infatuated with the idea that power reactors might
serve as the basis for an "Atomic Marshall Plan" for the world. Rockefeller
was anxious to implement the council's directive as boldly as possible by
offering research reactors to friendly countries and rapidly declassifying
power reactor information while providing assurances on the availability of
enriched uranium. Rockefeller envisioned the United States paying about
$15 million for at least forty research reactors, as well as aiding India,
Japan, Brazil (where there were important impending elections), and Italy
with immediate power reactor programs. Neither the Commission nor the
Department of State, however, was enthusiastic about Rockefeller's expansive plans. From the State Department came complaints that no one—
including foreign service officers, Commission staff, or prospective foreign
recipients—knew enough about technology to implement Rockefeller's
suggestion. Furthermore, with Strauss's concurrence, Gerard Smith objected to the temptation to push atomic energy beyond its technical possibilities in order to gain short-term psychological advantages.[16]

Rockefeller, nevertheless, prevailed upon the President to announce
during his commencement address at Pennsylvania State University on
June 11, 1955, that the United States had made important progress in
negotiating agreements with ten foreign countries. Furthermore, Eisenhower said the United States would "contribute half the cost" of building
research reactors abroad. In addition to announcing publicly the essence
of the National Security Council's decision to promote American-built nuclear reactors abroad, the President promised sufficient technological and
material assistance to support foreign development. Yet, for all of his opti-

mism, Eisenhower confessed to the graduates that the social and political problems accompanying nuclear power development could "be foreseen but dimly." The solutions, he suggested, might require the lifetime work of some of those present that day at University Park.[17]

In the face of the Administration's enthusiasm over small power reactors, Strauss had to resort to delaying tactics rather than overt opposition. Despite occasional prodding from Murray, Strauss avoided the subject for months. In July 1955 he told the National Security Council that the Commission was already involved in several projects to develop small reactors and that he did not think that the council should dictate the specific size or design. The precise size of the reactor was a technical matter that he thought the Commission should decide. When the President seemed to accept his argument, Strauss assumed that the council agreed, and he later confirmed with the council's staff his conclusion that the meeting had reduced the directive to a mere recommendation.[18]

246

## A SECOND INVITATION TO INDUSTRY

Strauss had broad support within the Commission and the staff for his opinion that a precise requirement for a power reactor did not make much sense. The most economically promising reactors appeared to be those several times larger in capacity than the 10,000 kilowatts now prescribed by the National Security Council, and as yet no one reactor type was clearly superior to any other for this application. A better approach seemed one the Commission was already considering: to ask industry to submit proposals for developing and building reactors smaller than those resulting from the first round of the power demonstration reactor program.[19]

Other considerations also recommended a second round. First, it would allay criticism that the terms of the first round limited participation only to teams of very large equipment manufacturers and utilities. Second, small electric cooperatives were effectively excluded by the Commission's refusal to contribute to plant costs under the first round. Third, some way was needed to accept the proposal from the Consumers Public Power District, which Libby considered technically superior to the others. And fourth, although it was never discussed explicitly in formal Commission meetings, Strauss was determined to keep the government out of commercial reactor development after Shippingport was built. So fixed was he on this point that he risked challenging Eisenhower's direct orders at the March 10 meeting of the National Security Council to give more weight to speedy development of nuclear power than to private participation by industry.

Strauss hoped that Commission approval of the second round would dissipate the criticisms from all sides. In addition to the kinds of assistance offered in the first round, the second invitation, announced on September 21, 1955, requested proposals in three specific output ranges, all less than 40,000 kilowatts, and offered broader assistance in providing that the Commission would take title to any portions of the plant constructed with government funds. In this sense, the second round represented a return to the type of joint government-industry project adopted for Shippingport. By establishing the deadline for proposals as February 1, 1956, the Commission also acknowledged the charge that the response time allowed for the first round had been too short to permit many companies to participate.[20]

Although announcement of the second round was received favorably in most quarters, it actually exacerbated relations with the National Security Council. Members of the planning board, led by Robert R. Bowie and other State Department representatives, insisted that the small-reactor requirement had not been rescinded. They were incensed that Strauss had chosen to ignore the President's order and cavalierly to assume that the Commission's judgment in this matter should prevail. Navy Commander Charles E. Nelson, who had replaced Snapp as the Commission's representative on the planning board, was frustrated by what he considered Bowie's sincere but wrong-headed notion that the small reactor could bring immediate success for the Atoms-for-Peace program and that there were unique aspects of small-reactor technology that the Commission was ignoring in the demonstration programs. So vigorous was the planning board's reaction that Strauss had to withdraw his original report on the small reactor, which had attempted to finesse the presidential requirement. Strauss tried to make light of the matter on February 9, 1956, when he told the Security Council that he was facing a "soft impeachment" on grounds of incompetence and insubordination. First, Strauss questioned whether the planning board was really qualified to select the type and size of reactor most appropriate for use abroad; second, Strauss contended that the Commission, through the demonstration program, had done far more to develop reactor technology than the single small-reactor project could hope to accomplish. The President agreed, and the requirement in the March 14, 1955, directive was revised to read that the United States "as rapidly as possible" would develop "power reactors of an appropriate size and design for use abroad." The implication was clear that the Commission, not the National Security Council, would determine what was appropriate.[21]

247

## DIXON-YATES AGAIN

During winter 1955 Strauss also faced renewed political conflict over the Dixon-Yates proposal. An early action of the new Democratic majority on the Joint Committee had called upon the Commission to cancel the contract, but that request in itself indicated that the Democrats still did not have enough votes to kill Dixon-Yates in a direct assault. Instead, they resorted to delaying tactics, attempted unsuccessfully to call hearings on the contract, and tried to put pressure on insurance companies to withdraw financial support from the project. Under the circumstances, Strauss took a hard line against the almost daily attacks on Dixon-Yates. He consistently turned aside Murray's attempts to get a formal Commission vote on canceling the contract and elected to consider Eisenhower's strong public statements of support as binding on the Commission. [22]

Failing to shake Strauss or the President, the Democrats quietly began probing every detail of the contract negotiations during the previous summer for any evidence of irregularity. Early in February a promising clue turned up in some sleuthing by Joseph Volpe, Jr., who had been retained by a group of intervenors opposing the waiver of certain debt-financing requirements by the Securities and Exchange Commission. Volpe, former general counsel at the Atomic Energy Commission and one of Oppenheimer's attorneys during the security hearings, knew how to use the Washington bureaucracy to gain information, and he had no compunctions about embarrassing Strauss. Following rumors that some "mystery man" had been involved in the contract negotiations between the Dixon-Yates group and the government, Volpe discovered that Adolphe H. Wenzell, a vice-president and director of the First Boston Corporation, had served as a consultant to the Bureau of the Budget on the Dixon-Yates project during the first four months of 1954, at the same time that he was advising the Dixon-Yates group on financing construction of the power plant. Volpe alerted Senators Clinton Anderson and Lister Hill, who asked the bureau for information about Wenzell's employment. When it developed that records of Wenzell's participation had not been included in supposedly complete chronologies prepared by the Atomic Energy Commission and the bureau on the Dixon-Yates negotiations, Hill in a Senate speech on February 18, 1955, charged the Administration with concealing important facts about Dixon-Yates. In the scramble to check their records, bureau and Commission officials found additional instances of Wenzell's participation, revelations that inevitably led to more charges of a cover-up. [23]

Both Eisenhower and Strauss, however, stood firm in the face of political sniping. Unless positive evidence of improper or illegal activities by Wenzell turned up, they thought Dixon-Yates would probably weather the storm. More serious at the moment were reports from Memphis that the city would not accept power from the Dixon-Yates plant even if it were built. During the early phases of contract negotiations in summer 1954, Memphis city officials had expressed no enthusiasm for the Dixon-Yates solution, mainly because the plant would be located across the Mississippi River from Memphis, in Arkansas; the city would have to rely upon another

248

state for rate and service regulations. There was also some sympathy in Memphis for the Tennessee Valley Authority, which had been providing power to the city for more than a decade. Two alternatives to Dixon-Yates were apparent: the city could join pro-TVA forces, overwhelming in Tennessee, to obtain construction of a TVA power plant on the eastern side of the river, or the city could build its own power plant. Walter Von Treschkow, a veteran promoter of electric utility financing, was urging the latter course on city leaders as a practical solution and on the Republican party as a way of halting TVA growth while avoiding the inevitable political damage to the party from a direct assault on TVA.[24]

As new charges in the Wenzell affair continued to fuel the Dixon-Yates controversy in Washington during spring 1955, Memphis leaders became more explicit in rejecting Dixon-Yates power, if only in private communications to the Commission and the Bureau of the Budget. General Manager Nichols took these seriously enough in March to start some contingency planning for terminating the contract. In June the issue came to a head when the Securities and Exchange Commission began hearings on debt-financing of the Dixon-Yates project. When Volpe announced plans to call Wenzell to testify, Sherman Adams of the White House asked the Securities and Exchange Commission to postpone the hearings for several days. They were not renewed until the House had voted on the TVA appropriations bill, which included funds both to build a transmission line from the Dixon-Yates plant across the river to TVA territory and to construct a TVA steam plant at Fulton, Tennessee, on the east bank of the river. When the House voted down the Fulton plant, the Memphis officials publicly declared their intention to build a municipal power plant.[25]

This decision, plus the Democrats' determination to call hearings before the Senate Judiciary Subcommittee on Antitrust and Monopoly, spelled the doom of Dixon-Yates. In response to a barrage of questions at a press conference on July 6, Eisenhower expressed his delight that Memphis was taking responsibility for its power needs at the local level. As Senator Estes Kefauver continued to make headlines and political capital out of Wenzell's testimony at the hearings, Strauss began to back away from Dixon-Yates. On July 16, Eisenhower accepted the recommendation from the Atomic Energy Commission and the Bureau of the Budget that the contract be terminated.[26]

Even then the political repercussions of Dixon-Yates did not end. A legal opinion from the Atomic Energy Commission and a ruling from the Comptroller General cast doubt on the validity of the Dixon-Yates contract on the grounds that Wenzell's activity had constituted a conflict of interest. The Commission's effort to negotiate a cancellation settlement with the Dixon-Yates group was thus aborted, and the company went to court in an effort to recoup up to $3.5 million already spent in the project.[27]

249

## REACTORS AT GENEVA

While Strauss and the Administration fought to save the Dixon-Yates plan in early summer 1955, the Commission was at the same time preparing for an unprecedented presentation of American accomplishments in nuclear technology. The United States had already taken the initiative in organizing the international conference on the peaceful uses of atomic energy that the United Nations was sponsoring in Geneva in August. In planning the conference the Commission had decided in the United States' presentation to highlight American achievements in developing commercial nuclear power. Mirroring the five-year reactor program, the American papers and exhibits presented at Geneva were impressive in the breadth and sophistication of the technology produced under the Commission's auspices. While some nations in Western Europe could cite experiments in reactor physics or vague plans for designing experimental reactors, the United States presented an astounding panoply of richly detailed information, not only in reactor technology but also in other areas of the nuclear sciences. American delegates described in full engineering detail reactors actually operating or under construction in the United States, including the full-scale Shippingport plant.[28]

The only nations potentially capable of challenging the United States in developing power reactors were the Soviet Union and the United Kingdom. Although the Russians described a small power reactor already in operation, questions by American delegates at the Geneva conference revealed that the plant was neither very sophisticated in design nor efficient in operation—smaller and much less efficient than the Shippingport plant, which would be far from economically competitive with conventional power plants. Surprising about the Soviet presentation in Geneva was the highly technical competence of Russian scientists and engineers generally and the large numbers of students in training in universities and technical schools.

The British reactor effort was miniscule by comparison with the five-year reactor and power demonstration programs, but it was sharply focused on commercial power. The British put their best efforts, not in the scientific and technical exhibit at the United Nations site, but rather in the commercial exhibit in downtown Geneva. Equally impressive were the British descriptions of the new Calder Hall reactors, then under construction. These dual-purpose reactors would produce both plutonium for weapons and power for civilian use; the plutonium subsidy and the relatively high cost of power in Britain were enough to make the Calder Hall plants look economically attractive as power producers. Thus, the British effort, although modest by comparison, commanded a sense of reality and directed purpose that the American program lacked. As one news magazine put it, the United States was ahead in the race for nuclear power "but not as far ahead as you might think." One American scientist was reported as saying: "If the United States vanished off the face of the earth tomorrow, the rest of the world could easily overtake our atomic science within three years."[29]

Overseas competition was developing, but Strauss continued to remind the Congress and the public that American achievements had been substantial. By late 1955 all four projects in the first round of the power demonstration reactor program were moving forward. The Detroit Edison consortium had formed the Power Reactor Development Company, which was planning to build a breeder reactor named for Enrico Fermi near Monroe, Michigan. Both the Consumers and Yankee proposals had been revised to conform with the terms of the first-round invitation, and the offer by the Nuclear Power Group had been replaced by a decision by Commonwealth Edison of Chicago to build a boiling-water reactor at Dresden, Illinois, independent of government support. Two other utilities in the East had already announced plans to build full-scale nuclear plants as independent ventures.[30]

251

Equally encouraging was the response to the second round. Six of the seven proposals received on February 1, 1956, were from small municipal power systems or cooperatives. There was at least one proposal for each range of capacities set forth in the invitation, and virtually every type of reactor under consideration by the Commission was represented. The response also nicely complemented the first round in terms of geographic distribution.[31] The Commission probably could not have done better if it had orchestrated the response itself. Indeed, it would have been remarkable if Strauss, Davis, and others did not steer some proposals into appropriate categories.

In the Commission's laboratories the five-year program was still the focus of attention as the five original experiments were supplemented by one new project at Oak Ridge and two at Los Alamos. Descriptions of the five-year program suggested that the Commission was exploring a remarkable variety of approaches, each intended to determine the engineering feasibility of a different design. Each was pictured as drawing on existing scientific and technical data and in turn contributing new information for the next generation of experiments or demonstration plants. The five-year program appeared rational and comprehensive, but it lacked focus; it offered no simple, direct, and predictable route to nuclear power.

## BUILDING THE REGULATORY STRUCTURE

Strauss could take some satisfaction in the staff's achievements in developing the administrative and regulatory structure necessary to support and control the new nuclear industry. The task had been far more difficult and time-consuming than most people had expected, but Harold Price had refused to be hurried as he erected the new structure. In the last six months of 1954, after the act had been passed, the task groups under Price's direction had drafted most new regulations required to govern private ownership of reactors and other facilities using fissionable material. Once the Commissioners had reviewed the drafts, Price arranged to confer with utility executives, scientists, engineers, and state officials to explain the drafts and gather comments. By summer 1955, Price's staff had been organized as a new Commission division of civilian application, which prepared new drafts of the regulations. By the end of the year, the Commission had approved most regulations in final form, and they were published for public comment before becoming effective in spring 1956. Even after this long process, Price had to admit to the Commissioners that the new regulations were little more than a beginning. Most of them had to anticipate the workings of a commercial technology that did not yet exist. The work required a delicate balance between protecting the public with effective regulations and giving private industry as much freedom from regulation as possible. Whether a proper balance had been struck could be determined only after industry had had an opportunity to test the new rules.[32]

252

Creating a new industry also required the wide dissemination of nuclear technology. Under new security regulations the Commission gave engineers from industry clearances to special categories of reactor data after only limited investigation. By late 1955 more than six hundred access permits had been granted to various companies, and more than three thousand security clearances had been processed in the last half of that year. Before the holders of these new limited or "L" clearances could use them, however, the Commission staff had to review thousands of technical documents and laboratory reports to determine which could be placed in the new classified category, which still contained secret restricted data, and which were unclassified. Of the twenty-five thousand reports reviewed by February 1956, more than one-third had been declassified entirely and about one-fourth had been downgraded to the "L" category.[33]

## THE RESEARCH BASE

In pursuit of the peaceful atom, Administration leaders and congressmen tended to measure success in terms of visible products of technology. Fully aware of this fact, Strauss and his colleagues justified the Commission's nonmilitary activities with statistics demonstrating technological achievements. But the Commissioners also believed that technical advances usually had their origins in basic knowledge amassed by scientists and research engineers. In his 1945 report, *Science, the Endless Frontier,* Vannevar Bush had presented the common wisdom growing out of the wartime experience: basic research was like money in a savings account; engineers could draw only so much from that investment for practical applications before it was necessary to replenish the account with more basic research. Bush's argument had been part of the rationale for the Commission's ambitious research program, which in the 1950s still overshadowed all other federally sponsored research except that in the Department of Defense.[34]

Sponsoring research, however, was more than an onerous task of keeping the accounts of knowledge and application in balance. The opportunity to foster activities that contributed positively to knowledge, that might even enrich the lives of people everywhere, was to the Commissioners and the staff a welcome relief from the harsh and unrelenting burden of producing more materials and nuclear weapons for the ultimate purpose of destruction. The millions of dollars the Commission lavished on research activities helped to salve the consciences of many who could not forget the potential for human disaster that lurked in the nation's growing stockpiles of nuclear weapons. Within the atomic energy establishment, the hope was probably all but universal that somehow the benefits of nuclear technology would eventually dispel the dark cloud of horror and destruction cast by the bomb. To bring that hope to reality was a strong and uplifting motivation.

253

Beyond these questions of conscience, there was the sheer delight in discovery, the excitement of exploring new realms of nature revealed by the powerful research tools of nuclear technology. The stunning successes within a single decade in applying scientific data and then adding once more to the store of basic knowledge raised the possibility that the world was on the brink of a new renaissance. For a man like Lewis Strauss, who stood in awe of scientists and their achievements, the chance to participate in and even to contribute to this extraordinary enterprise offered the ultimate in self-fulfillment.[35]

The Commission's research base rested on the national laboratories, university-based projects, special development laboratories, and a vast network of research activities performed by hundreds of colleges, universities, private research institutions, and other government agencies. By the time Strauss became chairman in 1953, the research base was firmly established. The three large multidisciplinary national laboratories—Brookhaven, Oak Ridge, and Argonne—all had roots in the Manhattan Project. All three were intended to be regional centers where resident scientists and others from nearby universities could work together on nuclear research requiring human resources and equipment beyond the capabilities of a single private institution.

Of the three, Brookhaven came closest to realizing the original model of a regional, cooperative research center. Managed by an association sponsored by nine universities in the Northeast, Brookhaven reflected, more than did Oak Ridge or Argonne, the interests of academic scientists in basic research. The only national laboratory with a large research reactor and a proton synchrotron in the billion-electron-volt range in 1953, Brookhaven could offer scientists a bountiful supply of subnuclear particles, fission products, and radioisotopes for a wide variety of nuclear research activities in both the physical and the biological sciences. The research reactor completed at Brookhaven in 1950 made the laboratory a natural center for a Commission-wide project to compile a complete set of data on the nuclear characteristics of the many materials used in atomic research and development. The cosmotron, capable of accelerating protons to more than three billion electron volts (GeV), was already producing in 1953 a variety of heavy mesons that gave Brookhaven at least a temporary lead in research in high-energy physics, a field that was capturing the attention of physicists throughout the world.[36]

254      Compared with Brookhaven, Oak Ridge National Laboratory had more of an industrial than an academic flavor. Originally built as a pilot plant for plutonium production during World War II, the laboratory had long been managed by an industrial contractor, more recently by the Union Carbide and Carbon Corporation. The Commission's contract with Union Carbide did not provide for the Brookhaven type of cooperative arrangement with university scientists in the region. Instead, the Commission supported the Oak Ridge Institute of Nuclear Studies, a consortium of twenty-four southern universities, which used laboratory facilities at Oak Ridge for research, training, and education.[37]

Well staffed by reactor physicists at the end of the war, the Oak Ridge laboratory had suffered a setback in 1947 when the Commission decided to make Argonne its center for reactor development; but under Alvin M. Weinberg's skillful leadership, Oak Ridge won from the Commission a series of assignments to study some of the more exotic reactor concepts. The laboratory was also the home of the aircraft nuclear propulsion project, supported by the Commission and the Air Force. The laboratory's principal research tools in the 1950s were the research reactor built during the war and an eighty-six-inch cyclotron. The reactor was the only one of its kind in the United States until the Brookhaven facility was completed. In addition to providing irradiation space and radioactive products for physical and biological experiments, the Oak Ridge reactor produced more than a dozen radioisotopes for distribution to industrial and research users. The reactor, the cyclotron, and other facilities at Oak Ridge made the laboratory a world center for the production and distribution of stable and radioactive isotopes. During the lean years in the 1950s when the Commission had little to boast about in advancing the peaceful uses of atomic energy, descriptions of the isotope distribution program filled Commission reports and press releases.[38]

Although the Commission in 1947 intended Argonne to be a regional research center accessible to universities in the area, the laboratory never achieved the degree of academic participation enjoyed by scientists at Brookhaven. Walter H. Zinn, the laboratory director, had himself been an academic physicist and appreciated the need for strong programs in basic research at Argonne. In fact, the laboratory under his direction pursued important areas of applied research in metallurgy, radiation chemistry, nuclear physics, and the biological effects of radiation. Zinn, however, felt even more keenly pressures from the Commission to develop nuclear power and meet defense requirements. Thus, Argonne had initiated some research on naval propulsion reactors for Rickover, had built the first breeder reactor, had completed design studies for the plutonium production reactors at Savannah River, and had developed the boiling-water reactor, which was fast becoming a credible approach to nuclear power. The facilities required for all these projects, and especially the experimental reactors built by the laboratory at Argonne and the Idaho test station, prompted the Commission by 1956 to pour more capital investment into Argonne than into the other two multipurpose laboratories.[39]

255

Important as these achievements were, they came at the cost of strong dissatisfaction among scientists in the thirty-two universities and research institutions in the Midwest that, on paper at least, were to have a voice in setting research priorities at Argonne. Zinn gave little more than lip-service to the board of governors, who represented the participating institutions, and proceeded as if all program decisions were to be made by the University of Chicago as the Commission's operating contractor at Argonne. By early 1948 the board of governors had abandoned all pretense of exercising any real influence over the laboratory's research program, and the Commission's revision of the laboratory's charter in June 1950 replaced the board with a powerless advisory body. The new charter suggested that the Brookhaven model of a cooperative regional laboratory was not to be duplicated at Argonne.[40]

While Zinn struggled for independence at Argonne, Ernest O. Lawrence already enjoyed a free rein at the University of California Radiation Laboratory in Berkeley. Lawrence had founded the laboratory before World War II with private and state funds and had made it a world center for research in high-energy physics before the Manhattan Project was created. Without hesitation Lawrence had thrown all his influence and all the laboratory resources into the war effort. He was thus in a strong position after the war to assure Berkeley its full share of federal funding for research without accepting either the designation of a "national laboratory" or a formal commitment to provide a research center for other universities on the West Coast.

Although the Radiation Laboratory conducted nuclear research in many areas of the physical and biological sciences, it primarily focused on high-energy physics centered on the bevatron and other accelerators, transuranium chemistry and the creation of transplutonium elements under Glenn T. Seaborg, and weapon research at Livermore. By 1956, the combined work force of more than four thousand people at Berkeley and Livermore made the Radiation Laboratory the largest of all the Commission's research facilities.[41]

Among the Commission's single-purpose research installations, the largest by far in 1956 was the Los Alamos Scientific Laboratory, also operated by the University of California. Virtually all the research and development at Los Alamos before 1956 was related to nuclear weapons, but the laboratory did perform basic research, for example on the physical, chemical, and metallurgical properties of materials used in weapons. Much basic research at Los Alamos was similar to that funded at other Commission laboratories, except that the work at Los Alamos was usually weapon-related and hence classified. Deeply concerned in 1954 that younger scientists would ultimately see little future in a laboratory devoted entirely to weapon research, Norris E. Bradbury, the director, urged Strauss to broaden the laboratory's charter. As a result, Los Alamos began investigating a very advanced concept for a power reactor in 1956 and, like Livermore and Oak Ridge, entered the new field of research on controlled thermonuclear reactions. At that time Los Alamos had the largest operating budget (more than $47 million) of any Commission laboratory and employed 3,300 persons. Comparable in size to Los Alamos were the two naval reactor laboratories: the Bettis Plant operated by Westinghouse near Pittsburgh and the Knolls Atomic Power Laboratory operated by General Electric near Schenectady.[42]

Other single-purpose laboratories were smaller than those already mentioned, but they still performed vital research functions for the Commission. The Sandia Laboratory in Albuquerque and the Mound Laboratory in Miamisburg, Ohio, had essential roles in weapon development and production. The Raw Materials Development Laboratory at Winchester, Massachusetts, and the Ames Laboratory at Iowa State College helped to improve processes for refining uranium ore and reducing it to metal. The Commission also supported medical and biological research using nuclear materials and equipment at the Universities of Chicago and Rochester and the University of California at Los Angeles and San Francisco. In all its laboratories in 1956 the Commission spent more than $51 million for research in chemistry, metallurgy, and physics and more than $30 million for research on cancer, medicine, and biology. During that same year, the Commission committed almost $19 million for more than eight hundred offsite research contracts, which included nearly every major research organization, college, and university in the country.[43]

## HIGH-ENERGY PHYSICS

This unprecedented commitment to scientific research was expected to contribute in hundreds of untold ways to the increase in human knowledge and the beneficial application of nuclear technology. By its very nature, however, research produced small increments of data, most of which could not be appreciated by the news media or the general public. To justify the value of research for the Administration's Atoms-for-Peace program, the Commission had to rely on a few projects that seemed to push the frontiers of science into exotic realms that somehow captured the imagination of non-scientists. Ernest Lawrence had learned in the 1930s that probes into the submicroscopic world of the atomic nucleus with the cyclotron elicited that kind of response. The discovery of the synchrotron principle during World War II had sparked new enthusiasm for high-energy physics after the war, and it became the research area in basic physics most generously supported by the federal government. Two products of that enthusiasm were the Brookhaven cosmotron and the Berkeley bevatron, which was expected to achieve proton energies above 6 GeV when the accelerator came into operation in 1954.[44]

257

Even before the bevatron was completed, physicists were looking for ways to reach even higher energies, which seemed necessary for fully exploiting the research possibilities already revealed by the cosmotron. Both the cosmotron and the bevatron, however, were approaching the maximum practical size of a synchrotron. Higher energies appeared to require that particles be accelerated over much greater distances than ever before. That meant that the vacuum-tight annular or "racetrack," through which the particles would move, would have to be considerably larger than those used at Brookhaven and Berkeley. As the radius of the racetrack was increased much beyond thirty feet, the cost of the steel and control equipment required for the magnets that focused the proton beam on its circular course became almost prohibitively large. Also, as the diameter of the racetrack increased, the volume of the doughnut-shaped race course to be evacuated with vacuum pumps became enormous.

In searching for a new approach to synchrotron design that would overcome these limitations, physicists at Brookhaven in summer 1952 investigated a design principle suggested by scientists at the European Center for Nuclear Research (CERN). The new idea was called alternating gradient, or strong focusing. Instead of flat, parallel pole faces on the focusing magnets, the European scientists proposed a curved surface. It had long been known that nonparallel or curved pole faces would cause variations in the magnetic field at different points in the cross section of the beam, but only relatively small variations or "shims" had been used. The scientists found that by introducing a relatively large variation or gradient and then alternating the orientation of successive magnets around the race-track, a focusing and defocusing effect was produced that sharply com-pressed the beam's cross section. A sharper beam meant that the aperture of a synchrotron could be reduced from a width of about 30 inches in the cosmotron to about 1.5 inches in a machine using strong focusing. The implications of strong focusing for accelerator design were dramatic. The smaller aperture made possible much smaller magnets and volumes; hence the diameter of the racetrack could be increased, and much higher ener-gies, perhaps as high as 100 GeV, now seemed possible. Strong focusing could also be used in Van de Graafs and linear accelerators, which served as particle generators and injectors for the large machines.[45]

The advantages of strong focusing, apparent to physicists, were likely to mean little to most government officials. It so happened, however, that the first studies of strong focusing in summer 1952 were an inter-national venture involving both European and American physicists. Fully appreciating the advantages of strong focusing, the European group made plans to use it in a cooperative effort to build a 30-GeV proton synchroton in Switzerland. Although scientists at Brookhaven saw strong focusing pri-marily as an opportunity for new research in high-energy physics, the Euro-peans' plans raised for Commission officials the specter of lost American preeminence in a preeminent field of science. The Commission proposal to build an alternating-gradient synchrotron at Brookhaven with a power of 25 to 35 GeV noted that "American scientists have held the lead in nuclear science since the invention of the cyclotron and they do not now wish to fall behind." Thus, the pace of American development in high-energy physics had become a measure of success in the Atoms-for-Peace program.[46]

The Commission's prompt decision to fund the Brookhaven accelera-tor, however, did not meet the expectations of many American physicists, particularly in the Midwest. With the cosmotron and bevatron in operation by 1954 and the first of a new generation of accelerators already approved for Brookhaven, scientists in the Midwest still had no prospects for an accelerator in the GeV range. Argonne was the logical location for such a machine. In January 1954, within weeks after Commission approval of the Brookhaven project, Zinn proposed to meet the growing demand for a large Midwest accelerator by building it at Argonne in cooperation with univer-sity physicists in the region. Reluctant at first to risk dilution of Argonne's work on reactors or to request additional funds from the tight-fisted Bureau of the Budget, the Commission in June 1954 approved a design study at Argonne, mainly to forestall attempts by the Midwest Universities Research Association to obtain federal funds for an accelerator project independent of Argonne. The core of the new association consisted of physicists who had been frustrated for years in trying to extract from Zinn and the Com-mission some role in establishing research priorities at Argonne. The depth of the scientists' disaffection with Zinn's high-handed methods became apparent in October 1954, when the association summarily rejected Zinn's offer to set up a separate accelerator division at Argonne and to give the Midwest group a voice in selecting the division director, who would have complete technical but not administrative control of the accelerator project. Drawing from experience, members of the association did not trust Zinn, and he looked upon the rejection of his proposal as another example of their unreasonable expectations.[47]

The uncompromising stance taken by both sides in autumn 1954 stalled for almost a year all attempts at settling the dispute. In the meantime scientists were publishing exciting results of experiments conducted with the cosmotron and bevatron. Most significant had been the discovery of the antiproton, which had been produced with high-energy protons in the bevatron and identified by Owen Chamberlin, Emilio Segre, and others at Berkeley with the recently developed liquid-hydrogen bubble chamber. With frustration and impatience growing on both sides in the Midwest, Lawrence A. Kimpton, chancellor of the University of Chicago, offered a compromise proposal, in which the university as the Argonne contractor offered significant concessions: namely, something similar to the Oak Ridge Institute of Nuclear Studies be established to design and build an accelerator at Argonne as an independent Commission contractor. The Midwest scientists welcomed the idea, but Kimpton had mistakenly assumed that he could convince Zinn to accept the compromise. Zinn instantly rejected it and submitted his resignation, to be effective within three weeks; only with difficulty did Strauss persuade Zinn to delay. The Commission now faced a quandary. On the one hand, the Commissioners did not want to lose Zinn or threaten the future of Argonne; they did not want to abandon the idea that Argonne was to become a regional multipurpose laboratory; and they also knew that it would be hard to obtain funds for two laboratories. On the other hand, the Commission knew that if Zinn stayed, the Midwest group would never agree to work within Argonne. Pressure from the Commission would free the group to seek an independent laboratory at another site. If the Commission refused to cooperate, the Midwest group might well seek funding from the Department of Defense and thus threaten the Commission's hegemony over basic research in the Midwest.[48]

A compromise solution emerged early in November 1955 with help from the general advisory committee: the Commission proposed to fund two accelerator projects but only one laboratory. Argonne was to be asked to build a 12-GeV scale-up of the bevatron, a machine that presumably would involve more engineering than high-powered physics and could be completed before the Soviet Union could operate a machine somewhat larger than the bevatron. Thus, Argonne could maintain the United States' lead in high-energy physics until the new Brookhaven accelerator took the lead in the world contest. The Midwest group would be offered funds to design

259

a truly advanced accelerator, to be built a year later at an unspecified site. Privately the Commission hoped that, by the time site selection became an issue, new faces might be on the scene and the Midwest accelerator might be built at Argonne.[49]

The Commission's compromise was acceptable to the Midwest group but not to Zinn, who insisted that Argonne was not staffed to build the 12-GeV machine and that in any case it could not be completed before the Brookhaven alternating-gradient accelerator. Instead, Zinn held out for an accelerator that would advance the state of the art. When the Commission formally assigned the 12-GeV project to Argonne, Zinn resigned.[50]

The turmoil that the Commission and Zinn experienced during his last two years at Argonne revealed the complex pattern of decision making in federal support of scientific research. It was by no means unusual that the quality of proposals and the ability of the scientists involved were not the only factors in determining which projects were accepted and which rejected. Regional interests, politics, budget limitations, bureaucratic competition, existing policy, and personality conflicts all played a part. In this kind of debate, it seemed inevitable that the appeal to national interest and even to national security should be involved. It was no accident that the solution to the Commission's dilemma should rest in part upon the argument that high-energy physics offered a significant battlefield in the Cold War.

## ENERGY FROM THE STARS

Secretly the Commission was supporting research that would challenge the United States' competitors in another race for nuclear power—harnessing the power of the hydrogen bomb for peaceful purposes. Since 1951, even before a workable thermonuclear weapon had been designed, the Commission had been supporting secret research on controlled thermonuclear reactions. In March of that year Lyman Spitzer, Jr., an astrophysicist at Princeton University, had begun to consider how he might design a reactor that would contain an ionized gas or "plasma" of hydrogen isotopes, which might be fused to release the enormous energy associated with the thermonuclear reactions that powered the sun and the stars. In order to fuse the hydrogen nuclei, the temperature of the plasma would have to be raised to one hundred million degrees, hotter than the interior of the sun and many times any temperature ever achieved in the laboratory. Because no material vessel could contain such a plasma, other methods of confining the gas would be required. Experiments with ionized gases in previous decades suggested that confinement might be accomplished with strong magnetic fields, and within a few weeks Spitzer conceived of a simple confinement system that would use an external magnetic field to confine the plasma within a vacuum chamber shaped like a doughnut twisted into a figure-eight. In summer 1951 the Commission funded Spitzer with $50,000 for a paper study of his idea.[51]

Spitzer's interest in fusion energy stemmed from the theoretical work that he was undertaking with John A. Wheeler on the design of a hydrogen bomb. Likewise, scientists at Los Alamos and Livermore saw fusion energy development as an offshoot of the thermonuclear research that they were already pursuing, and both laboratories staked out claims for other theoretically obvious but completely untested systems for magnetic confinement in 1952. Spitzer called his device the "stellarator," an optimistic reference to the stars as fusion energy systems. The Los Alamos approach was called the "pinch" and the Livermore concept the "magnetic mirror." By summer 1953, when Strauss became chairman, the Commission had spent about one million dollars on fusion energy research: 50 percent of it at Princeton, 30 percent at Berkeley and Livermore, and 20 percent at Los Alamos. Thirty scientists in the four laboratories were devoting part of their time to these projects, and the pace was unhurried and relaxed.[52]

261

When Strauss became chairman, he moved at once to enlarge and accelerate fusion research. Both Teller and Lawrence, whose opinions Strauss considered virtually unchallengeable, believed that the work deserved high priority. Strauss saw it as a priceless opportunity for the Atoms-for-Peace program and a telling refutation of the claims of fainted-hearted scientists like Oppenheimer, who, Strauss contended, had seen no redeeming or beneficial value in thermonuclear research back in 1949. What greater success could the Administration contemplate than to present the world with a new, clean, and limitless source of power while other nations were still striving to perfect the fission reactor? Fusion offered a "quantum jump" over fission reactors similar to that which the hydrogen bomb held over atomic weapons of the Hiroshima type.[53]

Under Strauss's leadership the Commission launched Project *Sherwood* and directed the staff to seek proposals from the laboratories for actual experimental devices, not mere paper studies, that would serve either as testing equipment or as prototypes for fusion reactors. Under pressure from Washington, Spitzer by June 1954 produced a plan for a full-scale operating stellarator even before bench-top experiments or a small-scale prototype could be completed. By summer 1955 the number of scientists engaged in fusion research had risen to one hundred full-time workers. Operating costs had reached almost $5 million annually. There was no shortage of enthusiasm for Project *Sherwood* in the chairman's office and no lack of funds in the laboratories. In fact, as one scientist remarked, "one gets the feeling in visiting the various sites that the number of dollars available per good idea is rather uncomfortably large."[54]

With his almost naive faith in the power of science, Strauss seemed to believe that with sufficient money and effort almost any technical goal, including controlled fusion, could be attained. But the fact was that in autumn 1955 scientists had not yet begun to understand the complex phenomena that would influence the behavior of plasma in a fusion reactor. By giving Project *Sherwood* a high priority, Strauss did raise morale among the scientists and put more of them to work, but the generous flow of funds from the Commission also had unfavorable effects. More money meant more reliance on cut-and-try methods of engineering design at the expense of systematic theoretical studies that were already in short supply. Big budgets also encouraged scientists to explore every idea that might conceivably work as long as money was available. And as the fusion projects in each laboratory grew in size and numbers of scientists, overhead increased and institutional requirements gained more importance.

Strauss had also handicapped the scientists by tightening the security restrictions on their work. In 1951 and 1952, when the first studies seemed closely related to weapon research, even the existence of the projects was classified secret; but many data on basic physics had been assigned to the confidential category, which permitted all scientists within the project to share the results of the several laboratories. Under Strauss the secret classification was imposed on all data and information compartmentalized in each laboratory despite appeals for declassification from both the scientists and the Commission staff. Not until the British and others described some of their work on controlled fusion research at the Geneva conference did Strauss agree to reveal the existence of Project *Sherwood*. Strauss had put more fuel in the research furnace, but he had closed the damper at the same time.[55]

## RADIATION AND LIFE

No Commission activity held greater promise for the peaceful uses of nuclear energy than did research in biology and medicine. Long before the discovery of nuclear fission, scientists had foreseen the possibility of using radiation in the treatment of disease, particularly cancer. Strauss himself had first acquired an interest in the nuclear sciences in the 1930s when he learned that the cyclotron, which Lawrence was developing at Berkeley, might be used in treating cancer, which had killed both of Strauss's parents. In the years after World War II, scientists and physicians in the national laboratories, universities, and other private research institutions clamored for various radiation sources to be used in biomedical experiments. Not only high-energy particles from accelerators were available but also a cornucopia of fission products and radioisotopes providing a wide variety of radiation characteristics. The Commission became the generous provider of these materials.[56]

From the outset the Commission allocated a significant portion of its funds for biology and medicine to cancer research. By 1955 the Commission was spending more than $2 million a year on cancer research and the distribution of radioisotopes for cancer therapy. The national laboratories took the lead in developing teletherapy units and radiation sources and finding new applications for radioisotopes. The Argonne Cancer Research Hospital, operated for the Commission by the University of Chicago, used both radioisotopes and high-energy radiation in investigating therapeutic applications and developing clinical techniques. Both national laboratories and university contractors used isotopes in a wide range of studies of biological systems, from studying antibody synthesis in blood proteins to measuring the effectiveness of drugs.[57]

One of the most exciting areas of biomedical research opened by the plentiful supply of radioisotopes was their use in tracer studies. Scientists found that they could introduce radioisotopes into biological systems without disrupting existing life processes and then use the radioactivity emitted to trace specific chemical compounds through the system. In physiology, tracers were used to study the rate of distribution of common elements in the body; in cytology, to study the turnover of biochemical compounds in living cells; in metabolic studies, to measure protein synthesis with carbon-14-labeled amino acids. Tracers were also used in various studies to measure the uptake and distribution of nutrients and other chemicals.

263

In devising new uses for radiation sources, scientists also had to give greater attention to radiation effects. For along with the therapeutic and diagnostic powers of radiation came many unknown effects on biological systems. From the earliest days of the Manhattan Project, the study of radiation effects was closely tied to industrial safety in nuclear technology. After World War II, studies were broadened beyond specific problems to include basic research on the biological effects of all kinds of high-energy radiation and scores of radioisotopes. In the early 1950s many animal studies were concerned with the gross effects of whole-body irradiation; in plant research scientists at Brookhaven and elsewhere measured the effects of exposing commercial plants to gamma radiation during the growing cycle.

After the *Upshot-Knothole* and *Castle* weapon test series in 1953 and 1954, research on radiation effects began to focus on phenomena directly related to the biological effects of radioactive fallout. In addition to research on whole-body effects of external radiation, scientists began giving greater attention to the metabolism and toxicity of radioisotopes entering the body, particularly the most health-threatening products of weapon testing: strontium-90, cesium-137, and iodine-131. Animal experiments were conducted to measure the effects of radiation on blood platelets, blood clotting, and embryos as well as the effects on life expectancy and productivity. In plant studies biologists followed radionuclides from fallout through dispersion in the soil to uptake by plants and then to ingestion by animals and humans. In addition to these studies of somatic effects, the Commission also funded genetic studies in an attempt to relate radiation exposure to mutations in germ cells. The Commission continued to support, through the Atomic Bomb Casualty Commission, studies of the only large human population exposed to heavy amounts of radiation—the survivors and offspring of Hiroshima and Nagasaki. The long generation span in humans, plus inevitable complexities in keeping track of large groups of individuals, made the studies in Japan difficult at best. To avoid some of these problems, the Commission funded genetic studies with mice, principally at the Oak Ridge National Laboratory, and with fruitflies at several universities.[58]

During the mid-1950s the Commission's budget for biomedical research hovered around $25 million per year. About 37 percent of this amount went to studies of radiation effects; 34 percent to investigating beneficial effects of radiation; 21 percent to research related to industrial health and safety; and 8 percent to experiments on combatting the detrimental effects of radiation.[59] Most of this research was fundamental enough to attract the interest of scientists in research institutions, many completely outside the context of nuclear technology. Basic knowledge generated under research contracts could then be used by scientists in the Commission's laboratories in studies directly related to Commission programs. Before 1955 many of these studies concerning the radiation effects of nuclear weapons were classified. Thus, as public concern over fallout hazards increased after 1954, it became difficult to evaluate the adequacy of the Commission's response. Critics could point to only nominal growth in the Commission's biomedical budget during the mid-1950s and to the fact that almost no funds were specifically earmarked for studies of the radiation effects of fallout. The Commission, however, could with some justification claim that the tens of millions of dollars dedicated to basic research represented an effective and significant response to the fallout problem. It was also true after 1954 that much fallout research related to testing was charged to the budgets for weapons.[60]

## GABRIEL *AND* SUNSHINE

Even more difficult for the public to appraise were the Commission's efforts to understand the larger implication of nuclear weapon testing and nuclear warfare. Obviously, estimates of the biological effects of fallout on large human populations were more likely to arouse fear and controversy than were small-scale experiments on laboratory animals. Thus, it was not surprising that initial studies of large-scale effects were highly classified and unknown to the public. The Commission's division of biology and medicine first sponsored a macrostudy in 1949, when one physicist at Oak Ridge undertook a theoretical calculation of the number of nuclear weapon explosions that would produce a significant radiological hazard. Revising his initial estimates in 1951 after the *Ranger* and *Greenhouse* test series, the scientist concluded that it would require the detonation of one hundred thousand weapons of the Nagasaki type to reach the "doomsday" level.[61] The likelihood of such an occurrence seemed so remote at the time that the Commission's biology and medicine staff could lightly give the study the code name Project *Gabriel.*

The 1951 weapon tests and quick estimates by the headquarters staff, however, indicated that the short-term, close-in effects of a nuclear detonation could have serious consequences for a densely populated area. At the request of the general advisory committee, the Commission supplemented occasional staff work and laboratory studies on Project *Gabriel* with a Rand Corporation contract in 1952 to make a systematic analysis of the "intensive, short-time hazard to residents of areas relatively close to points under attack with near-surface bursts or air-bursts in rainy weather." At that time the division of biology and medicine could find no contractor capable of undertaking a study of the long-term, widespread hazard.[62]

265

Within weeks after the conclusion of the *Upshot-Knothole* tests, which dumped significant amounts of fallout in localities beyond the Nevada test site, Willard F. Libby, then professor at the University of Chicago and a member of the general advisory committee, called a classified conference of Rand personnel, scientists from the Commission's laboratories, and military representatives in Santa Monica, California. Libby noted that Rand had divided Project *Gabriel* into two distinct studies: the first directed at short-term, close-in consequences; and the second at long-term, distant implications. The first study, Libby admitted, had to remain secret because the revelation of data gathered within the first few days of a weapon test would reveal classified information about weapon design. The study of long-term effects, however, could be unclassified, and Libby argued that gathering fallout data on a national and perhaps a worldwide scale could best be done in the open. Long-term studies were essential, Libby believed, because growth of the stockpile and recent Nevada tests made clear as never before that strontium-90 could pose a serious radiological hazard for the public.

In the original *Gabriel* studies the principal concern had been the potential toxicity of plutonium disbursed as particles in the radioactive cloud. But since 1950 scientists had become more concerned about the possible effects of strontium-90, which behaved much like calcium in plant and animal chemistry; hence it tended to concentrate in the bone, where, with its twenty-eight year half-life, it could cause bone cancer. Later *Gabriel* studies had used strontium-90 as the critical factor in determining the number of weapon detonations that constituted a radiological hazard. Not until the *Upshot-Knothole* tests in 1953, however, was it evident that strontium could be widely distributed over the northern hemisphere, not only by nuclear war but also by fallout from testing. Knowing that all previous work on *Gabriel* had been secret or top secret, Libby faced a skeptical audience in arguing for an unclassified survey.

Commission officials attending the conference found Libby's ideas "stimulating" but not very practical. To single out strontium for special attention in an unclassified study might easily arouse undue public alarm, while the cost and complexity of a worldwide sampling project seemed too ambitious to undertake without further study. Libby was encouraged to begin limited sampling and analytical work in his Chicago laboratory, but no extensive project could be authorized until more data had been gathered. In the meantime Project *Gabriel* remained classified.[63]

Although the Commission did not move as far or as fast as Libby recommended, a substantial effort had been organized by autumn 1953. In addition to Rand's theoretical studies, scientists from the University of California at Los Angeles were continuing to study soils, plants, and small animals collected within a few hundred miles of the test site. Data were available from the fallout monitoring network of more than one hundred stations established for *Upshot-Knothole*. Libby and other scientists were already analyzing the strontium content of materials collected from widely scattered locations. Possibly to suggest that strontium-90 could be as widely distributed over the earth's surface as solar energy, Libby and his colleagues began referring to their work as Project *Sunshine*, a name that unfortunately implied in later years an attempt to put a "sunny" connotation on a somber and frightening subject. By the end of 1953 the Commission was supporting Project *Sunshine* at a level of fifteen man-years and $140,000 per year. The division of biology and medicine estimated that it was also funding basic research related to Project *Gabriel* in about seventy projects costing $3.3 million per year. Although most basic research was unclassified, *Sunshine* and *Gabriel* were still considered secret.[64]

## THE MULLER FIASCO

The Geneva Conference in summer 1955 offered a potential opportunity for openly discussing the radiation effects of fallout. The purpose of the conference, after all, was to afford scientists from many nations an occasion to exchange information and ideas on the peaceful uses of atomic energy. A preliminary agenda drafted in November 1954 included eleven papers on "medical and biological applications": six on the use of tracers, one on radiation use in medicine, two on its use in plant physiology and morphology, and one on its genetic effects.[65]

It was all but inevitable that any session on the genetic effects of radiation would include a paper by Hermann J. Muller, who had won the Nobel Prize in 1946 for his work on this subject. First developing an interest in genetics as an undergraduate at Columbia University in 1909, Muller had embarked on a productive career as a teacher and researcher at universities and research institutes in Texas, the Soviet Union, and Scotland before going to Indiana University in 1945. Muller had startled the scientific world in 1927 with a paper describing experiments that proved it was possible to use radiation to induce mutations in genes. Always sensitive to the social and practical implications of his research, Muller never ceased before World War II to warn physicians of the genetic hazards of X-rays, although he believed that their therapeutic and diagnostic value was worth the risk if proper precautions were taken in using them.[66]

After the war Muller noted in several articles the potential genetic hazards posed by the atomic age, but his views did not attract widespread attention until April 1955, when he delivered a lecture at the National Academy of Sciences in Washington on "The Genetic Damage Produced by Radiation." The lecture caused alarm in government circles because it explicitly related genetic damage to nuclear testing and nuclear warfare and because Muller had already given a copy to the *Bulletin of the Atomic Scientists* for publication.[67]

Despite its bald title, Muller's paper must have seemed surprisingly moderate and judicious, especially to those who did not know his earlier publications. Muller challenged both those who discounted any genetic damage among the descendent populations of Hiroshima and Nagasaki and those who called, as he put it, "loudly, and in some cases in a suspiciously vitriolic tone, for an end to all nuclear test explosions, on the ground that even the tests are already seriously undermining the genetic basis of all mankind." Radiation, Muller admitted, did cause genetic damage, but he demonstrated that the potential effects of nuclear testing were exceedingly small and probably could never be traced to individuals. Much as he had done in warning physicians about X-rays, he urged great care to minimize radiation exposure from nuclear testing, but he took an unequivocal position that the national security requirements for nuclear weapons far outweighed the potential genetic damage of testing. Nuclear war would be a disaster, both genetically and otherwise, but nuclear testing seemed to Muller the best way to avoid it.

If Muller's lecture on the genetic effects of radiation upset some government officials, it did not seem to bother American scientists, both inside and outside the Commission, who were planning the Geneva conference. The Commission staff sent an abstract of Muller's paper to the United Nations early in May 1955, and the paper was promptly accepted for presentation at the conference. On June 6 the Commission's staff recommended that Muller be invited to the conference as a technical adviser

267

to the American delegation. On that same day, however, perhaps as a result of the staff's action, steps were taken within the Commission to remove Muller from the invitation list. Circumstantial evidence suggests that Strauss made this decision on security grounds after talking with Bryan LaPlante and Charles Bates, the FBI liaison officer.

The problem was that Muller's FBI file bulged with derogatory data. He had been an active socialist during his youth in New York City. During the Depression of the 1930s he had openly espoused communism as the hope of the future. He probably had not ever been a member of the American Communist party, but he had been active in organizations sympathetic to the communist cause. He had spent almost four years at the Institute of Genetics in Moscow, had many Soviet friends, and had come home from Europe, according to FBI reports, with bundles of communist propaganda. The facts that Muller after World War II had bitterly attacked communism and the genetic theories of Lysenko and that he advocated continued nuclear testing as a necessary defense against Soviet aggression were perhaps discounted simply as a cover for his communist sympathies. As a result, the Commission asked the United Nations not to accept Muller's paper for oral presentation, although it was to be printed in the conference proceedings.[68]

Muller, who was already in Europe on vacation with his family and counting on the invitation to pay for his own travel expenses, could hardly have welcomed the rejection, but he did not openly object. He did, however, attend the conference at his own expense and sat silently as he received a standing ovation from the scientists attending the session at which he was to have presented his paper. The incident did not have reverberations beyond scientific circles until a month later, when a *Washington Post* reporter called the Commission staff about the incident. A Commission press statement released the next day explained that Muller's invitation had been rejected because the full text of his paper "was belatedly found to contain material referring to the nonpeaceful uses of atomic energy, namely, the bombing of the Japanese city of Hiroshima."[69]

This transparent explanation at once raised an outcry of protest among American scientists, some of whom demanded an investigation by the National Academy of Sciences. Strauss attempted to defuse the protest by claiming personal responsibility for rejecting the paper when he did not read it carefully under the press of business. The public impression, however, was that the Commission was attempting to suppress any discussion of the potential genetic effects of testing, no matter how balanced such an account might be.[70] The truth was that a reappearance of the Oppenheimer security syndrome supplied the compelling reason for rejecting Muller's presentation. The fact, however, that Strauss apparently acted within days after Muller's academy lecture appeared in the *Bulletin of the Atomic Scientists* suggested that the popular conception was in part correct. The net

268

result, as in previous instances, was further to destroy the Commission's credibility on matters relating to the radiation effects of fallout.

## THE BALANCE SHEET

In the year following the adoption of the Atomic Energy Act of 1954 Strauss and other Administration leaders enjoyed some success in promoting the peaceful uses of atomic energy. Most prominent on the Commission's list of achievements was the impressive array of activities to develop nuclear power for commercial purposes. The five-year reactor program in the Commission laboratories, augmented by the first two invitations to industry in the demonstration program, at least gave the appearance of a concerted effort to develop a new energy source. Even more remote, but perhaps of even greater ultimate promise than power from fission reactors, were the Commission's programs to harness fusion energy and to probe the mysteries of the atomic nucleus with high-energy accelerators. Of more immediate and direct benefit to society were the results of Commission-sponsored research in biology and medicine; the growing use of radioisotopes in both clinical therapy and diagnosis was already producing dramatic results in treating cancer and other diseases. The Commission effectively presented all these benefits and achievements of nuclear technology, both in technical papers and exhibits, at the peaceful uses conference in Geneva in 1955; and the Commission hoped that they would be reflected in the report of the McKinney panel in early 1956.

269

Along with the benefits and accomplishments, however, came unexpected difficulties, disappointments, and public skepticism. For all Strauss's claims for the demonstration program, a practical nuclear power plant still seemed a long way in the future, and the American effort seemed to be lagging behind the British and the Russian. Strauss had yet to defuse growing Congressional demands for a massive government program, and the bitter, seemingly endless controversy over Dixon-Yates threatened permanently to politicize the nuclear power program. For the moment the United States appeared to have the lead in the international race for fusion energy and in high-energy physics, but research in neither area as yet seemed to have any important applications in nuclear technology.

In the biomedical sciences, where the results of Commission sponsorship had been most impressive, impending consequences were also the most sobering. The very technologies that brought enormous benefits to human welfare also revealed previously unknown and unpredicted hazards. Commission-sponsored studies following the *Upshot-Knothole* weapon tests in 1953 showed conclusively that the radiation hazards from fallout could be continental or worldwide. Research was revealing new and potentially serious hazards from internal emitters like strontium-90 and iodine-131 entering the human body through the food chain. Ironically, the ability to detect and measure such hazards came from research that had strikingly advanced knowledge of biochemistry in plants and animals. And just below the surface of public consciousness was the question of genetic effects, a subject politically so sensitive that even a world-renowned scientist could not approach it with impunity. Atomic energy did have peaceful applications; the question now was whether the accompanying disadvantages made it worth the effort.

## CHAPTER 10

# THE SEEDS
# OF ANXIETY

From Bikini the remnants of the gigantic cloud generated by the *Bravo* shot spread eastward, first over Rongelap, then on to Utirik and beyond, where white ashes fell like snow on the deck of the *Lucky Dragon*. A few hours earlier the same "snowfall" had silently descended on the unsuspecting islanders. Many of them suffered the skin lesions and discoloration and loss of hair that scientists had come to identify with radiation exposure at Hiroshima and Nagasaki. For the crew of the *Lucky Dragon*, the name of their vessel belied its fate. The fishermen already bore evidence of substantial radiation exposure when their ship reached port. As time passed, the superficial scars of radiation damage disappeared, and most of the crew could return home. But not radioman Aikichu Kuboyama, who languished without appetite or spirit week after week. By the time Kuboyama died in late September, the Japanese had their own name for fallout. They called it *shi no hai*—"ashes of death."[1]

The introduction to the nuclear age experienced by the Marshallese and the Japanese fishermen represented an extreme but highly localized example of the anxieties many people around the world would feel during the 1950s as they groped their way toward understanding nuclear weapons and their implications. For many Americans the stunning success of the atomic bomb in bringing a quick and merciful end to World War II engulfed concerns about the human toll in death and affliction. But the seeds of anxiety took root at *Upshot-Knothole* and began to flourish after *Bravo*. Scientists began to reexamine their earlier assumptions about the nature and significance of fallout and began gathering new data. Public officials, from Commission employees at the Nevada Test Site to the President in the White House, struggled to interpret the bloodless facts streaming in from the laboratories in technical reports and briefings. Politicians looked for ways to capitalize on the issues raised by fallout and testing while the public struggled to relate the controversy and growing anxiety to everyday life.

## EVALUATING BRAVO

Following a visit to the South Pacific test site and a briefing on the *Bravo* shot, Congressman Chet Holifield felt compelled to convey his deep concern to the President. "I believe it is imperative," he wrote Eisenhower in March 1954, "that the people know the effect of these weapons in order that they may be able to more realistically evaluate the gravity of international tensions and the necessity of making the financial sacrifices necessary to protect our free way of life." Holifield's call for "plain words" rather than generalities or confusing scientific explanations arose from his assumption that the American people were "mature enough to accept an authoritative statement of the facts without panic or hysteria." He believed that the facts about the hydrogen bomb would lead to a "surging and irresistible demand for peace."[2]

272

The facts about the hydrogen bomb, however, were not that easy to relate. Security considerations aside, it was not just a problem of collecting and analyzing fallout data. The *Castle* test series had upset fundamental assumptions about strategy and civil defense, a basic fact that took some time to sink in. Just a few months before, in January, John Foster Dulles had given his "massive retaliation" speech to the Council on Foreign Relations. Revised and qualified in the spring issue of *Foreign Affairs*, Dulles had outlined the basic defense policy expressed in NSC 162/2, which had formulated the "new look." Although not involved in developing the "new look," Dulles summarized the Administration's policy of relying upon rapid and overwhelming nuclear retaliation to deter or counter Soviet aggression against either the United States or its allies. Emphasizing collective security, the "new look," with its reliance on strategic thermonuclear weapons, was intended to meet the Soviet threat without seriously burdening the American economy. Yet the ink was scarcely dry on Dulles's *Foreign Affairs* article when the Administration faced nuclear tragedy in the Pacific without knowing exactly the consequences of the *Castle-Bravo* data.[3]

At his White House news conference on March 31, 1954, Strauss acknowledged the radiation injuries suffered by servicemen, the Marshallese, and the *Lucky Dragon* crew, but under questioning from reporters he also stated that the H-bomb could "take out a city" the size of New York. The fact that a nuclear bomb could wipe out a city, of course, was not new. Nevertheless, the *New York Times* understandably featured Strauss's devastating remarks and virtually ignored the fallout question. The fact that a thermonuclear bomb dropped on Washington might ravage the entire north-eastern seaboard with radiation was still secret information.[4]

Meanwhile, on March 27, Eisenhower had set in motion the establishment of a special Technological Capabilities Panel to study the dangers of surprise attack. Although the study was not directly related to the fallout problem, *Castle-Bravo* no doubt reminded Eisenhower that the United States was vulnerable to sneak attack from a hostile but closed nation, such as the Soviet Union. Thus, concurrently with the Commission's fallout studies, the President asked James R. Killian, Jr., president of Massachusetts Institute of Technology, to evaluate through a comprehensive review of weapons and intelligence technology ways of avoiding surprise attack. The Killian Report to the National Security Council in February 1955 would conclude that both sides would be vulnerable to a surprise attack by thermonuclear weapons, although the panel expected the United States to maintain the upper hand until 1960. Thereafter, attack by either side with thermonuclear weapons would undoubtedly destroy more than cities or devastate regions; it would result in mutual destruction of the combatants.[5]

273

Even while tests continued at the Pacific Proving Grounds in 1954 there were hurried efforts to evaluate fallout data from *Bravo*. This task fell to both Commission staff and scientists working with the Armed Forces Special Weapons Project, the Department of Defense organization primarily responsible for managing the military aspects of nuclear weapon technology. Established in 1947, the special weapons project had succeeded the Manhattan District in overseeing weapon development and production for the Defense Department. Before the end of May the special weapons project sent the Department of Defense and the Commission an analysis of "Radioactive Fallout Hazards from Surface Bursts of Very-High-Yield Nuclear Weapons." Faced with an unprecedented and alarming situation, the Commission, the Federal Civil Defense Administration, the Department of Defense, and the Office of Defense Mobilization formed a special interagency task force to revise minimum standards for dispersal of new industrial facilities from the ground zero of potential targets. Prior to *Bravo* the standard had been ten miles. Had it not been for fallout, the federal government would have found it comparatively easy, albeit sobering, to recommend new industrial guidelines based on information derived from the Bikini tests. But tripling the radius to thirty miles would not compensate for a fallout cloud forty miles wide and two hundred miles long.[6] After reviewing the dispersion standards on March 26, 1954, the President's Science Advisory Committee expressed its satisfaction with existing standards but stressed that there could be no fixed standards for absolute safety. On May 26, however, when the *Bravo* implications were somewhat clearer, Arthur S. Flemming, director of the Office of Defense Mobilization, requested Strauss's advice on establishing new criteria.[7]

For almost four months Strauss did not respond directly to Flemming's request for help. Instead, during the intervening summer of 1954, the Commission studied the fallout problem, evaluating data that it shared with its own scientists and other agencies. Meeting in late May, the general advisory committee not only endorsed continued fallout studies but also recommended that, when the fallout phenomenon was better understood, the public should also be informed of the facts. As General Advisory Committee Chairman Isidor Rabi's report to Strauss noted, it was hardly necessary to point out both the importance of and the ignorance about fallout from low-level thermonuclear bursts.[8]

During the months immediately following the *Castle* test series, the Commission was swamped with pressing problems of fallout evaluation, "clean up," and public relations. Through the torrid summer there was little time for calm reflection or plans for public education. There was no precedent, not even at Hiroshima or Nagasaki, for widespread contamination of human populations and habitats such as occurred after the *Bravo* shot. Data on acute or long-term radiation effects, both external and internal, on humans, pigs, chickens, dogs, coconut palms, papaya, tuna, and other flora and fauna were scarce or nonexistent. Immediate relocation and care for the sick Marshallese and negotiations with the Japanese government over compensation for the *Lucky Dragon* crew and its owners were the major post-test concerns.[9]

## A TEST MORATORIUM CONSIDERED

*Bravo* had also raised international issues. At the United Nations, the Soviet Union and India were pushing for a resolution to condemn the United States for testing in its Pacific trust territories. More astonishing, Commissioner Murray at home suggested the possibility of a comprehensive test moratorium. On February 2, 1954, just a month prior to the *Bravo* shot, Murray explained to Strauss and the President that he had raised the issue "for discussion and exploration only" in response to Eisenhower's Atoms-for-Peace initiative. Following Prime Minister Nehru's public call for a test moratorium on April 2, Murray's tentative proposal could no longer be brushed aside. Subsequently, Albert Schweitzer and Pope Pius XII in his Easter message joined the prominent persons who expressed moral concern over continued testing.[10]

At the April 6, 1954, meeting of the National Security Council, Secretary of State Dulles slipped the President a handwritten note. "I think we should consider whether we could advantageously agree to Nehru's proposal of no further experimental explosions." The Secretary of State offered the President assurances that "this could be policed—or checked—." Eisenhower thought for a moment, and then launched his Administration's first exploration of the test ban idea by jotting in reply: "Ask Strauss to study."[11]

Six days later, in response to the worldwide expression of fear, but especially to Nehru's proposal, United States Ambassador to the United Nations Henry Cabot Lodge asked Dulles whether the United States might agree to a partial moratorium on tests above one megaton.[12] Although there never was a serious possibility that the United States would suspend the *Castle* test series, the Murray-Nehru-Lodge proposals ultimately forced the President and the National Security Council to grapple formally with the issue.

On May 6, Dulles reported to the National Security Council that he had discussed the possibilities of a nuclear test moratorium with British Foreign Secretary Anthony Eden during the April talks in London. Dulles reflected that the United States ought to favor a moratorium on the grounds that the *Castle* series had placed the Americans well ahead of the Russians. Strauss agreed that the *Castle* tests were of utmost importance, but he expressed skepticism, which Secretary of Defense Charles E. Wilson shared, that the United States could satisfactorily police a test moratorium. Eisenhower countered that enforcement of the test ban was not a major issue; if the Russians violated a test ban, the United States could simply resume its own testing. More important, the President believed United States sponsorship of a moratorium would put the Soviet Union on the spot. Vice-President Nixon concurred by noting that the Russians had a greater need to test nuclear weapons than did the United States. Consequently, the President directed Foster Dulles, Strauss, Allen Dulles, and Acting Secretary of Defense Robert Anderson to report to the National Security Council on the possibilities for stopping or limiting atmospheric tests.[13]

275

Eisenhower's interest in a nuclear test moratorium, however, was not motivated simply by a desire to gain a propaganda advantage over the Russians. The President also fervently believed that it was wrong for the United States to view "this terrible problem" negatively. Noting that the world faced a bleak future overshadowed by the hydrogen bomb, Eisenhower could not envision a long-term solution to the danger of nuclear warfare without first establishing a test ban.[14]

Unfortunately Eisenhower's pursuit of a nuclear test ban was short-lived in spring 1954. After a month of study, Dulles informed the National Security Council that his committee was virtually unanimous in opposing a nuclear test moratorium. The recommendation reflected the power of logic over the power of will, Secretary Dulles wryly observed, because all members of the committee had professed their desire to end testing. Strauss, for one, had advised Dulles that a moratorium on testing large weapons would be advantageous to the United States, provided a dependable agreement could be worked out with the Soviet Union. The trouble, of course, was that Strauss believed that a reliable agreement with the Soviets was illusory.

Following advice the Commission had solicited from Edward Teller and Norris Bradbury, Strauss warned that it was feasible to conceal a low-yield test. Also worrisome to the Commission would be the deleterious effect on the weapon laboratories of a long-term moratorium. Dulles observed that the United States would enjoy an advantage over the Russians only in the short run, but that after January 1956 American weapon development would have to be significantly curtailed. [15]

Eisenhower was genuinely disappointed that a nuclear test ban appeared unenforceable at the time. On May 25, the United States had introduced into the United Nations Disarmament Subcommittee a proposal to establish enforcement committees to oversee any disarmament programs. Subsequently, the United States also supported an Anglo-French proposal of June 11, 1954, which called for a phased approach to disarmament through successive stages and for nuclear disarmament phased with reduced conventional armaments and forces. Although the President accepted the assumption that a test ban could not be effectively policed, he nevertheless categorically refused to link testing to an agreement on general disarmament. Putting the National Security Council on notice, Eisenhower informed his advisers on June 23 that if there were any way to negotiate an effective nuclear test ban or moratorium, he would do it. [16]

The gathering in the Red Room of the White House the following afternoon was unusually somber. Off by themselves, Strauss and Lord Cherwell were talking quietly. Surrounding the President and Prime Minister Churchill were Anthony Eden, Dulles, and a few other guests who had attended the Sunday luncheon in honor of the British delegation. Churchill spoke at length and with great feeling about his fears for the future of the British Isles. He had been told that two or three hydrogen bombs could wipe out all the inhabitants of England, Scotland, Wales, and Ireland. After viewing the movies of the *Ivy-Mike* shot Churchill had ordered all work on air-raid shelters abandoned, given that shelters would prove useless in a thermonuclear attack. Then reversing a position he had taken in Bermuda the year before, Churchill informed Eisenhower that the British would proceed to develop a hydrogen bomb. [17]

## TOWARD AN UNDERSTANDING OF FALLOUT

The Oppenheimer case and the debate over the Atomic Energy Act left the Commissioners little time to reflect upon the larger implications of fallout during June and July 1954, but there was growing concern elsewhere in the government, particularly in the Federal Civil Defense Administration. Late in June Robert L. Corsbie, chief of the Commission's civil defense liaison branch, briefed civil defense officials on classified aspects of the fallout data collected at *Bravo*. For a second opinion the civil defense group turned to the Armed Forces Special Weapons Project. The staff of the special weapons group included a number of prominent scientists, among them Herbert Scoville, Jr., a physical chemist who had worked at Los Alamos for two years after World War II before going to the Pentagon. From the group's report it was clear that *Bravo* had brought the world into a new era of nuclear weapons. *Bravo* represented as revolutionary an advance in explosive power over World War II atomic weapons as the Hiroshima weapon had over conventional bombs dropped in Europe during the war.

The enormous fallout pattern from *Bravo*, however, indicated that thermonuclear weapons were far more deadly as a radiation device than any explosive. Using fallout patterns from *Bravo*, the group estimated that detonating a fifteen-megaton weapon would deposit radioactive material in sufficient densities over a 5,000-square mile area to be "hazardous to human life. Indeed, if no passive defense measures at all are taken, this figure probably represents the minimum area within which nearly one hundred percent fatalities may be expected."[18]

The implications of *Bravo* reports were serious enough to warrant briefings of the National Security Council and the Joint Committee. Strauss took responsibility for the security council while Scoville briefed the Wedemeyer panel, which Congressman Cole had appointed to study the impact of nuclear technology on continental defense. The distinguished membership of the panel, which included Army General Albert C. Wedemeyer, Gordon Dean, and Charles A. Lindbergh, indicated the importance the Joint Committee attached to the study.[19] The panel was greatly disturbed by Scoville's report on fallout effects and asked to what extent the American public and the world at large had been informed of the new data available since Operation *Castle*. Paul F. Foster, a retired Navy admiral and former business executive who had recently joined the Commission staff to assist the general manager on international matters, saw at once that the panel's concern would soon spread to the Joint Committee itself. Foster warned Nichols that, despite injunctions of secrecy, there would be leaks to the press from someone taking it upon himself "to alert the public to the gravity of this, as yet unknown, danger."[20]

No doubt anticipating problems from the report of the Wedemeyer panel, the Commissioners met twice in September with the Joint Committee to report specifically what fallout information had already been provided to the Federal Civil Defense Administration. During these same weeks Strauss and Nichols, now convinced that a public statement was necessary, discussed how best to bring the matter before the National Security Council and the Operations Coordinating Board for a decision on issuing a full statement. Concurrently, the special interagency task force on dispersion standards, on which Foster represented the Commission, had been asked to develop a new policy on dispersion for recommendation to the cabinet. The task force completed its preliminary study in October.[21]

277

Speaking before an industrial health conference in Houston on September 23, 1954, John C. Bugher, head of the Commission's division of biology and medicine, presented the first public analysis of the medical consequences of thermonuclear warfare. Although Bugher minimized the effects of continued testing by estimating that fallout "would have to be increased by the order of one million times before an increased frequency of bone sarcoma from this cause could be recognized" in the United States, he candidly reviewed the awesome characteristics of the *Bravo* shot. After describing the elongated cigar-shaped fallout cloud that contaminated approximately 7,000 square miles in the Pacific, Bugher concluded that thermonuclear warfare would create unprecedented medical and social problems. Not only would the nation have to cope with blast and thermal casualties on a scale never before conceived of in warfare, but also, he warned, the radiological damage could create havoc far beyond the immediate attack zone. Although Bugher's speech received wide press coverage and was distributed throughout the United States by the Commission and the civil defense agency, its technical nature and guarded tone did not satisfy the increasing demands for public candor. [22]

On the day following Bugher's speech, Strauss finally answered Flemming's request for dispersion standards. Because it was impossible to predict what sort of weapon a potential enemy might develop within the next twenty years, for planning purposes the Commission estimated the effects of a sixty-megaton weapon as suggested by the Defense Department. Strauss stated that a distance of twenty-nine miles from the perimeter of the target area should provide reasonable protection from blast and thermal effects. Twenty-nine miles, of course, would not offer refuge from lethal fallout of even a fifteen-megaton weapon. Unless fallout patterns could be immediately and accurately forecast and citizens warned, mass evacuation after a nuclear attack could easily catch refugees in the open where they could be least protected from exposure to radiation. The most effective measure, Strauss suggested, would be to take shelter in basements or underground structures for a few hours or days until radiation levels decayed sufficiently to allow safe evacuation under escort. Thus, no matter what the dispersion radius, sheltering rather than evacuation would be required to protect the population against residual radiation if critical industries were to continue functioning after a nuclear attack. [23] Obviously, public education on the effects of fallout would be required to win public support for a large-scale civil defense effort to build shelters.

On October 1, Willard F. Libby replaced Smyth as the principal scientist on the Commission. Soon he would become the Commission's chief spokesman on fallout. Twelve days after Libby's appointment, the Commission briefed key State Department personnel, including Gerard Smith, on fallout from the *Bravo* shot. Several of Smith's advisers were worried about the expected adverse impact that publication of fallout infor-

278

mation would have on American foreign policy, and they recommended against immediate release of a public statement. Several others opposed any publication at all. Thereafter, on October 21, Smith notified Foster at the Commission that the State Department had reached an "informal consensus" that publication would be deferred for some months.[24]

It was already too late, however, to stop public discussions. Like the radioactive cloud that had swept over the Pacific, the fallout debate could not be contained: it spread beyond government circles. Perhaps taking advantage of Bugher's Texas speech or press coverage given to it, Joseph and Stewart Alsop were among the first journalists to recognize that the hydrogen bomb was a radiological weapon and not simply a gigantic version of the atomic bomb. Atomic bombs inflicted radiation casualties, the Alsops observed, but these hardly mattered since blast and heat damaged a larger area than that affected by radiation. The radiation effects from the thermonuclear bomb, on the other hand, far transcended the destruction caused by blast and fire. The Alsops clearly understood the strategic implications of this fact. They estimated that one hundred such super bombs could not only destroy most of America's major cities but could also temporarily paralyze much of the industrial eastern seaboard.[25]

279

Thereafter, in the October issue of the *Bulletin of the Atomic Scientists*, Harold A. Knapp, Jr., a Navy Department analyst and the civil defense director for South Woodley, Virginia, estimated the potential threat of thermonuclear war to his small suburban community. Located seven miles from the Pentagon and ten miles from the White House, South Woodley was easily within the range of a hydrogen bomb aimed at Washington, D.C. Although Knapp focused almost exclusively on blast and thermal effects, he stressed the need for more technical information, especially concerning fallout, so that effective civil defense plans could be formulated.[26]

## FALLOUT: WHAT THE PUBLIC SHOULD KNOW

From within the Commission and the interagency task force, Foster continued to push for full public disclosure. Foster identified the issue as one of the gravest problems facing the Administration—so important that no one less than the President could deal with it adequately. Foster conceded that disclosure by the government of the full dangers created by fallout was certain to create anxiety throughout the nation and abroad. Nevertheless, Foster believed it essential for Americans to confront "the stark facts of life" so that the public would support effective civil defense and dispersal of key industries. Acknowledging that recent press statements had hinted at the truth, Foster believed the public was prone to dismiss such reports as "journalistic exaggerations." Only with official sanction from the President would Americans be convinced that the thermonuclear age required a radical change in the physical structure of densely populated metropolitan areas.[27]

Foster anticipated several problems in releasing an official public statement of the effects of fallout. In Europe, he predicted, neutralist sentiment would almost certainly be strengthened, but at home the public might clamor for increased expenditures on continental defense at the expense of other military programs. Foster was also worried about the economic impact that such a statement might have on large cities where business interests could claim that property values were needlessly impaired by hysteria generated by disclosure. The political consequences were even more uncertain, and Foster speculated that an announcement could augment the ranks of either those who sought a retreat from containment or those who advocated preventive war on the theory that the United States might better survive an immediate conflict. Most seriously, he argued that without public disclosure the civil defense officials, ignorant of the potential dangers, could not organize effective programs. To minimize hysteria while properly emphasizing the dangers, Foster recommended that Eisenhower inform the American public in a fireside talk broadcast over television.[28]

Val Peterson, federal civil defense coordinator, did not wait to find out what the President's Cabinet planned to do. Three weeks after Bugher's Texas speech, Peterson startled state civil defense directors at a closed meeting in Chicago by warning that "many millions of lives" might be lost to fallout unless proper civil defense precautions were adopted. But the civil defense directors were not the only startled officials. With the assistance of several dramatic charts, Peterson had so graphically described fallout patterns that Commissioner Libby worried whether the civil defense administrator had compromised classified information. Reminding the Commission that fallout comes from fission not fusion, Libby observed that the government could not admit that several hundred square miles were contaminated without disclosing the fact that the thermonuclear bomb contained a fission component of real magnitude. Nichols quickly pointed out that both the *Lucky Dragon* incident and the injury to the Marshallese had already compromised this information to a considerable degree. Japanese analysis of the fallout debris collected from the *Lucky Dragon* would ultimately render Libby's objection moot. Nevertheless, the Commission decided to censor carefully a ten-minute film the Federal Civil Defense Administration was producing to describe the dangers of fallout.[29]

During November 1954 the Administration lost its chance to provide candid fallout information to the American public. Nichols told the general advisory committee that the British had already constructed an accurate map of a hypothetical fallout ellipse by scaling up known test data. Libby also noted that Knapp's article on South Woodley had underestimated fallout by factors of five to ten. Since 1953, Bugher reported, Project *Gabriel-Sunshine* had sharpened the Commission's understanding of fallout. After one big shot, for example, iodine-131 could be picked up anywhere in the world. Bugher estimated that every American received a dose to the thyroid equivalent to about 0.5 percent of that received by the Rongelap islanders. Without specifying localities, Bugher cautioned against the use of milk from heavily contaminated areas. Surveys also showed a consistent pattern of increasing levels of strontium-90 detectable in the New York milk supply. All this information on fallout, however, was still highly classified. In order to facilitate civil defense planning, Libby obtained a consensus from the committee that the Commission should increase the flow of information to the public despite the fact that fallout studies were still incomplete.[30]

Unfortunately Strauss was distracted by the Dixon-Yates hearings on Capitol Hill and was unable to attend a crucial luncheon conference at the Pentagon on November 8, 1954. Secretary of Defense Wilson, the highest ranking official present, strenuously objected to any recommendations involving presidential announcement of fallout hazards. Throughout the conference Wilson stressed the importance of allaying public anxiety about the prospects of thermonuclear warfare, particularly with reference to fallout. Too much had already been said publicly about fallout in his opinion; before the government outlined the danger's full extent, he believed that it should make civil defense plans to cope with an "atomic blitz." That was just the point, Peterson argued; he could not develop an effective civil defense program without popular support based on public understanding.[31]

281

Because he was the only cabinet-level officer present, Wilson dominated the meeting. Thus, instead of forwarding a recommendation to the President, as favored by Foster, the conference decided to establish a new working group organized by the Office of Defense Mobilization to study thoroughly the problems associated with "victorious survival in the event of atomic-nuclear warfare." Working in cooperation with the Commission, the Department of Defense, and the Federal Civil Defense Administration, the new working group was to confine itself to nonmilitary matters and report directly to Flemming, rather than to the public.[32]

Ironically, British Prime Minister Winston Churchill, not Eisenhower, first expressed public concern over fallout. Speaking to the House of Commons on November 30, 1954, Churchill expressed his worry that cumulative radioactivity released from nuclear explosions would have serious effects on the earth's atmosphere for five thousand years. As noted in the *New York Times*, Churchill's statement was technically and militarily "confused and confusing," yet it also addressed publicly one of the great mysteries and possibly one of the worst dangers of the nuclear age.[33]

As if to underscore Churchill's concern, Ralph E. Lapp published the first of his articles on fallout in the November issue of the *Bulletin of the Atomic Scientists*. What chance the Commission had enjoyed to lead public discussion on fallout was now gone. As a nuclear physicist who had worked at Los Alamos during World War II and later with the research and development board of the Defense Department, Lapp could write with some authority on nuclear weapons and their effects. Although Lapp referred to fallout as a "secondary hazard," he accurately observed that the fallout ellipses from *Bravo* had stunned civil defense planners and caused a major shift in policy. Lapp also demanded that the Federal Civil Defense Administration be given access to classified data on fallout so that the agency could accurately translate them into a realistic hazard assessment for the American public. Hanson Baldwin of the *New York Times* endorsed Lapp's plea. And in that same November issue the editors of the *Bulletin* reprinted Albert Schweitzer's appeal to scientists to speak out for a suspension of weapon testing. Thereafter, Eugene Rabinowitch, the *Bulletin*'s editor, in commenting on both Knapp's and Lapp's articles as well as Bugher's speech, stated that the American nation as a matter of right should be given "all the information needed to prepare intelligently for the defense of its cities, not only against blast and fire of an atomic war, but also against its radioactivity."[34] Clearly, public assessments and speculations were becoming more accurate and more insistent.

282

In its own way, the Commission continued to encourage studies of the effects of ionizing radiation. At a national conference on genetics sponsored by the division of biology and medicine at the Argonne National Laboratory in November 1954, more than fifteen leading scientists were invited to present research on the effects of radiation on genes, chromosomes, cells, tissues, organisms, and populations. Although the papers were mostly technical reports of experiments with mice, fruit flies, plants, or other organisms, Bugher reminded the conference of the geneticists' larger responsibility, as a consequence "of man's modification of his environment," to assist in replacing opinions with conclusions in the formulation of national policy.[35]

More directly related to the *Bravo* fallout, at the invitation of the science council of Japan, the Commission sent a delegation of six scientists headed by Paul B. Pearson, chief of the biology branch of the division of biology and medicine, to a United States–Japanese conference on radiology. The conference, a success far beyond the Commission's most sanguine hopes, met in Tokyo from November 15 to 19. It was apparent from the outset that the Japanese considered the conference of major international importance. Consequently, the Americans, including Morse Salisbury, the Commission's chief public relations officer, prepared carefully for the meetings. Despite considerable apprehension among the scientists arriving in Tokyo less than two months after Kuboyama's death in September 1954, a friendly atmosphere quickly developed between the delegates of both countries. At the end, the Americans were satisfied that they had provided the Japanese with a considerable body of useful information. In turn, the United States delegation was gratified to receive impressively extensive data concerning fallout from both American and Russian tests.[36]

In addition to these scientific conferences, with renewed support from the general advisory committee, Libby offered the Washington conference of mayors on December 2 the government's most definitive statement to that date on radiation hazards from fallout. Although Libby's speech was by no means alarmist, he took pains to emphasize the qualitative and unexpected differences between fallout and traditional hazards from blast and heat. Libby stressed that an unprotected populace would suffer seriously, but he was relatively optimistic that a sheltered citizenry, if beyond the immediate zone of detonation, could survive a thermonuclear attack. Skirting direct reference to testing, Libby did imply that the weapon tests had not added appreciably to worldwide natural background radiation.[37]

Considering the fact that neither the Cabinet nor the President had as yet approved a public statement on fallout, Libby's speech had been remarkably candid. Nevertheless, Strauss knew that the Commission could no longer delay issuing an official statement his colleagues had already approved. Citing the death of Kuboyama, Churchill's parliamentary speech, and recent articles by Baldwin, the Alsops, and Drew Pearson, Strauss also expressed his concern about the numerous alarming statements that had already been made by responsible American and foreign military authorities and scientists. Among the most serious, in Strauss's opinion, had been the widely quoted statements by Alfred H. Sturtevant, a professor of genetics at the California Institute of Technology, and by Louis de Broglie, the French physicist and Nobel laureate. They predicted that the H-bomb tests would inevitably increase future birth defects. De Broglie had warned that nuclear experiments had created a danger to the world's plant and animal life. Within security limits, Strauss insisted, the Commission simply had to be responsive to requests from the press for authoritative information on fallout hazards. Otherwise, the Commission would be accused of concealing vital information from the American public while at the same time it was attempting to counter fears that public health and safety were endangered by continued weapon tests in Nevada and the Pacific.[38] From Strauss's perspective, a policy of candor would provide the most certain protection for nuclear testing.

283

## INTERNATIONAL IMPLICATIONS

At the State Department Dulles and Herbert Hoover, Jr., were the major opponents of releasing the Commission's statement on fallout. Fearing severe damage to American foreign policy, Hoover cautioned the Operations Coordinating Board that even a discussion with the Cabinet might result in a disastrous leak. The French parliament, which had recently rejected the European Defense Community, was then considering ratification of the London Agreement rearming West Germany. Hoover thought French communists would use this fact to distort the fallout data in a propaganda campaign against the United States. In addition, it seemed likely that the information would stimulate pacifism, especially in Germany, and create additional strains between the United States and the new government in Japan. At Hoover's suggestion, the Operations Coordinating Board recommended that the Commission's statement not be circulated even within the American government until after Strauss, Dulles, and the President determined how best to present the issue to the Cabinet. [39]

Hoover had not categorically opposed release of the Commission statement, only its timing, although, as Foster put it, "the State Department never will think the time is propitious." Strauss and Nichols observed that the Commission's authoritative statement could not cause any more damage than had uninformed but sensational speculations in the press. When Dulles personally requested Strauss to defer publication until the North Atlantic Treaty Organization negotiations had been completed, the chairman acceded but not without carrying the matter directly to the President. At a Cabinet meeting on December 10, 1954, Eisenhower also noted, as Strauss put it, "the virtue of laying all the facts on the line before there is an inquisition." Encouraged, Strauss reiterated that the best way to combat sensationalism and alarm was "to put the full facts forward with frankness." [40] Another month was lost, however, waiting for Dulles to return from Europe.

In the meantime, the Commission searched for a way out of its dilemma. At his news conference on December 17, Strauss reported that the Commission staff was studying the fallout problem and expressed his hope that a public statement could be made at a later date. In support of the chairman, the general advisory committee at its mid-December meeting continued to favor the release of a concise statement. Thus, with the State Department, the Federal Civil Defense Administration, and the Operations Coordinating Board kibitzing in the background, the Commission in January 1955 struggled through at least five different drafts of its statement on "The Effects of High Yield Nuclear Detonations." [41]

During these deliberations Libby insisted that a fallout map be included in the press release. Gordon L. Dunning, health physicist with the division of biology and medicine, did not regard the map as either necessary or advisable but rather contended that an official fallout map would raise more questions than it answered. Because a fallout map would have to be constructed using data gathered from only a few points, Dunning believed that any such illustration could be easily misinterpreted. Consequently, the idea of providing an official fallout map was ultimately abandoned, leaving journalists and others to devise maps of their own. [42]

Ironically, foreign, not domestic, developments precipitated publication of the Commission's fallout statement. In London, Harold Macmillan, Minister of Defense, informed Deputy Secretary of State Dillon

Anderson that the Admiralty was obligated by law to report to Parliament on February 15 on the state of the United Kingdom's defenses. Churchill had directed that the report include a statement on the effects of thermonuclear weapons. Having learned that the Commission was considering the release of a fallout statement, Macmillan requested an advance copy to assure that British and American fallout data were compatible. Gerard Smith, in his critique of the Commission's statement, was especially concerned that the timing of the release be coordinated with the British and the Canadians so that even minor discrepancies could be reconciled rather than feed further speculations.[43] Foster seized this opportunity to emphasize how embarrassing it would be to the Administration if the American people received their first detailed official information on fallout from the British government.

From another perspective Foster also saw the necessity of a prompt release. With the five-power discussions on limitations of armaments scheduled to begin in London in late February 1955, Foster was anxious for the United States to take the initiative by firmly establishing the American position. Communist propaganda, he observed, had already branded the United States as the originator and principal proponent of atomic warfare. Nehru, Mendes-France, and perhaps even Churchill might support Russian demands for halting thermonuclear testing. In agreement with Strauss, Foster believed that testing could best be defended by outlining the United States' position before the communists organized another worldwide campaign against testing on the basis of distorted use of fallout information.[44]

285

## THE FALLOUT STATEMENT

Now that Whitehall had effectively made the decision for them, Eisenhower and the National Security Council finally saw the need to release the Commission statement. On February 2, 1955, the President personally reviewed and annotated the draft, principally by underlining key phrases in the report. The following day at a meeting of the National Security Council Eisenhower expressed his determination not to be scooped by the British. Strauss assured the President that the Commission's statement had been carefully worked out with the Operations Coordinating Board. The Federal Civil Defense Administration, he reminded the President, had been after such a statement for months. Despite continued fears expressed by Wilson and others, Eisenhower observed that his Administration had probably underplayed civil defense during a time when an informed citizenry was important.[45]

Eisenhower formally approved release of the Commission's statement on "The Effects of High-Yield Nuclear Detonations" on February 3;

whereupon the Commission immediately began preparations to publish its report. Before any action could be taken, however, Dulles returned from vacation. He complained that the Commission statement would stimulate neutralism and damage United States interests in West Germany and the Far East as well as feed the Russian propaganda mill, which had been churning out demands for outlawing nuclear weapons. After Eisenhower asked that the best public relations man be consulted on the advisability of releasing the statement, Strauss dutifully reported that William E. Robinson, president of the Coca Cola Company, recommended against issuing any statement at all, on the grounds that it might stimulate neutralism overseas. Undaunted, Strauss once again insisted to Eisenhower that, irrespective of international complications, the American people should be told the facts so that civil defense planning could proceed. In a personal appeal to Strauss, Val Peterson concurred that without the Commission statement, state and local civil defense officials lacked any planning base for protective measures.[46] At this late date Dulles could not block publication, but at his behest the Commission dropped the dramatic fallout map that Libby had thought important.

286

Finally, on February 15, 1955, the Commission issued its report accompanied by a statement from Strauss. After reviewing the effects of the *Bravo* shot, Strauss offered assurances that continental testing at the Nevada Test Site created no off-site safety or health hazards. Concerned that the statement might jeopardize United States testing, Strauss stated without qualification that the hazard had been confined to the controlled area of the test site. The highest actual dose of radiation at an off-site community, he observed, was estimated to be less than one-third that allowed yearly for atomic energy workers under the Commission's "conservative safety standards."[47]

To the satisfaction of the State Department, foreign reaction to the Commission's statement was surprisingly mild. Among the North Atlantic Treaty Organization countries the announcement was accepted soberly and without much comment, according to reports to the National Security Council. Other international news tended to obscure the immediacy of the Commission's story. In Switzerland, anticommunists seized the Rumanian legation. In London the United Kingdom announced plans to build the H-bomb and to construct twelve nuclear power reactors. The French were bedeviled by their continuing political crisis, while in Japan a fire in Yokohama and Soviet-Japanese talks preempted most headlines. The only communist nation even to mention the report was East Germany. The Soviet Union and the People's Republic of China pointedly refrained from noting the statement, emphasizing instead the communists' commitment to peaceful uses of atomic energy as well as to banning nuclear weapons. There were scattered sharp reactions in India, Japan, and France, while in London the *Daily Worker* played up the terror of fallout to support its continued

"Ban the Bomb" campaign. But aside from predictable criticism from the left, the National Security Council could discern no stimulus toward neutralism among America's allies.[48]

At home the Commission did not fare nearly so well. Before the Commission could release its statement to the public, Ralph Lapp on February 11 published his second and most alarming article on "Radioactive Fall-out" in the *Bulletin of the Atomic Scientists*. Lapp based much of his information on Libby's December 2, 1954, speech and on the Japanese reports about the radiological analysis of "Bikini ashes." At a time when most people had scarcely begun to comprehend the meaning of Hiroshima, Lapp conceded that it was still too early to appreciate the implications of the *Bravo* test. Nevertheless, he asserted that the new super bomb could be considered a radiological weapon that could "contaminate a state the size of Maryland with lethal radioactivity."[49] Lapp agreed with Libby that sheltering would provide substantial protection from radioactive fallout, especially if the government constructed an extensive system of fallout shelters on the periphery of the major cities. But he also criticized the government for maintaining tight secrecy on this vital issue. Prophetically, Lapp defined radioactivity as something mystical, understood by less than 0.1 percent of the American people; for their part, few scientists understood the terror that the "invisible killer" held for the nonscientist. Candor and education were the only antidote to this modern terror.[50]

Lapp's article in the *Bulletin* and another in the *New Republic* on February 14 placed the Commission in the worst possible light. Not only did the Commission fail to receive credit for its candor, but its own statement, long in preparation, subsequently appeared a reluctant response to Lapp's crusade. All along Strauss had feared just such an eventuality. Back in November he had predicted that the Commission might be left "holding the bag" just as in the Dixon-Yates controversy "where we wished to make all the information public long before."[51] Now for the second time within six months the Commission had to accept the responsibility and criticism for an Administration decision over which it had no control.

## THE KEFAUVER HEARINGS

Following a flurry of excitement in the press, the Senate Subcommittee on Civil Defense of the Armed Services Committee on February 22, 1955, quizzed Libby and Bugher on the Commission's weapon effects statement. Senator Estes Kefauver, chairman of the subcommittee, wanted to know why the Commission had not published official information about fallout until after the public was alarmed by Lapp's sensational disclosures. Neglecting to point out that most of the magazine articles were based on information taken from his own December 2 speech, Libby simply explained

287

that the Commission wanted to get the facts straight. Although Kefauver and Stuart Symington, who had joined the hearing, pressed for a more detailed explanation, Libby was not free to tell them the real reason for delay—that State and Defense had blocked publication for several months. Consequently, as Symington pointed out, public confidence in the government's assurances was shaken when Lapp's article was published before Strauss's official announcement. Lapp himself, first as a witness before Kefauver's subcommittee and subsequently in a follow-up article in the *Bulletin of the Atomic Scientists*, also accused the Commission of being dilatory and dissembling in informing the American people of fallout hazards. The year of secrecy maintained by the Commission resulted in a year of paralysis on civil defense preparedness, Lapp charged.[52]

288

Even as Kefauver's committee conducted its hearings, the Commission continued continental testing in Nevada with Operation *Teapot*. Libby assured the senators that the Nevada tests were being conducted "in accordance with health and safety criteria designed to insure that there will be no harmful effects on the public." Indeed, Libby continued, the Commission had detected no fallout hazardous to humans, animals, or agriculture beyond the immediate vicinity of the test site. Libby did not actually state that there were no risks in continental testing, but he certainly implied that the risks were minimal. In a speech delivered to University of Chicago alumni on June 3, 1955, and later submitted as an exhibit for the published civil defense hearings, Libby stated that the genetic damage caused by fallout from the *Teapot* tests would be so slight that no measurable increase in defective individuals would be observable.[53]

## FALLOUT MONITORING AT TEAPOT

Libby had every reason to speak with confidence about the effectiveness of fallout precautions taken at *Teapot*. In the two years since the *Upshot-Knothole* series the weapon laboratories at Los Alamos and Livermore had again accumulated a large backlog of tests that were urgently needed to develop various new weapons, especially small weapons, both fission and thermonuclear. Looking toward reducing the large amounts of fallout associated with tests in 1953 and 1954, the laboratories were also beginning to explore new designs that would reduce the ratio of fissionable to thermonuclear fuel in weapons so as to lessen fallout. The Commission had approved an ambitious program for fourteen shots at *Teapot*, but nine of these were less than ten kilotons, and all the high-yield shots were fired on towers 400 or 500 feet high. As a further precaution against heavy fallout, the new guidelines for continental test operations developed after *Upshot-Knothole* were now in effect. Among these was the decision to reduce the maximum permissible exposure for off-site personnel to three roentgens for an entire year.[54]

The most significant change in test procedures at *Teapot* was the increased attention given to off-site monitoring and the formal, largely independent role assigned to the U.S. Public Health Service. The service had first begun to respond to the health hazards of radiation in 1948; by 1950 it had organized a series of courses in radiation health training for its own officers and for other federal, state, and local agencies. About a dozen officers from the Public Health Service had assisted, at the Commission's request, in collecting fallout data at fixed stations in small communities just outside the test area during the *Upshot-Knothole* series. For the first time, complete fallout records were made for an entire test series in these communities. The Public Health Service officers, however, were under the complete control of the Commission and the test organization, and all the records they collected had to be turned over to the test group as classified information.

289

By the time of the *Teapot* tests, the Commission had signed an agreement with the Public Health Service to participate in radiation monitoring in a more formal way. Sixty-six officers from the service participated in *Teapot* and assisted in collecting information that was later published on each of the fourteen shots. During the series the officers were permitted to discuss their readings with residents and to provide them with information about the tests. These procedures not only produced more complete data than had been collected at earlier tests, but they also helped to assure nearby residents that potential fallout hazards were not being concealed by classifying the data.[55]

## THE NEVADA TEST SITE

Despite official assurances, concerns about the continued use of the Nevada Test Site increased after release of Libby's fallout statement. On the day after his testimony before Kefauver's subcommittee, Libby was shocked to learn that Senator Anderson had written Strauss to request another reassessment of using the Nevada site for testing any but the very smallest devices. Anderson's about-face coincided with second thoughts Strauss also harbored. The chairman now confessed to Murray and Libby that, if the decision were his, the two largest shots in the *Teapot* series would be fired in the Pacific. He had always been frightened, Strauss noted somberly, that something would happen to damage the Commission's public image.[56]

When Strauss observed, however, that both Las Vegas newspapers favored continued use of the Nevada site on the grounds that the tests promoted both national defense and local prosperity, Libby interjected that this was a most sensible point of view. "People have got to learn to live with the facts of life," Libby declared, "and part of the facts of life are fallout." Such a philosophy was all right, Strauss countered, "if you don't live next door to it," "or live under it," as Nichols ruefully noted. Nevertheless, Murray insisted, the Commission could not let anything interfere with the *Teapot* test series, "nothing." Bugher assured the Commission that residents of the area, and especially those living in St. George, Utah, were hypersensitive to low-level radiation from fallout. "It is not a question of health or safety with St. George," Bugher reported, "but a question of public relations." [57]

New developments continued to make the Commission look bad on the fallout issue. In March, radioactive fallout from the *Teapot* tests was reported in widely scattered locations in Colorado, Nebraska, Chicago, New York City, New Jersey, and South Carolina. Yet in his testimony before Kefauver's committee on March 4, Val Peterson complained that security considerations had hampered the Federal Civil Defense Administration in making available to state and local civil defense planners pertinent information on weapon effects and fallout. Even within the Federal Civil Defense Administration, Peterson could not discuss fallout data with officials cleared for access to top secret information because they did not also have a clearance for Restricted Data. Unintentionally, Peterson left the impression that the Commission had hindered the civil defense effort by being overly strict, inflexible, or both. In fact, the Federal Civil Defense Administration had difficulty analyzing classified fallout data provided by the Commission because Peterson had consciously kept the number of cleared persons as small as possible. This restriction proved shortsighted after several cleared staff members resigned rather than move to the agency's new headquarters in Battle Creek, Michigan. Although Peterson duly explained the problem to the Joint Committee, the press in the meantime had castigated the Commission for being uncooperative and secretive.

The Joint Committee's hearings on civil defense planning on March 24, 1955, enabled Strauss to explain for the first time why the Commission had delayed in releasing the fallout effects statement. By then, however, the Joint Committee was rather disinterested in the Commission's old dilemma, and Strauss's explanation for the delay was greeted with little comment or publicity. [58]

Of far greater interest to the Joint Committee were the possible effects of nuclear tests on both weather and human health. On April 2, ranchers around Sheridan, Wyoming, were mildly annoyed when a spring snow began to dust the semiarid range. Before it was over, the storm buried northern Wyoming under almost forty inches of snow, killing livestock and paralyzing the region. Severe weather also complicated Senator Anderson's life: returning home for Easter recess by air, Anderson could not land at

Albuquerque; later, continuing storms prevented him from catching his return flight to Washington. It was the first time in thirty years that the senator had experienced such weather in New Mexico. Moreover, the Rio Grande was dry in April, an unprecedented situation according to the records of the U.S. Weather Bureau. Harry Wexler of the U.S. Weather Bureau observed that it was almost impossible "to prove that something isn't so." From Wexler's point of view, weather conditions were essentially normal, but he admitted that there was always a slight possibility that the tests had affected the weather. Because of this possibility, he concluded, no matter how much evidence the weather bureau marshalled to the contrary, a segment of the public would always be convinced that testing had altered the weather.[59]

## FALLOUT: AN INTERNATIONAL ISSUE

While the public remained primarily concerned about the weather, which apparently still remained impervious to human will, scientists worried more and more about the health effects of fallout. On March 3, as a direct reaction to the Commission's February 15 statement, M. Stanley Livingston, a prominent nuclear physicist and chairman of the Federation of American Scientists, proposed establishing a United Nations commission to assess the radiation dangers from nuclear tests. Citing the injuries to the *Lucky Dragon* fishermen, the contamination of Pacific tuna, and the call of India's Prime Minister Nehru for an H-bomb test ban, Livingston observed that the implications of thermonuclear testing could not be limited to national considerations. On the heels of the federation's proposal, the Indian government sent a formal note to the United Nations Secretary General reiterating its intention to press for a moratorium on nuclear testing at the next meeting of the United Nations Disarmament Commission.[60]

That international fallout studies might be linked to demands for a cessation of nuclear testing was precisely what the Commission and the Defense Department had feared. Herbert B. Loper, Assistant Secretary of Defense (atomic energy), warned that a United Nations study "would place the United States in a position of recognizing and admitting that its weapons tests are endangering the lives and health of the peoples of other countries."[61] Although Loper did not think the tests had been inimical to public health, he did believe an international debate on fallout would damage United States national interests.

Similarly concerned, the British Embassy on March 18 advised the State Department that a United Nations scientific study of fallout would merely provide the Russians with a propaganda opportunity. As if to confirm the political sensitivity of the issue, four days later the Conservatives in the House of Commons beat back by forty votes a Labour motion for ceasing nuclear tests until an international conference of scientists had studied radiation effects.[62]

The Commission's initial strategy was to oppose the United Nations project while promoting an independent study by the National Academy of Sciences, funded by the Rockefeller Foundation. At the request of the Commission even before Loper expressed his opposition to a United Nations study, the National Academy of Sciences announced on April 8 its willingness to prepare a report with Rockefeller money and Commission cooperation. The Commission's division of biology and medicine had concluded that the National Academy of Sciences was not only a more appropriate group than the United Nations for this task but also that the American scientists could be given access to certain highly classified data that would lend greater public credibility to an academy report.[63]

The Commission's alternative was compromised, however, when
United Nations Ambassador Lodge, as a countermove in the face of growing international concern, urged the State Department to submit a resolution to the General Assembly calling for the United Nations to collect and disseminate national radiation health studies. Under Lodge's plan, the National Academy of Sciences study would become the United States' major contribution to the international data collection. Lodge obviously wanted the United States to seize the initiative so that the Americans could gain some control over what appeared to be an inevitable United Nations responsibility. That same day, April 13, Senator Frederick G. Payne of Maine, supported by twenty-one other senators, introduced a resolution supporting a United Nations study of the radiation effects from nuclear explosions.[64]

Again Strauss found himself at odds with the State Department. In his April 15 testimony to the Joint Committee he had planned to state flatly his opposition to any international study on the "radiation problem." On the preceding day, however, at the urging of Under Secretary of State Hoover, Strauss agreed to withhold his opposition and merely to note that the possibility of an international study at some future date was not ruled out. Nevertheless, in executive session before the Joint Committee Strauss clearly indicated his sentiments by reporting that the Commission had taken a position not favoring the federation's proposal. Repeating British opposition to the idea, Strauss frankly indicated his concern that a United Nations panel might become "a packed jury of scientists," many of them from Iron Curtain countries more interested in propaganda than fact.[65]

Despite Strauss's and the Commission's continued objections, Lodge adroitly secured the Administration's support for the United Nations radiation study. On April 20, 1955, Senator Payne, now with the support of twenty-five sponsors, formally introduced a joint resolution calling for the United Nations study. Shortly thereafter, on May 4, Swedish Foreign Minister Bo Osten Unden announced that Sweden might also propose a United

Nations study. Lodge was now convinced that some delegation—either Sweden, India, or Pakistan—would raise the issue. He was determined to gain control of the situation in order to protect United States security interests, as well as to reap public credit. By advocating international coordination of national studies, Lodge hoped to divert attention from American tests to those of the United Kingdom and the Soviet Union and at the same time reduce building pressures for a moratorium on testing. Indeed, unless the United States acted positively, Lodge feared, the Geneva peaceful uses conference might degenerate into an international debate on the effects of nuclear testing.[66]

Although even Gerard Smith remained skeptical of Lodge's position, Loper conceded in May that from a propaganda point of view the Lodge approach had considerable merit. Because the United Nations would serve only as a clearinghouse for collecting and distributing studies that might be produced anyway, the Department of Defense had no continuing objection.[67] With Loper's acquiescence, Lodge could now tackle the Commission head-on.

On May 20, 1955, Dulles, Strauss, and Lodge, with Smith and Hoover, met to resolve the impasse. Although preliminary meetings among Lodge, Libby, Foster, and Smith had laid the foundations for an agreement, Strauss at first seemed as adamant as usual. After Dulles reiterated Lodge's arguments, giving special emphasis to the assumption that the Swedes or Indians would act if the United States did not, Strauss confessed that he was willing to accept the onus of opposing anything proposed by these governments. Strauss observed that it might take two hundred years to document the effects of radiation on human genetics. In the meantime, the use of antibiotics in modern medicine might produce even more serious mutations than radiation. But Strauss did not oppose the international study simply because he believed it would produce inconclusive results. Fundamentally, Strauss and the Commission feared that an international investigation of radiation effects would lead into "dangerous paths where demands for cessation of nuclear tests and the disclosure of information concerning [United States] weapons would possibly result."[68]

Lodge reassured Strauss that, if adopted, the United States proposal would not call for any "judgment" on the part of the United Nations. In fact, Lodge suggested using the Disarmament Commission, on which the Soviet Union served as a minority of one, as a clearinghouse to receive national reports. Strauss understood all this, but he was skeptical that the United States could control either debates or amendments once the matter had been brought before the United Nations. When Gerard Smith next predicted that the Defense Department would object to linking radiation studies with disarmament, Dulles replied that the alternative, an ad hoc body, inevitably would raise the question of Indian membership. The consensus was that the Disarmament Commission, on which India was not repre-

293

sented, was the most readily controllable body available. With that under-standing, Dulles asked Lodge to prepare a revised draft resolution.[69]

Somewhat belatedly, General Loper, now with second thoughts, ex-pressed the Defense Department's objections to any language in the draft resolution that suggested guilt or implied any official uncertainty on the part of the United States. Loper wrote to Smith,

> While we recognize that many of our scientists, particularly those not directly connected with the radiation evaluation program, are critical, skeptical and uncertain, the official position of the United States Government, as expressed by the Atomic Energy Commis-sion, is that there is no basis for concern.

Accordingly, Loper insisted that the resolution make clear that the United Nations' only mission would be "to weigh the evidence and make known the facts."[70]

294

Throughout spring and summer 1955, the Commission contended that fallout from weapon tests had created a public relations issue, not a health and safety problem. Furthermore, along with the Department of De-fense, the Commission believed that national security might be endangered if public concern over fallout led to political pressure to suspend nuclear testing. Consequently, the Commission intensified its public relations of-fensive by encouraging Dunning to prepare a scholarly article on "The Ef-fects of Nuclear Weapons Testing." Dunning's highly technical paper, how-ever, not published until December 1955, did little to relieve public anxiety.[71] In a more popular vein, Commissioner Libby addressed the alumni at the University of Chicago on "Radioactive Fallout."

Although Libby's speech was also highly technical, it was straight-forward about the dangers of radioactivity while offering the public some assurances. If all the dosages from all atomic tests since 1945 were added together, Libby calculated, the total dosage for the American people would average considerably less than one-tenth roentgen or less than 0.02 percent of what was believed to be a lethal dose (400 roentgens). In actual fact, Libby estimated that as of January 1, 1955, the total dosage over the United States from tests was about 0.001 roentgen per year. The tests, he con-cluded, "therefore, do not constitute any real hazard to the *immediate* health." On long-range somatic hazards, Libby flatly stated that "natural radioactivities of the body, the effects of the cosmic radiation and the natu-ral radiation of the radioactivities of the earth's surface constitute hazards which are much greater than the test fallout hazards." Libby did not want to imply that there were no risks, but rather that the risks from testing were no greater, and indeed were less, than those naturally encountered.

Libby underscored this thesis in his section on the genetic effects of testing. Quoting from a May 1955 report of the advisory committee on bi-ology and medicine, Libby conceded that radiation produced by fallout from tests as well as from the peaceful application of atomic energy would produce additional mutations in human genes. But there would be "no measurable increase in defective individuals" as a result of the weapon tests because the small number of additional cases would not measurably change the ratio of forty thousand defective children to four million annual births. Of course, both somatic and genetic damage caused by all-out nuclear war could be catastrophic, an estimate Ralph Lapp confirmed simultaneously in his June 1955 article published in the *Bulletin of the Atomic Scientists*.[72] At the conclusion of his Chicago speech, Libby mentioned both the study by the National Academy of Sciences funded by the Rockefeller Foundation and a similar study in England by the Medical Research Council under the chairmanship of Sir Harold Himsworth. Without mentioning Lodge's proposal for a United Nations project, Libby simply expressed his hope that the American and British studies would be fully coordinated.

Finally reconciling the Commission and the Department of Defense to the wisdom of an American initiative at the United Nations, Lodge announced the United States proposal for an international pool of fallout data at the United Nations' tenth anniversary celebration in San Francisco. Approved in advance by several nations, including Britain and Sweden, Lodge's plan was to assemble all available information on the effects of nuclear test fallout "so that all nations can be satisfied that humanity is not endangered by these tests." Giving credit to the influence of Libby's June 3 speech in Chicago and thereby offering the Commission some welcome publicity, Lodge reaffirmed his conviction that fears about fallout had been greatly exaggerated. Because military topics were not to be considered at the Geneva peaceful uses conference in August, Lodge intended formally to introduce the American resolution to the General Assembly when it reconvened in September.[73]

## THE INSEPARABLE LINKAGE

The *Bravo* shot unexpectedly had forged inseparable links between the fallout issue and international demands for a nuclear test ban. With the exception of Murray, the Commission labored in vain to break the two issues apart. But as in tempering steel, the more the Commission threw cold water on the linkage, the harder it became. If anything, the Commission's February 15, 1955, statement on fallout and its spring public relations campaign on the safety of testing had only reinforced the interrelatedness of the two issues. The chain of circumstances that led inexorably to the nuclear test moratorium in 1958 was not singularly, or even primarily, the making of the Atomic Energy Commission. In fact, the Commission consistently opposed a nuclear test ban. Nevertheless, the Commission's role was not one of simple, mindless opposition; rather it was complicated by the fact that it served as the President's main source of scientific and technical information on nuclear issues. As such, the Commission was often obliged to provide information and opinions that actually facilitated test ban negotiations. The ambiguousness of the Commission's task was especially revealed in its relationship to Harold E. Stassen, whom Eisenhower appointed as special assistant for disarmament on March 19, 1955.

Eisenhower's decision to make a Cabinet-level officer responsible for developing basic disarmament policy was unprecedented. Stassen had become something of a political *wunderkind* after Minnesota elected him the nation's youngest governor ever at the age of thirty-one. Thereafter, he served as an American delegate to the San Francisco United Nations conference in 1945. Beaten by Thomas E. Dewey for the Republican presidential nomination in 1948, Stassen had vigorously supported Eisenhower in the 1952 elections. Subsequently, he was chosen to head the Foreign Operations Administration. Following Stassen's disarmament appointment, Eisenhower was delighted when the press referred to the former governor as the "Secretary for Peace."[74]

Stassen was given a delicate assignment requiring utmost skill in balancing conflicting interests represented by the State Department, the Pentagon, and the Commission, as well as by the Soviet Union and America's North Atlantic Treaty Organization allies. Stassen's appointment was announced in the midst of the London Disarmament Conference, which had convened in February 1955 only to be quickly deadlocked. Hoover, Acting Secretary of State while Dulles was in Bangkok, viewed the discussions as "only a debating exercise with the Communists using it for their usual propaganda purposes." Thus, Stassen was called upon to conduct a comprehensive review of American policy and strategy.[75]

In addition to his immediate White House disarmament staff borrowed from various agencies, Stassen established eight task forces to study the requirements and methods of effective international inspection and control. Ernest O. Lawrence headed the task force on the inspection and control of nuclear materials. Others included General James H. Doolittle on aerial inspection and reporting, General Walter B. Smith on inspection and reporting of Army units, Walker L. Cisler on power and industry, and James B. Fisk of Bell Laboratories on communications. The entire effort would parallel the Commission's search for international control of the peaceful uses of atomic energy.[76]

Stassen had hardly begun his work when the Soviet Union offered a new proposal to the London Disarmament Conference on May 10, 1955. At first American negotiators were uncertain whether the Russian initiative was genuine or simply another propaganda ploy. Nevertheless, the imperatives of the thermonuclear age seemed to require that the Russians be given the benefit of the doubt until otherwise proven disingenuous. The

Soviet proposals, which indicated much greater flexibility than ever before, essentially accepted the Anglo-French formulas for reductions in conventional and nuclear weapons and in armed forces. In addition the Soviet proposal called for the cessation of nuclear weapon tests as part of a ban on nuclear weapons. Although the Soviet Union continued to demand the elimination of United States bases abroad as well as abolition of nuclear weapons, the new proposal also recognized the scientific difficulties in accounting for nuclear material and in guarding against surprise attack.[77] From the American point of view, the Soviet initiative was unacceptable because it lacked provisions for effective safeguards and inspection.

By May 26, Stassen had prepared for the President his first report, which included an analysis of the Soviet proposal. Stassen believed that the Russians had placed disarmament in a "political package" that hinted at the possibility of a Russian withdrawal from central Europe in return for a United States pullback from Europe and the Far East. Although the Soviets had called for abolishing nuclear tests and weapons, the Russian plan did not provide for ceasing nuclear production. Furthermore, Stassen noted, the Soviet proposal offered only a "Korean-Armistice-Commission type of control over 'big' ports, railways, airdromes, etc." that was supposed to provide a crosscheck on nuclear capabilities and a warning against surprise attack. Significantly, however, Stassen did not dismiss the Russian overtures out of hand. Rather, he stressed the importance of finding some means of ending the arms race on terms compatible with American security interests.[78]

On June 30, 1955, having already received unfavorable comments from the Commission, the Department of Defense, and the Joint Chiefs of Staff, Stassen briefed the National Security Council on his suggestions for a United States disarmament policy. Stassen recommended that the United States seek an agreement with the Soviet Union to end the arms race by leveling off armaments, ceasing nuclear tests and weapon production, and establishing an International Armaments Commission to supervise an arms control agreement.[79] Eisenhower, generally sympathetic with Stassen's plan, thought the United States had to gain considerably more support from its allies, especially the United Kingdom, before any agreement could be reached with the Russians.

Defense Secretary Wilson explained that the Pentagon did not expect to settle all major issues with the Soviet Union before signing an arms control agreement. Nevertheless, without a significant change in Russian attitudes and policies on inspection and supervision, Wilson believed no agreement would be possible. The first order of business, Wilson suggested, should be to crack the Iron Curtain, perhaps through a movement toward free trade.[80] Speaking for the Joint Chiefs of Staff, Admiral Arthur W. Radford expressed their solid opposition to the Stassen proposal. He

297

declared that the plan was unworkable unless it included Communist China as well. Otherwise, Stassen's project would lead to the military inferiority of the United States.

Replying with some warmth, Eisenhower reminded the council that the Joint Chiefs of Staff had also rejected the Baruch plan in toto. As far as Eisenhower could see, Radford believed that the United States "should proceed as at present in the arms race despite the fact that this was a mounting spiral towards war." With withering scorn, Eisenhower wondered why the Joint Chiefs did not at once counsel preventive war with the Soviet Union. Taking another tack, the President argued that if the Russians failed to "play straight" on inspections, the United States could always abrogate the disarmament agreement. Radford demurred, by granting the theoretical possibility of the President's argument, but he doubted whether public opinion at home or abroad would allow the United States to counter Russian violations. Somewhat more patiently Eisenhower admitted that Stassen's proposal raised problems, but it also had the virtue of being a creative starting point for negotiations. Then essentially concurring with Wilson and Radford, he agreed that the crux of the problem was inspection.

Now Dulles captured the lead in the debate. If the United States did not make some bona fide move towards disarmament, Dulles predicted that Americans would lose allies and the right to use foreign bases. Not only was it impossible to stand still, but the United States could not wait for the settlement of political issues in Europe and the Far East. In Dulles's opinion, disarmament and political settlement had to proceed concurrently. Agreement was possible, the Secretary of State believed, because the Russians genuinely wanted some reduction in the arms race in order to deal more effectively with internal problems. Granting that inspection was the central issue, Dulles thought that no one had sufficiently studied the matter, including Stassen. Would the United States really be willing to allow Russian inspectors into American industrial and military centers? Dulles was skeptical and reminded the council that policing had seemed impossible to Baruch's planners. Since disarmament negotiations would most likely break down at this point, inspections would be the area in which the Department of State would put its greatest effort. Eisenhower was satisfied with Dulles's approach. Noting that the problem of inspection could not readily be separated from the substantive issues of disarmament, the President concluded with the obvious: the type of disarmament plan adopted would clearly dictate the type of inspection needed.

Throughout the debate Strauss sat glumly quiet. Opposed to a nuclear test ban, a key feature in Stassen's proposal, Strauss sought some means of supporting Wilson and Radford without incurring the wrath of the President. Finally he spoke pessimistically. Was it not possible, Strauss speculated wistfully, to pursue the approach first suggested by the President in his Atoms-for-Peace speech? Because the Russians could not be trusted, Strauss thought the best approach was the atomic pool that would drain off fissionable material from weapon stockpiles; this approach would take the heat off the United States while placing the Russians at a strategic disadvantage.

As the meeting concluded, Eisenhower ignored Strauss's irrelevant comments by returning to the main issue and asking Stassen to adjust his plan to an acceptable inspection system. Vice-President Nixon concurred with the comment that nothing was more important from a political point of view than an inspection system that would penetrate the Iron Curtain. The inspection issue, according to Nixon, was also the United States' most effective propaganda issue.

## THE GENEVA SUMMIT CONFERENCE

Always suspicious of Russian motives, Dulles had responded to the gradual thaw in relationships with the Soviet Union by remaining cool himself to a summit meeting until after the Soviets had demonstrated their sincerity by concluding an Austrian peace treaty. In May 1955, the Russians, as part of their post-Stalin revision of foreign policy, suddenly signed an Austrian treaty. Now on the spot and fearful that the Soviets might achieve a significant propaganda victory from their talk of "peaceful coexistence," Dulles, with the backing of the National Security Council, nevertheless continued to believe that the Russians would not deviate from their attempts to disrupt the North Atlantic Treaty Organization unity and to expand their influence, principally by subversion and insurrection, while avoiding direct confrontation with the Western powers. Dulles predicted that the Russians would use the Geneva summit conference, now scheduled for July 1955, to achieve considerable gains in moral and social stature over Western leaders. Unless the conference ended in utter failure, Dulles estimated that the Soviets would partially succeed in relaxing efforts at NATO build-up and German rearmament. In contrast, he did not believe that the Russians would achieve their disarmament goals by emphasizing "ban the bomb" at the expense of "the painstaking procedures needed to assure adequate safeguards." Dulles's confidence in the American ability to parry Russia's disarmament thrust was bolstered by the United States' plan to offer its own proposal designed to counter Soviet "ban the bomb" propaganda.[81]

Speaking directly to Soviet Premier Nikolai Bulganin at the summit meeting in Geneva on July 21, 1955, Eisenhower offered his Open Skies plan, which called for exchanging blueprints of military facilities and establishing bases for aerial photography and reconnaissance in each country. If adopted, Eisenhower's plan would have greatly lessened the danger of surprise attack. The President envisioned Open Skies as a confidence-building first step toward ending the arms race. Similar to ideas coincidentally developed by Nelson A. Rockefeller, the Open Skies proposal directly addressed the central issue of safeguards and inspection that the National Security Council held as the Administration's first priority. Because the Russians would almost certainly reject the Eisenhower plan on the grounds that it violated national sovereignty, Open Skies may have had a second purpose: to quiet European fears over stationing American nuclear warheads in Europe.[82]

On the same day that Eisenhower proposed Open Skies, Bulganin reiterated the Soviet proposal for establishing control posts at major sea and air ports, at railway junctions, and along main highways in order to prevent surprise attack. Khrushchev, on the other hand, virtually rejected Open Skies outright as nothing more than a spy system. The Russians, however, offered no new disarmament proposals at Geneva.

300

## "OPEN SKIES" OVER NUCLEAR FACILITIES

From the Commission's point of view, it was just as well that the Russians did not embrace the Open Skies proposal because the Commission had its own serious reservations about the President's plan. The Commission's concerns came to light when Arkady Sobolev, Soviet representative to the disarmament subcommittee, inquired whether nuclear weapons were included in Eisenhower's plan. The Russian's question was reasonable and, as Sobolev explained, consistent with the Soviet Union's desire to outlaw atomic and hydrogen weapons and to discontinue nuclear testing. Stassen, recently appointed to the U.N. Disarmament Subcommittee by the President and uncertain how to respond, announced that the United States had placed a "reservation" on all of its "pre-Geneva substantive positions" pending review of United States policies. Stassen's announcement was certainly candid, but it also squandered some of the President's hard-won propaganda victory by throwing in doubt American policies and Western solidarity.[83] Ironically, both the Russians and the Commission were able to exploit the uncertainty created by Stassen's faux pas.

When Stassen admitted that American disarmament policy was under review, he all but announced that the United States held "reservations" concerning its previous support of French and British positions. This apparent break in Western solidarity allowed the Russians to regain the initiative by offering numerous "first steps" to disarmament, confident that the North Atlantic Treaty Organization allies were in no position to respond positively. In his formal reply to Eisenhower on September 19, Bulganin pointedly noted that Stassen had been unable to clarify the American position. Did the United States still accept the 1952 Anglo-French proposals on force reductions? Was the United States willing to discuss control of atomic weapons? Would the United States also consider Soviet proposals for ground control posts? All Stassen would discuss, Bulganin complained, was aerial photography and exchange of "blueprints," which unfortunately included only the United States and the Soviet Union. To be workable, Bulganin suggested, Open Skies would have to include all allied nations, East and West.[84] By sly implication, Bulganin tweaked the Americans for refusing to recognize the Chinese communists and excluding them from the disarmament negotiations.

Sobolev's question and Stassen's "reservations" also enabled the Commission to seek exemption for its facilities and programs. First, Strauss was especially worried that if the United States were obligated to disclose nuclear stockpile figures, the Russians would be able to calculate production rates by extrapolating from any two stockpile reports. Second, Strauss was afraid that the Soviets might be able to improve their bomb design significantly by studying photographs of American thermonuclear weapons. He asked that the President be alerted to these problems so that Eisenhower's intentions for Open Skies could be clarified.[85] Before Strauss could take his questions to the President, disaster struck the Administration. On September 24, while on vacation, Eisenhower suffered his first heart attack.

301

Stunned, the National Security Council nevertheless met on October 13 to hear Stassen's recommendations based on his discussions with the disarmament subcommittee. It was possible, Stassen thought, that the Russians might initially accept limited Open Skies over a band of territory one hundred to two hundred miles wide. Under the circumstances, Strauss was hardly in a position to press vigorously the Commission's case against including nuclear weapons and facilities.

Dulles demurred, however, and virtually answered the Russians and the Commission by expressing doubt whether the President's Open Skies concept was "divisible." The problem with limited air inspection, Dulles suggested, was that the Russians might accept a modest plan with the hope that it would never have to be expanded. Obviously melancholy, perhaps discouraged, Dulles compared Open Skies with Atoms for Peace. Both ideas had been offered by Eisenhower primarily with the hope of improving the climate of international relations. In neither instance had the President fully appreciated the technical difficulties his proposals raised for inspection and safeguards. Vast technical problems would have to be solved, Dulles predicted, before any kind of worldwide system for arms inspection and control, including the exchange of blueprints and other military information, could be established. All the same, Dulles mused, the President's Geneva offer had "put the Russians on the hook." Dulles wanted to keep them there and thought it inappropriate to make any limited deal with Moscow until Eisenhower could make his own views of the matter known.[86]

Just prior to the Geneva foreign ministers' conference called in November 1955 to discuss arms control, Stassen submitted to the National

Security Council his "Proposed Policy of the United States on the Question of Disarmament." Stassen identified three priority objectives of the United States: (1) to open up the Soviet Union and other communist-controlled countries to effective inspection; (2) to prevent the proliferation of nuclear weapons to other nations; and (3) to inhibit the Soviet Union's development of intercontinental missiles capable of delivering nuclear weapons. To achieve these aims, Stassen endorsed Open Skies, a modest reduction in conventional armed forces, the prohibition of the production of nuclear material for any purpose other than peaceful uses, and expanded scientific and cultural exchanges. Stassen also suggested that space satellites and intercontinental missiles be developed only through international collaboration for peaceful purposes, precluding weapon testing and production. Although the United States should agree neither to reduce nuclear stocks nor to withdraw from overseas bases, Stassen recommended that a ban on nuclear testing should be part of a comprehensive agreement.[87]

302

Stassen's support of a nuclear test ban virtually insured that the Commission would seriously object to the proposed disarmament policy. The Commission supported Stassen's basic principles and premises, although Strauss noted that Stassen had not made clear whether his three priorities were offered in addition to, or as a substitute for, policy objectives outlined in previous reports. Confusion, however, was not the Commission's major concern. Writing on behalf of the Commission, Strauss outlined the chief deficiencies of Stassen's plans. Surprisingly, the Commission's first objection was that Communist China was not included in the proposed agreements. The Commission's motives in raising this sensitive issue may have been mixed. On the one hand, the Commission was on solid ground when it argued that no comprehensive inspection and control system could exclude the People's Republic of China. On the other hand, given the Administration's intransigence over diplomatic recognition of Communist China, the Commission's insistence that an effective agreement required Chinese participation virtually precluded a comprehensive treaty. Although the Commission's argument for including Communist China may have been a gambit designed to impede negotiations (the Russians had used the same tactic), the Commission was supported in this position by Allen Dulles of the Central Intelligence Agency.[88]

Strauss's second reservation touched closest to the Commission's fears. For political reasons, the Commission could not categorically oppose a nuclear test ban, but Strauss forcefully argued "that the suspension of nuclear tests should be listed as one of the items to which the United States will *not* agree except as part of the final phase of a comprehensive program for the limitation of armaments." On this point, the Joint Chiefs of Staff essentially concurred with the Commission, while Secretary of Defense Wilson more obliquely urged the implementation of Open Skies as the first and central objective of United States disarmament policy, subordinating all other goals to that end.[89]

On the question of inspection and verification, Strauss and the Commission were in accord with other commentators. Specifically, Strauss predicted that Stassen's plan would place too great a burden on the International Atomic Energy Agency, whose goal would include establishing safeguards to prevent use of nuclear materials for military rather than peaceful uses. Here, John Foster Dulles was closest in agreement with the Commission. Stassen's outline of an inspection and control system was so general, Dulles complained, that it did not provide the necessary details to evaluate the policy suggestions that should have been derived from the effectiveness of the inspection system itself.[90]

At the tenth General Assembly of the United Nations, Henry Cabot Lodge echoed Dulles's sentiments publicly. Inspection and control were the central issues in disarmament, Lodge stated, and had been ever since 1946. Lodge emphasized that the problem had now become more difficult and urgent because large stocks of nuclear materials could be hidden beyond the range of any known detection device. Nevertheless, India's delegate, V. K. Krishna Menon, introduced a resolution calling for the immediate suspension of nuclear testing. Although the General Assembly did not adopt the Indian resolution, it unanimously accepted one sponsored by the United States and seven other nations proposing that the United Nations establish a committee to study the effects of atomic radiation on human health. Thus, Lodge succeeded in his attempt to use a resolution to diffuse international anxiety over the health effects of radioactive fallout. By and large the American goals were achieved on December 16 when the General Assembly, by a vote of 56 to 7, against Russian opposition, urged the Disarmament Commission's subcommittee to give priority to such confidence-building measures as Eisenhower's Open Skies plan and Bulganin's ground inspection proposals while continuing to search for feasible measures that adequately safeguarded disarmament agreements.[91]

In the midst of the United Nations debate on disarmament Strauss urgently appealed to Eisenhower and Dulles not to endorse a test ban except as part of the final phase of disarmament negotiations. Strauss stated his unequivocal belief that the Soviet campaign for a testing moratorium was a "coldly calculated maneuver" to overcome America's superiority in nuclear weapons. Although Strauss believed that the United States held a lead over the Soviet Union in nuclear weapon technology, in event of a test ban he predicted that the Russians could overtake the United States through espionage, unimpeded research and development, and clandestine testing. Meanwhile the momentum and vitality of the American testing program would be lost. If a test moratorium were adopted as a first phase of disarmament, Strauss feared the Soviets would deliberately stall subse-

303

quent negotiations as a tactic to gain time for their own arms build-up. Even should the United States detect a violation of the test moratorium, Strauss believed it would be politically impossible to convince the world of Soviet duplicity in the face of denials from the Kremlin. Consequently, Strauss recommended aggressive opposition to a test ban until a "comprehensive program for the limitation of armaments" had been negotiated.[92]

Strauss's appeal contrasted sharply with that of Pope Pius XII. On December 24, 1955, the Roman Catholic pontiff called for an end to the nuclear arms race in his Christmas message to the world. According to the Pope, the great powers had to take three steps simultaneously: ban nuclear testing, outlaw the use of nuclear weapons, and control conventional armaments. The Pope's plea to end nuclear testing embarrassed the Commission. For once, Strauss could not dismiss a proposal as politically or ideologically motivated. In 1956 the question of a nuclear test ban would become a pressing public issue.

304

## CHAPTER 11

# SAFEGUARDS, EURATOM, AND THE INTERNATIONAL AGENCY

According to Lewis Strauss's recollection, President Eisenhower was the first head of state personally to operate a nuclear reactor. On July 20, 1955, in the midst of the historic Geneva summit meeting, the President visited the American research reactor assembled on the grounds of the Palais des Nations in preparation for the forthcoming conference on the peaceful uses of atomic energy. The reactor, which had been flown to Geneva from Oak Ridge, Tennessee, was the first nuclear reactor ever built in Western Europe. The President's inspection of the pool-type reactor created unusual excitement among the reporters, who were given their first opportunity to get close to the President since the opening of the Big Four meeting. In the noise and confusion, reporters and photographers jostled one another for a vantage point and even had to be restrained from climbing the platform on top of the reactor itself. Inside the glass-enclosed control booth where the President was insulated from the crowd, Eisenhower gradually withdrew the control rods by pressing a button. Slowly power built up in the reactor—first to ten kilowatts and eventually to one hundred.[1]

The President was delighted. He had always wanted to witness a nuclear weapon test but had never thought it politically advisable to do so. At Geneva Eisenhower could publicly express his interest in nuclear technology without associating himself in the slightest with atomic weaponry. Watching the control panel where three red sticks simulated the movement of the control rods, the President listened attentively while Oak Ridge scientists explained the principles of the controlled chain reaction, evidenced in the bottom of the cisternlike tank by the glow caused by the Cerenkov effect. At the conclusion of the demonstration, Eisenhower expressed his hope that private business and professional men throughout the world would assist in finding ways to employ the peaceful atom. In the meantime, he was confident that the demonstration reactor would teach all who saw it "that there are really many, many ways in which atomic science can be used for the benefit of mankind and not destruction."[2]


## THE DILEMMA OF PROMOTION AND CONTROL

As he stood at the controls of the first nuclear reactor exported to a foreign country, Eisenhower symbolized the dilemma of America's Atoms-for-Peace program. The President fervently believed that the world was doomed unless it could find peaceful uses for atomic energy. But thoughtful Americans also realized that without satisfactory controls and safeguards, the peaceful atom, especially when employed in research and power reactors or related technology, could also serve military purposes. During the two weeks of the 1955 Geneva peaceful uses conference several other political leaders and foreign scientists also operated the reactor under the watchful eyes of American technicians. It would be more difficult, however, to control nuclear technology, once peaceful uses had been successfully promoted throughout the world.

In 1955 and 1956 the Atomic Energy Commission and the State Department, with the guidance of the National Security Council, attempted to balance the President's Atoms-for-Peace policy against his determination to end the nuclear arms race. To this end, the United States enthusiastically supported numerous approaches to developing the peaceful atom: "selling" the nuclear option at Geneva, making nuclear technology and reactors available abroad, negotiating bilateral agreements that would assist other nations, pushing for an international atomic energy agency, and achieving the preeminence of the United States in atomic energy matters, particularly with respect to the Soviet Union, but also in terms of Britain and France. All these endeavors would promote the President's dream of redirecting nuclear research and resources from weapon activities to peaceful pursuits.

Nevertheless, under the President's direction, the United States' peaceful nuclear diplomacy was basically Europe-oriented. To some degree, the American policy was concerned with European and worldwide energy needs. The Suez crisis in fall 1956, and to a lesser extent the Hungarian revolution of the same year, would bolster Atoms for Peace by emphasizing Europe's need to develop atomic energy as rapidly as possible as an alternative to Middle Eastern oil. For the most part, however, the policy was born in the Cold War and was designed primarily to supplement American military security. Following the precedent of the Marshall Plan, Atoms for Peace was expected to forge even stronger economic and technical bonds between Europe and North America. Atoms for Peace, if coupled with an enforceable international moratorium on weapon development, would allow the United States to guard its near-monopoly over the military atom while promoting the peaceful atom.

At the same time, international control of atomic energy, a conflicting objective, required as much attention and effort as did promotion, even though nuclear management was less a topic for public discussion. If promotion of peaceful uses would inevitably place nuclear technology into more hands, it followed that the proliferation of knowledge would also increase the possibilities that the technology could be used for military purposes inimical to American interests. By its nature, control of atomic energy was negative and thus less attractive as an instrument of foreign policy. For that reason, and because it had implications for national security, the control objective was necessarily less visible. But behind the scenes, and to some extent in the public debate, control was a matter of serious concern to American leaders.

307

The problem was that international promotion and control of atomic energy were contradictory; the success of the one tended to hurt the cause of the other. After the Geneva conference the United States found it impossible to follow a consistent and steady course toward Atoms for Peace. Rather, the path that led toward one goal inevitably required a recharting of steps to reach the other. Consequently the search for a consistent policy on peaceful uses was hampered by apparent indecision within the Administration confronted with conflicting proposals, disagreements, and confusion about goals.

The turmoil and trials of the Atoms-for-Peace debates, however, were from a larger perspective dramatic symptoms of the deep moral question with which American leaders were struggling at the time. The specter of Hiroshima and Nagasaki, and more recently the *Bravo* shot and the *Lucky Dragon* incident, cast a shadow over the American conscience. The United States, in its drive to win World War II and save the world from totalitarianism, had developed the power of the atom for military purposes. Not until Hiroshima and Nagasaki were in ashes and the *Lucky Dragon* crew arrived in Yaizu, Japan, did the American people begin to understand the far-reaching implications of their accomplishments. Atoms for Peace was a sincere yet almost desperate effort to find some redeeming value in what seemed a uniquely American engineering triumph. This moral imperative provided a special incentive for the Atoms-for-Peace program. Without it, Atoms for Peace and Eisenhower's extraordinary dedication to that idea were not really understandable. At the same time, the sobering realities of thermonuclear warfare made international control of the atom a matter of paramount concern. The dilemma was that the two conflicting goals could not be separated.

## LAUNCHING THE INTERNATIONAL AGENCY

On his return from Geneva, Gerard Smith observed that the scientific conference had confirmed American leadership in the peaceful uses of atomic energy while refuting the Soviet allegation that the United States had concentrated exclusively on military applications. Although American dominance in peaceful uses of atomic energy was not as great as its leadership in atomic weapons, the United States' participation established a political fact that was expected to ease, somewhat, resistance to American economic promotion of nuclear energy.[3] Russian participation, however, had also been surprisingly strong, a fact noted by almost all American observers. Strauss and Libby, for example, reported that the Soviet Union had enjoyed disquieting success in training nuclear scientists and engineers.[4]

Smith also recognized that the Geneva conference, by increasing worldwide expectations for developing nuclear power, made it more difficult for the United States to limit its assistance programs. As he noted, the echoes from Geneva called for deeds rather than more words in the field of peaceful atomic development.[5] Realizing this fact, Commissioner Libby, on the last day of the Geneva conference, had outlined the steps already taken by the United States to implement Atoms for Peace. In addition to highlighting the various training programs sponsored by the Commission, Libby noted proudly that the United States had given the large technical library exhibited at the conference to the United Nations in Geneva. This same library, similar to a collection already presented to the European Center for Nuclear Research, would be provided to nations willing to share their collections of unclassified official papers.[6]

Although attracted by American training programs and libraries, most participants at the Geneva conference were more interested in obtaining direct American assistance than in sponsoring multilateral controls through the International Atomic Energy Agency. During and immediately after the conference, Smith reported that the United States had been approached by several countries, including India, France, the Netherlands, Italy, and Australia, seeking agreements for cooperation to build power reactors. In addition, the council of ministers of the European Coal and Steel Community had previously agreed in June 1955 to explore establishing a European common market and to discuss preliminary plans for EURATOM, a multilateral organization that would integrate European atomic energy development. At this same time, in part responding to Eisenhower's speech at Pennsylvania State University, the Organization for European Economic Cooperation, established in 1948 under the Marshall Plan, appointed a working group to study European cooperation in the areas of nuclear power and distribution.[7]

Even the Russians, according to Smith, had jumped on the peaceful uses "bandwagon." To Smith's surprise, politics were virtually absent from the scientific conference. Smith suspected, however, that the freedom with which Russian scientists had discussed their specialities was less attributable to the "Spirit of Geneva" than to a prior decision by the Kremlin to ride the "surge" of world interest in peaceful uses of atomic energy. His interpretation was borne out, Smith believed, by the course of negotiations between the United States and the Soviet Union on the International Atomic Energy Agency.[8]

Initially, the Russians opposed Eisenhower's plan for the agency by arguing that promotion of nuclear power around the world could only follow a ban on nuclear weapons because the widespread use of nuclear power would result in the proliferation of weapon-grade material. For its part, the Eisenhower Administration had contended that an "atomic pool" would siphon off weapon-grade material from national stockpiles, thus reducing theoretically the amount of enriched uranium available for nuclear weapons. Nevertheless, Eisenhower could hardly announce the Administration's subsequent position publicly without being accused of suggesting an atomic pool solely for the purpose of gaining control over Soviet fissionable materials.[9]

309

Having decided to establish the international agency without the Soviet Union, the United States limited its discussions to seven countries that had either developed raw material resources or maintained advanced atomic energy programs—namely, the United Kingdom, France, Canada, Australia, Belgium, the Union of South Africa, and Portugal. Anxious for his Atoms-for-Peace initiative to bear fruit, Eisenhower had asked Ambassador Morehead Patterson on September 15, 1954,[10] to negotiate the statute for the new agency while he also continued to conduct the bilateral negotiations. With Patterson responsible for both tasks, it had been evident that prior to the Geneva conference the Administration had not yet reconciled the inherent contradictions between international promotion and international control of atomic energy.

Patterson's job was to establish the international agency as quickly as possible while coping with the complicated details in the agency statute. His strategy was to support a constitutionally broad statute embodying general principles, leaving to a later date the solution of more technical problems that might delay the agency's establishment. Among the problems left for the agency itself to solve were the location of its headquarters and the functions it might assume under its broad grant of authority. On the basis of a British draft, the United States, the United Kingdom, and Canada adopted an initial outline that was presented to the entire working group on March 29, 1955.[11] It became clear as negotiations proceeded that, with the possible exception of France and Canada, and of course the United States, no member of the working group really wanted an international agency.[12]

At this juncture only the United Kingdom might have been able to scuttle the project. With Patterson concurrently negotiating the bilateral treaties, he assured the President that the British were not inclined to frustrate the American determination to implement Eisenhower's program. Also, Patterson successfully kept the points of disagreement between Washington and London to a minimum. He defined the agency's mission so broadly that both the United Kingdom and the United States could agree that the agency's principal task would be to act as a clearinghouse rather than an effective regulator.

Then on July 18, 1955, the Russians indicated their interest in joining the discussions. As an expression of good faith, Moscow offered to deposit fifty kilograms of fissionable material with the new agency as soon as its charter was approved. This offer confirmed Premier Bulganin's announcement made a few days earlier at the Geneva summit meeting that the Soviet Union would be willing to contribute fissionable materials. Despite their unexpected generosity, however, the Soviets also seemed to favor a clearinghouse rather than a "banking" function for the international agency.[13]

310

## DEFINING THE SAFEGUARD PROBLEM

As long as the Russians remained uninterested in the international agency, the control issue had not particularly troubled planners at the Commission or the State Department. Without Russian participation, in all likelihood there would be no international pool of nuclear materials requiring safeguards. It seemed that an effective system could be adequately established later on a bilateral basis. After the Soviet Union expressed a positive interest in joining the negotiations, however, the matter of controls took on new importance. From the outset, the Soviet Union had identified safeguards as a principal concern in promoting international cooperation in peaceful uses. Originally, Americans suspected that the Russians had merely seized the issue as a means of obstructing negotiations, or even of gaining greater technical insight into the American atomic energy program. The evident seriousness of the Soviet position had been underscored, however, when the Russians earlier agreed to meet with a panel of experts, as suggested by the United States on November 3, 1954, primarily for the purpose of discussing technical issues.[14]

Thus, in winter and spring 1955, while the National Security Council was hammering out its new policy on nuclear reactors abroad, the American Atoms-for-Peace initiative advanced on four broad but loosely coordinated fronts. As the Commission organized its exhibits and presentations for the peaceful uses conference in Geneva, Patterson was aggressively pursuing both bilateral and agency negotiations. Now with the Russians surprisingly receptive to a technical conference on safeguards, both

John Hall at the Commission and Gerard Smith at the State Department turned to drafting a tentative agenda for the proposed technical conference.

Already moving beyond the general policy on safeguards that the National Security Council would adopt, Hall had concluded in February 1955 that the size and number of research reactors requiring supervision from the international agency would be small. Furthermore, the stocks of weapon-grade material produced by the operation of research reactors would not be appreciably increased (and might well be slightly reduced). Nevertheless, some international supervision over the fabrication and reprocessing of fuel elements, even from research reactors, would be required to insure that the materials were not diverted for unauthorized purposes. More important, although the United States might not export power reactors for years, Hall realized that the Commission could no longer postpone formulating a comprehensive safeguard strategy.

Unhappily, the operation of large-scale power reactors would pose difficult control problems. For example, Hall pointed out to the State Department that reactors fueled with slightly enriched uranium produced significant quantities of plutonium, which could be diverted to weapons. In addition, it would be necessary to insure that neither thorium nor natural uranium was surreptitiously placed in the reactor for the production of uranium-233 or plutonium. In cases where power reactors were fueled by plutonium, uranium-233, or highly enriched uranium-235, safeguards would be required to prevent diversion of fuel in all stages of the fuel cycle from shipment and loading through removal and reprocessing. Consequently, Hall warned, the international agency would have to exercise very close supervision over reactor design, construction, and operation, maintaining even more stringent controls over preparation and extraction of fissionable materials.[15]

311

On April 14, 1955, in the midst of feverish preparations for Geneva, the United States finally suggested a tentative agenda for the technical discussion of safeguards. The Russians did not accept the American agenda until they simultaneously expressed their interest in participating in the international agency on July 19, just three weeks before the peaceful uses conference opened. Moving now with unusual swiftness, the State Department, with Commission concurrence, proposed that preliminary technical discussions on safeguards be conducted at the close of the peaceful uses conference. Although Strauss was worried that the safeguard discussions followed too closely after the larger scientific conference, the Commission consented to provide necessary technical support with the understanding that the talks would last no more than five days and would be scrupulously confined to technical issues, excluding all references to either the organization and the function of the international agency or disarmament.[16]

Initially, the Soviets asserted that peaceful applications would in fact increase the world's supply of weapon-grade materials. Although this fact was obviously true in a technical sense, no one was certain what kinds of specific controls would be required to prevent unauthorized diversion. In view of the short time available to prepare for the talks scheduled to begin on August 22, the Commission found itself confronted with several serious questions of tactics. For instance, concrete discussions of procedures for safeguarding advanced reactors might well instruct Russian scientists on the status of American programs, both peaceful and military. Furthermore, to outline prematurely the extent to which maximum assurance against diversion of materials would require supervision over design, construction, and operation of the reactors as well as the preparation and possession of fissionable materials might well discourage "have-not" nations from joining the international agency. Most embarrassing, perhaps, was the fact that the Commission itself had considered the matter only theoretically.[17]

General advisory committee chairman Isidor I. Rabi, already in Geneva attending the peaceful uses conference, was not officially appointed head of the American delegation until August 19, three days before the first technical session. Just three days before that, the Americans had assembled in Geneva to develop a technical position on monitoring power reactors. Rabi's group was instructed to explore with representatives from the Soviet Union, Canada, France, Czechoslovakia, and the United Kingdom technical safeguards that emphasized physical security of fissionable materials and detection of procedural violations as established by the international agency.[18] From the distinguished American delegation then present in Geneva, Rabi was able to obtain advice or assistance from Commissioner Libby, Warren C. Johnson, Eugene P. Wigner, and Richard W. Dodson, members of the general advisory committee; W. Kenneth Davis, director, division of reactor development; Alvin M. Weinberg, director, Oak Ridge National Laboratory; Walter H. Zinn, director, Argonne National Laboratory; several other top scientists from Oak Ridge and Argonne; and Gerard Smith, representing the State Department. The group agreed that continuous monitoring of small reactors might be feasible, but it conceded that it would be difficult to monitor large power reactors. Safeguarding fuel element fabrication posed an even greater problem, while satisfactory monitoring of chemical reprocessing was the most difficult, if not impossible, task. By and large, Rabi's working group advocated a stringent system of inspection and detection supported by tight physical security, accounting, and "leak" monitoring procedures.[19]

Consensus was frustrated, however, when Zinn expressed skepticism that the proposed "system" was practical. Zinn vigorously challenged the group's position, stating that most techniques attempting to trace elements through the fuel fabrication and reprocessing cycle were unreliable. He conceded that a material accounting system, based on the United States

312

model, might be feasible for safeguarding reactors. Yet even if adequate inspection and accounting procedures were technically possible, he thought the proposed safeguard plan "would require a tremendously complicated, elaborate, irritating, and expensive physical security system." Zinn predicted that the cost of maintaining such a system would place a severe economic burden on power production, perhaps doubling operating costs beyond the purchase of expensive nuclear fuel. Besides, Zinn concluded, "physical security is notoriously difficult and uncertain."[20]

Although not everyone agreed with Zinn, his critique of the safeguard proposals only five days prior to the technical conference's opening revealed to American scientists that the United States did not have a comprehensive plan it could confidently defend. In order to have something concrete to present to the technical conference, Zinn and others met in closed hotel rooms, usually at night, to thrash out a new American proposal for safeguarding the fuel cycle.[21] They discussed various means of tagging or "spiking" fissionable materials with an energetic gamma emitter so that the flow of nuclear fuel could be tracked through both the fabrication and reprocessing steps. The advantage of using an energetic gamma emitter over other tracing elements was that it would be almost impossible to shield the tagged fuel from detection. The American scheme, conceived in a Geneva hotel room, would use uranium-232, which decayed with the emission of a sufficiently "hard" gamma ray so that instruments, rather than personal search, might insure that what passed into the system eventually returned.[22]

313

## GENEVA SAFEGUARD CONFERENCE

On August 22, 1955, the opening day of the technical conference, Rabi was tired, a little irritable, and perhaps somewhat anxious. In preliminary discussions, Rabi had not succeeded in convincing the British of the need for infallible controls, nor was he certain that the British would support the tracer idea.[23] Indeed, the American proposal was so novel that when Dmitrii V. Skobel'tsyn, head of the Russian delegation, first learned of it on the morning of August 22 he was unfamiliar with the decay chain of uranium-232. Incredibly, the United States proposal would receive its first systematic analysis during the course of the six-nation conference.[24]

The American position presented by Rabi described a system of physical security supplemented by accounting procedures and detailed knowledge of plant configuration and operation. Although Rabi admitted it was extremely difficult to account for all material within a given site at a given time, a properly designed system would prevent unauthorized materials from entering or escaping the site. In the Americans' opinion, accounting systems were essentially supplementary; therefore, the tagging scheme was not intended to assist quantitative control but to facilitate security at a control point.[25]

Throughout the five-day conference, Skobel'tsyn pressed Rabi for details and concrete examples of how the American system, and especially the tagging idea, would work. The Russians' most aggressive questioning focused on the "dead period" in the decay chain of uranium-232. Skobel'tsyn noted that neither uranium-232 nor its daughter element thorium-228 are hard gamma emitters; not until the decay chain reached radium-224 would a sufficiently energetic gamma be released. Thus, if the thorium were removed by chemical separation, the marker would disappear for a considerable time. Although the Russians did not flatly reject the American idea, Skobel'tsyn was clearly skeptical that "spiking" would materially advance safeguard procedures. The main difficulty with the American proposals, Skobel'tsyn intimated, was that they relied too heavily on physical security (and consequently inspection) without providing effective quantitative controls for nuclear materials.[26]

314

The Russians were also disturbed by the fact that the American proposals were comparatively short range. In his opening remarks, Rabi stated that the intention of the safeguards was "to prevent diversion of sufficient amounts of nuclear material to constitute a hazard to world peace within a reasonable time, such as ten years." Skobel'tsyn questioned Rabi closely as to what the United States meant by this ten-year forecast. Rabi replied, somewhat vaguely, that the United States could not predict what technical developments might take place over the subsequent decade. In any system of inspection and control, Rabi admitted, there was always a possibility, because all human effort is fallible, of some sort of diversion. The United States sought a period of reasonable assurance, Rabi explained. "Ten years, it seemed to us, was a nice round number. . . . Clearly, one year is too short and one hundred years too long."[27]

## SAFEGUARDS REEVALUATED

If the peaceful uses conference had been a brilliant success, the discussions of safeguards proved something of a disaster. On their return from Geneva the Americans realized they no longer had an adequate safeguard policy. Smith candidly noted that the United States government had only a limited appreciation of the safeguard issue. The technology discussed at Geneva was, after all, common to both military and peaceful uses. As nations developed independent competence in nuclear power generation, they also became potential producers of atomic weapons; Smith emphasized that the Administration had not yet squarely confronted this major security problem.[28]

Although Smith had not entirely given up on the "spiking" technique, he observed that the talks had compelled the United States "to consider a number of difficult technical problems which will have to be solved if U.S. participation in an international atomic energy agency is to be consistent with U.S. security."[29] It was the first hint from the Department of State that United States membership in the international agency depended upon a successful technical solution to the safeguard problem. Indeed, Smith was even convinced that the safeguard issue should be resolved before the United States supported the construction of any nuclear power plants abroad on a bilateral basis. The next step, Smith recommended, should be an engineering study that developed the United States' technical control plan in greater detail.[30]

As Smith advised Dulles, Rabi had already suggested such an engineering study to Strauss. Rabi had returned from the safeguard conference no less shaken than Smith. Although he continued to believe that the American policy based on physical security supplemented by accounting procedures was feasible, Rabi stated that more data were necessary to make the American position secure. With W. Kenneth Davis, he bluntly informed Strauss that it was a matter of highest priority for the Commission to sponsor scientific and engineering studies on safeguard techniques before another such conference was held.[31] The Russians had been nit-picking, almost inquisitorially, Rabi felt, and had steadfastly refused to offer a safeguard proposal of their own. Still, the talks had been surprisingly free of politics; the Russians were especially careful to avoid any direct conflict so that the door would be left open for later agreement. In retrospect, both the United States and the Soviet Union had been unprepared for serious technical discussions.[32]

Despite inadequate technical planning, Rabi was confident in the strength of the American position—in terms of both the United States' near-monopoly of enriched materials and its ability to lend technological assistance. Unless the United States established firm controls to begin with, the situation would "shortly get out of control," Rabi predicted. Furthermore, he was confident that the United States and the Soviet Union shared a community of interest. Thus, he agreed with Smith that further planning for the international agency required technical engineering study by the Commission, accompanied by parallel political study on the feasibility of controlling diversion.[33]

For the engineering study, the Commission asked the Vitro Corporation to analyze the technical and economic limits of safeguard controls, to evaluate control techniques, and to recommend the best procedures to the Commission. Libby, who claimed credit for the "spiking" idea, was particularly anxious that the Vitro study be completed in time to assist American negotiators at the working conference drafting the international agency statute.[34] Unfortunately, the final Vitro report in September 1956 offered the Commission little technical comfort. Even with a 90 percent

315

probability of detecting unauthorized diversion of nuclear materials, Vitro estimated that within five years it would be possible to divert sufficient plutonium from a power reactor to build an atomic bomb. From a technical perspective, Vitro's conclusions questioned "the feasibility of any control scheme except for the initial years of operation." [35]

It became more and more apparent to both the Commission and the State Department that solutions would have to be political and diplomatic as well as technological. At the request of the Commission, the general manager appointed a broadly representative special task force to delineate policy issues relating to power reactor development at home and abroad. The task force subsequently reported that there was a "grave military problem inescapably bound up with the advancement of the atoms-for-peace program," especially as it related to building power reactors in foreign countries. The task force virtually conceded that any large or rich nation with sufficient commitment could eventually build a nuclear arsenal. More shocking was the conclusion, which the Russians had warned of all along, that Atoms for Peace might actually contribute to the proliferation of nuclear weapons among underdeveloped or small countries. [36]

Among its findings the Commission's task force concluded in December 1955 that the National Security Council's policy on safeguards was deficient in several respects. The National Security Council, anxious to woo potential customers away from the less restrictive Soviet Union or United Kingdom, had not examined how the United States would prevent the direct diversion of nuclear materials from power reactors. Furthermore, the council had failed to realize that direct diversion was not the most important source of a weapon potential. Rather, the task force noted, large quantities of fissionable material could be obtained from a blanket of readily available natural uranium or thorium that could capture neutrons escaping from the reactor core. Anticipating the Vitro study, the task force also doubted that the United States could achieve absolute protection against diversion. Even maximum assurance could be obtained only with an intensive and complete inspection system that included access to "*all* facilities, areas, and records of the country, and rights of unlimited aerial photography." [37] Obviously, such a safeguard system would entail an unprecedented infringement upon governmental, industrial, and personal privacy, unacceptable to both the United States and other countries.

In stark terms, the task force outlined the dimensions of the diversion problem. It was unlikely that fuel rods limited in enrichment to 10 percent would be diverted directly to weapon production. Rather, direct diversion would likely involve plutonium generated either in the fuel rods or more subtly in a blanket of natural uranium. If a foreign power reactor generated 100 megawatts of electric power, roughly 100 kilograms of plutonium could be produced each year. The most stringent controls involving round-the-clock surveillance of the facility would be required to prevent

316

the diversion of 15 to 20 percent of the plutonium produced, enough to build several nuclear bombs per year. In order to monitor a moderate-sized chemical plant employing two hundred workers on a twenty-four-hour shift, the staff estimated a full-time force of forty inspectors would be required. But even then the task force conceded "that a practical control system which accounts completely for all fissionable materials cannot be devised."[38]

Despite its pessimism about the feasibility of safeguard systems, the task force did not regard diversion of special nuclear materials as the most serious danger of proliferation. By far the greatest threat to international security resulting from the Atoms-for-Peace program came from training nuclear scientists and engineers in reactor construction and operation and in the technology of plutonium separation. Likewise, engineers and reactor technicians trained in nuclear power plants could be diverted to the construction and operation of plutonium production reactors using natural uranium.[39]

317

## THE RISKS OF ATOMS FOR PEACE

Ironically, the Atoms-for-Peace program, designed originally to circumvent the stalled disarmament talks, now confronted the old problems of inspection and control. The Russians, of course, had argued all along that Atoms-for-Peace discussions could not be conducted separately from disarmament considerations. The Americans, however, had assumed that peaceful development of atomic energy need not wait on disarmament because safeguards could be established to protect against nuclear proliferation. In the wake of the safeguard conference, when the Russians had finally abandoned their insistence on linking disarmament and peaceful uses negotiations, American officials admitted to themselves that the two issues were more closely related than they had earlier supposed. A basic difference, as Smith pointed out, was that safeguarding disarmament required universal control over international atomic energy programs, while detecting diversion from peaceful activities demanded, to a degree, less comprehensive measures.[40] But the tasks were similar, the chances of success were about the same, and the risks incurred differed only in magnitude.

Given the Commission's awareness in fall 1955 that atoms for peace could also provide atoms for war, did no one express serious reservations about the President's program? Actually John Hall met the question head-on: "In these circumstances, should the U.S. withdraw from its announced intention of furthering atoms-for-peace throughout the world?" The answer was clearly, "No!" The reasons given were not confined to the fact that a retreat from Eisenhower's offer would involve a serious loss of face for the President. Rather, withdrawal by the United States, according to the report, would merely leave the field open to the Soviet Union, the United Kingdom, and perhaps Canada, causing the United States to default on its political and economic advantages while watching the danger arise anyway. The problem, as defined at this time, was not how to abandon the goals set forth by the President before the United Nations but how to devise a way of achieving them that minimized the proliferation of nuclear weapons throughout the world.[41]

In December 1955, with Hall and Smith unable to resolve all differences of opinion, the Commission formally debated the safeguard issue. In view of the uncertainties, Libby inquired, was the United States firmly committed to "atomic foreign power?" Strauss thought "committed" was too strong a word; rather, the United States was "dedicated" to the worldwide use of atomic energy, carefully safeguarded. Should adequate safeguards prove impractical, the entire program would have to be restudied, the chairman believed. That was just the point, Libby asserted. "You see, sir, I rather think we are in that position."[42] For Libby, it was clear that even if a "perfect" safeguard system could be devised, it would be too expensive to be practical. He concluded, therefore, that the Commission should not delude itself by pursuing such an impossible goal.

Commissioner John von Neumann believed that international inspection and control should be administered by the international agency so that the onus of enforcement would not fall on the United States. Libby agreed and further suggested that inspections required under United States bilateral power cooperation agreements be conducted by the agency. Apparently believing that inspections were inconsequential anyway, Libby was inclined to rely upon atmospheric detection of weapon testing as the primary means of determining whether a nation was developing nuclear weapons. The Commissioners discussed at length the difficulties of conducting broad and elaborate inspections, as well as the problems of administering such an inspection system and insuring its long-term success. Von Neumann, supported by several staff members, even wondered about the practical wisdom of expecting the agency to fulfill these functions. Having called into question the United States' safeguard policy, the Commission decided to bring the matter to the President's attention rather than to proceed with further attempts to reach agreement with the State Department. To this end, Strauss suggested that Hall prepare a study outlining the major questions that should be presented to Eisenhower.[43]

In response, Hall noted that safeguards had not even been a major issue just six months before. He outlined options short of canceling the Atoms-for-Peace program. First, Hall insisted that the United States pursue a consistent safeguard policy in considering the international agency and bilateral cooperation agreements. If the United States and other "have" countries freely entered into bilateral arrangements in competition not only with each other but also with the international agency, the prospects of the agency's playing a major role as supplier of fissionable materials were remote. This difficulty could only be removed if to some extent all subsequent cooperation agreements were brought under the aegis of the international agency. To be effective, however, control required consensus among the "haves" that some measure of inspection was required in any agreement to supply nuclear materials.

Thereafter, Hall reviewed the political difficulties in establishing a control system. It would be hard to convince recipient nations to accept control and inspection in any form, especially if the supplying countries were not subject to similar controls. Because the efficacy of any system of control would have limited duration, a double standard between "have" and formerly "have-not" nations would be untenable within a decade. But, Hall emphasized, the bargaining position of the "haves" was at its maximum in 1956. If the nuclear powers formed a united front by insisting on controls as a prerequisite of assistance in any form, the "have-nots" might be willing to accept them. Moreover, a worldwide control system might be welcomed by nonnuclear powers as insurance against an atomic arms race with their neighbors. Although any inspection system would involve some sacrifice of national sovereignty, recipient nations were far more likely to accept examination by personnel of an agency of which they were members than they were to submit to inspection by a major power.[44]

319

How much control would be required, of course, was the salient issue. Hall thought it impossible for the international agency to require maximum assurance; that is, nations must pledge not to engage in the production of nuclear weapons, and they must permit large numbers of inspectors to go anywhere at any time to assure themselves that forbidden activity was not occurring. More practically, he speculated that the agency could require participating countries not to produce nuclear weapons or to engage in "sensitive" operations, and to allow intensive inspection of other areas for purposes of spot checking.[45]

The Commissioners generally agreed with Hall's analysis. They were now willing to take "a calculated risk" by providing nuclear materials for reallocation by the agency. Reemphasizing the expense of a comprehensive system, Libby was willing to compromise on an inspection system that might not be completely diversion-proof. In order to achieve the Commission's goal of installing one million kilowatts of power reactor capacity in foreign countries by the early 1960s, certain risks would have to be taken.[46]

The risks, however, were uncertain and incalculable at this time. In January 1956 the Commission was confident that it had auspiciously and safely launched the President's Atoms-for-Peace program as a major, positive element in United States foreign policy. At the State Department, Smith conceded that the Atoms-for-Peace program had been successful psychologically, but he warned that the Commission had also created expectations about nuclear power and American assistance that would be hard to realize. Although American firms were already announcing plans for substantial nuclear power facilities, including an 11,000-kilowatt reactor that Westinghouse was scheduled to build for the Brussels World's Fair, Smith predicted that unfavorable economics would slow the pace of nuclear power development. Given the serious problems of safety, security, and the availability of nuclear fuel, which would take some time to solve, Smith believed the economic disincentives were fortuitous. "For most countries," he noted, "right now training is the most important assistance."[47]

## EURATOM—THE GRAND DESIGN

320　The time and attention devoted to the numerous bilateral cooperation agreements and to international cooperation and control through the International Atomic Energy Agency, however, did not reveal the main thrust of America's peaceful atomic diplomacy. In fact, under direction from President Eisenhower, the United States placed its greatest support behind EURATOM, the European Atomic Energy Community embracing France, West Germany, Italy, the Netherlands, Belgium, and Luxembourg. As envisioned in 1956, EURATOM would develop an atomic energy industry similar to the European Coal and Steel Community. Although EURATOM would finance and coordinate research and development, it was primarily designed to promote generation of electrical power for industrial uses. With European coal production on the decline and the best hydroelectric sites already exploited, in the long run nuclear energy seemed to offer Europe its only indigenous source of industrial power.[48] Even that was somewhat limited by Europe's uranium resources unless supplemented by the United States. Of course, the Administration also expected American industry to profit from the sale of nuclear hardware to the EURATOM group.

　　Officially, the United States continued to support all approaches related to the international development of the peaceful atom—the international agency and bilaterals as well as the Organization of European Economic Cooperation (OEEC) and other regional associations—but under directions from President Eisenhower the major attention was given to EURATOM.[49] The President's determination to give EURATOM priority created severe strain between the Commission and the State Department throughout 1956 and gave credence to the charges that the Commission was "dragging its feet" on implementing Atoms for Peace.

　　On January 25, 1956, Dulles explained to the Commissioners the political factors underlying the President's desire, and incidentally his own, to promote European integration in the peaceful uses of atomic energy through the EURATOM approach. Eisenhower firmly believed that the unification of Europe along the lines of the North Atlantic Treaty Organization, the Brussels Pact, and the Coal and Steel Community was a prerequisite to a stable Western alliance and world peace. With the collapse of the European Defense Community, Eisenhower hoped to draw France and Germany together into a strong bulwark against the Soviet Union by giving American support to EURATOM. Additionally, Eisenhower thought EURATOM might well catch the imagination of the West Germans. Once European skills, resources, and purposes were channeled through EURATOM, the "burden of Europe" could be lifted from the "back of the United States" even if the United Kingdom did not participate in the European pool. According to Dulles, Eisenhower had first given "eloquent expression" to his vision of European unification in a speech to the English Speaking Union at London in 1951.[50] By 1956, only the Community of Six offered promise of opening the way to a genuine United States of Europe. If EURATOM succeeded, Dulles continued, the community could then proceed to other fields of activity. But if it failed, the integration movement itself would probably fall apart with little hope that it could be reconstituted, a possibility that presented a bleak outlook for the future.[51]

321

Dulles emphasized that the Atomic Energy Commission bore the responsibility for handling the technical aspects of the Atoms-for-Peace program, but in view of the McKinney report he also wanted the Commission to study the proposals in the broadest perspective. Anticipating legal and other objections from the Commission, Dulles asked the Commissioners not to think in terms of existing laws, regulations, or inhibitions but rather to define in maximum terms what lay within the realm of possibility. He reminded the Commissioners that if the Atomic Energy Act turned out to impede American support of EURATOM, then the law could be amended. In any event, because Congress supported European integration more vigorously than the Executive Branch itself, Dulles was confident Congress would approve a sound and prudent program sponsored by the Atomic Energy Commission. Livingston Merchant, Assistant Secretary of State for European Affairs, punctuated the Secretary's remarks by concluding that the Europeans were evidently determined to achieve atomic independence with or without the help of the United States. In that sense, American assistance to the Europeans was a wasting asset that bureaucratic dawdling could fritter away.[52]

## THE COMMISSION DISSENTS

Dulles's remarks were undoubtedly aimed directly at Lewis Strauss as well as the Commission. The Secretary's atomic energy advisers, principally

Smith, believed that Strauss was not fully sympathetic to the Administration's EURATOM policy. Although no one within the Administration publicly accused Strauss of thwarting the program, Smith and others were frustrated over the United States' failure to exploit fully its leadership in atomic energy affairs because the Department of State and the Commission had not spoken with one voice. How could Europeans or the American public know what the United States wanted when the State Department pressed for a supranational organization of atomic energy programs in Europe while the Atomic Energy Commission simultaneously encouraged the same European nations to come forward for bilateral negotiations?[53] Indeed, initial discussions of EURATOM at the Commission had raised the question of whether the United States could execute an agreement for cooperation with a group of European nations under Section 124 of the Atomic Energy Act. Obviously, such confusion provided ideal fuel for the political fires lit by the McKinney panel report and ultimately fanned by Anderson and Kefauver.[54]

322

In reply to Dulles, Strauss was forthright in stating the Commission's reservations about EURATOM. The Commission had already expressed considerable willingness to compromise on the safeguard issue, at least with respect to the proposed International Atomic Energy Agency. The Commission's comparative flexibility on the international agency had enabled the State Department to plan for the twelve-nation working conference—now including the Soviet Union, Czechoslovakia, India, and Brazil—scheduled to convene in Washington on February 27, 1956, to consider the latest draft statute of the International Atomic Energy Agency.

Strauss, however, was troubled that the United States by treaty would have to supply special nuclear material and technology to an entity that would not be a member of the international agency. More than likely, Strauss believed, an agreement with EURATOM would provide for transfer of classified information as well as nuclear materials. Under existing laws and regulations, the Commission had been unable to execute a power bilateral with France because French security procedures did not meet American standards. In negotiating a security agreement with EURATOM, Strauss observed, the United States might find that the Europeans insisted upon restrictions no greater than those acceptable to the French. Furthermore, to counter Dulles's veiled criticism, Strauss reported that the Commission objected to any "foot dragging" in the handling of the bilateral negotiations, but he assured Dulles he would cooperate with the State Department "to the hilt" within the legal limit.[55] With Eisenhower's directive backing him up, however, Dulles reiterated his request to the Commission that it not now concern itself with legal problems in order to consider all suggestions for United States cooperation, leaving for subsequent determination any decisions concerning what was safe, prudent, and lawful for the United States.[56]

Ironically, it became more and more difficult to distinguish "hardliners" from "softliners" on the safeguards and control issue. The Commission had been toughest on its stand concerning EURATOM given the likelihood that the industrialized nations, especially France, would obtain technical information that would directly aid weapon programs. Surprisingly, the Commission was not nearly so nervous about the International Atomic Energy Agency, no doubt because the agency would provide no competition, either commercially or militarily, to the United States. At a high-level meeting including Dulles and Strauss on February 3, Smith stated that the United States faced two basic policy choices concerning the international agency: whether to maintain limited controls designed to prevent diversion of nuclear materials for military purposes or whether to proscribe "fourth countries" from developing nuclear weapons. Strauss quickly responded that in the Commission's view, the international agency should require only minimum controls. The so-called "no-weapons pledge" that Smith sought would not be feasible, particularly because France would not accept it. More to the point, perhaps, Strauss observed that the United States would not accept sufficiently strict inspection and control of its own programs to satisfy prudent requirements for safeguards abroad.[57]

323

Arguing for strict controls, Harold E. Stassen, special assistant to the President on disarmament, believed the United States should try to prevent or retard the development of nuclear weapons in "fourth countries." From Stassen's perspective, the Americans should sponsor a comprehensive control system and let the Soviet Union bear the onus of rejection. In addition, Smith pointed out that the minimum controls advocated by the Commission might simply allow recipient nations to pursue peaceful uses with resources of the international agency while developing nuclear weapons of their own. In return for the "no-weapons pledge," Smith suggested that the United States should promise not to use plutonium recovered from foreign power reactors for military purposes.

Dulles, however, in support of Strauss, stated that it would be difficult to convince nations to forego permanently their right to build nuclear weapons while the United States, the Soviet Union, and the United Kingdom continued to make them. Furthermore, he was convinced that countries would not join the international agency if they were required to commit themselves to forego nuclear weapons for all time. The best the United States could do, Dulles thought, was to ask participating countries, as a matter of self-denial, not to complicate nuclear disarmament negotiations by manufacturing atomic weapons while the great powers tried to bring their own stockpiles under control.[58] Essentially, Dulles supported the Commission's position on safeguards, which required high reliance on the integrity of the nations participating in the international agency not to engage in clandestine nuclear weapon development. In order to exploit America's "wasting asset" of nuclear technology while its bargaining position was relatively strong and to fulfill the President's unswerving determination to find a peaceful alternative to the military atom, there seemed no choice but to plunge ahead with the Atoms-for-Peace program.

Toward this end, Eisenhower in February 1956 agreed to a second allocation of 20,000 kilograms of uranium-235, this time for foreign distribution.[59] The purpose was to implement the bilateral agreements, but the allocation also provided the President an opportunity to endorse both the international agency and EURATOM. Yet even as the Administration took steps to accelerate its promotion of international nuclear power, the Commission warned Eisenhower of the proliferation dangers inherent in the Atoms-for-Peace program. In a forceful letter written just two days before the public announcement of the allocation, Strauss expressed the Commission's apprehension. "The Commission wishes to point out," he wrote the President on February 20, "that the transfer of U-235 abroad and the subsequent production of fissionable material in power reactors increases the possibility of the development of weapon potential by those who receive our assistance." Nevertheless, having discharged its duty to warn the President, the Commission also expressed its determination to require "as a minimum, assurances and guarantees against diversion to other than peaceful uses."[60]

Reluctantly, the Commission fell in behind the Administration's policy as ordered by the President and the Secretary of State, who would assume leadership in formulating Eisenhower's nuclear foreign policy during the forthcoming election campaign. Although Strauss still functioned as the President's special adviser on atomic energy, Strauss, after EURATOM became a cornerstone of Eisenhower's grand design for a United States of Europe, increasingly relayed only technical and administrative assistance offered by the Commission. Even after the President had allocated 20,000 kilograms of uranium-235 for foreign power and research programs, Strauss, speaking for the Commission, insisted on two caveats: first, the Commission was not committed to specific programs such as EURATOM without additional discussion with the State Department, because, second, the Commission doubted that all proposals conformed with the Atomic Energy Act and National Security Council directives.[61]

When Eisenhower presented his Atoms-for-Peace proposals to the United Nations on December 8, 1953, he had prefaced his remarks with the observation that the world lived under the threat of nuclear danger—"a danger shared by all." The peaceful atom pointed the way "out of the dark chamber of horrors into the light . . . by which the minds of men, the hopes of men, the souls of men everywhere, can move forward toward peace and happiness and well being."[62] As he reflected on the world's collective hopes and fears for atomic energy, even Eisenhower could not have known just how prophetic he would be in his warning of universal dangers from atomic energy. In the aftermath of the *Castle-Bravo* shot, even as the President vigorously championed his Atoms-for-Peace program, the specter of global contamination from radioactive fallout revealed still another peril in the nuclear chamber of horrors from which Eisenhower sought escape. The light, toward which the President resolutely strode, was shadowed by an ominous radioactive cloud.

## CHAPTER 12

# NUCLEAR ISSUES:
# A TIME FOR DECISION

By the end of 1955 the Atomic Energy Commission and the Eisenhower Administration faced a wide range of policy issues that had emerged from efforts to develop nuclear energy for both peaceful and military purposes. On the military side, Cold War rhetoric continued to justify high priorities for developing and testing nuclear weapons, but the increasing tempo of atmospheric weapon tests both in Nevada and the Pacific had generated worldwide concerns over the dangers of radioactive fallout. Even more ominous was the specter of the thermonuclear weapon with its incredible potential for physical destruction and radioactive contamination. The enormity of this threat highlighted the difficult moral issues that had been created with the atomic bomb in 1945. Growing anxieties throughout the world and the rising sensitivity to the moral implications of nuclear warfare placed greater pressures on American leaders to consider both the feasibility of a nuclear test ban and the negotiation of nuclear disarmament.

Similar kinds of issues had arisen in the public consciousness since 1945 on the peaceful uses of the atom. The search for redeeming values in nuclear technology had prompted generous expenditures of public funds to develop various applications of radioisotopes in industry, agriculture, and medicine; some had been successful, but none had yet produced revolutionary effects. The greatest hope for peaceful applications was still nuclear power, but the dream of a cheap, clean, and reliable nuclear system still proved elusive. Thus, the old questions of the proper role of the federal government in developing nuclear power still remained to be answered.

No issue raised in the military or peaceful side was new. The Commission and the Eisenhower Administration had been struggling with the issues for three years, but in January 1956 they were taking a new dimension. By becoming more and more public issues of concern to people in everyday life, they were not just esoteric questions for high-level councils of government. In the face of this growing public concern the Commission and the Administration felt increasing pressure to resolve some of these long-standing conundrums. That 1956 was an election year promised to stimulate political debate of nuclear issues, and, as the months wore on, it became more evident that for the first time in American history nuclear matters would gain prominence in a presidential campaign.

## THE POLITICS OF NUCLEAR POWER

In 1955 Lewis Strauss had seen the Geneva conference as a triumph for both the American people and the Republican Administration, but, in fact, the conference had not provided the Commission with an enduring claim to superiority in power reactor technology. Within a matter of weeks after the conference the British made clear that Calder Hall, to be completed in 1956, would be only the first step in a startlingly ambitious plan to build twelve full-size nuclear power plants in Britain within a decade. When completed the nuclear complex was expected to produce 40 percent of British needs. In contrast, the first American plant, at Shippingport, would produce only 60,000 kilowatts and would not come on-line until 1957. Because the Americans would be relying on private industry to build nuclear power plants, there was no way that the Commission could commit itself to the British rate of nuclear power growth, or to any rate for that matter. By comparison, the Commission's predictions seemed little more than wishful thinking or the inflated claims of private industry. For Senator Anderson, Congressman Holifield, and other Democrats on the Joint Committee, Strauss's endorsement of industry's claims made them even less believable. In supporting the Dixon-Yates contract in 1954, Strauss had demonstrated to the satisfaction of Anderson and others his prejudice against public power. Anderson suggested that Strauss was working hand-in-glove with industry to thwart government projects.[1]

327

## THE MCKINNEY REPORT

For months Anderson had been planning to make nuclear power a central issue when Congress reconvened in January 1956. By this time Robert McKinney and his panel had completed their report on the potential impact of the peaceful uses of atomic energy. The panel, appointed in March 1955, had been charged to make a nonpartisan study of nuclear policy, but from the beginning Anderson expected the group to lay the foundation for atomic energy planks in the Democratic platform for the 1956 campaign. This ulterior motive, however, scarcely influenced the outcome. McKinney assembled a competent staff that worked diligently for the better part of a year with full cooperation from the Commission. The general manager funded a contract to support research for the panel and later estimated that the Commission's headquarters staff spent more than one thousand hours on the project.[2]

The panel's report in January 1956 did not criticize the Commission's efforts in reactor development as far as they went. McKinney and his colleagues, however, expressed strong doubts that the efforts of the Commission and private industry would be sufficient to develop nuclear power as fast as national security demanded. In that case, McKinney argued, "the Commission should support expeditious development, if necessary, even up to and including construction of one 'demonstration' plant of each major reactor size and type with public funds." This statement brought McKinney back to the position that Holifield, Price, and other Congressional Democrats had been holding for years. Even more, the report added fuel to the fire for a government-financed reactor program by setting forth assumptions about future national energy needs that constituted a dramatic imperative for quick action. "The growth of electric power," the report stated, "expresses in one simple index the American miracle of productivity and living standards." Thus, nuclear power could well be the key to the nation's economic future and "the most tangible symbol of America's will to peace." Forecasts of the annual growth rate of electrical generating capacity ranged from 4.9 to 7.5 percent over the next two decades. "The prospect of an indefinitely expanding national economy which may require as much as 600 million kilowatts of installed electric-generating capacity or more by 1980" seemed to give nuclear power a high priority.[3]

The panel also surveyed a wide range of other activities, including controlled thermonuclear energy, the uses of nuclear equipment and radioisotopes in medical, agricultural, and industrial research; and the application of nuclear power for the propulsion of commercial ships and aircraft, railroad locomotives, and motor vehicles. Not all these applications were yet feasible, but the panel urged that the federal government provide generous support for basic and applied research in university, industrial, and federal laboratories. Recognizing the many potential applications of nuclear technology, the panel concluded, however, that "atomic power may be the most tangible symbol of America's will to peace through the peaceful atom. . . . If we fail to act to bring atomic power to the free world, other countries will do so ahead of us, or progress will proceed at a slower pace."

## NEW DATA ON FALLOUT

By the end of 1955 the Commission's laboratories and headquarters staff were beginning to publish a substantial amount of data on radioactive fallout from nuclear testing. The Commission's *Nineteenth Semiannual Report to the Congress* in January 1956 contained a fifteen-page summary of recent findings on the long-term effects of fallout and brief descriptions of research sponsored by the Commission on radiation effects. More authoritative and detailed was a paper published in a scientific journal by Gordon M. Dunning, a health physicist in the division of biology and medicine. Dunning presented data on the blast, thermal, and radiation effects of nuclear detonating and discussed the radiation hazards posed by internal emitters such as strontium-90 and iodine-131. He concluded that the hazards of testing were negligible up to that time.[4]

Of much greater public interest was a paper that Libby presented at Northwestern University in January 1956 on "Radioactive Fallout and Radioactive Strontium." Libby's lecture was especially valuable to those outside the atomic energy establishment because for the first time it openly presented data gathered in Project *Sunshine*. In fact, Libby explained the background of the project and described the worldwide sampling network that had been created to gather data on fallout patterns for strontium-90. Libby contended that the major part of bomb debris from high-yield tests reached the stratosphere, where it would be suspended for about a decade before it slowly descended to earth. Because strontium-90 has a relatively long half-life—twenty-eight years—most test debris, Libby admitted, would eventually enter the earth's biosphere, where it could reach the food chain and potentially endanger children through cow's milk.

Libby reported a recent estimate that the maximum permissible concentration of strontium-90 in the human body was about one microcurie per 1,000 grams of calcium.[5] To help calculate total body burden, scientists had devised a convenient measure called a *Sunshine* unit, which was 0.001 of the permissible adult body burden. Thus, ten *Sunshine* units were comparable to natural background radiation. One thousand *Sunshine* units were not expected to produce any visible skeletal damage, but ten thousand units might be hazardous. Children under seven years of age were most susceptible to strontium-90, but absorption among adults over forty was negligible. Measurements made in Houston, Texas, on bones of deceased children indicated an average strontium-90 content of 0.4 to 0.6 *Sunshine* units.[6]

Libby sought to reassure his audience that the hazard from testing, if continued at the prevailing rate, would be insignificant. Despite the problems with the *Castle-Bravo* shot, Libby insisted that the weapon tests were conducted with great attention to the dangers of local fallout. In addition, scientists in Project *Sunshine*, who had collected fallout from gummed papers, milk and cheese, alfalfa, animal meat and bones, and even human cadavers, projected that worldwide fallout would be dispersed rather evenly, with slight concentration in the middle latitudes, principally by rains, morning mists, and fogs. Most fallout was dumped into the seas, drained into rivers and lakes, or washed into the top two or three inches of soil where it was held "very tenaciously." According to Libby's calcula-

329

tions, even if all the bomb debris distributed uniformly around the world were to reach the biosphere, there would be little risk to human beings. As it was, only a small fraction of the strontium-90 accumulated in human bones. "On the basis of the information [we have] obtained," Libby declared, "it is possible to say unequivocally that nuclear weapons tests carried out at the present time do not constitute a health hazard to the human population."[7]

Libby's "unequivocable" confidence in the safety of nuclear testing was not universally shared, however, even by the other Commissioners. Murray, for one, questioned the accuracy of some of Libby's information and openly challenged the wisdom of taking such a positive position in the Commission's semiannual report. Ultimately, the Commissioners adopted a much less categorical statement, noting in the section on "Long Term Effects of Fall-out From Nuclear Weapons" that the subject was "necessarily one in which the conclusions may vary over a wide range." The report conceded that estimates of injury from strontium-90 were based on data extrapolated from the known effects of radium on the human skeleton. Because injury due to strontium-90 had never been observed, there remained "degrees of uncertainty" over what concentration might actually produce damage.[8]

330

## FALLOUT AND THE HAZARDS OF TESTING

Health effects from fallout were not the only "degrees of uncertainty" that plagued the Commission in January 1956. The general advisory committee learned from Charles L. Dunham, the new director of the Commission's division of biology and medicine, that only 3 percent of the estimated debris from the *Castle* tests could be accounted for worldwide. The Commission estimated that 90 percent of the *Castle* fallout had dropped into the ocean, leaving only 10 percent for stratospheric deposition. The British, on the other hand, estimated that 60 percent of the strontium-90 produced from megaton explosions remained in the stratosphere. Furthermore, British figures were six to ten times greater than the American estimate if the concentration in temperate regions with high rainfall were considered. If the British calculations were correct, according to Dunham, maximum permissible body burden would be reached after exploding 110 to 170 megatons of fission weapons, rather than the American estimate of 11,000 to 17,000 megatons. Finally, Dunham concluded that health standards had been set for adults, but that effects on babies and children were not "known with equal certainty."[9]

Libby repeated his Northwestern University speech almost verbatim before a House subcommittee on government operations, which was receiving testimony on "Civil Defense for National Survival." Questioned closely by Congressman Holifield, Libby repeated his unequivocal assurances that nuclear weapon testing was safe. Later, when the Commission discussed the December 1955 program status report to be sent to the Joint Committee, Murray again suggested adding a qualifying introductory paragraph to the section on fallout to the effect that the information represented the best, but not necessarily the definitive, estimates of the staff. This time the Commission rejected Murray's amendment by a three-to-one vote.[10] For the time being Libby's public analysis of the global fallout hazard from testing went essentially unchallenged.

When Ralph Lapp testified before Holifield's subcommittee, he complimented Libby for his impressive statement. In fact, Lapp used Libby's data to estimate the strontium-90 hazard of local fallout. Urging the Commission to publish the actual measurements on Rongelap, Lapp postulated that local hazards from strontium-90 could be serious. He observed that the persistence of radiation effects were subtle and insidious. Madame Joliot-Curie had recently died of leukemia, and earlier her mother, Marie Curie, had succumbed to radiation effects. Lapp, nevertheless, was more concerned about the dangers of nuclear warfare than he was about the hazards of testing.[11]

331

As Lapp's testimony clearly indicated, the Commission was walking a fine line between justifying continued testing and informing the American people of the dangers of radioactive fallout in nuclear warfare. To counter increasing public opposition to further weapon tests, Libby proposed writing an unclassified technical paper on radiostrontium fallout that would outline the scientific data compiled by Project *Sunshine*. The Commission could not indefinitely argue that testing was safe, Libby stated, without declassifying the statistics upon which its conclusions were based. The general advisory committee agreed with Libby and recommended that "the flow of such information to the public domain be accelerated."[12] Such openness, Libby reminded the Commissioners, "has brought us the freedom to proceed with *Redwing*," the Pacific test series that included the first dropping of a hydrogen bomb from an airplane. Release of the *Sunshine* data, however, would also permit foreign governments to infer that American tests had yielded fission debris from at least twenty-four megatons of detonations. In the interests of the testing program, the Commission decided that neither American security nor the common defense would be jeopardized by releasing the *Sunshine* data through Libby's April 20 address to the American Philosophical Society in Philadelphia.[13]

## DULLES'S ASSESSMENT OF NUCLEAR ARMS

John Foster Dulles was becoming increasingly alarmed in January 1956 by what he described to Eisenhower as trends unfavorable to the United States in the development of nuclear weapons. The Soviet Union was already achieving the capacity to devastate the United States by surprise attack. In a few years, Dulles predicted, the Russians in a single stroke could virtually obliterate America's industrial power and seriously impair the nation's capacity to retaliate. Thus, the United States' own nuclear deterrent would be weakened. Conversely, Dulles also worried that the strategy of "massive retaliation" itself was becoming obsolete as the United States' ability to wage devastating nuclear warfare increased. He speculated that reluctance to use powerful nuclear weapons might begin to depreciate the value of the United States as an ally, undermine Western confidence in "collective defense," and reduce the availability of foreign bases to American forces.[14]

Most serious, Dulles acknowledged that nuclear weapon stockpiles were expanding at such a pace as to endanger human life on earth or at least vast segments of it. He told the President that the world cried out for statesmanship that would command nuclear power to serve humanity, not destroy it. Furthermore, Dulles thought that most people looked to the United States with its spiritual power, intellectual resourcefulness, and dedication to peace to lead the way to the peaceful atom. Dulles also believed that Eisenhower, who had inspired great hope with his Atoms-for-Peace and Open Skies proposals, was uniquely qualified to assume international leadership. The trouble was that both ideas had largely lost their popular influence because Atoms for Peace, for all of its promise, would not halt the nuclear arms race. Moreover, neither Open Skies nor any other inspection proposal had been linked to any broad American plan for nuclear disarmament. Thus, the Soviet Union, with its "ban the bomb" propaganda, had been able to challenge America's moral leadership by claiming that they wanted to end the thermonuclear danger. But the Americans were widely perceived as stalling on nuclear disarmament while trying to think up good reasons for continuing the nuclear race, or even expanding it. The irony for Dulles was that the communists, "whose creed denies moral principles," might subvert America's moral leadership.

Given the Soviet Union's unreliability and the lack of international controls and organization, the United States, in Dulles's view, had no alternative but to maintain an arsenal of nuclear weapons. Dulles saw virtually no possibility of finding a technical solution to the disarmament problem, and there was almost no chance that the Russians would submit to the comprehensive inspection system that the United States would demand before agreeing to substantial disarmament. Indeed, slim hopes vanished when Americans would not state categorically in advance that, should inspections prove technically feasible, the United States would, in fact, drastically reduce nuclear arms. Dulles concluded that the major obstacles to nuclear disarmament were not technical but political. To that end, Dulles hoped to expand the United Nations' peacekeeping role by outlawing national stockpiles of atomic weapons and providing the United Nations Se-

332

curity Council with sufficient atomic weapons to counterbalance any threat of nuclear attack by a single nation. Probably inspired by Stassen, Dulles's observations were still vague and speculative. Nevertheless, he shared them with Eisenhower, who apparently welcomed even the rough ideas of Dulles.

Eisenhower agreed with his Secretary of State that it was essential for the United States to recapture the political initiative in the debate over nuclear disarmament, although the President was not quite so willing to give up the search for technical solutions. Rather, Eisenhower suspected that political and technical proposals would have to complement each other. Certainly, technically feasible inspection schemes would strengthen any politically acceptable disarmament treaty. As anxious as Dulles was to counter Soviet propaganda, Eisenhower ignored the suggestion that disarmament might be enforced through the United Nations.[15]

333

## A NEW REJECTION OF DISARMAMENT

Despite rebuffs during 1955, Harold Stassen continued to develop a comprehensive American policy on arms control and disarmament. Sharing some of his views with Senator Hubert H. Humphrey's disarmament subcommittee on January 25, 1956, Stassen described testing as a necessary consequence of the arms race. As long as the Cold War continued, weapon testing would be "essential" for national security.[16] Although satisfied with Stassen's defense of testing, the Commission did not share his long-range hope that all nuclear material could be restricted to peaceful purposes. Not only would it be almost impossible to implement such a proposal, but, as Commissioner Harold S. Vance observed, Stassen's goal might also preclude developing military propulsion reactors for ships or other vehicles. In addition, Strauss pointed out that large amounts of nuclear materials would be needed for purely defensive uses in antiaircraft missiles.[17] When the National Security Council met the following day, January 26, it took no action on Stassen's report.[18]

## BRITISH MOVE TOWARD A TEST BAN

Testing became a major item of discussion when British Prime Minister Anthony Eden visited Washington in February. Eden asked whether, as a move in the Cold War, the United States and the United Kingdom could propose to limit, control, or restrict testing. He frankly admitted that the idea would help him politically in the United Kingdom where apprehension over fallout was mounting. Eden also believed that there was little chance that the Russians would agree to control testing.

Strauss did not like Eden's suggestion. He lectured Eden that all nuclear testing to date had added to the environment only a very small fraction of the radiation generated by natural sources; the differences, Strauss claimed, were no greater than the increases in exposure encountered in going from sea level to 5,000 feet. Furthermore, thermonuclear technology did not require the testing of ever larger bombs but rather the development of more efficient, lighter weapons such as those used against aircraft.[19]

When Strauss estimated that the National Academy of Sciences would require at least two years to complete all of its fallout study, Eden complained that lack of concrete conclusions in preliminary reports would probably increase pressures in the United Kingdom to stop testing. At a minimum, Eden wanted to reassure the British public that the United Kingdom and the United States were jointly studying the matter. Strauss reminded Eden that the two countries were cooperating in the study of radiation effects and promised to send the Prime Minister Libby's recent speeches on fallout and other pertinent information planned for release.

According to Dulles, there were two possible reasons for limiting testing: first to protect health, and second to advance arms control. Dulles reassured the British that the United States would stop testing if it were proven dangerous to humanity. Nevertheless, announcing that the United States and the United Kingdom were discussing a test limitation would only give credence to the belief that testing was hazardous. In Dulles's opinion, a joint study could not conclude that testing was safe without producing "a very bad public reaction." On the other hand, Dulles doubted that there would be serious technical difficulties in devising a workable test limitation if humanity was actually being injured by testing.

Dulles believed that any plan to limit testing as a first step toward arms control presented an entirely different set of problems. Unless testing were banned entirely, Dulles predicted great difficulty in distinguishing between permissible and nonpermissible tests and in establishing effective controls. The *Castle-Bravo* shot in 1954 had dramatically illustrated the difficulty in estimating yields. A cheating nation, Dulles speculated, could merely claim that a nonpermissible test had been the result of an unintended large yield. Cheating could also occur in China or Tibet where responsibility for the tests would not be clear. As a step toward arms limitation, Dulles vigorously concluded, "test limitation would be an extremely fallacious approach."[20]

## THE ARMS RACE: AN "AWFUL PROBLEM"

Following Eden's departure, Eisenhower called an impromptu meeting of the National Security Council to discuss Stassen's proposals. Although

334

Eisenhower complimented Stassen for his hard work, the President feared that there was nothing really new to propose, except possibly Strauss's idea of designating strips of territory in the United States and Russia where inspection could be tried on a small scale. Strauss also suggested that while earmarking 20,000 kilograms of enriched uranium for domestic use the President should designate an equal amount for peaceful uses around the world.

Eisenhower thought that these suggestions were useful, but he was disappointed at the lack of progress toward disarmament. With elaborate public announcements, radio addresses, messages to Congress, speeches to the United Nations, and high-level negotiations with the Russians, the Administration seemed to be using a sledgehammer to drive a tack. Profoundly discouraged, Eisenhower saw few ways to avoid the gradual drift toward war. Nonetheless, the President felt the moral obligation to seek some alternative to the arms race. He specifically asked the National Security Council to think about "this awful problem" and to offer ideas on how to channel mankind toward peaceful pursuits and the atom into peaceful uses. If the H-bomb could be banned, Eisenhower mused, the world would be better off. He also suspected that defense planning overlooked the fact "that nobody can win a thermonuclear war." In a nuclear war with the Soviet Union, what is left of either country after the first seventy-two hours? the President asked. Eisenhower implored his advisers to search their hearts and minds for some way out of the collision course on which the two nations seemingly were embarked.[21]

335

## OPEN SKIES: A FADING HOPE

Despite Eisenhower's plea, Stassen and Strauss squabbled over how best to answer Bulganin's letter of September 19, 1955, which had evaluated the President's Geneva proposals. Bulganin had characterized Eisenhower's ideas as "sincere," but he criticized Open Skies because the plan for aerial photography did not include the allies of each country. Furthermore, pushing the standard Soviet position, Bulganin complained that Eisenhower had ignored the reduction of armaments and the prohibition of nuclear weapons.[22] To respond to the Soviet's objections, Stassen suggested that the United States pledge its support to the eventual peaceful use of all nuclear material.

Strauss and the Commission objected vehemently to Stassen's proposal. Not only would a pledge to use nuclear material solely for peaceful purposes damage the weapon program, but it would also preclude the development of nuclear propulsion for submarines and surface ships. With Dulles moderating Strauss's strong protest, Eisenhower persisted in expressing his "ultimate hope . . . that all production of fissionable materials anywhere in the world [would] be devoted exclusively to peaceful purposes."[23]

In February 1956 infighting over Eisenhower's nuclear policies must have tried the patience of Administration insiders, who were not even certain whether the President would run for reelection. On February 8, Eisenhower told reporters he would announce his decision before the end of the month. On February 14, the same day that Nikita Khrushchev denounced Joseph Stalin at the twentieth Party Congress, doctors at Walter Reed Army Hospital advised the President that he should be able to lead an active life for another five to ten years. Buoyed by the good news and convinced by his close advisers that no other Republican could be elected in 1956, Eisenhower on February 29 announced his decision to run again for the presidency.[24]

Shortly thereafter, Stassen left Washington for London where the disarmament subcommittee would meet for almost two months, from March 19 to May 4. In London Stassen presented the American modified Open Skies plan, which melded limited aerial inspection with aspects of Bulganin's ground inspection proposal.[25] For Khrushchev, who was also present in London, Eisenhower's obsession with aerial photography was troubling. The Soviet Union did not even have a complete photographic record of its own country, Khrushchev admitted. Whimsically, he claimed that the Russians had little interest in aerial photographs, whether of the United States, Monaco, or Peru. Still, Khrushchev thought the Soviet Union could accept some aspect of Open Skies if the Americans insisted. In addition, he reemphasized that the Russians had dropped their position on banning nuclear weapons because they knew the United States would never agree. Moreover, Khrushchev complained that whenever the Russians had tried to move toward adopting Western proposals over the past years, they had discovered that the West kept moving away.[26]

## THE MORALITY OF MEGATON WEAPONS

Now a persistent goad to the Commission and the Administration, Commissioner Murray renewed his call for a limited test ban on February 23, 1956. Testifying before a closed session of the Joint Committee, Murray recommended that the United States unilaterally cease testing large hydrogen weapons, set an upper limit on the size of thermonuclear bombs to be placed in the stockpile, and intensify development of a wide range of small, tactical weapons. Murray feared that unless the Administration changed its policy, the United States would develop the capacity for destroying the world in a full-scale nuclear war. He had also seen estimates provided to the National Security Council that the Russians might produce a single weapon whose destructive power was greater than the entire American stockpile. To Murray, the arms race had become sheer madness. No matter what the Russians might develop, Murray was convinced that the United States did not need to experiment with larger, more destructive weapons. Murray was not against testing, whose risks he thought were slight; rather he opposed stockpiling huge numbers of megaton super bombs whose destructive capability might contaminate the entire earth.

Despite the efforts of the Commission's division of biology and medicine, Murray argued that not enough was known about radioactive debris, especially "one of its most insidious components, radiostrontium. . . . Uncertainties about the rate of fallout," he testified, "about variation in world distribution, about the mechanism of take-up into food and into the body, all combine to render definitive answers all but impossible at this moment." One could imagine, Murray warned, "the impact on the medical profession as a whole in this country if it knew the magnitude of our mounting stockpile and the potential hazards associated with its use."

337

Murray proposed that the United States unilaterally suspend thermonuclear testing. Conceding that this was his personal opinion, shared by neither the Commission nor the Joint Chiefs of Staff, Murray, for military and moral reasons, also opposed testing and stockpiling megaton hydrogen bombs. From the military perspective Murray contended that megaton-size weapons would not prove useful in warfare.

> Atomic superiority does not consist solely in the possession of bombs bigger than those possessed by the enemy. It also rests upon the possession of such a wide variety and range of small atomic weapons that we shall be able to cope successfully with all the various military contingencies that might arise. Superior strength means flexible strength; and this flexibility can only be achieved by advances in the field of small weapons.

Morally, Murray believed that "the traditional canons of justice that govern the waging of warfare are still valid in the nuclear age." Although he was not expansive on his moral arguments to the Joint Committee, Murray, like Eisenhower, saw the interrelationship between atoms for peace and atoms for war, or between nuclear weapons and industrial nuclear power. United States programs in both fields were directed toward the same ends—the furtherance of justice and peace. Virtually elaborating the President's own concerns, Murray identified America's most pressing problem as balancing military and peaceful programs in such a way that each individually and both together served the common purposes. Moreover, Murray believed that as the benefits of nuclear power became universally shared the world would come to appreciate that "God in His almighty power and goodness has given us the secret of atomic energy for purposes of peace and human well-being and not for purposes of war and destruction."[27]

Not surprisingly, Murray's testimony to the Joint Committee infuriated Strauss. Fearful that the issue might cause the President trouble at his next news conference, Strauss warned White House Press Secretary James Hagerty that Eisenhower might be questioned about testing. Murray knew perfectly well that the tests were not designed for large weapons, Strauss advised Hagerty, but for new applications, particularly in defensive and low-fallout weapons. The Atomic Energy Commission was run like a business, Strauss insisted, which included keeping Murray fully informed of all developments. For some reason, according to the chairman, Murray had a psychopathic obsession about being excluded from vital information.[28]

338

Strauss's warning was timely and helpful to the President. At his March 21 press conference, Eisenhower was asked to comment on Ralph Lapp's contention that it was possible to construct a suicide weapon so large that it could be carried only by a freighter. Lapp obviously had access to sources similar to Murray's. Although Eisenhower did not answer the question directly, he admitted that there was a practical limit to the size of thermonuclear weapons. There was an old saying, the President continued: "You do not drive a tack with a sledge hammer."[29]

Suspecting that the President supported his views on the development of tactical weapons, at least in principle, but receiving no satisfaction from the Commission or the Joint Committee, Murray took his case to the public on April 12, 1956, when he testified before Senator Humphrey's disarmament subcommittee. Because in open hearings Murray could not statistically document his arguments that American nuclear firepower and stockpiles were already dangerously high, his moral arguments for unilateral suspension of thermonuclear tests and the development of tactical weapons seemed even more accentuated. Acknowledging the military principle that armaments should be demonstrably useful in actual warfare, Murray described an even higher principle that the use of force is always subject to the dictates of moral conscience. In Murray's opinion the sheer brilliance of America's technical achievements in nuclear weapons had tended to dull the nation's moral sense. As a "nation under God," Murray testified, Americans should recognize their moral obligation to limit war and the use of force. Murray reiterated that he did not think testing as such was dangerous but rather that he was horrified at the ethical implications of Dulles's doctrine of massive retaliation. In retrospect, Murray even confessed that he did not believe that the use of the atomic bomb against "the city of Hiroshima and its multitudes of innocent people could be justified on moral grounds."[30]

## THE H-BOMB: A CAMPAIGN ISSUE

In early spring 1956, Adlai Stevenson, campaigning against Senator Estes Kefauver of Tennessee for the Democratic presidential nomination, spoke out against continued testing of hydrogen bombs. Inspired by Murray, Stevenson on April 21 proposed to the American Society of Newspaper Editors that halting H-bomb testing would be a dramatic expression of America's real concern for peace. Like Murray, Stevenson would end the tests unilaterally, but, unlike the Commissioner, he did not propose buttressing the tactical stockpile. Stevenson borrowed liberally from Murray's moral arguments while virtually ignoring the fact that Murray had also warned against simplistic "ban-the-bomb" schemes.[31]

Stevenson's proposal, offered to the editors on Saturday, was almost immediately smothered by Russian actions. On Monday morning Nikita Khrushchev informed British businessmen that the Soviet Union was building a ballistic missile with a nuclear warhead. Probably unaware of Khrushchev's announcement in London, Kefauver, uncertain on how best to parry Stevenson, conceded that he "saw no particular good in having further H-bomb tests." Stevenson himself asserted that the Russians had given every indication that they would "go along" with his suggestion. After lunch on April 24, however, Republican Senators Thomas H. Kuchel of California and Styles Bridges of New Hampshire sharply criticized Stevenson's test-ban proposals as misguided. By mid-afternoon, Kefauver had modified his morning statement by insisting that he favored only a reciprocal test ban with the Russians. Stevenson, now sensing that he had committed a major blunder, attempted to counterattack by reaffirming his test-ban proposal while charging that the Administration had been "dangerously dilatory" in developing guided missiles.[32]

339

Intentionally or not, the Russians had struck a major blow at Stevenson's campaign for the presidency without damaging his chances for the Democratic nomination. While campaigning vigorously for Florida's twenty-eight convention votes a week later, Kefauver tried to capitalize on the issue by underscoring the folly of a test ban in the face of Khrushchev's boast. But rather than reaping much benefit, Kefauver only succeeded in emphasizing the extent of Stevenson's political isolation on the question of nuclear armaments. In the long run, Eisenhower was the chief beneficiary of the issue.[33]

In his news conference on April 25, Eisenhower emphasized what he described as the paradox in Stevenson's position: that the United States should accelerate the development of guided missiles while stopping research on the hydrogen bomb. In the President's words, "If you don't work on one and get the right kind of explosive to use there, why work on the other?" Agreeing that the paradox simply made no sense, the *Washington Star* thought it analogous to fashioning an artillery piece without bothering to design and produce shells for it. Or, as the *Wall Street Journal* commented, Stevenson could hardly have it both ways. How could America's supposedly weakened defenses be strengthened by hobbling the nation's primary weapons?[34]

At this point, Stevenson might have escaped with but a few minor bruises. Indeed, with the strongest press support coming from the *Daily Worker*, Stevenson virtually ignored the issue as his campaign for the nomination rolled into high gear during May. But questions concerning testing and the health effects of fallout would not disappear. Without mentioning Stevenson, Ralph Lapp warned that indefinite testing of nuclear weapons would endanger world health. According to Lapp, the Atomic Energy Commission had sugarcoated the bitter facts about fallout and had been guilty of "double-talk with regard to the long-term hazards from nuclear detonations." Lapp praised Libby for publicly airing the issue on April 20 before the American Philosophical Society but sharply disagreed with his conclusions. In fact, the two men agreed only that strontium-90 was the chief long-term threat to human life. [35]

340

## THE NATIONAL ACADEMY REPORT

On June 12, 1956, the National Academy of Sciences issued its report on "The Biological Effects of Atomic Radiation." Simultaneously, in London the United Kingdom Medical Research Council presented similar findings to Parliament. Indeed, although the two studies had been conducted independently, their release was coordinated for simultaneous publication in the morning papers on the next day. [36]

According to Libby, neither report presented findings not already known to the Commission and available in open literature. There were minor differences over the effects of strontium-90, no doubt the result of different methods of measuring radioactivity. Libby was also gratified that the reports generally agreed with the Commission's views, with the exception that the studies recommended additional reduction in permissible lifetime exposure to radiation. Libby did not anticipate, however, that the reports would necessitate any change in the Commission's positions on nuclear weapon testing, the Atoms-for-Peace campaign, or any other atomic energy program.

Both reports identified the genetic consequences of radiation as a paramount consideration. Most experts agreed that there was no threshold below which radiation did not threaten genetic damage. Thus, geneticists recommended lowering permissible exposure rates as much as practicable. The National Academy of Sciences now advocated an upper limit of 50 roentgens for individual persons up to age thirty, or an average exposure of the population above natural background not to exceed 10 roentgens from conception to thirty years of age. In addition to natural background, the largest source of radiation to the population came from medical and dental X-rays and fluoroscopy. In comparison to the thirty-year dose to the gonads

that the average person received from natural background (about 4.3 roentgens) and from X-rays and fluoroscopy (about 3 roentgens), the dose from
weapon tests, if continued at the existing level, would have been 0.1 roentgen. Even if the test estimate was off by a factor of five—0.02 to 0.5
roentgens over thirty years—fallout from weapon tests was dramatically
less dangerous than radiation from medical uses. The academy did not
certify that nuclear weapon tests were safe but implied that the risks from
testing were minor. The academy did warn, however, that even low levels
of radiation could have serious biological effects directly proportional to the
amount of radiation. Thus, many of the disastrous consequences of nuclear
war could be implied from the lessons of peacetime use.[37]

The Commission welcomed the academy report and, with the exception of Murray, applauded its conclusions. When the Commission issued
its semiannual report to the Congress, Murray refused to concur on the
section pertaining to the hazards of fallout from radioactive strontium. The
Commissioners concluded that "at the present level of weapons' testing,
the present and potential contribution of strontium-90 to the world ecology
is not a significant factor." The Commissioners thereafter summarized the
findings of the academy and affirmed the need for additional research and
study, including continuation of Project *Sunshine.* Thus the report became
the basis for justifying Commission programs and accelerating research into
radiation effects. To the National Security Council the Commission emphasized the need for a broad research program on long-range hazards caused
both by nuclear weapon tests and power plants. Again citing the National
Academy of Sciences as well as the British Medical Council, the Commission advised the security council that there were still important data to be
gathered on the implications of testing and warfare.[38]

341

## THE DEMOCRATS AND NUCLEAR POWER

Much to the disappointment of Senator Anderson, the report of the McKinney panel in February 1956 did not give the Democrats ready ammunition
to fire at the Commission's civilian power program, but it did provide a firm
base from which to launch an attack. The ammunition was already available
in two forms. First, Senator Gore introduced a bill in July 1955 that "authorized and directed" the Commission to construct six demonstration
power plants, each of different design and located in a different geographical section of the country. Second, before the Joint Committee on February
23, 1956, Commissioner Murray proposed that the United States install at
home and abroad power reactors with a capacity of two million kilowatts.
Only in this way did Murray think that the nation could establish "a commanding lead in the atomic power race."[39]

By the end of April 1956 Anderson was prepared for a series of hearings on legislation designed to remove the roadblocks that the McKinney panel had found on the highway to civilian nuclear power. As the new executive director of the Joint Committee he had selected James T. Ramey, a veteran Commission attorney, who in a decade at the Chicago operations office had gained an intimate knowledge of both Commission and industry efforts in reactor development. For technical support Anderson had also obtained the temporary services of Walter H. Zinn, who had just resigned after ten years as director of the Commission's Argonne Laboratory. In May Anderson held a seminar and hearings on providing adequate insurance coverage for power reactor owners and equipment manufacturers.[40]

The big guns were reserved for hearings starting the following week on the Gore bill and other means of "accelerating the civilian reactor program." To prepare for the public hearings Anderson held two secret executive sessions on May 21 and 22 with officials from the State Department, the Commission, and the Central Intelligence Agency. In the closed sessions Anderson and his colleagues revealed their motivation for supporting the Gore bill. To be sure, the fight over public versus private power, growing distrust of Strauss, and a lack of confidence in industry's professed commitment to nuclear power were all involved. But the center of committee concern was Cold War competition with the Soviet Union. For hours the committee members tabulated and retabulated estimates of future nuclear power capacity in the Soviet Union and to a lesser extent in the United Kingdom and France. In the Cold War context the predictions were alarming. According to "intelligence estimates" the Soviet Union would have 400,000 installed kilowatts by 1958, 1,222,000 in 1959, and more than two million in 1960. In contrast the United States would have 60,000 kilowatts at Shippingport by the end of 1957. If all the power demonstration and independent projects were completed as proposed by industry, the United States would still have only 750,000 kilowatts of capacity by 1960. When it came out that the "intelligence estimates" were based on public statements by Soviet leaders, Strauss contended that these were not serious commitments reflecting Soviet capabilities. To use the Soviet figures to set the American goal might amount to chasing a chimera.[41]

In opening the public hearings later that week, Gore dramatized the Soviet threat. To lose that race, Gore said, would be "catastrophic." The United States had "a clear moral responsibility" to develop "this marvelous new source of energy . . . to dispel the Soviet propaganda that we are a Nation of warmongers." But as the hearings continued, the testimony followed the now familiar paths established in 1954 between the proponents of private and government development of nuclear power. Although Anderson, Holifield, and other Democrats supported the Gore bill, it soon became apparent that the proposal was too ambitious. Strauss pointed out that building six demonstration power plants, each of a different design and in a different geographic location, would be more costly in terms of money and talent than the huge Savannah River project. The idea of scattering reactors around the country also raised in Republicans the specter of a sinister attempt to build regional TVAs across the nation.[42]

Perhaps Gore had overstated the case for a federally supported nuclear power program, but there was no question that a ground swell of public sentiment was building for some kind of action to get the United States back in the international race for nuclear power. On the Democratic side Robert McKinney took up the issue in a ringing statement before the Overseas Press Club of New York on May 17 and later at the Joint Committee hearings. McKinney charged that the United States had been "backward" in promoting nuclear power, the most advanced, the most dramatic—perhaps even the cheapest—form of foreign aid. The problem, McKinney argued, was that the United States was too concerned about secrecy. "We have been afraid that other nations might misuse the information and the materials we would give them," he continued. But McKinney, who shared neither the Commission's sense of accomplishment nor the State Department's caution, thought risks from nuclear arms proliferation were small, particularly if the United States exported only nuclear power technology while keeping military application under lock and key.[43]

McKinney's speech seemingly stirred political embers. In reaction, C. D. Jackson, one of the original architects of Eisenhower's Atoms-for-Peace speech who was impatient with the subsequent pace of the program, offered Strauss an embittered history of failure and frustration since the President's glowing proclamation in December 1953. If Jackson's history was too harsh, he was not alone with McKinney in viewing the American program as too timid. Writing for the atoms committee of the Federation of American Scientists, Herbert J. Kouts expressed the opinion that the United States was not moving fast enough. "Probably you are motivated here by a desire to fulfill the program in a straightforward, orderly way, as free from mistakes as possible," Kouts wrote to John A. Hall. "We on the other hand think that some mistakes in detail are allowable, if only greater speed can be bought this way."[44]

Significantly, during spring 1956 the Democrats did not criticize Eisenhower because his nuclear power plan was environmentally reckless or socially dangerous. Rather, following the lead of Anderson and McKinney, they chastened the Administration for not charging ahead far enough or fast enough. In May, hammering away at the Dixon-Yates theme, Senator Kefauver, on the campaign trail for the Democratic presidential nomination, charged that the United States had "fallen woefully behind" the Soviet Union, the United Kingdom, and France because the Eisenhower Administration had insisted that private industry be the exclusive developer of

343

commercial atomic energy. Kefauver repeated his accusations a month later, more stridently blaming "Republican Freebooters" for falling behind in the international development of nuclear power.[45]


## THE GORE-HOLIFIELD BILL

The revised bill that Gore introduced in the Senate on June 29, 1956, reflected a more considerate and temperate position than the original draft. The new version, which Holifield introduced in the House, neither required that the plants be located in six regions nor specified the number or types of reactors to be built. Instead the Commission would be directed to build large-scale plants at existing Commission production sites to provide electricity for those installations, to construct smaller experimental reactors at Commission laboratories, and to assist other nations in developing their own power reactors. With these changes, the Democratic majority easily passed the bill in the Senate on July 12, 1956.[46]

As the election-year session of Congress churned to its end in the last weeks of the month, the House debates loomed as decisive for the Gore-Holifield bill. The Democrats, still firmly in control, used hearings before the House Appropriations Committee as an occasion to denounce both the Commission and the Administration for failing to mount a vigorous government program for developing nuclear power. When the committee submitted its report approving $440 million to fund reactor construction under the Gore-Holifield bill, it also published the transcript of the appropriation hearings, which contained more than three hundred pages of testimony, much of it excoriating the Commission and supporting the Gore-Holifield plan as a moral imperative. The Administration in the meantime marshaled its forces against the bill while private industry financed an advertising campaign against it.[47]

In seven hours of floor debate on July 24, 1956, the Democratic majority in the House struggled to maintain party ranks in support of the Gore-Holifield bill, but Congressman Cole's success in pushing through amendments favored by the Administration foreshadowed the final outcome. With twenty-seven Democrats not voting and an equal number siding with the Republican opposition, the bill failed by twelve votes.[48]

This unexpected defeat killed all hopes for a nuclear power bill in the Eighty-fourth Congress. Ever since the formation of the McKinney panel sixteen months earlier, Senator Anderson had harbored visions of a well-articulated federal program for nuclear power development that the Democratic members of the Joint Committee might propose as a key plank in the party's platform for the 1956 elections. Now that dream was in shambles. Frustrated by the Administration's refusal to accept any substantial increase in funding for the development of nuclear power, Anderson

344

became ever more suspicious of Strauss's motives. He even convinced himself that Strauss was really opposed to nuclear power on any basis because it would threaten the economic interests of the Rockefellers, who he believed had vast holdings in fossil energy resources. Bitterly disappointed by the defeat of the Gore-Holifield bill, Anderson angrily withdrew two other bills that he had shepherded through the Joint Committee to encourage private participation in nuclear development: one provided federal liability insurance for nuclear power facilities, and the other amended the Public Utility Holding Company Act to exempt from its provisions power companies participating jointly in noncommercial nuclear projects. Both bills probably would have passed with little or no debate, but Anderson was determined to hold them hostage pending Congressional action on a new version of Gore-Holifield in 1957.[49]

345

## REDWING *AND GENERAL GAVIN*

Throughout the spring and into July 1956 the Commission conducted its *Redwing* series of nuclear tests at the Pacific Proving Ground. More than one dozen tests, as described by Strauss, were designed to develop defensive weapons against air and missile attacks.[50] Nevertheless, *Redwing* also tested America's first airdrop of a multimegaton hydrogen bomb and provided the Commission its best opportunity since the ill-fated *Castle-Bravo* test to collect fallout data in the Pacific. The testing was unaffected by scattered protests in the United States and abroad. On May 21 over Namu Island at Bikini an Air Force bomber dropped its thermonuclear payload, which exploded at about 15,000 feet and created minimal fallout that drifted northward over uninhabited ocean. Somewhat embarrassingly, through navigational error the pilot had missed his target by about four miles, but the miss was of little consequence from either a military, diagnostic, or safety point of view. In multimegaton thermonuclear weaponry, a four-mile error did not mean that the target remained undamaged.[51]

A few days after the airdrop General James M. Gavin, Army chief of research and development, used the *Cherokee* shot to illustrate the radiological power and significance of the hydrogen bomb. Under questioning from Senator Stuart Symington, Gavin confirmed that a recent article in *Fortune* was essentially correct: a large-scale thermonuclear attack on the United States would kill or maim some seven million persons and render hundreds of square miles uninhabitable for perhaps a generation. Even more dramatically, Gavin predicted that American retaliation against Russia would spread death from radiation across Asia to Japan and the Philippines. Or if the winds blew the other way, an attack on eastern Russia could eventually kill hundreds of millions of Europeans including, some commentators added, possibly half the population of the British Isles.[52]

After the Air Force subcommittee of the Senate Committee on Armed Services released Gavin's classified testimony on June 28, 1956, America's allies, the press, and the general public began to understand the startling implications of thermonuclear warfare. The impact on allied nations in Europe, the Middle East, and East Asia could hardly be underestimated as America's partners in Soviet containment and massive retaliation came to realize that they could become devastated victims of a United States–Soviet Union war. Gavin's statement also evoked a sharp protest from General Alfred M. Gruenther, Supreme Allied Commander in Europe, a post once held by the President himself. At the White House, Dulles, Strauss, and others decided that Eisenhower should try to counter the disastrous effects of Gavin's testimony by minimizing the danger of fallout.[53]

346

## THE "CLEAN" WEAPON

The *Redwing* tests seemed to the President's advisers to offer an ideal opportunity to calm public fears by stressing American efforts to develop weapons with reduced radioactive fallout. The development of "clean bombs" presented the possibility of returning to the pre–*Castle-Bravo* era, when military planning focused on the blast and heat effects of nuclear weapons. There was a real question whether the clock could be turned back, but the White House gave the Commission the task of preparing a press release on clean weapons.

Although Strauss and his colleagues could appreciate the political and diplomatic considerations involved, the Commission was more concerned that any statement at all might compromise military secrets. Edward Teller warned that a reference to clean bombs could provide the Russians significant insight into the design of the United States' most advanced weapons. To reveal that the United States had developed a weapon that had very little fallout would alert the Russians to the fact that the United States had achieved a breakthrough in weapon design.[54]

White House desires to counter Gavin, however, overrode Commission reluctance to declassify some of its work on clean weapons. Strauss explained that a public statement would accomplish two purposes. First, the world would be assured that the United States was not obsessed with weapons of mass destruction. Second, Strauss believed that a press release would reduce public pressure for the cessation of weapon tests. The other Commissioners agreed that testing should be defended, but Libby remained leery of unnecessarily compromising design information. So did Eisenhower, who decided not to issue such an announcement himself because he did not want to field technical questions on nuclear weapons at press conferences.[55] The President had already mentioned in a press conference on April 25 that the *Redwing* series would test weapons with reduced fallout;

to that extent, American intentions had already been revealed. At an informal meeting when Murray was absent, the Commission acquiesced to an urgent appeal from Dulles that Strauss become the Administration's spokesman on clean weapons.[56]

Strauss issued a brief statement about the results of the *Redwing* tests that same evening. As cryptically as possible, he noted the progress that the laboratories had made in localizing fallout. The tests had achieved "maximum effect in the immediate area of a target with minimum widespread fallout hazard." After assuring the public that large thermonuclear weapons did not necessarily produce massive fallout, Strauss concluded hopefully that *Redwing* had proven "much of importance not only from a military point of view but from a humanitarian aspect."[57]

Unexpectedly, Strauss's "clean bomb statement," as it came to be called, caught a whirlwind. Opponents of nuclear testing might have been expected to dismiss it as the Commission's justification for further testing, but the bitterness of Anderson's and Murray's reactions were surprising. Anderson called the release of the statement without informing the Joint Committee a "studied insult" to Congress.[58] Murray was outraged because the Commission had approved the statement on July 19, after he had departed for a weekend at home in New York. For Murray, the incident was the latest and among the most egregious efforts by Strauss to grab all power in the chairman's hands. Within the week, Murray appeared before the Joint Committee to repudiate the press release. He did not object so much to what Strauss had said but rather to the fact that he had been hoodwinked into believing the President would make the statement. As it was, Murray had not been given the opportunity to express his views on an official statement by the Commission. Before the hearing ended on July 23, 1956, Anderson, Murray, and Strauss had exchanged bitter words on the issue.[59]

347

Troubled by the charges and countercharges that undermined the Commission's defense of the testing program, Libby proposed a joint statement acceptable to all the Commissioners. Both Strauss and Murray expressed their willingness to cooperate, but neither man ultimately could overlook the deep personal antagonism that divided them. Before they could reach any agreement at a subsequent Commission meeting, Strauss and Murray fell into bitter name calling: Murray accused Strauss of constantly twisting words, and Strauss blatantly denounced Murray as a liar.[60] Consequently, the clean bomb statement stood without further official elaboration.

Even had there been clarification, Strauss had already exposed the Commission to scathing criticism from the press. Ralph Lapp wrote a devastating critique in the *Bulletin of the Atomic Scientists*, when he observed that Strauss single-handedly had invented "humanitarian H-bombs." Lapp added a careful review of the available fallout data and a detailed analysis of the probable configuration of the hydrogen bomb. Lapp concluded that dirtiness was a relative thing. Superbombs could be designed to be rela-tively clean or very dirty. The former, Lapp assumed, were desirable for test purposes, while the latter could serve as a strategic weapon. "War is a dirty business," Lapp observed. "Part of the madness of our time is that adult men can use a word like humanitarian to describe an H-bomb."[61]

## STASSEN TRIES AGAIN

The Administration's attempt to exploit the clean weapon theme had back-fired, but it did show how seriously Dulles, Strauss, and others took the continuing demand for a moratorium or a permanent ban on testing nuclear weapons. Earlier in June 1956 both men had strongly objected to British plans to open negotiations with the Soviet Union on this subject.[62] But even more threatening was the test ban proposal that Harold Stassen included in the disarmament plan he sent to the National Security Council on July 29.[63]

348

Stassen based his proposals on the assumption that almost any na-tion, if it so desired, could fabricate an elementary nuclear weapon within three years. Thereafter, he assumed, a nuclear power could build a ther-monuclear weapon within another three years. Stassen also foresaw that the United States, the United Kingdom, and the Soviet Union would each have developed intercontinental missiles capable of delivering thermonuclear warheads within three to ten years. Thus, he predicted that in the relatively near future as many as twenty nations, both East and West, would possess nuclear weapons with the potential of igniting world war.[64]

To forestall uncontrolled nuclear proliferation, Stassen offered a complex ten-point plan designed to halt the spread of weapons while pro-moting peaceful uses. Incorporating key aspects of Eisenhower's Atoms-for-Peace and Open Skies initiatives, Stassen attempted to weave together the main threads of a comprehensive nuclear disarmament policy. The Commission could hardly take seriously Stassen's proposal that a test ban, a reduction of the numbers of nuclear weapons, and a cessation of all pro-duction of fissionable materials for weapons be accomplished by July 1, 1957. Stassen even suggested a "reasonable" nuclear posture for the United Kingdom and eventual inclusion of the Chinese communists within the terms of an international arms control agreement.

Whatever hopes Stassen may have had for his disarmament pro-posal, he had jeopardized his own future by stumbling into the quicksand of Republican politics. In a private meeting with the President on July 20, just before Eisenhower was to leave for Panama to confer with Latin Ameri-can leaders, Stassen announced his intention to support Christian Herter for the vice-presidential nomination at the forthcoming Republican national convention. According to Stassen, a private poll indicated that with Nixon on the ticket Eisenhower lost six percentage points and jeopardized the party's chances of recapturing control of Congress. With Herter, Stassen believed the Republicans could attract enough independents and Democrats to achieve Congressional victory.[65]

Apparently, Eisenhower offered no comment on Stassen's startling announcement. Recovering from ileitis and anxious to take off for his delayed trip to Panama, Eisenhower merely assured Stassen that as an American citizen he was free to follow his own judgment. Stassen interpreted the President's vague response as tacit approval of the ill-fated plans to "dump" Nixon from the ticket.[66] Whatever the President's motives or distractions that day—he was also very much involved in the annual civil defense exercise, Operation *Alert*, which simulated an attack over Alaska—he left Stassen with the impression that the President favored a truly "open convention." Stassen's miscalculations of both the President's intentions and Nixon's strength within the Republican party seriously undermined his role as the President's "Secretary of Peace." In the midst of renewed crisis in the Middle East prompted by Egyptian President Gamal Abdul Nasser's nationalization of the Suez Canal Company, tough budget negotiations with Defense Secretary Wilson, and planning sessions with Republican National Committee Chairman Leonard Hall about the forthcoming convention in San Francisco, Eisenhower was pestered by the "Stassen affair," as the President's personal secretary, Anne Whitman, called it. On July 31 Eisenhower met with Stassen, Ambassador Amos Peaslee, Deputy Special Assistant to the President, and Strauss to discuss progress on disarmament. During the meeting, Eisenhower decided to place Stassen on a month's leave-of-absence so that the disarmament adviser could continue his political activities as a private citizen.[67]

349

Inevitably, Stassen's political campaigning for Herter, who actually nominated Nixon in San Francisco, hurt Stassen's standing within the President's inner circle. Meeting with Dulles after the convention, Peaslee pointedly disassociated himself from Stassen's activities. Dulles lamented the unfortunate developments and predicted that they would create a real question of confidence in future disarmament negotiations. Senator William Knowland, a member of the Joint Committee, also confided in Dulles that Congress could no longer have confidence in Stassen's continuing conduct of disarmament affairs.[68] Nevertheless, despite his pique over Stassen's actions, Eisenhower stood by his "Secretary of Peace" even as opposition to Stassen's June 29 disarmament plan mounted within the Administration.

Despite the concerted efforts of the Administration and the Commission to resolve the pressing questions that the development of nuclear technology had created in domestic and international affairs, little was accomplished during the first six months of 1956. The resolution of nuclear power policy had stalemated with defeat of the Gore-Holifield bill. The President's hopes for halting the slide into the abyss of nuclear war had been thwarted by practical considerations of national security. By pressing too hard and blundering into political troubles, Stassen had hurt the cause of nuclear disarmament and the test ban more than he had helped it. Six months of opportunity had slid by. Now as Congress disbanded for the national nominating conventions, it seemed certain that nuclear issues would figure prominently in the presidential campaign.

CHAPTER 13

# NUCLEAR ISSUES:
# THE PRESIDENTIAL CAMPAIGN OF 1956

In contrast to their strategy in the 1952 presidential election, Dwight D. Eisenhower and Adlai Stevenson vigorously debated America's nuclear future in 1956. To be sure, as the Oppenheimer case, Dixon-Yates, and the *Lucky Dragon* incident had dramatized, atomic energy was no stranger to the political arena. Yet never before had presidential candidates stressed nuclear issues in a political campaign. In large part, the President himself was responsible for the debate. Throughout his first term Eisenhower had resolutely pressed his Administration to disseminate, within the limits of national security, all available information on atomic energy. Operation *Candor*, the President's 1953 United Nations speech, Atoms for Peace, the 1954 Atomic Energy Act, the Geneva peaceful uses conference, annual civil defense exercises, fallout reports, biomedical research and publication, and even the Commission's printed handbook on weapon effects were all part of his effort to inform the American public about atoms for war and peace. Eisenhower would have preferred to keep atomic energy out of partisan politics, and he was annoyed when Stevenson and others tried to capitalize on the test ban and other national security issues. The 1956 presidential campaign, however, reflected Eisenhower's belief that the American people should face up to both the hopes and fears of the nuclear age.

During the presidential campaign in 1956, political skirmishes began over domestic nuclear power, gradually spread to contention over international cooperation, and concluded in a spirited exchange over weapon testing and development. Eisenhower easily won the debates and the election, but not without paying a political price in terms of public confidence in the Atomic Energy Commission, its leadership, and programs.

## STRAUSS ON THE OFFENSIVE

The slim margin of the Administration's victory on the Gore-Holifield bill did not deter Strauss for a moment in his drive to develop nuclear power. Privately he considered Senator Anderson's suspicions of his long association with the Rockefellers preposterous, but he hoped that the incident would serve as evidence of Anderson's irrational hostility towards him. Anderson was correct, however, in his conclusion that Strauss was determined to keep the development of nuclear power in the private sector as much as possible. This bias was never more evident than in Strauss's efforts to expedite construction of the Enrico Fermi nuclear plant near Detroit.

The Fermi project had grown out of one response to the first invitation under the Commission's power demonstration reactor program. The proposal had come from a group of electric utilities headed by the Detroit Edison Company, whose president, Walker L. Cisler, had long been a spokesman for industry in nuclear power development. Cisler's plan had been to build a full-scale nuclear power plant in marshland on the shores of Lake Erie, thirty miles south of Detroit. The plant was based on the technology produced in operating the experimental breeder reactor, which had first produced electricity from nuclear energy at the Idaho test station in 1951. The breeder concept, which theoretically of all proposed reactor types offered the greatest efficiencies in using uranium fuel, also posed some of the most difficult engineering problems. The experimental plant in Idaho had provided much useful information, but it was far too small to serve as a prototype for the Fermi plant. Furthermore, operation of the Idaho plant had raised some grave questions about the safety of breeder reactors in general. In an experiment in November 1955, scientists at the Idaho station had deliberately subjected the test reactor to a power surge, revealing a short but definite positive temperature coefficient. This term meant that under certain conditions an increase in core temperature produced a rise in reactivity, which could lead to a power runaway and core meltdown. In fact, the core of the experimental reactor had been destroyed in this test.[1]

Under the high priority that the Commission accorded the Fermi project as part of the power demonstration program, Reactor Development Division Director W. Kenneth Davis and his staff pushed ahead with the administrative approvals necessary to begin construction of the plant. The core meltdown at Idaho was reason for concern, but the Idaho reactor engineers believed they understood the cause and could correct it. Without disagreeing with this assessment, the Commission's advisory committee on reactor safeguards warned Kenneth E. Fields, the general manager, in June that until much more information was available about the Idaho accident there was no assurance that a similar reaction could not occur in the Fermi plant. Estimates indicated that an equivalent reactivity surge in the Fermi plant could conceivably result in an explosion that would breach the containment building, and no one knew whether the Idaho failure represented the most serious accident theoretically possible. Before the Fermi reactor could be built with solid assurance of safe operation, the advisory committee concluded that the Commission would have to undertake extensive research, not only on the meltdown mechanism but also on fast-breeder reactors in general.[2]

This conclusion shocked Strauss and the Commission. Delay of the Fermi project pending additional research might seriously undercut the power demonstration program and give the Joint Committee new ammunition for a large federal reactor program. The same result could come from a Commission decision to put more money into breeder research and development. On the other hand, the Commission could not reasonably ignore the advisory committee's report and grant Cisler's group a construction permit. Under the circumstances the Commission could do no more than issue a conditional permit, pending the completion of additional research needed to assure safe operation of the reactor.

353

Before the Commission could make a formal decision, Commissioner Murray revealed the conclusions of the advisory committee's report in a hearing before a House appropriations subcommittee on June 29. Outraged that the Commission had withheld the report and then released it to a House subcommittee rather than the Joint Committee, Senator Anderson demanded a copy of the full report. Fearing that release of the report before the Commissioners had made a formal decision on the case would set a dangerous precedent for the Commission's regulatory process, Strauss consulted the staff in an effort to find a way around the Joint Committee's request. After several long discussions, the Commissioners agreed to send the Joint Committee a copy with a request that it be considered "administratively confidential." Anderson refused to accept the report with this condition and informed G. Mennen Williams, the Governor of Michigan, about the situation. When the Commission again balked at releasing the report, Anderson charged that the Commission had used "star chamber" proceedings and suggested that the new Congress in 1957 consider legislation that would separate the Commission's licensing and regulatory functions from its research and production responsibilities.[3]

Edward Teller had already warned Strauss that the Fermi reactor should not be built until the instability in the Idaho plant had been explained. Strauss also admitted privately that denial of the advisory committee report had been an error, but he had no intention of delaying the Fermi project. The Commission did not reconsider its decision to grant a conditional construction permit, and on August 8 Strauss participated with Cisler in ground-breaking ceremonies near Detroit. Strauss acknowledged that the Commission's action had precipitated "some rather violently voiced opposition in Washington," but he wrote this off simply as an "attack being directed against the free enterprise development of nuclear power in this country."[4]

Privately Strauss gave some thought to the stance the Administration should take on nuclear power in the impending presidential campaign. At his farm in Virginia he drafted for possible use by Republican members of the Joint Committee a statement denouncing Anderson for destroying the "committee's bipartisan tradition." This, he admitted to a White House aide, was a "labor of love," but on second thought he decided that it would do little more than anger Anderson. The White House agreed. As a campaign strategy Strauss apparently accepted the advice of one of his own staff that "a direct debate on the issue of public versus private power should be avoided, except to point out that the Commission is not doing business . . . exclusively with privately owned utilities."[5] Because Anderson and the Democrats had already abandoned the nuclear power issue, neither Eisenhower nor Stevenson made any extensive use of it during the campaign.

354

## POLITICS OF THE INTERNATIONAL ATOM

In spring and summer 1956, Atoms for Peace weathered international as well as domestic politics. The Atomic Energy Commission had assumed that in order to foster European political and economic integration, the United States would have to negotiate with the Community of Six on a most-favored-nation basis. That is, while promoting EURATOM partnership among the Six, it would be inconsistent for the United States to execute bilateral cooperation agreements with prospective members of the European Community on terms more favorable than it was willing to give EURATOM itself. For its part, the State Department was well aware of the potential embarrassment and inconsistency inherent in pursuing bilateral arrangements with individual members of the Coal and Steel Community, while at the same time trying to promote a common atomic energy institution among the Six. Bilateral negotiations with the European countries could have been discontinued, but at a price that might have damaged the United States' relations with EURATOM. Belgium's foreign minister, Paul-Henri Spaak, warned that EURATOM's opponents, especially in Germany, were encouraged by America's apparent willingness to undermine European unity by continuing to make bilateral arrangements with European countries. Spaak went so far as to predict "doom" for EURATOM should the United States indicate any willingness to conclude with Germany a power bilateral arrangement under which enriched uranium would be supplied from the President's February 22 allocation. The dilemma was not easy to resolve, particularly in view of the Commission's eagerness to pursue the bilateral route.[6]

Dulles decided it was inappropriate for the United States to refuse to negotiate bilateral agreements with the Six or to declare a moratorium on such negotiations pending the outcome of the EURATOM discussions. But he hoped to deemphasize the bilaterals by not concluding any long-term fuel commitments with the Six (Belgium being a possible exception) until after the future of EURATOM had been decided. Nevertheless, when the EURATOM negotiations bogged down in the summer of 1956, French, Italian, and German interest in discussing separate bilateral agreements with the United States increased to the point where American diplomats feared EURATOM itself was in jeopardy. To the State Department's alarm, at a particularly critical point of the EURATOM discussions between Spaak, Prime Minister Guy Mollet of France, and Chancellor Konrad Adenauer of West Germany, the Commission complicated matters by energetically promoting the bilateral agreements, which only encouraged German and French dissidents.[7]

355

## THE BRUSSELS CONFERENCE

Without seeming to meddle in the internal affairs of Europe, there was little the United States could do overtly to encourage the participants in the Brussels conference, which had convened on June 26, 1956, to study both the Common Market and the EURATOM projects. Jean Monnet, a French statesman and former chairman of the European Coal and Steel Community, had warned Strauss that the United States should not appear to pressure the Europeans into EURATOM with generous offers of enriched uranium. Because EURATOM's formation was primarily a matter for Europeans to decide by themselves, Monnet advised, the United States would do best not to indicate its position in the matter. The trouble with such reticence, however, was that EURATOM opponents had been encouraged by American silence. German industrialists who opposed EURATOM ownership and monopoly over fissionable materials had allied themselves with Franz Josef Strauss, minister of atomic energy affairs, against Adenauer. Led by Minister Strauss, this group advocated creation of an independent German atomic energy program, subject only to loose control by the German Federal Republic, with its international component resting on bilateral relations. The French were also divided between internationalists, led by Monnet, who wanted to check German industrial resurgence through European integration, and those who did not want to sacrifice French advantages in atomic energy to European economic integration. American observers of the debates in the French National Assembly during July 1956 were surprised by the recurring expressions of resentment toward the United States from both the right and the left. Sometimes oblique, but often quite blunt, criticism of the United States was voiced even by moderates favoring

EURATOM who argued that European integration provided France the best opportunity of attaining leadership in developing atomic energy without undignified dependence upon American help.[8]

As enthusiasm for EURATOM diminished following attacks from both German industrialists and French opponents, compromises inevitably weakened the original concept. Despite repeated diplomatic hints that the United States would like to sit down with the prospective EURATOM partners to discuss a strong agreement for cooperation, the Americans were consistently rebuffed by the Six, who assumed that any direct United States involvement in the negotiations would be highly damaging. At the same time, discussions at Brussels produced compromises that threatened to produce a weak and inconsequential European institution, incapable of advancing the United States' main political objective—tying Germany to Western Europe through economic integration. EURATOM supporters were not challenged by a direct assault but rather were undermined by proposals that emphasized cooperation rather than integration. This tactic would have left participating members free to pursue their own course. Left unresolved was the question of whether there could be private ownership of nuclear materials within the community and how the Common Market would be tied to the EURATOM treaty.[9]

## THE FRANCO-ITALIAN INITIATIVE

With EURATOM in the doldrums, the French and Italians independently approached the United States to request far-reaching classified bilateral agreements for cooperation: the French proposed an agreement involving 1,000 kilograms of enriched uranium, and the Italians sought an agreement covering 2,500 kilograms. The Franco-Italian maneuver was audacious, and when Dulles learned that the Commission had actually welcomed the overture he severely rebuked Strauss. Invoking Eisenhower's directive of January 11 and noting Ambassador James B. Conant's fear of the disruptive effects of persistent United States bilateral negotiations, Dulles stated unequivocally: "I believe it is incumbent on us to see that we do not take actions which might make more difficult the negotiating problems of the Six Nations." Pending the outcome of the EURATOM talks, Dulles curtly informed Strauss that the United States would suspend bilateral talks.[10]

Strauss, angered and no doubt hurt by Dulles's injunction, wanted to take the matter directly to Eisenhower, but instead he confined his reaction to Herbert Hoover, Jr., the Under Secretary of State. Not only did he believe the Administration was backing the wrong program in EURATOM, but he also thought that United States' inconsistencies had become a major impediment to the Atoms-for-Peace program. Strauss observed that the United States had already negotiated three bilateral agreements covering

356

power reactors with members of the Community of Six, namely, France, the Netherlands, and Belgium. Nevertheless, the Atomic Energy Commission was not authorized by the State Department to discuss power agreements with Italy or Germany, despite their desire to launch atomic energy programs. Meanwhile, the Commission was authorized to negotiate power bilaterals with Sweden, Norway, and Spain. Thus, as Strauss noted with some bitterness, the Commission's role was difficult and confused. It could negotiate rather freely with states in Western Europe outside the Community of Six; but the Commission was enjoined from immediate discussions with Germany and Italy, while at the same time the Commission was collaborating with all other members except Luxembourg. While Strauss professed support for the Administration's larger intentions embodied in EURATOM, he did not believe a discriminatory policy would advance Atoms for Peace in Western Europe.[11]

357

## THE SHADOW OF CALDER HALL

After Congress deserted Washington for the campaign hustings in August 1956, Strauss had an opportunity to reassess his position in his continuing contest with the Joint Committee over domestic nuclear power. The defeat of the Gore-Holifield bill gave him breathing space; at the very least it referred the whole question to the new Congress, which a big Eisenhower victory might well make Republican. But no one understood better than Strauss that the ultimate defeat of a government-financed power reactor program might well depend upon whether the accomplishments of private industry made federal support unnecessary.

In autumn 1956 it was by no means clear that a federal program could be avoided. On October 17, Queen Elizabeth II threw the switch sending electricity from the Calder Hall reactors into the national power grid. Anticipating the British achievement, Strauss and the Administration had tried to play down Calder Hall as essentially a plutonium-production facility, which it was, that generated power only as a by-product. But Calder Hall had an enormous impact on the fledgling nuclear industry in many countries, including the United States. Sir Christopher Hinton, director of the British project, announced flatly that "the Calder Hall reactor is giving us the initial lead in the use of nuclear power and we shall be able to retain that advantage for at least a decade by improvements in this type of reactor."[12] American industrial leaders were not quick to argue the point, and Strauss could reasonably expect that the British accomplishment would at the very least rekindle a new demand for federal construction of large dual-purpose reactors in the United States when the new Congress reconvened in January.

To make the British achievement even more impressive, the American entry in the international competition was more than a year from completion. Despite strong pressure from Strauss and the Administration, the Shippingport reactor could never have challenged Calder Hall's completion date. Rickover and his team had already applied extraordinary measures in their efforts to accelerate design and construction, but even in fall 1956 it was already apparent that Rickover would not meet his original target for completion in February 1957. There was only so much that more exhortation and money could do to reverse the effects of labor disputes and delayed deliveries of materials.[13]

## NUCLEAR POWER AT HOME AND ABROAD

Strauss still had high hopes for the power demonstration reactors, but there was cause for worry here, too. The question that Senator Anderson and others had raised about the safety of the proposed Fermi plant had sent a ripple of concern through the Detroit area. In September the United Automobile Workers, the American Federation of Labor, and the Congress of Industrial Organizations filed petitions for intervention and requests for public hearings on the Fermi license application. The experience that Westinghouse had gained on the Shippingport project made it possible for the company to move ahead on the design of the Yankee Atomic plant, but major decisions still remained before construction could start on the power plant at Rowe, Massachusetts. The third project in the first round, the Consumers project in Nebraska, was still struggling to be born. Almost two years after the Commission had authorized contract negotiations, the staff still had not arrived at a funding arrangement that was acceptable to both the public power district and North American Aviation, the design and development contractor. No proposal in the second round had yet been approved, and there was growing doubt within the staff that all of them could ever be accepted.[14]

Both Murray and Libby gained some measure of Strauss's determination to keep nuclear power development in the private sector when Commissioner Harold S. Vance raised the issue in a meeting in September 1956. It was perhaps surprising to Strauss that his long-time business acquaintance, a conservative midwestern Republican and industrial leader, should propose that the Commission construct at least two full-scale nuclear power plants to assure that the most promising reactor types were developed quickly. A self-educated engineer who had made his way to the top of the automobile industry to become president of the Studebaker Corporation, Vance had served with Strauss on several corporate boards of directors, and the two men had known each other on a first-name basis since World War II. Strauss had secured Vance's appointment to the Commission just a year earlier to fill Joseph Campbell's vacancy.[15] Vance not only had credentials acceptable to Strauss and the Administration, but he also seemed to possess personality traits likely to assure that he would not challenge Strauss's leadership. At age sixty-six Vance gave the impression of being a phlegmatic, soft-spoken, and rather colorless business executive.

Vance, however, soon proved himself capable of independent action. On September 13 he told his fellow Commissioners that they could not rely solely on industry to develop nuclear power, especially if the United States expected to win the international race with the United Kingdom and the Soviet Union. Vance believed government projects were necessary to develop some of the more promising and more difficult concepts, such as fluid-fuel reactors. Strauss immediately voiced his concern that, once the Commission opened the door, there would be no way to close it. Industry would thereafter expect the Commission to fund all development costs. Vance did not contradict Strauss directly but rather argued that winning the international race was more important than keeping the government out of nuclear power. This opinion delighted Murray, who at last saw the prospect of gaining support for his views within the Commission. Even Libby confessed some interest in Vance's arguments, particularly if the government were to fund development of pressurized-water reactors, the most promising type. For the first time since Strauss had become chairman, he rather than Murray faced the possibility of being a lonely minority of one on a major policy issue. Neither Vance nor Libby, however, was yet ready to break ranks with Strauss. The Commissioners agreed only to separate the domestic and international aspects of reactor policy and consider both at a later date.[16]

Given the delicate balance within the Commission, Strauss laid his plans carefully. As a short-term measure, he spurred the staff to expedite proposals under the power demonstration program. Before the end of September the Commission approved contract terms for two public power projects, Consumers in Nebraska and Piqua in Ohio.[17] This action blunted the charge by the rural cooperatives that the Commission was favoring big private utilities. On the policy issues, however, Strauss would not move until the November elections reliably forecasted the political future.

## THE POLITICS OF ATOMS FOR PEACE

During the summer the Democrats geared up for the fall campaign. The Democratic platform, published on August 16, gave full credit to Roosevelt and Truman for initiating the "atomic era" but condemned the Eisenhower Administration for plunging "the previously independent and nonpartisan Atomic Energy Commission into partisan politics." To recapture America's lead in "the world race for nuclear power, international prestige and world

359

markets," the Democrats pledged not only to accelerate the domestic civil-ian atomic power program but also "to give reality—life and meaning—to the atoms for peace program. We will substitute deeds for words." [18] Neither C. D. Jackson nor Gerard Smith could have quibbled with this plank.

As vice-presidential candidate, Kefauver kept up his hard-hitting attack on the Atoms-for-Peace program. Describing Strauss as that "baleful figure who is [Eisenhower's] chief atomic energy adviser," Kefauver re-peatedly asserted that the President and the chairman of the Commission wanted to keep America's atomic power production in private hands despite the fact that both the British and the Russians had forged ahead of the United States. [19] Consistent with the Democratic platform, Kefauver found no fault with the Atoms-for-Peace program except that the Administration had been too slow, too cautious, and too friendly toward big business.

Strauss accepted the major role in countering Kefauver's charges. The same October day on which the senator was railing against Strauss in New Hampshire, the chairman defended the Atoms-for-Peace program be-fore the New York Board of Trade. Strauss reiterated the accomplishments of the Geneva conference on peaceful uses and the provisions of the bilat-eral agreements for cooperation, but he highlighted the progress made to-ward establishing an international atomic energy agency. Predictably, he rejected Kefauver's sharp dichotomy between public and private power. In Republican terms, the Eisenhower Administration had stripped "the iron jacket of Government monopoly . . . from the atom," returning atomic en-ergy to the people. [20]

Both the florid rhetoric of the public-private power debate and par-tisan criticism that the Atoms-for-Peace program lagged behind foreign competitors to a large extent missed the point. All along the President's program had three clearly stated aims: to allocate fissionable materials to peaceful uses in medicine, agriculture, and research; to promote the pro-duction of power using atomic fuel; and to divert uranium stockpiles from the nuclear arms race. Under the stewardship of the Commission and the Department of State, the first two goals were successfully, if undramati-cally, advanced through bilateral agreements by summer 1956. The third objective, closely related to nuclear disarmament, required a significantly different negotiating strategy. Although Atoms for Peace was not a disar-mament proposal, the United States, to achieve cooperation with the Soviet Union in establishing nuclear safeguards through an international agency, had to sacrifice both speedy and efficient negotiations. Bernhard G. Bech-hoefer, a State Department officer involved in planning Atoms for Peace, later observed that the most successful East-West negotiations following World War II involved patient and confidential discussions with the Rus-sians. Unfortunately, this strategy also subjected the Eisenhower Admin-istration to charges of being too secret and too slow after 1955 when the

360

Soviet Union joined the discussions relative to the International Atomic Energy Agency.[21]

## DISARMAMENT AND THE TEST BAN: INTERNAL DEBATE

While the Democrats ineffectually probed domestic nuclear issues, sharp differences developed within the Eisenhower Administration over Stassen's nuclear disarmament proposals. Predictably, the Commission had responded warily to Stassen's June 29 disarmament plan. Asserting that it did not object to Stassen's intentions but only to his methods, the Commission offered the National Security Council a detailed critique of the disarmament plan as it affected nuclear weapons. To begin with, the Commission did not concur in Stassen's estimates concerning nuclear proliferation. Stassen was driven by the belief that as many as twenty nations might soon be armed with nuclear weapons. In dismissing this estimate as "speculative" the Commission tried to undermine Stassen's main premise.

361

The Commission objected to any proposal that limited testing and reduced the nuclear weapon stockpile without providing ironclad procedures for inspection and verification. There was unanimous opposition to setting July 1, 1957, as the deadline for halting the production of weapon-grade fissionable material. Not only was inspection an issue, but the date was also too early for the United States to reap full advantage of the weapon improvements tested at *Teapot* and *Redwing*. Even Murray concurred.[22]

The Commission was somewhat more conciliatory on testing. With the exception of Murray, the Commission continued to favor a test ban only as part of a general disarmament agreement that included "an effective and proven inspection system." Nevertheless, the Commission also recognized that overriding political considerations made it advisable for the United States government to propose negotiations toward an agreement for limitations on testing. The Commission's concession was stunning, even if Murray's continued advocacy of a unilateral test ban distracted somewhat from the significance of the moment. Still determined to continue the testing program, the Commission was at least willing to discuss limiting the size, number, frequency, and location of weapon tests.[23]

Of all the groups that wanted to ban testing, Libby believed by far the most numerous worldwide were those afraid of fallout. "They are just plain scared," Libby observed. Admitting that he did not like the thought of his children collecting strontium-90 in their bones despite his belief that it was essentially harmless, Libby suggested a strategy to limit worldwide fallout from testing. His idea was simple and probably unenforceable: to limit worldwide fallout to ten megatons of test detonations, divided more or less equally among the testing nations. The idea was impractical, but it did reflect the Commission's awareness that more than rhetoric was required to quiet public fears over fallout.[24]

Just when the Commission was willing to consider concessions on testing, the Soviet Union unexpectedly launched a major test series. In the past the Commission had not called attention to Russian activities, but after the Soviet Union began testing on August 24 Strauss pointedly contrasted Russian secrecy with the comparative openness of test announcements by the United States. On August 31, Eisenhower noted the second Soviet shot, and on September 3 the Commission reported still a third. Finally, on September 10, the Russians announced their own fourth test.[25]

Surprisingly, the Soviet's test series did not scuttle the Commission's search for an acceptable formula by which to limit testing. On September 5, the same day that Adlai Stevenson renewed his call for a test ban in a speech to the American Legion, the Commission organized an ad hoc committee chaired by General Alfred D. Starbird, director of military application, to study what might constitute an acceptable limitation on testing. Starbird's committee, which believed the Soviet Union was closing the gap in delivery capability, preferred no test limitation. Besides the inspection problem, the committee predicted that a test ban would have severe impact on morale and recruiting at the national laboratories. Through rigid controls over its scientists, the Soviet Union could maintain its testing capability despite drastic restrictions. Americans, on the other hand, could not expect to retain the best scientists and technicians without an active program. Starbird's group also feared that the Russians might stockpile improved nuclear weapons to be tested on the eve of a general war, too late for the United States to take countermeasures.[26]

Caution and skepticism aside, Starbird's committee weighed the pros and cons of several alternatives for limiting testing. All involved risk to American security in the committee's view, but the least risky was to "limit" testing to 1955–1956 levels. Should more stringent limitations be necessary, the committee recommended adopting some variation of Libby's plan, perhaps limiting total yield in any two-year period to thirty megatons of atmospheric testing. Such an agreement would still require some verification, and no doubt it would be only one step toward a more comprehensive test ban.[27]

Determined to find a workable disarmament formula, the President confined his discussions to Dulles, Wilson, Strauss, Radford, Stassen, and his own staff, Sherman Adams, William H. Jackson, and Amos J. Peaslee. With the possible exception of Stassen, Dulles most closely shared Eisenhower's sense of a moral imperative. As cautious as Strauss, Dulles nonetheless viewed the nuclear arms race as an "overwhelming moral issue" that required the United States to give "highest regard to world opinion." Although Dulles did not favor a total test ban, he was convinced that the

362

United States should "seek agreement on tangible forward steps toward as much as is possible to obtain." In contrast to the Commission, he did not want to defer negotiated agreements "merely for lack of an all-embracing perfect plan."[28]

Eisenhower's small inner circle of disarmament advisers, not the National Security Council, evaluated Stassen's proposals on September 11, 1956. Both Strauss and Radford now believed that Dulles was leaning towards Stassen's position. With Eisenhower present, Strauss wasted no time in arguing that a reliable inspection system could not be devised by July 1, 1957. Radford went even further, doubting whether an acceptable inspection system could ever be achieved. Against this pessimism, Dulles and Stassen reminded the President that the purpose of the meeting was to discuss whether the Administration should initiate quiet exploratory consultations, beginning with the British, to determine if Stassen's plan might serve as the basis for negotiations. Strauss and Radford, however, could not accept major portions of the proposal. Strauss stressed that the United States should continue to stockpile fissionable material at least through 1958. Production capacity had just reached the point where significant numbers of defensive weapons were being added to the stockpile. Radford concurred, observing that the United States would have to revise its war plans if nuclear stockpiling were halted in the next two years.[29]

363

As so often happened, Radford's hardline remarks provoked an impatient response from Eisenhower. If moral arguments were not persuasive, the President was prepared to use economic ones. Citing Secretary of the Treasury Humphrey, Eisenhower argued that some alternative had to be found to the arms race if only to preserve the American economy. From the President's perspective, mounting military expenditures, coupled with the threat of worldwide proliferation of nuclear weapons, represented threats to American security as significant as those from Russia itself.

When the discussion focused on testing, Strauss doubted that the United States could ever stop completely. Even if the United States did not want to develop more powerful or more sophisticated weapons, the Commission would have to guard against deterioration in stockpiled devices, improve control of fallout, and develop related technologies such as safety. When Strauss again objected that July 1, 1957, was an unrealistic deadline, Dulles proposed that December 31, 1957, "or as soon thereafter as an effective inspection system had been installed," would be just as acceptable. Dulles was trying to find some ground for realistic exploratory talks with American allies first, followed by negotiations with the Russians and Chinese.

Although the meeting broke up inconclusively, Eisenhower forcefully restated his determination to escape the disarmament impasse; he hoped to end or limit nuclear tests and to restrict the production of fissionable material to peaceful purposes. Those measures would calm escalating worldwide fears over fallout and nuclear war, but they could not be accomplished without effective inspection and assurances against surprise attack, both of which were also essential for a durable peace. He advised Radford to continue military planning on the assumption that no agreement would be reached. Eisenhower, however, also endorsed Stassen's proposal in principle, directing that the United States assume "affirmative leadership" toward an agreement. Recalling the seeming hopelessness of an agreement on reunification of Austria, the President still thought that persistence with the Soviet Union might pay off. Before adjournment, he requested that the Departments of State and Defense, the Atomic Energy Commission, and the Joint Chiefs prepare a joint paper, with dissenting views if necessary, for presidential approval by October 15, 1956.[30]

364

Eisenhower's hope for Soviet cooperation received a setback on the very day of the White House disarmament meeting. On September 11, Premier Bulganin rejected the idea of controlling the production of fissionable materials without at the same time outlawing the use of nuclear weapons. The one, Bulganin claimed, was useless without the other. Conversely, Bulganin argued against linking a test ban with a general disarmament agreement as Strauss insisted. In language not unlike that used by Dulles and Stassen, Bulganin described the termination of testing as the "first important step" toward eventual abolition of nuclear arms.[31]

While the President's disarmament advisers labored to meet the October 15 deadline, few outside Eisenhower's inner circle realized the depth of his commitment to end the arms race. Eisenhower believed the matter was too urgent, and delicate, for political bickering. As his sharp tone with Strauss and Radford had indicated, he lost all patience with attempts to exploit the issue for partisan advantage.

## THE STEVENSON CHALLENGE

On September 5, running on a Democratic platform that accused the Republicans of plunging "the previously independent and non-partisan Atomic Energy Commission into partisan politics," Stevenson thrust the test-ban issue into the presidential campaign during a foreign policy speech to the American Legion. Attempting to capture something of the peace issue for the Democrats, Stevenson told the Legionnaires that he favored an end to the draft as well as an end to testing megaton hydrogen bombs.[32]

Although Eisenhower's contempt was veiled, he did not hesitate to respond vigorously to his own political advantage. In what he called his first major address of the 1956 campaign, Eisenhower flatly rejected the possibility of ending the draft under current world conditions. Nor would he endorse any "theatrical national gesture" to end testing without reliable inspection. "We cannot salute the future with bold words," the President warned, "while we surrender it with feeble deeds."[33] Eisenhower's speech, however, was largely focused on other matters and revealed that disarmament and the test ban had not yet become major campaign issues.

When Stevenson responded to Eisenhower on September 21 in Silver Spring, Maryland, he elevated the rhetoric only slightly. Like the President, the Democratic candidate also addressed the broad issues of the campaign. Nevertheless, Stevenson gave highest priority to defense questions, including "the incalculable effects of unlimited hydrogen bomb testing." If he were guilty of grandstanding, Stevenson observed, then he was in the good company of Pope Pius XII, Sir Anthony Eden, representatives of the Baptist, Unitarian, Quaker, and Methodist churches, and Commissioner Murray among other sincere and thoughtful people. On the same day Murray issued his own press release denying that he had any partisan motives in raising the question of testing policy; he called for the end of multimegaton weapon testing and greater effort on smaller weapons.[34]

365

## THE PRESIDENT STANDS FIRM

To Eisenhower's distress, neither Stevenson nor Murray would abandon the test-ban question. In Minneapolis on September 29 and in New Jersey a few days later, Stevenson reiterated his proposals and challenged Eisenhower to debate the issues. Murray, in classified correspondence, once again goaded Eisenhower about limiting tests below one hundred kilotons. The President icily referred the letter to the National Security Council without a hint to Murray that Strauss was working on just such a proposal. Eisenhower was willing to allow Vice-President Nixon to counter Stevenson's offensive to a point, but ultimately the President was drawn into the public debate.[35]

Following his curt reply to Murray, Eisenhower issued a public statement on thermonuclear testing. He expressed regret that the issue had been raised in a matter that could only lead to confusion at home and misunderstanding abroad. Only his closest advisers could fully understand the context of the President's remarks. Ambiguously, he noted that while testing was, and continued to be, an indispensable part of the defense program, the United States had "consistently affirmed and reaffirmed its readiness—indeed its strong will—to restrict and control both the testing and the use of nuclear weapons under specific and supervised international disarmament agreements."[36] Only the most astute observer would have detected in the President's words the major shift in Administration disarmament policy.

Stevenson was still unaware that the Administration was preparing a major diplomatic initiative to limit testing. Eisenhower continued his broad defense of the Administration's record, including, but not featuring, comments on his defense record. Even former President Truman, who took great delight in lambasting Nixon, would not join Stevenson in criticizing nuclear tests. Hubert Humphrey, speaking in his role as chairman of the Senate Foreign Relations Subcommittee on Disarmament, urged that the United States "give careful consideration to seeking agreement on banning tests of large nuclear weapons." Humphrey's cautious announcement, however, scarcely helped the Democrats' cause. Stevenson's frustration mounted even as Eisenhower's advisers hammered out the new disarmament proposals. In Seattle on October 9, Stevenson brought the nuclear issue front and center by accusing the Republicans, including the President, of willful political distortion. Taking to heart the fact that Ralph Lapp had endorsed his position, Stevenson boldly attacked Eisenhower's entire nuclear policy and record, even Atoms for Peace. Reminiscent of earlier Democratic criticism, Stevenson tried to contrast the government's weapon program with the Commission's failure to build a single power reactor.[37]

On October 11, senior representatives from the Commission, State Department, and Defense Department worked toward a compromise on a new disarmament policy. The Commission continued to have reservations about the effectiveness of any inspection system acceptable to the Russians, but on testing it expressed its willingness to move "progressively" to limit nuclear and thermonuclear tests. As yet, the Commission had conceded little while endorsing in principle the idea of limiting testing, no doubt in the belief that any specific agreement would take years to achieve.[38]

Somehow the press caught wind of the fact that the Administration was entertaining new disarmament proposals. On the same day that his senior advisers were conferring, a reporter asked the President to confirm rumors that the Administration was considering elimination of the draft and halting thermonuclear tests. Eisenhower remarked that the journalist was telling him things about the Administration he had never heard. "I am quite sure no one has . . . suggested to me that we eliminate the draft in my Administration," he continued evasively. Then without even mentioning nuclear testing he declared, "Now, I tell you frankly I have said my last words on these subjects." The President had successfully sidestepped the issue, knowing full well that within four days he expected to receive a coordinated report on the implementation of the Stassen proposals. As a result, Stevenson continued to campaign blindly on the disarmament issue. In San Diego, he blasted Eisenhower for his failure in leadership and lack of new ideas. There could be no "last word" on the hydrogen bomb, Stevenson rebutted, until mankind had been freed from the menace of nuclear incineration.[39]

366

## GROWING SUPPORT FOR STEVENSON

To be sure, Stevenson did receive some support. Former Secretary of the Air Force Thomas K. Finletter, now chairman of Stevenson's New York state campaign, denied that Stevenson really wanted a unilateral test ban. Finletter, once so critical of Oppenheimer, claimed not to be alarmed by Stevenson's rhetoric; rather he did not see how anyone could object to the Democrat's promotion of arms control and disarmament. In addition, numerous scientists now began to speak out in Stevenson's behalf. In the *Bulletin of the Atomic Scientists*, Bentley Glass, a Johns Hopkins biology professor and member of the National Academy of Sciences' fallout committee, lent credence to Stevenson's fears by warning that carelessness with ionizing radiation could well lead to genetic bankruptcy from which "there might be no recovery, for nation or for mankind." From the California Institute of Technology ten scientists, led by physics professors Thomas Lauritzen and Matthew Sands, called for a "free and open discussion" of Stevenson's proposals. "Time is running out," the California scientists declared, "with an implacability that we ignore at our peril." Nevertheless, a street-corner poll by the *New York Herald Tribune* revealed that voters welcomed the lively discussion but generally sided with President Eisenhower in the debate.[40]

367

Encouraged by the public response to his speeches, and anxious to score a major breakthrough in the campaign, Stevenson decided to devote a televised address exclusively to the issues of disarmament, nuclear testing, and presidential leadership. He recruited Clinton Anderson and Stuart Symington to appear with him on the program despite the fact that both senators wanted him to tone down his remarks. Speaking from Chicago on October 15, ironically on the day Eisenhower had set for his disarmament advisers to report, Stevenson denied that his proposals for a thermonuclear test ban had been politically motivated. Still, he thought the issue appropriate for debate during a democratic election. He noted the power of a twenty-megaton bomb—as "if every man, woman, and child on earth were each carrying a 16 pound bundle of dynamite—enough to blow him to smithereens, and then some." He described the danger of fallout from strontium-90—"the most dreadful poison in the world." A mere tablespoonful shared by everyone in the world would produce dangerously high levels of radioactivity in bones, perhaps causing cancer or threatening reproduction. Stevenson added quickly that he did not want "to be an alarmist" or to claim that radioactive levels were too high. He wanted to stop the tests, however, before a maniac like Hitler or other irresponsible regimes fouled the atmosphere with tests of their own. Citing Stassen on the risks of nuclear proliferation, Stevenson then criticized Nixon, his favorite campaign target, for exaggerating the difficulty of establishing safeguards. According to Stevenson, scientists and even the President himself had already acknowledged that the United States could "detect any large explosion any-where." Ultimately, he scolded Eisenhower for wanting to shove the hydro-gen bomb under the table.[41]

With the election less than three weeks away, Stevenson had suc-ceeded in making disarmament and nuclear testing major campaign issues. Unfortunately for the Democratic candidate, the advantage was mostly with President Eisenhower. Stevenson's running mate, Estes Kefauver, almost burlesqued the issue a few days later when he predicted that H-bomb ex-plosions might blow the earth off its axis by sixteen degrees, drastically affecting the seasons. This bit of silliness was immediately refuted by Ralph Lapp, who pointed out that the earth's weight was so great that even millions of tons of exploding TNT would have little effect on the earth's rotation or attitude. Other unnamed scientists interviewed by the *New York Times* called Kefauver's claims "incredible."[42]

Kefauver's irresponsible claims aside, Stevenson's proposals on H-bomb testing sparked sharp debate within the scientific community, em-phasizing again how tightly the bomb had fused science and politics. Stevenson had enlisted Harold Brown, a geochemist from Cal Tech, to be his campaign adviser on the test ban and disarmament. Arrangements were also quickly made to obtain scientific advice for Kefauver by recruiting David L. Hill, a Los Alamos atomic scientist and former chairman of the Federation of American Scientists, to serve on Kefauver's staff. Henry Smyth, the Commission's lone dissenter in the Oppenheimer case and now a professor of physics at Princeton, also supported Stevenson's call for a test ban. Across the nation scientists signed petitions and letters calling for a test ban or public debate of the issue. As reported in the press, the number of scientists supporting Stevenson grew steadily. In addition to the ten scientists from Cal Tech, five nuclear scientists from Argonne National Laboratory endorsed Stevenson's efforts. In New York, eleven physics pro-fessors at Columbia University, where Eisenhower had once been presi-dent, took Stevenson's side on the H-bomb issue. Twenty-four scientists at Washington University in St. Louis, thirty-seven faculty members from City College of New York, and sixty-two nuclear scientists from Brookhaven National Laboratory variously subscribed to Stevenson's position.[43]

## THE ADMINISTRATION'S STANCE

The Eisenhower Administration could also enlist prominent scientists to support its position while it continued to assess the effects of nuclear ex-plosions. Early in October, while Stevenson was preparing his test-ban proposals, the Commission again reviewed estimates of the consequences of nuclear warfare. Spurred by General Gavin's testimony in the spring, preliminary studies by the division of biology and medicine confirmed that strontium-90 presented the greatest fallout hazard after a nuclear attack. In the short run, perhaps 50 percent of the crops might be contaminated and 35 to 60 percent of the unsheltered animals might be killed within the fallout area, with highest mortality closest to ground zero. Necessarily the vague estimates depended upon numerous factors, including bomb yield and weather conditions. The classified studies generally confirmed the National Academy of Sciences' projection concerning genetic mutations. Research conducted in cooperation with the U.S. Weather Bureau could not rule out the possibility that a massive nuclear exchange might usher in a new "ice age" should vast amounts of dust thrown into the stratosphere reduce the amount of solar radiation reaching the earth. Long-term effects, however, were considered negligible when compared with the immediate holocaust that would be unleashed in all-out nuclear war. The Commission's estimates, however, were limited by the fact that it did not have access to war plans and intelligence reports on prospective targets. Consequently, General Starbird recommended that the issue be referred to an interdepartmental group to be convened by the National Security Council.[44]

369

Despite the uncertainties of nuclear war, the Commission remained confident that nuclear testing was safe. On October 12, Willard Libby addressed the American Association for the Advancement of Science on "Current Research Findings on Radioactive Fallout." Libby also noted that strontium-90 was the most hazardous of the many radioactive elements found in fallout. But he did not believe that the total amount of radioactive debris in the stratosphere, estimated at twenty-four megatons of fission products, had increased since 1955. The *Redwing* tests, conducted from May into July, had successfully held thermonuclear fallout to a minimum, he reported.[45]

Building on Libby's report, Shields Warren, former director of the Commission's division of biology and medicine, lashed out at Stevenson's campaign. Warren, a prominent authority on medical radiology and scientific director of the Cancer Research Institute of the New England Deaconess Hospital in Boston, telegraphed Strauss that Stevenson's remarks on the dangers of testing needed correcting. Citing Libby's data, Warren asserted that testing could be continued for thirty years at the current rate without creating a significant genetic hazard or raising background levels more than a fraction. On the other hand, he argued, "to permit us to fall behind the Russians is disastrous. To wait for them to catch up to us is stupid."[46]

Strauss and Robert Cutler, the President's national security adviser, assumed the lead in preparing the Administration's counterattack. Strauss urged the general advisory committee to help disabuse the public of Stevenson's inaccurate campaign statements about the "biological effects of radiation, fall-out hazards from test activities, [and the] relative degree of progress in atomic power in Russia, England and the U.S." Without dissent from the committee, Robert E. Wilson suggested that his fellow members use their speaking engagements to present the correct technical information to the public. Warren C. Johnson, newly elected chairman of the committee, asked Strauss to provide a working list of erroneous and misleading statements. For his part, Cutler arranged for twelve distinguished scientists to meet the President and then to express their indignation over the unwarranted political exploitation of scientific issues. [47]

Ultimately, Eisenhower decided that only he could effectively counter Stevenson's campaign against testing. Perhaps recalling the usefulness of the thermonuclear chronologies that had been prepared by the Joint Committee and the Commission during the Oppenheimer crisis, Eisenhower on October 17 asked Strauss, Charles E. Wilson, and Dulles to draft a "complete history" of the hydrogen bomb, with limits set by security regulations. The history was intended to set the record straight regarding the Administration's commitment to both peace and security. James Hagerty admitted that he did not know whether the paper would become the President's "last words" on the subject. It all depended on the subsequent campaign. [48]

370

## THE INTERNATIONAL AGENCY: BORN AT LAST

As election day neared, delegates from eighty-one nations gathered at United Nations headquarters in New York, to debate the draft statute of the International Atomic Energy Agency. Convened on September 20, the conference was not a rubber stamp, even though most difficult negotiations among the nuclear powers had been completed by the twelve-nation working group during the previous spring. The Russians again unsuccessfully sought agency membership for the Chinese communists and reiterated their insistence that national sovereignty not be sacrificed to the international agency. For the most part, these demands were pro forma. More serious were the reservations on safeguards put forth by the Indians; this discussion occupied more than half the time of the conference.

The draft statute, which satisfied the Commission's minimum standards for safeguards, authorized the agency both to approve the design of any specialized equipment or facility and to require the maintenance of operating records accounting for source and fissionable materials. The agency would also have the right to request progress reports and to have access "to all places, persons, and data" necessary to determine whether diversion of materials had taken place. In the event of noncompliance the agency could suspend or terminate all assistance and withdraw both materials and equipment. To enforce these provisions, the agency was empowered to create a staff of inspectors who would also be responsible for enforcing health and safety measures. [49]

The Indians complained that even these relatively benign provisions might seriously interfere with the economic growth of member states. Specifically, India objected to provisions that included source materials in the accounting system and granted the agency virtually unrestricted rights over weapon-grade reactor by-products. Control over reactor "wastes" was considered essential to prevent stockpiling for weapon development. The eventual compromise involved some sleight-of-hand and judicious rewording of the technical language of the draft statute. In the end the agency retained the accountability for source materials but was limited in its control over reactor by-products so that member states could, under continuing agency safeguards, use by-products material as needed "for research or in reactors, existing or under construction." [50]

With compromise on safeguards accomplished, the conference on October 23 unanimously adopted the statute. Once again the stage was set for a dramatic American gesture. This time, Strauss, appearing on behalf of the President, announced that the United States would make available to the new agency 5,000 kilograms of uranium-235 to be taken from the 20,000 allotted to peaceful uses by Eisenhower in February, provided the agency and the United States could come to agreeable terms. Despite this offer, however, Gerard Smith reported that the American announcement had been received with apathy. Apparently, nations interested in developing nuclear power reactors preferred to work either directly with the United States through bilateral arrangements or through regional groups that might share the enormous costs of the plants. [51]

The successful negotiation of the statute just prior to the presidential elections and the numerous bilateral agreements of cooperation, however, did not reveal the main thrust of America's peaceful atomic diplomacy. Officially, the United States continued to support all approaches related to the international development of the peaceful atom—the international agency and bilaterals, as well as the Organization of European Economic Cooperation (OEEC) and other regional associations—but under directions from President Eisenhower, the United States would continue to devote major attention to the reluctant EURATOM group. [52]

## THE BULGANIN LETTER

On October 18, the same day that the President had offered his "last words" on testing, the complexion of the presidential campaign changed dramatically when Soviet Premier Bulganin wrote Eisenhower criticizing the Administration for its political stand on the subject. Bulganin professed understanding and implied forbearance of American electoral polemics, but he could not ignore what he claimed was deliberate distortion of Soviet policy. The Soviet premier was pointedly critical of Dulles, who was ac-

371

cused of making "direct attacks against the Soviet Union and its peace-loving foreign policy." Following additional polemics of his own, Bulganin renewed his offer of a test ban by endorsing the views of "certain prominent public figures in the United States." As far as the Russians were concerned, Bulganin charged, negotiation of a test ban had failed only because the United States and some of its allies had bargained in bad faith; the Americans, Bulganin charged, renounced their own proposals just when the Russians accepted them.[53]

Eisenhower was furious. Bulganin's public criticism of Dulles and his transparent support of Stevenson were bad enough, but his clumsy eleventh-hour meddling in American politics was intolerable.

Lewis Strauss was in Battle Creek, Michigan, on October 19 to address a meeting of the Joint United States–Canadian Civil Defense Committee. Dulles called him to arrange a meeting that evening, however late, to discuss the President's response to the Bulganin letter. Dulles, understandably indignant at both the tone and content of the letter, wanted the President to reject the note. Strauss, however, viewed the letter as a major windfall, which, if handled carefully, could be turned to considerable advantage for the President. First, Strauss thought it extremely important that Eisenhower, not the Soviets, release the letter to the public, even if a reply was not ready. By doing so the Administration could regain the propaganda initiative. Second, the reply should vigorously repudiate the Russian's personal attack on the Secretary of State and the shocking attempt of a foreign government to interfere in American domestic affairs. Above all, the letter must be answered, not rejected, because the American public might interpret such a formal diplomatic response as a presidential attempt to duck the issue.[54]

On Sunday morning, October 21, Strauss, Dulles, Milton Eisenhower, Under Secretary of State Hoover, and Hagerty gathered in the President's study on the second floor of the White House living quarters. The President and Dulles accepted Strauss's suggestions, but the hope of releasing the Soviet note in Washington had already been foiled when the Russians published it even before Eisenhower had a reliable translation in hand. Eisenhower used this as a pretext for immediately publishing his own reply. Eisenhower's withering temper, infamous among his inner circle but rarely witnessed in public, was directed squarely at the Soviet premier with little worry about the diplomatic consequence. Eisenhower wrote Bulganin that, were he a diplomat assigned to Washington, he would have been declared persona non grata and sent packing back to Moscow. Eisenhower insisted on taking the letter personally because it both attacked the Secretary of State and impugned the President's integrity. Still, Eisenhower expressed his willingness to keep lines of communication open despite the Russian's departure from accepted international practice.[55]

The exchange between Bulganin and Eisenhower was disastrous for

Stevenson, just as Strauss anticipated. The President's white paper on nuclear weapons and disarmament was now hardly needed and contributed little to the remaining campaign or to subsequent diplomatic negotiations. From Chicago, Stevenson attempted to disassociate himself from Bulganin's ploy by denouncing the Russian's interference. Somewhat lamely, Stevenson countered that in reality Bulganin preferred Eisenhower. More to the point, the Democratic candidate declared that the hydrogen bomb remained the real issue in the presidential campaign. Unfortunately, as the *Los Angeles Times* commented, Stevenson had been flanked, with no retreat. It was not, of course, that anyone really believed that Stevenson was a friend of communism or had intentionally played the Russian game. Rather, in the field of nuclear weapons, Eisenhower, former Army chief of staff, commander of the North Atlantic Treaty Organization, and President, obviously held an enormous advantage in both experience and access to information. A special public opinion poll conducted by George Gallup indicated that Americans opposed a nuclear test ban by a two-to-one margin. There is no question that Bulganin's heavy-handedness hurt Stevenson on the test-ban issue. Stevenson did not, as some had feared, derail Eisenhower's determination to seek a nuclear test ban.[56] Indeed, the presidential campaign, for all the sound and fury, probably did not delay the eventual test moratorium of 1958.

373

## SUEZ, HUNGARY, AND THE NATIONAL ELECTION

The remainder of the presidential campaign was virtually engulfed by foreign developments, greatly to the President's advantage. The Middle East exploded on October 29 when Israel assaulted the Sinai, followed by a combined British and French invasion of Egypt near the Suez Canal. Thereafter, on November 4, Russian soldiers marched into Hungary and ruthlessly trampled the revolution. Two days later on November 6 Americans reelected Eisenhower in a landslide victory that exceeded his 1952 win over Stevenson. Americans seemed both appreciative of Eisenhower for the "peace and prosperity" he had brought to the nation and confident that he would deal firmly with the Russians and other threats to international stability.

## NUCLEAR ISSUES IN POLITICS

For the first time atomic energy had become a major issue in a presidential campaign; it was no accident. Since Operation *Candor* and the Atoms-for-Peace speech in 1953, Eisenhower had self-consciously determined to include the American public in atomic energy discussions to the extent national security permitted. The awesome power of hydrogen weaponry and the great potential of the peaceful atom made it imperative that nuclear energy be a part of the nation's political agenda. Although Stevenson was unable to exploit the nuclear issue, by the same token he was not decisively hurt by his advocacy of a test ban and disarmament. With or without the nuclear debate, Eisenhower, who carried forty-one states with about 58 percent of the vote, would have won reelection handily. The 1956 presidential election, however, provided Americans their first opportunity to vote on political issues involving the future of atomic energy. If not exactly a national referendum on the subject, the election clearly endorsed the atomic energy policies of the Eisenhower Administration.

Atomic Energy Commissioners and the general manager at Washington Headquarters, fall 1953. Seated, left to right: Commissioners Eugene M. Zuckert, Henry D. Smyth, Lewis L. Strauss (Chairman), Thomas E. Murray, Joseph Campbell, and General Manager Marion W. Boyer. Photo by Elton Lord.

June 2, 1954. Dr. J. Robert Oppenheimer, seated at his desk in his office at the Institute for Advanced Study, Princeton, New Jersey, ponders response to the Gray board decision announced the previous day recommending withdrawal of his security clearance.

President Dwight D. Eisenhower signs the Atomic Energy Act of 1954 at the White House on August 30, 1954, a major step in opening the way for industrial participation and international cooperation in the peaceful uses of atomic energy. Seated, left to right: Senator William F. Knowland, President Eisenhower, Representative W. Sterling Cole, and AEC Chairman Lewis L. Strauss. Standing, left to right: AEC General Manager K. D. Nichols, Commissioner Henry Smyth, Assistant Secretary of Defense Donald A. Quarles, Military Liaison Committee Chairman Herbert B. Loper, Senator Edwin C. Johnson, Representatives Carl Hinshaw, James E. Van Zandt, Melvin Price, and Carl T. Durham, and Commissioner Thomas E. Murray.

March 17, 1953, civil defense experiment at Yucca Flat. In this series of pictures, the high-speed camera shows the complete destruction of House #1 by atomic blast, 3,500 feet from ground zero.

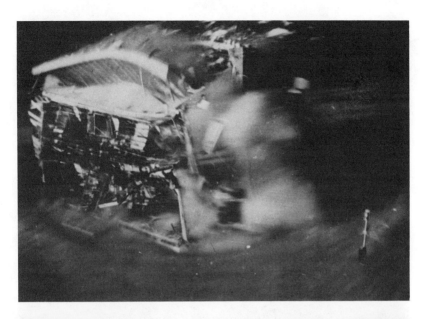

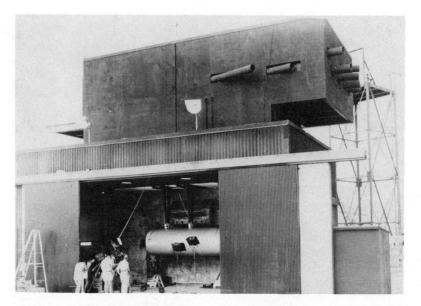

Last minute inspection of the *Castle-Bravo* device located in a small structure on a reef off Namu Island in the central Pacific. The March 1, 1954, detonation of the first shot in the *Castle* series demonstrated the feasibility of a "dry" thermonuclear weapon.

President Eisenhower confers with Administration officials at the White House on January 13, 1956, on the Atoms-for-Peace program. Seated, left to right: Secretary of the Treasury George Humphrey, President Eisenhower, Secretary of State John Foster Dulles, Special Assistant to the President Dillon Anderson, AEC Chairman Lewis L. Strauss, and Secretary of Defense Charles E. Wilson. Photo courtesy Dwight D. Eisenhower Library.

Utility company executives Edgar H. Dixon and Eugene A. Yates break ground in June 1955 for a power plant to supply power for Memphis, Tennessee. The contract between the utilities and the AEC was terminated by President Eisenhower when Memphis officials announced their intention to build a muncipal power plant.

Congressmen and other official observers watch the formation of a mushroom cloud following the firing of an atomic artillery shell from the Army's new 280mm artillery gun. Part of Operation *Upshot-Knothole* test series, the *Grable* shot was fired on May 25, 1953.

AEC Chairman Lewis L. Strauss confers with scientists from Livermore laboratory following June 24, 1957, meeting with the President to discuss "clean" weapons. Left to right: Ernest O. Lawrence, Strauss, Edward Teller, and Mark Mills.

President Eisenhower sets the cornerstone of the new Atomic Energy Commission building located in Germantown, Maryland, twenty-five miles northwest of Washington, D.C. Left to right: AEC Director of Construction and Supply John A. Derry, Representative Carl T. Durham, chairman of the Joint Committee on Atomic Energy, and AEC Chairman Lewis L. Strauss.

AEC Chairman John McCone describes the SNAP-3 device to President Eisenhower as it sits on his desk in the Oval Office of the White House, January 16, 1959. The small light-weight device is a radioisotope-fueled thermoelectric generator for use in space missions. Left to right: President Eisenhower, Major General Donald J. Keirn, assistant director for aircraft reactors (AEC), Chairman McCone, Colonel Jack Armstrong, deputy assistant director for aircraft reactors (AEC), and Lt. Colonel Guveren M. Anderson, project officer, missile projects branch, division of reactor development (AEC).

## CHAPTER 14

# IN SEARCH OF A
# NUCLEAR TEST BAN

Although the 1956 presidential election had clearly endorsed Eisenhower's "peaceful" atomic energy policies, the partisan debate over a test ban and disarmament had not clarified these sensitive issues. For the most part, official secrecy still shrouded the military atom so that beyond the President's inner circle few Americans knew of Eisenhower's diplomatic strategy. Only the President's 1953 Atoms-for-Peace speech, his 1955 Open Skies proposal, and periodic reports of the continuing disarmament talks gave any indication of the Administration's intentions.

One historian has speculated that by raising the test-ban issue Stevenson actually may have derailed a decision by the National Security Council to seek a negotiated test-ban agreement with the Soviet Union.[1] There is no evidence, however, that election rhetoric either slowed or deflected the test-ban strategy adopted by the President's disarmament advisers in mid-September 1956. Despite his great impatience with the public posturing of both Stevenson and Bulganin, Eisenhower remained determined to seek an end to the nuclear arms race. If anything, progress toward test-ban negotiations was impeded by internal strife within Republican ranks, not by Democratic campaign criticism. After Nixon's renomination and election as Vice-President, Stassen's position as Eisenhower's special adviser on disarmament became increasingly tenuous. Stassen did not lose the President's confidence immediately, but his open opposition to Nixon's candidacy helped Strauss and others to exploit resistance to Stassen's disarmament plans. Yet even as the President gradually lost confidence in Stassen's judgment, Eisenhower's commitment to a nuclear test ban remained unchanged.

The presidential campaign, however, did promote greater public understanding of radioactive fallout. Although public opinion polls indicated that Americans generally opposed a nuclear test ban, a survey of the presidents of scientific and technical organizations in the United States indicated that 57 percent of the respondents favored either halting or limiting the testing by all nations. In the October 1956 *Bulletin of the Atomic Scientists*, Ralph Lapp described the Commission, like Macbeth, as "haunted by the ghost of things which will not die." The specter in this instance was radioactive strontium-90, which Lapp reported was turning up in the bones of people all over the world. Using data provided by Libby and others of the Commission, Lapp concluded that some limitation of the test program was urgently needed "to preserve the sanctity of the biosphere."[2]

In the final days of the campaign, Senator Clinton Anderson charged that the Commission had purposely suppressed an unclassified report on the radiation effects of fallout from hydrogen bomb tests. Anderson's charges were blatantly partisan. Actually he was seeking an advance copy of the chapter on radiation effects of fallout in the *Weapons Effects Handbook*, due to be published early in 1957. Acting General Manager Richard W. Cook explained to Anderson that he could not release the draft chapter because it had not been cleared by either the Commission or the Department of Defense, a cosponsor of the handbook. Anderson insisted that the President order the Commission "to make the true facts public immediately while this important issue is being debated." Having made his point, Anderson later expressed his willingness to settle for the most recent fallout information if the draft of the *Weapons Effects Handbook* were unavailable.[3]

## EISENBUD'S "SUNSHINE SPEECH"

As a result of the political controversy and public debate over fallout, the Commission's general advisory committee, at the insistence of Edward Teller, decided to issue a statement on fallout to be published after the elections. The committee emphasized that radiation effects from tests at no time exceeded those from natural causes, a fact the National Academy of Sciences had already confirmed. Confidently, the committee noted that no "objective" criticism of the academy's report had yet been published. Furthermore, the committee pointed to encouraging progress made during the *Redwing* tests toward developing nuclear weapons with reduced fallout—the "clean bombs."[4]

Thereafter, on November 15, 1956, Merril Eisenbud, manager of the New York operations office, addressed the Washington Academy of Sciences on worldwide distribution of strontium-90. Eisenbud, in charge of the Commission's radiation monitoring program, acknowledged that strontium-90 was the most hazardous of the nuclides formed in the fission process. Project *Sunshine* had analyzed the physical and biological behavior of strontium-90 as it traveled from the nuclear fireball through the atmosphere into the soil, up through the food chain, and finally via human metabolism into bone.

Using research and sampling techniques slightly different from Libby's, Eisenbud came to the similar conclusion that through 1956 fallout from nuclear testing had not proven hazardous to human health. Libby had estimated that 4 to 10 micromicrocuries of strontium-90 per gram (mmc/g) of calcium could concentrate in bones in persons throughout the United States within ten to fifteen years. Using data gathered on the North Dakota milkshed, where the greatest concentration had occurred, Eisenbud predicted an eventual concentration of 25 mmc/g. Either value was less than the maximum permissible body burden of 100 mmc/g established by the National Committee on Radiation Protection and the International Commission on Radiological Protection. In his summary, Eisenbud noted that over a period of seventy years the highest estimate of skeletal accumulation that could be predicted from the devices already detonated was only 7 percent above the highest estimate received from natural background radiation. The *Sunshine* studies had indicated that the estimate could also be as low as 0.7 percent.[5] The implication of Eisenbud's speech was clear: testing had created only slightly greater hazards from radioactivity than had mother nature herself.

377

The importance that the Commission gave Project *Sunshine* was demonstrated a few days later when the general manager requested an additional $2 million for the biology and medicine program. Both Libby and Murray observed that Project *Sunshine* ranked next to the weapon program in priority. Libby even suggested that the Commission issue a staff directive stressing the high priority of *Sunshine*. Although not all the additional appropriation would go directly to *Sunshine*, over three-quarters of the funding would directly or indirectly support its activities. Curiously, given the project's high priority and the Commission's responsibility to keep the Joint Committee "fully and currently informed," the Commissioners also decided it was not appropriate to notify the Joint Committee of their action. Concurrently, Gioacchino Failla, chairman of the advisory committee on biology and medicine, called a special meeting, including the Commissioners and the general manager, to evaluate the status and implications of Project *Sunshine* with the hope of developing a public statement. Eisenbud's November 15 speech served as the basis of the advisory committee's discussions.[6]

## THE DANGERS OF FALLOUT

When the advisory committee on biology and medicine examined both Eisenbud's and Libby's statistics, a disconcerting conclusion emerged: Eisenbud's and Libby's studies analyzed only past testing, without considering continued or future testing. Although the committee members had no doubt that radiation levels from testing in the United States and the world were well within safe and established limits, they also noted that additional testing might well exceed permissible limits. H. Bentley Glass, a distinguished geneticist, was the first to observe that if testing continued at the same rate as it had for the past four years, the permissible limits would be exceeded within twenty-eight years; the implication of his simple arithmetic was so startling, however, that even he cautioned that he might "be entirely wrong."[7]

When Murray and Strauss joined the afternoon session, Failla explained the apparent dilemma. The advisory committee remained confident that there was "no appreciable danger" to world population from previous nuclear tests. On the other hand, some members were worried that additional international testing could increase the amount of strontium-90 in the bones of children above acceptable limits within fifteen to twenty years. In short, unless the standards themselves were altered or testing significantly reduced, body burdens of strontium-90 worldwide were likely to rise to levels that were too close to the limits. Murray brushed aside Failla's comments, reminding the advisory committee of the *Plumbbob* tests scheduled for Nevada in spring 1957. Murray had no data that the *Plumbbob* tests would add significantly to the fallout problem. "I would not want anything to happen that would disturb the going ahead with those tests in the spring," he warned the group. "That is our immediate problem, and I don't think anything will interfere with us going ahead."[8]

Strauss was far less categorical and infinitely more diplomatic with the committee members, but he hardly encouraged them to rush to judgment with their findings. When Failla asked how urgent it was for the committee to issue a public statement on worldwide fallout, Strauss replied that a statement was in order "whenever the committee is convinced that it has all the facts." Strauss thought there was no urgency for a statement that could not be supported "by facts in hand." Unfortunately, Failla continued, there would always be speculation, rather than absolute knowledge, concerning the effects of radioactive fallout because most data were obtained from animal experiments instead of human experience. Strauss carefully reminded the scientists that their professional responsibility required them to give the Commission the benefit of their "best judgment, whatever it may be." He then added that as far as he knew, the committee had received no urgent request from the Commission for a public statement. In effect, Strauss reenforced Murray's injunction against issuing a public statement without actually doing so. Not surprisingly, the advisory committee decided not to release a public statement on the hazards of worldwide fallout but instead offered an internal report to the Commission recommending continued studies of the biological effects of low doses of strontium-90. Given the

378

uncertainties and statistical limitations of the problem, the committee did not expect "to produce definitive results for many years."[9]

Throughout winter and spring 1957 the advisory committee on biology and medicine remained uncertain about how best to advise the Commission, the general advisory committee, and the public on the hazards of radioactive fallout. The general advisory committee was particularly anxious to have a statement it could endorse. Yet, even after two more long sessions on the subject in January and March, no one really knew what the effects of low-level radiation from strontium-90 might be. Failla speculated that there were no thresholds for various radiation effects such as bone tumor or leukemia, but this hypothesis could not be proven. At best, the Commission would have to continue to study the matter in hopes that within a year or two research would yield publishable results.[10]

When Senator Richard Neuberger proposed an independent institute responsible for nuclear health and related research and training, the advisory committee opposed the idea on the grounds that it would duplicate the Commission's existing programs and facilities. The committee was fully aware that Neuberger's proposal reflected criticism either that the Commission was not doing its job or that it was improper to combine weapon testing and public health protection in the same agency. Either way, the advisory committee declined comment on Neuberger's bill, confident that the Joint Committee on Atomic Energy would block any action.

379

Failla, however, was sensitive to the potential conflict of interest between those managing the weapon tests and those responsible for health and safety. When Failla suggested that Eisenhower should appoint an independent committee to advise him on the safety of testing, Strauss noted that it was already too late to review plans for Operation *Plumbbob*. Shields Warren objected to establishing an advisory committee between the President on the one hand and the Department of Defense and the Commission on the other, but he thought that there should be some way "to get word to the Commissioners" that the military's unlimited demands for testing were damaging world opinion. Warren, normally a staunch defender of the Commission, joined those who worried whether all atmospheric tests were militarily necessary.[11]

In his remarks to the *Sunshine* study group in February, Libby summed up the significance of the Commission's radiation studies. "Next to weapons," Libby stated, "Sunshine is the most important work in the Atomic Energy Commission." Libby believed that, unless the problems surrounding fallout were understood and clearly explained to the public, the testing program might be forced to stop, "which could well be disastrous to the free world."[12] Libby correctly sensed the urgency of the moment, but he missed completely the depth of Eisenhower's commitment to seek an end to testing. For Libby and the members of the advisory committee on biology and medicine, the most pressing issues were scientific, not moral. But for Eisenhower, the radiation studies, although important, would hardly be decisive in shaping his strategy for controlling the nuclear arms race. Even if *Sunshine* were to prove that atmospheric testing was safe, the President had set his own course to stop testing as an explicit step toward arms control and peace.

## STASSEN AND DISARMAMENT

In contrast to the fruitless efforts of the Commission's advisory committee on biology and medicine, the President's disarmament advisers gained headway after the national elections. Although the disarmament committee had missed its October 15 deadline, within a fortnight of Eisenhower's reelection Stassen had presented the President a revised version of his June 29 disarmament proposals.

By that time the Soviet Union also adopted new policies which were to pave the way for the 1957 disarmament negotiations. On November 17, Foreign Minister Andre Gromyko informed Eisenhower that the Soviet Union was willing to discuss the possibility of establishing Open Skies over both NATO and Warsaw Pact countries. Thus, although the "Spirit of Geneva" had been shattered by the Hungarian revolution, the Middle-East war, and the acrimonious correspondence between Bulganin and Eisenhower, the great powers were quietly seeking common ground for disarmament discussions.[13]

The pace of disarmament quickened after the American election. Euphemistically, Eisenhower called the three weeks between October 20 and November 8 "Twenty Busy Days." Preoccupied by war and politics, governmental leaders still made progress toward disarmament. On November 21, not yet two weeks since fighting ceased along the Suez Canal, Eisenhower approved Stassen's revision of the disarmament plan, which included a commitment to seek a nuclear test ban. At the United Nations, the Norwegian delegate suggested on November 27 that nations should register all nuclear weapon tests with the United Nations. Registration would not only serve as a first step toward test limitations but would also enable the United Nations to alert member states so that accurate measurements of worldwide fallout could be obtained. Canadian endorsement of the Norwegian proposal suggested that perhaps some limitations on testing could be established. On December 19, Stassen informed the Canadian ambassador that the United States was willing to explore the possibility of registering tests but that the Americans hoped Canada would consult with the United States before formally advocating test limitations.[14]

The President's disarmament proposals were officially made public on January 14, 1957, when Ambassador Lodge outlined them before a First

380

Committee of the United Nations General Assembly. Lodge offered five proposals for the disarmament negotiations scheduled to convene in London in March. The first was to control the production of fissionable material for weapons. Lodge expressed America's hope to reduce weapon stockpiles and to limit the production of fissionable material to peaceful uses under international supervision. If the nations could agree on international controls of fissionable material, then they might be able to limit, and eventually eliminate, all nuclear test explosions. Other proposals included reducing conventional forces and armaments, limiting outer space to peaceful research and exploration, and establishing international safeguards against surprise attack. All proposals, of course, were contingent on establishing acceptable provisions for inspections or verifications. Lodge also indicated the United States' willingness to seek a compromise between Eisenhower's air inspection system and Bulganin's plan for fixed ground observation posts.[15]

381

In contrast to his dramatic success in drafting the Administration's new disarmament policy with a commitment at least to discuss limiting nuclear testing, Stassen suffered serious political setbacks following the presidential election. His unsuccessful opposition to Nixon's renomination had already raised serious questions about his usefulness to the Eisenhower team. Dulles no doubt surveyed Stassen's liabilities and the Administration's options when he included the "future status of Mr. Stassen" on his agenda of "Matters to be raised with the President" on December 2, 1956.[16]

Several weeks later Eisenhower and Stassen had a long and, in the President's words, "brutally frank" talk about Stassen's conduct. Stassen assured Eisenhower of his unconditional support of the President and asserted that his troubles stemmed from the fact that he had been uncompromising in pursuing Eisenhower's disarmament goals, while others had dragged their heels hoping the President would change his mind. There was sufficient truth in Stassen's analysis to reassure Eisenhower of his disarmament adviser's good intentions. In a telephone call to Dulles shortly after his interview with Stassen, Eisenhower expressed confidence that Stassen was not then politically ambitious. Stassen may have made mistakes, Eisenhower confided to Dulles, but not because he was disloyal to the President.[17]

Dulles remained unhappy with Stassen's freewheeling style, and he told Stassen that same day that the Secretaries of State and Defense had been given presidential authority for public relations related to disarmament. Increasingly Dulles found Stassen's semi-independent status intolerable.[18]

Matters came to a head on January 28, 1957, when Stassen, unable to suppress his antagonism toward Nixon, publicly blamed the Vice-President for the Republicans' Congressional losses in the 1956 elections. Stassen reiterated that if Christian Herter had been Eisenhower's running mate, the Republicans would have not only regained a majority in Congress but also won more governorships and local elections. Predictably, Stassen's televised interview created a furor within the President's inner circle.[19]

With the London disarmament talks scheduled to begin in less than two months, Eisenhower had to decide how to deal with Stassen. Obviously, the President did not want to discredit his disarmament adviser on the eve of promising negotiations. Yet he could no longer ignore Stassen's open criticism of the Vice-President. Somehow, he had to find a way to discipline Stassen without destroying his effectiveness at the bargaining table. Eisenhower's solution was brilliant. With Stassen actually involved in United States diplomacy, the President decided that his disarmament adviser could be transferred from the White House to the Department of State. This meant not only that Dulles would now have more control over Stassen but also that Stassen would attend neither Cabinet nor National Security Council meetings unless the agenda specifically included disarmament questions. Thus, Eisenhower saved his disarmament adviser from dismissal, strengthened Dulles's hands in the forthcoming negotiations, and vindicated Nixon without causing any serious political damage.[20]

The President apparently mollified Stassen as well. Although transferred to the State Department where he ranked below the Under Secretary of State, Stassen was allowed to keep his original title as special adviser to the President. Eisenhower generously urged him gradually to reduce his attendance at Cabinet and National Security Council meetings so that there would be no abrupt or obvious change in Stassen's status. For his part, Dulles encouraged Stassen to attend his staff meetings. Rather pointedly, Dulles stated that he expected "complete loyalty to State Department policies" whether or not Stassen always agreed with them. Although he acquiesced to the changes, Stassen continued to protest that he always tried to be loyal and that reports of his disagreement with Administration policy were completely without basis.[21]

## PREPARATIONS FOR LONDON

Although Eisenhower had approved the Administration's new disarmament plan on November 21, 1956, the details had to be hammered out within the government and between the United States and its allies before confrontation with the Soviets in London. The Atomic Energy Commission was uneasy about the President's proposal to limit or eliminate testing contingent upon achieving agreement in other areas of disarmament and establishing an acceptable inspection system. In the meantime, the United States would propose that each nation announce its tests in advance and permit a limited number of international observers to witness the tests. When Stassen asked the Commission to develop recommendations for implementing the President's plan, the Commissioners were able to use the request as a way to contest the proposals without directly opposing the President.[22]

The Commission had ample reason for being nervous. Even without an international agreement, the President on the day after Christmas had expressed some doubt about the advisability of authorizing operation *Plumbbob*, a series of twenty-five tests that Strauss had indicated would be conducted in Nevada starting on May 1, 1957. Dulles explained that nearly all the tests would be small and confined to the continental United States. The Secretary of State anticipated no difficulty because recent Soviet tests had provoked little comment.[23]

The Commission was not enthusiastic about any testing proposal, and its fundamental position remained unchanged from that expressed to Stassen the previous July. On January 23, 1957, the majority of the Commissioners informed Stassen that they did not believe that the United States should agree to a moratorium on testing independent from a comprehensive disarmament agreement that included inspections and safeguards. They were less adamant about the possibility of placing limitations on testing. An ad hoc disarmament committee appointed to explore various options on limiting testing reported that it was impossible to predict what means might be technically acceptable in the future. Simply limiting the number of tests without at the same time restricting the amount of fallout allowable did not appear practical to the Commission's staff. But, assuming reciprocity from the Russians, the staff anticipated no great problems in admitting observers at the tests, provided they were not permitted to photograph or otherwise record observations that revealed design information.[24]

383

The British, too, were wary of the forthcoming disarmament talks. A delegation headed by Ambassador Harold T. Caccia proposed that the two nations adopt a common position in response to any Soviet offer. Thus, as the disarmament conference convened in London, Eisenhower flew to Bermuda for talks with Prime Minister Harold Macmillan, who had succeeded Anthony Eden after the Suez disaster. Nuclear testing was a major item on their agenda, and Eisenhower was inclined to be conciliatory toward Macmillan.[25]

Gerard Smith, State Department special assistant for atomic energy matters, recommended that the two leaders issue a joint statement reflecting Anglo-American restraint on testing. In their joint statement from Bermuda, Eisenhower and Macmillan affirmed the necessity of continued nuclear testing in the absence of an international disarmament agreement, but they followed Smith's advice by promising to contribute only a small fraction to permissible levels of worldwide fallout. Gratuitously, they assumed the Russians would do the same. Finally, in concert with the proposals Stassen was offering in London, they expressed their willingness to accept the Norwegian plan to register tests with the United Nations and to allow international observation of the tests if the Soviet Union would do the same.[26]

## LONDON DISARMAMENT CONFERENCE

When the United Nations disarmament subcommittee convened its longest, most significant, and final meeting in London on March 18, 1957, prospects for success were not bright. The Western alliance had been severely tested by the Suez crisis. The French were fighting in Algeria while suffering recurrent crises at home. The British, short of manpower and staggering under their defense budget, had already decided to rely primarily on their nuclear deterrent and had announced that they would be testing and manufacturing a megaton weapon during 1957. The Soviet Union, which had begun a new series of weapon tests in August 1956, exploded six devices in March on the eve of the conference, almost in cynical defiance of the negotiations. For its part, the United States planned to launch the *Plumbbob* series in May on schedule. All the while, with the Federal Republic of Germany as the new NATO partner, the Western alliance faced decisions on nuclear stockpiles and missile bases in Europe. The pall of the Hungarian revolution still darkened the prospects for peace, and, although Eisenhower was determined to persevere in "waging peace," few outside his inner circle were aware of the depth of the President's commitment.

To complicate matters more, just before departing for the conference, Stassen unaccountably announced that he would be seeking the Republican nomination for governor of Pennsylvania. Although there was no reaction to Stassen's announcement from either the White House or the State Department, the American delegation reportedly anticipated that the disarmament conference would end by late April.[27]

Within this bleak atmosphere there was reason for optimism on the American side, and for most outsiders it would have seemed to rest with an unlikely personage, none other than John Foster Dulles. Although infamous for having coined the phrase "massive retaliation," Dulles had not initially played a dominant role in shaping Eisenhower's "peaceful atomic diplomacy."[28] First, Strauss and then Stassen had that responsibility. Preoccupied by a series of international crises, Dulles had only gradually gained mastery of the moral and technical complexities of nuclear politics on the international level. By spring 1957, with Stassen transferred to the State Department and Strauss isolated by inflexible positions on testing, Dulles, despite his recent bout with cancer, emerged as the President's most dependable disarmament champion. While Stassen and Strauss increasingly voiced the extremes of disarmament and international nuclear policy, Dulles, under the shrewd tutelage of Gerard Smith, kept to the middle road occupied by the President.

384

Before the London talks opened, Dulles cautioned Stassen to limit his discussions to the proposals that the President and the National Security Council had approved on November 21, 1956. But before the London conference was two weeks old, reports began to filter back to Washington that Stassen appeared to have exceeded his explicit instructions. Alarmed, Gerard Smith confirmed that no one in Washington had cleared what appeared to be new proposals put forward by Stassen. Apparently, after Stassen offered the American proposals, Valerian Zorin, the Soviet representative, called for an "immediate and unconditional halt to tests, without any inspection." Stassen, eager to pursue any opening, did not preclude discussing the Russian's suggestion that a test ban might be the first step toward disarmament, not the last.[29]

Strauss was angered and alarmed by Stassen's willingness to discuss concessions on the testing issue before an agreement on inspection and verification had been made. He complained bitterly to Dulles, requesting that the Secretary of State call his emissary home for discussions during the Easter recess. Dulles conceded that Stassen was an "elusive fellow" given to overloading the Secretary of State with cables so that he could document that Dulles had been put on notice. Uncertain as to what was happening in London, Dulles agreed to call Stassen back "to find out what is going on."[30]

385

Captain John H. Morse, Strauss's special assistant, suspected that Stassen was either confused or intending to confuse. After analyzing disarmament cables from London, Morse concluded that Stassen wanted not only authority to abandon effective inspection, the keystone to the American position, but also personal freedom of action to negotiate the timing and extent of departure from the toughest American demands. Morse confessed, however, that Stassen's purpose, "if it exists, is well disguised—and perhaps accounts for the unusually obtuse wording of the proposal."[31]

## STASSEN RECALLED

Stassen returned to Washington under a cloud of suspicion to defend his actions on April 20. There had been an atmosphere of hopelessness in London when he first arrived, Stassen explained, and everyone anticipated short meetings and quick adjournment. Gradually, however, it became apparent that the Russians were interested in the possibility of reaching a "first step agreement." On April 12, Zorin had personally told Stassen that the United States' proposals were receiving serious consideration in Moscow. Three days later, Zorin announced he would return to Moscow during the Easter recess for consultation. Stassen anticipated that when Zorin returned to London the Russians would be amenable to an inspection system that did not undermine their regime either at home or in Eastern Europe. The Soviet envoy had already indicated willingness to negotiate separately on the major obstacles to a disarmament treaty, including outlawing nuclear weapons and abolishing foreign military bases. In general, Stassen was encouraged that the London conference might yet advance four American objectives outlined by the Secretary of State: (1) limiting the spread of nuclear weapons, (2) reducing the United States' vulnerability to surprise attack, (3) lifting the Iron Curtain slightly, and (4) setting the stage for further negotiations to ease Cold War tensions.[32]

Stassen did not believe that a first step toward disarmament involving a limited test ban and cessation of uranium enrichment for nuclear weapons would significantly reduce the nuclear weapon capability of either the United States or the Soviet Union. The greater problem, in Stassen's opinion, would be to get other countries, such as France, to go along. French Foreign Minister Jules Moch had informed him that France would be ready to test its first nuclear weapon by 1959 and, unless some agreement were reached in six months, would pass the point of no return in the development of nuclear arms. Because other nations would be certain to follow, Stassen now supported a twelve-month limited suspension of nuclear tests and production of fissionable materials, a delay that he thought would involve small risk until a reliable inspection system was adopted.

Strauss, supported by Abbott Washburn of the United States Information Agency, argued that once a test moratorium was established public pressure both at home and abroad against resumption of testing would be tremendous. According to Strauss, a year of testing would be lost just when the United States was on the threshold of developing a relatively clean thermonuclear weapon. Strauss expressed his willingness to negotiate a test limitation, but he adamantly opposed a test ban that would ultimately cripple the Commission's laboratories and permit top scientists and engineers to drift away. The Russians, who Strauss claimed could keep their laboratories at full strength by simple fiat, could break any agreement and end up far ahead of the United States. If tests were limited by number, size, or fallout, however, Strauss believed some agreement might be possible. While Strauss continued to minimize the health dangers related to atmospheric testing, Stassen reminded the group that a major international scientific debate on that very subject was far from settled.

First among Dulles's concerns at the April 20 meeting was the "fourth" or "n-th" country problem. Here Dulles observed, was an important common ground between the United States and the Soviet Union. Both countries were concerned about the implications of nuclear weapons in the hands of "irresponsible" powers, not because they could seriously threaten either the United States or the Soviet Union, but because rash actions might plunge everyone into all-out war. From Dulles's point of view, even if the United States and the Soviet Union failed to achieve substantial disarmament agreement, any successful steps toward eliminating the "fourth" country problem would justify taking some risks.

Following the meeting, Dulles asked to see Stassen privately. Alone, Dulles rebuked Stassen for offering "personal" proposals, which could prove highly dangerous should the Russians accept an idea that the President could not endorse. The Russians had already accused the United States of retreating from positions after the Soviet Union had accepted them. Dulles wanted no possible embarrassment to the Administration, especially since the Senate had not been thoroughly briefed on the progress of the London discussions.[33]

Later, Stassen also met with the President before returning to London. Covering much the same ground as he had on April 20, Stassen related his optimism over the Soviet Union's willingness to engage in serious negotiations. Stassen's report was obviously good news to the President, who expressed as much worry over the reactions of officials at State, Defense, and the Commission as he did over the response of America's allies or the Russians themselves. Especially on the testing question, Eisenhower thought that the United States might be the hardest nation to convince on the limitation of tests. Unlike other countries that tested for purely military reasons, Eisenhower observed that American scientists were fascinated by the basic research that the tests made possible—research that often transcended its military significance. Indeed, because peaceful and military research were often so interrelated, Eisenhower speculated that the unlimited right of inspection might be essential to any disarmament agreement.[34]

387

## STASSEN'S NEW PROPOSAL

By May 9, 1957, following his return to London, Stassen at Dulles's request prepared a new formulation of the United States' position on arms limitation and control. In a personal telephone call to the President at Gettysburg, Dulles commented that Stassen's new plan was "much too grandiose" and went far beyond anything practical at the time. Nevertheless, Dulles granted the need to revise the American position and recommended calling Stassen back to Washington for another round of interagency discussions.[35]

Dulles, Stassen, Strauss, Robert Cutler, Secretary of Defense Wilson, and Allen Dulles of the Central Intelligence Agency gathered on May 17 to review, paragraph by paragraph, Stassen's May 9 recommendations. Stassen reported enthusiastically that the Russians were genuinely interested in reaching an agreement and that the leaders of the other Western delegations also hoped for real progress in the negotiations. According to Stassen, during the crises in Suez and Hungary, the Soviets found themselves looking down the "barrel of atomic war." Much to the surprise of both Dulles brothers, Stassen reported that the Russian leaders were not worried about direct conflict with the United States; they believed that even an irresponsible administration in Washington would not attack the Soviet

Union unless the United States was prepared to follow through on land in Europe to finish off the Russians. What the Soviets feared most was that a crisis in Germany, Poland, Europe, or elsewhere might pull them into nuclear war with the United States. Although the Soviets appeared in no hurry to reach an agreement with the United States and its allies, Stassen did not think they were stalling. Rather, the Russians were constantly wondering whether the United States was stalling and whether the Americans were serious.[36]

In order to demonstrate clearly the United States' commitment to arms limitation, Stassen wanted to reformulate the President's November 21, 1956, disarmament policy to strengthen antiproliferation measures, increase international safeguards against surprise attacks, and, not incidentally, open up the Soviet Union and Eastern Europe. For the most part, where Eisenhower's November 21 disarmament policy had provided general guidelines for negotiations, Stassen sought to establish definite strategy and firm language. With respect to Open Skies, for example, Stassen proposed opening to aerial inspection limited portions of western Russia and Europe and all of the Soviet Union north of the Arctic Circle and east of Lake Baikal, matched by an equal area in the western United States, Alaska, and Canada. Stassen also developed similar details and proposed timetables concerning the establishment of ground control posts, exchange of military blueprints, reduction of armed forces and armaments, and sharing of information relative to movement of troops on land, sea, and air. All signatories—with the exception of the United States, the Soviet Union, and the United Kingdom—would agree never to manufacture or to use nuclear weapons. The three nuclear powers, for their part, would agree to a moral pledge not to use nuclear weapons except in self-defense; rather they would devote all future production of fissionable material exclusively to nonweapon or peaceful uses. All aspects of Stassen's new proposals but one required establishing satisfactory inspection systems before they would become effective. In a bold departure from previous American policy, Stassen now advocated that the United States accept Zorin's invitation to suspend all nuclear tests for one year without prior agreement on an effective verification system.[37]

## COMMISSION REACTIONS

For more than a week in mid-May 1957, the Eisenhower Administration once again labored over its disarmament policy. And again, Strauss struggled above all else to protect the Commission's nuclear testing program. As he informed Gerard Smith, if the aerial inspection proposals were "fuzzy" and made no sense, Stassen's call for a test moratorium without verification was completely unacceptable to the Commission. While the Atomic Energy

Commission limited its comments to nuclear-related issues, Secretary of Defense Wilson attacked on a broader front by declaring that, despite the prolonged study and deliberation that had established the outer limits of American disarmament policy approved by the President on November 21, 1956, Stassen's new draft went "well beyond" anything that was sound or realistic for long-term agreement.[38]

On the test moratorium, the Commission was unanimous in support of Strauss. Libby had already reported that the Commission had obtained "no useful fallout information in Operation *Redwing*." In addition to intensive fallout studies planned for Operation *Plumbbob* in fall 1957, Libby announced that a "prime objective" of Operation *Hardtack*, scheduled for 1958, would be to establish accurate data on local fallout so that it could be distinguished from worldwide fallout. Murray, who had angered his fellow Commissioners with an article in *Life* magazine criticizing the United States for its reliance on hydrogen bombs, reminded the Commission that he continued to believe that the United States should unilaterally abandon tests of multimegaton thermonuclear weapons. At the same time, without safeguard agreements with the Soviet Union and other nations, Murray actually favored "greatly accelerating" tests of small, tactical weapons. Commissioner Vance added that a test moratorium might actually obstruct a disarmament agreement because the United States would be severely hampered in developing small nuclear weapons as suggested by Murray. Major General Alfred D. Starbird, director of the division of military application, probably best summed up the Commission's perception by observing that not only would a moratorium jeopardize weapon programs and laboratory budgets but also, once a moratorium on testing was accepted, strong public opinion would probably prevent resumption of testing unless the United States was overtly provoked by a foreign country.[39]

389

## THE SCHWEITZER APPEAL

While the London Disarmament Conference met and the American and the Russian negotiators continued to search for policies acceptable to both their governments and their adversaries, international opposition to nuclear testing continued to mount. In March 1957, the Japanese government had sent Professor Masateshi Matsushita on a special mission to the nuclear powers to request an end to nuclear testing. In April, Prime Minister Nehru of India again called for an end to testing, while the British Labour party advocated halting thermonuclear testing by international agreement despite the fact that the United Kingdom was about to test its first hydrogen bomb. In the same month, leading West German nuclear physicists, including Otto Hahn, pledged they would neither construct nor test nuclear weapons.[40]

The most dramatic appeal came from Albert Schweitzer, the world-famous musician, doctor, and philosopher in French Equitorial Africa. At the urging of Norman Cousins, editor of the *Saturday Review*, Schweitzer requested the Nobel Peace Prize Committee to provide a platform that would permit him to speak his conscience on testing. Schweitzer, who had been awarded the Nobel Peace Prize in 1952, was granted his request, and on April 24, 1957, Gunnar Jahn, chairman of the Norwegian committee, read the great humanitarian's appeal over Radio Oslo. Although beamed around the world to fifty countries, Schweitzer's message was not heard in the United States. With the exception of the *Saturday Review*, which printed the verbatim text, his statement was largely ignored by the American press. In India, however, Schweitzer's words received wide circulation. Within a few days the Pope endorsed his stand, and on May 10 the West German Bundestag asked the nuclear powers at the London disarmament talks to suspend testing. As if to reply, the British detonated their first thermonuclear test at Christmas Island on May 15 with an assurance by Prime Minister Macmillan that the fallout from the test was "almost negligible."[41]

390

At the Commission, Willard Libby, also a Nobel laureate, assumed personal responsibility for responding to Schweitzer. In an open letter, which received more press attention in the United States than did Schweitzer's original broadcast, Libby appealed to Schweitzer's scientific objectivity. Reiterating the data he had already made public and would again summarize before the American Physical Society on April 26, Libby argued that radiation exposure from fallout was much less than that required to produce observable effects in the general population. As the *New York Times* noted, testing involved taking some risks. But, as Libby asked rhetorically, "Are we willing to take this small and rigidly controlled risk, or would we prefer to run the risk of annihilation which might result if we surrendered the weapons which are so essential to our freedom and our survival?"[42]

Although Libby's response did not satisfy everyone, he was addressing the key issues. American scientists were becoming more concerned that the long-term effects of fallout would be far greater than Libby estimated. Even before Schweitzer's appeal, five Yale University biophysicists expressed their concern over the irreversible effects of radioactive fallout. Although the Yale professors did not advocate an immediate test ban, one of Libby's former students, Harrison Brown, professor of geophysics at the California Institute of Technology, sided with test-ban advocates when he challenged his mentor in the same issue of the *Saturday Review* that reprinted Libby's reply to Schweitzer. Obviously hurt by his student's rebuttal, Libby wrote Brown that his article was "pretty unobjective" but nevertheless conceded that Brown had "put the question pretty squarely." The question, of course, was what risks should Americans take in the pursuit of national security.[43]

On the same day that the British thermonuclear test thundered over Christmas Island, Linus Pauling, another Cal Tech scientist and Nobel Prize winner, told an honors assembly at Washington University in St. Louis that he opposed nuclear testing on humanitarian rather than scientific grounds. Acknowledging his debt to Schweitzer, Pauling stated that no human life should be risked in developing nuclear weapons "that could kill hundreds of millions of human beings, could devastate this beautiful world in which we live." Encouraged by the response from the university audience, Pauling decided to circulate a petition among American scientists calling for an end to nuclear tests. With the assistance of biologist Barry Commoner and physicist Edward Condon, both professors at Washington University, Pauling obtained in a few weeks the signatures of almost two thousand scientists, including Nobel laureate Hermann Muller and Laurence H. Snyder, president of the American Association for the Advancement of Science.[44]

391

## THE COMMISSION MODERATES ON TESTING ISSUE

The Commission's testing program came under increasing pressure, not only from the White House and the scientific community but also from the Congress. On March 7, 1957, the Joint Committee had announced it would hold hearings "to educate the Committee and the public" about the origins and hazards of radioactive fallout. Although the committee repeatedly insisted that its only purpose in holding the hearings would be to gather scientific information, the Commission could see the obvious implications that the hearings might have for American negotiators at the London disarmament talks. Accordingly, the Commission decided to prepare a "fall-back position" rather than risk being forced by the President to accept Stassen's plan for a test moratorium as a first step toward arms control. Although unable to find an acceptable formula for halting weapon tests without reliable inspection, the Commission was prepared to accept a limitation on tests by the nuclear powers to fifteen megatons per year.[45]

Before the Commission could even offer its "fall-back position," however, Stassen once again seized the initiative by offering modifications and clarification to his May 9 proposals. He anticipated the Commission's shift by proposing that resumption of limited testing be permitted after a twelve-month moratorium, providing advance notice was given and all tests were conducted with due regard to health. Strauss now devised his own "fall-back position," which he shared with Libby: the United States should accept an unverified testing moratorium only on the condition that the

Commission would resume testing after twelve months if adequate inspection controls were not devised. In that way, Strauss believed the Commission could resume testing without appearing to violate the disarmament agreement.[46]

## THE STASSEN PLAN DEBATED

On May 23, 1957, Stassen presented his newest disarmament proposals to the National Security Council. With Eisenhower present, Stassen reviewed the progress of the recent negotiations in London. The great question yet to be answered, Stassen said, was whether the United States would be willing to take the necessary risks involved in the first steps toward disarmament. Dulles noted that considerable disagreement remained within the government, but he expected the differences could be ironed out before Stassen returned to London. Throughout the meeting, which Strauss silently attended, Eisenhower probed deftly into the details of Stassen's plan. He also repeated his determination to halt the arms race, not only for moral but also for fiscal reasons. Secretary of the Treasury George Humphrey had warned him of severe budgetary and financial problems if military spending were to continue unchecked. Risks with the Russians were great, Eisenhower conceded, but so were the risks to the American economy in inflated defense budgets. The negotiations in London were no mere intellectual exercise, he noted in closing; "we have got to do something."[47]

Economic imperatives were also beginning to motivate the Russians. From London, American Ambassador John Hay Whitney reported that, according to Prime Minister Macmillan, the Russians faced "real economic problem[s]" of their own. The Soviet leaders were beginning to talk seriously of disarmament, but Macmillan was pessimistic that anything constructive would come from the London conference. He predicted that only a summit conference devoted solely to arms control could break the disarmament deadlock.[48]

Shortly after Macmillan and Whitney talked at 10 Downing Street, Eisenhower and Dulles met alone late one evening at the White House to review Stassen's proposals. With the President scheduled to meet his disarmament advisers the following morning, May 25, Dulles was anxious to iron out his differences with Eisenhower ahead of time. By coordinating his presentation with the President, Dulles hoped to avoid the embarrassment of seeing his ideas "hacked away" before Eisenhower had time to focus on the issues. While Dulles discussed the agenda with the President, Strauss was also working behind the scenes to line up supporters for continued testing. General Herbert B. Loper and Admiral Radford assured Strauss that Deputy Secretary of Defense Donald Quarles would join the Commission in opposing Stassen's proposal to suspend testing prior to agreement on inspection and verification. Strauss may not have been optimistic about his chances on the testing issue, but he was confident that he had the solid support of the Defense Department.[49]

On Saturday morning, May 25, Eisenhower met with a large group of advisers to discuss disarmament policy. Working from Stassen's May 9 proposal as amended on May 22, Dulles in turn reviewed each issue with the exception of testing. With the toughest question temporarily set aside, Dulles led the group through the next most difficult maze: how to implement Open Skies through aerial inspections and exchange of blueprints. Eisenhower apparently favored opening all the United States and all the Soviet Union to mutual overflights, as well as exchanging comprehensive "blueprints" of military installations, stockpiles, and armaments. From the American point of view, the United States would have gained much and lost little from such an exchange. If the Russians insisted that to be comprehensive Open Skies would have to include American overseas bases and allies, the United States would insist upon including Communist China. However intractable, the issues were highly negotiable.[50]

393

Dulles gradually worked through the agenda until by the end of the morning only the testing item remained. To Strauss's surprise, Quarles left the room at that point, leaving him as the lone spokesman for continued nuclear testing within the Administration. Strauss described Stassen's proposal as a major departure from the policy established by the President in November 1956 and reaffirmed by the Chief Executive prior to the London talks. Stassen's proposal was wrong, Strauss argued, because it reversed the proper sequence of events by suspending testing before an inspection system was in place. This was the basic, and fatal, flaw in Stassen's plan. There were other problems, to be sure, and Strauss insisted that the United States could not negotiate with the Soviet Union except from a position of strength. Although the United States could maintain indefinitely numerical superiority in nuclear weapons over the Russians, in time the Soviets would obtain sufficient numbers to render the American "lead" relatively unimportant. Strauss believed that the United States could maintain real "qualitative" superiority but not without testing. Through their own development programs and espionage, the Soviets constantly strove to match American weapon technology. Strauss pleaded with Eisenhower:

> To maintain our position of strength, we must continue to improve. We cannot continue to improve with our laboratories shrunken and weakened, and we cannot put improvements into stockpiled weapons without tests to see that the improvements are practical.[51]

To Strauss's amazement, Dulles countered with a suggestion that the Secretary of State attributed to the absent Quarles. The rebuttal was, in fact, basically Strauss's own fall-back position that he had confided to Libby the previous day: the United States would suspend testing for twelve months, after which tests would be resumed if no inspection agreement had been signed. Future tests would be announced through the United Nations and would include limited attendance as had been suggested at the recent Bermuda conference. Libby had subsequently lunched with Quarles, with whom he shared Strauss's strategy, and now the chairman sat helpless, apparently "sunk by my own guns." Bail as he might, Strauss could not convince Eisenhower that the weapon laboratories were in jeopardy or that plans to develop small clean bombs for air defense would falter.

When the debate was virtually over, Quarles returned to the meeting but did not participate in the discussion. According to Strauss, no one spoke from the defense side of the table, although after the meeting adjourned both Radford and Loper privately expressed their distress. Thus, the meeting ended with the President endorsing Strauss's fall-back position on Stassen's proposal to end nuclear testing as presented by Dulles but attributed to Quarles. Again Eisenhower reaffirmed his willingness to make real concessions to end the arms race. At the same time, he expressed confidence that Strauss and the Commission would find a way to keep the laboratories strong and intact.

394

## LONDON CONFERENCE RECONVENES

As the Joint Committee launched its public hearings on the effects of fallout, Stassen returned to London with fresh instructions and renewed determination to secure a disarmament agreement with the Soviet Union. On May 28 and 30, he briefed British officials on the new policy, concentrating almost exclusively on provisions relating to nuclear arms control. Although Stassen did not outline the American position for the British in writing, he summarized the main points relating to testing, first use of nuclear weapons, transfer of special nuclear material to international stockpiles, and the cutoff of the production of weapon-grade nuclear material.[52]

Inexplicably, on the following day, May 31, despite instructions to the contrary, Stassen gave Zorin an "informal memorandum" that delineated the new American disarmament policy. Herter had warned Stassen not to engage in serious negotiations until the President had approved the policy statement in which all parties concurred. Stassen's incredible behavior can be explained by his eagerness "to do something" to end the arms race as directed by the President and perhaps by his political ambitions. Actually, he had prepared two documents: the first reflected his understanding of the meeting on May 25; and the second presented his "informal" interpretation of the new American position to Zorin.[53] Although he had not compromised an official document, his friendly memorandum to Zorin seemed to commit NATO allies to American policy without prior consultation, while at the same time actually misrepresenting the United States' new position.

Consternation was palpable on both sides of the Atlantic, although for very different reasons. In Europe allied leaders were incensed because Stassen, without their consent, had proposed opening most of Western Europe to Soviet aerial inspection. Earlier Dulles had assured West German Chancellor Adenauer that a European zone would not be included in an Open Skies agreement during the first stage of disarmament and certainly would not be established without the consent of America's European allies. Open Skies had been a relatively minor issue at the meeting on May 25. Now Stassen had not only aggravated the NATO allies, but he seemed to commit the Eisenhower Administration to policies not agreed to in Washington and to which the military and the Commission were strongly opposed. Dulles, Strauss, and others met to see how they could repair the damage Stassen had caused.[54]

395

For the Commission, Stassen's faux pas was fortuitous because it allowed Strauss to reopen the testing issue while impugning Stassen's reliability as a disarmament negotiator. According to Strauss, Stassen had oversimplified, glossed over, and outright misrepresented American policy. Although Strauss conceded that Stassen's memoranda were generally in accord with the White House agreements, he was distressed that Stassen had played down the inspection system as pro forma. For Strauss, safeguards remained the chief stumbling block to an arms control agreement, not the relatively simple matter that Stassen implied. Angered by Stassen's behavior, Dulles seemed to agree with Strauss's assessment when he privately criticized Stassen for observing "the letter of the law" but skewing it to create "a different impression."[55]

Once again, the famous Eisenhower temper roared within the safe confines of the White House. Furious, the President promised that Dulles would take the necessary steps to correct any misunderstandings. Eisenhower knew the wisdom of not overreacting, but at the same time he was determined to put both Zorin and Stassen on notice that the United States envoy had acted without sanction. Accepting Dulles's advice, Eisenhower bowed to a cooler approach in dealing with Stassen, the Russians, and America's NATO partners.[56]

While Dulles quietly mollified anxious diplomats and government officials at home and abroad, Eisenhower tried to clarify his arms limitation policy in a press conference on June 5. The continuing Joint Committee hearings had intensified public concerns about fallout. In response, Eisenhower told reporters he "would like to allay all anxiety in the world by a total and complete ban of all testing, based upon total disarmament." At the same time, he asserted the importance of testing to develop clean weapons. Clearly, Strauss had not labored in vain. A test ban could only be part of the first step toward disarmament, according to the President, if it were accompanied by an acceptable inspection system.[57]

In London, Stassen assured reporters that the United States had not yet presented official proposals to the Russians. All discussions had been "entirely preliminary," he asserted. Then, almost offhandedly, he mentioned that he intended to return to the United States to attend his son's graduation from the University of Virginia on Monday, June 10. The trip home would be strictly personal "with no official business," Stassen announced. He did not tell the press, however, that on orders from Dulles to withdraw his "informal memorandum" he had asked Zorin to return the paper. On June 8 Zorin further complicated matters by handing Stassen a formal Soviet reply to the as-yet-unofficial American proposals.[58]

## STASSEN REPRIMANDED

396

Stassen spent a busy "holiday" in Washington, after celebrating his son's graduation in Charlottesville. Both to Dulles and Herter, Stassen insisted that he had neither violated his instructions nor slighted NATO allies. On the contrary, Stassen countered, he had consulted with the Western delegations on "all points" prior to his meeting with Zorin. The trouble was that the Russians resented the fact that NATO partners, although not represented at the disarmament talks, were nonetheless privy to American policy. Impatient, Zorin had complained to Stassen that he was placed in an impossible position by being the last to learn about the new American proposals. When the Russian had intimated that he might be forced to break off negotiations, Stassen decided to brief his Soviet counterpart informally. Although he had committed no impropriety, he admitted he had angered the British.[59]

Stassen's explanation, however, hardly settled the matter. Zorin reportedly had cautioned that any withdrawal of Stassen's paper "would be detrimental to negotiations." Like a tar-baby, the Americans appeared to be stuck with Stassen's paper whether they liked it or not. As Dulles complained to Senator Knowland, there was even some danger that the Russians might make a commitment that would throw into the Senate's lap an inadequate arms limitation treaty to ratify or reject.[60]

On June 11, with Herter as his witness, Dulles severely reprimanded Stassen for his conduct in London. Acknowledging Stassen's good intentions, Dulles expressed his "shock" and worry over Stassen's apparent insensitivity to diplomatic protocols. Dulles demanded that Stassen refrain from circulating unauthorized documents "without advice and consent from the Department." As a further measure, Dulles informed Stassen that he was appointing a foreign service officer as Stassen's deputy with special responsibilities to provide liaison between NATO and the State Department. The following day Dulles sent almost identical assurances to Macmillan and Adenauer: "that with Presidential authority I have had a very thorough review of disarmament proposals with Governor Stassen and that the President and I feel certain that there will be no repetition of unauthorized procedures."[61]

Despite these assurances, Dulles did not intend to give America's NATO partners a veto over United States' disarmament policy. Unless disarmament progress was made soon, Dulles feared that several nations, including the United States, might begin unilateral disarmament under the pressures of public opinion and the high costs of military expenditures. He realized that the development of nuclear weapons was in its infancy and that the crude weapons then available were a deterrent only because they were weapons of mass destruction. With the development of more sophisticated tactical nuclear weapons, however, Dulles believed the eventual use of nuclear weapons in war would become inevitable. Ironically, as the era of massive retaliation ended, the likelihood of nuclear warfare increased, especially as fourth powers were able to obtain cheaper, smaller weapons. Dulles could see no way out of this dilemma. Gradually, NATO would become obsolete as the credibility of America's atomic shield diminished and France, and possibly others, obtained nuclear capability. For that reason, Dulles did not believe that NATO sensitivity over European inspection zones should be allowed to derail the disarmament talks.[62]

397

## THE SOVIET RESPONSE

Stassen's first task on returning to London in June was to build support among America's NATO allies for the United States' position on the first phase of disarmament. These NATO consultations, including deliberations of the Western Four and separate bilateral discussions between the Americans and the British, French, and Canadians, would build consensus on the issues of aerial inspection, test ban, cutoff of the production of special nuclear materials for weapons, and reduction of conventional armaments.[63]

No sooner had Stassen returned to London when, on June 14, Zorin announced that the Soviet Union was willing to accept a nuclear test ban with international control and supervision. Mindful that the Western powers would not agree to an unconditional test ban, Zorin proposed a temporary moratorium for a period of two or three years. Most significantly, the Soviet government, with a view to removing the major obstacle to a test moratorium agreement, proposed that an international inspection commission establish control posts in the United States, the United Kingdom, the Soviet Union, and the Pacific test area.[64] The Russians had made an important concession, and the Allies immediately recognized it. For the first time in the history of postwar disarmament talks, the Soviet Union was ready to consider establishing inspection posts within the Russian heartland. Stassen's foreign policy objective to breach the Iron Curtain now actually seemed obtainable.

At his June 19 news conference the President was clearly buoyed up by the prospects of a test moratorium. "I would be perfectly delighted," he told reporters, "to make some satisfactory arrangement for temporary suspension of tests while we could determine whether we couldn't make some agreements that would allow it to be a permanent arrangement." The President also reiterated the importance of reliable safeguards but noted that a test ban was not necessarily linked to an agreement on controlling the production of special nuclear material. Assuring the press that he was "intimately acquainted" with the American position presented by Stassen in London, he declined further detailed comment except to confirm his belief that the disarmament conference was not merely a sounding board for propaganda but a real possibility for general agreement.[65]

398

## THE COMMISSION'S CLEAN BOMB INITIATIVE

Both justifying further testing and answering international concern over fallout, the Atomic Energy Commission had been touting the clean bomb since the 1956 elections. Shortly after he returned from the Enewetak Proving Grounds in July 1956, Strauss had announced that the Commission had discovered new possibilities for perfecting nuclear weapons that concentrated maximum destruction on targets while reducing widespread fallout. Just weeks before his reelection, Eisenhower had reported that the *Redwing* tests had increased the United States' ability "to harness and discipline our weapons more precisely and effectively." As if to endorse the need for continued testing, the President concluded that "further progress along this line is confidently expected."[66]

When the Commission again boasted of progress in its "clean bomb program" on May 29, 1957, the Joint Committee called foul. Coming just four days after the President had approved his new disarmament policy and in the midst of the Joint Committee's fallout hearings, the Commission's announcement smelled of politics. With Senator Anderson's concurrence, Congressman Holifield charged that the Commission was misleading both the Joint Committee and the American people on the potential "cleanliness" of large, multimegaton thermonuclear weapons.[67]

Almost three thousand miles away in Livermore, California, Senator Henry Jackson spent Memorial Day visiting with Ernest Lawrence, Edward Teller, and the laboratory staff. Among other issues, Jackson was particularly interested in the future production requirements for plutonium and tritium at Hanford and Savannah River. His questions naturally led to discussions about the development of weapon systems, the necessity for testing, and the consequences of a test moratorium for the work at the weapon laboratories. As a result of their meeting, Jackson invited the scientists to share their views on production requirements with the Joint Committee's Subcommittee on Military Applications, which the Senator chaired.

At the hearings on June 20, Jackson introduced Lawrence, Teller, and Mark Mills from the Livermore Laboratory. Recalling his recent trip to California, Jackson reported that he "was particularly impressed with the progress that they were making in low-yield weapons, the possibility of making them smaller, the possibility of making them cleaner," and, as he noted, "the gleam in the scientists' eye of making them almost like Ivory Soap, [but] not quite."

In their testimony the California scientists presented a simple but powerful argument for increasing plutonium production and continuing testing. According to the scientists, plutonium weapons could be made smaller, cheaper, and more versatile than uranium weapons; and coincidentally, fusion weapons with very low fission yield would be cleaner than existing hydrogen weapons. As Teller explained it, the United States knew how to build "dirty" bombs of almost unlimited size, but smaller weapons using plutonium still remained to be perfected. For Lawrence the moral choice was stark and unambiguous. "If we stop testing," he warned the committee, "well, God forbid . . . we will have to use weapons that will kill 50 million people that need not have been killed." Somehow, Lawrence said, the American people had to realize the "crime" that would be committed if the United States had to use dirty bombs in war. No one described clean bombs as humane, but Lawrence, Teller, and Mills were moved by no less a moral imperative than Schweitzer or Pauling. Because they believed the fallout hazards from testing were negligible, they thought it would be "wrong," "misguided," and "foolish" to ban the development of weapons that might spare countless millions from nuclear holocaust.[68]

The next day, June 21, Lawrence, Teller, and Mills shared the same message with the full Joint Committee. Again Lawrence repeated his assertion that "it would be a crime against the people" to stop testing. Graphically, Teller described how an attack on Vladivostock might result in the death of thousands of Japanese as fallout drifted eastward. It was imperative for the United States to develop nuclear weapons that limited their destruction to the immediate area of the target. "Dirty" weapons, like poison gas, could contaminate friends and foes alike. In Teller's view, the United States would enjoy an enormous military and psychological advantage in a limited war if it could employ clean weapons while the Russians had no choice but to contaminate innocent populations with fallout from dirty bombs. Furthermore, the United States would be placed in an impossible position should the Soviets secretly develop their own clean weapons during a test ban while an international treaty prohibited the United States from doing so.

399

Alarmed, Senators Bricker and Pastore wanted to know whether the President, Strauss, or Stassen knew of the imperatives to develop clean weapons. Bricker was haunted by the belief that the recent Joint Committee fallout hearings simply fed Russian propaganda by focusing almost exclusively on the potential dangers of radioactive fallout. The President should know and the Joint Committee's report on fallout should reflect, Bricker said, that continued testing was necessary to perfect the clean bomb, which would "do more to preserve the peace of the world than anything we could do."

Teller next described various ways by which the Soviet Union could hide underground and upper atmospheric testing during a test ban. He explained how the Russians could muffle underground megaton tests so as to confuse seismic monitoring. Again the Joint Committee wanted to know whether the Administration was aware of this information. Lawrence was embarrassed because as Stassen's adviser he had a clear obligation to keep the Administration adequately informed of technical and scientific impediments to a test ban; instead, Lawrence and his colleagues were actually undermining Congressional confidence in the London negotiations. As diplomatically as possible, Teller explained that Stassen had been briefed on the general possibilities of hiding nuclear explosions, but he did not think that Stassen had heard of the most recent methods. How could he when Paul Foster, representing the Commission at the hearing, admitted that the Commission had learned only the day before about the possibility of an elaborate "clandestine subterranean explosion"?[69]

The Joint Committee members were shocked. On the one hand, everything about which Lawrence, Teller, and Mills had testified pointed in the direction of continuing nuclear testing; on the other, the reports from London all indicated that Stassen was moving in the opposite direction. Although the committee rejected the idea of recalling Stassen from London to testify, Congressman Cole by telephone personally arranged for the Californians to see the President.

Strauss, Lawrence, Teller, and Mills met with Eisenhower for forty minutes on June 24. For the third time that week, Lawrence repeated his litany that the United States' failure to develop clean weapons "could truly be a 'crime against humanity.'" On cue, Teller reviewed the arguments for developing small, tactical fusion weapons, including the psychological and propaganda onus of not producing them. Lawrence proposed inviting a United Nations team to the United States tests to verify that the Americans were testing clean weapons, and Teller outlined how nuclear explosions could actually be used for peaceful purposes.

In contrast to the Joint Committee's reaction, Eisenhower remained calm, albeit interested in the briefing. Tactfully, he agreed that no one could oppose the development program his visitors had outlined. Nevertheless, he reminded them of the mounting worldwide debate over testing.

Grimly, Eisenhower lectured the nuclear scientists that the United States could not "permit itself to be 'crucified on a cross of atoms.'" Furthermore, he emphasized that the test-ban proposals had been offered in the context of stopping war and were, after all, part of the disarmament package. When Mills and Teller tried to counter that a nuclear test ban could not be policed with certainty, Eisenhower responded that testing had not only fueled intense Soviet propaganda but also actually divided American public opinion. When Teller tried to discredit Pauling's open letter by noting how few scientists from the Berkeley campus had actually signed the statement, Eisenhower conceded that, although Pauling might be wrong, so many people were reading "fearsome and horrible" reports about fallout that they were having a substantial effect. Perhaps he could say something in his next news conference to clarify the matter by explaining that the United States wanted to continue testing principally "to clean up weapons and thus protect civilians in event of war."[70]

401

As the scientists were about to leave, Eisenhower wryly suggested that in the long run the United States might want "the other fellow" to have clean weapons, too—and perhaps it would be desirable for Americans to share their techniques with the Russians. The scientists were dumbfounded by this remark. To the President, and later to Andrew J. Goodpaster, White House staff secretary, just in case Eisenhower had not gotten the point, the visitors stressed that American weapons incorporated technical advances that the United States would not want to give to the Soviets. Teller again raised the ugly possibility that the Russians might secretly perfect a clean bomb as well as clean, peaceful explosives while the United States had no options but dirty weapons. Teller also noted, parenthetically, that it was comparatively easy to contaminate clean weapons with "additives."[71]

Lawrence, Teller, and Mills profoundly impressed both Eisenhower and the White House staff and temporarily succeeded in shaking the President's commitment to a nuclear test ban. Following the meeting, Eisenhower complained to Dulles that he had received suggestions from so many people that he was confused. He was especially upset that Strauss and his friends made "it look like a crime to ban tests." As Eisenhower recalled their argument, the most promising peaceful uses of atomic science ironically depended upon developing (and testing) a clean weapon. For the President the most painful dilemma was facing a future dependent on still another round of weapon development. Dulles admitted that the United States could not agree to a test ban independent of sound inspection requirements and other disarmament agreements.[72]

Writing to Strauss, Bromley Smith, National Security Adviser Cutler's assistant, summarized the disturbing implications of what the scientists had told the President. Smith acknowledged that the scientists not only had a professional interest in testing but also perhaps "an unconscious desire to reduce the horror of nuclear weapons which they are responsible in large part for creating." Yet, whatever the scientists' motives, they had convinced Smith that without reliable policing the risks of a test ban were too high. As he reported to Strauss, Smith now strongly urged Cutler to give Strauss another chance to present the case against a test ban to the President.[73]

Although Eisenhower understood the implications of the scientists' briefing, he was unwilling to abandon hope for success in the disarmament talks. As promised, at news conferences on June 26 and July 3 Eisenhower expressed his interest in developing clean bombs and peaceful nuclear explosives, but he did not preclude a test ban, as the scientists had wanted. Indeed, the President spoke as if clean bombs whose fallout had been reduced by 96 percent were an accomplished fact. Furthermore, he indicated that within four or five years, with adequate testing, the United States could develop an "absolutely clean bomb." If the President worried the scientists because he slightly exaggerated even their most optimistic claims, he must have satisfied them by adding his hope that the Soviets would also "learn how to use clean bombs."[74]

In New York, David Lilienthal could only shake his head in disgust over the newspaper reports of Lawrence, Teller, and Strauss meeting with the President to promote clean bombs. "The irony of this is so grotesque," he confided to his journal, "it is rather charming." Lilienthal recalled that the same trio had once been so certain that the super H-bomb, "big as all hell," would be the salvation of the country. Ruefully, he also noted that it had been people like himself, and Oppenheimer he might have added, whose patriotism or good sense had been questioned because they harbored doubts about the development of the thermonuclear bomb. Now with the weapon laboratories threatened by disarmament, the super-bomb scientists stumped for small, clean tactical weapons not too different from what Oppenheimer had advocated just four years previously. In sum, Lilienthal characterized the promoters of the clean bomb as pathetic, transparent, and greedy.[75]

## CHAPTER 15

# POLITICS OF THE PEACEFUL ATOM

The results of the 1956 election gave Lewis Strauss new incentives for promoting the development of nuclear power by private enterprise. On the one hand, the overwhelming endorsement of President Eisenhower at the polls led Strauss to believe that he had a mandate for assigning to private industry most of the responsibility and the financial burden for building the new atomic energy industry. Federal support, Strauss believed, should be confined only to those essential activities in research and development that industry could not or would not undertake. On the other hand, the Democrats had consolidated their hold on both the Senate and the House, and Senator Anderson, although no longer chairman of the Joint Committee, was still in a strong position of leadership. Strauss could anticipate another searching policy debate with the committee at the annual Section 202 hearings in February and another battle with the Democratic Congress over the Gore-Holifield bill. Rather than seeking compromise and conciliation, Strauss proposed to strike out boldly to complete the transfer of certain nuclear technology from government to private hands. If private industry could be induced to finance, build, and operate nuclear power plants incorporating each promising reactor design, there would be no need for the Gore-Holifield bill or "atomic TVAs."[1] Foreign affairs as well as domestic politics, however, frustrated Strauss at every turn.

## THE EURATOM CHALLENGE

The Suez crisis in fall 1956, and to a lesser extent the Hungarian revolution of the same year, revitalized EURATOM negotiations in Brussels by emphasizing the need to develop nuclear energy as rapidly as possible as an alternative to Middle Eastern oil. On November 6, the day after the initial French and British paratroop assaults on Port Said (and election day in the United States), the French and Germans settled their differences, paving the way for approval of EURATOM. The Germans agreed that EURATOM should have a monopoly on the purchase of nuclear fuel; and EURATOM would control but not fully own all fissionable material used in the reactors. The treaty would also allow the French to engage in nuclear weapon development with tests permitted four years later. Provided that the agency's inspection and control authority were acceptable, the community would have access to French weapon research and development as well as to the resulting weapon stockpile.[2]

Despite the international crisis and the election campaign, Eisenhower was kept well informed of the developments in Brussels. Dulles and Strauss urged the President to use the Middle East situation as a lever for immediate action on EURATOM. It was important, they advised, for Eisenhower to offer tangible support for EURATOM by advising Paul-Henri Spaak that the United States urgently wanted to discuss cooperative research and development that would help reduce European dependence on Middle Eastern oil. But as Jean Monnet, the veteran French diplomat, later noted, still unresolved was whether the United States would require international agency controls over nuclear materials provided by the United States Atomic Energy Commission. Not overawed by the Suez crisis, Monnet flatly stated that, if the United States had any intentions of imposing international controls over EURATOM activities, it would be better to abandon EURATOM at once. Smarting from military defeat, the French were in no mood to welcome visits from either Russian or Egyptian inspectors representing the international agency.[3]

Capitalizing on the sense of urgency generated by the Suez war in November 1956, the Brussels conference appointed a committee of three to formulate a politically and technically feasible nuclear power program that would contribute quickly to meeting the energy needs of the Community of Six. Designated as the Three Wise Men were Louis Armand, head of a technical committee of the French Atomic Energy Commissariat; Franz Etzel, vice-president of the Coal and Steel Community; and Francesco Giordani, former chairman of the Italian atomic energy commission. Their official assignment was to determine how quickly nuclear power stations could be constructed, to establish reasonable production targets, and to identify financial and budgetary problems. An equally important aim, however, was to stimulate interest in Europe and the United States. With these interests in mind, Dulles, with Strauss's concurrence, immediately invited the Three Wise Men to the United States to meet with the president, the Atomic Energy Commission, and the Joint Committee.[4]

The arrival of the Wise Men along with Spaak not only enlivened the Washington social scene but also forced the Commission and the State Department to hammer out a policy for EURATOM that would conform to the bilateral agreements already in force. Not wanting further to strain his relationship with Strauss, Dulles encouraged Monnet to explain the risks of negotiating a bilateral agreement with West Germany before consummating a EURATOM agreement. Echoing Spaak's belief that a separate power bilateral with West Germany would be fatal to EURATOM, Monnet played on Strauss's vanity by suggesting that Strauss would receive greater acclaim by waiting and concluding a major agreement with EURATOM than by making a smaller deal with the Germans alone. Meanwhile with Monnet's blessing, the State Department convinced the Germans, the Italians, and the French to confine their bilateral requests to specific projects, which could later be encompassed with the EURATOM community. As Gerard Smith later explained to Strauss, each ambassador had agreed to submit proposals for well-defined nuclear power projects with the clear understanding that any agreements reached with the United States would be only temporary pending establishment of EURATOM.[5]

405

Dulles received the Three Wise Men with enthusiasm. He told Strauss that their mission would be of great political importance to both Europe and the United States. Dulles was inclined to accept the Wise Men's opinion that a constructive relationship between Middle East oil-producing states and Europe was impossible as long as Europe was totally dependent on Arab oil imports. Without referring to the United States' corporate oil interests, Dulles saw the Wise Men's proposal as a "bold program of building nuclear power stations." Consequently, Dulles believed, American assistance would not only promote European economic solidarity but also reestablish friendship and cooperation between Western Europe and the United States following the strains that developed during the Suez crisis.[6]

## DOMESTIC IMPLICATIONS

For Strauss the key to developing nuclear power was not international cooperation but the domestic power demonstration program, launched by the Commission just two years earlier in the closing days of 1954. Although industry response to the first two invitations had been gratifying, progress in building the nuclear plants had been slow. To forestall renewed Democratic demands in 1957 for a massive federal effort, Strauss had encouraged the Commission to issue a third invitation late in 1956. The third round of invitations offered private industry more flexibility in developing engineering proposals and more liberal terms for government assistance than the two earlier versions had permitted. Strauss anticipated a prompt response from industry early in 1957, long before the Joint Committee could introduce a new version of the Gore-Holifield bill.

Strauss's plan for a self-starting nuclear industry, however, contained one dangerous flaw: its success necessarily depended upon the initiative of private business leaders acting in the interests of their own companies. In the face of new economic and political pressures, Strauss would have very little opportunity to respond in a way convincing to his antagonists in Congress. This inherent weakness in Strauss's leadership became apparent when the Commissioners considered their response to the EURATOM proposal. Commissioner Vance at once saw "the necessity that we develop and adopt as quickly as possible a separate and distinct policy for promoting the building of nuclear power plants abroad by American manufacturers—a plan . . . characterized by boldness and imagination." The nation's domestic plan for nuclear power, Vance observed, was quite properly based upon a careful and deliberate development of power reactor technology by government and industry. The energy crisis in Western Europe, however, demanded a quicker response than domestic needs required. Europe clearly faced the prospect of importing 100 million tons of coal annually at a cost of $2 billion. By 1975, the requirement might run to the "impossible level" of 300 million tons and $6 billion annually. [7]

To meet that demand, the EURATOM leaders were seriously proposing to bring into operation in the mid-1960s nuclear power plants with an aggregate capacity of fifteen million electrical kilowatts. Vance believed that the reactors selected to meet the European demand would be either slightly enriched, water-cooled reactors like those being built by Westinghouse and General Electric in the United States or a natural uranium, gas-cooled reactor developed by the British. Because electricity produced at nine to twelve mills per kilowatt of installed capacity would be competitive in Europe, Vance was confident that American designs could be made attractive to EURATOM. The United States could also offer help in improving the design of fuel elements, assure the Europeans of a reliable supply of enriched fuel, and offer the advantages of standardized, economical mass production that America's rapidly growing nuclear technology made possible.

No member of either the Commission or the Joint Committee was prepared to reject Vance's argument for a strong American bid, but there was broad disagreement about how the nation could or should respond. At the 202 hearings later that month, Strauss made his now familiar case for giving the responsibility to private industry. Commissioner Murray responded with his equally familiar argument that the national interest required the Commission to lead the way by building full-scale power plants using each promising reactor design. Two years' experience with the power demonstration program had proved to Murray that private industry could not finance such an effort, that industry had badly underestimated the difficulties involved in designing and building nuclear power plants, and that

406

industry opposition to any form of government development originated in an irrational fear of an "atomic TVA."[8]

Senator Anderson, Congressman Holifield, and other members of the Joint Committee used the hearings to bring out the fact that inflation and rising estimates of plant costs were already dampening industry interest in nuclear power. Compared to Britain's aggressive plan for building gas-cooled power reactors, the American program looked small and unfocused. The only full-scale nuclear plant then under construction in the United States was the Shippingport unit, but escalating construction costs at Shippingport threatened to push electrical rates from that plant to five to ten times those of fossil-fueled power stations. From the perspective of competitive economics, Shippingport was hardly an attractive selling point for American technology.[9]

407

## THE QUESTION OF SUBSIDY

Within the limitations of Strauss's private enterprise philosophy, the Commission could not do much more to meet the EURATOM challenge than advocate for American manufacturers forms of assistance that would make the United States competitive in the European market. During spring 1957, the Commission considered several staff proposals that would have given development allowances to American companies. These allowances would have covered research and development costs for all components of the plant so as to reduce capital costs charged to European producers. Similar allowances for manufacturing improved fuel elements and reactor cores would have helped to reduce operating costs, thereby making American reactors more competitive with British units. The assistance plan would have cost $200 million over twelve years and was intended to result in the sale and construction of at least one million kilowatts of nuclear capacity for EURATOM utilities by 1967, the target date established by the Three Wise Men.[10]

Strauss found it impossible to push the allowance plan through the Commission with only Libby's support. Both Murray and Vance had strong reservations about it, and with no one appointed to von Neumann's seat following his death in February there was no tie-breaking vote. Murray was pleased that the Commission was now prepared to advocate a million-kilowatt program, which he had urged a year earlier, but he did not believe private industry could meet the goal either with or without the allowances. Vance feared that both Congress and the public would consider the allowances a subsidy of European power stations, a move that seemed unacceptable when neither the Commission nor the Administration was prepared to grant subsidies for domestic projects. Vance also doubted that Congress would even appropriate enough money to support the program. In place of the allowance plan, Vance proposed much less costly measures that he believed would apply more directly to the needs of the European market: firm commitments to furnish enriched fuel for each reactor built, assurances that chemical processing facilities for spent fuel elements would be available, a commitment to purchase all plutonium generated in the power reactors, liberal terms for selling or leasing uranium or reactor materials such as heavy water, and some solution to the problem of third-party liability for American manufacturers. Such measures, Vance thought, would compete with potential British offers to reprocess or repurchase spent fuel elements for fixed amounts and to guarantee the performance of fuel elements. Neither Strauss, Libby, nor the Commission staff accepted Vance's proposals, and the whole question was put aside pending new appointments to the Commission.[11]

408

## NEW FACES ON THE COMMISSION

In June 1957, Strauss had an opportunity to fill two vacancies on the Commission. Despite determined efforts by the Democratic majority on the Joint Committee to obtain Murray's reappointment, Strauss's relentless antagonist was forced to retire from the Commission but not from the debate over nuclear policy. As a consultant to the Joint Committee he continued to speak out until the end of the Eisenhower Administration. Much as Strauss might have hoped to replace Murray and von Neumann with congenial colleagues, his deteriorating relationship with the Joint Committee suggested the need for at least a show of conciliation. Thus, neither seat went to a Republican or to a Strauss associate. To fill out von Neumann's term, the President appointed John S. Graham, a fifty-one-year-old lawyer who had served in the Navy during World War II and as Assistant Secretary of the Treasury during Truman's second term. A Democrat, Graham had been national treasurer of Volunteers for Stevenson in 1956. During the early Eisenhower years, he had made his way successfully in Washington as a financial and business consultant. Graham was prepared to assume Murray's role as spokesman within the Commission for the Democratic majority on the Joint Committee, but he lacked Murray's detailed knowledge of the Commission's program, his predecessor's technical knowledge as an engineer, and, most of all, Murray's stubborn partisanship. The full five-year term went to John F. Floberg who, like Graham, was a Navy veteran of World War II and a lawyer. Ten years younger than Graham, Floberg had been Assistant Secretary of the Navy for Air during Truman's second term, but he considered himself an independent. His only contact with the Commission had come during his Pentagon service, when he had supported Rickover in his fight for nuclear propulsion in the Navy.[12] Strauss could not count on either Graham or Floberg for automatic support, but neither would he have to endure the kind of persistent and sometimes spiteful opposition that Murray had brought to Commission meetings.

## THE CONGRESSIONAL INITIATIVE

The stalemate over reactor policy and the transition in Commission membership cost Strauss the initiative he had sought in his continuing struggle with the Democratic members of the Joint Committee. While Strauss was trying vainly to forge a credible response to the EURATOM challenge, Senator Anderson was moving ahead on all fronts to turn the Democratic defeats on atomic energy legislation in 1956 into solid victories in 1957. In March 1957 Anderson told Strauss that his failure to join the Democrats in a compromise nuclear power bill in 1956 had given Gore the chance to push his extreme measure through the Senate. This year, Anderson said, he planned to come up with a more workable solution, and he warned Strauss that the insurance indemnity bill, which the nuclear manufacturers demanded, would be bottled up until Strauss showed more signs of cooperating with the committee on nuclear power legislation.[13]

409

As things turned out, Anderson soon received help from an unexpected source. On April 16, Congressman Clarence Cannon, the crusty old chairman of the House Appropriations Committee, launched a blistering attack on the Commission's power demonstration reactor program. Cannon claimed that, because no project had been specifically authorized by Congress, the Commission—and in some instances the Joint Committee—had acted outside the authority of the Atomic Energy Act. Few people seemed to take seriously Cannon's charges of illegality, but the incident gave Anderson and the Joint Committee Democrats a new opportunity to gain leverage over the Commission's nuclear power program. Under existing law, the cooperative program was supported with funds from the operating budget and, hence, was not subject to Congressional authorization. If, as Cannon suggested, the act were amended to require authorization of demonstration projects, the Joint Committee would have a voice in determining which projects were approved and on what terms.

Anderson and his colleagues knew that open support of Cannon's position would expose them to charges of delaying the nuclear power projects, but they could offer to "cooperate" with the Commission by authorizing the projects as Cannon had demanded without changing the law. Although unhappy about establishing such a precedent, the Commissioners acquiesced in the process. Privately, in considering Strauss's plan for development allowances, they had concluded that the authorization process was the only way of both spreading the costs over several budget years and avoiding at the outset seeking all the operating funds needed for such projects. Thus, the act was not amended, and the Commission appeared before the Joint Committee to seek the authorization just as if it had been. The results were what both sides anticipated: the total authorization for the demonstration reactor program covered all the surviving projects in the first and second round and $30 million for the third round. The committee also added two new government projects: an experimental reactor to test the recycling of plutonium fuel at Hanford and engineering studies for a natural-uranium, graphite-moderated, gas-cooled power reactor.[14]

Once the authorization bill had been revised to the satisfaction of Joint Committee Democrats, Congressman Price and Senator Anderson introduced the insurance indemnity measure, which quickly passed both houses. The act required, among other things, that operators of large power reactors carry the maximum amount of insurance coverage available from private companies. The licensees and their suppliers were indemnified by the act for $500 million over the amount of private coverage available, and public liability was limited for each accident to the total amount of federal and private protection. Thus was established the Price-Anderson Act, which in the 1960s became a controversial issue in the nuclear power debate. Also, reflecting the Joint Committee's dispute with the Commission over the construction permit for the Fermi power reactor project, the new law made the Commission's advisory committee on reactor safeguards a statutory body and required that its reports be made public.[15]

## FADING PROSPECTS FOR NUCLEAR POWER

During winter 1957, Kenneth Davis, the Commission's director of reactor development, had tried to bolster the sagging spirits of American industrial leaders, who were becoming increasingly disillusioned by the fading prospects for nuclear power. Davis told the Nuclear Congress in March that his long-range estimates for nuclear capacity were somewhat higher than they had been two years earlier, more than 227,000 megawatts by 1980, compared to 175,000 predicted for that date in 1955. Nuclear power costs were certain to be high for first-generation plants like Shippingport, but Davis believed that economics of scale and standardization would likely bring costs into the range of nine to twelve mills per kilowatt-hour by the mid-1960s. Further improvements, Davis thought, might bring power costs down to six or seven mills by 1980.[16]

Despite Davis's optimistic prediction, achievement in the Commission's reactor program continued to be unimpressive in 1957. It was true that the five reactor experiments in the original five-year program had now grown to twelve projects, which included studies of a wide variety of reactor designs. Of the five experimental reactors that had been operated, however, two had revealed serious design problems, two were only in the initial

410

**Table 2**

**The United States Nuclear Reactor Program, Status in June 1957**

*GOVERNMENT PROJECTS*

| Reactor | Location | Design Power (ekw) | Status |
|---------|----------|--------------------|--------|
| *Five-Year Program* | | | |
| Experimental Breeder Reactor No. 1 | NRTS[a] | 200 | Shut down for new core |
| Experimental Boiling Water Reactor | ANL[b] | 5,000 | Initial testing |
| Homogeneous Reactor Experiment No. 2 | ORNL[c] | 300 | Shut down for leaks |
| Sodium Reactor Experiment | Santa Susanna, CA | 20,000 | Initial testing |
| Pressurized Water Reactor | Shippingport, PA | 60,000 | Nearing completion |
| *Experimental Power Reactor Program* | | | |
| Boiling Water Reactor Experiment No. 4 | NRTS[a] | 2,400 | Testing fuel rods |
| Argonne Boiling Water Reactor Facility | ANL[b] | None | Preliminary design |
| Experimental Breeder Reactor No. 2 | NRTS[a] | 20,000 | In development |
| Los Alamos Molten Plutonium Experiment No. 1 | LASL[d] | None | In development |
| Army Package Power Reactor (Pressurized Water) | Ft. Belvoir, VA | 1,855 | Operating |
| Los Alamos Power Reactor Experiment No. 2 (aqueous homo.) | LASL[d] | None | In development |
| Organic Moderated Reactor Experiment | NRTS[a] | 5,000–16,000 | Construction complete |
| Liquid Metal Fueled Reactor Experiment | BNL[e] | None | In design |
| Gas-Cooled Reactor Experiment | NRTS[a] | None | In design |

[a] NRTS  National Reactor Testing Station
[b] ANL  Argonne National Laboratory
[c] ORNL  Oak Ridge National Laboratory
[d] LASL  Los Alamos Scientific Laboratory
[e] BNL  Brookhaven National Laboratory

(continued next page)

### Table 2, cont.
### The United States Nuclear Reactor Program, Status in June 1957

#### GOVERNMENT PROJECTS

| Organization and Location | Type | Principal Contractor | Design Power (ekw) | Status |
|---|---|---|---|---|
| *Power Demonstration Reactor Program: First Round* | | | | |
| Power Reactor Dev. Company Laguna Beach, MI | Fast Breeder | PRDC[f] | 100,000 | Design & prelim. construction |
| Yankee Atomic Electric Co., Rowe, MA | Pressurized Water | Westinghouse | 134,000 | Design |
| Consumers Public Power District, Hallam, NB | Sodium Graphite | Atomics Int'l | 75,000 | Contract negotiations |
| Nuclear Power Group | Boiling Water | General Electric | 180,000 | Converted to an independent project |
| *Power Demonstration Reactor Program: Second Round* | | | | |
| Rural Cooperative Power Association, Elk River, MN | Boiling Water | AMF Atomics Inc. | 22,000 | Contract negotiations |
| Wolverine Electric Cooperative, Hersey, MI | Aqueous Homo. | Foster Wheeler Corp. | 10,000 | Contract |
| Chugach Electric Assoc., Anchorage, AK | Sodium Heavy Water | Nuclear Dev. Corp. of America | 10,000 | Preliminary design |

[f] PRDC   Power Reactor Development Company

stages of operation, and the fifth was really a test device. None had suggested a promising new approach to nuclear power. In the power demonstration reactor program, two of the three first-round projects were still alive but not yet in advanced design. Four of the seven proposals in the second round had been accepted for contract negotiation in fall 1956, but eight months later no agreement on contract terms had been reached. Only two proposals had been received in response to the third invitation, and only one of these seemed likely to survive.

## Table 2, cont.
## The United States Nuclear Reactor Program, Status in June 1957

### GOVERNMENT PROJECTS

| Organization and Location | Type | Principal Contractor | Design Power (ekw) | Status |
|---|---|---|---|---|
| City of Piqua, OH | Organic Moderated | Atomics Int'l | 12,500 | Contract negotiations |
| Power Demonstration Reactor Program: Third Round | | | | |
| Northern States Power Co., Sioux Falls, SD | Boiling Water | Allis Chalmers Mfg. Co. | 66,000 | Contract negotiations |
| Florida Nuclear Power | Nat-U, Heavy-Water Moderated, Gas-Cooled | | 136,000 | Under study |

413

### INDEPENDENT PROJECTS

| Organization and Location | Type | Principal Contractor | Design Power (ekw) | Status |
|---|---|---|---|---|
| Con. Edison of NY, Indian Point, NY | Pressurized Water | Babcock & Wilcox | 275,000 | Construction |
| Commonwealth Edison Co., Joliet, IL | Boiling Water | General Electric | 180,000 | Construction |
| General Electric, Vallecitos, CA | Boiling Water | General Electric | 5,000 | Construction |
| Penn Power & Light Co. | Aqueous Homo. | Westinghouse | 150,000 | Preliminary research |

During summer 1957 members of the atomic energy establishment maintained a tone of optimism in public, but behind the scenes there was growing concern. Walter H. Zinn, an old hand in reactor engineering and recently a consultant to the Joint Committee, privately expressed to Strauss his conviction that the United States was following the wrong path to nuclear power. In Zinn's opinion, the decision to concentrate on water-cooled reactors (pressurized or boiling) using enriched fuel had been a mistake. Zinn now favored natural-uranium reactors using a liquid coolant such as sodium. What bothered Zinn even more was the failure of the Commission's reactor development division to commit itself on any strategy while it waited for industry to make a decision by way of demonstration reactor proposals. In talking with Strauss, Zinn was careful to blame Davis and his staff for this failure to act, but he must have known that the fault rested more with Strauss than with Davis, who had heard similar complaints from others in the reactor industry.[17]

By autumn, signs of trouble were visible to the public. AMF Atomics announced that its estimated costs for building the Elk River plant now exceeded the ceiling established by the Commission. Similar difficulties had caused the Foster Wheeler Corporation to back out of the *Wolverine* project altogether. As *Nucleonics* reported that "confusion" had broken out in the nuclear power industry as a result of these announcements, the Commission reconvened its reactor advisory group for the first time in more than a year. The group included eleven prominent scientists and engineers representing the national laboratories and the university contractors, who joined two Commissioners, the general manager, and the headquarters reactor development staff for meetings in Washington during mid-October.[18]

414

## ECONOMIC REALITIES

The focus of the October meeting of reactor experts was on the economic potential of nuclear power. The group concluded that major reductions in both capital and fuel costs would be necessary if American manufacturers expected to sell reactors at home or abroad. Capital costs were likely to be reduced only if the water-reactor plants then being developed produced substantially more power than their design ratings. Fuel costs could be reduced, but only after substantial research and development over a period of years. In fact, the group believed that a long campaign of patient and painstaking development, rather than a dramatic technical breakthrough, was the likely road to nuclear power. And even then, the only hope seemed to be in very large reactor plants that took advantage of economies of scale. The group concluded that the Commission was working on too many types of reactors and that there was "too much breadth and not enough depth" in the reactor program.

Davis presented some of these same ideas in public two weeks later when he addressed the Atomic Industrial Forum in New York City. Although he believed that new types of reactors not yet developed would prove most economical in the long run, he thought that the best type for early achievement of a competitive plant rested with very large installations of water-cooled reactors. Without revising his earlier projection that as much as one-third of the nation's electricity might come from nuclear plants by 1980, Davis admitted that such a prediction would be realized only through hard work and close cooperation between government and industry. Perhaps nuclear power could not be competitive with conventional plants in the United States until the supply of low-cost fossil fuels began to decline, "at least 50 years" in the future. The real question was whether nuclear power could be made competitive within a decade or so. The next step, Davis believed, was "to obtain general agreement on a realistic program which would involve the necessary economic and technical incentives to reduce capital costs and particularly to reduce fuel costs."[19]

The twelfth American Assembly, meeting at Arden House in Harriman, New York, during that same month, agreed with Davis that, although nuclear power was not likely to be competitive domestically "for some years," long-range demand projections for electricity made research and development necessary. Such development, the Assembly believed, would come about only if the government continued to support private industry. The need for a partnership between government and industry raised the old specter of a public-versus-private power fight, a hazard that could be avoided, in the Assembly's opinion, by making government assistance equally available to public and private groups. The EURATOM plan announced by the Three Wise Men made an immediate response from the United States imperative; the new appreciation of the technical complexity and cost of developing nuclear power made federal participation essential, and that would require the Commission "to strengthen its internal administration of the program, with primary emphasis on positive accomplishment of its objectives in the power field."[20]

415

## THE LAST BEST HOPE

The report of the American Assembly carried a temperate but firm criticism of the Commission's performance under Strauss's leadership. Strauss indeed implied to Eisenhower that the report was simply a partisan attack by noting that Henry Smyth, Sumner Pike, and Robert Oppenheimer had participated in the conference. But, in fact, the assembly that year included more than fifty scientists, engineers, business leaders, and journalists representing a broad range of opinions. Perhaps Strauss did not know that Eisenhower had been interested in establishing the assembly as a nonpartisan group when he was president of Columbia University. About half the group, including Commissioner Vance, either had been or were still associated with the Commission.[21] Thus, the report was not easily dismissed, as Strauss hoped it would be. Even more important, it demonstrated a substantial consensus that the Commission needed a new approach to developing civilian power.

Strauss's last, best hope for avoiding a large government program was to rally American industry to the cause. Such a move would not be easy during those hectic weeks after the Soviet launch of *Sputnik I*, when the Administration was drafting plans for massive government support for science and technology. From the Joint Committee, Congressman Melvin Price was already appealing to the President to revitalize the development of a nuclear-powered aircraft with federal funds.[22] Strauss, however, was not about to be stampeded. Since summer 1953, he had resisted appeals from all sides, even from his own staff, that the Commission support the construction of nuclear power plants. As chairman, he easily quashed any such initiatives by turning his attention elsewhere and ignoring the reactor development division. Instead, he concentrated on private phone calls and meetings with industry executives who might be helpful in launching an impressive plan for private development of nuclear power. In this endeavor Strauss relied on Robert W. Zehring, an economist with both business and government experience who had joined Strauss's staff in spring 1956. An examiner in the Bureau of the Budget during World War II and the Korean War, Zehring had served as a consultant to Congressman John Taber, chairman of the House Appropriations Committee, during the early Eisenhower years. Zehring, who seemed to know everyone in the reactor industry, scouted lobbyists, trade organizations, and corporate boardrooms for bits of intelligence that might be useful to Strauss.[23]

416

The only concession that Strauss was willing to grant his colleagues was to agree to a series of three meetings successively with utility executives, equipment manufacturers, and atomic energy consultants on three days early in December. The scope of the meetings was to be limited, however, to technical aspects "and should avoid such topics as the political and financial factors." The Commission also insisted on personally reviewing the invitation lists, presumably to assure that the meetings did not become a forum for those supporting government action. The only exception came when the Commission, on Vance's request, agreed to invite Smyth, whose participation in the American Assembly conference had not enhanced Strauss's confidence in his former colleague.[24]

Strauss was probably even less enthusiastic about the forthcoming industry conferences when he received a confidential report from Zehring on November 4. In the corridors and barrooms at the Atomic Industrial Forum meetings in New York the previous week, Zehring had heard "moans and groans" about the high cost of developing nuclear power and the tough technical problems to be solved. Some equipment manufacturers were talking of dropping out of the nuclear business, and a few executives whom Zehring met thought it was "disgraceful" that large private utility groups had held back from supporting arrangements that could easily have financed nuclear projects. Zehring found the utility executives so gun-shy of nuclear power that there seemed little hope that the industry meetings would have any effect. The only way to save the situation would be for

Strauss to use his prestige in talking individually with selected utility executives to convince them to go nuclear.[25]

## DAVIS PROPOSES A NEW COURSE

The next day, Strauss attended a Commission briefing by Kenneth Davis and his staff. The agenda called for the Commission to discuss plans for the December industry meetings, but the real purpose was to hear an appeal from Davis for a major change of course in reactor development policy. Reflecting the views of the American Assembly, Davis declared that the Commission had reached a crossroads: "positive and effective action [was] absolutely necessary." Unless the Commission went beyond the "mere development of technology" to take the leadership in building power reactors, that task would be assumed by James T. Ramey and his staff at the Joint Committee, an eventuality that "could set the whole development back by years." The Commission, in Davis's opinion, needed to reach agreement with industry and the Joint Committee on a strong program, appoint someone to serve as its spokesman, and then seek the money and changes in the Atomic Energy Act that would be needed to accomplish it.[26]

417

Davis pulled no punches in describing the demoralized state of the nuclear industry. A new awareness of the costs and technical difficulties had come at a time when the economy was leveling off and investment money was tight. The rush to nuclear power by American industry, Davis said, had brought in more companies than could possibly survive, and some were already beginning to drop out. Most companies likely to build large-scale reactor plants had already announced their intentions, and some of these were already in trouble. In the meantime, Davis noted, the Commission had done nothing to support the economic development of water reactors, the one type likely to be useful in the next decade. Equipment manufacturers, Davis reported, saw no prospects of any help from the Commission. Financial and legal requirements imposed on the negotiation of power demonstration agreements left the manufacturers with no flexibility, and the Commission's failure to obtain construction funds for projects it had declared urgent had left contractors "despondent."

In analyzing the technical problems facing American industry, Davis followed closely the arguments he had used successfully with the reactor advisory group in October. The United States was not likely, in Davis's opinion, to be successful in selling abroad reactors that would not be economical at home. The nation's only hope, then, over the next decade was for water reactors, and these could come only with the building and operation of large-scale prototypes.

As Davis made clear in a second briefing three days later, the prototypes were not to be half-baked demonstration projects based on some utility's enchantment with an exotic reactor design but rather hardheaded engineering development efforts supervised by Davis and his staff under Commission contracts. All the projects, at least initially, would use water reactors, and all would be one hundred megawatts or larger in electrical capacity. Only after qualified architect-engineers had completed acceptable design studies and schedules under Commission contract would the Commission invite industry to design, build, and operate the plant. Davis proposed that the Commission adopt a ten-year program to develop and build large-scale prototypes.[27]

## STRAUSS AND STALEMATE

418

Davis's earnest appeal for a ten-year program did not move the Commission to precipitate action. Strauss failed to see why any change in Commission policy was needed. As for the most promising type of reactor for development, Strauss favored Zinn's choice of a large natural-uranium, heavy-water reactor. Vance agreed with Davis's choice of water reactors and the need for a prompt decision by the Commission, but he thought financial assistance from the government should be limited to research and development only, and most of that on improvement of fuel elements. Floberg did not agree that small reactors should be excluded, and his colleagues concurred. Strauss finally suggested that any decision on Davis's plan be postponed until the leading experts in the field could discuss the issues in a series of meetings during November and December 1957.[28]

Whether or not Strauss anticipated the outcome, the meetings of reactor experts tended to confuse rather than focus the issues. The two-day seminar sponsored by the Joint Committee on November 21 and 22 was off-the-record, but Strauss was able to get a detailed report of the discussion from some confidential source other than Zehring. The reactor designers and builders represented at the seminar agreed with Davis that the most urgent need was for a clear statement of reactor policy and preferably a ten-year plan. There were both considerable support for Davis's desire to encourage large-scale plants and strong objection to Davis's idea of concentrating on water reactors.[29]

The latter opinion became a repetitious theme in the three industry conferences held by the Commission early in December. Utility executives in particular complained that they did not yet know enough about the various types of reactors to be willing to commit themselves to one concept. The same group favored an orderly research and development program financed by the Commission to explore the alternatives to water reactors rather than rushing into the construction of large reactors that would produce very expensive power. The equipment manufacturers and consultants meeting separately later in the week added technical reasons opposing a concentration on one type of reactor. If Strauss needed any arguments to undercut Davis's proposal, the seminars sponsored by the Joint Committee and Commission provided them.[30]

At the same time, however, the seminars did little to advance Strauss's desire to keep power reactor development in the hands of private industry. Two weeks before the Commission's meetings with industry leaders, Zehring warned Strauss that the major utility companies were prepared to make a nuclear commitment only under certain conditions. A group of utility executives on November 22 had decided to cooperate only after rejecting a strong minority proposition that the industry organize an all-out fight against any government program. The majority decided that the utilities would put up some private capital to build two or three large nuclear power plants if the Commission announced in advance that the reactors were needed to bolster American prestige abroad or to promote national security. The Commission would have to tell the utilities what kind of reactors to build and how large they should be. The industry would expect the government to share research and development costs and to pay the difference between actual construction costs and those for an equivalent conventional plant. The utilities would own and operate the plants but would expect a government subsidy in the form of a steam price greater than the cost of steam from a conventional plant. The group agreed to assemble in Washington the day before the Commission meeting to clear its final statement, if the Commission should by that time announce its own intentions.[31]

419

Although forewarned by Zehring, Strauss made no move to commit the Commission to a nuclear power program that would have involved subsidies to industry. Lacking any word from the Commission on the day of the meeting, the utility executives delayed a final decision until it was clear that the desired commitment would not be forthcoming. During the morning recess in the meeting one member of the group told Zehring that the proposal was dead.[32] With that decision, Strauss lost his last chance for an expanding development effort by private industry. Apparently Strauss was unwilling to compromise his private enterprise principles in order to win a token of industrial participation. Now he would have to take his chances with the Democratic majority of the Joint Committee.

## SUCCESS AT SHIPPINGPORT

In the Commission's seminars with industry leaders, the most significant recent event in the development of nuclear power was scarcely mentioned—the initial operation of the pressurized-water reactor at Shippingport on December 2, 1957. Since the Commission had approved the project in summer 1953, Rickover and his staff had been engaged in a Herculean task to build the nation's first full-scale nuclear power plant and have it operating in a little more than four years. Detailed design and engineering studies had taken most of the time of the Westinghouse staff for the first eighteen months, and no significant construction had begun on the Shippingport site in western Pennsylvania until spring 1955. Then, with the design only 15 percent complete, Rickover had approved a schedule calling for finishing the entire plant in just twenty-four months. With relatively little experience in managing large construction projects, Rickover and his staff soon encountered such unfamiliar problems as jurisdictional disputes, slow-downs, strikes, and poor performance that frequently plagued labor relations in the construction industry. Steel shortages had delayed the project for three months in 1956, and a strike in South Philadelphia delayed delivery of the turbogenerator until February 1957, when the plant was scheduled to be virtually complete.[33]

420

Deeply concerned, Strauss had asked Rickover to do everything possible to have the plant in operation before the end of the year. Although it hardly seemed possible, Rickover further increased the tempo of the project during spring and summer 1957. Reorganizing both his own staff and the Westinghouse group at Bettis concentrated an enormous array of talent and resources on the project. While extraordinary efforts were made to complete the reactor core and instrumentation, Westinghouse tested every valve, every switch, and every inch of pipe and electrical cable on the site. Pipes were flooded with demineralized water until every trace of dirt had been washed away. Hundreds of valves and instruments already installed were found defective, ripped out, and rushed back to the manufacturers for repair or modification. On October 6, 1957, Westinghouse installed the reactor core. Then the head was bolted and welded in place; the control rod drives and the final instrumentation were installed. The reactor first went critical early on the morning of December 2, fifteen years to the day after Enrico Fermi in Chicago had achieved the world's first nuclear chain reaction. Sixteen days later, on December 18, the turbine was synchronized with the generator, and Duquesne personnel took over operation of the plant. At 11:10 a.m. on December 23, just eight days before the end of the year, the reactor reached its full net power rating of sixty megawatts of electricity.

Strauss was no doubt gratified that Rickover had completed the reactor in time to include the accomplishment in his year-end report, which stressed the Commission's accomplishments in developing power reactors. Strauss's enthusiasm, however, was tempered by the fact that Shippingport, for all its success, represented just the kind of reactor project that he was trying to avoid. A reactor completely financed by the government and built under almost total control by a naval officer was hardly a useful model for private enterprise. In fact, Rickover's heavy-handed methods in dealing with contractors had become so notorious that his name was now anathema among the industry executives who attended the Commission's December briefings. For example, one utility company executive reported to Zehring:

> Although there is a certain grudging respect for Rickover's engineering knowledge and dedication to the job, he is generally regarded as such an egotistical SOB that progress has been made on these contracts despite his personality rather than because of it. Some companies under contract with Rickover have taken the abuse in order to get the dollars. Others who might have the capacity to participate say "To hell with him" and stay away from the program because they will simply not stand his dictation or shift personnel as he frequently demands.[34]

421

Many industry leaders, especially those representing the electric utilities, were not overly impressed by Rickover's accomplishments. They tended to see the Shippingport plant as a simple and not very useful scale-up of the *Nautilus* power plant. For such men, the plant proved nothing because it had not been built by private industry to commercial specifications, and the high cost of the plant seemed to discourage rather than encourage further development. The heavy expenditures in 1957 to complete the plant before the end of the year had greatly increased total costs, which Rickover estimated at close to sixty-four mills per kilowatt of capacity as compared to six mills for existing conventional power plants.[35]

The significance of the Shippingport project was not yet wholly apparent to most people. Most readily evident was the exceptional performance of the plant at power levels far above its design rating and virtually free of operational faults or failures from the day of its first operation. As more information about the project became available to the public, it was obvious that the plant was not simply a scale-up of the *Nautilus* plant; rather it represented a fundamentally new conception of reactor design specifically for the production of electric power. Following the engineering practices that Rickover had developed in the Navy project, his staff and the Westinghouse engineers had painfully thought through the essential design characteristics of the plant and then translated them methodically and literally into the specifications for every component. The pressure vessel, towering almost thirty-five feet in height with a diameter of more than ten feet and a weight of 264 tons, approached the technical limits of steel fabrication at that time. Likewise, the required performance of the pumps, valves, and steam generators pushed design engineering and fabrication into unexplored realms of technology. The reactor core, consisting of almost 100,000 fuel elements, each meticulously encased in the little-known element zirconium and welded to standards of almost unprecedented quality, embodied scores of innovations in design and manufacture. Rickover's decisions to use uranium oxide and zirconium in the fuel elements and slightly enriched rather than fully enriched uranium were made only after months of exacting research and testing that produced fundamental engineering data for the future. All these data, carefully summarized in thousands of technical reports, were openly available to engineers throughout the world as the plant was being built. Perhaps no other engineering undertaking in history had been so thoroughly documented. After the plant went into operation, Duquesne organized a series of public training courses in reactor safety and operation. Over the next six years, more than one hundred engineers and technicians from the United States and ten other countries learned the rudiments of reactor technology at Shippingport.[36]

422

## BUILDING A NUCLEAR NAVY

During this same period, from 1954 to late 1957, Rickover's accomplishments in the naval reactor project as well as at Shippingport were ultimately to have a profound impact on the fledgling nuclear industry in the United States. While Westinghouse was straining to complete the Shippingport plant, Rickover was bombarding both the Bettis and Knolls laboratories with new requirements for submarine propulsion systems. As Rickover had anticipated, the brilliant success of the *Nautilus* had caused the Navy to shift its long-range planning strongly in the direction of nuclear power, especially for submarines. By the end of 1955, Rickover was faced with formal military requirements that far exceeded the existing capacity of his laboratories and contractors.

In addition to work on Shippingport, Bettis began designs of a new reactor smaller and more compact than that in the *Nautilus*, the S3W and S4W, for a new class of small attack submarine. The *Skate*, the first ship in this class, had been launched and was nearing completion by the end of 1957. Bettis was also at work on a new and larger reactor, known as the S5W, which would become the standard propulsion plant for twenty attack and twenty-nine *Polaris* missile-launching submarines to be authorized by 1962. The core and most components of the first S5W were ready for assembly by late 1957. In addition, Bettis was required to develop reactors for the surface fleet. The A1W built at the Idaho test station was the prototype for a multiple-reactor installation in an aircraft carrier. The C1W and F1W were to be smaller versions intended for use in a guided missile cruiser and a frigate (large destroyer).[37]

Likewise, General Electric scientists and engineers were engaged in several simultaneous development projects for naval propulsion systems. Knolls had cut its teeth on two sodium-cooled reactor plants, one a land-based prototype at West Milton, New York, and the second the shipboard plant for the attack submarine *Seawolf*. In 1955, Knolls received a new requirement to develop a water-cooled prototype (S3G) and a propulsion plant (S4G) ultimately used in the radar-picket submarine *Triton*. When the *Seawolf* plant developed leaks during summer 1956, Rickover decided to replace it with a water-cooled reactor, and Knolls began to convert its staff entirely to water-cooled technology. Combustion Engineering was also using water cooling in designing a prototype of a small propulsion reactor for a hunter-killer submarine.

Thus, by 1957 the major reactor manufacturers in the Navy program were no longer engaged in elementary studies of reactor technology or the design of simple reactor plants. They were now exploiting the advantages of multiple development, which enabled them to incorporate in successive designs the knowledge and techniques learned in building the first generation of water reactors. This capability made it possible for Rickover's contractors, particularly Westinghouse at Bettis, to respond quickly with new designs for water reactors and to build them without relying on the costly and time-consuming construction of prototypes.

Navy requirements for large numbers of nuclear ships also made it possible for Rickover's group and the manufacturers to realize the advantages of multiple production. Once Bettis had built the first S5G plant and standardized the design, it was feasible to farm out the manufacture of components for additional S5G reactors to a large number of fabricators and suppliers. In taking these first steps in creating a true nuclear industry, Rickover's staff encountered unprecedented problems in obtaining qualified subcontractors, training them to accept the extraordinary standards imposed by the specifications as both attainable and necessary, and then assuring that quality control was effective. By 1957, the production of zirconium had been transformed from a specialized laboratory technique into a commercial process performed by independent companies at a fraction of the cost incurred in fabricating the first *Nautilus* core.

The demand for components had become so large in 1956 that Rickover ordered Bettis to establish an independent procurement organization, which negotiated contracts with suppliers and manufacturers and monitored performance. Rickover saw to it that Knolls had a similar organization some months later. Within a short time, most reactor cores for naval ships were coming from the plants of five commercial fabricators under fixed-price contracts. No private utility executive who complained to Strauss about Rickover's insulting and outrageous behavior acknowledged or even understood that he was slowly and painfully building a national network of suppliers and fabricators capable of producing equipment that met nuclear standards. While the Commission debated policy issues, Rickover and his staff forged the commercial infrastructure on which the future of the nuclear industry in the United States would depend.

423

## STRAUSS'S LAST STAND

Early in December 1957, Strauss had in effect rejected all appeals for federal leadership and subsidy in building a nuclear power industry in the United States. On the thirteenth, Strauss told Eisenhower and the National Security Council that he still believed private industry would finance the development, without government assistance.[38] Under the circumstances, however, Strauss had no choice but to make at least a show of cooperation with the Joint Committee in devising a reactor program acceptable to both sides. He acceded to a request from Congressman Durham that the Commissioners meet on December 18 with the committee to discuss the opinions expressed at the recent industry meetings sponsored by both groups. Strauss did not attend the meetings himself, but he saw to it that all the other Commissioners and General Manager Kenneth Fields were present. In an effort to respond to repeated demands from industry for a clear-cut policy statement from the government, the two sides agreed on broadly stated objectives that would recognize the need for prompt achievement of competitive nuclear power at home, reassure the nation's allies of technical assistance to meet their power needs, strengthen the nation's position of leadership in the eyes of the world in the peaceful uses of atomic energy, and increase the nation's capacity for plutonium production by providing government assistance for building power reactors at home and abroad.[39]

424

Strauss could accept vaguely worded statements of intent such as these, but he had no thought of compromising on the specifics. His year-end summary of the Commission's accomplishments reiterated the usual long list of reactor projects, all set in a context of "progress." Zehring reported that the summary and a recent speech by Vance to utility executives in Chicago had done "more to encourage and stabilize views of the Company Presidents than any other events of the entire year." The source of encouragement was not the claim of accomplishment but the show of determination to avoid "large Government plant construction." The utility companies, Zehring reported, were reassured that the Administration policy would stay on the right track as long as Strauss served as chairman. Leaders of the industry had "already decided to plan a quiet and private campaign to keep Lewis Strauss on the A.E.C. job for another term."[40]

Such expressions of confidence in Strauss were not misplaced; however, in succeeding weeks Strauss proved too doctrinaire and inflexible in his views to control Commission reactor policy. On Friday, January 31, 1958, the day before a scheduled conference with the Joint Committee, the Commission still had not been able to reach a consensus on the outlines of a reactor policy. Strauss, insisting that private industry was showing more inclination to invest in reactor projects, saw no need for a government-financed program. Commissioner Graham, speaking in blunt language seldom heard since Murray's departure, called for a realistic approach to the political situation. Unless the Commissioners came up with specific proposals for the Saturday meeting, they would abdicate leadership in reactor development policy to Ramey and the Joint Committee. The committee was determined, Graham said, to see several new types of reactors constructed, and he urged the Commission to accept the inevitable. Strauss remained adamant that any new projects be undertaken within the power demonstration program. As consensus continued to elude them, Vance stepped into the breach. He reminded his colleagues that the final legislation on power reactor development would be written by the Joint Committee, not the Commission. As a compromise, Vance offered his own version of a Commission position.[41]

## THE VANCE PROPOSAL

For domestic purposes, Vance proposed that the Commission offer to continue to develop a number of reactor types, without focusing exclusively on water reactors, as Davis had recommended. On the need for more research on fuel elements, all were agreed. Following Davis's lead, the Commission would support design studies of improved water reactors. If these studies proved promising, the Commission would be prepared to build three prototypes—a large dual-purpose reactor for the production of plutonium or tritium and power, a moderate-size gas-cooled reactor, and a natural-uranium reactor—and additional test reactors, as Graham had proposed. As a concession to Strauss, the Commission would start construction only when convinced that private industry would not do the job. The Commission would also support construction of several small nuclear power plants at military bases overseas in cooperation with the Department of Defense.[42]

To support the development of nuclear power abroad, Vance proposed a comprehensive array of technical assistance and training programs and research support for friendly nations. As he had advocated a year earlier, Vance also proposed that the Commission cooperate with EURATOM in placing four to six large water-cooled plants with an electrical capacity of one million kilowatts in operation by 1963. This effort, plus continued support of the Atoms-for-Peace program in areas other than nuclear power development, would maintain the United States' world leadership in nuclear energy. At the end of his proposal, Vance added a new item, which had come into consideration only in 1958: that the Commission be authorized to buy plutonium produced in power reactors at home and abroad for periods of up to ten years of reactor operation. The trend toward smaller weapons, particularly for missile warheads, and toward weapons with greatly reduced fallout would likely increase requirements for plutonium and tritium, which were then produced in large quantities only in the Commission's production reactors.

With only hours remaining before the meeting with the Joint Committee on Saturday, the Commissioners had little choice but to accept Vance's proposal. After a few minor changes on both Friday afternoon and Saturday morning, the Commission adopted Vance's draft. As a general statement of intentions, the draft proved acceptable to the Joint Committee, and Strauss finally transmitted it on Monday morning.[43]

Although the plan seemed to mollify the Joint Committee, the Commission had no assurance that it could be effected. In attempting to comply with the President's ceiling for the 1959 budget, the Commission had severely pruned Davis's request for reactor development. In fact, the cuts had been so deep, for not only reactors but also production of nuclear materials and weapons, that the Commission was already considering a supplemental request that would have increased the proposed budget by almost one-third. Only the kind of psychological crisis created by *Sputnik* could have caused Eisenhower to relent in his determination to restrict federal expenditures. The Commission was not the only federal agency that saw in *Sputnik* an opportunity to recover some funding already pared from the budget.

A supplemental request, however, of about one billion dollars, half of which would be required to finance the new power reactor program, seemed far too large. As a tactical move, the Commission decided to exclude from its supplemental request any funding for the dual-purpose or gas-cooled reactors, on the grounds that the design studies mandated by the authorization act in 1957 had not yet been completed. If these studies, then being completed at Hanford, should conclude that the reactors were worth building, then the Commission might have to seek subsequent funding. Strauss explained all this in a letter to the Bureau of the Budget. Without mentioning the implied commitment to the Joint Committee to seek authorization for the two reactors, Strauss mentioned the informal discussions with the committee, and he added an admonition: "It is apparent that unless the Commission formulates and offers some program of acceleration it may be faced with a much larger program not of its own choosing."[44]

## HOLDING THE LINE

Under the circumstances, Strauss and his colleagues were not eager to have their informal agreement with the Joint Committee publicized, at least not until the Bureau of the Budget had acted on the supplemental request. For their own part, Ramey and members of the Joint Committee were perfectly willing to continue informal negotiations, which seemed to be producing better results than direct confrontations had in the past. Both parties therefore agreed that neither the informal meetings nor the draft plan would be discussed at the annual Section 202 hearings, which began on February 19. To this end, Congressman Durham announced that all discussions of power reactors would be deferred until the end of the hearings. In his opening remarks, however, Strauss could not resist the temptation to report that a West Coast utility had just decided to build a large nuclear power plant with no federal contribution. Senator Anderson exploded at what he considered a breach of the agreement to postpone discussions of the subject. Strauss later reported to the President that "the announcement literally infuriated the public power advocates on the Committee." Unfortunately, Strauss admitted, unfavorable economic conditions were tempting some large companies to testify at the hearings in favor of government construction or subsidies. Strauss added: "It is making it a little harder to hold the line."[45]

Strauss was indeed holding the line, but his unwillingness to compromise, even to the point of antagonizing his opponents, would cost him dearly. Early in February, in response to a discreet inquiry from the White House, Senate Majority Leader Lyndon B. Johnson saw no chance that Strauss could be reappointed without "a knock down, drag-out fight." Johnson reported,

427

> Some of my people are very upset about him. They consider him arrogant and resent his statements that they have tried to socialize the power industry through the use of nuclear reactors, whereas the Administration is represented as the only true friend of free enterprise in the field of power.

If Strauss behaved himself, Johnson predicted, Senator Anderson might still be able to squeeze through a new term for Strauss. But Strauss's performance at the Section 202 hearings twelve days later seemed to kill that possibility.[46]

Despite Strauss's breach, both the Commission and the Joint Committee continued to try informally to resolve remaining differences that stood in the way of a single nuclear power policy for the government. As the next step, the Commissioners invited the committee members to an informal luncheon on February 24 to resolve the last two points of difference: Should industry be given a chance to submit demonstration proposals for the three new prototypes? And what should be the specific terms of the plutonium purchase contracts? On the first point, Ramey and the committee members feared that the offer to industry would delay the projects for at least a year. On the second, Congressman Holifield was reported as suspecting that Strauss had designed the plutonium purchase idea to help out some utility companies that were overcommitted to uneconomical reactor plants. Strauss proposed a four-month time limit for industry proposals, and Fields was given authority to negotiate terms of the plutonium contracts with Ramey.[47]

By late March 1958, the remaining differences had been resolved to the satisfaction of both sides. The committee had accepted Strauss's insistence that private industry be offered a chance to submit proposals for constructing the prototypes under liberalized provisions of the third round of the power demonstration program. For its part, the Commission had agreed to drop its request for authority to negotiate plutonium purchase contracts. Vance's original statement had now been elaborated to justify fully the Commission's stand against unrestrained government financing, and the statement now set forth the specific development projects for which the Commission would seek authorization. The broad objectives at the beginning of the paper for domestic and foreign development had now been made more specific by providing goals to achieve competitive nuclear power in the United States during the next ten years and in friendly nations in the next five years.[48]

The agreement was not all that Strauss might have wanted. By admitting the need for the large prototypes, the Commission opened up the possibility that these might be built as government projects if private industry failed to take up the challenge. One way or another, however, Strauss had been able otherwise to retain the big features of the power demonstration program as a bulwark against unrestrained federal expenditures or subsidies.

Strauss and his colleagues also knew by this time that the Administration had no intention of approving most of the Commission's request for supplemental funding. They were astounded to learn early in April that the Bureau of the Budget had denied more than $220 million in their request for almost $260 million for reactor development projects. In the wide sweep of the budgetary scythe, the bureau had not only eliminated the proposed increase for the Commission's own power reactor projects and the Army package power reactors and cut the proposed estimate for fuel element studies by one-third, but it had also deleted all funding in fiscal year 1959 for the natural-uranium, the heavy-water, and the gas-cooled reactors, and for materials and test reactors. The third prototype, for which the Commission was already committed in its informal agreement with the Joint Committee, had not been included in the supplemental request. Because the Department of Defense refused to submit a formal requirement for additional production of plutonium and tritium, the Commission had refused to seek funding for the dual-purpose reactor.[49]

Given Strauss's lack of enthusiasm for the prototypes, it is difficult to believe that he was really as surprised by the bureau's action as he pretended to be; but in his discussions with Maurice Stans, the new director of the bureau, Strauss did not lose sight of the political realities. He feared that eliminating all the prototypes might push the Joint Committee too far. If the gas-cooled reactor were approved, Strauss thought he might be able to head off a new version of the Gore-Holifield bill in the Congress. Eisenhower agreed to include the project in the authorization bill, but he directed that any appropriated funds be held in reserve by the Bureau of the Budget

428

until private industry had a chance to submit proposals to construct the reactor with private funds. In the version sent to the Joint Committee, the draft authorization bill amounted to only $115 million: of that, $88 million was earmarked for the Commission's own research and development work, including $51 million for the gas-cooled reactor, and $27 million for the power demonstration program.[50]

Strauss could leave his post as chairman on June 30, 1958, with the satisfaction of knowing that he had stuck to his principles for five years through thick and thin. During his term as chairman, he had been able to thwart every effort by the Joint Committee and a Democratic Congress to enact a government-financed program to build nuclear power plants. In so doing, Strauss believed that he had successfully preserved for the private power industry what he saw as its traditional place in the American economy. For his considerable accomplishment Strauss had paid a heavy price, not only in terms of his personal career but also in mortgaging the future of the Commission. Strauss's determination to reserve the key decisions in nuclear power development to private industry excluded the Commission from exercising its role as an effective and active formulator of national policy. Prevented by Strauss from taking the initiative in the policy debate, the Commission appeared to defer first to industry, then to the Joint Committee, and finally to the Administration itself. However Strauss may have justified this strategy in his own mind, such actions of deference in the game of bureaucratic politics could only debase the Commission's prestige and authority as an independent agency of the federal government. In the process nuclear power had become a full-fledged political issue, and the Commission had lost the special status and advantage it had enjoyed since 1947.

429

## CHAPTER 16

# EURATOM AND THE
# INTERNATIONAL AGENCY, 1957–1958

The Atomic Energy Commission's role in setting America's nuclear power policy was complicated because much of the Atoms-for-Peace program required close coordination with the State Department and Congress. Another complication was that President Eisenhower insisted on personally monitoring the progress of Atoms-for-Peace negotiations and treaty making. EURATOM became a key element in Eisenhower's grand design for Europe. Following the precedent of the Marshall Plan, the President hoped Atoms for Peace would forge even stronger economic and technical bonds between Europe and North America. In this sense, the Administration's policy also stimulated foreign markets for American reactor manufacturers, who in the 1950s enjoyed only limited domestic prospects. As an instrument of American foreign policy, Atoms for Peace reflected Eisenhower's hope to promote international peace, prosperity, and security by providing an American atomic shield (NATO) behind which a coal-and-oil-poor Europe could establish nuclear-powered self-sufficiency through EURATOM.[1] To be sure, the International Atomic Energy Agency was important to American interests, but ultimately the Administration would place higher priority on European economic integration than on international cooperation on atomic energy. In the meantime, the second Geneva conference sponsored by the United Nations in summer 1958 gave the United States an opportunity to demonstrate its technical progress in developing the peaceful uses of nuclear energy.

## THE PRESIDENT AND THE THREE WISE MEN

During their visit in February 1957, the Three Wise Men from EURATOM met with Eisenhower, who was attended by Strauss but not by Dulles. The

President, however, shared with his visitors Dulles's ambitions for European economic solidarity. Recalling his vision of a united Europe as a third great force in the world, Eisenhower told the Wise Men that European nations had to learn the Biblical precept that to save their lives they must lose them. If the European nations did not join together, Eisenhower warned, "deterioration and ultimate disaster were inevitable." Offering the Wise Men his full support, Eisenhower asked Strauss whether the United States could supply sufficient enriched material to support the proposed EURATOM program. Without answering the President directly, Strauss replied that this matter posed a considerable problem because the projected needs of the EURATOM group were very large. Nevertheless, Strauss thought the Commission could guarantee delivery "for a very great deal" of what EURATOM needed.[2]

Undoubtedly still smarting from his earlier confrontation with Dulles over bilateral agreements, Strauss reluctantly concurred in the joint communiqué issued by the Department of State, the Commission, and the EURATOM committee. Despite his vague assurances to Eisenhower, however, Strauss would not offer the Wise Men an unqualified commitment to supply EURATOM with enriched fuel. At a luncheon with the Wise Men, Strauss had pointed out that the availability of nuclear fuels ought not be a limiting factor, provided the supplies of raw materials continued adequate and provided the requirements of the Defense Department for fissionable materials did not absorb too large a share of America's total production. But Strauss also made it absolutely clear to the Wise Men that the Commission's first responsibility was to supply the needs of the United States military, which were essential for the defense of not only North America but also the entire free world.[3] As far as Strauss was concerned, Atoms for Peace would not take precedence over Atoms for War.

## THE BRUSSELS TASK FORCE

Nevertheless, the Commission agreed to dispatch a task force of American experts to Brussels to offer technical and financial assistance to the Wise Men, who were preparing their final report to EURATOM. Arriving in Luxembourg on March 24, 1957, the staff members led by Richard W. Cook, deputy general manager, joined the work in progress, contributing principally to the section of the Wise Men's report dealing with "Nuclear Power Prospects."[4] The Commission group, working alongside a similar delegation from the United Kingdom, focused its attention on the feasibility of EURATOM's long-range plan, the projected estimated costs of nuclear power compared to conventional power, and the availability of enriched uranium fuel. The consensus among the Americans was that EURATOM's goal of 15,000 megawatts of nuclear power capacity by 1968 was overly optimistic but not impossible, especially if the Europeans purchased American light-water reactors and British gas reactors.[5]

The Commission experts also estimated that large European nuclear power plants could provide competitive power, excluding research and development costs, at a cost of eleven to fourteen mills per kilowatt-hour over the life of the plants with earlier costs high and later costs low. The Americans believed that fuel would be adequate, especially in view of the natural uranium available in France and the Belgian Congo and the Canadian government's assurances to the Wise Men. The American delegation returned to the United States hopeful of EURATOM's future and confident that the EURATOM treaty, which had been signed in Rome along with the Common Market Agreement on March 25, would be quickly ratified by participating governments.[6]

432

## THE EURATOM TREATY

The Commission offered no serious objections to the draft EURATOM treaty, which Paul-Henri Spaak sent to Washington for comments in April 1957. Speaking for his colleagues, Strauss noted that the Commission could not assure Spaak that there were no provisions in the treaty inimical to the relationship between the United States and EURATOM. Only experience and subsequent interpretation of the treaty could settle that question. The Commission was worried that the EURATOM agreement would permit member states to manufacture nuclear weapons. Murray endorsed a suggestion that all uranium-producing countries, such as the United States, Canada, and South Africa, require that uranium sold to EURATOM not be used in weapons. Despite the increasing availability of uranium, the Commission was also reluctant to release Belgium from its commitments to supply the United States with uranium concentrates through 1960. Spaak asked for this concession specifically because EURATOM's hopes for expansion rested in part upon Belgian Congo uranium resources. Again Strauss and the Commission relinquished the United States' options on Congo ore only under severe pressure from the State Department.[7]

## SURPRISE ATTACK FROM THE SENATE

United States participation in the International Atomic Energy Agency, not support of EURATOM, became the major issue before the Senate in 1957. Preoccupied by the EURATOM discussions, the Eisenhower Administration was caught by surprise when conservative Senate Republicans threatened to undermine American leadership of Atoms for Peace by challenging the United States' ratification of the statute of the International Atomic

Energy Agency. Adopted on October 26, 1956, at the eighty-one nation conference in New York, the statute became the key issue in the President's State of the Union message when he cited it as a demonstration of his "unalterable purpose to make of the atom a peaceful servant of humanity."[8] Unknown to the President, the Commission had already received a hint of the trouble ahead.

The day before the State of the Union message, Strauss learned that four influential senators held serious reservations concerning the International Atomic Energy Agency.[9] What Strauss did not know was that a campaign against ratification of the treaty had been gathering momentum since December 1956 when letters soliciting opposition to the "President's fantastic Atomic Energy giveaway plan" were sent to members of Congress, leading newspaper publishers, the National Association of Manufacturers, and the American Legion. At first the campaign against the treaty was conducted almost single-handedly by David S. Teeple, a disgruntled former deputy director of the Joint Committee and subsequent assistant to Strauss. Teeple had resigned as Strauss's aide in 1954 after protesting against "left-wing" advisers surrounding the chairman. He then carried his fight to the pages of the *National Review*, where he questioned the motives of the President, Strauss, and Dulles in sponsoring United States membership in an organization he thought contrary to national interests.[10]

433

Thereafter, opposition to the treaty mushroomed alarmingly. In a Lincoln Day speech written by Teeple, Senator Joseph McCarthy blasted the Administration for its plans to "give away" through the International Atomic Energy Agency sufficient enriched uranium to build 2,200 atomic bombs, which could "wipe every major American city off the map." McCarthy, who would die before the treaty was debated by the Senate, ultimately proved no threat. On the other hand, Senators Bricker, Knowland, and Hickenlooper, also assisted by Teeple, were reported to have fundamental objections to the statute, which Senator Pastore cautioned would have to be modified if the treaty were to have any chance of ratification. Within two weeks of Eisenhower's submitting the statute to the Senate, Teeple gloated that he had talked to at least twenty-two senators, and possibly thirty-six, who would vote against the statute. Indirectly, Pastore confirmed this gloomy estimate by warning that it was almost too late to save the statute unless the President appeared personally before the Senate to plead his case.[11]

The objections raised by the statute's critics, as Eisenhower well knew, were varied and often ill-defined. Hickenlooper presented Under Secretary of State Christian Herter with a booklet of questions prepared by Teeple and endorsed by Knowland.[12] With the President and Herter, Strauss reviewed the major challenges raised against the statute: the People's Republic of China might be admitted to the agency; American nuclear material would be shipped to the Russians or their allies; third world countries would be enabled to develop atomic weapons; the agency was not necessary because the United States had bilateral cooperation agreements; and the statute, once ratified, could be amended to include provisions adverse to American interests. No challenge was insurmountable, but Eisenhower's advisers agreed that the President would have to meet personally with Knowland and Hickenlooper, members of both the Foreign Relations Committee and the Joint Committee on Atomic Energy, if a bitter fight over the statute was to be avoided. Because the President had committed his personal prestige to the International Atomic Energy Agency, an American failure to ratify, or even a close Senate vote, would severely damage Eisenhower's political standing with immeasurable aftereffects.[13]

434

Embarrassment touched close enough on May 2, 1957, when Washington learned that the Soviet Union had already ratified the statute even before the Senate had begun its official consideration of United States membership. Not only had the Soviet Union successfully stolen the march on the United States, but it began to appear that the Eisenhower Administration could sell the program to every government but its own. According to the *New York Times*, Senate opposition to the international agency sprang mostly from a complex crosscurrent of isolationist, anti–foreign aid, anti-communist, and military-secrecy sentiments. There was, however, a new and unrelated current of uncertain strength—opposition from liberal Democrats to both the Administration's domestic power reactor program and the leadership of the Atomic Energy Commission. Although Senator Pastore provided invaluable intelligence and support, the Administration was hampered by the lack of strong proponents on the Republican side of the Senate. The danger was not so much that the statute would be rejected outright, but that without support from Knowland and Hickenlooper it would be encumbered with reservations that would make United States participation in the international agency impossible.[14]

Ultimately, the reservations proposed by the statute's critics were narrowed to two. Less damaging than a similar reservation offered by Bricker, Knowland demanded that all amendments to the statute be ratified by the Senate before becoming binding on the United States. More drastically, Bricker would have required the United States to withdraw from the agency in the event the Senate rejected an amendment to the statute. Bricker's unfortunate reservation would have emphasized withdrawal from the agency as a primary American concern and no doubt would have stimulated other countries to raise similar reservations. Nevertheless, some such caveat seemed to be the price for Senate support, and the Administration accepted the Knowland version, which simply stated that "the authority of the United States to participate in the IAEA would be terminated" should the Senate refuse to endorse an amendment to the statute.[15]

Potentially more damaging was Bricker's second reservation that modified the provisions of the 1954 Atomic Energy Act authorizing the transfer of United States nuclear material to the agency. Despite the fact that he was author of Section 124 governing the transfer of nuclear materials to groups of nations, Bricker was so fearful of communist nations obtaining American enriched uranium that he wanted to require Congressional approval of all transfers of nuclear materials to the international agency. In effect, Bricker proposed to cancel Section 124 as it applied to the agency and substitute direct Congressional oversight. Although the Administration successfully beat back the amendment during debate over the statute, Bricker's reservation was finally accepted by the conference committee, which approved the IAEA Participation Act following ratification of the statute on July 29, 1957. Because the act signed on August 28 granted the international agency 5,000 kilograms of enriched uranium and promised to match the contributions of all other member countries until July 1960, the Administration could swallow the Bricker proviso. It launched America's participation on a sour note, however, and created concern that the United States would be handicapped in competing against British manufactured fuel. With United States contributions dependent upon unpredictable Congressional action, *Business Week* suggested that foreign governments might well pass up the American-made reactor in favor of the British gas-cooled reactor, which did not depend on enriched uranium.[16]

435

## LAUNCHING THE INTERNATIONAL AGENCY

Having secured Congressional support for the International Atomic Energy Agency, the Commission and the State Department could focus their attention on preparations for the first general conference scheduled to convene in Vienna on October 1, 1957. Almost four years after Eisenhower's hopeful address to the United Nations, the fifty-two delegations gathered with optimism tempered by the anniversary of the Hungarian uprising and the Suez crisis. Although the United States was recognized as the instigator and leader of the conference, racial strife in Little Rock, the decline of the stock market, and the launching of *Sputnik* had tarnished America's reputation. If developing countries had overestimated the benefits from the peaceful atom and underestimated the time needed to gain them, the United States had underestimated the difficulties in organizing the International Atomic Energy Agency. As others have noted, the structure of the agency, with its balanced board of governors and limited authority for the director general, was obviously designed to protect the interests of the principal nuclear powers.[17] All in all, the climate at the opening of the conference was not as favorable as it had been when Eisenhower first presented his Atoms-for-Peace proposal in 1953.

The American delegation to Vienna was headed by Robert McKinney, who replaced James J. Wadsworth on the preparatory commission in anticipation of the conference. McKinney had had no prior diplomatic experience, but he had earned the confidence of the Senate Democratic leadership for his services to Senator Anderson. According to Strauss, Senator Lyndon B. Johnson, who wanted to be the "Vandenberg of the Eisenhower Administration" by stressing bipartisan peaceful atomic diplomacy, requested some kind of atomic appointment for McKinney. Almost certainly Johnson had in mind a Commission appointment to replace Murray, upon whom the Congressional Democrats could no longer rely. Horrified at the thought of one of Anderson's associates sitting beside him on the Commission, Strauss speculated that McKinney would not want to divest himself of his International Telephone and Telegraph interests in order to secure a Commission appointment. As an alternative, Strauss suggested that McKinney might be interested in leading the United States delegation to the international agency. With Herter's permission, Strauss made all the arrangements, recruited McKinney, and cleared the appointment with Johnson and Anderson personally. From Strauss's point of view, the appointment solved two problems at once: it blocked McKinney from a seat on the Commission while it gained powerful senatorial allies for the President's program. Strauss's only trouble came from the President himself, who was understandably miffed at the appointment of a Democrat who had personally attacked him during the 1956 campaign. Thus, political considerations not only sent an inexperienced diplomat to Vienna but also dictated the selection of a delegation chairman in whom the Administration was unlikely to place much confidence.[18]

## STAFFING AND SUPPORTING THE AGENCY

Even more inauspicious for inaugurating the International Atomic Energy Agency was American insistence that a United States national be selected to head the agency. Once again, political considerations forced the Americans to demand this concession from the surprised conference, which had expected the United States to honor the tacit agreement that the director general would come from a neutral country. In part, trouble came from the Senate where Knowland, reasoning that the United States might be the only country to contribute significant amounts of nuclear materials to the agency, suggested that the board of governors, if dominated by representatives from unfriendly countries, might distribute American uranium behind the Iron Curtain or to other unfriendly areas. Not only was it essential that the agency exercise tight safeguards, Knowland contended, but it was equally important to know who was going to be director general.[19]

On this issue, Knowland had allies in the Administration. As early

as September 1956, Strauss had considered seriously the possibility of recruiting W. Sterling Cole for the position. Although the President and
Dulles did not want Strauss to "push" for an American appointment, neither did they categorically oppose the idea. As Strauss explained to Dulles,
no one other than Cole could provide so much assurance of Congressional
support during the first critical years of the agency.[20]

The United States first hinted to the Soviet Union that it wanted
an American as director general on March 29, 1957, but it was not until
June 14 that Wadsworth formally broached the matter to Vasily S. Emelyanov, the Soviet delegate to the agency. The Soviets had expected to support the representative of a neutral country for the position, and they would
not agree to discuss the American appointment separately from other positions in the agency. The Americans, hoping to strike a deal, suggested that
a Soviet national might serve as the deputy director general for training and
technical assistance. It became clear that the the United States would have
to pay a price to obtain an American director general. The Soviet side
indicated, however, that it would also ask for other positions for Soviet
nationals.[21]

437

Piqued at having to haggle with the Russians over jobs, Eisenhower
told Strauss to make no deals until the Soviet Union had contributed its
share of fissionable materials to the international agency. Wadsworth was
instructed to inform the Russians that the United States intended to sponsor
Cole for director general but that further discussions of staffing would have
to await Soviet contribution of enriched uranium. The implication was
plain: Eisenhower would concede to the Russians only a level of representation appropriate to the amount of nuclear material the Soviet Union made
available to the new agency.[22]

Ultimately, Strauss was given the assignment to recruit Cole, who
after twelve terms in the House of Representatives was understandably reluctant to give up his safe seat for an uncertain tenure in Vienna. Nevertheless, because Cole was popular in the Congress, acceptable to the British, and unobjectionable to the Soviet Union, Strauss persuaded him to
serve by appealing to Cole's patriotic sense of duty while offering a salary
and perquisites second only to the secretary general of the United Nations.
Later Cole would have second thoughts about his decision, but on the eve
of the first general conference he believed the International Atomic Energy
Agency would become as important as the International Bank, collecting,
holding, and distributing nuclear material similar to the way the bank handled international funds.[23]

Notwithstanding the Administration's stance on placing Soviet nationals in operating positions, McKinney recognized that, if the Soviets
were going to participate in the agency, the United States could not expect
to isolate them entirely from positions of importance, especially given the
technical strength of the Soviet mission in comparison with the delegations

of the Western nations. Unless the United States matched the Soviet Union with a strong countervailing technical staff, McKinney feared the Russians would take full advantage of the vacuum created by the fact that NATO countries had sought mainly administrative posts.[24]

In further support of the agency, the Commission approved offering an unclassified technical library, a research reactor, and a radioisotope laboratory to the agency. Additionally, the Commission agreed to provide the agency free consultant services, to train 120 agency-selected fellows, to equip two mobile radioisotope training laboratories, and to assist the agency in its recruiting efforts by recommending fifty-four scientists and technicians. The total cost of the American contributions through 1959 would be $3,154,000. Finally, the Commission approved policies relating to the transfer of source and special nuclear materials to the agency. Financial assistance to the agency, however, was contingent upon the outcome of negotiations that were concurrently being conducted with EURATOM.[25]

438

## REDEFINING ATOMS FOR PEACE

Back in April 1957, the Commission and the State Department had submitted their joint progress report on implementing the National Security Council memorandum on "Peaceful Uses of Atomic Energy." Although the State Department reportedly considered writing its own report to offset the Commission's optimism, officially the two agencies expressed general satisfaction with the progress made in the Atoms-for-Peace program. Only Commissioner Murray, who favored immediate construction of large power reactors, publicly criticized the Commission's programs and policies in a separate opinion.[26] Taking note of the failure to make substantial progress with disarmament, the report nevertheless emphasized that the most significant achievement of the United States might have been in developing "an awareness of the vital necessity for international control over the peaceful uses of atomic energy" and in taking the first steps toward devising an acceptable safeguard system, especially as envisioned in the bilateral agreements. Yet, while the agency statute had established a broad safeguard policy, an effective multilateral control system had yet to be devised. In fact, because the United States had not yet shipped sizeable quantities of enriched materials to any country, the practical matter of implementing the safeguard provisions of the bilaterals still had to be resolved. Indeed, the initial policy of the National Security Council had sought only to prevent diversion of materials contributed by the United States, without anticipating the need to control fissionable by-products such as plutonium as well.

The Commission and the State Department agreed that the United States' original Atoms-for-Peace policy adopted in March 1955 had become obsolete. Since that time the United States had negotiated forty-three bilateral agreements of cooperation, sponsored the establishment of the international agency, and anticipated the ratification of the EURATOM community. In addition, the Organization for European Economic Cooperation, the Organization of American States, and the Colombo Plan nations in Asia had shown an interest in atomic energy. Both the Soviet Union and the United Kingdom had emerged as potential competitors with American industry in the field of nuclear power just when the need for alternative sources of power based on Middle Eastern oil had been demonstrated by the Suez crisis. Finally, as a matter of national policy, it became imperative to state unequivocally that projected national and regional nuclear power programs would increase the potential danger of nuclear weapon proliferation and radiation hazards.

Revision of the National Security Council's peaceful uses paper in autumn 1957 did not result in a major shift in American policy. Recognizing that the economics of nuclear power were not yet favorable in the United States and that large-scale development would proceed first in England and Europe, followed closely by Japan and the Soviet Union, the United States remained determined to maintain American supremacy in peaceful uses of atomic energy overseas and in nuclear technology, both in fact and in the eyes of the world. As long as the United States was regarded as the leading country in the field, friendly competition would not detract from that preeminence, which enhanced general acceptance of effective safeguards. Thus, the National Security Council concluded that loss of American preeminence in peaceful uses would damage not only the prestige but also the security of the United States.[27]

439

Perhaps most important, the revised National Security Council policy stressed the need to establish a safeguard system under the aegis of the International Atomic Energy Agency. To this end the Administration would try to persuade other governments to accept the international safeguard provisions in the agreements for cooperation, including the stationing of resident inspection teams at the larger and more complex installations. The council, however, rejected a State Department proposal to place certain United States nonmilitary atomic energy facilities under the inspection system of the international agency, provided the Russians and the British would do the same.[28]

## EURATOM PRIORITIES

Even as the Administration debated the new policy, Soviet *Sputniks* challenged American scientific and technical preeminence and created even greater political imperatives for the success of the Atoms-for-Peace initiative. According to the State Department, Russian scientific and engineering accomplishments had prompted the Atlantic community's serious and healthy reappraisal of the strength of Western technology. With Europeans wondering whether the United States would maintain its scientific and technical leadership in the space age, Douglas Dillon, Under Secretary of State for Economic Affairs, argued that the United States should exploit its nuclear capabilities as a rightful bellwether of scientific and industrial accomplishment.[29]

By spring 1958, however, United States support for EURATOM as a symbol of nuclear cooperation and a vehicle for Western European economic integration had proven incompatible with the American objective of sponsoring the International Atomic Energy Agency with broad safeguarding responsibility. Well before the Treaty of Rome established EURATOM on January 1, 1958, it was evident that the United States would have to choose between divergent foreign policy objectives. For John Foster Dulles and the State Department, European stability demanded that EURATOM be given priority over the international agency, should American policy toward the two organizations conflict. The fall of the Gaillard government in France in May 1958 and the assumption of power by Charles de Gaulle emphasized all the more, Christian Herter wrote to Strauss, "the need to build a strong, cohesive and responsible unit in Western Europe through economic integration."[30]

On January 28, 1958, the Commission and the State Department informed the President of their interest in developing a joint program with EURATOM that would bring on-line by 1963 about one million electric kilowatts of installed nuclear capacity. In comparison to the modest contributions to the international agency, the Commission anticipated providing to the EURATOM project long-term loans of up to $150 million, or more than one-third of the total capital cost, excluding fuel. To sweeten the pot, the United States also proposed to contribute $50 million in matching funds to EURATOM's research and development program. With presidential approval on February 6, a working party was established to negotiate a United States–EURATOM cooperative agreement.[31]

## SAFEGUARDS FOR EURATOM

Not surprisingly, two of the most serious concerns for the United States were safeguards and fuel-cycle guarantees. Safeguards created the greatest difficulty for American foreign policy, and fuel-cycle guarantees touched off further domestic political debates about the Atoms-for-Peace "giveaway." Of the two, the safeguard question was by far the more serious.

Recognizing the sensitivity of the issue prior to discussions with EURATOM representatives on March 20 in Luxembourg, Richard Cook, the leader of the American delegation to Brussels, suggested four alterna-

440

tives: (1) requiring EURATOM to accept the safeguard provisions normally included in bilateral agreements, (2) sharing safeguard administration and inspection with EURATOM on a joint basis, (3) seeking the same rights accorded in normal bilateral agreements but delegating partial responsibility for enforcement to EURATOM, or (4) foregoing expectations that EURATOM would conform to the Commission's normal safeguard requirements while acceding to European desires. According to the Commission staff, the first alternative was not politically feasible, and the last would represent an unacceptable reversal of United States policy. The State Department asked the Commission to authorize the American delegates to explore a compromise. For its part the Commission was willing to enter an agreement "which would recognize the supra-national position of EURATOM," provided the United States received assurances that no special nuclear material transferred to EURATOM would be used for military purposes.[32]

441

Although the EURATOM commission was willing to give the United States firm guarantees that all material, equipment, or devices provided by the United States would be used for nonmilitary purposes, the Europeans remained adamantly opposed to granting inspection rights to the United States or to any other country. The EURATOM commissioners stated their intention of granting United States representatives complete de facto access to facilities under the joint program, but they would not invest de jure inspection rights in any country outside the community. In short, the EURATOM commission did not think it should be treated less favorably than Canada and the United Kingdom with regard to safeguards and controls.[33]

The Commission was extremely reluctant to compromise on the safeguard issue. Although Cook had warned that there would probably be no agreement if the United States insisted on inspection rights, Commissioner Libby observed that any departure from normal safeguard requirements might well undermine existing bilateral agreements. Strauss also expressed his concern that in assisting EURATOM the United States might well weaken the International Atomic Energy Agency. He suggested that Cole be informally briefed in Vienna on the proposed EURATOM cooperation program before the Commission made its final decision. Commissioner Vance noted that Max Kohnstamm, chairman of the EURATOM commission, would shortly be conferring with the Commissioners in Washington. At that time, Vance recommended informing Kohnstamm that the United States had not changed its position on safeguards. Vance believed there was a "slight chance" that the Europeans might compromise, but even if they did not the delay would not seriously disrupt the program.[34]

On April 29, 1958, Kohnstamm left the Commission no doubt that EURATOM would not accept safeguard provisions imposed by a third party. He stressed the importance EURATOM placed on equality with the

United States and the need for a single international safeguard system operated by EURATOM without participation of the United States or any other non-EURATOM country, including the international agency. Although not exactly an ultimatum, Kohnstamm made it clear that EURATOM would not submit to inspections unacceptable to the United States, the United Kingdom, or the Soviet Union.[35]

Later that same day, the Commission reconsidered safeguards. Anticipating Kohnstamm's visit, the staff had recommended that the Commission accept EURATOM's determination to establish its own safeguard system with American assistance. Under the revised proposal, cooperation between the United States and EURATOM would depend on EURATOM's establishing and maintaining a mutually satisfactory and effective system, which the United States could review from time to time.[36] Strauss with Commission support favored this recommendation on the understanding that if the EURATOM system ultimately failed to meet Commission standards, American assistance would be terminated. Following the chairman's request that Cole be informed of developments, the Commission approved in principle the compromise on the EURATOM safeguard system.[37]

## REACTIONS FROM VIENNA

Strauss's concern about the reaction of the international agency to the United States–EURATOM arrangement proved well founded. Even before Cook could reach Cole, the American Embassy in Vienna cabled its alarm to the State Department. Noting the distress of both Cole and McKinney, the dispatch also outlined the consternation of other Western nations, which reportedly agreed that the Soviet bloc would never permit the establishment of effective international controls under the agency if EURATOM were allowed to establish its own system. Separately, the American and some other representatives were said to fear the creation of multisafeguard systems, with the most lenient dominating, should the EURATOM position prevail.[38]

Cook's attempt to mollify Cole failed utterly. On May 12, Cole expressed his dismay to Strauss. Thereafter, on May 18, he wrote directly to the President conveying essentially the same opinions. Defining the EURATOM safeguard proposal as "self-inspection," Cole predicted that such an arrangement would have "serious consequences on the effectiveness of the Agency" and strongly recommended to the President "that the safeguards or accountability aspects of EURATOM be assigned to the Agency."[39]

Independently, and far more bluntly, McKinney warned Acting Secretary of State Herter that, unless some compromise were reached between EURATOM and the agency, "we might just as well consider the IAEA finished and its basic purpose destroyed, along with the entire Atoms-for-Peace program which we initiated in 1953." Should the United States default on its leadership, as McKinney interpreted it, the Soviet Union stood ready to take over the leading role in the agency.[40]

The State Department had now begun to show mounting concern over the safeguard issue, which threatened to delay or even scuttle the agreement for cooperation with EURATOM at the moment the United States faced a critical political situation in Europe. On the one hand, the American diplomats wanted to seize an opportunity to encourage European integration while at the same time helping to free Europe from the uncertainties of Middle Eastern oil. On the other hand, in view of de Gaulle's lack of enthusiasm for the integration movement, any procrastination by the United States in supporting EURATOM would surely be interpreted as evidence of American disinterest in European unity. In a personal letter, Dulles urged Strauss's support so that the matter could be expedited for presidential approval. In deference to Strauss's loyalty to Cole, Herter agreed to discuss the matter directly with the two men if Cole could return from Vienna.[41]

443

At their decisive meeting on June 6, Cole began by stating his belief that EURATOM should not be permitted the right of self-inspection. Strauss agreed, stating that self-inspection by EURATOM would not only undermine the agency but also encourage other nations to form regional groups in order to secure immunity from international inspection. Herter searched for a compromise. Would it be possible, he asked, for Strauss to draft a letter to be sent by EURATOM to Dulles outlining American rights to verify that the EURATOM inspection system was working properly "by counting, weighing, assaying, etc.," the special nuclear material provided by the United States and the material derived from it? In addition, EURATOM would pledge to accept inspection by the agency, "if and when an international nuclear inspection system is agreed upon." Although Cole did not agree to Herter's proposal, neither did he object. When Strauss reported the meeting later to the Commission, Libby argued that EURATOM should accept inspection from either the United States or the agency, but Floberg advocated comprehensive United States inspection. Despite these reservations, Floberg agreed to draft the letter.[42]

Two days later, the *New York Times* accused the Commission of raising "last-minute objections" to the proposed EURATOM agreement, thereby jeopardizing, according to State Department and EURATOM officials, "the whole European movement toward economic and political unity." Although dismayed at the disturbing lack of coordination between the Commission and the State Department, the following day the *Times* editorially supported the Commission's position. The *Times* commented that if EURATOM were to establish the precedent of "self-inspection," the Soviet bloc could well establish a similar organization.[43]

The *Times* revelation of internal American disagreements proved embarrassing, but it may also have prodded all parties to resolve their differences. On the day the editorial appeared, Strauss assured the impatient President that a compromise could be struck. Herter, Strauss, Floberg, Cole, McKinney, and Philip J. Farley, who had succeeded Smith as special assistant to the Secretary of State for atomic energy matters, then met to hammer out a draft memorandum acceptable to everyone. With minor changes, including allowing EURATOM to assure itself that plutonium coming back to the United States would be used only for peaceful purposes, Herter conducted direct negotiations with Kohnstamm. By June 11, the Commission, the State Department, Cole, and Kohnstamm for EURATOM all accepted the same draft memorandum on safeguards, clearing the way for the Commission's approval of the agreement for cooperation the following day. The program was subsequently approved by the President on June 17, 1958.[44]

444

Thus, EURATOM had successfully maintained its refusal to submit to an externally administered safeguard system. The United States in pursuing its first priority in peaceful atomic diplomacy had been obliged to accept a system that included the right to audit but whose ultimate sanction would merely allow the United States to terminate the cooperative program if it were not satisfied that safeguards were effectively maintained. Verification of safeguard adequacy would be obtained by "mutually approved scientific methods" during "frequent consultations and exchanges of visits." And should the agency establish an international safeguard and control system, the United States and EURATOM would "consult" to arrange the agency's assumption of the safeguard responsibility. In Western Europe, therefore, where the Atomic Energy Commission would foster the first large-scale nuclear power generating facilities outside North America, the United States had failed either to establish unilateral inspection rights such as those included in the bilateral agreements for power reactors or to devise effective sanctions other than noncooperation with countries that violated safeguard undertakings.[45]

## CONGRESSIONAL APPROVAL

The safeguard issue, the source of so much difficulty in the international negotiations, raised few questions when the EURATOM agreement was sent to Congress for approval. The draft agreement, however, could not be sent to the Joint Committee until June 23, 1958, and the delay threatened loss of action in the rush of last-minute legislation. The Administration was confident that, once the EURATOM agreement cleared the Joint Committee, Congressional approval would be forthcoming. The key to the Joint Committee was Senator Anderson, whose personal feud with Strauss seemed to threaten the possibility of swift action.

In fact, Anderson virtually ignored safeguards but bore down instead on the financial aspects of the joint program. In order to minimize the economic uncertainties associated with the nuclear fuel cycle, the United States had offered EURATOM guaranteed pricing on both fuel fabrication and reprocessing as well as low interest loans. Anderson was reported to be skeptical of EURATOM's financial reliability and suspicious that the EURATOM agreement would be used to "bail out" Italian nuclear projects presumably in financial trouble. Raising a procedural question, Anderson wondered why the terms and conditions of the loan had not been negotiated before the program was submitted to Congress for approval. Besides Anderson, however, there was no concerted Congressional opposition to the program.[46]

Anderson's truculence no doubt reflected some of the exceedingly bad relations that existed between the Joint Committee and the Commission at that time. According to a State Department observer, the EURATOM proposal was sent to the committee at the very time the members had been infuriated by the treatment the Administration had given to the Joint Committee's unanimous recommendation pertaining to the domestic nuclear power program. Consequently, the committee members seemed so distrustful of the Commission that they were unwilling to accept the draft agreement as the best that could be negotiated in the time available; but instead, they looked upon it with suspicion that construed general provisions as an attempt to hide the details from the committee. Thus, the Administration regarded Anderson's expressed skepticism about the community's financial integrity and its political responsibility as secondary to his deep suspicion of the Commission and the Administration. In effect, the Administration won the substance of victory with none of its flavor.[47]

445

## THE SECOND GENEVA CONFERENCE

The second conference on the peaceful uses of atomic energy, which convened in Geneva on September 1, 1958, symbolically marked the culmination of Eisenhower's Atoms-for-Peace program. The conference was the largest scientific gathering of its kind ever assembled, Strauss noted afterward; he reported to the Secretary of State,

> One cannot examine the statistics of this Conference and the tons of technical papers, reports, transcripts, photographs, newspaper articles, magazine stories which it generated, without becoming aware of the fact that atomic energy has now become part of the fabric of our civilization.[48]

For years thereafter participants would remember the pride and excitement Americans shared at the conference. Yet, despite its great success as an international scientific convention and fair, the conference did not chart a clear course for developing nuclear technology. For Strauss, Geneva provided a final hour of celebration before his humiliating failure to win Senate confirmation as Secretary of Commerce. Among old-timers "Geneva '58" became a watchword for the heyday of the Atomic Energy Commission.

Just in statistical terms alone, American participation at Geneva overwhelmed that of all other nations. The United States exhibit occupied 36,000 of the 75,000 square feet of space utilized by the twenty participating nations, and, in substance, clearly surpassed all other exhibits. For the most part the displays of other nations used panels, photographs, models, and static displays of laboratory equipment; the United States exhibit featured full-size operating laboratories, including experimental devices, two research and training reactors, a radioisotope laboratory, a hydrogen bubble chamber, a whole-body radiation counter, and seven experimental working devices for research on controlled thermonuclear reactions. The exhibit was manned by nearly two hundred leading scientists and technicians from American laboratories, hospitals, and universities. Some scientists actually assembled portions of their laboratories and carried forward their experiments under the observation of foreign colleagues. It was common to find scientists from different nations engaged in animated conversation at blackboards around the exhibit hall. Not all the 100,000 visitors to the United States exhibit were scientists, and many people were counted more than once as they returned again and again to study the displays.[49]

The 572-member United States delegation, a virtual who's who of the nuclear community, was headed by Strauss and included other official representatives: Libby as vice-chairman, James R. Killian, Jr., chairman of the President's Science Advisory Committee, McKinney, and Isidor Rabi. American scientists contributed more than one-third of the 2,135 papers submitted to the conference and gave 231 of the 722 papers selected for oral presentation.[50] The United States also supplied seventeen of the fifty-one technical films presented by the United Nations and showed another twenty-eight short films on specialized subjects in four small theaters incorporated into the United States exhibit. At the Technical Information Center, located adjacent to the delegates' lounge on a specially constructed balcony, the United States distributed over 30,000 copies of technical literature.

The spectacular American show, set up in the shadow of *Sputnik*, which dominated the Soviet exhibit, was designed to demonstrate unqualified American leadership and preeminence in the nuclear field. From its inception in August 1955, when Strauss heard that the British were going to propose a second international conference and obtained the President's approval to "beat them to it," the second Geneva conference was destined to become an American extravaganza. Because of commitments to organize atomic energy exhibits for the Brussels World's Fair in 1958, Britain,

446

France, Italy, Belgium, and the Netherlands had all favored a more restrictive conference focusing on the problems of the International Atomic Energy Agency or confined to the theoretical and practical problems involved in the development of nuclear power. Americans serving on the secretary general's advisory committee accepted the idea that emphasis be placed on nuclear power, which would highlight American technology, but Ambassador Wadsworth also insisted that the agenda should be broad enough to include applications of atomic energy in industry, agriculture, and medicine.[51]

By mid-summer 1957, the Commission had decided to feature two special exhibits chosen as much for their propaganda value as for their scientific merit. In a technical tour de force, Argonne National Laboratory transported to Geneva an Argonaut training and research reactor that was assembled during the conference while delegates looked on as "side-walk superintendents." On the sixth day, Strauss brought the ten-kilowatt reactor to criticality by inserting a wand—containing some uranium from the original atomic pile constructed in Chicago by Enrico Fermi's team in 1942—into a mechanism that initiated the withdrawal of the control rods. Thereafter, the Argonaut was also dismantled in full view of the conference visitors, starting three days before the closing session.[52]

447

Even more ambitious was Strauss's dream to unveil at Geneva a working model of a controlled thermonuclear device. Unfortunately, scientists responsible for Project *Sherwood*, the Commission's name for its controlled thermonuclear program, held only scant possibility that such a machine could be developed in time for the conference. Consequently, the *Sherwood* steering committee decided to feature research projects from the principal laboratories at Princeton, Livermore, Oak Ridge, and Los Alamos.[53]

The launching of *Sputnik*s on October 4 and November 7, 1957, and the comparative failure of the United States *Vanguard* heightened the Commission's determination to prove at Geneva that American nuclear science and technology were second to none. On October 19 Strauss and Libby urged the Commission's division of research to mount "an exceptional effort" to obtain a device producing thermonuclear plasma as a central showpiece for Geneva. It was almost certain by February 1958 that a controlled thermonuclear device would not be among the American "firsts" displayed at Geneva, but Strauss urged that the United States plan to exhibit its most advanced devices and research so that American prestige would not suffer badly should the Russians include a device they claimed produced thermonuclear neutrons. Even after falling back to the original plan of the *Sherwood* steering committee, the fusion exhibit ultimately commanded almost half the space allotted to the United States.[54]

Perhaps the most significant achievement of this international competition was the declassification of Project *Sherwood*. On August 30, the day before the formal opening of the conference, the United States and the United Kingdom dramatically announced the joint declassification of all research on controlled thermonuclear reactions. Dag Hammerskjöld, Secretary General of the United Nations, hailed this action as the lifting of "some of the very last barriers" restricting the exchange of scientific information. The Anglo-American declassification no doubt also prompted the French to disclose their previously secret plans to build a gaseous-diffusion plant to enrich unranium.[55]

The Commission had not planned originally on participating in the commercial exhibits set up in the Palais des Exposition in downtown Geneva. The Americans, however, changed their minds in November 1957 when they learned that the British and French displays would occupy almost twice the space of that haphazardly reserved by United States firms. Consequently, the Commission contracted with the Atomic Industrial Forum to develop a representative commercial exhibition and to design, build, and manage an exhibit that would be a credit to the United States. The government's display was to be built around a model of a power reactor core, rising forty feet high. At the base was an information center telling the Atoms-for-Peace story. The Commission also supported the Atomic Industrial Forum in urging private industry to participate in the exposition.[56]

The crowning success of the Geneva conference tended to obscure the deeper conflicts in the United States' policy in Europe. For the moment Europeans could set aside their frustrations over the role of the United States in the affairs of their continent as they attended technical sessions in the Palais des Nations or enjoyed the breathtaking displays of American accomplishment in the nearby exhibition hall. But the inconsistencies in American policy represented by the Administration's handling of EURATOM and the international agency had not been resolved. The question remained: Would the United States place its economic interests in Europe above its concern to protect the world from the military threat of the atom?

## CHAPTER 17

# *TOWARD A NUCLEAR TEST MORATORIUM*

In summer 1957, the Atomic Energy Commissioners realized that nuclear testing and fallout continued to pose a serious public relations problem. With the President already committed to stopping tests if at all possible, mounting international anxiety over nuclear weapons and fallout only strengthened Eisenhower's resolve to negotiate a verifiable test ban with the Soviet Union. Although Eisenhower did not achieve his goal in 1957, the Commission thereafter had to cope with increasing skepticism from both the White House about the need for large numbers of atmospheric tests and the scientific community about the safety of those tests. The general public, meanwhile, clearly favored a test cessation of some sort. The number of persons who called for a unilateral halt to testing was small, but by mid-summer 64 percent of Americans favored a multilateral agreement.[1] Public support for a multilateral test ban would gradually decline as negotiations bogged down, but a majority of Americans generally continued to want some kind of test ban.

## THE PUBLIC RELATIONS PROBLEM

By and large, the Commission and the Joint Committee on Atomic Energy were satisfied with the outcome of the fallout hearings that had concluded on June 7. Shortly after Libby testified in June, he privately briefed the State Department staff on the effects and the significance of radioactive fallout, especially from testing. Commendably, Libby's briefing was consistent with his public testimony. Although he conceded that the Commissioners had learned a great deal about fallout since 1954, they still believed "that the risks involved in testing [were] infinitesimal."[2] At a Blair House party, James Ramey had confided in Gerard Smith that the Joint Committee was especially pleased at the amount of new information forthcoming at the hearings. Yet Ramey conceded "that a majority of the reporters [were] in way over their heads," resulting in a great deal of simplified or distorted reporting.[3]

Dwight A. Ink, a member of the general manager's staff, succinctly outlined the public relations problem. In May 1957, the Commission had received almost six hundred letters from people concerned about the hazards of testing. In addition, Ink noted that criticism in the press and from abroad had increased dramatically. Against this background the fallout hearings had progressed well, with the Commission presenting its testimony calmly and effectively—for the benefit of the congressmen. Nevertheless, headlines featuring the hearings had underscored the dangers of fallout or had emphasized the disagreements among the scientists. Because public opinion would be shaped by the press reports rather than the hearing transcript, Ink predicted that the hearings would prove of little help in educating the public despite the excellence of the testimony. Although Ink tried to be optimistic, it was impossible to escape the conclusion that a defensive Commission, facing the divided opinion of the scientific community and the momentum of the disarmament talks, would find it almost impossible to mount a successful public relations campaign.[4]

The advisory committee on biology and medicine generally agreed with Ink's assessment. In a special meeting with the committee on June 18, 1957, Strauss acknowledged that "the climate was undesirable and unfortunate." Strauss reflected the Commission's consensus that fallout was not a matter of health or science but rather a public relations problem. Indeed, from Strauss's perspective, the Commission could not have avoided its predicament; rather, it had been trapped when in February 1955 the State Department had forced it to delay reporting the results of the *Castle-Bravo* fallout study. Strauss also wondered why the National Academy of Sciences report on fallout had been "brushed aside" by so many people, including prominent scientists. He considered Albert Schweitzer's appeal as "a body blow to the testing program."[5]

Almost literally, the Commission saw itself on the ropes, the defensive victim, not of sloppy testing or bad science, but of a deepening public relations fiasco. Strauss continued to believe that Americans would support the Commission's need to test if only the public could receive a full and accurate assessment of radiation hazards. Believing that an active testing program significantly helped to deter Soviet aggression, Strauss would have balanced the radiation exposure risks from testing against the devastation that would result from atomic war. In fact, American insistence on careful testing created difficulties for the United States in the disarmament talks. If testing and weapon production were halted, Strauss argued, the Russians would gain a distinct advantage because of their willingness to produce weapons without the extensive testing required by American engineering standards.

450

The argument that weapon testing and development were actual deterrents to nuclear war would be heard over and over again.[6] Congressman Cole, for example, also believed it essential for the United States to develop "clean" tactical nuclear weapons to be used in limited wars. He did not think that the tactical use of nuclear weapons would inevitably lead to all-out, spasm nuclear war between the super powers. Cole granted that there was widespread public misconception that nuclear weapons were "wanton, indiscriminate and inhumane." On the contrary, he believed that nuclear weapons could be as precise, "humane," and limited in their use as any other weapon. The Russians, however, had constantly fanned the "flames of misconception" regarding the ruthlessness of atomic weapons. With its great manpower advantage it was in Russia's interest to outlaw nuclear tests and weapons through a campaign of fear, deceit, and propaganda. To Cole's dismay, the Soviets had been "astonishingly" successful.[7]

Cole's implication that advocates of a test ban were communist dupes, or worse, only reflected Eisenhower's comments at his June 5 press conference. Although the President later tried to soften his unfortunate remarks that the antitesting protests almost looked like "an organized affair," Congressman Francis Walter of Pennsylvania underscored Linus Pauling's association with communist-front groups. Furthermore, Representative Lawrence H. Smith of Wisconsin accused Norman Cousins of being a communist dupe by urging Schweitzer to join the test-ban movement. Cousins, in turn, scolded Eisenhower for his lack of generosity, noting that never before had Cousins known the President to impugn the good faith, integrity, or intelligence, let alone loyalty, of those who held views different from the Administration. Strauss wanted Eisenhower to send Cousins a long, blistering reply citing an article in the *U.S. News and World Report* that described how Pauling had organized his petition. Eisenhower did send Cousins the article, but in a tempered single-page note he merely assured the editor of the *Saturday Review* that he would continue pursuit of the peaceful atom but not at the expense of exposing Americans to unacceptable military risks.[8]

451

## ON THE BEACH

During the first two weeks of July, as Administration officials watched one of their most pessimistic nuclear war scenarios unfold in Operation *Alert* exercises at the Atomic Energy Commission, two dozen concerned scientists gathered at the summer home of industrialist Cyrus Eaton in Pugwash, Nova Scotia, to discuss ways of ending the nuclear arms race. Meeting from July 6 to 11, this first international Pugwash conference on science and world affairs attracted scientists from ten nations, including the Soviet Union. The conference prepared a report that, Linus Pauling noted, "covered the hazards arising from the use of atomic energy in peace and war, the problem of the control of nuclear weapons, and the social responsibility of scientists." As Pauling proudly reported, the three Soviet scientists at Pugwash signed the report; upon returning to Russia, they obtained the endorsement of 198 members of the Academy of Sciences and other Soviet academics. The Pugwash conference adjourned with an appeal for "the abolition of war and the threat of war hanging over mankind."[9]

Commission officials involved in Operation *Alert* at the Emergency Relocation Center, of course, were oblivious to the appeals of the Pugwash conference, but the secret results of the government's third annual disaster exercise were hardly less frightening than the published nuclear war scenarios that Americans would read in summer 1957. Most graphic was Nevil Shute's apocalyptic novel *On the Beach*, in which the entire world was laid waste by radioactive fallout. In Shute's fantastic book a spasm nuclear war between the great powers unleashed thousands of "cobalt" bombs that quickly rendered the northern hemisphere uninhabitable and slowly contaminated the rest of the world. Australians estimated that they had only nine months to live. Shute's hero was an American submarine commander who found temporary refuge in Australia. Drawn by the love of an Australian woman but determined to verify the fate of his wife and family, the commander sailed north, the only active remnant of the once powerful American Navy. Reconnoitering safely underwater where his crew escaped the effects of the deadly fallout, the commander cruised through the formerly lush Puget Sound to Seattle, which he found a lifeless desert. Ultimately, commander and crew had no choice but to return to Australia to await their fate.

One critic found Shute's novel banal, and others noted that it stretched scientific and military credulity to the point of science fiction. Nevertheless, the book became a best seller and, predictably, a popular movie. The popularity of *On the Beach* indicated that the American public now understood the strategic implications of the *Castle-Bravo* test.[10] Blast and heat from thermonuclear bombs could be horribly devastating, but even more fearsome was the threat from widespread fallout that, if unlikely to contaminate the entire world, might poison millions of square miles and kill additional millions of people.

## EFFECTS OF NUCLEAR WEAPONS

Although repeatedly accused of being too secretive and overly optimistic, the Commission published its own vision of nuclear war in summer 1957. If not as dramatic as *On the Beach*, Samuel Glasstone's *The Effects of Nuclear Weapons* was just as vivid and infinitely more accurate. In an earlier edition, *The Effects of Atomic Weapons*, published in 1950, Glasstone described the destruction caused by a single "nominal" twenty-kiloton bomb. In his update, Glasstone not only changed the title to reflect the thermonuclear age but also noted that it was "no longer possible to describe the effects in terms of a nominal bomb." Rather, Glasstone outlined the blast, heat, and radiation effects of twenty-megaton thermonuclear bombs, a thousand times more powerful than the bombs dropped on Japan in World War II. With the expectation that the handbook would be used by civil defense personnel, the government released *The Effects of Nuclear Weapons* just prior to launching Operation *Alert*. [11]

*The Effects of Nuclear Weapons* told its own grim story. Wood frame houses less than twelve miles from ground zero would be completely destroyed by a twenty-megaton blast. Houses as far as twenty miles away could have windows and doors blown in. Within six miles of ground zero, most multistory buildings would become rubble. Planes parked twelve miles away would be tossed about like toys. Within ten miles forests would be denuded, broken, blown down, or uprooted. In human terms, persons caught outside could suffer third-degree burns thirty miles away, and some individuals fifty miles away would receive first-degree burns. [12]

Reviewers noted that Glasstone did not mention "clean" weapons. Nevertheless, he included much information on radiation effects and fallout. Observing that a radiation dose of 700 roentgens spread over thirty-six hours would probably prove fatal, Glasstone, using fallout data from the *Castle-Bravo* shot, calculated the dosages persons would receive after an attack if they were caught in the open without shelter for a day and a half. A fallout plume nearly 20 miles wide at its base and 140 miles long would seriously threaten the lives of all persons who remained in the area unprotected; 220 miles downwind, deaths due to radiation would be negligible, although numerous victims would be temporarily incapacitated with radiation sickness. Soberly, Glasstone observed that true radiological warfare, although theoretically possible, was impractical with the old fission bombs. But after the development of thermonuclear bombs with high fission yields radiological warfare became "an automatic extension of the offensive use of nuclear weapons of high yield." Almost as if he anticipated *On the Beach*, Glasstone included a new chapter on worldwide fallout and long-term residual radiation. Glasstone's analysis was no more optimistic than an earlier study, *Radiation: What It Is and How It Effects You*, by Jack Schubert and Ralph Lapp. [13]

453

## KISSINGER ON NUCLEAR WAR

Henry Kissinger's book on *Nuclear Weapons and Foreign Policy* was also published in time to be included on 1957's summer reading list. Although not as graphic as Shute's *On the Beach* or Glasstone's *The Effects of Nuclear*

*Weapons*, Kissinger's portrayal of nuclear war and its social, political, and economic consequences was just as shocking. Sponsored by the Council on Foreign Relations, Kissinger had developed his theories roughly concurrently with the Eisenhower Administration's reassessment of nuclear strategy following the *Castle-Bravo* test. Drawing from nuclear war theorists, including Warren Amster, Bernard Brodie, William Kaufmann, Basil Liddell Hart, and Robert Osgood, Kissinger stated boldly what insiders and professionals already knew: the United States could not rely on the strategy of "massive retaliation" when its potential enemy also possessed thermonuclear weapons.[14] He analyzed the weakness of America's defense against conventional and thermonuclear attack and repeatedly stressed the need for a *credible* nuclear deterrent to contain Soviet expansionism. Kissinger believed the Russians would constantly nibble away at the West—first aggressively, then conciliatorily—but they would always be ambiguous. At no time would the United States be provoked into an all-out nuclear attack. Rather, the Soviet Union would confront Western powers with limited adventures, none of which would justify plunging the world into nuclear holocaust.

454

With Brodie, Osgood, and others, Kissinger struggled to develop a doctrine of limited nuclear war that would enable the United States to respond more flexibly to Soviet aggression in the nuclear age. Yet "limited war" and "limited nuclear war" could be easily confused. In summer 1957, no scenario stopped short of all-out nuclear war once nuclear weapons were unleashed. Although the Commission talked seriously of clean bombs and tactical weapons, nuclear weapons, however designated, could not be considered just another weapon in the American arsenal. Perhaps the terms clean and tactical reflected hopes to relate nuclear weapons to traditional warfare. Conventional wisdom held, nonetheless, that once introduced into battle the use of nuclear weapons could not be restricted.[15]

## HOLIFIELD AND FALLOUT

From the Commission's perspective the success of the fallout hearings chaired by Congressman Chet Holifield was measured by the more than 2,000 pages of testimony recorded by the Joint Committee. The Commission had been able to present its fallout data along with a plea for increased support for Project *Sunshine* without creating undue alarm or criticism from the press; however, the Commission did not escape completely unscathed.

Perhaps the Commission's most outspoken critic over fallout at this time was Holifield himself. In his report to Congress, Holifield complained that the Joint Committee had to "squeeze the [fallout] information out of the Agency." Had it not been for Congressional hearings, Holifield argued, the Commission would have withheld information important to the public. Even when the Commission did release fallout information on its own initiative, according to Holifield, the data were so technical or piecemeal that reporters and laymen alike had difficulty understanding their importance.[16]

More important, Holifield charged that the Commission had developed a "party line" on the hazards of fallout from nuclear testing—"play it down." Despite a responsibility to keep the public informed, the Commission was tardy in releasing information; but worse, according to Holifield, the Commission had selectively used information to support the Administration's political positions. Dredging up as well the conflict between Strauss's role as special adviser to the President and chairman of the Commission, Dixon-Yates, and the 1956 presidential campaign, Holifield linked these issues with the Commission's supposed muzzling of its scientists over the test-ban question.                                                          455

As Senator Anderson had previously questioned the Commission's role as both promoter and regulator of the nuclear power industry, Holifield saw a "conflict of interests" on the weapon side. "Is it prudent," he questioned rhetorically, "to ask the same agency to both develop bombs and evaluate the risks of fallout?" Later, writing in the *Bulletin of the Atomic Scientists*, Holifield supported greater research efforts on radioactive fallout and its effects on human health, but only under the auspices of the National Academy of Sciences.[17]

## THE ASSESSMENT OF SCIENTISTS

Holifield's charges that fallout information could be pried out of the Commission only by Congressional investigation was especially irksome to Strauss, who felt he had been double-crossed by the congressman. For the past year and a half, the Commission had cooperated with a United Nations scientific committee on radiation that had been proposed by the United States. The Americans' purpose, to be sure, was to allay international fear of radioactive fallout through the international scientific committee; but there was also a sincere interest in determining the dimension of the danger. Shields Warren, Austin Brues, and Merril Eisenbud were the United States delegates. In autumn 1956, Warren reported that the United Nations panel had made considerable progress in collecting and analyzing fallout data but nevertheless depended heavily on the United States and the United Kingdom for scientific information. Warren concluded with some satisfaction that "the willingness of the United States to share its information and, indeed, to assist other nations in collecting and analyzing fallout material, has certainly strengthened its position regarding the radiation problem."[18]

A year later the United States had submitted over thirty reports to the United Nations scientific committee, including papers on fallout, natural background radiation, genetic effects, occupational radiation hazards, generalized radiobiological effects, and waste disposal. The United States' first contribution had been the study prepared by the National Academy of Sciences–National Research Council, "The Biological Effects of Atomic Radiation." The Commission and the State Department considered the government's most recent contribution to be its testimony during the fallout hearings, which "provided the most exhaustive supply of data that has yet been compiled on this subject." In contrast to Holifield, the Administration viewed the Joint Committee hearings as part of the United States' continuing effort to inform the public and scientists throughout the world of the effects of fallout and radiation hazards.[19]

456

In response to the Joint Committee's fallout hearings and the work of the United Nations scientific committee, the Commission's advisory committee on biology and medicine reviewed the entire program of the division of biology and medicine and found it restricted, underfunded, and understaffed. In addition, through the summer and into fall the advisory committee prepared a "Statement on Radioactive Fallout" for the Commission. The advisory committee noted that since 1954 strontium-90 content of the soil had markedly increased while concentrations in milk had "increased steadily with time." Even if weapon tests were stopped, fallout would continue for a considerable period of time. Unfortunately, with continued testing, long-range estimates were at best only "intelligent guesses." The advisory committee also estimated that testing would contribute to a small increase in leukemia deaths and would cause some genetic damage in the world's population, which in the course of time could be "large in absolute terms."[20]

Although the members of the advisory committee on biology and medicine admitted that fallout from testing could be a problem, they nevertheless continued to believe that testing was necessary for national security. They urged the Commission to hold testing "to a minimum consistent with scientific and military requirements." It was unprecedented for the advisory committee publicly to request restraint from the Commission.[21]

## HARDTACK *REEXAMINED*

In August 1957 Eisenhower met with Strauss, Smith, and Cutler to discuss forthcoming weapon tests. The President was alarmed over both the large number and the excessive length of the tests scheduled for *Hardtack* in spring and summer 1958. Because of the disarmament discussions, the Commission and the military liaison committee had agreed to accelerate the testing program. Strauss told Eisenhower that he had cut in half the number of shots requested by the laboratories and the Department of Defense. Still, he agreed with the President that too many tests were scheduled. Strauss also admitted that four months—May through August—would seem like a long time, especially if disarmament talks were proceeding concurrently. Requirements that the weather be perfect for testing, however, dictated the lengthy schedule.[22]

The fallout issue no doubt caused Eisenhower to question the size of some proposed *Hardtack* shots as well. Strauss conceded that the Commission and the State Department saw no need to test very large weapons. The requirement to test multimegaton weapons had come from the Department of Defense, which wanted to determine what size and yield a B-52 could carry. In response to the President's skepticism, Strauss offered a compromise that would limit all *Hardtack* shots to a yield not larger than the 1954 *Castle-Bravo* test, a limitation that would become permanent. Although Eisenhower granted authority to continue planning for the *Hardtack* tests, if limited in size and condensed in time, he expressed his frustration at having to conduct extensive tests on the one hand while professing readiness to suspend testing in a disarmament program on the other. World opinion would be skeptical of the President's good faith in view of United States' paradoxical conduct.[23]

457

Strauss took the President's case directly to Donald Quarles, the Deputy Secretary of Defense. Uncharacteristically, Strauss was sharply critical of the weapon program. He compared it to the faltering missile program—too many designs, too much interservice rivalry, too much time spent on engineering refinements, and too little time spent on developing radically new approaches. The consequences were unhealthy and self-defeating. The laboratories were burdened with programmatic minutiae instead of original work. Scientists were so overloaded that they had little time for reflection or exploration. Before one test series was even concluded, the laboratories began planning for the next. Not only was the government spending unnecessarily large sums of money, but it was also aggravating United States and world sentiment to the extent that testing itself was endangered. Strauss admitted that the Commission was not free from criticism, but the greatest impetus for unnecessary tests came from the Department of Defense. Noting that he had assured the President that *Hardtack* would "not test beyond what is 'necessary,'" Strauss left no doubt that he hoped Quarles would make an honest man of him.[24]

Ultimately, Eisenhower authorized thirty-five tests in *Hardtack* Phase I, which featured six clean designs in a variety of yields; an additional clean test for United Nations observation was under study. Although worldwide fallout from *Hardtack* would be slightly greater than from *Redwing*, Strauss assured Eisenhower that it would be less than half of that from *Castle*.[25]

## LONDON REVISITED

The United States and its allies had welcomed the Soviet Union's acceptance of scientific inspection posts for fallout detection within the Russian homeland. In addition to Eisenhower's June 19, 1957, press conference, which hailed the prospects of a test ban, the allies officially acknowledged on July 2 the possibility of "a temporary suspension of nuclear testing as part of an agreement for a first step in disarmament."[26]

Despite public optimism, both the allies and the Eisenhower Administration remained skeptical that the Soviet Union would agree to an acceptable or a desirable agreement. In London, Stassen detected concern that a test moratorium could have unfavorable results. In Washington, Dulles was especially pessimistic about the London negotiations. Acknowledging Stassen's continuing optimism to British Ambassador Sir Harold Caccia, the Secretary of State discouraged Macmillan's proposal for private disarmament discussions with Eisenhower on the grounds that the timing was poor. Both the President and Dulles believed the negotiations would require much more time.[27]

Problems with Nikita Khrushchev and verification remained serious issues. During the first week of July 1957, Khrushchev emerged the victor in a Kremlin power struggle in which Malenkov, Molotov, Kaganovitch, and, ultimately, Bulganin were the losers. Khrushchev's rise to power with the full backing of the Soviet military establishment would raise questions in the Administration about the Soviets' commitment to disarmament. A few days later, Dulles told New Zealand's foreign minister, T. L. MacDonald, that he thought the London negotiations were simply a propaganda battle with little chance of success. In spite of the Soviet acceptance of inspections in principle, Dulles did not believe the new regime in Moscow would accept a workable system.[28]

Increasingly, the Administration felt trapped by the disarmament negotiations. By the end of July, Eisenhower wondered about the possibility of a recess in London, but Dulles responded that the talks "were in midstream and could not stop." Eisenhower's frustration was compounded by the fact that Strauss reported a steadily mounting campaign of letters and petitions addressed to the President demanding a ban on nuclear weapons and/or the cessation of weapon testing. Perhaps the best move, Eisenhower suggested, was for Dulles to go to London to take "command of the situation."[29]

As it turned out, Eisenhower's decision to send Dulles to London was shrewd. In the first place, only Dulles could shore up the allies' faltering confidence in American leadership. To be sure, Dulles's appearance again undermined Stassen, but it also enabled Dulles personally to assure the British, French, Canadians, and the NATO allies, including the West Germans (who were not a party to the negotiations), that the United States would not entertain aerial and ground inspection zones unacceptable to its allies. By August 2, having pulled together a unified front, Dulles was able to present an inspection working paper on behalf of the United States, Britain, France, Canada, and NATO. By further undercutting Stassen, Dulles served notice to the Soviets that the disarmament subcommittee's work in London would be fruitless. No doubt this move suited the Russians because Khrushchev apparently wanted to take disarmament questions to the summit.[30]

Returning to Washington, Dulles confirmed the importance of his mission to London. Without his presence, Dulles did not believe the United States could have obtained the concurrence of its NATO allies, especially West Germany, to the American inspection formula. Nonetheless, he confided to Strauss his pessimism that anything would come from the London negotiations, Stassen's persistent optimism notwithstanding. Dulles had no illusions that Khrushchev would ever allow mobile ground inspection teams from the West to roam freely around the Soviet Union.[31]    459

With the handwriting on the wall in London, it was evident to Dulles that the United States would have to revise its disarmament position by strengthening the link between a test moratorium and inspections. On the morning of August 9, the President, his son, Dulles, Gerard Smith, and Robert Cutler met to reassess the Administration's June 11 position. For a permanent test ban, the United States would continue to insist that satisfactory progress be made in negotiating inspections for testing, stockpiling, and producing special nuclear material. But Eisenhower also suggested that the United States announce its willingness to suspend tests for twenty-four months while the nuclear powers sought to solve the inspection dilemma. Should a solution not be found, testing could be resumed, or suspension might be extended beyond twenty-four months by unanimous agreement. If there were a violation of the testing suspension, of course, any party could begin testing again.[32]

Strauss joined the group for the afternoon session. On hearing the President's proposal, he protested that the best scientists would leave the Commission's laboratories if there could be no tests or experiments for two years or more. Eisenhower shrugged off his objection with the remark that the world situation was so difficult that Strauss's point was simply irrelevant. Ultimately, the President agreed to approve a twelve-month suspension of tests, with the possibility of an extension, after all parties agreed in principle to a cut-off of nuclear material production. Rebuffed by Eisenhower, Strauss pledged that the Commission would certainly support the President's decision and work for it. Not so certain about Stassen, Dulles and Smith decided not immediately to inform "the man in London" for fear that he would prematurely compromise the new policy on testing and disarmament.[33]

On August 15, Smith briefed the Humphrey subcommittee of the

Senate Foreign Relations Committee on the adjustment of the Administration's disarmament policy. Clearly, the Americans were not out to compromise with the Russians; rather they sought to quiet nervousness among the NATO allies while improving the United States' posture in the forthcoming United Nations debates. Smith explained that the Soviet Union had offered to suspend testing for two years, independent of disarmament agreements. The United States would now counter with a proposal to halt testing for twelve months, with an extension limited to twelve months if a cutoff to the production of nuclear materials were not established. To the senators' satisfaction, Smith explained that the new policy would strengthen the United States' position in the General Assembly debates on testing and would increase American freedom to continue testing in the future.[34]

In London, through most of August, Zorin remained calm while the American delegation consulted with its NATO allies. Word of the United States' revised position inevitably began to leak out in Paris and London. Consequently, on August 21 Eisenhower announced that the United States would be offering new "first-step" disarmament proposals, including a two-year test moratorium "under certain conditions and safeguards" and a permanent cessation of producing fissionable materials.[35]

For the Soviets, Eisenhower's offer was apparently the last straw. On August 27, two days before the West formally presented its new proposals to the London Disarmament Conference, Zorin launched a sharp attack denouncing the West for cynical delays and dishonesty. According to Zorin the Western powers virtually had given NATO a veto over the disarmament talks. With the denigration of Stassen, it was evident to the Soviet Union that the effective usefulness of the disarmament subcommittee was at an end. Zorin angrily anticipated that the Western powers were signaling their disenchantment with the London talks. Charging that the United States had been arming NATO "under cover of fruitless disarmament talks," Zorin's intemperate remarks left little doubt that the Soviet Union also sought another forum for disarmament negotiations.

Only Stassen remained optimistic about the future of the disarmament subcommittee. Hurriedly returning to the United States, this time ostensibly to attend his son's wedding, Stassen claimed that the major powers were closer together than at any time since the end of World War II. He conceded that Zorin's remarks posed a serious obstacle to an agreement, but he thought that the Russians were preparing to make concessions that they did not want interpreted as weakness. The United States should not overreact to Zorin because the Russian bluster was probably only a prelude to a propaganda alternative in the event of failure to agree. Eisenhower, of course, could only express indignation at the Russians' scornful attack while Dulles and Strauss felt some relief at Zorin's behavior. Dulles thought that perhaps the United States had already gone too far. Strauss, who wanted to avoid a test ban, hoped that when the talks seriously resumed the United States could go back to "first principles," rather than negotiate on the existing proposals.[36]

On August 29, the United States and its allies submitted a new test suspension proposal to the London Disarmament Conference as part of a comprehensive disarmament package. The proposal called for the suspension of nuclear tests for a period of twelve months provided that the conference reached agreement on the installation and maintenance of the necessary controls, including inspection posts with scientific instruments. Tests would be suspended for an additional twelve months if satisfactory progress was achieved in preparing an inspection system for ceasing production of fissionable material for weapon purposes. When the Soviets rejected the disarmament package in early September, there was little alternative but to adjourn the conference without setting a time or place for its next session.[37]

461

## NUCLEAR TESTING CONTINUES

Neither the Americans, the British, the French, nor the Russians were anxious for an immediate end to nuclear testing in summer 1957. The French had not yet tested their first weapon, and, with a test ban in the offing, the other nuclear powers wanted to complete all planned tests promptly. Throughout the London conference, the United States had continued testing in Nevada. On September 19, during Operation *Plumbbob*, the Commission fired the *Rainier* shot, a 1.7-kiloton device exploded in a tunnel drilled 2,000 feet into a mountain side. *Rainier* produced no atmospheric radioactive fallout or venting. Edward Teller had been a prime mover behind this first contained underground explosion, which demonstrated that testing could be continued underground without radioactive fallout. The Soviet Union began its 1957 series of six tests, some in the megaton range, on August 22, five days before Zorin verbally blasted the Western delegations in London. That same fall, the United Kingdom conducted tests in Australia, then concluded its experiments on November 8 with a thermonuclear shot at Christmas Island. After *Plumbbob*, the Commission intended to resume testing in 1958 with the Pacific *Hardtack* series scheduled to begin in the spring.

According to one calculation, in 1957 the three nuclear powers had exploded forty-two devices, compared to nineteen the year before. With more American tests planned in 1958, the international climate did not appear auspicious for a test moratorium. Yet there were signs that progress had been made. The major powers recognized the terrible, and unacceptable, destructiveness of nuclear warfare. In turn, they knew that the danger of nuclear war would be reduced by controlling nuclear proliferation and avoiding international confrontations and accidents. They would have to stop and then reduce the alarming buildup of atmospheric radioactive fallout. They hoped to ease the Cold War through confidence-building "first steps." Despite the denigration of Stassen and the tight linkage between a test ban and other disarmament issues, the United States had clearly signaled both its NATO allies and the Soviet Union that the United States was willing to negotiate on the testing issue. In turn, the Soviet Union had acknowledged the Western power's need for adequate safeguard and inspection systems. Although significant differences between the West and the East remained, the gap between the two on the test-ban issue had been narrowed. Control of conventional weapons and forces aside, agreement was possible in two areas. Given the ease of detecting large atmospheric tests, some limitation of nuclear tests seemed probable; given the fear of surprise attack, some combination of ground inspection and Open Skies was essential.[38]

## THE DISARMAMENT GENERAL ASSEMBLY

The twelfth session of the United Nations General Assembly became known as the "Disarmament General Assembly." As the State Department noted, seldom had so many nations placed disarmament issues so high on the General Assembly's agenda. Having failed to reach an agreement in the five-power disarmament subcommittee, the United States and the Soviet Union carried their propaganda battle to the General Assembly in September 1957.

In his opening remarks on September 20, Soviet Foreign Minister Andrei Gromyko again insisted on the importance of discontinuing all nuclear testing independent of any other disarmament agreement. As a measure of its concern, the Soviet Union would place the test-ban issue before the General Assembly as a separate and independent agenda item. In Gromyko's words, it would be a "first practical step towards the main goal—the absolute and unconditional prohibition of atomic and hydrogen weapons."[39] With this statement the Soviet Union had once again revived its old cry to "ban the bomb." All along, Strauss and the other Commissioners had argued that the Soviet Union ultimately sought to dismantle NATO's atomic shield; there was all the more reason for the United States to hold fast to its own linkage between testing, cutoff, inspection, and safeguards.

Dulles checked his own General Assembly address with Eisenhower. In his speech to the United Nations on September 19, 1957, Dulles reiterated the United States' determination to stand by its recent London proposal linking a test ban with a production cutoff. Dulles wanted to imply, but not actually say, that even without an agreement with the Soviet Union the United States was eager to develop with its allies a common position on arms control, nuclear proliferation, and test limitations, both in duration and yields. As he wrote to Macmillan the same day, "I tried to give the impression that we could, through our collective security systems, do something in the way of limitation of armament which would give us some financial relief and enable us to meet world opinion, all consistently with having collectively an adequate military establishment." Dulles evidently sought relief from both the press of public opinion and the weight of the defense budget.[40]

Stassen continued to press hard for moderating the London proposals; even Eisenhower began to grow weary of his disarmament adviser. Following Adenauer's success in the West German elections, Stassen urged another reassessment of the American policy and approach to disarmament, including a two-year suspension of testing without other disarmament conditions. "Informal quiet bilateral exploration of the USSR position, while keeping our Western partners advised, is the key for results," he advised Dulles. Stassen thought it desirable for Dulles to ask the Kremlin to send Zorin to the United Nations in New York so that informal discussions could be continued.[41]

Dulles was horrified. In sharp rebuttal, the Secretary of State rejected Stassen's overture. How could any consideration be given to altering a policy less than one month old, one that had been hailed by the President as "historic" and lauded by Dulles before the United Nations? Dulles contended that Stassen's ideas on testing ran counter to the positions of the Department of Defense, the Joint Chiefs of Staff, and the chairman of the Atomic Energy Commission.[42]

The reactions of Donald A. Quarles at Defense, Nathan F. Twining, chairman of the Joint Chiefs of Staff, and Strauss were predictable. Strauss summarized it very simply: "what is being suggested is a complete abandonment of our position," contrary to the security interests of the United States. All urged Dulles to hold fast to the August 29 London proposals. Each response was shared with Eisenhower and Nixon, who now began seriously to consider replacing Stassen; however, any such move would only further complicate an already messy situation.[43]

American and Russian maneuvering continued at the United Nations. In addition to their proposals to ban both weapons and testing, the Soviets asked that the membership of the disarmament commission be expanded to include all members of the United Nations. For their part, the Western powers sought an endorsement of the August 29 London proposals from the General Assembly. With twenty-four sponsors, the London proposals won endorsement, but over the opposition of the Soviet bloc and despite abstention of most Asian and African members. In turn, the disar-

463

mament commission was expanded to twenty-five members by a similar vote, after which the Soviets announced they would no longer participate in negotiations of either the commission or its subcommittee. On testing, the Soviet Union withdrew its resolution in favor of one sponsored by India. With the solid opposition of the NATO countries, however, the substitute test-ban resolution was defeated. The Western powers had "won" on each of the resolutions, but they did not achieve the propaganda victory sought by Dulles.[44]

## SPUTNIK

On October 4, 1957, *Sputnik I* stunned Americans. Since the dawn of the atomic age in 1945, Americans had believed that they had become pre-eminent in science and technology. At the 1955 peaceful uses conference in Geneva, American experts had gained a healthy respect for Soviet nuclear science and technology. Nor were American leaders naive about Soviet military capability or about the fact that the Russians were well advanced in missile development. Nonetheless the Russians' outstanding achievement during the International Geophysical Year took most Americans by surprise. When the Soviet Union followed up a month later by launching the half-ton *Sputnik-II*, which carried a live dog, shocked Americans knew they were behind in the space race. More ominously, it was also apparent that the Soviet Union was ahead in developing ballistic missiles capable of carrying a thermonuclear warhead.

To reassure the public, Eisenhower addressed Americans over television on November 7. Although the United States was second to none in military strength and scientific leadership, the President promised that his Administration would give high priority to government support of science and technology. To back up his pledge, Eisenhower announced that he had appointed James A. Killian, Jr., president of Massachusetts Institute of Technology, to be his special assistant for science and technology. Later, he enlarged the science advisory committee in the Office of Defense Mobilization and transferred it to the White House on December 1. The President's Science Advisory Committee, chaired by Killian, offered direct presidential access to scientists fundamentally antithetical to Teller, Lawrence, and Strauss. Not only did *Sputnik* provide "liberal" scientists renewed access to the White House, but the President's Science Advisory Committee also assured that new voices would join the internal debates over the Administration's nuclear testing and disarmament policies. Thus, as Stassen's influence waned, *Sputnik* ironically created a new circle of eminent advisers who would soon be deeply involved in test-ban negotiations.[45]

464

## THE GAITHER REPORT

The President received bad news of another sort on November 7 when the Gaither committee reported to one of the largest National Security Council meetings in history. The Gaither committee had been appointed in spring 1957 shortly after the Federal Civil Defense Administration had recommended to the President that the United States spend $40 billion over several years to build shelters against nuclear attack. Acting through the National Security Council, the President asked H. Rowan Gaither, Jr., chairman of the board at both the Ford Foundation and the RAND Corporation, to head an ad hoc panel to evaluate the civil defense proposal in relation to larger defense and national security issues. Robert C. Sprague, a Massachusetts industrialist and an expert on continental defense, was named codirector of the committee.[46]

According to one commentator, after the committee members had sifted through a mass of material, they concluded that the top echelons of the government did not know the full extent of the Soviet threat.[47] Actually, the exact opposite may have been the truth: by fall 1957, the corporate, scientific, and academic communities began to understand the President's deep concern about national security in the thermonuclear age.

Like the Killian report of 1955, the Gaither report stressed the vulnerability of the United States' deterrent, especially the strategic forces. Civil defense received secondary consideration from the Gaither committee, which concentrated on the danger of surprise attack on the Strategic Air Command and on the need to maintain an effective second-strike force. *Sputnik*, of course, heightened fears that the Russians held a significant lead in deploying intercontinental ballistic missiles (ICBM), against which the United States had no defense. The four years from 1959 to 1963 would be critical for developing ICBM deterrents and antimissile defenses. Once the United States had regained its retaliatory advantage on which the deterrence doctrine depended, the committee recommended that the United States concentrate on assembling a conventional force capable of fighting limited wars. This approach would require a vastly increased defense budget, which Eisenhower was committed to keep under control.

Regarding the Federal Civil Defense Administration's original request to build bomb shelters, the Gaither committee recommended against constructing blast shelters and set as a first priority spending several hundred million dollars on shelter and civil defense research. As a secondary priority, the committee endorsed spending $22 billion on constructing fallout shelters.[48]

Eisenhower was not happy with the Gaither report and complained to Dulles that it had been a mistake to call in an "outside group." Dulles agreed that such groups seldom took "a rounded view of the total situation," especially as it involved the Administration's attempt to control inflation in a sputtering economy. Eisenhower confided that he could not justify spending billions for shelters. For Dulles the issue was "largely a matter of temperament," and he was temperamentally unsympathetic to passive civil defense. Dulles believed that a strong offensive capability was the most effective deterrent. More important, the Gaither committee had confined itself to military problems although the international struggle against communism was not just military. Eisenhower found the Gaither report "useful," but he decided not to make it public on the grounds that advisory studies prepared for the President and the National Security Council ought to be kept confidential.[49]

## NATO, MACMILLAN, AND A CRISIS OF CONFIDENCE

466

The collapse of the London disarmament talks, the acrimony of the United Nations debates, the reaction to *Sputnik*, the creation of the President's Science Advisory Committee, and the reception of the Gaither report all reflected a deepening crisis of confidence within the Administration. If the Gaither committee had raised questions about the vulnerability of United States' defenses, there remained the even larger question about the state of the Western alliance. In late October 1957, Macmillan hurried to Washington to review the NATO partnership with Eisenhower. Strauss, who stopped in London on his way home from a meeting in Vienna, had already laid much groundwork for the discussion.[50]

At the British embassy on Massachusetts Avenue, Dulles and Macmillan shared a grim view of the future. The Western allies who themselves did not possess nuclear weapons or technology were uncertain, bewildered, and frightened. Who would decide how nuclear weapons would be used in their defense? In addition, as the cost of the nuclear deterrent increased, there would be less and less capacity, and perhaps even less utility, in maintaining the original "shield" principle. Originally NATO had been conceived as a bulwark of ready divisions sufficient to defend Europe while the nuclear powers mounted their counterattack. But the concept had never been realized, and it was increasingly anachronistic in terms of cost and military strategy.[51]

In fact, the Americans and the British had no choice but to shore up the NATO alliance as best they could. One consequence of *Sputnik* was that the Administration renewed consideration of integrating tactical weapons, including intermediate range ballistic missiles, into the NATO forces. A first step would be to negotiate a military bilateral with the United Kingdom allowing Americans to share their nuclear weapons with the British. To do so, however, would require an amendment to the Atomic Energy Act. At the conclusion of his meetings with Macmillan, Eisenhower announced he would seek an amendment "to permit . . . close and fruitful collaboration of scientists and engineers of Great Britain, the United States, and other friendly countries." As Senator Anderson observed, *Sputnik* not only upset Americans' complacency about their role in space but also their confidence in "winning" the arms race.[52]

Anderson and Durham on the Joint Committee were mystified, and just a little concerned, about what Eisenhower meant. Recalling the Klaus Fuchs spy case and the defection of Burgess and MacLean to the Soviet Union in 1951, they again raised questions about British security. Where would one draw the line between the British and other NATO allies in sharing nuclear weapon information? Strauss, who had consistently opposed sharing nuclear weapon information with the British, had a system: he would not give the British any information that the Russians did not already have. After Gerard Smith complained to Dulles that Strauss's restriction would nullify any agreement, Eisenhower privately assured Macmillan that he wanted genuine cooperation with the British. Strauss, feeling caught in the middle and very much embarrassed by Eisenhower, wondered if he should not resign. Dulles was quick to mollify Strauss by complimenting him on his skillful handling of a difficult matter.[53]

467

The extraordinary tension created by *Sputnik* also appeared in Dulles's attempt to enlist Adlai Stevenson in bipartisan support of the Administration's NATO policy. Dulles asked Stevenson to head a task force that would implement the President's plan for nuclear cooperation within NATO. Dulles shared with Stevenson NATO fears that the United States might misuse its nuclear power or, perhaps as bad, not use it at all in the defense of Europe. Appealing to Stevenson's altruism, Dulles foresaw a new international body that would control nuclear weapons "as a community asset and trust for the free world," rather than as a strictly national asset. Dulles would begin by creating a nuclear weapon stockpile for NATO as a way of assuring the allies that they could count on the United States in the face of the growing Soviet threat. At home, the Administration needed not only to amend the law but also to convince the Commission and the Department of Defense of the wisdom of trusting friendly powers with weapon information.

Stevenson was naturally wary of being compromised, and for four hours on the evening of October 30 he explored the matter privately with Dulles. He told Dulles frankly that he was unhappy with the Administration's emphasis on military preparedness over economic development. Furthermore, he thought the disarmament proposals were "unfair" to the Russians in that they had nothing to gain from reciprocal inspections. Like Stassen, Stevenson favored an inspected test ban independent from a cutoff of weapon production. Stevenson did, however, agree to help Dulles prepare several study papers.[54]

Eisenhower's stroke on November 25, 1957, upset this unusual bipartisan project between Dulles and Stevenson. At lunch the following day, Strauss told Stevenson of the President's most recent illness and relayed from Dulles that Eisenhower had only suffered a slight loss of speech. With a clear mind and no other impairments, Eisenhower planned to rest at Gettysburg for about three weeks. Still, his participation in the forthcoming NATO summit was in doubt. If Eisenhower could not attend, Stevenson believed the NATO meetings should be held on the ministerial level, not at the summit with Vice-President Nixon in Eisenhower's place. Stevenson continued to assist Dulles in the preparations up to the eve of the NATO summit, and then he quietly bowed out, in part because he felt unwanted but no doubt also because he disagreed with much Republican foreign policy.[55]

468

World attention was focused on Paris. On November 28, Indian Prime Minister Nehru appealed to both Eisenhower and Khrushchev to end nuclear testing and the arms race. "No country, no people, however powerful they might be, are safe from destruction if this competition in weapons of mass destruction and cold war continues," Nehru wrote. Subsequently, on December 10, Bulganin, now a mere figurehead for Khrushchev, wrote Eisenhower calling for a summit meeting on disarmament. In his letter, written less than a week before the convocation of the NATO conference, Bulganin also asked the United States and the United Kingdom to join the Soviet Union in a two- to three-year test moratorium starting January 1, 1958. In an obvious attempt to strain the NATO alliance, Bulganin included a proposal to create a nuclear-free zone in Western and Eastern Germany. The Bulganin letter seemed intended to embarrass Eisenhower prior to the NATO meeting, but it also served notice on the Western powers that the Soviet Union was willing to continue serious disarmament negotiations.[56]

It was evident from the American and British perspective that disarmament talks had reached a turning point after the collapse of the London Disarmament Conference and well before *Sputnik*. But *Sputnik* had precipitated the emergency meeting between Eisenhower and Macmillan in late October when the heads of state met in Washington to search out a common front. The Soviet satellites cast a pall over the December NATO summit in Paris, but so did the faltering Western economies, the President's uncertain health, and the miserable weather.[57] One can only speculate on whether or how *Sputnik* influenced the Soviet decision to abandon the disarmament subcommittee.

From Eisenhower's perspective, the NATO summit was a success. Most important, he was able to attend and to function normally. Each day confidence and mutual trust increased. In addition to agreements on nuclear warheads and intermediate range ballistic missiles for allied forces in Europe, the summit proposed a foreign ministers' meeting with the Soviets to try to break the disarmament impasse. In principle, the NATO powers endorsed a controlled reduction of arms in Europe on the condition that the

Soviet Union agree to adequate reciprocal inspections. They also decided to establish a group of scientists to advise on technical problems arising from proposals on arms control.[58]

Eisenhower's flexibility on disarmament was more fully revealed in his postconference correspondence with Macmillan. The British continued to endorse the four-power London disarmament proposal, but Macmillan urged Eisenhower not to dig in his heels. The President had no intention of doing so, and he pointed to the NATO summit, which already indicated the West's willingness to talk. For the United Kingdom, the biggest obstacle to a test ban was the comparative inferiority of British nuclear weapons. For that reason Eisenhower wanted to amend the Atomic Energy Act so the British could have access to whatever weapon information was necessary. With parity, the British would have no reason to continue testing. In his belated response to Nehru, Eisenhower gave no indication that he would break the link between a test ban and a production cutoff. As he wrote to Nehru on December 15, "to do so could increase rather than diminish the threat of aggression and war."[59]

469

By late 1957 most of those in the President's inner circle agreed that the United States was in a weak position on disarmament and the test ban. Reports from the Paris NATO meeting, from an International Red Cross conference in India, and especially from the United Nations in New York all indicated that the continuing deadlock was eroding America's moral leadership in the West. Stassen, for one, believed that the time had come for the United States to advance new proposals.

## STASSEN'S FINAL PROPOSAL

If Eisenhower was moving closer to Stassen's position on the test ban and disarmament, he was also steadily losing confidence in his disarmament adviser. Only four days after *Sputnik*, Eisenhower had authorized Stassen to explore just how open the Soviets might be to inspections, cutoff of weapon production, and other aspects of the London proposals. Eisenhower was keeping his options open by signaling his own flexibility. Yet a few days later, he complained about the heavy expenses of Stassen's office—about $500,000 annually—and expressed the hope that Stassen would accept an appointment as ambassador to Greece. Dulles was frank in telling Stassen that he would welcome the change because Stassen was so badly out of step with Strauss, the Joint Chiefs of Staff, and the Department of Defense. Dulles did not include Eisenhower among those who opposed Stassen's initiatives, but the President solidly supported Dulles's determination to sack Stassen. Although Stassen played a small role in preparing for Macmillan's visit, he had little access to the White House after his return from London. Yet by the Christmas holidays, Dulles confided in Nixon that the

Administration was heading for a "showdown" with Stassen when he presented a revised disarmament plan to the National Security Council on January 6, 1958.[60]

Stassen argued for three changes in the disarmament policy announced in London on August 29. All his proposals, he believed, would be acceptable to NATO. First, Stassen proposed dropping the linkage among the various disarmament proposals. The linkage, Stassen argued, was the major reason for the deadlock and only made the Americans appear intransigent. Second, he wanted to give the production cutoff a lower priority so that a twenty-four month test moratorium might become feasible. Finally, he suggested limited, confidence-building inspection zones for Europe, western Russia, Siberia, the Arctic, the Pacific Northwest, and western Canada with eight to twelve monitoring stations in both the United States and the Soviet Union; Stassen may have received some indication that the Soviets would be receptive to the new inspection plan. In any event, he believed his proposal would provide the basis for important first steps toward disarmament or a test ban.[61]

Unfortunately for Stassen, the Joint Chiefs of Staff, the Department of Defense, and the Commission were determined to stick by the August 29 proposals. Strauss presented the Commission's objections to a twenty-four month test moratorium, claiming that it would hurt both the development of the clean bomb and *Plowshare*, the peaceful uses program. Again, he stressed that the national laboratories would have great difficulty recovering from the negative effects of a test moratorium. Then speaking just for himself, Strauss objected to backing down from a sound disarmament position. He concluded by reporting that Teller and Lawrence believed that several score inspection stations, not a dozen, would be required to detect all tests in the Soviet Union.

Henry Cabot Lodge opened the way to further discussion when he supported Stassen's position. In responding to Lodge, Dulles revealed his own ambivalence about the United States' disarmament posture. The main obstacle to Western agreement on the issues was not NATO but the British and French, who opposed a test moratorium unless the United States would share information on nuclear weapons. Dulles also thought that the inspection zones proposed by Stassen would be politically unacceptable on all sides. At the same time, Dulles admitted that the United States had to consider public opinion. He worried that the United States could not retreat from the August 29 proposals without suffering a major propaganda defeat, but he acknowledged that the United States could not stand indefinitely on a rigid disarmament platform.

Eisenhower was as perplexed as Dulles. He agreed with Stassen and Lodge that public opinion was driving American disarmament policy. But without an amendment to the Atomic Energy Act allowing the United States

470

to share its nuclear technology, Eisenhower predicted that NATO would collapse. He concurred with Dulles that the time was not ripe for new proposals requiring coordination with NATO. Although Eisenhower did not like Stassen's proposed inspection zones, neither did he believe that these proposals retreated from existing policy. Most puzzling to Eisenhower was the conflict between his scientific advisers, especially Teller and Rabi, with Strauss supporting one side and Stassen the other.

From his "back bench," Killian interrupted to report that the Science Advisory Committee had already organized a technical study on the impact of a test ban on United States and Soviet weapon programs and on the feasibility of monitoring a test suspension. Eisenhower and Dulles were immediately interested. As Killian recalled, Dulles "had been looking for something to support his intuitive view that the United States should move toward a suspension of tests." Then and there, Eisenhower asked the National Security Council to sponsor the technical study on detecting nuclear tests. The President closed the meeting with the comment that the burden of the arms race hung heavy everywhere. For that reason, the United States should keep the world focused on nuclear disarmament.[62]

471

The National Security Council meeting on January 6 proved to be Stassen's "last hurrah" in the Eisenhower Administration. Perhaps more than anyone else on the President's staff, Stassen had worked to keep Eisenhower's test ban and disarmament options open. After the National Security Council ostensibly rejected his recommendations, Stassen knew he would have to resign. By February he was gone, but he had won a quiet victory. In its subsequent order, which established the technical panel on disarmament under the chairmanship of Hans Bethe, the National Security Council noted the Administration's adherence to the August 29 four-power proposals "for the time being." That is, the council would reexamine its policy should Congress amend the Atomic Energy Act allowing the United States to share its nuclear weapon information. The President and his advisers may not have realized it yet, but the Administration had forged, in effect, new linkages to a test suspension while greatly weakening the old. Obviously, it would be much easier to convince Congress to amend the Atomic Energy Act than it would be to negotiate a production cutoff with the Soviet Union.[63]

## THE BETHE PANEL CONVENES

The year 1958 began with little public indication of the Administration's shifting views on disarmament. In his note to Nehru and in his public statements to NATO, Eisenhower had already indirectly told the Russians that the United States was sticking to its August 29, 1957, proposals. On

January 12, in a letter to Bulganin, Eisenhower seemed to offer little more than a restatement of the August 29 principles. He agreed to meet with the Soviet leaders, but only after necessary groundwork had been laid at the ministerial level. Candidly, Eisenhower expressed his wariness of high-level meetings, such as the euphoric 1955 Geneva summit, which created great expectations and subsequently disillusionment, dejection, and even greater distrust. Eisenhower did, however, invite the Soviets to join American scientists in technical studies of the possibilities of verification and supervision of disarmament and test-ban agreements.[64]

Eisenhower's proposal for technical studies with the Soviet Union was neither unprecedented nor original, but it obviously reflected the National Security Council's decision to authorize technical disarmament studies of its own. At the conclusion of the 1955 peaceful uses conference, the United States and the Soviet Union had participated in a technical conference on the control of peaceful nuclear materials.[65] During the London conference in summer 1957, Britain's Selwyn Lloyd had advocated forming technical committees to study verification systems. Eisenhower's appointment of Killian as his science adviser and his advocacy of international technical studies indicated his seriousness in pursuing disarmament. In the last analysis, any disarmament agreement would rest on its technical feasibility.[66]

Following the National Security Council meeting on January 6, Killian and Cutler selected an interagency committee to conduct the technical disarmament studies. On the Bethe panel, as it was called, were representatives from the Atomic Energy Commission, the Department of Defense, the Central Intelligence Agency, and the missile panel of the President's Science Advisory Committee. In addition, the Bethe panel called on experts from the Los Alamos and Livermore weapon laboratories and from the Air Force Technical Applications Center. The State Department supplied observers. The Bethe panel focused on three major questions: Could the United States detect both atmospheric and underground Soviet nuclear tests? What were the comparative strengths of the Russian and American nuclear arsenals? What restrictions would a test ban place on the Commission's weapon laboratories?[67]

## INTERNATIONAL PRESSURES FOR A TEST BAN

While the Bethe panel launched its technical studies, international pressure for a test ban continued to mount. In Cairo, the Afro-Asian Solidarity Conference called for the end of nuclear testing. Shortly thereafter on January 13, Linus Pauling presented an antitesting petition to the Secretary General of the United Nations. Pauling had now collected more than 9,000 signatures from forty-four countries, including those of 36 Nobel laureates, 101 members of the National Academy of Sciences, 35 fellows of the Royal Society of London, and 216 members and correspondents of the Soviet Academy of Sciences. Because the President had consulted personally with Teller, Pauling requested an appointment for himself. As if to punctuate Pauling's request, on February 1 the Council of the Federation of American Scientists advocated a ban on all testing, even of the smallest weapons.[68]

During the period scientific data on fallout was continuously published. In New York, the fourth session of the United Nations' Scientific Committee on the Effects of Atomic Radiation met from January 27 through February 28 to draft its final report. On the whole, the United States delegation headed by Shields Warren was satisfied that the report on somatic and genetic effects of radiation would refute many exaggerated claims about the hazards of radiation. With the exception of the report's conclusion, the Americans had striven successfully to keep "political" comments from the draft. When the Soviets sponsored a condemnation of testing for the conclusion, the United States succeeded in blocking the move by tabling that part of the report.[69]

473

The *Bulletin of the Atomic Scientists* devoted its entire January issue to "Radiation and Man," with reports from Libby and Austin Brues as well as an article by Jack Schubert and Ralph Lapp. Under the aegis of Project *Sunshine*, J. Laurence Kulp and his associates from Lamont Laboratory, Columbia University, published new information on strontium-90 in the February issue of *Science*. Kulp and his colleagues concluded that the strontium-90 levels were not hazardous, but they also indicated that the levels of strontium-90 accumulated in human bones, especially children's, had risen measurably since 1956. Pauling then used the data to illustrate dramatically the cumulative millicuries of strontium-90 per square mile in New York City. Although not confirming Pauling's fears, General Alfred D. Starbird, the Commission's director of military application, forwarded to the Commission a warning from the division of biology and medicine that the *Hardtack* tests would produce more worldwide fallout than did Operation *Redwing* in 1956. Given the climate of world opinion, Commissioner Vance thought it unwise for the United States to conduct tests at levels so much higher than previous operations.[70]

## HUMPHREY SUBCOMMITTEE

Perhaps the most significant pressure to end testing at this time came from Senator Hubert H. Humphrey's subcommittee on disarmament, which held hearings on the issue from February into April. As early as November 1957, Humphrey had written Eisenhower asking for a more flexible disarmament policy. After discussions with Stassen, Humphrey suggested that the United States declare its willingness to negotiate separately on a nuclear test ban with the only condition being agreement on an effective inspection system under United Nations administration. Humphrey was supported in his position by Senators Anderson and Stuart Symington, a former Secretary of the Air Force.[71]

Humphrey opened his hearings on February 28 with testimony from Stassen, who had only recently left the Administration. Although Humphrey could not prove it at the time, he suspected that Stassen merely repeated his National Security Council briefing for the benefit of the disarmament subcommittee. Officially, Stassen kept the Administration's confidence, but in substance his Congressional testimony outlined his well-known disarmament plans. There was hardly any secret about Stassen's views or his optimism about the readiness of the Soviet Union to engage in serious disarmament negotiations.[72]

In subsequent hearings, the Humphrey subcommittee, with one exception, limited testimony to either representatives of the Commission and its weapon laboratories or members of the Bethe panel. Strauss, Libby, Starbird, and Spofford G. English, acting deputy director of research, all defended the Administration's official policy linking a test ban to other disarmament issues. As they stated repeatedly, the manufacturing and stockpiling of nuclear weapons, not their testing, threatened world peace. According to the Commission spokesman, a test ban would hurt the United States more than the Soviet Union because American testing emphasized the development of defensive weapons. Significantly, Humphrey did not call for testimony from either the State or Defense departments, a fact that no doubt underlined the Commission's increasing isolation on the disarmament question.[73]

Incredibly, in March 1958 both the Commission and the Russians strengthened the positions of the test-ban advocates; the former inadvertently, the latter perhaps deliberately. On March 6 while Libby testified before the Humphrey subcommittee, the Commission announced that the maximum distance at which its seismological stations had detected the *Rainier* shot was only 250 miles. The implications, if true, were immediately evident and appeared self-serving to the Commission's determination to keep testing. If detection of underground tests were so limited, policing an international test ban would be impossible. During the ensuing controversy the Commission hastily revised its estimates to 2,300 miles, but the damage had been done. In the eyes of Senator Anderson and others, the Commission and Strauss had been discredited by an apparently deliberate attempt to falsify the *Rainier* data. Humphrey, however, was inclined to accept Libby's explanation that the error was an honest mistake made while Strauss was on vacation.[74] But even an exonerated Commission would now find it much more difficult to argue the technical difficulties of monitoring a test ban.

The Humphrey subcommittee provided Edward Teller and Hans Bethe still another arena in which to debate America's nuclear weapon policy. Although Bethe was a Nobel laureate, Teller, who had recently become director of the Livermore Laboratory, was no doubt better known to the general public. In February, *Life* magazine had published a preview of Teller's and Albert Latter's *Our Nuclear Future*. In *Life* Teller and Latter also challenged Pauling and his 9,000 scientists who had petitioned the United Nations for a test ban. Before the Humphrey subcommittee, Teller repeated his familiar arguments for the need to test clean tactical weapons and to develop peaceful uses of nuclear explosives. Prophetically, he now raised questions about the reliability of detecting small underground tests and verifying a production cutoff in the Soviet Union. Perhaps unintentionally, Teller delivered a blow to the Administration's August 29 policy when he suggested that it might be more difficult to validate a production cutoff than it would be to monitor tests.[75]

Bethe's published testimony had been heavily censored, but it was clear in the published version that he acknowledged the difficulties of detecting both underground and high-altitude tests. He also agreed with Teller on the near impossibility of policing nuclear weapon stockpiles, although he was more optimistic about monitoring production. On the matter of testing, however, Bethe broke sharply with Teller and the Commission. Assuming that the United States was well ahead of the Russians in weapon design, variety, and stockpile, Bethe argued that a test ban would be greatly advantageous to the United States. Bethe admitted that if the Soviets cheated on a test ban, they would eventually overtake the United States. But Bethe did not believe the Russians could violate the test ban without incurring unacceptable risks of being detected.[76] Although Humphrey repeatedly professed his objectivity, it was clear that he was pleased with Bethe's remarks.

The Commission became increasingly nervous about the mounting pressure for a test cessation. During the Humphrey subcommittee hearings, Ramey requested the Commission prepare comments on a bill introduced in June 1957 by Congressman Charles O. Porter of Oregon, who was to become a major critic of the *Hardtack* tests. The bill would have halted United States testing as long as other countries refrained. Although Porter's bill stood little chance of passage, it irritated the Commission. Commissioner John S. Graham described his own opinions on testing as "tentative." Commenting on the Porter bill, Graham concluded that it was not wise to prohibit testing through legislation but that "some reasonable limitations on testing [were] so important that we should use every vehicle . . . to discuss these issues." At the Humphrey hearings Commissioners Gra-

475

ham, Floberg, and Libby agreed that disarmament and *imminent* test cessation were the most important issues facing the Commission.[77]


## TEST BAN ALTERNATIVES

Even Strauss recognized that a new disarmament policy was inevitable. To
complicate matters for the Commission, during the fall and winter of
1957–1958 Strauss moved to the periphery of the disarmament discussion,
almost as a messenger among Eisenhower, Dulles, and the Congress.
Shortly after the National Security Council meeting on January 6, Strauss
presented Eisenhower with an idea he had discussed with Dulles. Strauss's
new approach would retain the linkage between a test ban and a production
cutoff. He advocated closing down all production plants to ease the inspection problem and disassembling existing weapons to provide fissionable
material for power and other peaceful needs; therefore, all nuclear weapon
stockpiles would be reduced. According to Strauss, General Manager
Fields and Starbird agreed that the proposal could be "far more easily inspected" than earlier ideas. Strauss recommended trying the arrangement
for three years, after which, if the agreement worked out, testing could be
resumed "for peaceful purposes only." Eisenhower liked the idea and encouraged Strauss to pursue it.[78]

After reviewing sentiment in the United Nations and the Administration, even Fields acknowledged that the Commission should develop an
acceptable fallback position. He appointed an ad hoc disarmament committee of senior Commission staff to propose alternative policies. The committee identified ten possible alternatives, or variations thereof, but no two
committee members were able to agree on a single recommendation. From
the committee's perspective, all alternatives had considerable disadvantages. The committee concluded,

> Which one, therefore, is to be accepted is a function of how desper-
> ately we need make a new proposal and what we desire to achieve
> thereby:—taking a real disarmament step; making a proposal the
> Soviets might accept; making a proposal designed merely to give us
> propaganda advantage; or making a proposal to satisfy neutrals rela-
> tive to fallout; or a combination of these.[79]

The committee's note of desperation accurately depicted the Commission's
frustration at being unable to maintain its grip on the Administration's disarmament policy.

The Commission's first priority, obviously, was to continue testing as
long and as intensely as possible. Starbird outlined plans to conduct a
harbor excavation experiment in Alaska in 1959. Furthermore, he predicted that in the near future the United States would adopt a policy of

476

continuous testing, perhaps conducted completely underground. Libby enthusiastically endorsed greatly increasing underground testing. Yet even the possibility that the Commission might save the testing program by moving it underground was coolly received by Fields, who noted several limitations that could never be overcome—primarily the inability of testing complete weapon systems underground.[80]


## THE BETHE PANEL REPORTS

While the Commission searched ineffectively for a solution to the disarmament dilemma, the Bethe panel proceeded to evaluate the technical feasibility of monitoring a test suspension and the comparative losses to the United States and the Soviet Union as a result of test cessation. Given the interagency composition of the committee, the Bethe panel reached rather modest conclusions by late March 1958. The Commission's representatives who signed the report found little reason to complain. The Bethe panel described "a practical detection system" that would identify nuclear explosions in the Soviet Union, except for very small underground shots. The system would require observation stations, mobile ground units, and rights to fly over parts of the Soviet Union. The panel did not recommend suspension of the *Hardtack* tests and conceded that a test ban would result in some deterioration of the weapon laboratories. The United States, according to the panel, could benefit from additional testing—especially clean and small, inexpensive weapons. Finally, the panel was not able to estimate whether a test ban would be to the net military advantage of the United States.[81]

477

Clearly Bethe's thinking, supported by Herbert Scoville of the Central Intelligence Agency, dominated the panel. Starbird and General Herbert B. Loper firmly opposed even the panel's moderate report, but the Department of Defense failed to take a strong stand on the military consequences of a test ban, although in a separate action Quarles forwarded Maxwell D. Taylor's objection to breaking the disarmament linkage. As a result, the Bethe panel left the door open for the President's Science Advisory Committee to make its own estimate on the comparative consequences of a test ban.[82]


## THE SOVIET UNILATERAL TEST SUSPENSION

The second boost for the test-ban advocates in March came from the Soviet Union. On March 31, after completing one of the most intensive test series in history, the Supreme Soviet announced it would suspend all Russian atomic and hydrogen weapon tests and appealed to the United States and

United Kingdom to do likewise. From the American perspective, the Soviet announcement was a cynical, yet brilliant, propaganda ploy. Since autumn 1957 the Russians had been testing at an unprecedented rate, sometimes detonating two or more shots in a single day, so that global fallout levels had risen sharply by spring 1958. Bethe even speculated before the Humphrey subcommittee that the Russians had rushed to finish their tests before the United States began the *Hardtack* series. Nevertheless, the Soviet action won worldwide acclaim, especially in Asia and Africa.[83]

The United States was not caught unawares, but that fact hardly blunted the impact of the Russian announcement. On March 24, Eisenhower met with his senior advisers to work out a response to the impending Soviet declaration. Secretary Dulles suggested that the President beat the Russians to the punch by immediately announcing that the United States would suspend all testing for two years after the *Hardtack* series. Strauss and the Department of Defense representatives were strongly opposed, warning that the NATO allies would conclude that the United States was frightened. On second thought, Dulles agreed that Macmillan and Adenauer could be embarrassed if an apparently panicked United States were to play into the hands of its political enemies. Strauss now offered the plan that he had discussed with the President in February: a two-year test suspension and production cutoff accompanied by a pledge to reduce weapon stockpiles by using the nuclear material "to meet the needs of a power-hungry world." The trouble with Strauss's proposal was that it too would require prior consultation with the NATO allies. It was frustrating that, although the Americans knew the Russian announcement was imminent, the Administration could do nothing about it.

Stymied over how to soften the Russians' propaganda blow, Eisenhower nonetheless drew renewed resolve from the incident. For the first time in their history, he reflected, Americans were really "scared" by the tremendous power of nuclear weapons. For Eisenhower, it was "simply intolerable" for the United States to lose its moral leadership of the free world. For one thing, he speculated, the United States could confine its testing underground. For another, if Congress amended the Atomic Energy Act and the Soviets accepted inspection, a nuclear test suspension would be inevitable. Whatever the outcome, he directed his defense and security advisers "to think about what could be done to get rid of the terrible impasse in which we now find ourselves with regard to disarmament." The Administration was now on notice that the President would soon revamp the United States' disarmament and test-ban policies.[84]

Eisenhower met with the National Security Council on April 4 to discuss the Bethe panel's report. Noting that some areas of the Soviet Union have more than 140 earthquakes a year, Eisenhower asked Bethe whether underground tests in the ten-megaton range could be distinguished from earthquakes. Bethe could not provide a definitive answer, but he estimated that seismologists could tell the difference most times. Dulles was surprised that as many as thirty checkpoints would be required in the Soviet Union and wondered how many would be needed in the United States. Bethe thought perhaps fifteen. What if, Dulles interjected, the Soviets wanted to include all of the Western Hemisphere? Dulles was also skeptical that the Russians would accept the proposed overflights. Bethe did not think the number of checkpoints was critical so long as some kind of mobile inspection team could insure against cheating. Again Eisenhower voiced his worry about the tension gripping the free world over the nuclear testing issue. In the President's judgment, the United States faced a steady psychological erosion of its leadership on disarmament.[85]

In this climate of mounting gloom over America's ability to provide moral leadership to the Western alliance, Khrushchev asked Eisenhower to join the Soviet Union in a test cessation that would ease the fears of "all strata of society, from political personages, scientists, and specialists to ordinary people, the rank-and-file workers of city and village, to mothers of families." Gallingly, Khrushchev cited Pauling's United Nations petition signed by scientists from the United States and the Soviet Union as a testament against allowing continued nuclear tests, "thereby causing harm to the health of people throughout the entire world and threatening the normal development of coming generations." Hastily, Dulles prepared a presidential reply, little more than a holding action. In addition to the old formulas, the President's note repeated his January 12 proposal that technicians from both countries work cooperatively to develop workable control measures. To reporters, Dulles explained that the Soviet unilateral declaration was propaganda, pure and simple. Because the Russians knew of the planned *Hardtack* series, their promise to stop testing only if others followed suit was a transparent ploy requiring neither self-denial nor even hesitation in their own testing program. Nevertheless, by summarizing the Bethe panel's conclusions, Dulles also signaled that the Administration had its own technicians hard at work searching for an acceptable disarmament policy.[86]

When Eisenhower met with reporters on April 9, he had already reviewed his position on disarmament with Dulles. To questions about the Bethe panel and Killian's group, he replied with the characteristic vagueness that he often used with the press. But when asked directly whether he would consider a test suspension if the scientific reports were favorable, he answered "yes" without hesitation. In fact, he said he might even suspend tests unilaterally. Strauss was flabbergasted and immediately called Dulles to find out if the President and the Secretary of State were in collusion on the testing issue. Dulles assured Strauss that nothing was prearranged with the President. Angrily, Strauss complained that he was having great difficulty keeping "his ducks in a row." No doubt he was also upset that Killian and Bethe were steadily gaining influence within the President's inner circle.[87]

479

That same week the President's Science Advisory Committee met in Puerto Rico to evaluate the Bethe panel report. On the question of the comparative military advantage of a test suspension, the Killian committee filled the void left by the Bethe panel by concluding that an end to testing by both sides would "freeze the edge" the United States had in nuclear weapon technology. The committee did not challenge the need to complete the *Hardtack* series but believed that it would be in the United States' interest to break the linkage binding a test ban to other disarmament proposals. Finally, given the controversy over the reliability of technical detection systems, the Science Advisory Committee recommended further studies of monitoring techniques, perhaps in cooperation with the Soviets.[88]

## THE COMMITTEE OF PRINCIPALS

To provide guidance for a possible summit meeting, Eisenhower established a special Cabinet committee consisting of Dulles, as chairman, along with Strauss, Secretary of Defense Neil H. McElroy, and Secretary of the Treasury George Humphrey. In turn, on April 7 the White House appointed a committee of principals, a working group on disarmament policy comprising the Secretaries of State and Defense, the chairman of the Atomic Energy Commission, the director of the Central Intelligence Agency, and the President's science adviser. With Dulles in command, the State Department prepared a revision of the disarmament policy paper approved by the National Security Council on June 11, 1957; the paper was to guide subsequent discussions.[89]

The principals labored through mid-April without agreeing on specific new United States initiatives on disarmament. In general, they found the United States' policy adequate in scope and objective, but they differed on whether the various components of American disarmament policy could be separated. Consequently, United States policy appeared complex, rigid, and vulnerable in world opinion. The Department of State, the Central Intelligence Agency, and Killian's group favored a separate, inspected test ban. The Commission, on the other hand, indicating that it was bending, proposed a limitation on testing, rather than an outright ban. According to the Commission's formula, atmospheric tests would be limited to twenty per year having no greater yield than 100 kilotons each while underground tests would be unrestricted. The Commission also continued to insist that a test limitation agreement be linked to some other disarmament measure, although not necessarily a production cutoff. The Defense Department remained noncommital in the discussion.[90]

On his return from Puerto Rico, Killian met personally with Strauss to review his committee's recommendations. Strauss was surprised that Killian presented the views of the entire committee, not just the Bethe panel.

Killian quickly got to his major contention: that because the United States was technically ahead in weapons, a mutual test suspension would be advantageous to the United States. Bluntly, Strauss told Killian he could not agree. Although Americans believed they were ahead, Strauss was not convinced. In any event, the United States' lead was only relative, based on the development of smaller, lighter weapons. Because the United States was a democracy, Strauss argued, it was a defender nation, not an aggressor like the Soviet Union. Thus, while the Soviets could concentrate on developing large thermonuclear warheads, the United States would have to develop more sophisticated weapons. Historically, he continued, with the advent of new weapons, countermeasures were always devised but sometimes lagged for years. Strauss conceded that a test ban seemed attractive, but with "defensive atomic weapons . . . in their infancy" an end to testing "would be purchased at an intolerable cost to our security." According to Strauss, Killian was surprised, shaken, and uncertain as to what to do next.[91]

Killian's confusion, no doubt, was short lived, especially after his April 17 meeting with Eisenhower from whom he received encouragement for the Science Advisory Committee's recommendations. Killian hoped that the United States could suspend testing after the *Hardtack* series, but conscientiously he reported the continued opposition of the Commission and the Defense Department. The President confided in Killian that he had not been very impressed, or even convinced, by the pleas of Teller, Lawrence, and Mills for continued testing of clean and defensive weapons. Obviously, similar justifications from Strauss and Quarles were also wearing thin. Again, on April 22, Khrushchev wrote Eisenhower a long, stentorian letter in which he reviewed all past differences over disarmament and piously concluded with a call to "put an end to polemics on this subject."[92] This time, with advice and assistance primarily from Dulles, the President would be ready with a different reply for the Russian premier.

## DULLES'S DISARMAMENT ADVISERS

At his home on April 26, Dulles convened a critical meeting of his four personal disarmament advisers and the committee of principals. Dulles's advisers, all close friends of Eisenhower's, included General Alfred M. Gruenther, former NATO commander; Robert A. Lovett, Truman's Secretary of Defense; John J. McCloy, civilian head of German occupation; and General Walter Bedell Smith, Eisenhower's former chief-of-staff. Dulles set the tone in his opening remarks, stressing the urgency to do something to erase the widely held image of the United States as a militaristic nation. In Dulles's opinion, the continued military emphasis probably caused the United States to lose more friends than the gain from small technical military advances was worth. The United States, he said, now had no choice but to demonstrate the nation's interest in peace and arms control.

Dulles reviewed the various elements of the disarmament package. On testing, he summarized the views of the Science Advisory Committee, the Commission, and the Department of Defense. He also observed that the British were not only committed to complete their scheduled 1958 tests but also would not give up testing unless American weapon technology could be made available through an amendment of the Atomic Energy Act. On the production cutoff, Dulles reluctantly reported that the Strauss proposal for cannibalizing stockpiles for fissionable materials was dead. Strauss and Quarles repeated their objections to a test ban, while Killian reviewed the recommendations of the Science Advisory Committee. None of Dulles's four advisers took a clear-cut stand for or against a test suspension; indeed, they appeared to believe that suspension was a foregone conclusion. The forum was ideal for Dulles, however, because it enabled him to set a new course for the Administration without obtaining the formal concurrence of the Commission and the Defense Department through the National Security Council.[93]

Following his Saturday conference, Dulles worked rapidly on a reply to Khrushchev's latest note. By Monday, April 28, 1958, he had drafted Eisenhower's response. "The United States is determined that we will ultimately reach an agreement on disarmament," the President wrote. While he reiterated the United States' concerns for a production cutoff, a stockpile reduction, a test cessation, Open Skies, and the peaceful use of outer space, Eisenhower merely alluded to the "interdependence" of these issues without insisting upon their linkage. Rather, he stressed the need for technical studies of inspection and control, such as those called for by the United Nations General Assembly. Technical studies on test detection, for example, could serve as a vital first step to a political agreement. Significantly, the President made no mention of technical studies relative to production cutoff and left vague whether the United States was still bound to the August 29 disarmament proposals.[94]

## PLANNING FOR HARDTACK

While the Eisenhower Administration reevaluated its disarmament policies, the Commission continued its planning for Operation *Hardtack* at the Enewetak Proving Ground. On January 31, 1958, Eisenhower had approved modified plans for *Hardtack* that included several tests of various missile warheads. In the aftermath of *Sputnik*, the Commission and the Department of Defense considered these tests essential, but the two agencies disagreed on the advisability of two high-altitude shots. Strauss vehemently opposed detonating the high-altitude shots because the tests might

482

blind the islanders on nearby atolls. After the experience of *Castle-Bravo* the Commission did not want to risk another test fiasco. More important, mindful of the United States' role as United Nations' trustee for the islands, Strauss believed that it would be immoral to gamble with the health and safety of the Marshallese. He maintained that the cost of moving the two shots northeastward to Johnston Island would be minimal compared to the risks of testing at Enewetak. Despite Killian's support of the Defense Department, Quarles was unable to overrule Strauss's objections when they met with Dulles, McElroy, and Twining on April 7. The extra cost and delay notwithstanding, the two shots were eventually moved to Johnston Island.[95]

No sooner had agreement been reached on the Johnston Island tests than the Department of Defense proposed three additional high-altitude tests in a new series named *Argus*, to be fired 300 miles over the South Atlantic. The principal purpose of the *Argus* tests, scheduled for August and September 1958, was to test the "Christofilos effect," in which electrons from high-altitude bursts were captured by the earth's magnetic field resulting in some interference with radio, radar, and other communication systems. Eisenhower approved the additional *Argus* series on May 1, significantly with the concurrence of the Commission, the Departments of Defense and State, and Killian.[96]

483

The weapon laboratories also pushed hard to accelerate the testing programs through spring and summer 1958. With the prospect of a moratorium for two or more years, the laboratories stepped up experiments and expenditures wherever possible. When Eisenhower approved *Hardtack*, he had deferred a decision on an underground series for the Nevada Test Site during fall 1958. With continued pressure from the laboratories and the Commission, Eisenhower finally approved the underground series, originally called *Millrace*, on June 13. As the test suspension became more and more a certainty, the Commission and Defense carried forward requests for additional shots including balloon, tunnel, and safety tests in Nevada. The testing pace became so frenetic that Eisenhower did not finally approve *Hardtack II*, as the series was now called, until late summer.[97]

## DEMONSTRATIONS AGAINST TESTING

As the government intensified its weapon experiments, protestors also intensified their efforts to halt testing. On the twelfth anniversary of the bombing of Hiroshima, a small Quaker group, calling itself the Committee for Non-Violent Action Against Testing, set up camp outside the gates of the Nevada Test Site near Mercury. By twos and threes the protestors attempted to enter the test site but were stopped by the sheriff of Nye County, who arrested them for trespassing. During that fall, small groups of pacifists and political activists formed the National Committee for a Sane Nuclear Policy, later simply called SANE. In 1958 SANE was especially active in lobbying the Humphrey subcommittee for a Congressional test-ban resolution. Tactically, the leaders of SANE decided to focus their energies on the testing issue, rather than to confront the entire disarmament question.[98]

In February 1958, Strauss received reports that Lawrence Scott and the committee for non-violent action planned to sail to the Pacific Proving Ground in hopes of stopping the *Hardtack* tests. The voyage of the *Golden Rule* would obviously be symbolic with no chance of actually halting the shots. Nevertheless, by actually putting themselves at risk, the crew hoped to remind the world of the *Lucky Dragon*'s fate and thus quicken the world's conscience. The *Golden Rule* did not sail more than a mile and a half from Honolulu before it was detained by the Coast Guard on May 1. Although largely ignored by the Commissioners, the "voyage" of the *Golden Rule* succeeded in capturing public and press attention.[99]

484

Less dramatically, but more personally, the committee for non-violent action brought its protest to the Commission itself. On May 7, a group of pacifists led by David Dellenger and Theodore Olson walked into the lobby of the new Commission headquarters building in Germantown, Maryland, to announce that they would remain there fasting until they could speak to the Commissioners. Among the group were the wife and child of a crewman on the *Golden Rule* and a protestor who had fallen ill and failed to catch the boat before it left California. No doubt the demonstrators expected to be arrested for trespassing, but to mute publicity the Commission decided they could stay in the lobby or the adjacent auditorium indefinitely. Strauss even provided cots, blankets, a telephone, and a washroom for the group. Sandwiches, coffee, and soft drinks were offered, and the protestors, newsmen, guards, and employees eventually became friendly. Still, Dellenger and his colleagues pledged to maintain their fast and vigil in the lobby until they could speak personally to the Commissioners.

For a week they waited. First, Graham volunteered to see the group on behalf of the Commission. The meeting was cordial but not satisfactory for Dellenger. The demonstrators decided to hold out, in part to learn the fate of their family and friends on the *Golden Rule* but mostly to present their views to the entire Commission or at least to Strauss.

Finally, Strauss agreed to talk with the group in one of history's most unusual confrontations between antiwar protestors and a government official. Appealing to the moral force of the Christian-Judaic tradition and to the nonviolent principles of Ghandi, the pacifists asked Strauss and the Commission to abandon their preparations for nuclear war. For the most part, the exchange continued on this high moral and ethical level. Strauss's conscience was moved, and he reflected that prior to World War II when he was in the banking business he had refused, on moral grounds, to invest in either munitions or distillery businesses. But the subsequent holocaust of World War II had convinced him that only America's great nuclear deterrent had saved the world from communist domination.

The demonstrators disagreed, claiming that a nation under God should not have fought even against the Nazis. Strauss was nonplussed, and the courtly southern Jew rhetorically asked whether the Civil War, which freed the slaves, was justified. No, replied one northern pacifist; "the body is nothing," and only the freedom of the spirit mattered. Indeed, the blacks might have been freer had there not been a Civil War. No American war, not even the Revolution, had been justified. If the Commission could not by itself end nuclear testing, then mindful of the Nuremberg trials the pacifists stated that Strauss and everyone who worked for the Commission should resign.

Here the dialog virtually ended. Unknown to the demonstrators, Strauss had already resigned; and so with some irony he noted that America was still a free country, that Commission employees could work wherever they wanted but that most worked for the government out of a sense of duty as citizens. Not surprisingly, the confrontation ended inconclusively, albeit amicably. Within weeks, Dellenger and his friends were back in Washington, D.C., to protest in front of the White House and to rally near the Washington Monument where Pauling demanded an end to nuclear testing.[100]

485

## UNDERGROUND TESTING: A REFUGE

By May 1, 1958, even the most ardent supporter of nuclear defense knew that the days of atmospheric testing were numbered. Thus, while the protestors camped in the lobby of the Germantown headquarters building, the general advisory committee met in the Commission's Washington offices to discuss the future of nuclear weapons. Although Defense officials continued to support the Commission over the President's Science Advisory Committee, the Commission asked the general advisory committee: "How completely could our weapons program go forward if we were to be limited to underground tests only?" For two days the general advisory committee wrestled with that issue.[101]

Edward Teller took the lead in pressing the committee to consider the effects of a test moratorium after *Hardtack* upon the laboratories, the Commission, and the United States. Although Teller thought a complete moratorium would have serious consequences, he ventured that "an intermediate position," including underground, high-altitude, and a limited number of atmospheric peaceful tests might actually be desirable. Because absolute verification of a test ban would be impossible, Teller wanted the general advisory committee to endorse a position that would allow the development of peaceful nuclear explosives and anti-ballistic-missile warheads.

Speaking from the perspective of the President's Science Advisory Committee was James B. Fisk, a prominent physicist and former director of research at the Commission. Fisk emphasized the "broad" issues relating to a test moratorium; something would have to be done to calm public fears over atmospheric contamination. More important, Fisk viewed "some kind of test moratorium" as an initial step in reducing world tensions and stopping the arms race. Fisk had to leave, however, before the advisory committee adopted Teller's proposals for confining all tests underground with the exception of limited peaceful "ditch-digger" and antimissile tests. "The Committee is unanimously agreed that to go any farther than this in the restriction of testing would seriously endanger the security of the United States." [102]

486

Events were moving quickly on May 14 when Strauss met with the President. Already on May 9 Khrushchev had accepted Eisenhower's invitation to join technical disarmament studies. With Macmillan due to visit Washington in early June to confer on an exchange of nuclear weapon information, among other things, the prospects of a test moratorium were even more certain. The President and Strauss spoke briefly on the status of peaceful uses, whereupon Eisenhower asked Strauss to be his special adviser on Atoms for Peace under Dulles in the State Department following his term as chairman of the Commission. Strauss was delighted, especially if that meant he would remain within the "NSC family." On disarmament, Strauss reported that the general advisory committee was completely at variance with the conclusions of the Killian report, particularly on the matter of the superiority of American nuclear weapons. According to the committee, American defensive systems were not so advanced as Soviet offensive weapons. Eisenhower listened but offered no comment. [103]

Strauss gave Dulles a copy of the general advisory committee's report the following day. If the suspension of atmospheric tests following *Hardtack* were politically necessary, Strauss hoped that testing could be moved underground. Dulles commented that the British, too, would like to end testing by phases so that they could continue to develop "small" weapons of less than one megaton. Much depended on whether Congress approved an amendment to the Atomic Energy Act to permit exchanging weapon data with the British. Dulles also expressed his regret on Strauss's pending retirement from the Commission. With the President, Dulles encouraged him to become "ambassador-at-large" on Atoms-for-Peace matters. [104]

On May 24, Eisenhower wrote Khrushchev to propose convening the technical disarmament conference in Geneva within three weeks of the Soviets' acceptance of the invitation. He suggested inviting scientists from the United Kingdom, France, and other nations having experts on detecting nuclear tests. Eisenhower stressed the importance of selecting scientists "chosen on the basis of special competence, so as to assure that we get scientific, not political, conclusions." To minimize political maneuvering, he suggested that the conference draft an initial progress report within thirty days and prepare its final report within sixty days. When Khrushchev accepted on May 30, asking that Czechoslovakia, Poland, and India be included in the conference, the stage was set for the conference of experts, with the exception of India, to convene in Geneva on July 1.[105]

With the President now moving resolutely toward a moratorium and technical discussions of methods of policing such an agreement, the Commission made one more effort to keep open the option of underground testing. On May 28, the Commissioners met with laboratory representatives to discuss limiting weapon tests to underground shots. Commissioner Graham reviewed the recent events, including the reports of the general advisory committee and the advisory committee on biology and medicine. General Starbird asked the laboratory directors what technical problems were involved and what limitations would result should the Commission decide to test underground only.

487

Again taking the lead, Teller responded that scientists at Livermore had concluded that nearly all required information could be obtained from underground tests, which were easier to conduct than atmospheric tests. Even without an international moratorium, Teller was in favor of moving almost all tests underground, with exception of those for weapon effects and antimissile systems, which had to be atmospheric. He proposed to limit the amount of radioactive material released into the atmosphere by each nation to that produced by one-tenth of a megaton of fission weapons annually. He also noted that the development of peaceful nuclear explosives would be hampered by abandoning atmospheric testing.

Duane C. Sewell of Livermore saw considerable advantages to testing underground. It would allow the laboratories greater flexibility in scheduling tests and thus accelerate the development of new weapons. Instead of waiting for the annual test series, which was subject to the vagaries of weather, continuous underground testing would allow laboratory scientists to experiment when they were ready. Sewell envisioned that more radical weapon designs could be tested because the failure of an experiment would not be so important. Rather than waiting another year, the test would simply be rescheduled. Sewell predicted significant cost savings as well, particularly if the Commission eliminated the expensive biannual tests at the Pacific Proving Ground. According to Sewell, the cost of digging the tunnel for the *Rainier* shot was no more than the cost of a five-hundred-foot tower. Furthermore, the cost of additional tunnels would be about one-fourth the cost of the original. Finally, public opposition to tests because of the fallout danger could be eliminated by underground testing.

Norris Bradbury and Alvin C. Graves from Los Alamos were not as sanguine as their Livermore colleagues about the advantages of underground testing, but even Bradbury was not certain that the final "proof-test" of a missile system and its warhead was "absolutely necessary" if the two could be adequately tested separately. Although the Commissioners did not at this time actually decide to abandon atmospheric testing, the laboratory scientists, and particularly Teller and Sewell, had assured themselves that they could move all tests underground with little sacrifice to the weapon program.[106]

Within the atomic energy establishment underground testing seemed a viable, and perhaps preferable, alternative to a moratorium or an outright ban on nuclear tests. Eisenhower, however, was not ready to accept that easy solution. Five years in the White House had taught him that compromises of this kind merely postponed the realization of his fervent hopes to remove the nuclear threat that hung over the world. Underground testing might help the situation if a moratorium or test ban proved impossible, but in the meantime the President focused his attention on the technical conference of experts, soon to convene in Geneva. Perhaps the scientists could cut through the political tangle and determine whether limiting tests was technically feasible.

## CHAPTER 18

# A NEW APPROACH
# TO NUCLEAR POWER

On the last day of March 1958 Lewis Strauss wrote the President to acknowledge that his reappointment as chairman was not politically feasible. "Just as a ship too long at sea collects barnacles," Strauss noted, so had he "acquired the hostility of a small but vocal coterie of columnists" and of Senator Anderson. He offered to continue to serve as an adviser to the President, but for the good of the Administration he had decided not to seek reappointment as a Commissioner.[1] Although Eisenhower for the moment refused to accept Strauss's decision as final, the White House staff, with Strauss's assistance, began to search for a replacement.

## ENTER MCCONE

From the beginning of the search John A. McCone was a leading candidate. A Californian, McCone began his business career as a construction engineer for the Llewellyn Iron Works in 1922. When the Bechtel-McCone Corporation was organized in 1937, McCone became president and director. During World War II he was executive vice-president of the Consolidated Steel Corporation and president of the California Shipbuilding Corporation. As president of the Joshua Hendy Corporation after the war, he operated a fleet of merchant ships that transported chemicals, petroleum products, and ores. In addition to his business and financial activities, McCone served as special deputy to Secretary of Defense James Forrestal during 1948 and in 1950 became Under Secretary of the Air Force in charge of procurement. Early in 1954 Dulles appointed him to the State Department's public committee on personnel. McCone's technical background, his solid record as a conservative Republican businessman, and his government experience attracted Strauss's attention in 1957, when he was seeking a replacement for Murray. McCone in fact was offered Murray's seat; but he declined, as he explained forthrightly, because he would accept nothing less than the chairmanship.[2]

A year later that obstacle was removed by Strauss's decision to leave the Commission, and McCone readily accepted the appointment. Strauss had not been mistaken in his appraisal of McCone's political and economic outlook. As a self-made man, McCone had proved to himself that it was possible to do things in private enterprise without government assistance. McCone, however, was not doctrinaire on the subject. As one of his former assistants explained to a reporter, McCone was, if anything, more conservative than Strauss, but he was an "open-minded conservative." He preferred to let private business do the job, but, if government could do it better, McCone was not opposed to government programs. McCone's principal asset was "his razor-sharp intelligence that can pierce any proposal, reduce it to a skeleton of basics."[3]

McCone's other assets were his friendship with Eisenhower and the President's confidence in him. Unlike Strauss, a Taft supporter barely known to Eisenhower in 1952, McCone had worked with Eisenhower since 1947, first as a member of the Air Policy Commission and then as Under Secretary of the Air Force. Subsequently McCone had visited Eisenhower at Columbia University. With Strauss's departure, McCone had little interest in becoming Eisenhower's next special adviser on nuclear energy; rather he wanted to sit as a member of the National Security Council and the Cabinet. In this regard, with McCone the chairmanship of the Commission had reached its apogee.

Strauss's contention that most of the Commission's troubles with the Joint Committee stemmed from Senator Anderson's "almost psychopathic dislike for me" seemed to have some basis in fact when Anderson announced in mid-June that he was willing "to let the dead past bury its dead and go on to happier days." Despite Robert Zehring's fears that Anderson would hold the McCone nomination hostage in the committee's struggle with the Commission over the power reactor program, Anderson called the confirmation hearing on July 2 and completed the questioning in two hours. Anderson and Holifield asked McCone for his opinions on nuclear weapon testing, safeguards, and the development of nuclear power but did not press him beyond his straightforward but tentative replies. Some echoes from the Strauss period were heard when Anderson raised the question of McCone's conception of the role of the chairman in relation to the Commission and the White House and asked McCone about his understanding of the statutory requirement to keep the Joint Committee "fully and currently informed." McCone parried these thrusts without giving either ground or offense.[4]

McCone was fully sensitive to the need to improve the Commission's relationship with the Joint Committee and especially with Anderson, the touchy and hard-driving senator who would likely resume the committee chairmanship in 1959. McCone had no intention of letting slide the issues that Anderson had raised at the confirmation hearing; he was simply looking for a better forum for discussion. On July 16, two days before he was sworn in as chairman, McCone called on Anderson to see what could be done to clear the air. Anderson said he was confident that frank discussions of issues would avoid the kinds of problems that had damaged relations in the past. Without appearing overly conciliatory, McCone accepted the senator's premise; his demeanor suggested that he would not hesitate to state his views clearly and directly. That was a stance Anderson could understand.[5]

491

## THE FIRST TEST

McCone had an opportunity to use his forthright approach a few weeks later when he met privately with Holifield and then with Anderson to discuss Congressional action on the proposed EURATOM agreement and the authorization bill. On June 25, as Strauss was clearing out his office at the Commission's headquarters, the Joint Committee had reported out the authorization bill, precisely doubling the $194 million that the Administration had requested for power-reactor development. The total in the bill was close to the $400 million originally proposed by the committee in its private discussions with the Commissioners. The bill designated $145 million for a new plutonium production reactor, which both the Commission and the White House had opposed; $68 million for the design of four additional power reactors; and $37.9 million for basic research facilities. On August 4, when Eisenhower signed the authorization bill, he criticized the committee's action and urged "the Congress to guard more vigilantly against the ever present tendency to burden the government with programs, . . . the relative urgency and essentiality of which have not been solidly determined."[6]

Holifield interpreted the President's language as meaning that the committee had been irresponsible. The President had also implied that he might hold back from the Commission the funds authorized for not only the plutonium reactor but also the gas-cooled reactor, which had been included in the Administration's bill, on the grounds that the legislation had imposed an unrealistic time limit on the submission of private proposals. McCone reassured Holifield that the Commission had every intention to proceed on the gas-cooled reactor "energetically and . . . exactly in accordance with the legislation." On the plutonium reactor, however, McCone said frankly that the economics of the design, particularly its dual-purpose feature, were unacceptable to him, and he expected to make an independent study of the issues. Holifield seemed willing to await the results of that review.

McCone found Anderson equally resentful of the President's attack on the authorization bill, but the senator insisted that his opposition to the EURATOM agreement was substantive and not capricious. As he had stated during the public hearings in June, most of his objections to the proposed agreement related to financial issues rather than safeguards, but in the privacy of his office he could be more specific about his objections. He told McCone that he was concerned that the Commission had never even discussed the Export-Import Bank's loan, necessary to finance the construction of American reactors abroad. He questioned the feasibility of the plan for returning spent fuel elements to the United States for reprocessing. He did not like the provision of $50 million for research and development of reactor designs by the EURATOM countries; but most of all, Anderson objected to a $90-million item in the EURATOM authorization bill to cover cost overruns that might be incurred by American manufacturers in fulfilling performance guarantees on fuel assemblies for EURATOM reactors. Anderson claimed that the real purpose of the provision was to bail out Westinghouse, which at Strauss's insistence had given an Italian utility a very attractive guarantee for the SENN reactor. McCone listened patiently to Anderson's objections but made no promises.[7]

When the EURATOM package came before the Joint Committee on July 22, McCone assigned Commissioner Floberg and Deputy General Manager Richard W. Cook to present the Administration's case. The details of the bilateral agreement, the memorandum of understanding, and the assorted working papers were too intricate for McCone to master during the first weeks of his chairmanship. Fortunately Floberg was well versed on the subject and made impressive use of his considerable debating skills as a lawyer in explaining the text of the agreements during four days of gruelling testimony.

Anderson's private discussion with McCone proved an accurate indicator of the course the hearings would take. In negotiating the EURATOM agreement during spring 1958, the Commission had been preoccupied with the safeguards issue, particularly as it related to the International Atomic Energy Agency. Girded for battle on this subject, C. Douglas Dillon, the Under Secretary of State for economic affairs, was relieved to discover on the first day of the hearings that the Joint Committee had few questions about safeguards. Instead, the hearings followed Anderson's interest and concentrated on the dollar figures in the EURATOM authorization bill and on fine points of reciprocity in the agreement documents. In the end, Floberg's persistence and debating skill paid off. The committee with some grumbling accepted the agreements, trimmed back but did not delete the funds provided for research and development, and placed tighter restrictions on the use of funds for fuel guarantees.[8]

492

## FIRST IMPRESSIONS

Within the Commission McCone, perhaps to his satisfaction, discovered that he would have to chart his own course on a nuclear power policy. Both Kenneth E. Fields, the general manager, and Cook had resigned when Strauss's term ended; Cook stayed on only until the EURATOM hearings were completed. W. Kenneth Davis, the director of reactor development, had already announced his decision to leave during the summer as had his principal assistants in the division. Strauss had already selected Alvin R. Luedecke, an Air Force general, to be general manager, but Luedecke would not report to the Commission until after he had completed his assignment as commander of Joint Task Force Seven, which was conducting the *Hardtack* series of weapon tests in the Pacific. In the meantime Paul F. Foster, a former Navy admiral, engineer, and Chicago department store executive, would serve as acting general manager. In 1954 Strauss had brought Foster from the World Bank to the Commission, where he had served as a special assistant to the general manager for international affairs in 1956. Dependable, wise, and judicious in temperament, Foster at age sixty-nine was an ideal choice for this interim assignment.[9] Although Foster had been active on the staff for three years, he had no special knowledge of reactor development.

493

With Davis on his way out of the government, McCone relied on Rickover to give him his first inside glimpse of the Commission's reactor program. On a three-day trip with Rickover to Knolls, Bettis, Shippingport, and the Idaho test station, McCone had enough engineering experience to engage in technical discussions, and he quickly proved that he could identify the critical points of disagreement in a technical argument.

At Knolls, McCone was struck by the statement of one General Electric official that the company's commercial division did not give serious enough attention to designing reactor cores. This opinion led McCone to pursue the question of whether large equipment manufacturers like General Electric and Westinghouse accepted lower design standards on their commercial work than on the naval projects. At Bettis, McCone found that Westinghouse engineers denied any shortcuts in design that would produce a dependable power reactor. Yet McCone was surprised that the Westinghouse commercial division expected to produce power reactors at one-fourth or one-fifth the cost of Shippingport.

After visiting Shippingport and being greatly impressed by "its design, lay-out, safety and beautiful condition," McCone fully understood that the installation was not really a power plant but "a laboratory tool." In that sense it was unfair to dismiss Shippingport, as some industry leaders were doing, as irrelevant because its capital costs were so high. When McCone, however, excluded the expensive test equipment and heavy redundancy in design at Shippingport, he was still not satisfied. He noted that both Bettis and Knolls were concentrating on the problem of core design and that both laboratories expected vast improvement in core performance and a substantial reduction in costs within a few years. This McCone could understand because he realized that both the physics and engineering of core design were in a very early stage of development.[10]

What impressed McCone even more, however, was the fact that both companies were proceeding at once to install in commercial reactors fuel assemblies using cheaper and possibly less dependable materials than Rickover had specified in the Navy projects. McCone noted that the Yankee Atomic plant, which Westinghouse had designed, would use slightly enriched uranium-oxide pellets, which would be sealed in stainless steel rods. At first glance it seemed logical that these fuel assemblies for Yankee would be much less expensive than the fully enriched uranium, clad in zirconium, which the Navy was using. Rickover had already raised questions about the integrity and reliability of the commercial cores. McCone appreciated this concern, but he even had questions about the savings in cost. He suspected that the commercial divisions of the companies were overlooking the fact that the amount of energy used in enriching uranium (and hence the cost) was not proportional to the level of enrichment. Thus, enriching uranium to 3 percent content of uranium-235 took on the order of 50 percent, not 3 percent, of the energy needed for full enrichment.[11]

McCone found Westinghouse engineers vague on the amount of uranium or the level of enrichment they expected to use in their commercial plants. He was also suspicious of the statement that the value of the spent fuel elements would be so low that recovery of the uranium would not be worthwhile. McCone concluded that if the uranium was not recovered, actual fuel costs for the reactors would be very high, and he realized that this cost would be borne by the government under the power demonstration program. "There seemed to be an attitude," McCone wrote in his notes, "on the part of the commercial people at both Westinghouse and indirectly General Electric to ride on the fact that there was no fuel cost involved." For instance, it was obvious that the Westinghouse people were going to design the Yankee plant to produce the cheapest power, irrespective of the amount of uranium used, "because they do not pay for the uranium. . . . I am sure that General Electric is doing the same thing."

On the integrity and dependability of fuel elements McCone noted sharp differences in design philosophy between Rickover's group and the manufacturers. To achieve long core life, the Navy insisted on high integrity in every fuel element on the grounds that a slight break in one element would bring water in contact with the uranium and cause a swelling that would result in a chain reaction of damage. This reasoning explained the extreme care used in fabricating and inspecting fuel elements for the Navy projects. In contrast, McCone found that the commercial manufacturers took this matter "rather lightly." He noted that Westinghouse intended to place uranium in commercially manufactured tubes without knowing exactly how this was to be done. Although the Yankee plant was already under construction, there seemed to be no plans to inspect the tubes for imperfections or to determine what the results might be if a tube failed.

In his personal notes on the trip McCone wrote:

> As a result of these discussions, I am convinced that our reactor division must make the most penetrating study of how the commercial people intend to answer their core design and construction problems. It seems to me that it will be the center of our problem both from the standpoint of economics and ultimate success and safety.
>
> One receives the impression in travelling that so many companies have launched forward blindly into this field making huge investments in engineering organizations and plants and equipment that they now are rather desperately advancing exotic and extreme and sometimes unsound developments in the hope of gaining contracts against which to advertise their facility investment and to employ their organization.

495

McCone reminded himself that he would not proceed with "anything which is unsound," but he did intend to take a constructive approach to nuclear power.

## COOPERATING WITH THE JOINT COMMITTEE

McCone's open-minded approach to technical issues also carried over to political matters, particularly the Commission's relationships with the Joint Committee. The new chairman was not plagued by Strauss's nagging suspicion that every proposal by the committee's Democratic majority was motivated by a desire to socialize the electric power industry. Thus, McCone was not alarmed when he learned that James T. Ramey, the committee's executive director, had assembled a panel of reactor and utility experts to draft a long-term nuclear power policy. The panel, which included Walter Zinn and Henry Smyth, consisted of men who were above question in both knowledge and integrity. Working through the spring and into the summer of 1958, the panel hammered out four drafts of the policy statement before releasing it for public comment in August.[12]

In most respects the panel's draft contained few surprises for the Commission staff or the nuclear industry. Based solidly on the consensus reached by the Commission and the committee during their off-the-record discussions earlier in the year, the panel stated the objectives of its plan: "to demonstrate economically competitive nuclear power in the United States by 1970 and in 'high cost' free world nations by 1968." These dates reflected some relaxation of the ten- and five-year goals discussed by both groups in February, but the intention was the same. The goals were expected to "fortify" the nation's position of worldwide leadership in the peaceful applications of atomic energy, particularly in developing nuclear power. In other words, the panel recognized no immediate need for nuclear power in the United States to justify the proposal. Ultimately, however, nuclear power would be required at home as reserves of cheap conventional fuels were exhausted, particularly if the national demand for electricity continued to double every ten years.

The plan of action proposed by the panel also followed conventional wisdom. Through its research contractors and the national laboratories the Commission would continue to provide the general research and development needed to support engineering design and construction. As in the past the Commission would also be responsible for initial feasibility studies, reactor experiments, and prototype construction. Private industry would continue to participate by undertaking research and development for specific projects and by building full-scale nuclear power plants.

496

The panel, however, sharply rejected Strauss's policy of leaving to industry decisions about the course and speed of development. Going back to the American Assembly report and the industry seminars in autumn 1957, the panel echoed the need for "positive direction" by the Commission. The panel intended that the Commission should no longer permit the national laboratories and contractors to decide which types of reactors they would study but rather that it should establish a comprehensive plan for each reactor type. "Positive direction" also included the selection of reactors to be built under the power demonstration program and the setting of realistic dates for submission, approval, and negotiation of proposals for each project. And contrary to the Commission's practice during the Strauss era, the Commission "promptly would assume responsibility for construction" if industry did not respond with proposals for private construction in a reasonable length of time.

Getting down to specifics, the panel envisaged the construction of twenty-one reactors of diversified types over the next five to seven years. These included nine large, four intermediate, and three small power reactors, in addition to five reactor experiments by the Commission. Only about half of these were expected to prove worthy of full-scale construction. A rough estimate of the total cost of development and construction was $875 million.

One encouraging aspect of the Joint Committee's action was that there was no attempt to ram the program through Congress and down the Administration's throat. Rather Ramey sent copies of the plan to a large number of equipment manufacturers and electric utilities along with a questionnaire that encouraged frank views on every aspect of the plan. The questionnaires, dispatched on August 25, 1958, were to be returned by November 1 so that they could be tabulated and discussed at a seminar sponsored by the Joint Committee well in advance of the first session of the new Congress.[13]

McCone, who received the report a few days earlier, promptly sent it to the staff for careful appraisal. Before leaving for the peaceful uses conference in Geneva, McCone sent three copies to Rickover with a request that the admiral and his staff give them serious attention. McCone also informed Rickover that he had asked Foster to appoint an ad hoc committee to study the Joint Committee proposal and requested Rickover and his senior advisers to take time from "your important work" to discuss the plan with the advisory committee. In McCone's mind a key issue was one Rickover had discussed in a meeting with the Commissioners on the evening of September 17: Did industry's efforts to achieve economic nuclear power for central-station use constitute a threat to public safety? Rickover suspected strongly that it might, and McCone acknowledged that opinion. But he also reminded Rickover that there was "a division of thought" within both the Commission and industry on the question, and it was helpful to discuss the issues.[14]

497

## A NEW ADMINISTRATIVE STYLE

McCone's willingness to open policy issues for discussion revealed an administrative style sharply contrasting with Strauss's way. Strauss had seen issues largely in political terms; McCone viewed them in terms of technical and economic realities. Strauss dealt in personalities and liked to speculate on hidden motives; McCone was more interested in facts than opinions. Strauss took into his confidence only those whom he trusted and tried to exclude the influence of others; McCone sought ideas from many sources in the belief that he could select the best course of action from the diversity of opinion. In this sense McCone seemed more self-confident than had Strauss in his ability to make decisions. Once McCone had weighed the evidence, he was comfortable about his decisions and moved on to other things; Strauss, however, preferred to maneuver others into supporting his position without fully declaring himself, and he tended to brood over the motives of those whom he failed to win to his side.

Never one to spend much time discussing organization or management procedures, McCone quickly revealed by his actions a new approach to administering the Commission's reactor development program. While Strauss had relied on Kenneth Davis to translate administrative policy into specific programs, McCone chose to use the new ad hoc advisory committee established by Foster for this purpose. He made it clear that he expected the committee to do more than window-dressing. The membership list, which McCone approved personally, contained the names of eight highly regarded business executives, scientists, and engineers, including Henry

Smyth, former General Manager Marion W. Boyer, Harvey Brooks of Harvard, and Eger V. Murphree, an Esso engineer who had been serving on atomic energy advisory groups since 1941.[15]

As for Davis's replacement, McCone accepted Foster's recommendation of Frank K. Pittman, who had served as acting director for several months after Davis and his senior associates had departed. Unlike Davis, who looked upon federal service as a temporary tour of duty, Pittman was a career civil servant. Although just forty-four years old, Pittman had behind him fourteen years of government management experience, nine of them in the Commission's Washington headquarters. A chemical engineer who had studied and taught at the Massachusetts Institute of Technology, Pittman had served as deputy to Harold L. Price in setting up the Commission's regulatory program. In fall 1957, as an outgrowth of the industry seminars on nuclear power, the Commission had set up an independent division of industrial development with Pittman in charge. From that position he had moved into reactor development after Davis's departure.

In both positions Pittman reported to Alphonso Tammaro, former engineering officer in the Manhattan Project who was now assistant general manager for research and industrial development. Although volatile and often outspoken, Tammaro knew the atomic energy establishment like the back of his hand; he had a reputation for being both responsible and responsive to the Commissioners. Tammaro gave Pittman his chance to demonstrate his abilities as acting successor to Davis and saw that he received the permanent appointment in October 1958. By that time Pittman was fully in control of the job. Although he had little background in reactor technology, Pittman, like Tammaro, knew how the agency worked. He went about his job quietly and efficiently and tried as much as possible to stay out of the way of McCone, whom he considered a bloodless taskmaster. Despite being uncomfortable with McCone, Pittman fit perfectly into the new chairman's mode of operation. He was unemotional and objective in his approach to problems, disinterested in but not insensitive to political issues, adept in finding practical solutions, and perfectly willing to leave the headaches of policy making to McCone and the ad hoc committee.[16]

## GETTING THE FACTS

While Tammaro and the advisory committee members immersed themselves in the policy issues that would arise in drafting any national plan for nuclear power, Pittman and his division set about assembling the technical data that would form the basis for the plan. First to receive attention were the engineering studies for the heavy-water-moderated power reactor, two large-scale power reactors, and one intermediate-size prototype reactor mandated by the Joint Committee in the authorization act of August 4,

1958. To meet this requirement the Commission invited qualified companies to submit proposals for engineering studies and cost estimates for a boiling-water, a pressurized-water, and an organic-cooled reactor. Proposals were to be submitted by architect-engineering firms working with nuclear reactor manufacturers no later than October 15, 1958, so that initial results of the studies could be sent to the Joint Committee by May 1, 1959, as required by the Congress.[17]

The division issued similar invitations for proposals to study fuel-cycle problems and to provide space in test reactors for irradiating experimental fuel elements and materials. General studies of the fuel cycle received a $10-million allocation, including research on the properties of fuels and other materials, the design of fuel elements, new fabrication techniques, and testing. An additional $8.5 million in 1959 was earmarked for research relating to specific applications in power reactors being developed in cooperation with industry.

499

Responses to the invitations were excellent. On the reactor studies the Commission received 86 proposals from 32 architect-engineering firms, and from these it was possible to select 3 experienced and well-qualified contractors. For the fuel-cycle work, the Commission received 107 proposals from 39 companies. Before the end of 1958, 4 companies had indicated an interest in providing irradiation space in test reactors.[18]

Although McCone's open approach to nuclear power issues and the additional funding provided by the supplemental budget encouraged the use of outside contractors, Pittman did not rely on them exclusively. He wanted, in fact, to build a much stronger technical staff at headquarters than Davis had used. When severe limitations on personnel were imposed by the Bureau of the Budget, Pittman adopted the practice of creating task forces on specific technical problems. The task forces usually consisted of one or two members of the division's headquarters staff with five or six experts from the national laboratories or industry. By using task forces Pittman was able in autumn 1958 to undertake a systematic review of all the division's activities without substantially increasing the size of his organization. Again this device provided for an open investigation of technical issues from various perspectives.

The work of Pittman's task forces complemented the deliberations of the ad hoc committee, which began a series of two-day meetings in early October. Because the committee had been charged with developing both a policy statement and the specific programs to support it, the members had to delve deeply into the technology of all reactor types under consideration. Foster had charged the committee to begin its policy deliberations by considering the long-range plan that his predecessor had negotiated with Ramey during spring 1958 as well as the draft plan released by the Joint Committee panel in August. Because Smyth had been the principal architect of the Joint Committee's proposal and was now serving as the effective chairman of the Commission's advisory committee, there was little question that the new plan would reflect its forerunners. The favorable industry response to the Joint Committee's questionnaire gave the ad hoc committee added justification for drawing on the ideas of its predecessors.[19]

When the ad hoc committee reported in January 1959, it endorsed the common objectives of the two previous studies: the United States should "fortify" its position of leadership in nuclear power technology; and it should attempt to make nuclear power economically competitive in some areas of the United States within ten years and somewhat earlier abroad. To these aims the committee added two new ones: the first, to continue studies of reactor systems that offered possibilities of much greater cost reductions within twenty or thirty years but not within a decade; the second, to make the fullest possible use of uranium and thorium reserves by incorporating good neutron economy in reactor designs but more especially by developing the breeder reactor. Achieving these goals would require a broad program of applied research, not just on specific types of reactors but also on generic problems such as improvements in both the fuel cycle and the fabrication of fuel elements.

The committee also stressed the need for design decisions and the construction of many prototypes based on a wide variety of designs. In fact, the list of reactor types endorsed by the committee appeared to include every concept that the Commission had been considering over the past five years. In this respect the committee's proposal was more ambitious than the Joint Committee's, but, by concentrating on reactor experiments and prototypes with a generating capacity of no more than eighty electrical megawatts, the committee believed it would be possible to fund a research and development effort of unprecedented scope and magnitude at an annual cost of $200 million to $225 million, about $50 million below the Joint Committee's price tag.

The report seemed to attempt to build on the earlier Commission and Joint Committee proposals and to go somewhat beyond them but not so far as to make the new plan unacceptable. The advisers urged both the Commission and the Joint Committee to agree on a formal statement of objectives that would "explain the necessity for leadership by the Federal Government, in cooperation with industry" because "cooperation between the two groups is the most important single factor in the success of this country's nuclear power program."[20]

## POLITICAL REALITIES

In some respects the recommendations of the ad hoc committee supported McCone's strategies for developing nuclear power. Smyth and his colleagues acknowledged McCone's conclusion that the introduction of nuclear power would be more difficult and costly than many people had expected. The report also exposed the shallow reasoning of those who had urged the United States to join the "kilowatt race" by accelerating the construction of full-scale nuclear power plants. If big plants were not yet feasible as monuments to the nation's technological superiority, the pressures on the Commission's budget could be eased to that extent. Furthermore, the high quality of the report and its even-handed, if not unbiased, tone suggested that McCone had been correct in believing that it was possible to evaluate technical issues without becoming mired down in the personal and ideological disputes that had plagued the Strauss era.

McCone knew, however, by the time the ad hoc committee's report was completed that he could not escape the political realities of the enduring conflict between the Democratic-controlled Joint Committee and the Republican Administration. On December 29, 1958, Pittman told the Commissioners that shifting research and development from specific projects to a more general program of applied research would increase operating expenditures in 1960 by $15 million. The construction of prototypes recommended by the committee would increase construction requirements in 1960 by $45 million and mean an increase in the authorization request of $150 million. Cooperative programs with industry would require an additional $20 million. The chances seemed extremely remote that the Administration would authorize increases of this magnitude.

501

Since September the Commission had been in a running battle with the Bureau of the Budget in an effort to obtain adequate funding for fiscal 1960. In November the bureau had cut the Commission's budget request by $563 million in obligational authority, about $300 million below the 1959 level. Although most dollars would come from projects other than nuclear power development, the cuts did include elimination of funds for the gas-cooled reactor and one cooperative project, while all other reactor development expenditures were retained at existing levels. When the Commission appealed this decision, the Bureau of the Budget insisted on cuts of more than $250 million in nondefense programs. To meet this demand, the Commission had to find ways to trim an additional $60 million from the reactor development budget; this meant a reduction in some applied research areas where the ad hoc committee had recommended increases.[21]

Early in January 1959 McCone faced the unwelcome task of presenting these unpleasant facts to the Joint Committee at the annual Section 202 and authorization hearings. Pittman began work at once on a new statement of the Commission's reactor program that would save as much as possible of the ad hoc committee's recommendations. The statement went through several drafts during late January and early February. Trying to accommodate both the Administration and the Joint Committee was a painful process, but McCone had both the new program and a draft authorization bill in hand when he went to the Hill on February 17 to testify at the opening of the Section 202 hearings.[22]

It was no surprise to the Joint Committee that the Commission accepted the five objectives proposed by the ad hoc advisory group. After all, as Senator Gore and Congressman Holifield observed, objectives were easy to state; fulfillment was more difficult. Overlooking these barbs, McCone pressed on to assert his strong personal agreement with the ad hoc group's contention that power reactor development should concentrate on prototypes rather than full-scale plants. He also conceded that the Commission would have to take responsibility for deciding which reactor types were ready for the prototype stage. The Commission would invite both public and private utilities to submit proposals similar to those required in the power demonstration program but with one new feature: the Commission was now proposing to offer grants for capital costs. This new proposal was not lost on the Joint Committee, which had consistently opposed capital grants since 1954.[23]

502

When McCone's presentation turned to specific projects, it was apparent that the Commission had decided to make the best case that it could to adopt the broad approach to nuclear power recommended by the ad hoc group rather than to focus on only the most attractive designs. Thus, the 1959 program sounded much like those Strauss had presented in the past. In each of six reactor categories, McCone could list several projects— either reactor experiments funded by the Commission or cooperative projects with industry. As Senator Gore remarked, the statement sounded as if the Commission had left "no stone unturned." Yet, the senator said, it seemed to be the same proposal submitted in 1956 with two changes: adding capital grants and eliminating any deadline for submission of industry proposals. Even worse, Gore argued, the Commission had dropped five of the eight prototypes and all three reactor experiments proposed a year earlier. In some instances new projects had been substituted for those canceled, but Gore contended that the new authorization bill actually provided only $14.5 million for Commission reactor programs, compared to $74.5 million approved by Congress the year before. McCone could challenge Gore's arithmetic, but he could not refute the senator's premise that the Administration was cutting back the reactor program. Only a week earlier, in a private conversation with McCone, the President had made it clear that he wanted to keep the government from "getting deeper into this matter."[24]

While McCone was trying to make the best of a difficult situation, Holifield began to zero in on specific reactor items in the Commission's draft of the authorization bill even though the hearings on the bill would not start for another ten days. When an aide handed McCone a press release just issued by Holifield, the chairman exploded in angry accusation that the congressman was attacking the Commission's proposals before he had even completed his testimony. By the time McCone first appeared at the authorization hearings on February 27, however, both men went out of their way to admit a misunderstanding and to deny that the dispute had been personal. The incident impressed upon Holifield and his colleagues that McCone indeed was more interested in issues than in personalities, but at the same time the new chairman would not tolerate politically motivated abuse.[25]

## MOVING TOWARD A PROGRAM

The altercation with Holifield seemed to clear the air for productive discussions between McCone and the Joint Committee. In four additional extended appearances before the committee over the next ten weeks McCone patiently but firmly responded to every query and suggestion. Gradually the barbed questions and nasty implications that had peppered the committee's hearings during the Strauss era disappeared, and it was possible for McCone and his staff to discuss rather than debate items in the appropriation bill. McCone gave the impression that he was doing the best he could to accelerate power reactor development within the tight financial limits imposed by the Bureau of the Budget and the President. After all, these limits constituted a reality that the Congress as well as McCone had to face. Furthermore, the appropriation bill that McCone presented was far from a niggardly concession to the committee's demands but rather a positive and thoughtful proposal. In the bill the Commission proposed to start or expand five power reactor experiments at the Idaho test site, support five military reactor projects, and fund the construction of two experimental power reactors by the Commission and two prototypes to be built under cooperative agreements with either public or private utilities, a provision that effectively defused the old private-versus-public power fight.

McCone was careful in his presentation to explain the distinction he was making between experimental plants and prototypes, both in terms of size and function. He was forthright in stating that the Commission had an important role in building experimental reactors and in determining what kinds of prototypes were needed and when. After the Commission completed conceptual designs and general specifications for the prototypes, utilities would be invited to submit proposals for design, construction, and operation of the plants. The prototypes were not to be considered entries in a "kilowatt race" but rather sources of reliable data on construction costs and "statistically significant information on efficiency, performance characteristics, and other operating factors in a manner which will permit reliable projection toward central station powerplants." In short, McCone was seeking the kind of solid data that engineers and businessmen needed to make sound decisions about nuclear power.[26]

503

McCone's decision to focus reactor development on prototypes rather than full-scale power plants had several advantages. In addition to producing reliable data, prototypes could be constructed at less expense and greater speed than full-size plants. Thus, they made optimum use of the limited funding available and made it possible for the Administration to support more projects without breaking the budget. As long as the additional projects were well-conceived and well-executed, they also blunted the committee's interest in the "Gore-Holifield" approach, which seemed fiscally irresponsible to both the Administration and many Democrats. In fact, Senator Anderson and many of his committee colleagues liked to think of themselves as conservative on budget matters. By the time the hearings concluded on May 8, 1959, Anderson had gained so much confidence in McCone that he suggested that the Joint Committee could relax some of the cost controls included in previous authorization acts because "the Chairman of the Atomic Energy Commission is a very shrewd businessman and will watch it [the budget] carefully."[27]

504

Between his appearances before the Joint Committee McCone demonstrated that he was serious about evaluating the Commission's development projects and applying resources where they would do the most good. He did not exclude reassessments of projects for which contracts had already been let. When evaluation showed that two power demonstration projects for sodium-cooled reactors were not moving in a promising direction technically, McCone asked Pittman to explore with the contractors the possibility of terminating the work. In the first instance, the contractor agreed to cancel design work for one of these reactors, to be built at Chugach, Alaska. When Pittman discovered that cancelling the second sodium-cooled plant, at Hallam, Nebraska, would in the long run cost the government more than continuing it, McCone took the pragmatic course of extending the project even though recent experimental evidence indicated that the Hallam project would not produce engineering data of exceptional value. In both instances McCone was able to reach decisions without incurring outbursts of criticism from the contractors, the Joint Committee, or the nuclear industry.[28]

On the politically sensitive question of gas-cooled reactors, McCone proceeded cautiously but without equivocation. For more than two years the Joint Committee had been prodding the Commission to develop a gas-cooled power reactor, mainly in response to the British decision to commit its entire domestic and foreign nuclear power effort to that type of plant. Under committee pressure the Commission had agreed in 1958 to start design studies for a gas-cooled, graphite-moderated reactor and awarded a contract to Kaiser Engineers and American Car and Foundry Company (ACF) for that purpose. When the Joint Committee inserted a provision in the 1959 authorization act requiring the Commission itself to begin constructing the reactor if a satisfactory industry proposal were not received within ninety days after the bill became law, the Administration had denounced this requirement as a deliberate effort to force the Commission to build a full-scale plant. The Bureau of the Budget had approved only $30 million for the project rather than the $51 million authorized by the committee, a reduction that would make it possible to build only an experimental or prototype reactor.[29]

The Administration's decision had been based almost entirely on its desire to keep the government out of power plant construction and to balance the budget. McCone, however, was able to avoid another political fight with the Joint Committee by analyzing the Kaiser-ACF proposal and concluding that it did not warrant construction on technical grounds. Instead, McCone proposed to build a flexible prototype within the $30-million limit and to proceed with negotiations with the Philadelphia Electric Company, representing fifty-two utility companies, to build a high-temperature, helium-cooled prototype designed by the General Dynamics Corporation. Again for technical reasons McCone was not enthusiastic about the General Dynamics design because it represented a bold extrapolation of existing technology, but he was willing to commit some government funding if a reasonable compromise could be reached with the Joint Committee on authorization. As the committee was learning, McCone's idea of a reasonable compromise was to take only a calculated technical risk of failure after the proposal had been carefully analyzed for economic and engineering perspectives and to commit no more money than seemed necessary. Rather than confrontation, the McCone approach fostered discussion and joint decision.[30]

505

McCone was equally harsh in evaluating existing work on fluid-fuel reactors, which included the homogeneous and molten-salt reactors at Oak Ridge and the experiment with liquid-metal fuels at Brookhaven. Because Pittman's task force found that none of these experimental plants would contribute to the Commission's nuclear power objectives established early in 1958, all three projects were phased out in spring 1959, to be replaced by a long-range research effort to develop a breeder reactor using slow neutrons. On Pittman's recommendation and under McCone's leadership the Commission decided to focus its resources on water- and organic-cooled reactors, which still showed the greatest promise of producing economical nuclear power within the next decade. This decision was based in part on the results of the four reactor studies mandated by the Congress in the 1959 authorization act and completed in May 1959.[31]

McCone, Pittman, and the staff discussed all these and other studies at length with the Joint Committee during the course of the authorization hearings. As the weeks slipped by, Anderson, Holifield, and their colleagues came to appreciate the new spirit and attitude that McCone brought to decisions. Although the committee members did not always agree with the Commission's conclusions, they were persuaded that McCone and his associates were making an honest effort to get the facts and that they were acting in good faith. Thus, for the first time since the authorization procedure had been enacted in 1954, the committee's final recommendations represented a broad basis of agreement on the issues and a true compromise of remaining points of difference. The nine power reactor experiments and prototypes authorized for 1960 were more than the Commission had initially requested but less than the committee had sought. McCone could accept the outcome as consistent with the state of the technology and reasonable within the Administration's budget limitations. The chairman's only significant defeat was his failure to obtain approval of construction grants for prototypes, but he had the satisfaction of knowing that Senator Anderson shared his disappointment.[32]

506

## THE SAVANNAH CRISIS

One application of nuclear power that McCone could not afford to overlook was ship propulsion. In 1955 Eisenhower had personally conceived the idea of building a nuclear-powered "peace ship" that could tour the world with exhibits that would dramatize the peaceful uses of atomic energy. The President hoped that, by using a carbon copy of the Nautilus reactor and a cargo hull of standard design, it would be possible to have the "peace ship" in operation in a year or less. When both the Commission and the Joint Committee privately doubted the project's feasibility as the President had proposed it, Eisenhower's project was quietly scuttled after the Congress failed to authorize it in summer 1955. Eisenhower, however, had no intention of abandoning the idea, and in 1956 he directed the Commission and the U.S. Maritime Administration jointly to develop plans for the ship.[33]

Studies by the two agencies during 1957 resulted in a plan significantly different from the President's original conception. Instead of a "peace ship," which many members of Congress had criticized as little more than a publicity stunt, the two agencies now proposed to build a dry-cargo merchant ship, which would demonstrate the feasibility of using nuclear propulsion for commercial vessels. The second departure from the original plan was to use a nuclear propulsion plant designed specifically for the purpose by a private contractor rather than a copy of the Nautilus reactor. Rickover himself maintained that the Nautilus plant was not suitable, and the Commission staff estimated that a private contractor could provide a new reactor at about one-third the cost of the Navy plant. No doubt with Strauss's encouragement, the Babcock & Wilcox Company accepted a contract to design and build the reactor and the propulsion equipment while the New York Shipbuilding Corporation agreed to construct the ship. Both contractors started work in 1958, and on July 21, 1959, Mrs. Eisenhower attended the launching and christened the new vessel, the *Savannah*, after the first steam-powered transatlantic ship to be built in the United States.[34]

By the time McCone became chairman in summer 1958 the *Savannah* project was in high gear under the direction of Richard P. Godwin and the maritime reactors branch in the division of reactor development. As the new director of the division, Pittman probably knew little more about the project in autumn 1958 than McCone did, but it was only a matter of time before McCone's systematic evaluation of every Commission project would focus on the *Savannah*. Once he turned his attention to the project, it did not take McCone long to discover some troubling facts. First, there was far from a unanimous opinion among the Commission staff and contractor officials that all the design features of the propulsion plant were safe and reliable. Second, both Godwin and the contractors admitted that no one had clear responsibility for coordinating the installation of the nuclear propulsion plant in the hull and conducting plant tests and sea trials. Third, it was also evident that inadequate plans had been made for training the ship's officers and crew, particularly in reactor operation and maintenance.[35]

507

Serious as these differences were, McCone was even more concerned about the fact that the contractor had designed the nuclear propulsion plant without consulting Rickover, his staff, or the naval reactor laboratories. It was true that Babcock & Wilcox had been fabricating components for nuclear submarines for at least five years and had hired well-qualified reactor engineers to design the reactor plant, but McCone found it incredible that the contractor would deliberately ignore the mass of experience and knowledge that the Navy project had generated since 1946. After expressing his concerns to Rickover, McCone informed General Manager Luedecke that the naval reactors branch would survey the *Savannah* project and report its findings to the Commission. The chairman also suggested that the Commission's senior staff was not sufficiently supervising the project.[36]

When news of the survey leaked out, the press interpreted it as a power play by Rickover to take over the *Savannah* project. The facts could hardly be more contrary to that rumor. As a matter of principle, Rickover never wanted to bear any responsibility for a project over which he did not have complete control. He also must have realized that, with all the major decisions already made, it would be hard to offer positive criticism and thereby avoid appearing to confirm the press stories. When Rickover found it impossible to refuse McCone's request, he agreed to do the survey; but he stood firm that he would merely report the facts and make no recommendations. McCone accepted this condition and made clear to the staff and the press that there was no thought of transferring supervision of the *Savannah* project to Rickover. Obviously trying to minimize the role of his staff in the review, Rickover restricted his investigation to examining design documents and safety studies, and he completed the entire survey in one week. His report did not produce any new or startling information about the *Savannah* reactor. Rather, members of Rickover's staff explained ways in which a number of features in the ship's reactor differed from long-established design principles in the Navy project, and they suggested how these specifics might complicate operation and maintenance of the ship reactor. Godwin then addressed each of these points, mainly by elaborating upon the fundamental differences between the operational requirements for the merchant ship propulsion plant and naval propulsion plants. McCone's probing and Rickover's survey did not result in major redesign of the *Savannah* plant, but they did help to resolve issues over crew training and the division of contractor responsibility. Most important, Luedecke, Tammaro, Pittman, and Godwin, as well as the contractors, were now well aware that McCone had the facts and would hold these officials responsible for effective project management.[37]

508

## THE LONG-RANGE PLAN

McCone's down-to-earth review of the Commission's nuclear power plans with the Joint Committee during spring 1959 moved slowly in the direction of consensus. But McCone knew that the decisions incorporated in the authorization act of 1960 represented nothing more than a stopgap. The successful development of nuclear power required something more than piecemeal measures taken in the course of the annual authorization process. Three days after his final appearance at the authorization hearings in May 1959 McCone asked Luedecke to set up a special group to draft a long-range plan for further development of the reactor types most likely to meet the Commission's ten-year objective for economical nuclear power. Always with an eye on the practical, McCone wanted the staff to concentrate on prototypes for large central-station power plants and to evaluate each reactor type in terms of its current technical status and economic promise.[38]

It was also clear that McCone took seriously his commitment to the Joint Committee to complete the plan before the end of 1959. Within two weeks after receiving McCone's directive, Luedecke, Tammaro, and Pittman agreed on the scope and outline of the study, and Pittman's staff recruited contractor personnel to prepare the first two reports, which, in accordance with the McCone style, summarized the technical and economic status of each reactor type. By the time these reports were completed on June 30, Luedecke and Pittman had arranged for the Atomic Industrial Forum to organize a task force of engineers well known in the industry to establish the criteria for evaluating the reactor types.

A working subcommittee representing the organization of each principal was established to do the evaluations. Throughout summer 1959 the subcommittee worked closely with Pittman's staff and national laboratory engineers to assure that the evaluation criteria were sensible and uniform for all the reactor types under study. Criteria were carefully defined and, whenever possible, expressed quantitatively so that the evaluation would not unintentionally skew the result. When the nine evaluations were completed, Pittman discussed them with industry representatives and with the ad hoc advisory committee on reactor policies and programs, which had been reconvened for this purpose. The evaluations, together with recommendations for the future, constituted Part 4 of the long-range plan.[39]

The draft that Pittman submitted to the Commission on December 17, 1959, clearly reflected McCone's approach to technical management. The plan was direct, to the point, frank in its evaluations, quantitative where possible, and specific in its recommendations. It did not represent a radical or dramatic departure from the past but rather an extension and more precise definition of the proposals McCone had presented in the authorization hearings. Pittman tied the plan directly to the five objectives McCone had proposed to the Joint Committee early in 1959, but each objective was now carefully defined in quantitative terms where appropriate or properly qualified to reflect recent developments in the world's energy outlook.[40]

509

The most dramatic change had occurred in projections for conventional fuels in Western Europe. Early in 1957 the Three Wise Men from EURATOM had predicted that Europe would need to import 100 million tons of coal annually within five years unless electric-energy requirements could be met with nuclear power. Scarcely two years later, in spring 1959, Floberg reported to the Joint Committee that Europe had 50 million tons of coal above ground. The price in Europe had dropped five dollars per ton in the face of reduced shipping rates for American coal, new sources of natural gas, and new oil discoveries in the Middle East. All these factors had dampened at least the short-term urgency of nuclear power and thrown the long-term projections into question. "With fingers crossed and eyes raised heavenward," as a *Nucleonics* reporter put it, the United States and EURATOM had issued an invitation to European utilities to submit proposals by September 1, 1959, for six to eight reactor plants. With the coal glut and the leveling off of electricity demand, it seemed unlikely that more than one proposal would be submitted.[41]

The changing outlook for EURATOM had forced Pittman to modify the Commission's interpretation of its second objective, which was to assist friendly countries to achieve competitive nuclear power within five years. When the objectives were first formulated in 1958, the overseas market for nuclear power was the driving force behind the United States' civilian power program. Without the threat of British and Soviet competition for the European reactor market, there would have been little justification for accelerating the construction of power reactors at home. Now, in early 1960, with the European market all but vanishing, the objective was reinterpreted to mean only that the United States would assist friendly nations through cooperative arrangements on research and development directly related to the Commission's needs for its domestic power program. The less promising European outlook also required some modification in the fourth objective, which was to maintain the United States' position of world leadership in nuclear power technology. As competition for the European market declined, it was no longer essential that the nation maintain its preeminence in developing every reactor type. Now, in 1960, the nation could afford to pursue only the most promising avenues to competitive nuclear power, and these were being defined by McCone, Pittman, and the Commission.

The central focus of the long-range plan thus became the evaluation of reactor types for the domestic electric power market. Here the Commission's first, third, and fifth objectives were controlling. The first was simply stated: "Reduce the cost of nuclear power to levels competitive with power from fossil fuels in high energy cost areas of this country within ten years." The draft specified that the ten-year period would be counted from 1958 and defined what was meant by "competitive power" in quantitative terms, how the cost of fossil-fuel power was to be computed, and what were "high cost power areas." The third objective was interpreted to mean that the Commission would continue to support research and development over a longer term in order to reduce the cost of nuclear power even further. The fifth objective, which the ad hoc committee had long advocated, was to develop breeder reactors to make full use of the limited resources of fissionable material. The draft of the long-range plan noted that uranium reserves would probably be adequate "for at least the next fifty years." This conclusion meant that breeder development should be guided primarily by economic considerations and was therefore not a high priority.[42]

By the time the Commission approved the final draft in February 1960 the long-range plan had expanded from a concise internal policy paper into an encyclopedic public document that not only presented the Commission's recommendations but also protected the Commission's flanks against ambush by the Joint Committee or the nuclear industry. In addition to listing the projects directly related to nuclear power development, the plan also cited military projects and the *Savannah* as contributing to the effort. Like all Commission proposals since autumn 1958, the long-range plan placed the greatest emphasis on reactors moderated by light water and organic fluids. The Commission held to its conviction that pressurized-water reactors were the best understood of all reactor types. They were "safe, dependable, and reasonably easy to control." Now that one manufacturer was already offering a large central-station nuclear plant for a fixed price with some fuel guarantees, the Commission concluded that pressurized-water reactors would be competitive in high-cost areas of the United States by 1968. In addition to the experimental reactors and proto-

## Table 3
## Reactors Included in the Commission's Long-Range Plan,
### February 1960

| Project | Type | Design power (kwe) | Status |
|---|---|---|---|
| *Pressurized-Water Reactors* | | | |
| Pressurized Water Reactor Shippingport, PA | Co-op | 150,000 | Operating, to be modified |
| Yankee Atomic Electric Co. Rowe, MA | Utility | 110,000 | Construction |
| Consolidated Edison Co. of New York, New York, NY | Utility | 225,000 | Construction |
| Pennsylvania Power & Light Liberty, PA | Utility | 5,000 | Construction |
| Process Heat Experiment, CA | Government | — | Planned |
| Prototype | Co-op | 22,000 | Invitations issued |
| *Boiling-Water Reactors* | | | |
| Experimental Boiling Water Reactor, Argonne, IL | Government | 4,500 | Modification |
| Rural Co-op Power Assoc. Elk River, MN | Co-op | 22,000 | Construction |
| Vallecitos Reactor Livermore, CA | Manufacturer | 5,000 | Operating |
| Dresden Nuclear Power Station Morris, IL | Utility | 180,000 | Construction |
| Pacific Gas & Electric Humboldt Bay, CA | Utility | 48,000 | Site work |
| High Power Density Prototype | Co-op | 50,000– 75,000 | Design |
| *Nuclear Superheat Reactors* | | | |
| Borax-5, National Reactor Testing Station, ID | Government | 3,500 | Design |
| Pathfinder, No. States Power Co. Sioux Falls, SD | Co-op | 62,000 | Design |
| Bonus, Puerto Rico Water Resources Authority | Co-op | 16,300 | Design |
| *Organic-Cooled Reactors* | | | |
| Organic Moderated Reactor Exp. Nat. Reactor Test Station | Government | 150 | Modification |
| Exp. Organic Cooled Reactor NRTS | Government | 10,000 | Design |

*(continued next page)*

**Table 3, cont.**
**Reactors Included in the Commission's Long-Range Plan,**
**February 1960**

| Project | Type | Design power (kwe) | Status |
|---|---|---|---|
| *Organic-Cooled Reactors* | | | |
| Prototype, City of Piqua, OH | Co-op | 11,000 | Construction |
| Prototype | Co-op | 50,000–100,000 | Invitation issued |
| *Sodium-Cooled Fast Reactors* | | | |
| Exp. Breeder Reactor No. 1 Nat. Reactor Test Station | Government | 150 | Operating |
| Exp. Breeder Reactor No. 2 Nat. Reactor Test Station | Government | 16,500 | Construction |
| Consumers Public Power | Co-op | 75,000 | Construction |
| *Gas-Cooled Reactors* | | | |
| Exp. Gas Cooled Reactor Oak Ridge Nat. Lab. | Government | 22,000 | Design |
| Philadelphia Electric High Temperature Reactor | Co-op | 28,500 | Design |
| *Heavy-Water Reactors* | | | |
| Components Test Reactor Savannah River, SC | Government | 61,000 | Design |
| Florida East Coast & West Coast Groups | Co-op | 50,000 | Evaluation of concept |

| *Other Concepts* | | |
|---|---|---|
| Aqueous Homogeneous | Advanced Epithermal | |
| Fused Salt | Slurry | |
| Fluidized Bed | Pebble Bed Gas-Cooled | |
| Paste or Suspended Fuel | Solid Moderated, Steam-Cooled | |
| Supercritical Water-Cooled | Alternate Coolant Fast Reactor | |

types already under construction by the government and industry, the Commission announced its intention to build one additional prototype based on technology growing out of the operation of the Shippingport, Yankee, and Consolidated Edison pressurized-water plants.[43]

Boiling-water reactors, the Commission concluded from experimental reactors already operating, were technically feasible and would soon begin commercial operation in new plants of this type at Morris, Illinois, and elsewhere in the Midwest. The Commission intended to negotiate contracts with public or private utilities to construct, beginning in 1960, two prototypes to demonstrate technical improvements on boiling-water reactors. The need for further prototypes could not be determined until operating experience with all existing or planned boiling-water reactors had been evaluated, probably in 1963 or 1964. To achieve greater efficiency in both pressurized-water and boiling-water plants, the Commission was supporting one experimental reactor and two prototypes under cooperative agreements with industry.

The Commission predicted that organic-moderated reactors would become competitive in high-cost power areas of the United States by 1967 or 1968 and in most of the nation in the 1970s. A second reactor experiment at the Idaho test station and two prototypes—one under construction at Piqua, Ohio, and another planned—were expected to bring organic reactors into competition. Sodium-cooled reactors appeared capable of becoming competitive in large areas of the nation in the 1970s. A second experimental breeder reactor at the Idaho test station, the Enrico Fermi plant in Michigan, and development of auxiliary power systems for space vehicles were all expected to contribute to the technology of fast-neutron breeder reactors and might lead to a decision to build a prototype by 1963 or 1964. The future of sodium-cooled graphite-moderated reactors rested on results from continued operation of the sodium reactor experiment in California and the Hallam plant in Nebraska. No prototypes would be considered before 1963 or 1964.

513

Gas-cooled reactors were still considered promising for high-temperature operation but not until the 1970s. In the meantime the Commission planned to develop the technology with a new experimental reactor at Oak Ridge, the Philadelphia Electric prototype, and experimental reactors in Idaho. As for reactors moderated with heavy water, the Commission's long-range plan revealed that the United States would depend on a Canadian prototype and a full-scale plant in Ontario to carry the development burden. American efforts on heavy-water technology would be limited to a test reactor for components at the Commission's Savannah River plant and a cooperative prototype project with two Florida utility groups. Even farther in the future than the gas-cooled and heavy-water reactors were a dozen or more reactor types whose development had not progressed much beyond preliminary paper studies.

The long-range plan was admittedly ambitious. No one understood better than McCone that its accomplishment rested on a number of shaky assumptions. The most immediate uncertainty was whether the budget-tending Eisenhower Administration would provide the necessary funding. Even if it did, McCone knew that success also depended upon continuing financial and technical participation by private industry. It was not at all clear in spring 1960 that utilities would respond to invitations for prototypes, the essential step toward large central-station generating plants. The greatest uncertainty of all, however, was whether technological development over the next decade would fulfill the Commission's hopes. For many reactor types, technical feasibility was still an open question, and, even if the answer were positive, there would still be the much more difficult question of costs.

In just two years McCone and Pittman had made significant strides in bringing systematic evaluation and planning to bear on the Commission's amorphous and inflated programs for developing nuclear power. Realistic appraisal had helped to focus the Commission's efforts and to present a comprehensible and credible plan. That same appraisal, however, made clearer than ever before that nuclear power at prices attractive to electric utility companies in the United States was not yet assured. The dream that the power of the peaceful atom might solve the world's growing energy needs was still far from reality.

514

CHAPTER 19

# SCIENCE FOR WAR
# AND PEACE

The 1950s were a decade of spectacular achievement in nuclear science and technology. Less than twenty years after the initial experiments that had brought the world into the nuclear age, scientists and engineers were finding many applications for both military and peaceful purposes. This rapid transition from first experiment to widespread application seemed to have few precedents in the history of science and technology, but it was by no means unique. During this same decade other technologies were developing just as rapidly, and some of these were threatening to render obsolete some goals of nuclear programs. After years of desultory progress, the jet engine for aircraft was rapidly coming into its own. The invention of a practical transistor to replace the vacuum tube was revolutionizing the electronics industry and opening the way to the computer age. With solid-state circuits for use in guidance systems and steady improvement in the design of rocket engines, the Soviet Union and the United States were on the threshold of the missile age. These and other technologies were to have both dramatic and subtle effects on the practical application of research and development projects supported by the Commission.[1]

The most startling development during the 1950s outside the nuclear field had been the astounding progress in perfecting missile propulsion systems. The awesome symbol of that achievement had been *Sputnik I*, launched by the Soviet Union in autumn 1957. *Sputnik* shook the United States like no other Soviet accomplishment in the decade. The orbiting Soviet satellite proclaimed to the world the inferior position of the United States in missile development. Even worse, it suggested that the technological dominance that the United States had maintained since World War II was beginning to crumble. Most serious of all, *Sputnik* raised the possibility that the United States had missed the greatest technological opportunity of the decade and dedicated its resources to lesser projects.

The American reaction to *Sputnik* was a feverish effort to improve the nation's scientific and technical capabilities, all the way from restructuring secondary school education in the sciences to giving scientists a stronger voice in the highest policy councils of the federal government. During the last three years of the Eisenhower Administration the special assistant to the President for science and technology and the President's Science Advisory Committee gave scientists and engineers the greatest influence on national policy decisions that they have enjoyed before or since. Thus, Chairman McCone would find James R. Killian and his successor, George B. Kistiakowsky, persons to be reckoned with in his dealings with the White House.

Within the Department of Defense the new emphasis on science found expression in the appointment of Herbert F. York as director of the new office of defense research and engineering. A capable and personable physicist who had been director of the Commission's Livermore laboratory and the Advanced Research Projects Agency in the Department of Defense, York was to have an effective voice in policy decisions on both weapon development and test-ban negotiations. Thomas Gates, Jr., who served first as Under Secretary of Defense and later as Defense Secretary during McCone's chairmanship, recalled years later: "All of a sudden the scientists became very important. . . . They had great veto power. They became very important people. . . . The world really completely changed, in terms of military affairs. And foreign policy changed with it."[2]

The new role for the scientist did not just mean that McCone would have additional competitors for the ear of the President; it also meant that the substance of science would have a more prominent place in presidential decision making. Assessment of the Commission's military propulsion projects by scientists revealed the need for more attention to basic scientific research and less concern for quick demonstrations of hardware with little or no practical value. In international affairs, the President's long quest for a test ban and disarmament would move away from political considerations into new realms of thresholds and seismic decoupling that required sophisticated scientific analysis.

## AIRCRAFT REACTORS

An immediate consequence of *Sputnik* was a renewed effort by the Joint Committee to accelerate the development of nuclear propulsion for military aircraft. The committee's championing of Rickover's projects for a nuclear navy encouraged Democratic members, especially Congressman Melvin Price, to take a similar position on aircraft propulsion in hopes that it would lead to an equally spectacular success. Caught up in the *Sputnik* fever in autumn 1957, the Commissioners received Price's letter favorably and seized upon a proposal by General Electric to flight-test an aircraft reactor by 1960, provided that the government furnish additional funding for a "crash" program. Only Commissioner Libby demurred on the grounds that this approach would probably not lead to a useful propulsion system.[3]

In many respects there had been substantial progress in development since summer 1953. Experimental facilities at Oak Ridge had been greatly expanded, and private contractors had built large laboratories especially equipped for development of the two approaches: General Electric on the direct cycle near Cincinnati and the Pratt & Whitney Division of United Aircraft on the indirect cycle near Hartford, Connecticut. Both contractors had completed extensive design studies and component testing, and General Electric was operating a small reactor to test the performance of fuel elements.

The fact was, however, that more than $600 million and five years later, the United States was not much closer to an aircraft reactor than it had been in summer 1953. General Electric's test reactor appeared significant only if the Air Force were prepared to accept a nuclear-powered aircraft with low performance capabilities. Pratt and Whitney had just switched to a new concept for the indirect cycle and was only beginning to explore the problems of handling liquid-metal coolants at temperatures above 1,800 degrees Fahrenheit. Both contractors could suggest several military applications for the reactors they were developing, but in almost every case new designs of conventional aircraft offered superior performance at an earlier date.[4]

517

Armed with this information McCone joined the Department of Defense early in 1959 in recommending to the President a substantial cut in funding for the project, from $145 million for the Air Force and $95 million for the Commission in 1960 to $75 million for each agency. McCone, Killian, and others would have liked to eliminate one approach altogether, but in the post-*Sputnik* era that was unthinkable. Both approaches would be continued, but the contractors were instructed to concentrate on developing reactor components rather than complete engine prototypes.[5]

Price attempted to force the hand of the Executive Branch by calling a series of hearings before his subcommittee, one of which, in July 1959, was the first open hearing ever held on this topic. McCone favored further development if the project could be cut to one approach, but that was not feasible politically. When the Joint Chiefs of Staff refused to establish a clear-cut requirement for a nuclear-powered plane, Secretary Gates recommended to Eisenhower that the Administration scrap all plans for building prototype planes and limit development on both approaches to high-temperature research on reactor materials and components. On York's recommendation, the Department of Defense decided to terminate several unpromising development projects. With some reluctance the Commission accepted the reduction.[6]

McCone would have preferred to continue closely monitored research on both approaches and to make plans for a prototype of the indirect cycle, but the absence of a military requirement and opposition in the Bureau of the Budget precluded that course. Behind the scenes the influence of York and Kistiakowsky was decisive. York thought much of the research misdirected and tried to hold costs down to those politically necessary. Kistiakowsky sharply criticized General Electric for spending "about one-fourth of a billion dollars" on an engine that appeared useless; he considered the project "largely a political issue" and "definitely a technical failure." The President was inclined to take an even stronger position than did York and was not especially worried about the political implications.[7]

A further objection to nuclear-powered aircraft, one seldom voiced in public, was the potential radiation hazard. Even with extensive shielding the crew would be exposed to enough radiation to limit the number of hours that they could spend in the plane. Very expensive devices would be necessary to protect ground crews, and there was always the danger of radiation exposure of the public in the event of a crash. Another consideration was that the direct-cycle engine, which would feed the turbine with air coming directly from the reactor core, would continuously release measurable amounts of radiation to the atmosphere. Late in 1959 the Commission established an aerospace nuclear safety board to study the potential hazards of nuclear-powered aircraft and space vehicles.

518

By the end of 1960 virtually all support for nuclear-powered aircraft had evaporated except within the Commission and the Joint Committee. Probably hoping for better days in the Kennedy Administration, the Commission's aircraft reactors branch confidently announced plans for carrying both approaches forward to the operation of test reactors in the coming decade. One of President Kennedy's first decisions in 1961, however, was to kill the project after fifteen years of sophisticated and expensive research.[8]

## ROVER *AND* PLUTO

Since 1956 two weapon laboratories had been working on propulsion systems for unmanned air and space craft: Los Alamos on Project *Rover*, to develop a reactor for rocket propulsion; and Livermore on Project *Pluto*, to develop a nuclear ramjet that would propel a missile at low altitudes and supersonic speeds. Once the laboratories had investigated the high-temperature properties of various materials, experimental reactors were designed and built in a 500-square-mile area that the Commission acquired near the Nevada Test Site. Los Alamos completed the first test of an experimental reactor using gaseous hydrogen as a propellant on July 1, 1959. Two further tests using the Kiwi-A reactor with cores designed for higher power levels and more stringent operating conditions were completed in summer and fall 1960. Livermore operated the first test reactor in Project *Pluto* at the test site in December 1960. Although all the tests gave some promising results, fundamental problems remained in obtaining reliable performance with high-density, high-temperature reactors; and, as in the case of the manned aircraft, the fast pace of development in conventional propulsion systems was outstripping the nuclear approach. Thus, neither York nor Kistiakowsky was willing to recommend a high priority for these projects. Like the aircraft systems, *Rover* and *Pluto* did not survive the 1960s.[9]

## AUXILIARY POWER FOR SPACE VEHICLES

Although the Air Force had asked the Commission in 1955 to develop a 519 nuclear unit that would provide electric power for a missile, *Sputnik* sparked support for a full-fledged effort. An Air Force requirement for SNAP-1, a radioisotope-heated generator, had already been cancelled; but the contractor, the Martin Company of Baltimore, used the SNAP-1 technology to build a somewhat larger unit, SNAP-3, which President Eisenhower announced with much fanfare in January 1959. SNAP-3 weighed five pounds, had no moving parts, and produced 2.5 watts of electricity. Before the end of 1960 Martin had built and tested SNAP-5 and was working on SNAP-7A and -7B, 5-watt and 30-watt units to be used by the Coast Guard in light buoys. At the same time Atomics International was developing a family of SNAP devices that employed small reactors rather than radioisotopes as a power source. An experimental version of SNAP-2 reactor, designed to provide three kilowatts of electricity for a space vehicle, was completed in November 1959 and operated at full power for a year. By that time the turboelectric conversion equipment was being tested and the completed unit was scheduled for space flight in 1964. Two larger reactor generator systems, SNAP-8 and -10, were already under development. By comparison with aircraft propulsion, SNAP was still a miniscule project in 1960; total expenditures since 1955 had been less than $13 million. During the 1960s, however, the exceptional performance of SNAP-2 and its descendants in space missions would make the program the most successful of all the air and space projects.[10]

## REACTORS FOR THE ARMY

The reactors the Commission developed for the Army during the 1950s did not present the severe technological challenges of the aircraft projects. The initial aim was to create relatively small power reactors that could be assembled in remote areas to generate electricity for Army installations. With an emphasis on simple design and high reliability, the Army projects did not involve high risks in either government funding or international prestige. Thus, they did not command the attention of McCone, York, Kistiakowsky, or the President.

The first project was the Army package power reactor, a smaller and simplified version of the pressurized-water reactor derived from Shippingport technology. Completed in 1957 at Fort Belvoir, Virginia, the 1.9-megawatt plant continued to operate for more than a decade, first as an experiment and then as a training reactor and power generator. It was also the precursor of a larger stationary power plant at Fort Greeley, Alaska, and three portable plants—at Fort Sundance, Wyoming; Camp Century in Greenland; and McMurdo Sound, Antarctica—all completed and operated in the 1960s. Although these plants produced useful power for about a decade, they proved in the long run too difficult and costly to maintain and were eventually decommissioned. The Commission also sponsored research for the Army on small boiling-water and gas-cooled reactors, but neither of these was pursued beyond the experiment stage.[11]

520

## THE NUCLEAR NAVY

The spectacular performance of the *Nautilus* in sea trials and fleet maneuvers in the spring and summer of 1955 convinced Admiral Arleigh A. Burke, the new chief of naval operations, that all new submarines built for the fleet should be nuclear-powered. He promptly added three more to the three nuclear submarines authorized for 1956 and asked the bureau of ships to study the feasibility of using nuclear power in frigates, guided-missile cruisers, and attack carriers for the surface fleet. Then he spurred the Navy's lagging efforts in missile development and selected Rear Admiral William F. Raborn to head a special projects office in the bureau of ordnance to begin research on the Navy's launching system.[12]

Anticipating that the success of the *Nautilus* would lead to burgeoning requirements for nuclear ships, Rickover and his staff had already launched the development of new types of reactors to meet this demand. Using the technology produced in building the S2W propulsion plant for the *Nautilus*, Westinghouse was completing a new pressurized-water reactor, the S3W, which the Navy expected would become the standard reactor system for the submarine fleet. Despite the significant advances required over the *Nautilus* plant, Westinghouse was able to bypass the prototype and move directly into final design and procurement. The keel for the *Skate*, the first of three submarines to use the new reactor, was laid at Groton, Connecticut, on July 21, 1955; the same day the *Seawolf*, containing General Electric's S2G sodium-cooled plant, was launched at the same Electric

Boat shipyard. Rickover had also wheedled permission to resume design studies for an aircraft-carrier reactor at Westinghouse. Thus, he could respond promptly to Burke's interest in nuclear-powered surface ships by starting construction early in 1956 of the A1W, a land-based prototype, to be completed at the Idaho test station in 1958.[13]

It was also apparent, however, before the end of 1955 that the S3W (and its modification, S4W) would not take full advantage of the potential capabilities of a nuclear submarine as demonstrated by the *Nautilus*. Rickover and Westinghouse were suddenly required to shift emphasis from the S3W to a larger, more powerful plant, the S5W, which did become the standard reactor for the submarine fleet. The keel for the *Skipjack*, the first submarine to use the S5W plant, was laid at Groton in May 1956. Westinghouse received a steady flow of orders for S5W plants, not only for attack submarines but also for the missile-carrying Polaris ships, first authorized in the crisis response to *Sputnik* in 1958. By the end of 1960 the Navy had authorized thirty-seven submarines using the S5W plant: twenty-three attack and fourteen Polaris.

521

The A1W prototype, consisting of two propulsion reactors for surface ships, continued to operate during 1959 and 1960 to provide design data and crew training for the aircraft carrier *Enterprise*, which was launched at Newport News, Virginia, on September 24, 1960. The *Enterprise* would use eight A2W reactors, while the guided-missile cruiser *Long Beach*, under construction at Quincy, Massachusetts, would use two reactors. Work was in the early stages at West Milton, New York, on the D1G prototype for the frigate *Bainbridge*, also to be built at Quincy.

For many Americans the most impressive demonstrations of Rickover's accomplishment were the highly publicized sea adventures of the first nuclear submarines in the late 1950s. The *Nautilus* in July 1957 was the first submarine to maneuver for any distance under the Arctic ice. The following summer the *Nautilus* traversed the northern passage from west to east under the ice and surfaced at the North Pole. The new submarine *Skate* followed the same course in 1959, this time in winter, and surfaced ten times. By 1960 two more nuclear submarines had made the trip, and three Polaris vessels were operating. In May the radar-picket submarine *Triton*, powered with two S4G reactors, made a 36,000-mile voyage around the world without surfacing. These ventures were more than Jules Verne escapades; they had obvious implications for nuclear warfare in the missile age.

Some insiders, especially McCone, were impressed by Rickover's ability to get results. The admiral, it appeared, had succeeded where all others, including the Russians, had failed. He was not only actually building a nuclear navy years before most nations could even aspire to the idea but also creating the network of designers, suppliers, and fabricators needed to support a permanent technology. McCone appreciated these facts, and he was not about to sacrifice this advantage. He took a hard line in opposing the efforts of the Departments of State and Defense to honor a commitment made by Eisenhower in Paris in December 1957 to make nuclear submarine technology available to NATO countries. When the first request came from the Netherlands in spring 1959, McCone flatly opposed any cooperation and began reluctantly to draft an agreement only when Eisenhower ordered him to do so in September. Even then, McCone came up with a plan that would have delayed transmittal of classified information to the Dutch for two years. McCone, with the support of his fellow Commissioners and the Joint Committee, continued to drag his feet on the agreement for another year. By the time the President prodded him again in October 1960, it was too late to take any action on the agreement during the Eisenhower Administration.[14]

522

## HIGH-ENERGY PHYSICS

The Commission under Strauss's leadership saw American preeminence in the nuclear sciences as a key element in the Atoms-for-Peace program. To supplement the Berkeley bevatron and the Brookhaven cosmotron the Commission had approved construction of the much more powerful alternating-gradient synchrotron at Brookhaven, the zero-gradient machine at Argonne, the Cambridge electron synchrotron, and the Princeton-Pennsylvania proton synchrotron. At the same time the Commission was still entertaining a proposal from the Midwest Universities Research Association for another accelerator in the Great Lakes area. Behind these decisions lay the conviction that, by continuing to set the pace for all other nations in the most prestigious field of physical research, the United States could demonstrate its clear superiority over the Soviet Union. Thus, like other Atoms-for-Peace programs, high-energy physics had become an instrument in the Cold War.

McCone was just as enthusiastic as Strauss about staying ahead of the Russians in scientific research, but he was less easily swayed by the high-sounding appeals used by promoters of science to win Commission support for their projects. American preeminence in science was a worthy objective, but were the proposals from the national laboratories and the universities likely to serve that end? As he did in evaluating all Commission programs, McCone took nothing for granted; proponents were expected to show that their plans were realistic, their budgets reasonable, and the results worth the cost.

As an engineer, McCone tended to take a jaundiced view of scientists. Like Rickover, he understood the indispensable role that scientists played in establishing the base for technological innovation, but he did not quite accept the idea that turning scientists loose in the laboratory to pursue their own interests in basic research was always a good investment for the federal government. He visited the laboratories and questioned the scientists. By fall 1958 he was decidedly uncomfortable with the Commission's programs in high-energy physics. Were all those expensive accelerators necessary? Or had the Commission compromised in the face of competitive demands from the laboratories by giving each its own machine?

Willard Libby, who by this time understood McCone as well as his fellow scientists, suggested that it might be helpful to establish an interagency council to review federal policies for supporting high-energy physics. During summer 1958 Libby had met with Killian and Alan T. Waterman, director of the National Science Foundation, to draft a charter for the council. As a strategy, the group proposed that the Commission should assume responsibility for constructing large accelerators in the future and that the Department of Defense and the National Science Foundation should share funding with the Commission. The council, reporting directly to the President, would consist of senior officials from the three agencies, supported by technical staffs from the agencies and advisers from the laboratories and universities. Once established, the council would be expected to recommend to the President during fall 1958 "the construction of at least one new major accelerator."[15]

523

McCone accepted the proposal, probably because it promised financial help from other agencies and kept control in the hands of federal officials and not the scientists. It was hardly surprising, however, that the White House did not create a panel with the prestige and independence proposed. Instead, Killian appointed a panel of independent scientists under the President's Science Advisory Committee to make recommendations to him rather than directly to the President.[16]

The panel, headed by Emanuel R. Piore, a physicist who was director of research at the International Business Machines Corporation and a member of the Science Advisory Committee, lost no time in preparing its report. The panel urged sharp increases in federal support for high-energy physics from an annual rate of $59 million in 1959 to $125 million by 1963, without taking away funds from other areas of basic science. Highest priorities were for a linear accelerator capable of pushing electrons to energies as high as 10 billion electron volts (GeV) and a high-intensity proton accelerator of at least 8 GeV. For the linear accelerator, the panel recommended the proposal that Stanford University had been developing since 1956. The spark plug of the Stanford project was Wolfgang K. H. Panofsky, who as a graduate student had helped Luis W. Alvarez build the first linear accelerator at Berkeley in 1946. Talented and self-confident, Panofsky was accustomed to thinking big when it came to physics.[17]

The scale of Panofsky's plan matched his reputation. The accelerator, approximately two miles in length, would cost $100 million and would take six years to build. The accelerating tube would be placed in a tunnel ten feet wide and deep enough underground to provide necessary shielding.

A parallel tunnel, twenty-four feet in width and separated from the first by thirty-five feet of earth for shielding, would contain the 240 ultra-high-frequency klystron tubes that would supply power to the accelerating electrodes through which the electrons would pass on their way to the target. The proposed accelerator would provide an electron beam with the highest energy in the world and with fifty times the intensity of a circular machine.[18]

When Eisenhower met with Killian and the Piore panel on April 2, 1959, he reacted favorably to the proposal for the Stanford accelerator and to substantial expansion of high-energy physics in general, although it was not at all clear whether he approved the expenditure levels proposed in the Piore study. In a speech in New York on May 14, Eisenhower publicly committed his Administration to the project, but McCone took no precipitous action to carry out the decision. In August he asked General Manager Luedecke to make an intensive investigation of the technical, financial, and administrative plans for the project. These studies by a group of outside consultants led to other questions, including the possibility of a conflict of interest between Stanford University and some of its consultants.

McCone's greatest concern, however, was the skyrocketing cost of research in high-energy physics. He told members of the Joint Committee in Albuquerque on December 9 that accelerators posed "one of the most disturbing problems" that he had faced on the Commission, and he reported to his fellow commissioners that the increasing costs were "alarming" to both him and the committee members.[19]

Kistiakowsky, who by now had replaced Killian as the President's science adviser, grew more impatient as McCone continued to question the priority assigned to high-energy physics. When McCone suggested that the Commission appoint an independent advisory group to reexamine the question, Kistiakowsky and scientists at the Commission turned this suggestion into a decision to reconvene the Piore panel, which promptly reaffirmed the recommendations in its first report, including a high priority for the Stanford accelerator. Kistiakowsky wrote McCone that he could understand the chairman's concern over ever-increasing costs, but he observed that "the Federal Government [had] committed itself to support of science in order to further national welfare, health, security and prestige." In the space program, international prestige was sufficient justification alone. In high-energy physics "the selection [could] be based more on scientific grounds: the promise of the most fundamental contributions to human knowledge and therefore the anticipation of the most far-reaching effects on human future." Eisenhower found this argument persuasive when Kistiakowsky presented the Piore report to him on March 23. McCone later that day told the Commission that "while the President was impressed with the cost implications of this program, he felt that the work was so important to science and to the

524

prestige of the United States, there was no alternative but to go forward."[20]

This time McCone accepted the President's decision and set in motion the administrative actions necessary to start design and engineering in 1961. By working closely with Senator Anderson and the Joint Committee, he was able to thwart any efforts by the scientists to rush headlong into construction without extensive engineering studies. Although the Commission requested authorization for the entire project, McCone was probably not unhappy when the Joint Committee supported authorization for only one year and then only for design and engineering. McCone, however, was not yet ready to accept an open-ended commitment to high-energy physics in general. In September he asked Kistiakowsky to reconvene the Piore panel a third time, to examine the long-term needs for accelerators. After a series of meetings during fall 1960 the panel came up with sweeping recommendations for continuing expansion of high-energy physics with federal support. In addition to meeting the increasing costs for building and operating accelerators already under construction (estimated at close to $200 million by 1970), the federal government was asked to increase support for university research and to finance several new accelerators as the need arose. All these additional projects would push federal expenditures for high-energy physics close to $400 million annually by 1970. To assuage McCone's dismay, Kistiakowsky admitted that the recommendations represented an optimum program from the scientists' perspective and did not consider the needs of other research or budget constraints. Still, the panel report raised important questions about the role of the federal government in the new era of scientific development, questions that would continue to haunt succeeding administrations.[21]

525

## FUSION: A RETURN TO SCIENCE

During Lewis Strauss's term as chairman, Commission support of controlled thermonuclear research had grown rapidly from less than $1 million in 1953 to $10 million in 1957. The first three years had been a time of unrestrained optimism as scientists at Los Alamos and Berkeley joined those at Princeton in the search for a controlled thermonuclear reactor. While Lyman Spitzer and others at Princeton devised ways to circumvent technical difficulties encountered in experiments with the stellarator, James L. Tuck at Los Alamos and William R. Baker at Berkeley saw a possible shortcut to an operational system in the new linear pinch machines that they were developing. Tuck, who was usually cautious in his judgments, saw 1955 as "the greatest thrust forward" yet made in Project *Sherwood*.[22]

Before the end of 1957, however, the same kinds of "technical" problems that haunted Princeton were beginning to dampen enthusiasm in the western laboratories. When the Commission during the fall seemed determined to use fusion development as the centerpiece for the United States exhibit at the 1958 Geneva conference, few scientists involved were comfortable with the idea, especially when Strauss proposed that the fusion display should be the world's first demonstration of thermonuclear neutrons. The neutrons copiously produced in pinch devices in the United States, the United Kingdom, and the Soviet Union, which had elated scientists in 1955, had all turned out to be spurious; and there was little hope that such a demonstration could be accomplished at Geneva. Oak Ridge had now entered the field as the fourth laboratory pursuing the fusion goal, but the experimental work there was only beginning. Even a near doubling of the funding and Strauss's personal encouragement could not achieve his goal. The fusion exhibit at Geneva turned out to be a dazzling display of American ingenuity and commitment, but it failed to provide evidence that the successful extraction of energy from the controlled fusion reaction was imminent. The outcome was a clear example of the truism that politics and money cannot always drive technology.

526

Strauss, in his enthusiasm to recapture for the United States world leadership in scientific development, which the Soviets had seized with *Sputnik*, had ignored several trends that had been changing the character of thermonuclear research since 1956. First, there was growing realization that a practical fusion reactor would not be a simple extrapolation of an experimental device being operated in the laboratories. The troublesome "technical" problems were not the only obstacles to success. Behind them lay a failure to understand fully the physics affecting the process. The fusion scientists, if not Strauss, were convinced that they would have to give up cut-and-try efforts to finesse their way to a practical reactor and instead return to basic theory and experiments.

Second, closely related to the first trend was the growing realization among scientists that success depended upon declassification of the project and the opening of fusion research to the free exchange of ideas. The Commission staff had been advocating declassification since 1953. Although the scientists agreed in principle, they hesitated to take a strong stand on the issue in hopes that a successful reactor could be developed before the security wraps were removed. As that possibility grew more remote, the scientists took up the cause of declassification in 1956, only to encounter the unyielding opposition of Strauss. As a compromise the Commission had agreed to declassify basic research in fusion physics, so long as it did not relate to the design of practical reactors. Not until Strauss had left the Commission did it completely declassify all work on fusion and then mostly for a short-term political advantage on the eve of the Geneva conference.

Third, stemming directly from the second trend, was the movement of the fusion project away from exclusive Commission control toward the normal patterns established in academic and industrial research. With basic research declassified, some university scientists began to give more attention to plasma physics, and industry was ready to participate when the Commission made classified data available in 1956 to holders of access permits. General Electric promptly set up an ambitious program, Westinghouse kept two physicists working at Princeton, and Allis-Chalmers and the Radio Corporation of America received a contract to do detailed engineering for a new and larger stellarator at Princeton. In 1957 General Atomic, a division of General Dynamics, joined forces with a group of utility companies in Texas to study with private funding the long-range technology of fusion reactors.[23]

McCone, following the same course that he had adopted in high-energy physics, encouraged these trends in the fusion program. Declassification and the opening of research to academic and industry scientists impressed McCone as not only a healthy move but also one likely to reduce federal expenditures. Within weeks of becoming chairman, he instituted his standard procedure of asking the Commission staff for a complete review of the fusion program. His first observation was that annual expenditures had risen from $10 million in 1957 to $26 million in 1959 and were projected at $36 million in 1960. Much of the increase, he noted, was to support Strauss's intensive effort for the Geneva exhibit, and he suggested that costs could be cut for normal development. McCone also asked the staff to consider reducing the number of fusion experiments. Recognizing that a fusion reactor was now likely to be the product only of long-term basic research, an advisory committee of scientists accepted a 10-percent cut in funding but insisted upon continuing all four approaches. Under McCone, fusion no longer received preferred treatment from the chairman but rather became one of many research projects competing for Commission funding.[24]

527

Once the Commission had opened the doors to independent research on fusion, scientists in the universities began to establish the usual appurtenances of a conventional research field. Late in 1959 Melvin Gottlieb of Princeton took steps to create a division of fluid dynamics within the American Institute of Physics to replace the closed, classified *Sherwood* conferences that the Commission had sponsored until spring 1957. A steady stream of articles on fusion research appeared in the *Physical Review* until a new specialized journal, *Physics of Fluids*, could be published. The Massachusetts Institute of Technology, Princeton, and other universities soon organized graduate programs in high-temperature plasma physics and engineering. As the number of graduates increased in the early 1960s old-timers noted a gradual improvement in the quality of research. Perhaps the exciting "golden days" of fusion research were past, but, by the time

McCone left the Commission in 1961, the tortuous path toward the cherished goal of a virtually unlimited source of energy seemed to rest on much more solid ground than that explored in earlier years.

## PLOWSHARE

When Lewis Strauss for the second time took the oath of office as a Commissioner in July 1953, he marked his Bible at the familiar passage in Micah: "And they shall beat their swords into plowshares, and their spears into pruning hooks; nation shall not lift up sword against nation, neither shall they learn war any more."[25] Although the new chairman had often professed his dedication to developing the peaceful uses of atomic energy, he probably did not suspect in summer 1953 how directly the biblical words could be applied to nuclear technology. Within three years, however, the promise of such a transformation appeared within reach.

528

Late in November 1956 Herbert York, then director of the Livermore laboratory, had raised the possibility of using the energy released from nuclear or thermonuclear reactions to produce power or plutonium, to dig excavations, or even to accelerate rockets. York reported growing interest in such applications, not only at Livermore but also at Los Alamos and Sandia, and he suggested that scientists from the three laboratories be permitted to hold a classified conference to discuss the possibilities. The Commission approved the conference, with the proviso that work on peaceful uses not interfere with weapon development.[26]

Predictably the conference held at Livermore in February 1957 concluded that there was "a sufficient number of attractive possibilities" to warrant a few studies of "using clean nuclear explosive devices for nonmilitary purposes." The potential applications indeed appeared attractive, but the Commission saw certain hazards in the proposal. One, already noted, was the danger of diverting scarce scientific talent and resources from weapon development. Even more troublesome would be the common technical characteristics of peaceful devices and weapons. If nuclear explosive devices were to be used for peaceful purposes, they would have to be available eventually to the civilian economy, but their similarity to weapons would make declassification of their design and use virtually impossible. For the time being, then, studies of the new devices were to be limited to Livermore, and the project would remain secret.[27]

Still concerned about possible interference with weapon development, the Commission decided to limit the peaceful device project to $100,000 through fiscal year 1959; but by autumn 1957 Livermore was already advocating a vast expansion of the project to include designing special devices for excavation and mining applications, studying the possibility of extracting heat and tritium from underground detonations, and obtaining scientific data on underground shots. The proposal would require $450,000 in 1958 and $3 million in 1959. Although the Commission staff believed that Livermore was moving too fast, both Strauss and Libby advocated a program even larger than the laboratory proposed. In the end the Commission authorized the $3-million figure, primarily for an earth-moving experiment in 1959, and asked the Bureau of the Budget to increase the 1959 budget by that amount.[28]

Much of the Commissioners' enthusiasm stemmed from data just then available from *Rainier*, the first fully contained underground nuclear test. *Rainier* had demonstrated that no seismic or shock effects would interfere with mining operations following a nuclear detonation underground. Unable to contain his excitement, Libby told the *Washington Post* in December 1957 that he saw "very definite possibilities" in using nuclear explosions for peaceful uses. Referring to *Rainier*, Libby exclaimed, "I've not seen anything in years so exciting as this development." The Commission's semi-annual report to the Congress in January 1958 briefly described the Livermore project and named it Project *Plowshare*.[29]

Commission interest in *Plowshare* grew rapidly in 1958, not only in terms of its potential peaceful applications but also as an opportunity to put a better light on weapon development. As Strauss noted in February, *Plowshare* was intended to "highlight the peaceful applications of nuclear explosive devices and thereby create a climate of world opinion that is more favorable to weapons development and tests." Growing public demand for a nuclear test ban in spring 1958 also suggested that the Commission should move quickly to demonstrate the value of *Plowshare* devices while testing was still permissible.[30]

During his final weeks as chairman in June 1958, Strauss made certain that the future of *Plowshare* was in good hands. The Commission approved doubling the 1960 budget for the project to $6 million. Livermore personnel assigned to the project would increase to almost one hundred, and firm plans were made to bring industry into full participation in *Plowshare* experiments. Teller, now officially director of the Livermore laboratory, pushed forward with specific plans for *Plowshare* experiments still focused on excavation and the production of power and isotopes. The laboratory would continue to design devices for digging canals and harbors and to study the phenomena of underground detonations. These studies were intended to lead to two full-scale experiments: Project *Chariot*, to excavate a harbor on the northwest coast of Alaska in the summer of 1960; and Project *Gnome*, an underground shot to be fired in a salt dome near Carlsbad, New Mexico, in summer 1959, to test the feasibility of producing fissionable material by this method.[31]

Despite Teller's strong leadership and vigorous lobbying in Washington, schedules for *Plowshare* experiments continued to slip during the last two years of the Eisenhower Administration. As Commissioner John S.

529

Graham pointed out to McCone in September 1958, the President's announcement of a moratorium on nuclear testing was likely to stimulate
strong Soviet opposition and public sentiment against *Plowshare* experiments. Graham's prediction proved correct, and within a few weeks Soviet
protests forced the Commission to cancel a meeting with oil industry representatives to discuss oil-shale experiments with *Plowshare* devices. Although the Commission continued to plan *Plowshare* experiments, McCone
assured the State Department that no nationwide public announcements on
*Plowshare* would be made pending the outcome of the test-ban negotiations
scheduled to begin in October 1958. As those negotiations dragged on into
1959 and 1960, the schedule for *Chariot* and *Gnome* drifted with them.[32]

## INTERNATIONAL SCIENCE

530

By 1959 nuclear physics seemed the queen of the sciences. Kistiakowsky
saw high-energy physics as the key to understanding the nature of the universe and thus of "uniquely fundamental scientific importance." It had
"very high prestige value" and a "special appeal to many of the most able
and creative scientists." The United States could not afford to forfeit its
world leadership in a field that served as a touchstone of national superiority. Fusion experiments were considered equally critical, not so much for
their fundamental character but because of their enormous potential as an
energy source. These propositions, which the scientists continually invoked
to justify government support, gave both high-energy physics and fusion
special consideration in the Eisenhower Administration. Both fields offered
opportunities for competing with the Soviet Union in the Cold War while
advancing the Atoms-for-Peace program.[33]

If high-energy physics and fusion research held the promise of a
competitive advantage over the Soviet Union, they also generated proposals
for international cooperation between the two superpowers. The idea that
competitors could cooperate was nothing new to nuclear physicists, whose
discipline was born at the turn of the century in an international environment. In 1952 physicists at Brookhaven had welcomed colleagues from the
European Center for Nuclear Research and willingly shared with them the
strong focusing principle that made possible a quantum jump in the energy
capabilities of accelerators. The next step beyond the alternating-gradient
synchrotron posed enormous theoretical and engineering problems that only
the very best minds could hope to resolve. American physicists in 1958
took the lead in establishing a commission on high-energy physics within
the International Union of Pure and Applied Physics. The commission,
composed of two Americans, two Russians, and two physicists from Western Europe, laid plans for a series of international conferences to follow an
earlier one held in Rochester, New York, in 1956. The next meeting was

planned for Moscow in 1959 and the third for Rochester in 1960. More immediately, the commission was charged to encourage international cooperation among high-energy laboratories in all countries "to ensure the best use of the facilities of these large and expensive installations." This goal could be accomplished by arranging for the rapid exchange of the latest experimental results.[34]

International exchanges in fusion research were not so easy to arrange. Before 1955 everything related to fusion work in the United States had been classified, even the names of the laboratories where research was conducted. In 1956 the Atomic Energy Commission approved the exchange of scientists and information with Britain and then removed all restrictions on basic research not related to operating reactors. With complete declassification of the United States program on the eve of the 1958 Geneva conference, however, the doors were flung open for international cooperation. After Geneva not only British scientists but also Russians began to correspond informally with their counterparts in the United States.[35]

531

Even after declassification any significant exchanges with scientists in the Soviet Union required extensive diplomatic negotiations. Experience had already shown that, without a written agreement setting forth specific details for visits and the exchange of information, the Russians were not likely to grant fully reciprocal concessions. Fortunately the framework for exchanges in the field of nuclear physics already existed. In January 1958 the United States signed a two-year agreement with the Soviet Union providing for a broad range of exchanges in cultural, technical, and educational fields. Section 9 of the agreement permitted the exchange of "scientists and specialists for delivering lectures and holding seminars on various problems of science and technology."[36]

Isidor Rabi used the occasion of a meeting of a United Nations scientific advisory committee in Vienna in June 1959 to open discussion of a specific agreement with the Russians in the nuclear sciences. The Soviet delegate was Vasily S. Emelyanov, a metallurgist and government official already well known to Americans. Emelyanov, an intelligent and articulate man, chaired the Main Administration for the Utilization of Atomic Energy in the Soviet Union. He was responsible for all areas of the peaceful applications of nuclear energy; but he was subordinate to Soviet officials who directed the weapon and production activities, and he had no role in test-ban negotiations. Rabi and John Hall discussed with Emelyanov ways of reducing the tensions and suspicions that made the arrangement of scientific exchanges difficult. When Rabi suggested an exchange on nuclear power reactors, Emelyanov at once proposed a visit to the Soviet Union by McCone. Rabi reacted favorably, but he warned Emelyanov that the Americans were interested in visiting only large power stations, particularly those under construction, and not small experimental reactors. Emelyanov agreed to take up this issue with Chairman Khrushchev immediately upon his return to Moscow. On fusion research, Emelyanov was more optimistic about the possibilities than was Rabi, who noted that several American fusion projects were located at sites of weapon research.[37]

Before the McCone trip could be arranged, the Commission had to decide whether to permit Frol R. Kozlov, the first deputy premier of the Soviet Union, to visit Commission facilities during a visit to the United States in late June. With some hesitation the Commissioners agreed on the grounds that the visit would include facilities of low sensitivity: the nuclear ship *Savannah*, the Shippingport plant, and the Berkeley Radiation Laboratory. Another consideration was to ensure a warm Soviet reception for Vice-President Nixon, who was scheduled to arrive in Moscow in a few weeks.[38]

Nixon's trip to the Soviet Union took on significance for the Commission when McCone arranged to have Rickover join the Vice-President's party. No more awed by Kremlin leaders than he was by American presidents and senators, Rickover brushed aside diplomatic amenities and brusquely stated his intention to conclude an agreement to exchange reactor technology before Nixon left Moscow. Much to the later dismay of Commission officials, Rickover claimed that he was authorized by the President to include all American reactors in the agreement, even the production reactors at Hanford and Savannah River and the aircraft propulsion project, but not naval propulsion systems. As one official wryly noted, Rickover was willing to give away everything on all reactors except those for which he was responsible. Kozlov found Rickover's proposal intriguing and suggested that he discuss the details with the appropriate Soviet officials, in this case Emelyanov.[39]

By the time Rickover met with Emelyanov on August 2, he had ruffled more Soviet feathers. As the first American to visit the Soviet nuclear-powered icebreaker *Lenin*, Rickover had made a scene when Soviet officials tried to steer him away from specific details about the ship's reactor. Eventually the Russians gave in, but not before some of the press had picked up the incident. Rickover had also embarrassed his hosts by slipping away from his security escorts and spending several hours talking with private citizens without surveillance. McCone cabled Rickover a "well done" on the *Lenin* episode and urged him to gain access to nuclear power plants and "fully develop their views [on their] nuclear power program."[40]

Emelyanov was no doubt on his guard when Rickover arrived, and he soon learned that reports of Rickover's abrasive personality were true. Rickover began the conversation by saying there had been lots of talk about peace and friendship, but now was the time to do something about it. He pulled out a list of Soviet reactor projects and tried to extract a commitment from Emelyanov on each one. Emelyanov gave tentative reactions to each proposal but refused to say anything about production reactors or aircraft propulsion work in the Soviet Union. The meeting did not end on a congenial note.[41]

McCone had his first opportunity to meet with Emelyanov when Premier Khrushchev came to Washington in September 1959. With firm recommendations from the Commission staff that he proceed cautiously, McCone did not attempt to follow up Rickover's hard bargaining in Moscow, but rather accepted Emelyanov's suggestion that they consider first things first—namely, an exchange of visits by themselves. These visits might be followed by an exchange of information in selected fields and then possibly a joint project on thermonuclear reactors or accelerators.[42]

By the time Emelyanov had returned to Washington after the western tour of Khrushchev's party McCone had had a chance to discuss his tactics with the President. Eisenhower readily accepted the idea of cooperation with the Russians on peaceful uses but stressed that the exchange should be used to bolster the sagging image of the International Atomic Energy Agency. McCone admitted that he was neither as enthusiastic about a trip to Russia as his staff nor as hopeful that it would produce useful information, but he thought he should probably be able to say that he had at least visited Russian installations. Eisenhower suggested that McCone "do a good deal of listening" when he next met with Emelyanov. Keep the British and Canadians informed, the President told McCone, and do what you can to support the international agency.[43]

533

In a second meeting on September 25, McCone and Emelyanov quickly agreed on the types of facilities to be visited by each of them and on the kinds of information to be exchanged after the visits. The exchange was to cover eleven areas of the physical and biological sciences, including high-energy physics and fusion and power reactor development. McCone hoped that Khrushchev and Eisenhower would endorse the agreement the next day at Camp David, but other matters took precedence. The President later assured McCone that both leaders were aware of the proposal; Eisenhower seemed much more interested in Khrushchev's remark that the Russians had found the development of nuclear power far more difficult and expensive than they had anticipated and they were cutting back sharply on reactor projects. McCone wrote that the President "seemed to be telling me that I should take these views into consideration in connection with our budget."[44]

After some uncertainty about the proper timing for his trip to the Soviet Union, McCone departed on October 8 with Commissioner John H. Williams, a high-energy physicist; Alvin Weinberg from Oak Ridge National Laboratory and Frank Pittman to cover reactor development; Lyman Spitzer from Princeton to cover fusion research; and Kenneth S. Pitzer, a chemist from the University of California, to cover metallurgy research and uranium mining and processing. Arriving at Tallinn, Estonia, the group boarded the *Lenin* for a short cruise, visited two research institutes in Leningrad, and in Moscow saw the Russians' first research reactor, a fusion experiment, and several accelerators. At Dubna, outside Moscow, the group inspected five nuclear research facilities that housed several accelerators and other experimental devices. Then the group divided for separate visits to several nuclear power stations, a uranium mine, and a uranium reduction plant.[45]

When McCone met with the President on October 27 to discuss plans for Emelyanov's visit, he had almost an hour to describe his Soviet adventure. McCone found the *Lenin* a far more impressive piece of engineering than Rickover had suggested. He thought the Russians' nuclear power program was considerably behind the United States', but he admitted that the Russians had cut back their work in this area. Soviet fusion research was good and closely followed the American course. Soviet scientists were well trained, competent, and well treated. McCone thought the Russians' level of effort in the peaceful technologies was roughly equal to that in the United States but not as far advanced in any area.[46]

Emelyanov and eight distinguished Soviet scientists arrived in the United States on November 5, 1959, to tour nuclear facilities at eleven sites, mostly power reactors and national laboratories. By the time Emelyanov returned to Washington McCone had reviewed the draft exchange agreement with the Commission staff and had checked his proposed course of action once again with the President, who saw no reason to delay unless the exchange would actually hurt the United States. Impressed and gratified by the tour, Emelyanov engaged McCone in a wide-ranging and unusually frank discussion of their roles as agents of cooperation and understanding. He described to McCone how he had come to believe that Khrushchev, unlike Stalin, was sincerely dedicated to disarmament and peaceful coexistence. Emelyanov knew that McCone had his own problems with the politicians, but men in their positions had to expect such difficulties. "Everything," Emelyanov said, "depends on the two of us."[47]

The McCone-Emelyanov memorandum provided that specialists in small groups would be permitted to visit designated facilities in the host country for ten to fifteen days for conferences and examination of equipment related to fusion research, power reactors, high-energy physics, neutron physics, and the structure of the nucleus. The two nations agreed to exchange abstracts of unclassified work on peaceful uses of atomic energy, including both formal and informal reports, all of which were to be made available to the International Atomic Energy Agency. Both sides were to explore the possibility of setting up joint projects to build fusion reactors and accelerators and to study other technical problems.[48]

To top off Emelyanov's successful trip, the President invited him to the Oval Office for a brief visit after the formal signing of the memorandum on November 24. Eisenhower used the occasion to express his personal interest in the future of nuclear power and his hope that, working within the international agency, the two nations could pool some of their resources to develop peaceful uses. Emelyanov replied that the Soviet Union was looking forward to the President's visit in April 1960; he hoped Eisenhower could see some nuclear facilities while there.[49]

Arrangements for the first exchange visits proceeded slowly. During winter 1960 Emelyanov was scarcely ever in Moscow as he travelled with Khrushchev on several foreign trips. Not until late April did Emelyanov accept McCone's proposal to send five American scientists to the Soviet Union in May. Despite Khrushchev's outraged reaction to the U-2 spy plane incident a few days later and the cancellation of the long-planned summit meeting with Eisenhower, Emelyanov did not withdraw the invitation to a team of American physicists, who arrived in Moscow on May 12. Two weeks later, after a fruitful series of conferences at eight Soviet installations engaged in high-energy physics, the Americans were taken without prior notice to a meeting with Emelyanov. The high spirits of the Americans quickly faded as the bitter and discouraged official unburdened himself of a long list of resentments and complaints about American actions going back to 1956. The list included last-minute refusals by the American government to permit him to attend scientific conferences in the United States, Rickover's insulting remarks to prominent Soviet scientists at Shippingport, and provocative and persistent questions from American scientists as well as the press. The Americans did not seem to understand how such discourtesies could upset the tenuous status of the exchange program. Even more serious were the effects of the U-2 incident; it had confirmed the opinions of some Soviet officials who had long charged that the Americans could not be trusted and that Emelyanov had been naive and foolish in his quest for international cooperation.[50]

535

Emelyanov was in a friendly and cordial mood when he met privately with McCone in Vienna in September 1960. A Soviet fusion research team had visited five American laboratories in May and then in July a second pair of visits by an American fusion team and Soviet high-energy physicists had been accomplished, much to the satisfaction of all concerned. In Vienna McCone was able to resolve or postpone decisions on several issues that had first been raised in 1959. New difficulties with fast-breeder reactor experiments in both countries had caused the Russians to abandon their earlier insistence upon an exchange, which the Americans considered unfruitful, in this area. The Russians attending the high-energy physics conference in Rochester in August had been convinced that any decision to start work on a new accelerator in the 500-GeV range should be delayed for at least a year. Thus, Emelyanov gave up at least temporarily his hope expressed in spring 1959 that the two nations set up a joint project to build a new accelerator, probably near Vienna. The two leaders did agree that when such a joint project was established it would be a bilateral relationship with representatives of the international agency participating only as observers. Emelyanov accepted McCone's suggestion that they consider a joint study of the disposal of radioactive waste. Toward the end of the meeting Emelyanov again gave vent to the frustrations he had expressed to the American physicists. Because the Americans commanded an unbreakable majority in the international agency, Emelyanov had been unable as the Soviet representative to accomplish most missions assigned to him in Moscow. He complained that he was badgered by his associates at home who repeatedly asked him what five years of cooperation had accomplished. Emelyanov said it was hard to find a convincing answer.[51]

McCone met Emelyanov one last time in New York on November 19. John F. Kennedy had just been elected President, and McCone did not yet know what his future would be. Emelyanov's position in the Soviet hierarchy was by no means secure, as McCone already knew. With little to discuss on the exchange program, the two veterans indulged in a sharp but friendly debate over the proposed test ban and disarmament. McCone took strong issue with Emelyanov's charge that he was opposed to the cessation of nuclear tests. He insisted that he favored cessation with reasonable controls against cheating, but McCone believed that the Russians had no interest in controls. When Emelyanov complained that the U-2 incident made it hard to believe that the Americans were serious about friendship with the Soviet Union, McCone replied that the trouble lay in the Soviet insistence upon secrecy; until the Soviet leaders created an open society, there was only a limited base for mutual trust. Even after five years of frustration, Emelyanov could not bring himself to abandon the hope that somehow international cooperation among scientists might lead to peace, but McCone was probably too much a realist to believe that goal was within reach.[52]

## CHAPTER 20

# THE TEST BAN:
# A FADING HOPE

By the end of May 1958 President Eisenhower thought he had found a new path that might lead out of the nuclear nightmare. After months of fruitless sparring with the Russians and endless debate with his own advisers, the President had succeeded in extracting a commitment from the Soviet Union to participate in an international conference of scientists who would meet in Geneva on July 1. The purpose of the conference would be to examine the technical difficulties involved in policing a ban on the testing of nuclear weapons. The chances of success were indeed small, but the goal was more than worth the effort.

## PREPARING FOR THE CONFERENCE

On the eve of the Geneva conference certain restrictive provisions of the Atomic Energy Act remained an impediment to a test-ban agreement. Unless Congress amended the act, allowing the United States to share nuclear weapon information with its allies, the United Kingdom was unwilling to forgo its own plans for testing nuclear weapons. Following the December 1957 NATO meetings, Eisenhower had promised to promote greater integration of nuclear forces within the Western alliance. The Commission had subsequently submitted the necessary amendment to Congress, where the proposal ran into stiff opposition from the Joint Committee.

The Joint Committee, always the cautious guardian of nuclear weapon information, was skeptical about the wisdom of sharing restricted data with the NATO allies. Concerned about the stability of European governments, the committee was worried that friendly governments might decide to pass along American nuclear weapon technology to others. Commission and Defense Department officials tried to assure the committee that there was little danger of proliferation because the proposed amendments would restrict sharing of weapon information to countries, like the United Kingdom, that had advanced nuclear weapon programs. Strauss, however, whose relations with Senator Anderson continued to deteriorate, was no longer an effective spokesman for the Administration.

Ultimately, Dulles had to step into the breach to save the amendments. Unless the Atomic Energy Act was amended, he predicted, NATO would be weakened and NATO governments would either seek their own nuclear capability or take a neutral stance. Mindful of the proliferation danger, Dulles stressed the need for common defense planning, common training of nuclear equipped forces, shared naval nuclear reactors,and the exchange of information with allies that already have nuclear weapons. Dulles frankly asked the Joint Committee why the British should be "forced to follow the sterile course of reworking ground already covered by the United States and known to the Soviet Union." Then without mentioning a test ban, Dulles reiterated three times the linkage between the amendments and the disarmament negotiations. He concluded "that all our major planning, both in terms of disarmament, the limitation of nuclear testing, the limitation of the use of nuclear weapons, the building of NATO, all of those plans would be disastrously affected, in my opinion, without this legislation."[1]

538

Congress amended the Atomic Energy Act of 1954 on June 30, and Eisenhower signed the legislation on July 2. Under the new amendment the President could authorize the Commission or the Department of Defense to transfer nonnuclear parts of atomic weapons and special nuclear materials for military applications to nations that had "made substantial progress in the development of atomic weapons."[2]

## CONFERENCE OF EXPERTS, GENEVA

Throughout June, the American scientists prepared for the opening of the Geneva Conference of Experts to Study the Methods of Detecting Violations of a Possible Agreement on the Suspension of Nuclear Tests. At Killian's suggestion, Eisenhower had asked James B. Fisk, a member of the President's Science Advisory Committee and vice-president of Bell Laboratories, to lead the delegation. Other members of the delegation were Ernest O. Lawrence and Robert F. Bacher, former Commissioner, physics professor at the California Institute of Technology, and member of the Science Advisory Committee. Strauss had wanted to appoint Teller, but the outspoken scientist had been disqualified by his vigorous support of testing. None of the three members of the American delegation had been fierce partisans in the disarmament debates, yet they represented a satisfactory balance of the contending parties. To balance the delegation even more, Bethe and Harold Brown, associate director of the Livermore laboratory, were appointed advisers. The British named Sir John Cockcroft and Sir William Penney; the French, Yves Rocard of the École normale superieure de Paris; and the Canadians, Dr. Ormond Solandt, former chairman of Canada's Defense Research Board.[3]

When Dulles briefed Fisk, Lawrence, and Bacher on June 6, he emphasized the importance that he and the President attached to the Geneva conference of experts. He warned that the delegation's mission would be purely technical. The necessary political decisions would be made in Washington afterward, but sound technical recommendations were a prerequisite to a satisfactory political settlement. Dulles observed that the conference did not have to devise "a technically perfect system"; even an imperfect system would be satisfactory as long as violation created "an unacceptable risk" for the Soviet Union. Fisk, Bacher, and Lawrence were already aware of the need for more scientific data on detecting tests. Before their meeting with Dulles, they had asked Strauss whether the Commission could conduct another underground test in Nevada. Because *Rainier* had not provided sufficient information about detection, they wanted a larger shot. In what would prove a fateful decision for the future of testing, Strauss had promised to see what he could do.[4]

539

When the President's Science Advisory Committee met with Eisenhower on June 18, Fisk, Bacher, and Killian reviewed preparations for the Geneva conference of experts. Killian mentioned the potential difficulty of declassifying information for the meeting. Considering what the United States planned to accomplish in Geneva, Eisenhower hoped that the Commission would adopt a liberal policy on classification. Consequently, Strauss's special assistant, Navy Captain John H. Morse, Jr., armed with declassification authority, became the Commission's principal representative in the Western delegation.[5]

Almost simultaneously after arriving in Geneva, both the Americans and Russians voiced their expectations for the conference of experts. On June 24, the United States delegation outlined the technical factors it considered relevant to monitoring a nuclear test suspension. The Americans expected the discussions to include detection and analysis of nuclear tests at low and high altitude, undersea and underground, and on the earth's surface. The principal means of detection would be the analysis of nuclear debris and acoustic, electromagnetic, and seismic signals. For the United States, these four categories provided a natural agenda. The Soviets, however, wanted the Westerners to agree to a test ban a priori. Without such a commitment, the Soviets asked rhetorically, "what sense is there in general in convoking such a conference and what sense is there in sending to it experts?" On the very eve of the conference the American delegation waited in Geneva at the United States consulate wondering whether the Russians would actually appear.[6]

The Geneva conference of experts convened on July 1, 1958, the day after Lewis Strauss left the Commission. Although John McCone, as chairman-designate, professed to have no fixed opinions on testing, his appointment would neither upset the Commission's policies nor provide solace to test-ban advocates. During McCone's confirmation hearings, Senator Anderson had tried to test McCone on the issue by observing that much of the Commission's rhetoric had conflicted with the diplomatic objectives of the Secretary of State. When pressed for his own views, McCone replied that he favored a test suspension with "adequate and proper safeguards." Beyond that, he had "made no commitment" and had "no irrevocable conviction" on the matter.[7] Obviously, McCone was trying to buy time and improve relationships with Anderson and other Democrats on the Joint Committee. Meanwhile, Strauss, now on the State Department payroll as Dulles's special assistant for peaceful nuclear energy, continued to receive Morse's status reports from Geneva.

The Soviet delegation included two members of the Soviet Academy of Sciences: the Soviet Union's first Nobel laureate in physics and one of the nation's most distinguished nuclear scientists. The strategist of the Soviet delegation was one of the nation's most experienced negotiators. Former American diplomat Charles Thayer noted:

> When the Soviet delegation stepped from its plane it was headed by a shaggy-haired little man with an unprepossessing manner and a crooked smile. You could have searched in vain for his name in every register of Soviet scientific institutions. No American scientist had ever read one of his papers or heard him address a scientific gathering. But he was well known to many American diplomats as one of the Kremlin's toughest negotiators . . . with the name of Simyon [Semyon] Tsarapkin.

The Americans would ultimately call him "Old Scratchy."[8]

At the outset, the Soviets introduced political as well as scientific and technical issues. Their strategy was to question whether there was any purpose in exploring technical questions without prior commitments from both sides to stop testing. Fisk, however, insisted that the United States delegation would address only the "extremely difficult technical and operational problems" in detection and identification of nuclear tests. "These are not purposeless discussions," Fisk argued, "but are directed to provide Governments with one of the necessary parts of the whole material required for a political decision on whether or not nuclear tests shall be suspended." Attempting to draw from the United States' experience with prohibition, Yevgeni K. Fedorov countered by pointing out how silly it would have been

540

for American police to discuss means of enforcing prohibition without an actual law on the statutes. Quickly Fisk responded that before deciding on prohibition the United States might well have determined whether or not it was enforceable. Although the Americans were worried that the Russians might walk out of the conference, Fedorov, seeing that Fisk would not yield to political pressure, ultimately backed off so that the conference could continue.[9]

## THE GENEVA SYSTEM

Through July and into August the experts settled into the negotiations that created what came to be known as "the Geneva system." The Soviet delegates appeared much less concerned about details than did the Western delegates, and they were far more willing to hurry the discussions. When confronted with difficult technical problems, the Soviets expressed confidence that technical solutions could be found eventually if both sides would accept agreements in principle. Morse, who mistrusted the Russians, reported to Strauss that Fisk and Bacher had been swept away by the momentum of the discussions and become reluctant to press the Soviets with hard questions. Although both sides agreed that "further investigation" was necessary on detecting high-altitude and deep-underground tests, the Soviets carefully qualified their language so that no further tests were implied, while the Western representatives were equally careful to avoid committing to end testing completely.

541

The Geneva system was based on the assumption that nuclear explosions could be readily monitored through either radioactive debris (fallout) or seismic, acoustic, and electromagnetic waves. Detection of atmospheric testing had become relatively routine through sophisticated air sampling techniques. Acoustically, underwater testing would be difficult to conceal. High-altitude (outer space) and underground testing, however, were not so easily monitored. Prior to 1958 the United States had not conducted high-altitude tests. Because both the Americans and the Russians lacked experimental data for detecting high-altitude testing, discussions in this area were theoretical, and the Geneva system did not include specific techniques for detecting high-altitude tests.[10]

The greatest concern for both sides was detecting clandestine testing underground. On the basis of the data obtained from the *Rainier* shot and theoretical studies, Western scientists were confident that they could identify underground tests from seismic signals, provided a sufficient number of control posts were established. The conference of experts ultimately recommended a network of 160 to 170 land-based control posts and perhaps ten ships. About 110 posts would be located on continents, with the remainder established on oceanic islands. All posts would be equipped to detect fallout and seismic, acoustic, and electromagnetic waves; those located near oceans would monitor hydroacoustic waves. Each post would be manned by about thirty persons. Offshore air sampling by aircraft would continue, and some provision for on-site inspection would be required. With the exception of high-altitude tests, the experts were confident that the proposed control system would detect most tests larger than one kiloton.[11]

The report of the conference of experts left many issues open. The Geneva system did not specify the number of control posts to be located in the Soviet Union or the United States, nor did it settle who would operate the control posts. On the sensitive issue of on-site inspections, the West obtained an important agreement in principle, but the conference of experts defined neither the number nor the frequency of inspections that might be required. From the Western point of view, such details required "political" decisions beyond the mandate of the conference.

542

Killian spoke for many scientists in hailing the work of Fisk and the American delegation as a triumph, but some scholars later criticized the Administration for sending inexperienced scientists to negotiate with one of the Soviet's most seasoned and wily diplomats. Although Fisk and Bacher hardly matched Tsarapkin's diplomatic experience and skill, they succeeded in negotiating the basis for a technically feasible international monitoring system. If they failed to fill in details or define some terms, it was because many "details" involved sensitive political judgments as well as technical definition. The last month of discussions in Geneva was often dominated with just such political pulling and hauling. Fisk wrote Killian that the Russians repeatedly raised political issues concerning inspections and the organization of the control system. "We waste considerable time on such things," he reported, "but I refuse to be drawn in." In the end, the Geneva system would stand or fall on the operation and maintenance of control posts and the implementation of on-site inspections—both quintessentially political issues that the American scientists would leave for later discussions.[12]

## SEEKING AN ALTERNATIVE TO TESTING

During summer 1958 the Commission, with the support of Livermore laboratory, made a last-ditch effort to save the testing program from a moratorium. Through Philip Farley at the State Department, the Commission received working papers drafted at the conference. The Commissioners worried that the conference delegates had been too optimistic about detecting underground or high-altitude tests, where very little experimental evidence existed. Most seriously, the Geneva negotiators seemed to have overlooked the possibility of "energy decoupling" in underground shots in order to conceal the seismic evidence of a nuclear detonation. Seismic detection depended on the coupling of the underground explosion with the surrounding earth, which carried shock waves to monitoring seismographs. Decoupling involved firing a relatively small shot in a very large underground chamber, thus "muffling" the seismic waves sufficiently to escape or confuse detection by the control posts. Without on-site inspections of areas where violations were suspected, it would be difficult to differentiate certain tests from earthquakes. The Commission urged Farley to explore decoupling further before the United States agreed to any test ban.[13]

With the conference of experts obviously moving toward agreement, Libby and Teller personally asked McCone to appeal to the President and Dulles for a "test limitation." The ideal test limitation, according to Libby and Teller, would annually restrict atmospheric testing to one megaton of total fission yield per country. By limiting atmospheric testing, they hoped to halt the annual increase in worldwide fallout. As a contingency, Libby and Teller were also willing to limit testing to underground shots alone if that were the only alternative. They justified continued testing primarily on the need for the United States to develop small, "clean" defensive weapons.[14]

543

On August 7, at the height of the United States' involvement in the 1958 Lebanon crisis, Farley noted the State Department's objections to the Libby-Teller proposal. The proposal was unacceptable because it would retreat from the Administration's goal for outright suspension of tests. Not only would the efforts of the conference of experts become contradictory and illogical, but also under a test limitation the Soviet Union could continue to reap propaganda advantage with its own unilateral suspension while avoiding any commitment on production cutoff or on-site inspections. Furthermore, test limitation, difficult to enforce, would not inhibit the proliferation of nuclear weapons. Perhaps most important, according to the President's Science Advisory Committee, a test ban would freeze nuclear weapon development at a time when the United States retained important advantages in weapon technology.[15]

Although McCone supported the Libby-Teller proposal, he knew that any sort of test ban involved policy decisions beyond the Commission's authority. The Commission did have a role, however, in advising the President on the effects of a test ban on weapon development and production as they related to national defense requirements. McCone would do his best to convince the Administration that a test ban would seriously impair the Commission's ability to meet military requirements, but he was resigned to the fact that national policy on testing would be decided by the White House and the State Department. In fact, McCone confided to Strauss that he thought the President had already made up his mind.[16]

McCone was too pessimistic in assessing the Commission's ultimate role in the test-ban debate, but he realized that the Commission was virtually alone in advocating test limitation rather than suspension. Certainly he did not have the support of the "committee of principals," a group that usually included the Secretaries of State and Defense or their deputies, Killian, Allen Dulles, the director of the Central Intelligence Agency, and himself. When the committee met on August 8, Secretary Dulles announced that he was withdrawing his initial endorsement of the Libby-Teller proposal. Regretfully, Dulles explained that the United States could not make decisions on testing unilaterally without alienating its allies. Deputy Secretary of Defense Donald A. Quarles, who also backed away from the Libby-Teller proposal, now suggested that the United States suspend testing for two years, contingent on agreement by the conference of experts to establish a monitoring system. In Quarles's plan, the United States would test underground only devices smaller than the monitoring system could reliably detect. A permanent test ban would wait until the monitoring system had proven effective and on-site inspection for a production cutoff had been established. A subsequent meeting of the committee of principals failed to produce a consensus among the Departments of State and Defense and the Commission.[17]

544

McCone, Teller, and Bradbury were able to appeal directly to Eisenhower on August 12 when they briefed the President on the success of the *Hardtack* test series. Armed with sketches of the *Hardtack* devices, Teller emphasized the significance of a very small weapon that had been tested. He reported that *Hardtack* had improved weapons "by a factor two to five over the previously existing models." In the next year or two, Teller expected a similar rate of progress. Eisenhower admitted that he favored continued underground testing, but he observed that world opinion against testing could be even more powerful than thermonuclear weapons.[18]

The committee of principals met with Eisenhower on August 18 to discuss changes in the United States' policy on testing. Acting Secretary of State Christian A. Herter proposed separating the testing issue from the London disarmament proposals by suspending nuclear weapon testing for at least a year pending monitoring and inspection negotiations. Gordon Gray, the President's national security adviser, interjected that neither the Department of Defense, including the Joint Chiefs of Staff, nor the Commission had concurred with the State Department's proposals. Both McCone and Quarles were holding out for contained underground tests on the grounds that the political advantages of a test suspension did not outweigh the military disadvantages. Eisenhower recalled that Isidor I. Rabi, chairman of the general advisory committee, had claimed that Americans would benefit from a freeze because the United States was technically ahead of the Soviet Union, an opinion that Killian said the Science Advisory Committee shared. Eisenhower was sympathetic to making exceptions for *Plowshare* tests, but he did not believe the Russians would agree. For the record, McCone voiced the Commission's unanimous opposition to cessation of tests. Acknowledging the Commission's fears, Eisenhower doubted whether cessation would cause any key personnel to leave the national laboratories. In the end, Eisenhower accepted the State Department's proposal with a few changes of his own.[19]

The following day McCone assured Eisenhower that the Commission would accept his decision on testing. McCone expressed his own sympathy for the President's desire significantly to advance disarmament after five and a half years of frustration. Still, McCone hoped that some exception might be made for fully contained underground *Plowshare* explosions such as those that might extract oil from underground formations. McCone was willing even to subject these shots to United Nations agreement and inspection. Wanting to accommodate the Commission if possible, Eisenhower agreed to support the *Plowshare* exception provided it did not sabotage an agreement to suspend weapon tests.[20]

545

## STRAUSS'S APPEAL ON TESTING

Even as he prepared to end nuclear testing, Eisenhower kept his door open for last-minute arguments from both advocates and opponents of testing. Shortly after discussions with McCone on *Plowshare* testing for peaceful uses, Herter prevailed upon Eisenhower to reverse signals again and disallow underground peaceful shots unless the Russians specifically agreed to them.[21] Angry and discouraged, McCone reported to Strauss that his colleagues at the Commission were so disgruntled that they were threatening to resign. Could Strauss put on his "bullet-proof vest," McCone asked, and go to see the President?

Strauss lunched with Libby to learn that, while the Commissioners were deeply embarrassed and demoralized, Libby was certainly not thinking of resigning. Next Strauss went to see General Andrew J. Goodpaster, staff secretary to the President, to find out just where matters stood. While talking to Goodpaster, Strauss was summoned by the President, who had heard that he was in the White House. Eisenhower was obviously upset by the failure of the committee of principals to achieve consensus on the testing question. Yet with Dulles's fixation on the issue, the President explained, the matter had gone too far to reverse. Briefly, Eisenhower seemed sympathetic to the Commission, although he again discounted the impact of the moratorium on the weapon laboratories. The risk, Strauss countered, was that the very best scientists would leave. Strauss also argued that under a test moratorium the development of peaceful nuclear explosives would be impossible.

Eisenhower interrupted the conversation to call Press Secretary

James Hagerty for a copy of the forthcoming presidential announcement. Strauss admitted that the statement was not as damaging as McCone had predicted, but he hazarded the observation that the statement surrendered to the views of Stevenson and Stassen. Abruptly, Eisenhower dropped his conciliatory veil. He told Strauss that the Commission's alternatives led nowhere but to an indefinite arms race; at least Dulles's position might be a step toward general disarmament.

The President and his atomic energy adviser now stood face to face over the fundamental moral question that divided them. Political imperatives, diplomatic pressures, military advantages, laboratory stability, escalating budgets, and peaceful uses were all important in deciding the testing issue. But most important for both Eisenhower and Strauss was the moral question. For Eisenhower, the test moratorium represented a major milestone on the road toward the international control of atomic energy first mapped in his Atoms-for-Peace speech in December 1953. Perhaps for the first time, Strauss saw the depth of Eisenhower's moral commitment to a nuclear test ban. Strauss conceded that the President's course was correct if the West could live in peace with communism. In contrast, Strauss regarded communism as he did sin—there could be no compromise with it. Dolefully, Strauss observed that the arms race between good and evil was centuries old, with no end in sight. As he left Eisenhower, Strauss realized that their ethical discussion had brought him to the brink of a "permanent fundamental disagreement" with the President.[22]

## THE AMERICAN MORATORIUM

On August 22, the day after the conference of experts adjourned in Geneva, Eisenhower announced that on October 31, 1958, the United States would suspend nuclear weapon testing indefinitely, provided the nuclear powers could establish an effective inspection system and make substantial progress on arms control. He also made good on his assurances to McCone and Strauss by calling for an agreement on "detonations for peaceful purposes, as distinct from weapons tests."[23]

Although momentous, the President's announcement that the United States would suspend nuclear testing was both brief and general. He offered no indication that the United States had made a major change in its disarmament policy or had broken the linkage between nuclear weapons and disarmament established in the 1957 London disarmament proposals. At the President's news conference on August 27 most questions went to other issues. Only James Reston inquired about the Geneva conference and disarmament, specifically asking whether the United States had changed its policy. Eisenhower "muddled" through his reply by stating that the "principle" of the policy had not been abandoned at all. Insisting that the United

States had not changed its "general program or plan," he described the moratorium as a "step" along the route of disarmament negotiations.[24]

The President's evasive reply did not reveal his deep personal commitment to the test ban, and this was probably intentional. First, he was no doubt sensitive to the raw nerves the issue had exposed within the Administration and the Joint Committee and among laboratory scientists. McCone did not even brief the Joint Committee on the Administration's intentions until August 21 when it was too late to change the President's action. Having achieved his long-sought goal over the vigorous protests of many in the defense establishment, Eisenhower avoided salting wounds when he was uncertain that a permanent test ban could be negotiated. Second, Eisenhower had changed NATO policy almost unilaterally. None too happily, the British had simultaneously endorsed the report of the conference of experts and pledged to join the test moratorium.[25] The French, who would not be a party to the test-ban negotiations, remained silent after Foreign Minister Maurice Couve de Murville repeated French opposition to a test ban to Eisenhower on August 21. No other NATO ally had contributed significantly to the discussions. Furthermore, Eisenhower was not ready to face squarely the problem of Communist China. That nation could hardly be ignored if the nuclear powers established a worldwide network of control and monitoring stations, but China could not be included in negotiations without at least tacit diplomatic recognition. Finally, the President's vagueness assured him maximum flexibility in future negotiations and kept public expectations from rising too high.

547

## REACTIONS TO THE MORATORIUM

Certainly Eisenhower's caution was warranted by the Soviet Union's initial response to the Western offers to suspend testing. In an interview in *Pravda*, Khrushchev ridiculed the United States and Britain for placing "far-fetched" conditions on their proposals. According to Khrushchev a one-year moratorium would be "completely meaningless." Given Eisenhower's linkage of the test moratorium to verification systems and disarmament, Khrushchev wondered how it was "possible to lend credence to the statements of the United States and United Kingdom Governments concerning their alleged desire to discontinue tests?" Yet, in spite of his scorn, Khrushchev agreed to join negotiations in Geneva on October 31.[26]

When the United Nations General Assembly met again in September 1958, the Soviets proposed the immediate suspension of tests without inspections. The Soviet move was followed by an Indian resolution that in substance matched the Soviet proposal by calling for an indefinite suspension of tests prior to further negotiations at Geneva. Surprised, the Western powers offered a counterresolution urging the suspension of tests under effective international control. Although the Indian resolution with fourteen sponsors had the support of most African and Asian delegations, it was defeated in the General Assembly, as was the Soviet resolution. Following the adoption of the seventeen-nation Western proposal, India and Yugoslavia successfully moved to enlarge the disarmament commission to include all members of the United Nations General Assembly.[27]

Demands at the United Nations for an immediate end to testing prior to Geneva talks were not without some foundation. Eisenhower and Macmillan had no sooner announced their intentions to suspend tests than the two Western powers, later joined by the Soviet Union, rushed to complete as many tests as possible before the October 31 deadline. The United Kingdom launched its Christmas Island series on August 22, the day of the Eisenhower-Macmillan announcements. Although planned since spring, *Hardtack II* was not approved by Eisenhower until August 29. During the next two months at the Nevada Test Site the Commission conducted thirty-seven tests, concentrating on small devices and underground shots. Teller, especially, was anxious to obtain more data on the detection and monitoring of underground tests. As late as October 29, Eisenhower approved the final tests in Nevada providing they were conducted "prior to October 31."[28]

548

The Soviets were not as fastidious about completing their Siberian tests by the October 31 deadline. The last round of Soviet tests began on September 30 and, in contrast to *Hardtack II*, included several atmospheric shots in the megaton range. The tests were the most extensive ever conducted in the Soviet Union. They were so dirty, Libby later reported, that the total off-site fallout from Soviet tests in October 1958 equaled the total produced from United States tests in the preceding four years. Because the Russians had broken their self-imposed suspension, General Alfred D. Starbird, the Commission's director of military application, doubted that they could be trusted to maintain an indefinite, unsupervised moratorium. Starbird feared the Soviet Union would drag out negotiations in order to halt the United States testing program for an extended period of time. Consequently he urged the Commission to maintain readiness to resume tests within ninety days should the Russians break the moratorium.[29]

Even as the diplomats gathered in Geneva to resume disarmament negotiations, the Russians tested on November 1 and 3. Americans worried that, if the Soviet Union continued testing, the Geneva talks would collapse before they ever started. On November 7, Eisenhower issued the Russians a gentle warning. If the Soviet Union continued testing despite the United Nations resolution, the United States would be relieved of any obligation to halt its own testing program. But the President did not threaten to break off negotiations. When the Commission detected no further Soviet tests, the nuclear weapon test moratorium finally became effective. Eisenhower had achieved one of the cherished goals of his presidency.[30]

## HARDTACK *AND THE TEST BAN*

The apparent success of the Geneva conference of experts during summer 1958 led some prominent American scientists to suggest publicly that, by concentrating entirely on technical issues and excluding politics, the scientists in Geneva had broken down barriers that had stymied efforts to reduce the threat of nuclear war for more than a decade. According to Eugene Rabinowitch in the *Bulletin of the Atomic Scientists*, the conference had

> confirmed the belief of scientists that once an international problem has been formulated in scientifically significant terms, scientists from all countries, despite their different political or ideological backgrounds, will be able to find a common language and arrive at an agreed solution.[31]

Within weeks after President Eisenhower announced the one-year 549 moratorium on American testing on October 31, 1958, however, the heady optimism generated by the Geneva meeting began to dissipate. Early in December, Killian informed McCone that preliminary analysis of seismic data from the recent *Hardtack* tests in Nevada suggested that the assumptions used in Geneva to design a worldwide network to detect underground tests no longer seemed valid. The Geneva experts had relied upon data from the United States' first underground test, *Rainier*, in September 1957. On the basis of *Rainier*, the experts had devised a network they believed would detect very small explosions; more recent *Hardtack* data indicated that the network would probably not be as effective and that it would be much more difficult than previously thought to distinguish between a nuclear explosion and a natural earthquake.[32]

*Hardtack* had also undermined the experts' assumptions in another respect. During the summer the experts had concluded that at least for the immediate future the difficulties and expense of conducting nuclear tests at high altitudes made it unnecessary to establish a detection system for such tests. What the experts did not know, however, was that the United States had recently conducted three high-altitude tests during the Pacific phase of *Hardtack*.[33]

The instinctive reaction within the Administration was to attack the new difficulties with scientific studies. Killian with McCone's support immediately assembled a group of seismologists to examine the *Hardtack* data in light of the Geneva system. When the group concluded that the Geneva system indeed would have to be revised, Killian appointed two panels of eminent scientists to study the questions raised. The first panel, assigned to find ways to improve the seismic detection capabilities of the Geneva system, was directed by physicist Lloyd V. Berkner, president of Associated Universities Incorporated, which operated Brookhaven National Laboratory. The second panel, to investigate the feasibility of detecting high-altitude detonations, worked under the leadership of Wolfgang Panofsky, who was already well known to the Administration as the promoter of the Stanford linear accelerator. Thus, Killian and the Administration continued to rely upon what might be called "establishment" scientists to resolve policy issues related not only to international cooperation in nuclear research and development but also to the proposed test ban and disarmament. The group included scientists in the national laboratories, in universities with Commission contracts, and others who were convinced that the Geneva conference had opened an unprecedented opportunity to halt the nuclear arms race.[34]

550

As McCone soon discovered, however, others in the scientific community were sharply critical of the Geneva system and those who had negotiated it. Captain Morse charged that the *Hardtack* findings cast "doubt upon all 'scientific' conclusions of the experts" and confirmed Edward Teller's and his own predictions that these conclusions would prove invalid. Morse urged McCone to inform the Joint Committee at once that the technical basis for the test-ban agreement had been undermined. He also suggested that David M. Griggs, a seismologist at the University of California at Los Angeles, be appointed to the Panofsky panel in order to provide better balance. As Morse explained it, four of the six seismologists on the panel had been involved in the Geneva meetings. "While honest men, they may have an unconscious reluctance to admit that they were wrong." Morse reminded the chairman that Griggs had joined Teller three years earlier in proposing an underground test, a proposal that resulted in the *Rainier* shot.[35]

Morse might have added, as Teller did the following day in a meeting with Strauss, that "the group of Rabi, Bethe and Bacher, who are the prime movers of test suspension, are the same individuals who bitterly opposed the H-bomb program and that their advice, whether sincere or innocent, has been invariably wrong." Teller told Strauss that he was ready to make a public statement denouncing the Geneva system even if it forced his resignation as director of the Livermore laboratory. Strauss suggested instead that Teller take his concerns to McCone or try to write a letter to the President. Morse saw little hope of accomplishing anything through the Commission. As he saw it, McCone "had apparently given up the fight," the other Commissioners were "confused or not informed," and the many staff members who agreed with him were willing to leave foreign policy issues concerning nuclear weapons to the State Department.[36]

McCone did not miss the implications of the dispute. The emotional reaction of Morse, Teller, and others showed that the deep fissures in the scientific community created by the H-bomb controversy and the Oppenheimer case still existed. McCone would do well to defuse the argument before it became a public issue. He was too experienced to be swept off his feet by Teller's emotional appeals; yet he could see the incident as another example of how idealism could warp the judgment even of scientists. Killian, looking back on the episode years later, absolved the Geneva scientists and put the blame for the dispute on the Science Advisory Committee and himself for not "making clear the evolving nature of science and the inevitability of technical surprises" when the *Hardtack* data were presented. "It was quite natural that new seismic data would become available as underground tests proceeded, and it was quite natural that science would respond to the new data with new solutions."[37]

At the time, however, some scientists did not fully appreciate that the test-ban negotiations with the Russians involved political as well as technical issues and that the two could not be separated. Ambassador Wadsworth and others in the American delegation who met with the Russians in Geneva when the Conference on the Discontinuance of Nuclear Weapons Tests reconvened on October 31 soon became aware of that fact. The informal discussions that had proved helpful in reaching agreement with the Russians during the summer no longer seemed possible as Tsarapkin and the Soviet delegation took a legalistic, political approach to all issues. The American delegates had come home from Geneva in August believing that they had won a monumental victory in convincing the Russians to acknowledge the need for on-site inspection of suspected nuclear test sites. Now, by insisting that any member of the control commission could veto a proposed inspection, the Russians revealed that their true position was now what one historian has described as "self-inspection plus the veto."[38]

551

## BREAKING THE DISARMAMENT LINK

Faced with the inflexible stance of the Russians in the Geneva negotiations, the Administration began to consider ways of modifying the United States' position in order to improve chances of reaching an agreement with the Soviet Union. Senator Albert Gore, a member of the Joint Committee, had raised that possibility in a confidential memorandum to the President in November 1958. Fearing that the United States was "negotiating toward an unattainable goal," Gore urged Eisenhower to break the nuclear stalemate by announcing an "unconditional and unilateral cessation of all nuclear tests" in the atmosphere for three years and inviting other nations to join in negotiating a permanent ban on atmospheric tests. The Administration generally agreed that Gore's proposal conceded too much to the Russians, but it thought Prime Minister Macmillan's plan more plausible. Macmillan proposed that the two nations should "drop our condition that an agreement to stop nuclear tests should be subject to satisfactory progress towards real disarmament." Dulles liked Macmillan's suggestion because he believed that such a move might prevent the Geneva talks from collapsing. When McCone supported Dulles, Eisenhower wrote Macmillan that the United States would drop the condition "which the Russians may use as a screen to evade accepting responsibility for failure in the negotiations or to evade facing up to the control problem." In making the decision on January 12, Eisenhower expressed the hope that it would not be publicized, but Ambassador Wadsworth announced the decision eight days later. [39]

It was perhaps surprising to some members of the Administration that McCone acceded in this concession to the Russians. During his first six months as chairman he had closely followed the hard line laid down by Strauss. McCone, however, was motivated not so much by anticommunist dogmatism, as Strauss had been, but rather by a determination to drive hard bargains with the Russians in the interests of the United States. His willingness to concede the disarmament link was but the first step in an effort to reduce nuclear weapon policy into its constituent parts. Before Macmillan's letter arrived, McCone was already exploring within the Commission the wisdom of initially concentrating the Geneva negotiations on an atmospheric test ban while leaving high-altitude and underground testing for later resolution. Unlike Gore and others, McCone was interested not so much in improving the chances for some kind of agreement, however modest, but rather in sustaining the principle long held by the Commission that control was the essential feature in any test-ban agreement and that "only those tests which are detectable and identifiable are to be prohibited by treaty." The Commissioners reasoned that atmospheric tests could be banned at once because a capability of detecting all tests of this type already existed. The Commission wanted to exclude high-altitude and underground tests from negotiation until a reliable detection system had been designed and accepted by the Russians. Another argument for exclusion was that only atmospheric tests contributed to radioactive fallout. [40]

## THE ATMOSPHERIC TEST BAN

McCone continued to pursue his idea of concentrating Geneva negotiations on atmospheric testing. Although he found both Dulles and Under Secretary Herter sympathetic to his aims, there were objections to the proposal. Killian feared that it would leave the impression that the United States was conceding that fallout from atmospheric tests was dangerous and that the Commission was trying to find a loophole that would permit the laboratories to undertake high-altitude and underground tests. In fact, it became clear during these discussions that McCone proposed to begin a series of underground tests to develop more reliable data on detection capabilities. When Killian objected that the Berkner panel had found ways of substantially upgrading the Geneva system, McCone pointed out that the panel's suggestions were all theoretical; only extensive testing would show whether they were practical. Despite McCone's personal appeal to Dulles, the State Department rejected the proposal. Herter wrote McCone that he appreciated the chairman's concerns about an adequate detection system, but the department had concluded that there was an overriding need "to maintain pressure on the Soviet Union" on the key issues of the organization and functioning of the international control commission. "So long as the Soviets maintain their demands for a veto and for staffing of control posts in the Soviet Union with their own nationals, no technical control system, whatever its capabilities, could be effective."[41]

Over the next several weeks, however, new developments revived an interest in McCone's proposal. Philip Farley reported that the proceedings in Geneva were deadlocked over the veto. The situation was so discouraging that the department was giving some thought to seeking a recess in the conference and finding a fall-back position so that the Russians could not blame the United States for ending the talks. McCone's proposal was an obvious candidate for a new American strategy. The matter took on some urgency when Prime Minister Macmillan announced plans to meet Khrushchev in Moscow before coming to Washington. C. Douglas Dillon, Under Secretary of State for economic affairs, told McCone on February 12 that the department would keep the Geneva talks "on dead center" until Macmillan returned from Moscow.[42]

553

## TECHNICAL ASSESSMENTS

By mid-March the Berkner and Panofsky panels had completed their reports, which were promptly circulated as classified documents within the Administration. The State Department released a summary of the Berkner report containing all the essential information. From the *Hardtack* data the panel concluded that the Geneva system for distinguishing nuclear explosions from earthquakes was less effective than had been estimated and that there were about twice as many natural earthquakes equivalent to an underground explosion of a given yield than had earlier been estimated; these discoveries meant that the number of earthquakes indistinguishable from underground nuclear explosions by seismic means alone would substantially increase. With improved equipment and techniques the panel thought that the net of 180 seismic stations proposed in the Geneva system would acquire the capability to detect nuclear explosions at even lower yields without improvements. The Berkner panel stressed the very limited nature of the data on which the study was based and the need to support a vigorous research program in seismology. In a second report the panel described the kinds of research that would be useful.[43]

Perhaps of greatest interest to the Administration was a third report from the Berkner panel on concealing an underground test by decoupling. Albert L. Latter of the Rand Corporation prepared the study that was not released as an unclassified document until late 1959. In a similar study the Panofsky panel provided information on conducting tests in outer space, detectable only by satellites, and concluded that no nation was likely to be capable of using this method in the near future.[44]

## A NEW STRATEGY FOR GENEVA

When Macmillan arrived in Washington in late March 1959, he reported that Khrushchev considered the American and British proposal for an inspection system nothing more than "a military espionage plan." Tsarapkin had already complained at Geneva that Western proposals to upgrade the Geneva system in order to overcome the deficiencies revealed by *Hardtack* would make hundreds of seismic events subject to inspection in the Soviet Union each year. In response, Macmillan had suggested a limited number of on-site inspections, but he still wondered whether the *Hardtack* data had not rendered the Geneva system impracticable. Killian, as he had on other occasions, contended that the situation was not as bad as Macmillan believed and that the Berkner panel had come up with effective technical improvements. McCone was pleased that Eisenhower raised the question of limiting negotiations to an atmospheric test ban, which could be effectively policed, while underground testing continued in order to develop an effective detection system in that medium. There was general agreement that such a move would meet two of the original aims of the Geneva conference: to stop fallout and to limit weapon development; but it would not meet the third, to discourage weapon research by other countries. McCone noted that the President was emphatic that the West not enter into any kind of test ban that could not be reliably policed. After the meeting on March 22, he wrote: "I feel that the AEC's position is *now* pretty well recognized as the proper one by everyone concerned."[45]

With the Geneva talks resuming on April 13, 1959, the Administration needed to establish its strategy quickly and preferably in consonance with the British. The atmospheric test ban was a prime subject for discussion by the principals on March 26. Herter preferred to use it only as a fallback position and then only after another recess. Killian thought that the Berkner and Latter reports had introduced new complications and made an atmospheric test ban alone look more like the right approach. In the end, Herter, Killian, and McCone all agreed that the best course would be to propose continuing negotiations toward ending all tests along with an offer to stop atmospheric tests as the first part of the package.[46]

Herter's prudent approach did not entirely satisfy the President, who was determined to give "a note of hope" to the talks. "We cannot achieve this," Eisenhower cabled Macmillan, "merely by resuming interminable wranglings over the veto and the composition of inspection teams." The West should make clear, the President said, that important differences in approach should not be a bar to putting into effect those indisputable elements of a control system. He included a draft of a letter to Khrushchev proposing an atmospheric test ban as the first step. A few days later the President sent the same letter to Khrushchev.[47]

Ten days later Khrushchev rejected Eisenhower's proposal. A ban on atmospheric tests alone would mislead the public because tests would still continue at high altitudes and underground. Without mentioning the veto, Khrushchev pointed to the number of inspections as the chief stumbling block to agreement. He referred to his earlier discussions with Macmillan of the feasibility of setting a limit on the number of inspections in any one year. Thus, Khrushchev established the quota as the principal issue in the next round of Geneva negotiations.[48]

555

## THE QUOTA

Khrushchev's reply to Eisenhower opened the possibility that the Soviet Union might yield on the veto if some agreement could be reached on a quota of inspections to be permitted by each party in the course of a year. The possibility of a Soviet concession was heartening, but it also had its dangers, as McCone pointed out when he met on May 5, 1959, with the President and the principals. McCone reminded the group that a quota would compromise the long-held American position that any test ban had to be verifiable by an effective detection system. In light of the *Hardtack* data and the Latter report, only a ban on atmospheric tests as a first step would be consistent with that policy. The tenor of the group, however, was that some change was inevitable. The President volunteered that growing public concern over the arms race and fear of continuing fallout, especially from Soviet weapon tests, would eventually force the Administration to abandon atmospheric testing unilaterally. His reference to fallout was no doubt sparked by the announcement that the Joint Committee on Atomic Energy was beginning that same day a series of open hearings on the subject. As the principals' discussion continued, even McCone admitted that public opinion would probably force the United States to give up atmospheric testing. Thus the objective, as the President put it, was to reach an agreement with the Soviet Union that was more favorable to the United States than a de facto unilateral ban without any Soviet commitment to an inspection system. The crux of the matter then became the number of inspections allowed annually under the quota.[49]

The Joint Committee hearings amply justified the principals' conclusion that fallout had become a controlling factor in test-ban policy. The four days of testimony, but even more the thousands of pages of technical documents included in the printed record, showed clearly that the hazards of fallout had international dimensions. Scientists testifying at the hearings still considered strontium-90 and cesium-137 the greatest hazards of world-wide fallout (as distinguished from fallout near test sites). But several short-lived isotopes—such as strontium-89, iodine-131, barium-140, and zirconium-95—were also cited as potentially hazardous. The rate of deposition of strontium-90 had increased in spring 1959 in the northern hemisphere. Likewise, the content of strontium-90 and cesium-137 in food had risen since 1957, even more rapidly than the total fallout, suggesting that under certain conditions strontium-90 was being taken up directly by humans from food without going through the soil cycle. On the subject of biological effects of radiation, evidence was presented suggesting that the rate of dose might have some influence on the magnitude of genetic defects, but the biological significance of low levels of radiation was still unknown. No agreement was reached on whether or not there was a threshold of exposure below which there were no somatic effects such as cancer and leukemia.[50]

556

The thorny question of the quota number was not easily resolved. On June 17 the principals gave some consideration to specifying a percentage of suspicious events as the criterion, but opinion quickly reverted to the idea of a quota, particularly if each side had the right to choose which events it wished to inspect. As Allen Dulles pointed out, the use of intelligence data would help to assure that the most important incidents were inspected. Killian found the idea of "a quota with choice" promising and felt confident that one hundred inspections annually under that system would give a high probability of catching any violation, fifty inspections would provide a questionable capability, and twenty-five would be unacceptable. McCone was inclined to agree, but the question of arriving at a precise number remained. For that determination the principals turned to an ad hoc committee of scientists under Robert Bacher.[51]

Events during the following three weeks did not clarify the quota issue. On a trip to Geneva McCone found that the Soviet delegation had succeeded in diverting the negotiations into petty details of the inspection system. In informal meetings the Russians insisted that they would not discuss quota numbers until agreement had been reached on the quota system. When pressed, Tsarapkin had indicated that the Soviets would accept a quota of no more than fifteen with no reference to technical capability of the inspection system. Under such an agreement, McCone guessed that public opinion would force the United States to accept an inadequate number, something like twenty-five or less. Tsarapkin, according to McCone, had no intention of giving up the veto in any respect, derided the conclusions of the Berkner panel, and was obviously pressing for a complete test ban. When the Bacher panel reported on July 9, the feasibility of the quota became even more uncertain. Now even Killian concluded that the only safe policy for the United States was to accept an atmospheric test ban alone while further research was pursued. The Administration seemed to be reverting to the conservative position McCone first voiced in early 1959.[52]

## PRESSURES TO RESUME TESTING

As summer 1959 dragged on with no perceptible progress in the Geneva talks, pressures began to build within the Administration for resumed testing. During the moratorium the Commission's laboratories had accumulated various requirements for tests. They also needed to develop warheads for new types of missiles, to proof-test new weapons entering the stockpile, and to gather more information on weapon effects.[53]

Efforts by the Commission and the Department of Defense to obtain the President's approval for the resumption of testing, if only underground, received a setback when George B. Kistiakowsky replaced Killian as the President's science adviser in July 1959. The new science adviser was determined to take some fresh issues to the Geneva talks and to halt McCone's efforts, as he saw them, to undermine the test ban. He did succeed in the latter instance, when he arranged the appointment of a special panel under James W. McRae, a vice-president of Western Electric, to examine the need for weapon tests. The McRae panel promptly concluded that tests were not necessary in the immediate future, except for one minor category.[54]

557

In the meantime, both the Department of Defense and the Commission had to live with the fact that the voluntary moratorium was denying them the full potential of the nuclear stockpile. Just as worrisome to both agencies was the possibility that by the end of the year the President might once again extend the voluntary moratorium. In an insistent plea to McCone that bordered on insubordination, Starbird urged the Commission to make definite plans to resume testing soon after the first of the year and to convince the President to announce this decision promptly. With little effect McCone complained to the President that continually extending the moratorium would give the Soviet Union exactly what it wanted: an unpoliced ban of all nuclear tests.[55]

Eisenhower, however, was not yet willing to make any public statement that would damage the chances of negotiating a test ban. When the Geneva talks resumed on October 28 after the August recess, Ambassador Wadsworth urged the Soviet delegates to participate in technical discussions of *Hardtack* data and the Latter report. American hopes rose when the Russians finally agreed to discuss the data after ten months of delay. A panel of outstanding scientists under the leadership of James Fisk went to Geneva late in November. But it soon became apparent that the Soviet

Union did not intend to discuss the issues. Instead the Soviet scientists, obviously under strict political instructions, raised spurious technical objections about the American data and, when the conference broke up in December, impugned the integrity and competence of the American delegation. Outraged by the Soviets' behavior, Eisenhower directed the State Department to publish Fisk's refutation of the Soviet charges and instructed Wadsworth to admonish the Soviet delegation when the test-ban conference reconvened in January.[56]

## TEST-BAN STRATEGY FOR 1960

During Christmas week, 1959, McCone joined the principals for a trip to Augusta, Georgia, to discuss test-ban policy with the President. The primary purpose was to consider a response to the Soviet attack on the Fisk working group, but both McCone and Gates hoped to persuade Eisenhower not to extend the moratorium, which was due to expire in two days. Eisenhower, as usual, was reluctant to issue a formal policy statement. He preferred to wait until some inquiry made a statement necessary and then to have it come from the State Department. After much discussion, however, he approved a rather oblique statement, which the State Department released later that day. In it the President deplored the actions of the Soviet delegation at the Geneva technical conference, but he assured the world that "we will resume negotiations in a continuing spirit of seeking to reach a safeguarded agreement. In the meantime, the voluntary moratorium on testing will expire on December 31." The United States was now free to resume testing but would not do so without announcing its intention in advance.[57]

The principals' major concern in January 1960 was the proposal by Kistiakowsky and members of the President's Science Advisory Committee to come up with a fresh approach for the Geneva talks. The heart of the proposal was a new version of the old threshold idea. One idea considered in summer 1959 was to allay the Russians' concerns over a large number of inspections of seismic events by establishing a threshold in terms of kiloton yield, below which no inspections would be required. The new idea was to define the threshold in terms of seismic signal rather than yield. This change, which Kistiakowsky enthusiastically endorsed, offered the possibility of effective monitoring with about ten on-site inspections per year. The principals thought that a threshold of 4.75 on the Richter scale was reasonable, but the group recognized the possible need to adjust that figure in light of American interests. Too high a threshold might remove the justification for any seismic stations in the Soviet Union; too low a threshold might impair weapon development in the United States. McCone was in-

558

clined to accept the 4.75 threshold, but he wanted to explore its potential impact on American testing. After considering the views of several departments, the principals decided that the value of 4.75 was a reasonable compromise.[58]

The new American position, which Ambassador Wadsworth presented at the Geneva conference on February 11, 1960, proposed a ban on "all tests above ground up to the greatest heights to which effective controls can now be agreed, all tests in the oceans, and all underground tests" above the 4.75 threshold. The United States also proposed a joint research program involving Soviet, British, and American scientists to improve underground detection techniques so that the threshold could be lowered in time.[59]

The Soviet response, which Tsarapkin presented in Geneva on March 19, raised a number of problems, probably intentionally, for the Americans. The Soviet Union agreed to all the terms in the American proposal, including the 4.75 threshold, but added one of its own: all three powers would agree to forego all tests in all three media, including underground tests below the threshold, during a period of joint research. First, an executive agreement on a moratorium going beyond the end of Eisenhower's term as president on January 20, 1961, presented a legal difficulty; its remedy appeared to be a formal treaty binding Eisenhower's successor, but all the principals agreed that such a treaty could not be ratified. Second, and more serious, the length of the moratorium was a problem. The Americans believed that the joint research program on the seismic detection system would take about five years, and the Soviet delegates now privately acknowledged that fact. Could the United States forego testing for that long a time? Could the nation resume testing if the joint research program led to no agreement with the Soviets on the detection system? Herter, now Secretary of State, recognized the importance of all these concerns; but he also reminded the principals that, in the face of growing opposition to testing throughout the world, the United States had to come up with a positive response. The British considered the Soviet proposal a significant breakthrough, and their views could not be dismissed lightly.[60]

The Soviet proposal raised especially difficult problems for McCone and the Commission. McCone immediately objected, as all the principals must have expected, that the Soviet plan amounted to nothing more than a comprehensive test ban without safeguards; the United States' position had always been that it would not accept any test ban that could not be effectively policed. McCone also argued that, contrary to the Soviet contention, it would be impossible to construct an adequate detection system without some underground testing. Going one step further, he insisted that the United States should not give up the option to conduct underground tests in the interim. Two weeks earlier he had received a warning from Starbird

559

that morale in the weapon laboratories was sagging while the question of resuming testing hung in the air. On March 14, McCone had told Eisenhower that the laboratories could do all the testing they needed underground. He had mentioned to the President that important development work could be accomplished by using the experiments employed in safety tests. Eisenhower had asked for a written proposal, which he said he would probably approve, with the condition that "this experimentation does not constitute nuclear testing in the sense of the Geneva discussions, and that we do not regard it as nuclear testing."[61]

In a meeting with the principals on March 24, however, the President was still determined to "probe in every way the sincerity and intent of the Soviet declaration on disarmament." He thought some positive response was preferable to standing pat on the United States' position of February 11; for that purpose he intended to adopt the State Department's recommendation: The United States would agree at the time the treaty was signed to simultaneous declarations by the three powers that they would refrain from all nuclear tests not prohibited by the treaty for an agreed period while the joint research program was in progress, while the control system was being installed, and while there were no indications that the declarations were being violated. The length of the moratorium would not be specified in the statement, but the President said that he was thinking of one year or, if the Russians insisted, possibly two. McCone vigorously objected on the usual grounds. He proposed that the United States negotiate only on the basis of the threshold proposal already made. If the Soviet Union rejected this offer, McCone thought that the President should declare unilaterally that the United States would not test in the atmosphere or where significant fallout could occur but would reserve the right to test underground while proceeding to improve the seismic detection system. Eisenhower replied that he sympathized with McCone's argument, but he did not see how the proposed moratorium could harm the United States. When McCone continued to press the issue, the President informed him in a sharp tone that the State Department's position would be adopted.[62]

The following week McCone poured out his frustration in a conversation with Lewis Strauss. He said he was getting the kind of treatment that Strauss had received in 1958 and he was "pretty damned sore about it." McCone was particularly annoyed because he believed that the State Department was misrepresenting the Soviet proposal to the Joint Committee and was attempting to build support for the counterproposal through leaks to newspaper columnists. He was disgusted with the scientists, particularly Bethe, who did not seem able to separate political opinion from scientific fact. Eisenhower, McCone admitted, might want to give priority to political factors until the next presidential election, and in that case his usefulness to the Administration might be ended. Strauss urged McCone not to think of resigning because he was a valuable "balance wheel" in the debate.[63]

## FADING HOPES FOR A TEST BAN

McCone's worst fears failed to materialize, not because the President changed his policy, but because continued disagreement at the Geneva conference pushed hopes for a treaty, even of the limited scope proposed in March 1960, far into the future. Both sides stopped short of any action that would result in a final collapse of negotiations. The Soviet Union rejected the new position of the United States but continued to discuss the proposed joint research program, while a technical panel under Panofsky developed detailed plans. Then the U-2 spy plane incident and abrupt cancellation of the Paris summit conference in May momentarily threatened the future of the negotiations. Once both sides declared their intention to continue, the negotiations resumed at the usual tortuous pace as the Americans tried to iron out countless difficulties in formulating a joint seismic research program that would be politically and technically acceptable to both sides. The most serious obstacle was specifying the nuclear device that would be used in an underground experiment. The United States first proposed a "black box," a nuclear device so packaged that no weapon test data could be derived from it. When the Soviet Union rejected this idea, the Americans then considered using obsolete nuclear weapons such as the Hiroshima gun-type weapon, but this suggestion led to endless complications; most important, Congress for political reasons could not in an election year vote to give the Russians and British access to weapon information unless the other nations were willing to reciprocate, and the Soviet Union was not willing to do that.[64]

561

As the presidential election approached and Eisenhower's term drew toward its close, the ardent pursuit of a nuclear test ban gradually faded. Agreement with the Soviet Union still seemed as far away as it had in August 1958, when Eisenhower announced the moratorium and his determination to find a solution to the arms race. Now, in autumn 1960, it was clear that any agreement was at least years away, the responsibility of another president. And, wise to the workings of government, Eisenhower intended to leave that terrible problem to his successor.

## CHAPTER 21

# THE GREAT DEBATE

On the evening of January 17, 1961, three days before his second term ended, Dwight D. Eisenhower sat before a bevy of microphones and television cameras in the Oval Office for the last time as President to address the American people. It was eight years and one day since the President had met with the Atomic Energy Commissioners in that same room to hear a briefing on plans for enlarging the nuclear arsenal and then to learn about the loss of the Wheeler document. Since that day Eisenhower had been deeply immersed in the frightening issues posed by the bomb, and these issues were still very much on his mind in the closing days of his presidency.

As if to stress the serious import of his message, Eisenhower spoke slowly and deliberately as he struggled to make the words come out right. He spoke of "America's adventure in free government," of his efforts to keep the peace and "to enhance liberty, dignity and integrity among people and among nations. To strive for less would be unworthy of a free and religious people." But progress toward that goal had been threatened "by the conflict now engulfing the world." "We face," the President said, "a hostile ideology—global in scope, atheistic in character, ruthless in purpose, and insidious in method."[1]

To many in his electronic audience Eisenhower's words sounded like the clichés that he had repeated with little apparent effect in the recent presidential campaign, but the chief executive was clearly attempting in his farewell address to place squarely before the American people the momentous issues that would face the nation in the years ahead. Keeping the peace would continue to require a strong military establishment and an armaments industry unprecedented in America's peacetime history. Vital as these new developments were, they held grave implications for the future. The President warned,

In the councils of government, we must guard against the acquisition of unwarranted influence, whether sought or unsought, by the military-industrial complex. . . . Only an alert knowledgeable citizenry can compel the proper meshing of the huge industrial and military machinery of defense with our peaceful methods and goals, so that security and liberty may prosper together.

Of equal import for the future was what the President called the "technological revolution." Task forces of scientists, he noted, had replaced the solitary inventor in the nation's industrial and university laboratories.

Partly because of the huge costs involved, a government contract becomes virtually a substitute for intellectual curiosity. . . . In holding scientific research and discovery in respect, as we should, we must also be alert to the equal and opposite danger that public policy could itself become the captive of a scientific-technological elite.

563

Eisenhower could not end his address without one last reference to the continuing imperative of disarmament.

Because this need is so sharp and apparent I confess that I lay down my official responsibilities in this field with a definite sense of disappointment. . . . As one who knows that another war could utterly destroy this civilization which has been so slowly and painfully built over thousands of years—I wish I could say tonight that a lasting peace is in sight.

All he could offer was that war had been avoided.

Between the fall elections and January's inauguration, the nation's oldest President and its youngest President-elect met twice: on December 6 and January 19. Some discussion focused on administrative details and emergency procedures in case of a nuclear attack, but Eisenhower did not neglect the great issues of consequence that had plagued him for eight years. He spoke at length about the dangers of nuclear war and his hopes that the moratorium on testing would lead eventually to disarmament, both nuclear and conventional. Eisenhower also warned Kennedy of the potentially dangerous effect that partisan politics could have on national policy. Perhaps recalling events of eight years earlier, the President harshly criticized the Joint Committee on Atomic Energy and what he saw as its pernicious influence in both domestic and international affairs. He hoped that Kennedy, with the support of a Democratic Congress, could propose legislation abolishing the committee.[2]

Hovering over all the President's hopes and fears, however, was the dark shadow of the hydrogen bomb. He had first learned of its terrifying power at the secret briefing at the Augusta golf club a month before his first inauguration. The awesome results of the *Bravo* shot in 1954 had revealed the deadly terror posed by its potential radiation effects. Years of frustrating debate within his own Administration, dozens of proposals and counterproposals to the leaders of the Soviet Union, and his own personal appeals to the United Nations had merely postponed the cataclysm but had not dispersed the threatening cloud.

By 1960 Eisenhower's public statements had lost much of their earlier drive and focus. Like his farewell address, his speeches seemed to dissolve into a loose collection of platitudes. Inept as they often sounded, however, Eisenhower's words reflected the central role he had played in defining the place of the peaceful and military atom in American life. Unlike many politicians, he tended to look beyond the petty opportunities for advantage to the larger issues of war and peace. In fact, his proclivity for addressing such massive and intractable problems suggested a naiveté that hardened veterans of the political arena had learned to avoid. But Eisenhower seemed to sense that it was important to discuss these overriding issues of life and death, however unmanageable they appeared to be in their full dimensions, and to confront them in the simple and sometimes simplistic terms that the public could understand.

Likewise, the President's penchant for casting nuclear issues in moral terms again suggested naiveté at best or cynical manipulation of the public at worst. The truth, however, was that the development and control of nuclear technology did involve moral issues of great consequence, and Eisenhower was consciously trying to keep that truth before the eyes of the public.

In 1953 the military aspects of nuclear technology were not subjects for discussion even within the President's Cabinet, much less in the general public. Forcibly struck by top secret reports on the hydrogen bomb, Eisenhower had endorsed Operation *Candor* to give the American people a better understanding of the dangers of nuclear warfare. In the face of strong opposition from members of his Administration, the President continued to pursue that goal for almost a year, until he brought the issue squarely before the people of the United States and the world in his Atoms-for-Peace speech at the United Nations.

The United Nations speech in December 1953 gave new impetus to the effort already in motion to amend the Atomic Energy Act of 1946 in order to give private industry a role in developing nuclear technology and to encourage international cooperation in promoting Atoms for Peace. The debate over the new legislation, given added publicity by the Dixon-Yates fiasco, which itself resulted from a presidential decision, brought both the Atomic Energy Commission and nuclear issues into the political arena. During these same months in spring 1954 the transcript of the Oppenheimer security hearings, the result of another Eisenhower decision, became a public document and revealed more about the inner workings of the atomic energy establishment than *Candor* ever could have.

The Administration's attempts during the next two years to move the development of nuclear power technology from the government to the private sector, to establish the International Atomic Energy Agency, to support EURATOM, and to produce more efficient nuclear weapons through an accelerated program of atmospheric testing not only created political issues that brought nuclear weapons for the first time into a presidential campaign in 1956 but also generated anxieties that seemed to strike at the heart of human existence itself. Only a relatively few Americans could appreciate the economic and political arguments raised by the public-versus-private power fight that the debate over nuclear power revived, but parents everywhere in the nation, if exposed to the facts, could ultimately see the potential threat of radioactive fallout to the health of their children.

Thus, by 1957, the place of nuclear energy in American life, an issue that for almost a decade had been confined to the secret councils of the federal government, had become the subject of a significant public debate. Moreover, the enormity of the potential destructive capability of thermonuclear weapons had given that debate moral dimensions that few Americans could ignore. Did the threat posed by "a hostile ideology—global in scope, atheistic in character, ruthless in purpose, and insidious in method," in the President's words, justify the immediate hazards of atmospheric testing and the ultimate risk of global nuclear war?

565

Probably no American leader at the time wrestled harder with that dilemma than did Eisenhower. It fired his determination to find a way out of the nuclear nightmare by turning the genius of the world's scientists to the arts of peace. Nuclear disarmament became a cardinal objective of his Administration, and the failure to achieve it drove the President in 1958 to impose an unpoliced, unilateral moratorium on United States testing of nuclear weapons.

Underlying the rising public debate during the Eisenhower years was another moral concern deeply buried in the psyches of many who had brought the world into the nuclear age at Hiroshima in 1945 and at Enewetak in 1954: to expatiate that sense of personal guilt by finding in nuclear technology some redeeming values for the human race. Eisenhower, who himself did not share that sense of guilt, gave renewed hope to those who did when he launched the Atoms-for-Peace program. The search for redeeming values, as much as the desire to demonstrate the superiority of the American system over Soviet communism, explained the fervor with which the Atomic Energy Commission and its scientists and engineers pursued the shining dreams of Atoms for Peace.

Thus, by the time the President gave his farewell address on January 17, 1961, he had both consciously and inadvertently built up the foundations for the Great Nuclear Debate that would persist in the public arena for the next two decades and beyond. As the years passed, it would become a classic public debate in American history, of comparable historical importance to the debates over the ratification of the Constitution, the separation of church and state, the abolition of slavery, the free coinage of silver, the prohibition of alcohol, and the guarantee of civil rights. And while the Great Nuclear Debate continued, an anxious world awaited its outcome.

*Appendixes*

# Appendix 1
## *Personnel*

### United States Atomic Energy Commission

Name

| | | | |
|---|---|---|---|
| Gordon Dean, chairman | July 11, 1950 | – | June 30, 1953 |
| Henry DeWolf Smyth | May 30, 1949 | – | Sept. 30, 1954 |
| Thomas E. Murray | May 9, 1950 | – | June 30, 1957 |
| Thomas Keith Glennan | Oct. 2, 1950 | – | Nov. 1, 1952 |
| Eugene M. Zuckert | Feb. 25, 1952 | – | June 30, 1954 |
| Lewis L. Strauss, chairman | July 2, 1953 | – | June 30, 1958 |
| Joseph Campbell | July 27, 1953 | – | Nov. 30, 1954 |
| Willard F. Libby | Oct. 5, 1954 | – | June 30, 1959 |
| John Von Neumann | Mar. 15, 1955 | – | Feb. 8, 1957* |
| Harold S. Vance | Oct. 31, 1955 | – | Aug. 31, 1959* |
| John S. Graham | Sept. 12, 1957 | – | June 30, 1962 |
| John F. Floberg | Oct. 1, 1957 | – | June 23, 1960 |
| John A. McCone, chairman | July 14, 1958 | – | Jan. 20, 1961 |
| John H. Williams | Aug. 13, 1959 | – | June 30, 1960 |
| Robert E. Wilson | Mar. 22, 1960 | – | Jan. 31, 1964 |
| Loren K. Olson | June 23, 1960 | – | June 30, 1962 |

*Date deceased in office

569

## Joint Committee on Atomic Energy
### 83rd Congress, 1953–1954

W. Sterling Cole, chairman
Bourke B. Hickenlooper, vice-chairman

| | | |
|---|---|---|
| Senator | Bourke B. Hickenlooper (R) | Iowa |
| Senator | Eugene D. Millikin (R) | Colorado |
| Senator | William F. Knowland (R) | California |
| Senator | John W. Bricker (R) | Ohio |
| Senator | Guy R. Cordon (R) | Oregon |
| Senator | Richard B. Russell (D) | Georgia |
| Senator | Edwin C. Johnson (D) | Colorado |
| Senator | Clinton P. Anderson (D) | New Mexico |
| Senator | John O. Pastore (D) | Rhode Island |
| Representative | W. Sterling Cole (R) | New York |
| Representative | Carl Hinshaw (R) | California |
| Representative | James E. Van Zandt (R) | Pennsylvania |
| Representative | James T. Patterson (R) | Connecticut |
| Representative | Thomas A. Jenkins (R) | Ohio |
| Representative | Carl T. Durham (D) | North Carolina |
| Representative | Chet Holifield (D) | California |
| Representative | Melvin Price (D) | Illinois |
| Representative | Paul J. Kilday (D) | Texas |
| Executive Directors | William L. Bordon | |
| | Corbin C. Allardice | |

570

### 84th Congress, 1955–1956

Clinton P. Anderson, chairman
Carl T. Durham, vice-chairman

| | | |
|---|---|---|
| Senator | Clinton P. Anderson (D) | New Mexico |
| Senator | Richard B. Russell (D) | Georgia |
| Senator | John O. Pastore (D) | Rhode Island |
| Senator | Albert Gore (D) | Tennessee |
| Senator | Henry M. Jackson (D) | Washington |
| Senator | Bourke B. Hickenlooper (R) | Iowa |
| Senator | Eugene D. Millikin (R) | Colorado |
| Senator | William F. Knowland (R) | California |
| Senator | John W. Bricker (R) | Ohio |
| Representative | Carl T. Durham (D) | North Carolina |
| Representative | Chet Holifield (D) | California |
| Representative | Melvin Price (D) | Illinois |
| Representative | Paul J. Kilday (D) | Texas |
| Representative | John J. Dempsey (D) | New Mexico |
| Representative | W. Sterling Cole (R) | New York |

| Representative | Carl Hinshaw (R) | California |
| Representative | James E. Van Zandt (R) | Pennsylvania |
| Representative | James T. Patterson (R) | Connecticut |
| Executive Director | Corbin C. Allardice | |
| | James T. Ramey | |

## 85th Congress, 1957–1958

Carl T. Durham, chairman
Clinton P. Anderson, vice-chairman

| Senator | Clinton P. Anderson (D) | New Mexico |
| Senator | Richard B. Russell (D) | Georgia |
| Senator | John O. Pastore (D) | Rhode Island |
| Senator | Albert Gore (D) | Tennessee |
| Senator | Henry M. Jackson (D) | Washington |
| Senator | Bourke B. Hickenlooper (R) | Iowa |
| Senator | William F. Knowland (R) | California |
| Senator | John W. Bricker (R) | Ohio |
| Senator | Henry C. Dworshak (R) | Idaho |
| Representative | Carl T. Durham (D) | North Carolina |
| Representative | Chet Holifield (D) | California |
| Representative | Melvin Price (D) | Illinois |
| Representative | Paul J. Kilday (D) | Texas |
| Representative | John J. Dempsey[a] (D) | New Mexico |
| Representative | W. Sterling Cole[b] (R) | New York |
| Representative | James E. Van Zandt (R) | Pennsylvania |
| Representative | James T. Patterson (D) | Connecticut |
| Representative | Thomas A. Jenkins (R) | Ohio |
| Executive Director | James T. Ramey | |

571

[a]Wayne Aspinall was appointed March 17, 1958, to fill vacancy created by death of John J. Dempsey on March 11, 1958.

[b]Craig Hosmer was appointed January 15, 1958, to fill the vacancy created by resignation of Sterling Cole on December 1, 1957, to become director general of the IAEA.

## 86th Congress, 1959–1960

Clinton P. Anderson, chairman
Carl T. Durham, vice-chairman

| Senator | Clinton P. Anderson (D) | New Mexico |
| Senator | Richard B. Russell (D) | Georgia |
| Senator | John O. Pastore (D) | Rhode Island |

| | | |
|---|---|---|
| Senator | Albert Gore (D) | Tennessee |
| Senator | Henry M. Jackson (D) | Washington |
| Senator | Bourke B. Hickenlooper (R) | Iowa |
| Senator | Henry C. Dworshak (R) | Idaho |
| Senator | George D. Aiken (R) | Vermont |
| Senator | Wallace F. Bennett (R) | Utah |
| Representative | Carl T. Durham (D) | North Carolina |
| Representative | Chet Holifield (D) | California |
| Representative | Melvin Price (D) | Illinois |
| Representative | Wayne N. Aspinall (D) | Colorado |
| Representative | Albert Thomas (D) | Texas |
| Representative | James E. Van Zandt (R) | Pennsylvania |
| Representative | Craig Hosmer (R) | California |
| Representative | William H. Bates (R) | Massachusetts |
| Representative | Jack Westland (R) | Washington |
| Executive Director | James T. Ramey | |

572

## General Advisory Committee

| | |
|---|---|
| Isidor I. Rabi<br>chairman, 1952–1956 | Dec. 12, 1946 – Aug. 1, 1956 |
| Oliver E. Buckley | Aug. 2, 1948 – Aug. 1, 1954 |
| Willard F. Libby | Aug. 7, 1950 – Sept. 30, 1954<br>May 26, 1960 – Aug. 1, 1962 |
| Eger V. Murphree | Aug. 7, 1950 – Aug. 1, 1956<br>Apr. 4, 1957 – Aug. 1, 1964 |
| Walter G. Whitman | Aug. 7, 1950 – Aug. 1, 1956 |
| John von Neumann | Feb. 27, 1952 – Aug. 1, 1954 |
| James B. Fisk | Sept. 22, 1952 – Aug. 1, 1958 |
| John C. Warner | Sept. 22, 1952 – Aug. 1, 1964 |
| Eugene P. Wigner | Sept. 22, 1952 – Nov. 19, 1956<br>Dec. 3, 1959 – Aug. 1, 1962 |
| Edwin M. McMillen | Oct. 23, 1954 – Oct. 7, 1958 |
| Jesse W. Beams | Oct. 23, 1954 – Aug. 1, 1960 |
| Warren C. Johnson<br>chairman, 1956–1959 | Oct. 23, 1954 – Aug. 1, 1960 |
| T. Keith Glennan | Oct. 26, 1956 – Sept. 12, 1958 |
| Edward Teller | Oct. 26, 1956 – July 9, 1958 |
| Robert E. Wilson | Oct. 26, 1956 – Mar. 22, 1960 |
| Kenneth S. Pitzer<br>chairman, 1960–1961 | Oct. 27, 1958 – Aug. 1, 1964 |
| James W. McRae | Oct. 29, 1958 – Feb. 2, 1960 |
| Manson Benedict | Oct. 29, 1958 – Aug. 1, 1962 |

573

## Military Liaison Committee
### Chairmen

| | |
|---|---|
| Robert LeBaron | Oct. 1, 1949 – Aug. 1, 1954 |
| Herbert B. Loper | Aug. 2, 1954 – July 14, 1961 |

### Army Members

| | |
|---|---|
| Brig. Gen. Harry McK. Roper | Aug. 21, 1952 – Aug. 26, 1955 |
| Colonel Kenner F. Hertford | Nov. 1, 1952 – Oct. 5, 1954 |
| Brig. Gen. John P. Daley | Oct. 5, 1954 – Oct. 1, 1958 |
| Brig. Gen. Thomas M. Watlington | Aug. 26, 1955 – Dec. 29, 1955 |
| Major Gen. John S. Upham | Dec. 29, 1955 – July 13, 1956 |
| Major Gen. John E. Theimer | July 13, 1956 – Sept. 15, 1956 |
| Brig. Gen. Dwight E. Beach | Sept. 15, 1956 – July 1, 1959 |
| Major Gen. William W. Dick | Oct. 1, 1958 – July 11, 1960 |
| Brig. Gen. John T. Snodgrass | July 1, 1959 – July 18, 1961 |
| Colonel Walter T. Kerwin, Jr. | July 11, 1960 – Sept. 1, 1960 |
| Brig. Gen. David C. Lewis | Sept. 1, 1960 – July 9, 1962 |

### Navy Members

| | |
|---|---|
| Captain James S. Russell | Apr. 18, 1952 – Apr. 5, 1954 |
| Rear Adm. George C. Wright | Nov. 18, 1952 – Sept. 26, 1955 |

| | |
|---|---|
| Captain Paul H. Ramsey | Apr.  5, 1954 – Dec. 13, 1955 |
| Rear Adm. Courtney Shands | Sept. 26, 1955 – Dec. 27, 1956 |
| Rear Adm. David L. McDonald | Dec. 13, 1955 – Oct. 24, 1957 |
| Captain James H. Flatley, Jr. | Oct. 24, 1957 – Mar. 25, 1958 |
| Rear Adm. G. Serpell Patrick | May 10, 1957 – Mar. 17, 1958 |
| Captain Joseph A. Jaap | Mar. 17, 1958 – Sept. 23, 1958 |
| Captain Joseph D. Black | Mar. 25, 1958 – Nov. 25, 1958 |
| Captain Frederick L. Ashworth | Sept. 23, 1958 – July  2, 1959 |
| Rear Adm. William E. Ellis | Nov. 25, 1958 – Dec. 28, 1959 |
| Captain Harold G. Brown | July  2, 1959 – Sept. 21, 1959 |
| Captain John N. Shafer | Sept. 21, 1959 – Feb.  8, 1961 |
| Rear Adm. C.S. Cooper | Dec. 28, 1959 – Apr. 26, 1960 |
| Rear Adm. Frank A. Brandley | Apr. 26, 1960 – Apr. 16, 1962 |

## Air Force Members

| | |
|---|---|
| Major Gen. H.G. Bunker | Oct.  3, 1951 – Oct. 29, 1954 |
| Major Gen. J.E. Briggs | Mar.  5, 1952 – May  2, 1954 |
| Major Gen. H.B. Thatcher | May  3, 1954 – Sept. 24, 1956 |
| Brig. Gen. Richard T. Coiner, Jr. | Oct. 29, 1954 – Aug.  1, 1958 |
| Major Gen. John S. Mills | Sept. 24, 1956 – July  3, 1958 |
| Major Gen. Leland S. Stranathan | July  3, 1958 – May 29, 1959 |
| Major Gen. Charles H. Anderson | Aug.  1, 1958 – May 15, 1960 |
| Major Gen. Marvin C. Demler | May 29, 1959 – Nov. 23, 1959 |
| Brig. Gen. Paul T. Preuss | Nov. 23, 1959 – Mar. 28, 1960 |
| Brig. Gen. Ralph L. Wassell | Mar. 28, 1960 – Nov.  1, 1962 |
| Major Gen. Bruce K. Holloway | May 15, 1960 – Oct. 10, 1961 |

574

## Laboratory Directors
United States Atomic Energy Commission, 1953–1960

*Ames Laboratory*

| | |
|---|---|
| Frank H. Spedding | 1948–1968 |

*Argonne National Laboratory*

| | |
|---|---|
| Walter H. Zinn | 1946–1956 |
| Norman Hilberry | 1957–1961 |

*Brookhaven National Laboratory*

| | |
|---|---|
| Leland J. Haworth | 1948–1961 |

*Los Alamos Scientific Laboratory*

| | |
|---|---|
| Norris E. Bradbury | 1945–1970 |

*Oak Ridge National Laboratory*

| | |
|---|---|
| Clarence E. Larson | 1950–1955 |
| Alvin M. Weinberg | 1955–1974 |

*Radiation Laboratory-Berkeley*

| | |
|---|---|
| Ernest O. Lawrence | 1936–1958 |
| Edwin M. McMillan | 1958–1973 |

*Sandia Laboratory*[a]

| | |
|---|---|
| Donald A. Quarles | 1952–1953 |
| James W. McRae | 1953–1958 |
| Julius P. Molnar | 1958–1959 |
| Siegmund P. Schwartz | 1960–1965 |

*Livermore Laboratory*

| | |
|---|---|
| Herbert F. York | 1952–1958 |
| Edward Teller | 1958–1960 |

[a]The actual title was president, not director.

# Appendix 2

## AEC Ten-Year Summary of Financial Data
### (in millions of dollars)

|  | 1952 | 1953 | 1954 | 1955 |
|---|---|---|---|---|
| Cost of Operations[a] | 684.1 | 904.7 | 1,039.1 | 1,289.5 |
| Procurement of Raw Materials | 72.5 | 82.2 | 142.8 | 193.6 |
| Production of Nuclear Materials | 205.7 | 318.3 | 409.7 | 588.4 |
| Weapons Development and Fabrication | 229.2 | 257.5 | 250.0 | 258.7 |
| Development of Nuclear Reactors | 64.4 | 104.1 | 99.3 | 114.6 |
| Civilian | 1.6 | 6.4 | 16.2 | 21.4 |
| Military | 39.5 | 53.2 | 42.0 | 53.0 |
| Other | 23.3 | 44.5 | 41.1 | 40.2 |
| Physical Research | 34.7 | 41.8 | 43.6 | 48.2 |
| Controlled Thermonuclear | 0.2 | 0.8 | 1.7 | 4.7 |
| High Energy Physics | 5.9 | 8.6 | 7.8 | 8.6 |
| Other | 28.6 | 32.4 | 34.1 | 34.9 |
| Biology and Medicine Research | 24.5 | 26.3 | 27.0 | 28.9 |
| Community Operations — Net | 16.4 | 15.2 | 11.8 | 10.3 |
| Administrative Expenses | 31.4 | 35.5 | 34.7 | 34.0 |
| Other Expenses and Income Net | 5.3 | 23.8 | 20.2 | 12.8 |
| | | | | |
| Plant Construction and Equipment Costs Incurred During the Year | 1,082.2 | 1,125.6 | 1,215.1 | 842.5 |
| Total AEC Assets Excluding Inventories of Certain Products at June 30 | 4,692.6 | 8,014.5 | 8,144.4 | 8,077.8 |
| | | | | |
| Plant Investments at June 30 (Gross) | 3,496.8 | 4,579.1 | 5,705.3 | 6,487.4 |
| Production Plants | 1,327.3 | 2,118.1 | 2,957.8 | 4,645.8 |
| Research & Development Facilities | 338.8 | 548.0 | 616.5 | 707.1 |
| Other | 467.7 | 483.4 | 515.9 | 505.5 |
| Plant Construction in Progress at June 30 | 1,363.0 | 1,429.6 | 1,615.1 | 629.0 |
| Funds Appropriated — Net | 1,605.8 | 4,136.5 | 1,042.5 | 1,209.9 |
| Operations | -.- | 808.9 | 886.5 | 1,099.0 |
| Plant Acquisition and Construction | -.- | 3,327.5 | 156.0 | 110.9 |

[a] Includes depreciation.

| 1956 | 1957 | 1958 | 1959 | 1960 | 1961 |
|---|---|---|---|---|---|
| 1,608.0 | 1,918.2 | 2,288.6 | 2,496.6 | 2,619.1 | 2,615.8 |
| 278.9 | 397.8 | 596.4 | 700.0 | 716.5 | 636.8 |
| 731.0 | 762.8 | 750.2 | 713.2 | 731.3 | 732.5 |
| 280.8 | 337.2 | 433.5 | 492.0 | 505.5 | 515.5 |
| 168.9 | 255.7 | 306.2 | 355.6 | 399.2 | 437.3 |
| 33.5 | 42.0 | 52.5 | 78.3 | 100.1 | 102.3 |
| 97.0 | 158.4 | 173.1 | 180.3 | 186.7 | 201.2 |
| 38.4 | 55.3 | 80.6 | 97.0 | 112.4 | 133.8 |
| 56.5 | 69.6 | 87.7 | 112.3 | 132.8 | 154.1 |
| 7.0 | 11.1 | 19.0 | 27.7 | 32.1 | 30.1 |
| 12.0 | 17.6 | 19.1 | 27.5 | 32.3 | 47.5 |
| 37.5 | 40.9 | 49.6 | 57.1 | 68.4 | 76.5 |
| 29.8 | 33.1 | 36.0 | 42.8 | 48.9 | 53.9 |
| 9.0 | 8.9 | 11.2 | 9.9 | 7.1 | 4.5 |
| 38.2 | 38.5 | 46.4 | 50.1 | 51.2 | 57.4 |
| 14.9 | 14.6 | 21.0 | 20.7 | 26.6 | 23.8 |
| 301.7 | 317.0 | 289.7 | 299.0 | 331.5 | 432.7 |
| 7,368.3 | 7,397.9 | 7,652.8 | 7,764.8 | 7,689.4 | 7,802.4 |
| 6,713.1 | 6,907.9 | 7,110.8 | 7,292.8 | 7,344.8 | 7,664.8 |
| 5,212.8 | 5,392.5 | 5,494.4 | 5,552.7 | 5,458.2 | 5,453.6 |
| 753.5 | 792.6 | 937.7 | 1,124.5 | 1,271.3 | 1,435.0 |
| 499.8 | 411.6 | 407.5 | 365.8 | 288.6 | 313.4 |
| 247.0 | 311.2 | 271.2 | 249.8 | 326.7 | 462.8 |
| 834.2 | 1,898.7 | 2,334.0 | 2,635.3 | 2,649.6 | 2,666.7 |
| 1,146.4[b] | 1,740.4 | 2,225.5 | 2,385.4 | 2,387.1 | 2,456.2 |
| (312.2)[b] | 158.3 | 108.5 | 249.9 | 262.5 | 210.5 |

[b]Includes transfer to operations of $571 million appropriated in prior years as plant and equipment funds.

Source: U.S. Atomic Energy Commission, "Financial Report for 1961," Appendix 16 in *Major Activities in the Atomic Energy Programs, January–December 1961* (Washington: GPO, 1962).

# Appendix 3

## AEC Ten-Year Summary of Employment

|  | 1952 | 1953 | 1954 | 1955 | 1956 |
|---|---|---|---|---|---|
| Employment at June 30 | 149,443 | 148,846 | 142,021 | 112,618 | 110,197 |
| AEC Employees | 6,734 | 6,941 | 6,195 | 6,076 | 6,637 |
| Operating Contractor Employees | 58,101 | 71,775 | 73,312 | 82,936 | 90,238 |
| Construction Contractor Employees | 84,608 | 70,130 | 62,514 | 23,606 | 13,322 |

|  | 1957 | 1958 | 1959 | 1960 | 1961 |
|---|---|---|---|---|---|
| Employment at June 30 | 119,455 | 121,059 | 121,928 | 122,718 | 122,989 |
| AEC Employees | 6,910 | 7,107 | 6,855 | 6,907 | 6,846 |
| Operating Contractor Employees | 98,176 | 103,290 | 105,195 | 104,612 | 103,313 |
| Construction Contractor Employees | 14,369 | 10,662 | 9,878 | 11,199 | 12,830 |

Source: U.S. Atomic Energy Commission, "Financial Report for 1961," Appendix 16 in *Major Activities in the Atomic Energy Programs, January–December 1961* (Washington: GPO, 1962).

# Appendix 4

## Announced U.S. Nuclear Tests, 1953–1958

| Event | Dates | Location | Number of Shots | Purpose |
|---|---|---|---|---|
| *Operation Upshot-Knothole* | 3/53–6/53 | Nevada Test Site | 11 | Weapon Related |
| *Operation Castle* | 2/54–5/54 | Bikini | 6 | Weapon Related |
| *Operation Teapot* | 2/55–5/55 | Nevada Test Site | 14 | Weapon Effects/ Weapon Related |
| *Operation Wigwam* | 5/14/55 | Pacific | 1 | Weapon Effects |
| *Project 56* | 11/55–1/56 | Nevada Test Site | 4 | Safety Experiments |
| *Operation Redwing* | 5/56–7/56 | Enewetak/ Bikini | 17 | Weapon Related |
| *Project 57* | 4/24/57 | Bombing Range | 1 | Safety Experiment |
| *Operation Plumbbob* | 5/57–2/58 | Nevada Test Site | 30 | Weapon Related/ Weapon Effects/ Safety Experiments |
| *Project 58* | 12/57 | Nevada Test Site | 2 | Safety Experiments |
| *Project 58 A* | 3/14/58 | Nevada Test Site | 1 | Safety Experiments |
| *Operation Hardtack I* | 4/58–8/58 | Pacific | 35 | Weapon Related/ Weapon Effects |
| *Operation Argus* | 8/58–9/58 | South Atlantic | 3 | Weapon Effects |
| *Operation Hardtack II* | 9/58–10/58 | Nevada Test Site | 37 | Safety Experiment/ Weapon Related |

579

Source: U.S. Department of Energy, Office of Public Affairs, *Announced United States Nuclear Tests. July 1945 through December 1983* (Las Vegas: Nevada Operations Office, 1984).

# Appendix 5

## Procurement of Uranium Concentrates ($U_3O_8$)

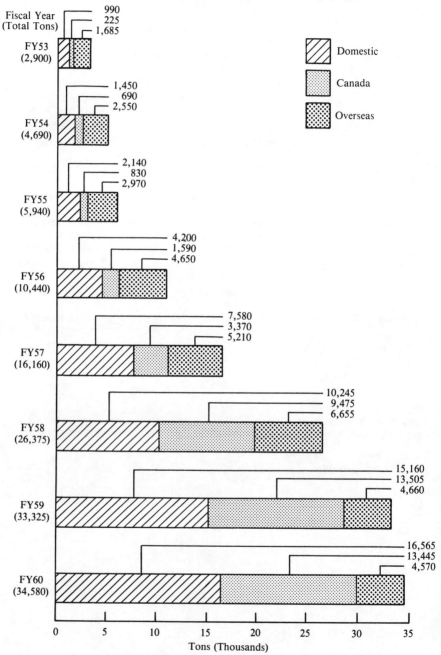

Source: U.S. Atomic Energy Commission, *Major Activities in the Atomic Energy Programs, January–December 1961* (Washington: GPO, 1962).

# Appendix 6

## Agreements for Cooperation in the
## Civil and Military Uses of Atomic Energy

| Coun-tries | Agree-ments | Country | Scope | Effective Date | Termina-tion Date |
|---|---|---|---|---|---|
| 1 | 1 | Argentina | Research[b] | 07-29-55 | 07-28-62 |
| 2 | 2 | Australia[a] | Research & Power | 05-28-57 | 05-27-67 |
| 3 | 3 | Austria | Research | 01-25-60 | 01-24-70 |
| 4 | 4 | Belgium[a] | Research & Power[b] | 07-21-55 | 07-31-65 |
| 5 | 5 | Brazil | Research[b] | 08-03-55 | 08-02-62 |
| 6 | 6 | Canada[a] | Research & Power[b] | 07-21-55 | 07-13-80 |
| 7 | 7 | China, Republic of | Research[b] | 07-18-55 | 07-17-62 |
| 8 | 8 | Costa Rica | Research | 02-08-61 | 02-07-66 |
| 9 | 9 | Cuba | Research | 10-10-57 | 10-09-62 |
| 10 | 10 | Denmark | Research[b] | 07-25-55 | 09-07-68 |
| 11 | 11 | Dominican Republic | Research | 12-21-56 | 12-20-61 |
| 12 | 12 | Ecuador | Research | 02-06-58 | 02-05-63 |
| 13 | 13 | France | Research & Power[b] | 11-20-56 | 11-19-66 |
| 14 | 14 | Germany, Fed. Republic of | Research & Power[b] | 08-07-57 | 08-06-67 |
| | 15 | West Berlin, City | Research | 08-01-57 | 07-31-62 |
| 15 | 16 | Greece | Research[b] | 08-04-55 | 08-03-62 |
| 16 | 17 | Guatemala | Research | 04-22-57 | 04-21-62 |
| 17 | 18 | Indonesia | Research | 09-21-60 | 09-20-65 |
| 18 | 19 | Iran | Research | 04-27-59 | 04-26-64 |
| 19 | 20 | Ireland | Research[b] | 07-09-58 | 07-08-63 |
| 20 | 21 | Israel | Research[b] | 07-12-55 | 07-11-62 |
| 21 | 22 | Italy | Research & Power[b] | 04-15-58 | 04-14-78 |
| 22 | 23 | Japan | Research & Power[b] | 12-05-58 | 12-04-68 |
| 23 | 24 | Korea, Republic of | Research[b] | 02-03-56 | 02-02-66 |
| 24 | 25 | Netherlands[a] | Research & Power[b] | 08-08-57 | 08-07-67 |
| 25 | 26 | Nicaragua | Research | 03-07-58 | 03-06-63 |
| 26 | 27 | Norway | Research & Power | 06-10-57 | 06-09-67 |
| 27 | 28 | Philippines | Research[b] | 07-27-55 | 07-26-63 |
| 28 | 29 | Portugal | Research[b] | 07-21-55 | 07-20-62 |
| 29 | 30 | South Africa | Research & Power | 08-22-57 | 08-21-67 |
| 30 | 31 | Spain | Research & Power | 02-12-58 | 02-11-68 |
| 31 | 32 | Sweden | Research[b] | 01-18-56 | 06-01-68 |
| 32 | 33 | Switzerland | Research | 07-18-55 | 07-17-65 |
| | 34 | Switzerland[a] | Power[b] | 01-29-57 | 01-28-67 |
| 33 | 35 | Thailand | Research[b] | 03-13-56 | 03-12-63 |
| 34 | 36 | Turkey | Research[b] | 06-10-55 | 06-09-65 |
| 35 | 37 | United Kingdom[a] | Research & Power[b] | 07-21-55 | 07-20-65 |
| 36 | 38 | Venezuela | Research & Power | 02-09-60 | 02-08-70 |
| 37 | 39 | Viet-Nam | Research | 07-01-59 | 06-30-64 |

581

| Mutual Defence Purposes Agreements[c] | |
|---|---|
| 1. NATO[a] | Mar. 29, 1956 |
| 2. Australia[a] | Aug. 14, 1957 |
| 3. Canada[a] | July 27, 1959 |
| 4. France | July 20, 1959 |
| 5. France[a] | Oct. 9, 1961 |
| 6. Germany, Fed. Rep.[a] | July 27, 1959 |
| 7. Greece[a] | Aug. 11, 1959 |
| 8. Italy[a] | May 24, 1961 |
| 9. Netherlands[a] | July 27, 1959 |
| 10. Turkey[a] | July 27, 1959 |
| 11. United Kingdom[a] | Aug. 4, 1958 |
| (Amendment to U.K. Agreement)[a] | July 20, 1959 |

Special Agreements[c]

1. European Atomic Energy Community (EURATOM) . . . Joint Nuclear Program . . . February 18, 1959.

2. European Atomic Energy Community (EURATOM) . . . Additional Agreement . . . July 25, 1960.

3. International Atomic Energy Agency (IAEA) . . . Supply of Materials, etc. . . . August 7, 1959.

[a]Classified Agreements.
[b]Denotes Agreement has been amended.
[c]Only the effective date shown for these agreements.

In effect: 25 research and 14 power agreements with 37 countries and West Berlin. 11 mutual defense purposes agreements, and 3 special agreements (IAEA and EURATOM). 5 other agreements had been signed. Of these, there were no plans for ratification for Cuba, Iraq, Peru and Panama. Brazil anticipated ratification.

Source: U.S. AEC, *Major Activities in Atomic Energy Programs, Jan.–Dec. 1961* (Washington: GPO, 1962).

# Appendix 7

## AEC Operations Offices
### *(with the area offices supervised by each)*

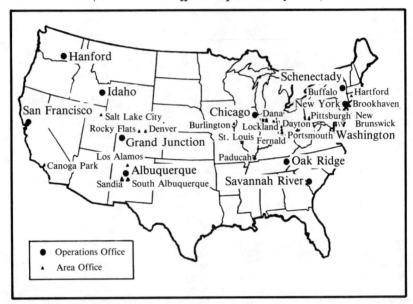

Albuquerque Operations Office
  Buffalo Area Office
  Burlington Area Office
  Dayton Area Office
  Los Alamos Area Office
  Rocky Flats Area Office
  Sandia Area Office
  South Albuquerque Area Office

Chicago Operations Office
  Hartford Area Office
  Lockland Area Office
  Pittsburgh Area Office

Grand Junction Operations Office
  Denver Area Office
  Salt Lake City Area Office

Hanford Operations Office

Idaho Operations Office

New York Operations Office
  Brookhaven Area Office

Oak Ridge Operations Office
  Fernald Area Office
  New Brunswick Area Office
  Paducah Area Office
  Portsmouth Area Office
  St. Louis Area Office

San Francisco Operations Office
  Southern California Area Office

Savannah River Operations Office
  Dana Area Office

Schenectady Operations Office

Source: U.S. Atomic Energy Commission, *Atomic Energy Facts* (Washington: GPO, 1957).

# Appendix 8
## AEC Organization Charts,
### May 1953–September 1958
*(see following pages)*

# AEC Organization Chart, May 1953

General Advisory Committee
Isidor I. Rabi
Chairman

Military Liaison Committee
Robert LeBaron
Chairman

Controller
Don S. Burrows

Office of Operations Analysis
David P. Herron, Chief

Office of Intelligence
Walter F. Colby, Director

Secretary to the Commission
Roy B. Snapp

Office of Classification
James G. Beckerley, Director

Office of Industrial Development
William L. Davidson, Director

Office of General Counsel
William Mitchell, General Counsel

Office of Special Projects
John A. Hall, Chief

Division of
Research
T. H. Johnson
Director

Division of
Biology & Medicine
Dr. John C. Bugher
Director

Division of Reactor
Development
L. R. Halstad
Director

Division of
Engineering
L. R. Halstad
Acting Director

Chicago
Operations Office
A. Tammaro
Manager

Idaho
Operations Office
L. E. Johnston
Manager

Schenectady
Operations Office
J. D. Anderson
Manager

San Francisco
Operations Office
J. J. Flaherty
Manager

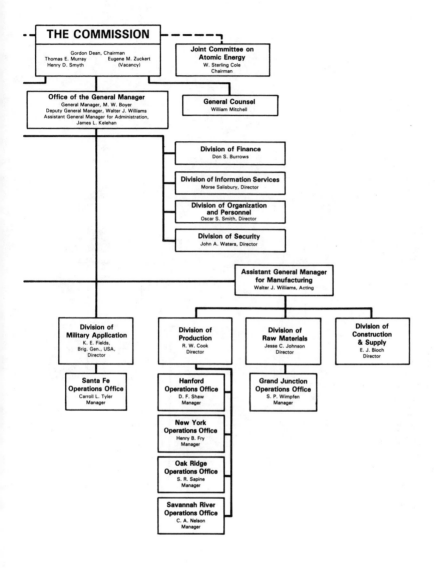

**THE COMMISSION**

Gordon Dean, Chairman
Thomas E. Murray          Eugene M. Zuckert
Henry D. Smyth              (Vacancy)

**Joint Committee on Atomic Energy**
W. Sterling Cole
Chairman

**Office of the General Manager**
General Manager, M. W. Boyer
Deputy General Manager, Walter J. Williams
Assistant General Manager for Administration,
James L. Kelehan

**General Counsel**
William Mitchell

**Division of Finance**
Don S. Burrows

**Division of Information Services**
Morse Salisbury, Director

**Division of Organization and Personnel**
Oscar S. Smith, Director

**Division of Security**
John A. Waters, Director

**Assistant General Manager for Manufacturing**
Walter J. Williams, Acting

**Division of Military Application**
K. E. Fields,
Brig. Gen., USA,
Director

**Division of Production**
R. W. Cook
Director

**Division of Raw Materials**
Jesse C. Johnson
Director

**Division of Construction & Supply**
E. J. Bloch
Director

**Santa Fe Operations Office**
Carroll L. Tyler
Manager

**Hanford Operations Office**
D. F. Shaw
Manager

**Grand Junction Operations Office**
S. P. Wimpfen
Manager

**New York Operations Office**
Henry B. Fry
Manager

**Oak Ridge Operations Office**
S. R. Sapine
Manager

**Savannah River Operations Office**
C. A. Nelson
Manager

585

# AEC Organization Chart, July 1955

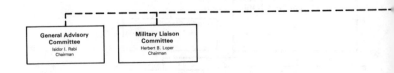

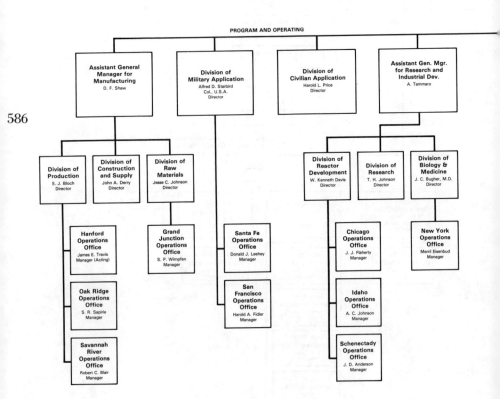

586

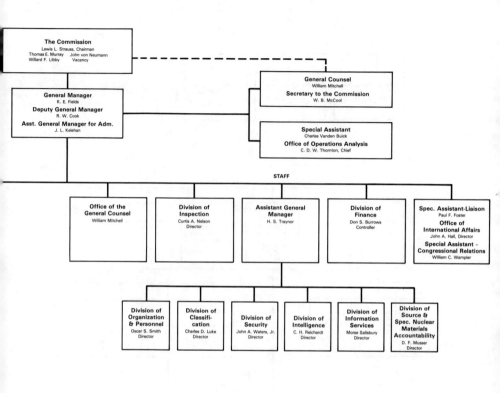

**The Commission**
Lewis L. Strauss, Chairman
Thomas E. Murray    John von Neumann
Willard F. Libby    Vacancy

**General Manager**
K. E. Fields
**Deputy General Manager**
R. W. Cook
**Asst. General Manager for Adm.**
J. L. Kelehan

**General Counsel**
William Mitchell
**Secretary to the Commission**
W. B. McCool

**Special Assistant**
Charles Vanden Buick
**Office of Operations Analysis**
C. D. W. Thornton, Chief

STAFF

**Office of the General Counsel**
William Mitchell

**Division of Inspection**
Curtis A. Nelson
Director

**Assistant General Manager**
H. S. Traynor

**Division of Finance**
Don S. Burrows
Controller

**Spec. Assistant-Liaison**
Paul F. Foster
**Office of International Affairs**
John A. Hall, Director
**Special Assistant – Congressional Relations**
William C. Wampler

**Division of Organization & Personnel**
Oscar S. Smith
Director

**Division of Classifi-cation**
Charles D. Luke
Director

**Division of Security**
John A. Waters, Jr.
Director

**Division of Intelligence**
C. H. Reichardt
Director

**Division of Information Services**
Morse Salisbury
Director

**Division of Source & Spec. Nuclear Materials Accountability**
D. F. Musser
Director

# AEC Organization Chart, September 1958

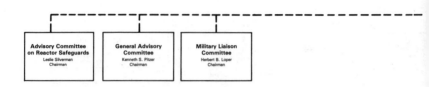

588

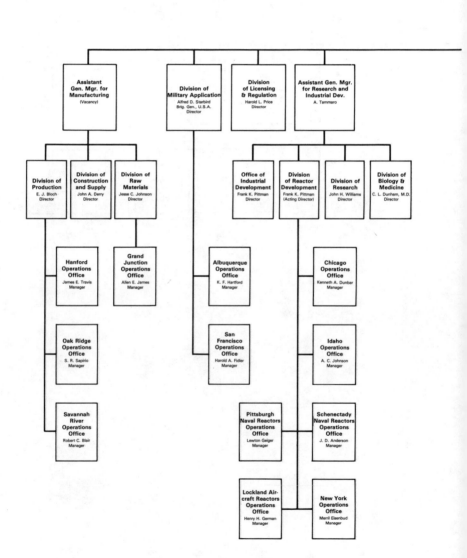

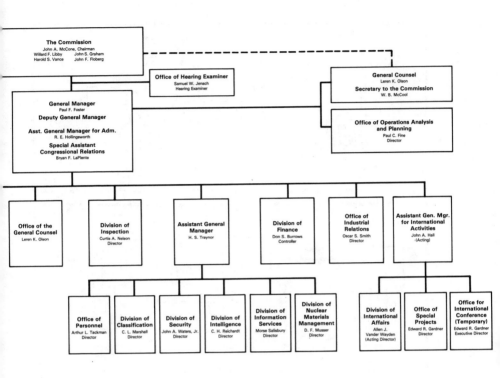

**The Commission**
John A. McCone, Chairman
Willard F. Libby    John S. Graham
Harold S. Vance    John F. Floberg

**Office of Hearing Examiner**
Samuel W. Jenach
Hearing Examiner

**General Counsel**
Leren K. Olson

**Secretary to the Commission**
W. B. McCool

**General Manager**
Paul F. Foster

**Deputy General Manager**

**Asst. General Manager for Adm.**
R. E. Hollingsworth

**Special Assistant
Congressional Relations**
Bryan F. LaPlante

**Office of Operations Analysis
and Planning**
Paul C. Fine
Director

**Office of the
General Counsel**
Leren K. Olson

**Division of
Inspection**
Curtis A. Nelson
Director

**Assistant General
Manager**
H. S. Traynor

**Division of
Finance**
Don S. Burrows
Controller

**Office of
Industrial
Relations**
Oscar S. Smith
Director

**Assistant Gen. Mgr.
for International
Activities**
John A. Hall
(Acting)

**Office of
Personnel**
Arthur L. Tackman
Director

**Division of
Classification**
C. L. Marshall
Director

**Division of
Security**
John A. Waters, Jr.
Director

**Division of
Intelligence**
C. H. Reichardt
Director

**Division of
Information
Services**
Morse Salisbury
Director

**Division of
Nuclear
Materials
Management**
D. F. Musser
Director

**Division of
International
Affairs**
Allen J.
Vander Wayden
(Acting Director)

**Office of
Special
Projects**
Edward R. Gardner
Director

**Office for
International
Conference
(Temporary)**
Edward R. Gardner
Executive Director

# Appendix 9
## Eight Basic Reactor Systems Being Developed

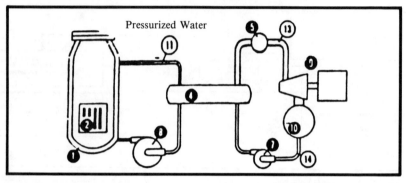

Pressurized Water

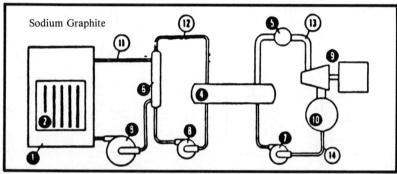

Sodium Graphite

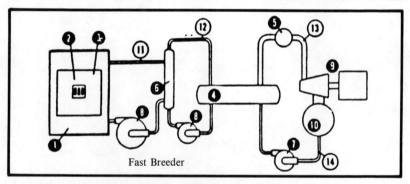

Fast Breeder

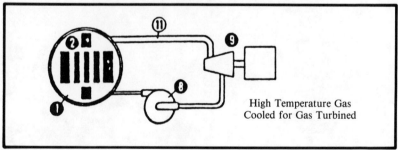

High Temperature Gas
Cooled for Gas Turbined

Source: U.S. Atomic Energy Commission, *Atomic Energy Facts*
(Washington: GPO, 1957).

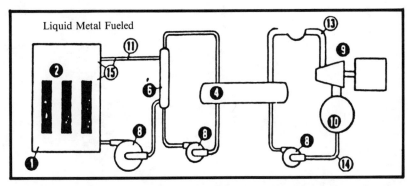

Liquid Metal Fueled

591

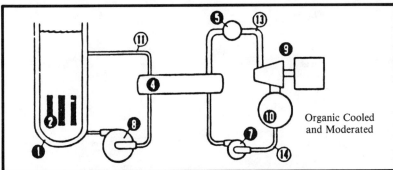

Organic Cooled and Moderated

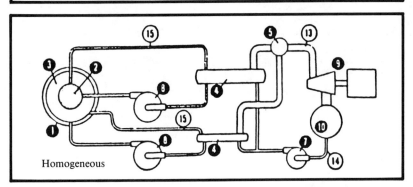

Homogeneous

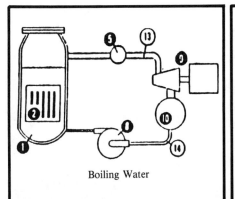

Boiling Water

| Features | | |
|---|---|---|
| **1** Reactor | **8** Circulating Pump | |
| **2** Core | **9** Turbo-generator | |
| **3** Blanket | **10** Condenser | |
| **4** Boiler | **11** Primary Coolant | |
| **5** Steam Drier | **12** Intermediate Coolant | |
| **6** Intermediate Heat Exchanger | **13** Steam | |
| | **14** Condensate | |
| **7** Feedwater Pump | **15** Circulating Fuel | |

# *ABBREVIATIONS*

| | |
|---|---|
| ACBM | Advisory Committee on Biology and Medicine |
| AEC | Records of Headquarters, U.S. Atomic Energy Commission, Washington, D.C. |
| BOB | Records of the Bureau of the Budget, Washington, D.C. |
| CDJ | Papers of Charles D. Jackson, Eisenhower Library, Abilene, KS |
| CM 1 | Commission meeting 1, U.S. Atomic Energy Commission |
| CR | Congressional Record |
| DDE | Papers of Dwight D. Eisenhower, Eisenhower Library, Abilene, KS |
| DOE | Records of the U.S. Department of Energy, Washington, D.C. |
| DOS | Records of the U.S. Department of State, Washington, D.C. |
| FBI | Records of the Federal Bureau of Investigation, Washington, D.C. |
| FCDA | Records of the Federal Civil Defense Administration, Washington, D.C. |
| FPC | Records of the Federal Power Commission, Washington, D.C. |
| GAC 1 | Meeting 1 of the General Advisory Committee to the U.S. Atomic Energy Commission |
| HDS | Papers of Henry D. Smyth, Princeton, NJ |
| IAEA | International Atomic Energy Agency |
| JCAE | Records of the Joint Committee on Atomic Energy, National Archives, Washington, D.C. |
| JRO | Papers of J. Robert Oppenheimer, Library of Congress, Washington, D.C. |
| LASL | Records of Los Alamos Scientific Laboratory, Los Alamos, NM |

LLS  Papers of Lewis L. Strauss, Hoover Library, West Branch, IA

NSC  Records of the National Security Council, Washington, D.C.

OMB  Records of the Office of Management and Budget, Washington, D.C.

PSAC  President's Science Advisory Committee

SNSC  Summary, National Security Council

TEM  Papers of Thomas E. Murray, Washington, D.C.

UCRL  Records of the University of California Radiation Laboratory, Lawrence Livermore National Laboratory, Livermore, CA (formerly LLNL)

# NOTES

These notes are intended as a guide to the material and records we consulted and should not be considered a rigorous citation of all the documentary evidence available. Neither should the citation of specific documents be interpreted to mean that the materials are necessarily unclassified or available to the public. We have, however, in the source abbreviations, indicated where the records we used are located. The Essay on Sources provides an additional guide to the archival and secondary literature pertinent to the history of atomic energy during the Eisenhower Administration. Except for those materials cited as being in the files of the Atomic Energy Commission, none of the materials are now available to the historical staff, and requests for access should be directed to the organization or archives cited in each note.

## FOREWORD

1. For helpful surveys of Eisenhower historiography, see Vincent P. De Santis, "Eisenhower Revisionism," *The Review of Politics* 38 (April 1976): 190–207; Gary Reichard, "Eisenhower as President: The Changing View," *South Atlantic Quarterly* 77 (Summer 1978): 265–81; Stephen E. Ambrose, "The Ike Age," *The New Republic* (May 9, 1981): 26–34; Mary S. McAuliffe, "Commentary/Eisenhower, the President," *The Journal of American History* 68 (December 1981): 625–32; Arthur M. Schlesinger, Jr., "The Ike Age Revisited," *Reviews in American History* 9 (March 1983): 1–11; Anthony James Joes, "Eisenhower Revisionism: The Tide Comes In," *Presidential Studies Quarterly* 15 (Summer 1985): 561–71; Steve Neal, "Why We Were Right to Like Ike," *American Heritage* 37 (December 1985): 49–64; Robert J. McMahon, "Eisenhower and Third World Nationalism: A Critique of the Revisionists," *Political Science Quarterly* 101 (1986): 453–73; Robert F. Burk, "Bibliographic Essay," *Dwight D. Eisenhower: Hero and Politician* (Boston: G. K. Hall, 1986); Richard A. Melanson and David Mayers, "Preface," *Reevaluating Eisenhower: American Foreign Policy in the Fifties* (Urbana: University of Illinois Press, 1987); Stephen G. Rabe, "Introduction," *Eisenhower and Latin America: The Foreign Policy of Anticommunism* (Chapel Hill: the University of North Carolina Press, 1988); Gary W. Reichard,

"Bibliographical Essay," *Politics as Usual: The Age of Truman and Eisenhower* (Arlington Heights, Ill.: Harlan Davidson, 1988).

2. McMahon, "Eisenhower and Third World Nationalism," 457.

## CHAPTER ONE

1. Richard G. Hewlett and Francis Duncan, *Atomic Shield, 1947–1952*, Vol. II of *A History of the U.S. Atomic Energy Commission* (University Park: Pennsylvania State University Press, 1969), p. 317 (hereafter cited *Atomic Shield*).

2. The following account of the meeting is based largely on Snapp's undated memorandum to file, probably written on Nov. 12, 1952, AEC.

3. *Atomic Shield*, pp. 437–38; *New York Times*, Nov. 11, 1952, p. 16.

4. Dean to Eisenhower, Nov. 7, 1952, AEC.

5. In the 1950s the name was spelled "Eniwetok," but the modern version "Enewetak" is used in this book.

6. AEC Press Release 374, May 25, 1951, AEC.

7. For background, see *Atomic Shield*, pp. 565–68.

8. Ibid., pp. 388–91.

9. AEC Briefing Book, Nov. 1952, AEC.

10. Not all these figures were in the Briefing Book; some come from AEC Monthly Status and Progress Report, Nov. 1952, AEC.

11. Dean, opening remarks for meeting with Eisenhower, Nov. 19, 1952, attached to Nov. 19 entry in Dean Diary, AEC.

12. Dean Diary, Nov. 18, 1952, AEC.

13. The following description of the Commodore meeting is based on Murray's notes on Discussion with President-Elect Eisenhower, Nov. 19, 1952, TEM.

14. Dean Diary, Nov. 24, 1952, AEC.

## CHAPTER TWO

1. Snapp to Scott McLeod, Jan. 10, 1953; Snapp to Styles Bridges, Jan. 10, 1953, both in AEC.

2. Herbert S. Parmet, *Eisenhower and the American Crusades* (New York: Macmillan, 1972), pp. 155–57.

3. AEC Controller, BOB Action on FY 1954 Budget Estimates, AEC 533/21, Jan. 21, 1953, AEC.

4. On the status of plant construction, see AEC Monthly Status and Progress Reports, Jan.–March, 1953, AEC. On plans for weapons tests, see D. Cooksey to K. E. Fields, Jan. 12, 1953, and N. E. Bradbury to Fields, Jan. 6, 1953, AEC.

5. Dodge to Dean, Feb. 3, 1953, AEC.

6. CM 826, Feb. 26, 1953; Division of Finance, Analysis of Special Review of 1954 Budget, Feb. 25, 1953; Smyth to Dodge, March 2, 1953, all in AEC.

7. National Security Council, Summary of Discussion (hereafter cited as SNSC), Meeting 134, Feb. 25, 1953, DDE; Military Liaison Committee Meeting 78, Feb. 18, 1953; CM 827, Feb. 27, 1953, both in AEC.

8. Dean to Wilson, March 13, 1953; Review of Military Requirements for Atomic Weapons, AEC 533/26, March 18, 1953, both in AEC; SNSC 137, March 18, 1953; Dodge to Strauss, March 19, 1953, both in DDE.

9. On Strauss's earlier career on the Commission, see Richard G. Hewlett and Francis Duncan, *Atomic Shield, 1947–1952*, Vol. II of *A History of the U.S. Atomic Energy Commission* (University Park: Pennsylvania State University Press, 1969), pp. 81, 109–10, 130–31, 283–99, 312–13, 373–74, 387–88, 394–95, 461–62 (hereafter cited *Atomic Shield*), and Lewis L. Strauss, *Men and Decisions* (Garden City, NY: Doubleday, 1962), pp. 201–30. For a recent biography of Strauss, see Richard Pfau, *No Sacrifice Too Great: The Life of Lewis L. Strauss* (Charlottesville: University Press of Virginia, 1984). For Strauss's account of his appointment, see Strauss, *Men and Decisions*, pp. 332–33. Announcements of Dean's intention to retire and of Strauss's selection appeared in *New York Times*, Feb. 11, 1953, p. 1, and March 8, 1953, p. 1.

10. Dean to Strauss, March 20, 1953; Dean to Eisenhower, March 20, 1953, both in AEC.

11. Dean to the Commissioners, Jan. 14, 1953, AEC.

12. *Atomic Shield*, pp. 494–98, 515; Richard G. Hewlett and Francis Duncan, *Nuclear Navy, 1946–1962* (Chicago: University of Chicago Press, 1974), pp. 175–79 (hereafter cited *Nuclear Navy*); W. H. Zinn, "Nuclear Power Generation Ad-

596

vances to Prototype Stage," *Electric Light and Power* 30 (Oct. 1952): 112–19; "The Breeder Reactor," *Scientific American* 187 (Dec. 1952): 58–60.

13. Joint Committee on Atomic Energy, *Atomic Power and Private Enterprise*, Joint Committee Print, 82 Cong., 2 sess. (Washington: Government Printing Office, 1952); Durham to Dean, Aug. 19, 1952; Dean to Durham, Sept. 4, 1952, both in AEC.

14. Director of Reactor Development, Overall Objectives and Program for Reactor Development, AEC 152/33, Dec. 9, 1952, AEC. For background on Hafstad, see *Atomic Shield*, pp. 209–20, 511–18.

15. On Davidson, see AEC Press Release 423, May 1, 1952, AEC, and "AEC Bids Business Join the Feast," *Business Week*, Dec. 20, 1952, pp. 140–43.

16. Directors of Industrial Development and Reactor Development, Development of Economic Nuclear Power, AEC 331/59, Jan. 23, 1953, AEC.

17. Dean to Eisenhower, March 4, 1953, AEC. Earlier versions of the proposal were issued: AEC 331/62, Feb. 2, 1953; AEC 331/64, Feb. 6, 1953; AEC 331/66, Feb. 19, 1953, all in AEC. For Commission discussions of the papers, see: CM 811, Jan. 28, 1953; CM 813, Feb. 3, 1953; CM 820, Feb. 11, 1953; CM 824, Feb. 25, 1953; CM 830, March 4, 1953, all in AEC.

18. SNSC 136, March 11, 1953, DDE. The proposal was distributed as NSC 145, The Development of Practical Nuclear Power, March 6, 1953, AEC. The Commission was formally notified of the NSC decision in James S. Lay to the AEC, March 12, 1953, AEC.

19. Preface of Statement, AEC 331/69, March 19, 1953; CM 835, March 11, 1953; CM 840, March 20, 1953; Dean Diary, March 13, 16, 18, 20, 1953, all in AEC.

20. Notes, Special NSC Meeting, March 31, 1953, DDE. See also Memorandum at a Special Meeting of the National Security Council, Tuesday, March 31, 1953, *Foreign Relations of the United States, 1952–1954, Vol. II, National Security Affairs* (Washington: Government Printing Office, 1984), pp. 264–81 (hereafter cited *FRUS, 1952–1954, II*).

21. Murray to Dean, April 10, 1953, AEC; underlined in the original.

22. The report is found as an attachment to

Hugh D. Farley to Robert Cutler, April 2, 1953, DDE. The seven consultants were Dillon Anderson, James B. Black, John Cowles, Eugene Holman, Deane W. Malott, David B. Robertson, and Charles A. Thomas. See CM 838, March 16, 1953, AEC and Lay to NSC, March 17, 1953, DDE.

23. From a Condensed Statement of Proposed Policies and Programs prepared by James S. Lay, executive secretary of the NSC, and sent to Dean by letter of April 3, 1953, AEC.

24. Thomas K. McCraw, *TVA and the Power Fight* (Philadelphia: Lippincott, 1971), pp. 1–66; Philip J. Fungiello, *Toward A National Power Policy; The New Deal and the Electric Utility Industry* (Pittsburgh: University of Pittsburgh Press, 1973), pp. 1–148; Harry S. Truman, Address before the Electric Consumers Conference, May 26, 1952, *Public Papers of the Presidents, 1952–1953: Harry S. Truman* (Washington: Government Printing Office, 1966), pp. 370–74; *Electric Light and Power* 30 (Aug. 1952): 39; 30 (Dec. 1952): 144.

25. *Newsweek*, April 13, 1953, p. 88; AEC Press Release 481, April 12, 1953; Atomic Industrial Forum, News Release, April 16, 1953; CM 859, May 1, 1953; Walker L. Cisler and Mark E. Putman to Dean, April 16, 1953, with attached proposals for revising the act, all in AEC. The Van Zandt bill was introduced as H.R. 4687, on April 20, 1953, *Congressional Record*, 83 Cong., 1 sess., pp. 3414, A2010. See also AEC General Counsel, Legislation on Atomic Power Development, AEC 615/3, April 30, 1953, AEC.

26. Alex Radin to Dean, April 14, 1953, in AEC 331/74, April 17, 1953; O. A. Knight to Dean, April 23, 1953, in AEC 646, April 30, 1953, both in AEC.

27. SNSC 140, April 22, 1953, DDE. See also Memorandum of Discussion at the 140th Meeting of the National Security Council, Wednesday, April 22, 1953, *FRUS, 1952–1954, II*, pp. 291–301. Dean, Memo on NSC Meeting, April 22, 1953; Lay to AEC, April 24, 1953, both in A C.

28. Murray to Dean, April 16, 1953, AEC; *Nuclear Navy*, pp. 196–98.

29. Rickover to Dean, May 15, 1953, AEC.

30. Snapp, Proposed letter to the President, April 28, 1953; Murray to Smyth, April

597

28, 1953; Smyth to Eisenhower, April 29, 1953; CM 859, May 1, 1953; Kyes to Cutler, May 4, 1953, all in AEC; "Thomas E. Murray and the PWR Project," typescript, p. 7, TEM.

31. SNSC 143, May 6, 1953, DDE; Smyth to NSC, May 6, 1953; Lay to Secretary of Defense and AEC, May 8, 1953; Joint Committee, Transcript of Executive Session, May 6, 1953, all in AEC.

32. Cole to Dean, two letters dated May 15, 1953, in AEC 331/81, May 19, 1953, AEC.

33. General Counsel, Draft letter to the Joint Committee, AEC 331/85, May 22, 1953; CM 868, May 25, 1953; CM 869, May 26, 1953; Joint Committee, Transcript of Hearing, May 26, 1953, all in AEC. The NSC policy statement appears in NSC Report 149/2, Basic National Security Policies and Programs in Relation to their Costs, April 29, 1953, *FRUS, 1952–1954, II*, pp. 307–16. The full NSC policy statement was transmitted by Smyth to Cole, May 29, 1953, AEC.

34. The Commission considered two versions of the bill: AEC 615/8, May 11, 1953, and AEC 615/9, May 21, 1953, both in AEC. Dean presented the latter to the Joint Committee. For Commission discussions, see CM 862, May 13, 1953, and CM 864, May 20, 1953, both in AEC.

35. CM 869, May 26, 1953, AEC.

36. Dean Diary, June 3, 1953, AEC.

37. Dean to Eisenhower, June 1, 1953; Strauss to Sherman Adams, June 8, 1953; Eisenhower to Dean, June 9, 1953; Strauss to Eisenhower, June 19, 1953; Mr. Strauss's Statement, June 24, 1953, all in DDE.

38. *Washington Star*, June 26, 1953; *Washington Post*, June 27, 1953; *New York Times*, June 25, 1953; Bob Considine in the *New York Journal-American*, June 29, 1953; *Denver Post*, June 29, 1953; *Schenectady Gazette*, June 29, 1953; *Cincinnati Enquirer*, June 26, 1953; *Oak Ridge*, June 26, 1953; Joint Committee on Atomic Energy, *Hearings before the Senate Section on Confirmation of AEC Commissioners*, June 1953–March 1955 (Washington: Government Printing Office, 1955), pp. 1–3 (hereafter cited as *Confirmation Hearings*).

39. *Confirmation Hearings*, pp. 5–8.

40. Joint Committee on Atomic Energy, *Hearings on Atomic Power Development and Private Enterprise*, June 24–July 31,

1953 (Washington: Government Printing Office, 1953), pp. 562–70.

41. Cole to John Phillips, May 20, 1953, in AEC 533/32, May 27, 1953, AEC.

42. *Nuclear Navy*, pp. 228–34.

## CHAPTER THREE

1. *Public Papers of the Presidents of the United States, 1953: Dwight D. Eisenhower* (Washington: Government Printing Office, 1960), p. 2 (hereafter cited *Public Papers, 1953, Eisenhower*).

2. Durham to Eisenhower, Jan. 29, 1953; Eisenhower to Durham, Feb. 14, 1953, both in AEC.

3. Richard G. Hewlett and Francis Duncan, *Atomic Shield, 1947–1952*, Vol. II of *A History of the U.S. Atomic Energy Commission* (University Park: Pennsylvania State University Press, 1969), pp. 369–408 (hereafter cited *Atomic Shield*).

4. Ibid., pp. 438–39, 529–41, 554–56, 569–71.

5. Joint Committee on Atomic Energy, Transcript of Hearing on Status of Atomic Energy Program, Feb. 6, 1952, AEC.

6. Joint Committee on Atomic Energy, Transcript of Hearing on Status of Hydrogen Project, Feb. 21, 1952, AEC.

7. R. A. Lovett to McMahon, March 9, 1952, AEC.

8. Foster to Acheson and Dean, March 28, 1952; Secretaries of Army, Navy, and Air Force to Secretary of Defense, March 27, 1952; Dean to Files, April 1, 1952, all in AEC.

9. Minutes, 30th Meeting of the General Advisory Committee, April 27–29, 1952, AEC (hereafter cited GAC 30).

10. Bethe to Dean, May 28, 1952, with attachment, Bethe to Dean, May 23, 1952; Teller to Garrison Norton, Aug. 15, 1952, transmitting comments on Bethe's history, both in AEC.

11. C. A. Rolander and R. Robb, Informal Interview with William L. Borden, Feb. 20, 1954, AEC.

12. Wheeler, Statement on Loss of Classified Document, March 3, 1953, AEC.

13. Joint Committee on Atomic Energy, Policy and Progress in the H-Bomb Program: A Chronology of Leading Events, Jan. 1, 1953, JCAE.

14. No copy of the Walker document was found in AEC files. Description of the

contents has been reconstructed from various reports and correspondence on the incident, e.g., Bethe, Bradbury, Teller, and von Neumann to the Commissioners, March 2, 1953, AEC.

15. Hoover to Waters, Jan. 9, 1953, AEC.

16. Chronology of Missing Document, AEC 634/1, April 16, 1953; Waters to File, Feb. 4, 1953, both in AEC.

17. Murray, Meeting with Eisenhower, Feb. 16, 1953, TEM.

18. Atomic Energy Act of 1946, P.L.585, 79 Cong., 60 *Stat.* 755–75, 42 *U.S.C.*, 1801–19, Sect. 15 (b).

19. National Security Council, Summary of Discussion (hereafter cited SNSC), Meeting 132, Feb. 18, 1953, DDE.

20. *Public Papers, 1953, Eisenhower,* pp. 40–41; *New York Times,* Feb. 12, 1953, p. 1. In late 1952 the Rosenberg case had suddenly become an international cause célèbre. Simultaneously the Supreme Court refused to review the case, leaving presidential clemency the Rosenbergs' only hope. See Ronald Radosh and Joyce Milton, *The Rosenberg File: A Search for the Truth* (New York: Holt, Rinehart, and Winston, 1983), pp. 330, 335, 347–49 (hereafter cited Radosh and Milton, *The Rosenberg File*).

21. The value of the data the Rosenbergs allegedly passed on is examined in Radosh and Milton, *The Rosenberg File*, pp. 432–49, and Roger M. Anders, "The Rosenberg Case Revisited: The Greenglass Testimony and the Protection of Atomic Secrets," *American Historical Review* 83 (April 1978): 388–400. Durham to Eisenhower, Jan. 29, 1953; Eisenhower to Durham, Feb. 14, 1953, both in AEC.

22. Department of State, Panel of Consultants on Disarmament, Arms and American Policy, second run, Jan. 1953, DOS.

23. SNSC 132, Feb. 18, 1953, DDE.

24. SNSC 133, Feb. 25, 1953, DDE; Dean Diary, Feb. 24, 1953, AEC.

25. John Major, *The Oppenheimer Hearing* (London: B. T. Batsford, 1971), p. 252 (hereafter cited Major, *The Oppenheimer Hearing*).

26. Borden to Strauss, Sept. 10, 20, 1952, LLS.

27. Philip M. Stern, *The Oppenheimer Case: Security on Trial* (New York: Harper & Row, 1969), p. 169 (hereafter cited Stern, *The Oppenheimer Case*); Joint

Committee Working Paper, Nov. 3, 1952, AEC.

28. Stern, *The Oppenheimer Case,* pp. 102–103; *Atomic Shield,* pp. 13–14.

29. Lewis L. Strauss, Men and *Decisions* (Garden City, NY: Doubleday, 1962), pp. 270–74 (hereafter cited Strauss, *Men and Decisions*).

30. Drew Pearson, *Newark Star Ledger,* April 20, 1954; Joseph and Stewart Alsop, *We Accuse!* (New York: Simon & Schuster, 1954), p. 7; Stern, *The Oppenheimer Case,* pp. 128–30; Joint Committee on Atomic Energy, *Hearings on an Investigation into the United States Atomic Energy Project* (Washington: Government Printing Office, 1949), pp. 277–315.

31. Stern, *The Oppenheimer Case,* pp. 178, 190–91, 204–05; D. M. Ladd to Director, FBI, Jan. 23, 1952; Hoover to Sidney W. Souers, March 26, 1952; L. B. Nichols to Mr. Tolson, March 28, 1952; Hoover to Souers, May 19, 1952; W. A. Branigan to A. H. Belmont, June 10, 1952, all in FBI; Major, *The Oppenheimer Hearing,* pp. 263–64.

32. Dean Diary, Nov. 24, 26, Dec. 1, 4, 1952, AEC; *Atomic Shield,* p. 519. Cotter sent Borden two memos on the Weinberg case, Dec. 2 and Dec. 8, 1952, JCAE. For Borden's interest in Oppenheimer's Berkeley activities, see Borden to E. O. Lawrence, Dec. 23, 1952, Jan. 13, 1953, and Borden to File, Jan. 17, 1953, all in AEC.

33. Joint Committee Working Paper, Nov. 3, 1952, JCAE; Hoover to Dean with FBI report on Wheeler incident, March 11, 1953; Transcript of Dean's testimony before the Joint Committee, March 24, 1953; Cole to the Attorney General, undated but about April 20, 1953; Cole to Dean, April 27, 1953, all in AEC 634/5, May 5, 1953; Attorney General to Dean, March 11, 1953, in AEC 634, March 24, 1953; Dean to Attorney General, April 3, 1953, all in AEC.

34. Strauss Telephone Log, April 28, 1953; Strauss Appointment Calendar, April 30, 1953, both in AEC. On April 28, Strauss talked with Trevor Gardner, Ernest Lawrence, Kenneth D. Nichols, Kenneth S. Pitzer, Luis Alvarez, and Leslie R. Groves.

35. "The Hidden Struggle for the H-Bomb," *Fortune* 47 (May 1953): 109–10, 230.

36. The Air Force's effort to remove Oppenheimer's influence over national military

policy has been extensively described, first in the Oppenheimer Hearings and more recently in secondary sources. See U.S. Atomic Energy Commission, *In the Matter of J. Robert Oppenheimer: Transcript of Hearing Before Personnel Security Board* (Washington: Government Printing Office, 1954), pp. 681–85, 744–54; Stern, *The Oppenheimer Case*, pp. 178–98; Major, *The Oppenheimer Hearing*, pp. 238–63.

37. The four were Ellis M. Zacharias, Oppenheimer, Isidor I. Rabi, and Charles C. Lauritsen. The FBI later tried to run down the source of the ZORC story. SAC, Newark, to Director, FBI, April 3, 1954; Branigan to Belmont, June 3, 1954; Hoover to Waters, June 4, 18, 1954; FBI Investigative Report, June 21, 1954, all in FBI.

38. Nichols to Tolson, May 11, 1953, and Hoover to Tolson et al., May 19, 1953, both in FBI.

39. Robert A. Divine, *Eisenhower and the Cold War* (New York: Oxford University Press, 1981), pp. 106–8; *Public Papers, 1953, Eisenhower*, pp. 179–84; NSC 151, Armaments and American Policy, May 8, 1953, AEC.

40. Waters to File, May 14, 1953, AEC.

41. Joint Committee Working Paper, May 29, 1953, AEC.

42. Ladd to Hoover, May 25, 1953, FBI.

43. R. B. to Mr. Stevens, May 18, 1953, President's Personal File, DDE.

44. R. W. Kirkman, director of AEC security at New York, to Waters, May 26, 1953, with encl., Oppenheimer to Mr. Marin, May 19, 1953, AEC.

45. SNSC 146, May 27, 1953, DDE; Lay to Dean, May 29, 1953, AEC.

46. Belmont to Ladd, June 5, 1953, FBI.

47. Dean Diary, June 5, 1953; W. J. Williams Diary, June 5, 1953; AEC Contract AT (49–1)–805, Mod. 1, June 5, 1953, all in AEC; Strauss, *Men and Decisions*, p. 275.

48. Edmund A. Gullion of the State Department began working on drafts of the speech in June. His first, third, and fifth drafts, dated June 16, 22, and July 17, 1953, are in DDE. James H. Lambie of the White House staff handled day-to-day contacts with the Advertising Council. See Lambie to Adams, July 9, 1953; Lambie to Cutler, July 29, 1953, both in DDE; Jackson to T. S. Repplier, presi-

dent of the Advertising Council, June 4, 1953; Jackson to Cutler, June 24, 1953; Cutler to Dean, June 26, 1953; Cutler to Jackson, July 20, 1953, all in DDE.

49. See statement by Jules Halpern, chairman, Federation of American Scientists, *Bulletin of the Atomic Scientists* 8 (Dec. 1952): 299.

50. J. R. Oppenheimer, "Atomic Weapons and American Policy," *Foreign Affairs* 31 (July 1953): 525–35.

51. Joint Task Force 132, Film on Operation IVY, uncut version, AEC.

52. Dean Diary, May 21, 22, 25, 29, June 1, 2, 1953; Cutler to the Commissioners, May 29, 1953, all in AEC.

53. Dean, Press Conference, June 25, 1953, AEC; *Christian Science Monitor*, June 27, July 1, 1953; *Washington Post*, June 19, 1953, p. 4; *New York Times*, June 19, 1953; *Los Angeles Times*, July 3, 1953; *Wall Street Journal*, June 30, July 1, 1953; *Memphis Commercial Appeal*, Aug. 7, 1953.

54. *Public Papers, 1953, Eisenhower*, p. 476. The Commissioners were given a copy of the transcript in AEC 111/26, July 16, 1953. *Washington Post*, June 27, 1953, p. 8.

55. Smyth, Analysis of Secrecy, AEC 111/25, June 17, 1953, AEC.

56. CM 889, July 17, 1953; CM 897, July 28, 1953, both in AEC.

57. Wiley to Strauss, Aug. 7, 1953, in AEC 111/30, Aug. 17, 1953; Strauss to Wiley, Aug. 19, 1953, in AEC 111/32, Aug. 24, 1953, both in AEC.

58. CM 887, July 14, 1953; CM 892, July 22, 1953; CM 894, July 24, 1953; CM 896, July 27, 1953; CM 898, July 29, 1953; CM 902, Aug. 5, 1953; CM 904, Aug. 13, 1953, all in AEC.

59. Strauss Telephone Log, May 25, 29, June 23, July 16, 1953; Strauss Appointment Calendar, June 23, July 10, July 23, 1953, both in AEC; Murphy, "The Atom and the Balance of Power," *Fortune* 48 (August 1953): 97, 202.

60. Jackson to Strauss, Aug. 5, 1953; C. D. Jackson Logs, Aug. 4, 1953, both in CDJ.

61. The full text of Malenkov's speech appeared in the *New York Times*, Aug. 10, 1953, p. 6. AEC Press Release 494, Aug. 8, 1953, AEC.

62. Draft press announcements, Aug. 14, 1953, AEC.

63. Strauss, Memo Files, Aug. 19, 1953; AEC Press Release 495, Aug. 20, 1953, both in AEC. The headline appeared in the *New York Journal-American*, Aug. 20, 1953. Similar headlines appeared in the *Washington Post* and *Washington Times-Herald*, Aug. 20, 1953. The *New York Times* carried a page-one feature story but no headline. C. D. Jackson Logs, Aug. 14–16, 1953, CDJ. The text of the Soviet announcement appeared in the *Washington Evening Star* and other papers on Aug. 20, 1953.

64. Cole to Eisenhower, Aug. 21, 1953, AEC; *New York Times*, Aug. 21, 1953, p. 1. Articles containing excerpts from Cole's American Legion speech appeared in the *New York Herald-Tribune* and many other papers on Oct. 13, 1953. Strauss's concern, expressed in MLC 84, Aug. 27, 1953, AEC, was confirmed many years later by Andrei Sakharov in an article quoted by Herbert F. York, *Oppenheimer, Teller, and the Superbomb* (New York: Norton, 1975), pp. 101–3. For Eisenhower's statement, see *Public Papers, 1953, Eisenhower*, p. 617.

65. American analyses of *Joe 4* appear in Carson Mark to John von Neumann, Sept. 4, 1953; Strauss to Cole, Oct. 27, 1953; Bethe, Summary of Preliminary Findings, Dec. 26, 1953; von Neumann to Cole, Nov. 23, 1953; Bethe to Strauss, Dec. 30, 1953, all in AEC. On the Commissioners' lack of information, see Zuckert to Strauss, Sept. 22, 1953, AEC.

66. Eisenhower to Jackson, Aug. 24, 1953; Jackson to R. G. Arneson, Sept. 2, 1953; John A. DeChant to Jackson, Sept. 3, 1953, all in DDE. See also Sherman Adams, *Firsthand Report: The Story of the Eisenhower Administration* (New York: Harper, 1961), pp. 109–10; Robert J. Donovan, *Eisenhower: The Inside Story* (New York: Harper, 1956), pp. 184–85 (hereafter cited Donovan, *Eisenhower*).

67. Cutler to Jackson, Sept. 3, 1953; Safety of the Republic, Sept. 9, 1953, both in DDE. A transcript of the June 3, 1953, television report is in *Public Papers, 1953, Eisenhower*, pp. 363–76.

68. Abbott Washburn to Jackson, Sept. 14, 1953, DDE.

69. Lambie to Arneson et al., Sept. 28, 1953, DDE; James Reston in the *New York Times*, Sept. 23, 1953, presented a detailed and essentially accurate story of *Candor*. Arthur Krock in the *New York Times*, Oct. 8, 1953; Strauss, Remarks for National Security Industrial Association, New York City, Sept. 30, 1953; Strauss to the Commissioners, Oct. 6, 1953, both in AEC; *New York Times*, Review of the Week, Oct. 11, 1953; *Newsweek*, Sept. 28, 1953, p. 28; Wilson, Excerpts from Press Conference, Sept. 29, 1953, p. 2, AEC.

70. SNSC 165, Oct. 7, 1953, DDE; Strauss to Eisenhower, Oct. 7, 1953; Lay to NSC, Oct. 8, 1953, both in AEC.

71. Hickenlooper's statement was reported in the *Baltimore Sun*, Oct. 5, 1953; President's News Conference, Oct. 8, 1953, in *Public Papers, 1953, Eisenhower*, pp. 644–48.

72. No copy of the Sept. 10 memo from Cutler to Jackson and Strauss was found in DDE, CDJ, or AEC. The memorandum is quoted in Strauss, *Men and Decisions*, p. 357, and Donovan, *Eisenhower*, pp. 185–86.

73. Stern, *The Oppenheimer Case*, pp. 204–5.

74. Hoover to Tolson and Ladd, June 24, 1953, FBI.

75. Murray Diary Memo, June 9, Aug. 18, 1953, TEM; Waters to Strauss, May 12, 1954; W. J. Williams Diary, Aug. 31, 1953, both in AEC; Ladd to Belmont, Aug. 28, 1953, FBI.

76. Belmont to Ladd, Sept. 10, 1953; Director, FBI, to SAC, Field, Sept. 14, 1953, both in FBI.

77. John Luter, Oral History Interview with Nichols, Oct. 12, 1967, DDE; Richard G. Hewlett and Oscar E. Anderson, Jr., *The New World, 1939–1946*, Vol. 1 of *A History of the U.S. Atomic Energy Commission* (University Park: Pennsylvania State University Press, 1962), pp. 649–50, 653.

78. Murray Diary Memo, Sept. 2, 1953, TEM.

79. CM 1007, June 15, 1954, AEC.

80. Strauss, *Men and Decisions*, pp. 357–58. For the development of Atoms for Peace from the President's perspective, see Stephen E. Ambrose, *Eisenhower, the President* (New York: Simon & Schuster, 1984), pp. 131–53.

81. Donovan, *Eisenhower*, pp. 186–87, refers to several documents that have not been found in DDE, CDJ, or AEC. The first draft of the Strauss memorandum,

601

dated Oct. 26, 1953, is in DDE; the second draft with a letter to Jackson, Nov. 6, 1953, is in CDJ.

82. Dulles to Cutler, Oct. 13, 1953, with State Department draft, "For Second Half of Atomic Speech"; Summary of Discussion of State Draft, Oct. 19, 1953, both in CDJ.

83. Copies of the five drafts, dated Nov. 3, 5, 22, 28, and Dec. 1, 1953, are in DDE. See also Jackson to Emmit Hughes, Nov. 6, 1953; Jackson to Strauss, Nov. 28, 1953, both in DDE, and C. D. Jackson Logs, Nov. 30, Dec. 3, 1953, CDJ.

84. Borden to Nichols, Nov. 7, 1953; Borden to Hoover, Nov. 7, 1953, both in FBI.

85. Belmont to Ladd, Nov. 19, 1953, FBI.

86. Murray Diary Memo, Nov. 23, 1953, TEM.

87. C. D. Jackson Logs, Nov. 27, 1953, CDJ.

88. Ibid., Dec. 2, 1953, CDJ.

89. Hoover to Tolson, Ladd, and Nichols, 9:22 a.m., Dec. 2, 1953, FBI.

90. Dwight D. Eisenhower, *Mandate for Change, 1953–1956* (New York: Doubleday, 1963), pp. 310–11 (hereafter cited Eisenhower, *Mandate for Change*).

91. Strauss incorrectly records his late afternoon visit to the White House as being on Dec. 3, not Dec. 2. The Dec. 3 date would suggest that the decision had been made before Strauss arrived. In fact, the evidence indicates that Eisenhower discussed his intentions with Strauss and others on Dec. 2 and made the decision the same day. Strauss, *Men and Decisions*, p. 267; Eisenhower, *Mandate for Change*, p. 311; Stern, *The Oppenheimer Case*, p. 220; Strauss Appointment Calendar, Dec. 2, 3, 1953; W. H. Haggard to R. M. Anders, Nov. 12, 1974, with encl., National Oceanic and Atmospheric Admin., Local Climatological Data, Washington, D.C., Dec. 2, 3, 1953, both in AEC; Anne C. Whitman, Memo for the Secretary of State, Dec. 3, 1953, Brownell Folder, DDE; Hoover to Tolson, Ladd, Nichols, and Belmont, Dec. 4, 1953, FBI.

92. Hoover to Tolson, Ladd, and Belmont, 4:52 p.m., Dec. 3, 1953; Hoover to Tolson, Ladd, and Nichols, 5:58 p.m., Dec. 3, 1953, both in FBI. Borden was interviewed in Pittsburgh on the evening of Dec. 3. In a telex to FBI headquarters early on the morning of Dec. 4, the spe-

cial agent reported that he found Borden "quite intelligent, extremely verbose and inclined toward generalities rather than specifics." Hallford to Inspector Carl E. Hennrich, Dec. 4, 1953, FBI.

93. Hoover to Tolson, Ladd, and Nichols, 4:26 p.m., Dec. 3, 1953; Hoover to Tolson, Ladd, Belmont, and Nichols, Dec. 14, 1954, both in FBI; Bryan LaPlante, Diary Memo, Dec. 3, 1953; Strauss to General Manager, Dec. 3, 1953, both in AEC.

94. Luter, Nichols Inverview, Oct. 12, 1967, DDE.

95. Eisenhower, *Mandate for Change*, pp. 310–11; C. D. Jackson Logs, Nov. 27–Dec. 2, 1953, CDJ; Major, *The Oppenheimer Hearing*, pp. 267–69.

96. C. D. Jackson Logs, Dec. 3, 1953, CDJ.

97. Dulles, Memorandum of Conversation with Churchill, Dec. 5, 1953, DDE; Donovan, *Eisenhower*, pp. 188–89; Strauss, *Men and Decisions*, pp. 358–59; J. M. Dunford to Murray, Dec. 18, 1953, TEM.

98. Bermuda Draft #3, Dec. 7, 1953, edited on the airplane, is in CDJ. See also first version of stenciled copy, Dec. 8, 1953, with handwritten notes by the President, in CDJ.

99. The final version of the speech appears in *Public Papers, 1953, Eisenhower*, pp. 813–22.

100. Ibid., p. 820. On reactions to the speech, see Henry Cabot Lodge to Jackson, Dec. 10, 1953, enclosing Summary of Reactions to President Eisenhower's Speech, Dec. 9, 1953, DDE.

## CHAPTER FOUR

1. Richard G. Hewlett and Francis Duncan, *Atomic Shield, 1947–1952*, Vol. II of *A History of the U.S. Atomic Energy Commission* (University Park: Pennsylvania State University Press, 1969), pp. 332–34 (hereafter cited *Atomic Shield*); Walter Gellhorn, *Security, Loyalty, and Science* (Ithaca, NY: Cornell University Press, 1950); Eleanor Bontecou, *The Federal Loyalty-Security Program* (Ithaca, NY: Cornell University Press, 1953); New York Bar Association, *The Federal Loyalty-Security Program* (New York: Dodd, Mead, 1956).

2. Henry D. Smyth, Answers to Questions in Stern Letter, Aug. 7, 1967; Mary Smyth Diary, Dec. 2–26, 1953, both in HDS.

3. Murray to Strauss, Dec. 10, 1953, TEM; page 2 was not provided.

4. Murray to Strauss, Dec. 7, 1953, AEC.

5. Murray Diary Memo, Dec. 8, 9, 1953; TEM.

6. Ibid., Dec. 10, 1953, TEM.

7. LaPlante, Implementation of the President's Directive, entry for Dec. 9, 1953; Strauss Appointment Calendar, Dec. 9–10, 1953, all in AEC.

8. Murray Diary Memo, Dec. 10, 1953, TEM.

9. AEC Press Release 470, Feb 18, 1953, AEC; Belmont to Ladd, Dec. 10, 12, 1953, FBI.

10. Philip M. Stern, *The Oppenheimer Case: Security on Trial* (New York: Harper & Row, 1969), pp. 225–26 (hereafter cited Stern, *The Oppenheimer Case*).

11. Hoover to Strauss, Nov. 27, 1953, FBI.

12. Stern, *The Oppenheimer Case*, p. 226.

13. Ibid., pp. 227–28; John Major, *The Oppenheimer Hearing* (London: B. T. Batsford, 1971), pp. 270–71 (hereafter cited Major, *The Oppenheimer Hearing*).

14. Hoover to Strauss, Dec. 18, 1953; Belmont to Ladd, Dec. 17, 18, 21, 1953, all in FBI.

15. Belmont to Ladd, Dec. 18, 1953, FBI.

16. Hoover to Tolson et al., Dec. 14, 15, 1953, FBI; Murray Diary Memo on Executive Session, Dec. 15, 1953, TEM.

17. Murray Diary Memo, Dec. 15, 16, 1953, TEM.

18. Nichols, Meeting with Oppenheimer, Dec. 21, 1953, AEC; Belmont to Ladd, Dec. 21, 1953, FBI. Nichols's memorandum, on which this account is based, does not square in all respects with the version presented in Stern, *The Oppenheimer Case*, pp. 229–31. Executive Order 10450, Security Requirements for Government Employment, April 27, 1953; Athan Theoharis, *Spying on Americans: Political Surveillance from Hoover to the Huston Plan* (Philadelphia: Temple University Press, 1978), pp. 210–18.

19. Oppenheimer claimed that Strauss first raised the possibility of resignation in U.S. Atomic Energy Commission, *In the Matter of J. Robert Oppenheimer: Transcript of Hearings Before Personnel Security Board* (Washington: Government Printing Office, 1954), p. 22 (hereafter cited *Hearings*). Nichols stated in his Dec. 21 memorandum that it was Oppenheimer. The disagreement seems trivial because Strauss had promised the Commissioners that he would raise the question in any event.

20. Nichols, Meeting with Oppenheimer, Dec. 21, 1953; CM 999, June 7, 1954, both in AEC; Lewis L. Strauss, *Men and Decisions* (Garden City, NY: Doubleday, 1962), pp. 276–78.

21. Strauss told Bates that he thought Oppenheimer really wanted to drop the matter quietly but was persuaded by his attorneys, Volpe and Marks, to ask for a hearing. Strauss suspected that their motive was lucrative legal fees. Belmont to Ladd, Dec. 23, 1953, FBI.

22. C. C. Hennrich to Belmont, Dec. 15, 1953; Ladd to Hoover, Dec. 21, 1953; Belmont to Ladd, Dec. 24, 1953; SAC, Newark, to Hoover, Jan. 5, 1954, all in FBI.

23. Belmont to Ladd, Jan. 5, 26, 28, 1954, all in FBI.

24. FBI, Newark, to Director, FBI, Jan. 5, 1954; Hoover to Strauss, Jan. 26, Feb. 1, 1954, all in FBI; Stern, *The Oppenheimer Case*, p. 241. Allen B. Ecker also joined Oppenheimer's legal staff before the hearings opened.

25. Garrison to Nichols, Jan. 20, 1954; Rolander to Nichols, Jan. 21, 1954; Rolander to File, Jan. 26, 1954, all in AEC.

26. Mitchell to File, Feb. 15, 1954; Nichols to Garrison, Feb. 12, 1954, both in AEC.

27. Mitchell to File, Jan. 19, 1954; Nichols, Memo for Record, Jan. 19, 1954; Garrison to Nichols, Jan. 20, 1954, all in AEC.

28. Mitchell to File, March 15, 1954, AEC.

29. Mitchell to Nichols, Jan. 12, 1954, AEC.

30. Mitchell to Morgan, March 9, 1954, AEC; Belmont to Ladd, Feb. 26, 1954, FBI.

31. Belmont to Ladd, Jan. 15, 1954; Hoover to Tolson et al., Feb. 1, 5, 1954, all in FBI; Joseph and Stewart Alsop, *We Accuse!* (New York: Simon & Schuster, 1954), p. 7. The Alsops neglected to mention that Robb had also served as a court-appointed attorney for Communist party leader Earl Browder.

32. It is interesting to note that when Drew Pearson charged that Strauss was primar-

603

604

ily responsible for instigating the investigation and hearings against Oppenheimer, he omitted any reference to Robb. Most likely Pearson had never heard of Robb either or, if he had, did not regard his appointment as significant. Drew Pearson, *Washington Post* and *Times-Herald*, April 20, 1954.

33. CM 962, Feb. 17, 1954, AEC.
34. A list of FBI reports sent to the Commission is attached to Virginia H. Walker to Harry S. Traynor, March 7, 1960, AEC. Most of these reports are available in FBI.
35. Worried about the propriety of providing Robb with such information, Strauss wrote Rolander: "I understand that you contemplate reproducing communications which I have received from the Federal Bureau of Investigation. This must not be done without the knowledge and consent of the Bureau, and I shall assume that unless I hear to the contrary, you have obtained this permission." Strauss to Rolander, March 9, 1954, AEC. No memorandum to the contrary was found in the files. Results of the telephone taps were reported daily to Washington. For example, see SAC, Newark to Director, FBI, February 24, March 1, March 25, 1954, all in FBI. For examples of surveillances while Oppenheimer was traveling, see FBI report on Rochester trip, Feb. 23, 1954; FBI Wash Field to Director, FBI, March 3, 1954; FBI Boston to Director, FBI, March 8, 1954, all in FBI.
36. During February and March 1954 Hoover sent Strauss up to three daily reports on the Oppenheimer case; copies are in FBI. See especially Hoover to Strauss, Feb. 18, March 3, 11, 16, 19, 25, 1954, all in FBI.
37. Rolander to File, Feb. 16, 1954; Rolander to Bates, Feb. 17, 18, 19, 1954, all in AEC; Belmont to Ladd, Feb. 2, 1954; Belmont to L. V. Boardman, March 29, 1954; Branigan to Belmont, March 31, 1954, all in FBI.
38. Rolander to File, Feb. 16, 1954; Rolander to Bates, March 1, 1954, both in AEC; Hoover to Strauss, Jan. 22, April 19, 1954, both in FBI.
39. Belmont to Boardman, April 6, 1954, *FBI*; Rolander-Robb-Borden interview, Feb. 20, 1954, AEC. Borden also supplied a list to the FBI bringing the total to about thirty-eight.
40. Rolander to File, Feb. 25, March 15, 22,

1954, all in AEC; *Hearings*, pp. 178–79, 266–70.
41. Rolander to File, March 15, 18, 1954, AEC.
42. Murray Diary Memo, Jan. 29, 1954, TEM.
43. E. R. Trapnell to Strauss, Oct. 26, 1953, AEC.
44. Belmont to Boardman, April 11, 1954, FBI; Major, *The Oppenheimer Hearing*, p. 9.
45. Stern, *The Oppenheimer Case*, pp. 243–44.
46. Hagerty Diaries, April 7–11, 1954, DDE.
47. Oral history interview with Gordon Gray by Robert Hopper, Washington, D.C., March 7, 1967, DDE.
48. Mitchell to File, April 5, 1954; Rolander to File, April 14, 1954; Strauss to Rolander, April 26, 1954, all in AEC. See also *Hearings*, pp. 527–28. Of the scientists mentioned by Gardner, Strauss noted: "In addition to being witnesses, [they] are also active workers on Oppenheimer's team. I think in their records in the future we can't overlook this." Telephone conversation between Strauss and Mitchell, May 10, 1954, *AEC*; Belmont to Boardman, May 10, 1954, FBI.
49. Rolander to File, April 12, 1954, AEC; Belmont to Boardman, April 24, 1954, FBI.
50. *Hearings*, pp. 565, 53–55; Stern, *The Oppenheimer Case*, pp. 263–64.
51. The Gray board proceedings, published by the Atomic Energy Commission, have been exhaustively analyzed by several scholars, including: Stern, *The Oppenheimer Case*; Major, *The Oppenheimer Hearings*; Charles P. Curtis, *The Oppenheimer Case: The Trial of a Security System* (New York: Simon & Schuster, 1955); Joseph and Stewart Alsop, *We Accuse!* (New York: Simon & Schuster, 1954); Cushing Strout, "The Oppenheimer Case: Melodrama, Tragedy, and Irony," *Virginia Quarterly Review* 40 (Spring 1964): 268–80. This account does not recapitulate the Gray board proceedings in detail.
52. Gray to Mitchell, May 10, 1954, AEC.
53. Dean Diary, Nov. 24, 1952, AEC; *Hearings*, pp. 16–17, 216, 306, 335–36; Branigan to Belmont, May 13, 1954, FBI.
54. *Atomic Shield*, pp. 391–92; U.S. Atomic Energy Commission, *In the Matter of*

J. *Robert Oppenheimer: Texts of Principal Documents and Letters of Personnel Security Board, General Manager, Commissioners* (Washington: Government Printing Office, 1954), p. 13 (hereafter cited *Principal Documents*); *Hearings*, p. 19.

55. *Hearings*, pp. 679–97, 742–70.
56. Garrison Norton to Finletter, July 1, 1952, AEC. See also *Hearings*, pp. 771–73.
57. Hoover to Waters, April 16, May 19, 1952, AEC. The scientist did not repeat his doubts about Oppenheimer's loyalty to the Gray board. *Hearings*, pp. 697–709.
58. Hoover to Waters, May 19, 1952, FBI; *Hearings*, pp. 328–29.
59. Rolander to File, March 15, 1954, AEC; italics added.
60. *Hearings*, p. 710.
61. *Ibid.*, p. 726; italics added.
62. FBI Field Report, George C. Eltenton, June 28, 1946, FBI.
63. Ibid.; FBI Field Report, Eltenton, July 3, 1946, FBI.
64. *Hearings*, pp. 14, 131, 137–39, 146–49, 285–300.
65. Hoover to Strauss, Dec. 18, 1953, FBI; LaPlante, Memo for File, Dec. 17, 1953, AEC; *Hearings*, pp. 167–68.
66. FBI Field Report, Eltenton, June 28, 1946, July 3, 1946, both in FBI.
67. FBI Field Report, Eltenton, Sept. 18, 1946, FBI.
68. *Hearings*, pp. 137–38, 145–46, 887–88.
69. Ibid., p. 263.
70. Ibid., p. 167.
71. Hooper interview with Gray, DDE; Summary of Oppenheimer Hearing, May 29, 1954; Director, FBI to SAC, San Francisco, May 28, 1954; Belmont to Boardman, June 2, 1954, all in FBI.
72. Gray to Nichols, May 27, 1954, in AEC 735, May 28, 1954, AEC.
73. Hooper interview with Gray, DDE.
74. Stern, *The Oppenheimer Case*, pp. 379–82; Major, *The Oppenheimer Hearing*, p. 187; Minority Report of Dr. Ward V. Evans, in AEC 735, May 28, 1954, pp. 34–36, AEC.
75. Mitchell to Nichols, May 20, 1954, AEC. The security clearance procedures in effect at that time had been adopted in September 1950. *Code of Federal Regulations*, Title 10–Atomic Energy, Part 4, Security Clearance Procedures.
76. CM 987, May 18, 1954, AEC.

77. Garrison to Nichols, June 1, 9, 1954; Nichols to Garrison, June 3, 24, 1954; CM 997, June 3, 1954; CM 999, June 7, 1954; CM 1001, June 9, 1954; Rolander to LaPlante, May 3, 1954, all in AEC.
78. Transcript, CM 1007, June 15, 1954, p. 61, AEC. Nichols's recommendation was published in *Principal Documents*, pp. 43–48.
79. Transcript, CM 1008, June 16, 1954, pp. 72–74, 78, AEC.
80. Smyth to the Commissioners, June 21, 1954, AEC.
81. Transcript, CM 1007, June 15, 1954, pp. 66–67, AEC.
82. FBI Field Report, Oppenheimer, Dec. 31, 1953, FBI.
83. Transcript, CM 1008, June 16, 1954, AEC.
84. Transcript, CM 1008, part 2, June 16, 1954, pp. 54–55, AEC. Kenneth E. Fields was the AEC director of military application.
85. Hagerty Diary, June 1, 1954, DDE. For published excerpts from the Hagerty Diary, see Robert H. Ferrell, ed., *The Diary of James C. Hagerty: Eisenhower in Mid-Course, 1954–1955* (Bloomington: Indiana University Press, 1983).
86. Hagerty Diary, May 29, 1954, DDE.
87. Ibid., June 1, 10, 1954, DDE; Belmont to Boardman, June 4, 1954, FBI.
88. Transcript of telephone conversation between Reston and Oppenheimer, June 11, 1954, JRO.
89. Gray to Rolander, June 9, 1954, AEC.
90. CM 1003, June 12, 1954; CM 1004, June 14, 1954; CM 1005, June 14, 1954; CM 1006, June 15, 1954; CM 1007, June 15, 1954; Smyth, Memo to the Commission, June 14, 1954, all in AEC; SAC, Boston, to Director, FBI, June 14, 1954, FBI.
91. Hagerty Diary, June 27, 1954, DDE.
92. CM 1011, June 28, 1954, AEC. All five opinions were published in *Principal Documents*. They were also published in the *New York Times*, June 30, 1954, p. 12.
93. *Hearings*, pp. 54, 365.
94. Ralph E. Lapp, "Atomic Candor," *Bulletin of the Atomic Scientists* 10 (Oct. 1954): 336.
95. Hoover to Strauss, June 18, 1954, FBI; Nichols to R. W. Scott McLeod, June 23, 1954; Warren Olney III to Mitchell, June 25, 1954; Hoover to Strauss, July 20, 1954, all in AEC; Hoover to Waters,

605

Aug. 11, 26, 27, 31, 1954, all in FBI; Rolander to Nichols, Aug. 10, 26 (two memoranda), 30, 1954, all in AEC; Hoover to Tolson et al., June 29, 1954; FBI Summary, July 2, 5, 14, 1954; Deputy Director, Plans, CIA, to Director, FBI, July 9, 1954; R. R. Roach to Belmont, July 9, 1954; CIA Memo I-2, Aug. 23, 1954; SAC, Newark, to Director, FBI, August 24, 1954; Belmont to Boardman, Aug. 24, 1954, all in FBI.

96. The letters are on file in AEC.

97. "Scientists Affirm Faith in Oppenheimer," *Bulletin of the Atomic Scientists* 10 (May 1954): 188–91; Bethe to Strauss, June 10, 1954; Merle Burgy et al. to Chairman and Commissioners, June 17, 1954; William Rubinson to L. J. Haworth, May 12, 1954; William Nelis to Strauss, June 25, 1954; Fred L. Ribe to Eisenhower, June 15, 1954; Authur H. Snell et al. to the Commissioners, Oct. 11, 1954; Robert Christy et al. to Strauss, June 21, 1954; Sidney Drell to Eisenhower, May 27, 1954; CM 1012, June 30, 1954, all in AEC.

98. *Santa Fe New Mexican*, July 18, 1954.

99. GAC 41, July 15, 1954, AEC.

## CHAPTER FIVE

1. James R. Newman and Byron S. Miller, *The Control of Atomic Energy: A Study of Its Social, Economic, and Political Implications* (New York: McGraw-Hill, 1948), p. 19.

2. Arnold Kramish and Eugene M. Zuckert, *Atomic Energy for Your Business: Today's Key to Tomorrow's Profits* (New York: David McKay, 1956), p. 130.

3. See Chap. 2, Nuclear Power and Private Enterprise.

4. General Counsel, Draft Legislation to Encourage Development of Nuclear Power, AEC 615/8, May 11, 1953, AEC. For the final version of the bill, see AEC 615/9, May 21, 1953, AEC.

5. Joint Committee on Atomic Energy, Transcript of Hearing on Nuclear Power Policy, May 26, 1953; Weeks to Dodge, June 23, 1953, in AEC 615/14, June 26, 1953; Excerpts from Executive Agency Comments on Proposed Legislation, AEC 615/11, June 15, 1953, all in AEC.

6. For background and evolution of the AEC position, see Patent Policy in Connection with Industrial Development of Atomic Power, AEC 615/10, June 1, 1953, AEC.

7. CM 872, June 3, 1953; CM 873, June 8, 1953, both in AEC.

8. CM 882, June 26, 1953, AEC.

9. CM 890, July 20, 1953, AEC.

10. Decision Summary on Topnotch II, Sept. 27, 1953; General Counsel, Proposed Legislation to Encourage Development of Peacetime Uses of Atomic Energy, AEC 615/22, Oct. 14, 1953; CM 930, Oct. 21, 1953, all in AEC.

11. The housekeeping amendments included changes in AEC organization and additional provisions for criminal prosecution in matters relating to security. Legislative Proposals by AEC, AEC 495/5, Feb. 24, 1953, AEC.

12. General Counsel, AEC Legislative Program for 1954, AEC 495/9, Sept. 28, 1953; CM 927, Oct. 14, 1953, both in AEC.

13. Richard G. Hewlett and Francis Duncan, *Atomic Shield, 1947–1952*, Vol. II of *A History of the U.S. Atomic Energy Commission* (University Park: Pennsylvania State University Press, 1969), pp. 283–314.

14. Strauss to Eisenhower, Robert LeBaron, and Dodge, separate letters with attachments, all dated Nov. 18, 1953, in AEC 495/11, Nov. 20, 1953, AEC.

15. General Counsel, Clearance of Atomic Power Legislation for White House, AEC 615/29, Dec. 7, 1953; General Counsel, Atomic Power Legislation, AEC 615/30, Dec. 9, 1953; CM 945, Dec. 10, 1953, all in AEC.

16. Draft Message on Amendments to the Atomic Energy Act, Feb. 3, 1954, AEC. Eisenhower's message appears in *Public Papers of the Presidents of the United States, 1954: Dwight D. Eisenhower* (Washington: Government Printing Office, 1960), pp. 260–69 (hereafter cited *Public Papers, 1954, Eisenhower*). Nuclear references in the State of the Union and budget messages are in ibid., pp. 10, 128–30.

17. The portions used almost verbatim are Sections 308(b) and 312(a) of the Communications Act of 1934, P.L.416, 73 Cong., 2 sess.

18. The preceding paragraphs are based in part on Cole's later description of these events, *Congressional Record*, 83 Cong., 2 sess., 1954, p. 11021 (hereafter cited *CR*); Harold P. Green and Alan Rosen-

thal, *Government of the Atom* (New York: Atherton Press, Prentice Hall, 1963), pp. 124–26; Corbin Allardice and Edward R. Trapnell, *The Atomic Energy Commission* (New York: Praeger, 1974), pp. x, 44–45.

19. The bill was published as "A Proposed Act to Amend the Atomic Energy Act of 1946," Joint Committee on Atomic Energy, Joint Committee Print, 83 Cong., 2 sess. (Washington: Government Printing Office, 1954). The bill was introduced in the House as H.R.8862 and in the Senate as S.3323 on April 15 and 19, 1954. All three documents were later published in AEC, *Legislative History of the Atomic Energy Act of 1954* (Washington: Government Printing Office, 1955), pp. 53–255 (hereafter cited *Legislative History*).

20. Joint Committee on Atomic Energy, Transcript of Hearing, May 3, 1954, pp. 14–33, 48–51, 58–62, AEC.

21. Mitchell to Strauss, Jan. 14, 1954; Strauss to Brownell, Jan. 18, 1954; Rogers to Strauss, Jan 29, 1954; Murray to Mitchell, April 30, 1954; Mitchell to File, May 3, 1954; Mitchell to Murray, May 2, 5, 1954, all in AEC.

22. Joint Committee on Atomic Energy, Transcript of Hearing, May 3, 1954, pp. 84–98, AEC.

23. Ibid., pp. 105–110B.

24. Ibid., pp. 111–75.

25. Ibid., May 4, 1954, pp. 315–16, 356–73.

26. Ibid., pp. 316, 375–78.

27. Joint Committee on Atomic Energy, *Hearings on S.3323 and H.R.8862, To Amend the Atomic Energy Act of 1946*, (Part I) May 10–19, 1954, Joint Committee Print, 83 Cong., 2 sess. (Washington: Government Printing Office, 1954), pp. 25–46, 58–60, 225–26, 326–29, 375–78, 421–22, 524–25, 537 (hereafter cited *Joint Committee Hearings*).

28. Ibid., pp. 61, 92, 170–74, 176–78, 218–21, 271–74, 306–21, 334–37, 401, 441, 467.

29. Joint Committee on Atomic Energy, Transcript of Hearing on Presentation of Casper Ooms, May 5, 1954, pp. 17–18, AEC.

30. *Joint Committee Hearings* (Part II), June 2–18, 1954, pp. 872–76.

31. *Public Papers of the Presidents of the United States, 1953: Dwight D. Eisenhower* (Washington: Government Printing Office, 1960), pp. 395–97, 433–34.

32. Aaron Wildavsky, *Dixon-Yates: A Study in Power Politics* (New Haven: Yale University Press, 1962), pp. 31–33 (hereafter cited Wildavsky, *Dixon-Yates*). This section relies heavily on Wildavsky's analysis and on the published documents cited in his footnotes, which should be consulted for a detailed study of the subject. The following notes contain only representative citations of the published documents to give the reader a sense of the documentation.

33. Wildavsky, *Dixon-Yates*, pp. 34–38; BOB Chronology, reproduced in Joint Committee on Atomic Energy, *Hearings on Exercise of Statutory Requirements Under Section 164, Atomic Energy Act of 1954*, November 4–13, 1954 (Washington: Government Printing Office, 1954), pp. 814–15 (hereafter cited *Section 164 Hearings*); *Public Papers, 1954, Eisenhower*, p. 169.

34. Wildavsky, *Dixon-Yates*, pp. 41–49; AEC Chronology, reproduced in *Section 164 Hearings*, pp. 922–25. See p. 280 for Murray's testimony. On the Commission's discussion of Strauss's role, see Notes on Executive Session, Jan. 19, 1954, AEC.

35. In summer 1953 Strauss had opposed an industrial reactor development contract with TVA on the grounds that it was inconsistent with Administration policy. CM 903, Aug. 6, 1953, and CM 906, Aug. 20, 1953, both in AEC.

36. Wildavsky, *Dixon-Yates*, pp. 50–64. The original Dixon-Yates proposal, dated Feb. 25, 1954, and the Commission's analysis, Strauss to Dodge, March 3, 1954, are in AEC 385/26, March 5, 1954, AEC. The documents also appear in *Section 164 Hearings*, pp. 931–35. See also Notes on Executive Session, March 2, 1954, and Snapp to Files, March 17, 1954, both in AEC.

37. Wildavsky, *Dixon-Yates*, pp. 65–78; CM 976, April 14, 1954; Strauss to Dodge, April 15, 1954, both in AEC. The letter is also in *Section 164 Hearings*, pp. 940–43.

38. Smyth and Zuckert to Hughes, April 16, 1954, AEC. Also appears in *Section 164 Hearings*, pp. 943–44.

39. Wildavsky, *Dixon-Yates*, pp. 85–86; *CR*, pp. 5370–72; Nichols to Leverett Saltonstall, April 17, 1954, in *Section 164 Hearings*, p. 827.

40. *Joint Committee Hearings* (Part II), June

607

2-18, 1954, pp. 760-61, 871-73, 945-65, 1004-7, 1034-37, 1041-42.
41. Ibid., pp. 945-1122.
42. The bill, introduced as H.R.9757 and S.3690, appears in *Legislative History*, pp. 541-748. The Joint Committee report on the bill appeared as Senate Report 1699 and H.R. Report 2181, 83 Cong., 2 sess. The reports are reproduced in *Legislative History*, pp. 749-886, 997-1134. For reasons of brevity we have not followed revisions of the April draft through the May 21, 1954, committee print of H.R.8862 to H.R.9757. The May 21 print appears in *Legislative History*, pp. 257-350. Bricker later explained the background of his suggested changes in *CR*, pp. 10088-93.
43. Holifield expressed his views on several occasions. The most complete exposition of his argument is in *CR*, pp. 10691-93. On Strauss's position, see Chap. 8, Worldwide Reactions and Atoms for Peace: With or Without the Russians.
44. Revised Section 11(c) in the Commission's bill was used by the Joint Committee. The Commission draft appears in AEC 495/14, April 8, 1954, AEC.
45. Max Isenbergh to W. B. Holton, May 10, 1954; Isenbergh to Mitchell, May 18, 1954; Isenbergh to H. L. Price, May 25, 1954; R. A. Anderson to Ooms, May 26, 1954; General Counsel, Proposed Patent Provisions As Suggested by Casper Ooms, AEC 495/26, June 9, 1954; CM 1001, June 9, 1954, all in AEC.
46. *New York Times*, June 23, 1954, p. 12; June 25, 1954, p. 6; July 9, 1954, p. 1; Gerard C. Smith, Note re: Discussion with Adm. Strauss, May 20, 1954, DOS; *CR*, pp. 8060-61, 11030-31, 11165-72.
47. *CR*, pp. 9247, 9251-58, 9556-57, 9924-25, 9928-48.
48. Wildavsky, *Dixon-Yates*, pp. 101-3.
49. *CR*, pp. 10017-18, 10109-12, 10158-202, 10210-21; *New York Times*, July 15, 1954, p. 1; July 17, 1954, p. 1.
50. *CR*, pp. 10231-37, 10252-62, 10278-94, 10584-96, 10615-17, 10715-66; *New York Times*, July 19, 20, 21, 1954, all front-page stories.
51. Eleven Democrats joined the Republicans in voting for the Ferguson amendment. Only two Republicans, Cooper of

Kentucky and Langer of North Dakota, voted against the amendment. *CR*, pp. 10770-72, 10783-88; *New York Times*, July 22, 1954, p. 1.
52. *CR*, pp. 10864-93, 10898-926, 10939-40, 10953-61, 11093-97; *Time*, Aug. 2, 1954, pp. 8-9; *Newsweek*, Aug. 2, 1954, pp. 16-17; *New York Times*, July 24, 1954, p. 1.
53. *CR*, pp. 11020-90, 11358-77, 11389-90; *New York Times*, July 24, 1954, p. 1.
54. *CR*, pp. 11352-53; Wildavsky, *Dixon-Yates*, pp. 114-15; *New York Times*, July 25, 26, 1954, p. 1.
55. *CR*, pp. 11488-97, 11532-38, 11554-55, 11565-66, 11573-74, 11703-13, 11739-52, 11754; *New York Times*, July 27, 28, 1954, p. 1.
56. *CR*, pp. 11771, 11872; Conference Report (H.R. Report 2639, 83 Cong., 2 sess.), Aug. 6, 1954, printed in *CR*, pp. 13056-71.
57. *CR*, pp. 13071-78, 13638-64.
58. *CR*, pp. 13982-85, 14043-48. The second Conference Report (H.R. Report 2666) was printed in *CR*, pp. 13873-88. Atomic Energy Act of 1954, P.L.703, 83 Cong., 68 *Stat.* 919.

## CHAPTER SIX

1. *Newsweek*, March 30, 1953, p. 31. Other reporters noted the same attitude among the troops: Robert Bennyhoff in *Las Vegas Review-Journal*, March 17, 1953, and Robert E. Baskin in *Dallas News*, March 22, 1953.
2. For earlier continental tests, see Richard G. Hewlett and Francis Duncan, *Atomic Shield, 1947-1952*, Vol. II of *A History of the U.S. Atomic Energy Commission* (University Park: Pennsylvania State University Press, 1969), pp. 535, 563-64, 571 (hereafter cited *Atomic Shield*).
3. Fields, Special Atomic Detonations for Weapons Effects and Training, AEC 487/2, Nov. 6, 1951; CM 624, Nov. 7, 1951; Fields to Dean, Jan. 3, 1952, with attachments, all in AEC.
4. The best reports on the diagnostic tests are classified. See Operation *Upshot-Knothole*, Report of the Deputy Test Director, Los Alamos Report WT-816, pp. 13-19; Summary of *Upshot-Knothole* Tests, June 4, 1953, both in AEC.

5. Goodwin, Description of FCDA Technical Program, undated but probably March 16, 1953; FCDA, Proposal for Civil Effects Test and Demonstration Program, June 1952, both in AEC.
6. FCDA, *Operation Doorstep*, published booklet, 1953.
7. There is an extensive collection of press clippings on this subject in DDE. The following are a representative sample: *Life*, March 30, 1953, pp. 24–25; *U.S. News & World Report*, March 27, 1953, pp. 38–40; *Minneapolis Star*, March 23, 1953; *Providence Journal*, March 17, 1953; editorials in the *Philadelphia Inquirer*, March 22, 1953, and the *Washington Post*, March 18, 1953, p. 12. On television coverage, see *New York Times*, March 18, 1953, p. 45, and *Variety*, March 18, 1953. Val Peterson's statement was issued in an FCDA press release, March 18, 1953, AEC. Eisenhower's endorsement is in *New York Times*, March 19, 1953, p. 1, and *Public Papers of the Presidents of the United States, 1953: Dwight D. Eisenhower* (Washington: Government Printing Office, 1960), p. 113.
8. AEC-DOD Test Information Office, Las Vegas, Background Information on Continental Nuclear Tests: The Spring 1953 Series, undated, AEC.
9. AEC-DOD Test Information Office, Las Vegas, A Fact Sheet on Continental Nuclear Tests, Jan. 14, 1954, AEC.
10. AEC, *Thirteenth Semiannual Report* (Washington: Government Printing Office, 1953), pp. 77–125 (hereafter cited *Thirteenth Semiannual Report*).
11. Committee on Operational Future of NPG, Summary of Minutes, Jan. 14, 1953; R. E. Cole to Fields, May 8, 1953, with Report of Committee on Operational Future of NPG, both in AEC.
12. Estimated yields were noted in Proposed Program for Operation Upshot, AEC 487/28, Feb. 2, 1953, AEC.
13. Summary of *Upshot-Knothole* Tests, June 4, 1953, AEC.
14. AEC, *Fourteenth Semiannual Report* (Washington: Government Printing Office, 1953), p. 49 (hereafter cited *Fourteenth Semiannual Report*). For a concise history of the development of radiation protection standards, see Lauriston S. Taylor, *Radiation Protection Standards* (Cleveland: CRC Press, 1971).

15. The pretest precautions monitoring system is fully described in *Thirteenth Semiannual Report*, pp. 96–112.
16. Test Director to Division of Military Application, March 18, 26, April 20, 27, May 9, 1953. These appear in AEC 487/45, AEC 487/46, AEC 487/50, AEC 487/52, and AEC 487/54, respectively, all in AEC. Richard G. Hewlett, "Nuclear Weapon Testing and Studies Related to Health Effects: An Historical Summary," in Interagency Radiation Research Committee, *Consideration of Three Proposals to Conduct Research on Possible Health Effects of Radiation From Nuclear Weapon Testing in Arizona, Nevada, and Utah* (Washington: National Institutes of Health, 1980), pp. 51–54, 78.
17. Operation *Upshot-Knothole*, Report of Deputy Test Director, Los Alamos Report WT-816, pp. 72, 78, 96–98.
18. AEC-DOD Test Information Office, Las Vegas, Press Releases 70, 71, 72, all on May 19, 1953, all in AEC. Weiss described his experiences in St. George in Transcript of Meeting on Statistical Considerations on Field Studies on Thyroid Diseases in School Children in Utah-Arizona, Dec. 3, 1965, pp. 3–5, Document 9735, PHS Archives. For another eyewitness account of incidents at St. George, see Frank A. Butrico to William Johnson, n.d., in House Committee on Interstate and Foreign Commerce, Subcommittee on Oversight and Investigations, *Hearings on Low-Level Radiation Effects on Health*, April 23–Aug. 1, 1979, Serial 96–129 (Washington: Government Printing Office, 1979), pp. 781–84 (hereafter cited *Radiation Effects Hearings*).
19. Oliver Townsend to Trapnell, May 20, 1953; Dean Diary, May 21, 25, 1953; Senator Arthur V. Watkins to Dean, May 23, 1953, all in AEC; *Washington Post*, May 21, 1953; *Baltimore Sun*, May 21, 1953; *New York Times*, May 25, 1953. AEC files contain many letters of inquiry addressed to the President about weather effects—e.g., L. D. Faunce to Eisenhower, June 11, 1953; Ruth M. Smith to Eisenhower, June 12, 1953, both in AEC. AEC received about 1,000 letters on weather effects. See Public Relations of Continental Tests, Sept. 23, 1953, *AEC*. For published articles, see *U.S.*

609

*News & World Report*, May 29, 1953, pp. 43–44; *Newsweek*, May 25, 1953, p. 37; *Newsweek*, June 1, 1953, p. 23; *Newsweek*, June 22, 1953, pp. 28–29; *U. S. News & World Report*, June 26, 1953, pp. 50–66. AEC files also contain numerous Congressional inquiries. See Sterling Cole to Dean, June 10, 1953, and Dean to Cole, June 12, 1953, both in AEC 652/1, June 16, 1953, AEC.

20. CM 862, May 13, 1953, AEC. The local fallout figure was reported in *Fourteenth Semiannual Report*, p. 50. The potential integrated dose was the theoretical *maximum* exposure that an individual remaining in that area would have received in the first thirteen weeks following the fallout. The amount actually received would depend upon whether individuals followed precautions to avoid fallout. The rainout at Troy was reported on p. 52. See also Bugher to Fields, May 14, 1953, AEC.

21. Many documents in AEC related to the sheep losses have been published in *Radiation Effects Hearings*, pp. 679–91, 717–36, 752–75.

22. Director of Military Application, Proposed Additional Shot for *Upshot-Knothole* Series, AEC 487/55, May 13, 1953, and CM 863, May 18, 1953, both in AEC.

23. CM 864, May 20, 1953; Zuckert to Dean, May 20, 1953; Dean to Zuckert, May 27, 1953; CM 866, May 22, 1953; Dean Diary, May 25–26, 1953; Dean to Strauss, May 26, 1953; Dean to Lay, May 19, 1953; Lay to Dean, May 27, 1953; Dean to Cutler, June 1, 1953, all in AEC.

24. AEC-DOD Test Information Office, Las Vegas, Press Release 84, June 4, 1953; Meteorological Criteria for Test Detonations at Nevada Proving Grounds, AEC 652, June 4, 1953; Zuckert to the Commissioners and General Manager, June 9, 1953; Zuckert to Fields, June 18, 1953; Fields to Zuckert, June 23, 1953, all in AEC.

25. Tyler to W. L. Guthrie, July 22, 1953; Elliott to Committee Members, Aug. 10, 1953; Tyler to Committee Members, Sept. 14, 1953, all in AEC.

26. *Radiation Effects Hearings*, pp. 692–93, 698–705, 709–16, 737–51, 776–79; CM 888, July 15, 1953; Director of Biology and Medicine, Sheep Losses Adjacent to the Nevada Proving Grounds,

AEC 604/3, Nov. 4, 1953; same title, AEC 604/4, Jan. 13, 1954, all in AEC; Bulloch vs. United States, 133 F. Supp. 885 (D. Utah 1955); Bulloch vs. United States, 145 F. Supp. 824 (D. Utah 1956); U.S. District Court for the District of Utah, Memorandum, Findings of Fact and Conclusions of Law, Aug. 4, 1982, DOE.

27. Tyler to Fields, Sept. 29, Dec. 21, 1953; Tyler to Committee Members, Oct. 19, 1953, all in AEC; Report of the Committee to Study Nevada Proving Grounds, Los Alamos Report SFO-LA-7 and 7A, Feb. 1, 1954, LASL.

28. Director of Military Application, Use of the Nevada Proving Grounds, AEC 141/22, Feb. 5, 1954; CM 962, Feb. 17, 1954; E. C. Stakman, chairman, ACBM, to Murray, March 25, 1954; GAC 39, March 31–April 2, 1954; I. I. Rabi, chairman, GAC, to Strauss, April 9, 1954; Director of Military Application, Use of the Nevada Proving Grounds, AEC 141/25, June 24, 1954; CM 1012, June 30, 1954, all in AEC.

29. Progress Report to the Joint Committee, Nov. 1953, in AEC 129/54, Dec. 1, 1953, AEC. On the 9,150-ton goal and its relationship to projected procurement, see Dean to Executive Secretary, National Security Council, June 10, 1952, in AEC 359/13, June 12, 1952; CM 723, July 16, 1952; and J. C. Johnson to M. W. Boyer, Nov. 7, 1952, in AEC 359/22, Dec. 3, 1952, all in AEC.

30. Director of Raw Materials, Uranium Ore Procurement, Draft Report to the NSC, Aug. 3, 1953, in AEC 359/27, AEC.

31. On developments before 1953, see *Atomic Shield*, pp. 426–27. See also Johnson's remarks to American Mining Congress, Sept. 23, 1954, AEC.

32. Press reports on the Colorado boom and to some extent on foreign sources began to appear in 1953. See articles: Burt Meyers, *Grand Junction Sentinel*, May 17, 18, 1953; Edward Hughes on South African developments, *Wall Street Journal*, June 1, 1953; John Worrall on South Africa, *New York Herald-Tribune*, Sept. 6, 1953; Herbert L. Matthews on Canadian boom, *New York Times*, July 24, 1953; on Wyoming ore discovery, *Washington Post*, Oct. 25, 1953. Charles Steen told his story in *American Weekly* in *Washington Times-Herald*, Sept. 27, 1953, pp. 4–5.

33. AEC Progress Reports to the Joint Committee, Nov. 1952, Nov. 1953; General Manager's Monthly Reports to the Commission, Raw Materials, Jan.–May 1954, all in AEC.

34. Murray to the Commissioners, July 8, 1952, in AEC 359/14; CM 723, July 16, 1952; Director of Raw Materials, Actions to Increase Uranium Production, AEC 359/30, March 25, 1954; Director of Raw Materials, Uranium Procurement Goal, AEC 359/31, March 25, 1954; CM 972, April 1, 1954; General Manager, Uranium Procurement Goal, AEC 359/33, Sept. 2, 1954; CM 1025, Sept. 15, 1954; Director of Raw Materials, Uranium Procurement, AEC 359/37, July 28, 1955; CM 1113, July 28, 1955; General Manager, Uranium Procurement, AEC 359/40, Jan. 13, 1956; CM 1169, Feb. 2, 1956, all in AEC.

35. This and the following two paragraphs summarize information in AEC Progress Reports to the Joint Committee, June–Nov. 1952, Dec. 1952–May 1953, and June–Nov. 1953; AEC Monthly Status and Progress Reports, Jan.–Dec. 1953, all in AEC.

36. The Princeton conference is described in *Atomic Shield*, pp. 542–45. Lithium Production Facility, AEC 458, Aug. 6, 1951, AEC.

37. CM 588, Aug. 8, 1951; Alloy Development Plant, AEC 458/8, April 3, 1952; CM 851, April 9, 1953; MLC 84, Aug. 27, 1953, all in AEC.

38. LeBaron to Dean, June 13, 1952, in AEC 493/4, June 17, 1952, AEC.

39. The quotation marks indicate that "true" and "semi" are not authentic terms but have been coined by the authors to protect classified information. For an authoritative but classified description of thermonuclear weapon technology, see Samuel Glasstone and Leslie M. Redman, *An Introduction to Nuclear Weapons*, WASH-1037, Rev., June 1972, pp. 100–41.

40. CM 776, Nov. 18, 1952; CM 793, Dec. 22, 1952; Operation *Castle*, Status of LASL and UCRL Programs, AEC 597/2, Dec. 10, 1952; MLC 75, Dec. 18, 1952; Operation *Castle*, AEC 597/4, Dec. 22, 1952; MLC 76, Dec. 23, 1952, all in AEC.

41. Graves to Clarkson, June 11, 1952; Tyler to Fields, Aug. 27, 1952; CM 746, Sept. 11, 1952; AEC Press Release 478, April 2, 1953, all in AEC. *Mike* is described in *Atomic Shield*, pp. 590–93.

42. CM 893, July 23, 1953; GAC 36, Aug. 17, 1953, both in AEC.

43. CM 917, Sept. 22, 1953; Draft Minutes of Executive Session, Sept. 23, 1953, AEC.

44. Revised Plans for ADP II, AEC 458/13, Sept. 22, 1953; CM 921, Sept. 30, 1953; CM 943, Dec. 2, 1953, all in AEC. Frederick C. Schuldt, Jr., to William F. Schaub, Sept. 16, 21, 1953; Schuldt to File, Oct. 20, 1953, all in BOB.

45. Arthur Radford, chairman, JCS, to Secretary of Defense, Dec. 15, 1953; Maj. Gen. James E. Briggs to Strauss, Dec. 16, 1953, both in AEC.

46. Modification of Loading in Hanford Piles, AEC 245/8, Aug. 18, 1953; CM 906, Aug. 20, 1953; Increased Capacity for Special Materials Production, AEC 458/23, Dec. 22, 1953; Program Reorientation to Meet New Military Requirements, AEC 706, Dec. 22, 1953, all in AEC.

47. Revised Program for Weapons Materials, AEC 706/2, Feb. 2, 1954, AEC.

48. For earlier instances of such discussions, see *Atomic Shield*, pp. 165–70, 559–72, 574–81.

49. CM 949, Dec. 23, 1953; CM 958, Feb. 4, 1954; CM 959, Feb. 5, 1954; Strauss and Wilson to Eisenhower, Feb. 5, 1954; Eisenhower to Strauss, Feb. 6, 1954, both in AEC 706/3, Feb. 9, 1954, all in AEC.

50. Detailed information on the planning and execution of *Castle* is found in Joint Task Force 7, *History of Operation Castle, 1952–1954*. Most information is included in the unclassified version in AEC; the unclassified version is cited below as *Castle History*. On early work at Bikini, see pp. 6–9.

51. *Castle History*, pp. 12, 60–62.

52. Ibid., pp. 47–50, 64–88.

53. Ibid., pp. 54–56, 90–93. An excellent summary of *Castle* meteorology is found in Appendix A, *Castle History*, pp. 151–72.

54. Ibid., pp. 42–46, 79–80.

55. Bugher to Radford, Commander in Chief, Pacific, May 15, 1953, and Radford to Bugher, June 26, 1953, both in AEC.

56. Col. Vincent G. Huston, acting director, Division of Military Application, to Nichols, March 30, 1954, with attachments, AEC, fully documents establishment of the exclusion area.

611

57. *Castle History*, pp. 57–58.
58. Report of Commanding Officer, Task Group 7.1, Report on Operation *Castle*, Los Alamos Report WT-940, p. 63.
59. *Castle History*, pp. 118–20.
60. Col. H. K. Gilbert, commander, Hqs. Task Unit 13, Task Group 7.1, to Distribution, May 12, 1954, AEC, includes charts and weather data used at the two weather briefings.
61. *Castle History*, pp. 120–23, 132; John C. Clark, "We Were Trapped by Radioactive Fallout," *Saturday Evening Post*, July 20, 1957, pp. 17–19, 64–66.
62. *Castle History*, pp. 123–31.
63. Earliest computed doses received at the atolls (in roentgens) were: Rongelap 100–130, Ailinginae 80, Rongerik 40–98, and Utirik 17. Clarkson, Memorandum for Record, March 19, 1954, LASL. Estimates cited in text and published in 1975 were only slightly different from the figures. See Robert A. Conard et al., A Twenty-Year Review of Medical Findings in a Marshallese Population Accidentally Exposed to Radioactive Fallout, ERDA Report BNL 50424, Sept. 1975, p. 7. Director, Division of Biology and Medicine, Return of Rongelapese to Their Home Island, AEC 125/30, Feb. 6, 1957; CM 1267, Feb. 21, 1957; Morse Salisbury to the Commissioners, April 15, 1957; Fields to Carl T. Durham, July 18, 1957, all in AEC.
64. The most detailed account of the incident is in Ralph E. Lapp, *The Voyage of the Lucky Dragon* (New York: Harper & Bros., 1957), pp. 27–70. The ship's position at the time of the detonation, as reported by Lapp, was established in an aide-memoire from the Japanese foreign office. See Merril Eisenbud to Bugher, April 9, 1954, in AEC 730/3, June 10, 1954, and George V. LeRoy to Bugher, March 16, 1954, both in AEC.
65. *New York Times*, March 16, 1954, p. 19; Charter Heslep to Rodney L. Southwick, March 15, 1954; CM 967, March 16, 1954; State Department Telegram 2048 to American Embassy, Tokyo, March 16, 1954; State Department Telegram 2243, Tokyo to Secretary of State, March 18, 1954; Morton to Bugher, March 28, 1954, with attachment, Preliminary Medical Report on the *Fukuryu Maru No. 5* Incident, all in AEC.
66. *Yomiuri Shimbun*, March 16, 18, 24, 1954; *Shukan Asahi*, March 17, April 7, 1954, and other translations of articles from the Japanese press in American Embassy, Tokyo, *Daily Summaries of Japanese Press*, microfilm in Periodicals Division, Library of Congress.
67. Eisenbud to Bugher, April 9, 1954, in AEC 730/3, June 10, 1954; Morton et al., Supplementary Medical Report on the *Fukuryu Maru No. 5* Incident, April 19, 1954; Morton and Jack J. Lewis, The Relationship Between the American and Japanese Scientists During the *Fukuryu Maru No. 5* Incident, May 27, 1954, all in AEC.
68. *Public Papers of the Presidents of the United States, 1954: Dwight D. Eisenhower* (Washington: Government Printing Office, 1960), pp. 320–21 (hereafter cited *Public Papers, 1954, Eisenhower*). For an excellent analysis of American and Japanese attitudes, see Herbert Passin, "Japan and the H-Bomb," *Bulletin of the Atomic Scientists* 11 (Oct. 1955): 289–92.
69. Teletype, Nichols to Strauss, March 17, 1954; teletype, Strauss to Nichols, March 19, 1954, both in AEC; *Public Papers, 1954, Eisenhower*, pp. 346–47.
70. Strauss Statement, March 31, 1954, AEC. The statement was reprinted in the *Bulletin of the Atomic Scientists* 10 (May 1954): 163–64. Hagerty Diary, April 2, 6, 1954, James C. Hagerty Papers, DDE. For published excerpts from the Hagerty Diary, see Robert H. Ferrell, ed., *The Diary of James C. Hagerty: Eisenhower in Mid-Course, 1954–1955* (Bloomington: Indiana University Press, 1983), pp. 40, 42.
71. *Castle History*, pp. 131–42. Technical aspects of the *Castle* shots are described in Report of Commanding Officer, Task Group 7.1, Report on Operation *Castle*, Los Alamos Report WT-940, AEC.
72. CM 971, March 30, 1954; MLC 97, March 31, 1954; Fields to Nichols, April 5, 1954; Commander, Joint Task Force 7, Final Report, Operation *Castle*, June 15, 1954; AEC Progress Report to the Joint Committee, June–Nov. 1954, all in AEC.
73. GAC 41, July 14, 1954, AEC. For a description of the Los Alamos program in 1954, see Bradbury to Fields, Dec. 11, 1953, AEC.
74. University of California Radiation Labo-

ratory, Livermore, Key Personnel and Functions, July 24, 1953, AEC; York to J. J. Flaherty, Dec. 18, 1953, LASL.
75. *Washington Star*, March 31, 1954, p. 1; *New York Times*, April 1, 1954, pp. 1, 20; CM 990, May 24, 1954, AEC.
76. Dulles's statement on "massive retaliation" first appeared in *Time*, Jan. 25, 1954, p. 17. The full text later appeared in *Vital Speeches* 20 (Feb. 1, 1954): 232–35. A modified, more qualified article appeared in *Foreign Affairs* 32 (April 1954): 353–64. Rabinowitch's article appeared in *Bulletin of the Atomic Scientists* 10 (May 1954): 146–47, 168.

## CHAPTER SEVEN

1. Joint Committee on Atomic Energy, *Hearings on Atomic Power Development and Private Enterprise*, June 24–July 31, 1953 (Washington: Government Printing Office, 1953), pp. 562–63 (hereafter cited *Atomic Power Hearings*).
2. Richard G. Hewlett and Francis Duncan, *Atomic Shield, 1947–1952*, Vol. II of *A History of the U.S. Atomic Energy Commission* (University Park: Pennsylvania State University Press, 1969), pp. 122–23, 435–38, 494–95, 512–13 (hereafter cited *Atomic Shield*).
3. See Chap. 2, Nuclear Power and Private Enterprise.
4. Hafstad to Snapp, Policy Problems in Reactor Development Program for Consideration at Topnotch Conference, Sept. 14, 1953, AEC.
5. On Hafstad's earlier career, see *Atomic Shield*, pp. 209–20, 420–518.
6. *Atomic Power Hearings*, pp. 127–30, 134–41, 177–81, 206–10; Cole to Strauss, July 31, 1953, in AEC 655/8, Aug. 3, 1953; Strauss to Cole, Aug. 14, 1953, in AEC 655/9, Aug. 17, 1953, both in AEC.
7. Richard G. Hewlett and Francis Duncan, *Nuclear Navy, 1946–1962* (Chicago: University of Chicago Press, 1974), pp. 88–92 (hereafter cited *Nuclear Navy*); *Atomic Shield*, pp. 189–93.
8. *Nuclear Navy*, pp. 93–120; *Atomic Shield*, pp. 197–99, 207–8, 418, 423.
9. *Nuclear Navy*, pp. 121–52.
10. Ibid., pp. 153–86.
11. *Atomic Shield*, pp. 71–74, 106–7,

120–21, 189–90, 419–20, 516–17; Director of Reactor Development, Reactor Progress and Status Report, AEC 152/46, Aug. 21, 1953, AEC.
12. Hafstad to Snapp, Policy Problems in Reactor Development Program for Consideration at Topnotch Conference, Sept. 14, 1953, AEC.
13. AEC 152/46, Aug. 21, 1953, AEC.
14. *Atomic Shield*, pp. 209, 214, 219, 421, 490–94; James A. Lane et al., *Fluid Fuel Reactors* (Reading, MA: Addison-Wesley, 1958), pp. v–vi, 1–11; AEC Press Release 474, March 9, 1953, AEC.
15. *Atomic Shield*, pp. 214–20, 429–30, 552–53. See also Irvin C. Bupp and Jean-Claude Derian, *Light Water: How the Nuclear Dream Dissolved* (New York: Basic Books, 1978).
16. *Nuclear Navy*, pp. 195–96, 204–7, describes the origins of the submarine advanced reactor and submarine fleet reactor.
17. Andrew W. Kramer, *Boiling Water Reactors* (Reading, MA: Addison-Wesley, 1958), pp. 1–19, 45–79; Samuel Untermyer, "Direct Steam Generation for Power," *Nucleonics* 12 (July 1954): 43–47.
18. Cole to Strauss, July 8, 1953, in AEC 649/4, July 9, 1953; CM 885, July 9, 1953, both in AEC; italics Cole's. *Nuclear Navy*, pp. 232–33.
19. Thomas E. Murray and the PWR Project, entry for July 13, 1953, TEM.
20. J. W. McAfee to Strauss, July 10, 1953, in AEC 666, July 21, 1953; Murray and the PWR Project, entry for August 20, 1953, TEM.
21. Director of Reactor Development, Participation in Reactor Development, AEC 666/1, Aug. 17, 1953; CM 906, Aug. 20, 1953; CM 907, Aug. 20, 1953; Murray to Strauss, Aug. 25, 1953; CM 914, Sept. 16, 1953; Murray to Strauss, two memos on Sept. 16, one on Sept. 18, 1953; CM 924, Oct. 6, 1953; Murray to Strauss, Oct. 12, 1953, all in AEC; Murray and the PWR Project, entries for Aug. 25, 31, Sept. 12, 14, 15, Oct. 5, 12, 1953, TEM.
22. Murray, "Far More Important Than War," AEC Press Release, Oct. 22, 1953, AEC.
23. *U.S. News and World Report*, Oct. 30, 1953; ibid., Nov. 6, 1953, pp. 49–50;

613

ibid., Dec. 25, 1953, pp. 28–29; *Time*, Nov. 2, 1953, p. 90; *New York Times Magazine*, Dec. 20, 1953, pp. 13, 38–41.

24. Director of Reactor Development, Policy Problems in Reactor Development Program for Possible Consideration at Topnotch Conference, Sept. 20, 1953, AEC.

25. Notes on Topnotch II, 3rd Session, Sept. 26, 1953, 4th Session, Sept. 27, 1953; CM 947, Dec. 17, 1953; AEC Press Release 509, Dec. 7, 1953, all in AEC.

26. AEC, Program Proposed for Developing Nuclear Powerplant Technology, undated but presented to the Joint Committee on Feb. 5, 1954; Snapp to Zuckert, Jan. 26, 1954; Director of Reactor Development, Nuclear Power Development Program, AEC 152/47, Feb. 1, 1954; CM 958, Feb. 4, 1954, all in AEC.

27. Research and Development Subcommittee, Joint Committee on Atomic Energy, *Report on Five-Year Power Reactor Development Program Proposed by the Atomic Energy Commission* (Washington: Government Printing Office, 1954). A transcript of the hearing on Feb. 5, 1954, is in AEC.

28. Nuclear Power Group Proposal for Participation in Pressurized Water Reactor Program, AEC 649/11, Nov. 23, 1953, AEC.

29. *Nuclear Navy*, pp. 236–39; CM 964, Feb. 24, 1954; Director of Reactor Development, PWR Participation and Site Selection, AEC 649/19, March 10, 1954; CM 966, March 11, 1954; Proposal by Duquesne Light Co., AEC 649/20, March 10, 1954; AEC Press Release 526, March 14, 1954, all in AEC.

30. Joint Committee on Atomic Energy, Transcript of Hearing on Power Reactors, March 12, 1954, AEC.

31. National Security Council, Cooperation With Other Nations in the Peaceful Uses of Atomic Energy, NSC 5431, Aug. 6, 1954, DDE.

32. National Security Council, Summary of Discussion (hereafter cited SNSC), Meeting 210, Aug. 12, 1954, DDE.

33. Snapp to AEC Staff, Dec. 10, 1954, transmitting draft of Report to the NSC on U.S. Policy on Atomic Power in Other Countries, distributed as AEC 655/25; Murray to Snapp, Comments on Draft Report, Jan. 7, 1955, both in AEC.

34. Snapp to the Commissioners, Sept. 29, 1954; Cutler, Comments on Draft Report,

Oct. 6, 1954; Snapp to Cutler, Oct. 6, 1954; Note on Planning Board Meeting, Oct. 12, 1954; U. M. Staebler, AEC reactor division, to Snapp, Nov. 29, 1954; Snapp to Strauss, Nov. 29, 1954; Snapp to Planning Board Subcommittee, Dec. 9, 1954; Murray Comments on Draft Paper, undated, all in AEC.

35. SNSC 236, Feb. 10, 1955, DDE.

36. Licensing Activities and Controls in Atomic Energy, AEC 23/14, Sept. 13, 1954, AEC; AEC, *Seventeenth Semiannual Report*, July–Dec. 1954 (Washington: Government Printing Office, 1955), pp. xi–xiii.

37. George T. Mazuzan and J. Samuel Walker, *Controlling the Atom: The Beginnings of Nuclear Regulation, 1946–1962* (Berkeley: University of California Press, 1984), pp. 65–75. Price was serving as deputy general counsel at the time of his appointment as special assistant to the general manager for licensing.

38. James L. Grahl, Bureau of the Budget, to File, Dec. 14, 1954, AEC.

39. William F. Schaub to the Director, Bureau of the Budget, Nov. 9, 1954; F. C. Schuldt, Memorandum on AEC Reactor Plans, Nov. 29, 1954, both in AEC.

40. Director of Reactor Development, Demonstration Power Reactor Program, AEC 777, Dec. 13, 1954, AEC.

41. CM 1049, Dec. 21, 1954, and Transcript of Discussion, pp. 21–24; AEC Press Release 589, Jan. 10, 1955, both in AEC.

42. Strauss to Sterling Cole, Nov. 11, 1954; Allardice to Strauss, Nov. 15, 1954, with copy of Joint Committee resolution, Nov. 13, 1954, in AEC 385/51, Nov. 18, 1954; AEC Press Release, Nov. 11, 1954; CM 1041, Nov. 11, 1954; Allardice to Strauss, Jan. 28, 1955, with copy of resolution, Jan. 28, 1955, in AEC 385/68, all in AEC.

43. P.L. 83–703; 42 *U.S.C.*, sec. 2252. The sixty-day period for the hearings was later changed to ninety days. The authorization power under section 261 is in 42 *U.S.C.*, sec. 2017.

44. Joint Committee on Atomic Energy, *Hearings on Development, Growth, and State of the Atomic Energy Industry*, Jan. 31–March 3, 1955 (Washington: Government Printing Office, 1955), pp. 30–31, 53–54, 270–80, 353–83 (hereafter cited *202 Hearings, 1955*); Clinton P. Anderson, *Outsider in the Senate: Sena-*

tor *Clinton Anderson's Memoirs* (New York: World Publishing, 1970), pp. 192–93; Aaron Wildavsky, *Dixon-Yates: A Study in Power Politics* (New Haven: Yale University Press, 1962), pp. 157–60.

45. *202 Hearings, 1955,* pp. 85–86, 152–55, 250–55.

46. Ibid., pp. 156–62. The discussion centered on the legislative history of Section 169 of the 1954 Act and the interpretation of the reference in that section to Section 31.

47. *202 Hearings, 1955,* pp. 253–54, 339.

48. Melvin Price to Strauss, March 2, 1955, in AEC 655/27, March 7, 1955; AEC Press Release, March 26, 1955, Statement by Strauss on the McKinney Panel, both in AEC.

49. CM 1073, April 6, 1955; Transcript of CM 1073, pp. 2–7; Strauss to Anderson, April 6, 1955; AEC Press Release 620, April 7, 1955, all in AEC.

50. Murray to Fields, May 18, 1955; Fields to Murray, May 23, 1955; Director of Reactor Development, Power Demonstration Reactor Program, AEC 777/11, June 30, 1955, all in AEC.

51. CM 1096 and Transcript, July 6, 1955, AEC.

52. *202 Hearings, 1955,* pp. 155–62; Transcript of CM 1096, pp. 24–28; J. J. Flaherty, Manager, Chicago Operations Office, to Fields, Aug. 16, 1955, in AEC 777/13, Aug. 25, 1955, both in AEC.

53. CM 1097 and Transcript, July 11, 1955, pp. 42–53, 75–77; CM 1107 and Transcript, July 21, 1955, pp. 45–83, all in AEC.

54. CM 1108 and Transcript, July 21, 1955, pp. 36–52, AEC.

55. AEC Press Release 674, Aug. 8, 1955, AEC.

## CHAPTER EIGHT

1. Lewis L. Strauss, *Men and Decisions* (Garden City, NY: Doubleday, 1962), p. 361 (hereafter cited Strauss, *Men and Decisions*); *Public Papers of the Presidents of the United States, 1953: Dwight D. Eisenhower* (Washington: Government Printing Office, 1960), p. 822 (hereafter cited *Public Papers, 1953, Eisenhower*); Corbin Allardice and Edward R. Trapnell, *The Atomic Energy Commission* (New York: Praeger, 1974), p. 201 (hereafter cited Allardice and Trapnell, *The Atomic Energy Commission*); Herbert S. Parmet, *Eisenhower and the American Crusades* (New York: Macmillan, 1972), p. 389.

2. Department of State, Official Foreign Reactions to President Eisenhower's Speech, Dec. 14, 1953; Department of State, World Reaction to President Eisenhower's Speech, Dec. 15, 1953, both in AEC. The Voice of America broadcast Eisenhower's speech over all eighty-two of its transmitters in thirty-three languages. Abbott Washburn to Jackson, Dec. 10, 1953, DDE; U.S. Information Agency, Impact of President Eisenhower's "Atoms-for-Peace" Proposal, March 2, 1954, AEC.

3. *Washington Times-Herald,* Dec. 9, 1953; *Newsweek,* Dec. 21, 1953, pp. 32, 34.

4. Murray to Smyth, Dec. 7, 1953; Joint Committee on Atomic Energy, Transcript of Hearing, May 3, 1954, both in AEC; Murray Diary Memo 371, Dec. 10, 1953, TEM.

5. Strauss to Hagerty, Dec. 14, 1953; Strauss, Suggested Draft Press Release, Dec. 12, 1953; Strauss to Jackson, Dec. 14, 1953, all in C. D. Jackson Papers.

6. *Public Papers, 1953, Eisenhower,* pp. 831–40.

7. For the 1946–1947 period, see Richard G. Hewlett and Oscar E. Anderson, Jr., *The New World, 1939–1946,* Vol. I of *A History of the U.S. Atomic Energy Commission* (University Park: Pennsylvania State University Press, 1962), pp. 531–619; and Richard G. Hewlett and Francis Duncan, *Atomic Shield, 1947–1952,* Vol. II of *A History of the U.S. Atomic Energy Commission* (University Park: Pennsylvania State University Press, 1969), pp. 261–73.

8. Office of Special Projects, Review of UN Plan for the International Control of Atomic Energy, AEC 226/28, Sept. 2, 1953, AEC.

9. David Bruce to Lay, Jan. 19, 1953, AEC.

10. Office of Special Projects, Review of UN Plan for the International Control of Atomic Energy, AEC 226/28, Sept. 2, 1953, AEC.

11. Smith to Strauss, Aug. 5, 1953, in Review of Scientific Developments, AEC 226/27, Aug. 10, 1953, AEC.

12. Smyth to Commissioners and General Manager, Nov. 25, 1953, in International

615

Control of Atomic Energy, AEC 226/30, Nov. 30, 1953, AEC.

13. Murray to Strauss, Oct. 2, 12, 1953; CM 924, Oct. 6, 1953; CM 928, Oct. 15, 1953; Notes on Executive Session, Oct. 20, 1953; Snapp, Memorandum to the Chairman, Dec. 10, 1953; CM 944, Dec. 9, 1953; Peaceful Uses Planning Board, "International Control of Atomic Energy—Chronology," n.d., all in AEC; Strauss, draft memo, Oct. 26, 1953, and Strauss to Jackson, Nov. 6, 1953, both in DDE; Smyth to Commissioners and General Manager, Nov. 25, 1953, HDS.

14. Memo of Conversation, Heads of Government and Foreign Ministers, Bermuda, Dec. 4, 1953, DDE.

15. Strauss, Informal Notes of Conversation, Dec. 5, 1953; Eisenhower Diary, Dec. 10, 1953, both in DDE; Dwight D. Eisenhower, Mandate for Change, 1953–1956 (Garden City, NY: Doubleday, 1963), pp. 254–55.

16. Bohlen to Dulles, Aug. 11, 1953, in AEC 240/5, Aug. 17, 1953; OCB Minutes, Dec. 11, 1953, both in AEC.

17. "Reply from U.S.S.R. on Atomic Energy Proposal," Department of State Bulletin, Jan. 18, 1954, pp. 80–82; Louis T. Olom to Nielson C. Debevoise, Dec. 23, 1953, DDE.

18. Jackson, Memorandum on President's Atomic Proposal, Dec. 28, 1953, DDE; B. G. Bechhoefer, Relationship of President's Proposal to the Remainder of the Disarmament Program, Dec. 22, 1953, DOS; Richard Hirsch, Memo for Record, Dec. 29, 1953, DDE; Summary of Meeting with the Secretary of State, Jan. 6, 1954, AEC.

19. Summary of Meeting with the Secretary of State, Jan. 6, 1954, AEC.

20. Eisenhower to Jackson, Dec. 31, 1953; Jackson to Dulles, Strauss, and Wilson, Jan. 7, 1954; C. D. Jackson Logs, Jan. 16, 1954, Jackson Papers, all in DDE; Dulles, Memorandum of Conversation with the President, Jan. 5, 1954, DOS; Summary of Meeting in the White House, Jan. 16, 1954, AEC.

21. R. R. Bowie, Memo of Conversation, Dec. 16, 1953; Meyers, Procedures for Implementing the President's Proposals, Dec. 24, 1953, both in DOS.

22. Snapp, Notes on Executive Session, Dec. 15, 22, 1953; Smyth to Bowie, Dec. 16, 1953, all in AEC; Summary of Meeting in

Commissioner Smyth's Office, Dec. 27, 1953, DOS.

23. Summary of Plan to Carry Out the President's Proposal, Jan. 21, 1954, AEC.

24. The question of patent rights was also raised but was deferred until the 1954 act was adopted. Summary of Meeting in Commissioner Smyth's Office, Dec. 27, 1953, DOS.

25. AEC, A Suggested Basis for a Plan to Carry Out the President's Proposal, Dec. 23, 1953, AEC. This is the Donkin-Trapnell proposal discussed in Allardice and Trapnell, The Atomic Energy Commission, p. 201.

26. New York Times, Dec. 27, 1953; David E. Lilienthal, The Journals of David E. Lilienthal, Vol. III, The Venturesome Years, 1950–1955 (New York: Harper & Row, 1966), p. 474.

27. Meyers, Procedures for Implementing the President's Proposals, Dec. 24, 1953, DOS.

28. Merchant, Memo of Conversation between Dulles and Makins, Dec. 22, 30, 1953, DOS.

29. Those present were Dulles, Robert Murphy, Bowie, and Merchant for State; Strauss and Smyth for AEC; Wilson, Kyes, Nash, and LeBaron for Defense. Summary of Meeting with the Secretary of State, Jan. 6, 1954, AEC.

30. Merchant, Memo of Conversation between Dulles and Makins, Jan. 7, 1954, DDE.

31. Note Handed to Ambassador Zaroubin by Secretary Dulles, Jan. 11, 1954; Note Handed to Secretary Dulles by Ambassador Zaroubin, Jan. 19, 1954, both in "Atoms for Peace Manual," Document 55, 84 Cong., 1 sess. (Washington: Government Printing Office, 1955), pp. 262–64 (hereafter cited "Atoms for Peace Manual"); R. C. Breithut, International Atomic Energy Conference: History of IAEA Negotiations, Oct. 2, 1956, DOS; Bernhard G. Bechhoefer, "Negotiating the Statute of the International Atomic Energy Agency," International Organization 13 (1959): 38–43 (hereafter cited Bechhoefer, "Negotiating the Statute").

32. Preliminary Views of the Canadian Government, Jan. 18, 1954; British Embassy Aide Memoire, Jan. 21, 1954; Robert Murphy, Memorandum of Conversation, Jan. 21, 1954; Dulles to Smith, Jan. 26,

31, 1954; Bidault to Dulles, Feb. 18, 1954, all in DOS; Draft Declaration Handed to Secretary Dulles by Mr. Molotov, Jan. 30, 1954; Aide Memoire Handed to Secretary Dulles by Mr. Molotov, Feb. 13, 1954, both in "Atoms for Peace Manual," pp. 264–66.

33. CM 953, Jan. 20, 1954, and Office of Special Projects, Outline of An International Atomic Energy Agency, AEC 226/32, Feb. 15, 1954, both in AEC.

34. Murphy to W. B. Smith, March 1, 1954, and Meyers, Memorandum of Conversation, Feb. 27, 1954, both in DOS.

35. R. H. Scott to Arneson, March 10, 1954; Comments of Canadian Government on the Outline of an International Atomic Energy Agency, March 11, 1954, both in AEC 226/35, March 17, 1954, AEC; Bechhoefer, Memorandum of Conversation, March 16, 1954; Arneson, Memorandum of Conversation with Scott, March 19, 1954; Arneson, Memorandum of Conversation with G. Glazebrook, March 19, 1954; Arneson, Memorandum of Conversation with Mr. Martin, March 8, 1954; Arneson, Memorandum of Conversation with Georges Carlier, March 8, 1954, all in DOS.

36. Jackson, Post-Berlin Thoughts on the Current Soviet Psyche, Feb. 22, 1954; Beam, Significance of Recent Soviet Press Treatment of Nuclear Developments, April 7, 1954; A. M. Bickel, Reply to Russian Proposal, April 23, 1954, all in DOS.

37. Outline of an International Atomic Energy Agency, March 17, 1954, in AEC 226/36, March 25, 1954, and Memorandum of Conversation, March 19, 1954, in AEC 226/37, March 25, 1954, both in AEC; Soviet Aide Memoire of April 27, 1954, in "Atoms for Peace Manual," pp. 269–73; Breithut, International Atomic Energy Conference: History of IAEA Negotiations, Oct. 2, 1956, DOS.

38. Bechhoefer, "Negotiating the Statute," p. 44; Bickel, Russian Note of April 27, 1954, April 29, 1954, DOS.

39. Informal Paper Left with Mr. Molotov by Secretary Dulles, May 1, 1954, in "Atoms for Peace Manual," p. 274; Merchant, Memorandum of Conversation, May 1, 1954, and Gerard Smith, Memorandum for the Acting Secretary, May 3, 1954, both in DOS; Department of State Memorandum handed to Zaroubin, July

9, 1954, in "Atoms for Peace Manual," pp. 274–78.

40. Murray to Strauss, Feb. 2, 1954; CM 957, Feb. 3, 1954; Murray to Eisenhower, Feb. 5, 1954, all in AEC.

41. Department of State, Memorandum of Conversation, April 12, 1954; G. C. Smith to Dulles, June 8, 1954, both in DOS. For the AEC analysis of Nehru's statement, see Office of Special Projects, Proposal by Government of India for Moratorium on Weapons Tests, AEC 226/39, May 3, 1954, AEC.

42. *New York Times*, Feb. 18, 1954, p. 1; Churchill to Eisenhower, March 12, 29, April 1, 1954; Eisenhower to Churchill, March 17, 1954, all in DOS. More than 100 Labourites presented a test moratorium petition to the British Government on March 25, 1954. *New York Times*, March 31, 1954, p. 1.

43. Department of State, Memorandum of Conversation between Dulles and Eden, April 12, 1954; Chronology of U.S. Study of Nuclear Test Moratorium, Oct. 21, 1956, both in DOS; CM 982, May 7, 1954; Radford to Wilson, April 30, 1954; J. A. Hall to G. C. Smith, April 22, 1954, in AEC 226/39, May 3, 1954, all in AEC.

44. G. C. Smith, Notes on Conversation with Strauss, May 11, 1954, and Smith to File, May 19, 1954, both in DOS; Strauss to the Commissioners and General Manager, May 21, 1954, AEC.

45. G. C. Smith to File, May 25, 1954, and Merchant, Memorandum of Conversation, June 27, 1954, both in DOS; Questions Concerning Weapons Tests, AEC 226/40, June 8, 1954, AEC; Smith, Memorandum of Conversation, June 8, 1954, DOS.

46. CM 999, June 7, 1954; CM 1000, June 8, 1954; CM 1002, June 11, 1954; CM 1006, June 15, 1954; Teller and Bradbury, Moratorium on Atomic Weapons Tests, AEC 226/42, June 24, 1954, all in AEC.

47. Strauss to Dulles, June 16, 1954; CM 1008, June 16, 1954; Murray to Strauss, June 18, 1954; Murray to Dulles, June 19, 1954, all in AEC; Chronology of U.S. Study of Nuclear Test Moratorium, Oct. 21, 1956, DOS.

48. G. C. Smith to Dulles, May 22, 1954; D. W. Wainhouse to Smith, May 17, 1954, both in DOS; Lodge to Dulles, June 2,

617

1954, in AEC 226/41, June 24, 1954, AEC.

49. Cutler to Strauss, May 1, 1954; G. C. Smith to File, June 4, 1954; Cutler to Dulles, June 9, 1954; Smith, Note for Churchill File, June 26, 1954, all in DOS; *Public Papers of the Presidents of the United States, 1954: Dwight D. Eisenhower* (Washington: Government Printing Office, 1960), pp. 631–32 (hereafter cited *Public Papers, 1954, Eisenhower*); Statement of President Eisenhower, Aug. 30, 1954, in "Atoms for Peace Manual," p. 252.

50. Dulles to Cutler, June 17, 1954, DDE; R. L. O'Connor to G. C. Smith, July 15, 1954; Smith, Exchange of Information, June 21, 1954; Merchant, Memorandum of Conversation held on June 27, 1954, July 14, 1954, all in DOS.

51. Strauss to Eisenhower, July 12, 1954, DDE; G. C. Smith to File, July 13, 20, Aug. 4, 1954; P. J. Farley to File, Aug. 9, 1954, all in DOS; Snapp to Smith, July 15, 1954, AEC; Strauss, VFW Address, Aug. 5, 1954, in *Department of State Bulletin*, Aug. 16, 1954, pp. 227–29.

52. G. C. Smith to File, Aug. 4, 11, 1954, DOS; NSC, Cooperation with Other Nations in the Peaceful Uses of Atomic Energy, NSC 5431/1, Aug. 13, 1954, AEC.

53. G. C. Smith to File, Aug. 11, 1954, DOS.

54. *Public Papers, 1954, Eisenhower*, pp. 840–41; CM 1019, Aug. 12, 1954; Farley to McCool and Hall, Aug. 13, 1954; Strauss to the Commission, Sept. 27, 1954, in Implementation of NSC 5431/1, in AEC 751/14, Oct. 5, 1954; Hall to G. C. Smith, Aug. 30, 1954, and Strauss to Cole, Aug. 26, 1954, both in Cooperation with Other Nations, AEC 751/5, Sept. 2, 1954, all in AEC; Smith, Telephone Call from Strauss, Sept. 4, 1954, and Smith to File, Aug. 19, 1954, both in DOS.

55. Dulles, Address to U.N. General Assembly, Sept. 23, 1954, in "Atoms for Peace Manual," pp. 259–60; McCool to Hall, Sept. 28, 1954, AEC.

56. Aide Memoire Handed to Ambassador Bohlen by Mr. Gromyko, Sept. 22, 1954, in "Atoms for Peace Manual," pp. 278–82.

57. G. C. Smith, AEC Briefing of Mr. Cole, Aug. 24, 1954; Dulles to W. B. Smith, Sept. 24, 1954; G. C. Smith, Status of Planning for Proposed Agency, Sept. 1, 1954; Farley, Planning for Agency, Sept. 7, 8, 20, 1954, all in DOS; G. C. Smith to Hall, Aug. 11, 1954, and British Embassy Memorandum Containing U.K. Views on Establishment of International Agency, Aug. 9, 1954, both in AEC 751/1, Aug. 20, 1954, AEC; Bechhoefer, "Negotiating the Statute," pp. 45–46.

58. Farley, Reply to Soviet Note of Sept. 22, 1954, Oct. 18, 1954; Smith, Problem of Continuing Negotiations with the Soviets, Oct. 1, 1954, both in DOS; Director of International Affairs, International Atomic Energy Agency, AEC 751/18, Oct. 19, 1954, and Director of International Affairs, Planning for International Agency, AEC 751/20, Oct. 25, 1954, both in AEC.

59. Director of International Affairs, Preliminary Outline of An International Agency, AEC 751/19, Oct. 21, 1954, AEC; G. C. Smith to Dulles, Oct. 26, 27, Nov. 1, 1954; J. R. Hamilton to Dulles, Oct. 27, 1954, all in DOS.

60. G. C. Smith, Conversation with Strauss, Oct. 13, 1954; Smith to Strauss, Oct. 13, 1954; Smith to File, Oct. 28, 1954, all in DOS.

61. G. C. Smith, Discussion with Strauss and Hall, Nov. 2, 1954, and Smith, Meeting with Dulles, Oct. 29, 1954, both in DOS; Jackson, General Comments on Ninth General Assembly, n.d., DDE.

62. Lodge to Eisenhower, Nov. 8, 1954; Lodge to Dulles, Nov. 9, 1954; Wainhouse, Peaceful Uses of Atomic Energy, Nov. 4, 1954; Hall to Strauss, Nov. 2, 1954; Smith, Discussion at Luncheon Meeting, Nov. 3, 1954, all in DOS.

63. Statement of Ambassador Lodge, Nov. 15, 1954, *Department of State Bulletin*, Nov. 29, 1954, pp. 832–36; Strauss to Eisenhower, Nov. 15, 1954, AEC; Jackson, General Comments on Ninth General Assembly, n.d., DDE.

64. Strauss, *Men and Decisions*, pp. 364–65; Churchill to Strauss, Aug. 19, 1955, C. D. Jackson Papers, DDE.

65. GAC 39, April 1, 1954, AEC; Strauss, "A First Step Toward the Peaceful Use of Atomic Energy," *Department of State Bulletin*, May 3, 1954, pp. 659–62.

66. GAC 40, May 27–29, 1954, AEC.

67. Strauss to W. B. Smith, April 23, 1954, AEC; G. C. Spiegel, Memorandum of Conversation, May 7, 1954; G. C. Smith

to Strauss, May 10, 1954, DOS; McKay Donkin, Memorandum of Conversation with Rabi, May 27, 1954, AEC; G. C. Smith to File, May 29, 1954; G. C. Smith, Draft Memorandum to Bowie, June 3, 1954; Spiegel, Memorandum of Conversation, June 4, 1954; Spiegel to G. C. Smith, June 12, 1954, all in DOS; G. C. Smith to Merchant et al.; Rabi's Prospectus for the International Conference, and a State Department memorandum on the Conference, all dated July 13, 1954, and included in AEC 729/1, July 20, 1954, AEC; David M. Key to G. C. Smith, July 16, 1954, DOS.

68. Rabi to G. C. Smith, Aug. 27, 1954; Record of meeting with Rabi in Cambridge, Aug. 24, 1954; Rabi to Strauss, Sept. 8, 1954; H. A. Robinson to Smith, Sept. 14, 1954, all in DOS; Cockcroft to Rabi, Sept. 1, 1954, AEC.

69. Gunnar Randers and Cockcroft to Rabi, Sept. 21, 1954, AEC. Discussions of the agenda are reported in Spiegel, Memorandum of Conversation, Oct. 21, 22, 1954, DOS. Charpie's agenda appears in AEC 729/8, Nov. 12, 1954, AEC. The agenda adopted by the Commission appears in AEC 27/103, Dec. 20, 1954, AEC. For a complete account of the classification problem see AEC 27/103 and AEC 729/10, Jan. 5, 1955. See also CM 1049, Dec. 21, 1954, and CM 1052, Jan. 5, 1955, all in AEC.

70. AEC 27/103, Dec. 20, 1954, AEC, describes the meetings with Hammarskjöld. Rabi's instructions were issued by David M. Key for the State Department, Dec. 27, 1954, DOS. Spiegel to File, Dec. 22, 1954; Wainhouse and G. C. Smith to the Under Secretary, Jan. 19, 1955, both in DOS.

71. Statement by President Eisenhower, Nov. 3, 1954; Excerpts of Address by Morehead Patterson, April 4, 1955, both in "Atoms for Peace Manual," pp. 291–92, 360–66.

72. Status of Implementation of NSC 5507/2—Peaceful Uses of Atomic Energy, AEC 751, 32, Aug. 19, 1955, AEC; Robert McKinney, *Background Material for the Review of the International Atomic Policies and Programs of the United States, Report to the Joint Committee on Atomic Energy* (Washington: Government Printing Office, 1960), pp. 843–44. In a few instances, agreements allowed for the transfer of twelve kilograms of uranium.

73. Joint Committee on Atomic Energy, *Hearings on Agreements with Turkey, Colombia, and Brazil,* June 8, 1955, AEC; AEC, *Progress in Peaceful Uses of Atomic Energy, July–December 1957* (Washington: Government Printing Office, 1958), pp. 189–221; CM 1079, April 29, 1955; CM 1080, May 3, 1955; CM 1082, May 18, 1955; JCAE Questions Concerning Turkish Bilateral Agreement, AEC 826/2, May 18, 1955; McCool to Hall, April 29, 1955; Libby to Pastore, May 19, 1955; Hall to the Commissioners and General Manager, June 10, 1955, all in AEC; Eisenhower to Libby, May 3, 1955, DDE. See Appendix 6 for a list of research bilaterals.

74. Joint Progress Report (State Department and AEC) on Implementation of NSC 5507/2—"Peaceful Uses of Atomic Energy," Aug. 13, 1956, April 22, 1957, both in AEC.

75. Report to the National Security Council on U.S. Policy on Atomic Power in Other Countries, AEC 655/25, Jan. 7, 1955; Joint Progress Report (State Department and AEC) on Implementation of NSC 5507/2—"Peaceful Uses of Atomic Energy," Aug. 13, 1956, both in AEC.

76. CM 1165, Jan. 19, 1956; Murray to the Commissioners, Jan. 17, 1956, both in AEC.

*619*

## CHAPTER NINE

1. Draft policy statements for NSC Planning Board, Jan. 18, 24, 1955; NSC 5507, Jan. 28, 1955; CM 1055, Jan. 19, 1955, all in AEC.

2. Draft policy statement for NSC Planning Board, Feb. 24, 1955, AEC.

3. National Security Council, Summary of Discussion (hereafter cited SNSC), Meeting 240, March 10, 1955, DDE. The paper considered was NSC 5507/1, Peaceful Uses of Atomic Energy. There is no copy in AEC, but the Planning Board draft of February 24, 1955, in AEC is probably very close to NSC 5507/1. The paper reflecting NSC revisions was issued as NSC 5507/2 on March 12, 1955, AEC.

4. On Libby's earlier career in atomic energy, see Richard G. Hewlett and Oscar E. Anderson, Jr., *The New World, 1939–1946,* Vol. I of *A History of the*

*U.S. Atomic Energy Commission* (University Park: Pennsylvania State University Press, 1962), pp. 99–100, 122–27 (hereafter cited *The New World*); Richard G. Hewlett and Francis Duncan, *Atomic Shield, 1947–1952*, Vol. II of *A History of the U.S. Atomic Energy Commission* (University Park: Pennsylvania State University Press, 1969), pp. 486, 537, 562 (hereafter cited *Atomic Shield*).

5. On von Neumann, see *The New World*, pp. 246, 313; *Atomic Shield*, pp. 176, 369, 439–41, 519, 529.

6. LaPlante to Strauss, Nov. 17, 1954; Strauss to von Neumann, Dec. 9, 1954; Strauss to File, Jan. 25, Feb. 12, 25, March 22, 1955, all in LLS; CM 1059, Feb. 5, 1955, AEC.

7. Joint Committee on Atomic Energy, *Hearings on Development, Growth, and State of the Atomic Energy Industry*, Jan. 31–March 3, 1955 (Washington: Government Printing Office, 1955), pp. 35–40 (hereafter cited *202 Hearings, 1955*).

8. Hafstad to Strauss, March 25, 1953; John J. McCloy to Strauss, Dec. 15, 1954; Strauss to McCloy, Dec. 16, 1954, all in LLS; AEC Press Release 582, Nov. 20, 1954, AEC.

9. CM 1055, Jan. 19, 1955; CM 1058, Feb. 1, 1955, both in AEC.

10. CM 1062, Feb. 23, 1955, AEC.

11. AEC Press Release 602, Feb. 25, 1955; AEC Press Release 648, June 17, 1955, both in AEC.

12. *202 Hearings, 1955*, pp. 61–65.

13. Schuldt to Schuab, Bureau of the Budget, March 14, 1955; Schuldt to File, March 14, 1955, both in AEC; SNSC 242, March 24, 1955, DDE. Strauss's briefing notes for the NSC meeting are also in AEC.

14. Lay to Strauss, March 26, 1955; Davis to C. E. Nelson, April 5, 1955; Draft Report on An Analysis of Factors Involved in the Installation of a Nuclear Power Reactor in a U.S. Merchant Ship, April 5, 1955; Final Report, April 7, 1955, all in AEC; SNSC 244, April 7, 1955, DDE; Lay to Strauss, April 9, 1955; CM 1074, April 11, 1955; AEC 653/3, April 13, 1955; CM 1075, April 13, 1955; Davis to Murray, April 15, 1955; CM 1077, April 27, 1955, all in AEC.

15. Hagerty Diary, April 25, 1955, DDE; CM 1077, April 27, 1955, AEC; Joint Committee on Atomic Energy, *Hearings on Authorizing Legislation, FY 1956*, May 2–31, 1955 (Washington: Government Printing Office, 1955), pp. 78–92; CM 1081, May 5, 1955; Libby to Strauss, Aug. 3, 1955, both in AEC; Richard G. Hewlett and Francis Duncan, *Nuclear Navy, 1946–1962* (Chicago: University of Chicago Press, 1974), pp. 186–93 (hereafter cited *Nuclear Navy*); Harold P. Green and Alan Rosenthal, *Government of the Atom: The Integration of Powers* (New York: Atherton Press, 1963), pp. 174–75.

16. Rockefeller to Herbert Hoover, Jr., March 9, 1955; Farley to File, March 17, 1955; Hoover to Strauss, March 25, 1955; Smith to Dulles, April 13, June 3, 1955, all in DOS; Don S. Burrows to Fields, July 3, 1956, AEC.

17. *Public Papers of the Presidents of the United States, 1955: Dwight D. Eisenhower* (Washington: Government Printing Office, 1959), pp. 593–600 (hereafter cited *Public Papers, 1955, Eisenhower*); Proposed Presidential Announcement on Atomic Power, AEC 751/29, May 24, 1955; Power Reactor Policy, AEC 751/28, May 13, 1955, both in AEC; Robert J. Donovan, *Eisenhower: The Inside Story* (New York: Harper, 1956), p. 192.

18. SNSC 255, July 14, 1955, DDE; P. F. Foster to the General Manager, Oct. 14, 1955; Strauss Statement to the Commission on AEC 655/39, Oct. 25, 1955; Murray to Strauss, Aug. 17, 1955; Fields to Strauss, Aug. 18, 1955, all in AEC.

19. Director of Reactor Development, Report on Status of Small-Output Civilian Power Reactor in 10,000 KW Range, AEC 655/36, Aug. 18, 1955; CM 1120, Aug. 25, 1955, both in AEC.

20. Director of Reactor Development, Power Demonstration Reactor Program, AEC 777/14, Sept. 9, 1955; CM 1122, Sept. 14, 1955; AEC Press Release 695, Sept. 21, 1955, all in AEC.

21. Nelson, Analysis of AEC 655/39, Oct. 17, 1955; Nelson to Strauss, Oct. 17, 1955; Director of Reactor Development, Report on Status of Small Output Civilian Power Reactor in 10,000 KW Range, AEC 655/39, Oct. 17, 1955; CM 1139, Oct. 17, 1955; CM 1143, Oct. 26, 1955; Strauss to Lay, Oct. 26, 1955; Schuldt to File, Nov. 3, 1955; Nelson to Strauss, Nov. 15, 1955; Director of Reactor De-

velopment, Report on the Background and Status of the Small Output Civilian Power Reactor, AEC 655/42, Jan. 3, 1956; CM 1161, Jan. 5, 1956; Strauss to Lay, Jan. 6, 1956; Nelson to Strauss, Jan. 18, 1956; SNSC 276, Feb. 9, 1956; S. E. Gleason to Strauss, Feb. 13, 1956, all in AEC.

22. Aaron Wildavsky, *Dixon-Yates: A Study in Power Politics* (New Haven: Yale University Press, 1962), pp. 223–27 (hereafter cited Wildavsky, *Dixon-Yates*); CM 1059, Feb. 5, 1955; News Bulletin, Feb. 1, 1955; Strauss to Gore, Feb. 8, 1955, all in AEC; Eisenhower press conference, Feb. 2, 1955, *Public Papers, 1955, Eisenhower*, p. 230.

23. Wildavsky, *Dixon-Yates*, pp. 229–33; *Congressional Record*, 84 Cong., 1 sess., Feb. 18, 1955, pp. 1714–16 (hereafter cited *CR*).

24. Wildavsky, *Dixon-Yates*, pp. 218–20.

25. Ibid., pp. 233–39; R. W. Cook to Nichols, March 22, 1955, in AEC 385/80, March 31, 1955, AEC; *CR*, 84 Cong., 1 sess., June 16, 1955, pp. 8469–95.

26. Correspondence on Memphis situation, in AEC 385/100, July 1, 1955; McCool to Fields, July 11, 1955; CM 1099, July 12, 1955; Rowland Hughes to Strauss, July 16, 1955, in AEC 385/104, July 18, 1955, all in AEC; *New York Times*, July 15, 1955; Sherman Adams, *Firsthand Report: The Story of the Eisenhower Administration* (New York: Harper & Brothers, 1961), pp. 311–17; Eisenhower press conference, July 6, 1955, *Public Papers, 1955, Eisenhower*, pp. 667–78; Wildavsky, *Dixon-Yates*, pp. 240–47, 251–66.

27. Strauss to Comptroller General, July 14, 1955, in AEC 385/106, July 20, 1955; David F. Shaw to Dixon, July 30, 1955, in AEC 385/110, Aug. 4, 1955; Correspondence on contract termination, in AEC 385/116, Aug. 26, 1955; CM 1119, Aug. 24, 1955; Frank H. Weitzel to Strauss, Oct. 3, 1955; McCool to Commissioners, Nov. 23, 1955; AEC Press Release 734, Nov. 23, 1955, all in AEC; Wildavsky, *Dixon-Yates*, pp. 267–92.

28. CM 1120, Aug. 25, 1955, AEC; SNSC 261, Oct. 13, 1955, DDE. For a comparison of national programs in reactor technology presented at Geneva, see *Proceedings of the International Conference on the Peaceful Uses of Atomic Energy*,

Vol. 3, *Power Reactors* (New York: United Nations, 1955).

29. Report of the U.S. Delegation to the International Conference on the Peaceful Uses of Atomic Energy, Geneva, Aug. 8–20, 1955, Vol. I, pp. 48–65, 119–30, 259–74; Vol. II, pp. 349–59; Confidential Supplement, pp. 20a–21a, AEC.

30. AEC Press Release 723, Oct. 27, 1955; J. J. Flaherty to Davis, Nov. 23, 1955, in AEC 331/106, Dec. 21, 1955; Davis to Fields, Feb. 2, 1956; AEC Press Release 779, Feb. 9, 1956, all in AEC.

31. AEC Press Release 777, Feb. 7, 1956, AEC; *New York Times*, Feb. 8, 1956; *Nucleonics* 14 (March 1956): 20–21.

32. These activities are richly documented in AEC files. The following is a sample: Acting General Counsel, Interim Orders To Be Issued Under the Atomic Energy Act of 1954, AEC 495/39, Aug. 24, 1954; CM 1021, Aug. 24, 1954; General Manager, Check-List of Actions Required Under the Atomic Energy Act of 1954, AEC 495/41, Sept. 9, 1954; General Manager, Industry Conferences on AEC Licensing Problems, AEC 23/15, Dec. 13, 1954; General Counsel, Report on Proposed Definitions of Production and Utilization Facilities, AEC 23/16, Dec. 22, 1954; Special Nuclear Material Regulations, AEC 784, Jan. 28, 1955; AEC Press Release 597, Feb. 10, 1955; Agenda, Electric Utilities Industry Advisory Conference, March 8, 1955; Draft Regulations for Use at Industry Advisory Conferences, AEC 23/19, March 3, 1955; AEC Press Release 606, March 9, 1955; AEC Announcement 305, March 25, 1955; General Manager, Proposed Regulations for the Licensing of Production and Utilization Facilities, AEC 23/22, March 30, 1955; CM 1073, April 6, 1955; AEC Press Release 622, April 12, 1955; Conference with State Representatives, AEC 23/25, April 27, 1955; AEC Press Release 638, May 19, 1955; AEC Press Release 656, June 29, 1955; General Manager, Proposed Rules of Practice Governing Licensees and Licenses, AEC 23/28, July 7, 1955; CM 1159, Dec. 21, 1955, all in AEC.

33. General Manager, General Access to Classified Non-Military Information and Use of AEC-Owned Facilities for Private Purposes, AEC 655/28, April 1, 1955;

621

CM 1073, April 6, 1955; AEC Press Release 626, April 20, 1955; Director, Division of Licensing, Promulgation of Regulations for Issuance of Access Permits, AEC 655/29, May 13, 1955; AEC Press Release 641, May 23, 1955; AEC Press Release 661, July 12, 1955; Director, Division of Civilian Applications, Regulations for Access to Restricted Data, AEC 843/3, Nov. 21, 1955; CM 1154, Dec. 7, 1955; AEC Press Release 770, Feb. 2, 1956; Joint Committee on Atomic Energy, *Hearings on Development, Growth, and State of the Atomic Energy Industry*, Feb. 7–23, 1956 (Washington: Government Printing Office, 1956), pp. 5–6, 52–77.

34. Vannevar Bush, *Science—The Endless Frontier: A Report to the President on a Program for Postwar Scientific Research* (1945; reprint, Washington: National Science Foundation, 1980), pp. 19, 28, 31, 74–78.

35. Lewis L. Strauss, *Men and Decisions* (Garden City, NY: Doubleday, 1962), pp. 163–80, 231–45.

36. Brookhaven National Laboratory Master Plan, AEC 645, May 21, 1953, AEC; *Atomic Shield*, pp. 38, 41, 224–25.

37. *The New World*, pp. 627, 635–36; *Atomic Shield*, pp. 103–4; ORINS Contract, AEC 267/41, July 5, 1957, AEC; AEC, *Sixth Semiannual Report* (Washington: Government Printing Office, 1949), p. 154.

38. *Atomic Shield*, pp. 199–201, 204–5, 224, 420–21; AEC, *Fifteenth Semiannual Report* (Washington: Government Printing Office, 1954), p. 39 (hereafter cited *Fifteenth Semiannual Report*); AEC, *Seventeenth Semiannual Report* (Washington: Government Printing Office, 1955), pp. 32–34.

39. AEC, *Sixteenth Semiannual Report* (Washington: Government Printing Office, 1954), pp. 38–39 (hereafter cited *Sixteenth Semiannual Report*); *Nuclear Navy*, pp. 54–55, 83–85, 94–97, 101–2, 145–50; AEC, *Twentieth Semiannual Report* (Washington: Government Printing Office, 1956), p. 96; Director of Reactor Development, Negotiations with the University of Chicago, AEC 324/10, Dec. 17, 1951; CM 637, Dec. 18, 1951, both in AEC.

40. Leonard Greenbaum, *A Special Interest: The Atomic Energy Commission, Argonne National Laboratory, and the Midwestern Universities* (Ann Arbor: University of Michigan Press, 1971), pp. 30–56 (hereafter cited Greenbaum, *A Special Interest*).

41. *The New World*, pp. 33–36, 46–47, 56–60; *Atomic Shield*, pp. 225–34, 248–51; Atomic Energy Commission, *Annual Financial Report, 1957* (Washington: Atomic Energy Commission, 1958), p. 20.

42. Bradbury's correspondence with Strauss was reproduced in a series of staff papers under the title, Role of Laboratories in AEC Program: Bradbury to Strauss, Oct. 27, 1955, in AEC 99/24, Nov. 14, 1955; Bradbury to Strauss, Feb. 7, 1956, in AEC 99/27, Feb. 14, 1956; Strauss to Bradbury, draft in AEC 99/28, July 24, 1956; Strauss to Bradbury, Aug. 14, 1956, all in AEC. On basic research programs at Los Alamos and Livermore, see Bradbury to A. D. Starbird, March 8, 1957, and Herbert York to H. A. Fidler, Jan. 22, 1957, both in AEC; *Fifteenth Semiannual Report*, p. 31; *Sixteenth Semiannual Report*, p. 37; *Nuclear Navy*, pp. 101–17, 142–47.

43. Atomic Energy Commission, *Annual Financial Report, 1956* (Washington: Atomic Energy Commission, 1957), pp. 22–23.

44. *Atomic Shield*, pp. 227–37, 249–51, 500–501.

45. M. Stanley Livingston, *Particle Accelerators: A Brief History* (Cambridge: Harvard University Press, 1969), pp. 60–75; E. D. Courant, M. S. Livingston, and H. S. Snyder, "The Strong Focusing Synchrotron—A New High Energy Accelerator," *Physical Review* 88 (1952): 1190–96; J. P. Blewett, "The Proton Synchrotron," in M. Stanley Livingston, ed., *The Development of High-Energy Accelerators* (New York: Dover Publications, 1966), pp. 295–99.

46. Director of Research, High Energy Accelerator Program, AEC 603, Dec. 1, 1952; AEC 603/1, Jan. 14, 1953; AEC 603/9, Oct. 8, 1953; CM 927, Oct. 14, 1953; CM 939, Nov. 12, 1953; AEC Press Release 513, Jan. 10, 1954, all in AEC.

47. Zinn et al. to T. H. Johnson, Director of Research, Jan. 30, 1953, LLS; Argonne Accelerator Project, AEC 603/17, June 3, 1954; CM 1001, June 9, 1954, both in AEC; Zinn to P. Gerald Kruger, Aug. 4, 1954; Kruger to Zinn, Oct. 11, 1954,

both in LLS; Greenbaum, *A Special Interest*, pp. 57–71.
48. Executive Session, CM 1135, Oct. 5, 1955; Executive Session, CM 1137, Oct. 11, 1955; CM 1138, Oct. 14, 1955; Executive Session, CM 1140, Oct. 21, 1955, all in AEC; Greenbaum, *A Special Interest*, pp. 72–83.
49. Executive Session, CM 1144, Nov. 1, 1955; CM 1148, Nov. 15, 1955; CM 1152, Nov. 23, 1955; Notes on Meeting with Argonne and Chicago Representatives, Nov. 15, 1955; Director of Research, Midwest Accelerator Program, AEC 827/7, Nov. 21, 1955, all in AEC.
50. CM 1153, Dec. 6, 1955; CM 1155, Dec. 13, 1955; Zinn to W. B. Harrell, Jan. 27, 1956; AEC Press Release 781, Feb. 10, 1956, all in AEC; *Chicago Sun-Times*, Feb. 10, 1956; *New York Times*, Feb. 11, 1956.
51. Joan L. Bromberg, *Fusion: Science, Politics, and the Invention of a New Energy Source* (Cambridge: MIT Press, 1982), pp. 13–21 (hereafter cited Bromberg, *Fusion*); Lyman Spitzer, Jr., "A Proposed Stellarator," AEC Report NYO-993, July 23, 1951, AEC.
52. Bromberg, *Fusion*, pp. 22–25; CM 582, July 26, 1951; Directors of Research and Classification, Research Program on Controlled Thermonuclear Processes, AEC 532, March 10, 1952; CM 678, April 2, 1952, all in AEC; Amasa S. Bishop, *Project Sherwood: The U.S. Program in Controlled Fusion* (Reading, MA: Addison-Wesley, 1958), pp. 15–64.
53. Joint Committee on Atomic Energy, *Hearings on Physical Research Program*, Feb. 3–14, 1958 (Washington: Government Printing Office, 1958), pp. 783–84; CM 916, Sept. 21, 1953; Zuckert To Strauss, Aug. 25, 1953, both in AEC.
54. Forthcoming Meeting with Messrs. Post, Spitzer, Tuck, et al., AEC 532/9, Sept. 16, 1953; Director of Research, CTR Program, AEC 532/10, Sept. 24, 1953; Paul W. McDaniel to Strauss, Oct. 2, 1953; CM 940, Nov. 20, 1953, all in AEC.
55. Bromberg, *Fusion*, pp. 36–44.
56. *Atomic Shield*, pp. 112–14, 251–55.
57. This and the following paragraphs are based on the AEC Semiannual Reports to the Congress, 1953–1957, and AEC staff papers in the 604 series, AEC.
58. Joint Committee on Atomic Energy, *Hearings on the Nature of Radioactive*

*Fallout and Its Effects on Man*, May 27–June 3, 1957 (Washington: Government Printing Office, 1957), pp. 170–267 (hereafter cited *Fallout Hearings, 1957*); *Atomic Shield*, pp. 242–45, 504–9.
59. AEC, Annual Financial Report, Fiscal Year 1955, in AEC, *Nineteenth Semiannual Report* (Washington: Government Printing Office, 1956), p. 180.
60. *Fallout Hearings, 1957*, pp. 21–23, 1380–88, 1391–408.
61. Director of Biology and Medicine, Status of *Gabriel* Studies, AEC 278/3, March 3, 1953; Nicholas M. Smith, Jr., Report of the *Gabriel* Project Study, May 21, 1949; Shields Warren to Carroll Wilson, Nov. 23, 1949, all in AEC.
62. Smith, *Gabriel* Project Reopened, Nov. 8, 1951; W. D. Claus to Murray, Dec. 11, 1951, both in AEC.
63. Director of Biology and Medicine, Rand *Gabriel* Conference, AEC 278/4, Aug. 10, 1953; Rand Report R-251-AEC, World-Wide Effects of Atomic Weapons, Aug. 6, 1953, both in AEC.
64. Director of Biology and Medicine, Status of Project *Gabriel*, AEC 278/6, Oct. 27, 1953; Supplementary Information on *Gabriel*, AEC 278/7, Jan. 19, 1954, both in AEC; *Fallout Hearings, 1957*, pp. 1198–200.
65. Director of International Affairs, Proposed Agenda for International Scientific Conference, AEC 729/8, Nov. 12, 1954, AEC.
66. Elof Axel Carlson, *Genes, Radiation, and Society: The Life and Work of H. J. Muller* (Ithaca, NY: Cornell University Press, 1981), pp. 26–36, 91–93, 120–27, 142–50 (hereafter cited Carlson, *Genes, Radiation, and Society*).
67. Ibid., pp. 315–18; George Spiegel to File, May 9, 1955, DOS; H. J. Muller, "The Genetic Damage Produced by Radiation," *Bulletin of the Atomic Scientists* 11 (June 1955): 210–12, 230.
68. Carlson, *Genes, Radiation, and Society*, pp. 352–67; P. W. McDaniel to H. S. Traynor, Sept. 26, 1955, with attachments, AEC.
69. Morse Salisbury to Fields, Sept. 19, 1955; Strauss Telephone Log, June 2, 1955; Strauss Appointment Calendar, June 6, 1955, all in AEC; *Washington Post*, Sept. 18, 1955.
70. George W. Beadle, editorial, *Science*, Oct. 28, 1955, p. 1; *Newsweek*, Oct. 3, 1955, p. 77; Senate Committee on Inter-

623

state and Foreign Commerce, *Hearings on the Nomination of Lewis L. Strauss to be Secretary of Commerce*, March 17–May 14, 1959 (Washington: Government Printing Office, 1959), pp. 1087–88 and 1093–99.

## CHAPTER TEN

1. Kuboyama died on September 23, 1954, of hepatitis contracted while he was recovering satisfactorily from radiation injury. Bugher to John A. Hall, April 6, 1955; Bugher to Masao Tsuzuki, April 5, 1955, both in AEC.
2. Holifield to Eisenhower, March 26, 1954, AEC.
3. Lawrence Freedman, *The Evolution of Nuclear Strategy* (New York: St. Martin's Press, 1981), pp. 81–88; Townsend Hoopes, *The Devil and John Foster Dulles* (Boston: Little, Brown and Company, 1973), pp. 193–201; John Foster Dulles, "Policy for Security and Peace," *Foreign Affairs* 32 (April 1954): 353–64; Note by the Executive Secretary to the National Security Council on Basic National Security Policy, NSC 162/2, Oct. 30, 1953, *Foreign Relations of the United States, 1952–1954*, Vol. 2, *National Security Affairs* (Washington: Government Printing Office, 1984), pp. 577–97.
4. Strauss later amended this statement to "put out of commission." Excerpts from President Eisenhower's Press Conference, Wednesday, March 31, 1954, AEC. *New York Times*, April 1, 1954, p. 1; Robert A. Divine, *Blowing on the Wind: The Nuclear Test Ban Debate, 1954–1960* (New York: Oxford University Press, 1978), pp. 12–13 (hereafter cited Divine, *Blowing on the Wind*).
5. James R. Killian, Jr., *Sputnik, Scientists, and Eisenhower: A Memoir of the First Special Assistant to the President for Science and Technology* (Cambridge: MIT Press, 1977), pp. 67–71.
6. ODM Planning for Dispersal of Facilities, AEC 540/15, June 4, 1954, AEC.
7. Flemming to Strauss, May 26, 1954, in AEC 540/15, AEC.
8. Rabi to Strauss, June 3, 1954, AEC.
9. Division of Biology and Medicine, Conference on Long Term Surveys and Studies of Marshall Islands, July 12–13, 1954; Compensation to the Japanese

Government on the *Fukuryu Maru* Case, AEC 730/4, June 11, 1954; ACBM 45, June 25–26, 1954, all in AEC.
10. Divine, *Blowing on the Wind*, pp. 21, 27–31; CM 957, Feb. 3, 1954; Murray to Strauss, Feb. 2, 1954; Murray to Eisenhower, Feb. 5, 1954, all AEC.
11. Dulles to Eisenhower, April 6, 1954, handwritten note in Eisenhower folder, LLS.
12. Proposal by Government of India for Moratorium on Weapons Tests, AEC 226/39, May 3, 1954, AEC. See also Statement by the Indian Prime Minister (Nehru) to Parliament Regarding Nuclear Tests [Extracts], April 2, 1954, *Documents on Disarmament, 1945–1959, Vol. I, 1945–1956* (Department of State Publication 7008), pp. 408–11 (hereafter cited *Documents on Disarmament*); Divine, *Blowing on the Wind*, pp. 18–31.
13. National Security Council, Summary of Discussion (hereafter cited SNSC), Meeting 195, May 6, 1954, DDE; Questions Concerning Weapons Tests, AEC 226/40, June 8, 1954, AEC.
14. SNSC 199, May 27, 1954, DDE.
15. SNSC 203, June 23, 1954, DDE; Teller and Bradbury to the General Manager, June 11, 1954, AEC.
16. Disarmament chronology and Memorandum—Disarmament Negotiations, Oct. 1956, LLS; SNSC 203, June 23, 1954, DDE.
17. Strauss to File, June 28, 1954, LLS.
18. D. C. Borg et al., Radioactive Fall-out Hazards from Surface Bursts of Very High Yield Nuclear Weapons, Technical Analysis Report—AFSWP 507, May 1954, p. iii, DOE History Division.
19. J. K. Mansfield to P. F. Foster, Aug. 19, 1954; Draft Statement by Chairman, Atomic Energy Commission, for Presentation in Executive Session, JCAE, March 24, 1955; Conference on Long-Term Surveys and Studies of Marshall Islands, July 12–13, 1954, all in AEC. The other panelists were Bernard Brodie, William W. Havens, Jr., Frederic de Hoffman, Lt. Gen. Elwood R. Quesada, Herbert F. York, and Col. Paul T. Preuss as executive secretary.
20. Foster, Memorandum for the General Manager, Sept. 2, 1954, AEC.
21. Draft Statement by Chairman, Atomic Energy Commission, for Presentation in Executive Session, JCAE, March 24, 1955; Flemming to Strauss, Sept. 24,

1954, in AEC 540/22, Sept. 28, 1954, both in AEC.

22. John C. Bugher, "The Medical Effects of Atomic Blasts," reprinted in Joint Committee on Atomic Energy, Subcommittee on Security, *Hearings on AEC-FCDA Relationship*, March 24, 1955 (Washington: Government Printing Office, 1955), pp. 10–20. Also see Divine, *Blowing on the Wind*, pp. 34–35.

23. Strauss to Flemming, Sept. 24, 1954, in AEC 540/22, Sept. 28, 1954, AEC.

24. Smith to Acting Secretary, March 18, 1955, DOS.

25. Joseph and Stewart Alsop, "Super-Super Bombs Leave Deadly Dust," *Washington Post*, Sept. 27, 1954.

26. Harold A. Knapp, Jr., "South Woodley Looks at the H-Bomb," *Bulletin of the Atomic Scientists* 10 (Oct. 1954): 306–11 (hereafter cited *BAS*).

27. Foster to the General Manager, Oct. 4, 1954; Foster to W. S. Paul, Oct. 8, 1954, both in AEC.

28. Foster to Paul, Oct. 8, 1954; Foster to the General Manager, Oct. 4, 1954, both in AEC; Foster to Strauss, Oct. 26, 1954, LLS.

29. FCDA Press Release PA #142, Oct. 15, 1954; Salisbury to Foster, Oct. 27, 1954; CM 1035, Oct. 21, 1954, all in AEC; Ralph E. Lapp, *The Voyage of the Lucky Dragon* (New York: Harper & Brothers, 1957), pp. 148–60; Foster to Strauss and Nichols, Oct. 29, 1954, AEC.

30. GAC 42, Nov. 3–4, 1954, AEC.

31. Foster to the General Manager, Nov. 9, 1954, in AEC 540/25, Nov. 16, 1954; Strauss to Murray, Campbell, and Libby, Nov. 8, 1954, both in AEC.

32. Foster to the General Manager, Nov. 9, 1954, AEC.

33. Hanson W. Baldwin, "Radioactivity—I and II," *New York Times*, Nov. 7–8, 1954.

34. Ralph E. Lapp, "Civil Defense Faces New Peril," *BAS* 10 (Nov. 1954): 349–51; Baldwin, "Radioactivity—I," *New York Times*, Nov. 7, 1954; Albert Schweitzer, "The Scientists Must Speak Up," *BAS* 10 (Nov. 1954): 339; Eugene Rabinowitch, "People Must Know," *BAS* 10 (Dec. 1954): 370, 398.

35. Summary, Conference on Genetics, Argonne National Laboratory, Nov. 19–20, 1954, AEC.

36. Bugher to Alphonso Tammaro, Dec. 8, 1954, AEC.

37. GAC 42, Nov. 3–4, 1954, AEC; Willard F. Libby, "Remarks for Delivery at the Washington Conference of Mayors, Washington, D.C., Dec. 2, 1954," in Senate Armed Services Committee, Subcommittee on Civil Defense, *Operations and Policies of the Civil Defense Program*, Feb. 22–March 8, 1955 (Washington: Government Printing Office, 1955), pp. 240–44 (hereafter cited *Civil Defense Hearings*).

38. Strauss to Flemming, undated, in AEC 540/26, Dec. 8, 1954, AEC.

39. CM 1047, Dec. 8, 1954; National Dispersion Policy—OCB Comments on Proposed Statement, AEC 540/29, Dec. 13, 1954, AEC.

40. CM 1047, Dec. 8, 1954; Strauss to Eisenhower, Dec. 10, 1954; Foster to the General Manager, Dec. 17, 1954, in AEC 540/31, Dec. 28, 1954; CM 1049, Dec. 22, 1954, all in AEC.

41. GAC 43, Dec. 20–22, 1954; Draft Release on Effects, AEC 540/32, Jan. 11, 1955; AEC 540/33, Jan. 18, 1955; AEC 540/34, Jan. 20, 1955; AEC 540/35, Jan. 28, 1955; AEC 540/36, Feb. 2, 1955, all in AEC.

42. Dunning to File, Jan. 20, 1955; CM 1055, Jan. 19, 1955, both in AEC.

43. Foster to Strauss, Jan. 19, 1955; Smith to Foster, Jan. 27, 1955, both in AEC.

44. Foster to Strauss, Jan. 31, 1955, AEC.

45. Eisenhower to Strauss, Feb. 2, 1955, and encl., AEC; SNSC 235, Feb. 3, 1955, DDE.

46. Strauss to Eisenhower, Feb. 7, 1955, DDE; Notes on Informal Meeting of Members of the Staff with the Chairman and Commissioner Libby, Feb. 7, 1955; CM 1059, Feb. 5, 1955; CM 1060, Feb. 11, 1955; McCool to Foster, Feb. 14, 1955; Peterson to Strauss, Feb. 10, 1955, in AEC 540/37, Feb. 16, 1955; Foster to McCool, Feb. 16, 1955, all in AEC.

47. Statement by Lewis L. Strauss, Feb. 15, 1955, AEC; *A Report by the United States Atomic Energy Commission on the Effects of High-Yield Nuclear Explosions* (Washington: Government Printing Office, 1955).

48. Foster to Nichols, March 3, 1955; Elmer B. Staats to Lay, March 2, 1955; Lay to the NSC, June 14, 1955, all in AEC.

49. Ralph E. Lapp, "Radioactive Fall-out," *BAS* 11 (Feb. 1955): 45–51.

50. Ibid.

625

51. CM 1047, Dec. 8, 1954, AEC.
52. *Civil Defense Hearings*, pp. 50–51; Ralph E. Lapp, "Fall-out and Candor," *BAS* 11 (May 1955): 170, 200; also see "Candor in Congress: The Kefauver Hearings," *BAS* 11 (May 1955): 181–84.
53. *Civil Defense Hearings*, pp. 5–7; AEC Press Release, June 3, 1955, Remarks prepared by Libby for the Alumni Reunion, University of Chicago, June 3, 1955, AEC.
54. Director of Military Application, Nevada Proving Ground Test Activities for Calendar Year 1955, AEC 707/3, Aug. 9, 1954; CM 1020, Aug. 18, 1954; Strauss to Donald A. Quarles, Asst. Secretary of Defense, July 1, 1954, in AEC 707/2, July 16, 1954, all in AEC. Details of the proposed test program were presented to the Commission in Operation Teapot, AEC 707/13, Dec. 20, 1954, and Proposed Program for Operation Teapot, AEC 707/17, Dec. 30, 1954, both in AEC. See also CM 1051, Jan. 4, 1955, AEC.
55. Richard G. Hewlett, "Nuclear Weapon Testing and Studies Related to Health Effects: An Historical Summary," in Interagency Radiation Research Committee, *Consideration of Three Proposals to Conduct Research on Possible Health Effects of Radiation from Nuclear Weapon Testing in Arizona, Nevada, and Utah* (Washington: National Institutes of Health, 1980), pp. 62–64. Extensive material on monitoring at *Teapot* is reproduced in Joint Committee on Atomic Energy, *Hearings on the Nature of Radioactive Fallout and its Effects on Man*, May 27–June 7, 1957 (Washington: Government Printing Office, 1957). See especially Reports of Off-Site Radiological Safety Activities, Nevada Test Site, Spring 1955, pp. 335–441.
56. Anderson to Strauss, Feb. 21, 1955, in AEC 141/28, Feb. 24, 1955; CM 1062, Feb. 23, 1955, both in AEC.
57. CM 1062, Feb. 23, 1955; CM 1063, March 1, 1955, both in AEC.
58. *Civil Defense Hearings*, p. 197; Joint Committee on Atomic Energy, Subcommittee on Security, Transcript of *Hearings on Civil Defense Planning*, March 24, 1955, pp. 4–6, 32–41; CM 1068, March 22, 1955; Foster to Strauss, March 21, 1955, all in AEC; Smith to Acting Secretary, March 18, 1955, DOS. See

also Divine, *Blowing on the Wind*, pp. 42–43.
59. Joint Committee on Atomic Energy, Transcript of *Hearings on Effects of Nuclear Explosions on Weather*, April 15, 1955, pp. 11–12, AEC (hereafter cited *Weather Hearings*).
60. "Proposal for a United Nations Committee to Study the Problem of H-Bomb Tests," *BAS* 11 (May 1955): 185–86; Lay to NSC, June 14, 1955, AEC.
61. Loper to G. C. Smith, March 17, 1955, in AEC 226/51, April 11, 1955; CM 1068, March 22, 1955, both in AEC.
62. Undated, unsigned note on stationery from British Embassy, AEC; Philip J. Farley, Chronology of Background Events Leading to Proposal for UN Exchange of Information on Fall-Out, May 19, 1955, DOS.
63. Foster to Nichols, April 13, 1955; Edward R. Gardner, Memorandum of Conversation, March 17, 1955, both in AEC.
64. FAS Proposal for U.N. Commission Study of H-Bomb Tests, AEC 226/52, April 11, 1955, AEC; Divine, *Blowing on the Wind*, p. 63.
65. Smith, Memorandum of Conversation, April 14, 1955; Smith to File, April 14, 1955; *Weather Hearings*, pp. 18–23, all in AEC.
66. Lodge to Dulles, May 3, 1955; Smith to File, May 5, 1955, both in DOS.
67. Smith and Wainhouse to Dulles, May 19, 1955; Farley, Chronology of Background Events Leading to Proposal for UN Exchange of Information on Fall-Out, May 19, 1955, both in DOS.
68. Smith, Memorandum of Conversation, May 12, 1955; Lodge to Dulles, May 16, 1955; United States Mission to the United Nations, Memorandum of Conversation, May 20, 1955, all in DOS.
69. Smith, Meeting in Secretary Dulles's Office, May 20, 1955, DOS.
70. Loper to Smith, May 25, 1955, DOS.
71. Gordon M. Dunning, "Effects of Nuclear Weapons Testing," *Scientific Monthly* 81 (Dec. 1955): 265–70.
72. AEC Press Release, Remarks Prepared by Libby for Alumni Reunion, University of Chicago, June 3, 1955, AEC (italics Libby's); Ralph E. Lapp, "Radioactive Fall-out III," *BAS* 11 (June 1955): 206–9, 230.
73. *Washington Post* and *Times-Herald*, June 22, 1955; *New York Times*, June 22 and

26, 1955; U.S. Initiative in U.N. on Radiation Effects, AEC 226/53, June 10, 1955, AEC; Alice L. Buck, "The AEC and the United Nations Scientific Committee on Radiation," manuscript, Historian's Office, DOE.

74. Hagerty Diary, March 21, 1955, DDE; Divine, *Blowing on the Wind*, pp. 60–61.

75. Hagerty Diary, Feb. 24, 1955, DDE; CM 1075, April 13, 1955; Snapp to Hall, Feb. 16, 1955, both in AEC.

76. Department of State, *Disarmament: The Intensified Effort, 1955–1958*, DOS Publication 7070, General Foreign Policy Series 155, Oct. 1960, pp. 8–10 (hereafter cited *Disarmament: The Intensified Effort*).

77. Ibid., pp. 14–15; Soviet Proposal Introduced in the Disarmament Subcommittee: Reduction of Armaments, the Prohibition of Atomic Weapons, and the Elimination of the Threat of a New War, May 10, 1955, *Documents on Disarmament*, pp. 456–67.

78. Stassen, Progress Report—Proposed Policy of the United States on the Question of Disarmament, Vol. I, May 26, 1955, AEC.

79. Ibid.

80. SNSC 253, June 30, 1955, DDE.

81. Walter LaFeber, *America, Russia, and the Cold War, 1945–1966* (New York: John Wiley and Sons, 1967), pp. 183–84 (hereafter cited LaFeber, *Cold War*); NSC, Basic U.S. Policy in Relation to Four-Power Negotiations, NSC 5524/1, July 11, 1955, AEC; Soviet Goals at Geneva, July 1, 1955; Estimate of Prospect of Soviet Union Achieving Its Goals, July 1, 1955, both in Dulles Papers, Princeton University.

82. Statement by President Eisenhower at the Geneva Conference of Heads of Government: Aerial Inspection and Exchange of Military Blueprints, July 21, 1955, *Documents on Disarmament*, pp. 486–88; LaFeber, *Cold War*, p. 185; W. W. Rostow, *Open Skies, Eisenhower's Proposal of July 21, 1955* (Austin: University of Texas Press, 1982); John S. D. Eisenhower, *Strictly Personal* (Garden City, NY: Doubleday, 1974), pp. 177–78; Stephen E. Ambrose, *Eisenhower, The President* (New York: Simon & Schuster, 1984), pp. 258–59, 264–65.

83. Bernhard G. Bechhoefer, *Postwar Negotiations for Arms Control* (Washington: Brookings Institution, 1961), pp. 308–15 (hereafter cited Bechhoefer, *Postwar Negotiations*); Stassen, Statement to the Disarmament Subcommittee, Sept. 6, 1955, *Documents on Disarmament*, pp. 510–14.

84. Bulganin to Eisenhower, Sept. 19, 1955, *Documents on Disarmament*, pp. 516–21.

85. R. I. Spiers, Memorandum of Conversation: Disarmament—Meeting in Mr. Hoover's Office, 4:15 p.m., Sept. 13, 1955, DOS.

86. SNSC 261, Oct. 13, 1955, DDE.

87. Stassen, Proposed Policy of the United States on the Question of Disarmament, Volume V, Nov. 1, 1955, AEC.

88. Strauss to Stassen, Dec. 2, 1955; Allen Dulles to Stassen, Dec. 5, 1955, both in AEC.

89. Strauss to Stassen, Dec. 2, 1955 (italics Strauss's); Radford to Wilson, Nov. 18, 1955; Wilson to Stassen, Dec. 7, 1955, all in AEC.

90. Strauss to Stassen, Dec. 2, 1955; Dulles to Stassen, Dec. 11, 1955, both in AEC.

91. *Disarmament: The Intensified Effort*, pp. 20–21; Bechhoefer, *Postwar Negotiations*, pp. 315–16; General Assembly Resolution 914 (X), Dec. 16, 1955, *Documents on Disarmament*, pp. 583–86; Memorandum—Disarmament Negotiations, undated but probably Nov. 1956, LLS.

92. Strauss to Dulles, Dec. 13, 1955; Strauss to Andrew J. Goodpaster, Dec. 14, 1955, both in AEC.

627

## CHAPTER ELEVEN

1. Laura Fermi, *Atoms for the World* (Chicago: University of Chicago Press, 1957), pp. 105–7.

2. Ibid.

3. Gerard C. Smith's Observations on the Geneva Conference, Sept. 23, 1955, DOS.

4. CM 1120, Aug. 25, 1955, AEC.

5. Smith, Observations, Sept. 23, 1955, DOS.

6. Willard F. Libby, "Increasing the Tempo of International Cooperation in Atomic Energy," address before the U.N. International Conference on the Peaceful Uses of Atomic Energy at Geneva on Aug. 20,

1955, *Department of State Bulletin,*
Sept. 5, 1955, pp. 381–84.

7. Smith, Observations, Sept. 23, 1955,
DOS; European Integration in the Field
of Atomic Energy, AEC 751/55, March
14, 1956, AEC.

8. Smith, Observations, Sept. 23, 1955,
DOS.

9. Morehead Patterson, Important Problems
Arising in International Atomic Energy
Agency Negotiations, Draft Report to the
President, n.d. but approximately Nov.
30, 1955, DOS.

10. International Atomic Energy Agency,
AEC 751/13, Oct. 1, 1954, AEC.

11. Richard C. Breithut, "International
Atomic Energy Conference—History of
IAEA Negotiations," Oct. 2, 1956, DOS.

12. Patterson, Draft Report to the President,
Nov. 30, 1955, DOS.

13. Memorandum received from Soviet Government, July 18, 1955; Breithut, History of IAEA Negotiations, Oct. 2, 1956,
both in DOS.

14. Soviet Aide-Memoire, Nov. 29, 1954,
DOS; International Atomic Energy
Agency, AEC 751/27, April 27, 1955,
AEC.

15. Hall to Those Listed, Feb. 7, 1955; Hall
to Smith, Feb. 17, 1955, both in AEC.

16. CM 1112, July 27, 1955; Foster to Mc-
Cool, Aug. 3, 1955, both in AEC; S/AE,
Conference on Safeguarding Peaceful
Uses of Atomic Energy, Aug. 11, 1955,
DOS.

17. Position Paper for Guidance of U.S. Par-
ticipants in Forthcoming International
Technical Discussions on Safeguarding
Peaceful Uses of Atomic Energy Under
Proposed Charter of International Atomic
Energy Agency, AEC 751/33, Aug. 23,
1955, AEC.

18. Robert Murphy to Rabi, Aug. 19, 1955,
DOS.

19. Richard W. Dodson, Notes on Meeting,
Aug. 16, 17, 1955, AEC.

20. Dodson, Notes on Meeting, Aug. 17,
1955, AEC.

21. Spofford G. English to Winston M. Man-
ning, Sept. 23, 1955, AEC.

22. Dodson, Notes on Meeting, Aug. 18,
1955, AEC.

23. Dodson, Meeting with British, Aug. 16,
1955, AEC.

24. Proposed International Atomic Energy
Agency, Meeting of Six Governments,
Verbatim Record of First Meeting, Ge-
neva, Aug. 22, 1955, AEC.

25. Text of Remarks of Dr. I. I. Rabi on a
Topical Outline of Basic Assumptions
and Tentative Suggestions for Inspection
and Control Under an International
Agency, Aug. 21, 1955, AEC.

26. Proposed International Atomic Energy
Agency, Meeting of Six Governments,
Verbatim Record of First, Second, and
Third Meeting, Aug. 22, 23, 25, 1955,
AEC.

27. Proposed International Atomic Energy
Agency, Meeting of Six Governments,
Verbatim Record of First and Second
Meeting, Aug. 22, 23, 1955, AEC.

28. Smith, Observations, Sept. 23, 1955,
DOS.

29. Smith to Dulles, Aug. 31, 1955, DOS.

30. Ibid.

31. Rabi and Davis to Strauss, Aug. 25,
1955, in AEC 751/34, Sept. 12, 1955,
AEC.

32. Ibid.; Rabi to Dulles, Aug. 27, 1955,
DOS; English, Notes, Sept. 13, 1955;
CM 1122, Sept. 14, 1955, both in AEC.

33. Smith to File, Sept. 14, 1955, DOS.

34. Diversion of Material, AEC 751/36, Oct.
19, 1955; Alphonso Tammaro to Fields,
Nov. 4, 1955, in AEC 751/39, Nov. 23,
1955; Norman A. Spector to U. M.
Staebler, Nov. 8, 1955; McCool to Davis,
Oct. 26, 1955, all in AEC. Although
Libby was present during the preconfer-
ence discussions, his authorship of the
"spiking" plan was challenged by Commission staff members. C. D. W. Thornton to R. W. Cook, Nov. 30, 1955, AEC.

35. Vitro Engineering Division, Inventory
Control Study, Final Report, KLX-1759,
Sept. 1, 1956, AEC.

36. Policy Relating to Peaceful Power Reactor Uses of Atomic Energy, AEC 655/40,
Nov. 28, 1955; Smith, Observations on
the Problems of Controlling Against Diversion of Fissionable Material from Nuclear Power Reactors, Sept. 17, 1955,
both in AEC.

37. AEC Staff Comments, Inspection and
Control Under an International Agency,
Dec. 9, 1955, AEC. Underlined in the
original.

38. Policy Relating to Peaceful Power Reac-
tor Uses of Atomic Energy, AEC 655/40,
Nov. 28, 1955; AEC Staff Comments,
Dec. 9, 1955, both in AEC.

39. Policy Relating to Peaceful Power Reac-
tor Uses of Atomic Energy, AEC 655/40,
Nov. 28, 1955; AEC Staff Comments,
Dec. 9, 1955; Knapp to Thornton, Oct.

24, 1955, all in AEC; Farley to File, Oct. 7, 1955, DOS.
40. Smith, Observations, Sept. 17, 1955, AEC.
41. IAEA Negotiations—Proposed U.S. Position on Control, Dec. 13, 1955, AEC.
42. CM 1156, Dec. 16, 1955, AEC.
43. CM 1157, Dec. 16, 1955, AEC.
44. International Atomic Energy Agency, AEC 751/41, Dec. 30, 1955, AEC.
45. Ibid.
46. CM 1160, Jan. 4, 1956, AEC.
47. Smith, Notes on the "Atoms for Peace" Program, Jan. 12, 1956, DOS.
48. European Integration in the Field of Atomic Energy, AEC 751/55, March 14, 1956, AEC; H. A. Robinson to Smith, July 6, 1955, DOS; André Fontaine, "Will the Atom Persuade Europeans to Unite?" *Reporter* 14 (March 22, 1956): 36–38; Secretariat of the Economic Commission for Europe, *Nuclear Energy and the Production of Electric Power in Europe* (Geneva: United Nations, Feb. 1956), p. 37; Electric Committee of the Organization for European Economic Cooperation, *The Electricity Supply Industry in Europe* (Paris: Organization for European Economic Cooperation, 1956), pp. 21–22, 57–58; Economic Commission for Europe, *The Electric Power Situation in Europe in 1955* (Geneva: United Nations, Feb. 1957), pp. 21–22, 57–58.
49. James S. Lay, Jr., Memorandum for the National Security Council, Dec. 1, 1955, DOS; United States Position on EURATOM and OEEC, AEC 751/62, May 7, 1956, AEC.
50. Dwight D. Eisenhower, *Waging Peace, 1956–1961* (Garden City, NY: Doubleday, 1965), pp. 125–26. For the administration's response to the collapse of EDC, see NSC 5433/1, Immediate U.S. Policy Toward Europe, Sept. 25, 1954, AEC. Stephen E. Ambrose, *Eisenhower the President* (New York: Simon & Schuster, 1984), pp. 48–49, 215–16.
51. Robert W. Barnett, Memorandum of Conversation, Jan. 25, 1956, AEC. See also NSC Action No. 1480. Dulles had indicated his support of the EURATOM project as early as July 1955. Dulles, Memorandum of Conversation, July 28, 1955; J. R. Schaetzel, Memorandum of Conversation, July 15, 1955, both in DOS; European Integration of Atomic Energy, AEC 751/43, Jan. 16, 1956, AEC.
52. Barnett, Memorandum of Conversation, Jan. 25, 1956, AEC.
53. Merchant to Smith, Dec. 6, 1955, DOS.
54. CM 1106, July 20, 1955, AEC; Smith to File, Jan. 5, 1956, DOS. For further discussion of the McKinney panel report, see Chap. 12.
55. Barnett, Memorandum of Conversation, Jan. 25, 1956, AEC.
56. Dulles to Eisenhower, Jan. 9, 1956; Eisenhower to Strauss, Jan. 12, 1956, both in AEC 751/43, Jan. 16, 1956; Barnett, Memorandum of Conversation, Jan. 25, 1956; CM 1167, Jan. 25, 1956, all in AEC; Davis to Farley, Jan. 10, 1956, DOS.
57. Farley, Memorandum of Conversation, Feb. 3, 1956, in International Atomic Energy Agency, AEC 751/56, March 20, 1956, AEC.
58. Ibid.
59. *Public Papers of the Presidents of the United States, 1956: Dwight D. Eisenhower* (Washington: Government Printing Office, 1958), pp. 258–59.
60. Strauss to Eisenhower, Feb. 20, 1956; Goodpaster, Memorandum of Conference with the President, Jan. 13, 1956, both in DDE; CM 1165, Jan. 19, 1956; Eisenhower to Strauss, Feb. 22, 1956, both in AEC.
61. Strauss to Dulles, April 13, 1956, AEC.
62. Address by President Dwight D. Eisenhower before General Assembly of the United Nations, "Atomic Power for Peace," December 8, 1953, in "Atoms for Peace Manual," Senate Document 55, 84 Cong., 1 sess. (Washington: Government Printing Office, 1955), pp. 1–7.

629

## CHAPTER TWELVE

1. Clinton P. Anderson, *Outsider in the Senate: Senator Clinton Anderson's Memoirs* (New York: World Publishing, 1970), pp. 154–55.
2. McKinney to Anderson, Sept. 23, 1955, and Anderson to McKinney, Sept. 27, 1955, both in CPA; J. L. Kelehan to Herbert I. Miller, executive director of the panel, Oct. 31, 1955, in AEC 152/64, Nov. 8, 1955; Manuscript of panel hearings with Commissioners and AEC Staff, Dec. 5, 1955, and Jan. 3, 1956; Civilian Power Reactor Development Program and Objectives, AEC 152/67, Feb. 28,

1956, all in AEC; Joint Committee on Atomic Energy, *Hearings on Development, Growth, and State of the Atomic Energy Industry*, Feb. 7–March 6, 1956 (Washington: Government Printing Office, 1956), p. 321 (hereafter cited *202 Hearings, 1956*); Corbin Allardice to Strauss, Aug. 11, 1955, July 8, 1960, both in LLS; Dwight A. Ink to Kelehan, Jan. 25, 1956, AEC.

3. Joint Committee on Atomic Energy, *Report of the Panel on the Impact of the Peaceful Uses of Atomic Energy*, Vol. I (Washington: Government Printing Office, 1956), pp. 1–2, 7, 29–49, 97. The panel published a large collection of supporting materials in Vol. II.

4. AEC, *Nineteenth Semiannual Report*, July–Dec. 1955 (Washington: Government Printing Office, 1956), pp. 69–81 (hereafter cited *Nineteenth Semiannual Report*); Gordon M. Dunning, "Effects of Nuclear Weapons Testing," *Scientific Monthly* 81 (Dec. 1955): 265–70.

5. Williard F. Libby, "The Radioactive Fallout and Radioactive Strontium," paper presented at Northwestern University, Evanston, IL, Jan. 19, 1956, AEC.

6. GAC 48, Jan. 12–13, 1956, AEC.

7. Libby, "Radioactive Fallout and Radioactive Strontium," AEC.

8. *Nineteenth Semiannual Report*, pp. 69–72; CM 1164, Jan. 18, 1956, AEC.

9. Rabi to Strauss, Jan. 17, 1956; GAC 48, Jan. 12–13, 1956, both in AEC.

10. House Committee on Government Operations, Subcommittee on Civil Defense, *Hearings on Civil Defense for National Survival*, Jan. 31–Feb. 9, 1956 (Washington: Government Printing Office, 1956), pp. 22–28; CM 1177, Feb. 21, 1956, AEC.

11. Robert L. Corsbie to Libby, Testimony of Ralph Lapp, March 20, 1956, AEC 604/15, AEC; *Washington Post and Times-Herald*, March 21, 1956.

12. Declassification of Certain Information on the Amount of Radioactivity in the Stratosphere, AEC 278/10, March 30, 1956; Review of GAC Recommendations, AEC 29/103, April 11, 1956, both in AEC.

13. CM 1190, April 4, 1956; McCool to Marshall, Commission Decision on AEC 278/10, April 5, 1956, both in AEC. Willard F. Libby, "Radioactive Strontium Fallout," *Proceedings of the National Academy of Sciences* 42 (June 1956): 365–90.

14. Dulles to Eisenhower, Jan. 22, 1956, Dulles/Herter Classified, Dulles Papers, DDE.

15. Dulles to Eisenhower, Jan. 22, 1956, Dulles/Herter Classified, Dulles Papers; Eisenhower to Dulles, Jan. 23, 1956, Dulles/Herter Classified, Dulles Papers, both in DDE.

16. Robert A. Divine, *Blowing on the Wind: The Nuclear Test Ban Debate, 1954–1960* (New York: Oxford University Press, 1978), pp. 67–68 (hereafter cited Divine, *Blowing on the Wind*); Senate Committee on Foreign Relations, *Hearings on Control and Reduction of Armaments*, Jan. 25–Dec. 12, 1956 (Washington: Government Printing Office, 1956), p. 15.

17. James S. Lay, Jr., to NSC, U.S. Policy on Control of Armaments, Jan. 13, 1956; Proposed Policy of the U.S. on the Question of Disarmament, AEC 226/69, Jan. 16, 1956; CM 1165, Jan. 19, 1956; Strauss, U.S. Policy on Control of Armaments, Jan. 23, 1956, all in AEC.

18. Strauss to Commissioners, Feb. 6, 1956; C. E. Nelson to Commissioners, Jan. 26, 1956, both in AEC.

19. Eden Talks, Washington, Jan. 30–Feb. 1, 1956, Memorandum of Conversation, Feb. 7, 1956, AEC; Strauss to File, Feb. 1, 1956, LLS.

20. Eden Talks, Washington, Jan. 30–Feb. 1, 1956, Memorandum of Conversation, Feb. 7, 1956, AEC.

21. National Security Council, Summary of Discussion (hereafter cited SNSC), Meeting 275, Feb. 7, 1956; Eisenhower, A. Whitman Diaries, Feb. 6, 1956, both in DDE.

22. Bulganin to Eisenhower, Sept. 19, 1955, *Documents on Disarmament, 1945–1959, Vol. I, 1945–1956* (Department of State Publication 7008), pp. 516–521 (hereafter cited *Documents on Disarmament*).

23. Eisenhower to Bulganin, March 1, 1956, *Documents on Disarmament*, pp. 593–95; CM 1173, Feb. 7, 1956; Comments on "Public Statement on U.S. Position on Disarmament," AEC 226/75, Feb. 8, 1956, both in AEC; Strauss to File, Feb. 10, 1956, Feb. 15, 1956, both in LLS; Goodpaster, Memorandum of Conference with the President, Feb. 15, 1956, DDE.

24. Dwight D. Eisenhower, *Mandate for Change, 1953–1956* (Garden City, NY: Doubleday, 1963), pp. 572–73.

25. Eisenhower to Stassen, March 10, 1956, DDE.
26. Amos J. Peaslee to Sherman Adams, April 23, 1956, DDE.
27. Statement of Commissioner Murray before the Joint Committee on Atomic Energy, Feb. 23, 1956, AEC.
28. Strauss to Hagerty, March 14, 1956, LLS.
29. Eisenhower, Press Conference, March 21, 1956, *Public Papers of the Presidents of the United States, 1956: Dwight D. Eisenhower* (Washington: Government Printing Office, 1957), pp. 333–34 (hereafter cited *Public Papers, 1956, Eisenhower*).
30. Murray, Testimony before the Subcommittee on Disarmament of the Senate Committee on Foreign Relations, April 12, 1956, pp. 713–96, AEC.
31. Divine, *Blowing on the Wind*, pp. 71–73; *New York Times*, April 22, 1956; *New York Herald Tribune*, April 24, 1956; *Milwaukee Journal*, April 30, 1956.
32. *New York Herald Tribune*, April 24 and 25, 1956.
33. *New York Times*, May 2, 1956; *Baltimore Sun*, May 2, 1956; *Washington Post and Times-Herald*, May 2, 1956.
34. Eisenhower, Press Conference, April 25, 1956, *Public Papers, 1956, Eisenhower*, pp. 434–35; A. Whitman Diary, April 25, 1956, DDE; *Washington Star*, April 27, 1956; *Wall Street Journal*, April 23, 1956.
35. *Daily Worker*, May 23, 1956; *Washington Post and Times-Herald*, May 22, 1956.
36. "The Biological Effects of Atomic Radiation: A Report to the Public," National Academy of Sciences—National Research Council, June 1956; Press Conference on "The Biological Effects of Atomic Radiation," National Academy of Sciences, June 12, 1956, both in AEC; "The Hazards to Man of Nuclear and Allied Radiations—Press Release," Medical Research Council; Roger Makins to Dulles, June 11, 1956, both in DOS.
37. Libby to Dulles, July 5, 1956; William Macomber to Gerard C. Smith, July 11, 1956, both in DOS.
38. AEC, *Twentieth Semiannual Report*, January–June 1956 (Washington: Government Printing Office, 1956), pp. 104–15; AEC Analysis of Reports on Radiation, July 18, 1956, Special Committee on Disarmament Problems, Stassen Papers, DDE; Annual Report to the National Security Council, Fiscal Year 1956, AEC 746/15, July 30, 1956, AEC.
39. *Congressional Record*, 84 Cong., 1 sess., July 30, 1955, p. 12198 (hereafter cited *CR*). The Gore bill was introduced as S.2725, 84 Cong., 1 sess.; Transcript of Joint Committee Hearing on Commissioner Murray's Statement, Feb. 23, 1956, AEC. An unclassified version of Murray's statement appears in *202 Hearings, 1956*, pp. 289–95.
40. JCAE Press Release 47, March 14, 1956; JCAE Press Release 48, March 14, 1956; JCAE Press Release 49, March 16, 1956; JCAE Press Release 52, April 26, 1956; JCAE Press Release 54, May 5, 1956, all in AEC; *CR*, 84 Cong., 2 sess., April 26, 1956, pp. 7054–63; *Wall Street Journal*, April 27, 1956; *Washington Post and Times-Herald*, April 27, 1956.
41. Joint Committee on Atomic Energy, Transcript of Hearings, May 21, 22, 1956, AEC.
42. Joint Committee on Atomic Energy, *Hearings on Proposed Legislation for Accelerating Civilian Reactor Program*, May 23–29, 1956 (Washington: Government Printing Office, 1956), pp. 5–8. For an AEC summary of the testimony, see Davis to Fields, May 29, 1956, in AEC 152/71, June 5, 1956; LaPlante to Fields, May 29, 1956, in AEC 152/72, June 15, 1956, both in AEC. The Commission's formal comments on the bill were presented on pp. 67–71 of the hearings. *Washington Post and Times-Herald*, May 26, 1956; *Baltimore Sun*, May 26, 1956.
43. Robert McKinney, Remarks, "Peaceful Uses of Atomic Energy As an Instrument in International Relations," May 17 and 28, 1956, AEC.
44. Jackson to Strauss, May 26, 1956, C. D. Jackson Papers, DDE; Kouts to Hall, in Recommendations of Committee to Consider the President's Atoms-for-Peace Program, AEC 751/71, June 21, 1956, AEC.
45. *New York Times*, May 13, 1956; *Baltimore Sun*, June 29, 1956.
46. *CR*, 84 Cong., 2 sess., July 12, 1956, pp. 12452–69; *New York Times*, July 13, 1956; *Washington Post and Times-Herald*, July 13, 1956.
47. House Appropriations Committee, *Hearings on Second Supplemental Appropriations Bill*: Part 2, *Investigation of Atomic*

631

*Electric Power* (Washington: Government Printing Office, 1956), especially pp. 78–96; *New York Times*, July 21, 1956; *Washington News*, July 20, 1956; *St. Louis Post-Dispatch*, July 20, 1956.

48. *CR*, 84 Cong., 2 sess., July 24, 1956, pp. 14246–88; *Wall Street Journal*, July 25, 1956; *Nucleonics* 14 (Aug. 1956): R1–R2.

49. Strauss to File, May 10, 1956; Harold S. Vance, Memorandum of Conversation with Senator Anderson, May 11, 1956, both in LLS; *Washington Star*, July 27, 1956; Senate Committee on Interstate and Foreign Commerce, *Hearings on the Nomination of Lewis L. Strauss to be Secretary of Commerce*, March 17–May 14, 1959 (Washington: Government Printing Office, 1959), pp. 514–17; George T. Mazuzan and J. Samuel Walker, *Controlling the Atom: The Beginnings of Nuclear Regulation, 1946–1962* (Berkeley: University of California Press, 1984), pp. 120–21.

50. Strauss to Eisenhower, March 5, 1956, AEC.

51. Eisenhower, Press Conference, May 23, 1956, *Public Papers, 1956, Eisenhower*, pp. 511–26; Divine, *Blowing on the Wind*, pp. 75–78.

52. Subcommittee on the Air Force of the Senate Committee on Armed Services, *Hearings on Airpower*, Part X, May 24–31, 1956 (Washington: Government Printing Office, 1956), pp. 856–62.

53. Strauss to File, July 13, 1956, LLS.

54. Teller to General Starbird, undated but about June 6, 1956; Teller to Libby, undated, but about June 6, 1956; Libby to Strauss, July 6, 1956, all in AEC.

55. CM 1214, July 11, 1956; CM 1215, July 12, 1956; Strauss to File, July 13, 1956, all in AEC; SNSC 290, July 12, 1956, DDE.

56. Informal meeting of the Commission, July 19, 1956, AEC.

57. Strauss, Press Release, July 19, 1956, AEC.

58. *New York Times*, July 20, 1956; *Washington Post and Times-Herald*, July 21, 1956.

59. Joint Committee on Atomic Energy, Transcript of Hearing to Consider H.R.12234 Re Transfer of Restricted Data on Military Reactors and Other Business, July 23, 1956, pp. 150–61, AEC.

60. CM 1221, Aug. 2, 1956, AEC.

61. Ralph E. Lapp, "The 'Humanitarian' H-Bomb," *Bulletin of the Atomic Scientists* 12 (Sept. 1956): 261–64. See also Eugene Rabinowitch, "Editorial: H-Bombs without Fallout," ibid., pp. 234, 264; *New York Times*, July 23, 1956, p. 6, July 29, 1956, p. E9.

62. Gerard C. Smith, Memorandum of Conversation: Possible U.K. Statement re Test Moratorium, June 2, 1956; Proposed U.K. Announcement on Test Limitation, June 6, 1956; Proposed British Announcement on Test Limitation, June 6, 1956, all in DOS.

63. Memorandum Dated June 29, 1956, to Members of the National Security Council from the Special Assistant to the President [Stassen], AEC.

64. Herbert S. Parmet, *Eisenhower and the American Crusades* (New York: Macmillan, 1972), pp. 450–51.

65. Ibid., pp. 451–52; A. Whitman Diary, July 20, 1956, DDE; David W. Reinhard, *The Republican Right Since 1945* (Lexington: University Press of Kentucky, 1983), pp. 130–32.

66. A. Whitman Diary, July 27 and 31, 1956, DDE; Dwight D. Eisenhower, *Waging Peace, 1956–1961* (Garden City, NY: Doubleday, 1965), p. 10; Richard M. Nixon, *The Memoirs of Richard Nixon* (New York: Grosset and Dunlap, 1978), pp. 173–75.

67. A. Whitman Diary, July 31, 1956, DDE.

68. Dulles, Memorandum of Conversation with Ambassador Peaslee, Aug. 28, 1956; Memorandum of Conversation with Senator Knowland, Sept. 8, 1956, both in Dulles Papers, DDE.

## CHAPTER THIRTEEN

1. R. O. Brittan, Some Problems in the Safety of Fast Reactors, Argonne National Laboratory Report ANL-5577, 1956; Gerald S. Lellouche, "The EBR-1 Incident: A Reexamination," *Nuclear Science and Engineering* 56 (March 1975): 303–7; Joseph R. Dietrich and Walter H. Zinn, *Solid Fuel Reactors* (Reading, MA: Addison-Wesley, 1958), pp. 40, 94; George T. Mazuzan and J. Samuel Walker, *Controlling the Atom: The Beginnings of Nuclear Regulation, 1946–1962* (Berkeley: University of

California Press, 1984), pp. 125–28 (hereafter cited Mazuzan and Walker, *Controlling the Atom*).

2. Reactor Safeguards Committee Report on Power Reactor Development Company Fast Power Reactor, AEC 331/111, June 20, 1956, AEC; Mazuzan and Walker, *Controlling the Atom*, pp. 129–33.

3. Williams to Strauss, July 16, 1956, in AEC 331/112; Fields to Williams, July 17, 1956, in AEC 331/113, both in AEC; Anderson to Williams, Aug. 3, 1956; JCAE Press Release 66, Aug. 4, 1956; Chet Holifield, Press Release, Aug. 4, 1956, all in Clinton Anderson Papers, Box 801, Library of Congress; Mazuzan and Walker, *Controlling the Atom*, pp. 135–40.

4. Teller to Libby, undated but with covering note, Strauss to Libby, June 7, 1956; Strauss to Anderson, Oct. 9, 1956, with covering note, Strauss to the Commissioners, Oct. 9, 1956; Director of Civilian Application, Issuance of Construction Permit and Allocation of Special Nuclear Material to PRDC, AEC 331/114, July 30, 1956; CM 1221, Aug. 2, 1956; AEC Press Release 865, Aug. 4, 1956, all in AEC; *Nucleonics* 14 (Sept. 1956), R3-R5; *New York Times*, Aug. 9, 1956.

5. Virginia H. Walker to Bryce N. Harlow, Aug. 14, 1956; Strauss to Harlow, Aug. 14, 1956; Draft Statement for Senator Hickenlooper and Congressman Cole; Earle D. Chesney to Harlow, Aug. 28, 1956; Chesney to Cole, Aug. 16, 1956, all in DDE; Paul F. Foster to Strauss, Sept. 8, 1956, LLS.

6. S. M. Cleveland, Spaak's Views on U.S. Atomic Energy Bilaterals and EURATOM, n.d., in Timmons to Merchant and Smith, March 28, 1956; Beam to Dulles, Oct. 15, 1956, both in DOS.

7. Schaetzel to Timmons, Oct. 1, 1956; Smith to File, March 29, 1956; Schaetzel to Smith, March 29, 1956; Beam to Dulles, Oct. 15, 1956, all in DOS.

8. Robinson, Memorandum of Conversation, April 28, 1956, AEC; Dulles to Strauss, Oct. 15, 1956, DOS. According to Ambassador James B. Conant, Heisenberg, Germany's most famous nuclear physicist who "has always had and still has strong nationalistic feelings," could also be counted among those Germans favoring an independent course. Conant to Merchant, Feb. 10, 1956, DOS. See also

European Integration in the Field of Atomic Energy, AEC 751/55, March 14, 1956, AEC; Dulles, Memorandum of Conversation, Feb. 9, 1956, DOS; Notes on EURATOM Debates, AEC 751/89, Oct. 3, 1956, AEC.

9. Schaetzel to Smith and Timmons, Aug. 2, 1956; Schaetzel to Strauss, Aug. 7, 1956; Smith and Elbrick to Bowie, Sept. 5, 1956; Smith and Elbrick to Dulles, Sept. 25, 1956; Yost, Status of EURATOM Negotiations, Oct. 10, 1956, all in DOS.

10. Dulles to Strauss, Oct. 15, 1956; Herbert Hoover, Jr., to Dulles, Oct. 24, 1956; Beam to Dulles, Oct. 15, 1956, all in DOS.

11. Strauss to Hoover, Dec. 19, 1956, in AEC 751/101, Jan. 3, 1957, AEC.

12. *New York Times*, Oct. 18, 1956, p. 1; *Nucleonics* 14 (Oct. 1956): 1; *Nucleonics* 14 (Dec. 1956): 51–54, S28-S29.

13. Richard G. Hewlett and Francis Duncan, *Nuclear Navy, 1946–1962* (Chicago: University of Chicago Press, 1974), pp. 247–53.

14. George Meany to Strauss, Sept. 12, 1956, in AEC 331/121, Sept. 19, 1956; PRDC Construction Permit, AEC 331/117, Sept. 4, 1956, both in AEC.

15. Strauss to Vance, March 21, 1946; Strauss to Edward T. Tait, Sept. 28, 1955, both in LLS.

16. CM 1224, Sept. 13, 1956, AEC.

17. Power Demonstration Reactor Program—Consumers Proposal, AEC 777/21, Sept. 24, 1956; Proposed Action on Piqua Demonstration Proposal, AEC 777/22, Sept. 25, 1956; AEC Press Release 898, Sept. 27, 1956; CM 1233, Oct. 11, 1956, all in AEC.

18. *New York Times*, Aug. 16, 1956.

19. *Baltimore Sun*, Oct. 10, 1956.

20. Strauss, Remarks to the New York Board of Trade, Oct. 10, 1956, AEC.

21. Bernhard G. Bechhoefer, "Negotiating the Statute of the International Atomic Energy Agency," reprinted from *International Organization* 13 (1959): 38–59 (hereafter cited Bechhoefer, "Negotiating the Statute").

22. Assistant General Manager for International Activities, Memorandum to the President from the Special Assistant to the President for Disarmament, AEC 226/88, Aug. 3, 1956, AEC.

23. CM 1217, July 18, 1956; Edward R. Gardner to Fields, Limitation on Testing

633

of Nuclear Weapons, Aug. 21, 1956, both in AEC.

24. Study Proposal by Commissioner Libby Concerning Limitation on Weapons Testing, AEC 859/3, Aug. 6, 1956, AEC.

25. Robert A. Divine, *Blowing on the Wind: The Nuclear Test Ban Debate, 1954–1960* (New York: Oxford University Press, 1978), pp. 85–87 (hereafter cited Divine, *Blowing on the Wind*); Memorandum on Weapon Tests Prepared for Release at the President's News Conference, Oct. 24, 1956, AEC (hereafter cited Test Memorandum, Oct. 24, 1956).

26. Limitations on Nuclear Tests, AEC 226/94, Oct. 1, 1956, AEC.

27. Report on Relative Effects of Test Limitations on Nuclear Weapon Programs of United States and Soviet Union, Oct. 1, 1956, AEC.

28. Memorandum of Conference at the Office of the Chairman of the Atomic Energy Commission, Aug. 16, 1956; Memorandum of Conference at the Office of the Secretary of State, Aug. 28, 1956; Peaslee to Eisenhower, Sept. 6, 1956, all in DDE; Strauss to File, Sept. 11, 1956, LLS.

29. Jackson, Summary of Conference at White House, Sept. 11, 1956, AEC.

30. Disarmament Proposals and Discussions, AEC 226/92, Sept. 19, 1956; J. H. Morse to Foster, Sept. 12, 1956; Jackson, Summary of Conference at White House, Sept. 11, 1956, all in AEC.

31. Bulganin to Eisenhower, Sept. 11, 1956, as quoted in Test Memorandum, Oct. 24, 1956, p. 9.

32. *New York Times*, Aug. 16, 1956. For an excellent summary of the test-ban issue and the election campaign, see Stephen E. Ambrose, *Eisenhower the President* (New York: Simon & Schuster, 1984), pp. 347–50.

33. *New York Times*, Sept. 20, 1956; *Washington Post and Times-Herald*, Sept. 20, 1956.

34. *New York Times*, Sept. 21, 1956; Statement of Thomas E. Murray, Commissioner, Sept. 21, 1956, AEC.

35. *New York Times*, Sept. 30, Oct. 4, 1956; *Washington Star*, Oct. 3, 1956; Walter Johnson, Carol Evans, and C. Eric Sears, eds., *The Papers of Adlai E. Stevenson*, Vol. 6, *Toward a New America, 1955–1957* (Boston: Little, Brown, 1976), p. 249 (hereafter cited *Stevenson*

*Papers*); Murray, Memorandum to the Commissioners, Limitations of Nuclear Tests, Oct. 3, 1956; Murray to Eisenhower, Oct. 4, 1956; Eisenhower to Murray, Oct. 5, 1956, all in AEC.

36. *New York Times*, Oct. 6, 1956; Chronology as found in Test Memorandum, Oct. 24, 1956, p. 9.

37. *New York Times*, Oct. 9, 10, 1956; Press Release, Senate Committee on Foreign Relations, Subcommittee on Disarmament, Oct. 7, 1956, Stassen Papers, DDE.

38. Foster to the Commission, Disarmament Proposals, Oct. 12, 1956, AEC.

39. *New York Times*, Oct. 12, 13, 1956.

40. *New York Herald Tribune*, Oct. 14, 1956; Bentley Glass, "The Hazards of Atomic Radiations to Man—British and American Reports," *Bulletin of the Atomic Scientists* 12 (Oct. 1956): 312–17; *Christian Science Monitor*, Oct. 17, 1956; Statement by Ten Scientists, Oct. 15, 1956, LLS.

41. Divine, *Blowing on the Wind*, pp. 93–95; *Washington Post and Times-Herald*, Oct. 16, 1956; *Washington Star*, Oct. 21, 1956; *Stevenson Papers*, pp. 281–86.

42. *New York Times*, Oct. 17, 1956.

43. *Baltimore Sun*, Oct. 22, 1956; *Washington Star*, Oct. 21, 1956; *New York Times*, Oct. 21, 1956; *Chicago Sun Times*, Oct. 21, 1956; Kenneth S. Davis, *The Politics of Honor: A Biography of Adlai E. Stevenson* (New York: G. P. Putnam's Sons, 1967), pp. 341–42.

44. Division of Biology and Medicine, Summary Discussion of Effects on Humans, Agricultural Products, and Weather of a Projected Nuclear War, Oct. 9, 1956; Study of the Biological Consequences of Atomic Warfare, AEC 604/22, Oct. 11, 1956; CM 1236, Oct. 17, 1956, all in AEC.

45. Willard F. Libby, "Current Research Findings on Radioactive Fallout," delivered before the American Association for the Advancement of Science, Washington, DC, Oct. 12, 1956; CM 1228, Sept. 25, 1956, both in AEC.

46. *New York Herald Tribune*, Oct. 18, 1956.

47. GAC 51, Oct. 29–31, 1956, AEC; Divine, *Blowing on the Wind*, p. 105.

48. A. Whitman Diary, Oct. 7, 1956, DDE; *New York Times*, Oct. 18, 1956.

49. Summary of 12-Nation Working Level Meeting on International Atomic Energy

Agency Statute, AEC 751/57, March 30, 1956, AEC.

50. Bernhard G. Bechhoefer and Eric Stein, "Atoms for Peace: the New International Atomic Energy Agency," *Michigan Law Review* 55 (April 1957): 765–66; Bechhoefer, "Negotiating the Statute," p. 57; Smith, Observations on the IAEA Conference, New York, Sept. 20–Oct. 26, 1956; David H. McKillop, "International Atomic Energy Agency Conference—Basic Position Paper," Sept. 14, 1956, both in DOS.

51. Smith, Observations on the IAEA Conference, New York, Sept. 20–Oct. 26, 1956, DOS; CM 1183, March 6, 1956; CM 1237, Oct. 18, 1956, both in AEC; Bechhoefer, "Negotiating the Statute," p. 57.

52. European Integration in the Field of Atomic Energy, AEC 751/55, March 14, 1956, AEC.

53. Bulganin to Eisenhower, Oct. 17, 1956, *Documents on Disarmament, 1945–1959, Vol. I, 1945–1956* (Department of State Publication 7008), pp. 694–96 (hereafter cited *Documents on Disarmament*).

54. Strauss to Dulles, Oct. 20, 1956, in Strauss to File, Oct. 21, 1956, LLS.

55. Telephone Call from the President, Oct. 21, 1956; Memorandum of Conversation with the President, Oct. 21, 1956, 11:00 a.m., both in Dulles Papers, DDE; Eisenhower to Bulganin, Oct. 21, 1956, *Documents on Disarmament*, pp. 697–98.

56. Eisenhower, White Paper on Disarmament and Weapons Testing, Press Release, Oct. 24, 1956, DDE; *New York Times*, Oct. 23, 1956; *Los Angeles Times*, Oct. 25, 1956; *Washington Post and Times-Herald*, Oct. 29, 1956.

## CHAPTER FOURTEEN

1. Robert A. Divine, *Blowing on the Wind: The Nuclear Test Ban Debate, 1954–1960* (New York: Oxford University Press, 1978), pp. 110–11 (hereafter cited Divine, *Blowing on the Wind*).

2. "Public Opinion on Continuing Hydrogen Bomb Tests," Public Studies Division, Department of State, Nov. 14, 1956, in Stassen Papers, DDE; Ralph E. Lapp,

"Strontium Limits in Peace and War," *Bulletin of the Atomic Scientists* 12 (Oct. 1956): 287–89, 320.

3. Anderson, Press Release, Oct. 30, 1956; Luna to Cook, Oct. 30, 1956, both in Anderson Papers, Library of Congress; CM 1243, Nov. 2, 1956, AEC.

4. "Statement by General Advisory Committee," Nov. 10, 1956, in Minutes, GAC 51, Oct. 29–31, 1956; Warren C. Johnson to Strauss, Nov. 9, 1956, both in AEC.

5. Merril Eisenbud, "Global Distribution of Radioactivity from Nuclear Detonations, with Special Reference to Strontium-90," delivered before the Washington Academy of Sciences, Washington, DC, Nov. 15, 1956, AEC.

6. CM 1248, Nov. 20, 1956; W. B. McCool to the Commissioners and General Manager, Nov. 21, 1956, both in AEC.

7. Special Meeting of the Advisory Committee on Biology and Medicine to the Atomic Energy Commission, Nov. 26, 1956, pp. 7–8, AEC.

8. Ibid., pp. 102–3.

9. Ibid., pp. 110–12; Advisory Committee on Biology and Medicine, "Committee Report—Operation *Sunshine*," Dec. 19–20, 1956, Washington, D.C., AEC.

10. GAC 52, Jan. 17–19, 1957, Oak Ridge, Tennessee; ACBM 60, Jan. 16–19, 1957, both in AEC.

11. ACBM 61, March 15–16, 1957, AEC.

12. Draft remarks made by W. F. Libby to *Sunshine* Group on Monday, Feb. 4, 1957, AEC.

13. Bernhard G. Bechhoefer, *Postwar Negotiations for Arms Control* (Washington: Brookings Institution, 1961), pp. 326–32 (hereafter cited Bechhoefer, *Postwar Negotiations for Arms Control*).

14. Joseph S. Toner, Executive Secretary of the President's Special Committee on Disarmament Problems, DPC Note No. 96, Nov. 27, 1956; U.S. Position on Testing, Appendix "B," Current International Proposals, AEC 226/98, Jan. 11, 1957, both in AEC.

15. "Statement by Ambassador Lodge, January 14," *Department of State Bulletin*, Feb. 11, 1957, pp. 225–28.

16. Dulles, "Matters to be raised with the President," Dec. 2, 1956, Dulles Papers, DDE; Richard M. Nixon, *The Memoirs of Richard Nixon* (New York: Grosset and Dunlap, 1978), pp. 174–76.

635

17. Dulles, Telephone Call from Eisenhower, Dec. 21, 1956, Dulles Papers, DDE.
18. Dulles, Memorandum of Conversation with Governor Stassen, Dec. 21, 1956; Dulles, Telephone Call to Gov. Adams, Jan. 2, 1957, both in Dulles Papers, DDE.
19. *New York Herald-Tribune*, Jan. 28, 1957.
20. Dulles, Telephone Call from the Vice-President, Jan. 29, 1957; Dulles, Memorandum of Conversation with the President, Jan. 30, 1957, both in Dulles Papers, DDE.
21. Dulles, Memorandum of Conversation with Governor Stassen at the Secretary's Residence, Feb. 9, 1957, Dulles Papers, DDE.
22. Stassen to Foster, AEC studies with respect to U.S. position on testing, Dec. 4, 1956, AEC 226/97, Dec. 27, 1956, AEC.
23. Memorandum of Conversation, Nuclear Tests, Dec. 26, 1956, Dulles Papers, DDE.
24. Strauss to Stassen, Jan. 23, 1957; CM 1260, Jan. 16, 1957; U.S. Position on Testing, AEC 226/98, Jan. 11, 1957; Ad Hoc Disarmament Committee Report on Testing, AEC 226/103, March 22, 1957, all in AEC.
25. Foster to the General Manager, Jan. 23, 1957; Libby to Strauss, Feb. 1, 1957; Memorandum for the Record on Meeting with British, AEC 226/100, Feb. 21, 1957; Foster to the General Manager, Feb. 5, 1957; New Draft Language for Disarmament Proposal, AEC 226/101, Feb. 25, 1957, all in AEC.
26. Smith to Strauss, March 21, 1957, AEC; Bermuda Statement by President Eisenhower and the British Prime Minister, March 24, 1957, *Documents on Disarmament, 1945–1959, Vol. II, 1957–1959* (Department of State Publication 7008), pp. 772–73 (hereafter cited *Documents on Disarmament*); Divine, *Blowing on the Wind*, p. 114.
27. Bechhoefer, *Postwar Negotiations for Arms Control*, pp. 332–34.
28. Samuel F. Wells, Jr., "The Origins of Massive Retaliation," *Political Science Quarterly* 96 (Spring 1981): 31–52.
29. NSC 1553 and annex as noted in NSC, Summary of Discussion (hereafter cited SNSC), Meeting 315, March 6, 1957, DDE; Notes on Secretary's Staff Meeting, March 29, 1957, DOS; Divine, *Blowing on the Wind*, p. 143.
30. Dulles, Telephone Calls from Strauss, April 17, 1957; to Radford, April 18, 1957; to Strauss, April 18, 1957, all in Dulles Telephone Log, Dulles Papers, DDE.
31. Morse to Foster, April 19, 1957, AEC.
32. Memorandum of Conversation, Disarmament, April 20, 1957, AEC.
33. Dulles, Memorandum of Conversation with Governor Stassen, April 20, 1957, Dulles Papers, DDE.
34. Goodpaster, Memorandum of Conversation with the President, April 23, 24, 1957, Dulles Papers, DDE.
35. Dulles, Telephone Call to Eisenhower, May 13, 1957, Dulles Telephone Log, Dulles Papers, DDE; Limitation of Armament, AEC 226/108, May 15, 1957, AEC.
36. Memorandum of Conversation, Disarmament, May 17, 1957, DOS.
37. Limitation of Armament, AEC 226/108, May 15, 1957, AEC.
38. Smith to File, May 15, 1957; Wilson to Dulles, May 17, 1957, both in DOS.
39. CM 1276, April 9, 1957, AEC; Thomas E. Murray, "Reliance on H-Bomb and its Dangers," *Life*, May 6, 1957, pp. 181–98; CM 1284, May 22, 1957; Limitation of Armaments—Draft Working Paper, AEC 226/110, May 21, 1957; Limitation of Armaments, AEC 226/111, May 21, 1957, all in AEC.
40. Harold K. Jacobson and Eric Stein, *Diplomats, Scientists, and Politicians: The United States and the Nuclear Test Ban Negotiations* (Ann Arbor: University of Michigan Press, 1966), pp. 20–21; *New York Times*, April 18, 19, 20, 22, 1957; Douglas MacArthur II to Dulles, March 28, 1957, in AEC 226/104, April 10, 1957, AEC.
41. Divine, *Blowing on the Wind*, pp. 118–25.
42. Libby to Schweitzer, April 25, 1957, AEC Press Release, AEC; Libby, Speech to the American Physical Society, April 26, 1957, as reprinted in Joint Committee on Atomic Energy, Special Subcommittee on Radiation, *Hearings on the Nature of Radioactive Fallout and Its Effects on Man*, May 27–June 7, 1957 (Washington: Government Printing Office, 1957), pp. 1519–37 (hereafter cited *1957 Fallout Hearings*); *New York Times*, April 25, 1957.
43. Ernest C. Pollard et al. to Senator Prescott Bush, Jan. 21, 1957; Bush to

Strauss, Jan. 31, 1957; Libby to Bush, April 5, 1957, AEC 604/24, April 10, 1957; Brown to Libby, May 21, 1957; Libby to Brown, May 24, 1957, all in AEC; Willard F. Libby, "An Open Letter to Dr. Schweitzer," and Harrison Brown, "What is a 'Small' Risk?" *Saturday Review*, May 25, 1957, pp. 8–10, 36–37.

44. Divine, *Blowing on the Wind*, pp. 125–28; *New York Times*, June 4, 12, 1957.

45. Carl T. Durham to Fields, March 7, 1957; Charles L. Dunham to Fields, Progress Report on Plans for Congressional Hearings on Fallout, March 6, 1957, in AEC 604/26, April 18, 1957, both in AEC; *1957 Fallout Hearings*; AEC 604/28, May 13, 1957; CM 1283, May 21, 1957; CM 1284, May 22, 1957; Holifield to Strauss, May 21, 1957; Ad Hoc Committee Report on Test Limitations, AEC 226/113, May 23, 1957, all in AEC.

46. Stassen to Dulles, May 22, 1957, in AEC 226/114, May 23, 1957; Disarmament Discussion, Agenda Planning Session, May 24, 1957, both in AEC.

47. SNSC 324, May 23, 1957, DDE.

48. Whitney to Eisenhower, May 24, 1957, Dulles White House Memoranda, DDE.

49. Dulles Telephone Calls to and from Eisenhower, May 24, 1957, Dulles Papers, DDE; Strauss to File, May 25, 1957, LLS.

50. Cutler, Memorandum of Conference at White House, May 25, 1957, DOS.

51. Strauss to File, May 25, 1957, LLS.

52. Smith to Dulles, June 4, 1957, DOS.

53. Stassen to Zorin, May 31, 1957, in Limitation of Armaments, AEC 226/115, June 4, 1957; CM 1289, June 5, 1957, both in AEC; Cutler, Conference in Secretary of State's Office, June 4, 1957, White House Office, Project "Clean-up," DDE.

54. Joseph N. Greene, Jr., Informal Record of Meeting in Secretary's Office, June 4, 1957, DOS.

55. Telephone Call from Strauss, June 4, 1957, Dulles Papers, DDE; Strauss to Dulles, June 5, 1957, in Limitation of Armaments, AEC 226/117, June 6, 1957, AEC. See also Arthur Larson, *Eisenhower: The President Nobody Knew* (New York: Charles Scribner & Sons, 1968), pp. 77–78.

56. Eisenhower to Dulles, June 4, 1957; Dulles, Telephone Calls to Eisenhower, June 5, 1957, Dulles Papers, all in DDE; C. Elbrick, Memorandum of Conversation,

June 5, 1957, Secretary of State Memoranda, DOS.

57. Eisenhower, White House News Conference, June 5, 1957, as transcribed by the State Department, Stassen Papers, DDE.

58. Whitney to Dulles, June 6, 1957, DOS; USSR Aide Memoire of June 7, 1957, AEC.

59. Stassen to Dulles, June 9, 1957; Stassen to Herter, June 9, 1957, both in DOS.

60. Smith to Dulles, June 10, 1957, DOS; Dulles, Memorandum of Conversation with Senator Knowland, June 10, 1957, Dulles Papers, DDE.

61. Herter to File, June 11, 1957, DOS; Dulles to Stassen, June 12, 1957; Dulles to Eisenhower, June 12, 1957, both in DDE; Harold Macmillan, *Riding the Storm, 1956–1959* (New York: Harper & Row, 1971), pp. 301–4.

62. Elbrick, Memorandum of Conversation, Disarmament, June 12, 1957, DOS.

63. Preliminary Draft Outline of Plan of Work of U.S. Delegation in London, June 12, 1957; Stassen to Herter, June 12, 1957, both in DOS; Foster to Commission, June 12, 1957, AEC.

64. Soviet Proposal Introduced in the Disarmament Subcommittee: Cessation of Atomic and Hydrogen Weapons Tests, June 14, 1957, *Documents on Disarmament*, p. 791; Bechhoefer, *Postwar Negotiations for Arms Control*, p. 354.

65. Eisenhower, Press Conference, June 19, 1957, *Public Papers of the Presidents of the United States, 1957: Dwight D. Eisenhower* (Washington: Government Printing Office, 1958), pp. 476–79 (hereafter cited *Public Papers, 1957, Eisenhower*); Divine, *Blowing on the Wind*, p. 146.

66. AEC Press Release, "Statement by the Atomic Energy Commission," May 29, 1957, AEC; Statement by the President Reviewing the Government's Policies and Actions with Respect to the Development and Testing of Nuclear Weapons, *Public Papers of the Presidents of the United States, 1956: Dwight D. Eisenhower* (Washington: Government Printing Office, 1957), p. 1000.

67. Joint Committee on Atomic Energy Press Release, May 29, 1957, AEC.

68. Transcript of Hearings on Plutonium and Tritium Requirements before the Joint Committee on Atomic Energy, Military Applications Subcommittee, June 20, 1957, AEC.

69. Transcript of Hearings on Technical As-

637

pects of Inspection before the Joint Committee on Atomic Energy, June 21, 1957, AEC.

70. Goodpaster, Memorandum of Conference with the President, June 24, 1957, DDE.

71. Divine, *Blowing on the Wind*, pp. 148–50; Robert Gilpin, *American Scientists and Nuclear Weapons Policy* (Princeton: Princeton University Press, 1962), pp. 168–69; Edward Teller with Allen Brown, *The Legacy of Hiroshima* (Garden City, NY: Doubleday, 1962), p. 68; Lewis L. Strauss, *Men and Decisions* (Garden City, NY: Doubleday, 1962), pp. 418–19.

72. Dulles, Telephone Call to Eisenhower, June 25, 1957, Dulles Papers, DDE.

73. Bromley Smith to Strauss, June 27, 1957, with attachment, Smith to Cutler, June 26, 1957, AEC.

74. Eisenhower, Press Conference, June 26 and July 3, 1957, *Public Papers, 1957, Eisenhower*, pp. 497–501, 519–20.

75. David E. Lilienthal, *The Journals of David E. Lilienthal*, Vol. IV, *The Road of Change, 1955–1959* (New York: Harper & Row, 1969), pp. 204–5.

## CHAPTER FIFTEEN

1. *New York Times*, Dec. 30, 1956; *Nucleonics* 15 (Jan. 1957): R1–R2.

2. Schaetzel, Current Status of EURATOM Negotiations, Dec. 3, 1956, DOS.

3. Gerard C. Smith and Elbrick to Dulles, Sept. 25, 1956; Draft, Dulles and Strauss to Eisenhower, Sept. 25, 1956; Draft, Eisenhower to Spaak, n.d.; Smith to File, Nov. 13, 1956; Schaetzel, Memorandum of Conversation, Nov. 12, 1956, all in DOS.

4. Smith and Elbrick to Dulles, Dec. 3, 1956, Jan. 23, 1957, both in DOS; Michel Gaudet, "EURATOM," reprinted from *Progress in Nuclear Energy, Series 10, Vols. 1 & 2—Law Administration* (London: Pergamon Press, 1959), pp. 140–79.

5. Strauss to Dulles, Jan. 2, 1957; Schaetzel to Linebaugh, Jan. 3, 1957; Dulles, Memorandum of Conversation, Jan. 10, 18, 1957, all in DOS; Obstacles Encountered in Promotion of Atoms-for-Peace Program, AEC 751/110, Feb. 12, 1957, AEC; Cleveland to Smith and Timmons,

Jan. 15, 1957; Smith to Strauss, Feb. 6, 1957, both in DOS.

6. Dulles to Strauss, Feb. 5, 1957, in AEC 751/110, Feb. 12, 1957, AEC.

7. Vance, Memorandum On a Foreign Power Program, Feb. 6, 1957, AEC.

8. Murray, Statement for 202 Hearings, Feb. 19, 1957, AEC. See also Joint Committee on Atomic Energy, *Hearings on Development, Growth, and State of the Atomic Energy Industry*, Feb. 19–25, 1957 (Washington: Government Printing Office, 1957), pp. 7–21, 55–74 (hereafter cited *202 Hearings, 1957*).

9. *202 Hearings, 1957*, pp. 22–54; *Nucleonics* 15 (March 1957), R1–R2.

10. The plan was presented in a series of staff papers entitled "Encouraging Nuclear Power Abroad," AEC 655/45, March 18, 1957; AEC 655/46, March 19, 1957; AEC 655/47, April 12, 1957, all in AEC. See also CM 1271, March 20, 1957, and CM 1272, March 20, 1957, both in AEC.

11. Vance, Remarks delivered before the Atomic Industrial Forum, New York, April 25, 1957; CM 1280, May 1, 1957; Deputy General Manager, Atoms for Peace Program, AEC 655/49, May 7, 1957; CM 1282, May 8, 1957, all in AEC.

12. Richard G. Hewlett and Francis Duncan, *Nuclear Navy, 1946–1962* (Chicago: University of Chicago Press, 1974), pp. 227–28 (hereafter cited *Nuclear Navy*).

13. Strauss to File, March 21, 1957, LLS.

14. *Congressional Record*, 85 Cong., 1 sess., April 16, 1957, pp. 5790–5801; Fields to Ramey, May 9, 1957, transmitting a copy of the General Counsel's opinion on Cannon's interpretation of the Atomic Energy Act, AEC. See also AEC 646/52, May 6, 1957; CM 1281, May 7, 1957; and Joint Committee on Atomic Energy, Transcript of Hearing on Legislative Authorizations for Appropriations, June 10, 1957, all in AEC. The Joint Committee's strategy was described in *Nucleonics* 15 (May 1957): 17–19. Section 111 of the FY 1958 Authorization Act, P.L.85–162 (71 *Stat.* 403) did require that all arrangements under the power demonstration program lie before the Joint Committee for forty days, but Section 261 was not amended to require authorization until 1963 (Sect. 107, P.L.88–72, 77 *Stat.*

84). For the Commission's views on authorization in terms of development allowances, see AEC 655/49, May 7, 1957, and CM 1282, May 8, 1957, both in AEC.

15. The Price-Anderson Act (P.L.85–256, 71 *Stat.* 576) added Section 170 to the Atomic Energy Act. For background see Insurability of Private Industrial Atomic Energy Installations and Undertakings, AEC 785/8, Feb. 17, 1956; Indemnity of Privately Owned Atomic Energy Facilities, AEC 785/12, April 30, 1956; CM 1199, May 16, 1956; Proposed Indemnity Legislation, AEC 785/18, Jan. 10, 1957; CM 1260, Jan. 16, 1957; Indemnity Legislation, AEC 785/28, May 21, 1957; CM 1283, May 21, 1957, all in AEC; Joint Committee on Atomic Energy, *Hearings on Governmental Indemnity and Reactor Safety*, March 25–27, 1957 (Washington: Government Printing Office, 1957), pp. 1–79.

16. *Nucleonics* 15 (April 1957): 17–19.

17. Zinn to Strauss, July 27, 1957, LLS.

18. *Nucleonics* 15 (Oct. 1957): 19–21; Meeting of Reactor Experts, Oct. 17–18, 1957, AEC.

19. Davis, "The Government's Program and Plans," delivered before the Atomic Industrial Forum, New York, Oct. 30, 1957, AEC.

20. *Nucleonics* 15 (Nov. 1957): 77, 186–91.

21. Strauss to Eisenhower, Oct. 22, 1957, DDE. The membership of the Assembly was printed in *Nucleonics* along with the report.

22. Price to Eisenhower, Oct. 24, 1957, JCAE.

23. Zehring to Strauss, March 2, June 1, 1956, LLS.

24. McCool to Davis, Nov. 5, 1957; Minutes, Agenda Planning Session, Nov. 1, 1957, both in AEC.

25. Zehring to Strauss, Nov. 4, 1957, LLS.

26. Davis, Reactor Development Program, AEC 152/83, Nov. 27, 1957, AEC.

27. Davis, Proposed New Prototype Power Reactor Program, AEC 152/81, Nov. 7, 1957, AEC.

28. CM 1314, Nov. 8, 1957, AEC.

29. Summary Notes on JCAE Seminar, Nov. 22, 1957, LLS. Summaries prepared by three participants are also on file in Box 104, JCAE. See also Joint Committee on Atomic Energy, *Hearings on Development, Growth, and State of the Atomic*

*Energy Industry*, Feb. 19–March 4, 1958 (Washington: Government Printing Office, 1958), pp. 583–85 (hereafter cited *202 Hearings, 1958*).

30. On plans for the Commission's industry meetings, see December Meeting With Industrial Representatives, AEC 646/56, Nov. 6, 1957, and Proposed Opening Statement for Industry-AEC Conference, AEC 152/82, Nov. 25, 1957, both in AEC. Zehring prepared a detailed summary for Strauss. See Zehring to Strauss, undated but ca. Dec. 9, 1957, LLS. *Nucleonics* 15 (Dec. 1957): 17–21.

31. Zehring to Strauss, Nov. 22, 1957, with a covering note: "After reading perhaps these written notes should be destroyed, I have no copies." LLS.

32. Zehring to Strauss, Dec. 5, 1957, 11:09 a.m., LLS.

33. *Nuclear Navy*, pp. 247–54.

34. Zehring to Strauss, Nov. 22, 1957, LLS.

35. *Nuclear Navy*, pp. 240–46, 254–57. Rickover's staff published a volume for the 1958 Geneva Conference, summarizing the design, construction, and operation of the plant: *The Shippingport Pressurized Water Reactor* (Reading, MA: Addison-Wesley, 1958), especially pp. 3–24 (hereafter cited *Shippingport Reactor*); Francis Duncan and Jack M. Holl, *Shippingport: The Nation's First Atomic Power Station* (Washington: U.S. Department of Energy, 1983).

36. *Nuclear Navy*, pp. 254–57; *Shippingport Reactor*, pp. 59–118; "PWR: The Significance of Shippingport," *Nucleonics* 16 (April 1953): 53–72.

37. This section is based on *Nuclear Navy*, pp. 258–96.

38. National Security Council, Summary of Discussion, Meeting 348, Dec. 13, 1957, DDE.

39. Durham to Strauss, Nov. 27, 1957; Strauss to Durham, Dec. 6, 1957, both in AEC. The letters also appear in Joint Committee on Atomic Energy, Subcommittee on Legislation, *Hearings on AEC Authorizing Legislation*, May 14–June 11, 1958 (Washington: Government Printing Office, 1958), pp. 210–12. McCool to File, Jan. 21, 1958, AEC.

40. Zehring to Strauss, Jan. 24, 1958; Zehring, Some Further Comments by "Mr. Blank," Jan. 29, 1958, both in LLS.

41. Director of Reactor Development, Program for Civilian Power Reactors, For-

639

eign and Domestic, AEC 152/88, Jan. 27, 1958; CM 1326, Jan. 28, 1958; CM 1329, Jan. 31, 1958; CM 1330, Feb. 1, 1958, all in AEC.

42. McCool to the Commissioners, Feb. 3, 1958, transmitting Vance's Informal Notes for Discussion Today, Feb. 1, 1958, AEC.

43. Strauss to Durham, Feb. 3, 1958, AEC.

44. Controller, FY 1959 Budget Estimates, AEC 939/6, Sept. 20, 1957; CM 1306, Sept. 27, 1957; Proposed Statement of Position at BOB Policy Hearing, Oct. 22, 1957, AEC 939/11, Oct. 18, 1957; CM 1328, Jan. 31, 1958; General Manager, Amendments to FY 1959 Budget, AEC 939/24, Feb. 10, 1958; Memorandum for Discussion with the Director, BOB, AEC 939/28, Feb. 14, 1958; CM 1332, Feb. 11, 1958; CM 1333, Feb. 11, 1958; CM 1334, Feb. 12, 1958; CM 1338, Feb. 28, 1958, all in AEC.

45. 202 Hearings, 1958, pp. 1–10; Nucleonics 16 (March 1958): 17; Strauss to Eisenhower, Feb. 25, 1958, DDE.

46. Bryce Harlow to Sherman Adams, Feb. 7, 1958, DDE.

47. CM 1336, Feb. 21, 1958; Fields to the Commissioners, Feb. 26, 1958, both in AEC.

48. Expanded Civilian Power Reactor Development Program, AEC 152/90, April 21, 1958; CM 1366, April 29, 1958, both in AEC.

49. CM 1353, April 9, 1958, with attachment, Analysis of Proposed BOB Allowance; CM 1355, April 14, 1958; CM 1356, April 15, 1958; J. E. Ammons to File, April 21, 1958, all in AEC.

50. Wilton B. Persons, Memorandum for Record, May 5, 1958, DDE; Nucleonics 16 (May 1958): 17–18; Nucleonics 16 (June 1958): 17–19.

## CHAPTER SIXTEEN

1. Jack M. Holl, "Eisenhower's Peaceful Atomic Diplomacy" (manuscript, History Division, Dec. 1977), DOE.

2. Goodpaster, Memorandum of Conference with the President, Feb. 6, 1957, DDE.

3. Foster to Strauss, Feb. 7, 1957; Foster to File, Feb. 8, 1957, both in AEC. Strauss's view also reflected the National Security Council. See Peaceful Uses of Atomic Energy, NSC 5507/2, March 12, 1955, AEC.

4. In addition to Cook, the American delegation included Paul C. Fine, Louis H. Roddis, and Allen J. Vander Weyden.

5. By 1968 the actual installed nuclear generating capacity for the EURATOM countries was 2,588 megawatts; for the United States, 2,743 megawatts; for the United Kingdom, 4,135 megawatts; and for the world, 11,324 megawatts. FPC, World Power Data: Capacity of Electric Generating Plants and Production of Electric Energy—1969 (Washington: Government Printing Office, 1972), p. 8.

6. CM 1263, Feb. 6, 1957; Status Report on EURATOM, AEC 751/102, Jan. 7, 1957; Visit of EURATOM "Wise Men," AEC 751/105, Jan. 29, 1957; Assistance to Three Wise Men—EURATOM, AEC 751/115, March 6, 1957; Visit to Luxembourg on EURATOM—Summary for Discussions with the Commission, AEC 751/117, March 6, 1957; Discussions with Wise Men and Staff on Their Report, "A Target for EURATOM," AEC 751/130, April 25, 1957, all in AEC.

7. CM 1269, Feb. 27, 1957; Letter to Department of State Concerning Proposed EURATOM Treaty, AEC 751/114, Feb. 25, 1957; EURATOM—Options to Congo Uranium, AEC 751/140, June 25, 1957; Strauss to Dulles, March 7, 1957, all in AEC.

8. Public Papers of the Presidents of the United States, 1957: Dwight D. Eisenhower (Washington: Government Printing Office, 1958), p. 27 (hereafter cited Public Papers, 1957, Eisenhower).

9. LaPlante to Strauss, Jan. 9, 1957, AEC.

10. David Shea Teeple, "Atoms for Peace—or War?" National Review, Jan. 12, 1957, pp. 35–37.

11. McCarthy's Lincoln Day Address was followed by a letter to Strauss also written by Teeple. McCarthy to Strauss, Feb. 15, 1957. Carl T. Durham and Strauss answered the letter. Durham to McCarthy, undated draft; Strauss to McCarthy, May 11, 1957, in AEC 751/120, March 14, 1957; LaPlante to Strauss and Fields, April 3, 4, 5, and 8, 1957, all in AEC; Staff Notes No. 95, April 9, 1957, DDE; Public Papers, 1957, Eisenhower, pp. 206–9.

12. The forty-eight questions covered thirteen typed pages. The answers required

forty-three pages. Hickenlooper to Herter, April 29, 1957; Replies to Questions Submitted to the Department of State with Respect to the Statute of the International Atomic Energy Agency by Senator Hickenlooper, May 3, 1957, both in DOS.

13. Goodpaster, Memoranda of Conferences with the President, May 2, 3, 1957, DDE; Wilcox et al. to Herter, April 11, 1957, DOS.

14. *New York Times*, May 2, 5, 1957; Spiers to Sims and Breithut, May 9, 1957, DOS.

15. AEC, *Progress in Peaceful Uses of Atomic Energy, July–December 1957* (Washington: Government Printing Office, 1958), p. 194; Wilcox et al. to the Secretary, June 4, 1957, DOS; CM 1284, May 22, 1957; CM 1289, June 5, 1957, both in AEC.

16. CM 1289, June 5, 1957, AEC; Breithut, Developments on IAEA Ratification During Week of June 3–7, 1957; Breithut to Sims, June 7, 1957, both in DOS. The Senate approved the treaty, 67–19, on June 18, 1957. *Congressional Record*, 90 Cong., 1 sess., June 18, 1957, p. 8534. Eisenhower signed the treaty in a Rose Garden ceremony on July 29, 1957. *Public Papers, 1957, Eisenhower*, pp. 571–72; Dulles to Fulbright, June 4, 1957; Secretary's Staff Meeting, July 10, 22, 24, Aug. 20, 1957, all in DOS; *Congressional Record*, 90 Cong., 1 sess., Aug. 19, 1957, pp. 15178–79; *Business Week*, Aug. 17, 1957, p. 130.

17. Corbin Allardice and Edward R. Trapnell, *The Atomic Energy Commission* (New York: Praeger, 1974), p. 203.

18. Herter to Strauss, March 22, 1957; Strauss to Herter, n.d.; Wadsworth to Dulles, June 10, 1957; Secretary's Staff Meeting, June 21, 1957; Breithut, Memorandum of Conversation, July 1, 1957; McKinney to Dulles, July 31, 1957, all in DOS.

19. LaPlante to Harlow, March 8, 1957, AEC.

20. Gerard C. Smith to File, Sept. 26, Oct. 6, 1956; Dulles, Memorandum of Conversation with Admiral Strauss, Oct. 22, 1956; Strauss to Dulles, Oct. 24, 1956; Herter to Strauss, Nov. 19, 1956, all in DOS.

21. International Atomic Energy Agency—Conversation with Members of the Soviet Mission to the United Nations, AEC 751/127, April 8, 1957; Hall to Strauss, July 19, 1957, both in AEC; Breithut, Memorandum of Conversation, June 14, 1957; Wadsworth, Memorandum of Conversation, April 4, 1957; Breithut, International Atomic Energy Agency Matters, July 1, 1957, all in DOS.

22. Herter, Conversation Between the President and Admiral Strauss, Aug. 2, 1957; Fisher Howe, Memorandum for the Record, Aug. 2, 1957, both in DDE; Farley to Murphy, Oct. 8, 1957, DOS.

23. Walmsley, Memorandum of Conversation, Aug. 13, 1957; Wilcox to Wadsworth, Aug. 13, 1957; Farley to Murphy, Oct. 8, 1957, all in DOS.

24. McKinney to Dulles, Nov. 11, 1957; McKinney to Breithut, Nov. 24, 1957; Outline of Official Report of the United States Delegation to the International Atomic Energy Agency, Dec. 1957, all in DOS.

25. Support for the International Atomic Energy Agency, AEC 986/1, Feb. 6, 1958; U.S. Assistance to the IAEA, AEC 986/2, May 1, 1958; Policies Relating to Source and Special Nuclear Material Offered by the United States to the IAEA, AEC 986/3, June 23, 1958; McCool to Hall, June 30, 1958, all in AEC.

26. Joint Progress Report to the National Security Council, AEC 751/125, March 26, 1957, AEC. One staff member from the Bureau of the Budget noted that "This report drafted largely by AEC appears somewhat optimistic and fails to present a very rigorous analysis of the problems which confront the U.S. in this program." James W. Clark to George Schwarzwalder, April 25, 1957, OMB.

27. Peaceful Uses of Atomic Energy, NSC 5725/1, Dec. 13, 1957, AEC.

28. Peaceful Uses of Atomic Energy, NSC 5725, Nov. 22, 1957; Foster to Strauss, Dec. 2, 1957; Statement of Policy on Peaceful Uses of Atomic Energy, AEC 751/150, Sept. 20, 1957; Revised Statement of Policy Concerning the Peaceful Uses of Atomic Energy, AEC 751/151, Sept. 27, 1957; CM 1302, Sept. 24, 1957, all in AEC; Farley to Smith, Oct. 30, 1957, DOS.

29. Dillon, Draft Opening Statement Before the Joint Committee on Atomic Energy with Respect to the US-EURATOM Joint Program, June 30, 1958, DOS.

30. Farley to Herter, April 16, 1958, DOS; Herter to Strauss, April 17, 1958, in

AEC 751/176, April 21, 1958; CM 1373, May 16, 1958, both in AEC.

31. Strauss and Herter to Eisenhower, Jan. 28, 1958, in AEC 751/160, Feb. 11, 1958; Goodpaster to Strauss and Dulles, Feb. 6, 1958, both in AEC.

32. Cooperative Arrangements with EUR-ATOM, AEC 751/162, March 13, 1958; CM 1342, March 13, 1958, both in AEC.

33. Controls and Safeguards—EURATOM, AEC 751/170, April 14, 1958, AEC.

34. CM 1359, April 21, 1958; CM 1361, April 24, 1958, both in AEC.

35. McCool to File, May 15, 1958, AEC.

36. Safeguards and Controls—EURATOM—Supplement to AEC 751/170, AEC 751/177, April 23, 1958, AEC.

37. CM 1366, April 29, 1958, AEC.

38. Matthews to Dulles, May 3, 1958, in AEC 751/183, May 8, 1958, AEC.

39. Cole to Eisenhower, May 18, 1958; Cole to Strauss, May 12, 1958; Farley to Herter, May 27, 1958, all in DOS; CM 1374, May 20, 1958; Cook to Strauss, May 20, 1958, both in AEC.

40. McKinney, Memorandum for Discussion with the Acting Secretary, May 8, 1958, DOS; McKinney to Dulles, April 21, 1958; McKinney to Dulles, May 26, 1958, in AEC 973/5, May 29, 1958, both in AEC.

41. Secretary's Staff Meeting, May 7, 1958; Farley to Herter, May 31, June 4, 1958; Farley to Dulles, May 20, 21, 1958; Dulles to Strauss, May 23, 1958, all in DOS.

42. CM 1380, June 6, 1958, AEC.

43. *New York Times*, June 8, 9, 1958.

44. Goodpaster, Memorandum of Conference with the President, June 9, 1958, DDE; Schaetzel, Memoranda of Conversations, June 9, 1958; Farley, Memoranda of Conversations, June 10, 11, 1958, all in DOS; Herter to Strauss, June 11, 1958; CM 1381, June 12, 1958; Proposed International Agreement, Memorandum of Understanding, and Agreement for Cooperation—EURATOM, AEC 751/185 and AEC 751/186, May 15, 1958; Joint US-EURATOM Cooperative Program, AEC 751/192, May 27, 1958, and AEC 751/197, June 11, 1958; Correspondence Regarding Agreement Between US and EURATOM, AEC 751/198, June 27, 1958, all in AEC.

45. Commission Policy on the Control of Special Nuclear Materials, 1946–1964, Oct. 1, 1965, pp. 71–80, AEC.

46. Cook to Ramey, May 21, 1958, AEC; Schaetzel to Farley, July 17, 1958; Schaetzel to Dillon, July 28, 1958, both in DOS.

47. Schaetzel to Butterworth, Aug. 14, 1958, DOS.

48. Strauss to Secretary of State, Dec. 4, 1958, as printed in AEC, *United States at Geneva, 1958—2nd International Conference on the Peaceful Uses of Atomic Energy* (Washington: Government Printing Office, 1959), pp. v–viii (hereafter cited *United States at Geneva, 1958*).

49. Office for International Conference, Executive Director's Report on the Second International Conference on Peaceful Uses of Atomic Energy, Geneva, Switzerland, Sept. 1–13, 1958 (hereafter cited Executive Director's Report), AEC.

50. As compared to ninety-nine papers given by the Russians, ninety-six by the British, and fifty-eight by the French.

51. Lodge to Dulles, Aug. 26, 1955, DOS; Rabi to Strauss, July 15, 1956, in AEC 930, Aug. 6, 1956; Strauss to Rabi, Aug. 6, 1956, in AEC 930/1, Aug. 17, 1956; Planning for Second International Conference on Peaceful Uses of Atomic Energy, AEC 729/38, Sept. 6, 1956; CM 1223, Sept. 12, 1956; Meeting of the U.N. Advisory Committee on the Peaceful Uses of Atomic Energy, AEC 930/5, May 27, 1957, all in AEC.

52. U.S. Technical Exhibit for 1958 International Conference on the Peaceful Uses of Atomic Energy, AEC 930/8, Oct. 7, 1957; Executive Director's Report, pp. 19–26, both in AEC; *United States at Geneva, 1958*, pp. 56–99.

53. U.S. Technical Exhibit for 1958 International Conference on the Peaceful Uses of Atomic Energy, AEC 930/8, Oct. 7, 1957; Accelerated *Sherwood* Activities, AEC 532/44, Nov. 15, 1957, both in AEC; Joan L. Bromberg, *Fusion: Science, Politics, and the Invention of a New Energy Source* (Cambridge: MIT Press, 1982), pp. 77–78, 86–88 (hereafter cited Bromberg, *Fusion*).

54. CM 1336, Feb. 21, 1958; *Sherwood* Exhibits for Geneva Conference, AEC 930/13, March 21, 1958, both in AEC.

55. Revised Classification Guide for the Controlled Thermonuclear Program, AEC 532/43, Aug. 21, 1957; Declassification of Project *Sherwood*, AEC 532/49, Aug. 5, 1958; CM 1394, Aug. 7, 1958; AEC

Press Release A-230, Aug. 30, 1958; Report by the United States Official Representatives to the Second United Nations International Conference on the Peaceful Uses of Atomic Energy, Geneva, Switzerland, Sept. 1–13, 1958, all in AEC; Bromberg, *Fusion*, pp. 89–93; Strauss to Secretary of State, Dec. 4, 1958, in *United States at Geneva, 1958*, p. v.

56. Executive Director's Report, pp. 43–46, AEC.

## CHAPTER SEVENTEEN

1. Eugene J. Rosi, "Mass and Attentive Opinion on Nuclear Weapons Tests and Fallout, 1954–1963," *Public Opinion Quarterly* 29 (Summer 1965): 281–83.
2. G. C. Spiegel to Gerard C. Smith, June 13, 1957, DOS. See Joint Committee on Atomic Energy, *Hearings on the Nature of Radioactive Fallout and Its Effects on Man*, May 27–June 7, 1957 (Washington: Government Printing Office, 1957).
3. Smith to File, June 1, 1957, DOS.
4. Ink to Robert E. Hollingsworth, June 17, 1957; Ink to Dunham, June 18, 1957, both AEC.
5. ACBM 63, June 18, 1957, AEC.
6. Robert A. Divine, *Blowing on the Wind: The Nuclear Test Ban Debate, 1954–1960* (New York: Oxford University Press, 1978), p. 140 (hereafter cited Divine, *Blowing on the Wind*).
7. Press Release, Remarks of Representative Sterling Cole (R., New York) in the House of Representatives, on July 1, 1957, AEC.
8. President's News Conference of June 5, 1957, *Public Papers of the Presidents of the United States, 1957: Dwight D. Eisenhower* (Washington: Government Printing Office, 1958), p. 429 (hereafter cited *Public Papers, 1957, Eisenhower*); Divine, *Blowing on the Wind*, pp. 140–41; Cousins to Eisenhower, June 7, 1957; Strauss to Eisenhower, June 18, 1957; Eisenhower to Cousins, June 21, 1957, all in DDE; "Scientists and the Fall-out Scare," *U.S. News and World Report*, June 21, 1957, p. 52.
9. Linus Pauling, *No More War!* (New York: Dodd, Mead, 1958), pp. 159–60 (hereafter cited Pauling, *No More War!*); Robert Gilpin, *American Scien-*

tists and Nuclear Weapons Policy (Princeton: Princeton University Press, 1962), pp. 156–57 (hereafter cited Gilpin, *American Scientists and Nuclear Weapons Policy*); Divine, *Blowing on the Wind*, p. 161.

10. Nevil Shute, *On the Beach* (New York: William Morrow, 1957); John Richard Young, "Mr. Shute Ends the World," *Milwaukee Journal*, July 28, 1957; Ed Hughes, "Fallout Novel Looks at Future," *Atlanta Journal and Constitution*, July 28, 1957; Divine, *Blowing on the Wind*, pp. 161–63.
11. Samuel Glasstone, ed., *The Effects of Nuclear Weapons* (Washington: Government Printing Office, 1957), p. xi (hereafter cited Glasstone, *The Effects of Nuclear Weapons*).
12. Frank Carey, "H-Bomb Effects Told in Book Issued by U.S.," *Washington Star*, July 12, 1957.
13. Glasstone, *The Effects of Nuclear Weapons*, pp. 424–28; Peter Edson, "The New Nuclear Handbook," *Washington News*, July 12, 1957; Jack Schubert and Ralph Lapp, *Radiation: What It Is and How It Affects You* (New York: Viking Press, 1957).
14. Warren Amster, *A Theory for the Design of a Deterrent Air Weapon System*, Report OR-P-29 (San Diego: Convair, 1955); Bernard Brodie, *The Atomic Bomb and American Security* (New Haven: Yale Institute of International Relations, 1945); William Kaufmann, ed., *Military Policy and National Security* (Princeton: Princeton University Press, 1956); Basil Liddell Hart, *Defense of the West* (New York: William Morrow, 1950); Robert E. Osgood, *Limited War: The Challenge to American Strategy* (Chicago: University of Chicago Press, 1957); Fred Kaplan, *The Wizards of Armageddon* (New York: Simon and Schuster, 1983)(hereafter cited Kaplan, *The Wizards of Armageddon*).
15. Henry Kissinger, *Nuclear Weapons and Foreign Policy* (New York: Harper & Brothers, 1957); Lawrence Freedman, *The Evolution of Nuclear Strategy* (New York: St. Martin's Press, 1983), pp. 102–19 (hereafter cited Freedman, *The Evolution of Nuclear Strategy*).
16. *Congressional Record*, 85 Cong., 1 sess., June 23, 1957, pp. 10569–573.
17. Ibid.; Harold P. Green and Alan Rosenthal, *Government of the Atom: The Inte-*

643

*gration of Powers* (New York: Atherton Press, 1963), pp. 205–6; Chet Holifield, "Congressional Hearings on Radioactive Fall-out," *Bulletin of the Atomic Scientists* 14 (Jan. 1958): 52–54.

18. Analysis of Voting in 10th General Assembly Consideration of Atomic Radiation, AEC 226/65, Dec. 5, 1955; United Nations Scientific Committee on Radiation, AEC 226/68, Jan. 11, 1956; AEC 226/76, Feb. 24, 1956; AEC 226/83, April 13, 1956; AEC 226/85, May 24, 1956; CM 1181, Feb. 28, 1956; Hall to Fields, April 2, 1956, all in AEC; Shields Warren, Official Report of the United States Delegation to the U.N. Scientific Committee on the Effects of Atomic Radiation, n.d., AEC.

19. Spiegel, Discussion of the U.S. Contribution to the Work of the UN Scientific Committee, Sept. 25, 1957, DOS. See also Divine, *Blowing on the Wind*, pp. 63–65.

20. AEC Press Release 1201, Statement on Radioactive Fallout Submitted to the U.S. Atomic Energy Commission by the Advisory Committee on Biology and Medicine, Oct. 19, 1957; ACBM 64, Sept. 13–14, 1957, both in AEC; Farley to Stassen, Wilcox, and Berding, Fallout report by Advisory Committee on Biology and Medicine, Oct. 4, 1957 (not sent), DOS; Helen C. Allison, "Strontium-90—Some Notes on Present and Future Levels," *Bulletin of the Atomic Scientists* 14 (Jan. 1958): 62.

21. AEC Press Release 1201, Statement on Radioactive Fallout Submitted to the U.S. Atomic Energy Commission by the Advisory Committee on Biology and Medicine, Oct. 19, 1957, AEC.

22. John S. D. Eisenhower, Memorandum of Conference with the President, Aug. 9, 1957; Dulles, Addendum to Memorandum of Conversation with the President, Aug. 3, 1957, both in DDE; AEC-MLC 112, June 27, 1957, AEC.

23. John S. D. Eisenhower, Memorandum of Conference with the President, Aug. 9, 1957, DDE; Strauss to File, Aug. 9, 1957, LLS.

24. Strauss to Quarles, Sept. 12, 1957, AEC.

25. Strauss to Eisenhower, Nov. 23, 1957, Jan. 29, June 12, 1958, all in AEC; Department of Energy, "Announced United States Nuclear Tests, July 1945 Through December 1982," Jan. 1983, NVO-209 (Rev. 3), pp. 8–9.

26. *Public Papers, 1957, Eisenhower*, pp. 468–80; Western Statement in the Disarmament Subcommittee on Nuclear Test Suspension, July 2, 1957, *Documents on Disarmament, 1945–1959, Vol. II, 1957–1959* (Department of State Publication 7008), pp. 802–3 (hereafter cited *Documents on Disarmament*).

27. Stassen to Dulles, June 20, 1957, DDE; Dulles, Memorandum of Conversation with British Ambassador Sir Harold Caccia, June 23, 1957, DOS.

28. Bernhard G. Bechhoefer, *Postwar Negotiations for Arms Control* (Washington: Brookings Institution, 1961), pp. 407–8 (hereafter cited Bechhoefer, *Postwar Negotiations for Arms Control*); Dulles, Telephone Call to Allen Dulles, July 8, 1957, DDE; J. G. Mein, Memorandum of Conversation, July 12, 1957, DOS.

29. Dulles, Memorandum of Conversation with the President, July 22, 1957; Strauss to Eisenhower, July 23, 1957, both in DDE.

30. Bechhoefer, *Postwar Negotiations for Arms Control*, pp. 406–7; Dulles to Herter, July 30, 31, 1957, DDE; Smith to Strauss, Aug. 12, 1957, DOS; Western Working Paper Submitted to the Disarmament Subcommittee: Systems of Inspection to Safeguard Against the Possibility of Surprise Attack, Aug. 2, 1957, and Statement by Secretary of State Dulles to the Disarmament Subcommittee, Aug. 2, 1957, *Documents on Disarmament*, pp. 837–45; Dulles to Herter for Eisenhower, July 31, 1957, DDE.

31. Dulles, Memorandum of Conversation with the President, Aug. 3, 1957, DDE; Strauss to File, Aug. 8, 1957, LLS.

32. Cutler, Morning Conference on Aug. 9, 1957, DOS.

33. Cutler, Afternoon Conference on Aug. 9, 1957, DOS; Smith Telephone Call to the Secretary in Utica (en route to Watertown, NY), Aug. 9, 1957, DDE.

34. Smith to Strauss, Aug. 15, 1957, LLS.

35. Statement by the President After Authorizing Inclusion of Nuclear Test Suspension Among Disarmament Proposals, Aug. 21, 1957, *Public Papers, 1957, Eisenhower*, p. 627; Dulles, Memorandum of Conversation with the President, Aug. 21, 1957, DDE.

36. Bechhoefer, *Postwar Negotiations for Arms Control*, pp. 408–13; Smith, Telephone Conversation with Stassen, Aug. 28, 1957; Spiers, Telephone Conversation

with Stassen, Aug. 28, 1957, both in DOS; *Public Papers, 1957, Eisenhower*, pp. 635–36; Dulles, Telephone Call from Strauss, Aug. 30, 1957, DDE.

37. Western Working Paper Submitted to the Disarmament Subcommittee: Proposals for Partial Measures of Disarmament, Aug. 29, 1957, *Documents on Disarmament*, pp. 868–74; Divine, *Blowing on the Wind*, pp. 155–56.

38. Divine, *Blowing on the Wind*, p. 159; Bechhoefer, *Postwar Negotiations for Arms Control*, pp. 433–34; Harold K. Jacobson and Eric Stein, *Diplomats, Scientists, and Politicians: The United States and the Nuclear Test Ban Negotiations* (Ann Arbor: University of Michigan Press, 1966), p. 17 (hereafter cited Jacobson and Stein, *Diplomats, Scientists, and Politicians*); *New York Times*, Oct. 14, 1957.

39. Jacobson and Stein, *Diplomats, Scientists, and Politicians*, pp. 28–29; Bechhoefer, *Postwar Negotiations for Arms Control*, pp. 413–14; Memorandum by the Soviet Government on Partial Measures in the Field of Disarmament, Sept. 20, 1957, *Documents on Disarmament*, pp. 874–84.

40. Dulles, Speech delivered to the United Nations 680th Plenary Meeting, *Official Records of the General Assembly, Twelfth Session: Plenary Meetings* (New York: United Nations, 1957), pp. 18–21; Dulles to Eisenhower, Sept. 16, 1957; Eisenhower to Dulles, Sept. 17, 1957; Dulles to Macmillan, Sept. 19, 1957, all in DDE.

41. Stassen to Dulles, Informal Memorandum, Sept. 23, 1957, DDE.

42. Dulles to Stassen, Sept. 27, 1957, DDE.

43. Strauss to Dulles, Sept. 28, 1957; Quarles to Dulles, Sept. 30, 1957; Twining to Dulles, Sept. 30, 1957; Dulles, Telephone Call to Eisenhower, Sept. 27, 1957; Dulles to Eisenhower, Oct. 1, 1957; Dulles, Memorandum of Conversation with Vice-President Nixon, Sept. 30, 1957, all in DDE.

44. Bechhoefer, *Postwar Negotiations for Arms Control*, pp. 413–39; Jacobson and Stein, *Diplomats, Scientists, and Politicians*, pp. 21–24.

45. *Public Papers, 1957, Eisenhower*, pp. 789–99; Gilpin, *American Scientists and Nuclear Weapons Policy*, pp. 176–77; James R. Killian, Jr., *Sputnik, Scientists, and Eisenhower: A Memoir of the First Special Assistant to the President for Science and Technology* (Cambridge: MIT Press, 1977), pp. 2–30 (hereafter cited Killian, *Sputnik, Scientists, and Eisenhower*); Jacobson and Stein, *Diplomats, Scientists, and Politicians*, pp. 32–33. Initial members of the science advisory committee were Robert F. Bacher, William O. Baker, Lloyd V. Berkner, Hans A. Bethe, Detlev W. Bronk, James H. Doolittle, James B. Fisk, Caryl P. Haskins, James R. Killian, George B. Kistiakowsky, Edwin H. Land, Emanuel R. Piore, Edward M. Purcell, Isidor I. Rabi, H. P. Robertson, Jerome B. Wiesner, Herbert F. York, and Jerrold R. Zacharias.

46. Seven members of the President's Science Advisory Committee had previously served on the Gaither committee or one of its subcommittees. They were: Lloyd V. Berkner, James H. Doolittle, James B. Fisk, James R. Killian, I. I. Rabi, Jerome B. Wiesner, and Herbert F. York.

47. Morton H. Halperin, "The Gaither Committee and the Policy Process," *World Politics* 13 (Oct. 1960–July 1961): 360–84 (hereafter cited Halperin, "The Gaither Committee").

48. Joint Committee on Defense Production, *Deterrence and Survival in the Nuclear Age (The "Gaither Report" of 1957)*, Joint Committee Print (Washington: Government Printing Office, 1976); Halperin, "The Gaither Committee," pp. 361–69; Freedman, *The Evolution of Nuclear Strategy*, pp. 160–63; Kaplan, *The Wizards of Armageddon*, pp. 129–32.

49. Dulles, Memorandum of Conversation with the President, Dec. 26, 1957, DDE; Eisenhower, *Waging Peace, 1956–1961* (Garden City, NY: Doubleday, 1965), pp. 219–23 (hereafter cited Eisenhower, *Waging Peace*).

50. Dulles to Eisenhower, Sept. 29, 1957, DDE; Strauss to File, Oct. 9, 1957, LLS.

51. Dulles, Memorandum of Conversation at the British Embassy, Oct. 22, 1957, DDE.

52. *Public Papers, 1957, Eisenhower*, pp. 768–72; Clinton P. Anderson, *Outsider in the Senate: Senator Clinton Anderson's Memoirs* (New York: World Publishing, 1970), p. 168 (hereafter cited Anderson, *Outsider in the Senate*); Harold L. Nieburg, *Nuclear Secrecy and Foreign Policy* (Washington: Public Affairs Press, 1964), pp. 137–38.

53. Anderson, *Outsider in the Senate*, p. 168; Dulles, Telephone Call from Smith, Oct. 26, 1957; Dulles, Telephone Call from Strauss, Oct. 26, 1957, both in DDE.

54. Dulles, Telephone Call to Stevenson in Chicago, Oct. 28, 1957; Dulles, Memorandum of Conversation with Governor Stevenson, Secretary's Residence, Oct. 30, 1957, both in DDE.

55. Dulles, Telephone Call to Strauss, Nov. 26, 1957; Dulles, Memorandum of Conversation with Governor Stevenson, Nov. 26, 1957, both in DDE. Correspondence relating to this episode can be found in Walter Johnson, Carol Evans, and C. Eric Sears, eds., *The Papers of Adlai E. Stevenson*, Vol. 7, *Continuing Education and the Unfinished Business of American Society, 1957–1961* (Boston: Little, Brown, 1977), pp. 96–137.

56. Statement by the Indian Prime Minister [Nehru] on Nuclear Test Explosions, Nov. 28, 1957, and Letter From the Soviet Premier [Bulganin] to President Eisenhower, Dec. 10, 1957, *Documents on Disarmament*, pp. 917–26.

57. Eisenhower, *Waging Peace*, p. 231. Divine, *Blowing on the Wind*, pp. 172–73, suggests that *Sputnik* caused only a temporary setback on a test ban.

58. Communiqué by the North Atlantic Council [Extract], Dec. 19, 1957, *Documents on Disarmament*, pp. 928–31; Eisenhower, *Waging Peace*, p. 232.

59. Eisenhower, Memorandum on letter of Prime Minister Macmillan (dated January 2, 1958), Jan. 3, 1958, DDE; *Public Papers, 1957, Eisenhower*, pp. 832–34.

60. Dulles, Memorandum of Conversation, Oct. 8, 1957; Dulles, Memorandum of Conversation with the President, Oct. 18, 1957; Dulles, Memorandum of Conversation with Governor Stassen, Secretary's Residence, Oct. 20, 1957; Stassen to Dulles, Oct. 21, 1957; Dulles, Memorandum of Conversation with Governor Stassen, Oct. 31, 1957; Dulles, Telephone Call to Nixon, Dec. 26, 1957, all in DDE.

61. National Security Council, Summary of Discussion (hereafter cited SNSC), Meeting 350, Jan. 6, 1958, DDE.

62. Killian, *Sputnik, Scientists, and Eisenhower*, p. 154; SNSC 350, Jan. 6, 1958, DDE.

63. James S. Lay, Jr., Memorandum for the National Security Council: U.S. Policy on Control of Armaments, Jan. 9, 1958; CM 1324, Jan. 8, 1958, both in AEC. Numerous documents in the Dulles papers concerning Stassen's last months in the Administration remained closed to research at the Eisenhower Presidential Library.

64. Eisenhower to Bulganin, Jan. 13, 1958, *Public Papers of the Presidents of the United States, 1958: Dwight D. Eisenhower* (Washington: Government Printing Office, 1959), pp. 75–84 (hereafter cited *Public Papers, 1958, Eisenhower*).

65. See Chap. 11, Defining the Safeguard Problem and Geneva Safeguard Conference.

66. Killian, *Sputnik, Scientists, and Eisenhower*, pp. 150–152.

67. Commission representatives were Brig. Gen. Alfred Starbird, Carson Mark, Harold Brown, and Roderick Spence. Department of Defense representatives were General Herbert Loper, Maj. Gen. Richard C. Coiner, Colonel Lester Woodward, and Doyle Northrup. The CIA representative was Herbert Scoville, Jr. Representatives from the Science Advisory Committee were Hans Bethe (chairman) and Herbert York. Representing the missile committee of PSAC were George Kistiakowsky, J. W. McRea, Herbert York, L. Hyland, and Robert F. Bacher. Designation of Members of Various Working Groups—NSC Meeting on Jan. 6, 1958, AEC 226/131, Jan. 23, 1958, AEC; Killian, *Sputnik, Scientists, and Eisenhower*, pp. 154–55.

68. Jacobson and Stein, *Diplomats, Scientists, and Politicians*, p. 34; Pauling to Eisenhower, Feb. 19, 1958, LLS.

69. Report of U.S. Delegation to the Fourth Session of the UN Scientific Committee on the Effects of Atomic Radiation, AEC 226/139, April 30, 1958, AEC.

70. *Bulletin of the Atomic Scientists* 14 (Jan. 1958): 9–61; Walter R. Eckelmann, J. Laurence Kulp, and Arthur R. Schulert, "Strontium-90 in Man, II," *Science*, Feb. 7, 1958, pp. 266–74; Pauling, *No More War!*, p. 102; CM 1280, May 1, 1957, AEC. See also Divine, *Blowing on the Wind*, pp. 184–97.

71. Humphrey to Eisenhower, Nov. 4, 1957; Eisenhower to Humphrey, Nov. 8, 1957, both in DDE; Jacobson and Stein, *Diplomats, Scientists, and Politicians*, p. 35.

72. Senate Subcommittee of the Commit-

tee on Foreign Relations, *Hearings on Control and Reduction of Armaments*, Feb. 28–April 17, 1958 (Washington: Government Printing Office, 1958), pp. 1336–64 (hereafter cited *Hearings on Control and Reduction of Armaments*).
73. Ibid., pp. 1365–615; Jacobson and Stein, *Diplomats, Scientists, and Politicians*, pp. 43–44.
74. AEC Press Release, Background Information on the Deep Underground Shot (*Rainier*) at the Nevada Test Site, March 6, 1958; AEC Press Release A-53, Libby to Humphrey, March 12, 1958; JCAE, Transcript of Hearings on Erroneous Statement in Press Release of March 6, 1958, Issued by AEC, Concerning *Rainier* Underground Atomic Detonation, March 15, 1958, all in AEC; *Hearings on Control and Reduction of Armaments*, pp. 1584–98; Gilpin, *American Scientists and Nuclear Weapons Policy*, p. 182.
75. Edward Teller and Albert Latter, "The Compelling Need for Nuclear Tests," *Life*, Feb. 10, 1958, pp. 65–72; Teller and Latter, *Our Nuclear Future . . . Facts, Dangers and Opportunities* (New York: Criterion Books, 1958); *Hearings on Control and Reduction of Armaments*, pp. 1453–60.
76. *Hearings on Control and Reduction of Armaments*, pp. 1526–43.
77. Comments on H.R.8269—A Bill to Prohibit Testing of Nuclear Devices, AEC 226/134, March 18, 1958; AEC 226/136, April 2, 1958; AEC 226/138, April 21, 1958; Graham to McCool, March 25, 1958; Graham to Commissioners, April 23, 1958; Graham to Durham, May 23, 1958; J. H. Morse, Jr., to Graham, March 3, 1958; Morse to Floberg, March 3, 1958; Morse to Libby, March 10, 1958, all in AEC.
78. Goodpaster, Memorandum of Conference with the President, Jan. 22, 1958, DDE.
79. Test Limitations, AEC 226/132, Feb. 24, 1958; CM 1337, Feb. 26, 1958, both in AEC.
80. CM 1340, March 7, 1958; Further Information Relative to Underground Testing, AEC 987/1, March 14, 1958, both in AEC.
81. Report of NSC Ad Hoc Working Group on the Technical Feasibility of a Cessation of Nuclear Testing, March 28, 1958, AEC.
82. Taylor to the Secretary of Defense, March 13, 1958; Quarles to Bethe, March 21,

1958, both in AEC; Morse to Strauss, May 2, 1958, LLS.
83. Decree of the Supreme Soviet Concerning the Discontinuance of Soviet Atomic and Hydrogen Weapons Tests, March 31, 1958, *Documents on Disarmament*, pp. 978–80; *Hearings on Control and Reduction of Armaments*, p. 1545; Jacobson and Stein, *Diplomats, Scientists, and Politicians*, p. 45.
84. Dulles, Memorandum of Conversation with the President, March 24, 1954; Goodpaster, Memorandum of Conference with the President, March 24, 1958, both in DDE.
85. SNSC 361, April 4, 1958, DDE.
86. Khrushchev to Eisenhower, April 4 and 8, 1958, and Eisenhower to Khrushchev, April 8, 1958, *Documents on Disarmament*, pp. 980–85; Secretary Dulles's News Conference of April 1, 1958, AEC; Secretary's Staff Meeting, April 1 and 8, 1958, both in DOS.
87. The President's News Conference of April 9, 1958, *Public Papers, 1958, Eisenhower*, pp. 294–304; Dulles, Telephone Call to Eisenhower, April 8, 1958; Dulles, Telephone Call from Strauss, April 9, 1958, both in DDE.
88. Killian, *Sputnik, Scientists, and Eisenhower*, pp. 156–57; Jacobson and Stein, *Diplomats, Scientists, and Politicians*, p. 49; Divine, *Blowing on the Wind*, p. 209.
89. Foster, Memorandum to the Secretary, Review of Existing Disarmament Policy, April 10, 1958, AEC.
90. President's Special Cabinet Committee on Summit Preparations—Report of Working Group on Disarmament, AEC 226/137, April 17, 1958, AEC.
91. Strauss to File, April 16, 1958, LLS.
92. Goodpaster, Memorandum of Conference with the President, April 17, 1958, DDE; Khrushchev to Eisenhower, April 22, 1958, *Documents on Disarmament*, pp. 996–1004.
93. Memorandum of Conversation, Meeting with Disarmament Advisers, April 26, 1958, DDE.
94. Eisenhower to Khrushchev, April 28, 1958, *Documents on Disarmament*, pp. 1006–7.
95. Strauss to Eisenhower, Jan. 29, 1958; CM 1351, April 4, 1958; CM 1352, April 7, 1958, all in AEC; Strauss to File, April 3 and 7, 1958, both in LLS.

647

96. Goodpaster, Memorandum of Conference with the President, May 1, 1958, DDE; CM 1359, April 21, 1958, AEC.
97. Letter to the President Regarding Test Activity, AEC 987/8, Sept. 2, 1958, AEC.
98. Morse Salisbury to Starbird, Action on United Press coverage of protestor groups at the Nevada Test Site, Aug. 7, 1957, AEC; Divine, *Blowing on the Wind*, pp. 160, 165–69, 178–81.
99. CM 1334, Feb. 12, 1958, AEC; Earle Reynolds, *The Forbidden Voyage* (New York: David McKay, 1961).
100. CM 1369, May 6, 1958; CM 1371, May 9, 1958; CM 1372, May 9, 1958; Meeting between Chairman Strauss and Members of National Committee for Non-Violent Action Against Nuclear Tests, May 13, 1958, all in AEC; Lewis L. Strauss, *Men and Decisions* (Garden City, NY: Doubleday, 1962), p. 413; Divine, *Blowing on the Wind*, p. 214.
101. GAC 58, May 5, 7, 1958; Quarles to Eisenhower, May 9, 1958; Loper to Strauss, May 8, 1958, all in AEC.
102. GAC 58, May 5, 7, 1958, AEC.
103. Goodpaster, Memorandum of Conference with the President, May 14, 1958, DDE; Khrushchev to Eisenhower, May 9, 1958, *Documents on Disarmament*, pp. 1036–41.
104. Dulles, Memorandum of Conversation with Strauss, May 16, 1958, DDE.
105. Eisenhower to Khrushchev, May 24, 1958; Khrushchev to Eisenhower, May 30, 1958; Eisenhower to Khrushchev, June 10, 1958, all in *Documents on Disarmament*, pp. 1043–44, 1050–51, 1051–52.
106. CM 1377, May 28, 1958, AEC.

## CHAPTER EIGHTEEN

1. Strauss to Eisenhower, March 31, 1958, LLS.
2. Strauss to File, Dec. 15, 1954, LLS.
3. *Nucleonics* 16 (July 1958): 20.
4. Anderson, "A Pattern for Nuclear Power," Joint Committee Press Release 167, June 19, 1958, AEC; Zehring to Strauss, June 13, 1958, LLS.
5. McCone to File, July 16, 1958, AEC.
6. *Congressional Record*, 85 Cong., 2 sess., pp. 12146, 12264. Identical bills, H.R.13121 and S.4051, were introduced

on June 25, 1958. Maurice Stans, director, Bureau of the Budget, to Eisenhower, July 1, 1958, DDE; Eisenhower's statement is in *Public Papers of the Presidents of the United States, 1958: Dwight D. Eisenhower* (Washington: Government Printing Office, 1959), pp. 582–83; *Nucleonics* 16 (July 1958): 17–19. The authorization act was P.L.85–590, 72 *Stat.* 490.
7. Holifield, President's Criticism of Atomic Authorization Bill Analyzed and Answered, Aug. 6, 1958, JCAE; McCone to File, Aug. 5, 1958, AEC.
8. Joint Committee on Atomic Energy, *Hearings on the Proposed EURATOM Agreements and Legislation to Carry Out the Proposed Cooperative Program*, July 22–30, 1958 (Washington: Government Printing Office, 1958). For Dillon's testimony, see pp. 22–82; for Floberg's testimony, pp. 88–128, 135–49, 182–223. The hearings also contain copies of all documents in the EURATOM package. The authorization bill was enacted on Aug. 28, 1958, as the EURATOM Cooperation Act of 1958, P.L.85–846. The EURATOM agreement was approved by Senate Concurrent Resolution 116, Aug. 23, 1958.
9. AEC Press Release A-165, June 30, 1958; AEC Press Release A-144, June 16, 1958, both in AEC; *Nucleonics* 16 (July 1958): 21.
10. McCone to File, undated but ca. Sept. 14, 1958, AEC.
11. McCone probably got these ideas from Rickover, who later presented them at a Joint Committee hearing. Joint Committee on Atomic Energy, *Hearings on AEC Authorizing Legislation, Fiscal Year 1960*, Feb. 7–May 8, 1959 (Washington: Government Printing Office, 1959), pp. 267–77 (hereafter cited *Authorization Hearings, 1960*).
12. Durham to Fields, June 18, 1958, in AEC 496/45, June 30, 1958, AEC; Joint Committee on Atomic Energy, *Proposed Expanded Civilian Nuclear Power Program*, Joint Committee Print, Aug. 1958 (Washington: Government Printing Office, 1958).
13. Durham to McCone, Aug. 21, 1958, transmitting JCAE Press Release 180, Aug. 25, 1958, in JCAE Press Release and Questionnaire on Proposed Expanded Civilian Nuclear Power Program, AEC 152/97, Aug. 29, 1958, AEC.

14. McCone to Rickover, Sept. 14, 18, 1958; CM 1403, Sept. 17, 1958, all in AEC.
15. Foster to McCone, Sept. 4, 1958; Ad Hoc Advisory Committee on Reactor Policies and Programs, AEC 1007, Oct. 7, 1958; AEC Press Release A-265, Oct. 8, 1958, all in AEC.
16. Tammaro to Foster, Oct. 14, 1958; Foster to the Commissioners, Oct. 21, 1958; AEC Press Release A-287, Oct. 29, 1958, all in AEC; *Nucleonics* 16 (Nov. 1958): 22.
17. Section 101(d) 13, P.L.85–590; AEC Press Release A-238, Sept. 15, 1958, AEC.
18. Director of Reactor Development, Fuel Cycle Development Program, AEC 152/96, Aug. 15, 1958; AEC Press Release A-269, Oct. 15, 1958; AEC Press Release A-322, Dec. 5, 1958; AEC Press Release A-329, Dec. 11, 1958, all in AEC; *Nucleonics* 17 (Jan. 1959): 24.
19. The committee's files in AEC contain verbatim transcripts of the twelve meetings held from Oct. 3, 1958, to Jan. 2, 1959, along with extensive correspondence. The Joint Committee published the replies to the survey as a committee print in November 1958. The originals of the replies are in Group 1, Box 44, JCAE. On Commission reactions, see CM 1429, Nov. 18, 1958, AEC.
20. Civilian Nuclear Power, Report by Ad Hoc Advisory Committee on Reactor Policies and Programs, Jan. 2, 1959, AEC. The complete report also appeared in Joint Committee on Atomic Energy, *Hearings on Development, Growth, and State of the Atomic Energy Industry*, Feb. 17–26, 1959 (Washington: Government Printing Office, 1959), pp. 510–40 (hereafter cited *202 Hearings, 1959*); *Nucleonics* 17 (Feb. 1959): 19–20.
21. Minutes, Informal Commission Meeting, Dec. 29, 1958; Stans to McCone, Nov. 26, 1958, in AEC 998/16, Dec. 1, 1958; FY 1960 Budget Estimates, AEC 998/17, Dec. 1, 1958, all in AEC; *Nucleonics* 17 (Jan. 1959): 23.
22. The plan was submitted to the Commission in four successive versions, all entitled Proposed Reactor Development Program: AEC 152/106, Jan. 9, 1959; AEC 152/107, Jan. 12, 1959; AEC 152/109, Jan. 26, 1959; and AEC 152/110, Jan. 27, 1959, all in AEC.
23. *202 Hearings, 1959*, pp. 38–48.
24. Ibid., pp. 77–79; Goodpaster, Memoran-

dum of Conference with the President, Feb. 11, 1959, DDE.
25. *202 Hearings, 1959*, pp. 99–104; *Authorization Hearings, 1960*, pp. 113–15; *Nucleonics* 17 (March 1959): 23.
26. *Authorization Hearings, 1960*, pp. 129–34, 142–44.
27. Ibid., pp. 658–59.
28. General Manager, The Chugach Program, AEC 777/81, Feb. 16, 1959; General Manager, The Hallam Reactor Project, AEC 777/82, Feb. 16, 1959; Director of Reactor Development, Consideration of the Hallam Project, AEC 777/84, March 5, 1959; Correspondence Regarding the Hallam, Nebraska, Project, AEC 777/83, March 2, 1959; CM 1472, Feb. 16, 1959, all in AEC; *Nucleonics* 17 (March 1959): 17–18; *Authorization Hearings, 1960*, pp. 181–87, 301; AEC Press Release B-103, July 2, 1959, AEC.
29. Sect. 110, P.L.85–590, imposed the ninety-day requirement. See Chap. 18, note 6. *Authorization Hearings, 1960*, pp. 329–30.
30. *Authorization Hearings, 1960*, pp. 1–55, 156–57, 335–41, 375–76, 402–15, 483–84, 636–48; AEC Press Release B-145, Aug. 27, 1959, AEC.
31. Director of Reactor Development, Fluid Fuel Reactors Program, AEC 152/128, May 28, 1959; CM 1533, Aug. 4, 1959; AEC Report on Four Power Reactors, AEC 152/125, April 28, 1959; Transmittal of Reactor Concept Report, AEC 152/126, April 29, 1959; McCool to File, May 5, 1959, all in AEC; *Authorization Hearings, 1960*, pp. 544–616.
32. *Authorization Hearings, 1960*, pp. 617–77; *Nucleonics* 17 (July 1959): 17.
33. Percival F. Brundage to Strauss, Jan. 25, 1956, in AEC 653/17, Jan. 30, 1956; CM 1170, Feb. 2, 1956; Strauss to Rowland Hughes, Feb. 10, 1956; Tammaro to Cook, March 16, 1956, all in AEC.
34. Clarence G. Morse, Maritime Administrator, to Warren G. Magnuson, June 27, 1956, in AEC 653/23, July 16, 1956; Eisenhower to Strauss, July 30, 1956, in AEC 653/24, Aug. 2, 1956; Director of Reactor Development, B & W Proposal for Nuclear Powered Merchant Ship, AEC 653/25, Sept. 21, 1956; AEC Press Release 1024, April 10, 1957; Selection of Construction Contractor for Nuclear Powered Merchant Ship, AEC 653/37, Nov. 13, 1957; AEC Press Release 1221, Nov. 19, 1957; AEC Press

649

Release B-56, April 9, 1959, all in AEC.

35. AEC Press Release 967, Jan. 25, 1957; H. D. Anamosa to Hollingsworth, Briefing on N. S. Savannah, July 13, 1959; R. V. Willit to File, Briefing Outlines, July 15, 1959; McCone to Luedecke, July 22, 1959, all in AEC.

36. McCone to Luedecke, July 30, Aug. 7, 1959; Dwight A. Ink to File, July 27, 1959, all in AEC.

37. *Nucleonics* 17 (Oct. 1959): 18; Luedecke to McCone, Aug. 10, 1959; Graham to Anderson, Sept. 30, 1959, with Summary Notes of Discussion with Admiral Rickover, Aug. 19, 1959, in AEC 653/55, Oct. 12, 1959, all in AEC.

38. McCone to Luedecke, May 11, 1959; Luedecke to McCone, June 8, 1959, both in AEC.

39. *Civilian Nuclear Power Program: Part I—Summary, Current Status of Reactor Concepts; Part II—Economic Potential and Development Program; Part III—Technical Status* (a series of mini reports); Notes on Nuclear Power Program, Oct. 30, 1959, all in AEC.

40. Minutes, Ad Hoc Advisory Committee on Reactor Policies and Programs, Oct. 27, Nov. 7, 13–14, 27–28, Dec. 5, 1959; Minutes, Informal Commission Meeting, Dec. 4, 1959; McCool to Pittman, Dec. 8, 1959; Pittman to McCone, Dec. 9, 1959; Director of Reactor Development, Program Recommendations for Development of Large Central Station Nuclear Power Plants, AEC 152/130, Dec. 17, 1959; Tammaro to McCone, Dec. 17, 1959, with attachment, Ad Hoc Advisory Committee on Reactor Policies and Programs to McCone, Dec. 14, 1959, all in AEC; *Nucleonics* 17 (Dec. 1959): 17–19.

41. *Authorization Hearings, 1960,* pp. 656–57; *Nucleonics* 17 (May 1959): 28–29.

42. AEC 152/130, Dec. 17, 1959, AEC. See Chap. 18, note 40.

43. Successive drafts of the long-range plan appeared in AEC 152/133, Jan. 16, 1960; AEC 152/134, Jan. 25, 1960; AEC 152/135, Feb. 1, 1960; and AEC 152/136, Feb. 3, 1960, all in AEC. See also McCool to Pittman, Jan. 15, 1960; CM 1584, Jan. 27, 1960; CM 1587, Feb. 2, 1960; CM 1590, Feb. 4, 1960; AEC Press Release C-20, Feb. 16, 1960, all in AEC. The long-range plan was published as *Civilian Nuclear Power Pro-*

*gram, Part IV, Plans for Development as of February 1960* (Washington: Government Printing Office, 1960); copies are in AEC.

## CHAPTER NINETEEN

1. Ernest Braun and Stuart MacDonald, *Revolution in Miniature* (New York: Cambridge University Press, 1978), pp. 54–72; Edward W. Constant II, *The Origins of the Turbojet Revolution* (Baltimore: Johns Hopkins University Press, 1980).

2. Oral history interview with Thomas Gates, Columbia University Oral History collection, as quoted in George B. Kistiakowsky, *A Scientist at the White House* (Cambridge: Harvard University Press, 1976), p. xxix (hereafter cited Kistiakowsky, *A Scientist at the White House*).

3. Price to Eisenhower, Oct. 24, 1957; CM 1313, Nov. 6, 1957; Joint Committee Press Release 183, Dec. 1, 1958, all in AEC; AEC, *Twenty-fifth Semiannual Report* (Washington: Government Printing Office, 1959), pp. 191–92.

4. Minutes, GAC Reactor Subcommittee on ANP Projects, Dec. 18–19, 1958, AEC. Expenditure figures appear in Joint Committee Press Release 235, July 21, 1959, AEC.

5. McCone and Quarles to Eisenhower, Jan. 2, 1959; R. X. Donovan to the Commissioners and General Manager, Jan. 26, 27, 1959, all in AEC.

6. McCone to the Commissioners, June 18, 22, 1959; Joint Committee, Transcript of Hearing, Jan. 26–27, 1959, all in AEC.

7. Director of Reactor Development, ANP Manned Aircraft Program Planning, AEC 17/175, Sept. 18, 1959, and AEC 17/183, Dec. 11, 1959; CM 1575, Dec. 19, 1959; Floberg to McCone, Dec. 21, 1959; McCone to Luedecke, June 30, 1960, all in AEC; Kistiakowsky, *A Scientist at the White House*, pp. 182, 204; Goodpaster, Memorandum of Conference with the President, June 23, 1959, DDE.

8. AEC, *Annual Report to the Congress, 1961* (Washington: Government Printing Office, 1962), pp. 155–56; AEC Press Release D-73, March 30, 1961, AEC.

9. Director of Military Application, Special Reactor Test Site, AEC 141/32, April 2, 1956; CM 1190, April 4, 1956; Brief History and Chronology of the Nuclear

Rocket Program, Dec. 12, 1962; Progress on the ANP Program, AEC 17/159, Aug. 25, 1958; Timetable on Project Pluto, AEC 564/29, Sept. 24, 1958, all in AEC; John S. D. Eisenhower, Memorandum of Conference with the President, Nov. 8, 1960, DDE; Kistiakowsky, *A Scientist at the White House*, pp. 122–23, 257, 303.

10. Pittman to McCone, May 23, 1960, AEC; *Washington Post*, Jan. 17, 1959, p. 1; AEC, *Annual Report to the Congress, 1959* (Washington: Government Printing Office, 1960), pp. 78–81 (hereafter cited *Annual Report, 1959*); AEC, *Annual Report to the Congress, 1960* (Washington: Government Printing Office, 1961), pp. 149–52 (hereafter cited *Annual Report, 1960*).

11. *Annual Report, 1960*, pp. 132–39.

12. Richard G. Hewlett and Francis Duncan, *Nuclear Navy, 1946–1962* (Chicago: University of Chicago Press, 1974), pp. 220–24, 259–67 (hereafter cited *Nuclear Navy*); Harvey M. Sapolsky, *The Polaris System Development: Bureaucratic and Programmatic Success in Government* (Cambridge: Harvard University Press, 1972), pp. 11, 22–23, 31, 132; Wyndham D. Miles, "The Polaris," *Technology and Culture* 4 (Fall 1963): 478–81.

13. *Nuclear Navy*, pp. 207–15, 270, 278–81.

14. Ibid., pp. 281–82, 310–18, 370–71; Director of International Affairs, Cooperation with the Netherlands in the Field of Nuclear Submarine Propulsion, AEC 1021/6, Oct. 27, 1959; CM 1564, Nov. 3, 1959; Eisenhower to McCone, Sept. 28, 1960; CM 1660, Oct. 7, 1960; McCone to Goodpaster, Oct. 7, 1960; Howard C. Brown, Memorandum of Commission Discussion, Oct. 21, 1960, all in AEC; Kistiakowsky, *A Scientist at the White House*, pp. 78–79.

15. Director of Research, Interagency Support of High Energy Physics, AEC 603/50, Oct. 7, 1958, AEC.

16. Director of Research, U.S. Policy and Actions in High Energy Accelerator Physics, AEC 603/53, Nov. 28, 1958; CM 1445, Dec. 17, 1958, both in AEC.

17. Special Panel of the President's Science Advisory Committee and the General Advisory Committee, U.S. Policy and Actions in High Energy Accelerator Physics, Nov. 25, 1958, AEC; Richard G. Hewlett and Francis Duncan, *Atomic Shield, 1946–1952*, Vol. II of *A History of the U.S. Atomic Energy Commission* (University Park: Pennsylvania State University Press, 1969), pp. 233–34.

18. *Annual Report, 1959*, pp. 152–53.

19. Goodpaster, Memorandum of Conference with the President, April 2, 1959, DDE; Killian to Eisenhower, April 2, 1959, in AEC 603/60, April 16, 1959, AEC; *Public Papers of the Presidents of the United States, 1959: Dwight D. Eisenhower* (Washington: Government Printing Office, 1960), pp. 399–406; McCone to Luedecke, Aug. 6, 1959; Luedecke to McCone, Oct. 24, 1959, in AEC 1036, Nov. 16, 1959; CM 1572, Dec. 11, 1959, all in AEC; Kistiakowsky, *A Scientist at the White House*, pp. 147–48.

20. Piore to McCone and Kistiakowsky, Feb. 5, 1960, in AEC 603/66, Feb. 17, 1960; Kistiakowsky to McCone, March 16, 1960, in AEC 603/69, March 25, 1960; Brown to File, March 23, 1960, all in AEC; W. B. Persons to Goodpaster, March 23, 1960, DDE; Kistiakowsky, *A Scientist at the White House*, pp. 223, 233.

21. Kistiakowsky to McCone, Sept. 27, 1960; Director of Research, High Energy Physics Program and Stanford Linear Accelerator, AEC 603/73, Dec. 16, 1960; Piore to McCone and Kistiakowsky, Dec. 15, 1960, transmitting the panel report; Kistiakowsky to McCone, Dec. 21, 1960, in AEC 603/74, Dec. 29, 1960, all in AEC. The panel report and other documents were published in Joint Committee on Atomic Energy, *Report on Background Information on the High Energy Physics Program and the Proposed Stanford Linear Electron Accelerator Project* (Washington: Government Printing Office, 1961).

22. As quoted in Joan L. Bromberg, *Fusion: Science, Politics, and the Invention of a New Energy Source* (Cambridge: MIT Press, 1982), p. 68 (hereafter cited Bromberg, *Fusion*). This and the following paragraphs depend heavily on Bromberg, pp. 68–88.

23. Ibid., pp. 89–105; AEC, *Twenty-second Semiannual Report* (Washington: Government Printing Office, 1957), pp. 96–105.

24. McCone to Luedecke, July 24, 1959; CM 1533, Aug. 4, 1959; Summary Notes of Briefings on Intelligence Matters and Project Sherwood, Oct. 5, 1959; Summary Notes on Review of Controlled

651

Thermonuclear Research Program, Jan. 10, 1961, all in AEC.

25. Lewis L. Strauss, *Men and Decisions* (Garden City, NY: Doubleday, 1962), p. 335.

26. Director of Military Application, Conference on Peaceful Uses of Atomic Energy, AEC 811/4, Nov. 26, 1956, AEC.

27. Director of Military Application, Non-Military Uses of Explosive Nuclear Devices, AEC 811/6, June 13, 1957, AEC.

28. Director of Military Application, Non-Military Uses of Nuclear Explosive Devices, AEC 811/7, Nov. 22, 1957; CM 1317, Nov. 27, 1957, both in AEC.

29. Ramey to LaPlante, Dec. 9, 1957; AEC Press Release A-203, Aug. 6, 1958, both in AEC; Joint Committee on Atomic Energy, *Hearings on Fallout from Nuclear Weapons Tests*, Vol. 3, May 5–8, 1959 (Washington: Government Printing Office, 1959), pp. 2198–99; AEC, *Twenty-third Semiannual Report* (Washington: Government Printing Office, 1958), p. 276.

30. Strauss to Gates, Feb. 27, 1958; CM 1353, April 9, 1958, both in AEC.

31. Director of Military Application, Non-Military Uses of Nuclear Explosive Devices, AEC 811/12, June 6, 1958; CM 1381, June 12, 1958; Teller to H. A. Fidler, June 27, 1958, in AEC 811/18, July 21, 1958; AEC Press Release A-136, June 9, 1958; AEC Press Release A-203, Aug. 6, 1958, all in AEC.

32. Graham to McCone, Sept. 19, 1958; Director of Military Application, *Plowshare* Program, AEC 811/27, Oct. 14, 1958; McCone to Herter, Oct. 21, 1958, in AEC 811/30, Nov. 11, 1958; Herter to McCone, Oct. 28, 1958, in AEC 811/29, Oct. 31, 1958, all in AEC.

33. Kistiakowsky to Floberg, Feb. 19, 1960, in AEC 603/67, Feb. 25, 1960, AEC.

34. See Chap. 9, High Energy Physics. Recommendations of IUPAP Commission for High Energy Physics, AEC 603/52, Nov. 6, 1958, AEC.

35. Bromberg, *Fusion*, pp. 91–93.

36. Department of State, Joint U.S.–U.S.S.R. Communiqué on Agreement on Exchanges, Press Release 33, Jan. 27, 1958, AEC.

37. Hall to File, June 19, 1959, AEC.

38. Director of Intelligence, Visit of Soviet Nationals to AEC Facilities, AEC 901/15, June 22, 1959; CM 1624, July 1, 1959, both in AEC.

39. Department of State, Memorandum of Vice-President's Conversation with Kozlov, July 25, 1959, AEC.

40. McCone to Rickover, July 28, 1959; Farley to Kohler, Sept. 10, 1959, both in AEC.

41. AEC, Memorandum of Conversation between Rickover and Emelyanov, Aug. 2, 1959; Transcript, Joint Committee Executive Session on Rickover Trip, Aug. 9, 1959, both in AEC.

42. Memorandum of Conversation between Emelyanov and McCone, Sept. 15, 1959, AEC.

43. Department of State, Memorandum of Conversation with the President, Sept. 22, 1959, DOS.

44. Meeting of McCone and Emelyanov, Sept. 25, 1959; AEC Press Release B-172, Sept. 25, 1959; McCone, Memorandum of Discussion, Sept. 26, 1959, all in AEC; Goodpaster to Herter, Sept. 28, 1959, DOS. AEC files contain a large collection of news clippings on the Khrushchev visit.

45. Luedecke, Memorandum for the Record, Sept. 30, 1959; AEC Press Release B-183, Oct. 7, 1959; McCone, Random Notes on Russian Trip, Oct. 19, 1959; AEC News Conference with McCone, Oct. 27, 1959; AEC, Visit of U.S. Team to U.S.S.R. Atomic Energy Installations, Report TID-6793, Oct. 1959, all in AEC.

46. Goodpaster, Memorandum of Conference with the President, Oct. 27, 1959, DDE; McCone to File, Oct. 27, 1959, AEC.

47. AEC Press Release B-199, Oct. 31, 1959; Raymond L. Garthoff, Memorandum for the Record, Nov. 19, 1959; AEC Proposal for Unclassified Exchanges with the U.S.S.R., AEC 1037, Nov. 14, 1959; CM 1568, Nov. 17, 1959; McCone, Memorandum for the Record, Nov. 19, 1959, all in AEC; Goodpaster, Memorandum of Conference with the President, Nov. 11, 1959, DDE.

48. Memorandum of Cooperation, Nov. 24, 1959, AEC.

49. John S. D. Eisenhower, Memorandum of Conference with the President, Nov. 24, 1959, DDE.

50. AEC Press Release C-89, May 11, 1960; Record of Meeting with Professor Emelyanov on High Energy Physics, AEC 828/24, June 3, 1960; George E. Kolstad and E. J. Lofgren, Visit of U.S. High-Energy

Physics Team to U.S.S.R., May 1960, AEC Report TID-6597, all in AEC.

51. AEC Press Release C-127, July 2, 1960; Hall, Memorandum of Conversation with Emelyanov, Sept. 26, 1960, both in AEC.

52. Hall, Memorandum of Conversation with Emelyanov, Nov. 19, 1960, AEC.


## CHAPTER TWENTY

1. Joint Committee on Atomic Energy, *Hearings on Amending the Atomic Energy Act of 1954*, Jan. 29–May 28, 1958 (Washington: Government Printing Office, 1958), pp. 446–75.

2. *Congressional Record*, 85 Cong., 2 sess., June 30, 1958, p. 12586.

3. Other members of the U.S. delegation included Perry Byerly, Norman Haskel, Spurgeon Keeny, Jr., J. Carson Mark, Doyle Northrup, George Olmstead, Carl F. Romney, Herbert Scoville, Jr., and Anthony Turkevich. Harold K. Jacobson and Eric Stein, *Diplomats, Scientists, and Politicans: The United States and the Nuclear Test Ban Negotiations* (Ann Arbor: The University of Michigan Press, 1966), pp. 54–55 (hereafter cited Jacobson and Stein, *Diplomats, Scientists, and Politicians*).

4. Spiers, Memorandum of Conversation: Meeting with U.S. Experts for Geneva Technical Talks on Nuclear Test Detection, June 6, 1958, DOS; CM 1380, June 6, 1958, AEC.

5. Goodpaster, Memorandum of Conference with the President, June 18, 1958, DDE· Declassification of Information for use at the Geneva Technical Conference on the Control of a Nuclear Test Moratorium, AEC 226/143, June 24, 1958, AEC.

6. Minutes, First Meeting, July 1, 1958, *Conference of Experts to Study the Possibility of Detecting Violations of a Possible Agreement on Suspension of Nuclear Tests*, Geneva, Joint Committee on Atomic Energy, AEC (hereafter cited *Conference of Experts*); Aide-Memoire from the Soviet Foreign Ministry to the American Embassy: Geneva Experts Conference on Nuclear Tests, June 25, 1958, *Documents on Disarmament, 1945–1959, Vol. II, 1957–1959* (Department of State Publication 7008),

pp. 1080–82 (hereafter cited *Documents on Disarmament*); Morse to Commissioners, Second Status Report—Geneva Conference, June 30, 1958, AEC.

7. Joint Committee on Atomic Energy, *Hearings on the Nomination of John A. McCone to Be a Member of the Atomic Energy Commission*, July 2, 1958 (Washington: Government Printing Office, 1958), pp. 21–22.

8. Charles Thayer, *Diplomat* (New York: Harper, 1959), p. 106, as quoted in Robert Gilpin, *American Scientists and Nuclear Weapons Policy* (Princeton: Princeton University Press, 1962), pp. 221–22 (hereafter cited Gilpin, *American Scientists and Nuclear Weapons Policy*). Scientists from Rumania, Czechoslovakia, and Poland also joined the Eastern delegation. See Aide-Memoire from the Soviet Foreign Ministry to the American Embassy: Geneva Experts Conference on Nuclear Tests, June 24, 1958, *Documents on Disarmament*, pp. 1078–79.

9. Minutes, Second Meeting, July 2, 1958, *Conference of Experts*; Morse to Strauss, July 2, 1958, LLS.

10. Jacobson and Stein, *Diplomats, Scientists, and Politicians*, p. 73.

11. Report of the Conference of Experts to Study the Methods of Detecting Violations of a Possible Agreement on the Suspension of Nuclear Tests, Aug. 20, 1958, pp. 1–26, in *Conference of Experts*. Regarding the location of control posts, the report suggested North America, twenty-four; Europe, six; Asia, thirty-seven; Australia, seven; South America, sixteen; Africa, sixteen; Antarctica, four; and sixty posts scattered on islands.

12. James R. Killian, Jr., *Sputnik, Scientists, and Eisenhower: A Memoir of the First Special Assistant to the President for Science and Technology* (Cambridge: MIT Press, 1977), p. 161 (hereafter cited Killian, *Sputnik, Scientists, and Eisenhower*); Fisk to Killian, Aug. 3, 1958, DDE. Fisk reported the findings of the conference of experts to the National Security Council. Summary of Discussion, Meeting 378, Aug. 28, 1958, DDE. For a critique of the "amateur scientist-diplomats" at the Geneva Conference of Experts, see Gilpin, *American Scientists and Nuclear Weapons Policy*, pp. 218–22.

653

13. Working Papers on System to Detect Nuclear Tests, AEC 226/155, Aug. 4, 1958; Comments on Draft Working Paper Relative to Systems to Detect Nuclear Tests, AEC 226/156, Aug. 6, 1958, both in AEC.

14. McCone to File, Discussions, Livermore, July, 22, 1958, AEC; Report by the General Manager, Consideration of Proposed Letter to Secretary of State Regarding Control of Nuclear Tests, Aug. 3, 1958, AEC.

15. Farley to McCone, Aug. 7, 1958, in AEC 226/157, Aug. 8, 1958, AEC.

16. CM 1395 and 1396, Aug. 8, 1958, AEC; Strauss to File, Aug. 8, 1958, LLS.

17. Starbird to Commissioners and Foster, Report of Meeting re Test Cessation, Aug. 9, 1958, and Further Meeting of 13 August Concerning a Position Relative to Test Limitation, Aug. 14, 1958, both in AEC; Summary of Meeting Held in the State Department from 4:00 to 6:20 p.m. on August 13, DDE.

18. Goodpaster, Memorandum of Conference with the President, Aug. 12, 1958, DDE.

19. Goodpaster, Memorandum of Conference with the President, Aug. 18, 1958; Proposal to Suspend Nuclear Weapons Testing, Aug. 18, 1958, both in DDE.

20. Goodpaster, Memorandum of Conference with the President, Aug. 19, 1958, DDE.

21. Goodpaster, Memorandum of Conference with the President, Aug. 25, 1958, DDE.

22. Strauss to File, Aug. 20, 1958, LLS.

23. Statement by the President Following the Geneva Meeting of Experts Proposing Negotiations on Nuclear Controls, Aug. 22, 1958, *Public Papers of the Presidents of the United States, 1958: Dwight D. Eisenhower* (Washington: Government Printing Office, 1959), pp. 635–36 (hereafter cited *Public Papers, 1958, Eisenhower*); Communiqué and Report of the Conference of Experts to Study the Possibility of Detecting Violations of a Possible Agreement on the Suspension of Nuclear Tests, Aug. 21, 1958, *Documents on Disarmament*, pp. 1090–111.

24. The President's News Conference of Aug. 27, 1958, *Public Papers, 1958, Eisenhower*, pp. 639–50.

25. Statement by the British Government: Experts' Report on Detection of Nuclear Tests, Aug. 22, 1958, *Documents on Disarmament*, pp. 1112–13.

26. Interview by the Soviet Premier [Khrushchev] With a *Pravda* Correspondent: Discontinuance of Nuclear Weapons Tests, Aug. 29, 1958; Note From the Soviet Foreign Ministry to the American Embassy: Negotiations on the Suspension of Nuclear Weapons Tests, Aug. 30, 1958, both in *Documents on Disarmament*, pp. 1114–20.

27. Bernhard G. Bechhoefer, *Postwar Negotiations for Arms Control* (Washington: Brookings Institution, 1961), pp. 458–61; Robert A. Divine, *Blowing on the Wind: The Nuclear Test Ban Debate, 1954–1960* (New York: Oxford University Press, 1978), pp. 234–35.

28. Teller to Strauss, Sept. 13, 1958, LLS; McCone, Notes on my discussion with Edward Teller . . . [on] Sept. 14, Sept. 17, 1958; McCone to Eisenhower, Oct. 2, 16, 24, and 27, 1958, all in AEC.

29. Fallout from the Last Russian Test Series, AEC 240/18, Dec. 16, 1958; Readiness for Nuclear Weapons Testing, AEC 226/172, Oct. 30, 1958; CM 1424, Nov. 12, 1958, all in AEC.

30. Statement by the President Concerning the Continued Testing of Nuclear Weapons by the Soviet Union, Nov. 7, 1958, *Public Papers, 1958, Eisenhower*, pp. 838–39.

31. As quoted in Gilpin, *American Scientists and Nuclear Weapons Policy*, p. 215.

32. Ibid., p. 226; Killian to McCone, Dec. 5, 1958; Killian to Quarles, Dec. 9, 1958, both in AEC.

33. Starbird to Foster, Oct. 27, 1958, in AEC 952/69, Nov. 4, 1958; Starbird to Foster, Nov. 14, 1958, in AEC 987/15, Nov. 24, 1958, both in AEC.

34. CM 1447, Dec. 19, 1958; D. L. Northrup to Chief, AFOAT-1, Dec. 22, 1958, in AEC 987/17, Jan. 14, 1959, both in AEC; Gilpin, *American Scientists and Nuclear Weapons Policy*, pp. 214–18.

35. Morse to McCone, Dec. 9, 1958, AEC.

36. Strauss to File, Dec. 10, 1958, LLS.

37. Killian, *Sputnik, Scientists, and Eisenhower*, pp. 170–71.

38. Conference on the Discontinuance of Nuclear Weapon Tests, Verbatim Record of Twenty-first Meeting, Dec. 8, 1958, pp. 25–52, AEC; Gilpin, *American Scientists and Nuclear Weapons Policy*, p. 229.

39. Gordon Gray to Dulles et al., Nov. 26, 1958, and Gore to Eisenhower, Nov. 19, 1958, both in AEC 226/179, Dec. 2, 1958; Evaluation of Test Suspension Proposal by Senator Gore, AEC 226/182, Dec. 9, 1958; CM 1451, Jan. 9, 1959;

CM 1453, Jan. 12, 1959, all in AEC; Macmillan to Eisenhower, Jan. 1, 1959; Eisenhower to Macmillan, Jan. 12, 1959, both in DOS; John S. D. Eisenhower, Memorandum of Conference with the President, Jan. 12, 1959; Gray to Eisenhower, Jan. 13, 1959, both in DDE; *New York Times*, Jan. 20, 1959.

40. Proposed AEC Position on Test Cessation, AEC 226/190, Dec. 22, 1958; CM 1448, Dec. 22, 1958; Vance to Herter, Dec. 23, 1958, in AEC 226/193, Dec. 31, 1958; McCone to Herter, Jan. 19, 1959; CM 1459, Jan. 26, 1959, all in *AEC*.

41. Department of State, Memorandum of Conversation, Jan. 26, 1959; McCone to Dulles, Feb. 2, 1959, both in AEC; Department of State, Memorandum of Conversation, Jan. 30, 1959; Herter to McCone, Feb. 16, 1959, both in DOS.

42. Bromley Smith, Meeting on Nuclear Testing, Feb. 12, 1959, DDE; Department of State, Memorandum of Conversation, Feb. 26, 1959, AEC.

43. Findings of the United States Panel on Seismic Improvement, March 16, 1959, *Documents on Disarmament*, pp. 1367–71; Report of the Panel on Seismic Improvement, March 16, 1959, encl., Killian to Herter et al., March 17, 1959, AEC; The Need for Fundamental Research in Seismology, March 31, 1959, *Documents on Disarmament*, pp. 1378–92.

44. A. L. Latter et al., A Method of Concealing Underground Nuclear Explosions, March 30, 1959, Rand Report RM-2347-AFT; W. K. H. Panofsky et al., Report of the Panel on High Altitude Detection, March 16, 1959, both in AEC.

45. Farley, Memorandum of Conversation, March 21, 1959; G. F. Reinhardt, Memorandum of Conversation, March 22, 1959; McCone to File, March 23, 1959, all in AEC; italics McCone's.

46. Department of State, Memorandum of Conversation, March 26, 1959, DOS; Herter to Eisenhower, March 28, 1959, DDE.

47. Eisenhower to Macmillan, April 4, 1959; Macmillan to Eisenhower, April 10, 1959, both in DOS; Eisenhower to Khrushchev, April 13, 1959, *Documents on Disarmament*, pp. 1392–93.

48. Khrushchev to Eisenhower, April 23, 1959, *Documents on Disarmament*, pp. 1396–98.

49. Goodpaster, Memorandum of Conference with the President, May 5, 1959, DDE; McCone to File, May 5, 1959; Department of State, Memorandum of Conversation, May 5, 1959, both in AEC.

50. Joint Committee on Atomic Energy, *Hearings on Fallout from Nuclear Weapons Tests*, May 5–8, 1959 (Washington: Government Printing Office, 1959), pp. 155–482, 949-1004.

51. Department of State, Memorandum of Conversation, June 17, 1959, DOS; Ink to the Commissioners, June 18, 1959, AEC.

52. CM 1526, July 2, 1959; Summary Notes of Briefing on the Bacher Panel Report, July 9, 1959; Department of State, Memorandum of Conversation, July 9, 1959, all in AEC.

53. Director of Military Application, Studies in Connection with Weapons Testing, AEC 226/213, July 2, 1959; CM 1529, July 17, 1959, both in AEC.

54. Starbird to McCone, July 13, 1959; Report of Ad Hoc Panel on Nuclear Test Requirements, Aug. 18, 1959, both in AEC; Statement by the Department of State: Extension of Voluntary Suspension of Nuclear Weapons Tests, Aug. 26, 1959, *Documents on Disarmament*, pp. 1439–40; Goodpaster, Memorandums of Conferences with the President, July 13, Sept. 22, 1959, DDE; Department of State, Memorandums of Conversations, Aug. 26, Sept. 22, 1959, DOS; George B. Kistiakowsky, *A Scientist at the White House* (Cambridge: Harvard University Press, 1976), pp. 55–56, 79 (hereafter cited Kistiakowsky, *A Scientist at the White House*).

55. Starbird to McCone, Oct. 26, 1959; Neil McElroy to Eisenhower, Sept. 14, 1959; McCone to Eisenhower, Dec. 24, 1959, all in AEC.

56. Department of State, Memorandum of Conversation, Nov. 17, 1959, DOS; Report of Technical Working Group II: Detection and Identification of Seismic Events, Dec. 18, 1959, and Statement of the United States Representative (Fisk), Dec. 19, 1959, both in *Documents on Disarmament*, pp. 1558–90.

57. Statement by the President, Dec. 29, 1959, *Documents on Disarmament*, pp. 1590–91.

58. Department of State, Memorandums of Conversations, Jan. 8, 12, 19, 1960, AEC; Kistiakowsky, *A Scientist at the White House*, pp. 222–23, 232–33.

655

59. White House Statement on the Cessation of Nuclear Weapon Tests, Feb. 11, 1960, *Documents on Disarmament, 1960* (Department of State Publication 7172), pp. 31–33 (hereafter cited *Documents on Disarmament, 1960*).

60. Department of State, Memorandum of Conversation, March 22, 1960, AEC; Kistiakowsky, *A Scientist at the White House*, p. 279.

61. Department of State, Memorandum of Conversation, March 23, 1960; Starbird to McCone, March 8, 1960, both in AEC; Kistiakowsky, *A Scientist at the White House*, p. 281; Goodpaster, Memorandum of Conference with the President, March 14, 1960, DDE.

62. Starbird to McCone, March 23, 1960; McCone to File, March 24, 1960, both in AEC; Goodpaster, Memorandum of Conference with the President, March 24, 1960, DDE; Kistiakowsky, *A Scientist at the White House*, p. 282; Joint Declaration, March 29, 1960, *Documents on Disarmament, 1960*, pp. 77–78.

63. Strauss to File, March 31, 1960, LLS.

64. Director of Military Application, Conducting Nuclear Detonations for Seismic Improvement, AEC 226/245, April 26, 1960; CM 1614, April 28, 1960; Department of State, Memorandums of Conversations, June 30, July 6, 1960, all in AEC; Kistiakowsky to Eisenhower, May 3, 1960; John S. D. Eisenhower, Memorandum of Conference with the President, July 7, 1960; Department of State, Memorandum of Conversation, Aug. 2, 1960, all in DDE; Joint Committee on Atomic Energy, *Hearing on Technical Aspects of Detection and Inspection Controls of a Nuclear Weapons Test Ban*, April 19–22, 1960 (Washington: Government Printing Office, 1960).

## CHAPTER TWENTY-ONE

1. *Public Papers of the Presidents of the United States, 1960–61: Dwight D. Eisenhower* (Washington: Government Printing Office, 1961), pp. 1036–40. The full text of the speech appeared in the *New York Times*, Jan. 18, 1961, pp. 22–24. Herbert S. Parmet, *Eisenhower and the American Crusades* (New York: Macmillan, 1972), p. 57.

2. Dwight D. Eisenhower, *Waging Peace, 1956–1961* (Garden City, NY: Doubleday, 1965), pp. 617, 712–16; Hagerty Diary, Dec. 6, 1960, James C. Hagerty Papers; Persons, Memorandum of Conversation, Jan. 19, 1961, both in DDE.

# ESSAY ON SOURCES

by

Roger M. Anders

Increasingly, major historical projects require the cooperative efforts of professional researchers and writers. This book was not only written by Hewlett and Holl but also supported by the research of Department of Energy staff historians. This team effort has enabled the historians to review extensive published and unpublished sources pertinent to the history of nuclear energy during the Eisenhower Administration. In this "Essay on Sources" I have especially tried to evaluate the principal record collections, books, and other sources used by the authors for their value and pertinence to understanding the history of United States nuclear energy policy.

## GENERAL NOTE ABOUT SOURCES

During the Eisenhower years the development of atomic energy in the United States left the exclusive preserve of the Atomic Energy Commission. Consequently, the record of atomic energy development of the period can be found in the collections of numerous public and private institutions. An expanding secondary literature reflects increased scholarly interest in the importance of atomic energy history. In addition, the volume and richness of sources on the Eisenhower years have provided the foundation for an extensive scholarly literature on the history of public policy.

As noted in the Preface, more than anyone Eisenhower set the national agenda for atomic energy issues in the 1950s. As one consequence of his strong presidential leadership, atomic energy policy was often made in the White House rather than in the Commission's conference room. Hence, for the historian of atomic energy policy, the papers of the President and his colleagues, assistants, and staff found at the Dwight D. Eisenhower Presidential Library are essential.

Despite Eisenhower's policy-making role, the files compiled by the Secretary of the Atomic Energy Commission remain the best source for day-to-day decisions made during the decade, as well as for evidence of the problems and controversies that plagued the development of atomic energy during the 1950s. We believe scholars will find the AEC secretariat files truly remarkable for the depth and breadth of issues, information, and decisions that the files captured. Reflecting the opening of atomic energy to American society, most Commission documents in secretariat files were no longer "born classified." An increasing percentage were "born unclassified," although areas such as weapon development and the production of special nuclear material remain largely classified even today.

In addition to White House and Commission files other sources provided essential information on the evolution of atomic energy policy. Published and unpublished State Department records captured the role of the Secretary of State and his special assistants in devising policy on international Atoms-for-Peace programs, arms control, and test-ban issues. Congressional hearings contained a wealth of basic information about atomic energy and were vital for depicting policy and philosophical differences between the Administration and the Joint Committee on Atomic Energy over civilian nuclear power programs.

As documentary declassification has released more data, an even greater variety of materials has become available for scholarly research. Building on the increasing availability of primary sources, a secondary literature pertinent to atomic energy has been expanding geometrically. This trend has been heartening, and historians and other scholars will profit from these developments.

## UNPUBLISHED SOURCES

### PRESIDENTIAL LIBRARIES

Consistent with President Eisenhower's strong leadership, the Dwight D. Eisenhower Presidential Library contains a number of essential collections for the historian of atomic energy. The most comprehensive source for Eisenhower's leadership is Dwight D. Eisenhower: Records as President, White House central files, 1953–1961, compiled by his secretary, Ann Whitman. Although many documents remain classified, the key documents in this collection are the memoranda of presidential conversations carefully prepared by Andrew J. Goodpaster and his successors at the White House.

The Goodpaster memoranda capture presidential thoughts, conversations, decisions, actions, and attitudes about atomic energy with a depth, subtlety, and comprehensiveness found in no other documentary source. If nothing else, the thoroughness and accuracy of Goodpaster's record keeping has assured Eisenhower a prominent place in the history of atomic energy. Another rich source for Goodpaster memoranda are the records of the White House Office, Office of the Staff Secretary: Records of Paul T. Carroll, Andrew J. Goodpaster, L. Arthur Minnich, and Christopher H. Russell, 1953–1961. Also of major value are the records of the White House Office, Project "Clean Up": Records of Gordon Gray, Robert Cutler, Henry R. McPhee, and Andrew J. Goodpaster, 1953–1961.

Indispensable at the Eisenhower Library are the minutes of National Secretary Council meetings found in Eisenhower: Records as President. Eisenhower used the council as a crucial policy making body; hence the minutes of its meetings also shed much light on policy formulation and presidential thinking. Unfortunately most documents in the collection remain classified, and access to them, even for historians with security clearances, has become increasingly difficult.

A number of other collections give important glimpses into the making of atomic energy policy by the President and his advisers. Particularly useful for tracing the development of policy in the Atoms-for-Peace and test-ban areas are the Dulles/Herter, Stassen, and C. D. Jackson papers. Less helpful are the Sherman Adams, Joseph M. Dodge, Gordon Gray, Bryce Harlow, Robert Merriam, Gerald D. Morgan, and Howard Pyle papers. Presidential Press Secretary James Hagerty's diary provides behind-the-scenes vignettes about the Administration; Robert H. Ferrell has edited it as *The Diary of James C. Hagerty: Eisenhower in Mid-Course, 1954–1955* (Bloomington, IN, 1983). Cabinet records provide some interesting material on the impact of nuclear weapon developments on civil defense procedures, although generally the Cabinet conducted few significant discussions of atomic energy. The oral history collection of the Library provided some material pertinent to atomic energy and the authors examined the interviews with Dwight D. Eisenhower (Columbia University oral history project), Gordon Gray, Jesse C. Johnson, John Davis Lodge, Kevin McCann, John A. McCone, Kenneth D. Nichols, James J. Wadsworth, and David W. Wainhouse.

Lewis L. Strauss created his own files of "personal" memoranda about atomic energy matters during his tenure as chairman of the Atomic Energy Commission. Until recently these materials remained in the custody of the Strauss family. Lewis H. Strauss graciously made his father's personal files available to the authors while the records were still in Washington. The Strauss files have since been donated to the Herbert Hoover Presidential Library and are open to researchers. They are vital for showing

659

Strauss's views on atomic energy issues and his role in both making and executing policy.

*COMMISSION RECORDS*

Files created by the Atomic Energy Commission are essential for any study of atomic energy in this period. Although the Commission was abolished in 1975, the Commission's official records, with the exception of those dealing with regulatory matters, were transferred to the custody of the history division in the Department of Energy. They form a rich source for both policy formulation and policy implementation.

The secretary's files are devoted to recording all decisions made by the five members of the Atomic Energy Commission. Occupying over 500 cubic feet, the secretariat files are one of the best organized collections maintained by a federal agency. They contain minutes of Commission meetings, information and decision papers organized into staff paper series, and copies of minutes of advisory committee meetings. Included in the files are documents showing policy implementation interspersed throughout with key press releases and speeches. Descriptions of the secretariat files also appear in the essays on sources of Richard G. Hewlett and Francis Duncan, *Atomic Shield, 1947–1952*, Volume II of *A History of the United States Atomic Energy Commission* (University Park, PA, 1969), and of George T. Mazuzan and J. Samuel Walker, *Controlling the Atom: The Beginnings of Nuclear Regulation, 1946–1962* (Berkeley, CA, 1984).

The subject files, which contain official copies of information and decision papers, are the heart of the secretariat collection. Adopting a format devised by the Joint Chiefs of Staff during World War II, the Commission organized its files according to a subject-numeric records management system. The Commission's decisions were thus recorded in the minutes by their approval or disapproval of a numbered staff paper. This numbering system has facilitated tracing Commission policy through the subject files and meeting minutes. In this volume the authors have provided the staff paper numbers in their endnote citations.

Other Commission files supplement the secretariat files. Individual Commissioners generally kept office files, although the extant files vary greatly in quality and quantity. Surviving Commissioner office files, understandably, are usually richest in matters in which the individual Commissioner took a personal interest. Willard F. Libby, for example, maintained extensive correspondence files on Project *Sunshine*. Commissioner Thomas E. Murray's office files are in the custody of family friends, who made only a portion of them available to the authors on a piecemeal basis. As previously noted, Lewis Strauss office files are at the Hoover Library. Typical of John A. McCone's thoroughness and drive, his office files are complete and particularly revealing about test-ban issues.

Some records below the top level of the agency are helpful in tracing policy development. The files of the general manager's office, although devoted almost entirely to implementing policy, contain occasional glimpses of policy formulation. Files of the division of biology and medicine contain valuable insights into the scientific and technical considerations on which policies were based. Particularly helpful among files of the division of international affairs is a collection containing materials on the establishment of the International Atomic Energy Agency. Not only is this group especially complete, but it also captures the activities of the State Department as well as those of the Commission.

Activities of the Commission's field offices and laboratories were usually too far removed from major policy issues for their files to contain much insight on presidential decisions. Extant Commission field office and laboratory files are, however, a rich and detailed treasure trove of technical information.

A boon to the historian is the massive effort that the Department of Energy is now mounting to declassify records pertinent to atmospheric nuclear weapon testing and fallout. One of the largest declassification projects ever conducted by a federal agency, the project has already declassified or released more than 100,000 documents. Commission records from the secretary's office to the weapon laboratories have been examined and processed by project researchers. Major topics for which documents have been declassified include weapon test programs, radiation standards, radiation injuries, weapon development, programs to detect and evaluate radioactive fallout, and other items pertinent to the fallout controversy of the 1950s. The record collection resulting from this project is available to the public through the Coordination and Information Center at Las Vegas, Nevada.

661

## OTHER GOVERNMENT ARCHIVES

Record collections important for tracing atomic energy policy making are found in the custody of several federal agencies. The State Department's records service center contains several collections pertinent to the international atom. General "lot" files are of some help but the most valuable are the atomic energy "lot" files containing office files of Gerard C. Smith and Philip J. Farley, both special assistants to the Secretary of State for atomic energy. Federal Bureau of Investigation records pertinent to the J. Robert Oppenheimer security case have been declassified via the Freedom of Information Act and detail the bureau's investigation and surveillance of Oppenheimer.

Of great potential value are the records of the Joint Committee on Atomic Energy. The unclassified Joint Committee files have already been transferred to the National Archives. They contain some materials pertinent to the Oppenheimer security hearing but reveal little of the internal workings of the committee. The classified files, when they were in the custody of the Senate office of classified national security information, were closed to the authors. The classified files might have shed light on the internal workings of the committee and the views of its individual members. Thus, the authors were not able to examine those files that might have contained revealing glimpses of the Joint Committee's role in a number of areas, including nuclear power policy. When this essay was written, the classified Joint Committee files were transferred from the Senate to the National Archives. We hope that the National Archives will be able to open the files to researchers in the near future.

*PRIVATE ARCHIVAL SOURCES*

662

Private papers pertaining to atomic energy vary greatly in quality and generally have been disappointing. The Dulles papers in the custody of the Princeton Library have a few items on the 1955 Geneva summit conference but little else pertinent to atomic energy. The Dulles Oral History Collection at Princeton contained helpful interviews, and the authors consulted the interviews with Sherman Adams, George V. Allen, Dillon Anderson, Robert R. Bowie, Herbert Brownell, Andrew J. Goodpaster, Richard M. Nixon, Lauris Norstad, and Arthur Radford. The J. Robert Oppenheimer papers at the Library of Congress have much on the early years of atomic energy but shed little light on Oppenheimer's security hearing. The Clinton P. Anderson papers at the Library of Congress are composed largely of constituent mail and were of little help. Also of little help were the Sherman Adams papers in the Dartmouth College Library and the Columbia University Oral History collection.

*PUBLISHED SOURCES*

*PERIODICALS*

The coverage of atomic energy news increased in the 1950s, but greater coverage did not always mean better quality or broader scope of reporting. Not surprisingly, most new periodicals covered the civilian nuclear power field. For historical research the most useful of the nuclear power journals is *Nucleonics*. The *Bulletin of the Atomic Scientists* followed the broadest range of nuclear issues with the most consistency and insight and gave close coverage of the fallout controversy. Other largely scientific journals such as *Physical Review, Scientific Monthly, Science,* and *Scientific American* contain occasional pertinent articles. Popular reactions to atomic energy and its controversies can be found in the standard news magazines, such as *Time, Newsweek,* and *U.S. News and World Report. Michigan Law Review, Business Week, Fortune, Foreign Affairs,* and *Vital Speeches* also provide items of interest. Of all major daily newspapers, the *New York Times* followed atomic energy issues with the most depth and consistency.

## GOVERNMENT PUBLICATIONS

Government publications, as well, were increasingly filled with information on atomic energy, and four Commission publications deserve special mention. The Commission's semiannual and annual reports to Congress, although designed to put the agency and its actions in the best possible light, expanded greatly during the 1950s with basic facts about the multitude of Commission programs and activities. Often these reports contain information that can be found nowhere else today. The drama and tension of the Oppenheimer security hearing has never been better captured than in the hearing transcript. Raw material for historians, *In the Matter of J. Robert Oppenheimer: Texts of Principal Documents and Letters of Personnel Security Board, General Manager, and Commissioners* (Washington, 1954) is the major source for details of the hearing itself, although it reveals little about the circumstances that led to the hearing. With perhaps more contemporary impact than the Oppenheimer transcript, *A Report by the United States Atomic Energy Commission on the Effects of High-Yield Nuclear Explosions* (Washington, 1955) published the Commission's official report on fallout from the *Castle-Bravo* shot as well as its justification of continental and Pacific testing. The 1957 edition of *The Effects of Nuclear Weapons* (Washington, 1957) presented the Commission's most complete summary of the then known facts about nuclear weapon effects.

663

Three other Executive Branch publications are also important for atomic energy history in this period. The *Public Papers of the Presidents of the United States, 1953–1960: Dwight D. Eisenhower* (Washington, 1958–1961) includes presidential speeches, addresses, messages, press conferences, and statements. The *Public Papers of the President* is frequently the best source for public statements and authentic text. Many key test-ban and disarmament documents have been published in the State Department's *Documents on Disarmament* series. The State Department's short pamphlet, *Disarmament: The Intensified Effort 1955–1958* (Washington, 1960), is a surprisingly helpful summary of disarmament negotiations.

Both Geneva peaceful uses conferences published extensive amounts of technical data. All papers submitted to the 1955 conference were published in *Proceedings of the International Conference on the Peaceful Uses of Atomic Energy Held in Geneva 8 August–20 August 1955* (New York, 1956), in seventeen volumes, and the papers submitted to the 1958 conference were published in *Proceedings of the Second United Nations International Conference on the Peaceful Uses of Atomic Energy Held in Geneva 1 September–13 September 1958* (Geneva, 1958), in thirty-three volumes. In addition, the United States presented a multivolume set of technical works to the second Geneva conference. Published by the Addison-Wesley Publishing Company of Reading, Massachusetts, in 1958, the set includes many works such as F. L. Cuthbert, *Thorium Production Technology*; Amasa S. Bishop, *Project Sherwood: The U.S. Program in Controlled Fusion*; Chauncey Starr and Robert W. Dickinson, *Sodium Graphite Reactors*; Joseph R. Dietrich and Walter H. Zinn, eds., *Solid Fuel Reactors*; Andrew W. Kramer, *Boiling Water Reactors*; James A. Lane, H. G. MacPherson, and Frank Maslan, eds., *Fluid Fuel Reactors*; and a reprint of Glenn T. Seaborg, *The Transuranium Elements*.

Congressional publications are another important, albeit voluminous, source. Much rich detail about the fallout controversy and the political battles over nuclear power programs was captured in Congressional hearings. Formal positions of opposing forces as well as occasional revelations about behind-the-scenes political compromises fill published hearing transcripts. Many hearings also contain appendices of related documents, which are sometimes the only source for the documents.

The most pertinent Congressional hearings were those held by the Joint Committee on Atomic Energy. Compiled by Commission personnel, the *Legislative History of the Atomic Energy Act of 1954* (Washington, 1955) reprinted all Joint Committee hearings on the draft act, as well as excerpts from the *Congressional Record*; it is the best single source for charting Congressional actions on the bill that became the Atomic Energy Act of 1954. The most sustained and revealing documents about the controversies in Congress over nuclear power programs are the published Joint Committee hearings held annually between 1954 and 1963 under Section 202 of the Atomic Energy Act. Rich in detail, much of it technical, the 202 hearings captured political differences over the appropriate role of the federal government in introducing nuclear reactor technology to American economic life. The Joint Committee's published hearings on civil defense, the effects of atomic explosions on the weather, the International Atomic Energy Agency, EURATOM, and the 1958 amendment to the Atomic Energy Act that provided for greater atomic cooperation between the United States and its allies contain vital information without presenting as sustained a picture of Commission programs as do the 202 hearings. A landmark in the fallout controversy, the Joint Committee's hearings on *The Nature of Radioactive Fallout and Its Effects on Man* (Washington, 1957) also form a virtual textbook of contemporary scientific knowledge about fallout and its potential hazards, mostly in layman's language. Less useful are the 1959 Joint Committee fallout hearings and the hearings the Joint Committee held on test-ban issues.

The Joint Committee, however, is not the only Congressional source for key atomic energy material. The Senate Armed Services Committee hearings on the *Civil Defense Program* (Washington, 1955) document the

664

public's initial realization that radioactive fallout from thermonuclear weapons was a serious hazard. Good sources for disarmament issues are the hearings held by a subcommittee of the Senate Foreign Relations Committee led by Hubert H. Humphrey. More focused on purely civil defense issues are the hearings on civil defense of the House Government Operations Committee. Providing the most comprehensive statement of the bitterness that developed between Clinton Anderson and Lewis Strauss are the Senate Interstate and Foreign Commerce Committee hearings, *The Nomination of Lewis L. Strauss to be Secretary of Commerce* (Washington, 1959). A primer of key documents relating to early Atoms-for-Peace programs is the *Atoms for Peace Manual, A Compilation of Official Materials on International Cooperation for Peaceful Uses of Atomic Energy, December 1953–July 1955* (Washington, 1955) published by the Senate Foreign Relations Committee. The famous Gaither report of 1957 has been published as a report of the Joint Committee on Defense Production. Contemporary views and fears about the hazards of atmospheric testing in the 1950s can be found in Joint Hearing Before the House Committee on Interstate and Foreign Commerce and the Senate Committee on Labor and Human Resources, *Health Effects of Low-Level Radiation* (Washington, 1979).

665

## LETTERPRESS DOCUMENTARY COLLECTIONS

Two letterpress documentary publications proved helpful. Adlai E. Stevenson's papers were published under the editorship of Walter Johnson and others in a multivolume set as *The Papers of Adlai Stevenson*. The authors found volume VI, *Toward a New America, 1955–1957* (Boston, 1976), and volume VII, *Continuing Education and Unfinished Business of American Society, 1957–1961* (Boston, 1977), the most useful, especially for the 1956 presidential campaign. Robert C. Williams and Philip L. Cantelon, eds., *The American Atom: A Documentary History of Nuclear Policies from the Discovery of Fission to the Present, 1939–1984* (Philadelphia, 1984) reprints some key documents of the Oppenheimer security hearing as well as other key documents in the civilian power, test-ban, disarmament, and fallout areas.

## PERSONAL NARRATIVES

Memoir literature for the period is the least satisfying of all sources. Dwight D. Eisenhower's two volumes, *Mandate for Change, 1953–1956* (New York, 1963) and *Waging the Peace, 1956–1961* (New York, 1965), convey his concern about atomic energy matters without revealing the overriding importance and urgency that he attached to them. Moreover, his memoirs are concerned with maintaining his benign public image and only occasionally reveal the private and decisive Eisenhower.

Robert H. Ferrell's *The Eisenhower Diaries* (New York, 1981) contains vignettes of atomic energy matters but does not present a sustained or comprehensive view of Eisenhower's attitudes about atomic energy.

Richard M. Nixon does not mention atomic energy issues in either *Six Crises* (New York, 1962) or *The Memoirs of Richard Nixon* (New York, 1978).

Several members of the Eisenhower Administration do, however, mention atomic energy matters in their memoirs. Sherman Adam's *Firsthand Report: The Story of the Eisenhower Administration* (New York, 1961) is helpful in sketching the impact of McCarthy on Eisenhower and the White House. James R. Killian's *Sputnik, Scientists, and Eisenhower: A Memoir of the First Special Assistant to the President for Science and Technology* (Cambridge, 1977) provides a view of the organization and operation of the President's Science Advisory Committee. Killian's successor, George B. Kistiakowsky, published his shrewd and penetrating insights in *A Scientist at the White House: The Private Diary of President Eisenhower's Special Assistant for Science and Technology* (Cambridge, 1976). One of the most revealing glimpses at the behind-the-scenes clashes within the Administration, Kistiakowsky's diary is a classic of the genre. With a keen and vigorous mind, Kistiakowsky penetrated issues and personalities and reported concisely on them. Of much less help is Emmet John Hughes, *The Ordeal of Power: A Political Memoir of the Eisenhower Years* (New York, 1963).

Harold Macmillan provides the British perspective to test-ban negotiations and mutual defense agreements in *Riding the Storm, 1956–1959* (London, 1971) and *Pointing the Way, 1959–1961* (London, 1972). Macmillan also makes revealing comments about John Foster Dulles, Harold Stassen, Lewis Strauss, and other members of the Eisenhower team. Anthony Eden presents his perspective on events, first as foreign secretary and later as prime minister during the 1951–1957 period, in *The Memoirs of Anthony Eden: Full Circle* (Boston, 1960). Eden, however, says little about atomic energy matters.

The memoirs of men closer to atomic energy are not helpful. Gordon E. Dean died before he could write his memoirs, and his *Report on the Atom: What You Should Know About the Atomic Energy Program of the United States* (New York, 1953) is written solely to introduce the layman to the atomic energy field. Lewis L. Strauss offers his version of events in *Men and Decisions* (New York, 1962) in which he is far more concerned about maintaining the rightness of his positions than in describing thoughts and rationales behind policy development. His antagonist, Clinton P. Anderson, has written his own breezy account of his career in *Outsider in the Senate: Senator Clinton Anderson's Memoirs* (New York, 1970), which contains little of depth about atomic energy policy. As might be expected, both

666

Strauss and Anderson continued their feud in their memoirs. In his memoirs, *The Road to Trinity* (New York, 1987), Kenneth D. Nichols includes a chapter on his tenure as Commission general manager in which he explained his positions on the Oppenheimer case, Dixon-Yates, weapon testing, and other matters. Although no longer a policymaker, David E. Lilienthal, the Commission's first chairman (1946–1950), maintained his *Journals* throughout the Eisenhower years and proved an astute critic of atomic energy policies. Thomas E. Murray's *Nuclear Policy for War and Peace* (New York, 1960) contains arguments for his views on test-ban, nuclear power, security, and other issues rather than recollections of his service on the Commission.

## SECONDARY ACCOUNTS

No longer can scholars complain of a paucity of secondary works pertinent to the postwar history of atomic energy. Although no good, single-volume history of atomic energy in the United States exists, there is a rich literature on more specialized topics. The literature on the Oppenheimer case or on nuclear strategy could well be the subject of separate bibliographic essays. The literature on the Eisenhower Administration continues to grow impressively. I mention only the most useful works here.

A literature depicting Eisenhower as a decisive leader and activist President has emerged during research on this volume. So far have scholarly views about him altered that Philip G. Henderson calls Eisenhower a model of presidential management in "Organizing the Presidency for Effective Leadership: Lessons from the Eisenhower Years," *Presidential Studies Quarterly* 17 (Winter 1987), and in *Managing the Presidency: The Eisenhower Legacy* (Westview, CT, 1988). Two excellent summaries of the "revisionist" literature on Eisenhower can be found in Mary S. McAuliffe, "Commentary/Eisenhower the President," *Journal of American History* 68 (December 1981), and in Steve Neal, "Why We Were Right to Like Ike," *American Heritage* 37 (December 1985). Perhaps the most thorough exploration of Eisenhower as an activist President is in Fred I. Greenstein, *The Hidden-Hand Presidency: Eisenhower as Leader* (New York, 1982). Greenstein discussed the major themes of *The Hidden-Hand Presidency* more succinctly in "Eisenhower as an Activist President: A Look at New Evidence," *Political Science Quarterly* 94 (Winter 1979–1980). Greenstein, though, says little about atomic energy matters. Richard A. Baker skillfully explores Congressional frustration at Eisenhower's "hidden hand" dominance in "A Slap at the 'Hidden-Hand Presidency': The Senate and the Lewis Strauss Affair," *Congress and the Presidency* 14 (Spring 1987).

Of the "revisionist" literature, Stephen E. Ambrose's *Eisenhower*, Volume 2, *The President* (New York, 1984), contains the most complete single-volume treatment of Eisenhower's presidential Administration and includes helpful, detailed accounts of Atoms-for-Peace negotiations and programs, nuclear weapon testing, the Oppenheimer case, and test-ban and disarmament negotiations. Ambrose also notes Eisenhower's early and profound commitment to slowing the arms race. His overall impression of Eisenhower's views on nuclear war as well as his conclusions about Eisenhower as a crisis manager agree with the impressions and conclusions of the authors of this volume. A short recent account that incorporates the latest findings of the "revisionists" is in Gary W. Reichard, *Politics As Usual: The Age of Truman and Eisenhower* (Arlington Heights, IL, 1988). Reichard includes brief discussions of the New Look, nuclear weapon policy, and the test-ban debate. Robert Griffith places Eisenhower's views on civilian nuclear power into the context of his political philosophy and thought in "Eisenhower and the Corporate Commonwealth," *American Historical Review* 87 (February 1982). Charles C. Alexander in *Holding the Line: The Eisenhower Era, 1952–1961* (Bloomington, IL, 1976) only superficially examines the Oppenheimer hearing, the Dixon-Yates controversy, test-ban negotiations, Atoms for Peace, and the fallout controversy in his reassessment of the Eisenhower years. Another comprehensive treatment of the Eisenhower Administration is Elmo Richardson's *The Presidency of Dwight D. Eisenhower* (Lawrence, KS, 1979). A volume in the University Press of Kansas American Presidency series, Richardson's study is both too broadly cast and too brief to say much about atomic energy matters. Herbert S. Parmet's *Eisenhower and the American Crusades* (New York, 1972) presents a well-balanced, detailed study of Eisenhower's first Administration but is much less thorough on the second. Stephen E. Ambrose with Richard H. Immerman in *Ike's Spies: Eisenhower and the Espionage Establishment* (New York, 1981) portrays Eisenhower as an activist President while saying little about atomic energy matters. Ambrose and Immerman do discuss the Oppenheimer case but say nothing new about it. Blanche Wiesen Cook's *The Declassified Eisenhower: A Divided Legacy* (New York, 1981) documents Eisenhower's conviction that nuclear war was unthinkable but says nothing about other atomic energy issues. An early "revisionist" view of Eisenhower that is still very useful, although silent about atomic energy issues, is in William L. O'Neill, *Coming Apart: An Informal History of America in the 1960s* (Chicago, 1971). Douglas Kinnard's *President Eisenhower and Strategy Management: A Study in Defense Politics* (Lexington, KY, 1977) contains a thoughtful analysis that aided discussions of the New Look and the role of nuclear weapons in national defense. Robert A. Divine's *Eisenhower and the Cold War* (New York, 1981) is an excellent study, although limited to specific topics.

Robert J. Donovan's *Eisenhower: The Inside Story* (New York, 1956) is occasionally helpful but was written too close to events to have historical perspective.

Two recent biographies of John Foster Dulles virtually ignore atomic energy matters. Townsend Hoopes in *The Devil and John Foster Dulles* (Boston, 1973) briefly describes Dulles's reprimand of Stassen and discusses Dulles's views on the New Look and massive retaliation but is silent about the Atoms-for-Peace program and test-ban negotiations. Michael A. Guhin, *John Foster Dulles: A Statesman and his Times* (New York, 1972), notes that Dulles supported a test ban in 1958 and discusses his views on the New Look and massive retaliation. Otherwise he, too, says nothing about atomic-energy-related matters. Dulles's early views on what later came to be known as "massive retaliation" can be found in "A Policy of Boldness," *Life*, May 19, 1952; his most complete discussion of the doctrine appears in "Policy for Security and Peace," *Foreign Affairs* 32 (April 1954); and his eventual retreat from the doctrine and his recognition of the possibilities of defenses based on tactical nuclear weapons is in "Challenge and Response in United States Policy," *Foreign Affairs* 36 (October 1957).     669

No complete short history of the Atomic Energy Commission exists. The first two works in this series, Richard G. Hewlett and Oscar E. Anderson, Jr., *The New World, 1939–1946*, Volume I of *A History of the United States Atomic Energy Commission* (University Park, PA, 1962), and Richard G. Hewlett and Francis Duncan, *Atomic Shield, 1947–1952*, Volume II of *A History of the United States Atomic Energy Commission* (University Park, PA, 1969), discuss in detail the history of the Commission through the Truman Administration. The history of regulatory matters is treated in a separate series. The first volume of the official history of the Nuclear Regulatory Commission, *Controlling the Atom: The Beginnings of Nuclear Regulation, 1946–1962*, by George T. Mazuzan and J. Samuel Walker (Berkeley, CA, 1984), is a well-written, detailed account of the entire spectrum of nuclear regulation from reactors to radioisotopes and includes accounts of the controversies over fallout, the Price-Anderson Act, and the licensing of the Fermi fast breeder reactor. Richard G. Hewlett and Francis Duncan, *Nuclear Navy, 1946–1962* (Chicago, 1974), includes a detailed description of the naval reactors program during the Eisenhower years. Although Corbin Allardice and Edward R. Trapnell wrote the *Atomic Energy Commission* (New York, 1974) for the Praeger series on federal agencies, their study lacks balance and fails to discuss many key issues and events. It does, however, give the lay reader a good basic view of the Commission and its functions.

Of the three chairmen who led the Commission during the Eisenhower period, only Lewis L. Strauss has a biographer. Commissioned by the Strauss family, Richard Pfau's *No Sacrifice Too Great: The Life of Lewis L. Strauss* (Charlottesville, VA, 1984) is well written and only occasionally reflects the family's partisanship. The best source for biographical details about Gordon Dean and an intimate view of the problems he faced as chairman under both Truman and Eisenhower can be found in Roger M. Anders, ed., *Forging the Atomic Shield: Excerpts from the Office Diary of Gordon E. Dean* (Chapel Hill, NC, 1987).

Many controversies engulfing the Commission are the subject of historical studies. The Oppenheimer case has spawned an extensive literature, much of it polemical. Dramatists have seen in the security hearing rich material for a study of the man and his hubris. Of the Oppenheimer books the authors found John Major's *The Oppenheimer Hearing* (New York, 1971) the most succinct and well balanced. Major is easily the best single-volume study of the Oppenheimer case. Philip M. Stern's *The Oppenheimer Case: Security on Trial:* (New York, 1969) is the most exhaustive study of the hearing, although it suffers from flaws in interpretation as does Charles P. Curtis, *The Oppenheimer Case: The Trial of a Security System* (New York, 1955). A penetrating examination of the advice Oppenheimer gave the Commission on the hydrogen bomb can be found in Herbert F. York's *The Advisors: Oppenheimer, Teller, and the Superbomb* (San Francisco, 1976). As a former director of the Livermore laboratory, York knew both Oppenheimer and Teller and has the technical knowledge to weigh their scientific advice. Thomas C. Reeves in *The Life and Times of Joe McCarthy: A Biography* (New York, 1982), the most scholarly study of McCarthy, notes that the senator had been quietly building a case against Oppenheimer but did not complete his work because of the Army-McCarthy hearings.

Even more extensive than the Oppenheimer literature is that devoted to the test ban and disarmament. The single most exhaustive study of disarmament negotiations in the 1950s is Bernhard G. Bechhoefer, *Postwar Negotiations for Arms Control* (Washington, 1961). The best single-volume study of the Geneva test-ban negotiations can be found in Harold K. Jacobsen and Eric Stein, *Diplomats, Scientists, and Politicians: The United States and the Nuclear Test Ban Negotiations* (Ann Arbor, MI, 1966). Robert Gilpin in *American Scientists and Nuclear Weapons Policy* (Princeton, NJ, 1962) examines political differences among the scientists on test ban issues. Walt W. Rostow studies the Open Skies proposal in detail in *Open Skies: Eisenhower's Proposal of July 21, 1955* (Austin, TX, 1982), and he explores the impact of Stalin's death on arms control policies of the Eisenhower Administration in *Europe After Stalin: Eisenhower's Three Decisions of March 11, 1953* (Austin, TX, 1982). The Soviet view of disarmament and arms control is thoroughly discussed in *Khrushchev and the Arms Race: Soviet Interests in Arms Control and Disarmament, 1954–1964* (Cambridge, MA, 1966) by Lincoln P. Bloomfield, Walter C. Clemens, Jr., and Franklyn Griffiths. Also useful is Edward Crankshaw, ed., *Khrushchev Remembers* (Boston, 1974). An absorbing popular account of the American U-2 program and the abortive 1960 Paris summit conference can be found in Michael R. Beschloss, *Mayday, the U-2 Affair: The Untold Story of the Greatest U.S.–U.S.S.R. Spy Scandal* (New York, 1986). The literature of

670

the proponents and opponents of the test ban is extensive, and an incomplete list includes Linus Pauling, *No More War!* (New York, 1958); Edward Teller with Allen Brown, *The Legacy of Hiroshima* (New York, 1962); Edward Teller and Albert L. Latter, *Our Nuclear Future: Facts, Dangers, and Opportunities* (New York, 1958); Philip Noel-Baker, *The Arms Race: A Programme for World Disarmament* (New York, 1958); Earl H. Voss, *Nuclear Ambush: The Test Ban Trap* (Chicago, 1963); James J. Wadsworth, *The Price of Peace* (New York, 1962); Norman Cousins, *In Place of Folly* (New York, 1961); Seymour Melman, ed., *Inspection for Disarmament* (New York, 1958); Bertrand Russell, *Common Sense and Nuclear War* (New York, 1959) and *Has Man a Future?* (New York, 1962); Thomas C. Schelling and Morton Halperin, *Strategy and Arms Control* (New York, 1961); Albert Schweitzer, *Peace or Atomic War?* (New York, 1958); Herbert F. York, *Race to Oblivion: A Participant's View of the Arms Race* (New York, 1970); Henry A. Kissinger, "Nuclear Testing and the Problem of Peace," *Foreign Affairs* 37 (October 1958); Freeman J. Dyson, "The Future Development of Nuclear Weapons," *Foreign Affairs* 38 (April 1960); Edward Teller and Albert Latter, "The Compelling Need for Nuclear Tests," *Life*, February 10, 1958; George Harris, "How Livermore Survived the Test Ban," *Fortune* 65 (April 1960); and Hans A. Bethe, "The Case for Ending Nuclear Tests," *The Atlantic Monthly*, August 1960.

671

The best single-volume study of the fallout controversy is Robert A. Divine, *Blowing on the Wind: The Nuclear Test Ban Debate, 1954–1960* (New York, 1978). In *The Voyage of the Lucky Dragon* (New York, 1958), Ralph E. Lapp recounts the Lucky Dragon incident and the fate of the Japanese fishermen. Earle Reynolds's *The Forbidden Voyage* (New York, 1961) is his account of his dramatic attempt to sail into the Pacific Proving Grounds during the 1958 nuclear weapon tests. In *Radiation: What It Is and How It Affects You* (New York, 1957), Jack Schubert and Ralph E. Lapp present for lay readers a summary of the hazards of radiation. Spencer R. Weart's *Nuclear Fear: A History of Images* (Cambridge, MA, 1988) contains an excellent and penetrating analysis of the popular perceptions of fallout, weapon testing, and the peaceful atom during the Eisenhower years.

Arnold Kramish's *The Peaceful Atom in Foreign Policy* (New York, 1963) is one of the few secondary works on Atoms-for-Peace programs. A series of recent studies of Atoms for Peace can be found in Joseph E. Pilat, Robert E. Pendley, and Charles K. Ebinger, eds., *Atoms-for-Peace: An Analysis After Thirty Years* (Boulder, CO, 1985). The most useful essays are James R. Schlesinger, "Atoms for Peace Revisited," Robert R. Bowie, "Eisenhower, Atomic Weapons, and Atoms for Peace," Richard G. Hewlett, "From Proposal to Program," and Jack M. Holl, "The Peaceful Atom: Lore and Myth." Bernhard G. Bechhoefer, "Negotiating the Statute of the International Atomic Energy Agency," *International Organization* 13

(1959), is especially valuable for the origins of the international agency. Irvin C. Bupp's and Jean-Claude Derian's *Light Water: How the Nuclear Dream Dissolved* (New York, 1978) contains an excellent analysis of Eisenhower's Atoms-for-Peace proposal and of the Eisenhower Administration's policy for power reactor development.

The literature of nuclear strategy is extensive and must begin with Bernard Brodie, *Strategy in the Missile Age* (Princeton, 1959), Henry A. Kissinger, *Nuclear Weapons and Foreign Policy* (New York, 1957), and Herman Kahn, *On Thermonuclear War* (Princeton, 1960) and *Thinking About the Unthinkable* (New York, 1962). Two recent excellent studies of nuclear strategy debates are Fred Kaplan, *The Wizards of Armageddon* (New York, 1983), and Lawrence Freedman, *The Evolution of Nuclear Strategy* (New York, 1983). Other valuable examinations of nuclear strategy or doctrines of limited war are Bernard Brodie, *The Atomic Bomb and American Security* (New Haven, CT, 1945), Basil Liddell Hart, *Defense of the West* (New York, 1950), William Kaufman, ed., *Military Policy and National Security* (Princeton, NJ, 1956), and Robert E. Osgood, *Limited War: The Challenge to American Security* (Chicago, 1957).

There is a growing literature on the history of scientific developments during the decade. Joan Lisa Bromberg's *Fusion: Science, Politics, and the Invention of a New Energy Source* (Cambridge, MA, 1982) is the definitive work on this program and a model for histories of specific governmental programs. M. Stanley Livingston has written an account of particle accelerator development in *Particle Accelerators: A Brief History* (Cambridge, MA, 1969) and has edited accounts of their evolution in *The Development of High Energy Accelerators* (New York, 1966). The best source for a fundamental understanding of how particle accelerators work is Robert R. Wilson and Raphael Littauer, *Accelerators, Machines of Nuclear Physics* (New York, 1960). Leonard Greenbaum's *A Special Interest: The Atomic Energy Commission, Argonne National Laboratory and the Midwestern Universities* (Ann Arbor, MI, 1971) and Daniel S. Greenberg's *The Politics of Pure Science* (New York, 1967) examine the controversies surrounding the Midwest Universities Research Association and its proposed particle accelerators from single perspectives. An excellent account of Herman Muller's work and times can be found in Elof Axel Carlson, *Genes, Radiation and Society: The Life and Work of H. J. Muller* (Ithaca, NY, 1981).

Two studies are especially valuable in the literature of atomic energy. Aaron Wildavsky's *Dixon-Yates: A Study in Power Politics* (New Haven, CT, 1962) contains a thorough and well-researched account of the battle over the Dixon-Yates contract and its impact on the 1954 Atomic Energy Act. Harold P. Green and Alan Rosenthal in *Government of the Atom: The Integration of Powers* (New York, 1963) present the best published account of the role of the Joint Committee during its early years.

## INTERVIEWS

The authors supplemented their documentary research with oral interviews of individuals who participated in the events described in the text. Although the extraordinary richness of the documentary evidence provided more than enough detail, often from several perspectives, the oral interviews also provided fresh insights, confirmed or refined interpretations based on documentary sources, and provided vivid detail unavailable elsewhere.

Former President Eisenhower and most of his immediate staff associated with atomic energy matters had died before research for this volume was completed, but the authors did receive valuable insights on White House deliberations from Andrew J. Goodpaster.

Among the men who served on the Atomic Energy Commission during the Eisenhower Administration, only Lewis L. Strauss, Henry D. Smyth, John A. McCone, John F. Floberg, and Eugene M. Zuckert were available for interviews. Each of them provided essential information for this volume.

673

Several key members of the Commission's staff also granted the authors interviews or related their recollections informally. These included Frank P. Baranowski, Edward J. Bloch, Howard C. Brown, Jr., W. Kenneth Davis, McKay Donkin, Edward R. Gardner, Dwight A. Ink, Alvin R. Luedecke, Woodford B. McCool, John L. McGruder, A. Bruce Mercer, Kenneth D. Nichols, Clarence C. Ohlke, Robert D. O'Niell, Charles A. Perry, Frank K. Pittman, Hyman G. Rickover, Louis H. Roddis, Jr., Roy B. Snapp, Alfred D. Starbird, Edward R. Trapnell, and Richard A. Willitt.

For a better understanding of the issues involved in weapon testing and the fallout controversy the authors interviewed Robert F. Bacher, Norris Bradbury, Richard Bice, Warren Donaldson, Neal O. Hines, Hal L. Hollister, Lewis Hopkins, Donald Kerr, William E. Ogle, Shields Warren, John C. Whitnah, and Herbert F. York.

Discussions of Atoms-for-Peace programs and the 1954 Atomic Energy Act were enhanced by Shelby Brewer, Robert R. Bowie, W. Sterling Cole, Philip J. Farley, Chet Holifield, John A. Hall, George Norris, Jr., and Gerard C. Smith.

For a better appreciation of progress in nuclear science during the decade, the authors turned to Glenn T. Seaborg and Gerald F. Tape.

Perhaps the single most controversial act of the Commission during the 1950s was the removal of J. Robert Oppenheimer's security clearance. Not only did the Oppenheimer case lend itself to greater clarity through oral history, but the authors also had the good fortune to find many key figures still active. For a better grasp of the case, they interviewed Luis W. Alvarez, Charles Bates, Hans A. Bethe, William L. Borden, Frank Cotter,

Harold P. Green, W. Lee Hancock, J. Kenneth Mansfield, Kenneth D. Nichols, Kenneth S. Pitzer, James Reston, Roger Robb, Roy B. Snapp, Henry D. Smyth, Edward R. Trapnell, Edward Teller, John A. Walker, John A. Wheeler, and Eugene M. Zuckert.


*CONCLUDING NOTE*

The wealth, number, and variety of sources discussed in this essay should amply demonstrate the vastness of sources with which the historian of the recent past is confronted. As an indication of the volume of collections, Dwight D. Eisenhower's White House Central files occupy 3,241 linear feet and the Atomic Energy Commission's secretariat files total nearly 500 cubic feet. These were the two collections of greatest value to this volume, yet the other collections that the authors had to examine amounted to several hundred additional linear feet.

674

The sheer size of documentary collections presented the authors with the problem of locating and selecting pertinent documents from among a vast universe of modern public records. As the Eisenhower years recede further into the past, increasing numbers of historians will face the same problem of reducing oceans of potentially pertinent data to islands of directly pertinent facts that can be analyzed. The methodology historians use for solving this problem will shape topics for research and influence conclusions drawn from that research.

As this series demonstrates, the authors have found team research and writing one method for digesting and analyzing large volumes of public documents. In the face of the explosion of post–World War II public records, the lone historian diligently making files of note cards seems as obsolete as the lone inventor tinkering in his basement. Increasingly it seems that sound professional history may become the product of teamwork, as has sound monograph production in other professions.

# INDEX

Acheson, Dean G., 42, 212
Adams, Sherman, 89, 249, 362
Adenauer, Konrad, 354–55
Advisory committee on biology and medicine.
  *See* Biology and medicine, Advisory Committee on
Agreements for cooperation: in JCAE bill,
  122; bilaterals, 227, 235–37; EURATOM
  agreement, 491–93. *See also* Bilateral
  agreements
Aircraft carrier reactors, 521
Aircraft reactors, 14, 25, 28, 416, 518
Air Force, U.S., 170, 174, 188–89
*Alert* Operation, 349, 451–52
Allardice, Corbin: on Oppenheimer hearing,
  86; on legislation, 120–21; on industrial
  participation, 125–26; on compulsory licensing, 142
Allary, Jean, 215
Allis-Chalmers Manufacturing Company, 527
Allison, John M., 177
Alsop, Stewart and Joseph, 84, 88, 279
Alternating-gradient synchrotron, 258–60,
  522
Alvarez, Luis W.: in Oppenheimer investigation, 93, 95–97; builds first linear accelerator, 523
Amarillo, TX, plant, 7, 19
American Assembly, 415–17
American Car and Foundry Company, 504
American Federation of Labor, 358
American Gas and Electric Service Corporation, 193
American Legion, 433
American Physical Society, 390
American Public Power Association, 27
Ames Laboratory, 256
AMF Atomics, 414

Amster, Warren, 454
Anderson, Clinton P.: on principal officer issue, 124; on JCAE bill, 138; on conference
  committee, 140–42; JCAE chairman, 202;
  Dixon-Yates, 248; Nevada Test Site, 289;
  EURATOM, 322; private vs. public power,
  327; power demonstration projects, 342,
  409–10; on Gore-Holifield bill, 344–45;
  on "clean bomb statement," 347; 1956
  election, 352, 367; demands reactor safety
  report, 353; questions Fermi reactor safety,
  358; *Weapons Effects Handbook*, 376;
  "clean bomb," 398; Senate leadership,
  403; Section 202 hearings, 407; on nuclear
  power, 409; reactor development program,
  427; on Strauss's reappointment, 427;
  U.S./EURATOM agreement, 444–45,
  492; opposes military bilateral, 467; supports test ban, 474; opinion of McCone,
  490–91, 504; high-energy physics, 525
Anderson, Dillon, 284–85
Anderson, Robert B., 224, 275
*Annie* test, 146–50, 153
Argonaut reactor, 447
Argonne Cancer Research Hospital, 263
Argonne National Laboratory: AEC laboratory, 8; designs submarine reactor, 186; reactor development, 190, 191, 195–96; in
  5-year reactor program, 195–96; as regional laboratory, 253–55; high-energy
  physics, 259–60; fallout studies, 282; scientists support Stevenson, 368; 1958 Geneva conference, 447; designs zerogradient synchrotron, 522
*Argus* test, 483
Armand, Louis, 404
Armed Forces Special Weapons Project, 149–
  50, 273

677

679

682

Graves, Alvin C., 148, 152, 157, 164–66, 173, 487–88
Gray, Gordon, 83, 89–91, 98–101, 544
Great nuclear debate, 562–66
Green, Harold P., 76–78
*Greenhouse* test, 265
Griggs, David T., 92, 550
Gromyko, Andrei, 380, 462
Groves, Leslie R., 1, 31, 96, 100
Gruenther, Alfred M., 346, 481

H-bomb. *See* Thermonuclear weapons
Hafstad, Lawrence R.: director of reactor development, 23; early views on nuclear power, 185–86; plans reactor program, 189; opposes PWR, 192; proposes five-year program, 195; reassures JCAE on PWR, 198; on power demonstration program, 200; planning for Geneva, 234; leaves AEC, 242
Hagerty, James, 71, 89, 338, 370, 372, 545–46
Hahn, Otto, 389
Hall, John A., 234, 311, 317–19, 343, 531
Hall, Leonard, 349
Hallam, NB, plant, 504, 513
Hammarskjöld, Dag, 235, 448
Hanford, WA, plant: new reactors, 19; production reactors, 161–62; waste storage and processing, 162; tritium production, 167; plutonium and tritium production, 398; reactor development studies, 426
*Hardtack I* test series, 389, 456–57, 482–83
*Hardtack II* test series, 483, 544, 548
*Harry* test, 154, 155, 156
Hart, Basil Liddell, 454
Hawkins, David, 51
Heavy-water production, 162, 167
Heavy-water reactors, 191, 197, 418, 513
Herter, Christian A.: 1956 elections, 348–49, 381–82; warns Stassen, 394; witnesses Stassen's reprimand, 396; Senate challenge to IAEA, 433; concurs in IAEA post for McKinney, 436; need for strong Europe, 440; IAEA and EURATOM, 442–43; and EURATOM agreement, 443–44; on test suspension, 544–45; questions atmospheric test ban, 552–53; plans for Geneva talks, 554–55; urges positive action on test ban, 559
Hickenlooper, Bourke B.: possible JCAE chairman, 39; in Oppenheimer case, 68; opposes information exchange, 118; reviews JCAE draft bill, 121; introduces JCAE bill, 133; faces opposition in Senate, 136–37; on conference committee, 140–42; role on JCAE, 202; challenge to IAEA, 433–34

High-energy physics, 257–60, 522–25, 530, 535
Hill, David L., 368
Hill, Lister, 137, 248
Himsworth, Harold, 295
Hinshaw, Carl, 140–42, 197, 202
Hinton, Christopher, 357
Hiroshima, Japan, 307
Holifield, Chet: promotes public power, 114–15; opposes industrial participation bill, 121; on principal officer issue, 124; on private ownership, 126–27; raises electric power issue, 128; attacks Dixon-Yates, 132–33; opposes Bricker amendment, 137; on conference committee, 140–42; questions industry's commitment, 185; cautions on PWR, 196; opposes power demonstration program, 204; N.S. *Savannah*, 245; weapon testing, 272; McKinney report, 327–28; chairs subcommittee on fallout effects, 331; "clean bomb," 398; Section 202 hearings, 407; plutonium purchase contracts, 427; criticizes AEC on fallout, 454–55; questions McCone in confirmation hearing, 490; criticizes McCone reactor program, 502–3
Holmes & Narver, Inc., 169, 170
Homogeneous reactor, 190–91, 195–96, 505
Hoover, Herbert, Jr., 284, 293, 296, 356, 372
Hoover, J. Edgar: informed of lost document, 38–40; meets with McCarthy, 48; cautions Strauss, 62; considers Borden letter, 67–69; cautions on Oppenheimer charges, 69–70; meets with Murray, 74; reviews statement of charges, 77; orders Oppenheimer surveillances, 80; sends Oppenheimer information to Strauss, 85
Hughes, Rowland R., 129–30, 131
Humphrey, George M., 18, 24, 52, 363, 392
Humphrey, Hubert H., 333, 366, 473–76
Hungary, 373

Idaho reactor test station, 255, 352, 422
India: small power reactors, 245; response to *Bravo* shot, 274; weapon test moratorium, 291; nuclear test suspension, 303; seeks power reactor, 308; amendments to IAEA statute, 371; hears Schweitzer appeal, 390; proposes test suspension, 547–48
Indiana University, 267
Industrial participation: favored by Eisenhower, 14; study groups, 21, 23; early legislative proposals, 114–15; AEC draft bill, 119–20; opposed by Holifield, 121; in reactor development, 184–86, 203–5
Information control, 117–19, 122, 159, 176
Ink, Dwight A., 450

683

Geneva, 300; complains of American duplicity, 336; Open Skies photography, 336;
ballistic missile with nuclear warhead,
339; comes to power, 458; proposes joint
test ban, 479; reopens disarmament question, 481; accepts technical studies proposal, 486; visits U.S., 533; ridicules moratorium, 547; rejects atmospheric test ban,
555
Killian, James R., Jr.: Report, 273; Geneva
conference, 1958, 446; appointed science
adviser, 464; proposes technical study,
471; appoints Bethe panel, 472; briefed by
Strauss, 480–81; Report, 481; special assistant to President, 516; evaluates high-
energy physics, 523–24; prepares for Geneva conference of experts, 539; hails
results of conference, 542; orders study
of *Hardtack II* data, 549–50; assessment
of "Geneva system," 551; questions atmospheric test ban, 552–53; supports Berkner
panel, 534; plans for Geneva talks, 554;
favors atmospheric test ban, 556–57; supports quota with choice, 556–57
Kimpton, Lawrence A., 259
Kissinger, Henry, 453–54
Kistiakowsky, George B., 516, 518, 524, 530,
557
Kiwi-A reactor, 518
Knapp, Harold A., 279
Knolls Atomic Power Laboratory, 187–88,
256, 422–23, 493
Knowland, William F.: leads Senate debate,
137–38; moves to end filibuster, 139–40;
on conference committee, 140–42; role on
JCAE, 202; critical of Stassen, 349; chal-
lenge to IAEA, 733–34; reservations to
IAEA statute, 432; on IAEA staffing, 436
Kohnstamm, Max, 441–42, 444
Kouts, Herbert J., 343
Kozlov, Frol R., 532
Krishna Menon, V. K., 316
Kuboyama, Aikichu, 271
Kuchel, Thomas H., 339
Kulp, J. Lawrence, 473
Kuykendall, Jerome K., 119
Kyes, Roger M., 27–28, 30, 66–67, 69, 71–
72, 215

Lamert, Rudi, 98
Langer, William H., 138
Laniel, Joseph, 71
Lansdale, John, Jr., 87, 95–96, 98, 100
LaPlante, Bryan F.: Augusta briefing, 2, 3;
NY trip, 12; liaison with FBI, 52; investi-
gates Oppenheimer, 63; on Oppenheimer
clearance, 70; assists on hearing, 86;
Muller affair, 267

Lapp, Ralph L.: on fallout, 281–82, 287;
Kefauver hearings, 288; testifies on fallout,
331; warns about "suicide" weapon, 338;
warns about risks of testing, 340; satirizes
"clean bomb," 347; on nuclear testing,
366; repudiates Kefauver's H-bomb warning, 368; AEC on fallout, 376; book on fallout, 453; article on radiation effects, 473
Latimer, Wendell M., 87
Latter, Albert L., 554, 557
Lauritzen, Thomas, 367
Lawrence, Ernest O.: consulted on secrecy,
56; interviewed on Oppenheimer, 86, 87;
supports Livermore, 181; director, Radiation Laboratory, 255; high-energy physics,
257; fusion energy, 261; disarmament task
force, 296; clean bomb development, 399;
testifies on weapon testing, 399–400;
questions inspection proposal, 470; delegate to Geneva conference of experts, 539
Lawrence Berkeley Laboratory. *See* Radiation
Laboratory, Berkeley
Lawrence Livermore Laboratory. *See* Livermore Laboratory
LeBaron, Robert, 217
Lehman, Herbert H., 138
*Lenin*, icebreaker, 532, 534
Libby, Willard F.: opposes Oppenheimer's reappointment, 46; on power demonstration
program, 206; nominated to AEC, 241;
second invitation to industry, 246; Project
*Gabriel*, 265–66; fallout spokesman, 278;
on fallout estimates, 280–81; radiation
hazards, 283; fallout statement, 284; Kefauver hearings, 287–88; Operation *Teapot*
fallout, 288; Nevada Test Site, 289; "Radioactive Fallout," 294–95; implementing
Atoms for Peace, 308; safeguards conference, 312; safeguards issues, 318–20;
Project *Sunshine* fallout data, 329–30; testifies on fallout effects, 330–31; on NAS
report, 340; proposes AEC statement on
"clean bombs," 347; on public power, 359;
on world fallout, 361–62; fallout estimates,
377–78; importance of Project *Sunshine*,
379–80; test moratorium at London conference, 389; answers Schweitzer, 390; drafts
Strauss's test ban strategy, 393–94;
federal subsidy for nuclear power, 407;
EURATOM safeguards, 441, 443; Geneva
conference, 1958, 446, 447; briefs JCAE
and State on fallout, 449; article on radiation effects, 473; testifies on disarmament,
474; urges underground testing, 477; questions aircraft reactor, 517; on high-energy
physics, 523; urges *Plowshare* research,
529; proposes test limitation, 543; reports
on Soviet tests, 548

685

691

693

695

Compositor: G&S Typesetters, Inc.
Text: Bodoni Book
Display: Bodoni Book and Aachen Bold
Printer: Maple-Vail Book Mfg. Group
Binder: Maple-Vail Book Mfg. Group

105409

QC
792.7
.H48
1989

Hewlett, Richard.
    Atoms for peace
and war.

## DATE DUE

GAYLORD                                      PRINTED IN U.S.A.